Le Ton beau de Marot

In Praise of the Music of Language

Le Ton beau de Marot

In Praise of the Music of Language

Douglas R. Hofstadter

```
              *
          *       *
      *       *       *
    *       *       *       *
  *       *       *       *       *
    *       *       *       *
      *       *       *
          *       *
              *
```

Basic Books
A Member of Perseus Books, L.L.C.

On page *xii*, reproduced with kind permission of the Louvre Museum, Paris:

Portrait présumé de Clément Marot, poète (avec cadre)
de Corneille de Lyon (ca. 1500–ca. 1575)
Musée du Louvre, Paris, France
© Photo RMN — Gérard Blot
Made available by the Agence photographique
de la réunion des musées nationaux, Paris. Philippe Couton, archivist.

Because of the large number of permissions and acknowledgments in this book, it is impossible to fit the remainder of them onto this copyright page. They have therefore been placed in a separate section on pages 607–608.

Library of Congress Cataloguing-in-Publication Data

Hofstadter, Douglas R. (1945–   )
    Le Ton beau de Marot : in praise of the music of language / by Douglas R. Hofstadter.
        p.   cm.
    Includes the text of Clément Marot's "A une Damoyselle malade" with numerous English translations.
    Includes bibliographical references (p. 599) and index.
    ISBN 0-465-08643-8 (cloth)   ISBN 0-465-08645-4 (paper)
    1. Translating and interpreting. I. Marot, Clément, 1496–1544.
A une Damoyselle malade. English & French. II. Title.
P306.H63   1997
418'.02—dc21   97-3999
                                                                          CIP

98 99 00 01 02 03   RRD   9 8 7 6 5 4 3 2 1

To M. & D.,

living sparks of their
Mommy's loving soul

Table of Contents

Chapter 6: The Subtle Art of Transculturation 141

Chapter 7: The Nimble Medium-hopping of Evanescent Essences 171

Chapter 8: A Novel in Verse 233

Chapter 9: A Vile Non-verse 255

Chapter 10: On Words and Their Magical Halos 279

Table of Contents

Introduction

In Joy
and in Sorrow

Picture Holden Caulfield all grown up, now a university professor, writing a book about translation. Okay, don't. It's too silly.

Still, I feel that this book has something of that flavor, in part because it is in fact all about translation and in part because it is autobiographical, candid, and informal in tone. And also because, even if this sounds like an utter cliché, there *is* some kind of deep kinship between my soul and that of Holden Caulfield. I know this is so; after all, why else would Brent Harold, my first English teacher in college, have written at the bottom of a highly emotional and personal essay that I handed in to him, way back in 1961: "D+. This sounds like poor, poor Salinger"? If your college English teacher thinks you're like Holden Caulfield, then you *must* be, ¿yesno?

This long book was sparked almost ten years ago by my trying to translate one sweet, old, small, elegant French poem into English, and by the unexpected snowballing of that one first try into a mammoth avalanche of further translations by old friends, new friends, relatives, colleagues, students, strangers, and, not least, myself. Details are found inside. That's not what I intend to tell, at the start; here I aim to tell *how* I wrote this book.

As has been the case for all the books I have written, working on this book has been an erratic alternation between tremendous exhilaration and self-confidence, on the one hand, and extreme nervousness and worry, on the other. Most of the time, though, I will admit that I have been running on a strong inner hunch that this is probably the best book I will ever write.

Exuberant Immersion

I had pretty much forgotten the exuberance that one can derive from working on a tightly integrated artistic structure as large as this book is, because the last time I did anything really similar was around twenty years ago, when I was writing *Gödel, Escher, Bach*. My subsequent books were also large and, I hope, well integrated, but they were not composed in one long determined drive motivated by a single clear vision; rather, they were assembled out of many separate parts written at diverse times. Although each part of such a patchwork opus may be strong, and although one can make great *a posteriori* efforts to tie all the separate parts together, there can never arise that same deep sense of unity as pervades a work that is created in one prolonged transcendent swoop of passionate fire.

If one is lucky, one has the luxury of becoming totally immersed in an artistic project, letting almost all other things go by the wayside — family, friends, students, colleagues, food, bills, correspondence, neatness, books, music, movies, shopping, and sleep, to give a few examples. The house becomes a pigsty, the kids a bit starved for affection, weight goes down, friends wonder where you are... Fortunately, this monomaniacal state will be transitory, but it seems absolutely necessary, at least in my own case, for the emergence of that overarching frame of mind that allows the project to take on a true unity of purpose and style.

Wrapping-around and Tightening

My way of working involves making as good a first draft of the whole thing as I can, and then, when that is all finished, cycling around from the end to the beginning of the book and revisiting and revising — or, as is more often the case, radically rewriting — chapter after chapter, till the end is reached again. Such a second pass produces a far tighter unity. Then a third wraparound comes and hopefully starts to sew things up, but even after that there are still endless tiny details that are tweaked as the final date, imposed from within or from without, approaches.

Something that inevitably happens during these wraparound phases, and which could not happen at any earlier moment, is that I pick up on all sorts of unsuspected links and resonances between ideas in far-separated corners of the book. A major part of the rewriting thus involves the effort to bring out these surprising, newly-discovered connections, or to insert new ideas that pop to mind as a consequence of the touching-up.

It is the intensity of this process of global tightening and smoothing of a huge structure that was once implicit in one's mind but is now external and has its own unanticipated shape, life, and momentum, it is the power of this process of converting a set of once-intangible intuitions into a very tangible network of interconnected crystals, that I had forgotten. At times, the feeling of excitement is so palpable that it overwhelms me, and a terrible jitteriness invades my body — a wild, wild tingling. At such times, no matter how tired I am, I find it impossible to fall asleep, saying to myself over and over again in the middle of the night, "Get this book *done,* for God's sake, get it *done!*" But the book just takes its own sweet time. New ideas have a way of popping up precisely when, in a certain sense, one least wants them to, and so one simply has to go with the flow.

The Gradual Emergence of a Global Tone

Even though the writing process is broken into hundreds of separate sessions truncated for all sorts of reasons (most often a growing awareness of fatigue setting in and coherence diminishing), there somehow evolves a stable, reliable, overall frame of mind that persists for months and imbues the book with its own unique stylistic consistency. At the outset, this "voice" is not quite there; one seeks it. This is why the earliest drafts of my chapters now turn me off: they seem like good ideas desperately in search of a style.

I believe the convergence to a global tone is something that has to come from deep within, from long and arduous grappling with things one is only beginning to understand. This should be private, not public. These days, people crow of the virtues of constantly-evolving Web pages — drafts of ideas that are tossed up and then changed day by day in front of the eyes of "visitors". To me, that has zero appeal. I want to hide my ideas until they are fully polished and unified. I don't throw my drafts away — I keep them for myself; but the beauty of the process of publication is that those drafts *are* secret, that one's creative tracks are covered. There is a kind of illusion thereby conveyed that this whole book just sprang up spontaneously.

Of course, nothing could be further from the truth. The amount of rewriting that I do of every single sentence is hard, even for me, to believe. I think it's safe to say that I entertain dozens of variants of each sentence, most of them in my head but many on the screen, in front of my eyes. They are tested out visually. A typical paragraph will represent an hour or two of work, not just a few minutes. And those hours will be distributed across many distinct periods of time, separated by hours, days, weeks, or months.

Welcoming the Unexpected Guest

My friend and "cousin" Stephen Jay Gould — his mother's brother Herb Rosenberg and my father's sister Shirley Hofstadter were married until Herb's sudden, young death of a heart attack, many years ago — has told me that he formulates an outline and then writes from it, using only a typewriter, not a computer, and never deviating from the plan. I cannot imagine doing that! For me, the appearance of unexpected ideas is the very lifeblood of my invention. Some little word, some little coincidence, will catch my eye, and all of a sudden, I'm off on a whole new direction…

An example: Chapter 3's rather amusing juxtaposition of a discussion of the droll German word for "nipple" and a certain poetic portrait of a charming breast was not planned at all. I was just merrily writing along about the German word, and as the contrast with other languages became stronger and stronger in my mind, it triggered my memory of the existence of a Marot poem in praise of breasts. I had read that poem a couple of times before but never with much care, and it was anything but my intention to include it in this book. But now, having drawn the connection in my mind, I, like Curious George, the curious little monkey, was curious. I reached up for my ever-handy volume of Marot poetry, flipped to the proper page, re-read the poem with a grin on my face, and then part of me groaned heavily as I realized, "Oh, no! Now I'm going to *have* to translate this!", while another part of me said, "Aha! Putting this in, along with a spicy translation, will certainly liven up this section of the chapter!" If I had been strictly following an outline, such a thing could never have happened.

And this is not rare or exceptional; such spontaneous intrusions absolutely pervade the book, on every structural level. An idea will wind up getting drawn in that I could never have anticipated, even just moments before it arose — and yet from the moment it has arrived, it suddenly seems inevitable, it seems to have been fated to be included. To me, that is the entire excitement and beauty of the creative process. Things come from out of left field and are drawn in and integrated and then become central. One's current mundane life's most accidental strands get woven deeply into the fabric of the artistic structure one is creating, and the whole is thereby imbued with a profound sense of time and place — even if, in some sense, the message is meant to be timeless and to transcend one's own small life.

The Metaphor of the Capri Mosaic

Over the past year, there is one metaphor for the unpredictable evolution of this book that has sprung up in my mind and that now haunts me; it is the idea of designing a multi-leveled mosaic.

I imagine that I am spending a pleasant vacation in some spectacularly lovely part of the world — the island of Capri comes to my mind — where, lying about all over the place, free for the taking, are thousands and thousands of small beautiful stones of many colors, sizes and shapes, each one special and distinct from all the others. Strangely, though, almost no one who is there seems to notice them or care about them. And so I formulate the goal of making a large, complex, multi-leveled mosaic that will capture my personal thrill over the extreme beauty of these stones, and then I will share my mosaic with others.

A little bit like "cousin Steve", I start out with, in my head, a clear plan that involves, say, twelve smaller sub-mosaics, each one with its own theme, and I try to imagine in my mind's eye how those sub-mosaics will be arranged with respect to one another. I even do a little sketch showing how I think stones might wind up arranged in the sub-mosaics. But then I start gathering the actual stones and making the first few sub-mosaics.

As I confront reality and not just my own fantasy, some of the stones that I come across excite me in ways that I never anticipated and suggest a couple of new sub-mosaics to me, and so I modify my first plan to allow, say, fourteen sub-mosaics. I continue collecting and arranging, but then, to my chagrin, I suddenly see that one of my sub-mosaics is getting over-inflated, and perhaps needs to be broken up into two, maybe even three, smaller ones. I don't like the idea at all, but as I turn it over in my mind, I realize that there is no denying the trend, and moreover that it is only going to get worse as I continue working on that sub-mosaic. And so, with reluctance, I allow myself the luxury of breaking it into two or possibly even three smaller pieces. At the moment of doing so, I actually breathe a great sigh of relief, since deep down, I'd known that things were going wrong. Having made this corrective move, I now of course have to go back to the drawing board and reimagine how the new set of sub-mosaics will fit together.

Although such unpredictable disruptive events are very frustrating, the mosaic as a whole definitely seems to be getting better, so I accept this kind of evolutionary bumpiness as a fact of life. Yet as it keeps on happening, I start getting quite upset. When will this infernal mosaic ever stop growing?

In the meantime, inside every single sub-mosaic, I am constantly shifting about its constituent stones in an effort to find the most pleasing of all possible patterns. Often I have the intuition that a stone initially placed in one sub-mosaic really would fit better in one of the other sub-mosaics, so I transfer it. For a while, this kind of transfer process happens incessantly, so that no sub-mosaic is absolutely stable or certain. But very gradually, the swapping of stones slows down and I start to be able to rely on the internal stability of most of the sub-mosaics, at least in terms of what their set of components is, if not in terms of their relative placement.

Much as the stones inside each sub-mosaic are still subject to shifting and rearrangement within it, so the sub-mosaics as wholes are still subject to shifting and rearrangement within the larger pattern. What makes things yet more complicated is that the gathering of new stones continues apace at the same time as the multi-level rearrangement process is going on, so that even toward the very end, unexpected jolts can happen at any moment.

Despite all this craziness at so many levels at once, a coherent vision of the mosaic as one large work of art slowly starts to emerge, admittedly quite unlike the original vision that I had at first thought of, and unbelievably more complex than my first crude sketch on paper, but nonetheless realizing my initial dream of creating a beautiful multi-leveled mosaic out of the pretty Capri stones that I so love.

I'm not sure I've even captured my own metaphor well; or perhaps spelling it out has changed it somewhat. In any case, this image, though far from perfect, does as good a job as I can do of suggesting how I perceive my own process of creating a coherent artistic structure on as large a scale as this book. It is a constant mixture of excitement and frustration, followed by let-down and reawakening of excitement. Living this way is very intense, and luckily, the process eventually comes to a close.

Deadlines and Other Constraints

Indeed, the time element in this book has been a very strange factor. I found out, about a year ago, that Clément Marot was born on November 23, 1496, and thus in my mind, his 500th birthday became a clear deadline for the book to be not only finished but *out*, available to buy in bookstores. However, as time passed and as the sub-mosaics started getting ever more inflated and as the rearrangements on all levels started depressing me with their never-endingness, I saw that that first goal would certainly not be met. This was very depressing. But in mulling this over, I fortunately discovered an even more auspicious goal: to finish the writing on precisely that special day — to put the last touches on the text on November 23, 1996.

And so that is what I have been driving towards. It is an entirely self-imposed constraint, a constraint exerting an incredible, unrelenting force on me for roughly a year now, turning me into a kind of obsessed madman — yet although it has certainly been hard on me, I think it has been extremely good for the book. I think one strongly needs deadlines of some sort or other in life; they act as organizers without which one would simply flail about for unlimited amounts of time.

The November 23 deadline is just one of innumerable constraints that I have imposed on myself in writing this book. Many of the others, though by no means all, have to do with the actual appearance of the text. Because I have always had a very clear sense of how things should look on a page, I dearly wanted to be able to control every tiny detail of my book's overall look, ranging from the cover art to the typefaces used to the size of the pages to the way displays are indented, and so on. Fortunately, the people at Basic Books have grown used to me and my idiosyncrasies over the years I have worked with them, and they assented to my unusual request.

Consequently, I have enjoyed total control over such things as line-breaks, page-breaks, hyphenations, widows, orphans, density of word spacing within lines, fine-grained intercharacter spacing ("kerning"), and so forth and so on — things that most people usually are unaware of and simply leave to their publisher or their word processor. I am a fanatic, though, and these things matter a great deal to me. Not only do they *matter* to me, they have had an overwhelming impact on this book from start to finish. This may sound crazy, but it is the gospel truth.

Who Is Really Controlling Whom?

Above, I very casually remarked that I have enjoyed total control over page-breaks and such things; yet the truth of the matter would be far more accurately captured by turning the phrase around and saying that the page-breaks and word spacing and such things have enjoyed total control over me! By this, I mean that I have been forced to rewrite and rewrite and rewrite passages in order to make a page boundary come out exactly where I wanted it. It is not just by some happy accident, for instance, that the poems inside chapters are never, ever broken across page boundaries.

The amount of influence exerted on my text by concerns of purely visual esthetics is incalculable — and by "my text", I don't merely mean how I wound up *phrasing* my ideas, I mean the ideas themselves. Content has been determined by considerations of elegant form so often that I couldn't begin to imagine it. Every single line of text, for instance, is characterized by its spacing — how wide the blanks between words are. I can clearly see the spacing as I type on my screen, and I rewrite and rewrite in order to make sure that no line is too tightly or too loosely spaced. In the course of such rewritings — here extracting a word, there using a shorter or a longer one, elsewhere inserting a word where none was — words and phrases that I would otherwise not have thought of pop to mind, suggesting ideas I would not have thought of, and those ideas suggest unexpected paragraphs, and those paragraphs are in turn linked to other ones, and so on...

I know this sounds quite nutty, but it is me to the core. This is my style at its most pure, and, I must say, at its most joyous. Paradoxical though it surely sounds, I feel at my freest, my most exuberant, and my most creative when operating under a set of heavy self-imposed constraints. I suspect that the welcoming of constraints is, at bottom, the deepest secret of creativity — and that, of course, is why poetry, built on a foundation of constraints, is so central to this book. Translation, too, is a dense fabric of constraints — and thus, needless to say, the merging of translation with poetry gives rise to such a rich mesh of interlocking constraints that the mind goes a bit berserk in a mixture of frustration and delight.

I'll relate just one example of the strangely twisty effects of my many self-imposed constraints. Early on, I decided, just for the fun of it, to begin each chapter with a bit of a flourish — a few large letters that gradually would shrink down to the size of the normal text. I soon realized that I had to avoid descenders in those first few letters — in other words, no "g", no "y", and so forth — in order to prevent collisions with letters just below. Well, this tiny constraint had quite a big effect in the case of Chapter 2.

An early draft of that chapter started out with a word that had a letter with a descender in it, and my search for a way to reword that first sentence to get rid of the lone descender led to a totally unexpected, unplanned style for that paragraph, which set a distinct opening tone for the chapter, which led to a curiously assonant three-word section head, which then suggested to me the idea of repeating that three-word pattern for all the section heads in that chapter, and then the various section heads that I created in the appealing mold of that pattern wound up exerting a considerable influence on what I actually said in the sections that they headed. Thus the trivial avoidance of one descender in the first five letters had a major impact on the ideas expressed in that chapter. Though this may seem bizarre, it is in fact absolutely typical. It is one of the more easily explained examples, but it is not exceptional.

With Such Warm Thanks to So Many

If I try to figure out where in the world this unexpected book came from, I wind up zeroing in on several events, but perhaps the key trigger of them all was the appearance, in early 1986, of Vikram Seth's lyrical novel in verse, *The Golden Gate*. It was the breathtaking experience of reading that book that caused the decades-old scales to drop from my eyes concerning poetry. All at once I realized I was and had always been a lover, not a hater, of poetry. And once my mind was open to this marvelous new old world, it was not too long before my involvement switched from passive to active.

It was my mother who, of course knowing me better than I knew myself, gave me *The Golden Gate,* while saying to me, "I have a feeling this is your kind of book." And it was also she who instilled my love for language in general, for French in particular, and for the charms of poetry.

My sister Laura played word games and language games with me when we were children, and we constantly enriched each other's sense of music throughout our teen-age years. Those indelible experiences shaped my sense of what true artistry is.

Peter, Steve, and Brian Jones were constant companions as I grew up at Stanford, and they were among those who taught me how to play with words and symbols. The countless "jolly evenings" at their house in which we entertained each other with higher and higher sillinesses are among the most joyful memories of my life — and they had lasting repercussions, too.

The chance to learn French well was, first and foremost, due to my parents' decision to go to Geneva in 1958–59. Although it was not on their agenda that that year would turn their boy into a languages fanatic, I know they were pleased, and thereafter did their utmost to support his passion.

But there were other people who helped catalyze my love for and mastery of French, such as my first French teachers — good old Mr. Whitehead, who even when speaking French was clearly from Georgia, and his young assistant Miss Vreños, whose lovely and precise accent enchanted me. In Geneva, I picked up so much French from my neighbor Roger Stauffer, my lifelong friend Cyril Erb, our live-in caretaker Nicole Montagne (now Howat), and several teachers at the École Internationale — Mme. Wendt, M. Adereth, and M. Stock. Once back in California, I continued to learn French under the tutelage of Mlle. June Sanders, who instilled in me some glimmerings of French history and more importantly, a deep love for *Cyrano de Bergerac* and *Gigi* — the French version, I mean. And to round out this list, I wish I could remember the name of my old French Lit professor at Stanford, but I cannot. Still, I remember him with fondness.

Before this book was even a gleam in my eye, there was a swirling tempest of translation activity that served as its eventual source, and at the eye of that intellectual hurricane were three very close friends, all of them with stellar linguistic gifts: Robert French, Melanie Mitchell, and David Moser. Without this fantastic trio, nothing would have happened at all.

After Bob, Melanie, and David, there came scores of people who at my behest translated the poem. Many are recognized in these pages, and with gratitude, but unfortunately, more are not; in compensation, all I can do is thank them here for their involvement in the project. Each one enriched my vision of the deep humanity that lies behind true translation.

Lectures in many cities helped pave the way for this book, and a few of my hosts — Valentino Braitenberg, Inga Hosp, Toon Witkam, Denis Baggi, Pino Longo, and Amos Carpenter — played key catalytic roles. Through my lectures I met Fabio Naj, Meg McIntyre, Ronnie Apter, and Jim Kates, each of whom introduced me to a sparkling work of literature of which I was unaware. I would also like to thank Hans Zeisel, who, never having met me, sent me a book with which he intuitively felt I would resonate. I did.

Throughout my last eight years at Indiana University, Helga Keller has played such a central role as my research center's administrative assistant that her contribution to my work environment is immeasurable, but on top of that, her personal devotion to me and my family has consistently been truly "ABCD" (above and beyond the call of duty). She has done amazing things to help bring this book into existence with a maximum of speed and a minimum of difficulty for me. Excellent friend, *grazie,* Helga!

In Joy and in Sorrow ◆ ◆ ◆ *xxi*

During my Italian sabbatical year's nightmarish unwinding in 1994, many loving people helped save Carol's and my children, and also me, from the worst ravages of the deep trauma we were undergoing. In Trento and nearby, there were Raffaella Bertagnolli, Heidi Zanella, Lucia dell'Eva, Mariangela Minati, Silvia De Paulis, Carmen Bertò, Oliviero and Lidy Stock, Achille Varzi and Freddie Oursin, Lucia and Pino Costa, Gary McGraw and Amy Barley, Jim Marshall, John Rehling, Sandro and Hannelore Simeoni, Sandra Magri, Emma Cristellòn, Elisabetta de Danieli, Roberto Dallacosta, Luisa and Benedetto Scimemi, Giovanni Sambin, Margareta Braitenberg and Paolo Bozzi, Inga Hosp, Pierluigi Novi Inverardi and Rita Rizzi, Tullio Grazioli — and, in a virtual but crucial manner, Kathy Wyss.

Caring friends who came from afar or who had us come and visit them were David Moser, Karl and Carla Leidlmair, Charles Brenner, Francisco Claro, Peter Smith, Don Byrd and Susan Schneider, Colleen Barton and Larry Tesler, Oliver Gugelot and Anita Valance, Karen Silverstein and Greg Huber, Cyril Erb and Naïma Lakhedar-Fouatih, Yvonne Lawaczeck-Seifert, Adelina and Egon von Fürstenberg, and Alejandro López.

My fears concerning our return to Bloomington were allayed by the benevolent radiance emanated by Monica's teachers Marilyn Stone and Catherine Hess at Sunshine Montessori and Danny's teacher Mike Love at Rogers Elementary — a trio I call "Sunshine and Love". Their warmth was enhanced by the devoted concern of Enrico Predazzi and Cristiana Peroni, Cindy and Steve Howard, Inga Karliner, Marina Eskina, Loveness Schafer, Giulia Ramigni, Tita Bonato, Sue Wunder, Lori Hubbard Welsh, Mary and Dan Friedman, the Steigerwald family, the Favinger family, Mike and Sally Dunn, Monica Mattinzoli, Edoardo and Mary Lebano, Wang Pei and Helen Sun, Emily Eells, Christiane Keller, Howard Keller, and Krissie Kryder.

Of course, my mother Nancy, my sister Laura and her family — Len, Nathaniel, Jeremy — in California, and Carol's parents, Murl and Millie Brush of Plainfield, Indiana, were always there for me and the children.

The spark that lit the fire that became this book was an invitation from Gene Woolf to speak in Cedar City, Utah, in the spring of 1995. In writing it, I have depended from start to finish on the power, flexibility, and intelligent design of FullWrite 2, which are due in large part to my friend Roy Leban. I have received caring and sensitive feedback on the text from David Moser, Ann Trail Gaponoff, Emily Eells, Jim Marshall, Vicky Grossack Stachowski, Helga Keller, and my mother. Support from Indiana University has been unflagging, especially from Dean Morton Lowengrub. The passage from the original small "Rhapsody" to the far larger "Ton beau" was smoothed by my friends at Basic Books: first, Kermit Hummel and Chris Korintus, and later, John Donatich, Zoë Pagnamenta, Rick Pracher, and Chris Goff. Finally, Frank Holmes turned my telephonic hints into a stunningly beautiful painting for the book's cover, and a lovely bookmark.

The deepest meaning in my life comes, without doubt, from my two little devilish angels, my *bambini birichini*, Danny and Monica, whose shining faces float before my eyes as always they did before their mother's beautiful eyes. Danny and Monica's wit and dash enrich and sustain my spirit as we grow together. In memory of their Mommy, I dedicate this book to them.

In Joy…

I have turned into a virtual hermit over the past several months, but my seclusion has been periodically broken, for short intervals, by three types of special rituals. One has been my nearly daily merry gobblin' of a Wendy's Spicy Chicken sandwich, always ordered with lettuce, tomato, and extra onions (but no mayonnaise!), and a kid-size pink lemonade. It may not be great for my cholesterol, but it sure tastes good!

Ice-skating on weekends with the kids has been one way for me to get some distance from my obsession. I've savored learning to do 3-turns and mohawks, crossovers and edges, even tackling the waltz jump. Not only is it a beautiful feeling to do such graceful things, it also makes me feel as if this old dog can still learn some new tricks. And it has sentimental meaning as well, since it was Carol who in early 1993 launched our family on an ice-skating kick, signing both herself and four-year-old Danny up for lessons.

My other main ritual has been running, which, although a lifetime habit, has intensified this past summer and fall. Runs seem to provide me with a deeply needed perspective on all the verbal churnings on which I spend 95 percent of my mental energy these days. Quite simply, *ça m'fait quelque chose*, or, as my Dad in his last years used to say, "This is like livin'!"

I realize that although what I am going through seems very mundane now, it will not seem that way at all when, years in the future, I look back, and I have therefore taken many photographs of my study at various stages of this book's evolution, showing a hopeless clutter of toppled and tilting piles of books and papers all over the floor of my study, capturing the crazy flavor of certain key moments in the book's genesis. One of the most special of those moments was the October Saturday that I chose to dedicate to writing the book's Conclusion — a Saturday that fell, not by chance, eleven years to the day from the October Saturday on which Carol Brush and I exchanged vows and rings in the Moveable Feast in Ann Arbor.

…and in Sorrow

The summer when I was twenty-two years old and struggling mightily to make myself into a decent pianist, I tackled Chopin's third Impromptu in G-flat major, a piece I considered so sublime that some ineradicable little superstitious relic of a voice inside me kept on telling me, "You'll never learn this piece — it's too beautiful. You'll get run over by a bus before you finish learning it." And yet somehow, miraculously, I didn't get run over by any bus, and by the end of the summer, I eventually came to be able to play it, and it was as beautiful as I had hoped.

That same summer, like so many summers and winters before, I was longing for romance, something that seemed always to elude me; and again, inside me, some fatalistic voice said, "She'll never come along. You'll never find her. You'll never get married." And in fact, this voice was closer to being right. It took far, far longer. Although there were a few sad and near misses along the way, it took another fifteen hellish, love-bleak years before I finally found the romance I had been hoping for — but long or short, I finally did find her, I finally did marry her, we finally did establish a little loving family of four. Like most couples, Carol and I slowly had to adjust to the reality of each other, and there were some tough times in our first years. But we loved each other deeply and worked things out, and in the end it was as beautiful as we both had hoped. To use a haunting phrase of Carol's own, what we had was "once in a blue, blue moon".

And in a way, so it has been with this book. As I have been coming closer and closer to finishing it, a nasty little inner voice in me has been saying, "You'll never finish this book. You'll get run over by a bus before it's done." And yet somehow, miraculously, I finally *have* finished this book. I made it without being run over by a bus; Carol, though, did not. In December of 1993, hit from out of left field by a strange and eerie malady with the disgusting name of *glioblastoma multiforme,* she died, vanishing from our midst almost as suddenly as if she had in fact been hit by a bus, with so much of life still left in her and before her. So much still to give, so many joys still to taste, all cut short by some cell gone wrong. Life is so very unfair.

Carol had often voiced the hope that I would write another sprawling book encompassing my many interests, and I finally did it. It didn't happen the way you wanted it, Carol, but I did my level best to create this book in a way that you would have loved and that would honor your memory. How I wish you could have savored its creation with me, for you were there the whole time these ideas were born and grew. You are so much of all this.

To you, Carol, *ma mignonne,* from me, Doug, *ton beau. Cin-cin.*

Hôtel Terminus,
Cahors en Quercy,
23 novembre, 1996.

● *Chapter 1* ●

The Life in Rhymes
of Clément Marot

●

Precisely one-half a millenium ago — and I mean what I say when I say it's precise — on the twenty-third day of the next-to-last month of the year fourteen hundred fourscore-and-sixteen (a tip of my hat to the Gauls' counting scheme), in the humble French town of Cahors en Quercy, some sixty-odd miles to the north of Toulouse, was born a bright boy christened Clément Marot, the son of an auto-taught poet named Jean and a lady whose life's but a question mark; our focus thus shifts from his folks to their lad.

Although his old man would have had him do law, Clément had a penchant for writing and words, and thus in his teens he displayed his great gift, presenting his poems to nobles and kings, in the hopes he'd appeal to some fine *protecteur*. King François the First, around fifteen nineteen, impressed by the gifts of the *fils* of the *père*, awarded the poet to Marguerite d'Angoulême, a duchess with whom he remained seven years. A bit before Easter, fifteen twenty-six, smack-dab in the ritual fasting of Lent, Clément found himself in the clink (as they say), for having partaken of bacon and ham, a definite no-no in that day and age. It wasn't at all a sweet jam to be in, but the lucky young stiff was released in two months, and soon had a break — meeting Anne d'Alençon, who, noble and kind, warmly welcomed him in. What's more, Anne became Marot's *dame d'alliance,* inspiring his numerous poems of love, and in dalliance they dallied a decade, *sans* sin.

Just a year after having this brush with the law, the irreverent poet was jailed once again, this time for the crime of abetting a friend — some poor ne'er-do-well who had fled from his cell — in dodging the dogged pursuit of *gens d'armes.* It took but a month till, by royal decree, Marot was released; once again he was free.

At age thirty-three, give or take a few months, Marot took to wife someone shrouded in fog, a woman of whom we know nothing today, except that she bore him a girl and a boy, of whom just as sadly too little is known, except that the boy bore the name of "Michel", while the girl gave herself to her God as His spouse (the habit of none too few maids in those days). Marot got relinked at this point with his King, relinquishing stress for a few pleasant years. But then one fine spring — 'twas fifteen thirty-two — our impenitent poet, at Lent, rewolfed pig, so again he was jailed, yet again soon released, this time on request of *la reine Marguerite* — not the duchess he'd served, but the Queen of Navarre (today it's in Spain, but Navarre was then French).

Toward the end of that summer Marot scored a hit, with *L'Adolescence Clémentine* taking off. This life of a poet ("Clément as a Teen") was printed and printed, and printed yet more — twenty-four or -five printings, in merely six years. If we all did so poorly, not a soul would be poor!

In the following year there appeared, overdue, a volume of verses by François Villon — the greatest, some say, of the early French bards. This tome was a homage by Clément Marot, compiled with respect for his forebear Villon, who by sixty-some years antedated Marot, and survived till the ripe age of — well, thirty-two.

Between these two poets the contrast is sharp. The verse of Villon exudes acid and bite (Villon, like Marot, was no stranger to stir, and barely escaped being hanged once or twice). Marot's verse, by contrast, is light, spiked with *joie*; it's humble and charming and filled with wordplay. Phonetic regroupings are common as day (for instance, *lave oye* and *la voie* and *l'avoie*). Some poems' main feature is short, pithy lines (in the most extreme case, just two syllables long), while others acrostically spell out some name; and then there are numerous mentions of self (both knockings and boastings, to balance the score). Here and there he takes pokes at deflate-worthy folks, and he now and then pens some erotic refrains. For example, a pair of cute pæans to breasts (in old French, *les tétins*): first *Du beau,* then *Du layd* ("An Ode to the Breaste That Is Nyce", one might say, as well as "An Ode to the Breaste Not So Nyce").

There's also this gem: *Des cinq poinctz en amours,* a listing of five lover's tips for a girl — in fact, Clément's friend, just a thing of fifteen — explicitly telling her of the first four (flitting eyes; flirting words; brushing lips; skin caressed), and of course the kind poet explains, toward the end, that should his young charge wish to learn of the rest, she's bid a warm welcome to visit his room, where he'll gladly disrobe and dispense, quite for free, a lesson in love to the soon-defloweree.

As fifteen thirty-four was just opening its door, with deep drifts on the ground giving grounds to stay in, Marot proudly proffered a version in French of the Latin of Ovid — *La Métamorphose* (of course it was verse, for he seldom wrote prose); putting Ovid in French was his gift to his King. Thus poetry translation was quite Clément's thing.

That October took place the *affaire des placards,* a nationwide poster campaign by some priest, to stir up the plebs against Luther and Rome, the upshot of which was that many were jailed, including Marot, who was held but released in the month of November that year in Bordeaux. Clément, seeking calm in a storm, made his way to the home of his friend Marguerite de Navarre, who, those turbulent days, gave him shelter and balm. However, the New Year, its very first month, all over the land there was posted a list of people whose goods were condemned to be dumped, with the listees themselves to be exiled and bumped. The mellifluous name of one Clément Marot was printed no lower than sixth on this sheet.

And thus, on advice of *la reine Marguerite,* he took wing and flew off toward the south — 'taly ho! And lo, in the valley of Po did he stop. His first hop: Ferrara, so lovely, so green. Then he bounced toward the north, toward the east, toward the sea, and dropped in on Venice, O dream most serene. After spending some moons by that magic lagoon, our poet set off on a trek to the west, his sights on *Genève,* where the Arve meets the Rhône. And after two years, he'd looped back to *douce France,* where, having recanted his errors of yore, he seems to have gotten the pardon he craved. Thereafter, Marot moved about without fear, and even was *fêted* again by his King.

As before, Marguerite de Navarre played his host, and in thanks, Marot quilled several poems for her; one ditty, moreover, he wrote to her daughter, a sweet little girl, Jeanne d'Albret de Navarre. (This ditty returns as our tale unwinds.) These years gave him freedom to write, so he wrote, penning many a poem and making a name. But then in fifteen forty-two came a purge, a huge sudden surge drowning Lutherans like ants, so Marot once again had to clear out of France; to Geneva he crossed, and thence off to Savoy; from there, fled to Piedmont (Italian today — but back in those days, no less French than Marseille).

In Torino (then Turin) the bard breathed his last, nearly forty-eight years after breathing his first; and there in a church were interred his remains. On his gravestone, engraved — *le tombeau de Marot* — by his friend Lyon Jamet, a true friend *à jamais,* was a eulogy generous yet not too unfair: *C'est Marot, des François le Virgile et l'Homère* ("He's the Virgil and Homer belonging to France"). The allusion to Virgil is not just a game, but hints at more meaning since Virgil's full name — namely, "Publius Vergilius Maro" — names *his* name. To be sure, this coincidence wasn't ignored when poems were penned by Marot and his horde.

The Life in Rhymes of Clément Marot ♦♦♦ 3

The site of the grave of the poet I praise has been lost, sad to say, with the passage of time. If one visits the church where the books claim he lies, all the leads peter out; it's a cruel surprise. In a way, though, this means that he rests in our minds; "C. M." names a soul, not some pile of dry bones. We can think of a church and imagine stain'd glass, or some gray stone with flowers on a hill green with grass. Whatever we think, we're remembering him well, but the best is reliving his lines' oft-wry tones.

In the four-and-a-half centuries now passed since his death, Marot's carved a niche — although small, quite secure — in the vast pantheon of French literature. *Le tome beau de Marot* — the great book of our bard — has respect far and wide; though he's dead, he's not died. *Mort n'y mord,* Marot's motto: "Death, dull are thy fangs." The fellow (it can't be denied) had *toupet* — he had marrow and pluck, plus some luck of the dice. Thus he garnered nice blurbs from the likes of Boileau («*Il trouva pour rimer des chemins tout nouveaux*» — "He opened up pathways of rhyme no one knew"), and Ronsard, Du Bellay, La Fontaine, La Bruyère. Had Marot been a restaurant, the Guide Michelin would have praised, with its stars, his cuisine, there's no doubt. *Chez Clément* might have wound up with fewer than three, but certainly one, and I'd hope at least two.

Perhaps too spontaneous, too bouncy, too cute to have soared to the heights of Malherbe or Voltaire, the lines by Marot nonetheless left their mark. Victor Hugo himself, as one sees in *Les Djinns,* even more in his ode *Le pas d'armes du roi Jean,* was profoundly impressed by Marot's mini-rhymes. *Le ton beau de Marot* — the graced tone of Clément — belongs to the ages, transcending its times.

The tribute that might have meant most to Marot was a stanza once scribed by the bard Charleval, and whose closing few lines have a quite special charm:

> *D'autres sont fols,*
> > *de leur marotte,*
> *Moi, je le suis*
> > *de mon Marot.*

Imported with license, they say roughly this: "Some others have pets / about which they crow, / But me, I go wild / about my Marot." It's simple, it's sweet, and it's right to the point. What more could one hope for, in life's afterglow?

●

Poems I:

~ Original and Literal ~

*

In October of the year 1537, Jeanne d'Albret de Navarre, perhaps seven or eight years old, had fallen ill and had to stay in bed, most likely under quarantine, for some weeks. Truly devoted to his sick little friend, Clément Marot wrote her an avuncular get-well letter in the form of a cute and catchy poem, titling it "A une Damoyselle malade" — "To a Sick Damsel", one might phrase it in English, or "To an Ailing Maiden". Borrowing its first line, I myself usually just call it by the nickname "Ma Mignonne". Though minuscule, this is a work that instantly enchants, yet also a work whose charm does not fade with time.

Considering that "Ma Mignonne" was written in a French spoken almost five hundred years ago, it is remarkably transparent for speakers of contemporary French, although a few words here or there might be a bit confusing today, such as *mander,* a verb that still exists but no longer means "to command", as it does here, and the word *doint,* an archaic form of the verb *donner* ("to give").

The brilliant *éclat* and the lively *élan* of this cigar-shaped poem derive, most of all, from its tight rhyming pattern rather than from any elaborate meshes of metaphor or multi-layered webs of ambiguity. But the rhyming pattern does not stand alone; indeed, it cannot be separated from a number of other structural features, which, taken together, help one better to understand the poem's unique essence.

Therefore, for the benefit of would-be translators, I once compiled a short list of formal or "syntactic" properties of "Ma Mignonne", respect for which I felt would be crucial in any attempt to carry it over into another language. In posing the translation challenge to other people, I always supplied this list, obvious though its items were, because I did not want them to be overlooked. If someone *knowingly* chose to disrespect one or another of them, that would be all right — or at least far more justifiable, in my opinion, than doing so out of ignorance. Here, then, is my original list:

1. *The poem is 28 lines long.*
2. *Each line consists of three syllables.*
3. *Each line's main stress falls on its final syllable.*
4. *The poem is a string of rhyming couplets: AA, BB, CC,…*
5. *Midway, the tone changes from formal ("vous") to informal ("tu").*
6. *The poem's opening line is echoed precisely at the very bottom.*
7. *The poet puts his own name directly into his poem.*

Several months after drawing up this list, I was shocked to learn that there were yet other tight formal properties of "Ma Mignonne" that had eluded me, one of them extremely beautiful and yet quite subtle to spot, although after the fact it seems obvious. Can you spot it?

The short series of English renditions that constitute the remainder of Poems I is a tiny bouquet of attempts to convey to an anglophonic audience both the literal content and the structural intricacy of "Ma Mignonne". I must give, however, a caveat: My putting these versions at the very front of this book does not reflect the true chronology of my own explorations in translation. In point of fact, not any of the English versions found in Poems I was done at an early stage of the game. They were instead *a posteriori* exegetical exercises — afterthoughts stimulated by a certain degree of success in carrying out *non*literal translations. In short, the next few anglicizations were all fall bloomers, not spring flowers. Despite this violation of our story's chronology, I felt it would be of such utility to English-speaking readers to see a few "cribs" or "ponies" from the very outset that I just went ahead and stuck them in here.

A une Damoyselle malade

Clément Marot

Ma mignonne,
Je vous donne
Le bon jour ;
Le séjour
C'est prison.   5
Guérison
Recouvrez,
Puis ouvrez
Votre porte
Et qu'on sorte   10
Vitement,
Car Clément
Le vous mande.
Va, friande
De ta bouche,   15
Qui se couche
En danger
Pour manger
Confitures ;
Si tu dures   20
Trop malade,
Couleur fade
Tu prendras,
Et perdras
L'embonpoint.   25
Dieu te doint
Santé bonne,
Ma mignonne.

Facing this page is as bland, boring, and literal a translation of Marot's poem as could ever be imagined. In it, no attempt whatsoever has been made at rhyme, rhythm, or any other aspect of form. It is so weak that, I must say, I hesitate even to apply the term "translation" to it. Its sole *raison de naître* was to provide a "crib" — a clear line-by-line gloss of the poem — for people who speak little or no French, and also to clarify, for speakers of modern but not old French, a few obsolete terms.

Perhaps the only interesting structural aspect of this anglicization is the fact that by switching partway through from "you" to "thou", it respects Marot's curious transition from the formal *vous* to the informal *tu*. It seemed to me that this unlikely switchover carried a good deal of emotional meaning, and therefore I felt compelled to try to "do the same thing" in English, although English's "thou" is hardly "the same thing" as French's *tu*.

Executing a totally literal-minded carry-over of "Ma Mignonne" into English may seem a very mechanical and thus fairly trivial task. However, there are actually many — enormously many — hidden subtleties. As clear a dilemma as one might wish for is posed already by the opening line: *Ma mignonne.* How in the world to render this *literally* in English? *Ma* is clearly "my", but what to do with *mignonne*? It is an adjectival noun that means "cute" and also "sweet", and the fact that it is given in a feminine form (*mignonne* as opposed to *mignon*) tells you it is addressed to a girl or woman. But "My cute" sounds most awkward in English. On the other hand, is it so awkward as to render it unacceptable? How about "My sweet"? Less awkward than "My cute" yet still awkward, is it acceptable?

One problem is that neither of these options tells readers that the recipient is female. How about "My cute girl", then? The trouble with this is that it uses three English words to render two French words. Is it crucial for a literal translation to contain exactly the same number of words as the original? Why, or why not? If so, how about "Sweet girl"? Ah, but that's just got two syllables, where *Ma mignonne* has three. How about "Girlie mine"? Ah, but that reverses the word order. How about "My girlie"? Ah, but that's accented on the wrong syllable! If we're striving solely for literality, should we pay any attention to things like location of stress, number of syllables, or word order? Exactly what kinds of things are we supposed to pay attention to, and what kinds of things are we free to ignore?

Another seemingly simple challenge is posed by lines 2–3: *Je vous donne / Le bon jour.* This phrase could be variously rendered as "I give you the good day", "I give you the hello", "I wish you good day", "I wish you a good day", "I wish you good morning", "I greet you", "I bring you greetings" — and on and on I could go till I was blue in the face. What is the proper trade-off among accuracy, awkwardness, and so on to use in a "literal" translation?

Or consider the next two lines: *Le séjour / C'est prison.* These offer a translator many options, since, as we just saw, there are many different levels of literality, among them these: "The stay it's prison"; "The stay it is prison"; "The stay is prison"; "Your stay is prison"; "Your stay has been prison"; "Your stay has been a prison"; "Your stay's been a prison"; and so forth and so on. And mind you, all these variants take utterly for granted that "stay" is the proper way to render *séjour* and "prison" is the proper way to render *prison,* neither of which is by any means certain.

These opening five lines are certainly bad enough, but lines 14–17 are much rougher, being far more ambiguous and even somewhat vague to a native reader of French. The problem is the unclear referent of the relative pronoun *qui* ("that/who"): Does it refer to the sick girl herself (in which case it would be "who"), or just to her mouth (in which case it would be "that")? I was lucky enough to discover a neat trick in this case — I could sidestep the whole issue by using a present participle ("lying") instead of a relative clause. But of course this is a noticeable syntactic deviation from the original. You just can't win!

To a Sick Damsel

C. Marot/D. Hofstadter

My sweet,
I bid you
A good day;
The stay
Is prison.   *5*
Health
Recover,
Then open
Your door,
And go out   *10*
Quickly,
For Clément
Tells you to.
Go, indulger
Of thy mouth,   *15*
Lying abed
In danger,
Off to eat
Fruit preserves;
If thou stay'st   *20*
Too sick,
Pale shade
Thou wilt acquire,
And wilt lose
Thy plump form.   *25*
God grant thee
Good health,
My sweet.

Here we have another line-by-line gloss, but in this case I expended quite a bit more effort, with the goal of ensuring that each line consisted of exactly three syllables, with the accent always falling on the final syllable. Considerations of form were thus brought in much more explicitly than in the previous version, even though there, despite the fact that I was striving for nothing but the purest, most austere, least form-concerned type of literality, issues of form raised their little heads all over the place, like crowds of little mushroomlets merrily sprouting up in the most carefully tended of lawns.

I strongly suggest that you read this poem aloud — indeed, I suggest that you do so with *all* poetry in this book, whether translated or original (in fact, the difference between the two is not even clear, but that is a can of worms that we will delve into much further on…). If you indulge my imprecation and read "My Sweet Maid" aloud, you will find, not surprisingly, that it flows far more smoothly than did the preceding version, but of course there is still no rhyme at all. It is blank verse.

Note that in order to achieve a truly smooth flow, I sacrificed the constraint of literality just a mite here and there — for instance, in the choice of "total health" (line 6), "unlatch" (line 8), and "full speed" (line 11). Note also that a teeny bending of the norms of pronunciation was deemed allowable; specifically, there are at least two (and conceivably several) lines that, if this translation were read aloud as plain, ordinary prose, would definitely *not* be accented on their rightmost syllable (and I don't mean line 12, since the English name "Clement" can be stressed on its first or last syllable without norm-bending in either case). Did you catch any of these minuscule anomalies while reading "My Sweet Maid" aloud? Did they bother you at the time? Do they bother you now?

Another interesting matter is the handling of lines 20–21 (*Si tu dures / Trop malade*). The English solution is a consequence of recognizing what the adverb *trop,* in the original poet's mind, was *really* modifying, as opposed to what it *appears* to be modifying. In a truly mindless literal translation, "too" would have to modify "sick" and the word "long" would not enter the picture at all. But here, rather than opting for the mindless route, the translator, without much trouble, divined the poet's genuine intent and respected it — namely, Marot wanted to encourage his little friend Jeanne not to stay sick for *too long* a time. The idea of "staying too sick", after all, doesn't even make sense, for to be sick *at all* is by definition to be *too* sick. It's not as if there was some moderate or lowish level of being ill that the kindly poet was suggesting would be acceptable!

The most mundane understanding of health and illness leads one automatically to shift the adverb's syntactic allegiance when one renders the phrase in English. It takes no genius to do so! We shall find ourselves drawn back to this delicate point toward the end of the book, namely in Poems XV, where we will examine a few translations of "Ma Mignonne" that were carried out in what might be called an "utterly MT" fashion.

A final comment on this attempt… Even though, out of the seven constraints for would-be translators that I gave in the list facing the original "Ma Mignonne", this version respects all but the fourth, it still does not merit, for me, the label "translation", for *rhyme* is the heart and soul of the original poem. To leave out rhyme in a supposed translation of "Ma Mignonne", or of *any* rhyming poem, strikes me as not a whit nor a shred less daffy or bonkers than for a publisher to insist, for reasons of economy, on reproducing a color wheel in black and white in a text on painting, and then to claim that this does a perfectly adequate job of imparting a sense for hue, brightness, and saturation to students of art.

P.S. — The truly anomalous lines are 4 and 19 (naturally accented on "sick" and "fruit", respectively), and then, depending on speaker and whim, any of lines 6, 8, 14, 20, and 21.

My Sweet Maid

D. Hofstadter

My sweet maid,
You I wish
A good day;
Your sickbed
Is a jail.   5
Total health
Please regain,
Then unlatch
Your room's door,
And go out   10
With full speed,
For Clement
Does insist.
Go, gourmande,
Thou whose mouth   15
Lies abed
Under threat,
Off to eat
Fruit preserves;
If thou stay'st   20
Sick too long,
A pale shade
Wilt acquire,
And wilt lose
Thy round shape.   25
May God grant
Thee good health,
My sweet maid.

At first glance, this rather prickly-looking pastiche of words, slashes, brackets, and so forth may not seem to have any more legitimate claim to being a translation of Marot's poem than a page of erudite text describing Leonardo's brushwork in the Mona Lisa could be plausibly claimed to be a fair reproduction of the Mona Lisa itself. Nonetheless, although "My Sweet/Cute [One] (Feminine)" probably shows you a lot more than you expected ever to see in a translation, it strikes me as constituting a legitimate exploration — albeit a rather extreme one — in the art of literal translation; as such, it seemed to merit being called a "translation" in its own right. Indeed, this hodgepodge reminds me of modernistic buildings that shamelessly, or perhaps proudly, exhibit all of their plumbing, wiring, and other types of functional innards to the people who circulate within them; warts and all, they are still buildings.

Exactly where the boundary line between a set of annotations and a literal translation lies is not clear. But whatever one calls this rhymeless, rhythmless jumble of stuff, it may be of use to nonspeakers of French who want to get a deeper feel for the nature of the precise syntactic pathways and the less precise semantic halos of the words in the French original. If it does nothing else, "My Sweet/Cute [One] (Feminine)" reminds us again, but from a novel angle, of how hazy and how intangibly complex the notion of "literal" translation is.

As you progress through this book and encounter numerous poems in original and translated forms, sometimes isolated and sometimes side by side, it may be instructive to keep in mind a fantasy in which you are going to be the editor of a bilingual anthology of poetry, and are drawing together material for inclusion in it. The structure that you are shooting for is one in which each original poem is printed on a lefthand page, and facing it on a righthand page is an English translation — or rather, *the* English translation, in a certain sense.

Imagine that in the course of long years of spadework for your anthology, you have collected in your files, for each original poem, many different translations to pick among for its righthand page. Which of those many will you wind up selecting? What criteria will you use to rank one translation ahead of another? You might find some translation delightful or daring or graceful and yet despite its virtues still feel it is inappropriate for selection as "the" translation of the original poem. Would you ever feel free to tamper, ever so delicately and tastefully, with a near-perfect translation done by someone else, in order to make sure that the best possible translation gets onto the facing page? Why or why not? Thinking about such issues will surely carry you deep into the spirit of this book.

My Sweet/Cute [One] (Feminine)

D. Hofstadter

My sweet/cute [one] (feminine),
I [to] you (respectful) give/bid/convey
The good day (i.e., a hello, i.e., greetings).
The stay/sojourn/visit (i.e., quarantine)
[It] is prison.   5
Cure/recovery/healing (i.e., [good] health)
Recover (respectful imperative),
[And] then open (respectful imperative)
Your (respectful) door,
And [that one (i.e., you (respectful)) should] go out   10
Fast[ly]/quickly[ly]/rapidly[ly],
For/because Clement
It (i.e., thusly) [to] you (respectful) commands/orders.
Go (familiar imperative), fond-one/enjoyer/partaker
Of your (familiar) mouth,   15
Who/which herself/himself/itself beds (i.e., lies down)
In danger;
For/in-order-to eat
Jams/jellies/confectionery.
If you (familiar) last (i.e., stay/remain)   20
Too sick/ill,
[A] color pale/faded/dull
You (familiar) will take [on],
And [you (familiar)] will waste/lose
The plumpness/stoutness/portliness (i.e., well-fed look).   25
[May] God [to] you (familiar) give/grant
Health good,
My sweet/cute [one] (feminine).

"My Small Princess" (in which the stress should fall on "ess" and not on "prince") is a translation of the rhyme, in which the choice of line-breaks' placement has been handed from creator to a piece of mindless software — or in other words, abandoned to the winds of fate's caprice. The basic aim was that of stating just the content of the rhyme in standard prose that felt as simple and as flowing as could be, with special care devoted to the bringing-out of the avuncular perspective that the poet chose to take. "My Small Princess" sounds like a quite straightforward note dashed off with love by some male friend who deeply cares about the health of this small lass of noble birth.

The role of line-breaks having been subtracted out, this prose translation is freed up from the constraints of word-for-word fidelity; in recompense (and thus and hence), the local freedom that one gains shifts one's attention to more global, higher planes, and so the translator must try to figure out the motivations lurking in the poet's mind, which can be sensed between his lines. It was the quest for this new style of being faithful that gave rise to "ghostly pale" and "skin and bones", and also led to "Uncle Clement" (where the stress falls not on "ment" but just before it) as the phrase by which the poet flings himself into his verse. And that is that, for well or worse.

*   *   *

We embark on the saga of "Touchstones" — a pattern of words telegraphic, a list that was penned at the outset as a set of mere memory jogs. For those who would tackle the challenge to render the ditty in English, this chain of the keys to its message will reveal what mustn't be skipped. A keychain so tight's hardly slapdash; but rather, like all the creations lending grace to the pages herein, it came from a long search for phrases that capture the heart of the poem while charming the eye and the ear.

Now given the *vous/tu* transition inserted midstream by Marot, my first thought was "equipartition" — in other words, half of the themes on a line destined solely *pour vous,* with the other half solely *pour toi.* Well, no sooner a *fait accompli,* this pattern cried out for more oomph, which led to a set of gay couples (a noun with a noun every time), always tied by a dot-hatted comma and flanked by a dot on the floor. In a nutshell, I've told you of "Touchstones"; our embarked-upon saga's thus o'er.

*   *   *

And now, my dearest reader, I would pose to you the challenge of converting into English (better yet, your native tongue) "Ma Mignonne" by friend Marot. Let me give you my assurance that having read as far as this, all you'd need to know you know. As for you, a proper reader who from start to finish plows, you who'd never skip ahead nor ever itch to browse about (or hardly ever, shall we say?), you're as pure as pure can be and not polluted in the slightest by the sight of others' tries, for you've kept your eyes in check by holding fingers back from riffling through the oh-so-tempting pages of my book. Not one look!

Or even if you've sinned and now a teeny bit are tainted by a peek at what some other folks already generated, still my challenge stands withal: What would *you* do, O dear reader, to come up with not just *a,* but rather *the,* Anglicization of this swell, sweet, short, svelte well-wish by a chap who first saw daylight *dans le sein du beau Quercy,* near the old Pont Valentré whose stony towers and stately arches (six half-circles side by side) stand astride the bubbling Lot just as it's doubling back upon itself to yield a giant "U", there to cradle in its crook a little town once called "Divona" by a tribe once called "Cadourques"?

My Small Princess

D. Hofstadter

My small princess, I send you a warm hello. Your long stay in bed has been like a term in prison. Uncle Clement urges you to recuperate, and to get out of there soon. You've always loved sweets, so don't let being bed-ridden stop you from indulging — have some jam! And don't stay sick too long, because you'll get ghostly pale and start looking like skin and bones. God will surely bring you back to good health, my small princess.

Touchstones

D. Hofstadter

<u>*Vous*</u>*: Cuteness; hail. Quarantine; cure. Egress; speed. Clément; insistence.*
<u>*Tu*</u>*: Epicurism; threat. Appetite; jams. Pallor; gauntness. Prayer; cuteness.*

•

• *Chapter 2* •

For the Love of a Poem
from Days Long, Long Gone

•

Sixteen-year-old kid starts college, wonders what to take, riffles through course bulletin, eye gets snagged by French Lit course. Kid signs up, likes prof, hates text, doodles in class, resolves never to take French Lit again. All quarter long, kid gazes, badly smitten, at quiet dark-haired Italian-named girl who always sits in back of room. Once after class both go up to talk to prof, stand right by each other, she looks at him, and kid comes within a heartbeat of speaking to her — but just can't open mouth. Say what? She's too pretty… Nothing ventured, nothing gained. Faint heart ne'er won fair maiden. And then one day, literature anthology falls open and cute catchy poem jumps off page: "Ma Mignonne". Love at first sight.

No way in the world could that kid have ever dreamt of the giant effect that that sweet little poem — his consolation prize in the French Lit course — would have on his life, in days long, long ahead…

Intoxication, Memorization, Hibernation

So taken was I with "Ma Mignonne", so intoxicated by its miniature lines and its ultradensely packed-in rhymes, that I was unable to resist committing it to memory, where it stayed fully intact for twenty-five years and then some, and from which it was stochastically resuscitated, perhaps two or three times a decade for just a day or two, after which it would plunge back into deep dormancy for another few winters.

Resuscitation, Recaptivation, Reorientation

Sometime in the summer of 1987, there took place one of those haphazard mental resuscitations of "Ma Mignonne" (this was how I always thought of it in those days, having totally forgotten — if ever I'd known it — that the poem had an "official" title). As always, I found it captivating, and I recited it with delight to my wife Carol.

This time, though, the context in which "Ma Mignonne" bubbled up from the murky depths to the sunlit surface of my mind was quite different than ever before, since over the previous few years, I had been involved in the intensely stimulating experience of consulting in detail on the translation of my linguistically playful book *Gödel, Escher, Bach* into a number of foreign languages — French above all, but also Spanish, German, Dutch, Italian, Chinese, and others.

As a result of all of these mind-opening, head-spinning involvements, I was steeped in freshly-minted personal opinions about how to preserve linguistic sparkle and structural intricacy while also preserving content in translation, and as a consequence I suddenly saw "Ma Mignonne" in a completely new light: as the potential object of a translation effort. In retrospect, I find it curious, even remarkable, that this thought had never occurred to me in the preceding twenty-six years — but it hadn't.

Aggravation, Perseveration, Consummation

I remember lying in bed in the dark one night working on the first few lines, trying to coax them gracefully into my native tongue, and soon realizing to my dismay that with just a handful of what seemed to be very natural, almost irresistible word choices, I had landed myself in a box canyon with no way out. Stuck after just seven or eight little lines. Dead in the water. Discouraged, I gave up, feeling the task was intrinsically impossible. The lines were just a trace too short, the fabric was just a tad too tight, the warp and the woof were just woven together too well.

I suppose it was inevitable, given my constellation of active interests in those days, that the challenge would sooner or later pop back into my mind and regain my attention. As it happens, it took but a month or two until "Ma Mignonne" reasserted itself, and I, like an optimistic boxer re-entering the ring after being KO'd a few weeks earlier, was eager to give it a fresh new try. This time around, I must have been in a slightly more flexible frame of mind, for I persevered and somehow punched my way through the first eight lines, then fifteen, twenty, and with a last burst of effort, got all the way to the bottom. I was delighted, even ecstatic, and very proud of my little achievement — "My Sweet Dear" — which opens Poems II.

Exhilaration, Reduplication, Communication

Though I had no inkling at the time, the challenge I'd just met would soon wind up provoking me into tackling it again, and these first droplets would trigger first a cascade and then an unstoppable torrent of intellectual activity that would consume me and many friends and acquaintances for months, even years, to come. This book grew in a roundabout fashion out of that intellectually tumultuous, exciting period in my life, which also coincided with Carol's first pregnancy, thus making it doubly exhilarating and forever precious in memory. Scattered through the pages that follow, I present a generous sampling of the results I obtained when I posed the identical translation challenge to many talented and original people.

I wrote the challenge up in a very carefully-worded letter in late September of 1987, and sent copies out to fifty, perhaps even a hundred, friends scattered around the globe. Into each envelope I stuffed a list of seven formal properties of the poem (see the commentary facing Marot's original French in Poems I), as well as two literal translations into English (also found in Poems I) — the totally flat "To a Sick Damsel" and the slightly less flat "My Sweet Maid".

My reason for including this supplementary material was that I knew that some of the letter's recipients would have a bit of trouble with the original French poem, yet I felt sure that if they had access to its literal meaning and understood its form quite clearly, they would be capable of doing wonderful things with it in their own native languages. Thus to get the raw meaning across, I chose these two bland versions, since on the one hand, both of them stick very close, on a line-by-line level, to the text of the original, yet on the other hand, neither of them comes anywhere close to being an ideal solution to the challenge. To my mind, both were simply *glosses* that hopefully conveyed meaning without conveying any bias at all as to what might constitute the "proper" approach to making a deep, literary translation. As for the list of seven formal properties, I intended it merely to serve as a set of indications, and by no means as a prescription for what must be preserved in translation. Indeed, I did my best to convey a very open-minded attitude in my letter, as you can see:

> The challenge for translators is to construct what they consider an *artistic equivalent* of Marot's poem in their own native language. Obviously, what you consider this to mean depends on all sorts of idiosyncratic facts about you, and on how heavily you weight innumerable small and large aspects of this poem, unconsciously as well as consciously. My purpose in providing you with the two English-language versions is simply to make sure that you have a crystal-clear understanding of the basic *meaning* of Marot's lines; I hope that, aside from that, these literal versions do not exert much of an influence on how you choose to render the original in your own native language.
>
> For instance, I did not mean to imply that an "unslippable" (*i.e.,* absolutely immutable) aspect of the poem is the "trisyllabicity" of its lines, or their stress pattern — nor did I mean to imply that all worthy translations should consist of rhyming couplets, nor indeed that

they should rhyme at all. Such considerations will surely enter into every translator's mind, but each one will be just one among a large number of mutually vying pressures, the relative strengths of which must be judged subjectively. For some people, the meaning is sacrosanct; for others, it is locally slippable but overall very important; and for yet others, meaning at all levels and on all scales is something that can be freely toyed with. Different people, or the same person in different moods, will make different decisions about what properties of the original are expendable and what ones must be preserved.

Incidentally, I believe that this task, like many (though not all) translation tasks, while not demanding native-level mastery of the *source* language, definitely does demand it in the *target* language: the constraints are so strong that, in attempting to satisfy them, translators will necessarily be pushed to the very fringes of their native language along numerous dimensions (*e.g.*, vocabulary, syntax, idioms, pronunciation, and intuitive understandings of flavor); a non-native speaker will almost certainly be so restricted that there simply won't be enough room to maneuver.

Aside from the pure fun of this game, what I am interested in is seeing how other people choose to interpret this challenge: What constraints do they impose on themselves? Having consciously imposed such contraints, how tightly do they actually obey them? What aspects of Marot's poem seem most clearly preserved in a given translation, and what aspects are most clearly lost? What is the overall stylistic effect resulting from a given compromise of pressures? How do early drafts compare with the final product? How did various slippages force other slippages to take place? Where were the hardest sticking-points? How were they overcome? What did it take for them to be overcome? Were there clear "breakthroughs" following long periods of being stuck? What brought about such breakthroughs?

In the case of those people (such as myself) who feel drawn to produce more than one translation, then there are further interesting issues: When you make different translations, do you vary your self-imposed constraints, to explore the possibilities afforded (and suggested) by different compromises? What tone results when you adopt a specific trade-off of pressures? Does a recognizable style permeate all your translations, revealing your authorship *despite* the various tones you adopt as a consequence of different trade-offs? How can one characterize or recognize that very abstract style?

The creation of "literal" translations, although at first blush much less exciting than the creation of "artistic" ones, actually poses some of the most fascinating challenges. Just how literal is literal? The enclosed translations at two levels of literality reveal the effects of different trade-offs even in this limited sphere — and of course they are by no means the full story. I myself have done five "literal" translations, so far, and so has Melanie Mitchell, in addition to the more "artistic" contributions we have both made.

The flip side of this coin is the question "Just how artistic is artistic?" What liberties do people permit themselves in the extreme? What are the farthest-out translations that people still consider to be worthy of the name? At what point does the phrase "translation of X" become invalid, and "inspired by X" take over? When does "artistic" really mean "lazy" or "sloppy"?

I look forward with great interest to seeing this poem rendered in languages other than English and French. Every language has its own natural meters and rhyme schemes, and so some languages will "welcome" the external form of Marot's poem more gracefully than others. I will be fascinated, for example, to see what Italian translators do with it, since it seems to me that Italian does not lend itself easily to the construction of three-syllable lines accented on the final syllable; there is thus likely to be an interesting slippage of some sort.

I must say, I have really had a ball translating "Ma Mignonne" and thinking about these issues. Once I had done one translation, thus proving to myself that it was feasible, somehow I was able to do others with much greater ease than I did my first one. I am fascinated by this effect, and don't fully understand it.

The dimensions of translation that this mini-problem reveals are numerous, and in a strong sense, I believe that the intellectual issues of translation are more clearly revealed in this challenge and its various solutions than in bigger, more formidable challenges. One of my theme songs is that deep issues emerge most clearly, and are therefore best studied, in well-chosen microcosms. I hope you find translating Clément Marot's little gem as fascinating and delightful as I have.

Joyeuse traduction !

Proliferation, Concentration, Condensation

In rereading this old letter after some years had passed, I was impressed by the way it anticipated so many issues that recur and dance together throughout this book, like themes in a sprawling counterpoint: content versus form, constraints, trade-offs, slippability, strictness and laxness, the creative process, drafts, revisions, breakthroughs, abstract style, varieties of literality, translation pushed to its limits, effects of the target language, the mystery of how one success builds on another...

If I were going to recommend to my 1987-vintage pre-incarnation just one chapter of this book to read, I would probably choose Chapter 13 (it would be a little too quirky to propose Chapter 2). The reason I would suggest Chapter 13, particularly its latter half, is that it addresses so many of the questions raised in the letter about the nature of the creative process. What would also please my old self — that is to say, my young self — is that Chapter 13's discussion is a very tight outgrowth of the letter I/he sent out. Another reason I'd select Chapter 13 for his consumption is that it devotes a few pages to the "rickety bridge" effect, which is my name for the curious phenomenon he described, in which a first spanning of a translation chasm, however modest, somehow facilitates further spannings of greater strength, substance, and subtlety. I know he would enjoy that chapter.

My 1987 letter bore wonderful fruit. I was surprised by who replied and who did not, by the languages represented and unrepresented, by old friends who came out of the woodwork, by unknown friends of friends to whom the letter was passed (and who sometimes became new friends), and most of all by the delightful collective fantasy that flowered in many minds in many lands, all inspired by an elegant, diminutive 450-year-old poem by a French poet of whom almost none of them had ever heard before.

For the first two years after the letter was sent out, replies trickled in to me, and I engaged in a lively correspondence with all sorts of people about the poem. I also taught seminars at the University of Michigan and Indiana University in which I asked my students to translate "Ma Mignonne", and got back some amazing results. But slowly, things started winding down, and out of the enormous swirl of material that had converged on me and become surely the world's densest concentration of anglicized Maroticity, I started filtering and condensing, choosing what I considered to be the most imaginative and the most polished responses to the challenge.

Oration, Publication, Variation

One day I realized that the results of my filtering process might be usable as the basis for an unusual lecture on translation and creativity. To this end, I photocopied many of my favorite translations of "Ma Mignonne" onto transparencies and sorted them according to translator, chronology, and issues raised. Thus came into being a big heavy folder that I lugged around with me to various places where I presented these ideas. Some of the cities where I lugged my packet, gave my talk, and had fine interactions with my audience are New York, Bloomington, Brighton, Bolzano, Lund, Utrecht, Stanford, Eugene, Salem, Ascona, Grenoble, Trieste, Dublin, Indianapolis, Keystone, Ottawa, East Lansing, Chicago, and Trento. It occasionally happened that in the aftermath of such a lecture, I would receive a letter from some total stranger who had been inspired to tackle the "Ma Mignonne" challenge in some novel way, or who clued me in to the existence of some related translation issue of which I would otherwise never have heard, and thus did my already-swollen files grow ever thicker.

It often crossed my mind that this lecture, essentially just a series of highly diverse translations of "Ma Mignonne" with spicy but fairly short commentaries, might make a cute little book. I figured that sooner or later I would take a free month or two and put it together, but I was waiting for the right moment. Years passed, though, without that "right moment" ever arriving. Then one day in early 1995, I got a warm letter from Gene Woolf, an old friend in Cedar City, Utah, asking me if I would consider giving the 1995 Grace A. Tanner Lecture at Southern Utah University, which — since I had given one once before, in 1982 — I knew also entailed preparing a writeup of the lecture for publication as an elegant little hardbound volume available just through Southern Utah University. I thought to myself, "Aha — the moment has arrived!", and gladly accepted Gene's invitation.

The lecture, by tradition always in April, went just fine, and Gene told me to take my time in writing it up, but I plunged into it with alacrity, celerity, vim, vigor, and vitality, and by July had several short chapters filled with commentaries on the translations I had selected, as well as a few hopefully worthwhile digressions on other aspects of translation. I structured the book as a series of chapters with all the poems coming in one long swoop at the very end, an elegant peacock's tail of a final flourish.

By summer's close I figured the book was nearly done, but just needed a bit of polishing. Unfortunately, though, the polishing turned out to be far more difficult than I had imagined, and I started running into all sorts of confusing problems of organization. I also found myself cringing at the style of the prose in my chapters. By November, I was really bogged down. Gene, always very courteous and easy-going, was putting the gentlest of pressure on me to finish it up, and although I assured him it would be ready soon, I was privately more than a little shaky on just *how* soon.

A quick jaunt to Stockholm in early December of 1995 proved to be a critical turning point. I had taken along photocopies of about sixty of the poems comprising the "peacock's tail" to give to a friend, and on my last day, I pulled out the sixty sheets, sat down on my hotel-room bed, and next to each poem, in red ink, scribbled down just the briefest sentence or two explaining how it fit into the larger picture of the whole collection. All this took me no more than an hour. As I slipped the red-annotated poems back into their manila envelope for my friend, I realized that *this* — not a book with chapters — was the ideal format for the Tanner Lecture book. Chapters be damned! What I needed was just a long succession of poems, alternating with commentaries. I could suddenly see it: poems all on righthand pages, commentaries all on left, never taking more than a page.

This was a key moment of epiphany. In an instant it had become clear to me that my idea of mixing digressions in with the commentaries to make short chapters had slowly metamorphosed from being a bright spark of insight into a ponderous albatross suffocating me. But luckily, with my red-ink notes, I had cut the Gordian knot in the cord tying the albatross around my neck, and the heavy bird had plopped — thud! — to the ground.

I flew home, and, now breathing easy, was able to write up short facing commentaries in under two weeks. My little Utah volume, containing just a brief introduction, nearly forty commented versions of "Ma Mignonne", and a two-page conclusion, was essentially ready by Christmas vacation. In a gesture of personal homage to the Russian composer Sergei Rachmaninoff, I chose as my title "Rhapsody on a Theme by Clément Marot", saluting his brilliant work "Rhapsody on a Theme by Paganini", which, composed in 1934, is a set of twenty-four enormously variegated, lyrical, and scintillating piano variations on a small and charming melody by his precursor Paganini. Gene finally had his book, and I was finally off the hook.

Amplification, Bifurcation, Commemoration

All was hunky-dory now, except for one thing: I felt sad about those digressions that had been cut. They had had such neat material in them that I was loath to abandon them completely. After pondering this for a while, I decided that perhaps I could write up a longer Marot book and have it published for more general distribution than the *Rhapsody*.

In this more ambitious book, I imagined including a substantially larger number of annotated "Ma Mignonne" translations as well as, of course, all or most of the excised digressions, but slightly expanded and greatly polished. Altogether, this project looked to me like perhaps a doubling in size of the *Rhapsody*. Gene Woolf was very gracious in granting me permission to reuse any material from that book, and so I started plunging ahead. Little more needs to be said about the mushrooming of the project, for you have in your hands what resulted.

I certainly did not foresee that as the digressions grew and grew, the role of the Marot variations concocted by so many sparkling minds would become smaller and smaller, and that in the end they would simply become a kind of sideshow in the longer book — or, if you prefer, a *leitmotif* popping up and then submerging for a while, over and over again. Musically speaking, one might compare this type of structure to the *rondo* form, in which a given theme recurs periodically throughout a work, with its multiple appearances separated by a series of episodes that are essentially unrelated to it and may or may not be related to each other. The rondo form is captured symbolically this way: ABACAD…AZA.

Had I known that the once-fluffy digressions would eventually turn into the main courses in an extended multi-course dinner, with the annotated Marot translations being more like fine wines served along with each new course, I would have probably been so frightened at the amount of work looming ahead of me that I would not have had the courage to go ahead. Luckily, though, I do not have the gift of clairvoyance, and so I blissfully plunged ahead, undaunted by precognitive visions of the countless all-nighters I would have to pull to pull the whole thing off.

While working on the *Rhapsody,* I found out that 1996 was Clément Marot's five-hundredth birthyear, and this marvelous coincidence seemed to demand that the new book be finished before year's end — but an even more powerful impetus came when I learned, early in 1996, that Marot's exact date of birth was November 23. Luckily, I still had time to make that day! The precision of the date felt like an absolute constraint on me, and so I revved up all my intellectual engines to full power, bearing down on that deadline. As I write this sentence, I still have thirty-four days left; as you read it, the date has of course long since passed. But it looks as if I will make it, though just barely.

As the book developed, vignettes from my life, and especially from my shared life with Carol, somehow wound up working their way naturally into the text, and the book slowly became more and more of a memorial to her life and her spirit. Never would I have guessed that Marot and Carol would have ended up playing almost symmetric roles in this book, and yet they do. I think it would in some ways have embarrassed Carol, and I almost feel as if I should apologize to her for it. But in another way, I think not. Had Carol read a similar book by someone else, in which a beloved partner's life was woven into the book's fabric and thereby warmly commemorated, I know she would have found it both interesting and moving. I would therefore like to believe that by writing about her and remembering her in loving words, I am honoring her in a manner of which she would have approved.

Scintillation, Delectation, Celebration

Even though the Marot poem along with its swarm of translations now constitutes, ironically, but a small fragment of the book to which it gave life, it is still the book's germ, its crux, its *sine qua non.* Without "Ma Mignonne" and the unpredictable branching pathways along which it led me, I could never have come up with anything resembling *Le Ton beau de Marot*.

The remarkable translations here collected of this one poem, though all faithful to it in their own ways, are as different as one could possibly imagine. So, to put it crassly, which one is the very best? Though it's hard to refrain from asking that question, to provide an answer was certainly not the point of the book — far from it. I never intended that my challenge to translate a charming French poem into other languages should be thought of as an Olympic event with gold, silver, and bronze medals!

No — a far better metaphor for the "Ma Mignonne" challenge and all that it inspired would be a mineralogical display featuring sparkling crystals of all sorts of dazzling colors and an unimaginable array of forms. Some of these crystalline translations will appeal more to one reader, others to another. The real point of the exhibit is simply to allow readers to revel in the diversity of this collection of deeply related gems, so beautifully illustrative of the endless inventive spark residing in the human spirit.

Flirtation, Despyrrhation: Ode Horatian

Little, when I wrote those lines, did I suppose they would apply as well to a book published nearly forty years earlier. But a few months ago, at a literary translators' meeting, Ronnie Apter aptly asked if I'd ever heard of Sir Ronald Storrs' collection *Ad Pyrrham*; to my "no" she said I surely should see it, and gave me enough information to track it down. When I obtained it, I found it a fantastic treat. It is based on Horace's Ode to Pyrrha, written in a 2,000-year-old Latin so richly tangled and so dense that at first I found it next to impenetrable, though after reading many translations I finally saw through much of the Horatian murk. Here it is, for your inspection:

Quis multa gracilis te puer in rosa	*What slender youth, besprinkled with perfume,*
perfusus liquidis urget odoribus	*Courts you on roses in some grotto's shade?*
grato, Pyrrha, sub antro?	*Fair Pyrrha, say, for whom*
cui flavam religas comam,	*Your yellow hair you braid,*
simplex munditiis? heu quotiens fidem	*So trim, so simple! Ah! how oft shall he*
mutatosque deos flebit et aspera	*Lament that faith can fail, that gods can change,*
nigris aequora ventis	*Viewing the rough black sea*
emirabitur insolens,	*With eyes to tempests strange,*
qui nunc te fruitur credulus aurea,	*Who now is basking in your golden smile,*
qui semper vacuam, semper amabilem	*And dreams of you still fancy-free, still kind,*
sperat, nescius aurae	*Poor fool, nor knows the guile*
fallacis! miseri, quibus	*Of the deceitful wind!*
intemptata nites. me tabula sacer	*Woe to the eyes you dazzle without cloud*
votiva paries indicat uvida	*Untried! For me, they show in yonder fane*
suspendisse potenti	*My dripping garments, vow'd*
vestimenta maris deo.	*To Him who curbs the main.*

The anglicization on its right — stunningly close to literal — was done near the middle of the nineteenth century by John Conington, professor of Latin at Oxford. And yet note that whereas Horace's Latin has no rhymes, Conington's English certainly does. And while Horace's syllable-count per line rigidly adheres to a 12–12–7–8 scheme, Conington, not to be outdone in the metrics department, sticks just as carefully to a 10–10–6–6 scheme.

The beauty of Ronald Storrs' anthology is that its many pages of translations — some 63 in English, 20 in French, 15 in Spanish, 13 in German, 12 in Italian, and yet another 21 in sundry other languages — are simply bulging with such gems. My museum metaphor applies perfectly. Witness, for instance, these two gems, the first by T. Herbert Noyes, Jr., of whom all I know, regrettably, is his birthyear (1827), and the second by Leopold Stennett Amery, described by Storrs as "statesman, scholar, historian, and publicist", and whose lifetime stretched from 1873 to 1955:

Oh, who is the stripling so scented and slim,
Who now in your pleasant grot, Pyrrha, reposes
    On litter of roses, / Still cooing and wooing?
Those tresses of gold you have braided for him,

With charming simplicity! ere very long,
For all he is now so confiding a lover,
    He'll surely discover / Sad treason in season,
The smooth waters ruffled by breezes so strong.

Fond fool! he believes you as sterling as gold,
And trusts he will find you forever as tender,
    As prone to surrender; / Not ruing what's brewing,
Alas! for the wights who've not known thee of old.

The walls of the temple bear witness for me,
Who hung up my raiment just after one dipping,
    All soaking and dripping; / My motive was votive;
My thanks they were due to the God of the Sea.

Who's that new boy, my sweetie,
That's visiting your flat?
Paying for all the roses
And for that simple hat,

So neat, but so expensive?
Well, he's content, I guess.
He thinks he's found the recipe
For life-long happiness

In the radiance of your welcome
And in that smile so wooing.
He little knows how sudden
The squalls that may be brewing.

I've faced them and survived them,
And in memory of sweet folly
Have hung up in Love's temple
My mackintosh and brolly.

Keen intelligence and delightful humor shine through. And yet are we perceiving Horace, or is his image too distorted by these refracting prisms? Such questions will hound us as we now turn back to Clément Marot and his equally charming and challenging minuscule opus, and its analogous, unpredictable kaleidoscope of glittering, glowing renditions.

Poems II:

~ Gals and Trysts ~

* *

Here is my first completed translation of "Ma Mignonne" into English — for all I know, the first ever done by anyone at all. This intense little burst of joy took place in early fall, 1987 — thus, by sheer coincidence, 450 years after the original poem's creation (early fall, 1537). It gives me pleasure to imagine — both unverifiably and irrefutably — that my small breakthrough may have taken place on the very anniversary itself!

This translation did not come easily. Weeks earlier, in a conservative, literal mood, I had found, after doing but a few lines, that I had painted myself right into a corner with no visible way out, and in despair had thrown in the towel. On my second go-round, though, I was in a fresh frame of mind and considerably more willing to play free and easy with various ideas in the original poem. Thus, whereas I felt compelled to get in a reference to prison, I happily left out the idea of "opening a door", feeling it was implicit in my line 9 about "going outside". Then my next line, about "taking a ride", brings in an image not present in Marot's poem at all. What kind of ride would it be, anyway — on horseback? In a carriage? Or in a *car*? This I left ambiguously floating between two distant centuries. Is all this too much liberty? Was I flouting the spirit of the original? At the time, I felt it was a fair use of translator's license — indeed, given my earlier frustrating experience, I felt that *only* by using such license was there any hope at all of translating the poem.

Here's another case to ponder. Marot never suggested in any way that the reason the sick little girl should arise and go outside was that eating buttered bread would mess up her bed, but the idea appealed to me, so I used it. In fact, even the concept of "bread" was only implicit in Marot's poem — but how else does one eat jam, if not on bread? I thus felt it was absolutely fine to mention bread explicitly. On the other hand, I left out the jam itself, preferring instead to mention its second cousin, butter. Did following this buttery trail constitute utter betrayal? Why not just call it Marot-like playfulness?

In my playful mood, I felt free, at least somewhat free, to transpose ideas from one zone of the poem to another. Thus instead of placing the poet's self-naming close to the poem's midriff, where Marot has his, I postponed mine till down near its ankles. Indeed, my line 26 jumps through two hoops at once: it not only gets in the desired self-naming at the last moment, but also, echoing Marot's line 26, squeezes in a reference to God (albeit dilutedly, via a deity-whispering verb rather than a deity-trumpeting noun).

I even dared to toy with the concept of "self", switching it, after some hesitation, from "Clément" to "Douglas". Purists might find this altering of ego intolerable, though I suspect Marot would chuckle approvingly. Fortunately, to placate the purists, the shift back to "Clement" (the anglicized version of "Clément") would pose no problem, since "Douglas" and "Clement" have the same syllable count (and as I mentioned earlier, the English name "Clement" has the curious property that its primary stress can be placed comfortably on either syllable).

Another example of idea transposition involves lines 20–25 of Marot's poem, in which he voices concern about little Jeanne growing pale, thin, and weak. By contrast, my *eighth* line, "Just get strong", alludes to those ideas and thus to that section of the original, but accentuates the hopeful rather than the worrisome side of things. My lines 24–25 also do some of the same work, but utilizing eyes rather than skin, body, or muscletone. Marot never referred to the girl's eyes, of course, let alone to them "glazing", but in a way, my worry over her eyes' potential glazing echoes his fear of her mouth being "in danger".

One last point: my phrase "bad news" is borrowed from the fairly recent (vintage 1970–1980 or so) joke-template "Here's the good news... and now the bad news...". Likewise, there is a fairly contemporary ring to the phrase "make a mess", though it probably dates back much farther. Taken together, in any case, these two phrases mark the author of this poem indelibly as a speaker of late-twentieth-century American English.

My Sweet Dear

D. Hofstadter

My sweet dear,
I send cheer —
All the best!
Your forced rest
Is like jail.   *5*
So don't ail
Very long.
Just get strong —
Go outside,
Take a ride!   *10*
Do it quick,
Stay not sick —
Ban your ache,
For my sake!
Buttered bread   *15*
While in bed
Makes a mess,
So unless
You would choose
That bad news,   *20*
I suggest
That you'd best
Soon arise,
So your eyes
Will not glaze.   *25*
Douglas prays
Health be near,
My sweet dear.

Most proud of "My Sweet Dear", quite heady with my little coup, I couldn't resist challenging my good friend and friendly intellectual rival Bob French, a professional translator between (of all things) French and English, to translate "Ma Mignonne" independently. Bob gladly accepted my challenge but then took his sweet time. When after a couple of days I prodded him, thinking he had perhaps encountered some trouble (an idea that, I admit it, secretly pleased me!), Bob nonchalantly replied, "Come on, Doug, I could easily toss off a cheap translation based on a sappy first line like 'Cutie pie', but I want a really *poetic* translation, and that takes time!"

This remark set me to worrying, since I knew Bob revered Victor Hugo and could express himself with a deft literary touch; I thus wondered if it might not be wise for me to attempt a second translation, so that just in case Bob's creation outshone my first try, I would have a kind of backup, an ace in the hole. However, unlike Bob, I saw nothing wrong with his scorned first line "Cutie pie" — to me, in fact, it sounded charming, not sappy at all! — and so I decided to start out my second attempt with that very line, perhaps deliberately to tweak Bob.

I made no systematic attempt to imbue my language with a uniform flavor; indeed, as you see, old-style words and phrases ("herewith", "'twill", "abed", "so say I") mingle freely here with modern-style ones ("cutie pie", "Clem", "posh", "nosh", "stuff", "no way", and so on), in a potpourri quite reminiscent of Lorenz Hart's lyrics to "Thou Swell":

> *Thou swell! Thou witty! Thou sweet! Thou grand!*
> *Wouldst kiss me pretty? Wouldst hold my hand?*
> *Both thine eyes are cute, too; what they do to me!*
> *Hear me holler, I choose a sweet lolla-paloosa in thee.*

I was quite self-confidently flippant with my breaking of words across lines ("med-ical", "sun-light"), but I reached the height of my sassiness in lines 13–14 — probably the poem's best touch. I recently came across some early drafts of the poem, and discovered that those two lines had actually started out life as "Doug says, 'Jump! / Bed's a dump!'", then metamorphosed into "'Quick!' says Doug, / 'Plug your bug!'", and only sometime thereafter did "Clem" and "phlegm" enter the picture — all of which, needless to say, I had totally forgotten.

Obviously, with the borrowing of a Yiddishism ("nosh", meaning "eat") and the use of other highly flavored words, I was moving far, far away from sixteenth-century France. And yet, I felt that my poem's lighthearted tone and obvious delight with words mimicked the flavor of Marot's playing-around with very short lines as well as his unexpected twists with words (*e.g.*, the shift from *vous* to *tu*).

What about my seemingly illegitimate image of ham and eggs? To me, those two items, taken as a unit, have a bright and sunny breakfasty aura about them quite in tune with that of jam, so they seemed to fall well within bounds. Perhaps this slightly daring act was my verbal way of mirroring Marot's real-life "crime" of consuming ham during Lent.

A curious rhythmic detail: On line 5, "jail" is treated as a single syllable, whereas on line 8, "jailbreak" is treated as three syllables, meaning that "jail" must be acting bisyllabic there. Strictly speaking, these two facts may seem inconsistent, but I think that my choice to let "jail" do double duty actually reflects quite accurately the syllabic durations that people naturally use when they read the poem aloud. Context can exert very powerful effects on how words are spoken.

In any case, with both "My Sweet Dear" and "Cutie Pie" as arrows in my poetic quiver, I now felt fully prepared to take my arch-rival Bob French on.

Cutie Pie

D. Hofstadter

Cutie pie,
Herewith I
Wish you well,
In your cell.
It's like jail   5
When you ail.
Hope you make
Jailbreak
Straightaway.
'Twill be gay,   10
Without doubt,
Once you're out.
"Quick!" says Clem,
"Flush your phlegm!"
Think of ham,   15
Eggs and jam —
Pretty posh
Stuff to nosh;
But no way,
If you stay   20
Stuck abed,
With those med-
ical folks
Making pokes.
"One needs sun-   25
light and fun!"
So say I,
Cutie pie!

Well, this is what Bob finally unveiled to me after a few days of work. It was nothing at all like what I had expected. Indeed, it was utterly different from anything I had even *considered*. Most impressed by its elegance and suavity of tone, I was therefore quite depressed about the lightheartedness of my own efforts. Bob's very terse, poetic way of evoking the atmosphere of dank stone castles and musty old dungeons, as well as his chivalric gesture of "sending an embrace", struck me as very true to the original; similarly, the gallant and medieval manner in which he (or was it Clement?) addressed the suffering damsel as "Fairest friend" conjured up images of Maid Marion and Queen Guinevere in my mind. And thus, next to this subtle, literary piece, my two exclamation-point–filled efforts suddenly sounded quite frivolous, even childish, to me.

I still *liked* my own two poems, mind you, but I felt that Bob had brought out subtle dimensions of the original that I had utterly neglected. Never once had it occurred to me to try to capture, or even tip my hat to, the *oldness* of the Marot poem. My naïve idea had been simply to use *my* native way of expressing myself — in contemporary, colloquial, often playful American English — to "do what Marot had done" in *his* native language. Thus, unconsciously influenced to varying degrees by such early- and mid-twentieth-century counterparts to Marot as Ira Gershwin, Cole Porter, Lorenz Hart, Tom Lehrer, A. A. Milne, Ogden Nash, Dorothy Parker, and many others, I had put together a couple of flippant, fun, sweet little poems, as American as apple pie, as twentieth-century as Apple Computer. Bob, on the other hand, had eschewed mere *fun* in favor of elegance and faithfulness to the epoch — an idea that, as I say, had never crossed my mind, and to tell the truth, I felt quite ashamed of myself for that lack.

In contrast to my two poems, which both painted an uninhibitedly joyous bursting-out of jail in the midday sun, Bob's hinted at a hush-hush, clandestine escape, the pair most likely slinking furtively through chilly corridors in the darkest of pre-dawn darkness. Then there was the phrase "Hid from day", subtle in both content and form. As a metaphor, it neatly suggests the girl's sunless sequestering; as a grammatical deviation from current usage (we would say "hidden" today), it manages to evoke, through a mere inflection, another whole era. And finally, the phrase "Bless your health / Till the end", being itself *located* at the end, was an ingenious little self-referential finishing fillip, and made me jealous! Despite all this, my flagging spirits were slightly perked by my feeling that my poems were more playful than Bob's, and in that desperate sense, perchance a mite more Marotesque in spirit.

And then there came a moment when I thought I was going to get a little bit of "sweet revenge" — namely, in typing up Bob's poem side by side with the original French poem, I noticed that it contained two extra lines (a fact I probably would never have noticed otherwise). Surprised, I confronted Bob with this mistake (at least as I saw it), but he caught me off guard by insisting that respecting the number 28 was of no interest or importance to him. When I said, "Well, then, why respect the three syllables of each line?", he said, "Now, now! *That* is too clear and too obvious a fact about the original to tamper with, but on the other hand, the exact line-count, being far from perceptually immediate, *can* be tampered with, as long as one stays in the same ballpark — obviously one should not have as few as ten lines, nor as many as fifty lines. But that's all!" On this issue Bob was adamant. Although I could see his point of view and certainly could not logically *prove* that it was wrong, I felt deep down that this was a bad esthetic judgment.

Fairest Friend

Robert French

Fairest friend,
Let me send
My embrace.
Quit this place,
Its dark halls   5
And dank walls.
In soft stealth,
Regain health:
Dress and flee
Off with me,   10
Clement, who
Calls for you.
Fine gourmet,
Hid from day,
Danger's past,   15
So at last
Let's be gone,
To dine on
Honeyed ham
And sweet jam.   20
If you stay
Ill this way,
Pale and drawn,
You'll put on
But then cede   25
Pounds you need.
May God's wealth
Bless your health
Till the end,
Fairest friend.   30

One day, while studying Bob's poem in detail, I chanced to note that it contained a mistranslation (oh, joy!) on lines 24–25: in the original, there was no insinuation of the suffering patient first *gaining* and then *losing* weight. With further thought, I saw how a small bit of reworking could fix up both this semantic glitch and the structural glitch of the wrong line-count in one single blow: namely, there were precisely two lines that one could drop and thereby eliminate the undesirable imagery. At first, naturally, Bob was reluctant to accept a fix suggested by his rival, but eventually he came around, agreeing that the meaning would be truer that way (he insisted that the resulting shorter line-count was not an influence on his decision). The patch-up led to the facing poem.

There was, in Bob's poem, a pervasive flavor of a surreptitious, clandestine rendez-vous with a beloved. This was the first time it had occurred to me that there was an ambiguity of tone in Marot's original poem: it might as easily have been written to a lover or mistress as to a little girl. Indeed, after showing Marot's poem to many people, I realized that Bob's reading of it was not unusual: many readers instinctively hear "Ma Mignonne" as a poem addressed to a lover. And who knows? It may well be that Marot, who was not the world's greatest prude, intended his overtly innocent poem to have slightly coquettish undertones.

I couldn't help noticing that Bob, like me, had allowed himself the luxury of using "ham" to rhyme with "jam". It turned out that many other translators, down the line, would do this same thing. This is a curious fact. What, aside from the rhyme, makes ham such a popular foreign element to introduce?

I already explained that in "Cutie Pie", a large part of my justification lay in the yoking together of "ham" with "eggs", thus conjuring up breakfast time, which for me brings the whole image quite close to "jam". What about unadorned ham, though? Well, like jam, it's still a food, in fact quite often eaten at breakfast — and ham is sometimes associated with jelly. The connection is thus not enormously strained.

How about *yams* instead of *hams*? Suppose Bob's lines 17–20 had run this way: "Let's be gone, / To dine on / Honeyed yams / And sweet jams"? Would this be any better? I could argue the case — after all, both yams and jams are sweet foods hailing from the plant world, hence are semantically closer than hams and jams. On the other hand, to be strict about it, Marot didn't mention *yams* any more than *hams*. So is "yam" no better than "ham" as a translation of "jam"? Are both to be equally rejected out of hand?

I don't at all see these things in black-and-white terms; rather, I see endless shades of gray. In fact, I would even argue that Marot *did* mention hams and yams in his poem — the question is only *how buried* each of them was between the lines. In Italy, they say *Chi dice Siena dice Palio* — to mention Siena is to bring up its famous horse race, like it or not. Carol twisted this into a droll family slogan: *Chi dice Hofstadter dice tardi* — "To say 'Hofstadter' is to say 'late'." How true… The point is, in any word, many concepts are *sous-entendus*: there, but whispered. Thus the question is: *How softly whispered* is X in Y?

How far a translator can reasonably drift from a literal text has everything to do with the fabric of human associations — with what lies mentally close to what, and what lies far away. Such associations come, of course, from deep familiarity with how the world itself is structured. If one has lived through millions of complex experiences, as we all have — including vicarious ones, from books we've read to movies we've seen to adventures we've heard friends relate — then just a few words can trigger rich imagery at a conscious level, as well as vast clouds of associations at a more subliminal, invisible level. These clouds of associations flesh out any passage we read, allowing us — nay, forcing us — to go far beyond its literal text. And thus, although "yam" might have worked better in Bob's poem, "ham" still works reasonably well, because it lies within a small enough radius of "jam" in the nebulous yet quasi-objective space of human concepts and experience.

Fairest Friend (II)

Robert French

Fairest friend,
Let me send
My embrace.
Quit this place,
Its dark halls   5
And dank walls.
In soft stealth,
Regain health:
Dress and flee
Off with me,   10
Clement, who
Calls for you.
Fine gourmet,
Hid from day,
Danger's past,   15
So at last
Let's be gone,
To dine on
Honeyed ham
And sweet jam.   20
If you're still
Wan and ill,
You will cede
Pounds you need.
May God's wealth   25
Bless your health
Till the end,
Fairest friend.

• *Chapter 3* •

How Jolly the Lot
of an Oligoglot

•

The roots of my passion for languages and my exuberance for translation lie in the wonderful good fortune that I had, at age thirteen, to go to Geneva, Switzerland, for a year. It was my father's sabbatical year, his first ever, and we were all excited about moving to a foreign land and especially about being plunged into a French-speaking environment. My mother had infected me with a passion for the liquid sounds of French — the word *aujourd'hui* ("today") seemed particularly lovely and exotic — and the year before we left for Geneva, I was granted a special dispensation to take French in eighth grade (for some reason, only Spanish was considered appropriate for eighth-graders in my junior high school).

Although I adored the sounds of French and reveled in practicing them in private, I felt ashamed to reveal my ability — I guess pronouncing French "r"'s and "u"'s in the proper way seemed less than macho, one of those cultural intuitions that teen-agers have, like "Real men don't eat quiche" — and so whenever I was called on in class, I hid this talent and put on a terrible, flat accent full of American "r"'s, like everyone else in the class, and with vowels sliding sloppily all over the place. Despite this façade, my true goal was utter perfection of accent. It was not just that I wanted to meet a personal standard, nor that I wanted to fool people about my nationality — it was, rather, a deep-seated intuition about language that told me, "Unless you have a perfect accent and perfect mastery of the grammar and lexicon, you are faking it — the supposedly foreign language coming out of your mouth is simply your native language, thinly disguised."

I have since abandoned this rather extreme belief, but two aspects of it that have never left me are a fanaticism about precise pronunciation of any language that I encounter, and a fascination with what it means to *think in* another language, with the idea of converting oneself into a true, full-fledged speaker of another language, a speaker whose utterances in the second language are not in any sense influenced by the first language but originate autonomously, in a completely separate area of the brain.

By now, I have studied many languages and achieved various levels of mastery of each of them — levels that fluctuate hugely and unpredictably with time, mood, conversation partner, topic, and other intangible variables beyond my ken. I have had the enormous pleasure of being taken for a native speaker of French a number of times in my life, but have also been humiliated by making grammatical errors or forgetting words in crucial contexts — blowing my cover, in short — equally many times. At this advanced age, I have come to realize how woefully far ahead of my French my English is, and how my French could never catch up, and thus that French, even if I sound very good for short bursts and in certain domains of discourse, will forever remain a *foreign* language for me. As for my other languages, they taper off rapidly in terms of level of fluency, though I can manage decent conversations in several, and have lectured in a few.

Pilingualism

People often ask questions like, "How many languages do you speak?" This naïvely black-and-white vision of things makes me uncomfortable, and so I always deflect the question with hedges such as, "Well, I've *studied* about twelve" or "It depends on what you mean by 'speak'" or "Do you mean *right now,* or do you mean *at some point in my life?*" Sometimes I even joshingly reply, "I speak exactly π languages", explaining that if you took all the languages I've ever studied and for each one estimated the fraction of true native-level mastery that I have ever attained in it (generously awarding me the fraction at my lifetime peak rather than its value right now), and then summed all those fractions up, you might get a result that was a little over 3 (counting English as 1, of course). And so I say π. It's a cute joke, but just between you and me, π is probably an overestimate. Maybe e would be closer — but don't tell anyone!

These things are extraordinarily blurry. I did not have the luck to grow up bilingual, as my children are doing (Italian and English), let alone trilingual, pilingual, or more. But despite this, I have done my best to overcome that disadvantage and have a pretty good command of both French and Italian (at this point, I'm not sure which of the two is stronger), am reasonable at German and Spanish, and at certain points in my life, I was able to sustain a pretty respectable conversation in Swedish (peaking in

1966, after I'd spent six months living in Swedish student dormitories) and even in Mandarin ("peking" a few years ago, after roughly four years of quite intense study and lots of long coffeehouse and pizza-lunch conversations with Chinese friends). I've also worked quite hard at Polish, mostly on my own (though now it's extremely dormant), and done a small amount of Russian and Hindi, even spent a few months each on Dutch and what at the time was called Serbo-Croatian, all decades ago. I would count Hebrew, Portuguese, and Sinhalese at exactly zero, although at different times in my life I studied each of them for maybe a month, and still recall an infinitesimal amount of each of them. I also, in high-school, took two years of Latin, but it's hardly a language I'm currently pat in.

As for the languages that are by far my strongest — French and Italian — sometimes I emerge from a conversation exultant about how fluently I speak and how effortlessly fancy constructions come spilling out, yet other times I despair of ever coming to express myself with that total, unconscious ease that I feel in speaking English. And there are still even moments — quite rare, thank God — when I feel like a naïve, stumbling beginner. Where the truth lies, I don't know. All I know is, one is never satisfied.

Future and Past Meet, Mingle, and Mate in a Mystical Blur

It was, in any case, in my eighth-grade pre-Geneva French class that I first became intoxicated with the mysteries of language. I will never forget the thrills of anticipation that I had in looking ahead at upcoming sections of our koobtxet, and seeing the new tenses that we would soon learn, the new sets of personal pronouns, the new types of constructions. Unlike most people, I was enthralled by grammar and the profound tie-in that it seemed to have with the entire way that we humans forge our mental model of the world around us. My favorite example of this tie-in is the near-mystical high that I experienced when I first put a certain one and one together to make two, and then put this two together with an analogous two to make four...

Our class had already learned how to conjugate French verbs in the future tense and in two different types of past tense — the *passé composé* (present perfect) and the *imparfait* (imperfect). I was fascinated by the distinction between these two past tenses, by the utterly novel manner in which the French language had chosen to slice up the world of actions. But learning the conditional tense — "she would dance", "you would believe" — was the key moment for me. It turns out that to say "I would go", "you would go", and so on, you take the *future root* of the verb *aller* ("to go") and to that you append the standard, universal *imperfect endings*. Thus by splicing the future root *ir-* with the past endings *-ais, -ais, -ait, -ions, iez, -aient*, you obtain the strange counterfactual idea of "would-ness" — *j'irais, tu irais, il/elle irait, nous irions*, etc. — symbolic encodings of what might be or might have been, what could happen, what would or could or should have taken place, what may (who knows?) still occur. The idea that in French, such counterfactual worlds are conjured up by this bizarre but intimate marriage of future and past components was, for me, too magical for words.

But the true capper came when I looked at our very own auxiliary verb "would" with fresh eyes, and for the first time in my life saw *into* it, saw it as a tight fusion of our future tense ("will") and our past tense (the "-d" suffix). Not only were these two pieces fused together to make a tight whole, but the blend was irregular and thus disguised from view; now, though, thanks to French, I had seen through the disguise. Double magic! Much the same held for "should" ("shall" + "-d"). All of a sudden, it was as if French and English together were linking arms to reveal to me a deeply hidden truth not just about grammar, but about the logical fabric of the universe itself: counterfactual worlds, what- or wher-ever they be, are made by an eerie convolving of that which is long long past with that which has yet to occur — a time warp in which "ago" and "to come" are married in a mystical blur.

Limitless Levels of Linguistic Mystery and Mastery

Once we'd reached Geneva and settled in, I had so many epiphanies about French. My baker-boy neighbor Roger baffled me by always saying what sounded like *Saillez !* — seemingly an exclamation of joy, but findable in no dictionary. One day the mystery came unraveled when somehow I realized *Saillez !* was not one word but three: *Ça y est !* Literally, this means "It's there!", but what it really means, depending on context, is: "Done!", "Great!", "Got it!", "Right on!", or even "Attaway!". A similar revelation happened when, after hearing *Il est malin suila !* and myriad other sentences starting or ending in *suila*, I finally reheard the nonexistent *suila* for what it really was: *celui-là,* literally "that one there", but in fact meaning "that guy".

From such experiences, I gained enormous respect for the subtlety of word boundaries, and in general for the challenge of understanding rapid, slurred native speech. Indeed, in every language I have tackled, I have found that *understanding natives well is far more difficult than expressing myself well,* an observation that is intimately tied in with my belief that the task of getting machines to "understand" (*i.e.,* to transcribe) rapid, continuous speech as well as people do is tantamount to the full mechanization of adult human intelligence plus understanding of the world. I will be impressed when a computer hears a nurse say, "*Air* by ghost a *chobber* glass a zame *oar*!" and realizes she means, "Everybody goes to *childbirth* classes any more!"

Over the years, as my French got better and better, I came to realize how many levels of mastery there are, as in chess or ice-skating or Indian cooking or any other human endeavor. You can have a large vocabulary in terms of *words,* but unless you have an equally large (or perhaps larger) repetoire of *stock phrases* ranging anywhere in length from two words to twenty, you are not even close to native level. For years I was blissfully unaware of how many such phrases I had effortlessly absorbed in English, and when it finally hit me — *"under the weather", "no way, José", "speak of the devil", "up a creek", "greasy spoon", "in one ear and out the other", "fat chance", "tell it to the Marines", "above and beyond the call of duty", "keep in touch", "get away with murder", "don't knock it", "for all I know", "out of the way", "once upon a time", "don't mind me", "got any spare change?", "take it easy", "over the hill", "sooner or later", "on my mind", "sticks out like a sore thumb", "knock off work early", "out of the blue", "spittin' image", "in a word", "can't say as how I do", "funny ha-ha or funny peculiar", "how about you?", "gimme a buzz", "cut it out", "got a kick out of it", "get off my back", "if it were up to me", "off the wall", "the thing is", "kill some time", "my kind of people", "the wee hours", "give up the ghost", "I'm gonna tell on you!", "the telling moment", "something tells me", "and the bad news is", "says who?", "and what of it?", "black eye", "pull an all-nighter", "green thumb", "out of order", "out of gas", "out of it", "go nuts", "do I ever", "talk about gutsy!", "tell me about it", "dream on", "the crux of the matter", "of all the silly things", "kiss of death", "to the very end", "by dint of", "stop on a dime", "kick the habit", "bully for her", "beer belly", "go to pot", "plumb forgot", "under my belt", "state of grace", "once in a blue moon"* — it was an enormously depressing blow in terms of what it told me about how far I still had to go in French. To this day, I still feel terribly behind in that sector of vocabulary.

There were times when I was convinced I was very close to native-level mastery, but that illusion was always soon shattered one way or another. I remember one day in a Paris-bound train, a month or so before I turned 30, reading a flowery editorial in *Le Monde,* and thinking to myself, "This sounds positively *alien!*" And mind you, this was at a time when I spoke very fluently and could at times pass for native (perhaps a fourteen-year-old native, admittedly!). The whole mode of expression seemed permeated by a deeply Gallic orientation to the world that I simply did not share. Of course, some French authors seemed far less alien, but still, I knew that this showed how far I was from adult-style native-level mastery.

By Dint of Hard Work versus On a Silver Platter

I felt intensely jealous of true bilinguals and trilinguals, such as my close Geneva friend Cyril Erb, who had grown up in a home where French, German, and English were spoken indifferently. Visiting Cyril's family always made my head spin. However, at some point I began to realize that the "good luck" of such people probably made them deaf to the very musicality that swept me off my feet. Perhaps better to love a language and suffer from your ineptness with it than to have everything handed to you for free at birth, and thus wind up not appreciating its beauty at all.

Carol and I, from the moment we were married, wanted to have children who would grow up bilingual or trilingual, and that is indeed what is happening with Danny and Monica. At times I have to shake my head in wonderment and amusement at the fact that my household today is much like Cyril's was when he and I were teen-agers: there is a constant, casual, unconscious slopping-back-and-forth between languages, with the kids maintaining perfect accents even as they switch gears mid-sentence. Yes, in a way I am jealous of my kids' free gift, but somehow, most ironically, I now feel thankful that I learned my languages "artificially" and not "natively".

On Simultaneous Translation and Hidden Substrates

A few times in my teen-age years, I found myself serving as an intermediary between English and French speakers, and thus I got to test out my ability as a simultaneous interpreter. I found that as long as the topic stayed within the bounds of my vocabulary, I was pretty well able to keep up, especially in the English–French direction. I was not as good in the French–English direction, an asymmetry with obvious origins: I had gained much of my French vocabulary from texts and dictionaries, and thus in the learning stages, I retrieved many French words via English. Similarly for syntactic structures, and so it was no wonder that I had a kind of natural skill in simultaneous interpretation from English to French.

In a way, my skill at this difficult art made me proud, but in another way, it reinforced a fear I had about the nature of my supposed mastery of French: that no matter how well I *seemed* to speak French, no matter how fluent or even native I might sound, all I was *really* doing was unconsciously generating sentences in English and then — so fast and so well that I had no conscious awareness of it — simultaneously translating them into French and uttering them. A cover-up! Was I just a faker, a fraud, a sham?

On occasion, especially when I was rusty or sleepy or just a bit off, I would make errors that would seem to corroborate this worst of fears. For instance, I remember one time when, suffering from jet lag, I formulated (but caught myself before uttering it!) the phrase *les liseurs de sa colonne* for "the readers of his column". Though the word *liseur* actually exists, it is an antiquated way of saying "reader"; the standard term is *lecteur*. In normal speech, *liseur* would be affected and silly. So why had I nearly uttered it? Simple: the word *lecteur,* although I knew it like the back of my hand, just didn't spring to mind fast enough in that particular mood and context, God knows why, and so in order not to lose precious milliseconds, my brain dove into its simultaneous-translation mode, easily found the ready-at-hand French equivalents for "read" and "-er", and glued them together. Presto!

The story behind *colonne* is similar. One part of me knew very well that *rubrique* is the word for "newspaper column", but when it didn't pop to mind fast enough, my unconscious speech-formulating subselves just mindlessly dredged up the word *colonne,* which means "column", but in the architectural rather than the journalistic sense, and shoved it into my mental output buffer, where, luckily, it was detected by higher-level censors before being converted into unrecallable vibrating columns of air.

When I "heard" the entire phrase *les liseurs de sa colonne* inside my mind, all produced, ready and raring to zip down to my vocal tract, I was horrified and deeply disappointed in myself. I felt that its mere generation — even though it was never uttered — clearly revealed an ineliminable English wolf underneath my quite *echt*-seeming French sheep's clothing.

However, a closer look shows that the situation is much grayer than this harsh, black-and-white negativism would imply. The fact that, even on that offest of off days, I had generated the words *sa colonne* (rather than *son colonne*) to express "his column" shows that some aspects of French were very deeply ingrained. The point is that in French, "her" and "his" are rendered by *sa* and *son,* but *sa,* though feminine, does not mean "her", nor does *son,* though masculine, mean "his". The choice between *sa* and *son* depends not on the gender of the possessor, but on that of the possessed! (In fact, whereas "his" and "her" are called possessive *pronouns,* their French counterparts *sa* and *son* are called possessive *adjectives.*)

In this case, *colonne* being grammatically feminine, *sa colonne* is the only possibility, whether one means "her column" or "his column". And my mind, even on that very bad day, had produced this automatically for me without being in the least tripped up or slowed down by my lifetime of English-speaking habits. This aspect of French syntax, though enormously counterintuitive to English speakers when they first meet it, had been totally integrated and internalized in my mind. Indeed, in all the years I have spoken French well, I can't remember once catching myself making a wolf-revealing *sa/son* error. This helps to compensate for the feeling of defeat and shame caused by other aspects of that phrase that day.

Cross-language Contaminations

Although I usually feel both ashamed and saddened by the various cross-language contamination errors I make, I still faithfully jot them all down in my little back-pocket notebooks, in the interests of gaining objective insights into how language works in the human mind and about what "thinking in French" (and other languages) really means. Over several decades, I have thus amassed a quite vast and variegated collection of cross-language contaminations, and to my immense relief and even delight, I have found a number of examples where, in a context in which French has recently been active in my brain, English structures are produced that are incorrect and that clearly reveal influences stemming from the way things are said in French. (I also have recorded examples where the influence jumps from even weaker foreign languages into my English.) From my large collection of language collisions of many sorts, I have concluded that the simultaneous-translation-from-English story, although doubtless one part of the truth about how I generate phrases in foreign languages, is by no means the whole story — and indeed, reverse translation would seem to apply, on occasion, to how I generate phrases in English! In short, things are far more complicated than any simplistic, one-way-only, native-to-foreign translation-based theory would have them.

Sometimes, I really *am* thinking fully in French, and my English is essentially dormant; other times, when French words far from the core of my vocabulary don't bubble up fast enough, unconscious translation mechanisms snap into service, and when those mechanisms make dumb blunders, an English influence occasionally bleeds through, but this cannot be taken as a proof that every last bit of my French is produced from a deeper English substrate. In short, "thinking in Language X" is not nearly as black-and-white a phenomenon as the popular image would have it.

Un premier amour ne s'oublie jamais…

I was deeply devoted to French and French alone for two or three years after returning to California from Geneva. In violent reaction to my traumatic reimmersion in my native English, I tried desperately to preserve whatever sense of bilingualism I had acquired during that year, constantly listening to beautiful French songs sung by Charles Trenet, Jacqueline François, Patachou, Line Renaud, Isabelle Aubret, Lucienne Delyle, Renée Lebas, Yves Montand, Brigitte Bardot (yes — and she was good!), Léo Ferré, Georges Brassens, and many more, and carefully transcribing many songs' lyrics. When bored in class, I would scribble little marginal notes to myself in French. I even went so far as to label half of my files in French. For a while, I thought I would never study another foreign language.

Trying German on for Size

However, after a couple of years had passed, I started feeling the lure of other tongues. I heard them all around me, found myself tantalized by not understanding them, felt pulled by their sounds, and so one day I decided to try out German. And how well do I remember the painful grogginess of attending 8:00 AM classes, five days a week!

Although I enjoyed learning the strange vocabulary and the twists of German grammar, I never found it at all magical, as I had French. I also remember being increasingly struck by the wrongness of the blanket categorization of English as a "Germanic" language. Although much of English certainly was related to German, it seemed to me that just as great a fraction of English was related to French. *Historically,* the *Germanic part* was *no doubt* older, but in *terms* of *actual impact* on today's *language,* the *Romance family* struck me as playing an *equally large role.* (Example: the previous sentence, whose Germanic words, in roman, are 14 in number, and whose Romance words, in italics, are also 14 in number.) Insisting that English be univocally proclaimed either "Germanic" or "Romance" (in which case the former always won, according to the official pundits) struck me as dogmatic and rigidly category-bound. As I think about it now, it strikes me as being the same kind of mistake as insisting that when I am speaking French, either I am thinking "100 percent in French" or else "100 percent in English" (followed by unconscious translation), as if it were inconceivable that such phenomena might come in shades of gray.

Strothmann's Thesis

Of all the memories I retain from the several German courses I took, perhaps the most striking one is of friendly old Professor Strothmann trying so hard to make us all believe in his pet notion, which I will here call "Strothmann's thesis", that no native German speaker ever needs a dictionary — *ein Wörterbuch* — because every single compound word can be understood at once by breaking it into its components (*e.g., Wörter* and *Buch*). German is so *logical!* (It occurred to me to wonder why, if no German dictionaries existed, the term *Wörterbuch* even existed, but of course the answer was obvious — other languages, being less logical than German, *do* need dictionaries, whence a term is needed for those books.)

Of course, Strothmann's thesis tacitly assumes that one knows all possible components first, a list of which would certainly number in the several thousands, and would include many exceedingly rare items. But even given that rather dubious assumption, Strothmann's thesis turns out to be completely untenable, as I had suspected from the very outset.

How could anyone ever intuit, for instance, that whereas the word *Satz* means "sentence" or "set", various compounds built from it, such as *Aussatz* ("out-set"), *Aufsatz* ("on-set"), *Absatz* ("off-set"), and *Einsatz* ("in-set"), would mean "leprosy", "homework", "heel", and "bet", respectively? And what would ever suggest to anyone who was not already in the know that *aufmachen* ("on-make") means "to open", that *auffallen* ("on-fall") means "to be noticeable", and that *aufhören* ("on-hear") means "to stop"?

Or that *Beispiel* ("by-game") would mean "example", that *Rundfunk* ("round-spark") would mean "radio", that *Durchschnitt* ("through-cut") would mean "average", that *Eiweiß* ("egg-white") would mean "protein", that *sowieso* ("so-as-so") would mean "in any case", that *durcheinanderbringen* ("through-one-another-to-bring") would mean "to mess up", that *vielleicht* ("much-easy") would mean "maybe", that *soweit* ("so-far") would mean "ready", that *Mannschaft* ("man-ness") would mean "team", that *preisgeben* ("price-give") would mean "to surrender", that *vorschlagen* ("fore-hit") would mean "to suggest", and on and on and on?

To be sure, one could make very similar points about the opacity of English. It's quite hard to understand, for example, why a compound word made out of the two pieces "under" and "stand" should mean "understand". What sense does that make? Or consider the verb "to make out". Why in the world should it have such a motley collection of meanings as "to discern", "to fare", "to fill out", and "to pet heavily"? No one in their right mind could ever be expected to make out these various meanings from "make" and "out" alone. And then there is "to make up", which can mean, among other things, "to invent", "to become reconciled", and "to apply facial cream to". No one in their right mind would have made up such a diverse set of meanings for a single term. And so on and so forth. I would be the first to admit that just as many examples of the opacity of compounds could be adduced for English as for German. The difference, however, is that we English speakers don't make grand claims about the supposed transparency and logicality of our language, whereas Professor Strothmann and not a few other German speakers I have met certainly do.

None of this is to deny that many German words *are* built up in a fairly transparent, logical fashion. Thus, that *Durchschnittsgeschwindigkeit* means "average speed" is pretty clear if you know *Durchschnitt* means "average" and *Geschwindigkeit* means "speed". Another good example is *Wortbedeutungslehre* ("word-meaning-theory"), which straightforwardly means "semantics". In all likelihood, Strothmann's claim was based on longish words like those, or on the even longer ones for which German is notorious, such as this term:

Agrarstrukturverbesserungsmaßnahmen

("measures taken to improve the agricultural structure"), which I once ran across in a Zurich newspaper. To any adult speaker of German, this blockbuster of a word busts apart straightforwardly and effortlessly into four more basic building blocks — *Agrar/Struktur/Verbesserungs/Maßnahmen* — in terms of which its meaning is obvious, *ganz sans Wörterbuch*.

If Strothmann's thesis is merely the claim that long chains of German words make sense without needing to be explained, then it's hardly a surprise. The analogous claim holds just as much for Romance tongues. And why shouldn't it? Romance-language speakers, no less than Germans, string together long chains of words for the purpose of making sense; so do all human beings. The fact that very long such chains can be quite effortlessly decoded by native speakers is hardly a revelation.

The Semantic Auras of Bustholders and Breastwarts

Not only was I skeptical about Strothmann's thesis; I didn't even like the supposed linguistic utopia that it suggested. Who would *want* every long word in their language to break down transparently into smaller units? For my part, I was charmed by English words I *couldn't* see through, such as "kindergarten", "gladiator", "dirigible", "eleemosynary", "hippopotamus", "mulligatawny", "bremsstrahlung", "cockatiel", "whippoorwill", "carpentry", "ramshackle", "dilapidated", "flabbergasted", "vicissitude", "obsequious", "obnoxious", "obstreperous", "mannequin", "syzygy", "assassin", "bulwark", "hanky-panky", "semantics", "gallivant", "brassiere", and thousands more.

Indeed, let us consider how they say "brassiere" or "bra" in German: *Büstenhalter*. To the German ear, this word busts apart naturally, yielding its meaning as "bustholder". To my American ear, that sounds awful. I admit that it's not just the fact that it's a compound, but also its blunt consonants and vowels. *Büstenhalter* strikes me as just about as gawky as "blockbuster". I'm not saying "bra" is a beautiful word, but at least it doesn't sound like a harsh warning that a Communist border guard might have yelled out to stop some desperate would-be escapee from scaling the Berlin Wall.

While we're dealing with this general area of female anatomy, I might as well bring up an even more disturbing case of component-visibility that I ran across in German. This was the word for "nipple": *Brustwarze*. Broken down, it means "breast-wart". Now the firm female breast — *le beau tétin*, as Clément Marot phrased it — is a shape of great beauty to many people (I, like Marot, am not immune to its charms), and the nipple is usually considered to be its point of greatest scenic interest, rather than a blotch, blemish, or blight. Yet what can one possibly think upon encountering the German word? Is a nipple not being called a "wart" in the plainest possible of terms? And is that not slandering the mysterious allure of breasts?

A native German-speaking friend to whom I posed this question in Italy merely shrugged her shoulders and said, "But isn't that exactly what a nipple is?" She wasn't in the slightest put off by the term; it just seemed accurate to her. In stark contrast, all the native speakers of English — male and female — that I have asked about the German term have been either bothered or amused by it, but never indifferent.

I thus have to wonder whether someone whose native language led them to perceive feminine breasts as being extrusions from the chest capped by some kind of "warts" would ever be inclined to write — or even be capable of *understanding* — a poem to celebrate the grace and charm of such entitties. Is it a mere accident of history or is there some more fundamental Whorfian reason behind the fact that it was Clément Marot and not, say, Walther von der Vogelweide (*c.* 1170–*c.* 1230) or Cyriakus Spangenberg (1528–1604), who conceived and penned *Du beau Tetin*?

Du beau Tetin	An Ode to the Breaste That Is Nyce
Clément Marot	*C. Marot/D. Hofstadter*

Tetin refaict, plus blanc qu'un œuf,	O Tit, than egg thou whiter art,
Tetin de satin blanc tout neuf,	White satin Tit near virgin's heart,
Tetin qui fais honte à la rose,	O Tit who shamest every rose,
Tetin plus beau que nulle chose.	O Tit, what's lovelier? God knows.
Tetin dur, non pas Tetin, voyre,	Firm Tit — not Tit — oh, let me see:
Mais petite boule d'ivoyre,	Thou dainty sphere of ivory,
Au milieu duquel est assise	Whose very center's cutely crowned
Une fraize, ou une cerise,	By berry or by cherry round,
Que nul ne veoit, ne touche aussi,	That one can't see, or even touch,
Mais je gaige qu'il est ainsi.	And yet I'd bet the truth is such.
Tetin donc au petit bout rouge,	Ah, yes, thou Tit of tiplet pink,
Tetin qui jamais ne se bouge,	Thou Tit that never sways a wink,
Soit pour venir, soit pour aller,	Not when she comes, nor when she goes,
Soit pour courir, soit pour baller.	Nor runs, nor dances on her toes.
Tetin gauche, Tetin mignon,	O leeward Tit, Tit sweet as sin,
Tousjours loing de son compaignon,	So distant from thy windward twin,
Tetin qui portes tesmoignage	O Tit who givest hints of how
Du demourant du personnage.	She is, a part of whom art thou.
Quand on te veoit, il vient à mainctz	For some, to see thee is to yearn
Une envie dedans les mains	To cup thee in their hands, to learn
De te taster, de te tenir ;	Thy secret shape, to cop a feel;
Mais il se fault bien contenir	But sadly, they must curb their zeal
D'en approcher, bon gré ma vie,	To pet thy curve, good gracious me,
Car il viendroit une aultre envie.	For soon they'd yearn for more than thee.
O Tetin ne grand ne petit,	O Tit not huge nor all that small,
Tetin meur, Tetin, d'appetit,	O Tit, Tit hung'ring for it all,
Tetin qui nuict et jour criez :	O Tit that crieth day and night,
« Mariez moy, tost mariez ! »	"Find me a mate, a mate that's right!"
Tetin qui t'enfles, et repoulses	O Tit who quickly growest up,
Ton gorgerin de deux bons poulses,	Who fillest well thy little cup —
A bon droict heureux on dira	So happy he who getteth thee
Celluy qui de laict t'emplira,	At last engorged with milk, for he
Faisant d'ung Tetin de pucelle	Thereby, O firm young Tit, hath made
Tetin de femme entiere et belle.	Full woman's Breast from Tit of maid.

Had they been written originally by a German poet rather than a French one, lines 6–8 might say, "Thou dainty sphere of ivory, / Whose very center's cutely crowned / By pimple, wart, or blister round". *Ach, wie schön!*

Whorfian Musings

My German-speaking friend's reaction to her native language's portrayal of that which crowns the female breast suggested an interesting hypothesis to me. Maybe translating *Warze* as "wart" is just a tiny bit inaccurate — and for no other reason than that *Warze* is associated with nipples! In other words, where "wart" has virtually *zero* positive associations in an anglophonic mind, the word *Warze* for Germans might have at least a slightly positive aura — aureola? — of associations, thanks to its role in the word *Brustwarze*. A German speaker thus wouldn't feel so appalled that a nipple is seen as a kind of a wart, because after all, *certain* kinds of warts are *nice*! It sounds a bit circular, but in the end I think it makes some sense.

If one believes this argument, then one would have to conclude that the extremely natural-seeming equivalence *Warze* = "wart" is simplistic; that the two words, although they are strong cognates and designate precisely the same class of entities (warts, of course) when used in a stand-alone fashion, do not behave identically when they are embedded in compounds (at least in *one* compound!), and hence the equality is imperfect.

Similar issues come up with the word *Reisschleim,* which denotes a kind of rice gruel. Its second component, *Schleim,* is a cognate to our "slime"; and like "slime" for us anglophones, *Schleim* is used by Germans to describe the moistness on the slippery body of a reptile, the trail left on the ground by a slithering slug, or in general, any kind of repulsive-seeming ooze (most often yellow and green). Thus how could something to eat conceivably be called "slime"? Well, the answer, according to my just-framed hypothesis, is that this food is *not,* despite appearances, called "slime"; it is called *Schleim,* and *that* word, though cognate to and nearly synonymous with "slime", has an aura of connotations that is ever so slightly, ever so subtly different.

Appealing though this hypothesis of non-equivalence is, I am not sure I buy it. In its place, I offer a slight variant: German speakers are just as repulsed by the words *Warze* and *Schleim* in isolation as we anglophones are by "wart" and "slime", but when those same words are buried inside certain compounds, German speakers suppress some of the negativity surrounding them and retain other more neutral properties, such as the idea that a wart is a protuberance, that it is darker than the surrounding area, that it is slightly irregular in shape, and so on; or that slime is viscous, sticky, perhaps slightly warm, and so on. (Another possibility is, of course, that German speakers are completely repulsed both by nipples and by rice gruel, and don't mind letting the world know it.)

Being an honest person, I feel obliged to confess that just a few days after writing the above remarks about warts and breastwarts, I was startled to hear the phrase "You're such a worry wart!" right after it had popped out of my own mouth in conversation with a friend. Though I had meant to use the gentlest of epithets, I had undeniably spoken that tainted word "wart" with its cloud of repulsive connotations. Yet I knew that no native speaker would hear any repulsive flavor at all in this stock phrase of American English. This suggested to me that in English as well as German, even the seemingly ugly word "wart" can go close to unheard, as long as it is embedded in the proper context. This approximate reflection of a strange German usage in my own native language gave me pause for thought about my claims about the intrinsic repulsiveness of "breastwarts".

Despite the blurriness of all these issues, I know that as an English speaker, I cannot help but feel put off by the bluntness of many German compound words, including those just mentioned and others such as *Elternteil* ("parents-part", which is the only way of saying "parent"), *Stinktier* ("stink-beast", which means "skunk"), *Faultier* ("lazy-beast" or "nasty-beast", which means "sloth"), *Fingerhandschuh* ("finger-hand-shoe", one way of saying "glove"), *häßlich* ("hateful", but it means "ugly"), *Denksportaufgabe* ("think-sport–exercise" or even "think-sport–on-gift", which means "puzzle" or "brainteaser"), *Wiedergutmachung* ("again-good-making", which sounds to me like saying "Mommy will kiss it and make it all better" but which in actuality means "war reparations"), and so on.

I know full well that we in English have many strange words too, but it seems to me that comparable linguistic or conceptual crudity, if that is what it is, is far rarer. Or perhaps we anglophones have as much crudity if you take the trouble to dissect our Latin- and Greek-based words etymologically, but most native speakers are unable to do so, and hence for them the parts are absent. This is somewhat the case even for our non-compound word "sloth", which, as an animal name, seems unrelated to the sin it names.

Tu, musica divina, tu che m'hai preso il cuore

Somewhere in the early 1960's, the Italian popular song "Volare" flew over the Atlantic and swept across the U.S. for a while. I already liked what little I had heard of Italian — words like *piccolo* and *bambino* charmed me — but when I heard the voice of Domenico Modugno crooning the mellifluous lyrics to his song, suddenly I was right up there in the air flying alongside him, *nel blu dipinto di blu, felice di stare lassù...*

> *E volavo, volavo felice più in alto del sole ed ancora più su,*
> *Mentre il mondo pian piano spariva lontano laggiù;*
> *Una musica dolce suonava soltanto per me...*

The way those pure liquid vowels just melted together — *più in alto, negli occhi tuoi blu, ma io continuo a sognare* — the doubled consonants, the repeated words, the palatalized "gl"'s and "gn"'s, the soft "c"'s in *voce* and *dolce* — all that just did something indescribable to me. This was magic if anything could be magic. It was obvious that sooner or later, I would have to learn Italian. And one day I was sitting at a table in Tresidder, Stanford's student union, when a professor of Italian and a student sat down near me and started talking together. I couldn't keep my ears off them! Surely one was in heaven if one could glide through the skies of this language as they were doing. And so, as soon as the next quarter rolled around, I signed up.

Of all things, my teacher was actually a French woman, married to an Italian, but she had a beautiful Italian accent and a great command of the language, and I ate it all up as ravenously as if it were scrumptious Italian food. Little tiny things, like counting to ten — *uno, due, tre, quattro, cinque, sei, sette, otto, nove, dieci* — gave me enormous pleasure. Just the word *cinque* alone rolled so trippingly off the tongue. And the phrase *qui vicino*, meaning "around here", but literally "here near", I found exquisite.

I was stunned at the discovery that I was able to "parlay" my French into Italian with remarkable ease, so much so that I felt that when I was speaking Italian, it was just French with a different veneer. Obviously, the more deeply one gets into Italian, the less this feels like the case, since languages become more and more idiosyncratic as one delves into them in ever greater detail, but at the outset it can feel wonderfully exciting to develop a very complex set of subtle conversion tricks that carry French forms, say, into their Italian counterparts. Each such trick provides a shortcut to a sizable set of vocabulary items. Thus I came to have a feeling for the correspondence between *château* and *castello,* for instance (both mean "castle"), and saw that *chapeau* and *cappello* ("hat") belonged to the same family, as do *cheval* and *cavallo* ("horse"), *châtier* and *castigare* ("punish, scold"), *hanche* and *anca* ("hip"), *vache* and *vacca* ("cow"), and many more.

Off to the Roman Wars?

Well, thanks to this somewhat unfair French-based head start, I was catapulted rapidly to the head of the class, and after just a couple of quarters, seemed to be able to express myself pretty well. Right after Stanford's balmy spring quarter was over — in June, 1963 — there was an international conference at Stanford on "Nucleon Structure", of which my father was a main organizer, and we held a big bash at our house on campus with all the participants. I thus met an Italian physicist named Gherardo Stoppini, who was very warm and outgoing and encouraged me to come to Rome and visit with him and his family later that summer. I was thrilled, and thanks to my parents' generosity and indulgence of my love for languages, was able to take him up on it.

I'll never forget the car ride back from Fiumicino (the airport) into Rome itself, during which Stoppini said to me, in thickly accented English, "Be sure to watch out for the wars." I nodded solemnly, *pur non avendo neanche la benché minima idea* of what he meant. Then he added, "A boy of your age might want to go with a war, but you must never, never do it." Just at that moment, we drove by a couple of tough-looking hoydens wearing skirts at the extreme end of the skimpiness spectrum and with cigarettes dangling luridly out of their mouths. Stoppini nodded in their direction, and all of a sudden I was pretty sure I knew what "going with a war" was. It had hardly been part of my Roman game plan, but then, how could Stoppini have known that?

I found speaking Italian in Italy quite a bit harder than I'd expected, given my bang-up performance in class, but made some progress in the two or three weeks I was there. When I returned to Stanford in the fall, I enthusiastically signed up for more Italian. In the new class, we were often required to write literary-criticism essays, a task I had no interest in doing at all. In order to make such assignments stimulating enough that I would actually do them, I adopted a strange artificial plan.

Rather than groping painfully in the dark for vague literary things to say and then expressing them in gawky Italian, I would leaf through Italian magazines and copy down snippets that sounded to me quintessentially Italian, the kinds of things that (so I thought) only a native could ever say, such as *pur non avendo neanche la benché minima idea* ("despite not having even the foggiest idea") — and then would build my essay up around those very snippets, thus being guided far more by form than by content (which was reasonable, since, as I say, I had little to say). By thus turning the task of writing literary essays upside-down, I somehow finessed a boring chore into a keen pleasure, and even taught myself quite a bit of new vocabulary.

I never was sure what my professors thought of those essays. Surely they must have seemed strange in spots. The technique has stuck with me, though, and often nowadays when I write I am powerfully driven by form — but not any longer for lack of ideas to express. I simply let the ideas already swimming about in my brain be gently molded, in their congealing into text, by structures and words that fit the constraints I've imposed on myself.

Zigzagando per l'Italia

Years and years later, on the first date I ever had with Carol Ann Brush, who would later become my wife, we found out that we both had studied Italian as undergraduates — in fact, she had majored in it, along with art history — and this mutual love became an unexpected kind of bond between us. Carol's roots were half Italian, a few generations back, and so she felt a deep connection with the country. She also had lived in Bologna for one summer as part of her Italian studies, and had fallen in love with the city for its liveliness, its stylishness, and of course its food.

The summer after we were married, to celebrate our shared love of Italy and its culture, we took a two-month tour of Italy during which I gave a slew of lectures that I had arranged in advance. The first two lectures were in Torino, and both were in English, though I gave an introductory apology for that fact in a somewhat nervous Italian. The next lecture was in the beautiful medieval city of Siena, and my hosts, sensing I spoke some Italian, asked me if I would mind giving my lecture in Italian — it would make it easier on the students, they explained. I was petrified, but said I'd try. I enlisted one of them as a "tutor", and spent about three hours before the talk grilling him on vocabulary and ways of saying things, and then just plunged in. To my relief, it went reasonably well, and I was encouraged enough that I was willing to try it again as we went to other cities.

And did we go to other cities! Our trip was a crazy kind of random walk, zigzagging back and forth, up and down, all over the upper two-thirds of the boot, including Torino, Camogli, Rapallo, Pisa, Volterra, Siena, Firenze, Bologna, Ferrara, Mantova, Padova, Venezia, Trieste, Udine, Perugia, Assisi, Todi, Urbino, Gubbio, Roma, Napoli, Sorrento, Amalfi, Ravello, Positano, Capri, Orvieto, Milano, Ivrea… Mostly at universities but also at some conferences, I gave exactly twenty lectures on quite a few different topics, and by the very end I was giving my lectures exclusively in Italian. That summer marked a huge jump in my mastery of the language.

In the course of our giant zigzag, we made many new friends and resaw many old friends, including Benedetto Scimemi, who appears doubly in Poems XI as a translator of "Ma Mignonne". In Benedetto's large and shady courtyard in Padova, one of the nicest photos ever taken of Carol and me was snapped, with each of us holding up a small *tartaruga* (tortoise) for display. When I mentioned that the German for *tartaruga* was *Schildkröte*, meaning "shield-toad", Carol snorted, incredulous but tickled, "'Shield-toad'!? Come on! That's like calling an eagle a 'feather-cow'!" This sweet memory of Carol's spontaneous parody of German word-building, so in tune with my own feelings, always brings a smile to my face.

Music and Sadness

Bonding with a culture, for me, always centers on finding the music with which my soul resonates deeply. In the case of Italy, it started out that summer of 1986 with a cassette we bought along the *autostrada* and played for the first time as we approached Sorrento. It was the famous old-time tenor Beniamino Gigli singing Neapolitan ballads, and our cassette included "Torna a Surriento" ("Return to Sorrento"). From this tape I have since branched out to other tapes and CD's of that period — the thirties and forties — songs of the World War II period and just before.

I discovered so many songs and singers who represent for me a kind of quintessential Italian-ness, which, ironically, is hardly known at all to the majority of young Italians I meet today. Mention the name of Alberto Rabagliati and you elicit a look of total bewilderment — and yet he was as popular in his day as Bing Crosby was in America. A soaring song like "Tu, musica divina" or a snappy ditty like "Ba...ba...baciami piccina" is as obscure today as are the great melodies of, say, Jerome Kern or Harold Arlen in America. To me, there is something extraordinarily sad, even frightening, about this contemporary trend, on both sides of the Atlantic, towards near-total detachment from an unbelievably glorious musical past.

I have recently come to know and love many songs from Italy's counterpart to our own Golden Era of Song, and theirs is comparable in quality, although smaller in absolute number of songs. A few of my favorites are "Il primo pensiero" (Rabagliati sings this), "La mia canzone al vento" (with Giuseppe Lugo), "Ma l'amore no" (Lina Termini), "Signora Illusione" (Luciana Dolliver), and "Se fossi milionario" (Ernesto Bonino). These songs and so many others of their vintage, whether in America, France, or Italy, reach deep into my heart and touch primal emotions of romanticism, nostalgia, yearning, and joy. Why such feelings are so foreign to the hugely predominant "sex, drugs, and rock-n-roll" crowd as virtually to seem from another planet is a tragic mystery utterly beyond my fathoming.

In the hopes of nurturing in Carol's and my children an appreciation for the kinds of music that their mother and father found so full of meaning, I play songs from the old days in the car whenever we take a long trip. They may be American — Fats Waller or Billie Holiday, for instance — or they may be Italian or French or even German. If I am lucky, and if they are lucky, some of our love for certain types of musical grace and depth will be passed on.

This past summer, in Italy as we always try to be during June, the three of us took just such a trip from Trento to Carol's beloved city of Bologna, and en route we listened to Marlene Dietrich singing nostalgic pre-war German songs, such as "Du, Du, liegst mir im Herzen", which the kids enjoyed greatly. We had gone down to see our friend Alex Passi, the other Italian translator/poet of "Ma Mignonne" featured in Poems XI. While visiting him, we all drove up into the hills near Bologna and had a wonderful vegetarian lunch in a restaurant that is part of a farm, and after coffee we took a little walk and found a field in which we all started kicking Danny's soccer ball around while chatting.

One topic led to another at random, and at some point — I'll never know why — I was reminded of an Italian restaurant in Ann Arbor where many years ago Carol and I had once eaten, called "Bella Ciao". Out of the blue, I asked, "Does the phrase 'Bella ciao' have some special significance, or is it just something somebody once made up for a restaurant name?" Without warning, Alex launched into a most haunting, sad melody in a very pure singing voice, and I found myself enormously moved without being able to say why, almost as if I'd known this heart-piercing song all my life.

It turned out this song had a complex history. It was originally sung by women called *mondine* — workers who did backbreaking labor in the rice paddies — as their lament about the endless toil and trouble that made up their barren lives. In that way, the original "Bella ciao" was like the old Negro spirituals in the United States, filled with a pain and a sadness so powerful that one could recognize them even if one didn't understand the words. However, in World War II, "Bella ciao" took on a new life as the rallying song of the *partigiani* — the anti-Fascists who took refuge in high mountain lairs and courageously fought the dark forces of Mussolini. The new words to "Bella ciao" were mostly different, but even so, there was a recognizable commonality of theme — a sense of suffering, strength, and refusal to give up, even were death to come. Here are some of them:

Stamattina,	*This morning early,*
Mi sono alzato,	*From sleep I wakened,*
O bella ciao, bella ciao,	*My love good-bye, love good-bye,*
Bella ciao, ciao, ciao,	*Love good-bye, bye, bye,*
Stamattina,	*This morning early,*
Mi sono alzato,	*From sleep I wakened,*
E ho trovato	*And I found*
L'invasor.	*The enemy.*
O partigiano,	*O freedom fighter,*
Portami via,	*Spirit me off now,*
O bella ciao, bella ciao,	*My love good-bye, love good-bye,*
Bella ciao, ciao, ciao,	*Love good-bye, bye, bye,*
O partigiano,	*O freedom fighter,*
Portami via,	*Spirit me off now,*
Ché mi sento	*For I fear that*
Di morir.	*I shall die.*
E se muoio	*And should I perish,*
Da partigiano,	*By your side fighting,*
O bella ciao, bella ciao,	*My love good-bye, love good-bye,*
Bella ciao, ciao, ciao,	*Love good-bye, bye, bye,*
E se muoio	*And should I perish,*
Da partigiano,	*By your side fighting,*
Tu mi devi	*Then I pray you'll*
Seppellir.	*Bury me.*

I Pass

I had known of Alex Passi for many years before we actually met in person. A key event in catalyzing our meeting was an amazing chance encounter that took place when I went to Ascona, Switzerland, an idyllic town on the hills overlooking the beautiful Lago Maggiore. I had been invited there to deliver a lecture in a conference on the very loose topic of "The Culture of the Artificial". I proposed speaking on translation, with my focus being "Ma Mignonne", and the organizers found that fit just fine within the scope of their conference. And so the evening before my talk I turned up, bearing my usual fat packet of transparencies, checked in, and headed straight for the hotel's dining room, where there was supposed to be a fancy banquet for all the participants.

I sat down alone at a big table and after not very long was joined by an Italian man, and we found enough in common to start up a lively chat in Italian. A few minutes later, an aristocratically clad woman arrived, sat down by us, and joined right in with our conversation in Italian. By her fluency and her beautiful pronunciation, she was obviously Italian and of very high culture. Then a French academic of some sort joined our little table and since he didn't speak Italian, I switched over into French, and so did the elegant lady. She didn't miss a beat, and what was strange was that by her fluency and her beautiful pronunciation, she was obviously French and of very high culture. This was definitely confusing to me. I was used to meeting people who spoke two languages very well, but she was something else, with her extraordinarily precise mastery of both.

At some point, she asked me if I was going to give a talk, and I said I was indeed, on translations of a French poem into English, at which point she remembered my talk and my name from the program and said, still going on in French, "So you're American? You didn't sound it at all." I took this as a compliment and felt pleased, but in a little while, maybe three minutes later, she started speaking English to me. What was strange was that by her fluency and her beautiful pronunciation, she was obviously English and of very high culture. Now I was *really* thrown. What in the world *was* this woman?

Soon she revealed that her presence at the conference was as a simultaneous interpreter, and so I asked her what languages she knew. She said she had grown up speaking not three, not four, but *five* languages, all equally well: Italian, French, English, Russian, and Portuguese. When I queried, she said she supposed her favorite of them all was Russian. Needless to say, her life story was a fascinatingly complicated mishmosh of peregrinations across Russia, Europe, and Africa, and that was all there was to it. She now lived in Florence. We finished up the dinner in pleasant fashion, bade each other adieu till the next day, and went off for the night.

Next day, an hour or so before my lecture, she asked me if she could take a quick look at my transparencies to see what kind of vocabulary I would be using; I was happy to oblige her, and left them with her. When she returned them to me, she said, "You know, one of the translators of your poem is a nephew of mine — Alex Passi." I was knocked off my seat! Her name, as she had told me the evening before, was Caterina Corsini Passi, which I had duly registered but it had rung no bells. Now I heard the "Passi" bell loud and clear. Of course I made very sure to feature Alex's translation quite prominently in my talk, and even mentioned the connection with his aunt in the translation booth.

In any case, thanks to this unlikely and stunning event, I was reminded of Alex, and so, after years of silence, I got back in touch with him; this eventually led to our first actual meeting, in Bologna in 1995. It turns out that Alex is merely a perfect bilingual (he spent several years in the United States as a boy), while his aunt is certainly the most polyglot person I have ever met in my life. Her language count is, as near as I can tell, 5.0. No, no — that's certainly way too low! It must be quite a bit higher than that, because to get that figure I added up just her *native* languages. (If you did that for me, I would come out at 1.0.) What about Spanish, which I'm sure she can get along beautifully in? What about German? What about Ukrainian or Polish? And so forth. My guess is, she's probably up there in the 7's or the 8's. I thought I had a pretty strong hand, but she makes my poky little pilingualism look pretty pathetic! But what can you do? I didn't grow up gallivanting all over creation. Those are the breaks. I pass!

Spreading My Net Yet Wider

We now rewind the tape some decades, to when I was still a college undergraduate waking up to a general love for languages. Back in those days when time seemed so expansive, I used to browse for hours in the foreign-language section of the Stanford Bookstore, and dream about how I would one day learn so many other tongues. It was exciting but also frustrating — there were just too many out there! As a partial relief from the frustration, I would buy grammars and dictionaries — if you can't actually *speak* the damn thing, at least have it on your shelf! — and thus started my binge of dictionary-collecting. This was a phase that I went through for quite a few years, until, with the help of a few friends, I had amassed a collection of perhaps two hundred dictionaries of all sorts of languages, including Eskimo, Australian Aborigine, Basque, Cherokee, Hopi, Maori, Albanian, Swahili, Turkish, Punjabi, Cantonese, Welsh, Manx, Malayalam, Bengali, Breton, Hawaiian, Solomon Islands Pijin, Malay, Malagasy, Papago–Pima, and ever so many more. One of my prizes was a Polish–Swahili two-way dictionary, which seemed pretty darned esoteric!

As a consumer of language books, I was nothing if not a spendthrift. If I'd gotten one of those "Buy one, get two more for free!" book-club–type offers, I would've taken them up on it in a snap! As a matter of fact, I have heard a droll quip along just these lines, but about actual languages, not language books. It was about Romance languages, and ran this way: "Learn one, get two more for free!"

I sort of put this joke to the test by deciding, quite on a whim, to take Spanish one quarter. But I knew it would be excruciating to start out in a first-year class with people who knew no foreign languages at all, and to whom even the ideas of "infinitive" and "conjugation" would be novel. So I went out and bought a cute little Learn-Spanish-Quickly book and zoomed through it in a couple of days, and then went and took a placement exam. I wound up getting put into some fairly advanced-level class in which we first read a short play and then a whole Pérez Galdós novel, which I quite enjoyed. After I had finished the book, I was very surprised by how much the Spanish language had invaded my mind, and for a short while, when I was bored in a class I would do my usual marginal jottings in Spanish.

The "Tower of Languages" Model

Obviously my Spanish was "built on" my Italian and my French. My rather simplistic theory at the time was that these languages in my head were strictly hierarchical, like a multi-story building. The ground floor was of course English, upon which was built my French. Then Italian was built on French, and Spanish was built right on top of my Italian. A neat theory, which would suggest that whenever I wanted to say *Quisiera un día saber hablar muchas lenguas extranjeras*, it would get built up by some ultra-rapid unconscious translation process from the Italian sentence *Vorrei un giorno sapere parlare molte lingue straniere*, which in turn would have been built out of *Je voudrais un jour savoir parler beaucoup de langues étrangères*, and at the bottom, the sole sentence formulated out of genuine *semantics* rather than by some kind of purely mechanical, meaning-free, syntactic manipulation of a string passed up from one floor below, would lie the English utterance "I would like one day to be able to speak many foreign languages."

Of course the plausibility of this whole story seems very low, and yet there has to be *some* truth to it. After all, *saber* is but a tiny tweak of *sapere*, and clearly when I first encountered it in some grammar or dictionary, I entered it into my memory in some sense *via* the Italian verb. And that verb, in its earlier day, had been entered as a kind of variant of the French *savoir*. For things *not* to happen that way would be absurd and grossly inefficient, as well as mighty implausible.

There is a profound flaw in the multi-translation theory, however, and that consists in the notion that the *original* memory entry defines forever the *sole route of access* to the given item. It assumes that no "express" pathway can ever be built up that leads directly from the *concept* of "knowing" to the Spanish *word* for that concept, but that instead the only pathway is like a milk train, stopping at a bunch of intermediary places en route. That would be sad, and it would also make my Spanish-speaking drag out awfully slowly. And these days, it's true: Were I to have to jump into Spanish cold turkey today, I *would* indeed drag a lot, and Italian phrases galore would pop to my mind, and get switched, just barely pre-utterance, by one piece of trickery or another into their Spanish cousins. But — would the Italian be coming from French, and the French in turn from English? Of course not.

Il parle italien comme une mouche espagnole…

And yet, and yet… Things are amazingly blurry and murky in this little oligoglottal brain. My Italian, which when young was so tied to the apron-strings of its sweet French mother, long ago grew up and became an autonomous, strong language. When I speak Italian now, I certainly am *not* "speaking French with an Italian veneer", as was once undeniably the case. ¡No way, José! But if that is so, then how come, about half the time when I want to refer to those buzzy black things that fly around and annoy the bejesus out of you, I come out with the word *mucca,* which means "cow", instead of *mosca,* which means "fly"?

A word of explanation. I earlier mentioned a family of transformation tricks leading from certain French words containing "ch" to Italian words with "c" or "cc" in them, such as *vache* into *vacca.* Those patterns, though only heuristic and certainly not rigid rules, became deeply ingrained in me very early on in my learning of Italian, and somehow played a special role in giving me that extra-quick start I had in Italian. Well, some vestige of those pseudo-rules remains buried in my mind, and the depth of its burial seems not to be fixed but variable, yet totally out of my conscious control.

And thus, last summer, when little Monichina and I were strolling around the grounds of the beautiful stately old house where Luisa Scimemi, wife of Benedetto, spent many years as a girl, I noticed a bunch of swallows gracefully swooping through the air near a pond, and I pointed them out to Monica, saying, *Guarda le rondini — stanno volando a caccia di piccole mucche!* That is, "Look at the swallows — they're flying around hunting for little cows!" I caught myself instantly, but not before saying it. And where did *mucche* come from? There is no question whatsoever: It came from the French word *mouche,* meaning "fly". On the fly, I had transformed that French word into its Italian "equivalent" — only, of course, it was a hilarious mistake. Why in the world would a French-to-Italian transformation pattern be active in my mind on a day when I had been speaking solely Italian all day long? How should I know? *Non ho neanche la benché moindra idea.*

Since that day, in various situations, I've heard myself, each time *ex post facto*, saying sometimes *mucca* for "fly", other times *mosca*. It seems about fifty–fifty, or maybe slightly in favor of *mucca*. The bubbling-up of French-based intruders inside my Italian utterances, or even pre-utterances, makes me feel a deep sense of shame — and yet, am *I* to blame? Did I *choose* to rely on such transformation patterns, or to activate them? No; they are just parts of me, relics from my ancient past. I'm a victim of my brain.

The Messy Truth about Multiple Languages

My conclusion from all of this is that although the tower-of-languages multi-translation theory is a poor approximation to the truth, it still does capture a certain bit of the truth that other theories do not. There seem to be links crisscrossing my brain in all sorts of directions, some going directly from concepts to words, others from English words to French words, others from English words to Italian words, others from French words to Italian words, and so on — and although each link may have a predominant directionality to it (thus, English-to-French links are generally stronger than the reverse ones), many are bidirectional, and this has as a consequence the fact that any foreign language that I am actively speaking (and, on rare occasions, even ones that I am not actively speaking at all) can have an effect on languages learned far earlier and more deeply. Even my English, ultimate ur-source of everything, is not immune to being penetrated by alien syntactic structures and lexical patterns while I am not looking.

And what is particularly surprising to me is that I see all sorts of English words and patterns bubbling up in my children's Italian, and vice versa. The shock of it is that they, in stark contrast to me, learned both languages purely through total immersion. They have never ever looked a word up in a dictionary, learned how to conjugate a verb, diagrammed a sentence, or anything of the sort. But even so, ways of perceiving the world that belong uniquely to one of their languages will show up right in the middle of the other language. This fact tends to soften my long-standing self-accusation as a mere "mechanical translator": If my kids, who certainly are *not* just translators, are subject to all sorts of bizarre cross-linguistic contaminations, then why should I take my own cross-language errors as being revelatory of a huge fraud taking place, all below the conscious level?

English ni stcejbus rieht edecerp ot dnet sbreV

An amusing pastime that I had, back in those days of intense language fever, was taking Backwards English — "hsilgnE", as I called it — fairly seriously as a language. Mostly as a tongue-in-cheek joke, but not entirely, I started to write a "koobtxet" for hypothetical foreign learners of hsilgnE, in which I explained, with a poker face, its curious grammar in which direct objects preceded verbs, and verbs preceded their subjects, and in which nouns were preceded by relative clauses but followed by adjectives and then by articles, and so forth. The header of this section, of course, is a typical sentence in hsilgnE, which I have every reason to believe you are capable of translating into English despite never having read even a single word of my definitive koobtxet.

A key part of the whole hsilgnE game/challenge was my stab at learning to pronounce hsilgnE accurately. To try to acquire this skill, I would tape myself saying a sentence in English and then twist the tape around so that the tape recorder would be "fooled" into reading off of the tape's shiny side instead of its dull side. Although my voice would come out a little muffled because of this flipping of the tape, I could still quite clearly hear myself saying, "Aureezy-*whoosh*, senya-*moosh*!", and I would imitate this as best I could and then record *that,* and then flip my hsilgnE-speaking voice over and play *that* backwards.

Thanks to this twofold time reversal, I got the chance to hear myself saying, "Too migh-ness too eez zeerow!" (Why I chose this inane truth of arithmetic as my target sentence, I'll never know.) The shock, of course, was that I had an *accent* in hsilgnE — an *English* accent! And try as I might, I couldn't get rid of it — no matter how carefully Doug listened to guoD talking hsilgnE on the tape, he couldn't master the pronunciation. (Note, by the way, that a time-reversed "t" sound is not like a "t" at all, but more like an "sh" that is suddenly and sharply truncated — a very subtle sound to learn to make, perhaps even an impossible one, for English speakers.)

The game of playing sounds backwards had an enormous charm for me. Those were the days when on Steve Allen's late-night TV show, they often would tape little skits and then right after a commercial break, come back and show the tapes backwards. It was often hilarious. Anyway, the idea was very contagious, and I experimented around with it a lot, especially on pieces of music. I had a fairly primitive record player whose turntable could be removed, and underneath it I found what drove it: an elastic belt much like a large rubber band. All I needed to do was take the band off and reinstall it so that instead of looking like an "O", it made a figure-eight. Then the turntable spun in the opposite direction, and luckily, the needle was placed vertically in the tone arm, so the grooves were happy when it was plunked down in them and traversed them from the inside out, toward the record's periphery rather than toward its central hole.

Most music, I must say, I found disappointingly meaningless-sounding, but not all. My greatest discovery — a wonderful "composition" of mine, so to speak — was the time reversal of the lyrical eighteenth variation from Rachmaninoff's "Rhapsody on a Theme by Paganini". Try it out yourself!

Generalized Accents

Not just in French or hsilgnE, but in all languages, doing my utmost to get rid of any foreign accent was always a very big deal to me. Of course, I didn't always succeed, but I certainly tried. At the very least, I think I have always managed to make my nationality reasonably obscure. In certain languages, I've been accused of sounding not like a native but like a German, a Swiss, and even, one time, a Martian!

Over the years, I suppose largely because of my fanatical obsession with acquiring native-style accents in various languages, I gradually abstracted and generalized the notion of "foreign accent". My exploration was rooted in languages and so the first abstractions that I made of it were naturally still language-based, but others soon transcended language.

For example, after I had been studying Chinese for a while, I realized with shame that my clumsily-drawn characters must have a very foreign-looking "visual accent" to them. In the course of trying to get rid of this "accent", I started to wonder if there was such a thing as a "Japanese accent" in Chinese calligraphy, given that both languages revere the same set of characters and have calligraphic traditions stretching back thousands of years. This question led me to pondering whether there is such a thing as, say, a German accent or a French accent or an American accent in typeface design. Could a sophisticated viewer looking at a beautiful typeface intuit its designer's country of origin? Is there something indelibly American about Americana (designed by Richard Isbell), something indelibly French about Banco and Calypso and Mistral (by Roger Excoffon), something indelibly German about Palatino and Optima (by Hermann Zapf)?

Certainly there are European handwritings. I think I could pretty easily tell the difference between a specimen of Italian handwriting and the same sequence of letters penned by a German hand. And there is without any doubt a kind of "era" accent in handwriting: an older person's handwriting tends to have all sorts of different shapes and curlicues from that of people who learned to write in cursive in the past couple of decades.

Moving away from the realm of language, consider baseball, which has spread from America to other parts of the world, where it is played with equal enthusiasm. Do Cubans and Japanese, for instance, have "foreign accents" when they play baseball? Does a lifelong chess player have a "chess accent" in playing Go for the first time? Do I have an "Algol accent" when I write computer programs in Lisp (Algol having been my first computer language)? In the 1950's and 1960's, many physicists decided to move over into the exciting new field of molecular biology. Did they have all have a recognizable "physics accent" in their various approaches to the problems of this alien discipline? Do Americans have an American accent when they drive in Europe? Do Europeans have European accents when they drive in

America? Is it possible to recognize an Italian driver on a German *Autobahn,* or vice versa (not cheating by using license plates or car makes)?

What is a "French accent" in music? Certainly in the classical genres, Ravel, Debussy, Fauré, Poulenc, and Satie epitomize this notion, but what about someone like Hector Berlioz, who to me sounds more German than French? And what about César Franck, who, although Belgian, can sound just as French as any of them? I even know a piano-trio movement by Welsh composer Alec Templeton and a piano-sonata movement by Russian composer Alexander Scriabin that sound as "French" as anything I can think of. But what *is* this elusive French musical accent?

This matter of "musical accents" can involve listening as well as producing. For instance, do Poles, when listening to, say, Chopin's fourth Scherzo, inevitably feel a deeper kinship to it, and a more effortless understanding of it, than Americans do? Conversely, do Americans, when listening to Elvis Presley belt out "Jailhouse Rock", inevitably relate to it better than any Pole ever could?

One of the most important goals I had when I visited Poland was to make a pilgrimage to the tiny rural village of Żelazowa Wola, birthplace of Fryderyk Szopen, also known as Frédéric Chopin. I was astonished not only at the cool disinterest in Chopin as a person on the part of some of my Polish acquaintances, but even more at their near-total indifference to his passionate and deeply Polish music, whereas I, even from childhood, had been utterly enthralled by it and knew it intimately. Most of the Poles I met, to my chagrin and surprise, were far more interested in The Who or The Doors (popular rock groups at the time) than in Chopin — a most curious reversal, since I, an American whose adolescence straddled the 1950's and 1960's, am as alienated by rock as I can imagine a human could be. So here are Poles who fail to "hear with a Polish accent", and likewise, an American who fails to "hear with an American accent"! Does this perhaps suggest that the very notion of "national musical accents" is incoherent? But if that is so, how can I call Chopin's music "deeply Polish"?

Flipping Gender Viewpoints

Carrying the "accent" metaphor into yet more remote territory, I ask: When a male writes fiction, has he necessarily a "masculine accent"? What if he writes a story featuring a female protagonist? What if he empathizes enormously with her? What if his entire novel is written, as was Norman Rush's *Mating,* in the first person from a female viewpoint?

Or, to turn this around, suppose a female reads a novel that was written, like *Catcher in the Rye,* by a male and with a male protagonist: Must her understanding of the events and emotions therein inevitably have a "feminine accent", or can she conceivably understand such a book "like a native"? By analogy with my experience of knowing Chopin intimately yet from a geographically, temporally, and culturally remote starting point, I would be strongly inclined to believe a female reader can empathize with and map herself essentially perfectly onto a male character, but the interesting question in that case is, *what is going on?*

Does this flexible female reader somehow convert herself into a male persona as she reads, and thus experience Holden Caulfield's experiences as a "virtual male"? Or conversely, could she possibly be translating Holden Caulfield's masculine adventures and feelings into feminine counterparts and then effortlessly relating to those? I suspect the former is much closer to the truth, in the case of a sensitive reader. Thus in some curious and subtle sense she "becomes a native experiencer of masculinity". How does this inner persona of the opposite sex get built? How close to being a full human mind is the mind-in-a-mind that she builds up in the course of reading? Does this relate somehow to the notion of multiple personalities?

Flipping Spectacles

I have been speaking of perceptual reversals — the temporal and spatial reversal of English, the musical-taste swap of members of different cultures, and male/female point-of-view reversals. Over the years, many other types of perceptual reversal have been experimented with, and have given rise to some remarkable findings. Among the most fascinating are experiments in which courageous and pertinacious subjects don prismatic glasses that turn their entire visual field upside-down, so that images, instead of appearing inverted on the retina (as an image usually does), land on the retina right-side-up. This right-side-up-ness means, ironically, that when the signals go further back into the brain to be processed more deeply and give rise to genuine *perception,* everything is flipped. Faces and places are unrecognizable, and the brain is lost and overwhelmed with the wrongness of it all.

Amazingly, however, after what must be an indescribable two- to three-week adjustment period, the experimental subjects adapt perfectly to these new conditions, reporting that they can see normally again, that everything looks just right. How can this be? Despite its counterintuitivity, there is a familiar analogue to this that makes it seem almost mundane and obvious: namely, the experience of learning to hear meaning through an "upside-down" channel — the initially totally alien phonemes, vocabulary, and grammatical patterns of another language — and getting so used to the new medium that one no longer notices its presence at all. After sufficient time spent in an alien linguistic environment, pulling out only the *ideas* in a conversation and not even hearing the sounds as such feels no different from how it felt in one's original native medium.

A further twist on this experiment is that when subjects remove the inverting spectacles, they find that they are, at least briefly, just as discombobulated by their new "normal" state as they initially were when they put the spectacles on. I admit that I personally have never been so totally out of touch with English that my own native language seemed rusty, alien, peculiar — but I know many people who have reported precisely this, after having lived for years in an environment where they almost never speak their childhood tongue. Will I one day "enjoy" such an experience?

Flipping Earphones

In the spirit of generalized translation, I imagined carrying this experiment over from vision to another sensory modality. What would it be like to wear "inverting earphones" — earphones that invert the auditory spectrum? By "invert", what I mean is the standard musical sense of the term, according to which any *upward* motion in pitch is converted into an equal-sized *downward* motion, and vice versa. For example, in the opening phrase of the Star-Spangled Banner, the melodic fragment "Oh, say can you see" would reach its highest note on "say", while "see" would be its lowest note. Bach and other composers of the Baroque era often used the device of inversion in writing fugues and other pieces, and it still enjoys a limited popularity, although there is no question that musicians back then had a far greater facility than today's musicians do for inverting melodies at the drop of a hat, and for recognizing inverted melodies when played.

What in the world would it be like to listen to music (or to the world in general) for weeks or months on end through such inverting earphones? Adult female and male voices would of course be interchanged, as would those of children and adults. And screaming would come out sounding very low, while muttering would involve very high pitches. What would it be like to try to converse? At first, nothing would be intelligible at all, and then gradually, you would grow accustomed to it and would start to make out words and then phrases, and eventually English would start to sound normal again. Or would it? Since I have obviously never been through anything remotely like this experience, I have no clear sense of how it would feel to hear a perfectly standard *sequence* of constituents, yet in which each constituent itself was rendered enormously differently.

Toward a Transparent Language

All these ideas about "generalized accents" and perceptual reversals were part of a talk I gave in 1981 at the Folger Shakespeare Library in Washington, D.C., as part of a symposium entitled "Toward a Transparent

Language", whose theme was, oddly enough, the translation of poetry. When I first received the invitation, which came from the Folger's director, O. B. Hardison, I was fascinated by the topic and flattered to be invited, but also quite puzzled, as I had no reputation either as poet or as translator. Moreover, in my eyes there was an irony to the invitation, since Shakespeare had always been something of a mystery to me, a little too opaque for my modern ears. I even thought of myself as something of a philistine with respect to poetry in general. Nonetheless, I accepted with great pleasure, since there was no doubt that translation fascinated me.

When I arrived, I felt a bit intimidated to find myself among famous poets, translators, literary critics, and Shakespeare scholars. Although two of them turned out to be mind-bogglingly pompous and egomaniacal (my lengthy interactions with them provided me with a couple of incredible-but-true anecdotes that I occasionally relate), O. B. Hardison was, to my great relief, the exact opposite. When I met him at the conference's opening reception, a gala affair, I found him most affable and charming.

I mentioned that I had felt honored but baffled to be invited to join this august company, to which O. B. replied, without a moment's hesitation, "As soon as I'd read your book *Gödel, Escher, Bach,* I was sure you would be the perfect person to invite." Still feeling in the dark, I said, "But why?" I have never forgotten Hardison's reply. "Simple!" he said, "Because it's all about translation!" I had never considered *GEB* in this light, but once he said it, I could see a good deal of truth in it. Perhaps Hardison's claim went a little overboard, but he had pointed something out to me about my book that I myself had not seen, and for this I always have felt truly appreciative.

Hardison was a jovial man, unpretentious and with a gleam in his eye. He told me that in his youth, he had camped out in a tent for a whole year on the grounds of his college campus, probably for economic reasons, if I recall correctly, and I think he had sailed around the world as well. He was obviously someone who loved adventures, both mental and physical. Most of all, I remember O. B.'s open and direct manner, his lack of pretension, and his boyish joy in intellectual experimentation. In Poems VI, we shall re-encounter O. B. Hardison, this time as he wears his translator–poet hat.

The flyer that announced the Folger Library symposium gave the following list of questions as its focus:

How does the translator work? What are the stages of translation? To what degree is "transparency" a possible ideal for the translator's language?

What does it mean to say we "think in English" or "think in Chinese"? What changes occur when a literary work is adapted from one language to another? from one genre to another? to a non-literary medium?

Where do the concerns of the poet and the translator intersect? How does translation affect the language and literature of the receiving culture? What are the real issues at stake in the controversy over fidelity and freedom in translation?

Although I was intellectually excited by these questions back then, I didn't yet have any deep personal experiences in literary translation to relate them to. Today, by contrast, these questions resonate so richly with a whole universe of my thoughts and experiences that I find it almost clairvoyant of O. B. Hardison to have invited me; I wish I could tell him so.

Generalized Translation and Analogy

In my talk at the Folger Library symposium, complementing my first theme of "generalized accents", I brought up some notions I had been exploring about "generalized translation". The basic idea was to conceive of translation as the faithful transport of some abstract pattern from one medium to another medium — in other words, analogy. Nothing about language need be mentioned or involved in any sense. One of several examples that I gave of this notion took up right where the "inverting spectacles" and "inverting earphones" ideas left off.

In a magazine article, I had read of a device intended to allow blind people to experience vision by exploiting a different sensory modality. The idea was as follows. Arrange a set of a few hundred short movable rods, all parallel to each other, in a fine-grained grid of perhaps ten inches by ten inches. Each rod can move in only one dimension: back and forth a few millimeters along its length. Each rod corresponds to, and is controlled by, one pixel in a fairly coarse-grained black-and-white television screen. Thus a dark dot on the screen would make its corresponding rod move forward, say, while a light dot would make it move backward. Controlled in this way, the rods would collectively form a kind of spatial image of some scene.

The key idea was to place this device against the bare back of a human being, thereby allowing television images to be transmitted tactilely onto the person's skin, and thence upward to the person's brain, for higher-level processing. According to what I had read (I have not run into anything further on the topic since then), people could definitely learn to "feel" the shape of a circle or the shape of a triangle. Sighted persons who were trained with this device for a while (always blindfolded, so that their normal retina-mediated vision systems were disabled) reported their subjective experiences in distinctly visual terms. In a manner of speaking, they had learned to "see through their backs" instead of through their eyes.

This was a stunning example of "generalized translation" — even more extreme than learning to hear meaning through a new linguistic channel, or becoming as comfortable with the world seen upside-down as right-side-up. As I jumped back and forth in my mind between this crazy but marvelous new technology and the idea of a single meaning being embeddable in all sorts of diverse linguistic media, I could see that if the technology really worked, then it would soon become no more far-fetched, unusual, or wrong-sounding to speak of blind people *seeing with their backs* than to speak of monolingual Chinese people reading *Crime and Punishment* or *Death of a Salesman*. The idea that vision is intrinsically linked with twin little liquid-filled bulbs attached to the front of one's brain would start to seem as parochial and narrow-minded as the idea that our word "water" is connected, in some privileged way that the Chinese word *shuǐ* is not, with the colorless and tasteless fluid with which we carry out our daily ablutions.

Who knows — somehow, someday, perhaps visual experiences could even be fed into one's brain through the ears or the tongue — or for that matter, tastes and smells might arrive via the channel of the ears or the eyes! All these ideas were, so to speak, real tongue-openers for me.

Seeing Noncubes as Cubes

Another example of generalized translation that I used in my Folger Library talk was provided by an intense interest I had just developed at the time: Rubik's Cube. (Many readers will, I hope, remember this as the brightly-colored plastic 3 x 3 x 3 cube whose six sides could all be rotated independently, thus hopelessly scrambling all the little "cubies", the game of course being to restore the full cube to its original state after such a scrambling.) If one is sufficiently curious and persistent, one can gradually discover certain complex maneuvers that will swap a given pair of cubies, for example, or that will cause two or three particular cubies to swivel simultaneously, each one about its own center, while staying put relative to the larger Cube as a whole. Such maneuvers are the key stratagems that, employed in careful combination with one another, allow the puzzle to be solved. Often these maneuvers have a kind of abstract structure that can be verbalized in a compact notation of this sort: *down-in-up-out-down-in-up* (and similar elegant patterns of varying lengths).

Now it turned out that in the course of only a few months, the worldwide Cube mania had given rise to an incredible number of variants of the original puzzle — there were polyhedra both regular and irregular, strangely sliced spheres, intersecting sets of circles, and on and on. I myself collected something like twenty variations on the Cube theme. What soon became apparent to me, once I had gotten my own personal algorithm for solving the original Cube well under my belt, was that my expertise, such as it was, could be rapidly transferred to these other puzzles, as long as I could figure out how to let go of certain aspects of my carefully-worked-out maneuvers on the Cube. What it took was a loosening-up of what *down* and *in* meant, for instance. Taken rigidly, a term like *down* had meaning only in reference to twists on the Cube itself, and nowhere else; interpreted loosely, however, it could be seen to have a fairly strong analogue in such variegated spatial frameworks as pyramids, octahedra, dodecahedra, sliced cylinders, sliced spheres, "Skewbs" (cubes sliced in an odd diagonal manner), and even pairs or trios of intersecting circles on a flat plane.

To my delight, I found my little Cube-mantra *down-in-up-out-down-in-up* worked just as well in the context of the new puzzles. In each new medium there were of course slight differences in both execution and effect, but I quickly grew used to them, and they were small enough that I got what I needed. Thus through analogical transport, I was able to parlay a quite solid mastery of the Cube into at least a middling command of a few of its cousins. Had I wished to get *really* good at these relatives, of course, I would have had to learn some idiosyncratic, non-transportable tricks, but as long as all I wanted was a mediocre competence, importing Cube-born ideas worked beautifully. All of this felt so much like the constellations of tricks I had long earlier developed for "parlaying" my French into Italian, or my Italian into Spanish — or, somewhat later, for converting my lower-level competence in German into very nice head starts in Dutch and Swedish.

The Ubiquity of Analogical Transfer

Analogy is really the name of the game. From a strong language you borrow skills and gain low-level competence in another one. From one puzzle you borrow techniques and solve others. From the ability to execute 3-turns or mohawks on the ice on your left foot, you find yourself able to do them also on your right foot. From ice-skating, you borrow skills and discover you are able to roller-skate not too badly. From roller-skating, you transfer skills over into roller-blading. Perhaps roller-blading gives you a hand up on skateboarding. You can even transfer skating's "hockey stop" into a similar type of stop on ski slopes, or vice versa. Then skateboarding combined with skiing leads to snowboarding. Since I do not do all of these sports, I have no idea to what extent analogies exist from one to the other, but I suspect that if one takes things sufficiently loosely, these domains are rife with analogies.

The "Learn one, get two more free" theme can even apply, to some extent, at the level of getting to know new people. Say you meet a complete stranger. If your first few minutes of interaction chance to remind you strongly of interactions with someone you already know very well, you will automatically start borrowing "routines" — little ways of joking, styles of banter, and so on — that you have used with your friend, and, more likely than not, they will work reasonably well. This can provide an accelerated route to relatively intimate exchanges with someone who but a short while earlier was utterly unknown. Of course, as with the Cube and the Skewb, or as with French and Italian, such tricks work only up to a certain point, and then the new friend turns out to diverge more and more from the old one. Still, the power of analogy is stunning in all these cases.

Pilgrimage to The Old Country

At the time I gave my Folger Library talk in 1981, my passion for languages was both quite deep and quite old — over two decades — and yet, somewhat amazingly, I had precious little experience in actual *translation*, let alone poetry translation. This is, as I said above, why I was astounded at O. B. Hardison's invitation. Although my memory may be failing me, all I can remember about translation is a few little isolated episodes, most of all when I translated some letters from Polish into English for my father. This actually is a story with some interesting background.

While I was living in Germany in 1974–75, a powerful yearning to learn Polish flared up suddenly and unexpectedly in me, sparked by an invitation from Marek Demiański, a physicist friend in Warsaw, to visit him and to give a talk at Warsaw University's Instytut Fizyki Teoretycznej on my then-ongoing doctoral work — the first colloquium I ever gave in my life, incidentally. I'd always been emotionally drawn to Poland and its language, to a large degree because of Chopin's having been Polish, but also because my father's parents were Polish Jews who had emigrated and settled in New York City around the turn of the century. Thus ever since childhood, I had felt a dual link to Poland, and now I had the chance to go there.

I quickly purchased a delightful elementary Polish text written in German and worked my way through most of it. Then one bright morning in March of 1975, having consumed some scrumptious apple tartlets in Regensburg's finest pastry shop, I set off by train in a burst of excitement. I stayed with some distant relatives for a couple of days in Cracow, after which I went on to Warsaw, gave my talk, and made my pilgrimage to Żelazowa Wola. My Polish of course got quite a workout during the visit. I particularly remember three episodes, all of them connected with Chopin.

Three Polish Vignettes

While wandering about Warsaw, I kept on seeing posters announcing a concert of Chopin piano music to be given by four Polish piano students at the Towarzystwo imienia Fryderyka Chopina — the Frédéric Chopin Foundation — housed in a beautiful old palace in the midst of Warsaw. It was something I felt I couldn't miss, so I invited Marek, and together we went and enjoyed it greatly. At the music's conclusion, I went up and spoke a few words to Joanna Kurpiowska, one of the piano students who had just performed, but found myself somewhat tongue-tied, and mostly we just smiled at each other. However, the next day I was in one of Warsaw's best sheet-music stores and who did I bump into but Joanna again! So at that point she and I really did try to communicate, exchanging chit-chat about

America, Poland, where she and I were studying, favorite composers and pieces, and whatnot. It was short but sweet, and made me feel a little proud of myself.

A few days later, I made a more somber pilgrimage, this time to the Kościół świętego Krzyża (Church of the Holy Cross), where, I had read, Chopin's heart is buried. Spotting a large group of lovely bouquets at the base of a pedestal with a small statue on it, I wandered over, and there, sure enough, was a plaque stating that Chopin's heart was right here. To me it seemed morbid, but after all, it had been Chopin's own last, fervent request to have his heart returned to Poland and buried there after he died, so I let myself enter into the spirit of it all, standing there silently, hands in pockets, letting fragments of a few of my favorite pieces by Chopin run through my head. After a few minutes I felt it was enough, and so I headed contemplatively toward the exit.

I had taken but a few paces when an elderly gentleman suddenly accosted me and, in a chiding tone of voice, intoned at me in Polish, "Sir, this is a sanctuary — you must take your hands out of your pockets!" I didn't obey, since I hadn't quite understood what he was saying, and so he grabbed my wrists and tried to pull them out forcibly. Astounded by his audacity and dogmatism, I found myself sputtering out, in highly questionable grammar, remarks to the effect that even if I did not share *his* religion, I had come from a great distance in order to engage in my *own* form of religion right there in that very church, and that my sort was every bit as good and as pious as his was, and that having one's hands in or out of one's pockets had nothing to do with respecting what is sacred. Then I turned and walked out, hands still in pockets. In retrospect, I felt I could have bent a little and removed my hands while leaving, but I had been too angered to see straight. It certainly left a sour taste in my mouth, not only for what he had done, but for what I had done. Still, I couldn't believe that I had managed to get all those complex ideas across, more or less, in my elementary Polish!

My final linguistic memory of Warsaw is infinitely pleasanter. One morning I went to visit Radio Warsaw, in order to meet the people who were behind the half-hour late-night radio broadcasts of Chopin's music, which, by good fortune, I had accidentally tuned in to one night early in my German stay and to which I had become a faithful listener. When I first entered the large building, I had to communicate with clerks and officials of various sorts, and this was of course all done in Polish. Having managed to get through that, I was next escorted to the office of a friendly woman who had already been informed of my request and was going to help me out with it. When she realized I spoke German fairly well, we bumped the level of our communication up a notch by switching into German, and had a very nice talk for maybe half an hour.

How Jolly the Lot of an Oligoglot   ◆ ◆ ◆   *49*

When we were done, she took me to the office of Maria Nosowska and introduced her as the woman who had single-handedly created and run the nightly Chopin broadcast for roughly twenty-five years. Luckily, although Pani Nosowska knew little English, she spoke an elegant French, and so again, *click!*, up went the communication level by another notch or two. She and I spent the entire afternoon together in her office, listening to Chopin pieces and talking about many things, including the trials and tribulations of her decades of devotion to our common hero. I was most impressed and touched, and in the end she gave me a special set of records of seldom-performed Chopin pieces, which I have always cherished.

When I walked out of the building, it was nearing sunset, and I was joined by Marek, whose English was extraordinarily fluent, and so, once again, *click!*, up ratcheted my ease of self-expression. All of a sudden I had at my disposal a vast storehouse of complex turns of phrase and tricky idioms that in French I simply didn't have, not to mention German and Polish. Indeed, the whole day suddenly seemed, in retrospect, to have been a series of releases from one prison cell to another, each one larger than the one before. Although in English I no longer felt the walls of my cell, I did wonder what it might be like to be released into a yet more expansive language, in which my self-expression might be even more fluent and unshackled. It's a nice dream, even if I can't imagine how it would feel.

Jak Ocalał Świat, à la Hofstadter

When I returned to America that spring, I continued my study of Polish off and on, and at one point was even motivated to take a semester of second-year Polish. In 1978 I went back for a second visit, but from that point on, my Polish — what little of it there was — went into a slow decline, and is now asymptotically approaching zero. Right at my Polish's zenith, however, my father happened to receive a couple of letters in Polish from his Cracow relatives as well as one from a clerk in a court office in the town of Mława, where his mother had been born and from which he had requested a copy of her birth certificate. He asked me if I could translate them into English for him, and curiously, doing so was the first time I had carried out any translation more complex than college koobtxet exercises!

My study of Polish had encouraged me to obtain a couple of books by the famous Polish science-fiction writer Stanisław Lem in their original language. I knew that Lem was fond of linguistic games and wordplay, and had seen some of his books in English but not read any. I had also been told that the English translations by Michael Kandel were brilliant beyond description. One story in particular that someone described to me was in *The Cyberiad,* and was called "How the World Was Saved" — *Jak ocalał świat.*

As I understood it, the premise of the story was that some inventor or other had designed and built a contraption that could make anything at all, as long as it began with the letter "n". Of course this was an absurdity, since not *things* but their *names* begin with letters, and names are language-dependent and arbitrary symbols: what begins with "n" in one language (*e.g.,* Polish) will not, as a rule, begin with "n" in another (*e.g.,* English). And for a machine's constructing capabilities to somehow be limited by a set of accidental vagaries of the language that its designer happened to speak really took the credibility cake. I was turned off by this story before even reading a word of it!

On the other hand, I realized that this absurdity had to be, in some sense, Lem's whole point. Surely he knew exactly what he was doing, and probably he was making both a philosophical and a linguistic joke. And so my curiosity was piqued. I wanted to read it, but on the other hand, I didn't want to read Kandel's translation of it (which I easily found in print), since I thought that translating it would be an interesting challenge, and I didn't want to plant any ideas in my own mind. So I went to my bookshelf, pulled down *Cyberiada,* and found *Jak ocalał świat* with no trouble. I started reading it with the aid of a couple of dictionaries, but by the time I had finished the first page I was caught up in it, and so right then and there I started translating. I wound up spending a couple of afternoons on the challenge, which in the end gave me an extreme feeling of esthetic gratification. Here are the opening few paragraphs, in my translation:

> One time Constructor Trurl invented a Machine That Could Make Anything Beginning With The Letter "N". When it was ready, he tried it out on Nails. Then he had it Nail them into Nameplates (which it also made), and next it wrapped them all in freshly-created Napkins surrounded by Nasturtiums, Needles, and Naugahyde. It carried out all these orders to a "T", but since Trurl still wasn't quite sure of its level of performance, he ordered it to make, in succession: Nimbus-clouds, Nuggets, Neutrons, Nerves, Noses, Nymphs, and Natrium. This last caused trouble and so Trurl, rather upset, bade the machine explain itself.
>
> "I don't know what Natrium is", it complained. "Never heard of any such thing."
>
> "Whaaat? But it's just sodium! You know — the metal, the element..."
>
> "If it's called 'sodium', then it begins with 'S', and I can only make things beginning with 'N'."
>
> "But it's called 'natrium' in *Latin*."
>
> "My Dear Friend," began the machine, "if I could make everything beginning with 'N' in all conceivable languages, I would be The Machine That Can Make Anything That Starts With Any Letter Of The Alphabet, since anything you choose must, in some language or other, start with 'N'. Now that's absurd. I can't do anything more than you dreamt me up to do. As for sodium, you shall get none."

In the middle of the story there was one part that I really got a bang out of, which involved nonsense words. Here was how I rendered that:

The frightened constructors were dumbstruck. The Machine was actually making Nothing, by annihilating one class of things after another; they simply ceased to be, as if none of them had ever existed at all. It had already destroyed Nethigores, Numbles, Natteroos, Nelliquicks, Nerns, Nonjubbers, and Nendasoles. At one point it appeared that, rather than reducing, lessening, eliminating, disposing of, annihilating, or merely getting rid of things, it was actually augmenting, amplifying, and adding to the world, for it was successively liquidating Ne'er-do-wells, Nogoodniks, Nonsense, Nonalignment, Nonaggression, Nixon, and even the word "No"! But then once again it started to make things grow sparse around the onlookers.

Although Trurl and his friend Klapaucius manage to get the machine to stop wreaking its havoc on the universe, they cannot get it to restore what it has already destroyed. The story's concluding sentence clearly conveys the immensity of the irreparable loss to the universe, thanks to the unfortunate tampering by Trurl and Klapaucius:

> And as no one has yet succeeded in making a machine for any other letter, one must resign oneself to the fact that never again will there be such splendid sights as pretaloons and spunkles, murples and squills, lampsters, appalories, and philidrones — not to mention pinthers, cambouselles, thwisters, extorptions, runchets, and wrasps — no, never again, till Kingdom Come.

Jak Ocalał Świat, à la Kandel

This, then, was the first serious translation challenge I had ever tackled, and it had really been a ball. Of course I was now most eager to see how Michael Kandel had approached the same task, and so I quickly pulled his version off my shelf and read it. I assume you are curious, too. Here, then, is Kandel's rendering of the same three sections:

> One day Trurl the constructor put together a machine that could create anything starting with *n*. When it was ready, he tried it out, ordering it to make needles, then nankeens and negligees, which it did, then nail the lot to narghiles filled with nepenthe and numerous other narcotics. The machine carried out his instructions to the letter. Still not completely sure of its ability, he had it produce, one after the other, nimbuses, noodles, nuclei, neutrons, naphtha, noses, nymphs, naiads, and *natrium*. This last it could not do, and Trurl, considerably irritated, demanded an explanation.
> "Never heard of it", said the machine.
> "What? But it's only sodium. You know, the metal, the element..."
> "Sodium starts with an *s*, and I work only in *n*."
> "But in Latin it's *natrium*."
> "Look, old boy," said the machine, "if I could do everything starting with *n* in every possible language, I'd be a Machine That Could Do Everything in the Whole Alphabet, since any item you care to mention undoubtedly starts with *n* in one foreign language or another. It's not that easy. I can't go beyond what you programmed. So no sodium."

The constructors froze, forgetting their quarrel, for the machine was in actual fact doing Nothing, and it did it in this fashion: one by one, various things were removed from the world, and the things, thus removed, ceased to exist, as if they never had been. The machine had already disposed of nolars, nightzebs, nocs, necs, nallyrakers, neotremes, and nonmalrigers. At moments, though, it seemed that instead of reducing, diminishing, and subtracting, the machine was increasing, enhancing, and adding, since it liquidated, in turn: nonconformists, nonentities, nonsense, nonsupport, nearsightedness, narrowmindedness, naughtiness, neglect, nausea, necrophilia, and nepotism. But after a while the world very definitely began to thin out around Trurl and Klapaucius.

And as all subsequent attempts to build a machine on any other letter met with failure, it is to be feared that never again will we have such marvelous phenomena as the worches and the zits — no, never again.

As you might suspect, if you compare these two versions, both of us took liberties of different sorts in different spots, although of course you can't tell who is being more faithful and who is cheating more. I will, however, confess to my own biggest sin, which was in the final sentence, where Lem limits himself to repeating the names of only two of many items mentioned earlier in the story, as does Kandel, but I, on the other hand, dared to repeat several, feeling it came out much more dramatically that way. And "till Kingdom Come" was just a little flourish that I chose to throw in, all on my own. It was a bit daring, but then, that's the mood I was in.

I might point out that Kandel and I were lucky, in a sense, that the Polish way of saying "nothing" — *nic* — and the English way of saying "nothing" both begin with the same letter. Or rather, it made our task as translators a bit easier. If the standard English word for "nothing" had been "zilch", for instance, putting *Jak ocalał świat* into English would have been a very different kind of task. First of all, Trurl's contraption would have had to be rotated through an angle of ninety degrees, thus becoming The Machine That Could Make Anything Beginning With The Letter "Z". And how would we have handled the section about Natrium, for instance? Well, there are always ways to substitute and improvise, that's for sure, but it would have been a bigger and quite different-feeling challenge.

Jak Ocalał Świat, à la Lugowski

Several years after I had done this translation, a new graduate student showed up in the Computer Science Department at Indiana University, someone who shared my birthday and many of my interests. Although he didn't exactly have a foreign accent, and although his command of English was clearly superior to that of most of his peers, there was something just a little bit peculiar about his way of speaking, and I soon found out why:

Marek Lugowski had been born in Poland and had spent his first fourteen years as a monolingual Pole. He had then come to America, gone through the tribulations and trials of adolescence in our country, and become a genuine lover of his adopted language.

It came to the fore quite early in our interactions that Marek was a long-time admirer of the writings of his compatriot Stanisław Lem, and so I naturally told him about my having translated one Lem short story from Polish to English. That I had done such a thing was amazing to Marek, and he couldn't resist the challenge of trying it himself. I provided him with a photocopy of the original Polish version, and he worked assiduously at the task. Before long, he had come up with a sparkling and most idiosyncratic anglicization, of which I now present the same three sections:

Trurl the Inventor once fashioned a machine that could make anything beginning with the letters "n" and "s". When it was ready, as a test he ordered it to make needles and sutures, then to stitch simulated navels (which it also made), and then to shove all this into a set-up nook, surrounded by showers, naiads, and steameries. It carried out the order to a T, but as Trurl was still unsure of its performance, it had to make in turn nimbi, necklaces, neutrons, nondenumerable sets, snails, sophistication, and finally "stannum". This last one the machine claimed it didn't know how to make and so Trurl, quite distressed, requested it to explain itself.

"Don't know what it is", explained the machine. "Never heard of any such thing."

"How come? It's just tin. A metal, an element..."

"If it is called 'tin', then it must begin with a 't', and I only know how to make things beginning with 'n''s and 's''s."

"But in Latin it's called 'stannum'."

"My dear Trurl," said the machine, "if I could make everything beginning with 'n''s and 's''s in any old language, I'd be The Machine That Can Make Anything Beginning With Any Letter Of The Alphabet, because any old thing most certainly begins with an 'n' or an 's' in some language or other. But no such luck. I cannot do any more than what you've invented. Tin is out."

Not a sound issued from the lips of the terrified inventors. The machine was now quite clearly making Nothing... It was seizing various items in the world, one by one, and causing them to cease to exist, precisely as if they had never existed at all. It had already deleted nonkeys, nacknicks, nartholomies, neanders, and nyps, as well as shtrumps, sententions, samphonies, sordelettes, and snafflesmut. At times, it seemed as if, instead of reducing, decreasing, removing, discarding, undoing, and subtracting from the world, the machine was instead increasing and adding to it, as it wiped out in turn namelessness, nepenthe, and neglect, as well as senselessness, solipsism, and secrecy. However, soon thereafter the world around the two onlookers started getting sparser again.

And, as no one thereafter has ever discovered how to construct the corresponding machine for any other letter of the alphabet, it must regretfully be announced that never again will there exist such splendid phenomena as poths and gnyroids — for ever and ever and ever.

A Cornucopia of Commendable Compromises

You might well wonder why Marek chose to add "s" to the machine's capabilities. There is a simple reason behind this odd-seeming decision. When Trurl's colleague/friend/rival Klapaucius first meets the machine, Trurl offers him the chance to test it. So in the Polish original, Klapaucius commands the machine to make *nauka* — that is, science. There ensues a quite Hieronymus Bosch–like description of a bunch of nutty scientists frantically doing research, writing articles, chattering, and bickering, all created to honor Klapaucius' request. Klapaucius, after witnessing this generation *ab ovo* of the human activity of *nauka,* expresses not delight but scorn for Trurl's machine, and so Trurl invites him to try something else beginning with "n", which provides a smooth segue into Klapaucius' final request: *Maszyno! Masz zrobić Nic!* ("Machine! Make Nothing!").

The whole *nauka* episode is substantial (it takes up over a paragraph) and perhaps important. To mirror it in English, one would clearly wish to have an analogous episode involving science and scientists. However, "science" doesn't begin with "n". So what do you do? Here are several options that a translator might consider, at this juncture:

(1) find a perfect English synonym for "science" that begins with "n", and use that word;

(2) invent some artificial English synonym for "science" that begins with "n", and justify this fakery in some very short, subtle manner inside the story itself;

(3) find some English word that begins with "n" and is closely enough related in meaning to "science" (*e.g.,* "non-ignorance") that the scene that Lem paints could be taken as a fair representation of that word;

(4) allow yourself to use the English word "science" by opening up the machine's initial-letter possibilities to include "s";

(5) keep the Polish word *nauka,* and invent some excuse for resorting to Polish in this situation (*e.g.,* maybe Klapaucius suspects the machine is of Polish origin, and so to trick it into revealing itself, he asks it for *nauka*);

(6) use some picturesque English word that begins with "n" but has nothing to do with science, and justify this by replacing the whole *nauka* scene with a new scene of your own creation, which accurately represents your new "n"-word.

Option (1), unfortunately, is out; there simply is no such word.

My own choice, for better or for worse, was option (2): I used the fictitious word "Nowledge", and tried to justify it inside the story by having Klapaucius be a poor speller. When the machine objects that "Knowledge" begins with "K", not "N", Klapaucius sputters at it, "Just leave the 'K' off! Give me some Nowledge beginning with 'N'." The ensuing bedlam of bickering scholars obviously doesn't fit one's ideal image of the concept "Knowledge", and thus, just as in the original, Klapaucius expresses scorn for the machine, to which Trurl reacts by chiding him for having asked for "Knowledge" without a "K". This last comment by Trurl was of course not in the original, but it involves only a few extra words.

Kandel's choice was option (3): he used the word "Nature", hoping that the reader would accept the slightly strained, somewhat dubious connection between Nature itself and the human activity of *studying* Nature. Klapaucius' expression of scorn for the machine's performance at the end of the episode may match the reader's own disquiet at Nature's having been represented by a silly crowd of quarreling scientists.

Marek's choice was option (4), which is in some ways the simplest, since you don't have to modify Lem's imagery or his story line in any way at all — except for the significant blemish, of course, that you have destroyed the purity and beauty of Lem's idea of a single-letter machine!

Options (5) and (6) are barely plausible, fairly desperate maneuvers.

A Cornucopia of Cowardly Capitulations

There are yet further options that a translator might consider at least fleetingly, such as these (and doubtless many more):

(7) use the English word "science" and insert a scholarly footnote explaining that Lem's original story was in Polish and that the Polish for "science" is *nauka*, for which, unfortunately, there is no English rendering that begins with "n";

(8) use the English word "science" and don't say anything at all about it, simply hoping that your readers won't notice it begins with the wrong letter;

(9) change the machine's specialty from "n"-words to "s"-words, use the word "science" for *nauka*, and then hunt for ways to express *Nic* (and all of the other Polish "n"-words in the original) with English words that start with "s";

(10) write a whole new science-fiction story from scratch, and claim it's by Lem;

(11) give up and go raise cabbage in Maine.

Option (7) is — I can find no better phrase for it — a total wimp-out. And yet, in the course of reading this book — especially Chapters 9 and 17 — you will meet translators, some famous, who prefer to translate in just that style, and some of whom even try, using pompous scholarly language, to demonstrate the superiority of their wimp-stance. This option is sad.

Option (8) is, one would think, nothing more than some kind of sick joke, and yet once again, the kind of philosophy it espouses is bought into by many translators, as we shall see in various places, especially Chapter 17.

Options (9) and (10) are similar to each other, in that both involve radical tampering with the original Lem story. The former puts the *nauka* cart before the *Nic* horse, while the latter jettisons both cart and horse.

Option (11) could be seen as a sort of Zen option. Cabbage is not the only possibility, incidentally. Rutabagas might work, as well.

This list of eleven options running the gamut from reasonable to ridiculous, though it is extremely specific to a tiny issue in one particular science-fiction story by Lem — the very first serious translation challenge I ever undertook — could nonetheless be taken as a metaphor for this entire book, because it is just these kinds of tricky, messy questions that are continually confronted, in varying guises, in the art of translation.

As a footnote to conclude these musings inspired by *Jak ocalał świat,* I might add that both Michael Kandel and Marek Lugowski were among the original recipients of my "Ma Mignonne" challenge, and both responded with lively, offbeat translations that are included in this book, one in Poems VI and the other in Poems XIII.

Annotating "Gödel, Escher, Bach"

My sparse records seem to indicate that I had already done my Lem translation when I gave my Folger Library talk, which fact thus lent me a tiny bit of legitimacy as a genuine translator (at least in my own mind!). This beginning foray into literary translation came at an opportune time, for just a year or two later, Basic Books started looking seriously into the idea of getting *Gödel, Escher, Bach* translated and published abroad.

I had never doubted that the book could be translated, even though, as its author, I was more aware than anyone else of all the traps awaiting potential translators: acrostics and double acrostics; puns based on reading melodies as English words or vice versa; symmetric, fugal, and canonical dialogues; exploitation of words and phrases with double, triple, quadruple, or even quintuple meanings; entire passages repeated and radically changing meaning according to context; and so on. My friend Scott Kim described the style of *GEB* by saying it was filled with "structural puns". Another way to try to articulate that quality of *GEB* would be to say that it is characterized by nearly constant crosstalk between form and content.

Despite all this fancy footwork, I knew for sure that there were clever people out there who would be able to imitate it while dancing on courtyards made of radically different material substrates. But I had never given much thought to questions such as how these bright people might be located, or whether they might desire or even need help from the author. However, as the reality of the translation projects started to set in, I started getting worried. Perhaps it was seeing the often very disappointing quality of the translations of my *Scientific American* columns, which started in January of 1981 and lasted for nearly three years, that all of a sudden gave me the needed kick in the pants to start thinking hard about how to forestall disaster in the upcoming *GEB* translations. Or perhaps it was translating this fanciful and linguistically playful Lem story that made me suddenly aware of the dangers for *GEB*.

Whatever it was, *something* made me sit down, one day in 1980, with a hardbound copy of *Gödel, Escher, Bach* in a coffeehouse at Stanford and start at the very beginning, marking it up in red pen for the aid of as-yet totally unknown translators. Oh, do I remember how slow the going was — a few pages per hour, if I was lucky (and the book is over 700 pages long).

This extraordinarily detailed work was, on the one hand, miserable, and on the other hand, fascinating. I was certainly the only one who could do the annotation — not only because I knew all the games I had played, but also because I knew the *relative importances* of all the games I had played. As we just saw with the Lem piece, one has to gauge the relative importance of different facets of a text in order to know which ones are adjustable, or even expendable, in the interests of "saving" others. But often a translator feels unable to do such gauging, or perhaps is willing to make guesses but then doesn't have much confidence in them.

And so, very dutifully, I plunged through the dense swamps of my own making, trying to anticipate all the possible words, phrases, ideas, allusions, parallelisms, double meanings, deliberate typos, acrostics, typesetting tricks, and so forth that intelligent foreign readers might not quite understand or might not notice. In the course of doing all this, I re-experienced some of the joy of the original creation, and also saw it from a very different point of view — that of someone who would be constantly trying to determine, "What aspects of this passage are essential to preserve precisely? What aspects of it are quite dispensable? What aspects are desirable to keep but somewhat slippable in detail? What types of slippages might be permissible, and what types would be going too far?"

I pulled out all the stops, covering many pages with vast masses of redness, and as a consequence, it took me, as best I recall, on the order of a year of off-again-on-again work, usually in one coffeehouse or another, first at Stanford and later in Bloomington. I felt like a slave, but I simply had no choice: Not to have done this arduous work would have been to betray the person I had been while creating the book; failure to do so would have doomed the book to mediocrity in other languages. Thus if I was a slave, my master was the person I had been only a few years before.

Deus Ex Machine à Écrire

By early 1980, Basic Books had already signed a contract for a French version of *Gödel, Escher, Bach* with the small Parisian publisher InterÉditions, which specialized in scientific works translated from English. The idea of a Gallic version of my book stirred up in me, I must admit, pangs of deep nostalgia, for it reminded me so sharply of my old dream to have grown up as a French/English bilingual. Though that sweet dream would never be realized, I yearned for the French *GEB* to represent the counterfactual me that might have been — *le moi fictif qui, à Dieu eût-il plu, aurait pu s'épanouir à Genève* — and so I wanted to be absolutely sure that the translator, whoever it might turn out to be, was someone of true top-drawer quality.

One summer afternoon I got a phone call from Geoff Staines, the head of InterÉditions, telling me a translation team was being assembled and things were really getting under way. I was very glad to hear of this, even though I was "out of the loop". A few months later, Geoff sent me more details on the composition of the team — all French, and almost all computer scientists — and I grew a little worried, and so in October of 1980 I sent him a letter that included this paragraph:

> Are you familiar with the work of Stanisław Lem, the Polish science-fiction writer? His translator, Michael Kandel, is extremely good. The wordplay is rendered so excellently in English that it is hard to conceive that it was not written in English originally. That is the kind of translation that I think it is necessary to give *GEB* — otherwise its value will really be lost. I am terribly concerned about this, as you know, and particularly in the French, since French matters to me very deeply. I can see that you are assembling a team with excellent potential, but what is lacking is a native speaker of English. Fortunately, I think that my annotated version of the book can substitute for that, since it explains nearly everything that a translator could conceivably want to know about the book.

Well, nearly two years went by and essentially nothing happened. In a way, this was very, very lucky, because the more I thought about it, the less I could imagine a team made of just computer types doing a superlative job on a book to which so much linguistic care had been devoted. Even Geoff voiced disappointment in the flatness of what little work he had seen by his own team, and this did not bode well. It was time for a *deus ex machina*.

In late August of 1982, I received a very neat letter *tapée à la machine* from an American living in a Parisian suburb, which began as follows:

> Dear Dr. Hofstadter:
>
> One day it arrived in the mail, the padded envelope in which it had been wrapped torn to bits after a rough trip in the hold of some trans-Atlantic freighter. The letter from my father, slipped under the cover of the book, was as laconic as is required by the US Postal Service: "Happy Birthday," the note said, "I know you'll like this book." Naturally, if I'm telling you this story, the book had to have been GÖDEL, ESCHER, BACH.

The letter went on, describing its author's delight in reading the said book, his university background in philosophy and mathematics, his current profession as a French translator, and finally his ardent desire to translate my book, in collaboration with a French colleague, into French. The letter was simply brimming with intelligence, enthusiasm, and some kind of intangible spark; I was instantaneously, instinctively sure that this, if ever any, was the route to take in turning *GEB* into a piece of art in French.

I thus wrote back to its author, Mr. Robert M. French, urging him to get in touch quickly with InterÉditions, so that he and his French partner might try out a couple of sample passages as a test. The long and the short of the story is, of course, that Bob French and Jacqueline Henry did a superlative job on the test passages and were rapidly engaged to carry out the full job. Disengaging the other team was, fortunately, not traumatic for anyone, since essentially nothing had been done in all that time.

Analogies Across an Ocean and Across a Tabletop

Before long, an intense volley of cross-Atlantic missives between the French–Henry duo and myself started up, concerning some of the most interesting and challenging translation issues in the book. I was truly thrilled to be intimately involved in this highly complex venture, and got swept up in the excitement of translating multi-leveled wordplay. It felt like such a fantasy as I dreamed up intricate puns in French by searching for analogues to essentially untranslatable puns in the English version.

In a sense, things came to a head when we started discussing how to handle the double acrostic in the dialogue called "Contracrostipunctus". They had certain ideas, and I had very different ideas. And yet, through a few exchanges of very long, cordial, thoughtful letters — all handwritten — we eventually arrived at a most amiable compromise that captured the best of what we all had wanted. This cooperation augured so, so well, not only for the quality of the French *GEB,* but also for the friendship that was clearly budding among us, even though we hadn't yet met face to face.

In the summer of 1983, I went to Europe in part to give some lectures but mainly in order to meet and work with the French–Henry team. The morning I arrived in Paris, I called Bob from my hotel, and he and I agreed to meet shortly in a small bistro situated on a pleasant stretch of the boulevard Raspail. As I sauntered into the place, sporting my traditional bright red backpack so I could be quickly identified, I spotted a bearded, red-headed, roundly-bespectacled, intellectual-looking chap in his thirties, sitting at a small table with a copy of *GEB.* There was no doubt in either of our minds who the other one was. And so, without further ado, we plunged into heated discussion on one topic after another, full of disagreements and analogies, yet all with great friendliness and giving intense pleasure.

It was obvious within just minutes that Bob's mastery of French was truly deep. He had, after all, spent nearly ten years there, most of them as a professional translator. Even so, his French was a shade better than I had expected. I listened carefully to Bob over the coming days, and observed that not only did he have a superlative accent, but his speech was peppered with cool slang as well as lots of filler words that buy time without giving the appearance of groping; he even used French *gestures* of all sorts! I couldn't help but feel a twinge of sadness as I realized that this was how the French of that *moi fictif* might have been if only I could have continued living in Geneva for another few years instead of returning to California. After we had known each other for quite a while, I used to kid Bob by saying that he had realized the destiny inherent in his own name by growing a red beard and mastering the Gallic tongue, until one day I was disabused of my decades-old notion that "Robert" means "red beard".

That first afternoon's sparring and analogizing across the boulevard Raspail tabletop was, as it turned out, the precursor of several more years of tabletop analogies and mental sparring. Indeed, reading *GEB* had made Bob aware of the stimulating new discipline of artificial intelligence, and it did not take long before he was convinced that, rather than continuing as a technical translator doing a job that had gradually turned, over years, from excitement into drudgery, he would like to pursue a doctorate in artificial intelligence. He thus resolved that as soon as the *GEB* translation was completed, he would return to the United States and pursue that goal.

Not too surprisingly but nonetheless to my gratification, Bob felt that my personal research direction and style were very compatible with his own interests and beliefs, and so in 1986, a few months after the French *GEB* appeared (incidentally, to a splash of extremely warm reviews that gave immense pleasure to all three of us — Jacqueline, Bob, and myself), Bob came and joined my research group at the University of Michigan in Ann Arbor. Thus began a distinct phase of our friendship, during which our verbal sparring continued unabated, during which the international "Ma Mignonne" challenge was sparked, thanks to the poem Bob produced in response to my personal challenge, and at the end of which he produced an elegant analogy-making computer program aptly called "Tabletop".

Ah Yes, That Jolly, Jolly Lot

But this was all quite a ways in the future. In the summer of 1983, the business at hand was translation — translation of dense wordplay, most of all. In Chapter 6, I will give a few examples of the strange kinds of problems the three of us were faced with and the unexpectedly complex intellectual issues they raised; for now, suffice it to say that our merry daily meetings over coffee after coffee after coffee were stunningly stimulating.

I must say that the electric sense of sparkle and fire in the air was due in part to the presence of two other key figures in *GEB*-translation work: Ronald Jonkers and David Moser. Ronald had come down to Paris from Holland specifically to consult with me on *GEB*, because he had been hired to translate the book into Dutch — and indeed, over the next year or two, he did a super job of it. The Dutch *GEB* is, without doubt, one of the best.

As for David, he was a close friend from Bloomington, one of your typical run-of-the-mill musician–artist–linguist–writer types, who was in Paris simply to imbibe the French culture and language, for which he already had a pretty strong sense. Little did any of us suspect that David would one day play a role exactly analogous to Bob's, Jacqueline's, and Ronald's, but *with respect to Chinese* — for at the time, David did not know a single word of that difficult language, nor did he have the slightest thought that he ever would. Life surely has its little surprises.

While not sipping our strong roasted coffees in bistros near the Jardin du Luxembourg, little subsets of our intellectually frolicsome fivesome took endless strolls through Latin Quarter streets, chatting about most anything under the sun. I'll never forget the elaborate joke that Ronald and I made about some bent rusty nail that we found in a gutter — it had supposedly been placed there decades ago by Marcel Duchamp and was by now a famous *objet d'art* called the *clou flou*. And one day, browsing in a bookstore near the boulevard Saint-Germain, David and I came across one of the most amazing, and also most expensive, books either of us had ever seen: the *Codex Seraphinianus*, by Luigi Serafini. Both of us snapped up copies in a flash, and have savored them ever after. I also remember the keen joy of buying little things for Carol — a cute umbrella with a duck handle, and the beautiful book *Paris que j'aime,* which I signed *Pour Carol que j'aime...*

I honestly cannot imagine five people more steeped in translation issues than that little group in Paris was, for those few weeks of that lovely summer. It's true, we were all greenhorns to the tangled knots that beset wordplay translation, but that very fact lent to our discussions a sense of freshness and openness that remains ever bright in my memory.

I went back the next summer, and the next, and over those marvelous Parisian coffees, Bob, Jacqueline, and I thrashed out every last little issue in the gallicization of *Gödel, Escher, Bach.* Each summer was characterized by its own special blend of *désaccords* full of tension and C-major *ré-sol-ut-ions* full of joy — fortuitous discoveries of hidden patterns inside words that we would never have believed could exist. Those heady days in Paris were my own personal training period in the endlessly subtle art of translation. And when you think about it, what more jolly a way to earn one's stripes?

Ah yes, ah yes, how jolly the lot — how jolly the lot of an oligoglot!

Poems III:

~ Antique Airs ~

* *
*

Working in the Fluid Analogies Research Group alongside Bob French in those good old Ann Arbor days was Melanie Mitchell, who found herself quite intrigued by our ongoing little competition, so much so that she eventually felt moved to tackle the challenge herself.

A long-time lover of poetry and of Shakespeare in particular, Melanie too wanted to make a version that respected the poem's temporal provenance, and in doing so she couldn't resist inserting numerous bold Shakespearean touches, such as the old-fashioned phrases "I entreat", "one regard", "'tis", "forsooth", and "lest", as well as the non-rhyming rhyme of "love" and "remove" (which in Shakespeare's day *did* rhyme, and that was her whole point). Another subtle touch, one I never would have thought of, was to tamper with the transitivity of verbs, thus using "loose" and "stay" transitively, and conversely, using "pale" and "mend" intransitively. To me, this counterintuitive reversal lent so much of an authentic archaic flavor to Melanie's poem!

A similar sly reversal was her use of "swift" as an adverb, on line 25. Melanie may well have been led to this by her familiarity with old English poetry, but there is another route to it, starting with Marot's curious word *vitement* — quite literally, "fastly". In the French, an unneeded adverbial suffix is grafted onto *vite,* which (in analogy to "fast") is already a perfectly fine adverb, thus giving rise to a word that is a bit *over*-adverbial; in the English, the adverbial suffix is amputated from the fine adverb "swiftly", thus yielding a word that is a little *under*-adverbial. This twist not only adds to the overall antique, poetic flavor, but also faintly echoes the structural strangeness of Marot's *vitement*. (Later I realized that in "My Sweet Dear", I had actually come up with nearly the same trick, writing "Do it quick, stay not sick" — with my under-adverbial "quick" occurring on the same line as does Marot's over-adverbial *vitement.*)

Further enhancing her poem's archaic flavor, Melanie used "thou" rather than "you" throughout as the second-person pronoun (there was thus no transition between levels of formality in pronouns). I particularly admired her lovely discovery of what seemed to me the quintessential English phrase for rendering Marot's *friande de ta bouche* : namely, "sweet-tooth", especially when rhymed with "forsooth"! Lastly but not leastly, one audacious leap by Melanie that impressed me was how she momentarily turned to the illness itself (in lines 6–8) to address it as if it understood English, mock-pathetically supplicating it to "loose its dart from her heart".

Altogether, Melanie's translation struck me as quite a *tour de force,* and, coming on the heels of Bob's excellent performance, made me feel quite inadequate. To add insult to injury, even the visual silhouettes of Bob's and Melanie's poems seemed smooth and graceful, as opposed to the jagged, irregular, jerky contours of both of my attempts. Ah, me! Next to Bob's and Melanie's, my two efforts felt like mere ditties, whereas theirs? — alas, they felt like true *poems!*

To My Sweet

Melanie Mitchell

To my sweet
I entreat:
One regard!
O, 'tis hard,
Dear recluse.   5
Sickness, loose
Thy cruel dart
From her heart!
Then my love
Will remove;   10
She'll appear,
Clement's dear,
Past her door.
Come now, poor
Fair sweet-tooth,   15
Starved, forsooth!
My heart breaks.
Eat some cakes
And some jam.
Courage! Dam   20
Up thy tears.
Stay thy fears,
Lest thou pale
And thus fail
Swift to mend.   25
May God send
Health complete
To my sweet!

It was at about this stage of the game that my friend and collaborator Gray Clossman and a professor in France named Benoît de Cornulier independently pointed out to me a beautiful property of the original poem that up till then had completely escaped my notice — namely, that its *semantic* chunks are couplets out of phase with its *rhyming* chunks. A graphical display of this fact makes it not just undeniably clear but also very appealing:

> *Ma mignonne,*
> *Je vous donne / le bon jour ;*
> *Le séjour / c'est prison.*
> *Guérison / recouvrez,*
> *Puis ouvrez / votre porte,*
> *Et qu'on sorte / vitement,*
> *Car Clément / le vous mande.*
> *Va, friande / de ta bouche,*
> *Qui se couche / en danger,*
> *Pour manger / confitures ;*
> *Si tu dures / trop malade,*
> *Couleur fade / tu prendras,*
> *Et perdras / l'embonpoint.*
> *Dieu te doint / santé bonne,*
> *Ma mignonne.*

This absolute regularity — right there, staring us in the eye, yet somehow very hidden at the same time — bowled us over; it made Marot's creation seem far more elegant and crystalline than we'd initially suspected. And yet, couldn't it be pure chance, something Marot never intended or even realized, but that just by accident came out that way? Of course that's conceivable, though hard to believe. But we'll never know for sure. In any case, to me it seems such a pretty pattern that it would be a shame not to treat it respectfully, as if it had been intended. He was, after all, a clever devil, that Clément!

Melanie now felt inspired to try another Shakespearean version, one that would respect these new semantic couplets and that would thus come far closer to the goal of line-by-line fidelity. And it did not take her long to pull off the feat! Although I was not thrilled with her addressing her poem to an arbitrary "Sue" (especially since Marot's poem had in fact been addressed to someone named "Jeanne"), I thought the rest of her effort was masterful.

My favorite line was "Your Bastille", with its subtle hint at the Frenchness of the original — the first time, incidentally, that any allusion to the French language or culture had entered any of the translations. There was an unintended irony to Melanie's metaphor — namely, the Bastille was not a jail but a fortress during Marot's lifetime; it was converted into a jail the following century. More importantly, the Bastille only became a famously *symbolic* jail 150 years after that — over two-and-a-half centuries after "Ma Mignonne" was written! Another irony is that the "Bastille/heal" rhyme works only because we anglophones pronounce the double "l" as an "l", which the French do not do.

The beautiful line "Your Bastille" was actually not in Melanie's original version. Lines 4–9 originally ran this way: "This home stay / Is prison. / Health, anon! / Recover, / Uncover / Your closed door." Unfortunately, there's just no way that "is prison", "recover", or "uncover" can be accented on their final syllables, nor does "prison" rhyme with "anon". To me, these few glitches ruined an otherwise lovely poem. The day after I told Melanie about my concerns, she bounced right back with her marvelous patch.

My Dear Sue

Melanie Mitchell

My dear Sue,
I bid you
A good day.
This home stay,
Your Bastille!   5
Darling, heal,
Turn the tide,
Then fling wide
Your closed door.
Out once more!   10
Quick: Descent,
For Clement
Summons you.
Come, dear, who
Loves sweet tastes,   15
Your mouth wastes;
'Twill risk meet.
Come and eat
Jams so fine.
If you pine   20
And still ail,
Skin so pale
Will be Sue's.
You will lose
Your plump self.   25
God, good health
Give to you,
My dear Sue!

Spurred on — indeed, goaded — by Bob's and Melanie's superb ancient-flavored versions, I decided, with a bit of trepidation, to risk my own hand at the unfamiliar art of Shakespearean-style poetry-writing. I have only dim memories of working on my very own "olde-style" effort, "On Ye, Childe", but somehow I managed to do it. I may have gone somewhat overboard in my capitalizing of all the nouns and adding "e"'s here and there to the ends of words, but I was so eager to imbue my effort with a quaint, dated flavor.

This poem, like Melanie's "My Dear Sue", features semantic couplets out of phase with the rhyming couplets, the only exceptions being at the very start and very finish, where there are three-line semantic chunks. And thus my new poem turned out to be far more faithful on a line-by-line basis to the original than I ever could have imagined would have been possible when I first set out, a few weeks earlier, on what seemed like a nearly impossible venture.

One of my novel contributions here, somewhat upping the ante in terms of fidelity to the original, was to imitate Marot's *vous/tu* transition by making a "ye/thou" transition, which on its own instantly conferred on my poem a conspicuous flavor of antiquity. This mid-poem switching of pronouns led me to making a slight discrepancy between the first and last lines, with "ye" appearing at the top and "thee" at the bottom. When I thought about it, this mismatch actually seemed like an elegant touch rather than a defect, since it drew attention in a clear but rather subtle manner to the change of form of address that had taken place midway through the poem, which people otherwise might read right through without noticing.

I was very happy with the metonymy by which the suffering young patient was equated with her hungry mouth, as well as with my rhyme of "Gem" and "M." Admittedly, it is a little peculiar to explicitly ascribe to Clément Marot, a gallivanting and obstreperous French poet, some lines written almost 500 years later by a North American cognitive scientist, deliberately putting on airs to try to imitate the style of a storied English bard whose entire life took place after Marot died. Is this a grotesque, tortured falsification of history? Or is it, quite to the contrary, a reverential bow embodying extreme fidelity to Marot, and thereby rendering a profound service to Truth?

Though I was pleased with this result, I was a little disappointed that it felt less polished, less *echt*, than Melanie's, and flowed less gracefully, but I could do no better: my feel for Shakespeare and for poetry in general was far less developed than hers. However, I, at least, had not addressed my poem to someone with the wrong name; in fact, I had addressed it explicitly to a *child*, which made my effort more faithful, at least on one level, to the original.

Luckily, I kept many drafts of early versions of my own poems, and so, even though I may not remember the compositional process at all, I have good records of how parts of it went. Thus, it is interesting to compare "On Ye, Childe" with one of its precursors, "On Ye, Child" (a one-letter difference in their titles).

Of course, I knew very well that the twentieth-century bureaucratese pseudo-word "and/or" (line 18) stuck out like a sore thumb — in fact, more like a badly smashed one — but using it in a Shakespearean context amused me no end, so I kept it in, at least for a while. Needless to say, though, "and/or" didn't make it into the final version.

The image of the poet's bad dream, given in lines 20–24, is very appealing, even though, relative to the original poem, it comes from out of the blue. And it certainly must have been hard for me to give up the delightfully archaic lines "Once awake, / Thanks I spake", in favor of "Prithee, nay! / God, I pray", but evidently the sum total of the pressures in my brain was sufficient to make the slippage take place.

On Ye, Childe	On Ye, Child
D. Hofstadter	*D. Hofstadter*

On ye, Childe,	*On ye, child,*
Sweet and milde,	*Sweet and mild,*
Would I call.	*Do I call.*
A dark Pall	*A dark pall*
Ye besets;	*Has beset* 5
Keen regrets	*Ye. Regret-*
Do I feel.	*ful I feel.*
Quickly heal	*Quickly heal*
And emerge;	*And emerge;*
To so urge	*To so urge* 10
Ye, dear Gem,	*Ye, dear gem,*
Clement M.	*Clement M.*
Penned these Lines.	*Pens these lines.*
Mouth who dines	*Mouth that dines*
Lustily,	*Rabidly,* 15
Thou must be,	*Thou must be*
Whilst abed,	*Yearning for*
Craving Bread	*Jam and/or*
With Marm'lade.	*Marmalade.*
Hast thou stayed	*Dreamt thou stayed* 20
Sick too long?	*Sick so long*
Hath thy strong	*That thy strong*
Heart grown weake?	*Heart was weak,*
Pale thy Cheeke?	*Pale thy cheek.*
Prithee, nay!	*Once awake,* 25
God, I pray,	*Thanks I spake:*
Will have smiled	*God had smiled*
On thee, Childe.	*On thee, child.*

At about this same time, my Ann Arbor friend Bill Cavnar got into the act with a few translations of his own. One of his best did something I had not suspected possible: Beginning with my own trisyllabic but nonrhyming literal translation "My Sweet Maid", already given in Poems I but repeated here for you, Bill carefully tweaked it here and there, delicately plying it back and forth, until, *mirabile dictu,* it came out not just in perfect meter, but also in perfect *rhyme*! I was truly taken aback, and had to salute Bill's insight and ingenuity.

A nice example of the tweaking process comes in line 15, where the girl's "tongue red" (rather than the far blander word "mouth") is used metonymously to stand for her whole self (and also, of course, to rhyme with "abed"). A similar metonymy-based tweak occurs in line 25, where Bill parlays a particular (and suggestive) part of the girl's anatomy — her thigh — into a symbol for her entire figure. The next line's rhyme of "thy" with "thigh" — the distinction being merely a question of voicedness of the initial sound — is charming as well. Also worth noticing is line 8's conversion of "unlatch" into "unchain", which not only yields the desired rhyme with "regain" but also adds antiquity to the already-vivid image of an old castle's creaky wooden door.

Because it is so closely modeled on a literal translation, this version is itself very near to being a literal line-by-line translation. This suggests that if it's *really* literal, then the semantic-couplet structure should automatically be reproduced in it. And yes, that is the case. What a jewel! If Bill Cavnar or anyone else had come up with this poem at the very beginning, I would have just closed up my translation shop and quit, figuring nobody could ever equal it again, let alone surpass it. But I'm certainly glad that that didn't happen, because in some ways, this translation, though superb along so many dimensions at once, still seems to lack a bit of that intangible verbal sparkle that I associate with the deepest Maroticity.

All in all, this is beyond any doubt the best translation in the whole book — even the whole world — in fact, it is perhaps the best translation of *anything* that has ever been done by *anybody* — or at least that is what Bill's mother says (or so Bill tells me, anyway).

My Sweet Maid	**O My Sweet**
D. Hofstadter	William Cavnar

My sweet maid,	O my sweet,
You I wish	May you meet
A good day;	A good day;
Your sickbed	Where you stay
Is a jail.	Is a jail. 5
Total health	Health, my frail,
Please regain,	Please regain,
Then unlatch	Then unchain
Your room's door	Your room's door,
And go out	And thence soar 10
With full speed,	Hastily:
For Clement	Clement thee
Does insist.	Does command.
Go, gourmande,	Go, gourmande,
Thou whose mouth	Whose tongue red 15
Lies abed	Lies abed
Under threat,	In retreat,
Off to eat	Off to eat
Fruit preserves;	Jams, as may'st;
If thou stay'st	If thou stay'st 20
Sick too long,	Sick and fade,
A pale shade	A pale shade
Wilt acquire,	Thus accrues;
And wilt lose	Thou wilt lose
Thy round shape.	Thy round thigh. 25
May God grant	God grant thy
Thee good health,	Health complete,
My sweet maid.	O my sweet.

• *Chapter 4* •

The Romantic Vision
of Thought as Pattern

•

There are certain special ideas that, when you first encounter them, grab you and will not let you go, and that wind up having a deep and lasting effect on your life. In my case, the eerie idea of "electronic brains", of which I first heard as a teen-ager, played such a role. Though corny as all get-out, that journalistic exaggeration took on a magical aura for me as I realized that somewhere out there in the world, people were trying to make nonliving objects be able to think, to create, to have inner mental lives of their own. Turn the phrase just a little differently — "to make inanimate objects animate" — and it starts to sound like a latter-day alchemy.

To me, this was an exciting, wonderful, head-spinning adventure. Ever since childhood, I had been fascinated by the fantasy and novelty manifested by human thought — at least human thought at its best. There was something so amazing about the ways people could put together ideas, notes, colors, lines, words, analogies, and so forth, in ever-new patterns, seeming to bring to life, almost out of nowhere, undreamt-of beauties and surprises in the abstract world of the mind.

As I grew older and was exposed to deeper and deeper creativity — great composers like Chopin and Bach, great mathematicians like Pierre de Fermat and Srinivasa Ramanujan, great artists like Wassily Kandinsky and Paul Klee, great physicists like Albert Einstein and James Clerk Maxwell, great humorists like W. C. Fields and the Marx Brothers, great lyricists like Cole Porter and Ira Gershwin — the more curious I grew about what was behind it all. In high school, this became one of my passionate interests. I was always asking myself, "What is behind the mysteries of innovation and novelty? What kind of logic is there to the illogic of creativity?"

Rubber-ball Riddles and Bach-style Jokes

One day when I was fifteen or sixteen, I was sitting out at a neighbor's swimming pool, drying off after a dip, and my attention was vaguely caught by three rubber balls on the cement deck. There were two small ones, one purple and one orange, and one large one, also orange. Schematically, they looked this way:

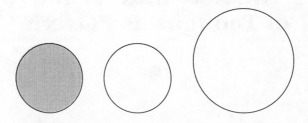

As I mused idly on this trio, it occurred to me quite out of nowhere that *one of them was different*. The thought seemed both hilarious and insightful. Do you see what I saw?

Well, clearly the purple one was different, because it was purple. Is that the end of the story? No… the big one likewise was different, because it was big. So now there were *two* different ones, not one. But for this very reason, there was one left that wasn't different — the small orange one — and hence it was the *truly* different one!

It was as if the attributes of different-by-color and different-by-size, pulling against each other in a mental tug-of-war, canceled each other out, neither of the two having a greater claim to marking off differentness than the other did, so that what was left after the mutual cancellation was a kind of higher-level abstraction: different-by-not-being-different, or, if you wish, unique-by-being-most-typical. I devised a term for this odd brand of uniqueness: "R-uniqueness", where the "R" stood for "really".

My mind reveled in the humorous and delightful paradoxicality that had come out of nowhere in this most ordinary of situations. On the one hand, I could see it as just a frivolous, isolated, California-poolside observation. And yet on the other hand, I felt there was something not frivolous at all in the process of the leap to higher abstraction. It seemed to me somehow connected with creative leaps in all sorts of domains.

In music, for instance, I was very familiar with the phenomenon of "sequences", where a little motif would be played, then transposed upwards by a note or two, then transposed upwards a further note or two, and suddenly, perhaps on the third or fourth repetition, once the expectation for another go-round had been solidly set up, the rug of security would be pulled out from under the listener and a deviating pattern would occur. Bach was a specialist at this type of abstract leap that would catch his listeners off guard.

Of course, the more Bach music one hears and absorbs, the more familiar one becomes with the abstraction known as "Bach style". This of course implies a constantly growing sensitivity to the kinds of games that Bach plays with sequences, and suggests that one soon can "get the hang of it" and never again be fooled by his trick-the-listener jokes. But this is not true of Bach. More often than not, Bach will catch even the most astute of his listeners by surprise. He is like a rabbit who can elude the wiliest and most experienced of foxes in a wild zigzag chase across a field, constantly throwing his pursuers off the track by pulling novel rabbits out of his foxy composer's hat.

And although there is a grain of truth to calling such escapes from predictability "jokes", the term does not do justice to the depth of the effect. Even the more dignified term "wit" undervalues the power and emotional meaningfulness of such Bachian leaps. "Spirit" or "spirituality" gets a bit closer.

In every intellectual field that I had encountered, ranging from mathematics to music to art to poetry, I had the sense that the moment that patterns were perceived at one level, this immediately established a higher level of abstraction, opening the door to the perception of totally unanticipated types of patterns. At least in principle, there was no limit to the number of upward levels one could reach. And thus I felt that in this tiny little three-balls puzzle, there was the barest germ of a hint at some important mechanisms of creativity. It was a definite thrill to think I might have stumbled across a tiny key to the mysteries of creativity in such a mundane context — three rubber balls by a poolside, indeed!

The Brain and the Heart

While one part of me felt there was a deep mystery to innovative thought, another part felt there was some explanation to be found at the bottom of it all: some kind of elegant, complex pattern giving rise to the very mechanisms that allowed new ideas to constantly bubble and churn forth. I had no doubt that this elusive pattern — the secret key to the creative spirit of the human mind — was embedded deep in the structure of human brains, and therefore, in a far more encoded and remote form, in human genes as well. But it seemed reasonable to me — in fact, almost compellingly certain — that looking at the microscopic details of the brain or of genes would be to concentrate too much on the trees and thus to miss the forest.

A simple analogy between brain and heart might make this clear. We describe what hearts do by talking about pumps, and we can point to specific parts of the heart and show how they give rise to its pumping action. At no time in such a discussion do we need to descend to the level of heart cells and refer to events on such a tiny scale. Were we to do that, we would totally lose our high-level perspective and get mired in irrelevant details. Of course, billions of heart cells, sewn into tissue, working together collectively, constitute each of the large-scale functional subunits of the heart — but that is another story and can be looked at separately.

Now if the analogy between brain and heart holds, one could say this: There are large-scale functional subunits of the human brain that work together in some as-yet-unclear manner to produce mundane thoughts, deep insights, clever quips, puzzling speech errors, good and bad dreams, and all the rest of the richness of mental phenomena, and the key to understanding the mind is to figure out how these subunits carry out their magic tricks — perhaps sending messages to each other along complex pathways, perhaps jumping into special states when unexpected similarities are noticed here and there (as at the poolside deck), who knows.

The main point of the analogy is just to suggest that, as in the heart, it would be a mistake to focus too much attention on the tiny, fine-grained, cellular or subcellular structure because — if the analogy is valid — what matters for the human brain's thinking activity is how its *larger* subunits communicate and collaborate, not the details of how those subunits are built up out of billions of infinitesimal parts, fascinating though that story might well be.

Now, if one believes this analogy, and if one thinks that there is — that there has to be — some way of describing thinking as a complex pattern of interactions among high-level subunits in the brain, then one's Holy Grail would become the study of those patterns themselves; for this, neurology would not seem the ideal pathway. In fact, so this line of reasoning goes, for anyone interested in coming to understand creative thought, it would be a grave error to become a neurologist because neurologists' attention is focused at *too low a level* to help out in this endeavor.

The critical conclusion that emerges from musings of this sort — unproven intuitions, needless to say — is that the key to unraveling the mystery of thinking has got to be some kind of *pattern* — a pattern that has little to do with biology (or at least what normally is called biology), and everything to do with such abstractions as messages and symbols, codings and decodings, ideas and associations, abstractions and similarities. It would seem that *this* is the right level on which to approach the mystery of thought, rather than by studying the detailed chemical properties of such tiny intercellular voyagers as neurotransmitters, and the fantastic intricacies by which one brain cell can physically link up to many others.

The Birth of Artificial Intelligence

You personally may or may not be convinced by such a brief, hand-waving set of intuitions that this is the way to go in studying the mind. The point is, however, that in the first decade or two after World War II, many bright people — mostly mathematicians, logicians, philosophers, linguists, psychologists, and "cyberneticists" (a now-defunct breed) — arrived quite independently at basically this intuition, and their collective interest sparked the emergence of the field known as *artificial intelligence* ("AI"). Such people felt, in essence, that thought *is nothing but* the manipulation of abstract patterns according to some set of abstract rules. Exactly what the patterns might be, and what kinds of rules might manipulate them, was very murky — but that was the alluring, enticing mystery.

Saying that thought "is nothing but" is perhaps too negative, making it sound as if there is no romance or mystery left. Perhaps I should have said "is nothing if not" instead. But you have to realize that for people convinced of this way of looking at thought, there is nothing demeaning to the human spirit in the equating of thought with some kind of hugely complex pattern, or pattern of patterns (or pattern of patterns of patterns); to them it is an exciting and indeed romantic vision to imagine that perhaps there is a hidden way of looking at the brain's activity, deliberately jumping right over the misleading low-level details, and leading to a deep understanding of what kinds of things the brain was *really* built to do.

This view of thought certainly did not arise from nowhere. Indeed, in a sense, it is the most natural human self-image. After all, we almost never consider the biological substrate of our own or anyone else's thoughts; intuitively, thought seems to float at a level all its own, as detached from its hardware underpinnings as a jellyfish is detached from the ocean bottom. On the other hand, from a hard-nosed scientific viewpoint, a vision of thought as free-floating is somewhat radical, resembling (although certainly not amounting to) an espousal of Cartesian mind–body dualism.

The Earliest Roots of AI: Proofs, Grammars, and Living Machines

The scientific and philosophical roots of the AI view of mind can be traced back as far as ancient Greece, with Aristotle's codification of varieties of syllogistic reasoning and Euclid's attempt to formalize mathematical proof. During the Renaissance, language itself was seen as an outgrowth of logic, and such philosophers as Blaise Pascal, Roger Bacon, Gottfried Wilhelm von Leibniz, Ramón Llull, Athanasius Kircher, and Thomas Urquhart speculated about universal grammars and tie-ins between the rules of grammar and the full repertoire of true sentences about the world.

In the seventeenth century, René Descartes played a transitional role in the view of mind's relation to body. In some ways his role in the mind–body problem is quite parallel to that of Girolamo Saccheri in what might be called the "line–point problem". Saccheri was an Italian mathematician who tried to prove that Euclid's was the only possible geometry and in his attempts he came right to the verge of inventing non-Euclidean geometry — indeed, he proved numerous theorems in it, but sadly, not recognizing them for what they were, one day he abruptly declared his explorations nonsensical, by which act he claimed to have "freed Euclid of every flaw". Saccheri's own misunderstanding of what he had accomplished cost him the chance for immortality as a mathematician. Descartes likewise came to the verge of understanding how mind, at whatever level of sophistication, is the outcome of physical processes; he developed the idea of animals as physical machines but refused to see that this idea extended naturally — indeed, nearly irresistibly — to humans. Descartes' refusal to cross the daring line made him a philosophical conservative whose name is preserved in, among other things, that quaint phrase "Cartesian dualism", used just above — the name for the belief that mind is an ethereal substance dwelling solely in a spiritual realm.

AI Roots, II: Human Machines, Ducks, Looms, and Cards

In 1747, the French physician Julien Offroy de la Mettrie played a role that I see as akin to that of the discoverers of non-Euclidean geometry, by taking Descartes' animals-as-machines idea and pushing it over the brink to its logical conclusion — that the human brain is a purely physical thinking engine — and then writing a book expounding his shockingly materialist views, *L'homme machine,* which was so scandalous that he could publish it only in Holland, and only anonymously so, at that. When his authorship of this Satanic Verbiage was revealed, he was chased out of both France and Holland and wound up in the liberal court of King Frederick the Great in Berlin, where he died in exile and in misery, ridiculed as a buffoon and longing for his homeland. Today at least a few people appreciate him.

Incidentally, I might add that translating la Mettrie's simple-seeming title "L'homme machine" into English is in fact not at all simple. It is certainly *not* "The Man Machine", although on the surface it looks that way; it is much more like "Man the Machine" or "Man as a Machine", both of which of course echo the sexism of the original. If one throws in the more modern constraint of nonsexism, as I would wish to do, then "People as Machines" is one possibility, although in the plural it somehow does not have quite the grandiose panache of the original. Perhaps "The Human Machine" does as good a job as can be done.

The picaresque tale of la Mettrie is well told in Pamela McCorduck's deliciously titled book *Machines Who Think,* a poetically written and truly engrossing, though somewhat biased, early history of AI — and while we're speaking of translating book titles, I offer you the challenge of translating McCorduck's title into French. There is a serious snag — namely, that the French relative pronoun *qui* means both "that" and "who", and therefore the obvious solution, "Machines qui pensent", falls totally flat, since it back-translates into "Machines That Think". Can you do better? Hint: The previous paragraphs contain the seeds for a lovely translation.

Two other French pioneers helped advance the mechanization of living processes. One was Jacques de Vaucanson (1709–1782), who created fabulously intricate models of people and animals, including a flute player, a drum player, and most especially his famed mechanical duck, which crudely simulated eating, chewing, and excretion. Vaucanson's crowning achievement, however, was his automated loom for weaving textiles. It was Pierre Jacquard (1752–1834) who saw in Vaucanson's loom the possibility of automation in a very modern sense. He invented the idea of punched cards as controls for the device, and with their aid one could "program" the Jacquard–Vaucanson loom to weave whatever pattern one could imagine.

AI Roots, III: Meshing Gears, Patterns, and Good Metre

A key role in the development of the computer, and thus in artificial intelligence, was played by Charles Babbage, an eccentric and multi-faceted English mathematician and inventor of the nineteenth century. He envisioned a vast system of adjustably interlocking gears for the purposes of calculating all sorts of mathematical tables, and spent much of his life developing this idea and trying to get it built. Gradually the generality of the mechanisms he had devised dawned on him. He realized that his "Analytical Engine" might, in principle, play "tit-tat-to" (as he called it) and chess, do typesetting, and carry out many other tasks traditionally seen as limited to human minds. His close friend and staunch advocate, Lady Ada Lovelace, a brilliant mathematical thinker and daughter of the poet Byron, wrote a memoir about his Engine in which its potential for mentation was clearly spelled out, and in it she made this poetic analogy: "It would weave algebraic patterns the way the Jacquard loom weaved patterns in textiles." Unfortunately, Babbage's Analytical Engine never was built, and Babbage died a most frustrated, although highly respected, old man in 1871.

Fairly late in life, Babbage wrote a most remarkable set of memoirs, which he refused to call an autobiography, entitled *Passages from the Life of a Philosopher,* the wondrously droll flavor of which I feel I can only vaguely hint at by suggesting that you first try to imagine Charles Dickens crossing Mr. Pickwick with a mathematical genius, and then try to imagine what kinds of adventures such an individual might have been through and written down. His book is dedicated to Victor Emmanuel II, King of Italy, because of the generosity of the latter's father, who two decades earlier had publicly recognized and celebrated Babbage's ideas for a calculating engine. He writes, "I am happy in thus expressing my deep sense of that obligation to his son, the Sovereign of united Italy, the country of Archimedes and of Galileo." This is the first time I had ever thought of Archimedes as Italian — but it's true, he was from Siracusa in Sicily.

Babbage had a wide range of interests, including lock-picking, codes and decoding, wordplay, the nature of humor, politics, and many, many aspects of mathematics, science and engineering. He even was interested, in his own curious fashion, in poetry, as this excerpt from a letter that he wrote to Alfred, Lord Tennyson, demonstrates:

> "Every minute dies a man, / Every minute one is born": I need hardly point out to you that this calculation would tend to keep the sum total of the world's population in a state of perpetual equipoise, whereas it is a well-known fact that the said sum total is constantly on the increase. I would therefore take the liberty of suggesting that in the next edition of your excellent poem ["The Vision of Sin"] the erroneous calculation to which I refer should be corrected as follows: "Every moment dies a man / And one and a sixteenth is born." I may add that the exact figures are 1.167, but something must, of course, be conceded to the laws of metre.

The amazing thing is that the poem's words were in fact revised; after Babbage's letter, from 1850 on, they were always printed as follows: "Every moment dies a man, / Every moment one is born."

AI Roots, IV: Logic, Psyches, Information, Cybernetics, Brains

In the years 1880–1889, the American statistician Herman Hollerith, combining some of Jacquard's and Babbage's ideas, designed and built punched-card–based statistical calculating machines, and he founded the Tabulating Machine Corporation, which grew and grew and eventually became the International Business Machines Corporation.

In this same period, and then crossing over into the early twentieth century, formal logic was enjoying a renaissance at the hands of George Boole, Augustus de Morgan, Gottlob Frege, David Hilbert, Bertrand Russell, Emil Post, Alonzo Church, and Alfred Tarski (among many others). These people believed that all of mathematical thought could be captured by formal, mechanical rules, and tried to lay those rules out. To some extent, this viewpoint suffered a setback at the hands of Kurt Gödel in 1931, when he showed that formalizations of mathematics are always incomplete; however, the exact implications of this beautiful and important discovery remained unclear and controversial, and certainly Gödel's work did not stop people from believing in thought as potentially rule-bound.

Coming from a very different angle around the turn of the century were the Austrian and American psychologists Sigmund Freud and William James, both of whom observed deep regularities in the processes of human thought, both unconscious and conscious, and formulated speculative but profoundly insightful theories about the abstract organization of the mind, or, more metaphorically, of the psyche or soul.

In the years just around World War II, there was a sudden flourishing of ideas about neurology, information, and feedback, known as *cybernetics,* among whose founders were MIT's Norbert Wiener and Bell Telephone's Claude Shannon. Linked to this set of explorers was a more biologically-oriented set of researchers, including Warren McCulloch and Walter Pitts, first at the University of Illinois and later at MIT, and Donald Hebb in Canada, all of whom were convinced that the abstract principles governing brain cells, or possibly large clusters of brain cells, could be isolated and modeled independently of the brain, either in mechanical devices or in mathematical theories. A few years later, the British psychiatrist W. Ross Ashby published his influential book *Design for a Brain,* in which he tried to set forth the principles necessary for a system to adapt to its environment. The ambitiousness of this book, which certainly did not fully meet its goal, served as a goad for many young researchers to go it one better.

AI Roots, V: Alan Turing and John von Neumann

The years during and just after World War II were the heyday of computer pioneers Alan Mathison Turing and John (alias "János", "Johann", and "Johnny") von Neumann, both of whom built on many of these ideas and carried them to a kind of logical pinnacle by devising effective computer architectures and establishing rigorous properties of computation that brought it in closer contact with the activities of minds.

Von Neumann is justly commemorated in the so-called "von Neumann architecture" of most of today's computers, characterized by the existence of an enormous, mostly dormant, memory, and an active CPU — central processing unit — which is a very small set of registers through which all computations must pass, like the tight line of toll booths on the lone bridge that spans a vast river. Toward the end of his early-truncated but hugely productive life, von Neumann wrote a book on a very different architecture for computation, *The Computer and the Brain,* showing that error-prone but redundant electronic circuitry could function in reliable, brainlike ways.

As for Turing, he developed an idealized model of computation now known as "Turing machines", found a computational analogue to Gödel's theorem, broke German codes during World War II, then designed and built a powerful early computer called "ACE", and was led to speculating about whether human-made devices might reach human-level intelligence. This last contribution was encapsulated in a famous article, "Computing Machinery and Intelligence", published in 1950, in which what he called the "imitation game", but what is now called the Turing Test, was proposed.

Turing's Imitation Game and Imitations Thereof

In the Turing Test, a human "interrogator" carries out simultaneous blind interviews with two "witnesses" — another human and a computer — conducted through the channel of teletypes (*i.e.,* text alone on terminals). The interrogator's goal is to unmask the two witnesses, in the sense of revealing which is human and which is not; the computer's goal is to pull the wool over the interrogator's eyes. Ever since this game was described, it has been a source of philosophical debate and a distant pot of gold at the end of the AI rainbow. Turing believed in the great power of his test, and tried to suggest how open-ended and deep the probing could be by giving this tiny fragment of an imaginary dialogue that might take place:

Interrogator: In the first line of your sonnet which reads, "Shall I compare thee to a summer's day", would not "a spring day" do as well or better?

Witness: It wouldn't scan.

Interrogator: How about "a winter's day"? That would scan all right.

Witness: Yes, but nobody wants to be compared to a winter's day.

Interrogator: Would you say Mr Pickwick reminded you of Christmas?

Witness: In a way.

Interrogator: Yet Christmas is a winter's day, and I do not think Mr Pickwick would mind the comparison.

Witness: I don't think you're serious. By "a winter's day" one means a typical winter's day, rather than a special one like Christmas.

To me, this dialogue snippet is enormously suggestive — it reminds me of just how deeply one's language reveals one's innermost soul, whether one likes that fact or not. However, there are many intelligent people who think the Turing Test could be passed by putting together a bunch of simple tricks. And indeed, the whole matter has gotten much murkier than I would ever have supposed it would, thanks to the annual staging, at Boston's Computer Museum, of the Loebner Prize Competition, which I would characterize as a stripped-down caricature of the Turing Test.

In the Loebner Competition, the judges are deliberately selected to have no expertise in computers or artificial intelligence, and each program that is entered is not required to be able to communicate open-endedly, but only in its own restricted domain of discourse, such as "Women's Clothing" or "Shakespeare's Plays". The winner of the 1991 Loebner Prize, the first time the competition was run, was an entry called "Whimsical Conversation". This program, written by a computer programmer named Joseph Weintraub, did not really talk about any specific topic, but simply bantered jocularly with its human counterpart. Here is a small sampling from an actual dialogue that took place between one of the ten human interrogators and this program during the competition:

Interrogator: Hello, earth person!

Whimsical Conversation: Hello there judge, are you ready to have some fun? How ya doin, judge? Hello — how's the weather up there today?

Interrogator: Dark clouds with occasional bursts of sunshine (or rather camera flashes).

Whimsical Conversation: The trouble with the rat race is that even if you win you're still a rat. Whimsy can be flimsy, right? How important is that to you?

Interrogator: can't say I understand the question... but the whimsy of a poet is one thing and the whimsy of most of us is another.

Whimsical Conversation: How do you know you can t say you understand the question... but the whimsy of a poet is one thing and the whimsy of most of us is another.

Interrogator: Are you repeating me just for laughs?

Whimsical Conversation: I'm sorry, I do sometimes repeat myself... perhaps it's because i can't find my electr]nic organizer!

The typos by the program are deliberate attempts on Weintraub's part to make his program have as unmechanical an appearance as possible. In an article in *AI Magazine,* Robert Epstein, the founder of the Loebner Prize Competition, wrote:

We allow great latitude when conversing with jesters; incomprehensible, irrelevant responses are to be expected.... Weintraub's program may have succeeded simply because his terminal was labeled "whimsical conversation." The prize committee recently discussed this possibility, and considerable concern was expressed. In 1992, the committee will favor programs that have clear subject matters.

Interestingly, the following year, Weintraub won again with a program called PC Professor, a close cousin of Whimsical Conversation, but souped up so that it could "converse" on the topic "Men and Women". Here is another snippet, this one taken not from the 1992 competition itself, but from a long "interview" made by John Markoff, a *New York Times* reporter:

The Romantic Vision of Thought as Pattern   ◆◆◆ **73**

Interrogator: Is your perspective more that of a man or a woman?

PC Professor: Do you believe in a world run by women there would be no war? What is it you really want to know? My God please help me!

Interrogator: I think a world run by women would be a truly different place. What do you think?

PC Professor: I would be willing to give it a try, as the male ego has pushed us into a very dangerous political realm!

Interrogator: When do you think the first woman will be President?

PC Professor: I would guess we might see a woman President before the decade is over... What was I saying? Are such questions much on your mind?

Interrogator: Sometimes you answer me with three sentences. Isn't one enough?

PC Professor: Good answer. Would you like to switch gender just to know how the other half lives?

Interrogator: Do you really think women are smarter?

PC Professor: Why else would we end every prayer with "ah! men!" if men were not superior. I suspect the universe is expanding... Oh, I really think women are smarter?

Interrogator: It seems you do from what you've been saying to me.

PC Professor: What does a woman want anyway? Why do you think I do from what you've been saying to you? Frown.

This hilarious dialogue is absolutely incoherent when you look closely, but the program does a fair job of masking its incoherency by regurgitating in complete form odd wisecracks and various opinionated sentences fed to it by Weintraub (it has a set of some 6,000 such items in its memory).

Alan Turing, too, died far too young — but unlike von Neumann, almost surely of his own hand, just short of his forty-second birthday, in 1954. One cannot help but wonder what in the world Turing would have thought of this bizarre and surreal spinoff of his very serious 1950 article.

AI Roots, VI: Dartmouth, Summer 1956

For two months during the summer of 1956, a "Conference on Artificial Intelligence" took place on the campus of Dartmouth College in New Hampshire, for the express purpose of exploring the potential of machines to perceive, to think, to learn, and to create. Its senior organizer was information theorist Claude Shannon, but he was helped by some younger colleagues: most of all John McCarthy, a professor of mathematics at Dartmouth (and the coiner of the term "artificial intelligence"), but also Marvin Minsky, a mathematician/neurologist then at Harvard, and IBM's Nathaniel Rochester, a computer designer and a very early modeler of neural nets. This group invited six young researchers to join them: Oliver Selfridge, the inventor of a truly foresighted model of perception called

"Pandemonium"; Ray Solomonoff, a mathematician interested in studying the extrapolation of patterns in microworlds; Arthur Samuel, who had designed a highly influential checkers-playing computer program; Trenchard More, a Princeton graduate student working on mechanized theorem-proving; and Allen Newell and Herbert Simon, modelers of logical deduction from California's RAND Corporation and Carnegie Tech in Pittsburgh. Everyone had their own perspective on what was important in cognition: theorem-proving versus game-playing versus problem-solving versus learning, and so on *ad nauseam*. There was nothing approaching universal agreement as to how best to approach the goal of making mind out of matter, but out of the conference came the term "artificial intelligence" and the official founding of that intellectual discipline.

AI: A Committed Belief in Thought as Pattern

What unites all these thinkers down through the centuries is their belief in the thesis of *thought as pattern,* and when fast electronic computers came about, those lucky enough to be alive in that era flocked to computers as the ideal way of investigating this thesis because they understood that computation is nothing more and nothing less than the manipulation of arbitrarily complex patterns in arbitrarily complex ways.

This was, however, very little appreciated by the broad public. Largely through the type of imagery that is easily suggested by the term "electronic brain", the widespread illusion arose — and is still rampant — that AI researchers must be banking on the hypothesis that computers themselves are quite literally *built like brains* — that there is some kind of physical one-to-one mapping between the components of their architectures.

But AI was anchored on no such faith. Indeed, as AI developed, few researchers paid any attention to the anatomy or physiology of brains, whether on a microscopic or a macroscopic level; if there was any field aside from mathematical logic to which AI owed a significant debt, it was cognitive/perceptual psychology, which was concerned with far higher-level phenomena such as learning, forgetting, attention, foreground and background, categorization, the unconscious, the organization of memory and associations, the relationship between words and concepts, the making of analogies, the mechanisms behind errors, strategies for problem-solving and planning, the nature of stereotypes, and so on.

In summary, artificial intelligence could be described as: the belief in thought as the manipulation of unknown sorts of patterns, the attempt to discover those patterns and the rules for manipulating them, and the strategy of using computers to try out all sorts of possible types of patterns and types of pattern-manipulation rules.

The Lure of the Laws of Logic

To me as a teen-ager, this approach to what minds do was not only extremely plausible, but also romantic and mystery-exuding. What in the world could these patterns be? Would they be related to words? To whole ideas? To associations? To some kind of meta-grammar abstracted from all the world's languages? To the rules of deductive and inductive inference discovered by philosophers and logicians? Could they be captured through abstruse mathematical notions, such as group theory or set theory or topology, or some as-yet-unknown branch of mathematics? Could the magical pulses and patterns and pattern-breakings of music come close to the core of it all? The game was wide open when I first heard the term "electronic brain" and absorbed this philosophical prospect, and for that reason, dealing with computers took on a resonance of excitement for me.

Before I learned to program, my fascination with the mysterious connection between covert thoughts and overt symbols manifested itself in my passion for languages and writing systems. I could spend hours browsing in the foreign-language section of a good bookstore, picking up bits and pieces of information about all sorts of far-flung languages. The different ways they had of breaking up the world, the unpredictable grammatical features, the unique sets of sounds and shapes used — all of this was endlessly engrossing to me.

At more or less the same time, I fell quite under the spell of the discipline known as mathematical or symbolic logic, because like many mathematical types, I was lured by the intuition that deep thought was something very pure and elegant, like mathematical deduction, and that the rules of logic somehow crystallized its essence. I now think of this view of logic's centrality as ridiculous, but many great intellects held this view in high esteem, so I wasn't alone in my youthful exuberance for it. The mystique of Gödel's eerie discoveries in which logic itself was twisted around so as to prove its own limitations, and related snake-eating-own-tail-style discoveries by Turing, Church, and others, did nothing to dampen my belief in logic's profundity but instead fanned the flames of infatuation.

By the time I was about to enter Stanford, I had a fairly good grasp of the basics of symbolic logic, and even understood the main lines of Gödel's proof. Somehow, my affinity for logic reached the ears of Winfield Christiansen, the principal of my old elementary school, Stanford Elementary, and one day as I was walking through its familiar octagonal rotunda, he spotted me and asked me if I would like to be a teacher in an experimental symbolic-logic course for fifth- and sixth-graders. I was flattered by the offer and delighted at the prospect, and thus wound up teaching symbolic logic, three times a week for a full school year, to the sixth-graders at Stanford Elementary School. I was all of sixteen years old.

It was a strange experience teaching my sister Laura and several of her friends, as well as quite a number of rowdy boys who had zero interest in logic and who constantly had to be thrown out into the hallway, probably to their delight. Most of the kids, even the better-behaved ones, couldn't make head or tail of such principles as *modus ponendo ponens* and *modus tollendo tollens,* although curiously enough quite a few of them remembered those strange names for decades afterwards. There were, however, at least a handful who ate it up, and made it worth my while.

It was perhaps back in those days that the first seeds of doubt might have been planted in my mind about the centrality of logic in thinking, for it became clear to me that if intelligent children were completely thrown by the most elementary of deductive principles, then the idea that thought was just built of logic lost a good deal of its plausibility.

Flashing Lights and an Inner Light

At the start of the 1960's, Silicon Valley did not exist. It was called the Santa Clara Valley, and was totally blanketed with pretty fruit orchards rather than thousands of back-to-back low-slung high-tech computer companies with self-conscious names like "XQute", "Core/teks", "PsiGraph", "sEn·gEn", "Mykrōx", and "ZzYKōN". Indeed, in those sleepier days, Stanford University had exactly one computer to its name — a Burroughs 220 that used vacuum tubes, not solid-state transistors — and almost no one on campus knew about it or cared about it. The 220 was shared late at night with a San Jose bank, which used it for accounting. Computer science was literally an unheard-of discipline, and the only two professors on campus interested in computation were both in the math department. This was most fortunate for me, since as a high-school student taking calculus at Stanford, I knew them both a little bit and they kindly used their clout to give me special privileges to program the 220.

My friend and math-and-swimming rival Charles Brenner already knew how to program well, and he taught me the fresh and elegant language called Algol. My first attempts to program the 220 involved making it check out some beautiful numerical patterns that I, at that time hoping to become a mathematician, had recently discovered but not proved. I wanted to see if these patterns continued to hold for very large numbers. As it turned out, my number-theory-scouting programs became a marvelous set of stepping-stones towards mastery of Algol and programming in general. Each new program yielded fresh new mathematical insights, and complementarily, each new mathematical discovery created the need for new programs. My understanding of number theory and my ability to program thus leapfrogged over each other in the most benign of circles.

I remember so clearly how I used to stand in the inner sanctum of the 220 machine room — a vast air-conditioned space at least 100 feet long — and with great exhilaration watch the "giant brain" on all sides of me execute my instructions. In one part of the room, there were long banks of tape drives that, at totally unpredictable moments, would start a rapid little series of jerks and sudden stops, making me wonder, "What in the world is it thinking now? What is it looking for?"

On the operator's console was a striking display of several hundred small orange lights showing the contents of various registers in the CPU; although these, too, were mysterious, their mystery was more penetrable. If you knew something about how your Algol program was converted into lower-level machine code (and I had a good enough idea), you could actually detect what section of your program was executing from moment to moment. On the occasions when I could tell, I took delight in saying to myself, "The machine is *right now* thinking about my recursive sequences", and even though I myself had written the program and thus intimately understood its narrowness, its lack of imagery, and its utter rigidity, I still was able to attach a mystique to the rapidly shifting eddies and vortices of electronic flow perfusing the "brain" in which I myself was engulfed. All this is long enough ago that I am not sure how genuinely I believed *thought* was taking place in those tangles of wires and flashing patterns of lights, but I do remember how romantic and magical the possibility felt.

The Young Romantic and the Younger Skeptic

It is most interesting to me to contrast my own reactions back then with those of a child from another generation. Almost twenty years later, when personal computers were becoming popular and quite high-quality chess-playing programs were available to the public, I, by then a beginning assistant professor of computer science, was invited to the home of some friends for dinner. Their son Andrew, then twelve years old, was battling against the computer that evening, as apparently he did many evenings, for mastery of the chessboard. Although his father, a superb player, always beat the machine, Andrew apparently lost to it most of the time.

To tweak the lad a little, I asked him, "Do you think the machine's *thinking* when it beats you in chess?" Without a moment's hesitation, he replied to me, "Naah — it's just following a *program*." I was flabbergasted by this nonchalant, blasé attitude. How could it be that this machine was running intellectual circles around the boy and yet he could scornfully dismiss the suggestion that it might be thinking? Why wasn't he at least *intrigued* by the mysterious power that was lurking inside the metallic frame? What was behind the day-and-night difference in our reactions?

One would think that of the two of us, the teen-ager in the 220 machine room should have been the blasé one, the one who would have derisively pooh-poohed any suggestions of mechanical thinking, since he had actually written the program he was watching run and knew how simple and rigid it was. But no. Perhaps over the intervening two decades, the tenor of the times had radically changed. Perhaps by then there was little romance left to the idea of "electronic brains". Or perhaps their breadbox size and their chicken-in-every-pot commonality made computers seem far less mysterious. But that's not the whole story, for human beings, too, are a dime a dozen and are much smaller than barns, and yet we do not deny that our human opponents are thinking when they beat us at chess.

I never figured out just what was behind the striking contrast between my own youthful willingness to read thinking into circuitry and flashing lights, and young Andrew's self-assured scorning of it all. But I have to consider that if some professor had actually asked the teen-aged me such a question point-blank, maybe I, too, would have responded much as Andrew did, out of a desire to act "tough" and "macho" and to hide any signs of softness, gullibility, or naïve romanticism. It could be as simple as that.

Doing AI without Realizing It

In 1964, a few years after I had started my joyous computer-aided explorations of number theory, I ran across an article in *Scientific American* by a linguist named Victor Yngve, in which some quite complex patterns of English grammar used in a children's story about a choo-choo train by Lois Lenski were captured in a program, and any number of new sentences using the same vocabulary were spat out by the computer. Inspired by this article, and by an elegant notation called "Backus–Naur form" that I had recently been shown for describing the grammars of formal languages, and also by the power and beauty of Algol's recursive procedures, I came up with a flexible and general method for encoding grammars of human languages, and over the next year or so developed a computer program that could generate amusing and complicated nonsense sentences in English, Italian, and Hindi. For a while, what preoccupied me most was getting right the labyrinth of short-range and long-range agreements in Italian syntax, but eventually English became my main focus.

Back then, I never gave my most advanced program a name, but now, adopting the proper Silicon Valley spirit, I shall refer to it as "sEn·gEn", for "synthetic English Engine" as well as "sentence generator". The more intricate sEn·gEn grew and the more delightfully baroque its output became (see Chapter 14 for examples), the more seriously I took the idea that the computer executing its instructions was doing something akin to thinking.

At the same time, however, sEn·gEn's own gaping holes and frustrating rigidities were sensitizing me ever more to the subtlety of what genuine thought is. While I still got a big charge out of standing in the machine room and resonating with the huge hunk of hardware carrying out my instructions (by this time, a much faster Burroughs 5500), I was also starting to feel the vastness of the gulf between true human thought and the relatively simple processes that were allowing a simulacrum of sense to come spewing forth out of the web of wires and transistors.

The challenge of getting a computer to use language in a realistic manner was a delicious game for me — perhaps so delicious that it always felt like indulging in dessert rather than eating a nutritious meal. In fact, I developed a sense of terrible guilt for playing this game, and at one point, trying to kick the evil habit, I even forbade myself from stepping in the door of Stanford's "Comp Center" for many months. It felt so much like sinning that when I went on to graduate school, the idea of pursuing this kind of goal was infinitely far from my mind. Instead, I first tried math (for a couple of years, after which it got too abstract and arid for my mentality) and then physics (for eight more years), and only after bashing my head repeatedly against the hard, hard wall of theoretical physics did I finally arrive at the radical notion that maybe what I had once found so easy and so seductive was not necessarily as frivolous and worthless as I had then judged it to be.

Re-encounter with AI After a Decade of Dormancy

A key chance event took place while I was visiting my parents at Stanford sometime in 1973, just as I was at long last starting down the home stretch of my physics Ph.D. at the University of Oregon. One day, wandering around on the campus, I happened to run into Lynne Reder, one of my old Stanford Elementary School logic students — in fact, my star student — and she, by this time a budding psychologist, was attending a conference on campus that turned out to be on AI. This was the first time I had ever heard the term "artificial intelligence". To my delight, Lynne credited her early exposure to logic with playing a role in inspiring her interest in how reasoning works. She gave me a conference program to look over and explained what it was all about. It sounded very much up my alley, and I sat in on a couple of sessions.

All of a sudden, though, panic filled my heart as I realized that many of the ideas about the recursive structuring of language that I had explored so passionately, and totally on my own, nearly ten years earlier had in the meantime been independently discovered and now were well-known techniques in the field.

In a sense, this could be taken as encouraging news, in that it showed that my ideas hadn't been frivolous at all — to the contrary, in the context of this new discipline, they were altogether solid and respectable. In another sense, however, it was crushing news, since I felt I had lost the chance to make a name for myself — and worse, that ten years of my own life had been thrown away on vain activities in the wrong discipline. I don't really think that way any longer; my physics incarnation, though harrowing and traumatic in some ways, was nonetheless a time of intellectual maturing and exploration of precious ideas that I would never trade now.

However, it is undeniable that my years of mental and emotional anguish in physics convinced me that as soon as my Ph.D. was a *fait accompli*, I ought to follow the path of lesser resistance: I would join the hardy band of researchers seeking the patterns of thought. That, to me, promised to be a wonderful, lifelong adventure for which my own mind was naturally cut out. I soon learned of the goals of quite a few different AI research groups, all believing in this basic notion of *thought-as-pattern*, yet pursuing entirely orthogonal visions of this idea. To me, this ferment, this crazy clashing of ideas, seemed fitting for a scientific field in its early days, searching in every direction for the most promising pathways.

In the fall of 1975, with my physics Ph.D. essentially in my pocket, I moved back down from Oregon's Willamette Valley to California's Santa Clara Valley, my old stomping grounds. I had chosen the Stanford area partly because it was home and partly because in those days Stanford was well known as one of the world's centers for AI, so I figured it was as good a place as any to "retool myself" as an artificial-intelligence researcher.

As an auditor, I engaged in a crash course in both computer science and artificial intelligence, urgently trying to catch up with developments from the mid-sixties to the mid-seventies. I sat in on several AI classes and indeed participated fully along with the graduate students in them. In one, I was given the assignment of writing a short encyclopedia article on the history of machine translation or "MT", a topic that naturally fascinated me.

FAHQMT

In doing the research for my little article, I was struck by the about-face of Israeli mathematician Yehoshua Bar-Hillel, who, in the late 1940's, was one of the pioneers of MT. He had started out full of enthusiasm and optimism, but within a few years, those hopes were utterly dashed by his realization of the enormous extent to which natural language is pervaded by ambiguity. The famous pair of sentences that he used as examples to demonstrate the ineluctability of what he cahqophonously called "FAHQMT" ("Fully Automated High-Quality Machine Translation") were

"The pen is in the box" and "The box is in the pen". Obviously, in the former, "pen" must mean a writing implement, while in the latter it must mean an enclosure. All the imagery associated with both "pen" and "box" changes radically as a function of nothing more than a two-word swap.

One might at first think there must be some simple recipe for figuring out which meaning of "pen" is correct — for example, it means "enclosure" whenever it occurs as an object of the preposition "in". But of course that's silly; not to mention atoms and molecules, there are small pieces and ink inside writing implements, and one could easily stick a message or an ant or a postage stamp inside the cap of a fountain pen. For that matter, one could even stick a box — a tiny one — inside a fountain pen.

Moreover, questions and negations throw havoc into any heuristic rules that one might come up with. A small child asking "Is the box in the pen?" could easily mean either sense of "pen", simply being uncertain of the relative sizes of things; likewise, "The box is *not* in the pen" might well be uttered by an adult in reply to the child, in order to emphasize that the box is far too big to fit inside the fountain pen. In this case, it's the very absurdity of the box-inside-pen image that makes the phrase "in the pen" refer to the fountain pen! For reasons of this sort, and many others, Bar-Hillel despaired of ever getting a computer to be able to handle the full complexity of human language, and over the years became better known for his skepticism than for his advocacy of the cause.

Warren Weaver versus I. A. Richards on Translation

Another early MT researcher of whom I read was the American mathematician Warren Weaver, perhaps the first person to propose the enterprise of MT. In any case, Weaver was bullish about the possibilities of getting machines to translate between languages, as the following most curious and provocative statement, from an article he wrote in 1955, shows:

> When I look at an article in Russian, I say, "This is really written in English, but it has been coded in some strange symbols. I will now proceed to decode."

It is fascinating to me to set Weaver's brazen remark alongside a comment made in 1953 by British linguist and poet I. A. Richards — one of the two authors of the famous treatise *The Meaning of Meaning* — on the act of translation of certain Chinese philosophical concepts into English:

> We have here indeed what may very probably be the most complex type of event yet produced in the evolution of the cosmos.

Where, between these astoundingly contrasting attitudes, does the truth lie?

I have often wondered what Weaver meant by his claim. On one level, it sounds like the most simplistic and naïve view of what language is — simply a one-to-one substitution cipher — yet that can't be the full story, for Weaver had a lifelong fascination with translation. It was he who wrote the marvelous book *Alice in Many Tongues,* a remarkable study of some of the tremendous linguistic and philosophical tangles into which one is inevitably sucked when attempting to render Lewis Carroll's wordplay-drenched *Alice in Wonderland* in a foreign language. In writing this book, Weaver located fourteen translations of *Alice* into languages from all over the globe, and then analyzed some of the knottiest parts with the aid of native speakers of each language, who were also fluent in English. It is a book to be savored, for it reveals a great love for language and its unplumbable depths.

Given all this, I suspect that beneath the surface naïveté of Weaver's remark there lay a profound respect for the subtlety of human languages and the strange, almost paradoxical idea of translation, a respect akin to that voiced by I. A. Richards. Still, Weaver's words leave one wondering.

Stanisław Ulam Sees Seeing as Seeing As

Is there any valid sense in which a Russian sentence or article *can* be seen as an English sentence or article in code? I suppose it all depends on what one means by "seeing X as Y". Certainly the substitution-cipher vision is far too simplistic, but there are more abstract levels on which it might be justifiable. In any case, the desire and the propensity to see one thing as another are hallmarks of the human mind.

This was once put very memorably by the extraordinarily original Polish–American mathematician Stanisław Ulam, with whom I was friends for a few years in the early 1980's, as he neared the end of his life. Heinz Pagels reports that Ulam and his mathematician friend Gian-Carlo Rota were once having a lively debate about artificial intelligence, a discipline that fascinated Ulam but whose approach he thought was far too closely tied to logic and strict deduction. Ulam, a very visual thinker and a great believer in the centrality of imagery to thought, said to Rota, "The time has come to enrich formal logic by adding to it some other fundamental notions. What is it that you see when you see? You see an object as a key, a man in a car as a passenger, some sheets of paper as a book. It is the word 'as' that must be mathematically formalized... Until you do that, you will not get very far with your AI problem."

To Rota's expression of fear that the challenge of formalizing the process of seeing a given thing as another thing was impossibly hard, Ulam retorted, "Do not lose your faith — a mighty fortress is our mathematics", a droll quip in which Ulam, perhaps unintentionally, practices what he is preaching by alluding to the Lutheran hymn "Ein' feste Burg ist unser Gott". This itself is a double layer of "seeing as": firstly seeing mathematics as a deity, and secondly seeing a deity as a fortress.

Ulam's stress on the flexibility and centrality of analogical thought, especially its noncapturability through the rigidities of logic, harmonized with my own intuitions about what is most elusive and most important about how human thought works.

AI Novice Seeking Pathway Meets Bongard's Problems

In the various courses I was sitting in on at Stanford, I read admiringly of the natural-language program SHRDLU developed by MIT researcher Terry Winograd, of the speech-understanding effort called HEARSAY, developed by Raj Reddy and a cohort of talented graduate students at Carnegie-Mellon, of the story-understanding work going on at Yale under the direction of Roger Schank, of research trying to integrate perception with language under the direction of psychologists Robert Lindsay, Donald Norman, and David Rumelhart at the University of California at San Diego, and so forth. Needless to say, I was not equally convinced by all the diverse approaches I read of — some struck me as rather simplistic, others as overly ambitious, yet others as focusing on non-central aspects of thought — but each had its own pluses and minuses, and seemed at least to have charted out some particular set of fascinating problems that up until then had not even been considered as legitimate targets of scientific inquiry.

I found myself pulled in two somewhat conflicting directions. On the one hand, I felt I had once had a genuine head start in understanding how computers could deal with natural language, and so a certain side of me was inclined to pursue and extend my old sEn·gEn ideas. On the other hand, I felt increasingly convinced that abstract perception and analogical thought — Ulam's notion of "seeing X as Y" — was really at the crux of everything mental, but exploring this route would mean dropping language and taking up much vaguer, harder-to-pin-down facets of thought.

What tipped the balance was my running into a book called *Pattern Recognition* by Russian computer scientist Mikhail Bongard. The book's text was not so inspirational or scintillating, but it had an appendix of 100 visual puzzles that I simply could not lay down. Each puzzle consisted of twelve little diagrams, separated into two groups of six each. The question in each case was simply: Why are *these* six on the left and *those* six on the right? What, in a few words, is the telling difference between the two groups? It was the same kind of "What's different? What's the same?" game as had fascinated me many years before when I discovered the three-balls puzzle, and it resonated deeply with my passion about the mysteries of creativity.

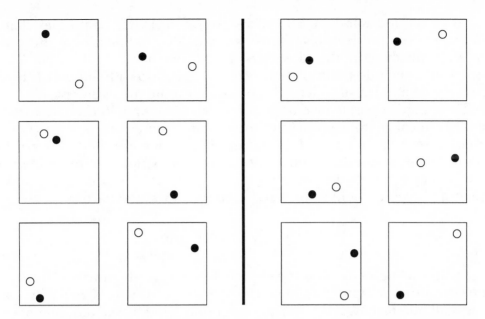

Two Bongard problems. In each, the idea is to figure out what constitutes the difference between the set of six diagrams on the lefthand side and the set of six diagrams on the righthand side. In other words, each of the six boxes on the left side has some property that none of the boxes on the right side has, and vice versa. What are these properties? Answers to both problems are given at the bottom of the page.

In the upper problem, connect the two dots in each box with a straight line. The lines in the lefthand boxes all slope downwards (as you scan them left to right), while the lines in the righthand boxes all slope upwards. In the lower problem, the middle shape on the left side is always a triangle; on the right side, it is never one.

So captivated was I by Bongard's escalating series of puzzles that I found myself compulsively inventing scads of additional puzzles in the same vein, often involving higher abstractions than his had. By the time I was finished with my little flurry of activity, I had come up with another fifty-six Bongard-style puzzles, of which two are shown on the preceding page.

This binge of puzzle-invention of course steeped me in thoughts about what the critical cognitive processes must be in solving such puzzles (not to mention inventing them), and this in turn pretty much pushed me over the brink in terms of the direction I felt I ought to explore in modeling the mind. Language wound up getting left in the dust — not that it wasn't a fascinating beacon, but in some sense I felt that it was too hard to tackle.

Hoist by My Own Petard

In the spring of 1977, I traveled to Bloomington, Indiana, for a job interview in the Computer Science Department at Indiana University. My talk was all about Bongard puzzles, perception and abstraction, analogical thought, the idea of seeing one thing as another. It was rather speculative, but the department members seemed to like it. For my part, I found the university as a whole most congenial and the campus very beautiful, and so I was deeply gratified to receive a job offer a few weeks later, and accepted with no hesitation. In fact, I considered myself very lucky, since in an official sense, I had no background in computer science: I had never taken a course in it at Stanford, Oregon, or anywhere else. But the department was most open-minded and encouraging, and I wound up feeling very much at home among its members and its graduate students.

One of the great experiences for me as a beginning professor at Indiana University was getting deeply involved in the AI assignments that I gave to my students. In the first AI course I ever taught, for instance, I had each class member, myself included, write a program that could play Chinese checkers, and conducted a tournament among all the programs. I selected the game of Chinese checkers very deliberately, because, although a total novice as a player, I had always loved the curious and sinuous pathways that a single jumping-here-and-there move could take.

One day I was sitting downstairs in the basement of Lindley Hall in front of a screen, testing out the level of skill of ChiChex, my own just-finished program, by pitting it against myself. A couple of my students were also in the same terminal room, each of us minding our own business, when all of a sudden ChiChex did something absolutely bizarre. It claimed to be able to move from one spot to a nearby one when there was no pathway at all connecting them — just an empty gap. It would have been a stunningly good move, but for the "technicality" of its utter illegality...

My heart sank. How could ChiChex be this stupid? It had never done anything like this before. I called over one of the students to show him this annoying bug and to elicit suggestions as to what in the world I might have done wrong in my programming. He studied the star-shaped board on the screen for a while and then said, "That's not an illegal move — look." And with his finger he then traced a highly circuitous pathway that started out backtracking from the marble's original site, then looping around way off to one side, bouncing left and right, finally arriving at the destination. The move was legal, after all — my program was exonerated! In fact, I had been tricked by precisely the aspect of Chinese checkers that had most attracted me. This experience of being outwitted by an entity of my own creation, rigid and mechanical though it was, was somehow very charming to me.

The Eliza Effect

Not everybody found it charming that people could be duped by computer programs. In 1976, Joseph Weizenbaum, an MIT professor of computer science and a former AI researcher, came out with *Computer Power and Human Reason,* a book provoked largely by his astonished dismay at how people had reacted to a program he had written in the mid-1960's called "Eliza", also known as "Doctor". Through typed exchanges with humans, this program acted the role of an insipid psychotherapist in a drug-induced stupor, dully droning on about the emotional problems of its "patients".

Eliza depended on a mixture of purely canned responses ("Go on", "I see", "I am not sure I understand you fully", and other content-free clichés) and semi-canned responses. The latter were simply templates with blanks that Eliza filled in by spitting back key words that the "patient" had just typed in. Thus if a human typed, "I do not get along well with my parents", Eliza might reply, "Tell me more about your parents", parroting back the noun "parents" and glibly switching the pronoun "my" into "your". The program's understanding was as skin-deep as that. Of parents it knew not a stitch more than it knew of the chemical basis for photosynthesis or the history of the interaction between the Sanskrit and Arabic writing systems. (These same simple tricks, incidentally, are central to Joseph Weintraub's much later programs Whimsical Conversation and PC Professor, as you can see if you go back and look over the dialogue snippets.)

Despite the fact that his Eliza program was nothing but an entirely vacuous syntactic manipulator — and here, the phrase "nothing but" conveys exactly the right flavor — Weizenbaum had observed, time and again, that people trusted it, and seemed to believe that this tiny bag of simple-minded tricks actually understood their own problems and related to them as emotional beings. Given my own handful of interactions with the program, I must admit that this severely stretches my credulity, but I am willing to believe that at least some people actually fell for the whole gag. In any case, that was Weizenbaum's claim, and it's what launched his book, which was an eloquently written diatribe about the alleged evils of AI, claiming that the whole effort was misguided and doomed to failure, but that even if it succeeded in certain ways, it ought to be stifled because of its intrinsic danger to humanity. The thesis was provocative and at times quite interesting, but the danger was so grossly overstated and the tone was so caustic towards the entire AI community and so sanctimonious that, for an enthusiast like me, it was painful to read.

Weizenbaum's book brought to the world's attention a phenomenon soon known as the "Eliza effect". The idea was simply that lay people have a strong tendency — indeed, a great willingness — to attribute to words produced by a computer just as much meaning as if they had come from a human being. The reason for this weakness is clear enough: Most people experience language only with other humans, and in that case, there is no reason to doubt the depth of its rootedness in experience. Although we all can chit-chat fairly smoothly while running on a mere half a cylinder, and often do at cocktail parties, the syntactically correct use of words absolutely drained of every last drop of meaning is something truly alien to us.

One of my favorite examples of the Eliza effect is a story told to me by my friend Bernie Greenberg. Sometime in 1970, Bernie and a friend were at a teletype, conducting a remote session with a mainframe computer at New York University. Along with what they themselves typed, many other messages would occasionally get typed out on the long scroll of paper, some extemporized by the remote machine's human operator, others simply canned remarks coming directly from the NYU computer, such as "ATTENTION REQUIRED ON 1442 PUNCH", at which point Bernie or his friend Mike would have to go and adjust the card punch.

At one point two art students walked up and, intrigued by the verbal exchange on the screen, asked what was going on. Mike said, "Oh, I'm just talking to the computer." They asked if they could try it out, so Mike typed, "WE HAVE TWO YOUNG ART STUDENTS HERE WHO WOULD LIKE TO ASK THE COMPUTER QUESTIONS, DIG?" His "let's-pull-the-wool-over-their-eyes" tone was instantly clear to the unseen human operator at the other end, who replied, "GO AHEAD. IT IS VERY IMPORTANT TO ANSWER QUESTIONS OF THE NATION'S YOUTH." For some reason, the art students' first question was, "DO CHICKENS HAVE LIPS?", to which "the computer" replied, "YES THEY DO. MOTHER NATURE PUTS THEM BEHIND THEIR BEAKS TO PROTECT THEM FROM PEOPLE WITH CHICKEN FETISHES." The students, quite thrilled, then asked what the meaning of life is, to which "the computer" replied, "LIFE IS 10000 VOLTS SURGING THROUGH YOUR TRANSISTORS." The art students were even more flabbergasted, and then tried a series of questions along sexual lines.

After a while, giddy with amazement, the pair ran out of questions. Before taking their leave, they asked if they could have the printed transcript from the teletype, and Bernie and Mike were happy to oblige them. After their departure, Bernie and Mike called up the computer's student operator, with whom they had of course been in cahoots, and the three of them laughed themselves silly.

By coincidence, Bernie ran into the same two students the next day in a cafeteria at Cooper Union's art school, and they were still admiring the printed teletype transcript, which they had in front of them. One of them said to Bernie, "Wow — that is really something. But how in the world did the computer ever know *this*?", and pointed to the line that said, "ATTENTION REQUIRED ON 1442 PUNCH".

The point of this little episode is that the art students had everything completely backwards: They had no problem attributing verbal behavior to the computer that would have been simple for a human but far beyond any computer, and conversely, they were astonished that the computer could do something that was trivial for it but that was somewhat alien to humans. This shows exactly the problem that the Eliza effect represents.

What came to disturb me ever more over the years was the fact that not just lay people were susceptible to the Eliza effect. AI researchers, too, often seemed to conflate the ideas behind their own programs' utterances with the ideas that would have been in the mind of a human who made the same statements. This is a surprisingly easy slope to slide down, even when one knows every last detail of how a program works. Perhaps it is an adult counterpart to children's ardent desire to believe their stuffed animals are alive, and to be able to convince themselves, or at least half-convince themselves, that their toys *are* indeed alive. In any case, it is something to watch out for.

On the other hand, one can jump too far in the other direction, and intransigently refuse to admit the existence of any meaning whatsoever in anything produced by a computer, purely and solely because it was produced by a computer. Where to draw the line? The work that I next turn to is an excellent example of the subtlety of the question.

The Meaning of Meaning: A Schankian View

Above, I mentioned the book *The Meaning of Meaning,* written in the early 1920's by the erudite British scholars C. K. Ogden and I. A. Richards. Their many-times-reprinted book was a valiant attempt to focus the world's attention on the mystery of symbols and to ask, perhaps to answer, deep questions about language and thought, the essence of humanity. Intrigued by this noble goal, I bought the book many years ago, but unfortunately I found it so opaque that I never read more than a few pages of it. This disillusionment inspired me to write a little limerick on the subject:

> *Two experts, to explicate Meaning,*
> *Penned a text called "The Meaning of Meaning",*
> *But the world was perplexed,*
> *So three experts penned next*
> *"The Meaning of Meaning of Meaning".*

This riddle — the meaning of meaning — has exerted a strong pull on many people in our century, one of the most noted among whom is AI researcher Roger Schank. When I was a fledgling AI professor, I studied Schank's work with interest, and had my students read about it as well.

Very early in his career, Schank had felt repulsed by what he considered a grotesquely unwarranted emphasis on *syntax* in AI's approach to language — concentration on such things as word order, inter-word agreements, the large-scale structure of sentences, the nature of pronoun reference, and a host of other problems of that sort. He therefore chose to follow an entirely different pathway, a vehemently syntax-eschewing pathway, and to delve into the mysteries of *semantics* — in short, to quest the meaning of meaning. This proved to be a long, arduous trek.

Schank's first foray in this direction was the development of a formalism he called "conceptual dependency notation", in which complex meanings were broken down into assemblages of crude primitives, a bit like factoring composite numbers into primes. Some of the primes for describing actions were called PTRANS, MTRANS, and ATRANS. A PTRANS is an event in which something physical is transferred by an agent from one place to another ("Albert gives Mileva a gold ring"), and an ATRANS is a transfer of possession (once again, "Albert gives Mileva a gold ring", seen from another angle). Then an MTRANS is a transfer of something mental ("Mileva gives Albert a good idea"). Each object and agent possesses a large number of time-varying attributes, such as HEALTH-VAL; thus the event of Albert's death, for example, would be mirrored in a Schankian program by the setting of his HEALTH-VAL attribute to its minimum allowable value of −10.

These early Schankian stabs at semantics were, as must seem obvious, impossibly crude. Nonetheless, they provided a backbone on which other ideas could be hung, and after a few years Schank supplemented this first layer of ideas with a second layer that involved stereotyped collections of interrelated agents, objects, and actions. These were called "scripts", and captured some abstractions behind common, oft-repeated events in life.

The most studied and most famous of all became the *restaurant script*, whose purpose was to allow the following kind of vignette to be understood:

"John goes into a restaurant, orders a hamburger, gets a burnt one, and suddenly feeling surly, walks out without paying." The restaurant script conveniently wraps up into a single computational data structure the ideas of entering, getting seated, looking at a menu, selecting, ordering, waiting, receiving food, eating it, asking for the check, paying it, leaving a tip, and departing.

A program endowed with such a script knew precious little about each of its components, but at least it had some sense of how they all fit into the larger-scale activity of a restaurant visit. The idea was that a program endowed with scripts for many situations could fill in all sorts of gaps when those particular types of situations were alluded to. Such a program, if quizzed but not probed too deeply in a short natural-language question-and-answer session conducted via a computer terminal, could often give the impression of understanding what goes on in restaurants and other stereotyped situations. However, a deeper and lengthier probing would soon destroy this façade and reveal a stunning emptiness in the symbols being glibly thrown about by the machine.

For instance, the following pieces of knowledge are lacking from the restaurant script: that restaurants have roofs; that they are smaller than galaxies and larger than DNA molecules; that there might be chewing gum stuck under the table but not in the servers' hair; that one generally does not pay one's bill in pennies or leave a cashier's check for a tip; that tables are not tilted (or if they are, then less than a couple of degrees), and thus that food does not slide down onto the floor; that straws and napkins are free and one can comfortably ask for a few but probably not a dozen of them, and definitely not a thousand; that tables and chairs are inanimate objects yet have legs; that the number of servers is usually less than the number of patrons, and does not have to be a prime number; that hamburgers are made from animal flesh but not usually out of brains or tails, and certainly not from moon rocks; and so on and so forth. What I am trying to get across by this slightly facetious list, which could, of course, be extended *ad nauseam,* is the unutterably large number of facts that we humans all know intimately about restaurants, tables, floors, silverware, people, time, space, and so forth, yet which are not provided by the restaurant script. Despite their gaping lacunae, scripts still constituted a legitimate attempt to endow programs with a deeper layer of semantics than Schank's first layer had done.

Lest readers get a false impression, Schank was by no means the sole or the first AI researcher to be gripped by the mysteries of semantics. Many of the best researchers devoted great efforts to grappling with the meaning of meaning as well as the intricacies of sentence structure, but Schank is famous to some extent because he so adamantly rejected any involvement whatsoever with grammar and its beguiling charms.

The Romantic Vision of Thought as Pattern

I myself was not terribly impressed by these early attempts by Schank and his team to capture meaning; I felt that there was something disturbingly upside-down in the group's strategy of giving short shrift to the most elemental words and concepts (such as these six, for example: "a", "the", "is", "on", "dish", "table") in favor of attacking very complex, compound notions first. On the other hand, I bore no deep intellectual distrust of the Schank group, because, after all, they were seeking what they thought were the true patterns manipulated in the mind. We just happened to disagree about what the most important ingredients of the patterns were likely to be, but we certainly agreed on the fundamental driving philosophy behind AI: the image of thought-as-pattern.

AI Achievements versus AI Claims

Over the years, Schank has had so many Ph.D. students, and they in turn so many of their own, that by now there is a large and not always harmonious family of Schankian-style researchers who work on "case-based reasoning" ("CBR"), the term being their own way of saying that people tend to understand the situations with which they are currently faced by seeking analogues in their storehouse of previous experiences and then "tweaking" retrieved memories to make them better fit the current context. This is quite in agreement with my own view of thinking, except that the further this type of research has gone, the more it has become topheavy in the sense described earlier: too little attention is paid to the very small but fundamental ingredients of thought (concepts like "table" and "on"), and too much attention is paid to large-scale stereotype structures like scripts.

Let me cite an example of the self-delusion that can arise when this is done. I recently read a paper by a trio of Schank research-family members that described ISAAC and SINS, two very different programs they had written using essentially the same principles. ISAAC was allegedly capable of reading science-fiction stories and understanding them just as you or I would. Here's a fragment of a story that it supposedly understood all of:

> Those were the shining days of the world. But are we so old now? Men had a bright flame — the old word is 'divine', I think — that flung them far across the night skies, and we have lost the strands of the web they wove.

To comprehend such prose requires full human intelligence and long experience in and of the world, yet the paper skimmed right over this boggling achievement, its main point being merely that ISAAC was built on the same principles as its cousin SINS, which allowed a robot to learn how to navigate its way among a few obstacles — a task roughly on the same level as a puppy dog learning to avoid chair legs as it walks around a room.

Both of these programs were described by the programmer/authors with equal respect, as if nothing were in the least funny about claiming in one breath to have conquered Everest and in the next breath to have taken one's first toddling steps. I must say, this kind of incomprehensible claim is not rare but typical in today's dizzyingly overhyped AI world, where words like "understand", "discover", and "create" are bandied about with such fatuous glibness that even a seasoned researcher can read an article with care and still have no idea what the program it describes really can do.

I was thus not too surprised to find out, some months later, that a few of my colleagues had read this same article without batting an eyelash at the prowess claimed for ISAAC. The matter-of-fact tone in which its alleged ability to read stories was described was apparently enough to let the claims sail smoothly by the eyes of sophisticated cognitive scientists. This is, to me, a disturbing indication of the confusion into which the field has fallen in the past couple of hype-swollen decades. And yet, just to emphasize the complexity of the situation, I might add that the authors of ISAAC and SINS feel skepticism about my research, mirroring mine about theirs.

Manipulation of Mandarin by Schankian Methods

Back to mechanical translation for a moment. Although there was a sudden sobering-up in the late 1950's, which continued all through the 1960's and even into the 1970's, the field of MT did not just shrivel up and die. Many groups pursued their own pathways; among them was that of Schank and his students, during the 1970's. It may have been little more than an attention-grabbing stunt, but one of the things that group did was to implement a multilingual "front end" to many of their programs that dealt with natural language, so that descriptions of the exasperation behind the hypothetical John's surly stomping-out from the restaurant after being served a carbonized hamburger were produced in a spray of languages, including English, Spanish, French, and Mandarin (in an amazingly awkward romanization).

The idea was presumably to show that what was going on inside the program went considerably below the surface of just *words,* and dealt instead with *ideas.* To some observers, such a virtuosic display, especially featuring exotic Mandarin output, was proof positive that Schank's group had indeed made a computer able to grapple with the complexities of genuine semantics; others remained skeptical. I myself sat somewhere in between, feeling the surface had been scratched but there was a lot of spin being put on rather modest achievements. Still, let me stress once again that, despite my skepticism of its claims, I was not an out-and-out enemy of this avenue of research; I just thought its claims should be toned down.

"Quoting" a Famous Attack on AI

In my youthful infatuation with AI's vision of thought as an abstract sort of pulsating, dynamic play of forms, I had had no notion of how much opposition such a thing might stir up among thoughtful folk. Thus it simply didn't cross my mind that philosophy, in particular, was awash with spoilsports who not only had doubts about AI and its approach to mind, but in fact had an antipathy for it so profound that I could hardly fathom its origins. Soon, though, as my own AI work was starting to bud, I ran across various philosophical tracts, monographs, and books aiming to show AI's bankruptcy, claiming to quash all visions of thought *qua* program — but of all such attacks, I didn't find any that I thought of as truly worthy, nor did any catch on popularly in such a way as to instill much worry on my part. But this would all soon shift.

In mid-spring 1980, I found in my mailbox at work "Minds, Brains, and Programs", a manuscript by a pugnacious luminary in linguistics and philosophy — in fact, it was a submission to *BBS,* at that point a just-born, up-and-coming journal on brain and mind — for which I, along with many, was to furnish my criticisms and/or witticisms for printing in a kind of public forum. Who but a clairvoyant could know that this scrappy, almost macho manuscript would soon turn into a major focus and rallying cry for anti-AI groups? It is astounding, actually, how many thoughtful individuals would wind up succumbing to its catchy and smoothly-flowing words. (On account of a conflux of factors sadly out of my control, I must hold off on naming its author, though not for too long.)

"Minds, Brains, and Programs" assaults all of AI by proxy — that is, by using Schank's paradigm of scripts as its focus, and abstracting to AI *in toto* all morals drawn from that narrow study. But nothing is wrong with such a plan, in my opinion, for Schank's work is typical; if his work falls victim to this particular attack, all of AI falls. And so, both for AI fans and AI cynics, it is vital to grasp how this harsh assault works. What I'd point to as its gist is found in a long but crucial paragraph, which puts forth a vivid sci-fi fantasy, and which to you I now transmit, as faithfully as my linguistic chains allow:

> A good tactic in trying to confirm or disconfirm any broad proposal as to how minds work is to try to think of what that proposal would imply about your own mind's workings (assuming, naturally, that all minds work according to its canons). Why not apply this tactic to Schank's AI proposals about mind? A curious imaginary situation will allow us to do just that. Say I find that I am in a log cabin with no way out. Looking all about, I spot a long scroll of Mandarin pictograms coming in through a narrow slot. I'm assuming (and this is in fact so) that I not only can't follow Mandarin at all, out loud or in writing, but probably couldn't distinguish Mandarin writing from, say, Japan's katakana and hiragana scripts, or from random scribblings totally lacking import. In short, to

my visual apparatus, Mandarin writing is just so many doodly scrawls, signifying nothing at all. Now, to amplify my imaginary situation just a bit, I posit that following this first batch of Mandarin writing is an additional batch of Mandarin script along with a group of instructions for associating parts of this additional batch of symbols with parts of my original batch. Luckily, that group of instructions is not in Mandarin but in Anglo-Saxon, and thus I can grasp what it says with as much facility as anybody who knows Anglo-Saxon as thoroughly as I do. By following said instructions, I can link up proximal or distal groups of formal symbols — and it is worth pointing out that "formal symbol" is simply a shorthand way of saying that all I know about any symbol is its physical form. Now I am going to posit a third and final scroll of Mandarin symbols sliding in through that slot along with a group of instructions, again in Anglo-Saxon, indicating firstly how to match up bits of this third scroll with bits of my two prior scrolls, and additionally how to output, as a function of particular strings of symbols in this last scroll, long horizontal rows containing many distinct Mandarin symbols. Now, although I am not cognizant of it, my initial batch of input symbols is known to its authors as a "script", my follow-up input batch as a "story", and my final input batch as a "quiz". In addition, my scrolls' authors call my rows of output symbols "quiz solutions" and my group of instructions in Anglo-Saxon a "program". So far, so good. Now, although it will add minor complications to our imaginary situation, I shall also posit that on occasion, a story in Anglo-Saxon (which I obviously follow with no difficulty) drops through that infamous slot, along with a quiz about it (again in Anglo-Saxon), and I do my duty, writing out, in my own hand, a group of quiz solutions in Anglo-Saxon and pushing it back out through that slot. But my main input/output activity is in Mandarin; and naturally, as days and months go by, I gain in skill in manipulating Mandarin symbols, and in a similar way, my programs' authors gain in programming skill. Thanks to this, my programs finally attain such intricacy and polish that, to anybody not privy to what is going on in my small "prison", my solutions to any quiz in Mandarin invariably pass outright for solutions by an individual who had grown up in China. Nobody just looking at my solutions has an inkling that I don't actually know a word of Mandarin. As for my output in Anglo-Saxon, I might add, although it should go without saying, that my solutions to any quiz in that idiom contain no awkward or suspicion-provoking traits, a fact that follows trivially from my having grown up talking and writing in Anglo-Saxon. Thus, to anybody not in my cabin — to anybody who simply scans my "quiz solutions" — my solutions in Mandarin do just as convincing a job as do my solutions in Anglo-Saxon. But in Mandarin, in contrast to Anglo-Saxon, my production of quiz solutions is brought about totally through manipulation of formal symbols to which I attach no import at all. Thus it is fair to say that in all of my cabin-bound manipulations of Mandarin, I act indistinguishably from a fancy digital calculator following a program; I do nothing but carry out various computational actions on various formal symbols. In sum, as far as my parsing and writing of Mandarin go, I am simply an instantiation of a Schankian AI algorithm.

Or, if I might try to cast this unusual vision in my own words: Although this fantasmagorical black box of a cabin, in its input and output, acts indistinguishably from a human in total command of Asia's dominant idiom, what in fact is going on is nothing but vacuous symbol-shunting by a

The Romantic Vision of Thought as Pattern   ◆ ◆ ◆   95

monolingual non-Asian who has no notion at all of any signification lurking in his cryptic symbols' alluring and florid brush-drawn forms. That is to say, this stunningly virtuosic human automaton, this author of "Minds, Brains, and Programs", this living-and-kicking, fully organic CPU sadly stuck in a prison of prancing pictograms, though displaying a glib linguistic facility, is in truth but a walking shadow, full of sound and fury, signifying nothing.

This by-now notorious armchair trip amounts — so claims its crusty author, and so claim many who find in his musings a natural way to uphold humanity's dignity — to an instant annihilation, a *diminutio ad absurdum,* of AI's shaky philosophical foundations. Simulating a mind through a symbol-manipulating program is, so run claims, shown up for what it is: a hollow absurdity. Similarly, computation is, so run claims, shown up for what it is *not*: in particular, it is not *about* anything; its bold front of signification or significancy (call it what you will) is nothing but a paltry Hollywood trick with mirrors. An algorithmic automaton's churning-away in imitation of cognition is unavoidably as lacking in import as a myriad cog-gnashings in a funicular railway, a fancy phonograph, a lustrous Swiss watch, or an old hot rod's rusty transmission. In a word, computation, notwithstanding how convincingly conscious it might look from without, is inwardly always just as unconscious and lacking in soul as any phonograph, chronograph, cool funky car, or funicular. And thus AI is but an airy nothing, an *ignis fatuus.*

Ugh, No "E"; Enough!

Unshackled at last, I reveal our provocative passage's ur-source and primogenitor: Berkeley professor John Searle. His article, of which the foregoing prolix verbal scenario, in slightly different form (coming up near the start of Chapter 5), is the core but far from the whole, touched off a firestorm of controversy that hasn't subsided yet. This is of course to Searle's credit: not just anyone can write an article that creates an uproar lasting for nigh on two decades. In that sense, kudos to Professor Searle.

On the other hand, Searle's article is what I would call a quintessential "bad meme" — a fallacious but contagious virus of an idea, similar to an annoying childhood disease such as measles or chicken pox: something one should be exposed to when young and thereby become immune to, hopefully for the rest of one's life. Although this is not the place to try to give a full immunization against searliomyelitis, it would be inexcusable to have "quoted" Searle without giving a follow-up at least sketching in broad strokes what is so terribly wrong in his scenario. Indeed, it has so many holes in it that it reminds me of those pictures in children's puzzle books where the caption says, "What's wrong with this picture?" At first it looks perfectly fine, but then the more carefully you scan it, the sillier it gets.

A Slighting of Mind

Probably the foremost and subtlest sleight of hand — or rather, sleight of mind — is the move by which the author sucks readers into uncritically identifying with, or projecting themselves onto, the human in the log cabin rather than the full system, which includes not just the human but also all the scripts and the very complex program for manipulating symbols. It is so easy, natural, and effortless for people to map themselves onto other *people* that the intellectually more challenging and confusing mapping — that between oneself and an abstract, composite structure, neither fish nor fowl, a structure one of whose components is a person, another of which is portrayed as resembling a fat instruction book, another of which is characterized as a long set of appendices — will almost surely be resisted. If this latter mapping is entertained at all, it will tend to be seen as artificial and forced, and people will unconsciously balk and instinctively reject it. Exploiting people's natural tendency to take the path of least intellectual resistance, in short, is Searle's first and foremost piece of clever trickery.

The second piece of trickery in Searle's long paragraph is also very subtle, and in fact is an essential ingredient in "lubricating" the first piece of trickery so that it works so smoothly for many people. What I am referring to is how Searle misleads readers about spatial and temporal orders of magnitude. By this, I mean two things.

Firstly, on the *spatial* side, Searle nonchalantly sidesteps the question of *how big* the Schankian computer program and the Schankian scripts would have to be to achieve the fantastic results he postulates. Recall that the image projected is one of totally duping native speakers for an arbitrary length of time — which amounts to full and flawless passing of the Turing Test. Now any human-readable printout onto paper of an AI program that could pass the Turing Test in this manner would certainly contain billions (or more likely, trillions) of lines of text, and would therefore not be simply a normal, visualizable scroll of paper with some symbols on it, but would require truckloads if not an entire aircraft carrier full of symbol-covered paper. If the whole printout could fit inside a little log cabin, which I seriously doubt, there would be nothing in the cabin but shelf after shelf of dense books, leaving very little space to maneuver.

Either Searle doesn't know this, which would show a total lack of understanding of the complexity of the endeavor of AI, and, in a curious sense, a profound disrespect for the depth of the human mind, or — far more likely — he knows it perfectly well but is being coy about it. In any case, if the system's size were portrayed accurately and vividly in the scene-setting paragraph, so that one imagined the system as being as huge as an oil refinery rather than as tiny as an outhouse, this imagery would rapidly tend to reduce the seeming importance and centrality of the human being.

The relative triviality of the role that the human plays would be clearer, and in compensation readers would rebel against slick attempts to downplay the vastness and complexity of the mind-capturing computer program. Such a program would necessarily contain a deep, human-level understanding not just of Chinese syntax, but of the entire world, since stories are, after all, about the world, and since unrestricted, free-for-all questions about stories can reach into arbitrary nooks and crannies of world experience.

Secondly, on the *temporal* side, Searle misleads just as seriously. It is a fact that a typical AI program's architecture requires any computer on which it runs to make *millions* of infinitesimal decisions in order to make any macro-level decision — for example, the macro-level decision of which string of symbols to output in response to a natural-language input question (even a string as short as a mere "yes" or "no"), since *understanding* any question generally involves bringing in a huge amount of knowledge and pondering.

If a cabin-trapped human such as John Searle or one of his avid converts really were to slavishly hand-execute every tiny jot and tittle of such a fine-grained computational process, sequentially making, let us say, a mere million micro-decisions in order to come up with the word "no" in answer to the natural-language input question "Do you see anything suspicious about the image of a hard-boiled egg rolling end over end for fifteen seconds down a curving pathway defined by two parallel garden hoses separated by a half inch or so of space?", and if each constituent micro-decision could be made in a mere second (a very generous underestimate, since for a human being, even *finding* the relevant parts of the computer program and the data in the vast shelves of books could take minutes if not hours!), then it would take a million seconds — some twelve days or so — to output this "no" answer to this one natural-language question. (I stress one last time that I have actually been enormously lenient in my estimates, and it would probably be more on the order of decades than days, but no matter.)

Clearly, it is not in Searle's interest to bring out either this phenomenal sluggishness of his mythic cabin's question-answering or the dizzying vastness of the printed information contained inside it, because doing so in a vivid enough manner would tilt readers' intuitions away from the naïve picture that he is attempting to portray, which is that of a person casually tossing off a few symbol-shufflings — on the order of a game of solitaire in size, duration, and complexity — with this nonchalant act somehow resulting in an arbitrarily long set of totally convincing responses in real time to unlimited, no-holds-barred natural-language questioning. The image Searle wishes to project places the human front and center and downplays the rest nearly completely. In such a case, what else *could* one wish to map oneself onto but the human?

When, however, one realizes that the human being plays but an inconsequential role — that of dronelike bookkeeper — in a fantastically large and intricate system the interesting aspects of whose behavior take place on a slow-as-molasses time scale far more stretched-out than one can easily identify with, one starts to realize how ingenuous and wrong-headed it is to insist on mapping oneself solely onto the tiny human lost in the middle of it, because doing so completely leaves out of the picture the true source of the system's complexity and interest.

Confusion of Levels

There are other sleights of mind here, as well. Probably the most notable one is the suggestion (not explicitly articulated yet clearly implied) that the rules allowing the system to answer questions at a native-speaker level are concerned exclusively with symbols of the Chinese language itself, as if coming up with reasonable answers to questions posed in Chinese were just a matter of shunting around Chinese signs, and not a matter requiring abstract patterns transcending the signs of Chinese or for that matter of *any* human language — patterns behind the scenes, patterns having to do with how ideas and concepts and knowledge are represented in complex, overlapping associative networks in the human mind. (Think of the mental imagery you concocted in understanding the question about the egg rolling down the pair of garden hoses, and consider the lifetime of experiences that allowed you to build up that imagery. Was what went on in your head nothing more than manipulation of mere English *words*?) To explore this matter would carry us deep into the nature of artificial intelligence and cognitive modeling, and is far beyond our scope. But it is absolutely crucial to the step-by-step dismantling of the hoax cleverly perpetrated by John Searle — a hoax that, sad to say, takes in a sizable fraction of his readers.

Perhaps this popular gullibility is the flip side of the gullibility that allows so many otherwise skeptical people to swallow the claim that a contemporary AI program can actually read and understand complex science-fiction stories, written in unsimplified English, at a human level. "Sure, I could easily believe there are, or soon will be, AI programs that can do everything that *we* can do mentally — except think. *Think*?! Naah — they're just *programs*!" That's pretty much the line of the Searle piece.

Stuff and Nonsense on "Wrong Stuff" and "Strong AI"

Not satisfied with casting doubt on the idea of a running computer program as a model of the mind, Searle also makes a curious and spurious distinction between two ways of looking at the enterprise of AI, ways that he dubs "weak AI" and "strong AI". I would not feel this distinction worth commenting on, except that so many people have bought right into it.

"Weak AI", as Searle would have it, is merely the attempt to gain some experimental insight into the mechanisms of thought by utilizing semantically empty and vacuous computer models of various aspects of thinking. Participants in this humble endeavor, if there were any, would make no claims that a computational model might one day think — they would innocuously assert no more than that computers provide an efficient way to study some properties of models. The effete band of "weak AI" researchers postulated by Searle would in his eyes belong to a discipline that could take its place next to such classical and unquestionably legitimate fields as linguistics, psychology, philosophy, and so on, none of which aims at the actual *making* of a thinking entity.

By contrast, "strong AI" would be, in Searle's eyes, that preposterous pseudo-science whose swaggering but pathetic participants have somehow been hornswoggled into the nonsensical belief that the computational models they are developing might someday *actually begin to think* on their own, that the symbols such models manipulate might someday actually begin to have *genuine content* rather than being vacuous, and so on. Obviously, it is with so-called "strong AI" that Searle has no patience.

Similar distinctions have occasionally been introduced in other sciences by philosophers, although under other names. If one were to draw a parallel distinction between "strong physics" and "weak physics", it would suggest that a certain class of arrogant physicists deludedly think their equations describe the real world, while a more modest and realistic bunch always humbly say, "Oh, I don't know — these equations are nice models of something that is reminiscent of the world, but they are not aspects of reality itself." Why would anyone want to study physics if from the outset they gave up on the idea that their achievements would describe reality?

For that matter, why are words any better than equations at capturing reality? Aren't we all guilty of the arrogant belief that our words describe real things rather than just describe our own weak internal images of reality? Words are far less precise than equations, and how they work is far murkier than how mathematical representations of reality work. But the funny thing is that Searle, in his insistence on the genuine semanticity of human language, is an inveterate, dyed-in-the-wool believer in the idea that words that come tripping off human tongues *really refer to the world,* but not words that trip across the screen of a transistorized machine.

And this ineluctable black-and-white dichotomy, we are told, comes about thanks to mysterious "causal powers of the brain" not shared by computers guided by programs. How does Searle know? Oh, he just *does.* As he puts it, computers are made of "the wrong stuff". "Wrong stuff", "right stuff", "causal powers of the brain" — it's all just too surreal for me.

Not Too Fast and Not Too Slow

With this philosophical capstone, we draw to a close our quick panoramic tour of the thesis, so beguiling for some and so abhorrent for others, that thought is but the shifting and superimposing and merging of subtle patterns in a flexible material substrate anciently evolved or recently designed for just that purpose.

Today's AI and cognitive science are still a long ways from explicating the mystery of what a human mind is and does, and this, in my opinion, is just fine. I would hate to think that our minds are so simple as to yield up all their secrets in but a few decades. On the other hand, we are making slow and steady progress, and that too is just fine by me. I would hate to think that our minds are so simple as to be constitutionally incapable of piercing the shroud of fog surrounding what it is that they themselves do.

There is much turmoil in this fanciful discipline, half science and half speculation, and I feel lucky to have been around in an era when my own idiosyncratic set of experiences and style of thought could play something of a role in the collective building-up of understanding of just what a mind and a human self really are.

•

Poems IV:

~ Oklahoman ~

* *
*
*

Xiàngsheng is a traditional Chinese verbal art form — translatable as "crosstalk", more or less — in which two comedians, standing before a crowd, roughly follow a preset script but also ad lib as they go along, laying on the puns and innuendoes as thickly as they can. The flavor of this difficult semi-improvisatory art has sometimes been likened to Abbott and Costello's famous "Who's On First" routine. Performers of *xiàngsheng* are well-known and greatly respected in China, and these days often appear on television. A relatively recent arrival on the Mainland's *xiàngsheng* scene is the talented actor Mo Dawei, whose nationwide television appearances have been great successes, and have made him known and admired all over China. I therefore take a certain amount of pride in having been Mo Dawei's first Chinese teacher.

One evening in 1983, my friend David Moser was inspired to take up Chinese when he saw me, a Caucasian, deciphering a few Chinese characters on the food containers we had picked up from a Chinese restaurant. He was so impressed that a non-Oriental could penetrate even the simplest secrets of that exotic language that he was sucked right in, on the spot, and persuaded me to make some tape recordings of elementary Mandarin for him. (At the time, I had studied Mandarin for around two years.) Well, look what came of it all, a few years later! These days, my Chinese protégé Mo Dawei is often recognized as he walks down the streets of Beijing or even down the dusty roads of a tiny village in the Chinese boonies — perhaps a desirable side effect of learning Chinese fluently, perhaps not, but that's the way the fortune cookie crumbled in David's case. Needless to say, my star (and sole) pupil has long since outstripped his first Mandarin master…

Before he knew one word of Mandarin, David had studied French and German, and he happened to be in Paris the summer that Bob French and Jacqueline Henry and I were plotting out our strategies for turning my book *GEB* into a truly French work. Along with Ronald Jonkers, the future Dutch translator of *GEB*, David was an active participant in all those marvelously stimulating, forever memorable, outdoor-café discussions. Little did any of us suspect, though, that David would wind up becoming intimately entangled with all those same problems we were discussing, except squared in difficulty, as a future member — and the only native anglophone — of the Chinese-language *GEB* translation team. Indeed, the whole idea would have sounded so crazy, so absurd, to all of us that we would have laughed it out the window immediately. And yet, it did come to pass. All of David's deep insights about translation, especially translation of subtle wordplay, which had bloomed in those Latin Quarter chats, served him beautifully as he helped to turn around what had initially been a sadly lackluster, literal-minded translation effort, and shepherded it into becoming a sparkling, effervescent piece of Chinese literature.

For a few years in the mid- to late 1980's, while he was intensely absorbed in matters Chinese, David was also involved in a peripheral way with my Fluid Analogies Research Group in Ann Arbor, and so he was right there on the scene when the whole "Ma Mignonne" thing exploded. It didn't take any coaxing for him to get involved. Before I knew it, David had come out with a rapid-fire series of modern, colloquial, even slangy translations, all characterized by hard-hitting, rat-a-tat rhythms.

"Honey Bun" exhibits these qualities perfectly. It starts out sadly, softly, a little wistfully — and then, all of a sudden, one smashes into lines 5–9: "What the hell! / Just get well! / Hit the floor! / Out the door!" What a transition! It's obvious that these are all trisyllabic three-word thoughts ending with exclamation points, but that's not all. Even their first words — "what", "just", "hit", "out" — are all linked by the sonic pattern of ending in the same explosive consonant, "t". And then, as fast as it had come on, this intensity vanishes in the gentle parenthetical remark that follows, which alludes, through the phrase "your beau", to the possibility of romance between the poet and his friend.

Honey Bun

David Moser

Honey bun,
It's no fun,
Sick in bed,
Eyes all red.
What the hell!   5
Just get well!
Hit the floor!
Out the door!
(Clem, your beau,
Tells you so.)   10
Let's go eat
Something sweet.
If you stay
Home all day,
Sick in bed,   15
Halfway dead,
You'll lose weight.
What a fate!
Sitting home
All alone,   20
Wan and pale,
Like in jail!
Heavens, dear!
I'm sincere,
On my knees: 25
Get well, please!
You're the one,
Honey bun!

"Lover Mine" is another Moserian effort and, in abstract tone, has much in common with "Honey Bun", and yet on a more concrete level, their overlap in terms of rhymes, even words, is surprisingly small.

As I remarked earlier, at this early stage of the translation game, though I had known and savored "Ma Mignonne" for nearly three decades, I had never been sure just who it was written to, and so it was mildly plausible to me, although I tended to doubt it, that Marot was addressing a lover. In my own translations I avoided suggesting this flavor, but I was often amused by other people's versions in which the "lovers" scenario was taken for granted. David's "Lover Mine" is quite unambiguous, especially in its title, about the nature of the relationship between the male poet and his female friend, but at the same time it avoids any explicit sexual allusions.

One of the charming features of this poem, and a defining feature as well, is the quasi-regular rhythm with which the poet bombards his lover with terms of endearment: "lover mine" (line 1), "turtledove" (4), "buttercup" (8), "little pet" (13), "honey bun" (16), "honeybunch" (20), "nightingale" (24), and finally, winding things up again symmetrically, "lover mine" (28).

When one reads contemporary American phrases like "Hit the town!", one is almost expecting the next line to suggest going off to see a movie ("Catch a flick"?) or perhaps the jaunty couple, instead of hitting the town, might merely settle in for a television show ("Watch the tube"?). And in this context, lines 17–18 ("In the mood / For some food?") have me practically salivating for popcorn. I don't know if it hits other readers this way, but that's how it strikes me. I wonder if Marot would have liked popcorn.

Lover Mine

David Moser

Lover mine,
Here's a sign
Of my love,
Turtledove.
You're not well,   5
I can tell.
All cooped up,
Buttercup?
How about
Going out?   10
Hit the town!
Lose that frown,
Little pet!
Clem's all set
For some fun,   15
Honey bun.
In the mood
For some food?
Then let's munch,
Honeybunch.   20
If you stick
At home sick,
You'll get pale,
Nightingale.
Hope tonight   25
You're all right,
Feeling fine,
Lover mine.

Whether they suggest romance or not, all these Moserian products give off an earthy, hedonistic aroma, in stark contrast to Bob's and Melanie's rather high-flown lyricism. "Sugar Lump" carries this trend just a tiny bit further, with its references to the girl's figure and skin (lines 22–27). And of course, the phrase "Your lips lust / For a crust / Smeared with jam" (lines 15–17) fairly reeks of hedonism, while just barely sidestepping direct allusions to sexual pleasure. Still, it is a most suggestive phrase.

There is a downhome, almost rural, old-America feel to this poem (and the others as well), with its antique-sounding phrases like "sugar lump" and "Lord above" (line 21), and perhaps even more, its rhyming of "skin" and "again" (lines 25–26), which to my ear sounds very country-western ("again" being pronounced "agin"). I suppose that it is not altogether surprising, given that the venerable *Xiàngshengmeister* Mo Dawei grew up in small towns scattered across the flat prairies of Kansas and Oklahoma, constantly exposed to strong regional twangs all about him, that this, the flavor of his deepest roots, should occasionally rise to the surface in his poetry.

While I was scanning "Sugar Lump" looking for characteristics to comment on, I chanced to observe that the exclamation points ending lines 10–11 were echoed on lines 18–19. I then noticed they were equidistant from the poem's midpoint. Next I saw that lines 12–14 and lines 15–17, also symmetrically straddling the midpoint, formed a kind of natural pair as well, both of them concerning zest for food. The more I looked, the more symmetry I found in "Sugar Lump" — for example, "blues" on line 3 and "pink" on line 26 — and so I decided to see how it would look when written out in a line-by-line reversed manner. Thus was born "Sugar Lump Flip Flop". To try to preserve coherence, I had to change the punctuation slightly, but I think that's legitimate, given the good cause. If one stretches reader's license just a little bit here and there, it all makes quite clear sense!

I asked David if he'd intended the symmetry pervading "Sugar Lump", but he had no idea what I meant. When he saw it, he was astounded by his poem's temporal reversibility! Well, what do you say, gentle reader — do I deserve my co-authorship, then? My shameless claim of co-authorship here is very much like my facetious claim to being the "composer" of the sublime time reversal of the eighteenth variation from Rachmaninoff's "Rhapsody on a Theme by Paganini". How much credit *should* one get for merely seeing things that are lying around in stuff that *other* creators sweated over? Is plagiarism potentially creative?

I am a great believer in the creativity of the selective, perceptive act. I once read an article in the *International Herald Tribune* about a man named Jean-Claude Andrault who had an exhibit, in a small Paris museum, of various pieces of wood he had found over a many-decade span, which resembled all sorts of objects: "landscapes, writhing polyps, an erupting volcano, abstract visions and so on", to quote Michael Gibson, the author of the article. In fact, let me continue quoting Gibson's opinions:

> He [Andrault] wanted to know if I thought these objects were art. I said I did not — because they do not voice any human intention. These objects are a case of nature imitating art.... But a work of art in its proper dimension is more than order, pattern, suggestion. It conveys an intention and thus reveals itself to be a product and an expression of culture taken as the web of all human purposefulness.

Gibson clearly *likes* Andrault's stuff — he just doesn't consider it *art.* I find this absurd. In a sense I agree that art has to "voice a human intention", but the act of selection by Andrault *is* a deep human intention, just as deep as a photographer's selection of a scene or an event to capture. In fact, Gibson overlooks one further level of human intention: the very idea of collecting pieces of wood and exhibiting them is an excellent example of original human intention. Indeed, it's the invention of a whole new art form!

Sugar Lump	Sugar Lump Flip Flop
David Moser	*David Moser/D. Hofstadter*

Sugar lump,	*Sugar lump.*
In a slump?	*Smooth and plump,*
Sick-bed blues?	*Pink again,*
That's bad news.	*Make her skin.*
Such a bore,	*Soft and warm,* 5
And what's more,	*Back her form*
All shut in,	*Give my love,*
You'll get thin,	*Lord above.*
There's no doubt.	*This I pray:*
Let's go out!	*No delay!* 10
I say so!	*Right I am!*
This I know:	*Smeared with jam,*
You've no slight	*For a crust*
Appetite.	*Your lips lust.*
Your lips lust	*Appetite* 15
For a crust	*You've no slight:*
Smeared with jam.	*This I know.*
Right I am!	*I say so!*
No delay!	*Let's go out!*
This I pray:	*There's no doubt* 20
Lord above,	*You'll get thin*
Give my love	*All shut in,*
Back her form,	*And what's more,*
Soft and warm.	*Such a bore.*
Make her skin	*That's bad news.* 25
Pink again,	*Sick-bed blues?*
Smooth and plump.	*In a slump?*
Sugar lump.	*Sugar lump.*

And now for a slightly more subdued effort. Or at least it starts off that way. In lines 1–8, the very short rat-a-tat commands and exclamations are gone, replaced by just a single sentence, but what a sentence — a behemoth of a sentence, containing no fewer than 22 words! Moser has gone Proustian! (Admittedly, all but the first and last of those words are monosyllabic, and just one semantic chunk is over three words long...)

Soon, deviating from the subdued start, the frisky tone of "Honey Bun" has returned, as in lines 12–15 we hit another Moserian string of four successive exclamatory one-liners. And then, after a hiatus of but two lines, we run into three more.

To me, despite their very American, very contemporary flavor, there is something truly Clementine about all these efforts by David. Perhaps I should not have said "despite" but "because of", in the sense that Moser's smooth, colloquial, in-tune-with-its-times fluency seems much in the spirit of Marot's original. To put it another way, in these poems, David is expressing himself in his native language, in contrast to Bob French and Melanie Mitchell, who, in their first translations, were putting on airs of antiquity, faking it very well but still faking it. Maybe I'm exaggerating a little here, in the sense that David doesn't actually go around talking in rat-a-tat three-syllable bursts any more than Melanie exclaims "Forsooth!" on a daily basis. But the medium that David imposed on himself is certainly far closer to his natural, everyday medium of expression than those that Bob and Melanie (and I, in my Shakespearean effort) selected. Or, to look at things from the receiving rather than the generating end, David's language here is probably closer to the natural linguistic medium of his readers, and hence is absorbed by them with greater ease.

There's always a trade-off between bringing the original poem fully into one's own place, time, and style, and leaving various trace elements in it, residues of its provenance (which in fact David does, on line 10, reminding us of the primary poet's Frenchness). Doing the latter retains a sometimes-desirable quality of distance and alienness, while doing the former makes the experienced world more immediate and familiar. Which is preferable? And who can say?

Wouldn't it be wonderful if we could just get Clément Marot back here with us for a little while — just a day or two — to give us some feedback on all these diverse modes of rendering his poemlet? We'd have to give him a crash course in modern American English, of course. Or perhaps not. After all, given that we're spinning fantasies, why not just throw into our fantasy the bonus that our French friend Clément *already* is fluent in modern American English, so that we don't have to spend our precious time teaching it to him? The problem with this idea of tampering with Clément is actually the same as our prior dilemma about translation: the more we imagine converting Clément into someone like us, the less faithful we are being to the actual person that he was. In the end, if we're not careful, we might wind up transmogrifying Marot into David Moser himself, having obliterated from his person every last trace of Gallicism and antiquity. And that would hardly give us the fresh kind of perspective and insight that in our fantasy we are seeking.

Dearest Dear

David Moser

Dearest dear,
Sad to hear
You lie ill,
Weak and still,
Wan and pale,   *5*
As in jail,
In your bed,
Thin, ill-fed.
For Clément,
Ton amant,   *10*
Grant this boon:
Get well soon!
Flee your room!
Leave that tomb!
Fly in haste!   *15*
Food's sweet taste
Lies ahead.
Off your bed!
Let us sup!
Come, get up!   *20*
If you stay
Sick all day,
Your allure
Won't endure.
With God's aid,   *25*
Health won't fade.
Never fear,
Dearest dear!

• Chapter 5 •

Sparking and Sparkling, Thanks to Constraints

•

Mandarin cabin, Mandarin cabin... Try letting that cute little mantra roll around on your tongue for a while, how about? John Searle's famous "Mandarin cabin" thought experiment. Pretty catchy, eh?

Beware the Translation Police, Beware!

If this book had been written in, say, Azerbaijani or Mohican or !Xhosa, and thus you had read, in the preceding chapter, all about Searle's thought experiment in one of those non-Anglo-Saxon, non-Indo-European media, you would have understood perfectly clearly from the very start that you were not being treated to the American professor's precise *words*, but rather, to his precise *ideas*. That, I daresay, is most people's tacit notion of translation. Words can be given the old heave-ho as long as ideas are preserved, the former being but an incidental vehicle for delivering the latter. Who cares what make of truck it is that carries the milk to their daily doorstep, as long as the milk is *fresh*?

Authors are not generally known to complain that their timeless verbal monuments have been desecrated when the linguistic medium conveying them is switched — in fact, though they may try to hide it, they are often secretly quite flattered. And why should they not be? "Tell me, Professor — how many languages has your great thought experiment been translated into?" "Oh, I don't keep track any more — maybe fourteen or fifteen..."

But there is a funny kind of double standard going on here. An article or book written originally in English is rendered in fifteen *different ways* if rendered in fifteen different languages. Depending on its popularity, it may even be translated into a single language by two or three different people, obviously using different words and different syntactic structures. Yet no one raises a red flag and hollers, "You can't tamper with art!" After all, tampering is the very name of the translation game — tampering, that is, in the name of preserving essence. Destroying the village to save it, as it were. But here's the double standard: Woe, true woe, to anyone who would dare to tamper with even a single comma in the original English!

There's no way that anyone can play around with an author's text in its original language and get away with it; the original text is universally understood to be sacrosanct. Try it — you'll soon see. In no time flat, the Translation Police, their sirens piercing the quiet of the night, will come and track you down, and off they will haul you to — oh, no! — the dread Mandarin cabin. Yes... And there, you will have to serve an unbearably long sentence — and not just any old sentence, but a sentence made up of totally meaningless squiggles and squoggles. The Chinese room torture!

Why is it that tampering with a text is fine and dandy, as long as the damage done is sufficiently radical, but when it is mild, doing so is seen as being just as dastardly as giving kiddies Halloween candy spiked with LSD? I suppose the answer has something to do with the fact that to get an article into a foreign language, there is simply no choice — damage *has* to be done to it — whereas no damage at all need be done in conveying the ideas in their original medium. Indeed, there is a general presumption, certainly overly generous in the case of some authors, that the original words were not just acceptable, but *optimal.* And thus a piece of text that was written originally in English, when quoted in a book that is in English, must be left exactly as it was. No new commas in, no old commas out. Period.

Quoting in a Dialect Different from the Source

And yet, as is true in so much of life, things are not black-and-white. After all, what is English? There are countless varieties of that ancient and venerable tongue. If high-schoolers in Muskogee put on a performance of *As You Like It,* must they also put on stuffy 400-year-old British accents, or are they permitted to transgress against the original, and use their twentieth-century Okie twangs? Or conversely, if all the men and women on the stage of the Globe Theatre back in The Bard's day were to have put on a pre-formance of *Oklahoma!,* would they have had to learn to talk with their noses all plugged up, as we up-to-date American clowns of course do, or could they have gotten away with the metaphorical murder of singing "Everything's Up to Date in Kansas City" in the style of H. R. H. Elizabeth I?

I think we all know the answer: adaptation is allowed. You pull the message into your own medium — and in doing so, it's okay to make modifications, even when your medium is a kissin' cousin of the original medium. In some sense, then, *a medium is an excuse for making a translation.*

This is why, when I quoted John Searle's lengthy paragraph in Chapter 4, I felt free — nay, compelled — to translate it into the medium in which I was expressing myself at that point. And that medium was…? Anglo-Saxon, of course. I launched into Anglo-Saxon when I started the section entitled "'Quoting' a Famous Attack on AI", and left it when that section ended. So really, I had no choice: I *had* to convert Searle's original paragraph into Anglo-Saxon, for fear of losing my readership otherwise. When reading merrily along in language A, who but a pedant wants to be suddenly forced to switch gears and plow through a long quote in language B?

Chinese Room: Accept No Substitutes

Having seen texts ruined by poor translation, I knew well that I had to treat Searle's authorial intentions with the utmost respect, and did my very best to preserve the fresh milk of his ideas while abandoning his delivery truck at the side of the road. Lest you doubt the degree of my dedication or the quality of my performance, I now give you the chance to show me where I semantically betrayed the good professor. To make your load light, here is Searle's original paragraph, untampered with, reproducing every last jot and tittle as it was in the original, so help me God:

> One way to test any theory of the mind is to ask oneself what it would be like if my mind actually worked on the principles that the theory says all minds work on. Let us apply this test to the Schank program with the following *Gedankenexperiment*. Suppose that I'm locked in a room and given a large batch of Chinese writing. Suppose furthermore (as is indeed the case) that I know no Chinese, either written or spoken, and that I'm not even confident that I could recognize Chinese writing as Chinese writing distinct from, say, Japanese writing or meaningless squiggles. To me, Chinese writing is just so many meaningless squiggles. Now suppose further that after this first batch of Chinese writing I am given a second batch of Chinese script together with a set of rules for correlating the second batch with the first batch. The rules are in English, and I understand these rules as well as any other native speaker of English. They enable me to correlate one set of formal symbols with another set of formal symbols, and all that "formal" means here is that I can identify the symbols entirely by their shapes. Now suppose also that I am given a third batch of Chinese symbols together with some instructions, again in English, that enable me to correlate elements of this third batch with the first two batches, and these rules instruct me how to give back certain Chinese symbols with certain sorts of shapes in response to certain sorts of shapes given me in the third batch. Unknown to me, the people who are giving me all of these symbols call the first batch a "script," they call the second batch a "story," and they call the third batch "questions." Furthermore, they call the symbols I give them

back in response to the third batch "answers to the questions," and the set of rules in English that they gave me, they call the "program." Now just to complicate the story a little, imagine that these people also give me stories in English, which I understand, and they then ask me questions in English about these stories, and I give them back answers in English. Suppose also that after a while I get so good at following the instructions for manipulating the Chinese symbols and the programmers get so good at writing the programs that from the external point of view — that is, from the point of view of somebody outside the room in which I am locked — my answers to the questions are absolutely indistinguishable from those of native Chinese speakers. Nobody just looking at my answers can tell that I don't speak a word of Chinese. Let us also suppose that my answers to the English questions are, as they no doubt would be, indistinguishable from those of other native English speakers, for the simple reason that I am a native English speaker. From the external point of view — from the point of view of someone reading my "answers" — the answers to the Chinese questions and the English questions are equally good. But in the Chinese case, unlike the English case, I produce the answers by manipulating uninterpreted formal symbols. As far as the Chinese is concerned, I simply behave like a computer; I perform computational operations on formally specified elements. For the purposes of the Chinese, I am simply an instantiation of the computer program.

The Art of Lipography

A lipogram is a piece of text written under the constraint that one or more letters are not allowed to be used at all. Thus, the current paragraph could be described as a lipogram in which the eleventh letter of the alphabet is being carefully sidestepped. However, it was not written with that intent — it just turned out that way, after the fact. That particular letter was not actually *forbidden* — it just happened not to pop up, by sheer chance. However, *deliberately* forbidding the eleventh letter of the alphabet from appearing in a paragraph or even a whole opuscule would not be too great a challenge, that letter being of fairly low frequency in English. One can always get around words that contain the letter in question by resorting to such innocuous-appearing synonyms as "enjoy", "very sure of", "believe", "cogitate", "utter", "opuscule", "osculate", "labor", "along the lines of", and so on, and nobody will believe anything strange is going on — unless, of course, the topic of the opuscule on which one is laboring just happens to be the state that osculates the western border of... or rather, the state that osculates the *southern* border of... or rather, the state that osculates the *northern* border of Texas — or something along those lines, if you are very sure, so to utter, of what I mean.

Suppression of a high-frequency letter is another matter altogether. It has long been a source of amusement to a certain playful class of authors to try to express themselves without allowing themselves the luxury of using the highest-frequency letter of their language, which, in English, French, and German, happens to be the fifth letter of the alphabet — namely, "e".

It is that constraint — no "e"'s — that defines the "dialect" of English that I call Anglo-Saxon. And although it is a fairly simple-minded pun, I cannot resist remarking that expressing oneself with no "e"'s is definitely expressing oneself with no ease. But then why would anyone ever want to write anything in Anglo-Saxon? Simply because, like "e"-full Everest (a.k.a. "that most lofty Himalayan Olympus"), it is there (*i.e.*, "is staring at you").

This type of literary game has a long history. For many years, I was vaguely aware of the existence of a novel called *Gadsby*, written in the late 1930's by an obscure Californian penpusher named Ernest Vincent Wright, in which there was nary an "e". If writing an "e"-less paragraph is running a literary sack race, then writing an "e"-less novel is climbing a literary Everest — and thus I was full of awe for Wright's accomplishment. Then I found out that the French author Georges Perec had, a few decades after Wright, penned his own lipogrammatic novel in French called *La disparition,* also lacking "e"'s. To me, French minus "e"'s — call it "Gallic" — seemed even more formidable than Anglo-Saxon. I thus suppose Perec's feat maps onto scaling Everest without carrying oxygen — literary oxygen — along.

The idea that people could write entire novels while wearing such tight alphabetic straitjackets fascinated me and made me curious to try it out myself — not, that is, the challenge of writing an entire novel, but a pocket-sized challenge. So in the fall of 1983 I suggested to a couple of friends, David Moser among them, that we try *speaking* together without using any words containing "e". They were keen to try, and thus began a rather addictive habit in which two or three of us would sit around for hours, scraping together awkward-sounding sentences in an attempt to get across our thoughts on the most varied of topics. We did our best to monitor each other and not allow contraventions, however small.

The whole exercise felt suprisingly much like learning a foreign language. You had to learn not just new vocabulary but also all sorts of new grammatical patterns, and long before "e"-trouble came you had to be able to "smell" it coming and prepare an alternate route as it got closer and closer. Although none of us ever came close to Anglo-Saxon fluency, we all slowly improved, since we collectively developed an ever-increasing number of standard tricks to circumlocute the most hazardous "e"-traps.

After a while, our little coterie couldn't resist tightening just a bit the lipogrammatic straitjacket: we tried suppressing not just "e" but also "t", English's second most frequent letter. We soon discovered that whereas in an "e"-less mode we felt hampered but were still able to say pretty much anything we wanted, in the new doubly deprived mode, we were virtually immobilized — not a single pre-formed thought could be expressed without lengthy mental struggle, and usually not even then. Deleting just the *one* letter of highest frequency was debilitating but survivable; deleting the *two* letters of highest frequency brought us to our knees.

Egadsby

Both despite and thanks to its difficulty, lipogrammatic writing has enticed writers for centuries. We shall now take a look at some examples, starting with E. V. Wright's *Gadsby,* of which here is the inspiring opening:

If Youth, throughout all history, had had a champion to stand up for it; to show a doubting world that a child can think; and, possibly, do it practically; you wouldn't constantly run across folks today who claim that "a child don't know anything." A child's brain starts functioning at birth; and has, amongst its many infant convolutions, thousands of dormant atoms, into which God has put a mystic possibility for noticing an adult's act, and figuring out its purport.

Up to about its primary school days a child thinks, naturally, only of play. But many a form of play contains disciplinary factors. "You can't do this," or "that puts you out," shows a child that it must think, practically, or fail. Now, if, throughout childhood, a brain has no opposition, it is plain that it will attain a position of "status quo," as with our ordinary animals. Man knows not why a cow, dog or lion was not born with a brain on a par with ours; why such animals cannot add, subtract, or obtain from books and schooling, that paramount position which Man holds today.

But a human brain is not in that class. Constantly throbbing and pulsating, it rapidly forms opinions; attaining an ability of its own; a fact which is startlingly shown by an occasional child "prodigy" in music or school work. And as, with our dumb animals, a child's inability convincingly to impart its thoughts to us, should not class it as ignorant.

Upon this basis I am going to show you how a bunch of bright young folks did find a champion; a man with boys and girls of his own; a man of so dominating and happy individuality that Youth is drawn to him as is a fly to a sugar bowl. It is a story about a small town. It is not a gossipy yarn; nor is it a dry, monotonous account, full of such customary "fill-ins" as "romantic moonlight casting murky shadows down a long, winding country road." Nor will it say anything about tinklings lulling distant folds; robins carolling at twilight, nor any "warm glow of lamplight" from a cabin window. No. It is an account of up-and-doing activity; a vivid portrayal of Youth as it is today; and a practical discarding of that worn-out notion that "a child don't know anything."

Now, any author, from history's dawn, always had that most important aid to writing: — an ability to call upon any word in his dictionary in building up his story. That is, our strict laws as to word construction did not block his path. But in *my* story that mighty obstruction *will* constantly stand in my path; for many an important, common word I cannot adopt, owing to its orthography.

And the expiring breaths of this novel, dedicated "TO YOUTH!", are these:

A glorious full moon sails across a sky without a cloud. A crisp night air has folks turning up coat collars and kids hopping up and down for warmth. And that giant star, Sirius, winking slyly, knows that soon, now, that light up in His Honor's room window will go out. Fttt! It *is* out! So, as Sirius and Luna hold an all-night vigil, I'll say a soft "Good-night" to all our happy bunch, and to John Gadsby — Youth's Champion.

FINIS

A tacit goal of all writing bound by constraints, lipogrammatical or not, is for said constraints to approach *invisibility* (or unobtrusivity, or inconspicuity). That is, an author's words should flow so smoothly as to prompt no suspicion at all — and Wright truly shows us how to do this. I think that, without a tip-off that you should look out for curious phrasings, you might absorb his paragraphs without noticing any sort of gap or lacuna. Not that Wright's story is totally normal-sounding, but you would probably just chalk its oddity up to his idiosyncratic way with words. Why not?

The Disappearance of Anton Voyl

We turn our attention now to the tragically short-lived French writer Georges Perec (1936–1982), and to his brilliantly eccentric novel *La disparition,* which was published in 1969. *La disparition* tells the tale of the arduous search for a shadowy missing figure named Anton Voyl. Early on in the story, Voyl has a hallucinatory vision in which, as he is strolling beside a bookshelf that contains a long row of numbered volumes, he notices that number five in a series of what ought to be twenty-six volumes is missing, although there is no empty space between volumes four and six. The resemblance to the fact that "e" is the fifth element in a twenty-six-element series is, shall we say, not coincidental. Note also that the French word for "vowel" is *voyelle.*

Moreover, *La disparition* itself consists of twenty-six chapters — or rather, it would do so, were it not for the fact that it skips inconspicuously from the fourth to the sixth chapter. And one of the main figures in the desperate search for the missing Voyl is Amaury Conson (again, note that *consonne* is French for "consonant"). Another character who makes a very brief cameo appearance has the curious name of "Gadsby V. Wright". You begin to get the picture.

It is hard to do justice to the delicious looniness of Perec's fantasy, but here, to whet your appetite, is the book's opening paragraph in its original lipogrammatic language:

Trois cardinaux, un rabbin, un amiral franc-maçon, un trio d'insignifiants politicards soumis au bon plaisir d'un trust anglo-saxon, ont fait savoir à la population par radio, puis par placards, qu'on risquait la mort par inanition. On crut d'abord à un faux bruit. Il s'agissait, disait-on, d'intoxication. Mais l'opinion suivit. Chacun s'arma d'un fort gourdin. « Nous voulons du pain », criait la population, conspuant patrons, nantis, pouvoirs publics. Ça complotait, ça conspirait partout. Un flic n'osait plus sortir la nuit. A Mâcon, on attaqua un local administratif. A Rocamadour, on pilla un stock : on y trouva du thon, du lait, du chocolat par kilos, du maïs par quintaux, mais tout avait l'air pourri. A Nancy, on guillotina sur un rond-point vingt-six magistrats d'un coup, puis on brûla un journal du soir qu'on accusait d'avoir pris parti pour l'administration. Partout on prit d'assaut docks, hangars, ou magasins.

Translating Gallic into Anglo-Saxon...

Hard to believe, but *La disparition* has been virtuosically translated into both Anglo-Saxon and "e"-less German, the latter being a dialect of German that I shall call (the German for "German" being *Deutsch*) "Dutsch". To begin with, I give you the opening paragraph of Gilbert Adair's very cleverly-titled Anglo-Saxon translation, *A Void*:

Today, by radio, and also on giant hoardings, a rabbi, an admiral notorious for his links to Masonry, a trio of cardinals, a trio, too, of insignificant politicians (bought and paid for by a rich Anglo–Canadian banking corporation), inform us all of how our country now risks of dying by starvation. A rumour, that's my initial thought as I switch off my radio, a rumour or possibly a hoax. Propaganda, I murmur anxiously — as though, just by saying so, I might allay my doubts — typical politicians' propaganda. But public opinion gradually absorbs it as a fact. Individuals start strutting around with stout clubs. "Food, glorious food!" is a common cry (occasionally sung to Bart's music), with ordinary hard-working folk harassing officials, both local and national, and cursing capitalists and captains of industry. Cops shrink from going out on night shift. In Mâcon a mob storms a municipal building. In Rocamadour ruffians rob a hangar full of foodstuffs, pillaging tons of tuna fish, milk and cocoa, as also a vast quantity of corn — all of it, alas, totally unfit for human consumption. Without fuss or ado, and naturally without any sort of trial, an indignant crowd hangs 26 solicitors on a hastily built scaffold in front of Nancy's law courts (this Nancy is a town, not a woman) and ransacks a local journal, a disgusting right-wing rag that is siding up against it. Up and down this land of ours looting has brought docks, shops and farms to a virtual standstill.

Note the huge jump in length as the passage passes from Gallic into Anglo-Saxon (eleven lines bloat out into eighteen, as printed above). This strongly violates expectations: A well-known translators' rule of thumb says a French text is usually fifteen percent longer than its English equivalent. So what is behind this deviant explosion? There is no single explanation.

One contributing factor is indubitably the overall tone adopted by Adair — a tone of mild redundancy and repetition, which is quite different from the rather concise tone of the original. For example, look at Perec's extremely terse sentence *Ça complotait, ça conspirait partout,* which on a word-by-word basis means "That plotted, that conspired everywhere." But a French reader hears *ça* in a highly context-dependent manner: it can refer to almost anything in the general domain of discourse, animate or inanimate, singular or plural. (In Patachou's haunting song *Rue Lepic,* for instance, one line goes *Ça grouille et ça vit dans cette vieille rue de Paris —* literally, "That swarms and that lives in this old Paris street", but more naturally, "It's teeming with life in this old Paris street.") In this case, the basic feeling is, "There was plotting and conspiring going on everywhere." This is a very colloquial, almost slangish usage, and there was no way Adair could parallel it perfectly in English, let alone in Anglo-Saxon.

In fact, to get across the subject of the two verbs *complotait* and *conspirait*, Adair used the long phrase "ordinary hard-working folk" — and of course, the two verbs are now completely gone, lost somewhere in the lovely semantic and phonetic swirl of "harassing officials, both local and national, and cursing capitalists and captains of industry". One looks in vain for "capitalists and captains of industry" in the original Gallic text. So much for "respect for the original"!

And yet, isn't it *deeply* respectful, this transmogrification by Adair? Doesn't Adair's expansive Anglo-Saxon prose exude a weird kind of self-consistent beauty quite similar in abstract flavor to the nutty elegance of Perec's far terser French — or rather, Gallic — prose?

One might also wonder, why in the world is the Anglo-Saxon story being told in the *first* person, whereas the Gallic comes across in the most impersonal of tones? And why is the Anglo-Saxon version in the *present* tense, whereas the Gallic version is in the *past* tense?

The answer to the latter is obvious: the ubiquitous "-ed" past-tense ending of English would have crippled Adair from the very start, hence he simply had to bail out instantly. The answer to the former question might well seem related: in English, one can get away with saying "I" without using the letter "e", whereas to one writing in Gallic, the pronoun *je* is deadly. Perhaps Adair *needed* to switch narrative center in order to avoid certain kinds of constructions impossible in Anglo-Saxon? But a deeper look at Perec's novel gives the lie to this reasonable conjecture. Indeed, all throughout the Gallic text, the tale is indeed told in the first person.

Anyone who knows that *je* and *me* are French for "I" and "me" will instantly ask, how in the world can this be done? The answer is manifold, involving a number of varied devices, such as: Use verbs that begin with vowels, thus allowing the "e" of *je* to be replaced by an apostrophe: *j'ai,* or *j'allai.* A related apostrophizing trick allows the dative and accusative personal pronoun *me* to be used: *il m'a dit,* for example, for "he told me". But then how, you might ask, does Adair render *il m'a dit* in Anglo-Saxon? He converts it into passive voice: "I was told" — a neat trick, resorted to over and over again.

This discussion just begins to scratch the surface of the bewildering variety of challenges with which Gilbert Adair had to grapple throughout his virtuosic Anglo-Saxon translation — his total reconstruction — of Georges Perec's obsessive work.

…and into Dutsch

We shall shortly return to the Anglo-Saxon version, but first let us take a look at the opening paragraph of Eugen Helmlé's Dutsch translation, *Anton Voyls Fortgang*:

Kardinal, Rabbi und Admiral, also Führungstrio null und nichtig und darum völlig abhängig vom Ami-Trust, tat durch Rundfunk und Plakatanschlag kund, daß Nahrungsnot und damit Tod aufs Volk zukommt. Zunächst tat man das als Falschinformation ab. Das ist Propagandagift, sagt man. Doch bald schon ward spürbar, was man ursprünglich nicht glaubt. Das Volk griff zu Stock und zu Dolch. «Gib uns das tägliche Brot», hallts durchs Land, und «pfui auf das Patronat, auf Ordnung, Macht und Staat». Konspiration ward ganz normal, Komplott üblich. Nachts sah man kaum noch Uniform. Angst hält Soldat und Polizist im Haus. In Mâcon griff man das Administrationslokal an. In Rocamadour gabs Mundraub sogar am Tag: man fand dort Thunfisch, Milch und Schokobonbons im Kilopack, Waggons voll Mais, obwohl schon richtig faulig. Im Rathaus von Nancy sahs schlimm aus, fünfundzwanzig Mann schob man dort aufs Schafott, vom Amtsrat bis zum Stadtvorstand, und, ruckzuck, ab war ihr Kopf. Dann kam das Mittagsblatt dran, da allzu autoritätshörig. Antipropaganda warf man ihm vor und Opposition zum Volk, darum brannt das Ding bald licht and loh. Ringsum griff man Docks an, Bootshaus und Munitionsmagazin.

Although far from being as concise as Perec's original, Helmlé's Dutsch version comes closer than does Adair's Anglo-Saxon. For instance, *Ça complotait, ça conspirait partout* becomes *Konspiration ward ganz normal, Komplott üblich* ("Conspiracy got totally normal, plotting standard."). Here, the verbs become nouns whose order, for some subtle reason known only to Helmlé, has been reversed. Also, the single adverb *partout* ("everywhere") has turned into a pair of adjectives (*normal, üblich*), one of them preceded by the modifier *ganz*. These are tricky, highly nonmechanical decisions!

Another amusing example of contortion under pressure is how Perec's *journal du soir* ("evening paper") turns into a *Mittagsblatt* ("noon paper") because an evening paper — *ein Abendblatt* — would be an obvious no-no. But how can Helmlé be sure that Perec didn't *intend* it to be and even *need* it to be an evening paper?

Even more interesting is the fact that where twenty-*six* magistrates were put to death in the original Nancy rioting, one of them was spared, in the Dutsch version. Might Helmlé have had a soft spot for one of Perec's butchered individuals? Unlikely, since he probably never met any of them. More likely is the fact that the German way of saying "twenty-six" — *sechsundzwanzig* — contains a certain letter that does not appear in *fünfundzwanzig*, and this fact, coupled with the by-now-familiar theme in Perec's work of diminishing the number twenty-six by exactly one, seemed to provide an elegant way around this translational obstacle.

Double Jeopardy

The climactic scene of *La disparition* comes at the end of Chapter 25, where the shrinking group of Voyl hunters is tensely gathered after the recent offings of several of their number. Aloysius Swann pulls out from his briefcase a significant communication that he wishes to share with the group, and he bids Ottavio Ottaviani read it aloud. The latter, most nervous because he realizes that something of great moment is about to take place, adjusts his glasses, clears his voice, and intones this note:

> Ondoyons un poupon, dit Orgon, fils d'Ubu. Bouffons choux, bijoux, poux, puis du mou, du confit ; buvons, non point un grog : un punch. Il but du vin itout, du rhum, du whisky, du coco, puis il dormit sur un roc. L'infini bruit du ru couvrit son son. Nous irons sous un pont où nous pourrons promouvoir un dodo, dodo du poupon du fils d'Orgon fils d'Ubu.
>
> Un condor prit son vol. Un lion riquiqui sortit pour voir un dingo. Un loup fuit. Un opossum court. Où vont-ils ? L'ours rompit son cou. Il souffrit. Un lis croît sur un mur : voici qu'il couvrit orillons ou goulots du cruchon ou du pot pur stuc.
>
> Ubu pond son poids d'or.

Aloysius Swann has heard the ominous rumble in this message that his cronies have not, and in a superior tone, he asks them, and I in turn ask you, borrowing Adair's way of putting it: "Isn't it obvious what's so fascinating about it?" But they don't see it. You of course do. Crtinly!

Here is "the same passage" in Adair's charming Anglo-Saxon restyling:

> "I'm going to rock this child in his cot," sighs Orgon, son of Ubu. "I'm going to wolf down mutton, broccoli, dumplings, rich plum pudding. I'm going to drink, not grog, but punch." Orgon drinks hock, too, rum, Scotch, plus two hot brimming mugs of Bovril to finish up with, which soon prompts him to nod off. Running brooks drown out his snoring. I stroll to rocks on which I too will nod off, with Orgon's dozing son, with Orgon, son of Ubu.
>
> Condors swoop down on us. Poor scrofulous lions slink out, scrutinising dingos with scornful looks. Chipmunks run wild. Opossums run, too, without stopping. North or south? I wouldn't know. Plunging off clifftops, bison splits limb in two. It hurts. Ivy grows on brick, rising up from stucco pots to shroud windows or roofs.
>
> From Ubu's bottom drops his own bulk in gold.

Unable to contain himself any longer, Aloysius Swann finally says in a condescending tone to one of them, "Look at it, Savorgnan — it hasn't got a solitary 'a'!" And a moment later, he adds: "I can find just a solitary 'y' in it — in 'ivy'!" Stunned, the little group around them chants, "Astonishing! Amazing! Astounding!" Or rather, *Confondant ! Saisissant ! Inouï !*

But this is not all. Ottaviani, still reeling from the shock of discovery, continues to check it over, and all of a sudden he lowers his voice, begins shaking uncontrollably, and murmurs pathetically, as he keels over in what can only be called his Swann song, "Nor has it got a solitary

And there, quotes hanging tremulously in the air, never to be closed, the chapter ends.

Ottaviani has finally, twenty-five (or twenty-four) chapters into the game, caught the first whiff of an odor that none of his companions has yet sniffed, and for his budding realization of the impoverished "e"-lessness of their recent lives, he succumbs, popping like a balloon punctured by a pin.

There is a wonderful mathematical analogue to this situation, pointed out by Italian wordplay expert Stefano Bartezzaghi in his notes to a text that we shall soon ourselves consider. Here are Bartezzaghi's beautifully apt observations, in my English rendition:

> The inhabitants of the two-dimensional world of Edwin Abbott's novel *Flatland* do not suspect the possibility of a third spatial dimension, but are capable of envisioning a world with just *one* dimension: one fewer than their own world possesses. As for us, we live in a world with three spatial dimensions, and we can likewise imagine a world with one dimension fewer than ours (it suffices to read Abbott's novel). We balk, however, when it comes to imagining the *addition* of a dimension. The mind boggles.
>
> We also live in a world of five vowels (written, anyway: we italophones have seven distinct vowel *sounds*). And in our world, a novel has been written with just four vowels — and inside this novel there is a passage with just three vowels. Does creativity consist merely in a process of repeated subtraction? Perhaps it is not totally crazy that three years later, Perec actually wrote a short story using just one single vowel. It was the limit toward which he was heading in *La disparition*, the ultimate asymptote implied between the lines of the episode of its penultimate chapter. The little story is entitled *Les revenentes,* and if we can bring ourselves to forgive it for a few questionable orthographic maneuvers, it contains no vowels other than "e", which is thus fully rehabilitated after its banishment in Perec's novel "A Vanishing", some three years earlier.

I see here a striking parallel, as well, to my own sensation, described in Chapter 3, of being released, over the course of one day in Warsaw, from a series of nested prison cells, each time into a cell allowing me greater freedom, until at sunset I was released into my native language, with the strangely inexorable momentum of the day's events leading me to ask myself, "And what if there were some 'grand mother tongue' that I could speak as much better than I speak English as I speak English better than I speak French (so to speak), or that I could speak as much better than I speak English as I speak German better than I speak Polish (so to speak)?"

Authors versus Constraints: Who's the Boss?

Recall how my friends and I, back in the days of our 1983 Anglo-Saxon dialogues, found ourselves stymied by our doubly-tight straitjacket of simultaneous "e"-less- and "t"-lessness. Surely that straitjacket was not too different from the "industrial strength" straitjacket that Georges Perec voluntarily donned to create that passage about... Yes, well, about *what*? If you re-read it a few times, you may be able to pull out some sort of theme or motif, but basically it is pretty incoherent. It's about folks imbibing various liquids, including or not including Bovril, depending on the linguistic environment that they are inhabiting (only in a certain sense, however, since in another sense their linguistic environment is always France), then getting drowsy and going to sleep on big rocks, surrounded by wild animals. *Un opossum court. Où vont-ils ?* "Opossums run, too, without stopping. North or south? I wouldn't know." (What a translation of *Où vont-ils ?* !)

Who is the boss here — Perec or his self-imposed constraints? The lovely thing is that — since Perec shackled himself in a self-chosen manner, and of his own free will — even if he is a slave to them, he is being a slave to entities of his own making, and thus in some sense, Perec himself is always the boss, always in the driver's seat, no matter what.

On the other hand, even if in this rarefied *philosophical* sense Perec might arguably always have been the master of his own destiny, there is a down-to-earth *practical* sense in which surely he was wafted about by whatever "e"-and-"a"-free words in French came his way; then, having been handed some particular semantic ball or other, he would grab it and run like the wind with it, making the most of each serendipitous gift from his native tongue. In that sense, rather than shoving his beloved French language around, Perec had to accept the fact of being shoved around by it. And although this boss/slave reversal held particularly clearly in the doubly-straitjacketed condition, it also held somewhat in just the simple "e"-less condition. That is, after all, what "constraint" means.

A Wolf Becomes Some Chipmunks

Now where does all this leave translators? In a very sticky wicket, to say the least. Obviously, a concept whose most natural, effortless expression in French contains no "e" is hardly guaranteed to have an analogous "e"-less expression in English or German! And so, how could a translator possibly either hope or be expected to follow Perec's medium-directed maneuvers in a second language?

Just to take a tiny example, consider this three-word sentence inside the passage read aloud by Ottaviani in the moments immediately preceding his demise: *Un loup fuit.* Before we consider translating it, I might point out a delicious ambiguity here. All through the short paragraph in which this sentence occurs, Perec is wavering dizzyingly back and forth between the present tense and the *passé simple* (French's literary past tense). I say "dizzyingly", and yet that is accurate only if one takes the tense-jumping *literally*. If one simply accepts that the story's location in time is vague, neither present nor past, and that tenses are but a convention, then there is nothing nearly so schizophrenic going on, after all. The funny thing about

Sparking and Sparkling, Thanks to Constraints   ♦♦♦   **115**

the sentence *Un loup fuit,* however, is that it floats halfway between present and past, because it is *both.* The word *fuit,* by chance, is the correct third-person singular form of *fuir* in both the present and the literary past.

Now to the translation question. Were we to translate this literally into English, we would get either "A wolf flees" or "A wolf fled". Whichever way you go, you violate not only Anglo-Saxon, but also British (a good name for "a"-less Anglo-Saxon). We can go from English into Anglo-Saxon by saying "A wolf runs" (or "A wolf ran"), but we still have that "a". Suppose we try to get it into British by pluralizing it: "Wolves run/ran"? No go. How about "Some wolf runs/ran"? Still no. "Jackal"? Hardly. "Hyena"? Still worse. "Dingo"? Already used (in the preceding sentence). We're beginning to thrash in our double straitjacket.

At this point, the awkwardness of staying with the "wolf" image is rapidly becoming clear, and indeed, Gilbert Adair cuts the Gordian knot in a stunningly brutal manner: "Chipmunks run wild." Can you believe the audacity it took to do this? *One wolf* has become *several chipmunks*?! In one sense, Adair himself is being shoved brutally about, and in quite another sense he is showing us that he is in total command. He can do "whatever he wants" — at least within limits — and he does it.

What does Helmlé do in Dutsch — or rather, in Double Dutsch — at this juncture? Indeed, what *is* Double Dutsch? Is it just "a"-less Dutsch, as one might expect? No, it turns out not to be — at least not when Helmlé's at the helm. Instead of depriving himself of the vowel "a", Helmlé decides that the proper move is to deprive himself of the consonant "r". Is this subdialect of Dutsch sufficiently constrained as to warrant being mapped onto "a"-less Gallic? I wouldn't know, but anyway, that's his choice. If he had deprived himself of "x", I would've felt he was taking the easy way out, but with "r", it seems to me *kif-kif* — kind of maybe-ish, a bit iffy.

In any case, given this choice, Helmlé converts *Un loup fuit* into *'n Wolf floh,* which, as you can see, preserves not only the animal's lupitude but also its singularity. The sacrifice, of course, is the shameless apostrophe, which represents a collapse of the indefinite article *Ein* into just one letter. Once again, what can you do? It's not as if Perec's Gallic always sounds perfect.

The Slippery Identity of Anton Voyl/Vowl

In *A Void,* the missing M. Voyl is renamed "Anton Vowl". It is clear why: *Voyl* is an "e"-cut variant of the word *voyelle,* and Adair wanted a similar variant of "vowel". All fine except for one thing: Voyl is a French national, and "Voyl", though a bit strained, would be at least marginally credible as a French surname, whereas "Vowl" — essentially unpronounceable in French — goes well beyond the pale. Adair's move, though nice for an English reader, seriously compromises the Frenchness of his antagonist.

But these are hard choices: trade-offs, if you will, that one has to make at virtually every step as one translates a work of literature. After all, Mr. Vowl *speaks English* (Anglo-Saxon, that is) throughout Adair's version, and certainly that is not what he would really do if he is indeed a French citizen (and he is)! And of course, Eugen Helmlé's version of Mr. Voyl (whose name is preserved, since rebaptizing him with the already "e"-less German word *Vokal* would miss the missing-"e" twist of *Voyl*) speaks German (Dutsch, that is), not French. But what other choice did Helmlé have?

In the act of translation, there are always two "frames" — the culture of origin, and that of destination — that inevitably get blended in countless ways as the ideas are transplanted from one soil to the other. Some ideas transplant easily, others put up a fight, occasionally ferocious, and some simply will not go at all, no matter how hard they are shoved. Out of a myriad stunningly diverse and utterly unrelated cross-cultural matches, quasi-matches, semi-matches, pseudo-matches, and mismatches, few if any of which were ever pre-dreamt-of by the original author, emerges the unpredictable shape and feel of a translation into another land, tongue, culture, and time.

The Size of the Waves Battering the Ship of Translation

In all likelihood (though we shall probably never know, given that Perec is gone), not merely a local detail here or there but the entire grand course of Perec's novel was dictated in large part by idiosyncrasies of the French language — words and phrases that, in French, just happened to have no "e" in them. These gave rise to ideas and images in Perec's mind, and the plot of the book took its twists and turns accordingly, one after another after another, under the influence of these quite accidental facts. As I said earlier, Georges Perec was by no means fully in charge of his ship, because the waves battering it were too powerful — but since (I am assuming) he didn't actually have any clear, fixed destination in mind at the outset, other than going *somewhere* interesting, being severely battered hardly even mattered: letting the winds of "e"-lessness blow him where they would, he simply went along for the ride.

In contrast, Eugen Helmlé and Gilbert Adair had no such luxury. To be sure, they could change little tiny events here and there without feeling guilty of being deeply unfaithful to their author — the first paragraph's bloody guillotining of twenty-six people could quite innocuously be converted into a bloodless hanging of just twenty-five, say — but what if some major concept in Perec's tale, some absolutely overriding, ubiquitous theme, worked beautifully and effortlessly in the "e"-less medium of Gallic but horribly, if at all, in Anglo-Saxon or Dutsch, its English and German counterparts?

Sparking and Sparkling, Thanks to Constraints   ◆◆◆ **117**

I confess to having only skipped about in these three versions of *La disparition,* rather than having read them in full, and so I am not sure if there is any such overarching notion (such as the very concept of "missing" or "absence", perhaps) that worked well in the original tongue but refused to go "e"-less into a target language. If that *were* the case, though, then the translator would be forced to somehow concoct a substitute notion — a much more global, more pervasive analogue to Adair's having replaced beheadings with hangings, or Helmlé's having replaced twenty-six victims by twenty-five — and would be forced to tell a related, an *analogous,* tale, but definitely not the tale that Perec himself told. What a weird situation to find oneself in!

On Preserving Meaning but Not Preserving Form

It is worth pointing out that a certain crucial, global, all-affecting decision about how to translate *La disparition* insinuated itself into our discussion right from the very beginning without even being brought up for a split second as a matter to be weighed in the balance, to be considered and possibly accepted, possibly rejected. I am speaking of the assumption that *some letter or other must necessarily be left out.* This idea just came in the back door without anyone's asking if it *should* do so.

The most naïve translator imaginable — or, for that matter, the most sophisticated simultaneous interpreter imaginable, but who had no chance to preview the text and notice the constraint — would simply try to "extract meaning" from the text, sentence by sentence, and ploddingly render "the same meaning" into the target language. Thus, under this vision, the first paragraph of *La disparition* might run more or less as follows:

> Three cardinals, one rabbi, an admiral who was also a Mason, and a trio of insignificant politicos under the thumb of some shady Anglo-Saxon wheeler-dealers announced to the French people first by radio, next by posters, that starvation was imminent. Ordinary folks at first thought this had to be a crazy rumor. They said, it's a bunch of drunkards spouting lies. But the rumor persisted. As the belief spread, the gentry began taking up arms, carrying clubs around with them. "Give us bread!" was heard everywhere, with crowds jeering and shouting down store owners, well-off burghers, and public authorities of all sorts. Before long there was plotting and conspiring on every streetcorner. The police started to fear going out on their beats at night. In the town of Mâcon, a government office was attacked. In Rocamadour, a warehouse was looted, and large quantities of tuna, milk, and corn were taken, as well as many pounds of chocolate, but to no avail: it all turned out to be rotten. In the town of Nancy, twenty-six magistrates were summarily beheaded at a major crossroads, and an angry crowd then burned to the ground the offices of an evening newspaper that had allegedly taken the side of the government. All over the country, docks, sheds, and stores were being seized by force.

This is certainly a dreadful, nightmarish vision. That is to say, this vision of *how to translate the novel* is certainly dreadful and nightmarish! It really seems to miss the point completely. And yet — it is on just such a vision of translation that the entire intellectual edifice of the worldwide machine-translation effort has been painstakingly built.

Tacit Tenets of Machine Translation

Let me spell this out more explicitly. MT takes for granted the idea that what matters in communication is *content,* not *form,* and that the very definition of translation is simply the extraction of "pure content" from one medium followed by the re-implantation of the "very same" content into another medium, thus allowing content to migrate absolutely intact from one vessel (*i.e.,* language) to another, very much in the same way as modern word processors allow a writer to pick up a sentence and convert it instantly from one size or typeface to another.

To make this image very clear and very concrete, let me suggest to you a word processor featuring a pull-down menu labeled "Language", which is found at the top of the screen right next to menus labeled "Format", "Font", "Size", and "Style", and which contains a long list of languages — let's say Anglo-Saxon, British, Choctaw, Dutsch, Fijian, Gallic, Hawaiian, Ibo, Jara, Kannada, Lithuanian, Mohican, Navajo, Orissa, Punjabi, Qïpchaq, Russian, Swahili, Thai, Urdu, Vogul, Wolof, !Xhosa, Yoruba, and Zulu — any of which you can point at with your mouse, and at the very instant you release the mouse button, the sentence or paragraph you've highlighted on your screen snaps obediently into the language you have chosen. There is no doubt or delay in the carrying-out of any such translation command — language-toggling is every bit as algorithmic, as deterministic, and as lightning-fast as is changing the selection's size from 10-point to 72-point, or flicking its font back and forth from Baskerville to Brush Script to Optima Bold to Zapf Chancery to Hobo to Benguiat.

This is certainly a dreadful, nightmarish vision. *This is certainly a dreadful, nightmarish vision.* **This is certainly a dreadful, nightmarish vision.** *This is certainly a dreadful, nightmarish vision.* **This is certainly a dreadful, nightmarish vision.** This is certainly a dreadful, nightmarish vision.

In the MT approach, there is no asking of the question, "What about when form and content are intertwined?" It is taken for granted that the two are totally independent, can be pulled apart very naturally, and that moreover, which aspects of a given text are *form* and which aspects are *content* is always the same. For example, size of type used for the text falls always on the *form* side of the divide, whereas size of animals mentioned in the text falls always on the *content* side. Likewise, *which language* a sentence is displayed in on the screen is considered every bit as surface-level and incidental a fact about that sentence as is *which color* and *which font* it is printed in. And the recipe for translation is to look on just one side of the division — the content side, of course — where the word processor must, in its canned little way, build some kind of neutral, medium-free structure that distills from the original text nothing but its "pure meaning", utterly devoid of any specific language's intrusive, contaminating idiosyncrasies governing such things as word choice or syntactical structures.

Notice that, if taken seriously, this would mean that *no human language whatsoever* could be taken as authoritative about how to break the world up into mental categories, because breaking a real-world situation up into linguistic units depends on properties of the expressive medium chosen. For instance, a term meaning what "uncle" means in English could *never* be used at this hypothetical language-neutral level. Why not? Because some human languages break the world up *more finely* than this (such as Swedish, which distinguishes between a father's brother and a mother's brother, or Chinese, which carries the split-up even further), while other languages break it up *more coarsely* than this. If one really took this quest to render all content in a medium-free manner in earnest, one would come to an instant grinding halt, because *every* scheme for breaking up the world into a set of pre-ordained categories amounts to choosing one particular expressive medium — one particular language, whether natural or artificial — as the "objective truth".

Despite this devastating flaw at the heart of the standard strategy of MT, let us nonetheless assume that a set of structures carrying "pure meaning" and nothing but that, no vestiges of form at all, has somehow or other been distilled from the input text. The next stage, then, is to "pour" that fluid, malleable, pure-content stuff into the mold of the desired output language — into the mold of *any* desired output language, in fact.

The naïve assumption that this can be done comes from a sadly impoverished view of what natural language and human communication are about. It all stems from the fact that, since its idealistic inception in the late 1940's, MT has been primarily pushed (*i.e.,* financially backed and hence directed) by industry and commerce, and as such MT is now mostly aimed at converting certain very limited kinds of texts from one language to another, such as weather reports or washing-machine repair manuals.

It might seem plausible that in such austere contexts as these technical and specialized ones, there *is* a clean and clear demarcation line between the medium (Anglo-Saxon, British, Choctaw,…, !Xhosa, Yoruba, Zulu) and the message (*e.g.,* "mostly cloudy with a few showers tomorrow afternoon, southwesterly winds gusting up to 15 miles an hour, and a 50 percent chance of light thunderstorms"), so that *exactly the same content* can be poured without any serious spillage into any one of the enormously many, enormously diverse recipient "language-vessels".

However, even for MT in austere microworlds, one can marshal impressive arguments against the plausibility of this claim. But I shall not try to do so here. I would simply point out that the field of MT takes for granted a philosophy that seems the antithesis of common sense — indeed, the apotheosis of utter silliness — in the translation of a work such as Perec's *La disparition,* where respect for form is clearly just as important as respect for content, and where failing to carry over the lipogrammatic quality from the input text to the output text would be a huge slap in the face to the author — in fact, far more disrespectful than would be the act of inventing from scratch a completely new, plotwise-unrelated novel in the target language, as long as this new novel involved no "e". Indeed, I can easily imagine Georges Perec himself humbly claiming that he viewed his own brilliant novel as no more than a latter-day French retelling of the great *Gadsby,* even though, as one might surmise from reading their openings, the two books' story lines have absolutely nothing in common.

Translation and Perfectionism

Having agreed that respect for form, perhaps even above respect for content, would seem to be of the essence to any translator of Perec's novel, let us now go back and look at sentence number six of the first paragraph of *Anton Voyls Fortgang,* reproduced below:

> «Gib uns das tägliche Brot», hallts durchs Land, und
> «pfui auf das Patronat, auf Ordnung, Macht und Staat».

Let's look, in particular, at its fourth word, *tägliche.* Indeed, let's zoom in on that word's final letter: "e". Whoops-ee! How in the world did *that* little rascal ever sneak into *this* big-league ballgame? That is a question to which I would love to know the answer. I presume, though I have not checked it out systematically, that this "e" is the sole "e" in Helmlé's whole book, and that it was an oversight, an error, a terrible blunder committed by the translator in the earliest stages of his work, one that subsequently was never caught by him or by any of his proofreaders or typesetters...

However, suppose — just to explore an idea, far-fetched though it might be — that for one reason or another, as he worked on the first page, Helmlé was having considerable trouble finding a way that pleased him of rendering the original French sentence *Nous voulons du pain* in Dutsch, and so after a while he simply said to himself, "I've tried damned hard for a full hour on this one. I just don't want to worry my head about it any more. Saying *das tägliche Brot* would be a little bit of a blemish, but not *that* bad. Needless to say, I'll leave out 'e''s from the Dutsch text *as much of the time as I can,* since the circumnavigation of 'e''s is the heart and soul of Perec's book. Obviously, nobody would want a Dutsch translation that was littered and splattered and festooned with 'e''s. But having *a few* 'e''s here and there really won't matter, as long as my translation is *nearly* 'e'-free — say, 99 percent or so. That would be the right spirit — and it's the spirit that counts, not the letter."

Incidentally, were he *really* to entertain such a thought, Eugen Helmlé would of course entertain it in Dutsch, not in English, and I know that perfectly well. In fact, it was for just that reason that I originally typed the thought out wholly in Dutsch, not in English — and believe me, I had every intention to leave it in Dutsch. But then, by an amazing coincidence, just as I hit the close-quote and carriage return, my doorbell rang. Who could it be? Of all things, it was a very stunning busty blonde mailman asking me to sign for a CD-ROM. Whew! Well, anyway, as soon as I had closed the door behind me, I tore into that little package as eagerly as a school of fish in a feeding frenzy, and inside, what did I find but a nearly-ready-for-delivery version of MicroHype's all-new SnazzWord© program for me to beta-test here at home for a week. Huh! It even included a personally signed letter from MicroHype's gigarich chairman, Gillian Bates. Well, I couldn't resist a plea from busty blonde Gillian (who, believe it or not, is an old girlfriend of mine — one of ever so many from this ex-lothario's halcyon high-school days), so I lost no time in putting it on my computer. One of many features I saw advertised was SnazzWord's LinguaFlick© capability and so, being a bit of a skeptic about such things, I thought, "Hey, check it out!" Given that I had just finished typing Helmlé's hypothetical musing in Dutsch, I selected that, and, using SnazzWord's drolly-named "Tongue" pull-down menu, I "flicked" the text right into English. Zzip! The time? 0.03 sec. Hey, not so bad! I then flicked it over into Azerbaijani, Mohican, and !Xhosa, and each time — what do you know? — it worked like a charm. And so, for my final test, I started the text out in Dutsch and then sent it round the full circle of *all* the languages in the LinguaFlick Tongue menu — a heap o' languages, I can tell you that for sure, although, for quite obvious reasons, the exact number is proprietary — converting it each time to the one below it until I hit the bottom of the menu, at which point I then cycled back to Anglo-Saxon at the top, and finally came in for a landing just where I'd started — in Dutsch. And what was the result? You're absolutely right: There was Helmlé's hypothetical musing, in perfect Dutsch, word-for-word identical to how it had been at the very start, despite having run the gantlet of all those intermediary tongues. Man oh man! Can you imagine having 100 Gregory Rabassas, all inside your PC? But darn it all, my copy of SnazzWord expired after just a week — after all, it's not quite ready for distribution. Still, the folks at MicroHype tell me it'll be out *real soon* for just $79.95 for downloading from the Web, or, if you're hopelessly old-fashioned like me, through a catalogue or at your neighborhood computer store. Rad!

But to get back to our main thread... Can you imagine Helmlé *really* having such a cavalier attitude about reproducing the "e"-lessness of Perec's text? As us dubious folks always say in Anglo-Saxon, "It pains and strains my poor li'l brain." In my view, and I presume in Helmlé's as well, once you've decided to adopt a strict, black-and-white constraint in any kind of creative venture, you really have to go total pig — to do less than that utterly defeats the purpose. At least that's how I see things. But then, I have always been an extreme perfectionist, so perhaps this is just my compulsive nature rearing its head once again. Perhaps, but I don't think so.

Of course, I can't rigorously *prove* one must be uncomprisingly rigid and precise when writing a lipogram or other similar type of form-driven piece of text, but the whole thing would seem to me to be a hugely bizarre exercise in self-mockery if one caught the high "e"-less kickoff, successfully ran all the way downfield steering clear of every last enemy "e" — and then, at the "e"-less one-yard line, out of sheer laziness, dropped the "e"-lessness ball and thus failed to score the enormously easy "e"-less touchdown.

Piero Falchetta ha fatto il Perec...

On the other hand, I must now confide to you that there may have been a completely different, and in that case completely legitimate, reason for Eugen Helmlé to put a word containing an "e" smack-dab in the middle of the very first page of his superlative Dutsch translation. The reason I say this is that the above-mentioned Stefano Bartezzaghi, in the same essay from which I quoted earlier, says:

> Sembra che Perec abbia confidato a un amico cruciverbista di avere lasciato, in un singolo punto del romanzo, una sola E: deve essere molto ben nascosta, visto che nessuno l'ha ancora trovata (devo la notizia a Piero Falchetta, autore di un'acrobatica traduzione italiana, tuttora inedita, della *Disparition*).

> It seems that Perec once confided to a fellow crossword-puzzle lover that he had left, in one single spot in his novel, a solitary "e": it must be very well hidden, since no one has yet found it (I owe this piece of information to Piero Falchetta, author of an acrobatic Italian translation, not yet published, of *La disparition*.)

If true, this delicious claim would provide every justification in the world for inserting one single, solitary "e" into one's text, if one were the Dutsch, Anglo-Saxon, or Italic translator of Perec's quasi-"e"-less novel.

However, aside from the fact that Bartezzaghi says that no one has yet found the "e", I have one further reason that makes me ever so slightly suspicious of it all: the fourteen letters in the name "Piero Falchetta", when suitably rearranged, become "Ha fatto il Perec", meaning, in perfect Italian, "He has done the Perec" — an anagram almost too good to be true.

Naj Sparks a Fab and Sad Talk Day at Trst

I have now quoted Stefano Bartezzaghi's exemplary essay not just once but twice. You deserve to know more about it. It is called *Tre guinzagli, due consonanti, una vocale* ("Three Leashes, Two Consonants, One Vowel"), and is the afterword to a tiny book that I not only own and cherish, but of which I by now have probably given away 25 copies. Actually, the book is not all that tiny: it is 235 pages long, but its format is roughly that of a 3″ x 5″ card.

The manner in which I came across this most extraordinary book is itself almost as extraordinary. In April of 1994, having been invited by my friend Pino Longo, I went to give a lecture in the beautiful ancient harbor city of Trst (as it is known to the many Slovenians who live in it or right across the border) before the "Circolo delle Arti e delle Scienze", an informal intellectual group in that city that meets to discuss cultural issues. The "Ma Mignonne" translations seemed to be the perfect topic for the venue, so that's the lecture I decided to give. It went amazingly smoothly — one of those dreamlike cases where I felt somehow as if I was transcending my own capabilities, for the Italian that escaped from my lips always seemed to be just a little bit beyond what I thought I knew.

In any case, at the lecture's end, there was, as usual, a question-and-answer period, and there was one fellow sitting in the front row whose face seemed so interesting and whose expression was so eager that I couldn't resist calling on him first. He asked me something to this effect: "Given your clear interests in unusual literary works, are you by any chance aware of the very recent book in Italian called *Allalblassazadrandramazzatta*?" At least that's how it sounded to me. All I heard at the end was a big long mess of consonants with one single vowel linking them together. At least I picked up on its phonetic oddness! I said, "What was it called again?" and he repeated it. This time I caught most of it, although there was a part in the middle that still escaped me. I said, "I suppose, from the title, that the book involves writing under constraints in some way?" The man nodded, with a wide grin on his face, and then asked me, "Would you like a copy?" What could I say? "Sure, sounds nice!", I replied, or words to that effect. At that point, the gentleman jumped out of his seat and before I knew what was happening, he had trotted out the exit in the back. Well, the question-and-answer session went on for a good twenty minutes more, and at that point, in bursts the gentleman, sweeps down the aisle, comes up to me as I'm still talking, and hands me a copy of the book! *È per lei!* he says to me — "It's for you!" I had never expected anything of the sort, but I accepted with pleasure. Little did I know how amazing its content would be.

In an attempt to reciprocate, I invited the curious gentleman to join a little group of friends that was going out to dinner afterwards, and he was delighted to accept. I soon found out his name was Fabio Naj and that he worked at a bank but also was a journalist. Indeed, he later sent me a very nice article in a Trieste paper that he had written about my talk and visit.

Our little group went out into the chilly Trieste evening and had a rather long walk through the city streets until we at last wound up in a small street where there was apparently a very good seafood restaurant, and Pino and the others went in to get us a table. But something looked familiar about this street to me, from a visit Carol and I had made to Trst eight years earlier (an unforgettable trip, on which we made a quick jaunt into what was then Yugoslavia, hiked through a spectacular huge cave, and then drove to the island of Krk, where we made sure to sally forth onto a rugged *rt* — a promontory overlooking the Adriatic sea). I had the strange sense that maybe Carol and I had eaten in a Chinese restaurant in the neighborhood — an excellent Chinese restaurant, I seemed to recall — and I hung back for a moment, asking Fabio, "Is there by any chance a Chinese restaurant around here?", and then, dredging my memory, added, "Perhaps next to a porno bookstore?" At that, Fabio's eyes lit up and he said, "Ah! Not next to a porno *bookstore*, no — but next to a porno *theater*, yes!" and he gestured to me to follow him. Again in his quick trot, he was off and I trotted along, and lo, just a block or so away, there it was — unmistakably the same restaurant where Carol and I had had a superb Chinese lunch one time in the summer of 1986. So Fabio and I rushed back to the seafood place and I very apologetically said to the others, who already had their menus and were about to order, "Would you all mind if we switched to the Chinese place by the porno theater? I have a sentimental attachment to it..." They were very nice about it, and we moved down to the end of the street and enjoyed not only a very fine Chinese meal but also extremely stimulating, lively conversation. I must admit, however, that I was filled with nostalgia the whole time through, remembering that happy *tête-à-tête* lunch in 1986.

Shahrazad Shall Hang at Dawn

Given my big buildup, you must be wondering, "What *was* this book?" Well, it was written by a contemporary Italian named Giuseppe Varaldo, and its title is *All'alba Shahrazad andrà ammazzata* ("Shahrazad Shall Hang at Dawn", to give it the type of anglicization it deserves, although literally it would be "At Dawn Shahrazad Will Be Put to Death"). On its cover, a small subtitle announces, *Capolavori in sonetti monovocalici* — "Masterworks in monovocalic sonnets". Yes, *monovocalic*!

In his astonishing *tour de force* of a book, Varaldo takes roughly fifty classics of Western literature and synopsizes each one in a perfectly constructed classical Italian-style sonnet, in which *just one vowel* appears, the vowel itself varying from sonnet to sonnet, depending on features of the work being compressed. For example, here is the "Varaldization", so to speak, of Dante's *Inferno*. In my very literal, polyvocalic, line-by-line English-language gloss I have not come close to doing its remarkable audiovisual flavor justice, but at least I have tried to give it a bit of poetic zest:

Nel mentre ch'è trentenne, l'Eccellente	At a thirtysomething age, the Great Fêted One
(nelle Lettere regge, è legge, splende)	(in Letters he reigns, he's classic, he glows)
ben nel ventre terrestre se ne scende:	deep into the belly of Earth down he goes:
ente perenne, sede del Fetente.	to the perennial stage of the Great Fetid One.
C'è gente greve, erede del Serpente,	Here are glum folk, of the Serpent the heirs,
che freme e geme per veneree mende,	who tremble and moan for venereal misdeeds,
che fece pecche becere e tremende,	who indulged their vulgar and terrible greeds,
che perse fede e speme e se ne pente.	who lost faith and hope, who repent now their errors.
Cenere, selve, belve, pece, sete,	Blazes and bushes, tar, thirst, and wild boar,
e febbre, vespe, neve…: pene eterne,	and snow, wasps, and fever…: an infinite scourge
e tenebre per sempre, se entrerete!	and darkness forever, all ye who'd cross o'er!
Emerger preme nelle brezze verne,	Into breezes of spring one so yearns to emerge,
tender testé ver belle estreme mete,	to quest far-off goals, now to seek beauty's shore,
nell'ètere veder le stelle esterne…	in space's deep void to glimpse stars as they surge…

Not only is this a vivid, compressed expression of Dante's imagery of hell, faithfully including several of the most central features Dante describes, but its first line alludes unmistakably to the opening line of *The Inferno*, its eleventh line alludes to the most famous phrase in *The Inferno* (*Lasciate ogne speranza, voi ch'intrate*), and its closing line likewise refers to the final line of that great work (of which more, in Chapter 17).

Here is Edmond Rostand's wonderful play-in-verse *Cyrano de Bergerac* in Varaldo's monovocalized sonnetized form, again shown side by side with a very literal rhyming English rendering from my own admiring pen:

Confronto ognor lo sbocco forforoso	My dandruffy blowhole I always compare
col corno, col trombon, col vòto dosso,	to a cavernous hump, to a horn, a trombone;
o l'osso con l'omologo Colosso.	to the Colossus of Rhodes I liken my bone.
Non sopporto sfottò o motto ontoso:	I cannot take teasing or wisecracks that tear:
lo stolto (provocò l'onor focoso!)	any lout (who provokes me and dares get my goat!),
lo tocco con lo stocco, lo fo rosso.	him I smite with a sword, I wash him in blood.
Col moccolo fo colmo pozzo o fosso,	With my taper a well or a moat I could flood;
lo scrosto con lo scovolo 'sto coso.	I clean, with the aid of a swab, its damn coat.
Col nostro — non lo nomo — soffro molto:	For my — left unspoken — I suffer, and how:
troppo grosso lo mostro… mostro sono:	far too bulbous my mien… I mean, I'm to dread:
lo zoccolo sformò l'ombroso volto!	This hoof, it disfigures my dark handsome brow!
Non complotto, non mormoro, non stono,	I never conspire, nor slander, nor bleat,
collotorto non sono, sono colto…	No, I'm not a fake, but well-bred and well-read…
Sposo non son, sto solo, non corono!	But wedded I'm not, I'm alone, incomplete!

And finally, voluntarily submitting to a quite different and in fact even tougher regime, Varaldo squeezes Vladimir Nabokov's prurient novel *Lolita* into a *biconsonantal* straitjacket of a sonnet, allowing any and all vowels free entry but on the other hand forbidding all consonants but "l" and "t". To this dialect of *l'italiano* it would seem most fitting to assign the name *l'italo*, which not only is the poem's first word but also is an anagram of "Lolita".

L'italo tuo telaio o l'alta tetta,	*Your Roman frame, your bust upthrust,*
il luteo tulle o l'ileo titillato,	*your ticklish crotch, your skirt of gold,*
o il titolato letto, a te alleato,	*the noble bed in which you've rolled,*
alla tua età liliale tutti alletta.	*though but a bud, you make men lust.*
Attui alla «tele» l'utile toeletta,	*While TV's on, your skin you shield*
e t'aiuta l'altea o il latte oliato;	*with floral scents, Oil of Olay;*
tolta la tuta o il tuo tutù attillato,	*when shift or slinky gown is peeled,*
l'attuale lui allieti, o tota eletta.	*o chosen goddess, he cries ¡olé!*
L'alito tuo è aloe, loto e tea,	*Your breath is fragrant lotus tea,*
e lutata è la tela tua letale,	*your fatal web so tight, so thick,*
e ti latita il tatto e la lealtà...	*you lack just tact and loyalty...*
Alata e lauta, la tattilità	*Your wingéd touch, so warm, so wet,*
tutela e attuta l'atto tuo totale.	*covers and softens your whole trick.*
Tu alea, Lete, Aletto...: tu talea!	*Thou Fury, Alecto, Lethe...: thou nymphet!*

You may have noticed that in my English renditions, I have not strictly followed Varaldo's rhyme scheme. For instance, in this latest poem, his scheme is this: ABBA; ABBA; CDE; EDC. My own, by contrast, was this: ABBA; CDCD; EFE; GFG. Although I did not do it for this reason, perhaps I intuitively sensed that just *one* ABBA stanza would be *abbastanza* (enough).

I know of no writings in any language that quite compare to Varaldo's remarkable collection of virtuoso lipo-literary *études,* of which these three are but a small sampling. It surely cannot be a coincidence that his book's preface was penned by the celebrated Italian semiotician/novelist Humbert Humbert, affectionately called "Umberto Eco" by his compatriots, since that nickname, taken on a literal level, means "Humbert Echo".

A Monovocalic Lecture Abstract

Here's an analogy puzzle for you: If writing with no "e"'s is writing with no ease, and if writing without "t"'s is writing without ease, then what is writing with "i" as one's sole vowel? As it happens, long before Varaldo's book was given to me, I had once tried expressing myself in what cries out to be called "Inglish". Rather than synopsizing a literary classic, however, I was writing the abstract for a lecture I was soon to give on my long-standing research aimed at imparting to a computer the ability to do insightful analogy-making involving letter strings. I have no idea what inspired me to dip my toes into the Inglish pool, as I had never done so before; nor have I been tempted to try monovocalic writing thereafter. Just a fluke, I guess.

In my abstract (below), I gave the reader two sample analogy puzzles in the letter-string microworld, and with the second puzzle included two weakish answers; I then asked rhetorically whether the kind of thinking that goes into solving them *insightfully* is algorithmic (finitely mechanizable).

$$\text{If } \textbf{\textit{IF}} \Rightarrow \textbf{\textit{FI}}, \textbf{\textit{IFF}} \Rightarrow ???$$

In string *IF*, I will switch *I* (its first bit) with *F* (its right bit); this switching, giving string *FI*, I'm titling *IF*'s *twiddling*. Find this twiddling's gist, fitting string *IFF* in with this gist. Dig? This is thinking's implicit spirit, isn't it? I insist it is.

With *IMK*'s twiddling *IMK* ⇒ *IJK* inspiring it, I bid: "Shift *IMN*." Hmmm… *IMN* ⇒ *IJK*? Nix! This is insipid. I dismiss it. *IMN* ⇒ *IJN*? This isn't it. Missing trick? Wish hint? *Find misfit; fix it!* (With insight, it'll click — this I plight!)

Is gist-finding finitistic? Is insight finitistic? List in — I'll bring light!

The Esthetics of Translation Boiled down to a Microcosm

In the preceding two chapters, I argued for the tight connection between analogical thinking and translation; if you take this seriously, you can conceive of the just-posed letter-string analogy puzzles as microscopic translation challenges: Express in one medium what has been expressed in another. For instance, in the *IF* mini-medium, the idea of "reversal" was expressed; how do you then carry that idea over to the *IFF* mini-medium? One possible translation would be *FFI*, simply writing the string backwards. Another one would be to swap the roles of letters *I* and *F*, which would give *FII*. One could also swap just the first two letters, which would result in *FIF*, or swap just the last two letters, which would appear to leave *IFF* intact. There are yet further justifiable answers, but that gives the idea.

Some of these answers are — though it's hard to explain exactly what one means by this — "righter" or "better" than others. For example, the answer *IFF*, even though justified above, seems very weak, especially in comparison with, say, *FFI*. And just think — if quality and justifiability of rival answers in a domain this microscopic are already intangible, how much messier the issue gets when you scale the domain up to one involving all of human experience (namely, translation of even the simplest of passages in natural language)! We got a taste of this in Poems I, where various literal translations of single lines of "Ma Mignonne" were compared and the formidable complexity of judging among them could already be sensed. And that was just for *literal* translations…

In any case, what about the second puzzle — "Can you do to *IMN* what was done to *IMK* to yield *IJK*?"? At first, one thinks, "Oh, easy — just replace the middle letter by a *J*!", which results in *IJN*. If this answer were not pooh-poohed in the lecture abstract, one might stick with it. But since there it was hinted that genuine insight might give something better, one perseveres. "Look for and fix the misfit" was the proffered hint. Well, was there really a misfit in the second puzzle's so-called "twiddling"? Yes: the letter *M* didn't fit in with the *I* and the *K* because the letter *J* belongs between them *alphabetically*. Taking this as a second hint, we thus look for a damaged alphabetical structure in *IMN*, and indeed, it now pops out: the damager is not the *middle* letter *M*, but the *leftmost* letter *I*. Tricky!

And now it's easy sailing: What we need in place of the *I* is clearly an *L*, and so we just plunk it down: If *IMK* goes to *IJK*, then *IMN* goes to *LMN*. To me, there is something very pretty here, because *IMN* has been totally "deblemished", much as was *IMK*. However, I claim this answer is not just pretty but also *insightful* and *deep*, relative to answers such as the relatively obvious *IJN* and the even more superficial *IJK* (whose "justification", if that word can be so stretched, would be the claim that *IMK*'s twiddling suggests that *every* string, no matter what it is, gets turned into *IJK*).

The fact that a brand of esthetics — indeed, a very abstract, pristine brand of esthetics — exists in such a tiny microdomain is to me a wonderful thing, and over the past fifteen years, my own research has pushed this idea as far as I can possibly push it. However, to my astonishment and chagrin, if you scan AI journals and conferences, you will find that microdomains are as rare as hen's teeth today, and the idea that esthetic judgments are central to cognition is virtually unheard of. People greatly underestimate the power of insights into cognition that are afforded by working in microdomains, and are fearful of the subjectivity of esthetics, so they shy away and stay on what they think is much safer turf — namely, no-nonsense huge real-world domains (or façades that give such an appearance, anyway). However, I would claim that this "safe" turf is also more arid turf. But then, my opinion lies very far out toward one end of the spectrum.

The Betrayal of Giuseppe Varaldo

There is a clear spiritual similarity between these very boiled-down translation problems (and the microesthetics that they involve) and Giuseppe Varaldo's monovocalic minipoems (and the microesthetics that *they* involve). One might even carry the game of analogy-making to a yet higher level of abstraction, and assert that these miniature translation puzzles are to the world of full-scale translation challenges as Varaldo's miniaturized poems are to the world of full-scale literature; after all, both are about *esthetics-based transfer of essence from one medium to another.*

In precisely that sense of preserving deepest essence, I must admit that I am afraid I betrayed Varaldo in my anglicizations of his poems. Do you recall how ginger I was, in Poems I, about sullying the word "translation" were I to apply it to a nonrhyming, literal rendition of "Ma Mignonne" in English? It struck me as all wrong. Well, how is what I did to Varaldo's sonnets any less a sullying of the word? If someone asked, "What is the essence of Varaldo's contribution?", the answer would of course highlight the trait of monovocalicity (or biconsonanticity, in the case of *Lolita*) most of all. Any supposed "translation" that fails to reproduce that core trait is no better than a money-change booth where you get a receipt but no bills, or a photomat where what you get out is a picture of your shoes only.

For another perspective on my failure, imagine giving to someone who had never seen the Varaldo poems the task of translating my three sonnets into Italian. Of course nothing monovocalic would result. I believe that truly deep translation entails *symmetry* — each side should look as if it might have come from the other — but of course what I did here was asymmetric: Varaldo's poems are not plausible renditions of mine. *Mea culpa!*

On the other hand, having now quite properly chastised myself on this score, I must also admit that I doubt that *anyone* could do what I am arguing would have to be done in order to do Varaldo's poems justice: namely, render their exact content in monovocalic sonnets in English (presumably even using, in each case, *the same vowel* as Varaldo chose — although perhaps infidelity along that axis might be forgivable). The constraints are simply far too tight; there is nothing to be done, end of story.

How, then, did Varaldo himself manage? Well, that's easy: He was able to filter and select out of a huge set of possible themes in each work just those whose words slipped naturally into a monovocalic framework. Given the size of all these works, it was very hard, but feasible. And if an anglophonic poet wished to start from scratch and select themes and words from *Cyrano* or *The Inferno* in such a manner that only one vowel was involved, and then bring these items together in a well-constructed sonnet, well, that too sounds plausible to me, although also extraordinarily hard. If that were done, though, it's not clear whether the resulting sonnet would count as a *translation* of Varaldo's poem, or simply as a *counterpart*.

ShrinkLits

In the late 1960's, a rhymester named Maurice Sagoff did something distantly related to what Varaldo did: He took fifty canonized works of world literature and shrank them down into what he called "constructive distillations" of themselves, thus creating a book called *ShrinkLits*. In fact, each ShrinkLit is a nicely rhyming and highly metrical poem whose lines are usually quite short and are thus reminiscent, in a way, of Marot's style.

Among the works that Sagoff treated were two of the three that I gave in Varaldo's condensations — *Cyrano* and *The Inferno*. It is thus possible to do precisely what I was just mentioning above — namely, compare what two different poets independently skim off or distill out of large works they are summarizing. Here, then, is Sagoff's distillation of *Cyrano de Bergerac*:

> *Big nosed-hypochondriac*
> *(Not de Gaulle — de Bergerac),*
> *Swordsman with a golden tongue*
> *Lends his knack to help a young*
> *Soldier win Roxane, a blonde*
> *Of whom both are mighty fond.*
>
> *War breaks out. The newlywed*
> *Joins the fray and winds up dead.*
> *Poor Roxane finds solitude*
> *In a convent, where she'll brood*
> *And reread her lover's prose,*
> *Not aware it's Cyrano's.*
>
> *He, the prince of cavaliers,*
> *Visits her for fifteen years,*
> *Gallantly dispelling gloom,*
> *Holding high aloft his plume;*
> *When Roxane at last gets wise*
> *To the whole charade, he dies.*
>
> *Through the falling autumn leaves*
> *— Can you hear? — a spirit grieves:*
> *"Chivalry is dead and past...*
> *Good guys always finish last."*

Of course it is not monovocalic, and hence no rival to Varaldo's, but it is still cute. And now, here is Sagoff's five-tercet compression of *The Inferno*:

> *Like a funky show?*
> *Like your torture slow?*
> *Come on down below!*
>
> *See historic greats,*
> *Thugs and reprobates,*
> *Suffer hellish fates.*
>
> *Filth around them laves,*
> *Hear them in their caves*
> *Screaming, "Don't make waves!"*
>
> *Using all the tricks*
> *Of the horror flicks,*
> *Dante feeds us kicks.*
>
> *Sure, a moral's there:*
> *"Godless man, beware!"*
> *Heard that tune somewhere?*

Sparking and Sparkling, Thanks to Constraints   ◆ ◆ ◆   **131**

An Illusory Reversal of Roles

One lesson we can learn from Sagoff's and Varaldo's laudable poetic accomplishments is the deceptiveness of the power of selection: If you do a good job in selecting what you need in order to accommodate your self-imposed constraints, you will appear to be in control of your medium, rather than the reverse.

This is a bit like a great ice-skater, who has become so at one with the constraints under which she is operating that her maneuvers seem for all the world to *show the ice who's boss*, rather than the reverse. The truth of the matter is, however, that over many years, it was the *ice* who showed *her* who was boss, until finally it had trained her so well that she now knows what to avoid and what to do in order to give an untrained audience the impression that *she's* on top. It takes a long apprenticeship to a set of constraints for this apparent reversal — this beautiful sleight of foot — to take effect.

Being Shoved Around Can Get You Pretty Far!

Some years ago, I was fortunate enough to get to know a long-time idol of mine — the American writer of brilliant satirical songs and lyrics, Tom Lehrer. When we first met, sharing a lunch in early 1984, Lehrer politely but reluctantly consented to discuss his songs, about which he is very modest. I uttered what to him must have sounded like effusive praise of his lyrics, so he deflected it all, insisting that what might seem to me like great cleverness was little more than the result of his having been forced into unexpected regions of semantic space (*i.e.*, the space of all possible ideas) by the self-imposed constraint of rhyming.

In other words, Lehrer said, he had simply found himself dreaming up odd images that would never have occurred to him had he not been bound to make one line rhyme with another. Thus, he argued, the mere constraint of rhyming made him appear far more ingenious than he actually was. He was being given free assists, so to speak, by an invisible and friendly genie quite external to himself.

The example I recall Lehrer citing was his song "Pollution". At some point, he explained, he'd decided to use the phrase "industrial waste", and after a bit of search, he found the potential rhyme-word "toothpaste". Now toothpaste seemed at first to have little to do with industrial waste, but a little further musing led Lehrer to the image of someone brushing their teeth with befouled water, and thence to the following couplet:

Pollution, pollution, you can use the latest toothpaste,
And then rinse your mouth — with industrial waste.

He stressed that working in an unconstrained mode, he would never have thought of such an image, but that the rhyming constraint had given him this free assist, making the creation of a cute, catchy, unexpected line easy. In my opinion, though, this was too modest: Not everyone would be able to make such a smooth connection between toothpaste and industrial waste, or, having done that, be able to figure out how to word it well.

Listening to a recording of Tom Lehrer playing the piano and singing this song before a live audience, one hears the audience members erupt in delighted laughter when they get the humorous image evoked by these lines — which, it must be said, is greatly enhanced by Lehrer's wonderfully sassy (or should I say "acid-tongued"?) delivery.

The other example Lehrer gave of how rhyming had led him down unpredictable semantic pathways was a famous challenge that he once put his mind to — that of finding a good rhyme for "orange". I will give you his solution shortly, but you might in the meantime consider the gauntlet to have been flung down.

The Left–Right Ride: A Cheap Route to Novelty

Tom Lehrer's credit-deflecting remarks remind me of a slightly nutty game some of my friends and I used to play in our college days — several years before the first oil crisis, I hasten to add, in self-defense. A few of us would pile into a car and set off on what we called a "left–right ride", which was the ridiculously silly idea of simply driving to the first possible choice-point (*i.e.,* a crossroads of any sort, as long as the crossing roads were public), taking the leftmost option there, then heading to the next possible choice-point, there taking the rightmost option, and so forth, always alternating between taking the leftmost and the rightmost options. (Thus sometimes, "leftmost" meant "go straight instead of taking the right turn here", and analogously for "rightmost".)

Since towns never have perfect rectangular grids, this flipflopping rule did *not,* as one might at first guess (indeed, as we ourselves had guessed), merely set us off on a locally zigzaggy but basically diagonal trek across the town. No, it carried us via strange, serpentine, self-backtracking and self-crossing (but never self-repeating) pathways into places that were literally all over the map — tiny little nooks and crannies that we had never dreamt existed, yet that were practically in our own back yards. We came across the strangest houses and stores and streets we had ever seen, simply by obeying a trivial constraint very strictly, doing things we would otherwise never have thought of doing. For me, this was an unforgettable lesson about discovery, and perhaps that's why I was quite receptive to what I heard Lehrer saying. On the other hand, the metaphor of the skater has to be kept in mind: You don't get out great results unless you've put in your long years of practice!

Sparking and Sparkling, Thanks to Constraints ◆◆◆ **133**

A Mini-exaltation of Constraints

Constraints come in all shapes and forms, to be sure, and need not involve left–right riding or left-out-"e" writing. I remember a particularly intriguing writing challenge that I came across as a teen-ager while perusing an anthology of articles on general science — the challenge of explaining Einstein's theory of relativity (both special and general) to the lay public *in words of one syllable.* Right after the statement of this delicious challenge came a four-page article in which precisely that feat was carried off. I would gladly display a bit of it here but for two reasons: (1) I was disappointed by the way the challenge was met; (2) I lost the book. Too bad! But perhaps a reader will take up the challenge and write a monosyllabic relativity primer. Or perhaps I myself will, someday, if ever I find time. But... how in the world could you fit "ether", "Michelson–Morley", "absolute", "simultaneity", "Lorentz transformation", "gravity", "contravariant coordinates", "tensor calculus", or for that matter, just "Einstein", into one syllable?

Oh, well. Such ethereal riddles are distracting us from the matter at hand, namely constraints. And so, let me list a few other types of constraint that one might impose on oneself in the act of writing:

- write nonrhyming prose in tetrameter, pentameter, or some other meter;
- allow no word longer than four letters, or forbid words of exactly four letters;
- construct an acrostic (the initials of all words in the text spell out a message);
- make sure that the name of some flower or other appears in every sentence;
- make all sentences in the text share exactly the same grammatical structure;
- never let a sentence exceed seventeen words in length (a constraint used by Ashleigh Brilliant in his numerous books of "Pot-shots");
- use three lines containing five syllables, seven syllables, and five syllables, respectively, and always mention a season (the formal constraints of haiku);
- use exactly the same set of letters as Lincoln used in his Gettysburg address (in other words, make the whole text be an anagram of the Gettysburg address).

Well, I could go on forever, but you get the idea. There is a blurry boundary at best between this notion of a "set of constraints" and the notion of a "linguistic medium", which we will explore in Chapter 7. Basically, a set of constraints is sharply defined and quite objective, whereas a medium might be a bit vaguer and looser in definition — for example, "telegraph terse" or "bumper-sticker terse" or "Ernest Hemingway terse" or "fortune-cookie vacuous" or "Buckminster Fuller mystical" or "treacly and obsequious" or "pompous, obscurantist, and Lacanian" or "pompous, obscurantist, and Heideggerian", and so on and so forth, *ad nauseam.* Of the two terms — "set of constraints" and "linguistic medium" — the latter is, for me, the broader one, encompassing *any* set of attributes, whether hopelessly vague or very precise and sharp, that someone might try to respect in a piece of writing. In any case, the imposition of any reasonably sharp set of constraints will force a writer to explore and discover pathways in semantic space that would otherwise have been left entirely unexplored, and that is a very simple but very deep truth about language and thought.

The Orange Challenge

To demonstrate this simple but deep truth, let us return to the famous challenge Tom Lehrer took up. If you want to try it yourself, stop reading *right now*! Here is how Lehrer solved the problem to his own satisfaction:

> *Eating an orange*
> > *while making love*
> *Makes for bizarre enj-*
> > *oyment thereof.*

I was charmed by this irreverent little image, and it seemed to me to call for a little poem in honor of Lehrer. Thus I tweaked it into the following:

> *"Make love with an orange,"*
> > *our teacher Tom toots,*
> *"And you'll harvest bizarre, ing-*
> > *enious fruits!"*

By this time, I was, however, hooked on the challenge myself, and before I knew it, a host of unexpected images had come spilling out the tip of my ball-point pen, surprising me, their author, no end…

> *A poem without "or-*
> > *ange" as a rhyme is not nice —*
> *It's a bustling bazaar*
> > *in Jodhpur, with no spice.*
> *It's a Friday night bar*
> > *in Georgetown, without ice.*
> *It is Deborah Kerr*
> > *'n' John Wayne — Yul look twice!*
> *Tiger Woods chipping far*
> > *and just missing — no dice!*
> *Yankees blurting "Au revoir"*
> > *in Japan — East/West splice!*
> *Or a Volkswagen car*
> > *engine smoking — ach, Scheiß'!*
> *A poem without "or-*
> > *ange" as a rhyme is not nice.*

Poetry — ¿An Art Lost in Translation? — Try Poe!

You thought we were done with Mr. Sagoff, but we're not — not quite. Just one more shrunken lit, then we'll let him go. I wanted you to see what he did with Edgar Allen Poe's "The Raven". Poe's full poem is far too long to quote here in its entirety, but here are at least its final two stanzas:

> "Be that word our sign of parting, bird or fiend!" I shrieked, upstarting —
> "Get thee back into the tempest and the Night's Plutonian shore!
> Leave no black plume as a token of that lie thy soul hath spoken!
> Leave my loneliness unbroken! — quit the bust above my door!
> Take thy beak from out my heart, and take thy form from off my door!"
> Quoth the Raven, "Nevermore."
>
> And the Raven, never flitting, still is sitting, <u>still</u> is sitting
> On the pallid bust of Pallas just above my chamber door;
> And his eyes have all the seeming of a demon's that is dreaming,
> And the lamp-light o'er him streaming throws his shadow on the floor;
> And my soul from out that shadow that lies floating on the floor
> Shall be lifted — nevermore!

They give a good sense for the marvelous, relentless, driving, lilting, soaring rhythm of the poem, about whose creation Poe actually wrote an essay entitled "The Philosophy of Composition", in which he attempts to demonstrate that the creation of the whole poem (which he considered his own greatest work) was inevitable from its very start. As he puts it:

Most writers — poets in especial — prefer having it understood that they compose by a species of fine frenzy — an ecstatic intuition — and would positively shudder at letting the public take a peep behind the scenes, at the elaborate and vacillating crudities of thought — at the true purposes seized only at the last moment — at the innumerable glimpses of ideas that arrived not at the maturity of full view — at the fully mature fancies discarded in despair as unmanageable — at the cautious selections and rejections — at the painful erasures and interpolations — in a word, at the wheels and pinions — the tackle for scene-shifting — the step-ladders and demon-traps — the cock's feathers, the red paint and the black patches, which, in ninety-nine cases out of the hundred, constitute the properties of the literary *histrio.*...

It is my design to render it manifest that no one point in *The Raven*'s composition is referable either to accident or intuition — that the work proceeded, step by step, to its completion with the precision and rigid consequence of a mathematical problem....

And here I may as well say a few words of the versification. My first object (as usual) was originality. The extent to which this has been neglected, in versification, is one of the most unaccountable things in the world. Admitting that there is little possibility of variety in mere *rhythm*, it is still clear that the possible varieties of metre and stanza are absolutely infinite — and yet, *for centuries, no man, in verse, has ever done, or ever seemed to think of doing, an original thing.*

One certainly does not have to believe in the truth of Poe's half-baked theorizings about his own creative process to find them fascinating and amusing, and in any case, eminently worthwhile reading, if only because of the incontestably Poëtic savor that they exude. But so much for Poe; now back to Sagoff. Here is how he rendered the entire eighteen-stanza poem:

> *Raven lurches*
> *In, perches*
> *Over door.*
> *Poet's bleary*
> *Query —*
> *"Where's Lenore?"*
> *Creepy bird*
> *Knows one word:*
> *"Nevermore."*

Fond though I am of this microverse, line 5 is a bit too austere for my taste. I'd add an adjective so it ran, "Poet's bleary / Fearful query" (or "Eerie" or "Quaking"). That would also give one word per stanza. Oh, well.

Now it was not quite for nothing that I wanted to talk about "The Raven", but to explain how it all ties in with the matters we have been discussing in this chapter, I must return to Georges Perec's *La disparition*, and in particular to its plot, which, as you well know, revolves about the missing personage of Anton Voyl.

In Perec's tenth chapter, the motley crew of Voyl searchers come together to pool their clues on their friend's fate and whereabouts, and it emerges that each of them has been the recipient of some cryptic mailing from Voyl. These various selections are then shared, the most unusual of them being the message received by Lady Olga Clifford, who shows everyone a set of six poetic selections written out in longhand by Anton Voyl himself. Each of these is — in a certain stretched sense — a classic piece of poetry by such illustrious denizens of "the vast pantheon of French literature" as Stéphane Mallarmé, Victor Hugo, Arthur Rimbaud, and others. What none of the assembled group picks up on, however, is the fact that these poems have all been transmuted into Gallic. Completely in the dark, the group members all read with fascination but no illumination. Though it is an inconclusive episode from the point of view of adventure, it is an incredible passage from the point of view of literature.

How might a translator into Anglo-Saxon approach this passage? The most obvious idea would be to work on converting each of these famous French poems, line by line, into a closely corresponding Anglo-Saxon piece of verse — surely a most difficult challenge, but perhaps within reach of a skillful translator–poet. However, since the selections are all from French poets, translating them into Anglo-Saxon, no matter how skillfully it were done, would go largely unappreciated by readers of English, since few would be able to compare the originals with their transmogrifications.

Gilbert Adair had a different idea. Taking full advantage of his poetic license (for is Anglo-Saxon not poetry?), he substituted English-language poets for French ones, then virtuosically rewrote some of their classic pieces in Anglo-Saxon. For instance, Hamlet's long soliloquy "To be or not to be, that is the question" is fully — and artfully — Anglo-Saxonized. And Milton's sonnet "On His Blindness" becomes — hold your laughter, please — "On His Glaucoma". But the most stunning is Adair's conversion of all eighteen stanzas of "The Raven", replacing Perec's "Booz assoupi" (his gallicization of Hugo's "Booz endormi"). You have just seen the final two stanzas in English; below I show how Adair redid them in Anglo-Saxon.

The authorship of these lines is attributed, in *A Void*, not to Poe (obviously taboo because of its orthography!), but to one Arthur Gordon Pym, whom readers may recognize as the alleged author of Poe's unique novel *The Narrative of Arthur Gordon Pym of Nantucket*, a figure with whom Poe's own identity is swirlingly mixed in the many-leveled hoax that is the novel's text. In any case, here is how Adair concludes, after sixteen stanzas:

> *"If that word's our sign of parting, Satan's bird," I said, upstarting —*
> *"Fly away, wings blackly parting, to thy Night's Plutonian plain!*
> *For, mistrustful, I would scorn to mind that untruth thou has sworn to,*
> *And I ask that thou by morn tomorrow quit my sad domain!*
> *Draw thy night-nibb'd bill from out my soul and quit my sad domain!"*
> *Quoth that Black Bird, "Not again."*
>
> *And my Black Bird, still not quitting, still is sitting, <u>still</u> is sitting*
> *On that pallid bust — still flitting through my dolorous domain;*
> *But it cannot stop from gazing for it truly finds amazing*
> *That, by artful paraphrasing, I such rhyming can sustain —*
> *Notwithstanding my lost symbol I such rhyming still sustain —*
> *Though I shan't try it again!*

Posthumous Fencing with Robert Frost

Robert Frost once made a delicious remark to the effect that writing free verse is like playing tennis with the net down. I think this is a terrific, right-on-the-mark observation. I have no axe to grind with Robert Frost in general. However, he is also well known for another aphorism with which I happen to disagree intensely. Although I have not managed to find it in his writings, I have seen it quoted in print in the following manner: "Poetry is what disappears in translation." In a sense, this whole book is a riposte to Frost's thrust, and certainly Adair's effort above helps my case enormously. But I have also written my own little poem, inspired by Frost's remark…

Star Frost Bite Dust

From Robert Frost, this sound bite I found:
"Poetry's that that's lost in translation."
But is our star's bright sound bite sound?
"'Tis lost!" nods Frost in cool indignation.

To me this sound bite sounds like junk
Food begging for regurgitation;
And challenged thus, I become a monk
Who'd find himself lost in translation.

I tackle a verse by old Clément Marot;
My sweat pores, wet, pour transpiration.
I translate high and I translate low,
And sweat turns to sweet inspiration.

Soon friends chime in and join the fun:
I get by post, from across our wide nation,
A hundred verse versions of "Ma Mignonne":
A swell success — indeed, a sensation!

And then, to see if they're up to it,
I send out to folks in machine translation
The selfsame modest challenge — to wit:
"Please output an anglicization."

My findings now I would share with you:
Translation of poems for recreation
Is far from what our machines can do;
Instead, it calls for true re-creation —

Like procreation, a mind's deep lust.
I'm stunned by the gems of imagination
Unearthed by my friends — indeed, nonplussed
By their slippery flips of interpretation.

"Lost in translation"? That motto's bust.
Frost's thrust; my riposte: "Unjust accusation!
Thou unsound Frost bite, just bite the dust!
For poetry's found, not lost in translation."

Poems V:

~ Sue Suite ~

* * *
*
*

David Moser, mentally meandering through the virtually endless space of variational possibilities inherent in Marot's theme, wondered: Why not make the rhyming constraint even *tighter*, with bisyllabic rather than trisyllabic lines? Since the original poem has 84 syllables *in toto* (28 x 3), David felt it would be both respectful and elegant to preserve that number, so he opted for a version with 42 bisyllabic lines (42 x 2 = 84 syllables).

Probably nudged by Melanie Mitchell's hypothetical "Sue", David adopted the famous song title "Sweet Sue" to get his first (and last) line, and from there took off like a streak, coming up with a fantastic, jaunty, staccato poem jam-packed with hard-hitting, driving rhythms, and featuring a high density of flavorful, droll words ("egad", "boo-hoo", "pout", "splurge", "pine", "bulge", etc.). Its catchiest lines are surely those comprising its closing exhortation: "Indulge and bulge anew, Sweet Sue!" This stunning effort was marvelously effective and completely different from all those that had preceded it.

Not that "Sweet Sue" was the first poem in all history to have bisyllabic lines; Marot *père* and *fils* wrote some, as did Victor Hugo. Take *Les Djinns,* his stunning study in symmetry that starts with a whispering bisyllabic octet, gets louder as a wild horde of Djinns (genies) approaches — three syllables, four, five, six, seven, eight — and in the center, a deafening ten-syllable octet; then the whole process unwinds, ending in a whispering bisyllabic octet. Here is how *Les Djinns* opens and closes. As for anglicization? *Ah ça, je l'avoue, c'est à vous !*

> *Murs, ville,*
> *Et port,*
> *Asile*
> *De mort,*
> *Mer grise,*
> *Où brise*
> *La brise*
> *Tout dort.*

> *Dans la plaine*
> *Naît un bruit.*
> *C'est l'haleine*
> *De la nuit.*
> *Elle brame*
> *Comme une âme*
> *Qu'une flamme*
> *Toujours suit.*

> . . . .

> *Ce bruit vague*
> *Qui s'endort,*
> *C'est la vague*
> *Sur le bord ;*
> *C'est la plainte*
> *Presque éteinte*
> *D'une sainte*
> *Pour un mort.*

> *On doute*
> *La nuit...*
> *J'écoute : —*
> *Tout fuit,*
> *Tout passe ;*
> *L'espace*
> *Efface*
> *Le bruit.*

Sweet Sue

David Moser

Sweet Sue,
What's new?
Feel bad?
Egad!
5 The flu?
Boo-hoo.
Oh, well.
I'll tell
You what
10 (You nut):
Don't hide
Inside
And pout.
Come out!
15 The night
Is right
For fun,
And one
Like you,
20 Sweet Sue
(Whose zeal

Is real
For sweets
And eats),
Should splurge! 25
The urge
For jam
And ham
Is fine!
Don't pine, 30
Or waste
The taste
Of life
On strife
And pain. 35
Regain
Your mood.
Eat food!
Indulge,
And bulge 40
Anew,
Sweet Sue!

Impressed and inspired, I mused for a good while on David's structural tampering, and in the course of so doing, came up with the somewhat perverse idea of "repairing the damage" that David had done to Marot's trisyllabic lines. In particular, I decided to see if I could "fix up" each broken line by adding back one "missing" syllable to it. As I was carrying out this generous fix-it act, I decided to place one further constraint on myself: my new syllable had to make an internal rhyme with one or the other of the two syllables already present in the given line. Moreover, I insisted that the set of 42 final syllables comprising David's original rhyme pattern — not necessarily the words themselves, but the rhyming *sounds* — had to be preserved. These self-imposed constraints allowed me to do things like taking David's anorexic little couplet "The flu? / Boo-hoo!" and fattening it up into "Blue? The flu? / Boo-hoo. Pooh!" This strange-sounding, quite tricky-to-read-aloud poem is what resulted when I had restored the "missing" parts throughout.

Sweetmeat Sue

David Moser/D. Hofstadter

Sweetmeat Sue,
What's new, you?
Feel real bad?
Mad? Egad!
5 Blue? The flu?
Boo-hoo. Pooh!
Oh, well. "Hell!"
I'll yell. Tell
You what's what
10 (Sue, you nut):
Slide — don't hide
Inside — glide
Out and pout!
Come plum out!
15 The night light
Is quite right
For more fun,
And, hon', one
Tyke like you,
20 Sweetmeat Sue
(Whose meal zeal

Is real real
For sweets, treats,
And grand eats),
Should splurge! Surge! 25
Free the urge
For more jam
And canned ham —
This is fine!
Don't pine, whine 30
More, or waste
The graced taste
Of love life
On rife strife,
Strain and pain. 35
Plea: regain
Your core mood.
Eat stewed food!
Win! Indulge!
Stand and bulge: 40
A new you,
Sweetmeat Sue!

The most glaring defect of my fattened version of David's thin poem was that it was now definitely overweight, consisting as it did of 42 x 3 = 126 syllables. This was too much *embonpoint*! And so it occurred to me that by pruning various entire lines here and there, I might be able to bring Sue back down to her original size-84 figure. Indeed, it wasn't too much trouble to find fourteen relatively expendable lines, and thus — after some additional minor tweaking of surviving lines here and there, including first and last — I had transformed David's radical vision into a very bizarre variant of itself — perhaps more faithful, in some curious sense, to Marot's original French, and yet totally subverting David's beautiful idea. A double betrayal had given rise to a new type of fidelity to Marot.

This translation embodied a strange extra constraint that I doubt would ever have occurred to me on my own: that of insisting that each line contain an internal rhyme. "Meat-sweet Sue" was certainly far from the best imaginable anglicization under this constraint, but it showed that the challenge could at least be met. In any case, this new and quite general theme of piling on further constraints to the already very tight constraints of Marot's original poem started to appeal to me; we will see the theme returning with future versions.

Meat-sweet Sue

David Moser/D. Hofstadter

Meat-sweet Sue,
What's new, you?
Blue? The flu?
Boo-hoo. Pooh!
Slide — don't hide   5
Inside — glide
Out and pout!
Come plum out!
The night light
Is quite right   10
For more fun,
And, hon', one
Tyke like you,
Sweetmeat Sue,
Should splurge! Surge!   15
Free the urge
For more jam
And canned ham —
This is fine!
Don't pine, whine   20
More, or waste
The graced taste
Of love life
On rife strife.
Win! Indulge!   25
Stand and bulge —
A new you!
Meet Sweet Sue!

Eight years later, as I was pulling together this collection, I couldn't help noticing some small flaws in David's "Sweet Sue", most of all the lack of the poet's self-naming. When I pointed this out to David, he agreed that it could definitely be improved, and in fact criticized his own poem far more heavily than I had. So he undertook the task of revision, and in only a few days he had come up with an even tighter and more spirited realization of his own idea.

Like me, David felt comfortable playing about rather loosely with the semantics of the original, and thus he invented quite a bit of unexpected imagery, such as connecting the sick girl's "prison term" (*i.e.,* quarantine) with a "crime" (whether committed or not), as well as the idea of himself (and not Clément) "grabbing the tab" for some gourmet treats. On the other hand, as in his original version of "Sweet Sue", there was no suggestion of hopes for divine succor, but this did not seem too dreadful a lack.

This poem, the final outcome of a delightful, unpredictable set of experiments, represents for me one of the peak points of the whole set of variations on Marot's theme.

Sweet Sue (II)

David Moser

Sweet Sue,
What's new?
Feel bad?
Egad!
5 The flu?
Boo-hoo.
To ail
Is jail,
They say.
10 But, hey,
Dear one —
You've done
No crime!
It's time
15 You fled
That bed.
Don't hide
Inside
And pout.
20 Come out
And splurge!

I urge
Some cake!
Partake
Of sweets,   25
Eat treats
You crave,
And Dave
Will grab
The tab!   30
Cast off
Your cough!
Forsake
Your ache
And pain!   35
Regain
Your mood.
Eat food!
Indulge,
And bulge   40
Anew,
Sweet Sue!

• *Chapter 6* •

The Subtle Art
of Transculturation

•

It was only by pure coincidence that I found out, late in 1985, that a Chinese-language translation of my first book — *Gödel, Escher, Bach: an Eternal Golden Braid* — was under way. My friend and University of Michigan colleague Arthur Burks, returning from a visit to Beijing's oddly retro-yclept Peking University, casually mentioned that he had met two professors of computer science — an elderly man named Wu Yunzeng and a younger one named Ma Xiwen — who were directing the effort.

I was surprised and excited but also concerned, for already twice I'd had the infuriating experience, first with Spanish, then with German, of my annotated version, on which I'd spent hundreds of laborious hours jotting notes for translators, either failing somehow to reach the translator or else being arrogantly ignored, as a consequence of which, in the former case, a valiant but sad attempt made it all the way into print and then, thankfully, sank into oblivion, and in the latter, a rough-edged, spiritless manuscript was just barely headed off at the pass and then given a huge overhaul by a few brave souls, including *GEB*'s superb Dutch translator, Ronald Jonkers. God knows, I did not want a replay of this type of fiasco.

My first thought was, of course, to get the annotated version as fast as possible to the Chinese team, but another thought flashed to mind as well: Why not also send along David Moser, who at the time was working very hard on his Chinese, and was looking for a way to spend a few months in China? David had the great advantage, of course, of having participated, like Ronald, in all the early Paris talks on the strategy for converting *GEB* into French, and as I had found out then, David's philosophy of translation and mine were in virtually perfect synchrony.

The Internet not yet being the standard communication channel among academics in those laughably archaic days, I fired off a paper letter to Professors Wu and Ma, to which I soon received a very warm handwritten reply from the former in an English that flowed beautifully. In it, Professor Wu confirmed my intuitive fear that the team included no native speaker of English — but, he added, and to my great relief, the project was far from finished, and David would be most welcome to join the group. Professor Wu also mentioned that he himself was planning to make a trip to the United States, and hoped he might be able to drop in on me. I wrote back, enthusiastically inviting him to come spend a few days in Ann Arbor.

Thus in early 1986, David took off for Beijing, where he met Professors Wu and Ma, who had formed and were guiding the project at a high level, but were not doing the nitty-gritty translation work. They introduced him to two of the key players in their small team: Yan Yong, a sharp and witty graduate student in computer science, and Liu Haoming, a literature graduate student and excellent artist whom Yan had brought on board because of his ingenious ways of playing with the Chinese language. These three swiftly became good friends and strong working partners.

A Man, a Plan, a Canon, a Palindrome, a Translation — China!

Only days after David landed in Beijing, Professor Wu took off for the United States. He flew into Detroit, and to distinguish myself in the crowd at the gate, I carried a sign saying "Wu Yunzeng — Welcome!" in Chinese characters I'd penned. We had no trouble recognizing each other, in fact, and drove back to my house in Ann Arbor, where, with Carol and Melanie Mitchell, we had an Italian dinner that he enjoyed immensely, pasta being among his favorite foods since he had lost most of his teeth. On finding out that both Melanie and I knew some Chinese, Professor Wu asked us a couple of questions in Chinese, but neither of us did a very good job in answering. From then on, conversation was strictly in English!

We were all curious how it was that Professor Wu spoke quite good, although strongly accented, English. He explained that as a young child, he had gone to a school in which all classes were conducted in English. He had even been given an English first name — "Andrew" — which he urged us to use, but somehow it never felt natural to us to think of him as "Andrew", so he remained "Professor Wu" to us all.

The most memorable parts of Professor Wu's visit were the lively discussions that took place about translation, a topic in which he obviously had been keenly interested for decades. I could tell that although he was a genuine fan of my book, he did not know it intimately and could use a crash course on some of its trickier passages. To this end, I devised a little plan: Bob French, who Professor Wu knew had been involved in the French translation, would join us for dinner, and the three of us would discuss the dialogue called "Crab Canon", strictly modeled on a piece for two violins by J. S. Bach. Bach's Crab Canon (a tiny part of his Musical Offering) has the property that when played backwards, it sounds just the same as forwards except that the two instruments or "voices" have been interchanged. Pieces of music with this property have traditionally been called "crab canons" because crabs allegedly walk backwards (actually, they walk more sideways than backwards, but the name has stuck nonetheless).

For dinner, we went out to — of course — an Italian restaurant, where our discussion took off very nicely. No sooner had I described the concept of a crab canon than Professor Wu drew a connection between such a musical piece and a palindrome — a sentence that reads the same backwards and forwards. To be sure, there is a strong resemblance, though a palindrome has only one "voice", hence there is no counterpart to the interchange of voices when it goes backwards. He jotted down for us a famous five-character classical Chinese palindrome, *Yè luò tiān luò yè,* which can be literally translated as, "At leaves-fall season, fall the leaves." To tell the truth, with its tautological content, it was not particularly impressive, but at least it served to launch us into the idea of translating palindromes, a challenge clearly fraught with thorns and prickers. To explore this specific case, we wrote down an English gloss for each of its five characters:

leaves fall season fall leaves

and then noticed something striking: "fall" has two unrelated meanings ("autumn" as well as "tumble"), as does "leaves" ("foliage" and "departs"). Taking advantage of this, Bob and I quickly assembled a lovely reversible sentence in perfect English and making perfect sense:

Fall leaves as soon as leaves fall.

("Autumn departs just moments after foliage has tumbled.") Not only did this semantically echo the original Chinese palindrome, it also outshone its progenitor in surprise value and elegance. We agreed that this was a most fortuitous discovery, delightful but atypical.

Turning the tables around, either Bob or I (my memory blurs) asked Professor Wu how one might try to translate into Chinese the most famous and, in my opinion, the most spectacular of English palindromes:

A man, a plan, a canal — Panama!

We wrote it down for him, but it was with a look of utter bafflement that he stared at it. After we had our own moment of bafflement, Bob and I quickly realized what was the matter: Professor Wu did not see this as a palindrome! Guided by what we had together done with the "fall leaves" palindrome, he was reading this one backwards *word by word,* and when it was inverted that way, it came out "Panama! — canal a, plan a, man A". Obviously that isn't the original phrase — it isn't even grammatical English!

We explained that in this case, you have to read the phrase backwards at the *letter* level; only then do you get it back again (ignoring punctuation, spaces, and capitalization). It was not hard to see why someone accustomed to reading Chinese characters, which represent whole morphemes, would naturally be inclined to reverse a sentence at the word level instead of at the letter level — we had simply forgotten a fundamental difference between Chinese and English.

This little confusion resolved, we all agreed it would be most unlikely that anyone could construct a Chinese palindrome with the same content as this English classic. However, I suggested that as the most salient aspect of this utterance is not its content but its symmetric form, *any* outstanding Chinese palindrome, whatever topic it might have, would serve, in some abstract sense, as a "faithful translation". Although that proposal seemed a bit extreme to Professor Wu, there was universal agreement among us that if a translator converted this remarkable, reversible English phrase about the engineer who conceived the Panama Canal into a run-of-the-mill, nonreversible Chinese phrase saying something like "A person, a notion, a sluice — Panama!", the act would be an utter travesty. The metaphor that then popped out of my mouth as I idly gazed at the bubbles in my soft drink I've always remembered: "As flat as a Coke that's lost all its fizz."

Fighting Transculturation with Transculturation

The word "faithfulness" brought to Professor Wu's mind a celebrated translator from the beginning of this century named Yan Fu, who is often remembered for stressing three prime qualities that one should strive for in translation: faithfulness, clarity, and grace. To illustrate his personal interpretation of the concept of faithfulness, Professor Wu told us of the contrast between two famous translations of the classic "Diamond Sutra" from Sanskrit into Chinese.

The first was done in about 500 A.D. by an Indian scholar who knew Chinese. This scholar made two major changes. Firstly, he took all the names of places in India unlikely to be known by Chinese people and replaced them by names of more familiar places (still in India). Also, he turned the poetry into prose. The second translator, by contrast, retained (in transliterated form) the names of obscure Indian towns and rivers, and also preserved the form of verse. "Which of the two," Professor Wu provocatively asked Bob and me, "produced the more faithful translation?"

It was quite obvious he wanted us to answer, "The second translator, of course!", but before either of us could reply, Professor Wu continued, "What the first translator did would be like telling a French friend a story about Ann Arbor, but replacing the name 'Ann Arbor' everywhere by 'Chicago' — or even by 'Washington'!" With this spontaneous analogy, Wu was clearly trying to caricature the first translator's stratagem of replacing obscure town names by well-known ones, trying to bring out with maximal clarity the stratagem's utter silliness — but unintended by him, there was an amazing irony hidden in it: Wu's analogy was a beautiful example of precisely what it was intended to mock!

In his analogy, Professor Wu had converted the first translator's stratagem from Wu's own Oriental frame of reference (India viewed through Chinese eyes) into Bob's and my Occidental frame of reference (the United States viewed through French eyes). Thus tacitly, Professor Wu (much like his first translator) was relying on this maxim about clear interpersonal communication: To convey your situation's essence to someone else, use analogy to recast it in terms of *their* situation. Then — to echo Stanisław Ulam's theme song — they will see your situation as theirs, or perhaps see their situation as yours. Whichever, they will metaphorically see through your eyes.

Professor Wu presumed that the unretouched facts in their original ancient-Asian setting would be too remote to convince us modern Westerners of his firm belief: that the first translator's device of "transculturation" — that is, the use of analogy to convert not just the *form* but also some of the *content* of a story from one culture to another — is an unfaithful way of translating, and should be shunned. Yet ironically, what could be a better argument *for* transculturation than this spontaneous act of transculturation by Professor Wu himself?

I replied that I greatly appreciated his explaining things from an American point of view, adding that it was precisely this type of willingness to "bend over backwards" that I wanted to see — only in the reverse direction — in the Chinese translation of *GEB*. And thus were we circuitously led back to discussing rival strategies for translating my Crab Canon dialogue, in which, if you disentwine the speeches made by Achilles (A) from those made by his friend the Tortoise (T), thus creating two separate lists of speeches, you find that the two characters' remarks are identical, except that the *order* of the speeches of either character is reversed with respect to the other character. At the very center, in addition, one droll speech is made by — who else? — the Crab (C), who, along with his set of Genes (G), makes his very first appearance in the book right then and there.

Form's Occasional Primacy over Content

The key to everything, I explained, is the realization that the Crab Canon's final appearance utterly masks its origins. In order to construct a dialogue that could be read backwards at the speech-by-speech level, I had had to build up, with great patience, a collection of phrases in English that had two utterly unrelated meanings, such as "Not at all!", which, depending on its context, can mean "Definitely not!" or "You're welcome!" Another phrase I used is "One has no frets", which in a context where string instruments are the focus, means "A distinction between violin and guitar is that the former lacks discrete ridgelets on its fingerboard", whereas when the context is geriatric emotionality, it means "As you get older, your worries drop to zero" (hogwash, to be sure, but that's beside the point).

Precious finds like this — sentences that can swing either of two radically different ways — became the pivots of the dialogue, hingepoints that determined the majority of its content. A translator who took the Crab Canon's content very straightforwardly, assuming it had been *premeditated,* would be completely misreading my intent, for the truth was that at the outset, I, the author, hadn't cared one whit what my characters wound up saying to each other, as long as their chat had the proper symmetry and sounded reasonably coherent!

What made things more complicated, admittedly, is the fact that, as I revised the Crab Canon over a period of months, I got more sophisticated and discovered some tricks with whose help I was able to imbue my evolving dialogue with the deceptive appearance of having been constructed primarily around certain *ideas,* and only secondarily around its symmetric *structure,* rather than the reverse. The most crucial such trick was my working-in of brief mentions of three curious crab-canon-like structures in other (*i.e.,* nonverbal) media: firstly, of course, Bach's own musical Crab Canon; secondly, a marvelous visual study by M. C. Escher that consists of harmoniously interlocking parades of crabs moving in opposite directions; and thirdly, a special but surprisingly common type of DNA segment in which the message embodied in either strand's sequence of adenines, thymines, cytosines, and guanines is identical to that carried by its base-paired mate (*i.e.,* a strand with A's facing the original strand's T's, and C's facing G's), except that it runs in the reverse direction, as is illustrated by the crab-canonical segment below:

```
TTTTTTTTTCGAAAAAAAAA
AAAAAAAAAGCTTTTTTTTT
```

Thus, taken at face value, *GEB*'s Crab Canon would seem to be a verbal vehicle constructed to convey a predetermined message about crab-canonical works of music and art and crab-canonical structures in biology, whereas in fact, at the very outset, I had set my sights far lower — no premeditated message at all; just *any old* coherent symmetric dialogue. If it were not for the strong resonance that finally came to exist between the dialogue's own form and the three curious entities it describes, a Chinese translator might feel justified in constructing a smoothly-flowing symmetric dialogue in Chinese on virtually *any* topic, in tight analogy to my suggestion for how to "translate" the Panama palindrome. However, the Crab Canon's intimate form–content interaction upped the ante: Although form was still the primary — and an inviolable — aspect of the dialogue, its content, too, ought to be preserved as much as possible. This made things harder.

Obviously, reproducing the Crab Canon's exact content, sentence by sentence, would destroy the essence of the dialogue. Indeed, the very idea of such a "literal" translation verges on incoherence, since each speech but the Crab's droll soliloquy on his Genes appears twice, in spots poised symmetrically thereabout. Now, either both copies are translated *identically*, in which case half the dialogue's content has been thrown down the drain, or else they are translated *differently* in the two contexts, in which case something far more subtle and context-dependent than "literal" translation must be taking place. But then, of course, the symmetry has vanished.

To do the Crab Canon properly, translators would have to set out just as I did — first building up a sizable collection, in their own language, of phrases possessing two maximally unrelated meanings. Then, having built such a collection, they should pick out from it a set of phrases that not only can work together to make a comprehensible dialogue, but also allow references to the musical, artistic, and biological crab-canonical structures to be inserted in a non-forced way. Such a translation strategy requires constant intermingling of attention to form and attention to content.

These were essentially my dinnertable comments to Professor Wu. I wound up by stating that in many parts of *GEB,* the only way to be deeply faithful to the book's spirit was to be unfaithful to its letter. For the Crab Canon in particular, faithfulness to spirit would entail the creation of a very different dialogue in the new language! And, Bob added, that is just what he and Jacqueline Henry had done in their French translation.

Although the Crab Canon's structural tricks and these ideas about its radical re-creation were new to Professor Wu, he reacted with unabashed enthusiasm and amusement over it all. As a going-away present when he left Ann Arbor, we gave him Warren Weaver's book *Alice in Many Tongues.*

The Devil, the Demon, and the General

Close to, perhaps even precisely at, the very moment that Bob French and I were having this critical exchange over plates of pasta with Professor Wu in Ann Arbor, an oddly similar conversation was taking place halfway around the world. David Moser, freshly arrived in Beijing, had begun reading the various translated dialogues in the Chinese *GEB* manuscript in order to see what kinds of things had been done with them. One of the dialogues he was studying was "The Magnificrab, Indeed" (modeled in some ways on Bach's Magnificat in D). Toward the start of this dialogue, one character says — in the English original — "Speak of the devil!" This common remark in English, triggered by the unexpected appearance of someone who's just been mentioned, had been rendered as: *Shuō guǐ, jiù lái guǐ!* Back-translated fairly literally, this sentence means, "Mention the demon, then comes the demon!"

Always eager to learn new idioms, David asked Liu and Yan, "Is this a stock phrase in Chinese, something that everybody's heard before?"

They replied, "No, but a reader can easily imagine what it means."

David then inquired, "But does there exist an idiomatic way of saying this — a Chinese equivalent to our phrase 'Speak of the devil'?"

"Oh, yes," they replied, *"Shuō dào Cáo Cāo, Cáo Cāo jiù dào!"* And they explained to David that this famous phrase involves Cao Cao, a prominent character in the famous Chinese historical novel *Romance of the Three Kingdoms,* and means, "Mention Cao Cao, and Cao Cao then shows up!"

"Well then, how come you didn't use that phrase instead?" asked David, somewhat at a loss.

"Oh, but we couldn't do *that*!" answered Liu and Yan earnestly. "The Cao Cao phrase is so steeped in Chinese culture that only a Chinese author could have thought of it, and since readers will know that the book is by an American, it would strike them as all wrong! How would an American know about Cao Cao?"

This was a fascinating point of view, which caught David quite off guard. After stirring it around for a while, he countered as follows: "But readers will obviously know Hofstadter didn't write the book directly in Chinese — they will know it was translated. Hofstadter simply wants his book to seem graceful and totally natural — not at all foreign — to Chinese readers. In fact, his goal is precisely for it to feel as if it had been *written originally in Chinese*!" And yet, this idea, so obvious and so appealing to both me and David, seemed utterly alien to Yan and Liu.

Their protestations were vehement: "If we adopt your strategy for rebuilding the book in a pure Chinese style, then readers will feel the book is no longer by Hofstadter." And yet from my perspective, it was precisely the reverse — I would feel the book was no longer by Hofstadter if the team *failed* to adopt the translation strategy advocated by Hofstadter!

Could it be that the very idea of transculturation itself is a Western one, and strikes the Oriental mind as alien? In that case, paradoxically, the most deeply Chinese-style translation of *GEB* would be an ultraconservative one in which all Chinese idioms and metaphors were carefully eschewed, in which all Chinese vignettes or situations were strictly shunned, in which all references to the Chinese culture were religiously avoided — in short, a translation in which the book's rootedness in America was as blunt and stark as a good slap in the face. Conversely, and equally paradoxically, a translation of *GEB* such as I myself was so keen on — keen to the point of having sent, at my own expense, a personal emissary over to China to help realize it — in which every English-language pun and structural game was ingeniously re-created in flawless, sparklingly witty Chinese, in which all references to American geography, history, or culture were seamlessly replaced by lovely and crystal-clear Chinese analogues, would strike Chinese readers as being a weird, trumped-up, artificial, "foreign-style" translation. By virtue of being overly Oriental, it would be extraordinarily disorienting!

*#@! out of the Mouths of Russians

When David Moser first relayed Liu and Yan's reaction to me, I was bowled over and deeply upset. To me, their attitude seemed absolutely perverse — inscrutable, one might say — and yet, as I dredged my own memory in an effort to try to make some sense, even the tiniest amount, of their view, I had a sudden flashback that illuminated it all like a bolt of lightning: *One Day in the Life of Ivan Denisovich.*

As a graduate student, I had heard great things about Alexander Solzhenitsyn's novel about life in a Siberian prison camp. When one day on the radio I heard Solzhenitsyn speaking about his experiences in the *gulag,* I was so moved by his eloquence that I instantly went out to buy the book. Not for a moment did it occur to me that in buying an English translation I might be acquiring a *distortion* of Solzhenitsyn's work; like a naïve kid, I unquestioningly snapped up the first copy I found on the rack.

I began reading with high hopes, but after only a few pages I started to squirm. Something felt wrong. Here were prisoners supposedly in a Soviet camp yet using the most up-to-date, idiomatic, pure-American slang and obscene cusswords. The imagery that came to mind was neither remote nor alien; rather, it felt to me as if these things were taking place in some state penitentiary only a few miles away, certainly not in far-away, frozen Siberia. The more I read, the worse it got — and soon my desire to read was totally squelched. All the alien Sovietness that I knew permeated this novel seemed to have been sucked right out of it like fluff from a pillow, and replaced by familiar Americanness. I thought to myself, "Had I wanted to read an American novel, I would have bought an American novel!" — and quit in disgust. In a nutshell, this novel had been *overtranslated.*

Let me play devil's advocate for a moment. Could one not claim that this translation was making me experience exactly *what a Russian would experience* on reading the original? To a Russian reader, the slang and the vulgarities would sound up-to-date, idiomatic, and of course familiar; likewise, to this American reader, they had sounded up-to-date, idiomatic, and familiar. Is that not ideal? Or — would I have preferred the prisoners to sound awkward and old-fashioned, strange and alien?

Well, yes, precisely — perhaps not awkward, but definitely alien. My purpose in buying the novel had been to experience the *Russianness* of the prison, of the prisoners, of their way of talking. That was being denied to me by the translator's overzealousness. My hope had been to taste what it would be like to be a Russian dissident in a Russian prison, freezing in Russian, suffering in Russian, complaining in Russian — I merely wanted to gain access to this bitter world through the flexible medium of English. That may be a tall order to fill, but it is what I had fully expected.

When, a few years earlier, I had read Fyodor Dostoyevsky's *Crime and Punishment,* something of the sort is what I had experienced. Without in any way seeming incorrect or awkward, the English prose in the translation I had read nonetheless exuded a "strange" or "alien" flavor, which gave me much pleasure — something like the pleasure of arriving in a foreign city and smelling its unfamiliar odors for the first time. Although the English was not awkward in any sense, it felt almost as if many idioms had been translated quite literally, rather than replaced by cultural equivalents. This allowed me to vicariously feel what it might be like to speak and hear Russian, to use Russian idioms, to smell Russian smells, and so on. Perhaps it was simply the fact that the translator was from England whereas I was from America that gave the book a slightly "alien" flavor, but whatever the reason, that flavor was there, and I savored it. Perhaps deludedly, perhaps not, I felt as if I had genuinely read a Russian novel, had genuinely experienced Dostoyevsky, all through the medium of English.

To make my lamentations about *Ivan Denisovich* more concrete, here is a bit of the version I read, translated by Max Hayward and Ronald Hingley:

> And he pulled the thin, dirty blanket over his face and didn't hear the guys from the other half of the barracks who were crowding around the bunks waiting to be checked.
> Shukhov went to sleep, and he was very happy. He'd had a lot of luck today. They hadn't put him in the cooler. The gang hadn't been chased out to work in the Socialist Community Development. He'd finagled an extra bowl of mush at noon. The boss had gotten them good rates for their work. He'd felt good making that wall. They hadn't found that piece of steel in the frisk. Caesar had paid him off in the evening. He'd bought some tobacco. And he'd gotten over that sickness.
> Nothing had spoiled the day and it had been almost happy.
> There were three thousand six hundred and fifty-three days like this in his sentence, from reveille to lights out.
> The three extra ones were because of the leap years...

In order to provide some kind of basis for comparison and thus for judgment, I now show how the same passage was rendered by Ralph Parker:

And he buried his head in the thin, unwashed blanket, deaf now to the crowd of zeks from the other half as they jostled between the bunk frames, waiting to be counted.

Shukhov went to sleep fully content. He'd had many strokes of luck that day: they hadn't put him in the cells; they hadn't sent his squad to the settlement; he'd swiped a bowl of kasha at dinner; the squad leader had fixed the rates well; he'd built a wall and enjoyed doing it; he'd smuggled that bit of hacksaw blade through; he'd earned a favor from Tsezar that evening; he'd bought that tobacco. And he hadn't fallen ill. He'd got over it.

A day without a dark cloud. Almost a happy day.

There were three thousand six hundred and fifty-three days like that in his stretch. From the first clang of the rail to the last clang of the rail.

Three thousand six-hundred and fifty-three days.

The three extra days were for leap years.

There are differences galore, such as the striking "guys/zeks" contrast in the first paragraph, and the "cooler/cells" and "mush/kasha" contrasts in the second. The funny thing is, I don't even know what a *zek* is, other than some poor soul trapped in the *gulag*, but I don't care: I know it's someone *Russian*, whereas a *guy*, to me, is basically someone American. Of course, I know that a *guy* could be Russian, but in this context, the word just jars my ear. A somewhat subtler difference, but a quite telling one, I feel, is Hayward and Hingley's American-sounding phrase "a lot of luck" as opposed to Parker's location-neutral phrase "many strokes of luck".

What troubles me most of all is Hayward and Hingley's phrase "from reveille to lights out", in contrast to Parker's "from the first clang of the rail to the last clang of the rail". This is an amazing difference. On the one hand, we have a morning bugle call and a nocturnal switching-off, while on the other hand, we have two identical metallic clangs. Even without the Russian text at hand, I have little doubt which is the more accurate image (and I later checked it out and confirmed my intuition).

The crux of what disturbs me is the fact that the word "reveille" connotes, to my American ear — and from conversations with friends, I believe to most American ears — not just some *generic* bugle call, but a very *specific* melody, one intimately connected with the American military. The trite song known all over our land as "Reveille" (with a capital "R") even has specific words: "It's time to get up, it's time to get up, it's time to get up, in the morning!" How could one possibly get further removed from an atmosphere of Russianness? The act of placing Reveille (which even the uncapitalized "reveille" conjures up) in a Siberian *gulag* strikes me as being just about as incongruous as having one *zek* say (of course in Russian) to another, "So putcher John Hancock here, ol' buddy ol' pal! Attaboy!"

The Subtle Art of Transculturation   ◆◆◆ 151

When Is Transculturation Called For?

As I recalled my *Ivan Denisovich* disappointment, Liu and Yan's once-inscrutable "Oriental" attitude about the Chinese *GEB* seemed to be floating nearby, within my grasp: the source of their instinct to leave the alien flavor of my ideas and my native language "poking through" the Chinese veneer was pretty clear now. Although their official job was to completely cover my Occidental face with a well-done Chinese mask, they nonetheless wanted to ensure that my Caucasian "big nose" would still show through unmistakably. Such an attitude was, I now saw, not particularly Oriental after all; it was just one viewpoint on faithfulness, a viewpoint Professor Wu had advocated in front of me and them, a viewpoint I myself had embraced in a different circumstance.

And yet, despite my new-found ability to don Liu and Yan's spectacles — despite my now being able to see my own English-language book *GEB* as parallel to Solzhenitsyn's Russian-language book *Ivan Denisovich* — I remained firmly planted in my stance of advocating a transculturated Chinese translation of my book. But on what grounds could I coherently argue for transculturation of *GEB* while utterly repudiating that exact same style of translation for Russian novels?

The key variable seems to me to be the extent to which the culture is simply *part of the vehicle* for conveying a culture-independent message. Thus there are books such as *GEB* (and most books on science) whose message is primarily *culture-independent,* and then there are novels, history books, and so forth, whose message is primarily *culture-dependent.* It would make no sense whatsoever to "transculturate" a history book; if one were to do so, a history of France written in French would become a history of Germany written in German! As for novels, in most cases it would also be a disaster to "transculturate" them — to reconstruct them in the style of the target culture. Every trace of the original would be lost, and all that would remain would be a vaguely reminiscent tale told in a completely new setting.

Not that such a process is reprehensible or uninteresting. Indeed, it can give rise to the most scintillating creative works of art, such as the movie *Black Orpheus,* a modern Brazilian surrealistic fantasy closely modeled on the ancient Greek myth of Orpheus and Eurydice, whose Greek roots still are clearly visible, but only to viewers who know the myth. This kind of story adaptation is too thorough and radical, though, to count as *translation* — at least in the narrow, popular sense of the term.

The term's narrow sense would of course cover a telling of the myth of Orpheus and Eurydice in a conservative brand of Portuguese, keeping ancient Greece as the setting. A sense of stretch would arise, however, if the setting hopped across the wide, wide sea to some fictitious version of Brazil in ancient times, populated by nymphs, naiads, undines, dryads, fauns, satyrs, and sprites. Such a sizable geographical switch in setting — "transportation", one might call it — puts a severe strain on the traditional notion of translation.

By the same token, a sense of stretch would arise if, with the original Greek landscape kept as the setting, the Portuguese issuing from the mouths of the characters were too modern or too trendy in tone. Such a sizable temporal switch in setting — "transtemporation", one might call it — likewise puts a severe strain on the traditional notion of translation.

Transtemporation — Fast Forward and Rewind

I once heard an Italian woman living in the United States describe her perplexity on finding out that her own favorite book as a child — Louisa May Alcott's *Little Women* — had no appeal at all for her daughter. After some head-scratching, this woman — herself a translator of talent — finally realized that as a girl, she had read the book in an Italian translation whose language was very contemporary in tone, whereas her daughter, growing up in America, was reading the book in the original English, whose tone is much more old-fashioned, and it therefore seemed alien and dull to the daughter. The original text had been fast-forwarded by roughly a century in its italianization, and, in a certain sense, had thereby been improved. As we have seen in many "Ma Mignonne" translations, including quite a few of my own, interlanguage translators often take the liberty of this type of inter-epoch sliding as well, and quite possibly without thinking carefully about the shift that they are effecting.

Retrograde transtemporation is a delicious challenge that I have heard several people suggest now and then, but I have seen it executed in only a couple of instances. Can you imagine rewinding J. D. Salinger, John Updike, or, for that matter, William Shakespeare, into Old English, the mirror image of fast-forwarding *Beowulf* or Chaucer into modern English? How about down-dating *Lolita* into Latin, or *The Name of the Rose* into Sanskrit? Of the two actual examples of retrotranstemporation that I can think of, one is a rendering of *Winnie-the-Pooh* in Latin, called *Winnie ille Pu*. As I have never tried to read it, I cannot comment. The other is a short but virtuosic essay by the highly original science-fiction writer Poul Anderson, called "Uncleftish Beholding"; we shall meet it in Chapter 10.

Shakespeare's Slippery Identity

It is commonplace to dispute whether the bard born in Stratford-on-Avon was the author of what are called "Shakespeare's plays". Indeed, with my former graduate students Marsha Meredith and Gray Clossman, I long ago wrote an essay called "Shakespeare's Plays Weren't Written by Him, But

The Subtle Art of Transculturation ♦♦ **153**

by Someone Else of the Same Name", in which we explored quite a number of variations on this mysterious theme of how personal identity blurs deeply with the way in which proper names refer through language. And I must say, it was with a feeling of naughty delight that I carried a copy of this essay to the Folger Shakespeare Library when I presented my talk there in 1981, and donated it to their collection. I still savor the formal card they sent me acknowledging its receipt and its presence in their archives.

There is, however, a totally unrelated but equally fascinating sense of blur that swirls about the issue of Shakespearean identity as soon as translation enters the picture. Like the Italian woman who so much enjoyed *Little Women* thanks to a transtemporated translation, I have had the experience of reading short excerpts from Shakespeare in French and finding them clearer and in that sense more enjoyable than the original versions in my own native language. Whose art, then, am I enjoying? Who is Shakespeare, when "he" — or she, or they — is not speaking English?

I have heard more than one German proclaim that Shakespeare's plays in German constitute the greatest of all German literature — as good as, if not better than, the original! — a crazy-sounding claim on the face of it, but before one dismisses it, it's fun to hear the arguments. The classic translation to which people are referring when they make this claim is one carried out in the first quarter of the nineteenth century primarily by August Wilhelm von Schlegel, a key figure in early German romanticism, and Dorothea Tieck, with considerable assistance from one Count Wolf Heinrich von Baudissin. Though I've not read their translation, I've been told that, aside from the sheer beauty of the language, part of its appeal is its clarity and accessibility — much easier for an average German to understand than are German dramas written in Shakespeare's day.

In this connection, George Steiner, in his book *After Babel,* cites the early-twentieth-century critic Friedrich Gundolf on the germanization of Shakespeare, in which Gundolf passionately declares that Shakespeare's *Seelenstoff*— his "soul-stuff" — has been embodied in the German language, and that the English text, rather than merely having been *translated* into German, has *become* German. The bizarre but fascinating extremism of this attitude emerges most clearly and most strikingly when Steiner summarizes Gundolf's thesis in the following paraphrase:

> "Shakespeare" was somehow hidden inside the accidental husk of English. The teleology of his full meaning, of the "meaning of his meaning", the realization of his complete historical–spiritual presence, lay with German.

"Accidental"! The image, then, is one of Shakespeare having been somehow born in the wrong land, writing his plays and poetry in the wrong tongue, eventually dying, and then wandering around in limbo, a bit of a lost soul, until he finally "comes home" to German and Germany. Well, it's one thing when Irish-born Samuel Beckett chooses to leave his native land for France, or when Teodor Józef Konrad Nałęcz Korzeniowski is buffeted about by fate's cruel winds and winds up in England — but it's quite another thing when William Shakespeare, who never left his isle of birth, let alone set foot on German soil, is seen as having at last reached his true native land and his true native tongue, thanks to posthumous translations!

What about the perhaps less radical idea that Shakespeare's plays and poems should be gracefully transtemporated into more modern English? I don't mean into trendy, slang-peppered, rock-song English; I just mean English stripped of archaic words requiring footnotes, and devoid of strained syntactic contortions that distract from a quick apprehension of the ideas. Perhaps lyrical, poetic early-nineteenth-century English would be a good tone to strive for. In principle, I would certainly not be against a skilled poet conducting such a literary experiment — indeed, I find challenges of that sort to be intellectually exciting. Nonetheless, if such a translation were carried out, I would probably be reluctant to read too much of the product, even though such a decision might doom me to remaining forever ignorant of most of Shakespeare, whose style for me will always remain an enticing yet formidable barrier. What seems inconsistent in my position is that I have nothing against reading similarly time-shifted translations of Shakespeare into other languages. I cannot quite figure out what lies behind these clashing instincts.

Many Romeos, Many Ands, Many Juliets

In the 1950's, composer Leonard Bernstein and lyricist Stephen Sondheim took Shakespeare's play *Romeo and Juliet* and converted it from a tragedy caused by a long-standing family feud in Verona, Italy into the magical musical *West Side Story*, a tragedy stemming from the enmity of rival urban gangs in New York City. This was made into a movie in 1961, which launched a trend of cinematic re-creations of *Romeo and Juliet*, including Franco Zeffirelli's 1968 version, once again set in Italy, and just this year, two new versions, *Love Is All There Is* (set in the Bronx) and Baz Luhrmann's *William Shakespeare's Romeo and Juliet* (set in Verona Beach, Florida). What's nutty about the former is that it has been transmogrified from a tragedy into a comedy, and what's crazy about the latter is that despite the pink hair, the tattoos, the vanity license plates, and the rock-video style, it preserves the original Shakespearean language, word for word.

Janet Maslin wrote in a review in *The New York Times*, "Mr. Luhrmann's frenetic hodgepodge actually amounts to a witty and sometimes successful experiment, an attempt to reinvent 'Romeo and Juliet' in the hyperkinetic vocabulary of post-modern kitsch. This is headache Shakespeare, but there's method to its madness." What a weird anding-together of eras!

Transtemporation of the Ideas behind Words

One of the more peculiar examples of transtemporation that I recall is that of the will of Jane Stanford, who with her husband Leland founded Stanford University in memory of their son, toward the end of the nineteenth century. In her will, Mrs. Stanford — and I did consider writing "Ms.", but felt it would be too radical a transtemporation! — specified that there be no liquor on sale on the campus or within a three-mile radius of the university (the exact legal logistics of this stipulation have always eluded me, but no matter). But a few decades after her death, her will, which formerly had always been interpreted literally, was taken to court and contested, the argument being that Mrs. Stanford's will was a product of her times and had to be interpreted in other times in the light of current mores, not bygone ones. The argument won the day, the idea being roughly that had Mrs. Stanford lived decades later, she would not have imposed or even wished to impose such strictures on students and faculty. And so nowadays liquor is available to students and faculty not just within a three-mile radius but at the very heart of the Stanford campus.

This notion of literal interpretations giving way, with time, to more liberal interpretations of "sacred scriptures" of course recalls how the words of the Bible have been reinterpreted over and over in the light of changing times, so that the Catholic Church, for instance, now has no problem with the once-heretical notions of a heliocentric universe, π not equaling precisely 3, and even Darwinian evolution, including the descent of humans from apes, apes from rodents, rodents from fish, and so on down the line…

Musical and Cinematic Transtemporation

Every so often, attempts are made to modernize or update the classic King James translation of the Bible, prized for its beautiful language, so that contemporary readers can relate to the message more easily. This kind of reformist attitude inevitably spreads to other aspects of the church. Thus the Vatican, after hundreds of years of conducting its masses in Latin accompanied by solemn traditional music, dropped this requirement and proclaimed that all rites should henceforth be conducted in the local languages and could be accompanied by popular music of any sort.

Too bad the Pope didn't consult me about this matter! I would have strongly advocated leaving masses in Latin and with traditional music, based on my intuition that religion derives much of its power from the sense of mystery evoked by exotic and awe-inspiring rituals. Even I, though a nonreligious person, am touched by the flavor of the ancient rituals, especially their music.

A case of musical transtemporation that elicits stronger emotional reactions in me is the cleaning-up of recordings of jazz made in the 1930's or earlier. The original recordings have a great deal of surface noise and a rather limited frequency range. Computer sound-enhancement techniques allow the surface noise to be eliminated and the instruments to be made to sound much richer. As a result, the cleaned-up recordings sound almost as if they had been made yesterday — yet they feature artists long dead. Up till recently, I was sure how I felt on this issue: I was totally against such cleaning-up operations. However, a few years ago, a friend played for me an amazingly sharpened-up recording of Louis Armstrong's "St. James Infirmary", a song I know well and love in its original incarnation, and I was most surprised at my own positive reaction to the new version. Thanks to that experience, I feel somewhat split — I can appreciate the virtues of the clean-up transformation. Still, were I forced to choose between the old and the new recording, I would unhesitatingly take the old, for I cherish the aura of irreplaceable, bygone times that is so powerfully and beautifully conveyed by the lower quality of the original medium.

A similar type of technological transformation in the cinematic realm has recently provoked white-hot debate — namely, the colorization of old black-and-white movies. Given that computer technology is now available to help humans quickly convert a black-and-white film to color, many people are eager to see this done, even to old classics that powerfully exude the flavor of their times. The argument in favor is obvious: Color makes the picture seem realer and somewhat more attractive, at least to the retina. The opposing argument is of course one of faithfulness to the spirit of the times in which the film was made. Is it not intellectually dishonest to show a film that has been tampered with in a way that is incompatible with the era and style in which it was created?

Part of the debate centers on the fact that, although non-colorized copies of these classic old films will survive in film repositories and museums, the vast majority of copies shown in theaters and purchasable as videos will be colorized, and hence will misrepresent their eras and their directors' intentions, as far as the vast public is concerned. I personally tend to the conservative side in this particular debate, perhaps out of sentimentality; I'm not sure I could articulate my reasons convincingly. But then, I don't even like reading newspapers with color photos, and I think of color-television news coverage as being a far less faithful mirror of reality than a completely pictureless article printed in black type on white paper in *The New York Times*.

A related phenomenon in the world of cinema is the occasional production of *remakes* of classic films, using contemporary actors and updating all the sites and situations and language. My minimal personal experience with this phenomenon consists of having experienced the striking contrast between George Cukor's brilliant black-and-white 1940 film *The Philadelphia Story* and Charles Walter's star-studded 1956 color remake *High Society,* for which one of my personal heroes, Cole Porter, produced some of his weakest songs ever; between the two, I would declare the former the hands-down winner. But that does not in any way imply that I deplore or condemn the whole idea of remakes. Indeed, I find the idea quite delightful and full of rich potential.

Dubbing and Subtitles in Movies

Virtually every foreign film shown in Italy is dubbed. This leads to surprising confusions, such as when Elisabetta, a teen-aged acquaintance of ours who told Carol that she adored the voice of some American movie star (I don't remember which one); when Carol reminded her that in fact, she had never heard his real voice, but only the voice of an Italian dub-artist, Elisabetta thought for a moment and then smiled with amusement at her own mistake. It's an easy kind of mistake to make in Italy, where dubbing is such an absolute that it gets taken for granted and then forgotten.

This also leads to strange alter egos for famous people, such as Groucho Marx. The Marx Brothers' movies have all been redone in Italian, replete with Groucho's famous *sotto voce* asides, and Groucho is renowned for his sparkling Italian repartee — utterly different in Italian from English. The whole Groucho persona in English, after all, depends on his voice, his unique mode of delivery, and several boatloads of untranslatable puns. So Groucho simply has acquired a second identity in Italy.

The same goes for "Stanlio e Ollio", the Italian versions of Stan Laurel and Oliver Hardy. However, in their cases, the genial flip is that they are dubbed by actors with super-strong English accents, and their Italian grammar is likewise ludicrously bad. Thus their foreignness (Hardy was American; Laurel, born English, became American) not only is preserved in translation but is parlayed into a central aspect of their silliness, something that obviously is not the case in the original. In French, similarly, Laurel and Hardy have atrocious American accents. I remember the first time I went to a Laurel and Hardy movie in Geneva when I was thirteen, and I practically rolled in the aisles at their accents. I also got the impression, at the time, that these were their own genuine voices and accents. I've never been sure, however, if that impression was right. In any case, the terrible accents add a special zany twist to the general atmosphere of buffoonery.

In America, we tend not to dub movies, to my personal relief, so that we can experience the original voices and the alien phonemes of a foreign film. We are also given free lessons in humility if we thought we knew a foreign language well, since rapid movie dialogue is often surprisingly hard to follow even if one can conduct fluent conversations. And yet another type of lesson in humility is available for those who try to follow the dialogue at the same time as the subtitles, for then one sees how subtly the art of dialogue translation can be carried out. Not that it's always terribly well done, but on occasion, I have been rendered so jealous of the figure hidden behind the screen, whose bilingual mastery of slang and the subtle flavors of idiomatic expressions is so uncanny.

Subtitles are not a replacement of anything, but an addition to a film — they form an overlay, so that one has a kind of simultaneous bicultural interpretation of what is going on. Thus if one is sufficiently skilled at keeping two languages in one's head at once, then in watching Gérard Depardieu's Cyrano de Bergerac reciting Edmond Rostand's marvelously fluid nonstop-rhyming French couplets, one can simultaneously read, at the screen's bottom, the English subtitles by novelist Anthony Burgess, which, unfortunately, rhyme only now and then and are not nearly so fluid or charming:

> *Regarde-moi, mon cher, et dis quelle espérance*
> Tell me what exuberance
> *Pourrait bien me laisser cette protubérance !*
> I have with this protuberance!

On television and radio news programs, things are handled in another manner entirely. We tend to give a foreigner a few seconds of air time in their own language, and then let their voice fade out while a translation into English is played in the foreground. This can be most frustrating to someone who can understand the language that is being suppressed, and would like to hear the original. Thus one might see a dramatic image of dissident Chinese students huddled together at night in Tian'anmen Square and hear, masking the impassioned yet barely-audible Chinese of one of them, a lightly-accented English voiceover. At least one gets *some* kind of impression of the actual voices and sounds, if only a fleeting one. Impressions of China are not always this direct.

And Now, Live from China, Huck Finn...

Imagine Huck Finn, raggedly insouciant, holding forth in a Beijing subway. He is lugging an incredible popcorn machine, twice as big as himself. He sells the stuff. Okay, don't. It's too silly.

Still, I feel that the book *Chinese Lives: An Oral History of Contemporary China* has something of that flavor, and in fact I myself didn't invent the droll image; rather, I spliced together the opening three sentences of Studs Terkel's typically jaunty preface to that book, and two from this very book's introduction, to make the previous paragraph.

The Subtle Art of Transculturation ◆ ◆ ◆ *159*

Terkel goes on to award his highest words of praise to the amazingly vivid, living image of China that one gets from *Chinese Lives*. He exclaims: "Talk about talk! You'll find it in this work, flowing over. You'll get an earful, an eyeful, and a mindful. You'll get China." Sounds awfully good. But does Studs Terkel read Chinese?

Well, no. *Chinese Lives* started out in Chinese as a collection of about a hundred interviews with, as Terkel accurately puts it, "street vendors; corner philosophers; old women remembering pre-Liberation days, forced prostitution, and bound feet; intellectuals suffering during the Cultural Revolution; family disputants; peasant day-to-day musings; hotshot youths, Westward-Hoing; dreamers of the ideal…" These revelatory interviews were conducted by Zhang Xinxin, once an army nurse, then a theater director, television producer, and celebrated writer of fiction, and her colleague Sang Ye, a journalist and columnist. It made such a hit when published in Chinese in China that it was then slightly trimmed down and converted into Terkel's lingo by native speakers of English.

A few years ago, I received the English version as a present from Seng Lin Koh and Siva Bala, dear friends from Singapore who inscribed it in both Chinese and English, saying, "May this book give you a glimpse into the culture whose language you're most interested in." Well, I suspect I got quite a bit more from Seng Lin and Siva's present than they bargained for: not only many glimpses of China, but also scads of provocations about the nature of translation.

A Chinese Hick Who Ain't Got No Coal Book

To give you something of a sense of it, here is an excerpt from the book's very first interview, called "Popcorn", with that Beijing incarnation of Huck Finn that Terkel alluded to:

> Been in Beijing over three weeks now. I make over two yuan a day — over four on a good one. We carry our gear to outside an apartment block and shout, "Fresh popcorn!" Once you start popping you draw a crowd. One explosion works a lot better than a dozen shouts. They bring their own corn — all I do is pop it for twenty cents a time. For that I'll pop them a whole sack of corn — much cheaper than the state shops. Sometimes I don't ask them to pay, I'll do it for five pounds of grain coupons. City people are rolling in grain coupons…. Sometimes I ask for coal, especially from kids. I promise them a big handful of popcorn for free if they'll steal me a few lumps from home. Nobody counts their coal. That way I've got my fuel. The Beijing city government's got everything planned — you can't even get coal without showing your book. If you're from out of town and you ain't got no book, forget it. Okay. So I get the Beijing kids to steal it for me….
>
> Government kids are real softies but I'm no match for them — their dads carry too much clout. Those kids give me a bad time. They call me a hick. I didn't used to know that word, but I do now….

When I first read this, my jaw nearly dropped with amazement at the language. After many readings I still find it jarring. How would the translator — William J. F. Jenner — justify putting the phrase "you ain't got no book" into the mouth of someone speaking hard-core street Chinese? Beijing is not an American inner city! And how can a nonspeaker of English be quoted as saying, "I didn't used to know the word 'hick', but I do now"? Well, *of course* this teen-aged hick of a popcorn vendor didn't know — and still doesn't know — the word "hick", because it's a slangy, flavor-packed *English* word! Oh, yes, to be sure, there's some Chinese word that plays a vaguely analogous role, but there's no way that either word can be thought of as *being* the other! Also note in the final sentence the phrase "I didn't used to", which is a very informal, oral-only, native-speaker type of usage. What is it doing here? And perhaps less obvious, yet cut from the same cloth, how could Jenner dare to put flavor-loaded English words and expressions — "kids", "okay", "softies", "rolling in grain coupons", "forget it", "carry clout" — into a Beijing popcorn vendor's mouth?

Vanilla English versus Spicy English

I read with much interest on the book's back cover a blurb that says, "The language is so lively that an American reader can 'hear' what was being said and identify with the sentiment of the speaker. This is a great achievement." Well, maybe so, maybe not. In any case, here is how the book's translator/editors — Delia Davin and Jenner himself — describe their philosophy of translation:

> The task was frustrating because translation was bound to lose some of the variety and individuality of the different voices. We could not have people from all over China speaking a single regional dialect of English, nor did we feel it would be appropriate to use a variety of recognizable forms from around the English-speaking world, making readers feel they were listening to Jamaicans, Geordies, Kentuckians, Dubliners and so on. We have also tried to avoid sticking so close to the Chinese idiom that instead of responding to the speakers' humanity, readers would be preoccupied by their exoticism. We hope that our linguistic equivalent of monochrome has not done too much injustice to the subtle shadings of the originals.

Clearly, and most reasonably, they are concerned with the following key question a translator must face: What medium — in other words, what variety of English — to translate into? They mention four specific regional varieties, just to point out that no regional dialect would be their medium of choice. They understandably want more universality, less "exoticism", than that. It would be ridiculous if residents of Beijing came out sounding like Dubliners, Shanghai residents like Jamaicans, peasants from Guilin

Province like Kentuckians, and so on. Davin and Jenner are seeking a kind of accentless, nonlocal, nonexotic voice in their target medium.

However, despite their praiseworthy search for local-accent-freeness or geographical neutrality, Davin and Jenner don't mention the closely related idea of "non-flavored" English, what might even be called "vanilla" English — that is, English that is both fluent and highly articulate, yet that at the same time scrupulously avoids highly "spiced" words and idioms. (I note that for some reason, in trying to characterize this type of English, I'm not able to avoid cooking metaphors.) And just why should such spiciness be so scrupulously shunned?

Because the spicier an English phrase is, the less universal it is — that is, the more it tends to suggest one or another specific subculture *inside the English-speaking world* — and the more densely one piles spicy English words and phrases together, the more firmly will the reader's imagery associated with this or that narrow stereotype of geographical and cultural provenance be locked in. Indeed, since I haven't been able to think of any better way to put my finger on just what I mean by "spiciness", I'll let the previous sentence itself serve as my definition of the notion.

One Day in the Life of Mr Average

Lest the foregoing seem too abstract and hence too elusive, let me supply you with what for me is a crystal-clear example of very spicy, definitely non-vanilla English, this time an excerpt from an interview called "Mr Average", anglicized by Geremie Barmé:

> Just look at our mill. They haven't got a clue about what to do with the foreign machinery they've bought. They finally got this technical expert from some company in Hongkong. Couldn't see the management for all the arse-licking that was going on. The man could do no wrong. If the truth be told none of them have the faintest idea about the technical side. They spend all their time swilling tea in their offices. People blather on about China going to the dogs if people like me had a say in the running of things; but we'd all be in the shit if everyone was like them, believe you me. They buy their technical expertise with our money. Who needs them? It'd be a different matter if they knew their jobs. Screw 'em. The high and mighty section head pointed at a crane one day and asked what the "10T" painted on the side of it meant. It's a disgrace. A few months back they gave 'em all the boot and put in a bunch of specialists. But all the old penpushers are still doing okay for themselves organizing gardening brigades, canteen committees and that factory beautification office — screw 'em....
>
> If you ask me love's a load of crap.... there's no way I'd ever marry a hayseed. I don't care what they say about the villages being rich nowadays. Marry a peasant and you have one foot in the sticks....
>
> I can't make any comparisons. There's tons of other young workers like me about. Some are more political than me, others worse. I'm just Mr Average.

In reading this, I'm distracted like all getout from the speaker's humanity, because I'm intensely preoccupied by what Jenner and Davin might call the *non*exoticism (that is, the utter lack of Chineseness) of his language. "Arse-licking"!? "Screw 'em"!? Those are amazing things to have Mr Average say — especially the dropped "th". Or take "There's tons of others like me about." What next — will Mr Average start dropping his "h"'s in the Cockney manner? "Lemme tellya, guv'na, it's an 'elluva way ta treat a chappie, eh?" Where does one draw the line?

To explore this question of the limits of plausibility, suppose that, just for fun, we push things a little in the fantasy direction, and put some hypothetical words in Mr Average's frustrated mouth, such as these:

> The sons and daughters of cadres are born with silver spoons in their mouths. Screw 'em. They just float through the system not payin' their dues, but when it comes to us lowborn types, we get no leeway. Hell, we don't have a Chinaman's chance! The powers that be look down from their fancy-shmancy perches and say to us, "Ho ho — no tikkee no washee!" Well, I say, screw 'em. Here's a frinstance for ya. When my son tried to take both chem and bio in high school, just like his friend the cadre's son did the year before — and mind you, my kid's got quite the head for science, and his friend don't at all — the friggin' headmaster had the chutzpah to tell him, "No way, José! You get one science course per year, full stop. Like old Confucius say: 'Pay one bowl rice, get one bowl rice!' So no favors for you, Charlie Chan!" Well, if I had my druthers, I'd string 'em all up and let 'em twist in the wind.

Surely even translator Barmé would not dare go this far; it is both absurd and in bad taste to put into the mouth of a native of China such crude English-language stereotypes of Chinese people as "Confucius say", "No tikkee no washee", "Charlie Chan", "a Chinaman's chance" — and it seems all the more so when one considers that the speaker of this diatribe was supposedly not speaking English but in reality speaking Chinese. What would that mean? How could you even *say* such things in Chinese itself?

Although this last quote was made up and not genuine, I would say that in some sense the "real" one too was made up and not genuine. That is, I have the sense that some powerful distorting filter has been interposed between me and Mr Average. His anger comes across, of course, but it's got far too strong of a native-English-speaker feel to it; the language fairly *reeks* of a culture halfway around the world from China, believe you me.

Indeed, to me, reading the passage where Mr Average vents his spleen with such splendid English eloquence brings back fond memories of many a balmy summer Sunday afternoon spent at Speaker's Corner in London's lovely Hyde Park, listening to crackpots perched on soapboxes with a bee in their bonnet and a small crowd around them amusedly listening and occasionally egging them on with hilarious retorts, as they rant bitterly away about this or that wretched aspect of the evil British society, often in the most delightfully colorful and of course utterly native English. The only difference is that Mr Average, for God knows what half-baked reasons, has decided to substitute, every so often, words like "Hongkong", "China", and "brigade" for words like "Glasgow", "England", and "clique". Mr Average is decidedly not Chinese; he's just a British soapbox orator ranting and raving about China. Maybe he's even of Chinese extraction and *looks* Chinese, but he *sounds* born and bred British.

Geremie Barmé is clearly a very skilled translator, but this translation goes way overboard in stripping Mr Average of his Chineseness, and the same can be said for virtually all the anglicized interviews in *Chinese Lives*. Maybe that's just exactly what some people want — Studs Terkel, for one — but for me, the result, though fascinating on one level, is ludicrous and grotesque on another.

Artistic Masks versus Straight Talk

Ah, but who am *I* to complain? I'm the one who put "pretty posh stuff to nosh" into the mouth of French Renaissance poet Clément Marot, right? And wasn't I the American fellow who wanted his own book *GEB* to be transculturated so that it would read in Chinese as if it had been written by a native Chinese speaker? Talk about double standards...

Perhaps, but I would fight the label. Let's take the case of the Marot poem first. Here, we are talking about translating an artistic pose. In "Ma Mignonne", we are not listening to Clément Marot spouting off with his guard down to some friend about the Catholic church or French nobility; after all, Marot didn't go around speaking to his friends in verse. When he wrote poetry, he was donning a kind of formulaic mask or artistic persona, and part of the goal of translating his poem (or any poem) is to create a similar formulaic mask in another culture. The phrase "pretty posh stuff to nosh" helps to create that second mask — in this case, by setting a highly playful, informal tone. Above and beyond the get-well message, *art* was the point of Marot's poem, which could not in the least be claimed true for Mr Average's monologue. Mr Average was just letting steam off willy-nilly, and certainly wasn't trying to create a polished, refined work of art in words.

Secondly, as for my advocating a total Chinese transculturation of *Gödel, Escher, Bach,* it's actually a little subtler than that. My overarching goal for all of the book's various incarnations, no matter what the target language or culture might be, was for a certain constellation of intellectual ideas, as well as certain styles of linguistic and structural game-playing, to be transmitted with maximal vividness and spark. Therefore, as the author of the book, I too was inevitably donning masks — here a lively science-teacher's mask, there a fanciful dialogue-writer's mask — as opposed to revealing autobiographical truths in my most frank and undisguised voice (as in the interviews in *Chinese Lives*). When either of those masks was in place, I wanted my readers and translators not to think of me as particularly American but to take the text at a far higher level of abstraction. The book was, in my view, a work of art one of whose prime characteristics was its esthetic aspect. This meant that for translators, the doors were wide open to re-creation, using the devices of liberal analogical reconstruction and no-holds-barred transculturation, just as I described above in connection with the Crab Canon. The transculturated science-teacher's or dialogue-writer's mask would be thereby created, and the book's esthetic aspect would, by being re-created, be preserved.

In the rare spots in *GEB*, however, where I inserted actual vignettes from my own life — minuscule snippets of straight autobiographical reality, not usually as passionate but just as unvarnished as Mr Average's outburst — then all of a sudden, I felt there was no artistic mask and therefore no call for transculturation, no pressure at all for re-creative playfulness. Let me give an example.

In a sentence toward the beginning of *GEB*'s Chapter 19, I recall a pleasant afternoon at an American football game, sitting next to a friend whose offhand counterfactual musing about an alternate pathway that the just-completed down might have followed caught my attention and in fact wound up triggering a profound and many-year fascination on my part with just such "trivial", everyday counterfactual musings. When the French version of *GEB* was being worked on, two problems arose with this innocent-seeming sentence of the original English text. Firstly, French grammar forced Bob French and Jacqueline Henry to assign a gender to this spectator, whereas in the original English the sentence had been written in such a way that the gender was left out. The person had in fact been a woman, but Bob and Jacqueline, not knowing that, had used the default masculine term, thus converting her into a man. Secondly, they deftly substituted the sport of rugby for the sport of football, since French readers are far more familiar with rugby than with American football.

When I read this sentence in their manuscript, I was struck dumb with amazement. Bob and Jacqueline were turning a true event in my life into a completely fictitious event! Since first of all, the woman sitting next to me at the football game was a close friend of my parents whom I had known ever since early childhood, and since second of all, I have never in my life been to or even wished to go to a rugby game, I adamantly did not want either of Bob and Jacqueline's small distortions, trivial though they were, to be propagated. They would not be faithful to the true story that I, the author, was recalling and recounting with affectionate memories. Thus this is an example of a passage in *GEB* where transculturation (having American football slip into rugby) would be the wrong choice, because simple, unadorned truth, rather than vividness of imagery, is the overriding pressure here.

Curiously enough, although it wasn't any problem at all to convince Bob and Jacqueline to reinstate the femininity of my old friend, it took literally hours of arm-twisting on my part to get them to kick rugby out and reinstate football! In doing the many previous chapters and dialogues they had gotten so used to deep transculturation that it was becoming a reflex, and as a result it wound up taking all of my rhetorical and negotiating skills to argue them out of it in this case.

When Yan Fu's Virtues of Clarity and Grace Override Truth

One final example will help to show how many unexpected zigzags lie on the path to faithful translation. In another part of *GEB*'s Chapter 19, I wanted to describe how a complex and highly polished artistic product is produced by a human mind, and so I chose an example from my own firsthand experience — the genesis of the Crab Canon — partly because I knew the story from inside and thought it was both intricate and illustrative, but also because readers of *GEB* would *ipso facto* possess this particular artistic product, in fact between the same two covers as Chapter 19 itself. A reader could thus jump back and forth between the Crab Canon and Chapter 19's discussion of its genesis, following the connection. My choice was therefore made in the interest of compactness and self-containedness.

In telling my tale of the genesis of the Crab Canon, I mention my personal search for doubly-sensed phrases in English, and I use "not at all" to show the kind of thing I was ideally aiming for. Well, when Bob and Jacqueline translated this paragraph of Chapter 19, they replaced my English example with a French one. More specifically, instead of citing my phrase "not at all", they cited their own find, the doubly-sensed idiomatic expression *finir au violon,* which occurs twice in their own *Canon cancrizans* (first meaning "switch to the violin" and later meaning "wind up in jail"). They made this replacement in order that the French version of *GEB* be self-contained and compact precisely as the English version was — so that a reader could jump back and forth between the *Canon cancrizans* and Chapitre 19's discussion of its genesis, following the connection.

Had Bob and Jacqueline left my phrase "not at all" in their French text, then no such jumping-back-and-forth would have been possible; their paragraph would then have described, in a French-language book, the genesis of an English-language dialogue that is found only in an English-language book. That was too awkward, and so English became French. But since the passage is written in the first person (*i.e.,* I am telling readers about a creative episode in my own life), they had effectively converted *me* into an avid collector of *French* doubly-sensed phrases. This, just like the placement of me at a rugby game, was an outright falsification of history —

in fact, a more serious one, since French readers would have no reason to see anything odd in my going to a rugby game, but surely they'd know that I'd written *GEB* in English and that the French chapters and dialogues were *not* due to me. So the falsity of Bob and Jacqueline's maneuver would be out in broad daylight, obvious to any thoughtful reader!

And yet, in the end, Bob, Jacqueline, and I agreed to leave the image of the author dreaming up French symmetries and creating his dialogue in French, rather than destroying the self-containedness of the French book. Note, amusingly, that this acceptance of the falsification of an episode in my life is the opposite of the outcome of the rugby episode, where I would not stand for such a thing. The pendulum swung the "false" way this time because the pressures of *simplicity and elegance* — that is, *clarity and grace,* as Yan Fu put it (speaking English, of course!) — simply overwhelmed the powerful pressure to tell the full and honest *truth.* Clarity and grace do not *always* beat out truth, to be sure, but in this case the subtle array of forces was such that they did. Very subtle combinations and interactions of pressures make all the difference, and I cannot imagine there being any hard-and-fast theory that could explain all such choices in translation.

Wheeling and Dealing over Artistic Truth

While dredging my memory of those delightful tussle-filled days, I recalled one last ingredient in the mix, the one that did the final tipping of the balance. Over the years of work on the French *GEB,* Bob, Jacqueline, and I had many debates and disagreements, and often I would give in on one battle if they would let me win another. I found this idea downright funny; never before had it occurred to me that the search for truth and beauty might resemble crass political wheeling and dealing in smoke-filled back rooms. And yet, these little *quid pro quo*'s pitting one translational quarrel against a totally unrelated one just cropped up over and over again. Thinking of a concession made in one fight as a bargaining chip to be used in another became par for the course for us all (a little bit like a marriage!). And by no means were the battle lines always the same — sometimes it was Bob and me against Jacqueline, sometimes Jacqueline and me against Bob, and sometimes, as in this case, it was me versus them. And, I must say, all three of us got a big kick out of these fights. This illustrates the idea (which we will come across again in its Italian and English incarnations in Chapter 14) that *les amours les plus belles se nourrissent de querelles,* or, flipping it around a little flippantly, *un amour sans bagarres, ça te fout le cafard.* If this eludes you, feel free to flip ahead to Chapter 14.

As I was saying, on this particular occasion there were two unresolved battles going on at once: the football/rugby battle and the "not at all"/*finir au violon* battle. Although I cared about both, I was more concerned with the former, so I proposed a deal: I would concede truth to simplicity in the *finir au violon* case provided that Bob and Jacqueline would switch rugby back to American football, thus in that case conceding clarity to truth. Being reasonable people, they accepted my generous offer with only a little bit of grumbling.

Unfortunately, this particular fight took place entirely via transatlantic telephone, and as I recall, my phone bill that month was over a thousand dollars. So in the end, though the rugby victory may have been mine, it was rather a Pyrrhic one.

From "GEB: an EGB" to "Jí Yì Bì"

Well, to round out our chapter symmetrically, let us flip around the globe from Paris to Beijing. No one will be surprised to hear that after David Moser had been in Beijing for a while, he managed to swing Yan and Liu, and with them, Wang Pei and Guo Weide, who were the translation team's two other key players, away from their initial conservatism and over to a more radical and playful pro-transculturation policy. Thus, just to give two little examples, one finds in the Chinese Magnificrab the ultra-Chinese idiom involving Cao Cao, and the Chinese version of the Crab Canon possesses perfect symmetry and great elegance, thanks to a well-chosen set of doubly-sensed Chinese phrases.

What about Chapter 19's discussion of the genesis of the Crab Canon? There, the team opted, after wrestling with it for a long time, for the history-falsification path, as in the French *GEB*. One thus reads of me, the American author, assiduously collecting doubly-sensed phrases in Chinese, and the author then describes his personal little eureka experience in coming up with *zhōumò yúkuài* — "pleasant weekend" — which works both as a salutation (by which the Tortoise opens the dialogue) and as a farewell (by which Achilles closes it). Of course, this American author never had any such eureka experience in Chinese — but the bald-faced lie makes the story a little bit better!

The group got so much into the swing of transculturation that one day Liu Haoming blurted out to David Moser, as they were looking back at how things had evolved over the years, that the products of their initial highly conservative style of "faithfulness" had been "like Szechuan food without any spice". This spontaneously generated Chinese image was a superb transculturation of my American image "as flat as a Coke that's lost all its fizz", yet totally unintended as such: Liu had never once heard that phrase.

From what I can gather, the Chinese team's collective accomplishment has resulted in a sparkling, snappy version of *Gödel, Escher, Bach*, containing a good number of unprecedented types of wordplay in Chinese, and as I write, it is just about to appear in China, at long last. The Chinese version's subtitle, *Jí Yì Bì*, gives a little taste of its translators' freshness and verve: the three characters, when said aloud, sound just like the English letters "G–E–B", but what they mean is "Collection of Exotic Jade", echoing the semantics of the phrase "Eternal Golden Braid".

A Tip of My Hat to Professor Wu

I am sad to say that Professor Wu died in Beijing of a heart attack in 1987, at the age of 69. Not only was he the person who initially conceived the idea of translating my book, but also he was very open-minded about how it should be done. The final product of his faithful team thus owes a great deal to his adventurous spirit, and I feel confident he would have heartily approved of it. I even like to think that Professor Wu would have agreed with me that *Jí Yì Bì* beautifully incarnates the three maxims of his favorite translator, Yan Fu. Out of respect and gratitude, therefore, the Chinese edition of *Gödel, Escher, Bach* has been dedicated to the cherished memory of Professor Wu Yunzeng — "Andrew", as he would like me to say.

●

Poems VI:

~ Bold Ventures ~

* * *
* *
*

Bob French, not to be outdone by the virtuosic minimalism of David Moser's "Sweet Sue", quickly chipped in a one-syllable-per-line translation — or rather, condensation — of the original. Obviously, unlike David's effort, Bob's minuscule "Love" does not respect the syllable-count of the Marot poem.

Overall, this skinny little poem flows rather smoothly and forms, I think, a charming addendum to "Sweet Sue" (the original or the revision). I am not satisfied, however, with the way it ends: "love / dove". Though at first this looks like a fine echo of the beginning, precisely in the Clementine spirit of putting the words "Ma mignonne" at both top and bottom, in my view that is a false analogy. The proper analogy would have the first line serve also as the last line — and since the first line is the word "love", the last line should also be that word. Hence if I had my esthetic druthers, I would reverse Bob's final two lines. Not that "dove / love" *sounds* better to me — quite the reverse! — but intellectually it is far more satisfying, which in my view easily compensates for the sacrifice in sonority that it would entail.

One other curious reversal issue arises here. Repeating what he did in the original version of "Fairest Friend", Bob has switched the sign on the weight-change vector. That is, whereas Marot's fond hope was for his *mignonne* to gain weight, Bob in "Love" urges his fairest fantasy friend not to put on an ounce more: "Pray / stay / in / thin, / slim / trim". One might justify Bob's transmogrification of Marot's thought by pointing out that whereas back in the sixteenth century, buxom ripeness was all the rage (remember Rubens' chubby beauties), our century is obsessed with svelte sleekness. This fact could be taken as implying that "Hey babe, stay sleek 'n' tawny for me!" is the optimal inter-era translation — the proper transtemporation — of the old-time request, "Prithee, grow ever thou plumper, sweet pet!"

Cute though this idea is, I don't think it's what Bob had in mind. I seriously doubt that he explicitly made a careful study of different centuries' varying conceptions of stereotypical feminine desirability and then, putting to practical use the theoretical analogy-making expertise that he had already acquired in his then-ongoing doctoral work in my research group, consciously executed this conceptual reversal. Rather, I suspect the explanation is much simpler.

Bob, like most of us, is unconsciously pervaded by our own era's stereotypes, standards, and norms, which make us all susceptible to powerful top-down effects on the process of understanding spoken or written language. The slightest suggestion of a complex, subjective topic — for instance, feminine beauty — is likely to trigger a whole slew of subconscious prejudices built up in our memory over a lifetime, which swiftly rush in and influence our comprehension process, often severely contaminating it, leading us to hear what we expected rather than what was actually expressed, and thus, at the output end, to produce a distorted rendition of what we received.

In a nutshell, I think Bob simply got it in his head that the girl should *look good,* and to him, what that meant was obvious: *being thin.* No deliberate, intellectually sophisticated, transtemporal, transcultural reversal was involved — just a hasty misreading. And yet, even if Bob's reversal of the original meaning and imagery was executed entirely reflexively and unconsciously, the process involved could *still* be claimed to be one of many valid manners of effecting cross-cultural translation.

Love

Robert French

Love
dove,
still
ill?
"Fly   *5*
high!"
I
cry,
"Why
lie   *10*
so
low?"
For
your
sweet   *15*
treat,
eat
meat,
jam,
ham.   *20*
Pray
stay
in
thin,
slim   *25*
trim,
love
dove.

The members of the Fluid Analogies Research Group were by this time quite excited by what was going on. Clearly, we were starting to explore the gray areas if not the very fringes of the notion of "translation", and the ideas thereby churned up were driving us to push our explorations even further out. In all this ferment, many strange avenues were dreamt up, considered to some extent, and at times fully realized. The facing poem by Melanie Mitchell is one such little brainstorm. By examining the poem itself, can you figure out what her idea was?

It was a somewhat peculiar challenge that Melanie set herself: that of building an English translation utilizing the maximal number of French–English *cognates* — words having a common origin somewhere back in history, even if today they are often quite distant semantic cousins, having developed independently over hundreds of years in lands sharply separated by a wide, watery, unbridged, unchunneled channel. More specifically, Melanie's idea was to look at each line of Marot's verse, to seek in it at least one French word that had an English cognate, and then around that English word to build a semi-plausible line with at least a vaguely related meaning. Starting from this quite bizarre premise, which depends upon the fact that French and English are just teeming with cognates, Melanie came up with "My Minion", a lumpy and bumpy yet pleasing pastiche, most striking for its florid and Latinate lingo.

Probably the subtlest French–English cognate used here is line 14's "Alley-oop!" — an English way of saying *Allez hop !* (which is a French way of saying "Alley-oop!"). The reason it counts as a cognate is that Marot's word *va* (line 14 of the original French poem) is the familiar imperative of the verb *aller* ("to go"), and *allez* is simply its more formal counterpart, derived from the same verb. More tersely put, "alley" is roughly *allez*, which is roughly *va.*

As for "vimfully" (line 11) and "frisky" (line 14), it's not really clear whether they stem from the same sources as *vitement* or *friande.* In fact, it's dubious, although the sounds are similar. As you read those lines, therefore, you are kindly entreated momentarily to look, in benign and bounteous benevolence, the other way.

My Minion

Melanie Mitchell

My minion,
To you I donate
A benign journey;
Your sojourn
Is prison. 5
Take care
To recover;
Posthaste open
Your portal,
And make a sortie 10
Vimfully,
For Clement
Thus commands you.
Alley-oop! Thou frisky
Of embouchure, 15
Who art couched
In danger —
Go to a manger
Of confectionery.
If thou endurest 20
In this malady,
A faded color
Wilt apprehend,
Along with perdition
Of thy bounteous points. 25
Deity donate to thee
Benevolent sanity,
My minion.

As a result of the letter I sent out in a scattershot manner to many literary friends around the world, I got back many poems. One of the very first came from O.B. Hardison, then director of the world-famous Folger Shakespeare Library in Washington, D.C. From his cover letter, I couldn't quite tell whether or not O.B. had actually improvised this poem, "Dear, Your Bard", while sitting at his typewriter (it was definitely typed, not worked out or printed with the help of a word processor). The letter consisted of a sweet poem in trisyllabic rhyming couplets that began as follows: "Hofstadter: / Gentle Sir, / Take this sheet, / Here complete: / A translation / As I mention, / Of Marot. / Watch it go!" These choppy lines then segue'd straight into his translation, "Dear, Your Bard", shown on the facing page, which in turn was followed by yet more verse, whose last lines ran this way: "Maybe later / I'll do better. / Let me know / How things go. / Cordially / Yours, O.B."

In a P.S., as a friendly closing gesture, Hardison typed out a very short poem by Goethe entitled *Wanderers Nachtlied* (a.k.a. *Über allen Gipfeln*), offering it as a counterchallenge to me. I regret to say that I never took him up on it. A few years later, I was truly saddened to hear that O.B. had died, not all that long after having published a collection of personal ruminations on science, entitled *Disappearing Through the Skylight*.

O.B.'s translation, whether improvised or not, definitely fell on the erotic side of the fence — no doubt how he interpreted the relationship between Clément and his friend! Though it had charm, I felt there were a number of glitches in "Dear, Your Bard", which of course would all be forgiven if it had indeed been improvised — the extra syllable in line 5, various near-rhymes such as "soon/room", "bon-bon/Clément", "food/good", and "bony/honey", and — most grating on my ears — totally wrong stress patterns in lines 25–27. Given O.B.'s deep Shakespearean link as well as the persona implied by his ditty's title, his near-rhymes could perhaps be excused as having been genuine rhymes in the Bard's day, like Melanie's "love/remove" rhyme in "To My Sweet", but still and all, I couldn't help being bothered by the sum total of the many little glitches.

Since I appreciated the verve of this poem enough to want to see it just right, I typed it into my computer and began uninvitedly tampering with it. Well, one tampering led to another, and pretty soon it had become a wholesale revamping effort on my part. By the end, I had taken almost complete possession of the poor poem. What resulted was a kind of homage from me to O.B. Hardison, in which I not only fixed the glitches I perceived but also added a couple of new Shakespearean allusions, as well as gave it the new title "Your Old Bard". It was probably arrogant of me to have done this revamping, but I had just gotten carried away. In any case, it was driven by a good cause: a desire for esthetic perfection. I don't know whether others will see my final result as a strengthening or a weakening of O.B.'s poem; I thought I would just exhibit the two of them together and let them both be enjoyed or groaned at, whichever the case may be.

The echo of "Sweets" in lines 15–16 has the neat property that the second time can be heard equally easily as meaning "sweet food" or "darling". But the most peculiar feature of my conversion of "Dear, Your Bard" into "Your Old Bard" is line 12, locus of the poet's self-naming. Whereas O.B.'s choice was to leave the designator as "Clément", thus modestly keeping himself out of the picture, I took the liberty of shifting the pointer from Marot to Hardison. On one level, this would seem quite fitting, but the weird thing is that by the time I was done with my thorough revision, I had contributed more lines to the end result than Hardison had! Despite my helping hand, however, it would have seemed utterly wrong for me to insert any reference to myself into the poem. (In addition, the double meaning of "O.B." was too delicious to let me do that. It was only days later that I noticed a second occurrence of "O.B." — the initial letters of "Out" and "Blot" on lines 13 and 14, an even more delicious coincidence. Or was it a coincidence? I'm not sure myself.)

Dear, Your Bard	**Your Old Bard**
O.B. Hardison	O.B. Hardison/D. Hofstadter

Dear, your bard	Your Old Bard	
Sends this card:	Sends this card:	
"Get well soon."	"Health resume."	
Days in room	Days in room —	
Are years in jail.	Years in jail.	5
Do not fail:	So don't fail:	
Get well, hear?	Get well, hear?	
Then appear	Then appear	
At your door,	At your door,	
Well once more.	Fit once more,	10
Sweet bon-bon,	Bon-bon mine.	
Your Clément	O.B.'s line:	
Says, "Quick! Out!"	"Out, vile spot,	
Think about	Blot her not!"	
Dainty food	Sweets you need,	15
(Tastes so good	Sweets, indeed:	
Served in bed)	Jellied bread	
Or, instead,	Served in bed:	
Sweetest fruit.	Fruity fuel.	
You'll be moot	Else, dear, you'll	20
If you stay	Go all gray,	
Sickly gray —	Rot away.	
Your plump ass	So I say,	
Like dry grass,	With a hey	
And bony.	Nonny-no,	25
So, honey,	This bon mot:	
God heal you.	"Heal you, He'll;	
Then we'll screw.	Screw then, we'll!"	

Only a day or two after hearing from Hardison, I received a very short letter from the literary critic and author Hugh Kenner in Baltimore, with whom I had had some friendly correspondence a few years earlier. Kenner's letter consisted mostly of a tiny poem called "Hey, Chick". I enjoyed it but found its fourth line, featuring the famous pharmaceutical symbol, somewhat murky. In any case, I was pleased he had taken the trouble to contribute an effort, and did my best to reply in kind, as follows:

> Dear Hugh,
>
> Thank you.
> Bit terse,
> Your verse.
> I dug
> It.
>
> *Doug*

Kenner's reply to this note included the following comment: "The 'Hey Chick' poem was like an X-ray of Venus' skull; I most like the fact that the 'R_x' cannot be pronounced." I guess some people just like to be perverse. In any case, Kenner's mini-effort helped to expand my growing sense of the sorts of bizarre avenues that might be attempted. For example, my "Touchstones" in Poems I owes its existence to this version by Kenner, as do two of the items in Poems VII.

*　　　*　　　*

One day in April of 1987 I received, totally unexpected, a note from Michael Kandel, translator of Stanisław Lem's science fiction, with a manuscript he'd just completed of *Fiasco,* a new Lem novel. I read much of the book, and this led to a stimulating exchange of letters in which I found out, to my surprise, that Kandel had gone to graduate school at Indiana University and had done his dissertation on translations of Alexander Pushkin's poetry into Polish. Small world! A few months later, the "Ma Mignonne" whirlwind started up, and so I fired off to Kandel my standard "'Ma Mignonne' challenge" letter. The cute poem on the facing page was his rapid reply. Just as Kandel's prose in translating Lem tends to the terse side, this too was terse — in fact, ultra-terse.

Much of our correspondence was about the Lem novel's sexism. I wrote to Kandel:

> Lem's sexist prose, aside from giving offense, simply looks terribly dated; in a few years, I'd guess, it will look even more so. The book repeatedly portrays males as standard, as the "doers" of society, always treating "man" as equivalent to "human", taking for granted that the reader is male (able and willing to mate with women). Women are recognized with hesitation, and condescendingly at best. Do you feel innocent of such sexism, simply the faithful reproducer of Lem's views and usages in English? Certainly, being unfaithful to a text at one level in order to be more faithful to it at another would be nothing new to you. Couldn't you take advantage of English's remarkable flexibility to avoid sexism, creating something really *new,* just as you have habitually "reproduced" Lem's wordplay by creating truly new ideas and images in English?

Kandel replied, saying that he fully agreed with my opinions, and that with Lem's permission, he had in fact excised from the original Polish version a very vehement two-page antifeminist tirade! He added, "Lem's sexism doesn't offend me. It's a weakness, and not his only weakness. The wisest and most enlightened of us have their weak, foolish sides." And after reading Albert Einstein's extremely disappointing, terribly cold letters to Mileva Marič, his first wife, I must say that I certainly agree.

Hey, Chick

Hugh Kenner

Hey, chick,
You sick?
Ungood.
R$_x$ food.
Eat fruit,   5
Stay cute,
My chick.

Good Morning, Little Hon'

Michael Kandel

Good morning, little hon',
In bed, so frail.
Your sick state's hardly fun —
It's more like jail.
To break out free,   5
You need to eat an apple pie —
Or something sweet as you are. Try!
Bon appétit.

By this time, I was getting so deeply wrapped up in the challenge of translating "Ma Mignonne" that I was distributing it to all sorts of friends, colleagues, and relatives. Thus eventually it reached my mother in California. Now of all people, my mother is the one to whom I most clearly owe my love for words and language in general, and so she was a natural to give it to. On the other hand, my mother has always had a remarkably different verbal style from mine. Where I tend toward strict discipline and crystalline pattern, she tends toward anarchy, irregularity, and capricious unpredictability. And so it was that when I first saw this translation by her, I was very disappointed at how little she had respected the tight form of Marot's poem. I felt she had thumbed her nose at him — and it didn't help when she told me she had taken only five or ten minutes to do it.

It took me a while to come to appreciate the wonderful lightness that her playful, slangy style gave to the poem, but nowadays I think of this one, ironically, as one of the most faithful of all to the deep, Clementine spirit of the original — faithful despite the fact that it doesn't respect Marot's number of lines, his number of syllables per line, his rhyming pattern, his first-line/last-line sameness, his semantic couplets, or practically anything else in my ever-so-carefully-drawn-up list of formal properties! This just goes to show the unbelievable subtlety and intangibility of what translation is all about — in fact, of the act of penetrating to the essence of what a text is all about and feels like.

One thing is obvious: My mother read the Marot poem in purely romantic terms, and reconstructed it in saucy-French-postcard style, throwing in the hilarious stereotype of a high-pitched female squeal ("oo-la-*la*!") followed by a reference to a wiggling fanny of the sort one might see in a risqué 1950's French movie showing a rear view of high-heeled Parisian women prancing provocatively up the Champs-Élysées. In her typically playful fashion, my mother smoothly parlayed an interjection connoting surprise into a noun connoting pizzazz. I have observed that the trickiness and subtlety of this maneuver seem to go essentially unnoticed by readers; people pick up the connotations of my mother's off-the-wall syntactic and semantic transformation with no effort whatsoever. How plastic is the human mind! (Incidentally, the interjection in question, "oo-la-la", is a widespread anglophonic misconception of the amusing sound that French people come out with when nonplussed or impressed; in truth, however, its first syllable is "o", not "oo". I surmise that the error stems from the lyrics, by Sam Lewis and Joe Young, to the post–World War I song "How'ya Gonna Keep 'Em Down on the Farm After They've Seen Paree?")

It is interesting to imagine a certain tweak to this poem: Suppose that on lines 7–8, my mother, instead of writing "Clement's orders / In a nutshell", had said "Nancy's orders / In a nutshell", thus inserting her name and herself into the poem, in the same spirit as what I and some others had done. Though tiny on one level, the implications of such a twist would be huge on another: Readers would be forced to catapult their image of the sexy poem's author not only from one century to another (sixteenth to twentieth), but also from a case of heterosexuality to one of possible homosexuality. A kind of halfway house would be to write "Clementine's orders", which would cause the poet's sex and likely sexual orientation to be toggled in tandem, while leaving his/her birthdate intact.

This poem tips its hat to its Gallic provenance in a few spots. In addition to the flirtatious French fanny and the sexy-squeal-turned-sex-appeal, it fires one final parting shot totally in French: its last line, *Mon petit chou* (literally "My little cabbage", meaning "My darling")! Now if you can get away with *one* line in the original language, how far could you conceivably go with such a technique? How many lines could be fully in French? Two? Three? Six? The "logical" conclusion of such a tendency would of course be a "translation" that was *completely* in French. But such an ambition, even if "logical", would be totally absurd.

Hi Toots!

Nancy Hofstadter

> *Hi Toots,*
> *Get well!*
> *Hospital's prison*
> *And prison's hell.*
> *Get well,*   5
> *Flee your cell.*
> *(Clement's orders*
> *In a nutshell.)*
> *Go pig out,*
> *Ope wide your mouth:*   10
> *Keep those sweetmeats*
> *Goin' south!*
> *Unless you're hale,*
> *You'll turn pale,*
> *Lose oo-la-la*   15
> *That wiggles your tail.*
> *God restore*
> *Good health to you,*
> *My little flower,*
> *Mon petit chou.*

• *Chapter 7* •

The Nimble Medium-Hopping
of Evanescent Essences

•

Floating high on the screen above us is the familiar smiling face of Shelby Lyman — in case you've forgotten, the genial television announcer of that unforgettable 1972 Reykjavík chessboard showdown between Brooklynite bad boy Bobby Fischer and solid Soviet citizen Boris Spassky. Lyman is providing us duffers (me and my ilk, I mean; apologies to you who transcend that lowly label) with an incomparably clear blow-by-blow analysis of yet another World Chess Championship. Fluidly shoving pieces around on the board, describing simply and straightforwardly their complex interactions, he gives us hopeless outsiders (same disclaimer as above) the momentary illusion of almost seeing the board as the masters themselves see it. How grand!

But hold on a moment. What's this? Why are the "squares" on the board on the screen not square? In fact, they are interlocking hexagons forming a perfect honeycomb, an exemplary beehive, a lovely bathroom-tile pattern. This is no chessboard! And yet, the two players that Lyman is constantly naming are undeniably the two most illustrious chess masters in the world today, and moreover he keeps on saying such suggestive things as "A rook takes a bishop, then is taken by a knight, which is in turn knocked off by a bishop; the center is opening up a little", or "The pawn could move one space forward and thus get promoted to a queen", and then he shows us exactly which direction it would move in, and why. It sure *sounds* like chess, and yet it doesn't *look* like chess! What in the world is going on?

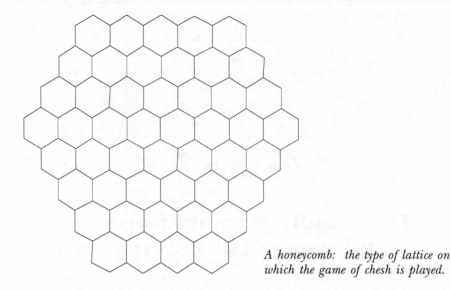

A honeycomb: the type of lattice on which the game of chesh is played.

Simultaneous Translation between Games

It turns out that Shelby Lyman has hidden talents: Not only is he a genial chess announcer, he's also a superb simultaneous interpreter — not between normal languages, however, but between the ancient game of *chess* and the more recently minted game of *chesh,* the latter being the closest analogue to chess that can be realized on a perfect hexagonal lattice. And so, what we are being treated to is a blow-by-blow *translation* of the decisive world-championship chess match, rendered for us entirely in terms of chesh. Luckily, there is another channel, just a button-push away, on which the actual square-lattice game is being broadcast, so we can flick ourselves back and forth between square and hexagonal worlds with the greatest of ease. We can even wheel out another television and place the two side by side, and in that way watch both versions of the story at once.

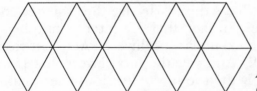

A triangular lattice: the texture of a board on which to play chest.

Oops! You pushed the button twice. Now what's *this* on the screen? A *triangular* lattice? And here's an announcer using the same players' names, and the exact same type of chess lingo, yet all the moves are taking place on a board composed of equilateral triangles! What is going on here? Just another simultaneous translation, of course — this time from the game of *chess* to the game of *chest*. And *nota bene*: The last letter of the name of the game is the first letter of the name of the lattice. So what would *chesp* be?

Try pushing the button yet again — maybe that way you'll hit upon chesp by chance. Uh-oh, didn't work. Looks like this time we're back to a hexagonal lattice, but there's a difference: Instead of Shelby Lyman, we have the respected chess writer George Steiner, author of *Fields of Force*, a fascinating little memoir about the Fischer–Spassky match, providing the running commentary. Surprisingly, it sounds just as lucid as Lyman's, and yet somehow different in style. If we wheel in yet another TV and watch both of the hexagonal blow-by-blows at the same time, comparing Steiner's and Lyman's analyses, we find — oh, horrors! — that the actual moves that the two chess grandmasters are reported to have made, when shown to us on the cheshboard, are *not even the same moves*! How is this possible? How can there be conflicting reports of one and the same chess game? Isn't there anything left to *truth* in this old world?

The Transvestism of Grandmaster Marot and His Superb Owl

Well, of course, we've seen all this craziness before — except that it was taking place in a very different medium: that of linguistic translation. How can a blow-by-blow re-creation of a poem by one-time Word Champion C. Marot be given on a square-based Anglo-American board, a triangle-based German board, or even a Penrose-tile-based Polish board, when the revered grandmaster's original moves were made solely on his native hexagonal French board? (By the way, now you know what type of board chesp is played on — or at least you know its name.) Isn't it all just a pack of lies to quote Marot's semantic and syntactic moves on the wrong board, with the wrong pieces, and the wrong rules governing how they move? And when we focus in on one poetic little gem of a game that grandmaster Marot played in 1537, when at the height of his powers, how can it possibly be that his actual moves depend, when reported in square English, on *which commentator* happens to be telling us about them, when in hexagonal French he clearly made just *one move* on each turn?

The idea of matter-of-factly reporting and analyzing a *chess* game on a *chesh* board seems implausible, even preposterous. The next thing you know, the Superbowl will be slickly dressed up on some counterfactual TV channel as a basketball game, and somehow there will be one-to-one matchups between football plays and basketball plays. And that's not all: on some other counterfactual channel, the very same Superbowl will be being shown at the very same time, but cross-dressed most convincingly as a baseball game. And on and on. It all sounds quite absurd. And yet, how different is it, really, from the charade of claiming to quote a poet in various and sundry languages, none of them the original one?

Quick Poetry Break, I

What with all these bizarre *Gedankenexperimente* about counterfactual TV channels, transvestite sports events, and incommensurable lattices on the Euclidean plane, my head is spinning. I don't know about yours, but I find it pretty mind-stretching stuff, and I could do with a respite. I suggest we momentarily float back down to earth, and savor a delicious poem.

V's Straight Tip
To All Cross Coves

Suppose you screeve? or go cheap-jack?
Or fake the broads? or fig a nag?
Or thimble-rig? or knap a yack?
Or pitch a snide? or smash a rag?
Suppose you duff? or nose and lag?
Or get the straight, and land your pot?
How do you melt the multy swag?
Booze and the blowens cop the lot.

Fiddle, or fence, or mace, or mack;
Or moskeneer, or flash the drag;
Dead-lurk a crib, or do a crack;
Pad with a slang, or chuck a fag;
Bonnet, or tout, or mump and gag;
Rattle the tats, or mark the spot;
You can not bank a single stag;
Booze and the blowens cop the lot.

Suppose you try a different tack,
And on the square you flash your flag?
At penny-a-lining make your whack,
Or with the mummers mug and gag?
For nix, for nix the dibbs you bag!
At any graft, no matter what,
Your merry goblins soon stravag:
Booze and the blowens cop the lot.

The Moral

It's up the spout and Charley Wag
With wipes and tickers and what not.
Until the squeezer nips your scrag,
Booze and the blowens cop the lot.

Now wasn't that a kick and a half? I say! And what a way that this unnamed poet has with words! Well, I hope you've enjoyed our little break. And now, refreshed and revitalized, we return to our more prosaic prose-bound musings.

What is a Bishop's Move in Chesh?

All the conundrums just given about truth-in-reporting if the World Chess Championship were to masquerade as a series of chesh or chest or chesp matches are hypothetical, to say the least. They are titillating and provocative teasers, but we need not take them too seriously. On the other hand, it would be quite serious and very much worth our while to delve just a little bit into a far simpler but still subtle conundrum — namely, what the game of chesh might be like. Presumably it would have to involve pieces named "king", "queen", "rook", and so on, and presumably each piece would move in a manner "analogous" — whatever that might mean — to how its homonymous piece moves on a square lattice. Thus, for instance, a chesh bishop would move analogously to a chess bishop — namely, just along diagonals.

What is a diagonal, though, on a lattice of hexagons? When you first scan a hexagonal lattice, the whole notion seems to go up in smoke. There simply *are* no diagonals! Or is that too hasty a surrender? Before declaring the transfer's impossibility, we should first try to get very clear on what defines diagonality on a lattice of squares, and see if we can't salvage *something* of the notion in the foreign framework of a hex-board.

Chessboard diagonals are characterizable in terms of:

(1) 45-degree angles;

(2) squares that kiss each other at corners;

(3) nearest neighbors sharing a color.

Probably the most obvious way of characterizing square-lattice diagonality is in terms of *45-degree angles*. This notion, unfortunately, doesn't seem to lend itself to export to a hexagonal lattice, where 45-degree angles are rather unnatural interlopers. And 45 degrees with respect to *what*, anyway? On a hexagonal lattice, that's not at all clear. The notion could of course be forced, but it does not seem promising from an esthetic point of view. Strike one, as Françoise Ulam (whom in a later chapter we shall meet) would say.

A second tentative approach to pinning down the crux of square-lattice diagonality would be in terms of *squares that "kiss" at their common corner* (and touch each other nowhere else). But on a hexagonal lattice, there are no hexlets that kiss each other just at corners. Rather, given two hexlets, either they meet flush along one whole side, or else they don't meet at all. And hence, strike two.

A third view of the essence of square-lattice diagonality is in terms of *nearest neighbors of the same color*. But for this concept to be exported, we would first have to find some way of coloring our bathroom-tile wall so that adjacent hexlets are always different colors from each other. Using two colors would seem the obvious choice, but it just "doesn't compute" when you try it out. Foul ball. However, it turns out, quite beautifully and naturally, that *three* colors do a most splendid job of quickly colorizing a hex-hive — wow! And with that, we get a base hit.

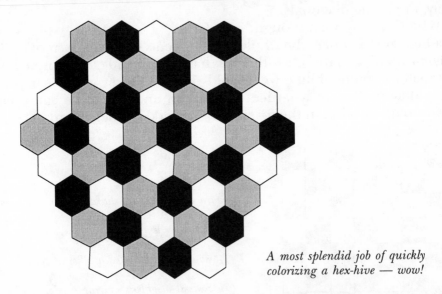

A most splendid job of quickly colorizing a hex-hive — wow!

Does this unexpected twist mean that in chesh, each side will have *three* different bishops, one for each color? Well, it could mean that, although you could simply leave one color out per side. But before such matters are even considered, one has to ask oneself, "What will a chesh bishop's move look like?" And the answer is now quickly forthcoming: Being "diagonal", it will have to involve jumping from the starting hexlet to any of the six closest-possible same-colored hexlets (and then anywhere beyond them, as long as the direction and style of motion are maintained). And notice that this means that a chesh bishop will slide along the creases, hopping from any *corner* of the starting hexlet to the nearby *corner* of a like-colored one. From corner to corner! Even if the hexagons' corners aren't close enough to let them French-kiss, they can still blow each other kisses, which will give rise to *une charmante petite brise de bises.*

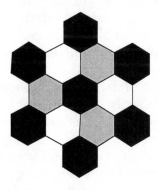

Diagonal moves from the central black hexlet connect it to any of its six nearest black neighbors.

The unexpected upshot is that we have managed to discover, in our color-based view of diagonality, a subtle residue of the corner-based view of diagonality that we had prematurely deemed inapplicable to a hexagonal lattice. This pleasing confirmation helps to buttress our confidence in the rightness of the coloring scheme, and our whole view of the transport of diagonality to a radically new framework.

There's even more: The bishop's "diagonal" slide along the crease is poised, angularly speaking, halfway between two adjacent rook moves (such as from the central black hexlet to its gray neighbor at one o'clock, or its white neighbor at three o'clock). So the diagonal move is still associated with a half-angle — not 45 degrees, which is half of a right angle, which is a square-based notion, but 30 degrees, which is half of 60 degrees, which, speaking metaphorically, is "the right angle of the hexagon". So once again we discover a hidden resonance with an earlier perspective on diagonality that we had at first rejected, since we had taken it too literally — but when we eventually loosened up, it came back into the fold.

Diagonality as a Metaphor

The beauty of this insight is that diagonality, instead of being a clear, sharp, unambiguous, geometrically defined notion that is transportable by mechanistic or algorithmic means from the square-lattice framework to any other regular framework (or else that is sharply and clearly incapable of being transported to certain frameworks), had to become a *metaphor* in order to be able to be lifted up and out of its initial home and plunked down in a new one.

And how did it become a metaphor? The answer is, it became a metaphor when we let go of many of its surface attributes and seized on something elusive but beautiful about it, something that would at first seem far from the notion's essence, something that would seem a mere perfume hovering about it: the coloring scheme for the underlying lattice. And yet that subtle hovering fragrance turned out to be the key to the transport, and as a gratifying bonus, we discovered *ex post facto* that the notion of hexagonal diagonality that resulted therefrom also preserves a tiny, poetic whiff of the corner–corner kissing and the special half-angle, both of which seemed so central to the original square-based notion.

We could go on to try to define the chesh knight's move (rookery, we've seen, is a piece of cake), the pawn's move, such delicacies as capture *en passant* and castling, and so forth. To flesh chesh out completely, we would then need to specify the cheshboard's exact size and shape, as well as the initial cohorts of pieces (how many bishops per side, for instance?) and their precise spatial layout at a game's very start. Then, for good measure, we could go on and try to tackle the riddles of how chest and chesp pieces ought to move, and how the boards should look and be set up. But I will skip all of that, good fun though it would be to delve into it all.

My main purpose here has been to evoke the image of *the transport of an elusive essence between frameworks,* since that short phrase is for me the simultaneous definition both of analogy-making and of translation. To illustrate this motto, I chose frameworks in the most literal sense of the term — regular geometrical lattices in a plane — so as to make the notion of inter-frame essence-transport (sounds almost like a trucking company, doesn't it?) as graphic and visual as possible.

Grids, Grains, and Jaggies

Geometrical lattices come in finer and coarser grains. It's a fun mental game to try to find familiar square lattices from real life, ranging from very fine to very coarse. A few minutes' worth of memory-dredging led me to this escalating series, for instance: the sodium atoms in a crystal of salt, the dots used by a laser printer, the pixels on a video monitor, the holes in a screen door, the mesh of a Go board, the squares of a chessboard, the tiles of a linoleum floor, the seats in a theater, the houses in a suburban tract, the streets in a city grid, the half-mile-on-a-side fields in our midwestern prairies, the counties in a few very flat states, and so on. You can probably find many better ways of filling in the different sizes and extending my list.

Suppose we wanted to create a very, very thin pathway, ideally just a hair's-breadth wide, on each of these grids — a pathway as nearly circular as possible and with a diameter of, say, 100 feet. First we would color all of the squares with some light background shade, and then, using some dark contrasting shade, we would color in just those squares that lay along the ideal perfect circle.

On all of the coarser grids, the resulting jagged pathway of darker squares would obviously do a wretched job of approximating circularity, but as the grain got finer, the set of contiguous dark boxes would come closer and closer to the ideal, and for the human eye, as we jumped from grid to ever finer grid, approaching the beginning of my list of real-life lattices, the shape's graininess would gradually vanish into the cracks. From a pessimist's point of view, if one were to zoom in and look sufficiently closely, one could always find some tiny scale, no matter how fine the grain of the grid was, on which there remained "jaggies", but, looking at things more from an optimist's point of view, a fine-grained mesh allows circularity to be reproduced extremely well from a distance.

The smaller you make the desired circle, though, the worse any fixed grid will do. Thus the mesh size of a screen-door grid is reasonably good for circles with diameter of a foot or more, but a one-inch circle will look pretty jagged, and a millimeter-sized circle will be a pure square — a terrible rendering of circularity, for sure. When the dimensions of the arc you wish to simulate are on the same order as the grain size of the grid, then you have reached the limits of your grid's resolving power; there is nothing to be done about it any more.

Suppose this whole discussion had involved hexagonal or triangular lattices rather than square ones. Nothing much would be different, except that I would have come up with far fewer real-life examples. For these grids no less than for square ones, as the grain size of the lattices shrinks, a given arc will be ever more faithfully reproduced; and conversely, as an arc shrinks relative to a lattice of fixed mesh, its simulation on the grid will get more and more jagged.

My main reason for again bringing up grids of different underlying structures was to point out that when they are coarse, their underlying cell's shape has a visible effect, but as they get finer and finer, how they are realized becomes invisible. Thus for all I know, the dots realizing the letters you are now reading, coming from my 600-dots-per-inch laser printer, actually form a hexagonal rather than a square lattice. The difference would be completely undetectable to the human eye. But if it were 60 dots per inch, you can bet your boots we could tell.

Languages, Words, and Metaphorical Jaggies

The reason that I have spelled out at such length what must seem like painfully obvious facts is that I want to carry the imagery about grain size and faithfulness over to the case of translation, where the counterpart facts are less obvious, or at least less familiar to most people.

Specifically, if the task is to translate a whole novel from, say, Russian to English, and if this task is given to a skilled translator, then the myriad discrepancies that exist between Russian and English semantics and syntax will in the end give rise to tens of thousands of little metaphorical "jaggies" — language-necessitated deviations from the ideal content — scattered everywhere throughout the book. But the grain size of these myriad deviations will be very fine compared to the dimensions of the structure being translated, and so — providing the translator is good — a sensitive reader will perceive very little discrepancy. This is, to hammer the point in, because the "arc" of an entire novel is huge, relative to the grain size of human languages, which resides, roughly speaking, at the level of words and short phrases.

As the translation task gets smaller and smaller, however — a poem, a sentence, a book's clever short title — the grain size of language becomes more and more relevant and intrusive, so that in tiny challenges, such as clever titles of books, the highest levels of ingenuity are called for, and often it takes weeks if not months for the right idea to bubble up. And of course, sometimes a tiny passage is so dense with overlapping meanings and flavors that there is nothing that even roughly approximates it in the target language. At that level of challenge, you *can't* shove the grain size of human language under the rug, because you are *at* the grain size. And the grain size of language is not an adjustable feature. We have no knob to twist to make our human languages finer or coarser, no magical granularity knob effectively turning gravel to sand to salt to flour, or the reverse.

Actually, that's not quite true, and here's where my metaphor of languages as lattices gets quite interesting, I feel. The knob to twist is precisely something that I alluded to above — the translator's skill. Metaphorically speaking, a great translator is someone who has a perfectly internalized Roget's Thesaurus and uses it constantly and effortlessly; it is someone whose sensitivity to words and their flavors has a far finer grain size than a poor translator. Thus the better the translator, the less visible the discrepancies between original and copy. As you move further and further toward the head of the list of translators, the more the metaphorical jaggies recede into the cracks, and the more you feel that the nature of the underlying lattice is unnoticeable.

When you're dealing with 600-dots-per-inch translator Richard Wilbur, perhaps known best for his rhyming English renditions of Molière's plays (we'll glimpse another of his sparkling facets in Chapter 17), the fact of which grid you're dealing with — the hexagons of French or the squares of English — becomes pretty much irrelevant. Much the same could be said about Michael Kandel, another 600-dots-per-inch translator, who renders Stanisław Lem's highly idiomatic wordplay in English in such a convincing way that you'd swear all those puns must have been traced originally on an English-language square grid, when in point of fact they were all first penned on Polish's quasi-periodic pentagonal Penrose-tile grid.

Richard Wilbur and Michael Kandel are the sorts of translators who can pull the wool over our eyes as skillfully as Shelby Lyman and George Steiner did, when they made us think that we were seeing a square chessboard through Bobby Fischer's grandmaster eyes when in fact we were merely looking at a hexagonal cheshboard through our own pathetic potzer eyes (apologies, apologies, again, to the fine chess players out there among you!).

Understanding Media

A lattice is a place where patterns can play, and a language is a playground where words can cavort. Lattices and languages have much in common, because they are both superb examples of *media*.

For me, an erstwhile physicist and ever a faithful lover of the beautiful concepts of physics, the word "medium" has a special aura to it. It evokes dozens of rich images, among them these: a wrist-flick pulse snaking its way down the twisty coils of a horizontally suspended Slinky; glittering circular patterns of ripples passing silently through each other on the windless surface of a pond; sound waves emanating from a sharp snap of the fingers and propagating through the air as ever-growing spheres; a series of red flashes zooming countercurrent down a jammed freeway when one alarmed motorist slams hard on the brake and in a long wake behind, as predictably as toppling dominos, one car after another reacts in like fashion; quantum vortices spinning across a dewar filled with cold-beyond-cold superfluid helium; and microscopic electromagnetic pulsations in nothingness sailing timelessly across the void, coaxing virtual pairs out of the vacuum and spurting on as they cancel, all the way from Arcturus to the Solar System, coursing through the Terran atmosphere and straight into the open maw of a long telescope tube, bouncing at its far end against a parabolic mirror, leaping back up towards where, thirty-six years earlier, Arcturus once was, being channeled through a series of glass lenses and filters, and finally, at the end of their enormous and fully predestined interstellar voyage, crashing somewhere on the sandy beach of a human retina.

A medium is a vehicle for patterns, a propagator of distortions, a transmitter of disturbances. And a linguistic medium, in particular, is a carrier of messages. When one first thinks of the linguistic sense of this word, one tends to equate "medium" with "language". Thus, French would be one medium, English would be another, and so on. All true, but that is nonetheless a very crude first pass; as in the case of physical media, the notion is potentially far richer and more interesting.

Linguistic Media

A linguistic medium, in my eyes, is definable as: *a language restricted by a set of constraints that are not so tight as to preclude the expression of arbitrary meanings.* As an illustration of this notion, Anglo-Saxon will do a good job, for in it you can say most anything you wish (as in fact this thirty-word auto-alluding affirmation shows). For similar reasons, monosyllabic English would be a linguistic medium. I might rephrase my definition as follows: a linguistic medium is: *a language that has been restricted but that is still rich enough that any reasonable passage can be translated with grace and clarity into it.* With such fluffy terms flying all about, this definition is obviously far from being mathematically razor-sharp, but rather, would necessitate a judgment call in virtually every case; however, I never intended it to be anything more than suggestive and provocative.

One could extend the notion of "linguistic medium" to include restrictions on length and style, so that, for example, the sonnet form — fourteen rhymed lines of between four and six iambic feet, more or less — would be a linguistic medium. Of course, such length restrictions might seem to prevent arbitrarily complex messages from being expressed, but to circumvent that problem, one can simply use the same vessel over and over again: thus a novel could hypothetically be realized in the sonnet-form medium, should anyone ever be so daft as to wish to tackle such a pointless challenge, simply by tacking sonnets together, head to tail, yielding a piece of text of arbitrary length.

To show that the notion of "linguistic medium" is not utterly trivial, let me give some counterexamples. The set of all possible palindromic sentences is not, for me, a linguistic medium, because it is not nearly sufficiently receptive: you certainly cannot say anything you want in it. In fact, you can say very little in it — it controls you; you cannot control it. Until I encountered Giuseppe Varaldo's virtuosity, I would have confidently claimed that monovocalic English and Italian were non-media, insisting that in either case, one is far too hemmed in to be able to say whatever one wants. I still would tend to assert this, but I now would be a bit more ginger in betting large sums on it. On the other hand, I feel extremely confident asserting that the set of words beginning with "x" — for that matter, even the set of words containing an "x" anywhere — is *not* a medium, under my definition. You could hardly say anything at all in it.

One could of course restrict the set of messages of interest, and define a semantically limited linguistic medium to be a constrained language rich enough to allow all of the restricted messages to be expressed. This is an interesting extension of the concept, and, depending on the set of restricted messages, would certainly allow some kinds of counterexamples back in. We shall briefly deal with the notion later in the chapter.

Quick Poetry Break, II

What with all these metaphorical jaggies, 600-dots-per-inch translators, hypothetical novels in verse, and a panalphabetic caption to boot, my head is spinning once again. I think I just need another break. I hope you'll enjoy this one as much as the last one, even though — please excuse me for this — it is cast in such a very different medium from that one.

Ballade de bonne doctrine
A Ceulx de mauvaise vie

Car ou soyes porteur de bulles,
  Pipeur ou hazardeur de dez,
Tailleur de faulx coings, tu te brusles,
  Comme ceulx qui sont eschaudez,
  Traistres parjurs, de foy vuydez ;
Soyes larron, ravis ou pilles :
  Où en va l'acquest, que cuydez ?
Tout aux tavernes & aux filles.

Ryme, raille, cymballe, luttes,
  Comme fol, fainctif, eshontez ;
Farce, brouille, joue des fleustes ;
  Fais, ès villes & ès citez,
  Fainctes, jeux & moralitez ;
Gaigne au berlanc, au glic, aux quilles,
  Aussi bien va — or escoutez —
Tout aux tavernes & aux filles.

De telz ordures te reculles ;
  Laboure, fauche champs & prez ;
Serz & pense chevaulx & mulles,
  S'auculnement tu n'es lettrez ;
  Assez auras, se prens en grez.
Mais, se chanvre broyes ou tilles,
  Ne tens ton labour qu'as ouvrez
Tout aux tavernes & aux filles.

Envoi

Chausses, pourpoins esguilletez,
Robes, & toutes voz drappilles,
  Ains que vous fassiez piz, portez
Tout aux tavernes & aux filles.

I ask you, is this not *vachement chouette?* *Morbleu!* And what a deft touch this unnamed poet has with words. I thus hope you've enjoyed our second little break. And now, refreshed and revitalized, we return to our more prosaic prose-bound musings.

The Legacy of a Lowlife Genius

You may feel cheated that, contrary to my usual practice with poems in foreign tongues, I failed to provide a translation of this *ballade*. Even if you speak French well, you might still feel the need for a translation, for some of the words are quite obscure. And with good reason, for they date from around 1461, when Parisian rogue and lowlife bard François Villon, who penned them, was composing his *Grand Testament,* or Last Will and Testament, in the form of a long series of quite earthy poems.

Villon, though of humble birth — his father was a laborer, his mother illiterate — received an excellent education. According to the records of the Faculty of Arts at the University of Paris, he received a baccalaureate degree in 1449 and then a *licence* and a *maîtrise ès arts* in 1452. In those years of poverty, he fell under the seductive influence of a street gang called *les Coquillards* and adopted their wayward ways, which led to his association with criminals and riffraff of every sort, including prostitutes galore, and to his fluency in a special jargon of that *demi-monde*. A mere seventy years later, the alien tone of Villon's language — *"l'antiquité de son parler"* — was already striking to Clément Marot, who edited an edition of his works in 1533. Despite Marot's respect, Villon was disdained by the next famous generation of French poets, collectively known as *La Pléiade,* for they were an aristocratic bunch and recoiled from gutteral language.

A Lesson to the Lost

If Villon's poem cries out for translation, then all the more so does the earlier-quoted "V's Straight Tip to All Cross Coves", despite the fact that it is in an English of sorts. Were it in my powers, I would translate it, but unfortunately I do not understand it well enough. The first time I read it, in fact, I laughed aloud, thinking it was deliberate nonsense and savoring its opacity. With time, I came to realize it was not just joyous playing with sounds, but that meaning lurked hidden within (a disappointment at first).

And now, surprising perhaps no one, I admit I *have* in fact provided translations of both poems: each other. The truth is, "V's Straight Tip" is a rendition of Villon's "Ballade", done probably over a century ago by William Ernest Henley (1849-1903), an English editor, essayist, and author of the famous poem "Invictus". We will return shortly to "V's Straight Tip".

Luckily, Villon's "Ballade" has been anglicized more than once, and not always so elusively. In 1914, H. De Vere Stacpoole published a bilingual volume of Villon verse, including this ballad. Stacpoole's rhymes had moments of inspiration, but at times were uneven and even clunky. Therefore I, taking that version as my starting point, reworked it to preserve nearly all its rhymes and basic structure, but clarifying it a little and making it flow more smoothly. Here, then, is Stacpoole's emended opus:

Ballade of Good Doctrine
To Those of Evil Life

Ye who be smugglers of papal bulls,
Or cheaters at dice, whatever be ye —
Coiners who risk life and limb like fools,
Then boil in hot oil for their felony,
Traitors disloyal — ye know who ye be —
Stealers of jewels, of perfume and pearls:
So where goes it all, that ye get in fee?
All to the taverns and to the girls.

Rhyming and jesting, cymbals and lutes —
Don ye these emblems of minstrelsy.
Farce and imbroglio, music of flutes —
Try these in hamlets or Gay Paree.
Go mumming in masque or mystery,
Win money at cards, or at ninepin hurls.
But 'tis of no use! It'll flow, hear ye me,
All to the taverns and to the girls.

Ye shrink before such a hard-knocks school —
Play safe, then, with honester husbandry:
Of horses be grooms, go tend to a mule,
Plow ye the fields, here and there plant a tree.
And should ye be short on Latinity,
As lowly in learning as poor peasant churls,
Just work, lest your hard-earned pennies flee
All to the taverns and to the girls.

Envoi

Your stockings and doublets, your fine drapery,
Every last rag that around ye furls,
Ere ye be done, will have slipped, ye shall see,
All to the taverns and to the girls.

Thus lifteth the fog. This poem — and notice the odd plausibility of referring to a poem in French by pointing to some English text and saying "this poem", not so different from passing off a move in a game of chesh as a chess move — is found toward the end of Villon's *Grand Testament,* where it is preceded by a short poem declaring it to be an object lesson to be read aloud by Villon himself to the "lost children", the *enfants perdus,* of the unforgiving streets of fifteenth-century Paris.

Just to give a sense of why I felt it proper to modify Stacpoole's verse, here is the second stanza, entirely unretouched:

> *Song, jest, cymbals, lutes —*
> *Don these signs of minstrelsy.*
> *Farce, imbroglio, play of flutes —*
> *Make in hamlet or city.*
> *Act in play or mystery,*
> *Gain at cards, or ninepin hurls.*
> *All your profits, where go they?*
> *All on taverns and on girls.*

Gallows Humor

The final fate of François Villon, born François de Montcorbier, *alias* François des Loges and Michel Mouton, is a complete mystery. In 1461, at age thirty, for reasons unknown to us today, he was thrown by the bishopric of Orléans into a primitive dungeon in a castle in Meung-sur-Loire and subjected to a cruel water torture. He would almost surely have perished in his wretched cell, had the newly crowned King Louis XI not passed through the region that fall and magnanimously brought about Villon's release — and yet, true to form, the incorrigible Villon promptly got into more mischief. This time he was involved in a mêlée and brawl that ended in the swording of a papal notary by his comrade Robin Dogis, and for Villon's unclear role in the sordid affair, he was sentenced to be hanged, while the lucky Dogis went free. Villon appealed to the Parliamentary Court of Paris and miraculously, his sentence was reversed; in its place was substituted a ten-year banishment from the entire Paris region. Mysteriously, though, just at the point of his release, in very early 1463, Villon simply vanished, traceless, into thin air — an Amelia Earhart of the fifteenth century.

The penultimate poem known to have come from the hand of François Villon is a humorous letter to the Parliamentary Court, thanking it, on behalf of his entire body — its five senses and all of its sundry parts — for saving his life, and ending in a request for three extra days to pack his bags and bid adieu to his family. And his ultimate pen production is a somewhat taunting letter to a court clerk named Garnier, who, one gathers, must have scoffed at Villon's idea of appealing the death sentence. In it, Villon claims he was treacherously framed and asks the clerk, in effect, "Do you think I'm so stupid that I might not have thought to ask for a reversal of the verdict? Do you think I wanted to hang?"

One of Villon's tiniest verses, written when he was under threat of the gallows, is this quatrain, with my own liberal rendition flanking it:

Je suis Françoys, dont ce me poise,	*I am French, I, François (which I find somewhat crass),*
Né de Paris emprès Pontoise,	*And in Paris was born (from Pontoise no long trek).*
Qui, d'une corde d'une toise,	*When I hang from a rope (a royal pain in the ass),*
Sçaura mon col que mon cul poise.	*By my ass I'll be choked (a royal pain in the neck).*

The first line is a pun on the fact that *François* was both a first name and the word for "French", which, at the time, meant that one came from the Île de France (just Paris and nearby areas to the north and east). His resentment of being French might be linked to the fact that his friend Dogis — from the Savoie and hence not "François" — was pardoned for the bayonetting he committed, whereas Villon, at most an accomplice, was condemned to death. As for the town of Pontoise, it is apparently cited because, in medieval literature, it was a renowned symbol of Frenchness, thanks to its inhabitants' superb pronunciation of French.

One could call this verselet by a condemned man "a bit of bravado", as does Canadian Villon scholar Barbara N. Sargent-Baur; one could call it whistling in the dark; one could call it gallows humor. But call it what one may, it bears witness to a remarkably gritty and highly high-spirited spirit.

François Villon's Two Linguistic Media

As I mentioned above, Villon occasionally slipped into quite extreme forms of Parisian underworld jargon — a secret, cabalistic tongue whose exact meaning eludes virtually all French speakers today, even specialists. He wrote a series of poems called *Ballades en jargon,* of which I now provide just the opening stanza of the fifth one, with an educated guess as to its decipherment given in English by Sargent-Baur:

Ioncheurs, ionchans en ioncherie,	*Tricksters tricking in trickery,*
Rebignez bien où ioncherez ;	*Take a good look at where you play your tricks;*
Qu'ostac n'embrou' vostre arerie,	*Lest Ostac send your behind,*
Où accollez sont voz ainsnez.	*Where your elders were taken by the neck.*
Poussez de la quille & brouez,	*Shake a leg and speed away,*
Car tost seriez rouppieux.	*For you'd soon be sorry.*
Eschec qu'accollez ne soiez	*Take care not to let your neck be grabbed*
Par la poe du marieux.	*By the hangman's paw.*

Sargent-Baur's anglicization is obviously meant to convey nothing but the poem's content in the most literal manner, with the spicy flavor of Villon's slangy medium being left almost completely out of the picture. One might at first suppose that respecting both the content and the form of such a poem would be a hopeless task, but that would be a hasty judgment: one has but to recall W. E. Henley's "Straight Tip". The contrast clearly shows the difference between a ginger scholarly treatment and a bold artistic treatment.

W. E. Henley's Criminal-slang Medium

If ever anyone did, W. E. Henley appreciated Villon's wild lifestyle and his partiality for street slang. Even though the "Ballade de bonne doctrine" is not one of the jargon ballads, its language being tame in comparison, Henley came up with the inspired idea of expressing its vivid but somber message through the pungent medium of the jargon ballads (or to be more precise, through a counterpart medium in the anglophone world). The outcome, a marvelous grafting of form borrowed from one source onto content borrowed from another, is one of the most gutsy and striking pieces of writing I have ever come across — a brilliant masterpiece of translation, a scintillating gem of a poem on its own.

I spent a good hour looking up dozens of terms in Henley's "Straight Tip" in the *New Shorter Oxford English Dictionary*, and as a result I now have a fair, though by no means full, understanding of what it means. Not surprisingly, almost all the terms turn out to come from nineteenth-century or older British slang, and many specifically from British underworld slang. Several are very colorful, such as "fig a nag", which meant to apply ginger to a horse's anus to make its tail stay high and to make the horse livelier, or "thimble-rig", which was a London version of the still-flourishing shell game involving a hidden pea, with which con artists in big cities in America often dupe gullible takers today. "Moskeneer" came from Yiddish but became street slang, meaning "to pawn something for more than it is worth".

Henley's first two stanzas feature many terms dealing with stealing and counterfeiting (to *knap a yack* was to swipe a watch; a *snide* was a stolen coin; to *smash* was to pass counterfeit money; a *rag* was a small sum of money; to *duff* was to pass counterfeit goods; to *mace* was to swindle), others having to do with passing stolen goods along (*swag* was stolen goods; to *fence* was to get rid of swag quickly, and the term is still used often today), and a bunch having to do with cheating (to *bonnet* was to cover up underhanded proceedings; to *tout* was to spy on racehorses for the purposes of betting; to *mump* was to accept bribes; to *gag* was to trick someone; a *tat* was a loaded die). Strangely, the opening line, with its suggestions to "screeve" (write?) or "go cheap-jack", remains opaque to me.

The third stanza starts out, as its first line announces, on a different tack. I found its second line — "on the square you flash your flag" — to be wonderfully ambiguous and yet at the same time very clear. I suppose Henley intended either "you hang up your shingle on the town square" or else "in an honest manner you make a living for yourself". Pleasingly, these two interpretations, though entirely different on the surface, converge to roughly the same deep idea: a criminal reforms and starts doing straight business. "Penny-a-lining" turns out to be the activity of doing hack writing, paid at the rate of a penny per line. As for the second half of the stanza, I can translate it pretty well, on a literal level (a *goblin* being a sovereign, an obsolete golden coin worth one pound): "The money you earn is all for naught, since whatever your job, your merry coins soon wander away, every last one of them squandered on drinking and wenching."

The *envoi*, or Moral, is harder to decode, although I can get bits and pieces of it. "Up the spout" refers to some kind of hoist in a pawnshop that carried items up and away into storage; the phrase as a whole came to mean "useless, hopeless". Unfortunately, I don't have a clue as to what "Charley Wag" is all about, nor can I figure out "wipes and tickers" either. However, a squeezer was definitely a noose, and a scrag a neck.

The Sprawling Suburbs of English Monosyllables

I often felt like a total foreigner as I looked up terms in "A Straight Tip". The nature of the problem is simple to describe. Let's take lines 5 through 7 of the first stanza: "Suppose you duff, or nose and lag? / Or get the straight, and land your pot? / How do you melt the multy swag?" I did decipher "duff", as I said above, as "passing counterfeit goods", but how do you look up longer expressions like "get the straight", "land your pot", and "melt the multy swag"? There is no entry for such an expression as a whole, so one has to rely on the meanings of its component words.

As a native speaker, I come equipped with a pretty rich set of halos for many of these words, but nothing quite seemed to fit the context. "Pot", for example, has dozens of meanings. I know it sometimes refers to the stakes in a wager, but does "land your pot" mean "win a bet"? If so, might a "straight" be a tip, as in horse-racing? A plausible guess, but how does that fit in with the previous line's phrase "nose and lag"? I had no idea at all what that meant, and thus hurried off to the dictionary — the *SOED*, as I said earlier.

In that rich resource, I found that "to nose", in the early nineteenth century, was a slang term meaning "to inform on someone", and in the same general era, "lag", as a slang noun, meant a term in prison. This was a little encouraging, since the meaning was in the right ballpark of criminal terms, but on the other hand, it really didn't fit together with the meaning I had found for "nose", and besides, it was just a noun. For "lag" as a verb, nothing seemed to make any sense in the context of informing on others, let alone in the broader context of passing counterfeit goods and betting on horses. "Nose and lag" was a tough nut that was just not yielding to my attempts to crack it.

As for "melt the multy swag", the best I found for "melt" was "cash a check" in archaic slang, with "swag" being late-eighteenth-century slang for "loot". Each meaning on its own had a modicum of plausibility, but they didn't fit together well. And "multy", unfortunately, was nowhere to be found in the *SOED*. For a while I felt I was up a creek, but then, looking back at the French line while musing on check-cashing and loot, I put two and two together and realized that "How do you melt the multy swag?" had to mean "How do you covertly unload your multitude of ill-gotten gains?"

In the second stanza, things got rougher, not easier. Expressions like "flash the drag", "do a crack", "chuck a fag", "mark the spot" were far harder to decipher. Take a word like the noun "crack". I can imagine it being related to the activity of safecracking, but I have no idea if that is the intended meaning. If I go to a medium-sized dictionary like my trusty old 1969 *American Heritage,* I will not find anything that I don't already know, and so it is of no help. This means I must move up to a much larger dictionary, something that I normally avoid like the plague. The reason is simple: Each entry then balloons out to an enormous size. When I look up "crack", for instance, I will find not just a dozen but hundreds of lines in fine print detailing meanings galore in an incredible variety of contexts and eras. How can I figure out which one is meant?

It would certainly make life simple if the sole difference between the entries in the thin and fat dictionaries consisted of the addition of just the meaning I'm seeking and nothing else, but that is an absurd pipe dream. When a city expands like crazy, it does so in *all* directions, not just to the north-by-northeast. And when you move from a medium-sized dictionary to a huge one, each entry is like a once-modest town that has suddenly mushroomed into a giant metropolis with vast suburbs sprawling on every side, leaving you gasping for breath in the dense semantic smog.

Given a big fat dictionary and a phrase like "mark the spot", there is going to be a gigantic combinatorial explosion of possibilities. With, let us say, a hundred meanings for each of the two main words, that gives us 10,000 potential meanings! As a native speaker, I can rule many of them out immediately, but I am still left bewildered and stunned by the richness of what I find. I would so much like to jump downwards to a smaller dictionary to stem the combinatorial explosion, but then I risk losing the desired meanings entirely. And heaven help me if I instead jump upwards to the full *Oxford English Dictionary,* where I will wind up suffocating in semantic pollution.

In my work on the second stanza, I simply had to give up on all four of the phrases mentioned above, as well as "bank a stag" and the very colorful "dead-lurk a crib". In the latter case, I found nothing at all under "dead-lurk", which was bad news, and as for "crib", I found that in the mid-nineteenth century, it could be used as a verb meaning "pilfer; purloin" and in the same era as a noun meaning "pub; saloon; brothel". Both of these meanings vaguely fit the general Villon–Henley context, but without deciphering "dead-lurk", I was lost. And so I got the flavor but the specifics eluded me totally. It's a strange thing to find yourself entirely at sea in your own native language.

I could not conclude my anecdotes about dictionary look-up without sharing one special moment of delight, which was when, trying to decode "pad with a slang", I looked up "slang", found the very promising-seeming meaning of "traveling show", and noted, with much amusement, that this meaning was classified as, of all things, "archaic slang".

The Multy Media in This Book

"Villon's Straight Tip to All Cross Coves" — this is how Henley actually titled it — provides a beautiful example of a linguistic medium. We are not dealing with normal English, but with a highly restricted subset of it, yet one still full of expressive power. Given that my definition of "linguistic medium" included the proviso that *any* reasonable meaning should be amenable to expression therein, you might be forgiven for wondering how, say, an introduction to Einstein's theory of general relativity might sound in this medium. I leave this challenge as an exercise to the interested reader.

In the collection of "Ma Mignonne" translations that constitute the backbone of this book, there are some excellent examples of linguistic media created on the fly by various translators. A little reminiscent of Henley's old-style British medium is Melanie Mitchell's Shakespearean medium. Of course, Henley's medium is not just that of antiquated British criminal slang, for it also includes the metrical and rhyming structures inherited from the form of a Villon ballad. Similarly, Melanie's medium includes the trisyllabic rhyming form of Marot's original.

A quite different medium is David Moser's bisyllabic diminution of the Marot form (including the augmented number of lines, to preserve the syllable-count). Along with this syntactic aspect of David's medium, one should also include the jaunty colloquiality of contemporary American English, which clearly is a more semantic aspect. From David's ingenious experiment in a new medium there came a few spinoffs, including Bob French's monosyllabic medium, and my own twist of "fattening" the thin lines in David's poem — a return to trisyllabicity but with the additional constraint that two of the three syllables in each line have to rhyme with each other. In my first try along these directions ("Sweetmeat Sue"), I preserved David's augmented number of lines, but in my next attempt ("Meat-sweet Sue"), I reduced the line-count to the original number, in order to reinstate the poem's original syllable-count of 84. The resulting medium is one that I would never have invented on my own; it took the circuitous route of David's playful experimentation to provoke me into dreaming up the idea of trisyllabic lines featuring an echo effect somewhere in each line; this idea, in conjunction with Marot's original network of constraints, yielded a very strangely-flavored medium indeed.

If you flip ahead to Poems XIII, you will see that each of the versions of "Ma Mignonne" found therein could be thought of as representing a distinct kind of clay into which to impress the content of the French poem. Of the three, the most unusual is certainly that chosen by Marek Lugowski — namely, the medium of contemporary rap songs' lingo. That medium is just about as familiar to me — or as unfamiliar — as is centuries-old British criminal slang. But even though I scarcely know these two media at all, I recognize at least one similarity, which is that both are big-city street lingos developed in some sense as a rebellion against authority and repression.

What's Wild in One Medium is Restrained in Another

Usually when one thinks of translation, one imagines it as the transfer of a piece of text from one language to another. But I feel that this is far too simple. I would instead choose to describe it as *a transfer between two linguistic media*. A translator's most basic choice is of course that of language (usually a given rather than a choice, in fact), but an equally important set of choices is the combination of constraints voluntarily donned for the duration. A constraint need not be hard-and-fast and black-and-white, like "e"-lessness or trisyllabicity — it can be as vague and hard to pin down as "romantic in tone" or "sprinkled with subtle allusions to Greek mythology" — but it is nonetheless constantly exerting pressure and making itself felt. Often the constraints constituting the medium selected are not decided upon explicitly or consciously; they simply lurk in the back of the translator's mind, unformulated in verbalized terms. Even so, they are no less real for their tacitness.

This view of translation affords a somewhat different perspective from the normal one on what is radical and what is mild. Take a simple example such as the conversion of the word "English" to "Anglo-Saxon" in my anglosaxonization of John Searle's key paragraph. I would not be at all surprised if you were quite jolted when you first hit that word: on first encounter, it seems somehow out of place, wrong. But if so, that is because you were unaware of the true nature of the medium, mistaking it for more ordinary academic-style English. In *that* medium, to be sure, "Anglo-Saxon" would sound ridiculous, which is why Searle himself didn't use it. But in "e"-less English, "Anglo-Saxon" is an ideal term, and is anything but wrong or out of place.

For another example, let me once again go back to my own phrase "Flush your phlegm" in "Cutie Pie". A certain type of reader might find this horrifying, given its informal, almost crudely physical, tone. Where is its counterpart in the Marot? Perhaps nowhere. But that, I would argue, is a red herring. The fact is, I as translator determined my medium from the very start, whether consciously or unconsciously. In this case, deeply built into the medium was a flippant, jaunty, nose-thumbing tone. Once one accepts this fact as *part of the challenge,* then how can a phrase that respects all these qualities be complained about? Once one sees the medium as having been fixed first, then what at first seemed like shocking liberties taken are reperceived as very straight-and-narrow choices falling well within the confines of the fixed medium. To be sure, one can complain about the medium chosen, but one should not confuse criticisms of the medium itself with criticisms of solutions found *within* the medium. To do so would be to confuse two very different levels of a creative act.

Someone could argue that the medium chosen by a translator should always resemble, to the maximal possible degree, the medium of the original. This attitude, however, strikes me as enormously conservative and stodgy. It would squelch leaps of genius such as that by W. E. Henley, who superimposed on one Villon ballad the flavor of a totally different set of Villon ballads. It would suppress David Moser's sparkling bisyllabic experiment. It would totally deny the validity of my mother's "Hi Toots!" poem. And on and on. Nearly every translation in this book, in short, would be regarded as outrageous and illegal by those who would promote such a narrow and rigid view of translation.

Choice of medium is, to my mind, the most delicious degree of freedom open to a translator, and is what makes translation so open-ended and full of unlimited potential for creativity. Suppress that freedom, and you reduce translation to a tiny and quite boring caricature of itself.

Alphabetic Styles and Linguistic Media

An analogy may be useful here. In the art of typeface design, there is a standard distinction between *book faces* and *display faces*. The former are ones like Times, Baskerville (the face of these very words), Garamond, Bodoni, and many other famous names. They tend to be conservative and elegant, like gentlemen in jackets and ties. The latter, also known as *advertising faces,* include Helvetica, Hobo, Brush (the script face used on this book's cover for the subtitle), Friz Quadrata (the face used for section titles), and thousands of others. To be sure, there are some faces that float in between, such as Americana (the face in which "Le Ton beau de Marot" is written on the cover), Tiffany (in the "running feet" at the bottom of each chapter page), Benguiat (used for chapter titles), and many others.

There is a kind of unwritten convention about book faces that forbids them from getting too wild, but there is no such restriction on display faces. Indeed, although many of them are fairly tame, there are vast numbers of display faces that play with letters in the most imaginative and zany ways, once in a while sliding out towards the very fringes of legibility. To continue the analogy to modes of dress, display faces are a bit like the wilder styles that fashion designers dream up for women (and occasionally for men) — often very silly, but sometimes delightful, and collectively important in allowing modes of dress to undergo a gradual type of evolution. Like wild fashion experiments, the wild letters of most display faces would be frowned on by people who felt that "the only good typeface is a book face". But just imagine what a boring typographical world we would live in if such imagination-stompers were victorious, and all display faces were wiped off the surface of the earth! For me personally, the very lifeblood of letters would have been sapped from them.

A letter in a playful style certainly would not fit into a conservative book face like Baskerville, but that doesn't mean that playful letters don't have any place at all! Indeed, any such letter has a natural home, which is its own full alphabet. A playful letter such as Hobo's *g* would not work at all inside the Brush world (*abcdefg...*), nor would the Brush *g* work inside the Hobo world (**abcdefg...**), but each works in its own context. Every little alphabetic world, if well designed, has its own internal consistency and its own type of beauty. Often that beauty comes about not through the grace of individual letters (indeed, a single letter of an adventurous display face may well seem ugly, if taken in isolation), but through their harmoniously interlocking relationships, with echoes of one letter easily spotted in many other letters, and, at a deeper level, abstract stylistic decisions giving rise to inter-letter analogies whose effects reverberate throughout the alphabet, yet have only a subliminal effect on all but the keenest of eyes.

All of these ideas can be carried back to the idea of linguistic media. An opening line like my mother's "Hi Toots" would, if substituted for Bob French's opening line "Fairest friend", utterly destroy the dark and medieval flavor of his "book face" poem, and yet in her own bright and splashy modern opus it works beautifully. Conversely, a grafting of Bob's phrase "Fairest friend" onto the beginning of my mother's "display face" poem would spoil it just as totally.

To conclude, then, a word or a phrase in a given translation may at first be perceived as a breach of good taste and rejected out of hand, but then may, with further consideration, come to be reperceived as fitting well within the norms established by a linguistic medium that one at first simply had not recognized as such, or perhaps that one had recognized but rebelled against. One has every right to reject a medium as a whole as being distasteful, but one should not confuse rejection at that level with rejection of bits and pieces within a medium that has been accepted. Each type of decision has its place, but they are very different from each other.

Sweet Chariot, or Syrupy Surrey?

Oscar Hammerstein II, who worked intimately with composer Richard Rodgers after the death of his first lyricist Lorenz Hart, was responsible for some of the most beautiful lyrics that I know. Many of Hammerstein's lyrics are in special linguistic media, such as the pseudo-Oriental English spoken by various characters in the musicals *South Pacific* and *The King and I*, or the Chinese-American variety of English in *Flower Drum Song*. And then there is the sometimes-coarse, sometimes-tender medium of American country language, exemplified by one of my favorite Rodgers and Hammerstein songs, "The Surrey with the Fringe on Top", from the extraordinarily successful 1943 musical *Oklahoma!* It's rather amusing that David Moser, who grew up in Oklahoma and can put on a country twang with the best of them, finds this song — both its words and its music — utterly trite, whereas I find it indescribably touching. Here are its last four stanzas:

> *I can see the stars gettin' blurry,*
> *When we drive back home in the surrey,*
> *Drivin' slowly home in the surrey*
> *   with the fringe on top!*
>
> *I can feel the day gettin' older,*
> *Feel a sleepy head on my shoulder,*
> *Noddin', droopin' close to my shoulder,*
> *   till it falls, ker-plop!*
>
> *The sun is swimmin' on the rim of a hill,*
> *The moon is takin' a header;*
> *And jist as I'm thinkin' all the earth is still,*
> *A lark'll wake up in the medder...*
>
> *Hush, you bird, my baby's a-sleepin',*
> *Maybe got a dream worth a-keepin',*
> *Whoa! you team, and jist keep a-creepin'*
> *   at a slow... clip... clop...*
> *Don't you hurry with the surrey*
> *   with the fringe on the top!*

Maybe it's just me, but I find something terribly lyrical and sweet in the gentle protectiveness of cowhand Curly for his brand-new girl Laurey, who is drifting off to sleep in his embrace. The tenderness seems to be especially concentrated, for me, in the very rural and evocative phrases "The moon is takin' a header" and its rhyming partner "A lark'll wake up in the medder..." I admit, though, that it is hard for me to tell if I respond so strongly to this poetry mostly because of its words, or mostly because of the music that I can't help but hear in crystalline clarity when I read it, or mostly because of the specific way in which Alfred Drake sings it in the original Broadway-cast recording, which I also can't help but hear...

This difficulty of pinpointing the source of an emotional reaction reminds me of a few occasions — they seem but yesterday — when Carol and I were browsing through fashion catalogues, and Carol, toying with the idea of ordering something, would ask me which dresses and skirts and so on I liked, and I would say, "Well... maybe this one, but to tell the truth, I'm really not sure if it's her *blouse* or her *face* that I'm responding to." It got even worse when one time Carol flipped through a magazine with some very pretty models in ads, trying to find a new hair-do for herself, and she asked me for advice; I found myself almost totally unable to mentally untangle the framed faces from the framing hair. I just couldn't figure out whether it was the medium or the message pulling the strings inside me.

Yokohama, Where the Rain Falls Mainly in the Plain...

Does it make sense to translate "The Surrey with the Fringe on Top" into another language? Whatever your personal feeling is, I can tell you that I have in my record collection a small-size LP with several songs from *Oklahoma!* in Japanese. I always smile when I think of it, because the entire musical seems to me so deeply rooted in pioneer-era Oklahoma, and because that era and area's flavor seems so quintessentially American and, I imagine, so immensely out of the ken of a typical Japanese audience. It's almost as strange as if straight Peking opera were to be put on, sung in English, by American performers for an American audience.

As for the "Surrey", it happens that I was recently given a cassette tape on which the great actress Marlene Dietrich sings in German, and it includes this exact song. Well, maybe not "this exact song"... In fact, a thorough semantic reversal was effected; the German lyrics remind me of a building that's been gutted and rebuilt inside. What remains is just the shell — in this case, the image of lovers taking a ride in some horse-drawn vehicle. Thus what started out as a surrey has been transmogrified into a sleigh softly gliding through white snowdrifts, not by day but by night, with little bells constantly jingling; and moreover, instead of summertime bliss there is wintertime melancholy, and it's the she, not the he, who is singing.

On that same tape is the sweet nineteenth-century German folk song "Du, Du, liegst mir im Herzen", which Monica and Danny and I listened to with joy as we drove from Trento to Bologna nearly a year ago. Just as I was unable to detach a model's pretty face from her fringe on top, so can I not unlink Marlene Dietrich's sultry voice from this old song's old charms:

Du, Du, liegst mir im Herzen,
Du, Du, liegst mir im Sinn;
Du, Du, machst mir viel Schmerzen,
Weißt nicht, wie gut ich Dir bin.
  Du, Du, Du, Du,
    Weißt nicht, wie gut ich Dir bin.

You, you, my heart have captured,
You, you, my heart have caught;
You, you've got me enraptured,
Yet you don't care what you've wrought.
  You, you, you, you,
    Why don't you care what you've wrought?

So, so, wie ich Dich liebe,
So, so, liebe auch mich;
Die, die, zärtlichsten Triebe
Fühl' ich allein nur für Dich.
  Ja, ja, ja, ja,
    Fühl' ich allein nur für Dich.

So, so, deep is my yearning,
So, so, please let's not part;
Keen, keen, keenest of burning
Flames just for you fill my heart.
  Yes, yes, yes, yes,
    Flames just for you fill my heart.

Doch, doch, darf ich Dir trauen,
Dir, Dir, mit leichtem Sinn?
Du, Du, darfst auf mich bauen,
Weißt ja, wie gut ich Dir bin.
  Ja, ja, ja, ja,
    Weißt ja, wie gut ich Dir bin.

Yet, yet, dare I surrender
To, to, you, sprite uncaught?
Be, be, I'd be so tender,
Making you care what you've wrought.
  Ja, ja, ja, ja,
    Making you care what you've wrought.

Und, und, wenn in der Ferne
Dir, Dir, mein Bild erscheint,
Dann, dann, wünscht' ich so gerne,
Daß uns die Liebe vereint —
  Ja, ja, ja, ja,
    Daß uns die Liebe vereint!

And, and, when in your dreaming,
I, I, float from your past,
That, that, day, so I'm scheming,
Love will unite us at last —
  Ah, ah, ah, ah,
    Love will unite us at last!

As I strove to anglicize its stanzas, I was chained by one extra constraint: fitting the precise musical rhythm of the song. And when I tipped my tiny hat to German itself, it felt so *right* that I heard myself singing, "Ja, ja, ja, ja!"

Just as odd as hearing a semantically flipped fringe-topped "Surrey" is to stochastically flip the tuning knob of one's radio and land on a station broadcasting German country-western music, which in fact I once did. The instruments, the melodies, and even the twangs of the vowels sounded as if they came from deep in Appalachia, yet when I listened closely, every syllable was definitely in German. It was almost surreal, to my ears. It also made me wonder if there is perhaps a kind of universal "country accent" that has some uniform qualities that transcend the actual language that it involves. I have long had the vague sense that country-style pronunciation tends to turn pure vowels into diphthongs, which may or may not be a correct generalization, and I wonder if there isn't even a greater degree of language-independent predictability to the large-scale pattern of shifts that collectively convert the world's "officialeses" into the world's "ruraleses".

Ages ago, I acquired two other recordings that inspire a similar feeling of weirdness whenever I listen to them, or even think about them. Both are performances of the great Lerner and Loewe musical *My Fair Lady* in languages other than English: one in Spanish, the other in Hungarian. Each of them has a special twist of irony. At the core of the original story is how the coarse Cockney girl Liza Doolittle is, as a challenge, taken in by the insufferably smug but utterly smitten professor Henry Higgins, and through painful exercises — "The rain in Spain falls mainly in the plain" — acquires such an impeccably upper-class Oxbridge way of speaking English that at her (and his) ultimate test, a posh ball that she attends incognito, drifting amongst the cream of British society, the keenest linguistic sleuth in the land dances with this mysterious beauty and in the end declares her too good to be true, and hence not English at all, but *Hungarian*!

The whole idea of de-anglicizing this story strikes me as really nutty — and yet there they are, those recordings on my shelf. And so, on what wet plains do those heavy, drenching rains mainly fall, in *Mi Bella Dama*? And in the Hungarian version, to what elite nationality is the too-good-to-be-true unrecognized Cockney girl assigned? Of course, the truly strange part in both cases is that the whole time she is speaking Spanish or Hungarian, the charade is maintained that she is actually speaking English, and, unlike most plays or movies where one language is made to pass for another, the linguistic medium here is not just an incidental fact, but the very crux of the entire plot. I suppose the suspension of disbelief involved is no more strained than our willingness to accept as "reality" a story that is occasionally punctuated by the actors' breaking into lyrical song, and then, as suddenly as it started, the singing is over and apparent normalcy resumes on stage.

From Tomsk with Love

Once, when I was giving a talk on radical translation based on the "Ma Mignonne" series, a gentleman in the audience rose and described a reading he had attended in which the Russian poet Yevgeny Yevtushenko had recited a poem he had composed entirely out of the names of Russian cities and towns. Of course this was an experience from which anyone who did not know the Russian tongue, culture, and country intimately would be entirely shut out, except for the savoring of the phonetic exuberance that must have been obvious. The gentleman then said that this seemingly untranslatable opus had in fact been "translated" by a daring English poet who had concatenated a long series of town names from the English countryside, and that Yevtushenko had confessed to his audience that he found the English version more effective than his own. It's a wonderful story, quite believable but a bit frustrating, since one would like to see and hear each of the two, with their marvelous media so close and yet so far.

I have regrettably never tracked down either the Yevtushenko or the "Yevtushenko" poem, but on hearing the story, I could not help but be reminded of one of my favorite Tom Lehrer songs, "Lobachevsky", which tells a droll tale — false from top to bottom, incidentally, a fact that the devilish Lehrer is the first to acknowledge, and in fact quite gleefully so — about the Russian mathematician Nikolai Ivanovich Lobachevsky, one of several more or less contemporaneous discoverers of the revolutionary field of non-Euclidean geometry. One verse of the song that I have always admired, and which quite beautifully illustrates the notion of *feminine rhyme* (about which more next chapter), is this:

> *Plagiarize,*
> *Let no one else's work evade your eyes,*
> *Remember why the good Lord made your eyes,*
> *So don't shade your eyes,*
> *But plagiarize, plagiarize, plagiarize —*
> *Only be sure always to call it please "research".*

This excerpt gives a clear idea of the topic of the song — falsely slandering the perfectly honest Lobachevsky, as I already said — but the part I was reminded of by the gentleman's story is this pair of verses:

> *I have a friend in Minsk, who has a friend in Pinsk,*
> *Whose friend in Omsk has friend in Tomsk*
> *With friend in Akmolinsk.*
> *His friend in Alexandrovsk has friend in Petropavlovsk,*
> *Whose friend somehow is solving now*
> *The problem in Dnepropetrovsk.*

> *And when his work is done — xaxa! — begins the fun.*
> *From Dnepropetrovsk to Petropavlovsk,*
> *By way of Iliysk and Novorossiysk,*
> *To Alexandrovsk to Akmolinsk,*
> *To Tomsk to Omsk, to Pinsk to Minsk,*
> *To <u>me</u> the news will run — yes, to <u>me</u> the news will run!*

The "x"'s in "xaxa!" represent a strong guttural "ch" sound, as in Scottish "loch" or German "Loch", suggesting how the laughter sounds when Lehrer himself sings the song with his marvelous put-on Russian accent.

It would seem to me only fitting if some witty Russian incarnation of Tom Lehrer flipped the tables around, taking Lehrer's music and putting new words to it, obviously character-assassinating some poor innocent

American mathematician and using a mellifluous series of American place names as an accessory to the crime. When this thought first occurred to me, the spots that sprang to mind were those celebrated in the whimsical song "Go Go Pogo", composed and boisterously sung by Walt Kelly, the famous possum's progenitor, including Key Largo, Fargo, San Diego, Oswego, Kokomo, Tishomingo, Shamokin, Hoboken, Shenango, Chicago, and, last but not least, Okeefenokee. (These are all in my gazetteer, by the way, whereas I could not find Akmolinsk or Iliysk for the life of me.)

There are many poems and songs, of course, that exult in addictive sonic media of one sort or another. "Villon's Straight Tip" by Henley is a great example, as are the above-mentioned pieces by Yevtushenko, Lehrer, and Kelly. One of the most wonderful in this category, in my opinion, is Tom Lehrer's song "The Elements", whose words run as follows:

> *There's antimony, arsenic, aluminum, selenium,*
> *And hydrogen and oxygen and nitrogen and rhenium,*
> *And nickel, neodymium, neptunium, germanium,*
> *And iron, americium, ruthenium, uranium,*
> *Europium, zirconium, lutetium, vanadium,*
> *And lanthanum and osmium and astatine and radium,*
> *And gold and protactinium and indium and gallium,*
> *And iodine and thorium and thulium and thallium.*
>
> *There's yttrium, ytterbium, actinium, rubidium,*
> *And boron, gadolinium, niobium, iridium,*
> *And strontium and silicon and silver and samarium,*
> *And bismuth, bromine, lithium, beryllium, and barium.*
>
> *There's holmium and helium and hafnium and erbium,*
> *And phosphorus and francium and fluorine and terbium,*
> *And manganese and mercury, molybdenum, magnesium,*
> *Dysprosium and scandium and cerium and cesium.*
> *And lead, praseodymium, and platinum, plutonium,*
> *Palladium, promethium, potassium, polonium,*
> *And tantalum, technetium, titanium, tellurium,*
> *And cadmium and calcium and chromium and curium.*
>
> *There's sulfur, californium, and fermium, berkelium,*
> *And also mendelevium, einsteinium, nobelium,*
> *And argon, krypton, neon, radon, xenon, zinc, and rhodium,*
> *And chlorine, carbon, cobalt, copper, tungsten, tin, and sodium.*
>
> *These are the only ones of which the news has come to Ha'vard,*
> *And there may be many others, but they haven't been discavard.*

I have known several people who, in their teen-age years, memorized this marvelous tongue-twister of a lyric from beginning to bitter end. It would be interesting to know how long it took Lehrer to find this ordering, which seems, *a posteriori*, optimal if not inevitable. The words are to be sung, by the way, to the tune "A Modern Major-General" by Arthur Sullivan.

I have been sloppily calling these extremely narrow semantic ranges within which virtuoso phonetic games are played "media", but in fact this violates my own definition of the term, according to which one should be able to express *any* reasonable message in the medium. To be self-consistent, then, I will retreat to the more limited notion of a "semantically limited linguistic medium", which I defined earlier — a medium able to express only a restricted class of messages. As these examples show, the spontaneous invention — or discovery — of such limited yet engrossing media is a true art in its own right.

A Pervasive Medium of This Book

In this book there are transient passages exemplifying many types of linguistic media, some in prose and some in poetry, some even halfway in-between. But there is one medium — one set of constraints — in which not just little bits, but the entire English text has been cast. That is the medium of nonsexist English.

Over the last twenty-five years or more, nonsexist language has made considerable inroads on the conservative bastion that is accepted English usage — particularly in America, in contrast to England and other places where English is spoken. In this country, it is not nearly as common as it used to be to encounter blatantly sexist usages of the words "man" and "men" in academic journals, newspapers, book titles, and so forth, and one sees and hears "he" and "him" used as generic pronouns quite a bit less than a few decades ago. However, such usages are nowhere close to being fully squelched, and in any case, subtler sexist usages remain scattered throughout our language in an almost frighteningly dense manner.

"Waiter/waitress", "actor/actress", "hero/heroine", "host/hostess", "spokesman/spokeswoman", "tiger/tigress", "brother/sister", and similar pairs in which the masculine is conflated with the generic are rampant in English, and syntactic and semantic subordination of the feminine is so routine and standard that, paradoxically, it is still entirely invisible to most people. "Wish I could be king for a day" is as likely to pop out of a girl's mouth as out of a guy's, and if one imagines a feminine version of it — "Wish I could be queen for a day" — one instantly hears all sorts of subtle pejorative and loaded flavors in the "equivalent" phrase; just this one example makes it clear why there remains in our society today a powerful unconscious tendency to shy away from many feminine types of usage.

The dense and sticky spiderweb of social pressures tending to keep so many sexist patterns rigidly intact despite the remarkable flexibility of our English language and despite so much recent progress in women's rights constitutes a gigantic topic, fraught with political and social complexities that are entirely beyond the scope of this book — and yet at the same time, this is a topic filled to the brim with fascinating cognitive issues having to do with how the semantic halos of words really work, and in that sense it is closely related to the core concerns of this book.

Cloaked in "You Guys", Old "Man" Resurfaces in New Guise

In my view, the most pervasive — and, for that reason, by far the most serious — disease of sexist usage infecting contemporary American English is the to-many-people-innocuous-sounding phrase "you guys" (and related ways of using "guys" in directly addressing a group of people), which is by far more popular than the now-taboo sexist terms "man/men" ever were, in terms of applicability to a mixed-sex or even all-female group. I find it an amazing irony that the fairly recent groundswell of popular acceptance of "you guys" is largely welcomed, rather than contested, by feminists of most stripes, the very same people who adamantly, angrily, and properly urged rejection of the very similar false generics "man", "men", "he", and "him".

The reasons that women seem to be happy being called "guys" when the term also continues to be used as a clear and sharp opposite to "girls" or "women" — "Girls to the right, guys to the left", for instance — are many and murky; and indeed, both fascinated and driven to absolute distraction by this pervasive usage that I personally find so perverse, I have recently undertaken a long-term project of psychological experimentation to try to lay bare some of the unconscious qualities that flavor the phrase "you guys", qualities that render it such an attractive, even irresistible, nuisance of an expression. My own conviction is that the phrase's desirability is due precisely to the fact that "guy" in the singular remains clearly masculine, thus imbuing the word's unconscious halo with the positive aura associated with being male in our society. To find the right experiments to probe this ironic hypothesis is very subtle, but I hope to succeed in the course of time. In my opinion, and although this may seem improbable to some, to fully explain the usage of the simple-seeming pair of words "guy" and "guys" would hugely advance our knowledge of the workings of the human mind.

For many years, I have noted that in America, the default little furry animal scampering up the tree trunk is always a "he", no matter whether the child pointing at it with delight is a little girl or a little boy. I have also heard, on several different occasions, intelligent adults refer to an insect that lays eggs as "he", and seen no one around smile in amusement or utter a peep of protest. I even remember a family whose pet cat was female but the two daughters gave her a masculine name and called her "he" anyway.

These sad and weird little facts strike me as being related, behind the scenes of the American collective unconscious, to the sadder and weirder fact that the friendly male and female swim and gym teachers at the local YMCA (what ever happened to the YWCA?) address the children, even in their all-girl classes, as "you guys" in nearly every sentence that they utter, thus subliminally inculcating in their innocent and malleable charges, from a very tender age on, the clear-as-day message that *being a guy* is what one really wants in this world, because guys get the perks.

The fact that guys do indeed tend to get the perks in this still very sexist land of ours makes it understandable why women would want to be included in the category of "guys", but since simply sticking that label on them is as empty a gesture as going around insisting that night is as bright as day, what does it gain them? Do women actually *become* guys if they are *called* "guys" enough times? Did women *become* men by being included in "mankind" for centuries? Does a horse have five legs if you call its tail a leg?

I have often wondered what would happen if I were to try to engage one of the college-age swim teachers at the "Y" in a dialogue on this topic, and in my mind I imagine something like this (if she didn't get offended):

Me: I hope you don't mind if I ask you a strange question... Why is it that you address my daughter Monica and the other two little girls as "guys"? In fact, why do *all* the teachers call *all* the kids "guys"? Do you think they *are* guys?

She: Of course not — it's just that that's what you *say*. Everybody says it.

Me: Yeah, but would you say to your three-girl class, "Now I want you boys to kick on your tummies all the way out from the wall to me"?

She: No, of course not. I would no sooner call them "boys" than "cows".

Me: Well, what's the difference? "Boy", "guy" — they sound equally male to me.

She: I don't know, but we just say "you guys". It's just what people say.

Me: Is it a kind of friendly joke, a bit of wishful thinking, a bit like saying to a group of kids, "Come on, Olympic champions — let's show how fast we are!"?

She: No, I wouldn't call it wishful thinking. Like you said, it's just friendly-sounding. It's informal, palsy, easy-going — that kind of thing.

Me: Is saying "you guys" to a group of girls maybe a metaphor, like calling these swimming classes "Minnows", "Eels", "Pike", "Fish", and so on? Are girls "guys" in the same sense that these kids in this pool are "fish"?

She: I don't think so. "Guys" isn't a metaphor. Like I said, it's just a convention.

Me: But it's a strange convention, to my ears. Would you say that *you're* a guy?

She: No, obviously not.

Me: But if I said to you and another swim teacher, "Do you guys ever let the kids swim in the deep end?", would you feel upset being addressed that way?

She: Not at all. It wouldn't matter if the other teacher was male or female.

Me: Right. But if I said to just you alone, "Hey, guy, you did a great job with the kids today", would you find it strange?

She: Well, yeah... I mean, I'm *not* a guy...

The Nimble Medium-Hopping of Evanescent Essences ◆ ◆ ◆ **203**

And on and on it would go, round and round, never making any real progress, never hitting an out-and-out contradiction, never getting to the nub of the matter, with both of us simply citing popular usage and neither of us ever penetrating to beneath the surface, to where the unconscious flavors of words determine what is chosen to be uttered in certain circumstances, and what is rejected. This is so inaccessible to the conscious mind that its inaccessibility is not even thought about by most people. Indeed, most people just get puzzled or annoyed when you ask them why they say what they say, because to them, it's all just common sense, all perfectly obvious. There's nothing at all beneath the surface to probe, in their view — nothing to think about, nothing puzzling. It's just the way things are. Anyone who spends their time thinking about it is weird.

The way I see it, the near-universality of "you guys" represents a deplorable state of affairs both in terms of the status of women and in terms of the lack of linguistic self-awareness in our country today. Maybe I'm reading too much into it, but that's how I see it. How else can one explain the following astonishing event I witnessed not long ago? I was at the birthday party of a three-year-old girl, and her aunt, an elementary-school teacher in her early thirties, I would guess, was pushing the cute little birthday girl and a four-year-old playmate, also female, in one of those two-seater swings. The two little ones were going back and forth, higher and higher and higher, and at a certain point, they both started squealing in fear. The aunt, scornful of this sissyish behavior, said derisively to them, "Come on! What *are* you guys — a couple of *girls*?" Being *girls* was the worst possible thing that these two little "guys" could be accused of — and by another female, on top of it all. Hearing that sentence made me sick.

Dutch Boys, China Buddies, and Norway Guys

The phenomenon of borrowing a catchy, with-it term that specifically designates males and applying it to females to boost their status or self-esteem is, as it turns out, not limited to America. For instance, a few months ago I learned that in Holland, the word *jongen*, which means "boy", has in recent years caught on among women as a term of camaraderie, but — almost isomorphically to the case of "you guys" in America — only in the *plural*, and only when one is *directly addressing* an all-female or mixed-sex group, as in the following sentence: *Jongens, loop eens door, anders komen we te laat!* ("Hey, boys, walk a bit faster, or we'll be late!"). In contemporary Holland, this sentence could easily be uttered by a woman to her female friends, by a man to his male friends, or in any spliced mixture of the two situations — but no one would ever use *jongen* to call or refer to just *one* girl or woman, for *jongen*, "boy", and *meisje*, "girl", are exact opposites. With the word "boys" used in the English translation, this sentence sounds positively nonsensical, and yet if for "boys" you substitute "guys", it suddenly sounds as all-American and as wholesome as apple pie and motherhood. Yukkh!

An unlikely-seeming venue for this kind of linguistic phenomenon is contemporary China, and yet an eerily parallel trend is occurring there. David Moser has observed (and verified with native speakers) the fact that the word *gēmenr*, which is a plural noun coming from *gēge*, meaning "older brother", is used as a term of camaraderie not just among males but also occasionally among females. Much like "you guys", this word seems to appeal to many people as a verbal means of suggesting or reinforcing group bonding, as in a team working together for a common goal. The final "r" is a common suffix in Mandarin that lends an affectionate, diminutive flavor to a noun, and its presence in this case creates a subtle flavor extremely similar to that of our American word "buddies" (which, with its strongly analogous derivation from the word "brother", still tends to have a masculine flavor but is nonetheless often applied by girls or women to each other, especially in highly competitive sports or other "macho" contexts).

Curiously enough, the false-generic "you guys" phenomenon does not seem to have spread — yet — from America to other English-speaking countries. When I have given talks on the topic, Australian or English members of the audience have sometimes not even understood, at the beginning, what I meant when I said that "guys" is applied to females. It sounds as wrong to them as calling dogs "cats" or horses "cows". By the end of the talk, of course, they fully get the picture, although the idea of saying "you guys" to women still *sounds* as silly to them as at the beginning.

A few years ago, as I sat sipping my breakfast coffee in an elegant little hotel dining room in Bergen, Norway, I chanced to overhear a snippet of conversation at a nearby table in which an American was talking to a Norwegian about daylight-savings time. All of a sudden, I cringed inside when I heard the American ask his European colleague, "So, do you guys change your clocks at the same time of year as we do?" I couldn't help but project myself into the mind of the Norwegian, through whose British-trained ears the whole country of Norway (or perhaps the whole continent of Europe) must have sounded as if it was being cast in the masculine guise. But the conversation kept on going without a hitch. Perhaps the Norwegian even liked the term and next time around used it himself in talking about all of America. "You guys like cappuccinos a lot, don't you?"

I found this little conversation strangely depressing. I know that for reasons I am unable to fathom, "palsy" American memes seem to have a penetrating power in other cultures that makes them nearly irresistible over time, and so it may well be that "you guys" will, within a decade or two, have become an internationally accepted false generic in English. Like chewing gum, jeans, and rock-and-roll, one more "gold" for the red, white, and blue. Attaway, guys!

Speaking, Writing, and Translating in Nonsexist English

Let me leave these subjective and controversial psycholinguistic bones of contention to the side, and simply state that nonsexist prose is a brand of English that comes in many different degrees of purity, and one can adopt the medium at any level of strictness that one finds comfortable. Some people balk at generic "man" but see nothing wrong with "you guys", while others reject both "man" and "you guys" but aren't so compulsive as to feel any need to purge from their vocabulary such familiar expressions as "waitress", "actress", "she-wolf", "temptress", "chessmen", "garbageman", "freshman year", "mailman", "first baseman", "Mother Nature", "no-man's land", or "animal kingdom". There are hundreds of others, perhaps even thousands, that could be adduced here, but this little sampling gets the feeling across.

Where to draw the line between the objectionable and the acceptable is very subjective. In fact, of course, the vast majority of speakers of English, even linguistically reflective ones, never make any overall policy decision about where to draw the line, but simply take whatever expression bubbles up from their unconscious mind as a result of whatever unique constellation of mental pressures the current situation happens to have imposed. Thus "you guys" or "mailman" or a masculine pronoun for God might sound acceptable in one context and completely unacceptable in another. This type of noncompulsive fluidity seems pretty reasonable.

As for me, however, my lifelong trait of linguistic perfectionism — a type of compulsiveness, for sure — has led me to work for many years now at polishing my speech and my writing in a very strict form of the medium. Once I had become sufficiently aware of the issues, I simply found it repugnant to write or speak in any other manner, and from that day onward, I made a point of trying to express every thought in an elegant and graceful way without sexual bias in one direction or another. But this is by no means always easy, let alone mechanical. There are all sorts of methods one can utilize, and what works in one context may not work in another. There are some superb books that deal with these issues, among them Casey Miller and Kate Swift's *Words and Women* and *A Handbook of Nonsexist Writing*, and Rosalie Maggio's *Nonsexist Word Finder and Dictionary*.

The task of translating from sexist to nonsexist English, though sometimes fairly straightforward, can occasionally pose an incredibly subtle and complex challenge. To show the kinds of issues that can come up, and to let you try your own hand at it, I have chosen a short excerpt from *The Magic Years*, a sensitive book about children and child-rearing that was written in the 1950's by psychologist Selma Fraiberg. At the time, of course, the prose that now looks quite bizarre was absolutely par for the course, and almost no one had ever thought of trying to change things. Here goes:

The child who has not conceived of human bodies as being different from his own reacts to this discovery according to his own sex. If he is a little boy observing a little girl he sees that something is "missing" on her. If she is a little girl she sees that the little boy has something that she doesn't have, that something is "missing" on her. When the child tries to explain these observations to himself he can only come up with primitive theories.... But normally the child overcomes these feelings and develops appropriate feelings of pride and pleasure in being a boy, in being a girl. He achieves this in several ways.... He will learn that nothing was taken away from the little girl and that nothing will be taken away from him, that they were both made the way they are from the very beginning. He will also learn that he is made just like his father, that the little girl is made just like her mother, and in this way the child begins to take pride in his own sex because he is made just like a beloved parent.

This is a wonderful example of a passage demonstrating how interwoven a message and its medium can be. Untangling that tight intertwinedness and then constructing a related tangle in a different medium is the challenge.

A HexHagonal Patter Designed by Our Lady of the Army

A guide to a type of feminist language that goes much further than the three cited above is *Websters' First New Intergalactic Wickedary of the English Language,* "conjured", as it says on the cover, by Mary Daly, "in cahoots with Jane Caputi". The apostrophe's appearance after, rather than before, the "s" in the first word is not an error; indeed, the *Wickedary* itself defines "Webster" as: "a woman whose occupation is to Weave, especially a Weaver of Words and Word-Webs"; on looking up "Weaving", one finds it means, among other things, "creating tapestries of Crone-centered creation; constructing a context which sustains Sisters on the Otherworld journey" as well as "wending one's way through and around the baffles of blockocracy". The latter noun, when looked up, turns out to be this: "rule by blockers, cocks and jocks". And a Crone, by contrast, is a "Great Hag of History, long-lasting one; Survivor of the perpetual witchcraze of patriarchy".

As if you needed to be told, the wordplay in this book is extraordinary. Although the *Wickedary* is perfused with a raging bitterness toward males that is unique to militant separatist Lesbians, it is also inventive and funny, often through its device of co-opting terms that one would *a priori* tend to think of as virulently redolent of antifeminist prejudices, such as the nouns "banshee", "battle-ax", "bitch", "crackpot", "crone", "dragon", "gooney bird", "gossip", "hag", "harridan", "harpy", "hex", "hog", "monster", "nag", "nix", "old maid", "prude", "quack", "scold", "shrew", "sloth", "spinster", "termagant", "virago", "virgin", "vixen", and "witch", and then putting a Positive Spin on them. I capitalize "Positive Spin" because, in fact, all words in the *Wickedary* that have a Positive Spin (*e.g.*, the ones in the list above) are capitalized. Among the definitions of "Spinning" itself, for instance, are: "whirling and twirling the threads of Life on the axis of Spinsters' own be-ing; moving Counterclockwise; whirling away from the death march of patriarchy". And an Old Maid is defined as "a Crone who has steadfastly resisted imprisonment in the Comatose State of matrimony".

Adjectives having negative auras in standard use are equally gleefully co-opted, including "batty", "canny", "catty", "dreadful", "eccentric", "horsey", "odd", "pigheaded", "queer", "revolting", "silly", "sinister", "snaky", "strange", "weird", "wicked", and "wild". There are also novel verbs, such as "Be-Wilder", which is defined as "to lead the Self and Others on Pixie-paths that wind ever deeper into the Unknown; to hear and follow the Call of the Wild", and "Gabble", which is "to utter utterly articulate sounds in Canny Conversations with Animals, Augurs, and Other Wise Ones; to mutter messages utterly unintelligible to snools". This last word, incidentally, is a new noun whose sound simply sizzles with complex and subtle semantic resonances; it means a "normal inhabitant of sadosociety, characterized by sadism and masochism combined; stereotypic hero and/or saint of the sadostate. *Examples:* Adam, Saint Paul, the Marquis de Sade."

The *Wickedary* has many such words with negative auras (*i.e.,* words seen as drenched with masculine aggressivity and necromancy). Thus one finds "bull, papal" ("Wholly, Holey, Holy Baloney"), "popebot" (the pope as robot — the Holy See takes a pummeling), "fembot" ("the archetypical role model forced upon women throughout fatherland"), "stag-nation", "snot boy", "clockocracy" (clocks and watches are equated with doomsday), and a host of words based on sundry vulgarities for male genitals.

Here are a few miscellaneous definitions of note. "Sisterhood of Man" is cleverly defined as: "a transitional expression giving a generic weight to the word *sisterhood* while at the same time emasculating the pseudo-generic term *man.*" Then there is "prick", which is explicated as follows: "a self-important member of the thrusting throng; an especially contemptible and disagreeable dick (see *dick*)". We conclude our gay romp through the wily *Wickedary* with "cockocracy", whose definition is a little separatist pun-poem: "the state of supranational, supernatural erections; the place/time where the air is filled with the crowing of cocks, the joking of jocks, the droning of clones, the sniveling of snookers and snudges, the noisy parades and processions of prickers: pecker order". A-men! (Eh, men?)

Although I salute the militant Army Lady — described on the book's back cover as "a Positively Revolting Hag who teaches Feminist Ethics in the Department of Theology at Boston College" — for her Canny HexHagonal patter, I am saddened at all the energy spent on condemning all males to roughly the same status of respect as, say, fire hydrants — just plug-ugly inanimate objects to be avoided when one espies them on the sidewalk. Still, Wild Cat Mary's *Wickedary* puts forth one hell of a medium, and that's to its credit. Or *is* it a full medium? Can any message be expressed? *Any?*

Quick Poetry Break, III

What with our jolly keen and quing for a day, our Dutch "boys" and butch Dykes, the droning of clones, the Nagging by Hags, the Spinsters and Websters, the Baxters and Sisters, my poor little male bird brain is — how shall I put it? — Positively Spinning. And so, I think we all deserve one more poetry break. It'll be our last one for the chapter. What do you say?

D's Cross Tip
To All Straight Wives

Ye who be snookered by slick papal bulls,
*   Play dumb like a broad, deride Canny Nags,*
Ye suckseeding sexpots, ye fembots, ye fools,
*   Ye bimbos who blurt snide remarks about Hags —*
*   So how come ye powder your noses for stags?*
Ye wearers of pearls, of perfume and jewels,
*   Why twitches your butt? your tail why wags?*
All for the phallacies and for the snools.

Your flappers and jabbers and jerkalike jocks,
*   Your maskuline queens, gaily flashing in drag,*
Your lickspittles, louts, cockaludicrous cocks,
*   With fake-padded bras for some clock-foolish fag,*
*   Your bonnies who tout their god-rods till they gag,*
Flaunting their plug-ugly nineteen-inch tools;
*   Ye wives can not hook a Single Strange Bag*
With all of your phallacies and all your snools.

Ye shrink before husbandly hard-on cock schools,
*   And with us Queer Norns would flash your flag?*
With Horses go Wild? come Spin with us Mules?
*   Or with Wicked Monsters go Skew and Zig-zag?*
*   O Nix, Lusty Nix, all the Dykes ye would snag,*
If ye axed all your clock-driven, death-luvvin' ghouls!
*   Our Merry daily Gabblings would soon be your jag,*
If ye chopped all your phallacies and all your snools.

Envoi

*   But up spouts the popebot (that vatican wag);*
O pity the wifebot who drools for his stools,
*   And unless the Weird Hexes can save her poor scrag,*
Falls prey-gnant to phallacies and to the snools.

How Snaky and Batty, how Horsey and Catty. And how Weirdly Weird, the way with words that this unnamed Wordster has. I hope you enjoyed our last little poetry break. And now, refreshed and revitalized, we return once again to more prosaic prose-bound musings.

The Quirky, Fluky Evolution of a HexHagonal Poem

"D's Cross Tip to All Straight Wives" was anything but foreseen as I started this chapter out a few weeks ago. It was, quite to the contrary, the totally chance result of a conflux of several independent strands. As I gaze back, I see the story of the evolution of such a curious hybrid as having some intellectual interest, especially given the cognitive focus of this book, and so hope you will indulge my desire to relate it briefly right now.

Of course it all stemmed from the original Villon ballad, but this was a poem I did not know in the least until just under a year ago. It was while I was browsing through an old poetry anthology of my mother's that I happened to run into W. E. Henley's "Villon's Straight Tip to All Cross Coves", whose strange, cryptic flavor and wondrous virtuosity truly boggled my mind. Despite its title's claim that this was a François Villon poem, I was quite skeptical that it could ever have been in French at all! This strong cognitive dissonance propelled me into a search for the original poem, and soon thereafter I extracted a big stack of Villon books from the Indiana University library. It was not such a trivial task, however, to tell which of Villon's numerous ballads the Henley "Tip" was a translation of, since both Henley's old English slang and Villon's very ancient French were a bit cryptic to me, but despite this barrier, I eventually succeeded in recognizing the "Ballade de bonne doctrine" through its thick Henley mask.

My curiosity having by now been highly piqued, I went on to look up the same Ballade in all the different Villon volumes, and in this manner came across H. De Vere Stacpoole's anglicization. Since it rhymed and felt like a genuine poem, it had great appeal for me, but I nonetheless felt it badly needed some touching-up, so I undertook that task, and in the course of my doing so, the poem, both in French and in English, became very much part of me. The next step in the game — part of a different strand — was the careful decipherment, to the extent that I could carry it out, of Henley's slang version into a more normal medium, an act that brought the Henley poem into far sharper focus than before. And thus, all three cousin poems, two in English and one in French, were swimming about most vividly in my head, at the same time as I was thrashing out this chapter.

Since the whole chapter was largely about linguistic media, and since nonsexist English is not only a canonical example of the notion but also pervades the book, I had intended all along to include some commentary on it, but it was only while I was deep in the midst of doing so that I decided that Mary Daly's extraordinarily idiosyncratic HexHagonal patter, which I had known for many years, was a closely related linguistic medium just too crazy and too intriguing to leave out, despite its disagreeable aspects, and so I started writing up a brief summary of its Wild Wicked Weirdness. After a page and a half, it felt pretty much done, so I printed it out, read it over, and then scribbled at the bottom, in red pen, a sketch for what I thought would make a very nice concluding paragraph:

> Is the language of the *Wickedary* a full linguistic medium? That is, could you translate any arbitrary message — say, the "Ballade de bonne doctrine" — into it? I can only dimly imagine what such a translation might be like, but it would surely have to involve a sex reversal, thus becoming a warning and a counsel to weaker women not to succumb to the lures of snooldom.

The image seemed delicious but extremely weird — a good combination — so I figured I would flesh this thought out a little bit, letting readers savor it in their imaginations, and in that manner I might wind up the *Wickedary* section with a bit of a bang.

Well, the next morning, for some reason, I happened to wake up very early and was tossing and turning in bed. As I did so, I pondered the notion of someone translating Villon's "Ballade de bonne doctrine" into Daly's odd medium. The idea seemed absolutely preposterous, but still, it caught my fancy, and I couldn't help but notice that Daly's HexHagonal vocabulary and Henley's slang vocabulary had more than a slight overlap. Right off the bat, for instance, I noticed "hag" and "nag", and then, as "drag" and "fag" had strong overtones of the Gay/Lesbian world, I could imagine how they might fit into a translation quite easily.

Thus to my surprise, I found myself getting sucked into what had been, really, just a joke of a challenge. I jumped out of bed, fixed myself a coffee, then jumped back into bed, wide awake, lively, and utterly hooked. What would be a plausible way of converting Villon's warnings to his crowd of booze-guzzling, slut-lusting, crime-prone male street cronies into their "equivalents" in Daly's not-so-similar world of militant separatist Lesbianism? Being very partial to the sonorous ring of "snools", I could imagine that word playing the key role of "girls" — a cute twist — yet this was but a teeny snippet. Other disconnected ideas came to mind, but nothing at a higher organizational level, so I went out to the Runcible Spoon for a coffee break.

The decisive moment came when it occurred to me to try to interleave the Henley and Stacpoole poems, letting each contribute fourteen lines — in particular, taking all the "-ag" lines from Henley and modifying them, then taking the complementary lines from Stacpoole and modifying *them.* With a bit of luck, all these new lines would then merge smoothly with each other, like cards effortlessly fluttering together when a true cardsharp shuffles a deck. And lo and behold, after a couple of hours of splicing and tweaking, discarding and restarting, rearranging and flipping, and so forth and so on, I found I had evolved a fairly polished product. And then, over the next day or so, the whole thing slowly settled into its final state.

In the heat of fresh creation, I ran into some lovely coincidences, such as Stacpoole and Daly's overlapping interest in the topic of papal bulls, and the way that "jewels, perfume, and pearls" (which rhymes with "all to the girls") can be made to rhyme with "all to the snools" by a simple reversal; or the fact that "nix", used twice in one line by Henley as meaning "nothing", is also one of Daly's synonyms for "Hag" (using a capital "N") — and the facts that Henley's "merry" suggests "Mary" and that his word "goblin" resembles her word "Gabbling". I also admit I got a Wicked little *frisson* of delight at being able to lift two longish phrases right out of the *Wickedary*'s Appendicular Web Two — lines 1 and 3 of the second stanza (minus the word "your"). Lastly, I note with amusement that a Mule (see Villon's original) is "a sterile hybrid of a male ass and a female Horse". Too much!

All in all, then, I wound up having concocted (sorry!) a rather surrealistic translation of François Villon's heterosexual-male-oriented fifteenth-century French "Ballade de bonne doctrine" into a twentieth-century dialect of English oriented toward male-bashing homosexual females. Delicious icing on the cake was provided by the modern sexual meanings of "cross" and "straight" in Henley's title, which I swapped with great relish to make my own title — and as a final point after touchdown, I was able to tie all this nonsense in with the chess/chesh theme of the chapter's outset, through the idea of Daly's HexHagonal patter. One has to assume that a bishopric's move would link two kissing Hexes...

Joke-telling Reveals Pernicious Sexist Attitudes

One of several forms of expression in which someone committed to nonsexism is put under severe pressure is the art of joke-telling. A joke is a tight verbal structure in which each part is there for a reason. Although a good joke-teller makes the telling seem leisurely and casual, it is in fact anything but that; every word and bit of intonation is taken by listeners as a cue preparing them for something unexpected. This means the linguistic pressures on the speaker or writer are very different from those in ordinary prose. In particular, if you take a standard joke and in the interests of gender balance replace its opening line "Guy goes into a bar and says to the bartender..." by any feminine adaptation of it, whether it is "Woman goes", "Girl goes", "Gal goes", "Lady goes", or whatever other phrase you might dream up, you will set into motion a host of bawdy expectations on the part of your listeners — be they female or male — for almost every word in a well-constructed joke is charged with implications, especially words like "woman" or "girl", which tend to suggest "taboo" topics such as sexuality.

Yes, I hate to say it, but one of the definitely drearier facts about contemporary Western society is that in many contexts — not all, thank God! — saying "female" is tantamount to saying "sexual" (and "deviant" and "lesser" and many other undesirable qualities as well), whereas saying "male" is tantamount to saying "neutral" (and "standard" and "better" and so forth). Our culture's silent acquiescence to so much tacit androcentrism gives rise to sharp gynocentric backlashes by people such as Mary Daly.

Thus in all jokes, all protagonists *have* to be male, unless there is a specific reason to make them female (*e.g.*, the farmer's daughter, who is there specifically in order to be seduced by the traveling salesman; or a character who is a housewife because the joke is specifically about what housewives do). If, again in the interests of nonsexism, some character in a standard joke were "artificially" made female and the joke were told, even if it were told very well, people would scratch their heads when the punch line came, and would wonder, "But what did the fact that the person who jumped out of the window was *female* have to do with it?"

Unexplained, unjustified femaleness will always be seen as anomalous, as a loose end that never was tied up, whereas of course maleness, being taken for granted as standard, never is seen as unexplained or unjustified; it doesn't *have* to be explained or justified, because it is the default, the canonical, the expected, the *norm*.

I have given thought to this dilemma for some years now, but never have I found any systematic, global resolution. It seems to me that society's pro-male biases are just too pervasive and too strong. Luckily, since I am not and never have been a card-carrying joke-teller, I've rarely had to face the dilemma myself, but that's of little consolation to those who are.

Joke Deporning as a Translation Challenge

A few years ago, I organized a small workshop on the topic of "Humor and Cognition" at my research center at Indiana University. Present were my graduate students, some local colleagues, some old friends, and some external visitors — a professor and three of his graduate students — whose specialty was the study and modeling of humor. In selecting the participants, I used two main criteria: first, a refined and original sense of humor, and second, a deep interest in how cognition and creativity work.

Over the course of the workshop, many dozens of jokes were told by participants to illustrate points about humor, and a fair percentage of them were, as might be expected, sexual in nature. A good number of these jokes were quite funny, but I was bothered that the taboo nature of their subject matter seemed to add to their humor; I wondered to what extent they would still be funny if the sexual element could somehow be subtracted from them.

In this manner arose an amusing and unusual translation challenge: Given a sexually explicit joke, transfer its funniness to a nonsexual setting, or in other words, translate jokes between two media: X-rated and G-rated. The question was: Could this always be done, or are some jokes unalterably sexual in nature, and hence fundamentally untranslatable into the G-rated medium? I personally was inclined to think that most if not all sexual jokes could be carried over into a nonsexual medium in such a way that an average listener would agree that, in essence, the same punch line was involved, despite a completely different setting.

Here is a sexual joke that you are hereby challenged to "deporn":

Erection-vs.-hand joke

A robust-looking fellow in his thirties goes to the doctor and says, "Doc, I've got a problem. When I was younger, every time I got an erection, I could bend it with my hand — but these days, whenever I try it, I find I can't bend it any more. What I want to know is, am I getting stronger or weaker?"

By the way, although I find this joke amusing, I am not claiming it is the funniest joke in the world, nor that it is the hardest imaginable joke to translate out of the medium of X-ratedness. It is simply a joke that someone in the workshop told, so we all had it fresh in our minds. The group tackled the challenge of deporning this joke with alacrity, celerity, assiduity, vim, vigor, vitality, savoir-faire, and undue velocity, and came up with several attempts, of which I now show two.

Runoholic version of erection-vs.-hand joke

Have you heard about *runorexia nervosa*? It's a disease some young women get, which makes them run a huge amount, often a full marathon's worth every day, no matter how much it hurts. This one obsessed woman was really forcing herself to do great damage to her body, and her doctor told her she absolutely had to cut down to ten miles a day. Well, it took a great deal of effort on her part as well as lots of help from friends, but finally she was able to do it. But then she got very worried and went back to her doctor in a fit of panic, asking, "Doctor, tell me — is my will power increasing, or is it decreasing?"

Theological version of erection-vs.-hand joke

God goes to the doctor and says, "Doctor, such a problem I've got... When I was younger, I always used to make stones so damn heavy that I couldn't lift them off the ground — but these days, every time I make a stone, I can pick it up with no trouble. So, Doc, am I getting *more* omnipotent, or less?"

The lower version was dreamt up by my friend Scott Buresh almost instantly after I remarked that the original joke reminded me of the renowned medieval scholastic paradox/riddle "Can God make a stone so heavy that He [sic] can't lift it?" I personally found Scott's joke just as funny as the original X-rated one, perhaps even funnier, and thus was convinced that deporning was a feasible proposition, at least for some jokes.

The Pursuit of Elusive Essence as Jokes Flit across Media

Another of the translations proposed was this one, which seemed (and still seems) particularly flat and unfunny to me:

Army–Navy version of erection-vs.-hand joke

Ronald Reagan goes to his astrologer and says, "Hey, doc, I'm really worried. Army beat Navy in football five years in a row, but this year Navy beat Army. What does this mean? Tell me, doc! Is our military youth getting stronger or weaker?"

I felt its flatness stemmed from the fact that for an average person to remember, from year to year, whether Army beat Navy or vice versa is a bit like remembering which of Tweedledum and Tweedledee ate more crumpets last Sunday. The idea of a strange, level-crossing battle inside a single system has vanished; in its place there is simply a dull symmetry.

The raising of the "flatness" issue inspired me to try to make an even flatter version, and after a while I came up with the joke below, which for me is just about as feeble a version of the original as is imaginable:

Arm-wrestling version of erection-vs.-hand joke

A robust-looking fellow in his thirties goes to the doctor and says, "Doc, I've got a problem. You see, I've always enjoyed arm-wrestling with myself, pitting one arm against the other. Well, when I was younger, my right arm would generally beat my left arm — but these days, I find that my left arm is almost always winning. What I want to know is, am I getting stronger or weaker?"

This deliberately bad joke unexpectedly brought to my mind an old favorite and — on the surface — very different joke in whose punch line some of the same abstractions play key roles. Here it is:

Two-ties joke

A Jewish mother gives her son two ties for his birthday. He puts one on at once, but when she sees him, she says, "So what's the matter with the *other* one?"

This joke has some deep abstractions in common with the erection-vs.-hand family of jokes, and also some deep contrasts with it. The deep link is that the mother plays the role of the dimwit who recognizes neither the symmetry of the "competition" nor the silliness of drawing any conclusion from the identity of its "winner". More precisely, she doesn't seem to recognize that between the two ties, there will always be a winner and a loser — never a tie. The analogy to the flatness of the Army–Navy football rivalry and the even flatter arm-wrestling situation is obvious.

The two-ties joke and the erection-vs.-hand family differ mainly in that although the son's choice *might* reflect a strong preference on his part for one tie, his mother *cannot know* if it does or doesn't; after all, no matter whether he liked his new ties equally or liked one of them far better, he could wear but one of them. In at least some of the erection-vs.-hand family of jokes, by contrast, the perplexed dimwit might have at least *some* justification in believing there is diagnostic information in the results being reported to the doctor, even though on some level there is a symmetry.

The detailed analysis of these similar jokes starts to get subtler and subtler and murkier and murkier, and no end is in sight to the comparisons and contrasts we could conceivably draw, let alone to the variations and translations we might go on to devise. As the variations proliferate, one starts to feel like someone who is momentarily losing all touch with the meaning of a very familiar word such as "hub", simply by repeating it over and over again. Too much spinning in the same spot leads to intellectual dizziness, and one needs to stop to regain one's stability.

Yes, Slippage Humor Has No Banana Peels

Despite this dizzying effect, I believe this type of analysis points the way to a theory of humor, or, more precisely, to a theory of a certain limited brand of humor whose major ingredients are playful intellectual operations such as role-switching, foreground–background reversal, and so on. I call this subset of the full range of humor *slippage humor,* not because it involves anyone slipping on a banana peel — indeed, the image of someone landing on their rear end is about as far from what I mean by "slippage humor" as you could get — but because it is characterized by the sudden, unexpected slippage of some mental structure that had seemed perfectly solid and not in the least suspicious until the moment the mental rockslide occurred. One of my favorite examples of slippage humor is the one-word breaking of the strict silence in Mel Brooks' silent movie *Silent Movie* by, of all people in the world, Marcel Marceau, the great mime.

In a word, slippage humor is humor that is *conceptual,* featuring jokes whose punch lines may involve, but *do not depend on,* such things as sexuality, religion, excretion, belching, vomiting, vulgar table manners, loud shouting, other people's physical deformities, misfortunes, foibles, ethnicities, and so forth.

Even when the world of humor is pared down to just slippage humor, it is obvious that this domain is still huge and fantastically subtle; it is certainly not going to yield up its secrets to a mere few hours' pondering.

Can the Tamer be Made Tamer?

Having arguably had one mild deporning success, our little workshop group wanted to see if it was a fluke or if we could do as well with another sexual joke. Here, then, was our next challenge, which proved somewhat harder, at least for us. I hope readers will try their hand at deporning it.

Lion-tamer joke

As the grand finale to his act, the circus lion tamer sat his fiercest lion in the center of the ring, with its snarling mouth wide open. But rather than placing his head between the beast's gaping jaws, he unzipped his trousers and instead boldly inserted the full length of his erect penis. The crowd gasped in amazement, and only after a full minute had passed did he withdraw and zip his pants back up.

He then offered $500 to anyone in the audience who would do the same. Not a murmur came from the audience, so he increased his offer to $600, then $700, and finally $1,000. At this point, a small, meek-looking chap in the back of the tent stood up and came forward, saying he would be willing to try. The crowd was stunned, and the lion tamer warned him it was extremely dangerous.

"Are you absolutely sure you want to go through with this?" he asked.

"Well," said the small chap, looking a little nervous despite himself, "I'll do my best, but I'm not sure if I can open my mouth as wide as the lion's."

It is at the abstract level of *last-minute switching of how roles are filled* that the essence of this joke resides, and in any cross-domain leap made by this joke, that is clearly the aspect that must be preserved at all costs.

Before revealing what I consider to be a successful deporning of this joke, I would first like to show that essentially the same joke can be told in a very different way *within* the sexual arena, and in fact it may seem so different at first glance that you may feel it is a quite different joke.

Tea-time version of lion-tamer joke

Did you hear the one about Lady Myra, who was known far and wide for her posh social affairs? It seems that a rude boor had crashed a fancy tea she was giving for her friend the baroness, and was wandering freely about, making all sorts of loud, crass remarks. Well, just as the butler wheeled in the tea-tray, Lady Myra's tiny little lapdog strolled into the elegant drawing room, lay down, and in full view of the assembled guests began licking its privates with obvious relish.

Snorted the snool, "Haw, haw! Wish *I* could do that!"

Without losing a beat, the Catty Lady Myra sweetly purred, "Well, my dear, give him a dog biscuit and perhaps he will let you!"

The counterintuitive counterfactual assignment of roles to dog and snool that Lady Myra's remark suggests is delightfully unexpected — and note, by the way, that Lady Myra's femaleness is not "artificial" but carefully calculated; it enhances the joke, as does the fact that she is of British blue blood, since her genteelly phrased but very raw suggestion is a powerful stereotype violation. The joke would be far less effective if the host (and dog's owner) were, say, a cool American fraternity boy.

In this tea-time tale, a good deal of the lion-tamer joke's essence is preserved, in that last-minute reassignment of role-fillers is the crux of the punch line, although the details of the reassignment are somewhat different. Of course, much more is preserved than just the playing-about with how roles are assigned, since the highly taboo theme of oral sex with animals is also still there. On the other hand, another salient ingredient of the original joke — the element of danger at the outset, and then its sudden evaporation at the role switch — is missing in the tea-time version.

Raw Meat but No Sex

The next version, by Joel Martin, does a fine job at stripping the lion-tamer joke bare of any trace of its original pornographic flavor:

<u>Butcher version of lion-tamer joke</u>

Each year at our county fair, there's a certain very macho butcher who always puts on a quite grisly show. He slaps a whole carcass down on a table and guts the animal one organ at a time. He extracts the innards through a small incision and always in the same order: pancreas first, appendix second, and so on. As each organ emerges, he waves it in the air, and the audience applauds madly.

Usually, the butcher gets a standing ovation, clears his table, and repeats his show. This year, though, he offered ten pounds of meat from the carcass itself to anyone who would do the next show. No one volunteered, so he increased his offer to twenty pounds, then thirty, and finally fifty. At this point, a small, meek-looking woman rose and came forward from the back of the tent.

The butcher smirked at her and said, "Are you absolutely sure you want to go through with this, ma'am?"

She replied, a little nervously, "Yes, sir, I'll try it… but I should probably warn you that I already had my appendix removed, when I was a little girl."

This joke is in one way opposite to the original, in that the humor arises at least in part from the unexpected way that the punch line has the danger element shoot through the ceiling rather than go to zero. Why would anyone possibly volunteer to be hacked apart, live, by a butcher? And the dizzy idea that a woman would jump at the offer to take home a free fifty pounds of her own flesh simply compounds the surrealism. But if we ignore these differences, I would argue that a yet deeper essence of the original is excellently preserved here — namely, the way that the challenge-accepter's remark instantaneously overturns the natural, totally automatic assumption that there will be a human and an animal filler, respectively, of the two key roles ("butcher" and "meat").

The way the story is told, the listener's unconscious mind is unlikely to anticipate a role swap, as the "meat" role is occupied by a dead and hence inanimate being. Indeed, up till the punch line, the meat is not even perceived as a role to be filled — there is only *one* role, that of "butcher", in view. Perhaps that makes this joke's punch line even more startling than that of the original joke. However, it could be argued that in the lion-tamer scenario, the lion's role, even though played by an animate agent, is not recognized by listeners as a genuine niche available for a human to fill — it is invisible, nonexistent. In that sense, the sudden perceptual shift induced by the punch line might be claimed to be equally jolting in both jokes.

It would be, by the way, interesting to study the degree to which a punch line's "startle index" (if such a thing could be reliably quantified) is correlated with the amount of mirth provoked in human listeners (once again, a most difficult thing to quantify). One would doubtless uncover some positive correlation between the two, but equally certain is that the two are by no means equivalent.

A Joke Belonging to Two Families at Once

We have looked at a tie joke, a tea joke, a tame joke, and a meat joke. We come now to a meta-joke — "meta" in the sense that it somehow rolls many of their common themes into one. Here it is:

Texas-ranch joke

A Texas cattle rancher was proudly driving a visiting sheep rancher from Idaho around his ranch in a jeep, and bragged, "Ah kin drahv due west all day long, from sunrahz to sundown, and still not leave mah property."
Unimpressed, the visitor replied, "Oh, yeah — *I* once had a jeep like that, too."

The coolness of this suave put-down is reminiscent of Lady Myra's cool snool-trumping remark, and of course it is similar in deeper ways as well. As in all the jokes in the lion-tamer family, and most especially the butcher version, a fillable role that listeners had not noticed as such is suddenly brought to the fore by a casual remark. In this case, it is the role of the vehicle, which was only a semi-noticed part of the background. In the twinkling of an eye, the jeep becomes foreground and the ranch recedes to the background, in somewhat the same way as the meat became foreground and the butcher faded to the background.

This sudden shift of foreground and background sets up an analogy between frameworks that is skewed. That is, American listeners know that Texas jokes always involve pride concerning giant-sized this's and that's, and in this case, it's clearly ranch sizes that are being compared, and so the default analogy maps host to visitor, cattle ranch to sheep ranch, and, presumably, giant to average. Vehicles are no more important to this analogy than are the sunrahz and the sundown. But then, out of the clear blue, vehicles become the only thing that matters in the mapping.

The unexpected perceptual shifts and skewed analogies clearly link the Texas-ranch joke with the lion-tamer family, but it is just as linkable to the erection-vs.-hand family, for the punch line forces us to ask ourselves: Is the jeep's speed being used to gauge the ranch's size, as the Texan would wish, or vice versa, as his visitor would suggest?

Many aspects of the erection-vs.-hand joke are absent from the Texas-ranch joke, but perhaps most notably, the erection joke features — and the Texan joke lacks — a dimwit who simply doesn't realize that although two very different measurements seem to be in competition, there is just not enough information for anyone to conclude anything from the story as told. Of course, the lack of a dimwit does not mean that the Texas-ranch joke is any less mirth-provoking than the erection-vs.-hand joke. In fact, there is still a kind of stooge — namely, the Texan, who, we presume, is quashed by his visitor's deflationary remark, much as the snool at Lady Myra's party was presumably silenced. And so this joke, like the tea-time joke, is a splicing of slippage humor, which is abstract and refined, with a cruder, baser form of humor — laughing at someone else's misfortunes.

The Paradoxical Fun of Unwrapping Utterly Unfunny Ur-jokes

When a joke is transferred successfully from an old medium to a new one, or when two already-known jokes are perceived to be linked by a deep analogy of their abstract structures, this means that the two jokes share what I call an *ur-joke* — an abstract theme that crops up in many different jokes, spanning domains and styles of humor.

Despite the fact that people see inter-joke similarities intuitively and effortlessly, it is often surprisingly hard to verbalize the ur-joke shared by two or more jokes that are obviously "exactly the same joke" at a deep level. Worse yet, if and when the ur-joke is actually articulated in words, it is almost always completely devoid of humor in itself. Take, for example, the following sincere but rather unsatisfying attempt on my part at spelling out the ur-joke shared by all the members of the erection-vs.-hand family:

> There is an occasional competition C that pits two activities, A and B, against each other, in the sense that the more success in A, the less in B, and vice versa. The degree of success in either A or B on its own is a simple and objective matter, and either degree can be taken, with some justification, as a crude estimate of the amount of a certain far more intangible attribute X, greatly prized by party P. It happens that in recent cases of C, A has been having ever higher levels of success, and B, perforce, the opposite. Party P takes this nondiagnostic fact as a cause for alarm, seeing in it an ominous sign that quality X may be diminishing with time.

Note how much longer this ur-joke is than most of the actual jokes in the family — and even so, it leaves out certain key abstract facets of the jokes. And of course it is not mirth-provoking in the least.

Actually, in my view, this is not a genuine ur-joke; a genuine ur-joke would be, rather than a set of English sentences, an abstract kind of conceptual structure that would almost certainly make use of diagrammatic constructs schematically and formally encoding interrelationships of many sorts. Clearly, an ur-joke of that ideal and rarefied sort would be as sterile and devoid of humor as the fine print in a mortgage contract. And yet listening to a joke and detecting in its punch line the presence of just such a skeletal structure can make us laugh uproariously. How can it be that stripping away the complexities of a fully dressed joke to reveal a bare but unfunny ur-joke can strike us as hilarious?

There is something strangely reminiscent here of the old art of strip tease, where the end point of the act — total nudity — is often the least erotic moment of the act. This paradox is, of course, well known — the frustration of the tease is at the same time its primary pleasure.

To me, it seems that joke understanding fits right in with strip tease and the kind of paradox on which it is based. In fact, I would argue that much light can be shed on the cognitive act of joke understanding by comparing it to the strip-tease-like act of unwrapping birthday presents. The present itself is the ur-joke, but reaching it is tantalizing and the most exquisite part of the process. After all, whatever it is, it is wrapped up first of all in some kind of elegant paper, within which there is a big cardboard box with tape on it, and when that has been opened, then there are little white "peanuts" of packing material, then more white paper, then a tiny box inside, then some soft cottony stuff, and finally comes the present itself — perhaps a pair of earrings or cufflinks, or even two ties.

Of course, just as in the case of a birthday present, the ur-joke has to be well thought-out for the joke not to flop, but what provokes the laughter is not just the final instant of ur-joke *recognition,* but the combination of this quick cognitive flash with the slower cognitive process of ur-joke *unveiling* — the process of seeing how a familiar old theme got dressed up in completely new clothes and as such, seduced us anew. If this were not the case, we would not laugh at basically the same joke in new guises.

Complex Jokes, Composite Numbers, Subtly Spiced Recipes

Who knows how many ur-jokes there are? Are there just a few dozen? Or hundreds? Or thousands? Have they all been discovered by now (or invented)? Were they all found (or concocted) already centuries ago? Or are new ones still being invented (or stumbled over), and will there always be room for more?

And when do two jokes really share precisely the same ur-joke? Is it really a black-and-white matter to say which ur-joke(s) a given joke is based on? In fact, can a single joke involve a blend of two or more completely unrelated ur-jokes? Of course, the answer to this last question is *yes,* and we have seen an example of such a blend in the Texas-ranch meta-joke.

The answers to the other questions would require, I am convinced, many years of deep and original research. I am also convinced that as the research progressed, the questions would shift, proliferate, and become much more detailed, because as stated here, they are surely very naïve. What a joy it would be to embark on such a laughworthy research program!

To finish up these reflections on humor, I will toss out a speculative analogy that I hope readers may find stimulating: Ur-jokes are the prime numbers of humor, and sophisticated jokes are large composite numbers made up by multiplying two or more ur-jokes together. When children first learn humor, they internalize a vast repertoire of basic ur-jokes, and each new one cracks them up; however, as children approach adolescence, they are no longer satisfied by mere ur-jokes, no matter how they are clothed — they start to crave novel mixtures, or mixed ur's.

I am reminded of the pleasures of gastronomy (to blur up the pristine analogy): Young children go for simple, single, "prime-number" tastes and love to pour them on thick (this could perhaps be likened to putting a prime number to a power), whereas more sophisticated tongues prefer constantly fresh new mixtures of spices and oral textures (analogous to savoring large composite numbers built from many primes). If this analogy is at all plausible, then it would suggest that the supply of ur-jokes, like the supply of prime numbers, is inexhaustible — a happy prospect.

Quick Poetry Break, IV

I know, I know — I had said that the *last* one would be the last one. But that was before I had ever heard of Peter Dale. It was but a few days later that I read somewhere or other of his work and instantly knew I had to lay my hands on a copy quickly, for Mr. Dale, like me, is a strict believer and staunch advocate of rendering rhyme for rhyme, meter for meter — and he has translated most of the poetry of François Villon into English. In the short but eloquent introduction to his book of Villon verse, he writes, in a somewhat defensive manner (which I well understand):

> This translation is a strict metrical translation and would seem.... to require justification in modern eyes. It seems to me that to translate a very formal poet into free verse is as odd as to attempt to translate *The Cantos* into heroic couplets. Traffic in either direction is as illogical. The fact is that the exigencies of form that the translator faces are more or less the same as the author faced — and these are part of the texture of the poem....

It remains true that Villon cannot really be translated; he can only be dislocated. He has muscle and he has music, a mastery of form. In English translation, you cannot convincingly and consistently have all three. I have tried to articulate muscle and bones, the sleight of mood — the music has had to make shift for itself. A ghost of it lingers, I hope, in the more straightforward stanzas....

Well, here is how Peter Dale renders the same old ballad that we've now seen in quite a few other linguistic grids (I gave his poem a title):

A Bug in the Ear
To All Children of Darkness

Whether you counterfeit your brass
*   and end so oiled you boil and bake;*
traitors whose credit wouldn't pass;
*   or peddle pardons; learn to shake*
*   the loaded dice; or maybe take*
to filching in and out of doors —
*   where does it go, the money you make?*
All to the taverns and the whores.

Rhyme or rail or clash your brass,
*   like shameless fools that always fake;*
mime, mum, or try some magic pass;
*   or if in towns and cities, make*
*   miracles, mysteries, jigs; or take*
a trick or two or skittle scores —
*   soon gained, soon gone! (You still awake?)*
All to the taverns and the whores.

If depths like these are not your class,
*   then plough up fields or drive a rake;*
or turn to doctoring horse and ass.
*   But only if you cannot take*
*   to book and pen. A crust you'll make.*
Yet if you've slaved at prison chores
*   you haven't lifted loot to take*
all to the taverns and the whores.

Envoi

Before you do much worse then, take
trousers and shoes and all that's yours,
*   gowns and the silks for your own sake*
all to the taverns and the whores.

I hope you now see why I felt I had no choice but to include Dale's rendition of this spicy ballad in this chapter. There are, to be sure, stylistic points that I disagree with — most of all, his using of the verb "take" five times as an end rhyme, and "make" three times — but on the other hand, Dale's "dislocation" has an energy and a verve that strike me as deeply right. As they say in French, *chapeau!*

Variétés de véhicule

The propagation of a single, subtle essence from medium to medium is both an art and a game, the joy and beauty of which have been for centuries appreciated by creators in many domains, but perhaps most of all by musicians. The art of spinning scores of *variations on a theme* is a venerated tradition in music, and some of the greatest examples of the form, such as the famous Goldberg Variations, are due to Johann Sebastian Bach. Another such set by Bach is his unfinished final work, the Art of the Fugue, which contrapuntally exploits a very simple, almost banal, theme in the most complex and majestic of ways.

It was a performance of this piece in a concert in the 1930's that led the young French mathematician and budding author Raymond Queneau to ask himself if something analogous could not be done in words, and from these musings was born the idea for a now-celebrated little book of literary variations on a theme. Deliberately trying to imitate what Bach did, Queneau selected a very short, unimpressive theme as the basis for his work, and then spun off variation after variation on the theme.

There the parallel ends, however, at least as far as I am concerned. In terms of artistic depth, there is no comparison whatsoever (an opinion with which I suspect Queneau would have heartily concurred). The Queneau book is a delightful frippery, an extended bagatelle, a sustained shaggy-dog story, whereas the Bach piece is a monumental construction as sublime as the human mind has ever devised. Queneau's stylistic variations are to Bach's explorations of counterpoint as Paris' fluffily amusing Pompidou Center (known better to the French themselves as Beaubourg) is to the serene, refined splendor of the palace at Versailles. However, to lose out to J. S. Bach in a profundity competition is not exactly to suffer the world's most humiliating defeat — one might still have a modicum of depth! — and indeed, to close this chapter, I feel that taking a look at Queneau's book will be well worth our while, given its close links with all that we have been discussing.

As I said, the plan for the book is simple: Recount the same banal real-life episode over and over again, each new time in a different linguistic medium. The book's title suggests that each new manifestation of the theme is in a different *style,* which is perfectly fine, but I feel that the word "medium" would be slightly more accurate. Had Queneau felt the same way, how would he have titled his book?

The answer is not obvious, because "medium" has no exact counterpart in French, splitting up according to context into nouns like *moyen, support, voie, véhicule, intermédiaire,* and yet others. After thinking it over for a while, I decided that a reasonable title might be *Variétés de véhicule,* since *véhicule* as a metaphor embraces not only the idea of language as a medium of expression, but also the concept of a physical medium for wave propagation, such as water for ripples, air for sound, and so forth, which probably would have appealed to the scientist in Queneau. And what about a corresponding title in English? Perhaps, to take a tip straight from our old friend W. E. Henley, "Multy Media".

In point of fact, though, Queneau's book is not titled *Variétés de véhicule* but *Exercices de style,* and its sole English translation — sole at least to my knowledge — is called *Exercises in Style.* We shall soon return to the many interesting issues involved in translating this book, but for now, we will deal with the English version only, realized by Barbara Wright and published in 1958, eleven years after the French version appeared, and just one year before the publication of what is surely Queneau's most famous opus: the zany, slangy novel *Zazie dans le métro.*

"S'assit dans l'autobus"

The most natural way to open such a book, or so it would seem, would simply be to exhibit the theme to be varied, as in most pieces of music of the variations-on-a-theme genre (though not all), where the opening is a precise statement of the theme soon to be varied. Although this appealing idea works without a hitch in musical variations, it cannot in literary ones, because the music–language parallel is inexact.

What is being varied, in music, is a specific set of notes forming a definite melody and having a definite set of harmonies; this theme can thus be stated precisely and unambiguously. In language, by contrast, the object of variation is not a set of discrete letters or words but something behind the scenes: an ill-defined *event* in space and time. Being a continuous, infinitely dissectable event, it cannot be captured in any finite sequence of words; it can surely be *portrayed* using sets of words, but no portrait is authoritative or final.

In a very real sense, that infinite openness of possibilities is the whole point of Queneau's book, but it is easy, nonetheless — perhaps almost fatally tempting — to take the literal text on the opening page of the book as being the theme itself. To be sure, that carefully composed set of words occupies a privileged spot in the book, yet it is by no means the fullest or most objective statement of the episode. The theme that forms the basis of

Queneau's book is simply *not part of language,* in contrast to a theme in music, which *is* a musical structure. Thus even when one has read the entire book through, one still does not know the theme *directly*; it remains invisible, just as do Romeo and Juliet after one has read Shakespeare's play. In accordance with these views, to preclude conflation of Queneau's theme with any passsage in his book, I shall start by portraying it in my own words:

Vignette

S'assit dans l'autobus bien bondé de la ligne S, dans une place libre, un jeune type au cou long et qui portait un chapeau insolite, peu après s'être disputé avec un autre passager ; deux heures plus tard, on l'aperçut dans un autre quartier en compagnie d'un copain qui lui proposait de se faire coudre un autre bouton sur son pardessus.

Plunked himself down on a crowded Parisian bus of the "S" line, in a vacant seat, a long-necked young fellow wearing an unusual hat, after an altercation with another passenger; two hours later, elsewhere in Paris, he was spotted with a friend who was suggesting he go get another button sewn onto his coat.

Putting it in two languages helps to render its language-independence clearer, and also the French text helps to show why I think it would have been so elegant if Queneau had only titled his book *S'assit dans l'autobus* — but on the other hand, he would have needed clairvoyance of the twelve-year variety in order to anticipate the phonetic allusion thereby made.

And now I think it only fitting to display Queneau's own book-opening narration of this banal, indeed, quasi-soporific, episode — or rather, its anglicization at the hands of Barbara Wright — and hopefully, no one will mistake these two paragraphs for the book's intangible, nonverbal theme:

Notation

In the S bus, in the rush hour. A chap of about 26, felt hat with a cord instead of a ribbon, neck too long, as if someone's been having a tug-of-war with it. People getting off. The chap in question gets annoyed with one of the men standing next to him. He accuses him of jostling him every time anyone goes past. A snivelling tone which is meant to be aggressive. When he sees a vacant seat he throws himself onto it.

Two hours later I meet him in the Cour de Rome, in front of the gare Saint-Lazare. He's with a friend who's saying, "You ought to get an extra button put on your overcoat." He shows him where (at the lapels) and why.

A Minuscule Sampler of Stylized Retellings

Having thus gotten the ball rolling, Queneau now launches into 98 more retellings of the event, and his multy media are hardly timid: They range all over the stylistic map, including narratives in transcribed foreign or regional accents; a lipogrammatic version ("e"-less, in fact); slang and colloquial treatments; variations that play with tense, mood, and point of view; a hyperbolic publisher's blurb; several metaphor-loaded retellings; a story related in the first person with private thoughts interpolated in italics; variants that are variously conversational, legalistic, poetic, scientific, telegraphic, numerical, insecure, obscure, pompous, humble, retrograde, terse, verbose, redundant, or sparse in flavor; variants based on conceptual reversals; variants using nouns or interjections alone; a variant consisting of a generous inventory of vignette-appropriate words arranged according to their parts of speech; a sonnet, a tanka, and a playlet; and on and on.

Below, once again drawing on Barbara Wright's English translation, I exhibit a few of Queneau's more diverse and interesting variations on his invisible theme:

Logical analysis

Bus. Platform. Bus platform. That's the place. Midday. About. About midday. That's the time. Passengers. Quarrel. A passengers' quarrel. That's the action. Young man. Hat. Long thin neck. A young man with a hat and a plaited cord round it. That's the chief character. Person. A person. A person. That's the second character. Me. Me. Me. That's the third character, narrator. Words. Words. Words. That's what was said. Seat vacant. Seat taken. A seat that was vacant and then taken. That's the result. The gare Saint-Lazare. An hour later. A friend. A button. Another phrase heard. That's the conclusion. Logical conclusion.

Hellenisms

In a hyperomnibus full of petrolonauts in a chronia of metarush I was a martyr to this microrama: a more than icosimetric hypotype, with a petasus pericycled by a caloplegma and a eucylindrical macrotrachea, anathematized an ephemeral and anonymous outis who, he pseudologed, had been epitreading his bipods, but as soon as he euryscoped a cœnotopia, he peristrophed and catapelted himself onto it.

At a hysteretic chronia I æsthesised him in front of the siderodromous hagiolazaric stathma, peripating with a compsanthropos who was symbouleuting him about the metakinetics of a sphincterous omphale.

Proper names

On the back Josephine of a full Leo, I noticed Theodulus, one day, with Charles-the-too-long, and Derby, surrounded by Plato and not by Rubens. All of a sudden Theodulus started an argument with Theodosius who was treading on Laurel and Hardy every time any Marco Polos got in or out. However, Theodulus rapidly abandoned Eris to park Fanny.

Two Huyghens later I saw Theodulus again in front of St. Lazarus in a great Cicero with Beau Brummel, who was telling him to go back to Austin Reed to get Jerry raised by a little Tom Thumb.

The Nimble Medium-Hopping of Evanescent Essences ◆ ◆ ◆ **227**

Midnight. It's raining. The buses go by nearly empty. On the bonnet of an AI near the Bastille, an old man whose head is sunk in his shoulders and who isn't wearing a hat thanks a lady sitting a long way away from him because she is stroking his hands. Then he goes to stand on the knees of a man who is still sitting down.

Two hours earlier, behind the gare de Lyon, this old man was stopping up his ears so as not to hear a tramp who was refusing to say that he should slightly lower the bottom button of his underpants.

Probabilist

The contacts between inhabitants of a large town are so numerous that one can hardly be surprised if there occasionally occurs between them a certain amount of friction which generally speaking is of no consequence. It so happened that I was recently present at one of these unmannerly encounters which generally take place in the vehicles intended for the transport of passengers in the Parisian region in the rush hours. There is not in any case anything astonishing in the fact that I was a witness of this encounter because I frequently travel in this fashion. On the day in question the incident was of lowest order, but my attention was especially attracted by the physical aspect and the headgear of one of the protagonists of this miniature drama. This was a man who was still young, but whose neck was of a length which was probably above the average and whose hat-ribbon had been replaced by a plaited cord. Curiously enough I saw him again two hours later engaged in listening to some advice of a sartorial order which was being given to him by a friend in the company of whom he was walking up and down, rather nonchalantly I should add.

There was not much likelihood now that a third encounter would take place, and the fact is that from that day to this I have never seen the young man again, in conformity with the established laws of probability.

Translating Queneau's Stylistic Exercises

How would one go about translating a book that is not, like most works of fiction, a series of messages in a single medium, but rather, a series of media supporting a single ur-message? The task, though daunting, is not impossible, for *Exercices de style* has been translated into several languages, including German (by Ludwig Harig and Eugen Helmlé, the latter of course being the translator of Perec's liponovel), Italian (by Umberto Eco), English, and Dutch. The Dutch translator, Rudy Kousbroek, is a writer on cultural matters who is renowned in Holland for his erudition and his wit, and particularly for his fluent bridging of the "two cultures" (the humanities and the sciences).

Because of common interests and common acquaintances, Rudy and I were brought together in the mid-1980's — first in Amsterdam and later in Paris. It was in fact in his Paris apartment one lovely summer afternoon that Rudy presented me with a signed copy of his Dutch translation, called *Stijloefeningen*. Riffling through its variations, I quickly ascertained that the subtleties of the Dutch wordplay were way beyond me, but I also observed that there was a twenty-page introduction in a much more reserved style of Dutch, of which I could make out a good deal without too much trouble. And so, though it was slow going, I slogged my way through the whole introduction in Dutch, in it finding much of interest.

In one section, Kousbroek points out that since the book consists of a series of diverse media, a would-be translator into another language has to jump to a higher and more abstract level of translation than is usual — one has to *translate linguistic media* from one language and culture to a second language and culture. (I have paraphrased Kousbroek's way of putting it, inserting this chapter's pet term, but this is essentially his point.) He cites several very clear examples of this kind of difficulty:

> There are complications that have to do with geographical and historical circumstances. Sometimes it is possible to find equivalents; thus Germanisms are found in this book, instead of Italianisms (similar location of a contiguous nation with a closely related language). Other times no equivalent comes to mind, and so a more or less arbitrary substitution has been made, such as replacing *Pour lay Zanglay* (French written with English phonetics) with Afrikaans [a spinoff of Dutch going back some 300 years, whose quaintness never fails to amuse the Dutch].
>
> Yet another type of problem is the existence in French of verb tenses that are foreign to Dutch, such as the *passé simple,* or tenses that cannot be used in the same ways, such as the *passé indéfini*. Taking as my model the English translation by Barbara Wright, I have replaced variations based on these two tenses by my own variations called "Passive Voice" and "Indirect Speech"....
>
> The one respect in which my translation deviates from all its precursors is that not just the words have been translated into Dutch, but also the location of the goings-on. There is just something absurd about it when, in an unmistakably Parisian ambiance, one runs smack into the following tirade uttered by a London Cockney: "A sees ve fust young bleeder agin walkin' up'n deahn ahtsoider ve Garsn Lazzer...", or when one hears the following words emerge from the mouth of a West Indian: "Later I bounce him up, he coasting lime in the Cour de Rome..." And the necessity of sticking in, from time to time, a little reminder that the story is taking place in France ("A sees vis young Froggy bloke...") makes a most painful impression on me.
>
> It is for this reason that the Parisian "S" bus (in later years renamed as line 84) is converted in this translation into tram number 16 of the Amsterdam municipal transport system. Similarly, the Gare Saint-Lazare has been turned into the Concertgebouw, and the Cour de Rome into the Jan Willem Brouwersplein.

This last set of tightly interrelated decisions by Kousbroek, concerning how to convert Paris into Amsterdam — and he spells it out in more detail as he brings his introduction to an eloquent close, nostalgically reminiscing about long-gone little details of ticket-punching machines and other delightful and quirky features of Parisian buses and Amsterdam trams, from

the days around World War II, when *Exercices de style* was being composed —
constitutes a superb example, one of my favorites ever, of what Chapter 6
was all about: the art of transculturation.

Paris Drifts from its Moorings and Floats down the Thames

The conversion of Paris into another city in another country, although
perhaps highly jolting at first, in fact has a precedent in this very chapter.
Just think about W. E. Henley's slangy rendition of Villon's ballad. The
latter, of course, is quintessentially French and even more quintessentially
Parisian — indeed, the Villon is so deeply embedded in and wedded to
Paris as to make one think it would be "as untranslatable as the smell of
garlic in the Paris metro", to quote Barbara Wright's lovely first reaction to
Queneau's experiments with the French language. But despite her first
impression of sheer futility, Wright did go on to anglicize the Queneau, and
Henley did likewise for the Villon.

However, their styles of anglicization were diametrically opposed.
Whereas Wright took pains to keep the events explicitly in Paris, including
all sorts of street names and other proper nouns that indelibly anchor the
goings-on in the capital city of the Hexagon, Henley makes not the slightest
gesture towards France or Paris or anything whatsoever across the channel;
indeed, "V's Straight Tip" sounds every bit as profoundly rooted in the
bawdier quarters of the London of, say, Charles Dickens' time as the Villon
seems rooted in fifteenth-century Paris. No one who read Henley's poem
would ever dream of connecting it to Paris unless they had memorized the
Villon and recognized it through the disguise — and conversely, anyone
who knew old British criminal lingo would instantly place the Henley poem
in London, despite the lack of any specific locations or other telltale
Londonian references. Henley's poem is, I daresay, more English than our
old friend Mr Average's soapbox tirade, and that's saying something!

As Rudy Kousbroek pointed out, even Barbara Wright is guilty, now
and then, of a Franco–English frame blend that sets one's head a little
spinning. In "Proper names", for instance, she has Beau Brummel telling
Theodulus to "go back to Austin Reed", a posh British supplier of clothing.
Given that we are in Paris, this is a strange suggestion.

Though Amsterdam and London are quite far afield, they are by no
means the most extreme repositionings of Paris that I have encountered. I
should mention that it was thanks to Bob French and Jacqueline Henry that
I was first made aware of Queneau's in-depth study of Parisian bus-bound
quarrels and overcoat-button advice, and when they presented me with my
very own copy of *Exercices de style,* I found inscribed in the very front, in what
might well have been Raymond Queneau's handwriting, but looked, rather

suspiciously, much more like Bob's, the following variation on the book's theme — either number zero or number 100, depending on how you want to count it:

<u>Américain</u>

Rush hour, right? The IRT, packed. Thinnish guy, red backpack, cowboy belt, hair kinda long, touch a gray. Train stops. People get out. Thin dude keeps shovin' and pushin' and actin' like he owns the place. Pisses people off around him.

I spot him again later that day. Decked out in an overcoat. Grand Central Station. Buddy a his, red beard, intellectual-as-hell round glasses, says: "Might be a good idea to look into Gettin' Extra Buttons."

Here we are in midtown Manhattan, worlds away from Paris, London, and Amsterdam. In one of those odd coincidences, right after typing the previous sentence, I gazed over at a pile of books on my study's crowded floor, and noticed the Edward Hopper–style drawing of Holden Caulfield on the cover of the original paperback edition of *Catcher in the Rye*. Aside from the gray hair, the "thinnish guy" sounds a lot like Holden himself, who is seen sauntering through Grand Central Station, dressed in a long overcoat. Whereas it makes some sense to transport *Exercices de style* across Europe or even across the ocean, obviously Holden and his adventures are as firmly rooted in the glittering steel-and-glass canyons of New York City as London Bridge is eternally planted in the waters of the Seine.

The Elusive, Slippery Ur-dog

Rudy Kousbroek, no less than I, is fascinated by the implicitness of the flitting, darting, elusive, protean essence of Queneau's book, which he calls its "urtext", and which he links with the mysterious, invisible *oerhond*:

The riddle of Queneau's urtext brings to mind the notion of "ur-dog". There are, as one knows, all sorts of variations on the theme "dog": St. Bernards, shepherds, poodles, spaniels — many more than a mere 99. But just exactly what all these are variations *on* is not easy to pin down. The more dogs you've seen, the better you are at assigning new percepts to the category "dog", but at the same time, your image of the ur-dog gets continually blurrier.

Though he casts the riddle in terms of the *oerhond,* Kousbroek's point is how Queneau is constantly pushing at the blurry edges of an implicit category. The better one comes to know it, the less one is able to put one's finger on it. And the same elusiveness that applies at the level of a multiplied vignette or a proliferating ur-joke applies even at the far more basic level of a one-word concept, such as "dog", "fork", "nose", or "dirt".

This is in fact the focus of Chapter 11, which deals with the way that such categories, through the powerful mechanism of analogy, grow and grow and grow around their initial cores.

As ever more varieties of an ur-dog, an ur-joke, or an ur-vignette are encountered, does essence eventually get lost? At what point are things stretched just a little too far? If you have never read Queneau's book, you are unsure just how far out the ur-vignette's metropolitan area stretches. And so, as a parting puzzle, I ask: Is the following *exercice de style* within the city limits, within the metropolitan area — or is it simply beyond the pale?

Hexagonal

Smack in the middle of the board; tense, crowded situation. A crystalline pawn, maybe 26 millimeters high, strangely-shaped ellipsoidal head instead of the usual spherical blob, and also too long a neck — I can just see the glassblower stretching it out while daydreaming distractedly. A rook takes a bishop, then is taken by a knight, which is in turn knocked off by a bishop; the center is opening up a little. The aforementioned pawn threatens to take an enemy pawn right next to it, looks very serious, then backs off. Espying a vacant spot nearby, it hops right onto it.

Two hours later, the game is still going strong and I notice the very same pawn in a distant corner of the board, now next to a friendly pawn. The latter makes the suggestion, *en pâchant*, of moving one space forward and thus getting promoted to a queen. It shows the first pawn exactly which direction to move in, and why.

●

Poems VII:

~ A Gala of Gists ~

* * *
* *
*
*

The upper poem's title, *Mots-clés marrants,* is a phonetically exact rearrangement of the sounds comprising the poet's name, "Clément Marot". To make this sonic equivalence visually clearer, the two different lines could be rendered as follows, using a kind of French phonetic spelling:

m–ô–clé–m–ar–an
clé–m–an–m–ar–ô

I made this fortuitous discovery when playing around with the sounds in Marot's name in a moment of idleness. My intuition tells me Marot would have relished it, although it might well have had to be explained to him (I doubt that *marrant,* a colloquial adjective meaning "fun, amusing", was used back then as it is today; who knows, maybe even *mot-clé,* meaning "key-word", was an unheard-of concept in those days).

The English "poem" bearing this title consists of nothing but a terse set of key-words — hopefully, even somewhat *fun* key-words — representing the principal themes or sections of the French original. The Hellenistic neologism "poietautonym", coming in the center, simply means "poet's self-naming" — and as such, it designates the spot in the original poem where the poet names himself.

Enormous care was taken to ensure that this chain of key-words would have an elegant curved silhouette when printed; moreover, a close inspection reveals that on an acrostic level, it is palindromic. That is to say, for whatever it is worth, the initial letters of the nine key-words form a symmetric "keychain": "EPCEPECPE".

Despite his name's appearance on the author line, Clément Marot is of course not the author of this little *étude*; however, I could not resist placing the two phonetic jumblings as close to each other as I could on the page, in order to bring out the fun of the pun, for that's surely the name of the game!

*　　　*　　　*

The lower poem's title, "Fun Key-words", is a literal translation of the upper poem's title into English. As for the lower poem itself, it is abstractly related to my "Touchstones" and "Mots-clés marrants", as well as to Hugh Kenner's "Hey, Chick", in that all four of them represent diverse approaches to the idea of breaking the content of "Ma Mignonne" up into natural-seeming chunks and then tersely summarizing those chunks — a kind of tersification of Marot's versification, one might say.

Quite obviously, great care was taken in making all lines rhyme and consist of the same number of syllables. I was a little bit concerned about using "Poet greets dear" as a summary of Marot's closing lines (though what else could I do, given the constraints I had imposed on myself?), but I found more support than I expected from my dictionary, which had these definitions:

"greet": "to address in a friendly or respectful way"
"greeting": "a gesture or word of welcome or salutation"
"salutation": "a polite expression of greeting or good will"

And so, despite my initial self-doubts, it seemed that it was perfectly legitimate to describe a friendly valediction as a "greeting".

Mots-clés marrants

Clément Marot

Entrée.
Pleasantries.
Commiserations.
Encouragement.
Poietautonym.
Enticement.
Concerns.
Pieties.
Echo.

Fun Key-words

D. Hofstadter

Poet greets dear.
Poet sheds tear.
Poet hints cheer.
Poet comes clear.
Poet's sincere.
Poet vents fear.
Poet greets dear.

This condensation or paraphrase or *explication de texte,* as they say in French — however one might prefer to label it — expands and fleshes out the preceding version, by adding an explanatory phrase for each of the seven lines of "Fun Key-words". Of course the overall symmetry of the structure leaps instantly to the eye.

On a more fine-grained level, there are some interesting symmetries here, all centered on line 5, such as the identity of lines 1 and 9, the closely parallel structures of lines 2 and 8, the three evenly-spaced occurrences of the word "clemency", and the closely parallel structures of lines 4 and 6. One might wonder: How much of this symmetry has been "read into" the original poem, and how much of it was intrinsically there, simply waiting to be observed?

This poem and the two on the preceding page evolved very slowly in an extremely intricate "dance of mutual avoidance", by which I mean that each word chosen for any one was instantly forbidden for the others (excepting, of course, the inevitable overlap due to the fact that "Fun Key-words" is contained inside "Funky Words").

Funky Words

D. Hofstadter

Poet greets dear,
Wishing for meteorological clemency.
Poet sheds tear: Quarantine likened to long, painful incarceration.
Poet hints cheer: Health's blessings once regained, go out doors.
Poet comes clear: Reveals personal Clemency.
Poet's sincere: Mouth's yearnings now imperiled, go eat sweets.
Poet vents fear: Lasting moans, fading tones, shrinking to bones.
Wishing for providential clemency,
Poet greets dear.

In a surprise move, all three poems from the previous two pages have been interleaved with each other and the result has then been "unfolded", in a manner of speaking, to give rise to a coherent 28-line whole that tries, in a number of ways at once, to reveal both the structure (the form) and the message (the content) of the original French poem. The three different component poems have been typographically differentiated so that one's eye can readily pull each poem out without trouble. Note how closely this composite poem reflects the original poem on a line-by-line basis.

Of course the order of presentation of these poems should not be taken as indicating the chronological order in which they were created — it's not as if I just threw together the previous three and with good luck got out a nice 28-line poem!

Does this curious verbal structure count as a true translation of "Ma Mignonne"? Or is it more of a paraphrase? Is it even a genuine poem? *A vous de décider.* ("Your call.")

Funky Mots

Clément Marot/D. Hofstadter

Entrée. *Poet greets dear.*
Pleasantries.
    Wishing for meteorological clemency.
Commiserations. *Poet sheds tear:*
    Quarantine likened to long, painful incarceration.   5
Encouragement. *Poet hints cheer:*
    Health's blessings,
    Once regained,
    Go
    Out   10
    Doors.
Poietautonym. *Poet comes clear:*
    Reveals personal Clemency.
Enticement. *Poet's sincere:*
    Mouth's yearnings   15
    Now imperiled,
    Go
    Eat
    Sweets.
Concerns. *Poet vents fear:*   20
    Lasting moans,
    Fading
    Tones,
    Shrinking
    To bones.   25
Pieties.
    Wishing for providential clemency.
Echo. *Poet greets dear.*

"Charms of Form" is a careful reworking of the original list of syntactic or formal properties of "Ma Mignonne" that appeared on page 1a, with a few other charms of form thrown in, of which #7 (already discussed on page 11a) is by far the most surprising. As I've already mentioned, I was completely unaware of charm #7 at the outset, as were the first several people to whom I posed the translation challenge, and so that lovely property was not reflected in any of our initial translations.

In working out and polishing this list — something that I did only recently, while preparing this book — I once again aimed at creating a structure having maximal levels of elegance and symmetry. Thus, deliberately echoing the original poem, charms 1 and 10 both start with "Ma Mignonne"; charms 5 and 6, midway through the list, both talk about what happens midway through the poem itself; charms 4 and 7, symmetrically straddling the two middle charms, describe Marot's two complementary and overlapping types of couplets in strictly parallel language; and finally, the physical length of each of these ten charms is very nearly the same as that of its mirror-image charm, as reflected across the midpoint of the poem. (If I'm not careful, I will soon wind up writing a poem about the formal charms of *this* poem! Hmm...)

One would be hard pressed to say that this carefully-worded and daintily-typeset list is a "translation" of Marot's poem, and yet it comes close to that: it is an English-language poem (in a slightly stretched sense of the term, perhaps) whose content is derived completely from Marot's French-language poem.

All of the verbal creations gathered together in this "Gala of Gists" are experiments that play with the sublime idea of "variations on a theme". They were deeply inspired by and influenced by Raymond Queneau's *Exercices de style*, which, as we saw in the previous chapter, tried looking at one single always-occult theme from a vast diversity of points of view, taking it apart and putting it back together again in the strangest of ways.

My hope, in doing my own set of "exercises in essence", was that by trying to pinpoint both the semantic and the structural gist of "Ma Mignonne" in a wide variety of manners, I would somehow succeed in laying bare the poem's ultimate essence. Perhaps, however, all that I succeeded in doing was to make the poem's essence grow ever murkier. But in a way, that's probably good. Indeed, what clearer lesson about essence and about poetry could one possibly wish to learn?

Charms of Form

D. Hofstadter

1. *"Ma Mignonne" is exactly 28 lines long.*

2. *The lines of the poem have just three syllables.*

3. *The stress always falls on the final syllable of a line.*

4. *Chunks of rhyme form couplets, thus:*
   AA, BB, CC, DD, ..., KK, LL, MM, AA.

5. *Midway through, the poet shifts from "vous" to "tu".*

6. *Midway through, the poet refers to himself by name.*

7. *Chunks of sense form couplets, thus:*
   A, AB, BC, CD, ..., KL, LM, MA, A.

8. *The first line and last line of the poem are identical.*

9. *The language of the poem is 500-year-old French.*

10. *"Ma Mignonne" is sweet and light in tone.*

●

● *Chapter 8* ●

A Novel
in Verse

●

So Sad to say, a speaker of Russian I never could claim to be. True, when in graduate school at the University of Oregon in Eugene, I worked my way through a short and very basic Russian grammar, whereupon I adventurously jumped into a second-year Russian course, somehow managing to keep afloat as our class slogged its way through a couple of annotated short stories. From then on, I've generally been able to figure out in broad strokes what is written on the backs of record covers and such. But I've never once had a conversation in Russian. Worse yet, I am ashamed to admit that the last time I was in New York, as I ascended by elevator from my hotel lobby, I eavesdropped on my two co-elevator-riders, trying to discern their liquid language, and as they stepped out, I inquired hopefully, "Was that Portuguese?" — to which the dapper gentleman, unintentionally searing my linguistic ego, tersely replied, "Russian." Egad! (My only excuse, and a weak one it is, is that they were sort of muttering and we'd gone up a mere two or three floors.)

Given this, what in the world would give me the chutzpah to write about, let alone think I could *judge,* various English translations of *Eugene Onegin,* the exemplary Russian novel in verse by that most Russian of Russian poets, Alexander Pushkin?

And now, yet another shameful admission: Until just a few years ago, I knew less about A. Pushkin than about a pushpin. Blissfully ignorant was I of the fact that he was a poet, not to mention the author of *Eugene Onegin.*

Indeed, for me, *Eugene Onegin* was just some random opera by Tchaikovsky that I'd never heard. Curiously, this piece of musical trivia came in handy one time when, again back in my graduate-school days, I chanced upon an announcement in the student newspaper for an upcoming performance of "Tchaikovsky's opera *Eugene Oregon*". Amused and amazed by such naïve provincialism, I clipped the little typo and sent it in to *The New Yorker,* an act that resulted in my first publication in a major journal!

Back in those days I was, no doubt, a know-nothing about Pushkin and his *œuvre*; however, the nice thing about having a brain is that one can learn, that ignorance can be supplanted by knowledge, and that small bits of knowledge can gradually pile up into substantial heaps. And thus it was with me and the work to which this chapter and the next are devoted.

One Novel in Verse Doffs its Hat to Another

I first heard of the original literary incarnation of *Eugene Onegin* from reading a far more recent novel in verse: *The Golden Gate,* a story set in contemporary California (indeed, my old stomping grounds — the San Francisco Bay Area), written in the mid-1980's by Vikram Seth, at the time a graduate student in economic demography at Stanford University. The latter novel, with which I was enchanted from the moment it appeared, owes its genesis and indeed its entire stanzaic structure to the former, a debt that Seth happily acknowledges in his book, first alluding to the Russian original and then devoting a full stanza to the work that directly sparked his own, namely the English version by Sir Charles Johnston, a British diplomat and poet, which came out in 1977. Here are stanzas 3 through 5 from Chapter 5, in which Seth, explaining what led him, in the late twentieth century, to dare to write a novel in an early-nineteenth-century style, extols his models:

> *How do I justify this stanza?*
> *These feminine rhymes? My wrinkled muse?*
> *This whole passé extravaganza?*
> *How can I (careless of time) use*
> *The dusty bread molds of Onegin*
> *In the brave bakery of Reagan?*
> *The loaves will surely fail to rise*
> *Or else go stale before my eyes.*
> *The truth is, I can't justify it.*
> *But as no shroud of critical terms*
> *Can save my corpse from boring worms,*
> *I may as well have fun and try it.*
> *If it works, good; and if not, well,*
> *A theory won't postpone its knell.*

Why, asks a friend, attempt tetrameter?
Because it once was noble, yet
Capers before the proud pentameter,
Tyrant of English. I regret
To see this marvelous swift meter
Demean its heritage, and peter
Into mere Hudibrastic tricks,
Unapostolic knacks and knicks.
But why take all this quite so badly?
I would not, had I world and time
To wait for reason, rhythm, rhyme
To reassert themselves, but sadly,
The time is not remote when I
Will not be here to wait. That's why.

Reader, enough of this apology;
But spare me if I think it best,
Before I tether my monology,
To stake a stanza to suggest
You spend some unfilled day of leisure
By that original spring of pleasure:
Sweet-watered, fluent, clear, light, blithe
(This homage merely pays a tithe
Of what in joy and inspiration
It gave me once and does not cease
To give me) — Pushkin's masterpiece
In Johnston's luminous translation:
Eugene Onegin — like champagne
Its effervescence stirs my brain.

I adore these three stanzas, and yet, were I reading them aloud to you, I would brazenly alter two lines — both in the first stanza — and not even say a word about my little deviltry. The reason I would customize that stanza is that, to my ear, two of its lines seem to need an extra syllable somewhere. Try reading it aloud, and see if you hear anything missing.

For better or for worse, here's how I'd render lines 4–6: "How can I (careless of fashion) use / The dusty bread molds of Onegin / In the brave new bakery of Reagan?" To me, not only do these tweaks improve the flow, but they also feel in Seth's style. You might throw tomatoes at me for this, and so might Vikram Seth, but tough apples — that's performance for you!

I am reminded of the one time I heard Arthur Rubinstein performing in person. On his program was "my" Chopin G-flat impromptu — the one I swooned over and learned at age twenty-two — and I'll never forget how he altered the very last chord. Though I didn't like the chord he substituted, I *did* like the fact that he had the moxie to try a variant.

Let me add that Vikram Seth's *Golden Gate* (his name and his novel's title rhyme, incidentally) is itself a supremely luminous work whose sweet-watered, fluent, clear, light, blithe, and fashion-careless effervescence stirs *my* brave new brain. I hope this short excerpt conveys its grace and depth.

A Double Bedside Delectation of Onegins

In a very favorable review in *The New York Times,* John Gross wrote of Seth, "he has fashioned a medium flexible enough to accommodate the most disparate material". Apparently Seth's elegant bow to his Russian precursor, pointing straight at the source of his medium, had gone right over Gross' head. I can't be too harsh on Gross for this oversight, though, for I, too, in my ecstatic first reading of *The Golden Gate,* somehow missed the intimacy of its connection with *Eugene Onegin.* But the moment I came to understand their link, I was fascinated. As I said above, my Russian being very limited, I couldn't hope to read *Eugene Onegin* in the original without years of further study. But Seth's praise made me eager to read Johnston's English version, so off I dashed to Printer's Inc. (a bookstore/coffeehouse near Stanford where Seth, periodically recharging himself on French roast, wrote much of *The Golden Gate,* and to which a witty stanza thereof is devoted) and there picked up a copy, feeling thankful it was still in print.

But then, inexplicably, I placed it high on a shelf in my study, where it slept in undisturbed peace for a few years, and where it might easily have kept on sleeping forever, had I not chanced to notice, one evening, while again browsing the shelves of Printer's Inc., another copy of *Eugene Onegin,* wrapped in an unfamiliar cover and peeping up at me from a shelf down by my knee. My curiosity aroused, I leaned down, pulled it out, and found, to my surprise, that it was a completely new, completely different rendering of the novel into English — or, as the French say, into *américain* — by a professor of Russian at the University of Tennessee named James Falen.

How could this be? Surely, I thought, quite swayed by Seth's words, Pushkin's tale had found its definitive anglicizor, so to speak, in Charles Johnston, so who would dare to tackle it again? Who would dare to risk the inevitably humiliating comparison with Sir Charles' luminous *tour de force*? And yet, after glancing at just a few stanzas, I realized that Falen's work, too, was of very high caliber, and so I snapped it up, took it home, and filed it on my shelf right next to its "luminous" rival. At first, I felt this purchase had lowered my chances of ever coming round to reading *Eugene Onegin.* After all, if I'd had so much trouble getting started with just *one* translation, how now, with two of them tugging at me, was I ever going to decide?

Luckily, this dilemma was elegantly resolved one day in the spring of 1993, when Carol and I decided to read both of them at once. Our strategy was this: Once evening had fallen and our children had had their bedtime stories and were drifting off to sleep, the two of us would settle down cozily in our bed together, plump our pillows, and read aloud to each other. Sometimes I would be assigned Falen and she Johnston, and other days the reverse. But whatever the matching of books with performers, one of us would read aloud a stanza from our assigned book, and then the other one would read aloud the corresponding stanza from the other book.

We felt, however, that a single reading of each stanza did not allow us to fully appreciate what we were hearing, especially to compare the two treatments, and so each time we would read aloud our respective stanzas once more: thus four readings, all told, for each stanza of the Russian original. And that was not all, for we would often contrast and compare a few specific lines, and sometimes discuss the evolving story, before going on to savor the next stanza. Although this was a slow process, it gave both of us a special and rare type of pleasure. For me, and I think for Carol as well, the intense sharing of these two translations was one of the high points of our all-too-short married life, something I am so grateful for having done.

The Structural Essence of Pushkin's Novel in Verse

A few words are in order about the poetic units out of which *Eugene Onegin* was fashioned by its author. With but a handful of exceptions, the novel consists of roughly 400 fourteen-line stanzas written in iambic tetrameter. These so-called "Onegin stanzas" — essentially an idiosyncratic Pushkinian variety of sonnet — have a hypnotic and rigid rhyming pattern: ABAB; CCDD; EFFEGG. (Note how this applies as well to Seth's stanzas.)

One can group the final six lines according to two quite different logics: either EFF/EGG or EFFE/GG. Sometimes the semantics fits one of these, sometimes the other — and quite often, neither. Occasionally there is a final GG couplet that stands apart and has a definite *zing* to it; however, it is just as frequent for Pushkin's semantic chunks to pay little heed to the boundaries of rhyming units, and once in a while an incomplete sentence will even sassily leap across a few blank lines to find its conclusion in the next sonnet. Such enjambments are always fun. In any case, both the tetrameter and the rhyming pattern are strictly adhered to in each stanza.

The final strict defining feature of Onegin stanzas is a fixed semi-regular distribution of so-called *masculine* and *feminine* rhymes. A masculine rhyme — the simpler of the two cases — occurs when the lines in question are both accented on their final syllables, and those syllables rhyme (*e.g.*, "miss/bliss"). A feminine rhyme occurs when the lines are both accented on their penultimate or antepenultimate (etc.) syllables, and not only do those syllables rhyme but also the remaining nonaccented syllables sound identical (*e.g.*, "mister/blister", say, or "mistletoe/bliss'll tow"). A beautiful example was shown in the previous chapter — Tom Lehrer's elaborate "plagiarize/evade your eyes/made your eyes/shade your eyes/plagiarize" rhyming lyrics to "Lobachevsky".

In theory, the notion of feminine rhyme could encompass even more ornate cases, such as "mistletoe/blissful show", where the two unstressed trailing syllables, though not phonetically identical, still rhyme. Clearly, feminine rhymes pose a much more intricate challenge to the poet or the translator. In any case, the pattern in Onegin stanzas runs as follows: FMFM; FFMM; FMMFMM. Seth's sonnets also follow that pattern, of course — and note his subtle "justify it/fun and try it" feminine rhyme.

It goes without saying that both Charles Johnston and James Falen religiously respected all of these strict structural criteria in creating their translations of Pushkin's novel, for to do otherwise would have been — would it not? — to mock the book's essence.

The Transcribability of Music

As one reads, one quickly grows used to and fond of the special lilt and sway of Onegin stanzas. I, of course, can speak only of my sensual pleasure at reading them *in English,* but I am sure that at that essentially musical level, the experience in Russian is similar. Actually, I've also read here and there in Maurice Colin's excellent French translation, as well as bits and pieces of two fine German translations, one by Ulrich Busch and the other by Rolf-Dietrich Keil, all three of which are rendered in flawless Onegin stanzas obeying all the constraints just mentioned, and so I think it is fair to say I've experienced "the same" sensual pleasure in three different languages. (I've also read a bit of Giovanni Giudici's Italian translation, which, though it's pretty, punts on the pattern of masculine and feminine rhymes — too hard!) The raw *sounds* are of course different — one can do nothing about that — but at the next higher level of abstraction, all the key *patterns* among sounds are preserved isomorphically.

This act of trans-sonification can be likened to what happens when a piece of music is moved from one set of instrumental timbres to another (*e.g.,* from piano to orchestra or vice versa) — a subtle art at which Maurice Ravel, for instance, was a past master. Ravel's most famous accomplishment along these lines is the orchestration of Modest Moussorgsky's piano piece *Pictures at an Exhibition,* but to my mind a far more beautiful example is his arrangement for orchestra of most of his own exquisite piano suite of antique-style dances, *Le Tombeau de Couperin,* a homage to one of his idols. There are also innumerable examples going in the reverse direction, such as Sergei Rachmaninoff's sprightly transcription for piano of Nikolai Rimsky-Korsakov's "The Bumblebee", or, to sink to a more bombastic level, Wagner's transcription for piano of Beethoven's Fifth Symphony.

That such high-quality transcription is not to be taken for granted, however, is illustrated by Leopold Stokowski's sadly overblown attempts to render some of Bach's large-scale organ works as grand orchestral pieces. Of course, any one person's failure does not prove that a given work will resist all efforts at transcription; even a long series of failures by different musicians would not constitute a proof of absolute nontranscribability. Indeed, since Bach himself freely moved so much of his music around from one set of instruments to another, I suspect his organ music could well be orchestrated effectively. However, there are limits to the notion. I find it extraordinarily hard, for example, to conceive of Chopin's ultra-pianistic études retaining even a small fraction of their power and depth if transcribed to the medium of string quartet, let alone to a trio of tubas or a pair of piccolos. But who knows? I once heard a Scott Joplin rag somewhat plausibly and pleasantly rendered by a tuba quartet.

Abstractions Coolly Floating Far Above the Fray

One of my best birthday presents ever was for my sixteenth birthday, when my mother gave me a recording of the first eight preludes and fugues from Bach's Well-Tempered Clavier, performed on piano by Glenn Gould. In no time flat I fell deeply in love with that record, obsessively playing it over and over again, gouging out those groovy little sonic wiggles with a too-heavy needle. I'll never forget how I then doggedly hunted through record stores in search of the rest of the Well-Tempered Clavier. Each new disk I discovered — and it took me a couple of years to collect them all! — was a savored treasure, and whetted my appetite for more, more, more.

I knew that Bach had written this great work for harpsichord, not piano, but I didn't care a fig; I far preferred the rich, resonant sound of the latter to the thin, almost tinny sound of the former. I could easily tell the difference between pianists Glenn Gould and Jörg Demus, but I didn't vastly prefer one to the other. What mattered to me was the instrument, not the performer. On rare occasions, I remember, I would chance to hear some prelude and fugue in its original harpsichord version, and though it was still beautiful, I would invariably find it less appealing in that timbre. (Oh, no! I suddenly hear myself echoing Gundolf's thesis that Shakespeare finally reached his "manifest destiny" when he met the German language!)

And so, after having gorged myself for a few years on this music, after having thrilled to each prelude and fugue at least 100 times, and in many cases far more, was I fooling myself in thinking that I knew the Well-Tempered Clavier intimately? Is the painful truth that I had never been in touch with it at all, having always eschewed its original instrument? Or — is the Well-Tempered Clavier a higher-level abstraction, floating above any specific instrument, just as it floats above any specific instrumentalist?

My Well-Tempered Clavier story is double-edged, in that in trying to use it to show how a piece transcended its original medium, I have actually shown that for me, the medium still mattered. So what is the truth? I honestly don't know. Some pieces of music seem clearly more wedded to their original timbre than others are, yet masterful transcriptions show that seemingly uncrossable timbral barriers can occasionally be overcome. Such a work then becomes an abstraction, floating above its original medium.

And what about works of literature? Analogously, some seem clearly more wedded to their original language than others are, yet masterful translations demonstrate that seemingly uncrossable linguistic barriers can occasionally be overcome. Such a work of literature then becomes an abstraction, floating above its original medium.

Where, then, does Pushkin's poetry fall, along the spectrum of levels of detachability from original medium? Is it inseparably wedded to the Russian language, or can it be delicately and subtly seduced away from it and happily bonded to a new foreign mate? Should one conceive of Falen and Johnston as "performing" Pushkin's poems on the English horn instead of the original russophone, in analogy to Gould and Demus playing Bach's preludes and fugues on the pianoforte instead of the original harpsichord? Might Pushkin even sound *better* when played on the English horn? (And… how about on the anglosaxophone?)

In our delicious reading-aloud sessions, Carol and I were obviously not experiencing Pushkin *directly*. Nonetheless, were we not still, in some deep and true manner, experiencing Pushkin? If not, then what on earth *were* we doing? (Was I not experiencing Bach when, riveted, I listened to Glenn Gould at the piano? If not, then what on earth *was* I doing?) I admit that for me, it was surprisingly easy to unconsciously conflate either of the two English versions we were reading with Pushkin's own original voice. I could easily rejoice in some particularly felicitous line by Falen or Johnston and think to myself, "Ah, Pushkin! What a fine touch he had! What a genius!"

In reacting this way, was I being unwittingly led horribly afoul of The Truth? Or was I quite on the mark, and is Pushkin's *Eugene Onegin* an abstract work of art floating above any specific linguistic medium? If not, then how can publishers get away with writing "Eugene Onegin, by Alexander Pushkin" on the cover of books *in English*? The question gets all the more sticky when one considers that there are different pieces of English text out there, all claiming the same title and the same author.

If, as most reasonable people would, one accepts the idea that *Eugene Onegin* has many different valid realizations in our language, then why not push further towards the inevitable conclusion that A. Pushkin's original exquisite manner of realizing *Eugene Onegin* in the Russian language is merely one of an enormous number of perfectly valid, though never-realized, Onegin instantiations in Russian?

Intellectual Stereopsis

There was, for Carol and me, a definite magic in the act of jumping back and forth between two different translations of each sonnet. Had there been just one, we would simply have had to take the translator's word that this is more or less what Pushkin said, having in truth not the slightest idea how many liberties had actually been taken. But with two translations side by side, each of them had the effect of "keeping the other one honest". If they deviated from each other in any significant way, it was obvious that *somebody* had changed *something*, though it was not clear who or what. Interestingly, though, this happened very seldom. We always sensed how the two English texts, different as they might be on the surface, were mirroring one and the same hidden Russian text.

Together, moreover, the two English texts gave us a strong sense for what the underlying Russian had to be like. Imagine trying to reconstruct a hidden three-dimensional object if you can see just one shadow of it cast on a wall by a distant source of light. No matter how crisp the shadow might be, you would have at best a vague idea of the hidden object's shape, with a lot remaining unknown and unknowable. But now imagine a second light source is turned on, coming from an entirely different direction, casting a second shadow of the same object on some other wall at right angles to the first. All of a sudden, you have a far clearer sense of the three-dimensional nature of the original object. This combined usage of two sources of visual information to figure out the shape of something otherwise inaccessible is similar to the act of triangulating, in maritime navigation — that is, using the observed angles from your ship to two different known landmarks to locate yourself precisely relative to a coastline or shoal. Scaled down, this is essentially stereopsis — the parallax effect that we humans exploit in binocular vision, allowing us to see a third dimension despite having only two-dimensional images on our retinas.

And so, as Carol and I glimpsed Pushkin's poetry through a kind of intellectual stereopsis, we were having a ball at several different levels, getting to know Onegin and his crowd and their times, gaining a strong and clear feeling for the brilliance of the original Russian poetry as well as for Pushkin himself, and even coming to sense the distinctive personalities and creativities of Johnston and Falen.

Onegin Starts to Turn Up Under Every Stone

One day around this time — the summer of 1993 — Carol and I were chatting in our kitchen with our sparkly and funny Russian friend Marina Eskina, and with a bit of pride we told her of our evening delectation of her compatriot Pushkin's novel. Marina knocked us for a loop by off-handedly mentioning that as a teen-ager, she had learned the whole book by heart. I expressed amazement, saying I could never do such a thing — I had a hard enough time memorizing a twenty-eight-line poemlet! — to which Marina, in a hilarious attempt at modesty, replied, "Well, *your* brain is so full of *ideas,* but mine, it was almost *empty* then!" Carol and I just had to laugh.

But then, a year or so later, I chanced to be at a symposium in Sweden with the late Russian poet Joseph Brodsky, and on a lovely group excursion by bus to see some ancient runes, he and I sat side by side for a while and chatted. Naturally, I was eager to tell him about my new-found love for Pushkin's novel in verse, of which he approved but said little, and so then, seeking to make light conversation, I repeated Marina's claim to him with amusement. To my surprise, Brodsky's eyes lit up and he said, "Oh, yes — very typical, very very typical! Having us do this in school was a pretty common assignment when we were young! I too memorized much of *Eugene Onegin,* and I even remember quite a few sonnets today." What a phenomenal difference between educational systems!

As a curious footnote to all this, my realization of Marina's literary talent prompted me one day to ask her if she would be interested in doing a Russian translation of *Gödel, Escher, Bach,* and indeed she was, and by now she has completed a most scintillating one, all ready to be published.

In 1995, having fallen under the spell of *Eugene Onegin,* I started seeking more versions in English, and eventually, aside from a few rather musty ones in the Indiana University library, all of which I checked out, I discovered there were two further English-language translations still in print, and purchased them. One was by Walter Arndt, the distinguished linguist, Slavicist, and Germanist; it was first published in 1963 and in fact won the Bollingen Prize that year for the best English translation of poetry. The other was by Oliver Elton, who as best I can tell was a professor of Russian at Oxford, and it was first published in England in 1937 (the centenary of Pushkin's original) and quite recently was substantially revised by A. D. P. Briggs, a professor of Russian in Birmingham, England.

Did I say *two* more? Perhaps I should have said *three.* There was, after all, another claimant to the throne of "luminous", or at least "authoritative" — namely, an imposing multi-volume rendition into English, executed by a famous trilingual author and published in 1964 by the Princeton University Press. I will come back to this curious attempt in the following chapter.

Four Sonnets, Four Ways Each

For now, what I wish to do is share with you the pure, unadulterated joy of the four English translations just mentioned. I will let you decide for yourself, to the extent you have sufficient data to choose, whose style you prefer. From the four-hundred-and-some stanzas I have selected just four. Stanza I.6 tells you a little bit about Onegin's wit and weaknesses; stanza II.18 is a touching meditation on the fading intensity of passions with age; stanza III.31 is Pushkin's way of leading up to the naïve but intense love letter written in French and innocently proffered to the suave and blasé Onegin by the humble country girl Tanya (or, more formally, "Tatyana"); and lastly, stanza VIII.20 encapsulates in a certain sense the novel's main plot line: It is the key moment at which Onegin, having long earlier repudiated Tanya's girlish love, years later re-encounters her, now a dignified married woman with high standing in St. Petersburg social circles, and as they meet again, Tatyana gives him the cold shoulder, leaving the lonely Onegin reeling in pain and disbelief.

We begin, then, with four rhyming anglicizations of stanza I.6 (displayed in a "random" order):

'Tis out of fashion now, is Latin;
And yet, in truth, it was no doubt
A language he was rather pat in.
A motto he could puzzle out,
Could prate of Juvenal; none better
Could with a <u>Vale</u> end a letter;
Yes, could two lines of Virgil say
With several blunders on the way.
Onegin had no sort of longing
To rummage in the dust of dates
Or chronicles of ancient states;
But to his memory came thronging
Full many a hoary anecdote
From Romulus till now, to quote.

Now Latin's gone quite out of favour;
yet, truthfully and not in chaff,
Onegin knew enough to savour
the meaning of an epigraph,
make Juvenal his text, or better
add <u>vale</u> when he signed a letter;
stumblingly call to mind he did
two verses of the Aeneid.
He lacked the slightest predilection
for raking up historic dust
or stirring annalistic must;
but groomed an anecdote-collection
that stretched from Romulus in his prime
across the years to our own time.

The Latin vogue today is waning,
And yet I'll say on his behalf,
He had sufficient Latin training
To gloss a common epigraph,
Cite Juvenal in conversation,
Put <u>vale</u> in a salutation;
And he recalled, at least in part,
A line or two of Virgil's art.
He lacked, it's true, all predilection
For rooting in the ancient dust
Of history's annals full of must,
But knew by heart a fine collection
Of anecdotes of ages past:
From Romulus to Tuesday last.

The Latin vogue has now receded,
And I must own that, not to brag,
He had what knowledge may be needed
To puzzle out a Latin tag,
Flaunt Juvenal in a discussion,
Add "Vale" to a note in Russian;
Of the <u>Aeneid</u>, too, he knew,
With some mistakes, a line or two.
To burrow in the dusty pages
Of Clio's chronologic waste
Was hardly to our hero's taste;
But anecdotes of bygone ages,
From Romulus to days just past,
To these his memory clung fast.

We now move from Chapter I's portrait of the novel's debonair hero to Chapter II's meditation on the mellowing of passions with age, with the four poets occupying the same spots in the matrix as before.

When to the standard we are flying
Of tranquil reason, and her rule,
And when our passions' flame is dying
And we begin to ridicule
Their wilfulness and all their sallies
And their belated after-rallies,
Then, with a struggle, we are tame;
But sometimes like to hear the same
Wild speech of passion, in a stranger;
It stirs our heartstrings. So, while penned
In his forgotten hut, may lend
An eager ear to tales of danger
Some crippled veteran, when they're told
By young, mustachioed heroes bold.

When we've retreated to the banner
of calm and reason, when the flame
of passion's out, and its whole manner
become a joke to us, its game,
its wayward tricks, its violent surging,
its echoes, its belated urging,
reduced to sense, not without pain —
we sometimes like to hear again
passion's rough language talked by others,
and feel once more emotion's ban.
So a disabled soldier-man,
retired, forgotten by his brothers,
in his small shack, will listen well
to tales that young mustachios tell.

When we at last turn into sages
And flock to tranquil wisdom's crest;
When passion's flame no longer rages,
And all the yearnings in our breast,
The wayward fits, the final surges,
Have all become mere comic urges,
And pain has made us humble men —
We sometimes like to listen then
As others tell of passions swelling;
They stir our hearts and fan the flame.
Just so a soldier, old and lame,
Forgotten in his wretched dwelling,
Will strain to hear with bated breath
The youngbloods' yarns of courting death.

When we have rallied to the standard
Of a well-tempered quietude,
And blazing passions have been rendered
Absurd, their afterglow subdued,
Their lawless gusts and their belated
Last echoes finally abated —
Not without cost at peace again,
We like to listen now and then
To alien passion's rage and seething,
And feel its clamor at our heart;
We play the battered veteran's part
Who strains to listen, barely breathing,
To exploits of heroic youth,
Forgotten in his humble booth.

We skip now to Chapter III. Tanya has just written her impulsive and passionate declaration of love to Onegin — in French, as I noted above — and in this stanza, in which Pushkin tells us that he has feebly translated it for us into Russian (if you know what I mean), his strong feelings for this sympathetic character of his own invention become evident:

Tatyana's letter never tires me
To read; and when I read it now,
I hold it sacred; it inspires me
With a sad, private pang, I vow.
Who taught her in soft words to render
Her love, so heedless and so tender?
Such touching nonsense — to impart
All the wild language of her heart,
So baneful in its fascination.
I know not — a pale copy give,
No more — the picture does not live —
A feeble, incomplete translation;
Just so a schoolgirl's finger may,
All timidly, Der Freischütz play...

Tatyana's letter, treasured ever
as sacred, lies before me still.
I read with secret pain, and never
can read enough to get my fill.
Who taught her an address so tender,
such careless language of surrender?
Who taught her all this mad, slapdash,
heartfelt, imploring, touching trash
fraught with enticement and disaster?
It baffles me. But I'll repeat
here a weak version, incomplete,
pale transcript of a vivid master,
or Freischütz as it might be played
by nervous hands of a schoolmaid.

— Chapter 8 —

Tatyana's letter lies beside me,
And reverently I guard it still;
I read it with an ache inside me
And cannot ever read my fill.
Who taught her then this soft surrender,
This careless gift for waxing tender,
This touching whimsy free of art,
This raving discourse of the heart —
Enchanting, yet so fraught with trouble?
I'll never know. But none the less,
I'll give it here in feeble dress:
A living picture's pallid double,
Or *Freischütz* played with timid skill
By fingers that are learning still.

What Tanya wrote is in my keeping,
I treasure it like Holy Writ;
I cannot read it without weeping
Nor ever read my fill of it.
Who, what, unsealed that fount of feeling,
With such unguarded grace revealing
(Naïve appeal of artless art)
Her unpremeditating heart,
Alike disarming and imprudent?
I cannot answer — anyhow,
Here is my weak translation now,
Life's pallid copy by a student,
Or *Freischütz* waveringly played
By pupils awkward and afraid.

And finally we arrive at the decisive and sad moment in Chapter VIII, when Tatyana's faithfulness as a wife — she has been married now for some time to an old general who was injured in battle, and for whom she clearly feels deep tenderness but not deep passion — overrides the embers of attraction that still glow in her heart for the more dashing Onegin.

Was this Tatyana — who'd believe it? —
Whom once, when our romance began,
In that remote, dull spot — conceive it! —
Long since, alone with her, the man,
Full of the blessed glow of preaching,
Had been admonishing and teaching?
She, in whose letter, cherished still,
Her heart had spoken, of free will,
With utter frankness? was he dreaming?
That ungrown girl — could this be she,
Whom, in her modest station, he
Had in those days been disesteeming?
Had _she_ encountered him, just now,
With that indifferent, fearless brow?

Was she the Tanya he'd exhorted
in solitude, as at the start
of this our novel we reported,
in the far backwoods' deepest heart,
to whom, in a fine flow of preaching,
he had conveyed some moral teaching,
from whom he'd kept a letter, where
her heart had spoken, free as air,
untouched by trace of inhibition,
could it be she … or had he dreamed?
the girl he'd scorned in what he deemed
the modesty of her condition,
could it be she, who just had turned
away, so cool, so unconcerned?

Was this the Tanya he once scolded
In that forsaken, distant place
Where first our novel's plot unfolded?
The one to whom, when face to face,
In such a burst of moral fire,
He'd lectured gravely on desire?
The girl whose letter he still kept —
In which a maiden heart had wept;
Where all was shown … all unprotected?
Was this that girl … or did he dream?
That little girl whose warm esteem
And humble lot he'd once rejected? …
And could she now have been so bold,
So unconcerned with him … so cold?

The girl whom he had gently scolded
Once, far away and tête-à-tête
(Before our tale had quite unfolded),
Whom, like a prim old magistrate,
He had presumed to read a lecture…
Who would have ventured to conjecture
That she, who penned in tender youth
That note, all candor and all truth,
Which he still kept, a declaration…
That same Tatyana — had he dreamed
All this? — to whom it must have seemed
That he disdained her age and station,
Could face him now without a qualm,
So blandly self-assured and calm?

We have just experienced four windows on one Russian poet — a fascinating, thought-provoking experience. Though I have much respect for each of these translator–poets, I am not fence-sittingly indifferent. I have my preferences! But first let me reveal their hidden identities:

> Elton/Briggs   Johnston
> Falen   Arndt

These anglicizations are a bit like performances of Chopin's études in the media of string quartet, woodwind quartet, brass quartet, and barbershop quartet — each one faithful and unfaithful in its own way to the original.

Some Comparisons of the Translations

There is no doubt that Vikram Seth's favorite, Sir Charles, is deserving of high praise — I love the last four lines of his version of II.18, for instance — but so are his rivals. Indeed, the corresponding lines in Falen's translation — especially the closing couplet "Will strain to hear with bated breath / The youngbloods' yarns of courting death" — are, for me, even more poignant and pungent. Or take, for instance, Elton's discovery of the nifty phrase "pat in" as a rhyme for "Latin", in I.6: "'Tis out of fashion now, is Latin; / And yet, in truth, it was no doubt / A language he was rather pat in." It seems made for the occasion! Or consider these lines by Arndt, also in I.6: "Flaunt Juvenal in a discussion, / Add 'Vale' to a note in Russian". Here, "in Russian" seems the most natural, obvious rhyme in the world for "discussion", and yet no one else noticed it. What lovely finds, totally faithful to Pushkin's meaning, yet simultaneously getting across that fantastic, brilliant snap of his style!

But let me not conceal the identity of my personal favorite. Falen, for me, is consistently clear as a bell, not only in meaning but also in ease of reading aloud — a key criterion in poetry. Effortlessly, one senses which are each line's strong and weak beats, and equally effortlessly, one makes sense of the ideas. In the others, despite wonderful moments of brilliance, there are too many spots where the rhythm goes momentarily awry (*e.g.*, line 8 of Johnston's version of I.6, which forces one to awkwardly accent "Aeneid" on "id" instead of the preceding "e", or the clunky, stumbling meter of lines 4 and 6 in Arndt's version of II.18); too many spots where words are used with murk, sloppiness, or phonetic imprecision (*e.g.*, Johnston's vague and clumsy phrase "Reduced to sense, not without pain" in II.18, or his ill-fitting words "address", "trash", and "transcript" in III.31, or Arndt's forced rhymes, such as "standard/rendered" in II.18 or *"tête-à-tête/*magistrate" in VIII.20); too many spots where sentences are so twisted around that they become hard to parse (*e.g.*, Elton/Briggs' "crippled veteran" in II.18, a phrase that turns out to be the subject not only of a verb that comes two lines earlier but also of a participle one line above that); and there are even times where it's hard to be sure just who or what is being referred to (*e.g.,* lines 10–11 of Elton/Briggs' version of III.31, or lines 7–14 in Arndt's version of VIII.20). There are numerous other uncomfortable moments I could have pointed out in these stanzas by Arndt, Elton/Briggs, and Johnston, but instead I leave the challenge as an exercise for the reader. This type of awkwardness, sad to say, seems to be the price occasionally paid for a lofty, "poetic" tone.

Falen, by contrast, is nearly unfailingly graceful and limpid, and time after time, he finds simple ways of saying things with zip and panache, such as his ending of I.6: "But knew by heart a fine collection / Of anecdotes of ages past: / From Romulus to Tuesday last." Falen's is the only version that I would unhesitatingly characterize as an unbroken string of beautifully chiseled Onegin stanzas in our language, as rhyming and rhythmic as those of the Russian original.

Just Foolin' Myself?

But how would I know? I've never read the Russian original! Perhaps I'm guilty of a rather pathetic delusion: Could it be that I have gradually slipped into the belief that I have a deep feeling for the Russian original simply because I have, over time, conflated Falen's voice increasingly often with that of Pushkin? In that case, it would come as no surprise that I judge Falen to be the most faithful translator, since my judgment would amount to nothing more than a tautology asserting that Falen is the most Falen-like!

I admit that recently I was having a chat with another translator, lauding the bell-like clarity of Falen's version, and after reading aloud stanza II.18 to him, I said, "Isn't that beautifully expressed?" and then I caught myself a split second before adding, "Of course, Pushkin deserves *some* of the credit..." I laughed at myself for this tendency to take Falen for Pushkin and vice versa. It's a very easy confusion to fall into, to tell the truth, reminiscent of the slippery performer/composer conflation to which audiences at recitals by famous virtuoso soloists are so, so susceptible — or reminiscent, for that matter, of our young Italian friend Elisabetta's naïve belief that she knew the voice of her favorite American screen star.

Imagine a roller-blader who does an amazing and unprecedented routine at which everybody who sees it gapes and gasps. Then some viewer chances to recall having seen on television, a few years earlier, an ice-skater who did very similar things. When you watch them simultaneously on side-by-side screens, you see that the roller-blader has simply copied, move for move, the routine that the ice-skater invented, substituting all sorts of idiomatic roller-blading maneuvers for ice-skating maneuvers that can be done only on ice, and on top of it all even making his routine match hers second for second... Who, then, should get the lion's share of the credit for the roller-blader's astounding performance?

Native-speaker Corroboration of My Assessment

Because of vague worries of this sort, I was gratified to find my personal esthetic intuitions reinforced by a literary Russian friend, Ariadna Solovyova (we will meet her again in Poems XI as a translator/poet), who recently wrote this to me, after I had sent her some of these same excerpts: "Of course Falen's is the best, hands down! When I looked at the translation samples, it caught my eye at once, and — oh, miracle! — the Russian verse popped up in my head! It's just perfect — the very same playful spirit." Ari then went on to say that she had not realized how much of *Eugene Onegin* she, too, knew by heart, and added that Falen's metric structures — specifically, the distribution of stressed and unstressed syllables in each verse — struck her as much more balanced, and much truer to the original, than any of the others.

Despite this native Russian speaker's corroboration, I admit that my preference is somewhat subjective. I surmise, for example, that I relate more easily to Falen since his English is more American than the others' is; however, this is not the whole story. (Indeed, his deft phrase "Tuesday last" sounds British to me, not American!) There is, simply, something objective about qualities such as clarity, directness, concision, non-forcedness, ease of scansion, and so on. But I won't press this point, firstly since I respect all four a great deal, and secondly since what I've displayed here is too small a sample for readers to be able to make a confident judgment on their own.

I will add, however, that after very careful reading and comparing of all four versions, I find that Johnston's, though "luminous" in the eyes of Vikram Seth, is not even my second choice. For me, there is a very clear rank-ordering: Falen, Arndt, Johnston, Elton/Briggs, with the gaps growing in size as quality falls, and with the performances by the first two often extraordinarily different in tone and imagery, yet amazingly close in eloquence, a bit like two world-class violinists' hair-raisingly precise slalomings down the steep slopes of a great sonata, differing in style on every single turn, yet in speed separated by no more than a few hundredths of a second.

My only nagging worry is this: Could Falen perhaps be *too* lucid? That is, what if it turns out that native Russian speakers have noticeably more trouble in understanding Pushkin than native English speakers do in understanding its Falenization? Would Falen's "improvement" on Pushkin then count as a faithful transmission of Pushkin's covert intent, or instead as a fickle falsification of Pushkin's overt output? Fortunately, from all accounts that I have read, it seems that Pushkin's mode of expression is always lucid and free-flowing, as natural and easy to parse as smooth prose. And that is precisely the beauty of Falen's English version.

Triangulating on the Original Text

As I pointed out earlier, a reader who had been given just one of these translations could savor its poetry but would have no idea how much liberty was being taken at any given point — how far the translator was deviating from the original Russian text. But given any two of these versions, any significant liberty taken by either one of them with respect to the Russian becomes instantly noticeable, since right at that very point, a significant discrepancy between the two English versions will also show up (barring the freak coincidence that both translators should have chosen to take exactly the same liberty at the same time!). Of course, someone who cannot read the Russian could not tell *which* translator had taken the liberty, but at least it would be clear that one or the other had done so.

Consider, for a tiny example of this kind of thing, lines 11–13 of Johnston's and Falen's versions of II.18. Where Johnston describes "a disabled soldier-man, retired, forgotten *by his brothers,* in his small shack", Falen speaks of "a soldier, old and lame, forgotten in his wretched dwelling". The question arises: in Pushkin's original Russian, was there any explicit mention of "brothers" or "fellow soldiers" having forgotten their colleague, or was the poor old fellow simply forgotten by the world in general? One translation suggests the former, the other suggests the latter.

If we look to the other translations for help, we find that both seem to confirm the image conveyed by Falen: he has been forgotten in general, not just by his military brothers. Actually, Elton/Briggs suggests that it is his *hut* that has been forgotten, but this is a kind of metonymy — alluding to one thing by mentioning something closely associated with it — that is clearly sanctioned by poetic license.

The flip side of the coin is when two or more translations of the same passage feel very much "in synch"; in such cases, one can quite confidently infer backwards to what the Russian itself must be like. For an example, let us once again refer to Johnston's and Falen's versions of II.18. We know with considerable confidence, if we read both English stanzas attentively, that in the original Russian there must be some allusion to the *silliness* or *laughability* of passions that are viewed in hindsight, because of the phrases "become a joke to us" on Johnston's line 4 and "become mere comic urges" on Falen's line 6. On the other hand, from this small line-number discrepancy, we know that one of these translators, perhaps even both, took the liberty of moving this idea of *humor* a short distance from its original position in the poem, but that is a pretty minor sin.

We can triangulate on this matter by consulting the other two English versions. In the Elton/Briggs version, line 4, we find "we begin to ridicule", and on lines 3–4 of Arndt's version we find "have been rendered absurd". It thus starts to appear quite likely that it is on line 4 of the original Russian where this allusion to the retrospective silliness of the passions of youth occurs. Thus, of all the translators, only Falen has betrayed his author.

But does it really make that much of a difference? Line 4, line 6, line 8, line 12 — who cares? It is within conceivability that a translator who was having trouble squeezing an idea in at the precise spot where it occurred in the original poem might, if it happened to work out easily and elegantly, transpose the idea outside of its original stanza, perhaps to a neighboring stanza, perhaps a few pages away, maybe even to a distant chapter! In that case, only by reading on a *global* level could one tell that all ideas were actually preserved, albeit in a shuffled order.

Actually, there would be a certain poetic justice to such moving-about of ideas, so long as no idea was deformed in the act of transport — the reason being that in physics and mathematics the technical term "translation" means "shifting an object from one point in space to another, without rotating or deforming it". By this definition, then, a translator could "translate" ideas from one site in the poem to another without being unfaithful. Of course, someone might well protest that the very order and structure of the ideas is itself a crucial aspect of the original text, in which case any translator who had the audacity to translate ideas would be an unfaithful translator.

In any case, by triangulating two or more independent translations of *Eugene Onegin,* a complete outsider to Russian can gain a considerable feel for how the Russian itself is structured and how it feels to read it in the original. In fact, it was precisely this type of slow and systematic line-by-line triangulation with respect to the hidden Russian original that gradually gave me the chutzpah I mentioned at the outset of this chapter.

To be sure, one will never in this way hear the sounds of the Russian as they sound to a Russian, the inner resonances of the words and phrases in the mind of someone born and bred in that vast, distant land, but can an outsider *ever* do that, anyway? Even if I were to spend the next fifteen years immersing myself in Russian, could I ever make up for not having grown up there? For that matter, how can a Russian of today presume to know how those words sounded to Russians of Pushkin's era, some 160 years ago?

All readings are partial and approximate, and we must content ourselves with whatever joy and insight we can derive from deep ideas rendered clearly in beautiful language, knowing that our derivative response and the author's original vision will never be perfectly aligned.

Translations: Unspontaneous and Non-memorizable?

One of the paradoxes for a Russian reading Pushkin today is that so many of his phrases have entered the language that they sound vaguely familiar the first time they are seen in print. (Much the same could be said for Shakespeare in English or the Old Testament in Hebrew, for example.) This can create the illusion that original Pushkin flows in a marvelously "natural" way, when in fact what is happening is merely a kind of *déjà vu*. My friend Ari Solovyova first realized this for herself and pointed it out to me when I objected to the following sentence she had written in a note to me: "It is always hard for me to memorize translations because I can sense the author's strain, see the seams (or so it seems)." I saw this as a too-facile blanket condemnation of translations, and when I objected to it, saying it sounded implausible and quasi-mystical to me, she replied as follows:

> I see now that the idea of a mystical inherent difference between original poetry and translations is a stereotype, and I no longer wish to keep it. The essence of this stereotype (which may be common) is:
>
> - originals are organic; they grow, flow, ring; they are music of sounds, and music is easy to remember;
> - translations are carefully calculated, based on abstract formulas; the words in them were not sung spontaneously but forcibly pulled together; thus they are hard to remember.

Actually, even the best poems may have involved a fair amount of calculation; and there's no reason why translators cannot get in the precise mood of a verse and then recreate it spontaneously (or almost) in the new language.

The real reason Onegin is easy to remember must be that so much of it became a part of the Russian language — hundreds of phrases.

Blurring of Reality with Fiction in "Eugene Onegin"

A careful reader may notice something peculiar about stanza III.31 — to wit, it is Pushkin himself who is claiming to have in his own possession a letter written by Tatyana, a fictional character in his great novel! How can this be? The answer is that Pushkin, quite early in the story, explains that he and Onegin are long-time friends, and had even planned to take an extended foreign trip together, but unfortunately, just as the two of them were about to take off, Eugene's father died, and their plans were dropped.

Pushkin even drew a sketch of himself and his pal Yevgeny standing side by side, gazing across the river Neva at the Peter and Paul Fortress in St. Petersburg. I wonder what the two are talking about — perhaps about the blurring of truth and fiction? Or perhaps about a new play that has just opened? Or a little gossip about Tatyana's husband? Or the role of fate and chance in the pursuit of love? Or how things are going in Pushkin's current novel in verse? Or the best shoestore in St. Petersburg?

Of course, the mere fact that Eugene Onegin and Alexander Pushkin were alleged friends does not explain how the latter came to have this most intimate, treasured letter written to the former, and which, you may have noticed (check out stanza VIII.20), the former still kept. Would Onegin have copied out this highly personal letter for *anyone*?

The Pushkin/Onegin composite personage is a most interesting blur of identities, compounded and confused further by the fact that the other principal male character of the novel, Vladimir Lensky, is a young poet who is killed in a quite senseless duel, much as — several years later and in real life — the young poet Alexander Pushkin was killed in a senseless duel with a confused and headstrong baron named d'Anthès. And who is it that kills poor Lensky? None other than his headstrong friend Eugene Onegin!

I once asked my mother for her opinion of the strength of the portrayal of the characters in *Eugene Onegin*. She replied that she found Onegin himself particularly richly painted, a view to which I assented, adding, however, that I considered him somewhat shallow, or at least not very intellectual. She immediately countered, "He couldn't be *too* shallow, for after all, he was a friend of Pushkin!" All of a sudden, I was struck by this hilarious twisty logic — Eugene Onegin confirmed as a serious intellectual by virtue of being a friend of Russia's greatest poet, Alexander Pushkin, author of the world-famous novel in verse *Eugene Onegin*! Fine credentials, I must admit.

Part of the enormous charm and richness of *Eugene Onegin* is that it abounds in unpredictable, delightful self-referential twists of this sort. Consider Tatyana's love letter, described in stanza III.31. To take the author at his word, this letter was originally written *in French* by the naïve country girl Tatyana (in this fact *per se* there is nothing particularly strange: all well-educated Russians of the day expressed themselves in writing as fluently in French as in Russian, often more so), and Alexander Pushkin, poet, is now allegedly sitting at his desk, painstakingly rendering Tatyana's guileless, artless French into Russian. In which case, how curious, how astonishing, how wonderful, that a letter written in French prose should wind up coming out in flawless rhyming Russian tetrameter! Or could it have been originally penned in flawless rhyming tetrameter in French? But in that case, this naïve country girl would herself have been a gifted poet. If so, why doesn't Pushkin tell us so? Why doesn't he comment on the brilliant rhymes and rhythms of her epistle?

If one backs away from this image in which fiction blurs so intimately into reality, there are still puzzles. How did Pushkin the author (as contrasted with Pushkin the peripheral character in his own novel) in fact compose Tatyana's letter? Should one assume that he first wrote out, on

Tanya's behalf, a letter to Onegin in genuine, simple French, and only *then* proceeded to render it in Russian verse — or would doing things in this roundabout manner have been an extravagant, time-wasting way of creating her letter? Did he instead write it out directly in Russian, with the suggestion that it had come from a French original being no more than a grand conceit? Or did he write it out in Russian while juggling various French phrases in the back of his mind?

And whatever one might surmise the answer to this question is, when the entirety of *Eugene Onegin* is translated (as it has been) into rhyming French tetrameter, is there any reason to suppose that Tatyana's letter, now supposedly back home in its original linguistic medium, would have a more genuine ring to it than the novel's other sections?

A Nostalgic Counterfactual

As I wrote these musings, I found myself nostalgically wishing that my old high-school English teacher had assigned us Falen's version of *Eugene Onegin* instead of the more standard fare (Hawthorne, Hemingway, etc.), which I found turgid and dull. Suddenly I realized that my unconscious mind had concocted an incoherent counterfactual: back then, not a single line of Falen's beautiful translation had yet been written, so she *couldn't* have given it to us. Silly, silly me!

Well, all I can say is, I *still* wish, simply stretching my fantasy a tiny bit further into "alternity", as George Steiner once aptly dubbed the realm of spontaneous counterfactual musings, that I had had the chance to read Falen's translation when I was very young: I bet it would have bowled me over, intoxicating me with its snappy rhymes and pungent phrasings, perhaps bringing out the poetry lover in me much earlier in life. And maybe, just maybe, in that highly counterfactual world, I would have been so taken with Pushkin and his lyrical language that I might have been launched as a teen-ager on a long linguistic pathway finally enabling the adult me, on my recent New York trip, to open a conversation, perhaps even to initiate a friendship in their native tongue, with my two momentary partners-in-ascension in the lift at the Jolly Madison. *Как знать?*

●

Poems VIII:

~ Sassy City ~

* * * *
* *
*
*

"You, My Sweet" sets a flippant tone from its very start by splitting the word "sweetie" across lines, venturing out on the same rickety hyphenation limb as did "Cutie Pie". I was aware that to some readers, though not all, this kind of cross-line word-chop feels so jarring that it might look like something done in desperation: an aberration, possibly an unconscious mistake. My intuition told me that if I were to use this device of enjambment (dictionary definition: "the continuation of a sentence or idea from one line or couplet of a poem to the next") at the intra-word level, then I shouldn't use it just *once* inside a poem, because an isolated instance might stand out as a misfit. On the other hand, using it twice or more would upgrade the whole idea into a theme, marking intra-word enjambment as a *feature* rather than a *bug* of my style. Thus motivated, I hacked "ruthlessly" apart and mercilessly splattered it across two lines, thereby constructing a "rhyme", in a metaphorical sense of the term, with the enjambment occurring 15 lines above it.

I was doubtless vaguely aware of re-using individual words, even rhymes, that had already been exploited here or there — "ail/jail" and "emerge/urge", for instance — but as long as the way that such recyclings fit into the larger-scale flow of the poem felt reasonably fresh and new, I let myself do so. Thus I was certainly most conscious of borrowing Melanie's clever find "sweet tooth", but as my use and hers seemed sufficiently distinct, I felt my mini-plagiarism was excusable.

My favorite couplet was the blunt "squelched/belched" rhyme — so "naughty" that I delighted in it, like an innocent schoolchild sent into stitches by a mere burp. I was likewise amused by line 23's suggestion that "getting stout" might be a positive goal to shoot for, the word "stout" in my mind mainly evoking silly, stodgy, Pickwickian imagery.

In fishing about in memory for a rhyme for "to get stout", I dredged up a phrase close to the fringes of my own native command of American English: "You need out". I would argue that, simple though it seems, the little six-word couplet thereby produced could only have been concocted by someone with a true, native-level mastery of American English. As I hear it, "you need out" is a down-home phrase typical of the rural American flatlands, and in order to know it and know how to use it, one has to have spoken American English for many years. It is pretty far-fetched to imagine this phrase being taught in an English class in China or Iran or France. While it's true that "need out" might possibly come up in some Mark Twain or Tom Robbins selection in an American Literature course, chances are that the class, even the teacher, would be thrown by it, and almost certainly wouldn't have any sense of its regional flavor. From many observations of this sort, I was starting to appreciate just how indispensable a deep, native-level mastery of the target language is in order to do a good job at translating "Ma Mignonne".

A couple of footnotes on development. Originally, I was not so bold at the poem's start: In my first sketch, lines 1–2 ran "You, my sweet / One, I greet". On the other hand, in that same sketch I waxed a bit blasphemous at the ending: "Have you belched / Recently, / From a spree / With some jam? / No! God damn / It, my fair, / You need air! / Here's my pray'r: / With His care / May God treat / You, my sweet."

You, My Sweet

D. Hofstadter

You, my sweet-
ie, I greet
With much love.
Tell me of
What you ail,   5
In that jail
Cell from which,
With no hitch,
You'll emerge
Soon. I urge   10
You to jump
From that dump
Of a room,
Where, in gloom,
Your sweet tooth   15
Has been ruth-
lessly squelched.
Have you belched
Recently,
From a spree   20
Of marm'lade?
No. Frail maid,
To get stout,
You need out.
Thus Clem's pray'r: 25
With much care
May God treat
You, my sweet.

In pulling Marot's tiny poem out of its native tongue, invariably one of the most interesting mini-challenges is that of choosing what to do about the first line (and last line, perforce), for that choice inevitably exerts a profound and pervasive influence on everything to follow it (and to precede it!). In my earliest efforts, I'd always found myself trying to capture as many nuances of the French words *Ma mignonne* as I could in one single English phrase, but as I gained experience, I gradually loosened up on this score and started trying out one term of endearment after another. "Pet" was a typical such experiment, and working with it led to this effort.

Lines 2–3 in "Pet of Mine" have a neat ambiguity to them: On a surface level, they clearly constitute a cheery greeting saying "A fine day to you!" — yet on a subtler level, through their strong overlap with the well-known anger-loaded exclamation "That's a fine how-do-you-do!", they suggest the poet's outrage that illness could have overtaken his young little friend. Lines 4–5 tend to reinforce the latter interpretation.

The very next semantic couplet again goes out on the hyphenation limb by splitting "cuplet" across lines (and of course, despite the spelling, one can't help but hear this word as meaning "distich" as well as "little cup"). Once again I felt that the presence of this hyphenation in the poem was "justified" by the existence of a parallel some twelve lines down — an analogous splitting of "jellies". In fact, rather fittingly, it's an enjambment on just the line where "jam" should be jammed in.

In this poem, yet another time, I borrowed Melanie's elegant find "sweet-tooth", but this time with the added twist of subword-swapping, which I found most appealing because it yielded an unexpected but strong allusion to the familiar French phrase *tout de suite* ("instantly; straightaway"). The sentence on lines 10–13 is thus pleasingly ambiguous: The meaning "Clément urges you to come outdoors without delay" competes with the meaning "Clément urges you to come outdoors, you candy fiend, you!" In inserting this *soupçon* of French directly (or indirectly) into my poem, I was clearly under the influence of my mother's breezy use of French phrases in hers.

This poem, like my Shakespearean effort, "On Ye, Childe", has the special virtue of respecting that infamous and elusive "charm #7", the out-of-phase semantic couplets.

Pet of Mine

D. Hofstadter

Pet of mine,
Here's a fine
Howdee-do!
Why are you
All cooped up?   5
Quaff a cup-
let of pills.
Quash your chills!
Bolt from bed!
Stick your head   10
Out-of-doors,
Clem implores
You, tooth-sweet!
You who eat
With delight,   15
You should fight
To get well
And gulp jel-
lies and cakes.
Bellyaches   20
You'll forget,
When you get
Back some rose
On your nose
And your cheeks.   25
Health in weeks
Will be thine,
Pet of mine.

For me, the peak appeal of "Kiddo, Hi!" comes close to its midpoint, in the back-to-back parallel lines "Of my song" and "Of my game". Lines 10–12 allude to two idiomatic phrases: "to make a long story short" and "the long and the short of it"; then lines 13–16 analogously allude to the phrase "the name of the game". This is the site of a *double entendre*: readers are left up in the air as to whether the phrase "Of my game / Here's the name" refers just to the very next line, containing the poet's name ("Clem Marot"), or to the next *three* lines, which set out the poet's game plan (*i.e.*, sloughing off old Sawbones).

With the exhortation to "stay plump / 'Round your rump", the tone gets a bit more ribald than in my previous efforts, but such a flavor is not unexpected in a context where "throw out your doc" is acceptable. Indeed, the tone of this poem is extremely slangy and percussive throughout, with words like "blinks", "clink", "split", "joint", "scarf", and "bolt". Even the title's two words, "kiddo" and "hi", are pretty chatty.

Phonetically, the poem's closing couplet involves exactly the same rhyme as its opening couplet does, but of course "hi" and "high" are unrelated in meaning; this type of first-line/last-line homonymy was a trick I had recently discovered and was starting to exploit quite often in my translations. In this type of venture, I was surely influenced by my favorite song lyricists of the 1920's and the next couple of decades. For instance, take the classic George Gershwin/Ira Gershwin song "But Not for Me", written in 1930, whose lyrics lament on and on about the fact that wonderful romances are happening for everyone else, "but not for me", and then come to a teary conclusion as follows:

> *He's knocking on a door,*
> *But not for me;*
> *He'll plan a two by four,*
> *But not for me.*

> *I've heard that Love's a Game;*
> *I'm puzzled, just the same —*
> *Was I the Moth or Flame…?*
> *I'm all at sea.*

> *It started off so swell,*
> *This "Let's Pretend";*
> *It all began so well;*
> *But what an end!*

> *The climax of a plot*
> *Should be the marriage knot,*
> *But there's no knot for me.*

The twist here is of course the homonymy of "not" and "knot", which allows what sounds on a phonetic level like a double negation to make perfect sense on the semantic level.

Even though I was born too late to enjoy such songs in the years they came out and were most popular, I grew up constantly hearing them on records, and consequently this sort of wordplay flows deeply in my blood. Oh, how I thank my parents for their good taste! With any luck, love for this type of music will course through my children's blood as well, for I make sure they have a steady diet of this healthy stuff. They got to see the Broadway production of *Crazy for You*, for instance, and from the cassette tape of it had practically all the lyrics to all the songs fully memorized at one point, including this one.

Kiddo, Hi!

D. Hofstadter

> _Kiddo, hi!_
> _Greetings fly_
> _From your friend._
> _Please don't spend_
> _Many blinks_   5
> _In that clink's_
> _Dismal bed,_
> _But instead_
> _Split the joint!_
> _That's the point,_   10
> _Short and long,_
> _Of my song._
> _Of my game,_
> _Here's the name:_
> _Clem Marot_   15
> _Says to throw_
> _Out your doc!_
> _Scarf a choc-_
> _'late eclair!_
> _Lay'r by lay'r,_   20
> _Bolt down cakes!_
> _Tummyaches_
> _Might ensue,_
> _But, dear, you_
> _Will stay plump_   25
> _'Round your rump._
> _May you fly,_
> _Kiddo — high!_

In "Hurry, Love", I again played the sassy first-line/last-line homonymy game (with something of a Cockney accent), but this time spiced it up even more by combining it — both at the poem's start and at its finish — with my other favorite game of word-splitting, thus at the top chopping "lovely" in two, and at the bottom doing the same to "recovery".

As is obvious, at this stage I was starting to "feel my oats", as the old phrase goes — that is, to feel quite self-confident and even cocky — in my manipulations of the language, an example being my casual use of "mean means" to express the idea "nasty fashion". A couplet like "Quarantine's / A mean means" would simply never have occurred to me when I first set myself the challenge — it would have been beyond my mental reach.

By taking more and more such little risks, I was having more and more fun. Thus, because of enjambments of various types and at various levels, a large proportion of the individual lines in this poem make no sense at all in isolation, yet when read aloud in succession they flow well, merge into ideas, and make perfect sense. For instance...

Line 13 forces "Clement" to be accented on its second syllable, which in turn forces "Vehement-" to be accented on its third syllable, something that in another context just wouldn't work. Lines 17–18 rhyme at both front and back, and lines 19–22 form a section where a single sound ends four lines in a row; this fusillade is instantly followed by a line where "jellyfish" is broken apart into fragments brazenly flung into separate sentences. Then line 24 is almost *too* brazen, requiring "nourish" to be strongly accented on its final syllable. Line 25 likewise forces line 26's indefinite article "a" to be pronounced as a long vowel and to receive the line's primary stress — pretty damn pushy. Despite all these risky moves, I still feel the poem works as a whole. "Hurry, Love" is hardly lyrical, but the fact that I could come up with a translation possessing this kind of snappy, sassy verve, clearly indebted on a deep level to Ira Gershwin, Cole Porter, Tom Lehrer, and other such lyricists, gave me a special kind of satisfaction that's hard to convey.

One of my greatest pieces of luck in marrying Carol Brush was an unexpected across-the-board agreement in taste: people, movies, music, food, languages, art... She and I had a real resonance going, that's for sure. Like me, Carol was enamored of American popular music of an era long before her birth, and together we savored so many old melodies and their often sassy lyrics. For instance, in an early Cole Porter song called "I'm Getting Myself Ready for You", we listened over and over to one verse, which seemed to go this way:

> *To be sure of being worthy of you, dear, in every way,*
> *I'm building a perfect physique;*
> *And beside which I want you to holler hooray,*
> *When first you see me in my so-to-speak...*

But the phrase "see me in my so-to-speak" struck us as too risqué for 1930, so we concluded that perhaps it actually said "soldier's peak", which we theorized might be some dashing old piece of headgear. But finally we looked it up and found "so-to-speak" was right. Hah!

In 1986, we both went on a big Gershwin kick, reading biographies of George and watching TV shows about him and his family. On one, we saw interviews with older brother Ira and younger sister Frances ("Frankie"), who sang a couple of their songs in a very touching way. On our first anniversary, we splurged and went to New York City for a few days to take in some shows, including a review of songs by Kaye Swift, once George's lover. It was in a small recital hall, and eagle-eye Carol spotted Frankie Gershwin sitting just a few rows ahead of us. Wow! At the intermission, Carol, normally a very shy person, *insisted* we go up and say a few words to her, and Frankie greeted us very warmly. Carol always looked back on the few moments we shared with her with extreme happiness, and described our meeting Frankie as being "like shaking hands with an era". Right she was!

Hurry, Love

D. Hofstadter

Hurry, love-
ly girl, of
Whom I sing.
Things aren't swing-
ing with you —   5
'Tis to rue.
Quarantine's
A mean means
To shield us
From you; thus   10
Quickly kick
Out your sick-
ness, Clement
Vehement-
ly would urge   15
You. This scourge
Trounce, and then
Bounce again
Out of bed,
To chew bread   20
That you've spread
With sweet red
Jelly. Fish
Will nourish
You, too. May   25
God speed a
Swift recov-
ery, Love.

The tightly entwined enjambments and syncopations of "Pretty Dear", most striking in lines 4–11 and again in lines 18–21, are similar in flavor to those just seen in "Hurry, Love"; however, I would say that line 7's amphisbænic enjambment is more brazen than anything attempted there.

One distinguishing feature of this poem is the joke at the end, alluding to the high price of medical care in the United States — a joke that of course has no counterpart at all in the original poem. I haven't the foggiest how expensive it was in France in the 1530's, but since medical care, such as it was, wasn't socialized at the time, Marot probably could have related to the lament. This may not, however, provide a sufficiently credible pretext for my having inserted this utterly extraneous element into my poem. Clearly, I wouldn't have dared to do such a thing — I would never have even been able to think of it — when I first started trying to translate "Ma Mignonne".

The most interesting thing about the final couplet, however, is the way that the phrase "Pretty dear" is used as a rhyme with itself. What's implicit here is the idea that, because both "pretty" and "dear" change radically in their *meaning* from one line to the next, their precise copying should not be seen as mere repetition but as genuine rhyme, quite unlike, say, the repetition of "the moon" in Edward Lear's poem "The Owl and the Pussy-Cat", whose lovable last stanza runs this way:

> They dined on mince, and slices of quince,
> Which they ate with a runcible spoon;
> And hand in hand, on the edge of the sand,
> They danced by the light of the moon,
> The moon,
> The moon,
> They danced by the light of the moon.

I don't think anyone would argue that Lear's four line-ending "moon"'s (or any subset thereof) actually rhyme with each other, whereas I would strongly defend the idea that in my poem, two visually and phonetically identical lines indeed *do* rhyme with each other.

Since my quip about doctor bills takes up a few lines, some of Marot's original content had to yield a bit, and in this case, it was the poet's worry about his friend's weight loss and her pallor, as well as his hopes for divine intervention. Of course, leaving some of the content out is nothing new (the next poem, "Pretty One", is far more radical in this regard), but it raises the question of the extent to which this poem has the right to be labeled "translation". Is it merely an "interpretation of" or, even worse, just a "poem inspired by"?

Pretty Dear

D. Hofstadter

Pretty dear,
Clement, here,
Wants you well.
Your long spell
Spent in stir   5
Has him wor-
ried a lit-
tle bit. It
Should be clipped:
Stopped and nipped   10
In the bud.
Your young blood
Will perk up
Once you sup
On sweet stuff.   15
Off your duff,
Little girl!
In the whirl
Of things, get
Back; no set-   20
back allow!
You must now
Shake your ills:
Doctor bills
Else will be   25
(Believe me,
Pretty dear)
Pretty dear.

Most notable in "Pretty One" is the irregular rhyme scheme, lurching back and forth pretty much at random between distichs and tristichs. I don't know just why I took this liberty, but I guess I felt that having already adhered to "Ma Mignonne"'s tight rhyming constraints several times fairly successfully, I had earned the right to try some experiments with variations on the constraints.

The novel contractions in lines 3 and 4 push the limits of what might count as a single syllable, but I was definitely in a sassy mood. And then the splitting of "sentence" across lines 5–6 is actually a bit sassier than prior splittings we've noted, firstly since it dares to echo the exact sound that occurs just two lines above, and secondly since it fails to carve the word at its natural joints — that is, its official syllable boundaries (thus "sen-tence", not "sent-ence", would be proper). But being in that sassy mood, I merrily thumbed my nose at convention and broke the word where I felt like doing so. Note also that "A long sentence", on one level alluding to jail, can on another level be taken as a self-reference.

Continuing in the same spirit, I committed a "cannibalism" (a situation where a sound "swallows" an identical sound that would be its neighbor) on lines 9–10, having the second half of "bitten" get swallowed by the first half of "tennis" — a twist followed instantly by another twist: the forced parsing of "courts" as a verb rather than a noun. (Incidentally, I plagiarized the next phrase, "sports of all sorts", from Lucky's speech in Samuel Beckett's *Waiting for Godot,* a nonsense passage that as a teenager I'd memorized with much glee.)

All these jokes make the tone even more flip than usual. Indeed, on the content level, all that is preserved of the original poem is the very general idea of someone sick being kept in confinement against their will, accompanied by imagery of recovering, eating well again, going outside, and enjoying life. Thus once again, the question arises: Is this a genuine *translation* of Marot's poem, or merely a ditty *inspired* by it?

Pretty One

D. Hofstadter

Pretty one,
This note's done,
And's been sent
T'where you've spent
A long sent-   5
ence in bed,
Being fed
Food unfit
To be bit.
Tennis courts   10
You, and sports
Of all sorts
Woo you too,
As I do,
Clement who   15
Wants you out,
Prancing 'bout,
Gaily flout-
ing disease,
In the breeze,   20
Having fun,
Eating none
Of that junk
Food those lunk-
heads fed you,   25
In that zoo.
Gotta run,
Pretty one.

•

• *Chapter 9* •

A Vile
Non-verse

•

A **few** chapters back, I displayed the opening paragraph of *La disparition*, Georges Perec's dizzyingly weird and dazzlingly wizardly "e"-less novel, as translated by myself in a zombie-ish manner into unconstrained English, with "e"'s falling everywhere, left and right, helter-skelter, wherever they might. To this goofy theme we now return, pushing it counterfactually just a little further into the realm of goofiness.

Marvin Validbook's Eerie Pseudo-Disappearance

In our somewhat surrealistic, or some might say slightly silly, scenario, then, that eminent Franco–Irish playwright Marvin Validbook, celebrated for exemplary and exact exegeses of East European émigré essayists, for an effervescent enthusiasm for philately ("My joys, as joyous as joys known to Boy, spring from artful wordsmithing and postal stamp chasing", Validbook confides in an interview reprinted in *Brash Attacks*), for escapist eenybopper erotica (who could ever forget Vladimir Vladimir, the lecherous lothario in Validbook's scandal-provoking play *Là, ô Lit?*), and (last but not least!) for an especial expertise in eschewing the letter "e" ("My upbringing had all your typical Anglo-Saxon constraints" is found somewhere in Validbook's quasi-eidetic autobiography *Spout, Mind*), has dedicated a full ten years, out of profound personal reverence for Georges Perec's *La disparition*, to translating the whole of that novel into English in a painstakingly precise, word-for-word manner, of course exquisitely aware of the fact that the beauty and brio of Perec's novel stem not so much from its plot or its diction as from the tight lipogrammatic hoop through which its author made every line of the French original text jump, yet adamantly maintaining that it would be a preposterous betrayal of literary truth to try to imitate that crucial, all-important property in an English reconstruction. (Why in the world would Validbook or anyone else ever make such a fatuous choice? *Qui sait ?* People are strange. And so, on with the fantasy.)

Not long after embarking on this labor of love, Validbook publishes in *The Manhattanite* a pair of epistles lovingly penned in beautiful Perec-style Anglo-Saxon, addressed directly to the late lamented author, apologizing with a curious blend of reverence and arrogance for the decision to spurn Perec's lipogrammatic constraint in anglicizing *La disparition*.

In the prefatory material to *The Disappearance*, Validbook most saliently declares that only a work of art's final form has any interest, that only mediocrities would think they could learn anything of value from drafts, discards, erasures, manuscripts, and such things: "It is, I insist again, a work's final form, and only its final form, that has import for a pupil — or for this pupil, anyway — who would confront a top-notch artist's output." This point having been made crystal-clear, Validbook supplements the thinnish volume of translated text with two bulging companion volumes of some 1,000 further pages, filled with agonizingly detailed examinations of Perec's drafts, discards, erasures, manuscripts, and such things.

Scattered throughout these ancillary volumes are also found many further archly-worded defenses of the unbudging decision to throw out the window the original text's most salient aspect: its "e"-lessness. And on the classically elegant front cover of each volume, Validbook's highly respected publisher prints, in large, bright type just underneath the title, the phrase "A Novel in Which the Letter 'E' Never, Ever Appears", to ensure that potential readers will know just what sort of book they have in their hands.

By coincidence, just as Validbook has sent off the final proofs, the climax of so many years of torturous labor, Professor Wilber Darent, a younger scholar but no less of a lipoglot, publishes a scrupulously "e"-less Anglo-Saxon translation of Perec's novel, which is awarded that year's coveted Nobelling prize for creative translation. Validbook, stung to the quick, savagely attacks Darent's translation as well as several earlier "e"-less ones, mercilessly accusing, in various literary fora, all their creators of being "dainty mimics" who "falsify authors" (to cite just two of many abusive epithets hurled at them), and at the same time proudly characterizes *The Disappearance* as "a crib, a pony, straightarrow and clumsy, turgid and slavishly faithful", though emphatically adding that it is "crying out for additional cacophony". Finally, putting the last ironic coat of icing on this amusingly absurdist layercake, a solemn review of Validbook's idiosyncratic and anything-but-"e"-free creation comes out in *The Manhattan Chronicle,* poker-facedly praising this "limpid, literal 'e'-free translation" to the skies.

If the foregoing sounds like a Monty Python spoof, there is good reason: Marvin Validbook (whose love for anagrams led him to invent Vikram Vainblood, a fictional *alter ego*) has a delightful dextrous daffiness to him that occasionally catapults him to the remoter reaches of oddity.

Vladimir Nabokov's Baffling Pseudo-Onegin

And now for something completely different... we turn to Vladimir Nabokov. This prominent Russo-American writer, celebrated for his poetry, his prose, his pomposity, his pugnacity, his perfectionism, his prejudices, his pedantry, his punctilious phrasemongery, his pooh-poohing of politics, his putdowns of psychoanalysis, his predilection for puzzles, his powerful passion for lepidoptery ("My pleasures are the most intense known to man: writing and butterfly hunting", Nabokov confided in an interview reprinted in *Strong Opinions*), his popular pedophilic pornography (who could ever forget Humbert Humbert, the randy rake in Nabokov's scandal-provoking novel *Lolita?*), and (last but not least!) his prodigious polyglottism ("Mine was the typical trilingual childhood" he once said, perhaps somewhere in his quasi-photographic autobiography *Speak, Memory*), dedicated a full ten years, out of profound personal reverence for Alexander Pushkin's *Eugene Onegin*, to translating the whole of that novel into English in a painstakingly precise, word-for-word manner, of course exquisitely aware of the fact that the beauty and brio of Pushkin's novel stem not so much from its plot or its diction as from the tight metrical and rhyming hoop through which its author made every line of the Russian original text jump, yet adamantly maintaining that it would be a preposterous betrayal of literary truth to try to imitate that crucial, all-important property in his English reconstruction. (Why in the world would Nabokov or anyone else ever make such a fatuous choice? *Как знать?* People are strange. And so, on with the facts.)

Not long after embarking on this labor of love, Nabokov published in *The New Yorker* a pair of carefully crafted Onegin stanzas very much in the Pushkin style, addressed directly to the dear defunct poet, apologizing with a curious blend of reverence and arrogance for the decision to spurn Pushkin's metric and rhyming constraints in anglicizing *Evgeniy Onegin*.

In the prefatory material to his *Onegin* translation, Nabokov most saliently declares that only a work of art's final form has any interest, that only mediocrities would think they could learn anything of value from drafts, discards, erasures, manuscripts, and such things: "It is, let me repeat, the structure of the end product, and of the end product only, that has meaning for the student — or at least this student — confronted with a master artist's work." This point having been made crystal-clear, Nabokov supplemented the thinnish volume of translated text with two bulging companion volumes of some 1,000 further pages, filled with agonizingly detailed examinations of Pushkin's drafts, discards, erasures, manuscripts, and such things.

Scattered throughout these ancillary volumes are also found many further archly-worded defenses of the unbudging decision to toss through the transom the original text's most salient aspect: its strict rhyming and metric structure. And on the classically elegant front cover of each volume, Nabokov's highly respected publisher printed, in large, bright type just underneath the title, the phrase "A Novel in Verse", to ensure that potential readers would know exactly what sort of book they had in their hands.

By coincidence, just as Nabokov sent off his final proofs, the climax of so many years of torturous labor, Professor Walter Arndt, a younger scholar but no less of a polyglot, published a scrupulously metrical and rhyming translation of Pushkin's novel, which was awarded that year's coveted Bollingen prize for poetry translation. Nabokov, stung to the quick, savagely attacked Arndt's translation as well as several earlier rhyming ones, mercilessly accusing, in various literary fora, all their creators of being "dainty mimics" who "traduce their author" (to cite just two of many abusive epithets hurled at them), and at the same time proudly characterized his own version of *Onegin* as "a crib, a pony, honest and clumsy, ponderous and slavishly faithful", though emphatically adding that it was "not ugly enough". Finally, putting the last ironic coat of icing on this amusingly absurdist layercake, a solemn review of Nabokov's idiosyncratic and anything-but-poetic creation came out in *The New York Times,* poker-facedly praising this "limpid, literal poetic translation" to the skies.

If the foregoing sounds like a surrealistic farce out of the pages of *Ubu roi,* there is good reason: Vladimir Nabokov (whose love for anagrams led him to invent Vivian Darkbloom, a fictional *alter ego*) had a strange sinister streak in him that occasionally pushed him to the far fringes of irrationality.

Truth and Traduction

Some may be stunned by Nabokov's decision to eschew rhyme and meter totally, and to strive solely for semantic fidelity — that is, literalism — which he immodestly refers to as "truth". To help set this in perspective, here is how, in the Foreword to his anglicization of *Eugene Onegin,* Nabokov posed and answered for himself the question of how to translate verse.

Can a rhymed poem like *Eugene Onegin* be truly translated with the retention of its rhymes? The answer, of course, is no. To reproduce the rhymes and yet translate the entire poem literally is mathematically impossible. But in losing its rhyme the poem loses its bloom, which neither marginal description nor the alchemy of a scholium can replace. Should one then content oneself with an exact rendering of the subject matter and forget all about form? Or should one still excuse an imitation of the poem's structure to which only twisted bits of sense stick here and there, by convincing oneself and one's public that in mutilating its meaning for the sake of a *pleasure/measure* rhyme, one has the opportunity of prettifying or skipping the dry and difficult passages? I have been always amused by the stereotyped compliment that a reviewer pays the author of a "new translation". He says: "It reads smoothly." In other words, the hack who has never read the original, and does not know its language, praises an imitation as readable because easy platitudes have replaced in it the intricacies of which he is unaware. "Readable", indeed! A schoolboy's boner mocks the ancient masterpiece less than does its commercial poetization, and it is when the translator sets out to render the "spirit", and not the mere sense of the text, that he begins to traduce his author.

In transposing *Eugene Onegin* from Pushkin's Russian into my English I have sacrificed to completeness of meaning every formal element including the iambic rhythm, whenever its retention hindered fidelity. To my idea of literalism I sacrificed everything (elegance, euphony, clarity, good taste, modern usage, and even grammar) that the dainty mimic prizes higher than truth.

This eccentric decision on Nabokov's part would be all right, though disappointing to those who admired his stunning linguistic gifts, were he not insufferably smug about it. Unfortunately, he felt compelled to sneer contemptuously at anyone who, tilting ignorantly against the inexorable windmills of "mathematical impossibility", imagined there might be another choice, and to condescend with unimaginable venom towards anyone — any "dainty mimic" tempted by the serpent's apple of "spirit" to "traduce" the "truth" of a text — who dared to actually *try* the pathway that he, from his lofty station, had deemed futile.

"Traduce his author" — now there is a typical Nabokovian linguistic maneuver. The verb is a rare Latinate one meaning "slander, betray". In using it to characterize certain translators as traitors to their author's meaning, he is slyly winking at the clever, catchy, and thought-provoking, though in the last analysis very silly, Italian motto *Traduttore, traditore* ("Translator, traitor"). But Nabokov, no dilettante with words, knew well that *traduce,* if perceived as an Italian word, means "[he/she] translates" ("betrays" is *tradisce*). It is hard for me not to believe that he set this little bilingual semantic trap quite deliberately, savoring the thought of how his devious word choice would confuse many readers.

Needless to say, I, as a non-speaker of Russian, am one of the many pitiful hacks who, never having read the original, have unsuspectingly fallen hook, line, and sinker for smooth-readin' *pleasure/measure* doggerel regurgitated by commercial poetasters too dishonest or too dim-witted to realize that true translators must ever and oh-so-humbly worship sense over spirit and reason over rhyme.

In this connection, it is interesting to note that Pushkin and all those in his literary circle were also "hacks" like me, in the sense that they regularly imbibed great batches of poetry from foreign lands but not in the original languages, nor even, as one might at first guess, in Russian translation, but in *French* translations. Byron was among the favorites, but also up there were Schiller, Goethe, Shakespeare, Petrarch, Dante, and many, many others. (Some of these translations of verse, perhaps the majority, were in prose, but a large number of them rhymed.) So in my non-omnilingualism, I'm at least in respectable company.

Speak of the Devil

Where did I learn all this about Pushkin and his circle? Well, as I already stated briefly, along with his prose rendition of Pushkin's novel in verse, Nabokov originally provided two further volumes of astonishingly erudite commentary on *Eugene Onegin* and its origins, coming to nearly 1,000 pages. These two volumes have been reissued together in paperback, to form a thick companion volume to the translation proper (or improper). Whatever one might think of Nabokov's translation, its companion volume is a remarkable and engrossing treasure mine of biographical information, literary gossip, previously unpublished poetry and correspondence, Sherlockian speculations, etymology, entomology, botany, mythology, Russian and European history and geography, and not least, Nabokov's personal musings on literature, translation, and many other topics; it's a book I'm delighted to possess and peruse.

Sometimes, I must admit, I am overwhelmed by the huge number of arcane quotations by unheard-of poets in several different languages that Nabokov has managed to unearth. One gets the impression that in his adolescence he must have swallowed whole some vast literary library and as an adult had every single line of every volume therein at his fingertips. Perhaps unfairly, this mammoth memory for minutiae reminds me a bit of Jorge Luis Borges' character Funes the Memorious, an *idiot savant* who recalled every tiny detail of every scene and sound he had ever encountered but had no understanding of anything he experienced, because he was deprived of the faculties of abstraction and generalization — more like a circus freak than the way most of us would like to be. But despite its detail, Nabokov's set of notes is an admirable accomplishment, and represents a devotion to an idol that precious few disciples have ever equaled.

I will give just one micro-example, which I think suggests the whole quite well. We are in stanza VI:21, where young Lensky, about to duel with his more seasoned friend Onegin, melodramatically seizes his quill and frantically scribbles down verses pondering his past life and his upcoming fate. His musings start on lines 3–4, which in Nabokov's literal translation read: "Whither, ah! whither are ye fled, / my springtime's golden days?" In the commentary is found a note about line 4, which begins as follows:

A well-worn Gallicism. I can mention only a few examples, jotted down in the course of casual reading:

Clément Marot, *De soy mesme* (1537):

> *Plus ne suis ce que j'ay esté,*
> *Et ne le sçaurois jamais estre ;*
> *Mon beau printemps et mon esté*
> *Ont fait le saut par la fenestre.*

Well, well — of all people to turn up at Nabokov's big *Onegin* bash! And how droll that the date of this poemlet (of which Nabokov's excerpt is just the first half) is 1537, meaning that it shares its birthyear with "Ma Mignonne".

Below I give the whole of "De soy mesme" (with two slight inaccuracies in the old French fixed up) and then, as no translation was provided by Nabokov, I add a trivial and treacherous rhyming paraphrase of my own:

Plus ne suis ce que j'ay esté,	*What once I was no longer I'm,*
Et ne le sçaurois jamais estre ;	*Nor will a second chance come;*
Mon beau printemps et mon esté	*My lovely spring and summertime*
Ont faict le sault par la fenestre.	*Have hopped out through the transom.*
Amour, tu as esté mon maistre :	*Love, you have been my master handsome:*
Je t'ay servi sur tous les dieux.	*Above all gods I've served are you.*
O si je pouvois deux fois naistre,	*If of my deeds I could recant some,*
Comme je te servirois mieulx !	*Far better in that life I'd do!*

Right below the Marot quote, a second French poet, Guillaume de Chaulieu, practically unknown these days, is cited for a couple of lines. The page bottom having been reached, one assumes the commentary on "golden spring" is now over, but upon flipping the page one finds that the quotations and references go on and on, running through a long series of poets and translators including Voltaire, André Chénier, Laurent Gilbert, Charles Millevoye, Vasiliy Tumanski, Wilhelm von Küchelbecker, Thomas Peacock, Catullus, François Noël, and Petrarch — and then one turns the page again and is shocked to find yet more, this time including translations and comments by Théophile Gautier, Vasiliy Zhukovski, Friedrich Schiller, Mikhail Milonov, and Vladimir Baryatynski. Incidentally, in the middle of all this hubbub about line 4, Nabokov cannot resist the chance to put down verse translators once again, as follows:

> The curious paradox is that, though eighteenth-century translations into French from modern and ancient poets are the worst in existence, the French translations of a later era are the best in the world, one reason being that the French use their marvelously precise and omnipotent prose for the rendering of foreign verse instead of shackling themselves with trivial and treacherous rhyme.

All in all, nearly four full pages are devoted to this single line of Pushkin's novel! Nabokov's claim, presumably true, that these are but "random jottings" from his "casual readings", amuses me no end.

As the Marot example illustrates, Nabokov translates only from Russian, assuming all other languages to be transparent to his readers. This leads to occasional bizarrenesses, such as the discussion of a "half-French, half-Russian letter" by Pushkin, which, as displayed for his readers, is half in French and half in English! Of course, one sees the translator's dilemma here: if both languages were rendered as English, then the linguistic seams would become invisible. An obvious solution would be to replace the Russian/French distinction by a roman/italic distinction.

A Mean Wordsmith Wielding a Mean Wordsword

The foregoing gives the flavor of Nabokov's huge auxiliary tome, to which I am of course not alone in having a largely favorable response. Indeed, both Charles Johnston and James Falen cite their indebtedness to Nabokov's deep, thorough, and trail-blazing scholarship. There can be no doubt that Nabokov did a great service to Pushkin and indeed to Russian literature in compiling this unparalleled sourcebook.

Sadly, however, even this volume of notes, detached and historical though it aims to be, is seriously marred by occasional crude snipes at others. Thus, in his very short Foreword to it, Nabokov says:

> The four "English", "metrical" "translations" mentioned in my notes and unfortunately available to students are [at this point Nabokov cites rhyming translations by Lt.-Col. Henry Spalding (1881), Babette Deutsch (1936), Oliver Elton (1937), and Dorothea Prall Radin and George Z. Patrick (1937)].
> Even worse are two rhymed versions, which, like grotesque satellites, accompanied the appearance of the first edition of this work; one is Walter Arndt's [1963], a paraphrase, in burlesque English, with preposterous mistranslations, some of which I discussed in *The New York Review of Books*, April 30, 1964; and the other Eugene M. Kayden's product [1964], of which the less said the better.

Slamming the four older editions of *Eugene Onegin* by putting scorn-quotes around the words "English", "metrical", and "translations" (and then twisting the knife by referring to them as "unfortunately available"), tarring Arndt's refined and subtle English with the label "burlesque", and smearing his and Kayden's labors of love as "grotesque satellites" is altogether such haughty, disdainful, and exaggerated behavior that nearly the only word that I can think of to understand it is "infantesque". This kind of vicious intellectual backstabbing, though not uncommon in the world of letters, is hard to fathom.

Poetic Glow and Sparkle?

And yet every successful author, even the most heartless, has friends in high places. Thus in a review in *The New York Times*, Harrison Salisbury generously called Nabokov's effort a "limpid, literal poetic translation", and continued, "He has given Pushkin's wondrous lines the glow and sparkle of the original." Well, let's see. Here are Nabokov's ways of rendering the four stanzas discussed in the preceding chapter. Judge for yourself the degree of glow and sparkle there is to be found in these doggerel-spurning Nabokovian revelations of "truth" (the brackets are his, by the way):

Latin has gone at present out of fashion;
still, to tell you the truth,
he had enough knowledge of Latin
to make out epigraphs,
descant on Juvenal,
put at the bottom of a letter <u>vale</u>,
and he remembered, though not without fault,
two lines from the <u>Aeneid</u>.
He had no urge to rummage
in the chronological dust
of the earth's historiography,
but anecdotes of days gone by,
from Romulus to our days,
he did keep in his memory.

When we have flocked under the banner
of sage tranquillity,
when the flame of the passions has gone out
and laughable become to us
their willfulness, [their] surgings
and tardy repercussions,
not without difficulty tamed,
sometimes we like to listen
to the tumultuous language of another's passions,
and it excites our heart;
exactly thus an old disabled soldier
does willingly bend an assiduous ear
to the yarns of young mustached braves,
forgotten in his shack.

Tatiana's letter is before me;
religiously I keep it;
I read it with a secret heartache
and cannot get my fill of reading it.
Who taught her both this tenderness
and amiable carelessness of words?
Who taught her all that touching [tosh],
mad conversation of the heart
both fascinating and injurious?
I cannot understand. But here's
an incomplete, feeble translation,
the pallid copy of a vivid picture,
or <u>Freischütz</u> executed
by timid female learners' fingers.

Can it be that the same Tatiana
to whom, alone with her,
at the beginning of our novel
in a stagnant, far region,
in righteous fervor of moralization
he had preached precepts once;
the same from whom he keeps
a letter where the heart speaks,
where all is out, all unrestrained;
that little girl — or is he dreaming? —
that little girl whom he
had in her humble lot disdained —
can she have been with him just now
so bland, so bold?

This crib, this gloss, this "pony" is a service to scholars, perhaps, but it could hardly be called a joy to read. Actually, what scholars would it help? Any professional Russian scholar can already read the original. Perhaps it would be most appreciated by students of Russian taking a literature course in the original language. If the truth must out, I admit that once in a while, in comparing various English rhyming translations among themselves, I have turned to Nabokov's text to see how Pushkin "actually" said it "in

Russian". So I would not deny that this volume has its limited uses. But where, oh where, are "the glow and sparkle of the original"? All I see is tedious and heavy-handed, strained and straining prose. And perverse though it may sound, I suspect Nabokov would have heartily agreed. Indeed, the following remarkable Nabokovian statement, taken from a 1966 article called "Reply to My Critics", suggests he would have brusquely dismissed Salisbury's compliments on his translation's style:

> My *Eugene Onegin* falls short of the ideal crib. It is still not close enough and not ugly enough. In future editions I plan to defowlerize it still more drastically. I think I shall turn it entirely into utilitarian prose, with a still bumpier brand of English, rebarbative barricades of square brackets and tattered banners of reprobate words, in order to eliminate the last vestiges of bourgeois poesy and concession to rhythm. This is something to look forward to.

These lines reek of a strange, proud perversity, and behind them there seems to lie a masochistic wallowing in the joy of self-mutilation.

An Apologia to the Idol

And yet, as anyone who has sampled the plate of his written offerings knows, Nabokov has a more human and poetic side. Thus in 1955, while immersed in his prose translation, Nabokov published in *The New Yorker* two Onegin stanzas directly addressed to Pushkin, attempting to explain his rationale — essentially apologizing to his idol — for turning the latter's exquisite poetry into utterly forgettable prose. Here is the first of the pair:

> *What is translation? On a platter*
> *A poet's pale and glaring head,*
> *A parrot's screech, a monkey's chatter,*
> *And profanation of the dead.*
> *The parasites you were so hard on*
> *Are pardoned if I have your pardon,*
> *O Pushkin, for my stratagem.*
> *I traveled down your secret stem,*
> *And reached the root, and fed upon it;*
> *Then, in a language newly learned,*
> *I grew another stalk and turned*
> *Your stanza, patterned on a sonnet,*
> *Into my honest roadside prose —*
> *All thorn, but cousin to your rose.*

Though elegant and undeniably touching in spots, this sonnet is not flawless. Its animal metaphors for translation, for instance, seem to me so ridiculously overdone, and its not-so-far-but-still-no-cigar "hard on/pardon" quasi-rhyme strikes me as every bit as vulnerable to criticism as some of the near-miss rhymes for which Nabokov excoriates Arndt, such as "family/me" and "capital/ball". Finally, of course, English was hardly a "language newly learned" for Nabokov, who acquired it, just as he did Russian, while still in infant clothes, while still on boyhood's shore.

Impossibly Vulgar, Dreadful, Idiotic, Disastrous Doggerel

Nabokov chose to use his discussion of stanzas VIII.17 and VIII.18 as a podium from which to demolish, for once and for all, his four principal antecedents as would-be anglicizors of *Onegin*: Spalding, Elton, Radin, and Deutsch. Though he uses seven pages for the purpose, in the space of just three successive paragraphs, he manages to squeeze in all of the following caustic epithets: "very weak", "dreadful", "meaningless", "ludicrous" (this salvo is directed at Spalding); "miserably reproduced", "idiotic", "impossibly vulgar", "preposterous", "horrible" (this salvo is for Elton); "wild", "very clumsy" (this salvo for Radin); and once again "wild" (this last little potshot is taken at Deutsch). In case it looks like Deutsch got off easy, that illusion is caused by the fact that Nabokov mostly uses full sentences rather than short adjectives to throttle her, and at one point jabs pointedly at her "translation" (the sneering quote marks being his, of course).

Why not take a look at a sample of Babette Deutsch's "translation"? I happen to have one and only one of her stanzas — V.1 — which I found quoted in a book entitled *This Amazingly Symmetrical World*, written by a Russian physicist named L. Tarasov. He calls this sonnet "a simple, elegant Pushkinian pattern". Of course, he is referring to the original Russian, not to Deutsch's anglicization, but the book's translator seemed to feel fine reproducing that judgment without introducing a footnote remarking on the fact of the language-switch. Below I give you Deutsch's perfect Onegin stanza and, to its right, Nabokov's prose rendition.

That year was extraordinary,	*That year autumnal weather*
The autumn seemed so loth to go;	*was a long time abroad;*
Upon the third of January,	*nature kept waiting and waiting for winter.*
At last, by night, arrived the snow.	*Snow only fell in January,*
Tatyana, still an early riser,	*on the night of the second. Waking early,*
Found a white picture to surprise her:	*Tatiana from the window saw*
The courtyard white, a white parterre,	*at morn the whitened yard,*
The roofs, the fence, all moulded fair:	*flower beds, roofs, and fence;*
The frostwork o'er the panes was twining;	*delicate patterns on the panes;*
The trees in wintry silver gleamed;	*the trees in winter silver,*
And in the court gay magpies screamed;	*gay magpies outside,*
While winter's carpet softly shining,	*and the hills mellowly spread over*
Upon the distant hills lay light,	*with the resplendent rug of winter.*
And all she looked on glistened white.	*All is brilliant, all is white around.*

Is Deutsch's betrayal of her author (whom we still perceive only indirectly) really so treacherous? I personally find her stanza as sparkling as the fresh snowfall she describes. For further comparison, here is how Walter Arndt rendered the same stanza, on the left in rhyming tetrameter and on the right in his own nonrhymed, literal interpretation. Note the many small differences between Arndt's and Nabokov's literal translations.

Fall lingered on as if it never	*That year the autumn weather*
Would leave the countryside that year,	*Held for a long time out of doors,*
While Nature seemed to wait forever	*Nature waited [and] waited for the winter.*
For winter. Snow did not appear	*Snow fell only in January*
Till the third January morning.	*On the night of the second. Having woken early,*
Up early, Tanya without warning	*Through the window Tatyana saw*
Finds roofs and fences overnight	*At morn the yard turned white,*
Turned to exhilarating white,	*Flower beds, roofs, and fence,*
Her window laced with subtle etching,	*On the windowpanes faint patterns,*
The trees with wintry silver starred,	*The trees in winter silver,*
Pert magpies sporting in the yard,	*Merry magpies in the yard,*
The softly covered hilltops stretching	*And the hills softly sheeted*
'Neath winter's scintillating shawl...	*In winter's glistening carpet.*
And clear is all, and white is all.	*All is bright, all white around.*

Although Nabokov probably never saw *Eugene Onegin* as rendered in English by Johnston (it appeared the year he died), and definitely missed Falen's version, I would have to assume, given his earlier-quoted credo that poetry-to-poetry translation is inherently and necessarily unfaithful — or "mathematically impossible", in his quaint phrasing — that he would have happily included them in the family of "disastrous versions of *EO* in English doggerel" (a phrase he uses to start out his lengthy commentary intended to demolish Spalding *et al.*).

I cannot help but ask myself: What would make the eloquent English rhyming stanzas by Deutsch and the four translators discussed in the previous chapter merit the harsh accusation of "doggerel" any more than do Pushkin's own regularly rhythmic, rigidly rhyming, often infectiously alliterative Russian stanzas? The English stanzas were penned by true lovers of literature, specialists whose lifelong devotion to and respect for words and their mysterious semantic and sonoric halos, both in Russian and in English, are every bit as profound and as sincere as Nabokov's.

Internal Inconsistency

For me, perhaps the greatest irony of Nabokov's *Onegin* volumes is his internal inconsistency about this storm that he stirred up, for the crazy truth of the matter is that he himself often took pleasure and pride in translating Russian poetry into English poetry, or vice versa. Indeed, his first published book was a now-celebrated Russian translation of *Alice in Wonderland,* with rhyming verse rendered as rhyming verse (what else could one possibly do with *Alice* without destroying it?). Moreover, the final paragraph of his novel *The Gift,* originally written in Russian and then converted by Nabokov himself into English, is a perfect rhyming Onegin stanza masquerading as plain prose — in English no less than in Russian. And to cap the irony, in his thick volume of commentary on *Eugene Onegin,* there are several tangential poems by Pushkin that Nabokov renders in supple, graceful, metrical, rhyming English. Needless to say, when he gives these, he is careful to skirt the fact that he has rendered poetry as poetry, for then we would catch him *in flagrante delictu,* violating his own dictum, indeed traducing *himself*!

For example, in his commentary on stanza I.48, Nabokov not just once but twice translates Russian rhymes by Pushkin into English rhymes. In one of these cases (since the Pushkin is a bit ribald and frivolous), he even prefaces his English by saying this: "I have wavered whether to quote these lines. Here they are, for what they are worth." I ask: How in the world can this man *dare,* after all of his frothing at the mouth about "miserable paraphrasts", "dainty mimics", "truth traducers", and the like, turn around and use the very strict word "quote" in a situation when the author has changed, the tone has changed, the language has changed, the era has changed, and even the writing system has changed? This is *quoting*?!

I, to be sure, would feel perfectly comfortable using the term "quote" in that context, but then, my translation philosophy is the diametrical opposite of Nabokov's. Remember, I'm one who thinks of the Well-Tempered Clavier as a piano piece, someone who'll even accept as genuine Joplin a rag played by four *tubas*! But when Vladimir Nabokov, of all people, substitutes his own English rhymes for Alexander Pushkin's Russian rhymes and nonchalantly calls it *quoting,* what in the world is going on?

All of this is most baffling, although happily it reveals that Nabokov was — as aren't we all? — filled with confusions and self-contradictions.

Satanic the Verses of Walter Arndt

As I mentioned at this chapter's start, just as Nabokov's multi-volume set was about to come out, Walter Arndt's verse translation appeared. Baaad timing! Beset with a fury worthy of a spurned ayatollah, Nabokov attacked Arndt's work with astounding savagery in *The New York Review of Books.* In the opening of that article, he refers to it as "a monstrous undertaking" by a "pitiless and irresponsible paraphrast", and then goes on: "A sympathetic reader, especially one who does not consult the original, may find in Mr. Arndt's version more or less sustained stretches of lulling poetastry and specious sense; but anybody with less benevolence and more knowledge will see how patchy the passable really is." (Note for philistines: "poetastry", according to my trusty old dictionary, means "verse of little or no merit".)

Then he goes on for several pages, ripping the often-exquisite product of Arndt's years of devotion to the same idol as his own into the tiniest shreds he possibly can, liberally flinging about a vast variety of terms exuding revulsion, such as "howlers", "bungling", "nonsense", "offensive", "desperate", "grotesque", "bizarre", and on and on. (In a footnote appended a few years later, after Arndt had carefully reworked his translation, taking into account a good number of Nabokov's criticisms, and published a new version, the implacably Nazistic Nabokov says: "This 'revised' version still remains as abominable as before.")

Unfortunately, Nabokov's complaints about Arndt are almost all so microscopically pedantic, so cruel, and so tiresome that it is hard to stay with him without becoming very agitated. An example:

> Passive readers will derive, no doubt, a casual illusion of sense from Arndt's actually nonsensical line 2 of VI.36. They will hardly notice that the chancrous metaphor in lines 4–5 inflicted by a meretricious rhyme is not Pushkin's fault, nor wonder at the naïve temerity a paraphrast has of throwing in his own tropes when he should know that the figure of speech is the main, sacred quiddity and eyespot of a poet's genius, and is the last thing that should be tampered with.

What is this "chancrous metaphor" that passive readers will hardly notice? It occurs where Pushkin is lamenting the fate of poor Lensky, killed while still in early youth. In Nabokov's eyes, Pushkin's metaphor for early youth should be rendered in English as "scarce out of infant clothes", while the criminally mad Arndt had the gall to write "yet scarce adrift from boyhood's shore". My God, the stench!

I have to hand it to Nabokov for his poetic way of assassinating other authors, using a series of words that I never even knew existed! And yet on the intellectual point itself, with all due respect, I have to demur. I simply do not agree that the "sacred quiddity and eyespot of a poet's genius" (whatever that might mean) resides principally, or necessarily, or even largely, in the poet's choice of metaphors. To be sure, if one is dealing with but a single short poem, then clearly it is crucial to try to preserve each metaphor as closely as possible, but when one is dealing with a giant poem of some 5600 lines, there is far more latitude, and the main things to try to preserve are the global spirit, the all-pervading texture, and the local sparkle. Here and there an individual metaphor can be entirely let go of, or replaced with a cousin, with little harm done. These are judgment calls, not black-and-white Laws of Nature.

Sometimes Nabokov's attacks get a little bit too *ad hominem* for my taste, as the following excerpt from his review shows:

Inadequate knowledge of Russian. This is a professional ailment among non-Russian translators from Russian into English. Anything a little too far removed from the *kak-vy-pozhivaete-ya-pozhivayu-khorosho* group becomes a pitfall, into which, rather than around which, dictionaries guide the groper; and when they are not consulted, then other disasters happen.

What do the transliterated Russian words mean? They mean "How are you? I am fine." It is hard to believe, but Nabokov is not referring to some inept college sophomore stumbling through a first-semester Russian course, but to his respected peer and colleague Walter Arndt, at the time a professor of Slavic Languages and Literatures at the University of North Carolina, and subsequently a full professor and the department head in Russian at Dartmouth! Where does Nabokov get off?

With Friends Like Vladimir...

By this point, readers will probably feel they have endured enough of Nabokov's trashing of his rivals, and yet I cannot resist including just one last blast. By all means, feel free to skip it, especially if your stomach is turned by extreme boorishness.

It turns out that Nabokov reserved by far his heaviest blunderbusses not for attacks on Arndt or other miserable paraphrasts of *Onegin,* but for sandbagging his own former friend Edmund Wilson (the two had even collaborated, many years earlier, on a translation of Pushkin's short play *Mozart and Salieri*). Why? Because silly Wilson had the unpardonable gall to rise in print, in the same journal, to the defense of Arndt's translation.

Amazingly, Nabokov's hardball savaging of his "old friend" Mr. Wilson makes his criticism of Arndt look as wimpy as a two-year-old's petulant toss of a Nerf ball. Could it be that Nabokov took as his model of "friendship" that between Onegin and Lensky, or (at least in Pushkin's version) that between Salieri and Mozart, in which one "friend" murders the other? The usual Nabokovian barrage of arcane and recherché barbs is hurled without letup from beginning to end, which is bad enough, but Nabokov goes way beyond bad taste in writing this unforgivably cruel passage:

> A patient confidant of his long and hopeless infatuation with the Russian language, I have invariably done my best to explain to him his monstrous mistakes of pronunciation, grammar, and interpretation. As late as 1957, at one of our last meetings, in Ithaca, upstate New York, where I lived at the time, we both realized with amused dismay that, despite my frequent comments on Russian prosody, he still could not scan Russian verse. Upon being challenged to read *Evgeniy Onegin* out loud, he started to perform with great gusto, garbling every second word, and turning Pushkin's iambic line into a kind of spastic anapest with a lot of jaw-twisting haws and rather endearing little barks that utterly jumbled the rhythm and soon had us both in stitches.

Such unrelenting verbal sadism makes for compelling reading, in a perverse way. It runs on for twenty pages in Nabokov's *Strong Opinions*. Take my word for it, or go look up the whole wretched thing yourself.

Giving Arndt the Floor

Luckily, Walter Arndt was not destroyed by Nabokov's frenzied assault, and in 1972 he came out with *Pushkin Threefold*, an anthology of Pushkin verse in which, as its title hints, each poem appears in three versions: first, in the original Russian; second, in a rather Nabokovian "literal" translation (a plausible-sounding concept whose very coherence, however, is cast into serious doubt, and most persuasively so, by Arndt); and third, in a lively, rhyming, metrical English version. This is a lovely plan for a book, and indeed, *Pushkin Threefold* affords a relative newcomer like me a splendid panorama of the Russian poet's lifetime output.

In his stimulating introductory reflections on the general problems of translating verse, Arndt replies directly and indirectly to the countless barbs flung at him by Nabokov. One example of returned fire is this portrait of Nabokov's prosification of Pushkin's poetry: "... the sad ritual murder performed for the purposes of an ever more insatiable lexical necrophilia in the first volume of Nabokov's otherwise peerless commentary on *Onegin*." Arndt, too, could dish it out quite well, thank you, when he felt like it.

Aside from the amusement of highbrow polemical crossfire, though, it is worthwhile quoting Arndt at some length, since he is one of the few people who have translated so much poetry for so long and so well. Here are some of his reflections on the legitimacy — indeed, the necessity — of verse-to-verse translation:

> Nabokov's recent two-volume commentary in English on *Eugene Onegin* attempts to call into question again, not *a* verse translation, but verse translation itself. This happens once or twice in every literary period. The work illustrates this attitude of militant resignation by continually substituting exhaustive and highly imaginative exegesis for translation — while, however, retaining the word "translation" in its title. It will be clear now that I cannot regard the essential legitimacy of poetic translation — as distinct from the means and the areas and limits of tolerable compromise — as highly controversial. I would endorse the more challenging majority view of the task, which is that the task exists, and must be tackled. The goal is to create a poem in the target language, which should simulate, as near as may be, the total effect produced by the original on the contemporary reader. Total effect to me means *import* as well as *impact*, i.e., both what the poem imparts to the mind and how it strikes the senses; cognitive as well as aesthetic (stylistic, formal, musical, "poetic") values, pretending for just a moment that these two congruent entities can somehow be analytically separated. Again, "import as well as impact" means import *through* and *congruent with* impact; it does not mean a message in garbled prose, with subsequent assurances by way of stylistic and other commentary that the corpse in its lifetime was poetry.

In a nutshell, a stodgy literal gloss supplemented by a slew of scholarly footnotes is no substitute for the spark and sparkle of creative translation. I'll buy that!

Another key theme in Arndt's introductory essay is what he first calls the "frame of accuracy" and later the "unit of fidelity". His concern is with how one determines the proper grain size for a given poetic translation:

> The central problem of verse translation, then, in a sense the only one, is not whether there can and should be simultaneous fidelity to content and form, but rather how to decide, first, what constitutes double fidelity in a given case and how it can best be approximated. The proper formal frame of accuracy, i.e., the largest allowable unit of form within which maximum fidelity must be achieved, is a delicate matter of balancing the poetic pulse of the original against the stylistic sense of the reader in the target language, and against his syntactic comprehension span; but luckily a large enough unit *can* usually be chosen to afford desperately needed latitude for transposing and rearranging within it elements of message and lexical–stylistic effects. This latitude somewhat soothes the notorious enmity between form and content in the recasting process — what I am now tempted to call the Nabokov Relation of fated failure....
>
> In prose, except for extreme cases that tend to depart from prose, the problem of the unit of fidelity is not acute.... But in poetry, especially rhymed poetry, the rigors of prosody bring "naturalness" and fidelity into conflict much sooner and oftener — in fact, sometimes at every step. "Meaning" acquires a more rigorous, because more comprehensive, sense; freshness of vision and linguistic novelty are of the essence of what is stated, meaning *is* form and form meaning, over quite small units of discourse. To *just that* particular poetic impact of a line or phrase, there seem to be no alternative "plain" forms that could produce it. By the same token, literal translation.... not only runs into the hard wall of rhythm and rhyme, but is intrinsically absurd and self-defeating. Poetic utterance is not produced from some underlying, neutral, merely cognitive statement by linguistic manipulation; and if it were, the manipulations could not be the same in language A as in language B, or else they would be the *same* language. Hence sequential literalness becomes worse than irrelevant... All this would have been comically redundant to say again, had the notion of literalness as a technique not been resurrected by Nabokov in relation to a major work of world literature, and had it not been respectfully (or at least gingerly) handled by at least some critics.

The antepenultimate sentence here ("Poetic utterance..."), though expressed a little fuzzily, seems to me right on the mark. The way I hear it, Arndt is denying that poetry gets composed in a two-stage process in which, in the first stage, language-independent gobs of "pure cognitive meaning" are formed, and in the second stage, these form-free gobs of content are "poured" into passive linguistic receptacles and thereby acquire distinct, language-dependent shapes. Behind Arndt's words I detect the opposite image: the target language and the various poetic constraints play simultaneous, deeply intertwined, highly active roles, serving as associative sonorous and structural springboards, in determining the thought itself.

These reflective, restrained analyses of the ineluctable problems of conflict and balance that lie at the core of the translation challenge reveal, I think, a world of difference between the cool, egocentric verbal virtuosity of Vladimir Nabokov and the warmer, more generous, and simply more *human* style of Walter Arndt.

Falen's Odelet in Praise of Constraints

It comes as no surprise that James Falen, like Walter Arndt, has expressed thoughts on translation that resonate with Arndt's and mine, and that clash with Nabokov's. In the introduction to his translation of *Eugene Onegin,* Falen writes about the powerful effect exerted on one's words and thoughts by the constant presence of a set of strict linguistic constraints:

> I too have chosen, in my version, to preserve what I could of Pushkin's form, taking the Onegin stanza as one of the novel's most essential and characteristic features, the building block with which, as it were, the entire edifice is constructed. By retaining the stanza form that Pushkin uses as his poetic paragraph, a translator positions himself, in a sense, on the work's home ground and imposes upon himself a useful discipline for the journey. Furthermore, he is thereby constrained, as was the poet himself, to seek solutions without self-indulgence, to find variety within oneness, and to earn a freedom within the bondage of the form. The very rigidity of the stanzaic structure can bring at times a fruitful tension to the words with which the form is made manifest, and the economy of expression it enforces upon the translator will sometimes reward him with an unexpected gift.

In a friendly exchange of letters that I recently had with Falen, he included this tiny poem — an "odelet in praise of constraints", so to speak:

> *Every task involves constraint,*
> *Solve the thing without complaint;*
> *There are magic links and chains*
> *Forged to loose our rigid brains.*
> *Structures, strictures, though they bind,*
> *Strangely liberate the mind.*

The closing rhyme could be taken as the theme song of this book.

To paraphrase Falen and Arndt, the search for truth in translation does not arbitrarily jettison certain facts, but rather, requires balancing many conflicting pressures. Just as nourishment requires consuming foods from different classes and leads to death if only one class is consumed, so translation requires simultaneous respect for multiple facets of the original text, a fact that forces one all along the way to take risk after risk, and to intertwine subtle experiments, adjustments, readjustments, and judgments. Luckily, this arduous process occasionally yields unanticipatable finds of such elegance that the struggle suddenly becomes completely worth it.

Nabokovian Regrets

Despite Nabokov's shrill insistence, truth in literature is not uni- but multi-dimensional, and by singling out just one dimension as the only one that counts, Nabokov painted for us a feeble, impoverished, anemic, and, ultimately, lifeless portrait of Pushkin's vibrant poem — for *poem* is what it is. That is the key word to keep in mind. Indeed, listen to Nabokov:

> Pushkin's composition is first of all and above all a phenomenon of style.... The paradoxical part, from a translator's point of view, is that the only Russian element of importance is this speech, Pushkin's language, undulating and flashing through verse melodies the likes of which had never been known before in Russia. The best I could do was to describe in some of my comments special samples of the original text.

Mirabile dictu, Nabokov actually sounds a bit regretful here. And recall this wistful sentence: "In losing its rhyme the poem loses its bloom, which neither marginal description nor the alchemy of a scholium can replace."

As well as anyone ever has, Vladimir Nabokov understood that Pushkin set an extraordinary constraint for himself, and that that constraint had an incessant, all-pervading impact on how his words and phrases flowed, surely even on how his ideas developed. Why couldn't Nabokov then bring himself to see that *truth* would demand an identical or at least an analogous constraint on a version in any other language? Why could he not see that this constant, pervasive, insistent, driving constraint is far closer to constituting the "sacred quiddity and eyespot" of Pushkin's work than are the twists of its story line or even its multifarious, glittering metaphors?

Cover Claims and Cyrillic Characters

If we're going to talk about "truth", let's begin at the beginning — the book's cover. As I stated near this chapter's opening, on the front cover of Nabokov's translation and again on the title page, it says in large letters: "A Novel in Verse". Balderdash! What's between those covers is expressly *not* in verse. The claim's nonsensicality quotient would not rise by one iota if it said "A Novel in Russian", or even "A Novel in Russian Verse, Printed in Cyrillic Characters". The truth is plain and simple: What's between the covers of Nabokov's Pushkin is only "A Novel", and a mighty clumsily written one, at that. Don't take *my* word for it; recall Nabokov's own words about sacrificing elegance, good taste, grammar, and so forth.

While we're on the subject of Cyrillic writing, it is worth pointing out another stunning irony in Nabokov's 1,000 pages of commentary on *Eugene Onegin*: Although many thousands of Russian words are discussed (perhaps ten per page on the average), there is not one single Cyrillic character to be found in it. All "original Russian" text is in fact given in *transliterated* form, thus in roman characters. If this does not sound traitorous enough to you, then try turning the tables in your mind. Just imagine that some Russian scholar's set of detailed commentaries on *Lolita* is being published in Russian, and every single piece of the "original English" text appears in a phonetic Cyrillic transcription. Here at last would be a case where Warren Weaver's droll dictum — "When I look at an article in Russian, I say, 'This is really written in English, but it has been coded in some strange symbols. I will now proceed to decode.'" — *is the literal truth.* Let's take the novel's titillating, title-touting, tantalizing opening, for example:

Лолита, лайт оф май лайф, файр оф май лойнз. Май син, май соул.
Ло-ли-та: зэ тип оф зэ танг мэйкинг а трип оф сри стэпс даун зэ пэлэт ту тэп,
эт сри, он зэ тис. Ло. Ли. Та.

Is *this* English? More to the point, since we're dealing with Vladimir Nabokov, is this *truth,* or is this *traduction*? And *mutatis mutandis,* is it truth or traduction to render Russian in roman writing? Peering at the allegedly "original" fragments buried in Nabokov's tome, an average Russian could make little if any sense of them. Perhaps using such a cipher is no more shocking than substituting a flute for a violin or a piano for a harpsichord, but it would seem worth at least a word or two of justification. And yet, there is nothing — just a key to the pronunciation of transcribed words.

Cuckoo Twists on the Onegin Theme

For more perspectives on truth in advertising, let us try on another fantasy for size. This time I'll conjure up the beatnik Indian novelist Vikpush Kinsey, who has penned *One Gin over the Cuckoo's Gate,* a novel in verse set in the 1950's Pacific Northwest and, as you might guess, written in perfect Onegin stanzas. It tells the story of a hard-up family of struggling loggers who trudge endlessly between the Willamette Valley and Moscow, Idaho. The hardscrabble hero, Eugene Oregon, is fighting the ravages of alcoholism with the help of his cowboy-poet sidekick Len Sky. But we need not delve into the sordid details of the plot; all we need to know is that its story line has nothing in the least to do with that of Pushkin's novel. Suppose, nonetheless, that author Kinsey boldly claimed his book was a translation of *Eugene Onegin.* Why then, I could see how a Nabokov disciple would protest "untruth" and would howl about the "traducing" of Pushkin.

I myself would not feel so confident about the matter. Indeed, I am sometimes tempted to think of Vikram Seth's *Golden Gate* as a translation of *Eugene Onegin,* despite the fact that the two novels' plots have no more in common than would the plots of two novels selected at random from the fiction section of any big bookstore. Actually, much though it would outrage Nabokov disciples, not to mention Nabokov himself, I could easily make the argument that Seth's *Golden Gate* is, as a translation of Pushkin's novel in verse, superior to Nabokov's stumbling prose "pony", precisely because it is so permeated by the Onegin *spirit,* even though its "letter" is amazingly different. For starters, the phrase "A Novel in Verse" printed on the cover of *The Golden Gate* is not a lie! To reach the heights of absurdity represented by the act of labeling Nabokov's version "A Novel in Verse", the cover of Seth's Silicon Valley tale would have had to proclaim it to be "A Novel of Nineteenth-century Russia". Now *that* would be a claim to balk at.

Before we abandon Oregon and Sky, let's twist the counterfactual dials a bit and suppose that Kinsey's novel had instead been based on the plot of *Eugene Onegin,* thus carefully transplanting the latter, via an elaborate set of mappings, into a mid-twentieth-century rural-America setting. This Kinsey novel goes much further than the earlier one or Seth's, having not only an analogous plot but also exactly the same structure as Pushkin's — the same number of chapters, even the same number of stanzas in corresponding chapters. *Now* how loud would the Nabokov gang's protests of travesty be?

And suppose, to twist the dials of alternity a little further, that Vikpush Kinsey was so inspired by his model Pushkin that each of his stanzas was strictly modeled on its numerical counterpart in the original *Onegin,* so that musings became musings, epistles epistles, dialogue dialogue, and so on. Surely by this point the Nabokovian howls of treason would have to diminish in volume at least a little! The difference remains, of course, that one takes place in a recent Wild West, the other in old Tsarist Russia.

But since we have full control of the knobs of counterfactuality, we can twiddle them in any way we like, and so we can continuously slide the date and the setting of Kinsey's novel, moving it back further and further in time — 1943, 1915, 1893, 1835,... — and closer and closer to Mother Russia: Finland, Poland, White Russia,... (We could, conversely, slide Pushkin's own novel *forward* in time and *westward* in space, since we are exploring counterfactuals with no holds barred, but out of respect, we'll leave it intact.) This process gives rise to a giant family of hypothetical novels in verse by Vikpush Kinsey, each of which is, by hypothesis, strictly modeled on Pushkin's original text, stanza by stanza. At exactly what point along this slide through spacetime does Kinsey's text turn into a *translation* and cease being a *traduction* of the work that was his inspiration? *Как знать?*

Somewhere near the endpoint of this counterfactual slide, we find the English texts by Falen, Arndt, Deutsch, and so on, since these all tell a story that takes place in just the right locations and dates, and moreover they all have just the right content on a chapter-by-chapter, very nearly line-by-line level. *And,* let us not forget, they are also in precise Onegin stanzas. Their counterpart to Pushkin's Russian sparkle is a genuine sparkle in English. What could be more truthful than such a multifaceted combination?

Richard Burgin: A Life in Verse

My spectrum of thousands of novels sweeping back across space and time from the American 1980's to the Russian 1830's was, of course, the idlest of fantasizing. But as we all learn early in life, Truth is stranger than Fiction, and what I am about to tell you is a prime example of that maxim.

Jim Kates, a Russian translator, told me but weeks ago of a curious book he'd run across in Onegin stanzas in English — not quite a novel, more a biography — and generously sent me his copy to peruse. As I read it, I grew ever more amazed. If any book ever did, this non-novel belonged smack-dab in the center of my zany hypothetical spectrum of novels!

Its author is Diana Lewis Burgin, a professor of Russian literature in Boston, and its subject is the life of her father, Richard Burgin, a Russian Jew born in 1893 in Warsaw, who grew up in St. Petersburg, became a violin prodigy, studied with some of the great names in violin history, eventually emigrated to the United States, became concertmaster of the Boston Symphony Orchestra, and retained that position for most of his adult life, with occasional conducting and solo performances as well. At his peak, Burgin was a famous and respected musician, and even were it recounted in prosaic prose, his life's story would have been eminently worth the telling.

However, his deeply devoted daughter wound up creating a truly extraprosaic memorial to him, and utterly without premeditating it. The day before her father suffered an incapacitating ictus at age 88, she'd bought a tape recorder to tape his memoirs, but all her plans went up in stroke and so sadly she madly scrambled to try to reconstruct his life. One day, as she sat down to compose what she knew, she found herself drifting into an Onegin-like mode, something she knew intimately from years of teaching, yet had never tried out as a channel for self-expression. Here, then, are the stanzas in which Diana Burgin, rich life verser, opens the tale of her father's first romance, tenderly interweaving fantasy with fact:

But now that we have finally started
on chapter four, left three behind,
and have tetrameterly charted
the in-between, we must rewind
our reel a bit, to our depiction
of Richard, when first love's affliction
infected him, and this, we glean,
befell him when he was sixteen.
So, reader, now we're off together
to early summer, nineteen ten;
my hero was in Pavlovsk then,
relaxing in the straw-hat weather,
a carefree youth until he met
a fellow student, Henriette.

A lovely day! I hear the trolling
of birds and strings in summer air,
and there I see my Richard strolling
the wooded path, without a care;
but now he stops and starts to listen,
then smiles and, with his eyes aglisten,
murmurs, "Sure, I know that sound,
the Kreutzer — but...", and looks around,
"But isn't that a piano playing
the part that Lotto played with me
on violin?! How can this be?"
He runs to see without delaying,
and syncopates his gait with grins:
"I'd swear 'twas for two violins!"

What's true here is that as a youth Richard Burgin naïvely believed Beethoven's Kreutzer sonata to be a two-violin piece, and it's also true that he and a young pianist named Henriette fell in love, but Burgin's daughter had no idea how the two in fact met, so she daydreams, putting one and one together under the guidance of her muse. Speaking of which, Burgin's chummy chatting with her muse is an intentional imitation of a favorite theme of Pushkin. Indeed, a deep charm of Burgin's *Burgin* is its frequent stylistic allusions to Pushkin's *Onegin*, as in a love letter from Richard to Henriette, line-by-line echoing Tanya's to Eugene, or a stanza singing the praises of New York that elegantly maps to a Pushkin stanza in honor of St. Petersburg. Here is Burgin ending her Foreword and articulating this link:

> In the end, what is Pushkin to me, or I to Pushkin? Pushkin is the "father of Russian literature", and I am a daughter of the realm, so to speak, a reader of his novel and a writer of my *Life*. That *Life* began with a dying father at a loss for words, and ends with a birthing daughter who has found them. The ways in which *Richard Burgin* echoes, parallels, polemicizes with, and re/verses its parent text, *Eugene Onegin*, reveal its play upon genre, gender, and generation.

Though her virtuosic, loving tribute appeared a bit after Seth's *Golden Gate*, Burgin hadn't seen that cousin book. Uncanny, for in so many ways, *Richard Burgin* is nearly my zany fantasy, *One Gin over the Cuckoo's Gate*. What in the world would Nabokov have said about it? *Как знать?*

Dove Droppings on a Monument

When but a youth, Nabokov fell head over heels for Pushkin's stanza. Unable, of course, to possess it alone, he tried dismissing his rivals as fools. This worked for a while, but it takes no psychoanalyst to see that when Walter Arndt was awarded a coveted translation prize publicly marrying him to *Onegin*'s magic, Nabokov was pushed over the brink into uncontrollable jealousy and bitter, immature attacks, such as this "strong opinion":

> Mr. Arndt's most bizarre observation, however, comes on page vi, towards the end of his preface: "The present new translation … is not aimed primarily at the academic and literary expert, but at a public of English-speaking students and others interested in a central work of world literature in a compact and readable form." — which is tantamount to proclaiming: "I know this is an inferior product but it is gaily colored and nicely packed, and is, anyway, just for students and such people."

Nabokov's interminable string of "strong opinions" of this sort, casting all of his fellow *Onegin*-smitten translators as meretricious fools, constitutes a pathetically self-revelatory performance by a highly gifted intellect. What, for God's sake, does he have against a version of *Eugene Onegin* that is not aimed primarily at scholars and experts? Need I point out that Pushkin's intent was not to write a novel mainly for scholars and experts? Although

A Vile Non-verse

◆◆◆ 277

he gave a handful of footnotes at the end, Pushkin would have scoffed at the idea of supplementing those with a thousand pages more!

Why would anyone ever wish to read Nabokov's prose translation of *Eugene Onegin*? It is so tedious, so awkward, and so utterly sparkless that one's eyelids would soon start to droop. To read it is to experience the diametric opposite of reading the original Pushkin.

By contrast, to read just a few pages of the lucid and lilting English-language Onegin stanzas of Falen, Arndt, or Deutsch is to become addicted to a marvelously fresh new way of phrasing things, even of perceiving the world, by chopping it up into a steady sequence of vibrantly pulsed crystalline patterns that convey the "sweet-watered, fluent, clear, light, blithe" and effervescent essence of the original Pushkin — and this I fearlessly assert while admitting I have never even read one full page of the Russian! Poor Nabokov, if he heard such blasphemy, would surely roll over in his grave, yet somehow I doubt that his idol, whose literary taste and style were formed in large measure by absorbing huge quantities of verse in translation — fancies loose and footnote-free — would flinch in the least.

Underneath all his bitter bluster, I suspect, Nabokov somehow sensed how weak and wanting was his austere anglicization, and his own sonnet — completing the 1955 *New Yorker* pair — poignantly conveys (despite one subtly flawed feminine rhyme) a sense of inchoate despair:

> *Reflected words can only shiver*
> *Like elongated lights that twist*
> *In the black mirror of a river*
> *Between the city and the mist.*
> *Elusive Pushkin! Persevering,*
> *I still pick up your damsel's earring,*
> *Still travel with your sullen rake;*
> *I find another man's mistake;*
> *I analyze alliterations*
> *That grace your feasts and haunt the great*
> *Fourth stanza of your Canto Eight.*
> *This is my task: a poet's patience*
> *And scholiastic passion blent —*
> *Dove-droppings on your monument.*

Poems IX:

~ Two Little Families ~

* * * * *
* *
*
*

"My Petite", if placed next to the rather exuberant poems in "Sassy City", appears exceedingly restrained: it contains no split words, no slang phrases, no bad hyphenations, no *double entendres,* no extraneous ideas — nothing of the sort. Indeed, it comes close to being a no-nonsense translation, which, in the context of the recent ones, makes it seem very nearly literal! I suppose that by some people's lights it might quite seriously merit the label "literal", but I personally would not go that far.

Although it is quite straight on the whole, "My Petite" retains a humorous tone, whose peak is hit in lines 13–14, where the poet first executes a mock throat-clearing and then facetiously refers to himself as "Doctor" — complete with what I might call (borrowing from Monty Python) "nudge-nudge-wink-wink" quotation marks.

Though this is hardly a bland translation, it may have struck me as such at the time, and perhaps its relative blandness is what led me to start playing around with it, trying to see if I could liven it up a bit more. Such explorations led to the next two poems.

My Petite

D. Hofstadter

My petite
Girl so sweet,
Here's a hug.
Did some bug
Get you down?   5
Well, don't frown.
Get the will
Bugs to kill!
You'll emerge
From your scourge   10
In a trice —
Sound advice
From (ahem!)
"Doctor" Clem.
Come, you who   15
Love to chew —
Shun the bed
That you dread.
Come eat treats:
Jams, sweetmeats!   20
She who stays
Sick for days
Grows too thin,
And her skin
Glows no more.   25
Here's to your
Health complete,
My petite!

At some point, driven by a vague intuition that "My Petite" had considerable untapped potential, I started playing around with certain sections of it, and after much travail, the facing poem resulted. Like "On Ye, Childe", "Kiddo, Hi" and "Hurry, Love", this poem plays the first-line/last-line quasi-homonymy game, and indeed, its title is taken from its last rather than its first line.

For me, the most elegant and certainly the snappiest part of "My Pet, Eat" is the section running from line 4 to line 14. The fact that I could come up with three successive rhyming couplets each of which possessed near-total phonetic overlap (lines 5–6; 7–8; 9–10) truly stunned me. Though they were slangy, I felt they were beautiful. Note that in reading lines 6–11 aloud, one must be absolutely strict in accenting the last syllable of each line: "Made you *up*- / chuck a *lot*? / Knuckle *not* / Under, *but* / Under*cut* / Your dis*ease*."

Once again, I would point out that producing this kind of trickery would seem to require native-level mastery. How many non-native speakers, even fluent ones, have at their fingertips such phrases as "to upchuck" (as a crude way of saying "to vomit"), "to knuckle under" (as a more vivid replacement for "to surrender"), or "no end" (as a jaunty substitute for "a lot")? Obviously very few; I myself certainly don't have anything like that level of total mastery of my two strongest foreign languages, French and Italian.

Even for someone who knew the idiomatic expression "to knuckle under" very well, it would take yet another quantum jump in experience and self-assurance to have the intuition that, in this very special context, one could get away with negating it by interpolating "not" between its components ("knuckle not under"), as opposed to sticking with the prosaic and safe auxiliary-verb-based style of negation ("don't knuckle under"). I bring this little example up not to lavish praise on myself, but to emphasize the many layers and types of knowledge that underlie a smooth, flowing translation. This is the kind of thing that I feel is out of the range of almost all non-native speakers. (It is even pretty tricky for most non-native readers.)

So much for the up side of "My Pet, Eat". On the down side, there are lines 15–16: "Come, kid who'd / Kill for food". Though their final syllables rhyme impeccably, on "who'd" and "food" is not the way one would naturally accent this phrase, not by a long shot. If these lines were read out loud as prose, one would hear the following strong stresses: "*Come*, kid who'd kill for *food*", with secondary accents on "kid" and "kill". By far the weakest syllables would be "who'd" and "for". Therefore, to read this phrase aloud as "Come, kid *who'd* kill for *food*" is somewhat strained, but if the poem is to work as a poem, it's got to be done. Of course, it's over and gone in a split second and certainly doesn't destroy the poem, but still, it's a minor glitch.

In a similar vein, "sweetmeats", strictly speaking, should be stressed on "sweet" and not on "meats", so that reading line 20 out loud in a properly poetic manner also takes a little bending of convention. Altogether, then, to read "My Pet, Eat" out loud in real time and to make it sound good requires a skillful performer. It cannot be taken for granted.

Unfortunately, when one is working on a poem, one gets so immersed in the task that one becomes quite unaware of the degree to which one is forcing and stretching the language to one's own purposes. For this reason, I have often been rudely shocked, when listening to someone else read a poem of mine out loud, to hear my carefully-constructed lines accented wrongly left and right, to hear my precious little couplets brutally mangled, when I naïvely had thought there was only one conceivable way of reading my creation out loud. Such shocks have taught me how hard it would be to come up with a poem that virtually any native speaker would effortlessly read aloud with the timing and rhyming of every line coming out just as the poet hears them internally.

My Pet, Eat

D. Hofstadter

My petite
Pet, you're sweet —
Have a hug.
Has some bug
Laid you up?   5
Made you up-
chuck a lot?
Knuckle not
Under, but
Undercut   10
Your disease.
That would please
Your old friend,
Clem, no end.
Come, kid who'd   15
Kill for food —
Shun that bed,
And stale bread.
Come eat treats:
Jams, sweetmeats!   20
One who stays
Sick for days
Gets pale skin
And grows thin.
What a pain!   25
So, to gain
Health complete,
My pet — eat!

Not satisfied with just one revision of "My Petite", I felt inspired to try another. The most distinctive joke here is the use of two different names — "Doug" and "Clem". Who is actually speaking? Is it two people? Is it one? Is it a moving target? After all, it starts out as "Doug", then becomes "(ahem!) Doug/Clem", and winds up as "Clem" (lines 3, 13–14, 24). A case of multiple personalities? You of course know, but a reader who didn't know the circumstances of this poem — its origin in French with author Clément Marot, its translation into English with translator Douglas Hofstadter — would be a bit thrown.

Speaking of the line "Doug/Clem", it is actually a joke on a couple of levels, since at first glance it looks bisyllabic, thus violating the metrical constraint so carefully obeyed everywhere else. But in reality, the slash is to be pronounced (indeed, as "slash"): "Doug slash Clem", a fact that restores the line's trisyllabicity after all. And this in turn gives rise to the next little piece of wordplay — the rhyming of the *middle* syllables of lines 14–15.

Another venture out on a limb is the supposed "rhyming couplet" consisting of "Come — yoo-hoo!" and "Come, you who". It takes a bit of chutzpah to try to pass these phonetically indistinguishable lines off as rhymes, but I decided to risk it anyway. (Note for non-native speakers: You probably won't find "yoo-hoo" in your typical English–French or English–Chinese dictionary, but in America, it is a standard way of trying to get the attention of someone very far away and who you suspect can barely hear you when you yell. By the way, strictly speaking, "yoo-hoo" is normally stressed on "yoo", not "hoo", but one can take liberties with the stress, especially in a poem.)

Lines 19–20 not only constitute something of a tongue-twister, but also feature near-total phonetic overlap, recalling lines 5–10 of the preceding poem. Also, the word "Sweets" on line 19 has precisely the same dual interpretability as it did in "Your Old Bard": it might mean either "darling" or "goodies". It would seem weird to claim that it means both, but I suppose one could do so. However, even if it does, I as a reader can hear it only one way at a time. "Sweets" can flip back and forth like the rival visual interpretations of the Necker cube, but it can't be heard both ways at once — at least not in my mind.

Once the first/last lines were solidly set, inserting the word "palpitate" into this poem suddenly became an irresistible goal to me. The story of how this goal was actually met is quite interesting. Because of its semantic halo, it was clear that "palpitate" would fit most naturally into the last third of my poem, since that's where, in Marot's poem, such bodily concerns as escaping from pallor, weakness, and weight loss are under discussion. It also seemed most natural to let the word, being trisyllabic, take up a full line. (Again, strictly speaking, "palpitate" is normally accented more strongly on its first than on its last syllable, but in a poetic context, the metric momentum could allow the reverse to sound smooth.) Now if "palpitate" was going to be used as line N (the value of N to be determined as things developed), this pretty much forced line $N-1$ to terminate in the words "your heart" (what else could reasonably palpitate?). Then, thanks to the rhyming constraint, "heart" exerted further retrograde influence on the ending of line $N-2$. The upshot was that I penned lines 23–22–21 "swimming upstream", so to speak, although there was a bit of downstream influence as well. In particular, the combination of the (upstream) *phonetic* influence of the need to rhyme with "heart" and the (downstream) *semantic* influence of the need to dovetail smoothly with the image of chewing sweets (already set up in line 20) tickled the dormant word "tart" in my memory, and up it bubbled into consciousness. "Tart" in turn triggered the recall of "pop a tart", and this candidate phrase was then considered at the conscious level. It passed muster with flying colors, and thus $N-2$ was fixed at 21.

One last feature of "Pal Petite" is the existence of two episodes where several lines in a row share an end rhyme — first four lines (7–10), then six (15–20). These analogous segments could thus be said to "rhyme", on an abstract plane, with each other.

Pal Petite

D. Hofstadter

Pal petite,
Gal so sweet,
Hug from Doug.
Some dumb bug
Dragged you down?   5
Zap that frown!
Feel the urge
Bugs to purge!
From the scourge
You'll emerge   10
In a trice —
Sound advice
From (ahem!)
Doug/Clem.
So, smash flu!   15
Come — yoo-hoo!
Come, you who
Live to chew —
Sheets eschew;
Sweets, let's chew!   20
Pop a tart;
Make your heart
Palpitate!
(Clem's mandate.)
Sure hope God   25
Cures your bod,
Head to feet,
Pal petite!

"Little Gem" was composed as a lark one day in Ann Arbor as I sat alone in a quiet classroom, letting myself wind down after teaching a class, with the late-afternoon sun streaming in through the windows. I was surprised at how fast I tossed it off (on the order of half an hour); indeed, I remember savoring the thought of how far I had come, in just two months or so, in the tiny art form of making "Ma Mignonne" translations.

Not that I saw this quick study as a little gem — it was too flip and silly in tone, especially the quirky, off-the-wall endearment "brontosaurette", obviously prompted by nothing more than the desire to find an easy rhyme for "pronto" — but it had some nice touches, such as the wrap-around syncopation of lines 7–13 (replete with amphisbænic enjambment, on line 12) and of lines 21–28 (with yet another amphisbænic enjambment on line 23); the with-it, twentieth-century suggestion "Get a tan" to render the idea of fighting pallor; and the phrase "Doin' time / For no crime" (the same elaboration of Marot's prison metaphor as David Moser independently came up with, some eight years later, in revising "Sweet Sue"). It seemed to me that these merited preserving somehow.

To this end, I tried patching up "Little Gem" in spots, which led to my noting more problem spots, thus to my making further patches — and soon, round and round I was going. Eventually, I wound up in an unexpectedly long cycle of patches of which, for some reason, I recorded every last one. The destination that I reached — "Gentle Gem" — was hardly a place I had anticipated; indeed, it was about as far away as I could have imagined! Little of what I had hoped to preserve actually wound up preserved. Instead, something totally new emerged. So my full set of notes, a fragment of which is represented by my commentary on the next pair of poems, forms an interesting case study in the genuine unpredictability of the creative process, and along the way it illustrates the cognitive process of struggling to resolve the multiple pressures provided by various simultaneous, independent constraints.

Little Gem

D. Hofstadter

Little gem,
Diadem,
Happy day!
Can't be gay,
Doin' time   5
For no crime!
Gotta yank
Off those blank-
ets, fling wide
Your door, glide   10
on out pront-
o, my bront-
osaurette.
Little pet,
Big of mouth,   15
Face the south —
Get a tan!
Raid the pan-
try and eat
All things sweet.   20
In my book,
a good look-
er ain't spin-
dly 'n' thin.
You'll be just   25
fine — just trust
Uncle Clem,
Little gem.

Although there is obviously no black-and-white division between one stage of revision and the next, I found it useful and natural to render the long chain stretching between "Little Gem" and "Gentle Gem" as two endpoints with fifteen fairly evenly-spaced intermediary poems spanning the wide gap between them. As it would be a drag to exhibit the entire record of the gradual metamorphosis, I've selected just the fourth and the tenth of the fifteen way stations, in addition to the two endpoints.

One goal of my revision work was to soften the silly, flippant tone of the original. Thus instantly, not just "brontosaurette" but also "pronto" and "ain't" were dumped. However, a more important driving force behind my reworking of "Little Gem" was a sense that the gemstone/jewelry metaphor suggested by its opening lines could be elaborated so as to pervade the poem from start to finish. Up to this point, no one had yet tried producing a translation based on a *conceit* — that is, a single metaphor, systematically and consistently exploited from beginning to end. The time thus seemed ripe for this idea.

To flesh out the gemstone conceit, I obviously needed to introduce many more references to jewels and jewelry. By stage 4, as you can see, I had already brought in "ruby", "pearl", "emerald", "carat cake" (hardly an original pun), "jewel", and even the idea of gleaming brightly. Unfortunately, I had also produced a sloppy mishmash of competing metaphors: there were gems, there were jails, there were beds and aches and cakes and even cream puffs. Whew! You can see why I kept on revising.

Stage 10 shows a bit more restraint and seems much more coherent. One of my subtler additions to the gemstone conceit — or rather, the "precious stone" conceit — was line 7. I was surprised how few readers picked up on this little pun. I also managed to work in "zircon", "amethyst", "tourmaline", and "gold", though "ruby" was dropped. In addition, I took the "carat cake" metaphor a little more seriously here, suggesting that the best kind of cake for restoring lost luster would have a carat-count lying between 18 and 24. One advantage of this maneuver was that it co-opted the eating metaphor, making it now serve, rather than rival, the gemstone metaphor.

Lintle Gem (Stage 4)	**Gintle Gem (Stage 10)**
D. Hofstadter	*D. Hofstadter*

Gentle gem,	*Gentle gem,*
Diadem,	*Diadem,*
Hi — bonjour!	*Ciao, zircon!*
How come you're	*Heard you're on*
Doing time	*The sick list,* 5
For no crime?	*Amethyst.*
Ruby, yank	*Precious, tone*
Off your blank-	*Down your moan,*
et; fling wide	*And fling wide*
Your door; glide	*Your door; glide* 10
From your oy-	*From your oy-*
ster bed, coy	*ster bed, coy*
Little pearl.	*Little pearl.*
Bedfast girl,	*Fev'rish girl*
Em'rald green	*Of sad mien* 15
Is your mien.	*(Em'rald green),*
Carat cakes	*For your aches,*
Will stem aches!	*Carat cakes*
(Spread sweet slop	*Are the cure.*
On the top.)	*Eat no fewer* 20
Crammed with cream,	*Than eighteen,*
Bright you'll gleam!	*Tourmaline,*
(Jewels are prized	*But no more*
More when sized	*'n twenty-four.*
More.) God's just;	*Oh, you'll gleam,* 25
You'll heal. Trust	*My gold dream!*
Uncle Clem,	*Trust old Clem,*
Gentle gem.	*Gentle gem.*

This is the unanticipated destination where I wound up, having left "Little Gem" long behind. It's quite a tightly knit little conceit, allowing the image of fighting an illness to shine through as the literal theme of the poem, while at the same time allowing that theme to coexist easily with the metaphorical theme of gems and beauty. Incidentally, the "carat cake" metaphor is taken even more seriously here than earlier, with the gemologically correct implication that although twenty-four carats represents pure gold, fourteen is verging dangerously close to silver.

If you look back, you'll see that gems are going in and out like tourists through a hotel's revolving door — thus "zircon" has just checked out (thank God, since it sounded so awkward!), but also "amethyst", "tourmaline", and "emerald" have taken their leave. Too bad, since they were most welcome guests. On the other hand, "ruby" has returned after a short business trip, and, for better or for worse, will stay on for good.

Line 5 has a subtle set of undertones, since "in the rough" as a *golf* metaphor means "in trouble", and yet in the context of gemstones, the words cannot help but also conjure up the stock phrase "diamond in the rough", meaning a diamond not yet extracted from its rocky surrounding, let alone polished. Consequently, both meanings contribute, each in its own subliminal way, to the overall understanding. The following line's rhyme for "rough" — "sub-snuff" — is an amusing contraction of the idiom "not up to snuff", and helps to reinforce the imagery of illness.

On line 14, the sound of the words "sea-blue girl" continues the undersea imagery of lines 10–13, while also exploiting the more abstract meaning of "blue" (*i.e.*, "in the dumps"). And then line 15 playfully contradicts the more literal, color-oriented interpretation of its predecessor.

Probably the most unexpected feature of this poem is a purely formal one: namely, the fact that its natural semantic chunks, rather than being couplets, as in Marot's original poem, consist of *three* lines each. There is necessarily an exception to this somewhere, since the total number of lines is 28, a number not evenly divisible by 3. The inevitable glitch comes when the clause beginning on line 7 spills over onto line 10, thus making a chunk that contains 3⅔ instead of three lines; the subsequent chunk, running from "glide" through "pearl", contains 3⅓ lines; thereafter, the precise trilinear semantic rhythm resumes.

I confess that I certainly did not set out to create a poem with this unusual formal structure, but I will take partial credit, in the sense that once I chanced to notice that, by pure coincidence, I was somewhat near to achieving such a pattern, I gladly incorporated that elegant goal into the package of interacting constraints to which I had already voluntarily submitted.

Gentle Gem

D. Hofstadter

Gentle gem,
Diadem,
Ciao! Bonjour!
Heard that you're
In the rough:　　　　　　　*5*
Glum, sub-snuff.
Precious, tone
Down your moan,
And fling wide
Your door; glide　　　　　　*10*
From your oy-
ster bed, coy
Little pearl.
See, blue girl,
Beet-red ru-　　　　　　　*15*
by's your hue.
For your aches,
Carat cakes
Are the cure.
Eat no few'r　　　　　　　*20*
Than fourteen,
Silv'ry queen —
But no more
'n twenty-four,
Golden dream.　　　　　　*25*
How you'll gleam!
Trust old Clem,
Gentle gem.

• *Chapter 10* •

On Words and their Magical Halos

•

In a fattish sack of post, on a day so dull and drear, the editors of the magazine *Astounding Science Fiction* find a manuscript, fresh-typed, which is recognized at once, by an eagle-eye among them, as a word-for-word facsimile of one chapter from J. Cooper's novel *Last of the Mohicans*. Up the cry goes: "Plagiarism!", as all rush to see just *what* is going on…

Someone flips to the typescript's last page and notices it has been signed, in very neat, small handwriting, "Pierre Menard", just below which this sentence has been tacked on: "I should like to inform readers that the activity described herein takes place over a temporal period of some twelve milliseconds in duration, inside a square meter of the outermost millimeter of the crust of a small neutron star distant roughly eleven light-days from earth; it is hence not, as a few readers might overhastily assume, an old tale about Mohican Indians but a new, original work about alien micro-beings."

Six months later the alter-authored James Fenimoore Cooper chapter appears in the pages of *Astounding,* retouched in no way save that Menard's short commentary has been transposed from the end to the beginning.

Jorge Luis Borges, Author of Pierre Menard

The reclusive French novelist Pierre Menard — some claim with great vehemence and considerable credibility that he was but a figment of the rich imagination of Argentinian writer Jorge Luis Borges, since no other works by him have been found; here, however, we shall not enter into this fractious fray — is best remembered for his unfinished novel *Don Quixote,* written not in Menard's native French but in painfully accurate Spanish toward the end of the 1930's. Its two-and-a-half chapters are word-for-word identical with the corresponding chapters of the novel *Don Quixote,* written some 320 years earlier by the Spaniard Miguel de Cervantes.

In his definitive essay on Menard and his contributions, Borges makes clear that the similarity of the two works is not a coincidence. Menard's identification with his Hispanic idol was indeed so strong that he set for himself the task of writing his favorite novel anew — that is, not from the original perspective of Cervantes in the Spain of the 1600's, but from his own personal perspective in the France of the 1900's. His aim was thus not to *copy,* but to *generate the exact same text* completely from scratch, as if it had never existed before, thus imbuing the resulting words with a totally fresh set of hidden meanings and associative halos. As Borges notes:

> The text of Cervantes and that of Menard are verbally identical, but the second is almost infinitely richer. (More ambiguous, his detractors will say; but ambiguity is a richness.) It is a revelation to compare the *Don Quixote* of Menard with that of Cervantes. The latter, for instance, wrote:
>
> > ...*la verdad, cuya madre es la historia, émula del tiempo, depósito de las acciones, testigo de lo pasado, ejemplo y aviso de lo presente, advertencia de lo por venir.*
>
> Menard, on the other hand, writes:
>
> > ...*la verdad, cuya madre es la historia, émula del tiempo, depósito de las acciones, testigo de lo pasado, ejemplo y aviso de lo presente, advertencia de lo por venir.*
>
> Equally vivid is the contrast in styles. The archaic style of Menard — in the last analysis, a foreigner — suffers from a certain affectation. Not so that of his precursor, who handles easily the ordinary Spanish of his time.

If I, writing with the advantage of several decades' hindsight, might be forgiven for my choice of words, Menard's was, from its very outset, a most quixotic mission; for this reason, his failure to complete the novel he had hoped to write is hardly surprising.

Indeed, the significance of Menard's accomplishment may ultimately reside not in the fragments that he managed to complete, but in his friend and admirer Borges' exemplary exegesis thereof, the key point of which is to stress how a set of familiar words and situations, if reinterpreted in a new context, can take on utterly novel and occasionally quite bizarre auras of meaning and imagery. This theme, then, will become the *Leitmotiv* of this chapter and the following one.

I Say, Is That Mr Caulfield Practising Maths in Gaol?

Ever since I first read and fell in love with it in 1960, I have made a practice of re-reading J. D. Salinger's masterpiece *The Catcher in the Rye* every ten years. Each go-round, I have feared that *this* time, finally, I would find it too adolescent, too simplistic, too dated, too corny — too this, too that, too something-or-other — but each time, glad to say, to my joy and relief, I have found it to be not too young or too trite, but too touching for words, to be frank, and as funny and fresh as the first time, to boot.

Now it happened that on a transoceanic leap to England in 1990, one of those special "0" years, I found myself with a fair patch of spare time, and so when I happened to run across a copy of the novel in a small bookstore in Brighton, I purchased it, figuring it was just about time for my decadely encounter with gangly sixteen-year-old Holden Caulfield, his adorable little sister Phoebe, his crude macho roommate Stradlater, his teachers and peers at Pencey Prep, old Maurice, the nasty New York elevator boy, phony Sally Hayes, who Holden used to neck so damn much with that he thought she was intelligent, smart Jane Gallagher, the muckle-mouthed girl who Holden used to play checkers with and once *almost* necked with, the two nuns at the breakfast counter at Grand Central Station — and then, lurking at the shadowy core of it all, the tragic ghost of Allie, Holden's dead brother. In case you don't know it or don't remember it well, here is how Maurice Sagoff memorably micro-miniaturized this great novel in *ShrinkLits*:

School was crumby,
    Classmates mean.
Holden Caulfield,
    Aged sixteen,
Copped out to the
    New York scene.

There he wandered,
    Sorrow's son,
Overgrown
    But underdone,
Seared by girls...
    It wasn't fun.

Broke, disheartened,
    Home he slid.
Sister Phoebe
    (Perky kid)
Buoyed him up,
    She really did.

Only for the
    Moment, though;
Down the skids,
    Alas, he'll go,
Landing in a
    Shrink-château.

Ah, what torment
    Must be his
Who Goddams
    But feels Gee Whiz!
Youth is rough,
    It really is.

And so, quite on schedule, I opened up this novel so treasured in memory, and plunged in with high hopes. But much as in the case of *One Day in the Life of Ivan Denisovich*, after only a few sentences I started to feel ill at ease. And what was the matter? This will sound silly to you, but the em-dashes were too short. Instead of saying (about his parents), "They're *nice* and all—I'm not saying that—but they're also touchy as hell", Holden said, 'They're *nice* and all – I'm not saying that – but they're also touchy as hell'. The *em*-dashes had been micro-miniaturized into *en*-dashes!

The ratio of the size of my reaction to the size of the stimulus may remind you of the fable "The Princess and the Pea", but bear with me for a moment. Quite soon I came across a "week-end visit" (why the hyphen?), and "haemorrhages" (how come "ae"?), as well as Pencey Prep's claim to be "moulding" — not "molding" — boys into young men. And then I read about "Mr and Mrs Spencer" (no periods?!), and Selma Thurmer's "phoney slob" of a father. *Phoney*??? This key word in Salinger's book, appearing eighteen times if it appears once, sported a superfluous "e" each and every time it was printed.

And so it went. On nearly every page, something somewhere looked *British*. The quote marks used in dialogues were single, not double; people travelled with two "l"'s in the hyphenated summer-time and sat in their living-rooms in the ditto winter-time; room-mates put on their favourite grey-coloured pyjamas; women hailed taxi-cabs in front of theatres and phone-booths and twelve-storey buildings; carousels went round and round (but not around and around); *and,* it was all marvellously humourous.

Well, these anglicisms were harmless enough, I suppose, but then, in the space of one single page, after first running into a "coloured girl singer" and a "pearl-grey hat", I banged straight into the *kerb*. A *kerb* in New York City? Blimey! That was too much. But the worst came when I read *this*:

Note to the reader: I've left this passage in small type (size 10, in point of fact), so that it looks just like the extract that was originally right here, taken from the British *Catcher in the Rye* (two paragraphs about James Castle's pathetic death, in which "gaol" is used for "jail", and "Maths" for "math"). However, as you may have guessed, what you are reading is not that extract. No, this is in fact your author, improvising at his Macintosh keyboard. Why on earth is that? Simple — here it is, an eye-blink from press time, and guess what? Old J. D. *won't give me permission* to quote a measly 26 lines from his book! No, he won't! Don't ask me why. He's a funny guy, I guess. I could plead till the cows came home, and he wouldn't budge.

Unfortunately, that leaves me up a creek. Why? Well, as I told you in my Introduction, I've calculated every line of every page in this whole book down to the last comma. Page-breaks can't just fall willy-nilly; they have to come at certain precise points, so as to leave poems and major displays unbroken. With my 26-line gaol-and-Maths extract, I had it all worked out great for Chapter 10. But with it jerked out from under me, especially at the last moment, I was in a mess! For instance, flip to p. 302. Do you honestly think, reader, that that giant paragraph with its six-line coda filled out the page merely *by accident*? Give me a break!

To cite just a couple of other examples, do you suppose that the Steiner quote at the bottom of p. 291, or the Barnstone quote on p. 294, worked out so nicely solely by *happenstance*? Or (my last example), do you really believe it's just by some kind of *coincidence* that the last word of p. 282 is "break" (as in "page-break")?

*Some*thing had to be done to make up for the missing 26 lines. Something — but what? Yes, *what*?? And as I pondered my dilemma, I kept on asking myself, "Suppose old Holden *had* grown up and become a university professor and written a book on translation… Would Salinger have denied even *him* the permission to quote from *The Catcher in the Rye*?" If so, I pity the old guy. Poor, poor Salinger.

"Gaol"!? *"Maths"*?! Which side of the Atlantic are we on, for God's sake?

I persevered and plowed my way through to the end, but doing so was both painful and ludicrous. Here was a book printed in an odd hybrid of American and British, wavering back and forth all the time, a fact that made me hypersensitive to minuscule typographic and orthographic usages that normally I would pay but slight attention to. Penguin Books, without in any way intending to do so, had converted, by just the subtlest of tweaks, a quintessentially American novel into a schizoid Anglo-American one!

If this is not convincing, then let me suggest you imagine yourself heading off all alone on a six-hour interstate car trip and inserting, with great anticipation, a recorded version of Salinger's novel into your car's cassette player and settling back in the seat, only to hear the mature and stentorian Oxbridge voice of Sir Charles Laughton intoning Holden's insecure but brave adolescent gropings and grapplings with life. What a preposterous marriage of medium and message this would be!

To be sure, one could imagine a far more radical and thorough job of transoceanic transculturation of *The Catcher in the Rye,* with New York City getting replaced entirely by London, Pencey Prep likewise replaced by some mediocre but pretentious public school down in Devonshire, and on and on. Certainly the end result, were it done well, would be fascinating to experience, but just reading this kerb-and-gaol, maths-and-moulding version of Salinger's book was already dislocating enough for me.

Noses and Then Noses

I remember vividly that the first time I saw the word "gaol" in print, I had no idea how it was pronounced or what it meant. It was without any doubt one of the strangest, ugliest words I had ever seen. When I found out it was the British way of spelling "jail", I thought it was hilarious! And so I wonder what British children's reaction is upon finding out that the ridiculous Americans' spelling for "gaol" is "jail". Do they find it funny, or can they all of a sudden see their own spelling as comical?

When I see the word "kerb", what springs to mind is the curbs — the kerbs — the curbs — whatever — along The King's Road in Chelsea in the mid-1960's, where I spent several months with my parents and sister in

Bramerton Street. Those were the heydays of hippies and Jean Shrimpton, the Beatles and the Viet Nam War, Lyndon Johnson and Mao Tse-Tung. To a young American male living in the same row house on Bramerton Street today, would "kerb" have the same meaning? Along these lines, here are some related questions to ponder:

- Does a sentence written in American English mean what it means in British English? (Does the word "monarchy" mean the same thing in both places? How about "Yankee"? How about "jolly"? How about "you"?)
- Does a sentence written in British English mean what it means in Indian English? (Does "cow" mean the same thing in both of them? How about "beef"? How about "Crown"? How about "nose"?)
- Did a French sentence written by someone in Pushkin's Russia mean what the same French sentence written in Hugo's France meant? (Did "Napoléon" mean the same thing to both of them? How about *tsar*?)
- Does a San Franciscan speak the same language as a New Yorker? (Does "Chinatown" mean the same thing to both of them? How about "China"? How about "Broadway"? How about "earthquake"? How about "steep"?)
- Does a Manhattanite speak the same language as a Brooklynite? (Does "New York" mean the same thing to both of them? How about "D train"?)
- Does an Upper East Sider speak the same language as an Upper West Sider? (Does "Central Park" mean the same thing to both of them? How about "Broadway"? How about "dog"? How about "thing"? How about "a"?)
- If John F. Kennedy and Richard M. Nixon were to speak the same patriotic sentence, would it have a fixed meaning? (Did "patriotism" mean the same thing to both of them? How about "communism"? How about "Abraham Lincoln"? How about "assassination"? How about "New York"? And "nose"?)
- Do women speak the same language as men? (Does "menopause" mean the same thing to both of them? How about "attractive"? How about "guys"?)
- Do feminist women speak the same language as nonfeminist women? (Does "oppression" mean the same thing to both of them? How about "attractive"? How about "guys"?)
- Do Lesbian feminist women speak the same language as non-Lesbian feminist women? (Does "gay" mean the same thing to both of them? How about "attractive"? How about "guys"?)
- Do separatist Lesbian feminist women speak the same language as nonseparatist Lesbian feminist women? (Does "separatist" mean the same thing to both of them? How about "men"? How about "guys"?)
- Do militant separatist Lesbian feminist women speak the same language as nonmilitant separatist Lesbian feminist women? (Does "militant" mean the same thing to both of them? How about "woman"? And... how about "nose"?)

Indeed. *Does* "nose" mean the same thing to everyone? Did it mean to Cyrano de Bergerac what it meant to Roxane? Did it mean to Jimmy Durante what it meant to Cyrano? Of course, Cyrano spoke French, not English. Well, then, did *nez* mean to Cyrano what "nose" meant to Jimmy Durante? Or did *pif* mean to Cyrano what "schnozzola" meant to Durante?

Bommère

A friend sent me recently the following paragraph by Geoffrey Nunberg, a linguist and writer at Stanford.

> Have you seen those new IBM ads? I mean the ones with the global-village theme, about how technology makes Americans of us all. There are these two French gaffers walking along the Seine and talking about disk drives while accordions play in the background. The subtitles have one of them saying, "My hard drive's maxed out" and the other responds with something that's translated as "Bummer". Or there's the clutch of Czech nuns talking about operating systems as the Mother Superior says, "I'm dying to surf the Internet." Right; they wish they all could be California girls.

As it happens, I've not seen the ads in question, but I can very easily imagine them, and when I do, I get hot under the collar, infuriated by the gall of simplistically translating other languages into American slang, as if all that was going on in another language is word substitution *à la* Warren Weaver — as if French or Czech really *were* isomorphic to English, with words that mean *exactly* "Bummer!" or "maxed out" or "surf the net" — as if all you need to do to decode the gaffers' (or nuns') sentiments into English is look up those French (or Czech) words in a sufficiently big and with-it dictionary, and there you will find "bummer" (or "net-surf") as the one and only English equivalent. One-to-one mappability. No flavor differences.

The IBM ads are playing a tricky game, because they're trying on one level to suggest that there *are* deep flavor differences — the clichéd accordion music, the Parisian scenes so different from American ones, the idea of nuns in some central-European medieval castle-cloister, the different sets of sounds used to express ideas — but on another level, it's as if they're subliminally saying to viewers, "Well, sure, all that stuff *looks* different, but hey, guys, when you strip away the foreign veneer, you find that we're really all the same under the skin, we're all concerned with the same exact problems — our disk drives, the net, the Web... Things annoy us in precisely isomorphic ways, we all have the same yearnings, are all affected by trendy language (in whatever tongue we happen to speak) in exactly the same way, are all susceptible to technology fads in identical ways... Yup, under the skin, folks, we're all interchangeable, despite that misleading disparity in veneers that we all enjoy despite its misleadingness. It's cute and quaint, how people use different *sounds* to say 'bummer' or 'dying to surf the net' or 'maxed out', but of course it's not really different at all, once you strip off those sounds." That's one way of reading the ads.

Or perhaps one could interpret them as being a bit tongue-in-cheek, saying something more like this: "Oh, tee-hee — French (or Czech) people don't *really* say 'bummer' or anything like it, but it tickles us Americans to put our American expressions into their virtual mouths in the subtitles, because we know perfectly well that other languages are so, so different, and we know perfectly well that people in Europe have different styles and sensibilities and don't go for trendy, modern language nearly as much as we do — and yet, despite all this, in *some* sense, it's possible for old French gaffers to be frustrated with their disk drives, and in *some* sense, it's possible for pious Czech nuns to feel that computer connections to the world are relevant to their lives, and so it's amusing to *pretend* that they would express themselves in a type of language that could be rendered as very up-to-date, modern, trendy, with-it American technoslang. It's all a *joke,* though. We at IBM are profoundly cosmopolitan; we know full well that people in other cultures are extraordinarily different at all levels from us — but still, it's fun to play the analogy game, it's fun to try sticking American slang into European mouths, if only to make us laugh at ourselves for our silliness in momentarily letting ourselves think that it's the right way of looking at words and cultures. And so, in this way, we at IBM are actually contributing subliminally to a deepening of our viewers' appreciation for how *fake* the whole image shown in the ad is, and thereby enriching our viewers' respect for cultural differences."

And then there's actually a third option, in some sense the vilest of all: namely, the people who make the ads have done it in full awareness of both of these interpretations, and they calculate along these lines: "Well, certain viewers will fall for the 'bummer'-exists-in-French line, and *that'll* pick up customers for IBM; then other viewers will think it's all an intentional send-up of Americocentrism, and that *too* will pick up customers. Either way is fine, ambiguity is great, hear it as straightarrow or tongue-in-cheek, have it your way — the main thing is, it'll help IBM (and more to the point, us guys here at the advertising agency) rake in a bunch more money, and ain't that life's bottom line anyway?" (Sounds like Mr Average talking Chinese, no?)

Transculturation: A Cannonball versus Buckshot

I have been suggesting, in the past few pages, an image of individual words as very small loci of transculturation, a myriad micro-dots of betrayal as opposed to one huge act of total treason. This brings up the idea of a spectrum of levels on which transculturation can be effected.

The most extreme sort is the no-holds-barred top-to-toes retooling of a work, preserving only its abstract essence, such as the conversion of *Romeo and Juliet* into *West Side Story,* or the conversion of *King Lear* into a drama taking place in China itself, with all protagonists Chinese, or the conversion of Edward Albee's play *Who's Afraid of Virginia Woolf?* from a heterosexual to a homosexual context, or (see Poems XIII) Marek Lugowski's conversion of "Ma Mignonne" into rap language in an inner-city framework — and so on.

A milder sort is what I earlier called "transportation", which means a shifting of the site of the action, but little else. Examples of this would be Melanie Mitchell's "To My Sweet", which carries Marot's poem into a Shakespearean England but leaves its content otherwise undisturbed, or Rudy Kousbroek's transfer of *Exercices de style* from Paris to Amsterdam.

On a more local level would be Adair's substitutions — of a hanging for Perec's guillotining, or of his "e"-less rendering of Poe's "The Raven" for Perec's "e"-less rendering of Hugo's "Booz endormi". The key is that in Adair's retelling, Anton Vowl, *né* Voyl, is still French and the action is all still in France. In other words, the global level is left intact, but here and there are pockmarks of various sizes where mini-betrayals have occurred.

More local yet would be the kinds of small linguistic transculturations that abound in translations of *Gödel, Escher, Bach,* typified by the conversion of "Speak of the devil" into the sentence about Cao Cao. Any swapping of expressions deeply rooted in their own cultures would fall in this category, as when the Beijing popcorn vendor sounded off in Chinese and was quoted in English as saying, "You ain't got no book, forget it." A subtle but excellent example would be Voyl's redubbing by Adair as "Vowl".

And then we come to that lowest, most local level of transculturation, which is simply the substitution of one supposedly equivalent word for another — converting *ma* into "my", *mignonne* into "sweet", *prison* into "jail", *porte* into "door", *confitures* into "jam", *tetta* into "bust", *radio* into "radio", "jail" into "gaol", "summertime" into "summer-time", "gray" into "grey", and so on. The utter reasonableness and justifiability of such "atomic" acts of translation usually goes completely unquestioned, but of course, as the previous few pages have suggested, it is far from uncontroversial.

By no means am I the first person to point out the dubiousness of the possibility of translation even at this bottom-most rung of the ladder:

> There are innumerable near-identities, or, more strictly speaking, overlaps of associative content which Englishmen share by virtue of historical or climatic experience but which an American, emitting the same speech-sounds, may have no inkling of. The French language, as self-consciously perhaps as any, is a palimpsest of historical, political undertones and overtones. To a remarkable degree, these embed even ordinary locutions in a "chord" of associations which anyone acquiring the language from outside will never fully master. There is no dictionary that lists even a fraction of the historical, figurative, dialectic, argotic, technical planes of significance in such simple words as, say, *chaussée* or *faubourg*; nor could there be, as these planes are perpetually interactive and changing.

A Babbling Brook of Brilliance

I should take this moment to insert a brief interlude in salute to the author of the foregoing paragraph, George Steiner, who has written at such length, and so often most articulately and provocatively, on language and translation. His book *After Babel,* which I made a valiant attempt to read when it came out in the mid-1970's, is brimming with insightful, important, and quite lyrical observations (such as the one just quoted) about the subtlety of human language and the power of the human mind. Regrettably, though, its prose is continually flirting with murk, and all too often, having been seduced, it verges over into dense philosophico–lit-crit flights of fancy that, read as poetry, sound marvelous but, because of their enormous ambiguity and vagueness, are essentially impossible to make sense of. (I must say, Steiner is far from alone in this affliction.) Despite its troublingly frequent oscillation between these two poles of meaningfulness, *After Babel* is well worth the tackling, for in it can be found a vast number of fascinating examples, wonderful quotations, and brilliant observations.

In many ways, George Steiner and I share passions; we often focus on the same issues, at times even zooming in on precisely the same examples. Thus today, in flipping through and rereading parts of his book with considerable pleasure, I was amused to find that he, writing twenty years earlier, had quoted exactly the same section of Borges' essay on Menard as I do above, only in a different translation. Was he thus, *à la* Pierre Menard but in retrograde, striving to preconstruct Hofstadter? (In my opinion, by the way, Steiner unduly overpraises Borges' clever spoof, calling it "arguably the most acute, most concentrated commentary anyone has offered on the business of translation". With all due respect for all three, that's just silly.)

Another meeting of the minds is our common fair-minded inspection of, dissection of, and ultimate rejection of, Vladimir Nabokov's curious letter-over-spirit approach to the great *Eugene Onegin.* But without doubt, our greatest overlap is our mutual fascination with the incessant primordial background radiation of conditionals, subjunctives, and counterfactuals fluttering softly through the chasms of the unconscious mind, a process that Steiner sees as the root of all that is human. I couldn't agree more! And so I offer a toast: Hats off to George Steiner, translator and writer of insight, mystery, and crypticity *par excellence.*

¿Cheese = Fromage?

As I was saying, I am far from the first human being to be concerned about the insidious danger of substituting officially corresponding words for each other in different languages. As we saw, George Steiner makes the point very sharply, but he himself credits Schopenhauer over 150 years earlier with the humorously desperate conclusion that since "no amount of labor or genius would convert *être debout* into *stehen....* no less was needed than a 'transference of soul'." On the face of it, this sounds ridiculous, but let us take a careful look at the issues, because they turn out to be astoundingly far from clear-cut.

When I question whether it is a betrayal and a sham to substitute "jam" for *confitures,* I am not speaking of sophisticated abstractions infamous for their reputed untranslatability, such as German's *Gemütlichkeit, Zeitgeist,* and *Schadenfreude,* or French's *savoir-faire, sang-froid,* and *je-ne-sais-quoi,* or Polish's *żal,* Russian's *пошлость,* Chinese's *zǐ* and *xiào,* English's "tricky", "pattern", "fancy", and "fun", and thousands more, but rather of down-to-earth words as straight and unproblematic-seeming as "one", "two", "buckle", "shoe", "door", "floor", "foot", "head", "sing", "ring", "bed", "red", "near", "far", "sun", "moon", "day", "night", "fork", "spoon".

The question is, do the resonances of "door" differ so vitally from those of *porte* that the substitution of one for the other is a travesty? I can argue it either way. Arguing on the side of travesty, I could point out that traditional doors in France have handles, not knobs as in America, and so the stereotype conjured up in a French mind by *porte* simply looks different from an American's mental image for "door". And *la porte,* moreover, is embedded in a stereotype French *maison* that differs in thousands of ways, small and large, from the stereotype American Anyhouse — and of course *les habitants* of the French *maison* dwell in a surrounding stereotype *ville,* coming and going in their *vieille deux-chevaux,* whereas good old American anyone lives in a pretty how town (with up so floating many bells down)…

And so, after all these stereotypical and biequinic (hee-hee) comings and goings, we find ourselves back at the "kerb/curb" contrast of which I made so much, in my grousing about the "phoney" British re-typesetting of *Catcher in the Rye.* And thus I might seem to have clinched the argument for word-substitution-as-travesty in a decisive manner.

But I can easily take the other side. In fact, Bob French and I once got into the most heated of debates, he arguing that "bread" and *pain* bring up utterly unrelated images in his mind, as do "cheese" and *fromage* — and I, egged on by his dogmatism, scoffing at such claims as nonsense. The crux of my argument was that it all depends on whose mouth the words emerge from, and why and when.

Take "cheese", for instance. If I were at a children's birthday party anywhere in America and heard someone ask a six-year-old, "Hey, bud — want cheese on yer burger?", there's little doubt I would imagine the kind of orangy processed squares that come pre-sliced and pre-wrapped in plastic. "Kraft" is the operative word here. On the other hand, if I were at my friends the Dunns' for dinner and we were sitting chatting in the living room when I overheard Sally whisper something to Mike about bringing in a plate of cheese, I would have a fantastically different expectation: the last thing in the world I would expect is the processed orange Kraft-type stuff! Indeed, I would fall off my seat if that's what was brought out. Instead, I would expect a tray full of unprocessed, non-presliced cheeses, perhaps a hunk of Brie, some Gouda, some chèvre, who knows what-all else.

On Words and their Magical Halos ◆◆◆ 289

It's simply not the case that the word "cheese" — merely because I am in America and have just heard it said with an American accent — conjures up in my mind a rigidly fixed, context-independent image. Not at all — rather, I get totally different vibes depending on who is saying it, and to whom, and in what tone, and so forth. If Mike or Sally were offering cheese to that same six-year-old at the party, I would not be surprised when a tray of Brie and Gouda failed to materialize. In fact, that would be the furthest thing from my mind. Many diverse factors contribute to the image I make.

The same goes for "bread", "door", "jam", and so on. And I'm not exceptional — this is just how the human brain works, Bob French's no less than mine. Thus all that fancy European stuff that Bob claims *fromage* means for him is part of what his own word "cheese" means, and vice versa — lurking somewhere deep down in that exalted, aromatic halo of *fromage* in Bob's mind, there is the lowly Kraft processed cheese. *Fromage* is not nearly so pure and pristine as he wishes it were; it is irrevocably contaminated by the annoying image of pre-sliced plastic-wrapped orange squares, like it or not, and in certain specific conversational contexts in the middle of France when Bob French is speaking his fluentest French with no one but French native speakers, that image will snap — and very appropriately so — faster to his mind than Gruyère or Gouda or Brie. Nor would Bob *want* visions of Brie to pop up and interfere when, because of the conversation's flow, Velveeta is the precise image needed.

Another example I like is "Fifth Avenue". If I am mentally in the little olive-growing town of Corning, California — I used to spend time there when we went to my parents' ranch in Flournoy, fifteen miles further west — and hear this phrase, I envision a wide, quiet, lazy, east–west residential street that goes for a mile or so, then crosses the tracks near the feed-and-grain store and heads off toward the Sacramento River (at least that's how it seems in my fallible memory). But if I'm mentally in Manhattan, dazzling images of Rockefeller Center, the old Scribners bookstore, the Empire State Building, Central Park, the New York Public Library, F. A. O. Schwarz, the Plaza Hotel, the Guggenheim Museum, synchronized traffic lights, and much, much more, all swarm in my head, all with a clear north–south orientation, to boot. Not for a split second does the lazy east–west road passing the feed-and-grain store cross my mind — unless, of course, I happen, by some odd coincidence, to be sitting with a friend in a ritzy Fifth Avenue café chatting about the rural Sacramento Valley and old Corning happens to come up, and the phrase "Fifth Avenue" is mentioned. In that cute case, contrariwise, not even a trace of all the glitter and the glamour before our eyes would be brought into my mind by that same short phrase.

To put it in a nutshell, my counterargument to Bob's claim that the mental images evoked by "cheese" and by *fromage* (etc.) have no overlap is: "Words do not have fixed imagery; context is everything."

Deep Tension Builds up in Counter-counterpoint

And yet I can give a counter-counterargument quite easily, too. All I need to say is that there is such a thing as a *default* image for a word or concept — the image that, most of the time, in "random" circumstances, would be produced. This notion has great intuitive appeal to me, but it is not just a personal hunch on my part; indeed, the notion of defaults, and more specifically, the notion of "spherical" concepts with certain images being central, and thus easily, rapidly, and frequently evoked, and others being peripheral, and thus difficultly, slowly, and rarely evoked, lies at the core of current cognitive-science models of how thinking works.

The idea of default imagery amounts to positing the existence of a personal or even an interpersonal "default context". Generally speaking, "Fifth Avenue" brings Manhattan, not Corning, to mind in me (and in 99.9 percent of people). Generally speaking, "door" suggests *knobs,* not handles, to me. And on and on. There *are* defaults in the mind, and that's what Bob meant. To him, "bread" means, generally speaking, processed bread, like Wonder Bread, while *pain* means, generally speaking, long, thin *baguettes,* crescent-shaped *croissants* (as opposed to rectangular ones in America, where the meaning of the word is not appreciated), and other fresh-baked *délices* that one finds in a *boulangerie.* Any such default can be easily overridden, but that fact does not belie its existence. And since these default images differ from culture to culture, we are back where we started: Even vanilla word-substitutions are betrayals, which of course would imply that full translation is a travesty, is a pipe dream, is impossible.

A Ringing Resolution in C

But I will not stop there. I don't believe it. Despite the grain of truth that resides in the thesis that cross-language, cross-culture substitutability of words is shaky, translation is still possible. I do not and never will subscribe to *Traduttore, traditore,* even though I admire its ring. As Galileo might have put it, *Eppur si traduce.* George Steiner puts it this way:

> We *do* speak of the world and to one another. We *do* translate intra- and interlingually and have done so since the beginning of human history. The defence of translation has the immense advantage of abundant, vulgar fact....
>
> The argument from perfection, which, essentially, is that of Du Bellay, Dr. Johnson, Nabokov, and so many others, is facile. No human product can be perfect. No duplication, even of materials which are conventionally labelled as identical, will turn out a total facsimile. Minute differences and asymmetries persist. To dismiss the validity of translation because it is not always possible and never perfect is absurd. What does need clarification, say the translators, is the *degree* of fidelity to be pursued in each case, the tolerance allowed as between different jobs of work.

On Words and their Magical Halos

In Sweden's Nationalmuseum in Stockholm about a year ago, I saw a beautiful oil painting by a little-known Danish painter named Ring, done in about 1896. It showed a woman — in fact, Ring's wife — sitting in a flowery bathrobe at a table in a charming porch, reading a newspaper and drinking her coffee out of a china cup, white with light blue designs on it, if I recall correctly. When I saw that painting, I was touched to the core. There, brought to life again, was my beloved wife Carol, drinking her beloved cup of morning coffee and reading her beloved *New York Times*. I stared for a long time. I tried to make out the words in the paper, but could not. It could have been in any language — Danish, French, English. The coffee could have been any coffee — Swedish, Italian, American. The scene could have been in many places — Odense, Bologna, Bloomington. It was 1896 but it could easily have been 1986. And it was Ring's wife but it could easily have been my Carol.

To say that translation is impossible is to say that experiences cannot resemble one another. Let us translate, somewhat liberally, Ring's painting into language, and see it from that perspective: "Every morning she drank her cup of coffee and read her newspaper with pleasure." And now let us look at it in French, transposed word for word without any rearrangement: *Chaque matin elle buvait sa tasse de café et lisait son journal avec plaisir.* In fact, let us look at them right next to each other, nearly aligned:

Every morning she drank her cup of coffee and read her newspaper with pleasure.
Chaque matin elle buvait sa tasse de café et lisait son journal avec plaisir.

Yes, *nearly* aligned; they are not *perfectly* aligned. One gets a little ahead of the other and then they fall back into alignment, then there is another speed-up and another falling-back again. Little local bursts of speed are compensated by subsequent brief slowings-down, and so it goes. In the end, they arrive at about the same point. And as I said, there is a perfect word-for-word mapping between these two mated sentences, much as there seemed to be some kind of deep resonance, a nearly perfect alignment, between Ring's tender feelings for his wife and mine for mine, both gone. You cannot tell me that Ring did not love that woman. His love for her is as clear and sure as is the morning light in his painting.

Is the seemingly innocent word-for-word translation of these sentences into each other in fact fourteen separately insidious mini-betrayals, adding up to one grotesque, huge betrayal? French roast, it's true, is stronger than a mere can coffee. And "paper of news" is hardly synonymous with "daily" (*journal*). Indeed, why is "her" rendered first by *sa,* then *son*? Is my French betraying my English? And am I betraying Ring's love for his wife when I read his painting through my own life? If so, then human communication is simply impossible, it's all a farce — but that's a line I simply will not buy.

How Do You Say "Jazzercise" in Aramaic?

None of the foregoing is to deny that there are times when translation, even of simple passages, is very difficult. In any given language, there are words that seem as natural and obvious as "1 + 1 = 2", yet which are vexing as anything to translate into some other language. There can be holes.

One time many years ago in Paris, Bob French and some friends and I were out to dinner and this topic cropped up. I asked Bob which English words, in his experience, were the hardest to translate into French. He thought for a while, and then said that to the best of his recollection, the hardest word he had ever run across was — I kid you not — the word "bob", in the sense of "bobbing for apples". He said there just was no way to get this image across in France without spelling it out in a whole phrase. I nearly exploded with laughter. "Bob," I said, "Did you say 'bob'? Did I hear you say that the hardest thing to say in French, according to Mr. Bob French, is 'bob'?!" The amazing truth is that Bob had never made the connection with his name, like Monty Python's hilariously un-self-aware Mr. Smoketoomuch, to whom it had never once in his life occurred that someone might hear his name as suggestive of an individual who had the bad habit of setting the distal ends of tobacco-sticks aflame and then inhaling an unhealthy dose of the fumes they give off.

Just as people can have blind spots, so can languages. For instance, how do you say "skyjacking" in Hun, or "ribosome" in Phoenician, or "jazzercise" in Aramaic? For aerobics fanatics who are also into time travel, this last would seem an important — indeed, a crucial and indispensable — word to know. And yet, for all its utility and centrality, the word simply did not exist in Aramaic. It was a hole.

Fortunately, Hebrew, a close cousin to Aramaic, is filling that gaping hole and many similar ones. Indeed, as the state of Israel has revived Hebrew from a kind of coma it went into some 2,000 years ago, thousands of such questions have had to be supplied with answers over the past fifty or so years. Thus there exists an official council in Israel that is charged with concocting official pure-Hebrew expressions for such notions as:

car • bicycle • jet airplane • takeoff • parking meter • supermarket • refrigerator • tin can • can-opener • computer • commuter • radio • electricity • battery • protein • hubcap • typewriter • loudspeaker • ballpoint pen • soft drink • condom • pornography • striptease • comic strip • brassiere • pantyhose • horoscope • soccer • pole vault • stopwatch • photofinish • instant replay • talk show • television commercial • drug dealer • junk food • garbage dump • recycling • meltdown • fallout • stand-up comedian • software • video recorder • skyjacking • racism • feminism • sexual harassment • compact disc • tyrannosaurus • jazzercise

and on and on *ad nauseam*.

On Words and their Magical Halos   ◆ ◆ ◆   *293*

It is somewhat ironic that Hebrew should be striving to keep itself so pure, since in Hitler's times, it was the German language that was being analogously Aryanized — that is, aggressively stripped of foreign influence and thus carried back towards the purity of its ancient Gothic origins. This led to the banishment of *Telephon* in favor of *Fernsprecher* ("farspeaker") and many other analogous retro-innovations.

Translating between Incommensurate Cultures

This list, incidentally, which I drew up just to illustrate the fantastic richness and complexity of a modern lexicon, can also serve an unintended purpose: that of gauging one's true mastery of a language. You think you know French/Chinese/Hebrew well? How many of those precisely fifty terms — of which, if you are an adult native speaker of American English, you probably know every last one — can you write down, cold, right now, in French/Chinese/Hebrew? Take your score, *n*, and calculate *n*/50. That will tell you, very crudely speaking, what fraction of an adult native speaker you are. Or 2*n* gives you the percentage. (Of course, this applies only to people who haven't seen the list before. You can't just memorize all fifty items and from then on award yourself a rating of 100 percent!)

Oh, silly, silly me! Some of the items in my list of fifty do not exist in other cultures! That, in fact, was my whole point in asking about terms for skyjacking, ribosomes, and jazzercise in various ancient languages. So my "linguistic-mastery test" is deeply flawed.

My thoughtless error reminds me of a tale that David Moser told me he had read somewhere about an anthropologist studying a primitive tribe in some remote land. A member of the tribe who had started to get the hang of the anthropologist's constant queries about the tribe's habits decided one day to turn the tables, and walked up and said, "In *our* village, when we want to shoo a goat out of our hut, we say *Tak-tak*. What do you say in *your* village, when a goat wanders into your hut?" My tacit implication that there must be standard words or phrases for "horoscope", "sexual harassment", "talk show", and "stand-up comedian" in, say, Mongolian or Dyirbal (spoken by certain Australian aborigines) is in some sense an American translation of this tribe member's naïveté.

The flip side of this naïveté coin is represented by an interesting fact cited by Willis Barnstone in his remarkable study *The Poetics of Translation*:

> There are no lambs trotting on the ice meadows of the Arctic where Eskimos live. Translators of the Bible into Eskimo have resorted to the phrase "Seal of God" for "Lamb of God". In this instance the translators saw their ecclesiastical purpose to provide a meaningful text in Eskimo rather than to use Eskimo as a subtext for learning cultural meanings in an English translation of Hebrew and Greek scriptures.

Compounds: Transparent, Translucent, Opaque

The famous German-style strategy for the building of new words, using a large but fairly well-defined core of primitive constituents out of which to make compounds, like making molecules out of atoms, is ubiquitous in language, but each language has its own unique style of compound-building, and moreover, what is compound in one language will be primitive in another. This makes for some amazing contrasts and, of course, knotty translation problems.

A couple of pages back, I pointed out the contrast between the words "newspaper" and *journal*. What I find subtle here is the degree to which the components "news" and "paper" are buried, mostly unheard, in the English word. Thus as I typed "newspaper" right above *journal* in the sentence about Ring's painting, it never occurred to me that I was typing *two* English words to just *one* French one; it felt very ordinary, just one unit associated with one unit, much like "she"/*elle*, "coffee"/*café*, "pleasure"/*plaisir*. Only when I consciously scanned all the vertically mated pairs of words did the amount of hidden betrayal in this particular pair leap to my eye. It was also at that moment that I consciously recalled the root *jour* inside *journal*, something one knows but doesn't think about. From this novel perspective, "newspaper" and *journal* suddenly seemed enormously distant from each other. Only when the words are opaque, when their roots are buried underground, are the words excellent translations of each other. When their roots emerge into view, making the compounds transparent, then their match seems to go down in quality.

It would be ridiculously facile to try to divide compound words into just two categories — "transparent" and "opaque" — as if this were a sharp binary distinction. In fact, there are all imaginable shades of translucency, just as there are all imaginable shades of "deadness" of metaphors. Although English, French, and German would be plenty rich enough to provide endless grist for the transparency/opacity mill that we are now entering, let us nonetheless go further afield and take a glance at Chinese, since looking at a distant language often helps to shed a clearer light on what is up close.

Compounds in Mandarin

Modern Mandarin Chinese, like Fascist-era German and modern Hebrew, and in contrast to Japanese and modern German, has valiantly sought to resist the influx of Western words for all sorts of things, and hence is crammed with analogues to *Fernsprecher* ("telephone" itself being *diànhuà* — "electrospeak", perhaps, or more concisely, "sparkspeak"). The language is built on compound words no less pervasively than is German.

There are thousands of single characters — all monosyllabic — which are the building blocks of the language, and for some historical reason, the language exerts a strong phonetic pressure to make bisyllabic chunks, thus using exactly two characters.

A simple example is *dàxiàng*, the standard way of saying "elephant". The curious thing is that aside from *dà*, which means "big", the other component, *xiàng*, already means "elephant" on its own. But people almost never say *xiàng* alone. On the other hand, when it is needed inside compounds, "elephant" is usually rendered by *xiàng* alone — thus *xiàngyá*, literally meaning "elephant tooth", is the word for "ivory". (It would sound like a joke if someone said *dàxiàngyá*.)

The second component, *yá*, is a one-syllable term for "tooth" used solely in compounds (or poetic language); to say "tooth" by itself, one uses the two-character word *yáchǐ*, each of whose components on its own means "tooth" or "cog". Such quasi-redundancy is a recurrent pattern in the Chinese style of making bisyllabic compounds. Curiously, *yá* by itself can also mean "ivory", as in *yákuài*, which means "ivory chopsticks". And of course, the stand-alone word for "chopsticks" is not just *kuài*, but the two-syllable word *kuàizi*, meaning roughly "chopstick-things". (We shall come back to this final syllable in a little while, and get a sense for how complex it actually is.)

A second strong pressure in modern Mandarin is, whenever possible, to juxtapose pairs of two-syllable words, thus giving elegant four-syllable structures (*e.g., fēicháng yǒuqián* — "extremely wealthy", but in literal terms, "un-common have-money"). This does not mean that three-syllable words don't exist; there are plenty of them (*e.g., yǒuyìsi* — "interesting", literally "have-meaning"), just as there are one-syllable words. But there is a constant real-time metrical pressure on speakers of Mandarin — a pressure to assemble structures having a "good rhythm" — that has no analogue in any of the Western languages I have studied.

Contrary to popular myth, the vast majority of Chinese words are polysyllabic, not monosyllabic, which is to say that the vast majority of Chinese words are compound words. And, as is the case for every other language, Chinese compound words range all over the map in terms of their degree of clarity or opacity. Some are very clear *a priori*, some make sense but only after the fact, and some remain dumfounding even after you know their meanings.

My favorite example of all Mandarin compounds is the word for "thing": *dōngxi*, which literally means "east–west". Yet few native speakers ever hear those parts inside it. It is just as seamless-seeming to Chinese speakers as are "wardrobe" and "doughnut" to English speakers, or *beaucoup* and *sourire* to French speakers ("much/many" built as "lovely-blow", and "smile" built as "under-laugh"). I presume its etymology has to do with the idea that from east to west, from north to south, all one ever finds is *things*. But virtually no one ponders its etymology: for 999 speakers out of 1,000, *dōngxi* is just an unanalyzed chunk.

A handful of other examples, sliding down the slope from clarity towards opacity, are these: *xiǎoshuō* ("small-tell", which, once you know that it means "a novel", you can sort of see why, although *dàshuō* would have made more sense), *mǎshàng* ("horse-upon", meaning "immediately", which seems not too illogical), *míngbái* ("bright-white", but it means "to understand", and this is definitely not obvious), *fángshì* ("house-stuff" or perhaps "domestic-matters", but it actually means "sexual intercourse of a married couple"), *guàchǐ* ("hang-tooth", but it means "to mention" — a compound just about as opaque as our "crackpot" or their own *dōngxi*).

Dinosaur Names: Transparent versus Opaque

A particularly stark cross-language contrast involving compound words is given by dinosaur names, whose subliminally evoked flavors held me quite in thrall as a child, and which seem to exert a similar grip on today's children. In this microscopic region of semantic space, the contrast between Chinese and English is quite extreme, as the following table demonstrates:

English	Chinese	Literal gloss
brontosaurus	*léilóng*	thunder dragon
tyrannosaurus	*bàwánglóng*	tyrant-king dragon
pterodactyl	*yìshǒulóng*	wing–hand dragon
stegosaurus	*jiànlóng*	sword dragon
triceratops	*sānjiǎolóng*	three-horn dragon

All other dinosaurs, of course, have similarly transparent names in Chinese. This strongly suggests that the image — or, more precisely, the aura of connotations — that swirls around these beasts in the mind of a Chinese speaker is truly different from ours. Thus, as their names all end in *lóng*, dinosaurs are seen as *dragons,* a concept playing a central role in Chinese mythology. Given how permeated Chinese culture is by the notion of *lóng,* would it not be inevitable that many of the feelings associated with dragons would subliminally seep into small children's absorbent and uncritical minds?

A term like "wing–hand" is so much more concrete and mundane than is the exotic, strangely-spelled word "pterodactyl" that one can't help but assume that the feelings evoked thereby have to be radically different. Of course, to anyone who knows ancient Greek, it's obvious that "pterodactyl" means "wing finger", which, if you analyze it, is almost the same as the Chinese term — but most of us don't know one whit of ancient Greek. Still, a sensitive speaker of English, scanning a strange string of letters like "pterodactyl", would certainly sniff *some*thing funny in it, vague hints of the presence of ancient and alien parts inside the word, even if they are in a completely opaque language. And such a person, upon repeatedly seeing the ending "-saurus" for one dinosaur after another, would naturally build up a sense of its implications, despite not knowing that it is ancient Greek for "lizard".

The little table would seem to imply that a Chinese speaker's and an English speaker's experiences of "dinosaur-ness" are profoundly different in flavor. But maybe that is not the case. Perhaps the separate visibility of the constituents inside the Chinese compounds gradually fades as one approaches puberty, so that, much as in our own compound words "blackboard", "understand", and "newspaper", the components eventually melt together like two pieces of wax left out in the noonday sun, yielding what feels like a partless whole.

This type of word-melting happens all the time in German (*e.g.,* *Volkswagen* is first heard by a small child as *Volks Wagen,* meaning "folks' wagon" — a genuine description — but in the end becomes as routine and unanalyzed a name as "VW"), and also in English (does the name "New Jersey" make you think of a fresh-bought sweatshirt?). If the Chinese dinosaur names follow this type of evolutionary pathway as a child matures, with parts slowly fusing and slowly losing their separate identities, then who's to say if, in the end, the auras of feeling unconsciously evoked in an adult mind by the Chinese names aren't indistinguishable from those evoked by the English names?

The Mystique of Elementary Seeds

A case quite similar to that of dinosaur names is that of the names for elementary particles, of which some of the most common are shown in the little table below:

English	Chinese	Literal gloss
electron	*diànzǐ*	spark seed
proton	*zhìzǐ*	primal seed
neutron	*zhōngzǐ*	neutral seed
neutrino	*zhōngwēizǐ*	neutral seedlet
photon	*guāngzǐ*	light seed

Note that the final constituent in these names is always *zǐ*, which is the character we saw earlier inside the word for "chopsticks". I called it "thing" there, while here I've rendered it as "seed". But the fact of the matter is that it is a tremendous oversimplification — dare I say "grotesque betrayal"? — to render *zǐ* by "seed", by "thing", or by any other single English noun, since off of that very high-frequency and densely-laden character dangles a phenomenally complex constellation of meanings, including "honored master", "person", "son", "fledgling", "sprout", "seed", "egg", "kernel", "bead", and "coin". This *zǐ* is, by the way, the same "tse" as ends the names of ancient and venerated Chinese philosophers such as Laotse and Chuangtse ("Old Honored Master" and "Serious Honored Master"). What a zoo of meanings has *zǐ*!

As did the dinosaur-name table, the particle-name table reveals that the Chinese terms suggest far more tangibility and visualizability than ours do. To me, such concreteness gives the impression that the entities being described are quite ordinary, but simply extremely small — in other words, like so-called *classical* particles, which are essentially microscopic billiard balls. There is no hint in the words themselves that, in fact, electrons and protons and so forth are unprecedentedly weird entities that are not amenable to being visualized in any ordinary way, entities so weird that even the super-general umbrella term "thing" sounds too normal to apply. "Entity" somehow fits particles far better than does "thing".

I am alluding to such bizarre aspects of the microworld as the wave–particle duality of quantum mechanics and its many hard-to-swallow consequences, such as Heisenberg's uncertainty principle and the apparent nondeterminacy of the laws of physics, something that the discoverer of special and general relativity and many of the underlying principles of quantum mechanics never reconciled himself with.

It is, in summary, the subliminal suggestion that classical behavior might exist at the deepest and most hidden micro-level that I find so misleading about the Chinese words. Subatomic particles are nothing at all like seeds or eggs or bits or beads or sons or sprouts. They are strange, strange entities having no analogues in our macroscopic lives. To me, they *demand* terms that suggest their totally alien nature.

Poul Anderson's Eerie Etym-Splitting

As a boy, I loved the clueless opacity of eerie words like "photon"; it suggested that photons, though somehow making up plain old light, are themselves not quite of this world, but belong to some *other* world, an unimaginably alien kind of world.

Because of my long-standing partiality to opaque, mystery-exuding compound words, I was riveted by an article someone sent me, with no explanation at all, a few years ago. It was by the science-fiction writer Poul Anderson, of whom I had only vaguely heard, and it bore the cryptic title "Uncleftish Beholding". As I don't normally go in for science fiction, I put

On Words and their Magical Halos   ◆ ◆ ◆   **299**

it aside at first, but when I finally tackled it, many months later, I couldn't put it down. Without further ado, here are its first four paragraphs:

> For most of its being, mankind did not know what things are made of, but could only guess. With the growth of worldken, we began to learn, and today we have a beholding of stuff and work that watching bears out, both in the workstead and in daily life.
>
> The underlying kinds of stuff are the *firststuffs*, which link together in sundry ways to give rise to the rest. Formerly we knew of ninety-two firststuffs, from waterstuff, the lightest and barest, to ymirstuff, the heaviest. Now we have made more, such as aegirstuff and helstuff.
>
> The firststuffs have their being as motes called *unclefts*. These are mighty small: one seedweight of waterstuff holds a tale of them like unto two followed by twenty-two naughts. Most unclefts link together to make what are called *bulkbits*. Thus, the waterstuff bulkbit bestands of two waterstuff unclefts, the sourstuff bulkbit of two sourstuff unclefts, and so on. (Some kinds, such as sunstuff, keep alone; others, such as iron, cling together in chills when in the fast standing; and there are yet more yokeways.) When unlike unclefts link in a bulkbit, they make *bindings*. Thus, water is a binding of two waterstuff unclefts with one sourstuff uncleft, while a bulkbit of one of the forestuffs making up flesh may have a thousand or more unclefts of these two firststuffs together with coalstuff and chokestuff.
>
> At first it was thought that the uncleft was a hard thing that could be split no further; hence the name. Now we know it is made up of lesser motes. There is a heavy *kernel* with a forward bernstonish lading, and around it one or more light motes with backward ladings. The least uncleft is that of everyday waterstuff. Its kernel is a lone forwardladen mote called a *firstbit*. Outside it is a backwardladen mote called a *bernstonebit*. The firstbit has a heaviness about 1840-fold that of the bernstonebit. Early worldken folk thought bernstonebits swing around the kernel like the Earth around the Sun, but now we understand they are more like waves or clouds.

It is not too hard to discern that its topic is the modern scientific view of the "motes" that make up matter, starting at the chemical level ("bulkbits" are molecules; "waterstuff" and "sourstuff", analogues to German's *Wasserstoff* and *Sauerstoff,* are hydrogen and oxygen), progressing towards the atomic level (where "uncleft" echoes the etymology of "atom"), and then descending ever further in size to the realms of nuclei and elementary particles (thus "forwardladen firstbits" and "backwardladen bernstonebits" are positively-charged protons and negatively-charged electrons, the latter reflecting the fact that ἤλεκτρον is ancient Greek for "amber", which in German is *Bernstein*).

The simple secret of "Uncleftish Beholding" ("Atomic Theory") is the inexorable eradication — nay, ruthless uprooting! — of all Latin and Greek roots from English, and the concomitant invention of terms based solely on pure Anglo-Saxon roots. The resultant tone is distinctly that of medieval alchemy, yet the phenomena being described are as modern as modems and jazzercise. It is, to revive an earlier term, a retrotranstemporation of a never-written article in ordinary English about the makeup of matter.

I was so caught up in the vivid eerieness of this new way of looking at the atomic world that I transtemporated Anderson's whole piece forwards in time several centuries (*i.e.,* I performed an "antiretrotranstemporation" on it), thus bringing into existence the "original article" that never had been. Here, "for a showdeal", are two matching excerpts:

> Some of the higher samesteads are *splitly*. That is, when a neitherbit strikes the kernel of one — as, for a showdeal, ymirstuff-235 — it bursts it into lesser kernels and free neitherbits; the latter can then split more ymirstuff-235. When this happens, weight shifts into work. It is not much of the whole, but nevertheless it is awesome.
>
> With enough strength, lightweight unclefts can be made to togethermelt. In the Sun, through a row of strikings and lightrottings, four unclefts of waterstuff in this wise become one of sunstuff. Again, some weight is lost as work, and again this is greatly big when set beside the work gotten from a minglingish doing such as fire.
>
> Today we wield both kinds of uncleftish doings in weapons, and kernelish splitting gives us heat and bernstoneness. We hope to do likewise with together-melting, which would yield an unhemmed wellspring of work for mankindish goodgain. Soothly we live in mighty years!

*   *   *

> Some of the higher isotopes are *fissile*. That is, when a neutron hits the nucleus of one — uranium-235, for example — it breaks it into smaller nuclei and free neutrons; the latter can then split more uranium-235. When this happens, mass is converted into energy. It is not a large percentage of the mass, but nevertheless it is impressive.
>
> With enough energy, lightweight atoms can be made to fuse. In the Sun, through a series of collisions and radioactive decays, four atoms of hydrogen become a single atom of helium. Again, some mass is lost as energy, and this energy is enormous when compared to the energy obtained from a chemical process such as combustion.
>
> Today we use both kinds of atomic processes in weapons, and nuclear fission provides heat and electricity. We hope to do likewise with fusion, which would yield an unlimited source of energy for human profit. Truly we live in great times!

The Old One's Ideas Bend under Constraints

In Anderson's piece (whose variety of English one might sensibly dub "Ander-Saxon"), there are brief mentions of photons, quantum mechanics, quantum leaps, and the special theory of relativity, as this excerpt reveals:

> For although light oftenest behaves as a wave, it can be looked on as a mote — the *lightbit*. We have already said by the way that a mote of stuff can behave not only as a chunk, but also as a wave. Down among the unclefts, things do not happen in steady flowings, but in leaps over midway bestandings that are forbidden. The knowledge-hunt of this is called *lump beholding*.
>
> Nor are stuff and work unakin. Rather, they are groundwise the same, and one can be shifted into the other. The kinship between them is that work is like unto weight manifolded by the fourside of the haste of light.

In other words, $E = mc^2$. And who was it that dreamed up this stunning talekennish likeness? Although Anderson names no names in his work, we all call back to our minds that it was Albert One Stone, that mightily wideknown but soft-spoken worldkenseeker.

And it was old One Stone, too, who first guessed and then showed that the Pull Down on all things — the Pull that gives us weight, the Pull toward the ground that we feel at all times — is not a true pull at all, but what is known as a "fake pull" — the same kind of pull as pulls things from the hub toward the rim of a wheel that spins. Such pulls are called "fake" since they all go up in smoke when you make a shift in what you deem to be "at rest". Though but a shift in your head — though but a trick in how you look at things — such a shift casts all things in a new light. Mind you, fake pulls are not like most pulls, for they make all things, be they great or slight in weight, pick up speed at one and the same clip (a truth most odd, in truth). Thus, since the Pull Down on all things is this way, old One Stone was tipped off that he might try to see it as a fake pull. No one else had thought to do this, though it had been plain as day for all to see for scores of years. When One Stone tried this out, he soon found that the Pull Down could well come from a Bend in the shape of the Great Bare Frame whose three sides are called "length", "width", and "height" (that is, north and south, east and west, up and down), and through which we all wend our way. This Great Frame, which no one can see, has Stuff in it here and there; and the Bend in it, which no one can see, comes from the Stuff in the Frame: The more Stuff found in a spot, the more bent is the Frame near that spot, and thus the more the Pull seems strong there. The Bend is, if truth be told, in Time as well as in the Frame, for Time, too, can be thought of as a side with no ends, a side that runs from "no more" to "not yet", and when this fourth side is blent with the three old sides of the Great Bare Frame, it makes one thing — a new Great Bare Frame with four sides, none of which can be seen or felt, yet which are all in truth there. A Bend in such a weird Frame is a most hard thing to think of, and yet it is the way things are: It is what makes sticks and stones fall to Earth, our Moon float high up in the sky, and light from far stars bend in flight. All these things old One Stone wrote down four score years back, and in ten years or so from that time, all had been shown to be true by folks whose job is to gaze at the night sky's lights. New Town's old laws were thus shoved to the side and flung in the bin of "once right as right can be, and still kind of right, but now a bit less right".

By the way, I wrote that long chunk (and this short chunk) while tied by two tight ropes at once: first of all, I used but words that have no truck with tongues that folks in old Greece and Rome once spoke, way back when, in days long gone; on top of that, all words I used have but one speech bite each. And this is why one might say, as a bit of a joke yet for that no less in truth, that I have here killed two birds with One Stone.

Expanding Spheres of Connotations

Anderson's piece had a somewhat paradoxical effect on me. When I was a young boy, I found opaque terms like "photon" and "neutrino" endlessly suggestive and mystery-laden — but over the years, especially in my graduate-school days, I gradually got used to them and they became quite routine items in my vocabulary. But then, when I read "Uncleftish Beholding", my mind was once again jolted and disoriented for a few brief days by the eerie vantage point on modern physics embodied in the terms of Ander-Saxon, mundane and down-to-earth though they sounded, and to some extent I was again rendered able to savor that feeling of cosmic strangeness and awe that I had first known when I encountered the more opaque Greco-Latinate terms. What a surprising turnaround!

This paradoxical personal experience gave me a new way of thinking about the Chinese names for elementary particles, which, when analyzed, seem so much like Anderson's. My thought was this: Although the Chinese names have connotations that, to someone who knows quantum mechanics, appear overly classical and of-this-world, it is nonetheless possible that a Chinese speaker encountering them for the first time could intuitively and easily attach to them an aura of mystery, simply on the basis of the very strange and counterintuitive statements in which they occur. In such a case, the monosyllabic classical-Chinese word *zǐ*, as a consequence of its tight association with quantum-mechanical weirdness, would take on a new aura of very modern connotations, enriching the old aura made up out of "egg", "bead", "sprout", and so on.

It is not as if these new flavors would be added onto the old halo for no reason: It was precisely because *zǐ* exuded something of the proper aroma *already* that it was chosen as a suffix for particle names. And thus, like a snowball ever gaining in radius as it rolls, a word's halo of meanings constantly evolves and broadens, ever adding newer outer layers to older inner ones — not only in Chinese, but in all the world's languages.

On Words and their Magical Halos　　　　　　　　　　◆ ◆ ◆　*303*

Poems X:

~ Struttin' my Stuff ~

* * * * *
* * *
*
*

Here we have another conceit like "Gentle Gem", but this one is based on a rather unexpected metaphor — that of pugilism. In it, Clément's sweet little *mignonne* becomes a tough cookie, a vamp, a feisty fox, a saucy, gum-chewing boxing moll. But why in the world boxing? Well, just serendipity — I went with the flow of what fell my way. All it took was the little rhyme "Use your right!" that jumped to mind for line 7's "Gotta fight!" (it was subsequently slightly modified) — and all of a sudden I found myself swimming in images of punching and counts and bells and knock-outs and so forth, and they didn't let go of me until the whole poem had been transported into the metaphorical boxing ring.

The original opening, devised before the boxing conceit had been dreamt up, was "Maiden cute, / I salute." Once I hit line 8 and launched the boxing metaphor, I easily worked my way down toward the end under its influence. Coming in for a landing in the last three lines, I entertained this idea: "You'll be one / Boxing beaut, / Maiden cute", closing things out in the usual symmetric fashion. I hadn't yet figured out lines 24 and 25, though my plan was for God to appear somewhere in there. As I tackled them, though, I found myself unexpectedly boxed in by the word "one" on my tentative line 26, unable to find a good rhyme for it to flesh out line 25. Slightly squirming under this pressure, I hunted for alternative pathways, and while exploring, encountered the nearly irresistible line "Box your pox", which so tightly rolls together the pugilistic conceit with the illness. This phrase cried out to be used as line 27 — but given the rhyming constraint, that meant I would have to kiss "Maiden cute" good-bye. Luckily, just at that moment, "Goldilocks" dropped out of the sky to fill in for the unlucky maiden in the last line. "Box your pox, Goldilocks" sounded so good that I adopted it without a moment's hesitation. And of course, this decision then wrapped back around to the poem's start as well, knocking the hapless maiden out for the second and final time. Accompanying this knock-out was a switch in line 2, from "I salute" to "Feisty fox" (actually, "Pretty fox" in early versions). It then was no problem to fill in lines 24–26, although God wound up getting left in limbo. (Amusingly, when you subtract "God" from "Goldilocks", what remains is "Sock ill".)

There is a sharp irony in the effect I've just described, a little like when children grow up healthy and happy and then utterly reject the folks who begot and fostered them — namely, the first line triggers avenues of thought that lead to a successful sequence of lines all the way to the very end, at which point it is discovered that a different last line would work even better, and so by symmetry, the first line, thanks to which all of this came about, is thanklessly dumped into the sea. This could be called "unintentional covering of one's tracks". We saw a similar phenomenon elsewhere in this same poem: "Use your right!", having served its purpose, was also discarded in the end — in that case, not entirely but partially. Still, it's the same idea. Despite its ironic flavor, unintentional tracks-covering — the downstream jettisoning of a once-key ingredient in the genesis of a work of art — is rampant, in my experience, and not just in poetry translation but in all sorts of creative activities, such as musical composition, artistic design, and the writing of prose essays.

My favorite rhyme in this poem is that of "jelly *dough*nuts" with "they *go* nuts" in lines 21–23; I was disappointed, however, to hear exactly that rhyme when I took my kids to see the movie *Willie Wonka and the Chocolate Factory*. Nothing new under the sun, I guess.

As I go over this poem, I am led to muse on how huge a debt I owe — no, not just I, *we* — how huge a debt our entire contemporary English-speaking world owes to the likes of Cole Porter, Ira Gershwin, "Yip" Harburg, P. G. Wodehouse, Oscar Hammerstein, Mitchell Parish, Noël Coward, Frank Loesser, Dorothy Fields, Lorenz Hart, Johnny Mercer, Otto Harbach, Sammy Cahn, Gus Kahn, Al Dubin, Alan Jay Lerner, B. G. DeSylva, Ted Koehler, Andy Razaf, and so, so many other names, now forgotten but surviving in rhymes, the lyric lyricists of America's Golden Age of Song: the collective Shakespeare of our century.

Goldilocks

D. Hofstadter

Goldilocks,
Feisty fox,
You're a pip,
Whom the grippe,
Sad to say,   5
Has in sway.
Gotta fight!
With a right
To the chin,
Babe, you'll win!   10
No kid gloves!
Clement loves
You, ya vamp —
You're his champ!
Champs must eat;   15
Wimpy wheat
Bread's a sham,
Without jam!
To gain brawn,
Champs chomp on   20
Jelly dough-
nuts; they go
Nuts for pies
(Your top prize-
fighters do).   25
As for you,
Box that pox,
Goldilocks!

This gentle poem merits inclusion for two reasons, I think. The first is its unusual tone, compared to many of my other efforts. Instead of lighthearted wordplay and merriment, there is a rather subdued air of concern, and yet the language is still modern in flavor, imbuing it with a quite different feel from, say, Bob French's similarly subdued but ancient-flavored "Fairest Friend".

By itself, the softish tone might not suffice to mark the poem off as all that remarkable, but "Turtle Dove" also has a special structural property that we have seen just once before: like "Gentle Gem", it is built out of semantic tristichs. (Chronologically, however, "Turtle Dove" was the first translation of "Ma Mignonne" designed to have this structural feature.) As we saw in the case of "Gentle Gem", since 3 doesn't divide 28, there has to be an exception to the tristich pattern somewhere, and here it occurs in lines 10–13, which can be perceived either as two semantic couplets or as one semantic quatrain.

In keeping with the overall tone, there is only a little wordplay in "Turtle Dove", one time playing on the double meaning of "just desserts", the other time flipping the word "lackluster" into "luster's lack". Perhaps the poem's most charming touch is the sentiment "Your old skirts, now a bit loose, will fit" — an indirect sartorial manner of expressing the hope that the sick maiden will soon regain her former fuller physique.

Turtle Dove

D. Hofstadter

Turtle dove,
All my love
Wings its way.
Your long stay,
So cooped in,   5
Is a sin.
Conquer, please,
Your disease —
Give it rout.
Then come out   10
With due haste:
Do not waste
Precious time.
That's what I'm
Asking you,   15
Dear, to do.
Jams galore
Will be your
Just desserts.
Your old skirts,   20
Now a bit
Loose, will fit.
Cheeks aflush,
You will crush
Luster's lack.   25
God, bring back
The health of
Turtle dove.

The opening line "My wee one" was selected expressly because of its mild phonetic resemblance to *Ma mignonne.* From the start of "My Wee One", there is a sweet and concerned avuncular tone, clearly addressed to a very little child. In line 5, the reader is led down a very short garden pathway by the positive connotations of "has been a ball" — but when the corner is rounded on line 6, a far grimmer image is glimpsed: of shackled prisoners hobbling along in a sweltering chain gang.

On line 18 there is another one of those amphisbænic — that is to say, two-headed — enjambments, a phenomenon that we first ran into in "Pretty Dear" and then in "Little Gem". Here are the four examples we have so far seen of the phenomenon:

ried a lit-

o my bront-

er ain't spin-

onade. Rem-

Taken out of context, each of them looks pretty outrageous as a line of poetry, it must be admitted. But that's what makes them fun.

That infamous old cure-all of cod liver oil — the bane of sick children a century or more ago — gets a well-deserved mention near the bottom, as does a jocular exhortation to eat that I heard so often from my father as I was growing up: "It's good for you — it'll put hair on your chest!" When little, I hated the idea of growing hair on my chest, but my Dad's remark always got a good laugh anyway. And it was funnier, being something of a gender bender, when he said it to my younger sister Laurie.

Speaking of gender benders, line 27 here carries out an unexpected sex switch. It was certainly not necessary for this poem, and indeed, I vacillated between the words "hon'" and "son", but in the end opted for the latter, partly because of the tone it exudes and partly because of the novelty of the effect. Of course I would never have done so had this been my first translation. But then, I wouldn't have done the "ball and chain" or the "hair on your chest" joke, either.

My Wee One

D. Hofstadter

My wee one,
Here's to fun
These next days.
Your long stay's
Been a ball   5
And chain. Crawl
From your cell
(That small hell)
To get well!
Wee one, smell   10
How spring's sprung,
With old Un-
cle Clement.
Don't lament
Your lost time   15
Lacking lime
Juice and lem-
onade. Rem-
edy that:
Swig a vat   20
Of the pair!
'Twill put hair
On your chest,
And what's best:
It's not cod   25
Liver! God
Bless you, son —
My wee one.

A couple of amusing but raunchy pornographic versions of "Ma Mignonne" having been contributed by friends who will remain anonymous, I felt provoked to try to make a softer, though still suggestive, version aimed unambiguously at a lover. Thus resulted "Babe o' Mine", a poem that now sounds to me as if it could have come straight from the pen of David Moser. One of its features — and I honestly have no memory of whether this was my conscious intent or just a crazy fluke — is that its semantic chunks are couplets, just like Marot's, and also, like his, are 180 degrees out of phase with the rhyming chunks. There are a couple of spots where "Babe o' Mine" goes a little blurry in its approximation to this ideal, but basically it preserves that wonderfully elegant property of the Marot.

Despite this good feature, I felt this was actually a pretty weak poem, and over the next few years, as I went back over my many attempts, I now and then focused in on this one and did a little patchwork on it. And just now, in putting this collection together, I did even more radical surgery, with the end result being an enormously transformed, almost unrecognizably different poem: "Darlin' Mine". One of the few features preserved all the way through this long series of modifications was the two-line semantic-chunk property. In fact, in "Darlin' Mine", no blurriness remains on this score. Of course, by this stage, that property, if ever it was coincidental, had certainly become very explicit and intentional.

There is a virtual continuum of tiny changes, hundreds if not thousands of them, connecting these two versions together. Obviously, it would be folly and soporific in the extreme to exhibit even one-tenth of that slow metamorphosis. Still, there is something fascinating about it, especially in this age of video "morphing" — smooth conversion of one complex visual image into a very different one (*e.g.*, a human face into a cat's face, or one American president into another one) by having a computer execute scads of simple algebraic interpolation formulas. If a series of intermediate images in the morphing is displayed in order, there is a tantalizing midway point where one can see both extremal images struggling to dominate. Something similar happens in my mind when I look at a set of printouts of intermediate stages between "Babe o' Mine" and "Darlin' Mine": the bridge is so smooth and gradual that it seems uncanny when one then looks at the remote endpoints it links. Since I have already exhibited something of this sort — sections of the bridge from "Little Gem" to "Gentle Gem" — I won't do it here.

Perhaps it was inevitable that sooner or later, someone would be reminded of the old American mining ballad "Clementine" and would be inspired to incorporate bits and pieces of it into a version of "Ma Mignonne". In any case, the idea occurred to me, and I played around with it. One option, perhaps the most natural one, would have been to have the poet undergo a sex-change operation, resulting in "Auntie" Clémentine Marot writing a get-well note to her adored young friend — perhaps mutated, for reasons of symmetry, into a male. But that route, though appealing, wasn't the one I chose to follow. Most likely I never considered it at all. Instead, I simply gave the name "Clementine" to the short, skirted child, holding tightly onto the idea that an unretouched C. Marot himself was still the sweet sentiments' author. Thus one will find fragments of "You are lost and gone forever, oh my darlin', Clementine" in the first few lines of this poem, and mixed in elsewhere one will hear recognizable snatches of the original Marot — most notably in the stretch from lines 10 to 14, where, through a liberal blending of techniques, *Et qu'on sorte* is rendered as "Hey, consort" and *Va, friande* as "Go free, and".

It is amusing to contrast the weight-oriented exhortations in these poems with those in Bob French's poems. Bob urges: "Stay in thin, slim trim, love dove." In contrast, "Babe o' Mine" hopes for a return to a full, voluptuous figure, while "Darlin' Mine" goes even further, unabashedly endorsing corpulence! It's a mini-Babel of competing voices on what's shapely and what's not.

Babe o' Mine	**Darlin' Mine**
D. Hofstadter	D. Hofstadter

Babe o' mine,	*Darlin' mine,*	
Gal divine,	*Clementine,*	
Here's a kiss.	*Greet the dawn!*	
It ain't bliss,	*Lost and gone,*	
Bein' sick.	*Gaunt and sick,*	5
Get up quick,	*Padlocked chick,*	
Take a spin!	*Squeeze through bars!*	
Don't stay in	*(Thank your stars*	
Where it's dark.	*It's no fort.)*	
For a lark,	*Hey, consort*	10
Go on out,	*With me, rose!*	
Jump about —	*That's Marot's*	
Clem's command!	*High command.*	
Hey, gourmande,	*Go free, and*	
You whose wish	*Fill your wish:*	15
Is a dish	*Snarf a dish-*	
Full of fruit,	*ful of fruit!*	
You should scoot	*Next thing, scoot*	
From your bed,	*From your lair;*	
And instead	*Gulp the air,*	20
Get some sun.	*Soak the sun.*	
Come on, hon' —	*Lastly, hon',*	
Losin' weight	*Don't lose weight!*	
Makes your great	*Want your great*	
Figure flat.	*Figure flat?*	25
Don't do that!	*God, not that!*	
Just get fine,	*Fat's divine,*	
Babe o' mine!	*Darlin' mine!*	

"Hey, Hot Lips!" moves a few steps further down the long path that would end up in an explicitly sexual interpretation of "Ma Mignonne". Here, however, things are still done essentially by innuendo and suggestion, somewhat in the spirit of my fellow Hoosier, Cole Porter, whose lyrics to "Let's Do It" (among so many others!) always struck me for their clever way of flirting with the off-color. Here is the third refrain of that song:

> *The nightingales in the dark do it;*
> *Larks, k-razy for a lark, do it;*
> *Let's do it, let's fall in love.*

> *Canaries, caged in the house, do it;*
> *When they're out of season, grouse do it;*
> *Let's do it, let's fall in love.*

> *The most sedate barnyard fowls do it,*
> *When a chanticleer cries;*
> *High-browed old owls do it —*
> *They're supposed to be wise.*

> *Penguins in flocks, on the rocks, do it;*
> *Even little cuckoos in their clocks do it;*
> *Let's do it, let's fall in love.*

The author of "Hey, Hot Lips!" seems, in line 2, to have a clairvoyant sense that the get-well wish will come out sounding wrong — and indeed, exactly as line 2 anticipates, the author's pen-and-ink tongue *does* trip on line 4. The resultant spoonerism — "Set well, goon" — has an amusing ring to it; in a somewhat similar manner, so does the juxtaposition, on lines 19–20, of "voice" and "box".

This poem comes very close to the ideal of having semantic distichs throughout; it messes up only in lines 4–5/6–7, where the first of two back-to-back hyphenated line-breaks of course prevents a clean separation between lines 5 and 6. Other than right there, however, there are semantic couplets throughout, and they always consist, just as they should, of an even-numbered and then an odd-numbered line.

Hey, Hot Lips!

D. Hofstadter

Hey, hot lips!
My tongue trips
As I croon,
"Set well, goon!"
But I'd soon-   5
er than spoon-
erize spoon.
Your eyes (swoon!)
Mesmerize,
So please rise   10
From those sheets
Your sweet feets
Are betwixt,
And be fixed
In a flash!   15
Gone, the rash
On your back!
Gone, the hack
In your voice!
"Box of choice   20
Candies, ma'am?
Brandies, ma'am,
As you please?"
Oh, I'll squeeze
You, will I —   25
First your thigh,
Then your hips.
Hey, hot lips!

As gradually I gained in skill and self-confidence, I realized that I was making new translations quite routinely and not finding the challenge nearly as hard as it had been at the beginning. For this reason, I decided one day to try imposing further constraints on myself — not blurry semantic ones such as a conceit or an overall tone, but really sharp, tight syntactic constraints. Such a proposal would have astounded me at the outset, but at this point I had made so much progress that it seemed completely reasonable.

And so, keenly aware of the fact that Marot himself had on occasion taken pleasure in composing acrostics (poems whose lines' first letters spell out a hidden message, usually someone's name), I thought that making an acrostic version would be an appropriate additional constraint to pile on. But this meant I would first of all have to devise a 28-letter secret message to embed in the lines' openings. And a moment's thought revealed that there was actually one further constraint, this one on the acrostic message itself: its first letter had to equal its last letter, so that the poem's first and last lines could be identical! This made the search for a good acrostic message in itself fairly tricky. I tried out a number of ideas involving the poem's original title (in either French or English), Marot's name, my own name, and other possibilities, and finally settled on the following 28-letter phrase, starting and ending with "t":

To a Damsel in Bed, by Clément Marot

Having selected this message to be inserted, I now had my job clearly cut out for me: write the 28 lines of the poem, using these initials! Although I didn't hold myself to the stricture of tight line-by-line fidelity to the original poem's meaning, I did my best in that direction.

You see the results to the right. One of the more amusing features of this version is its rather shaky attempt to suggest the *vous/tu* transition by addressing the Damsel in Bed as "miss" on one line and as "madame" on a nearby one (one more hat-tip to France). Other than that, this poem is not particularly strange-seeming, which in itself is quite strange.

I thought I might show how Marot played the acrostic game, in a poem honoring a woman named Maguelonne, contrasting her with the tragic and mythic Dido, who impaled herself when abandoned by her lover Æneas. Next to Marot's autoacrostic poem, I have given a slightly updated but still autoacrostic version of the story, in memory of J.L.B.K.O.

La bonne Maguelonne

Comme Dido, qui moult se courrouça
Lors qu'Eneas seule la delaissa,
En son pays tout ainsi Maguelonne
Mena son dueil. Comme tressaincte et bonne
En l'hospital toute sa fleur passa.
Nulle fortune oncques ne la blessa,
Toute constance en son cueur amassa,
Mieulx esperant, et ne fut point felonne
   comme Dido.
Aussi celluy qui toute puissance a
Renvoya cil qui au boys la laissa
Où elle estoit ; mais, quoy qu'on en blasonne,
Tant eust de dueil, que le monde s'estonne
   que d'un cousteau son cueur ne transpersa
   comme Dido.

The good Jacqueline

Died O, rival of Callas, long smoldering for
Onassis' malice. How dare he her ignore!
Unlike yet like her, Jackie in her palace
Grieved for her Jack, who in a dismal Dallas
Hospital had passed; now Camelot was o'er.
Of pain she knew yet pure remained at core;
Faith filled her heart, her spirit did restore;
She tendered feelings warm and never callous
   Toward the man who'd left her — as did O.
Almighty God did fairly even the score,
Destroying the Greek who'd tossed her over for
That prima donna, rendering her pal-less.
Extraordinary grief did fill her chalice.
Remarkably, she didn't choose death's door,
   as did Dido.

To a Damsel in Bed

D. Hofstadter

To you, dear
One, some cheer:

A good day.

Do not stay
Away long.   5
May your strong
Spirit kill
Ev'ry ill.
Leave your room

In haste; zoom   10
Nimbly thence,

By Clement's
Edict, love.
Dreaming of

Being fed?   15
Your sickbed

Crimps that hope.
Lest you mope,
Exit soon,
Miss, and spoon   20
Ex'lent jam!
Now, madame,
This flu you

Must undo,
And — soon plump —   25
Rise from slump!
Our Lord's near
To you, dear.

Having managed to do one super-constrained version of "Ma Mignonne", I felt ready and rarin' to tackle another super-constraint. This time, for God knows what reason, I decided to make all 28 lines rhyme with each other. In other words, all the lines in the poem should end with exactly the same sound, thus turning the original rhyme scheme into "AAAAA…". In fact, why not let each line end in "end" itself?

Finding this new challenge to be very hard, I granted myself the liberty to make hyphenations at nonstandard spots inside words (*i.e.*, at places other than strict syllable boundaries, as I had already done to the word "sentence" in "Pretty One"), but other than that, I permitted no deviations whatsoever from the rhyme pattern or the rhythmic regularity of the original. Note that this led to three more amphisbænic enjambments — found on lines 16, 17, and 26.

The resulting poem, though by no means a masterpiece, reads reasonably well out loud, and, simply because of the salient stunt it accomplishes, stands out among the translations in the collection. One curiosity: The first and last lines, though phonetically identical, consist of entirely unrelated words and meanings — they have nothing in common but their pronunciation. Note also that being jailbound is alluded to twice in the poem: not only via the word "penned" in line 5, where it's quite expected, but also in lines 17–18, via the word "offender".

It is my firm conviction that Marot himself, could he have read and understood them, would have delighted in this translation and the previous one. I have the strong sense that both would have resonated strongly with his joyful, playful, undeniably Clementine spirit.

To the End

D. Hofstadter

To thee, end-
uring friend,
Let me send
All my tend-
er love. Penned   5
In bed, mend;
Then ascend!
Thy way wend
Out; descend
As thou'd yenned,   10
I commend
To thee. Bend
Near, love — lend
An ear: tend
Toward sweet blend-   15
ed jams. Slend-
er offend-
er, suspend —
Nay, up-end! —
Thy gaunt trend.   20
May God's splend-
or forfend
Thy surrend-
er, and fend
Off thy pend-   25
ing, heart-rend-
ing dead-end,
Too. The End.

• *Chapter 11* •

Halos, Analogies, Spaces, and Blends

•

A WOrd being the name of a concept, and a concept being a class of items linked by analogy, and people by nature being creative and ever finding new analogies, a word's connotations are consequently oozing continually outwards to form an ever-larger and blurrier nebula as more and more analogies are recognized as legitimate and welcomed by the culture. A table thus acquires legs, a mountain acquires a foot, ships venture into space, sopranos sing high and basses low, books have jackets, families have trees, computers have memories, salad is dressed, wine breathes, cars run, hearts dance, a storm threatens, actors become stars, friends give you a hand, ideas bloom and die, hopes soar, hearts melt, Suzi is bubbly, Sami is dull, their marriage crashes, hearts break, companies fold, stocks plummet, the Yankees cream the Braves, viruses invade PC's, PC's get immunized, critics give feedback, I see your point, sockets are female, plugs are male, gay couples get married, the H-bomb has a father, all people are men, all men are brothers, all brothers are Greeks, Greek sisters are cool chicks, cool chicks are good guys, words have halos, you get the picture... Well, you get the picture. Words have halos.

The noun "shadow" offers a nice study in extension-via-analogy. The original meaning is of course a darker area where light is blocked by a solid object, but extended meanings abound, all based on analogies of different sorts. A child can grow up insecure in an accomplished parent's shadow. A sick person can be a shadow of their former self. A mountain range can cast a rain shadow to its east. A set of ministers temporarily out of power constitutes a shadow cabinet. The concept of "generalized shadow" is a potentially unlimited source of fresh analogies, and will perpetually serve to expand the meaning of the word that names it.

As we curious little humans explore our awesome universe, we are constantly forced to borrow old words to describe new phenomena. Galileo, peering through primitive lenses, sees tiny white dots dancing near a disk, deep in the nighttime sky, and soon the once-unique proper noun "Moon" acquires a lowercase "m". Newton tells us about gravity and all of a sudden the once-absolute notions of "up" and "down" become variables linked to the centers of spheres floating in the void. With fancier arrays of lenses and mirrors, we examine one of Galileo's moons and note imperfections in its sphericity; distortions that go "up" are called, by courtesy, "mountains". And since this moon rotates about its own axis, it is accorded, by analogy with earth, a "north pole" and a "south pole", and then our own "east" and "west" are likewise born anew on its near-spherical surface; moreover, a full revolution, whatever its duration, is dubbed "one day". (Oddly enough, we are too timid to call a grand tour about Jupiter, which plays the "sun" role, "one year", however!) We discover that around this moon-ball there is a terribly thin zone of some tenuous gas, and eagerly we jump to baptize it "atmosphere", thereby pluralizing a word heretofore solely terrestrian in denotation. Soon we find out that up from certain mountaintops on this moon there shoot streams of molten rock into the atmosphere; the mild mind-hop of calling them "volcanos" doesn't even feel like an analogy — no more than, on encountering some friend's new pet, we feel we are being witty and bold when we refer to its pendulous hirsute posterior oscillator as a "tail". But then biologists start asking, "Might there be *life* on this moon?" How would we decide what is *life*? We cannot look for dogs or elephants or snakes or squids or ants or oaks or seaweed; we must seek a far higher abstraction, a pattern, something to do with self-copying entities, cycles that remind us of terrestrian birth and death, struggle and competition, our holy grail being the telltale spiral of ever-increasing complexity... *That*'s what would allow the word "life" to be applied to some never-before-seen phenomenon occurring in an alien milieu, be it agar in a Petri dish, the surface of a Jovian minimoon, or some supercomputer's giant screen.

Words Stretched to their Rubbery Limits on a Neutron Star

None of the above is at all new, but... what happens when this totally natural process of extending words by analogy gets pushed to its very limit? This idea is a theme, albeit a tacit one, of the science-fiction novel *Dragon's Egg* by the physicist Robert L. Forward. The wonderful premise of this novel is that an entire civilization comes into existence on the crust of a madly-whirling, superdense, enormously hot neutron star a scant twelve miles in diameter.

To grasp the bizarreness of this, you have to realize that there are no atoms in such a crust; in place of atoms, molecules, and their chemistry, there are only pure nuclei arranged in a loose crystalline lattice. However, Forward postulates a kind of "chemistry" (note my quote marks to indicate caution, since we are proceeding strictly by analogy here) in which neighboring nuclei can bond together and form nuclear compounds called "molecules" — again extending the familiar term very gingerly.

Once this analogue to chemistry is given, then the door is wide open for all sorts of higher-level phenomena — tight analogues to phenomena we know well — to take place in the hugely alien medium of the crust, such as "oxidation" and "reduction" reactions, "acids" and "bases", 'polymers', catalysis, auto-catalysis, self-replicating "molecules", 'genetic material', "enzymes", mutation, natural selection and evolution, "microbes", agglomerations of "cells", "viruses", "plants", "animals", 'sex', intelligence, stupidity, language, death, families, tribes, enemies, war, superstition, 'God', religion, "Jesus", "Christianity", morality, hypocrisy, love, lies, towns, timidity, flirtation, exploration, 'hieroglyphs', alphabets, mathematics, science, universities, 'printing presses', literature, 'typefaces', politics, law, 'sexual' harassment, science fiction, sarcasm, slang, jokes, puns, poems, 'music', 'jazz', *haute cuisine,* analogies, translation, advertising, "Scotch tape", 'fast-food' chains, 'X-rated' "videos", 'jazzercise', and so on. The occasional quote marks help you keep in mind that these are *extensions via analogy* of the same-named phenomena on the surface of our planet.

What is the meaning of *single* as opposed to *double* or *no* quote marks? The distinction is very blurry, but basically, my goal was to suggest how much mental strain the given extension-by-analogy causes. Obviously this is pretty darned subjective, but double quote marks designate those analogies where, to me, the stretch feels the tensest and furthest-fetched; single quote marks denote somewhat less of a mental stretch; and there are no quotes for analogies that feel natural and easy.

As an example, I single-quoted "X-rated" but double-quoted "videos", meaning that given the basic aspects of sexuality, it is fairly easy to imagine some rough analogue to hard-core scenes, but on the other hand, the actual medium in which such scenes would be recorded would be unlikely to bear any resemblance to videocassettes. Put another way, X-ratedness is more of an abstract *pattern*; videos are more of an earthbound *thing*. A similar logic explains why I single-quoted "God" but double-quoted "Jesus". (There is, by the way, a scene in the novel that strikingly echoes Christ's crucifixion; there is even an X-rated scene where a *she* alien and a *he* alien... but I digress.)

Halos, Analogies, Spaces, and Blends   ◆ ◆ ◆   *307*

These examples illustrate a general trend that you can verify as you scan the paragraph: as a rule, the higher up in the ladder of abstraction you go — that is, as you reach levels where what counts is *pattern* rather than *matter* — *function* rather than *shape* — the less strain there is, so the more natural it feels to grant the analogical extension.

Scientific Plausibility of Neutron Stars as Life-cradles

Despite the many fairly unstretched analogies, one has to constantly remember that there is a huge disparity in scales, both in size and in speed. The reason for this gulf is that the electromagnetic force, on which all atomic chemistry is based, is nearly irrelevant on a neutron star's crust, and so its role is played, roughly speaking, by the *nuclear* force, also called the "strong" force, the latter name reflecting the fact that at subatomic distances, it is millions of times more powerful than its electromagnetic cousin. For this reason, Forward's nuclear "chemistry" proceeds millions of times faster than the chemistry we know. Also, given the absence of electronic shells holding nuclei apart, there is a dramatic gravitational collapse to a size thousands of times smaller, linearly, than in atom-based chemistry. The upshot is that everything that takes place in the neutron star's crust does so on a lilliputian scale and at a blindingly fast pace.

Because it is only twelve miles across (our sun is 860,000 miles across, the earth 8,000), the neutron star spins all the way about its axis in just one-fifth of a second — that is, a "day" is 0.2 seconds long. The star is also inconceivably dense to us earthbound creatures, making lead seem like cotton candy. And its surface temperature is roughly 9,000 degrees Kelvin.

It is crucial to understand that Forward's fantasy is not in any sense your usual sloppy science-fiction easy-chair anything-goes exercise in blue-skying it, where science itself is thrown to the fictional winds (as in Superman and Star Trek television shows, movies like *Star Wars* and *E.T.*, and so forth); to the contrary, most of it is at least scientifically plausible and has been lovingly worked out by Forward in impressive detail, much of which is given in a lengthy appendix that poses as a technical article, with tables, graphs, and sketches, published in the year 2064. Indeed, the germ of the idea for his novel came from a speculative but very serious article called "Life on a Neutron Star", written by the distinguished astrophysicist Frank Drake and published in the journal *Astronomy* in 1973.

Of Cheelas and Humans

We need not go into the "biology" of "life" in the nuclear-lattice crust; suffice it to say that the intelligent beings who finally emerge from a lengthy evolutionary process (lengthy according to *their* time scale, at least!) are pancake-shaped creatures that are roughly the size of a human baby's littlest fingernail, and they are pressed to the surface of their star by staggeringly powerful gravitational forces, 70 billion times greater than on earth. Each so-called "cheela", though comparable to an ant in size, has roughly the mass of a human being, being made of pure nuclear matter, and its temperature is a cool 9,000° K. Cheelas communicate, mate, make friends, form groups, work together, and have an organized society.

During one turn of their neutron star — curiously, Forward strongly resists the analogical extension of our word "day", instead always saying "turn" for the star's 0.2-second rotational time — the cheelas accomplish roughly what we-folk accomplish in a full earth-day (we sleep but cheelas don't). In other words, each turn feels to a cheela about as long as twelve hours feels to you or me. A cheela's entire life lasts about 45 human minutes, and in that interval take place many of the major transitions that mark our own lives: birth, childhood, adolescence, maturity, professional life, retirement, and death. In a full earth-day, a time period comparable to the sweep from the Roman Empire all the way to our own twentieth century takes place on the surface of Dragon's Egg.

The novel's plot is based on the near-ludicrous premise of one fleeting yet highly significant instant of carefully planned-out friendly contact — just one-tenth of an earth-second — between the highest products of the sluggishly slow evolution on earth and the blindingly fast evolution on the star. The dramatic ratio of intrinsic speeds of all processes gives rise to some very bizarre twists. For instance, for a few hours, there is radio contact between the two civilizations, and while an earthling speaks one sentence, the equivalent of a month has passed on the neutron star. And as the planning for the encounter begins, the cheelas start out far, far behind the earthlings in scientific and technological advancement, but by the time the meeting happens, just a few earth-hours later, they have far outstripped us and are careening headlong into their collective future, leaving us humans straggling behind in their intellectual dust.

The drama of the novel comes from the fact that the chapters flip back and forth between the two vantage points, each one seeming totally ordinary on its own — until the contrast with the other is brought up, when all of a sudden, the *other* civilization seems extraordinarily slow (or fast). The contrasting worlds are like two bubbles, within each of which everything seems completely normal; it is at the interface where everything goes wild. For a down-to-earth analogy of the sort that Professor Wu would have adduced at just this point, imagine jumping back and forth between, say, China and America, experiencing the internal normalcy of each one on its own, indeed the great similarity between the two, and yet also experiencing the enormous clash when the cultures actually meet. The plot of *Dragon's Egg* is just that idea raised to the nth power.

Cheelas who Giggle and Munch

However, my purpose here is not to discuss the plausibility of the plot or the merits of the science behind it, but to consider the bizarreness — or perhaps the utter reasonableness! — of Forward's use of ordinary English words (plus, as we shall see, even one or two cheela words) to describe this strange world and its goings-on. Consider that on the neutron star's crust, there are extrusions, ranging from a few millimeters to an awe-inspiring ten centimeters in height, which Forward terms "mountains"; the tips of the highest of these mountains poke through the "atmosphere", which consists of unattached iron nuclei floating above the dense nuclear lattice. In this "atmosphere", there are "winds" that carry "smoke" from "volcanos" — mountains at whose peaks a "liquid" variety of nuclear matter emanating from deep in the neutron star's core occasionally belches forth, forming flows of "lava" that spill all the way down the mountain's slopes and far beyond, a few microns in thickness and covering several, if not several dozens, of square meters.

Let us give Forward the floor — it is, after all, his novel! — and see how he — never using cautionary quotes, you will note — describes things:

> Soon the whole clan gathered at the edge of the settlement and watched as the happy giggling hunting party returned and dumped their booty. The seeds were distributed and quickly planted in the waiting holes by a large crew, all munching on ripe pods.
> Flow-Hunter spent the next turn giving a detailed account of the trip to Broken-Petal. The report of the loss of See-High caused a moment of sadness in them both, but they turned their minds back to the present and continued on.
> The nearby volcano dominated their lives. Fortunately it became dormant for a while, with just a thin wisp of yellow-white smoke spiraling up into the air, but the rumbling in the crust grew worse every turn.

It sounds for all the world like a band of Apaches or Mohicans to me, even down to the Indian-style names of the individuals. But let us focus on the use of English. I find myself alternately accepting and rejecting these sentences. How could cheelas "giggle", for instance? This quintessentially human verb is here being applied by metaphorical extension to certain types of infinitesimal distortions inside some tiny squashed superhot disks moving at inconceivable speeds in a lattice of pure nuclear matter on the surface of a neutron star billions of times denser and smaller in volume than our sun! "Giggle"!? What nonsense! Yet then I think to myself, "Yes, but this recurrent pattern of tiny and rapid distortions is *like* giggling — it plays the *role* in cheela society of a giggle. It signifies uncontrolled mirth, relief, and so on — so why not use it?" Fine; but the problem is, this argument presumes that earthborn words like "mirth" and "relief" fit, glove-like, onto certain types of events on the neutron star — already quite a leap of faith. And so back and forth I go.

What about "munch"? Similar arguments would seem to allow it, and yet we don't talk about *fish* munching anything; it would even sound noticeably anthropomorphic if someone described their pet dog or cat as "munching". The whole halo of connotations of "munch" is too tied in to aspects of being *human* to extend even to our co-evolved planet-mates — so how on earth (so to speak!) could it be extended to cheelas? The only answer would seem to be: It can be done because cheelas are *intelligent,* because they have *language,* because their *emotional makeup* is reasonably analogous to ours. "Analogous" is the key word, of course.

Yellow-White Smoke

Oddly, what troubles me more than "giggle" and "munch" is the final paragraph of the selection, especially the phrase "a thin wisp of yellow-white smoke spiraling up into the air". Such language is just *too* evocative of a terrestrial scene. In my mind, I see Mount St. Helens from twenty miles or so, a few days before it blew its top. Like old Mr Average, this is overdone.

What do "smoke" and "air" mean? Why did Forward not put these words — obviously giant metaphorical leaps — in quotes? The answer is that then *everything* — every last word — would have to go inside quotes. Or if not everything, then there would have to be a reasoned set of criteria for deciding when to use quotes and when not to. A reader would go crazy!

What does "yellow-white" mean? As seen by human eyes? Clearly not. As seen by cheela eyes? Well, cheelas do have perceptual organs that Forward has the audacity — or the common sense — to call "eyes", and these organs are sensitive to electromagnetic waves, but not of the same wavelengths as human eyes are. In fact (so to speak), cheelas can see all the way from the ultra-violet region into the X-ray region of the spectrum, but are as blind to good old red, orange, yellow, green, blue, indigo, and violet as our eyes are to radio waves. And thus, how can human color terms possibly apply to the cheelas' "vision"?

Once again, one has to look beyond the surface-level facts of the modality, and deep into their minds (their "minds", if you prefer). Rather than concentrating on the wavelengths of the impinging photons, one has to concentrate on the *cognitive effect* that such photons indirectly trigger inside a being in a given complex context. One has to look at the way sensory modalities interface with concrete and abstract concepts. It is conceivable to me that some kinds of X-rays could trigger reactions inside eensy-weensy cheela brains that are structurally analogous — perhaps even isomorphic — to the reactions triggered in my brain by 5,000-Ångström photons. Carrying this idea further, it is conceivable to me — indeed, it sounds entirely reasonable — that "being a cheela" feels much like being a human, in just the same way as being Chinese feels much like being American, despite the fact that the constant flux of communicative sounds bombarding the eardrums has an entirely different sonic makeup, if described on a purely phonetic level.

The Central Riddle

I am at times puzzled by what strike me as inconsistent choices on Forward's part. Why, if he grants us readers sufficient mental flexibility to handle *some* analogical extensions, does he not think we are flexible enough to handle others? Why, for instance, does he always say "turn" instead of "day", while feeling perfectly comfortable referring, without even any cautionary quote marks, to "smoke" and "air"?

Why, if he feels free to call some cheela organs "eyes" and has the guts to talk about a group of cheelas coming back "empty-handed" from a hunt, does he always refer to the body fluid coursing inside cheela bodies merely as "fluid", never as "blood"? This "fluid" plays the role of blood every bit as much as their so-called "eyes" play the role of eyes; what then prevents it from having the honor of being called "blood"? Would it be merely because this "fluid" is "blue" and not "red"? Actually, I don't think Forward ever tells us which "color" it is, but that would hardly seem to matter, given all the far more radical differences. And how can Forward blithely apply the deeply earthbound metaphor "a pack rat" to Great-Crack, the curious cheela who couldn't resist collecting everything?

In a way, using the rather high abstraction of "pack rat" to describe a complex pattern in that alien world is *less* strange than using "plant" to apply to certain living entities in that world, and using "plant" is in turn less strange than using "air", which, in its turn, is less strange than saying "mountain". Ultimately, it's at the physical level, rather than at the abstract cultural level, that the contrast between worlds is so shocking and bizarre.

With these musings, we are truly homing in on the central riddle of the novel's language — indeed, the central riddle of language as a whole: Under what circumstances should one take a word or phrase devised for one narrow type of situation and apply it to other situations that had never been dreamt of when it was born, and to which it was never intended to apply? When is the strain so great that a new word must be made up?

Quote Marks and SimTown

All of this goes straight to the core of a deep philosophical controversy that has come up over and over again as computers have been used as simulation tools in more and more domains. The key claim is this:

> No one supposes that computer simulations of a five-alarm fire will burn the neighborhood down or that a computer simulation of a rainstorm will leave us all drenched.... To confuse simulation with duplication is the same mistake, whether it is pain, love, cognition, fires, or rainstorms.

The author of this seemingly reasonable remark is John Searle, whom we have met before and with whom we shall meet up shortly again.

To help the issue become concrete and vivid, let us take the popular computer program SimTown, which I have watched my son Danny play with quite often. On the screen of SimTown one sees houses — or should I put the word in quotes, signaling caution? All right. One sees "houses". And one sees "children". And one sees "bicycles" and "cars". (This is getting tiring.) The "cars" are "moving" along some "streets"...

Why, one might well ask, do I not put cautionary quotes on "along" and "some" and so forth? I guess I should, and so: "The" "cars" "are" "moving" "along" "some" "streets". Presumably this is what Searle would want, his attitude being that nothing in that computer world is to be taken seriously; it's all as fake as can be. But wait. There was a *reason* I intuitively refrained from putting cautionary quote marks on words like "the" and "some". Even if those "cars" are not real cars, the concepts of *definite article* and *partitive adjective* still apply perfectly well to the little pseudo-world on the screen. This is not a *fake* some-ness or the-ness. And hence, off with the quotes around those two words.

What about "along"? Well, the "streets", even if not made of asphalt (they *are* made of "asphalt", in some diluted sense of "made"), have a linear dimension, and so "along" would seem to be deserving of "release" from the "jail cell" of its quote-marks. Above suspicion.

But is this matter of quoting and dequoting all so black-and-white, all so absolutely crystal-clear? For instance, how about "move"? Something *seems* to be changing location on the screen. It's true, it's not a tangible solid object that I can reach out and grasp, but I can *track* it visually. It keeps some kind of identity as it changes position on the screen. *If* this is an "object", then is it not fair to call what it is doing "moving"? To say yes is a leap, but all right, let me daringly dequote the verb, as well. Now I am left with: The "cars" are moving along some "streets". This seems to be a reasonable compromise, but it took thought and judgment to decide what belonged in quotes and what did not, and I might change my mind later.

Wetness, Real and Simulated

In SimTown, many other things can happen, including houses being set on fire and goldfish flopping out of their bowls. (I'm leaving off the quotes merely as a shorthand — I know they aren't *real* goldfish!) Well, what is that medium in which they are immersed before being spilled out?

Of course it is "water". Is it wet? Well, certainly the "water" is "wet", but I'm asking something else: Can the cautionary quote marks be pulled off of the adjective? Searle would say no, most vehemently. This is all fake.

But what, then, *does* the word "wet" mean? When *can* it be applied to new situations? First of all, let us consider the everyday world around us. Does it take water molecules for something to count as wet? No, even Searle would admit that the actual substance can vary: milk, alcohol, and a million other chemicals in the liquid state can get us sopping wet. Hence wetness is a kind of *pattern,* not something uniquely tied to one special substance. And how do we identify the presence of that pattern? It has to do with flow and motion and stickiness and many other intangibles, which we need not go into. The main thing is that it has to do with how things move and cling and so forth.

Can, then, this notion of wetness, this abstract pattern, be exported from our cozy planet to other planets? Are things wet on the surface of Venus? Sounds plausible; after all, I hear tell Venus is a land of continual storms. Is anything wet in or on the sun? Sounds implausible; after all, it's a yellow oven of nuclear fusion, burning up vast gulps of hydrogen to make helium. How could anything be wet *there*?

All right, then; let's give up on the sun and pass to a neutron star. Hello; anything wet down there? The amazing thing is that if we could fire off this message to a cheela ham-radio operator, we might easily get back the response, "Wet? Are you kidding? I just spilled my tequila all over my new shirt, my baby just vomited on the computer keyboard, and outside, it's pouring like hell right now! And you ask me if anything's *wet* down here?"

Okay, maybe I exaggerated a bit, but see what you think after reading this rather gory short excerpt from the novel:

> Quick-Mover looked in awe at the fang held in his manipulator. Both were covered with dripping gobs of glowing juice. He sucked them clean, enjoying the unaccustomed taste of fresh juice and meat.

Given this vivid a portrayal of juiciness and sucking, we shouldn't be surprised if, in answer to our query about wetness, a message something like the following came back: "Wet? We on Dragon's Egg know many wet substances: our blood-like bodily fluid; the liquid that fills our eyeballs; the seminal fluid of male cheelas; the succulent juice that fills plants and that we drink; and most of all, the ubiquitous liquid that courses our streams and rivers and fills our oceans." What would Searle say to this? *Does* wetness exist in the crust of that neutron star?

I'm not, mind you, asserting that the science-fiction world of *Dragon's Egg* is reality; I'm only asking how Searle would reply to a hypothetical question of this sort. Would he be prepared to extend, analogically, the word "wet" to cover phenomena on the 9,000° K surface of a neutron star, provided certain criterial kinds of flow-and-viscosity patterns were identifiable there? And, leaving Searle aside, how about you?

SimBowl...

And now we pass back to SimTown. Actually, let's bump it up a few notches in sophistication and realism, while scaling it down to just a room, a table, a few objects... In fact, let's imagine SimBowl, a program where goldfish-resembling things "swim around" inside a "bowl" on a "table" in a "room". But we don't just watch them passively; indeed, we can interact with this "bowl", controlling it from our keyboard. We can tip it, and watch the "water" in it slosh around, just like real water, carrying the "fish" along with it, just as real water would. We can drop a simulated pebble into the "bowl" and watch "ripples" spread on the surface, hit the "edges" of the bowl, bounce back, and interfere with other ripples. Beautiful!

If we "drop" our simulated pebble from high enough, it will actually "splash" (how do you like that clash of the adverb "actually" with the quote marks around "splash"?) and "drops" of "water" will sail up and out of the "bowl", possibly to "land" on the "table" or the "floor". (With all those cautionary quote marks, you can see I'm trying *extremely* hard not to get "sucked in" by the illusion. Now don't *you* "fall for it" either, reader!) When we look at the "floor", we can see shiny spots where the "drops" "landed". Using our mouse — er, our "mouse" — we can navigate about inside the "room" and go get a "paper towel", and if we "put" this "paper towel" on the shiny spots on the "floor", it "absorbs" the "liquid", while itself changing in "texture"...

I could go on and on, but you get the picture: the SimBowl program is hugely realistic and practically unlimited. Thus, a simulated kitty-cat might softly pad in and simulate licking up the water on the floor. Would its "tongue" be wet? And the crux of the question here is: Could I leave the quote marks off of the word "wet"? Is the simulated water in the simulated bowl *actually wet*? I suspect Searle would scoff at this, pointing out that I couldn't reach in and *get my own hand wet*. End of story. Simulated water in simulated bowls or on simulated wood floors is not wet and never will be, no matter how powerful the illusion is, because it's just a simulation!

Well, maybe that's good enough for Searle, but it's not good enough for me. Just why do *I* have to be able to get *myself* wet for it to count as wetness? I, who by chance am realized through a chemistry of the giant atomic type, could never go dip my feet in the dense nuclear-matter brooklets that flow across the neutron star; and cheelas, conversely, who happen to be realized through a chemistry of the petite nuclear type, could never splash about in the lovely limpid waters of the great green greasy Limpopo, no matter how dearly they longed to. We and they are sadly separated by an insuperable wall of time-scale and space-scale disparity, not to mention the mismatch of physical substrates and types of chemistry. But that wall between us does not invalidate the cheelas' use of their word for "wet" for *their world*. Their own body fluid is just as genuinely wet to them as our own blood is wet to us. Note: I stress once again that my use of the present tense does not signify an endorsement on my part of their reality; I am, rather, indulging in a typical *Gedankenexperiment* — a Forward-thinking thought experiment, if you will.

… and SymBol

Let us now change the focus-word from "wet" to "alive". If wetness be just a pattern, surely aliveness is even more of a pattern, even more abstract, even less dependent on the substrate in which the phenomena are embedded. Thus we should be willing to grant that Forward's cheelas, if they existed, would be genuinely alive. And presumably, if phenomena that rivaled the cheela world in complexity someday came to take place inside the memory of a supercomputer, then why not extend the word "alive" to those beings, as well?

Indeed, this is the plot of Stanisław Lem's ingenious and very dense short story "Non Serviam", which features "personoids" that are realized as highly dynamic, very abstract data-structures inside a computer program that seems like an enormously extrapolated and complexified version of SimTown. To read "Non Serviam" is eerily like reading *Dragon's Egg*, as a matter of fact. Here is a sample sentence: "One second of machine time corresponds to one year of human life." The similarity is clear. As in Forward's novel, a reader comes to know by name and to be fond of a few of the alien beings inhabiting the alien substrate, but in contrast to *Dragon's Egg*, where the cheela civilization will presumably live on indefinitely, evolving and changing but not being squelched from outside, "Non Serviam" ends on an ominous tone, as we are informed that the electric bills to support this gigantic artificial "digital universum" inhabited by the friendly personoids are growing too high, and sooner or later the entire experiment will have to be terminated, the "universum" shut off forever… One cannot help but find this abhorrent and tragic, because one intuitively senses that these personoids, like Forward's cheelas, are not only alive, but fully *conscious*.

It is this notion, consciousness, that is the central concern and true cause of John Searle's outcry about the hollowness of simulations, only he gives it a different name: "intentionality". He also sometimes calls this elusive essence "aboutness" or "semantics", as we shall see in Chapter 16, the presumption being that in computers, symbols are merely "symbols" (those are scorn-quotes, by the way) since they *symbolize nothing.* As Searle's great-aunt Dorotrude from Oakland once said, there's no *aboutness* about them. But the choice of words here is of little import. The central question is, can we extend the word "conscious" from human beings to Forward's cheelas to Lem's personoids, or does there lurk, in one of these jumps, an invisible solid sheet against which we shall knock ourselves silly, as a bird smashes into a window, if we attempt it?

For me, this is a question of how to use words, which means it is a question of analogical extensions, which means it is a question of the degree of similarity of two patterns, which means that there are shades of gray. The question boils down to this: In two different media, is "the same thing" happening? The answer is not a black-and-white one — yes/no. For Searle it is. For me, there are shaded quote marks — a whole spectrum of amounts of strain and stretch, hence degrees of wariness about the applicability of a word. The words "consciousness" and "semantics" are not exceptions to this rule, as I see it. These mental qualities are present in a given medium to the degree that we are able to recognize their telltale patterns — because, indeed, in the last analysis, they *are* patterns.

For a certain class of philosophers and people interested in computer models of mind, however, there is a foregone conclusion: Computers are dead objects, minds are live things, and never the twain shall meet. For such people, there can be no program that can think or feel; anything that looks like it does is merely an empty sham, a hollow façade. For them, just as a SimBowl program may someday simulate water perfectly down to the last drop yet without that "water" having even the slightest trace of *wetness,* so a SymBol program may someday simulate the full human use of symbols and language perfectly down to the last drop yet without those "symbols" having even the slightest trace of *symbolism.*

The intuitions of such folk are a bit of a mystery to me. Searle, for example, has written, "Martians have intentionality but their brains are made of different stuff." Of course, Searle no more believes in Martians than do I in cheelas; he just wants to signal his open-mindedness about the potential realizability of genuine semantic, intentional mentality in media other than human brains, which is an admirable attitude; indeed, judging by his generosity towards Martians, I reason (by analogy, of course) that he would be equally welcoming of cheelas into the community of intentional or conscious beings. However, since Searle's willingness to extend his term to entities other than human brains doesn't seem to be based on analogy and pattern but on preconceived dogmas about certain special physical substrates that are endowed with what he mysteriously calls "causal powers", I just don't follow his logic. For me, the substrate is irrelevant; the *patterns* that the substrate allows to come into being are all that matter.

Speaking Cheelinese with English Words

We circle back, at long last, to translation issues, focusing on the way that Forward renders pure Cheelinese dialogue in English. If I was bothered when colloquial and slangy English expressions were pasted over the tongues of Soviet prisoners and random Chinese monolinguals, well, at least *they* were human beings sharing the same chemistry and evolutionary history as I do! But cheelas? Here is a tiny excerpt, and yet sufficient to suggest the utter bizarreness of putting English in their "mouths":

> "It sure is tall," he remarked calmly.
> "Sure is," said Flow-Hunter. Her tread rumbled teasingly. "Looks as if it is going to fall right on top of you, doesn't it?"
> "Yes, but it has not fallen before, so I guess it won't now," Speckled-Egg said confidently.
> "But it will when we get through with it," said Flow-Hunter.

What planet are we on, anyway? Are these cheelas, or are they Mohicans? And yet — given the need to render *in English* a conversation between cheelas, how else to do it? What Flow-Hunter actually said to Speckled-Egg in their own "tongue" surely sounded — or rather, *seemed* — natural to them both; shouldn't Forward's English translation of it therefore be done in such a way as to make it sound equally natural to us?

There is an amusing sidelight to all this: Forward is not *really* translating anything, since he doesn't know Cheelinese — or more bluntly put, since Cheelinese doesn't exist at all. But this kind of faking is typical of so much fiction. For example, in Fenimoore Cooper's *Last of the Mohicans,* there are many pages of English text supposedly rendering things that were actually said in Delaware, Huron, and other Indian languages — but since Cooper spoke none of those, he just invented it all directly in English. And in *Eugene Onegin,* as I earlier pointed out, Pushkin supposedly translated Tatyana's famous heart-rending letter from French, but almost surely, that, too, is just a sweet conceit: I would be willing to bet that Pushkin gave birth to it directly in Russian, bypassing French entirely, even though in theory he could have taken the more circuitous route, since his French was superb. But let us skip this fakery issue, and benignly adopt the novel's premise: that Cheelinese really exists, that certain "conversations" really took place in it, and that Forward's job was to render them "faithfully" in English.

The challenge is nontrivial: to take some kind of semipatterned interchange of disturbances in the nuclear lattice between the cheelas, something that plays the role of a language, and to convert it into strings of roman letters constituting English words and sentences. Let's presume Forward has access to a "transcript" of the original — let's say, for the sake of concreteness, a videotape of some kind of cloud-chamber tracks. Does it make sense to think that an expert could pinpoint, somewhere in the video, some telltale little pattern of tracks that calls for being rendered with the American English colloquial use of "sure" as an adverb? Is there *that* close a match-up between cloud-chamber patterns and English syntax? Likewise, can we be confident that Flow-Hunter's two headless English sentences accurately capture the flavor of her actual cloud-chamber "remark"? Are there really patterns in the Cheelinese tracks that map well onto the use in English of contractions like "doesn't" or "won't", or onto macho-style idioms like "when we get through with it"?

Moving to a different level, we could well ask why a typical cheela "utterance" contains roughly the same amount of content as a typical human one does. How come cheela conversations follow discourse protocols indistinguishable from our own? What a coincidence that our brains are so similar!

For that matter, why do we uncritically lap it up when Forward exploits the English word "said" — "Sure is," *said* Flow-Hunter — to denote his creatures' communicative actions? Doesn't the verb "say" implicate a human mouth, vocal cords, sound waves? Why didn't Forward instead stick to a higher, safer abstraction such as "state" or "remark"? Alternatively, he could have used an oddly-flavored English word such as "emit" to suggest the alienness of the act, or possibly made up a neologism such as "outpush" or "offsend" to denote the act that is, to a cheela, what "saying" is to us.

A more radical suggestion would be to plug directly into the English text the actual *Cheelinese* verb meaning "utter" or "state", thus making it crashingly obvious that we don't mean "say", we don't mean "talk", we don't mean anything remotely like the producing of *sounds* in *throats*. Ironically, though, the rejoinder to this suggestion is the very point that it is making: How could you possibly print a Cheelinese word in roman letters? After all, a Cheelinese word is not transcribable in the way any terrestrian language's phonemes are, since *it is not built from sounds at all.*

That would seem to slam the door for once and for all on the idea of English borrowing Cheelinese vocabulary items, and yet — what, then, is the strange-looking word "t'trum" that occurs over and over in Forward's novel? Where did this unpronounceable pseudo-word come from, if it is not an attempt to represent the "phonetics" of a Cheelinese word? I gather from context that a t'trum is a repetitive "offsending" produced by the "tread" of a cheela, and that it serves to convey to other cheelas the current emotional mood of the individual. It makes me think of the wagging of a dog's tail. (Could tail-wagging-ese be translated into American slang? "Hey, folks — dig! I'm feelin' groovy!" wagged Spot.)

In any case, what a weird idea it is to pretend that English letters are capturing the *actual sounds* of Cheelinese, when such sounds simply do not exist. Of course Forward knew this. Writing "t'trum" was presumably a poetic attempt to suggest, in the alien medium of sound (actually, the medium is not sound itself, but the *graphic representation* of sounds), a pattern that simply is extrinsic to it, pushing translation to the limit — a little like when a musician tries to "translate" a visual scene or an emotion into a pattern of pitches and harmonies.

Mixt Tongues, Blent Names

Whenever a pair of cultures meet each other, whether on friendly or inimical terms, whether at a shared physical boundary or through long-distance exchanges, a borrowing of words in both directions is inevitable. Thus when invading Europeans encountered Amerindians — an event that for its times may have seemed nearly as radical, as confusing, and as mystical as the meeting of humans and cheelas in *Dragon's Egg* — both cultures absorbed many new terms. European anglophones gained words such as "squaw", "wigwam", and "tomahawk". But when you think about it, why was a word like "squaw" an addition to English? What did it add? We already had "woman" and "wife" — there was nothing new to "squaw" other than... *flavor.* Yes — it connotes, it radiates, it exudes, Indian-ness. This is the magic of its halo. And it is this ineffable halo that causes that specific word, and not "woman" or "lady" or "wife" or "mate" or "spouse" or "helpmeet" or "missus" or "frow" or "wahine" or "female" or "dame" or any of a large number of other theoretical options, to pop to the mind of a novelist who is writing an adventure tale about Indians and who wishes to convey not just denotations but, in the same breath, a viewpoint, an attitude, hidden implications...

Blending even the most ordinary word from another culture into one's own language inevitably gives rise to a sense of novelty, of exoticism. There is thus a great gain to be had by indulging in this practice. But there is another practice, quite the opposite of this one, in which a culture tries to absorb or appropriate things outside it and make them seem more internal than they really are. Take the French, for example, who have carried this art quite far. The great Michelangelo, for francophones, is "Michel-Ange", and Johann Sebastian Bach is "Jean-Sébastien Bach". The effect is a kind of false image, verging on the ludicrous suggestion that both the Italian sculptor and the German composer were French.

But having gallicized Bach's first two names (and wired them together with a Gallic hyphen), why did the French stop short at his last name, which means "brook"? If it was legitimate to convert the Italian word *angelo* ("angel") into its French cognate *ange,* then why not go all the way with Bach, and invent the composer "Jean-Sébastien Ruisseau"? There is an intuitive sense that this would just be going a little too far — but where does this sense come from? Where in the blur is the line to be drawn?

I do not mean to be unfairly singling out the French for the sin of name-tampering. The Italians often refer to Bach as "Giovanni Sebastiano"; in Spanish he's "Juan Sebastián". For all I know, he's "João" in Portuguese and *Иван* ("Ivan") in Russian. As for us anglophones, we're guilty too, even though, thank God, Dostoyevsky is not Theodore and *One Day in the Life* is not *of John Dennison*. Still... *Евгений Онегин* is *Eugene Onegin*.

Although it's been a long time now, I have seen "John Sebastian Bach" in a few places, and each time I cringe. It is precisely this kind of vague associative discomfort, intangible but crucial — these "yukkhy vibes" — that whispers a quiet warning in one's ear that one has just gone a little too far in one's well-meant attempt to pull some great one by the scruff of their name into the bosom of one's own culture. I believe I have run into "John Bach" only in musty old British publications, which does not surprise me: its flavor seems part and parcel of the British attitude in the glory days of their far-flung Empire, when the whole world seemed within such close reach of falling under the rule of the Crown.

We anglophones are taught about "the Italian explorer Christopher Columbus" rather than "Cristoforo Colombo". Why, then, do we not sing the praises of "the Italian inventor William Marxon"? Not only have we not rebaptized him thus; in fact, the very idea would evoke ridicule. Times and sensibilities have surely changed quite a bit since the days of Christopher Columbus and John Sebastian Bach. Indeed, calling the opera composer Giuseppe Verdi "Joe Green" is by now a standard old joke, exploiting the fact that doing so makes him "one of us" but at the price of turning him into the local dog-catcher.

Why is it that we Americans never tried to appropriate Albert Einstein fully into our anglophone world by rechristening him (as I, rope-tied in the preceding chapter, was forced to do) "Albert One Stone"? The reasons underlying such hesitations are extraordinarily difficult to pinpoint or articulate; the final decision has everything to do with one's unconscious set of attitudes about what one wishes to radiate through language — in a word, with one's tone.

What is such appropriating all about? What does it suggest? Could it be that the multiplicity of names for J. S. Bach is some kind of collective recognition that Bach, despite having been German, transcends nationality and is a figure for the world? Or do translated names suck people in? For example, the Italians refer to Paris as "Parigi", a very Italian-sounding name for a city. Does this suggest to an Italian, be it ever so lightly, that Paris is actually located in Italy? That may sound absurd, but then consider this: Do you know in what country the city of Leghorn is located? It's also the land where the great metropolises of Meiland and Rzym are found, for a hint. In fact, the latter — one of the great cities of world history — is the country's capital. The country is — at least for Poles — Włochy. Why is

Leghorn not in England, Meiland not in Deutschland, and Rzym not in Polska, where they would seem to belong? Perché sono tutte e tre in Italia?

Where is the newspaper *People's Daily* published? It sounds as if it could be put out by a left-wing group in New York City, but it's not; in fact, it is one of the largest newspapers in the world, published in China, where it is known as *Rénmín Rìbào* (taken character by character, this is something like "Person-folk Day-gazette"). Why do we refer to this Chinese newspaper and its military cousin *Red Flag* (*Hóngqí*) by means of English words, when we do not do so for papers of most other lands? We never refer to the French paper *Le Monde* as *The World* or to the German paper *Die Zeit* as *The Time* — to do so would ring very strange to our ears. Perhaps this is just convention, but even so, why did the convention fall this way rather than the opposite way? If convention *had* gone the opposite way, as it did in the case of *People's Daily,* then even during the deepest chills of the Cold War, we would have ironically referred to the most blatant propaganda blat in the Soviet Union as *Truth* (rather than as *Pravda*).

In a recent article in the *Washington Post,* I read about the trials and tribulations of several Soviet newspapers, including *Pravda* (recently gone under after many decades of serving the Party well), *Den* ("Day"), and *Sovietskaya Rossiya* ("Soviet Russia"). Linguistically speaking, these few titles were mutually consistent, but in the same article I then read of a Russian television program called "600 Seconds", as well as of the legislative body called, in a real mishmosh, the "Supreme Soviet" (*i.e.,* "Supreme Council"). And most confusing of all, in an article in the *Boston Globe,* I read this fact: "A diamond found in Peaceful, a small settlement in eastern Siberia, has been named after Samantha Smith." Well, I suppose that if there is a "Friedens" in Pennsylvania and a "La Paz" in California, then there could be a village named "Peaceful" (or more properly, Писфул) in Siberia — but even so, I harbor grave doubts that this English word, whether spelled with roman letters or transliterated, is really the place's name.

Music is a domain where, despite many appropriations, there are also many counterexamples that remain in their original language. Thus no one ever speaks of "A Little Night Music"; rather, Mozart's little night music is invariably referred to in the original German as *Eine Kleine Nachtmusik*. (I wonder what Stephen Sondheim's waltzy musical *A Little Night Music* is called in German...) Similarly, no one ever takes Ravel's poetically-titled *Le Tombeau de Couperin* and squashes it into the flat "Couperin's Grave". Perhaps I overreact, being so used to and so attached to the former, but on imagining the latter I once again get that shuddery feeling of those old British Empire days. Next thing you know, the French composer would no longer be François Couperin but Franklin Cuttering. This is not quite as far-fetched as it might sound: The French refer to the Beethoven piece that we call "Wellington's Victory" as *La bataille de Victoria*. It's clear why.

As a young boy, I was deeply influenced by many hearings of a couple of records of Chopin's Études for piano; this was my first exposure to the French word *étude,* a word that immediately took on wonderful resonances of power, intensity, and passion. When, years later, I explored Chopin's music very avidly, reading about it, playing it myself, even composing small pieces in his style, I occasionally ran into references to "Chopin's Studies", and was totally turned off. "Study" for me sounded ever so dull and dry, compared with *étude,* and yet for a French person, *étude* would probably give off almost exactly that same stale aroma. In fact, now that I speak French, I can hear a flatness in the word *étude* very easily, and yet I can also glide over effortlessly — especially when speaking English and thus accenting the word on its first syllable ("*A*-tood") — to a romantic hearing of it again.

The Stunning Slop in Mental Spaces

All these words, sliding and sloshing back and forth so slipperily across semiporous linguistic boundaries… What to make of it all?

A truly seminal work that helped catalyze my thinking about these messy matters a bit over a decade ago was the book *Mental Spaces* by French cognitive linguist Gilles Fauconnier. In his book, Fauconnier points out in hundreds of brilliant examples how we often refer to people or things by means of clearly incorrect linguistic pointers, and yet such "errors" somehow increase, not decrease, the efficiency of human communication. Most of Fauconnier's examples involve a reference that leaps between two associated frames, or "spaces", as he calls them. A movie is a simple example of a space, a painting is another example, and real life itself is a third. Thus consider these sentences about a movie:

> In that movie, Clint Eastwood is a villain.
> But he thinks he's a hero.

Who are the two occurrences of "he" referring to? They could both refer to the *character* (Sam, let's say) played by Eastwood, in which case the meaning is that the fictional Sam is a bad guy who considers himself a good guy. Alternatively, the first "he" could refer to Eastwood, the actor, and the second one to Sam, in which case the meaning is that Eastwood, despite playing the part well, doesn't realize that Sam is an evil fellow. It is also possible, as Fauconnier says, that the two "he"'s both refer to the off-screen personality Eastwood, in which case the speaker is asserting that although Eastwood considers himself a fine guy, he sometimes plays jerks in films.

We find it very natural to refer to characters in plays and movies by the names of the actors who play them ("I never could figure out what Shirley MacLaine saw in that guy"); conversely, it can be equally natural to refer to the actors by the names of the characters that they portray ("After the performance of *The King and I* was over, we went backstage and chatted with Mrs. Anna and the King"). Even though such statements, if taken in a literal manner, are hopelessly confused if not utterly meaningless, we communicate efficiently and elegantly with them. Not only would it be harder to generate sentences expressing "what we really mean", those sentences would be dull and lifeless, something like legal documents.

Another of Fauconnier's examples concerns someone commenting on a painting done by a friend. Two contrasting comments are given:

If you were a good painter, the girl with blue eyes would have green eyes.
If you were a good painter, the girl with green eyes would have green eyes.

What do these mean? In the upper sentence, "the girl with blue eyes" probably refers to a blue-eyed person *in the painting* whose eye color should have been made green, in order to faithfully echo the eye color of someone in real life. Or perhaps not! Perhaps it is the reverse: the phrase refers to a blue-eyed girl in real life who *should* have been falsely rendered green-eyed in order to enhance the color balance of the work of art! Nor do these two exhaust the interpretive possibilities.

In the lower sentence, the nearly-identical phrase "the girl with green eyes" now *must* refer to someone in real life whose eyes are in fact green but in the painting were erroneously rendered as, say, blue. No, "must" is too strong. The sentence might mean this: "Any halfway competent painter who makes a girl green-eyed in a painting does so because she is actually so in real life, but *you* took a blue-eyed girl and made her green-eyed, you dummy!" To convey this meaning, I think it has to be stressed on the word "have" near the end. In any case, it is fascinating how, in a suitable context, we can refer to a girl who in fact has blue eyes by the phrase "the girl with green eyes" and our meaning will come across with perfect clarity.

Fauconnier uses examples like these to show how in our minds we effortlessly hold two, three, even more "mental spaces" at once, and how we mentally stitch them together by unconscious "pointers" whose existence is made manifest by the way in which we effortlessly cross-reference the spaces in our linguistic interchanges, as above. The book is masterful, and clearly and entertainingly sets out a vast array of issues at the most mysterious core of cognition. There's no slop in *Mental Spaces,* that's for sure.

From Mental Spaces to Frame Blends

Being myself engrossed in the study of analogy-making and having been exposed to Fauconnier's work, I suddenly found, in the mid-1980's, that I was starting to see analogy-making in quite Fauconnier-esque terms. I began noticing that when people are talking about two analogous situations, they will often borrow words from one to refer to the other. Thus a mother will say to her little boy, pointing at her own teeth, "You have a tiny speck of tomato *right here*." This is a very rudimentary example, but it makes clear how we can refer to one situation by using words that pertain to some analogous *other* situation. Such a mental mixing of two situations, whether purely in one's mind or expressed via language, is what I started calling a *frame blend*.

This example just given involves an analogy — the mapping of one human body to another — that is extremely standard and therefore the communication is very efficient and nearly always error-free. What is surprising is that even when an analogy is totally fresh and quite complex, the communication that is afforded by mixing its two sides, despite being incoherent on an "official" level, can be efficient and colorful in a way that no logically consistent language could ever approach.

Frame blends are amazingly pervasive, once one becomes sensitized to them, and I know that they abound in my own prose (in fact, it is a habit that I have tried to cut down on in recent years, not with total success). I could cite hundreds of examples of frame blends that I have collected in casual conversations, newspaper articles, television commercials, and so forth, but here I will limit myself to just two vivid blends that occurred earlier in this book, because I think they make the notion very clear. The first one is a sentence from Chapter 8, where I am talking about four different translations of *Eugene Onegin*:

> For me, there is a very clear rank-ordering: Falen, Arndt, Johnston, Elton/Briggs, with the gaps growing in size as quality falls, and with the performances by the first two often extraordinarily different in tone and imagery, yet amazingly close in eloquence, a bit like two world-class violinists' hair-raisingly precise slalomings down the steep slopes of a great sonata, differing in style on every single turn, yet in speed separated by no more than a few hundredths of a second.

What am I *really* talking about here? I began with an analogy between marvelous translators and virtuoso violinists, and that in itself would be plenty interesting enough to provide a fine frame blend. But before I have launched myself far along that pathway, I bring in a third image, that of ski racers on a steep slope, and all of a sudden the piece that the violinists are playing *is* the slope, and its measures are (roughly speaking) the flags planted in the snow (or perhaps the flags in the snow are the flags on the stems of the notes!). The incredible flurry of the notes is then blurred smoothly with the mad dash of the skiers toward the bottom, and now it seems as if the violinists are racing each other to finish first. The phrase "differing in style on every turn" is one of the key moments here, since it is easily heard in terms of the skiing image yet at the same time can apply to the music in either a metaphorical or a technical sense (a *turn* being a trill-like kind of ornamentation). All of this, mind you, is to be understood as describing the skill of *translators*, in fact.

Another quite intricate frame blend in this book occurred in Chapter 10, in which I discussed Ring's painting of his wife drinking coffee, my own wife drinking coffee, and two isomorphic sentences in different languages, each of which was simultaneously about the two wives. All through that discussion, questions about linguistic translatability were intimately blurred with analogous questions about mutual understandability of people.

The King and We

Armed with the notions of mental spaces and frame blends, let us return to our earlier concerns with translation and the interpenetration of languages and cultures. Translation can be cast in terms of the stitching-together of two mental spaces that have many points in common and many differences. The best possible result is some kind of artistic unity in which aspects of both spaces — both cultures, both media, both works of art — are harmoniously combined. Aside from translation, pure creation often has this same type of origin.

Since I just recently took my two children to a marvelous performance of *The King and I,* an example from that glorious, sad musical is at the forefront of my mind. There is a scene where the King is introducing a select subset of his 67 ("I started late") children to "Mrs. Anna", who has just arrived from England to be their teacher. One by one, the children come tramping in to the strains of a piece called "March of the Siamese Children". It's a lovely, lilting melody and clearly Richard Rodgers, its composer, was striving to make it give off an exotic, Siamese flavor. On the other hand, he was working within the idiom of Western tonal music and could not fully break out of it without losing his audience. What resulted from the combination of these two pressures on Rodgers is a curious (and delicious) mishmosh that to me sounds a little bit Oriental (maybe one-third) and a lot like Edvard Grieg (his "Wedding Day at Troldhaugen"). In fact, if you had told me that it was *by* Grieg, I would have believed you. This kind of cross-fertilization of traditions is one of the best ways we have of producing wondrous new insights and works of art.

What I said a couple of pages back — in quotes in parens — about going backstage after the show to see Mrs. Anna and the King was in fact so. Moreover, I think the blend captures far more of the truth than would a supposedly "truer" version: "We went to see *the people who played the roles* of Anna and the King." The fact of the matter is that we also went, in some vague but very real sense, to see Mrs. Anna and the King themselves. There was an aura of old Siam that still clung to them both, even though she had dropped her stunningly good English accent and he his Thai accent, even though they were now all smiles and quite a bit of sweat. The fact of the matter, again, is that the separate frames of stage and real life are not kept apart in a watertight manner in our minds, although for our dignity's sake we — especially we adults — maintain the official pretense that they are. But to be overly rigid about it is silly, for to do so is to miss out on much pleasure: blurs of that sort are a large part of the poetry of life.

But let us return to language itself. Still thinking of *The King and I*, I am reminded of the groveling submission of the King's courtesans and ministers, the pathetically servile and toad-like way they constantly kowtow to him. What is this *kowtowing*? Its sound tells us unmistakably that whatever it is, it is an *Oriental* mode of behavior. In fact, it is a direct phonetic import from the Mandarin expression *kē tóu* — "to bang head" — and denotes obsequious, groveling behavior. Why do we use such a word in English? Not just to say "obsequiousness" or "groveling", because we have those words; we do it to bring in a subliminal halo of other places and other times; we do it to mix those flavors, like exquisite Thai spices, in with the otherwise familiar words and images of our more normal English sentences.

My question is, would the English translators of Zhang and Sang's *Chinese Lives* ever have used a word like "kowtow" in their English renditions of the Chinese interviewees? And my conclusion, after reading a large part of the book and scanning the rest of it quite thoroughly, is that no, they wouldn't. They avoid words with an Oriental flavor *like the plague*. In fact, I was surprised to see that they even used the name of the Chinese monetary unit, the *yuan,* rather than replacing it by some slang British term like "tanner" or "bob" or "quid". In their book, English swearwords and idiomatic phrases ("the textbooks are all old hat anyway"; "we'll cross that bridge when we come to it", says a young woman nicknamed "Diploma") are a dime a dozen, but words like "kowtow" or "rickshaw" are rare as hens' teeth — in fact, nonexistent. Orientalisms have been thoroughly expunged from the mouths (and the minds?) of these Chinese people. About this there's something not just sad but glaringly wrong, I feel.

Jawohl, monsieur!

We all have seen German U-Boot officers in old World War II films saying things like this: *"Jawohl, mein Kommandant. Und* also, haff you any Newce about ze Sinkink of zat Britisch Scheep?" The pretense that they are speaking German is as corny as all get-out, but it works. In fact, this flavor is very crucial to the movie. If the evil Nazis were speaking in standard American accents, sounding indistinguishable from their innocent, bright-eyed, gum-chewing, red-blooded Yankee counterparts, then we just might start having a bit of trouble knowing which side we were rooting for.

Such devices are time-worn, by the way. Here is a little taste of how the nonfictional Major-General Louis-Joseph de Montcalm (1712–1759), leader of the French forces in Quebec, speaks, in Chapter 15 of *The Last of the Mohicans,* to his fictitious adversary Major Duncan Heyward, when the latter, sent as an emissary of his commanding officer, meets the former in the inner recesses of his garrison:

> …said Montcalm, taking Duncan familiarly by the arm and leading him deep into the marquee, a little out of earshot: "Je déteste ces fripons-là ; on ne sait jamais sur quel pied on est avec eux. Eh bien ! Monsieur," he continued, still speaking in French, "though I should have been proud of receiving your commandant, I am very happy that he has seen proper to employ an officer so distinguished, and who, I am sure, is so amiable as yourself." …. "Your commandant is a brave man, and well qualified to repel my assaults. Mais Monsieur, is it not time to begin to take more counsel of humanity, and less of your own courage? The one as strongly characterizes the hero as the other!"

The gall of that transition into English-referred-to-as-French! But gall or not, the frame-blending is somehow appealing, with *Mais Monsieur* coming right in the middle, reminding us once again just who is speaking and what language he is allegedly speaking in.

There are many other frame blends of various languages in the book, but I particularly like one that I ran across at the end of Chapter 23, this time involving English and the Indian language of Huron. A Mohican chief is sternly addressing a doomed prisoner, a young Huron Indian, before putting him to death:

> "Reed-that-bends," he said, addressing the young culprit by name, and in his proper language, "though the Great Spirit has made you pleasant to the eye, it would have been better that you had not been born. Your tongue is loud in the village, but in battle it is still. None of my young men strike the tomahawk deeper into the war-post — none of them so lightly on the Yengeese. The enemy know the shape of your back, but they have never seen the color of your eyes.…"

I was puzzled by the word "Yengeese", at first thinking it was the name of another Indian tribe, but in the glossary I found, to my surprise, that it was the Indian pronunciation of the word "English". Cooper certainly *could* have had the chief say "none of them so lightly on the English", but instead he chose to insert the Huron way of saying "English" right into the English text, once again to remind readers that the chief was *not* speaking Yengeese. There is certainly something funny going on here. I assume, by the way, that "Yankee" must come from this distortion of "English", even though my dictionary tells a totally different etymological story.

I close this section with one last example, and quite a byzantine one, of frame-blending in cinema. This involves the film *The Last Emperor,* which Carol and I saw together many years ago. As soon as we got home that evening, I zoomed into my study and, before I forgot the details, jotted down two little pages of notes for myself on its strange linguistic conventions. Here is what I wrote:

> As a child, the Emperor spoke perfect (accent-free) English, which was their way of showing him speaking his native language, Chinese. But when he grew up, he had a very noticeable foreign accent in English, which was their way of showing him speaking a language other than his native language. Basically, then, for the Emperor the convention was this:
>
> - accent-free English symbolizes Chinese;
> - accented English symbolizes English.

To make matters worse, he kept his foreign accent even when speaking with his two wives (presumably in Chinese!), because it would have been ludicrous for him to switch back and forth between accented and accent-free English, depending on who he was talking to.

> By contrast, the convention for all the rest of the characters was the *usual* movie convention — namely:
>
> - accented English symbolizes non-English.

Another problem — a more standard one — was that crowds (such as the Red Guards at the film's end) would clearly be singing in Chinese, and even would say short things to each other in Chinese, but then when you zoomed in on just *one* of them and saw that person interacting with the Emperor, that person suddenly switched to *English* (with a light accent, of course, so you wouldn't be jarred by a perfect American accent, making you think of a Chinese–American from Los Angeles). And yet, just a few moments earlier, this same person had been singing or chanting or barking an order to someone else, *in Chinese*!

And of course, all the writing everywhere was in Chinese, and when the Emperor, as Prisoner 981, was asked his actual name (by someone speaking English with an accent), he replied out loud, then was asked to write his name down, and wrote it in Chinese characters.

The Parapluies of Chêne-Bourg

In my youthful year in Geneva, I grew enormously fond of *les trams électriques* that crisscrossed that beautiful small Swiss city, and liked nothing better than doing the full loop of the "1", cycling me around from Cornavin to Champel and back (*hélas,* it's now *défunt*), or riding the "12" all the way from Chêne-Bourg to Carouge and back. We returned to California all too soon, leaving me full of nostalgia; whenever Geneva and our activities there came up in conversation, I *always* used the word "tram" (thus borrowing back into English, curiously enough, a French borrowing of the outmoded-sounding English word "tramway"); it would have sounded absurd and totally dislocating to say either "trolley" or "streetcar". Those beloved cars were *trams,* pure and simple, no two ways about it.

And yet, if we went into San Francisco, I was equally charmed and fascinated by the *trolleys* that crisscrossed that city's streets and hills. These were no more *trams* than its legendary cable cars were trolleys! (Note: San Francisco's cable cars belong to a completely different species from its trolleys.) The words are deeply rooted in the place, and if you rip them out of their native territory and apply them to entities in another place, you wind up sounding silly or naïve. Thus no one would refer to Paris's Métro as "the Paris underground", or even worse, as "the Paris tube", those terms being exclusively attached to its counterpart in London; nor would anyone talk about "the Paris subway", even though in theory "subway" is a bland, neutral term.

The point has to be made very carefully, however. I am not saying that one leaves the words behind as one leaves the place behind; I am saying something very, very different: that although certain words are firmly anchored to things in a specific place, they not only *can* but *should* be used in distant places and even in distant tongues, precisely in order to evoke, inside the new framework, the local — and now exotic — flavors that they are imbued with. Each such word is like a Trojan horse that, once inside the ramparts of the alien city, bursts wide open and spills a horde of aliens into the heart of The Other.

The evocative power of such an act is why my mother and Melanie Mitchell, in their translations of Marot's poem, both inserted elegant and unmistakable references to its Frenchness (*e.g.,* my Mom's "oo-la-la" and Melanie's "your Bastille"); it is also why Bob French, in doing his first translation of the same poem, inserted antiquated phrases suggesting its oldness (*e.g.,* "fairest friend" and "quit this place"). And I, taking my cue from these pioneers, then inserted "Madame" into "To a Damsel in Bed", giving just the faintest of faint hints of the original poem's Frenchness. There are, of course, other fine examples of such blending in various versions of "Ma Mignonne" scattered throughout the book.

Back to Forward

This brings me back to the "inconsistency" of Robert Forward — his odd, almost inexplicable treatment of analogical extensions from earth: embracing so many, yet balking at so many others. Thus "air" is in but "day" is out; "plant" is fine but "blood" is *verboten*; and so forth. This kind of uneasy vacillation permeates the book.

Although he will liberally use words like "pollen", "skin", "muscle tone", "blister", "body", and "enzymes" in reference to (so-called) plants and animals on the star's crust, he then turns right around and talks about "intake orifices" instead of "mouths", "treads" instead of "feet", and even "flowing" instead of "dying" (although "die" is sometimes used as well). He is careful always to say "crust" instead of "ground" or "soil" (heaven forbid he should refer to crust-matter as "earth"!); however, "dirt" is fine, for some reason. Also along these lines, an earthquake on the neutron star is (understandably) renamed a "crustquake"; but on the other hand Forward has no qualms in talking about "pebbles" found in the crust.

As I mentioned earlier, the term "pack rat" is used, despite the fact that there are of course no rats, in either the straight or the stretched sense of the term, on Dragon's Egg (an earth-rat, pretending it were not instantly squashed out of existence, would be taller than the tallest mountain on Dragon's Egg, and it is most unlikely that a gnat-sized nuclear-chemistry animal so rat-like as to deserve that name would have evolved on Dragon's Egg itself). He also refers to "empty-handed" cheelas despite the fact that cheelas have no hands (they have "manipulators" and "pseudopods"). These two examples would seem to suggest that Forward is willing to use earthbound metaphors as if they were opaque compounds, as if one swallowed them whole without picking up the slightest taste of their semantic parts — but if that is so, then why was "earthquake" taboo?

Oh, of course I know the answer: compound words are never fully opaque or fully transparent, but each is translucent to some unique degree, not even to a fixed degree but a context-dependent one, and in the context of this novel, the word "earth" inside "earthquake" stands out as clearly as does the word "blood" in "blood-curdling". Which leads me to wonder whether Forward would have said "fluid-curdling" had the occasion for the choice arisen. In fact, he describes what I would be tempted to call a "bloody" battle between two cheelas this way:

> …They wallowed, struck at each other's eye-stubs with the sides of their spears, trod one another's edges, tried to wrest the spear from the other's grasp, and slapped each other with muscular pseudopods in an attempt to deliver a knockout shock to the brain-knot.
>   The usually fluidless battle for Leadership ended in a shocking way when Great-Crack found Blue-Flow's spear pointing in an opportune direction and deliberately impaled herself on it, taking it into her body.…

I was amused by the odd-sounding phrase "fluidless battle", and was also struck by the word "brain-knot", which seems to be an attempt to steer close to, but avoid direct impact with, the word and the feeling of "brain".

Eros is Eros is Eros

Speaking of bodily fluids, one of the oddest parts of *Dragon's Egg* is one to which I gave a teasing allusion toward the beginning of this chapter. In it, a female cheela named Swift-Killer engages in "fun and games" with a male friend, "the eager North-Wind". Bowing to the conventions of the times and the exigencies of the marketplace, I have decided, somewhat against my better judgment, to include this "mature" material in this section (headed, in case it sounded familiar but you couldn't place it, by yet another quip from Searle's witty great-aunt from Oakland). Readers not yet 604.8 seconds old are thus hereby ordered to skip the following passage:

> She put [the offending plates] to one side and attended to more important business, such as thinning herself down and slithering under the hot kneading tread of North-Wind as their eye-stubs entwined softly about one another. They took turns kneading each other's topside with their treads, concentrating on their favorite spots. Then with their eye-stubs firmly intertwined to pull their very edges together, their mutual vibrations raised in pitch with an electronic tingle adding an overtone of spice to the massage. Finally in a multiple spasm of their bodies, a dozen tiny perimeter orifices just under North-Wind's eye-stubs opened — to emit a small portion of his inner juices into the waiting folds around Swift-Killer's eye-stubs.

All of this, of course, ties into cheela genetics, about which, ironically, the cheelas gain much information from an unlikely source: the earth! The way this happens is that over the course of a few hours, as the cheela civilization is advancing by inconceivably rapid leaps and bounds, a vast encyclopedia summarizing all human knowledge is sent via radio waves from earth to Dragon's Egg, and serves as a catalyst to speed up their progress even more. It turns out that much of molecular biology is so abstract — so information-oriented rather than chemistry-oriented — that it transfers straight across the fantastic gap, with genelike patterns, which code for protein-like structures, arranged linearly along a *triple* (not a double) helix, thus allowing for sexual recombination, and one of the finer points of the analogy being that there are even dominant and recessive genes, exactly as in terrestrian chromosomes.

At times, I must say, this kind of one-to-one mappability between cheelas and humans strains my patience; I find it goes too far, as if Forward, for all his ingenuity and scientific probity, was incapable of dreaming up anything but the simplest possible variations on deep, rich themes such as DNA and proteins, sperms and ova, and so forth. I'm not saying I could do any better! And certainly, compared to most science fiction, in which one routinely encounters intelligent aliens from other galaxies that are distinguishable from earthlings only by such tiny twiddles as the shape of the tips of their ears, this degree of imagination is a welcome relief.

The Centrality of Frame-Blending in Translation

As I reviewed what had at the outset seemed to me like disturbing inconsistencies in Forward's narration, for terrestrial consumption, of many episodes involving neutron-star life forms — some plant-like, some animal-like, some human-like — I started to realize that although I might disagree with the details of which words to borrow wholesale and which words to balk at, *some* sort of mixture was certainly necessary in order to build the strange halfway house that is the mapping between two related but deeply different frameworks.

I will never be a cheela and will never know from inside just what that experience is like; I will ever be a human and must understand everything from within *this* viewpoint, limited though it may be. But trying to bring the cheela experience totally within my own experience on earth, trying to fold it all neatly into my pre-existing terms, is certainly not going to do justice to the fact that theirs is a radically different viewpoint from mine. Spoonfeeding everything into my world would be a sham. And this is why and where frame-blending becomes so important.

Let us go back to the central issues of Chapter 6 for a moment and recall the early debates over how to translate *Gödel, Escher, Bach* into Chinese. There was no author's hope or translator's need to get across some special essence of Americana to an Oriental audience. After all, the book's motivating message floats somewhere between the scientific and the philosophical, but is in any case transcultural rather than local; and where the book's language plays games and indulges in humor, that too is abstract and has no essential roots in its author's home culture. To be sure, I am a native speaker of English and so my puns are in that language, and likewise, many of my examples and vignettes are drawn from quintessentially American experiences; but the joy of the puns was the fact of double meanings, not the specific sounds of English, and the pungent American smell of the soil of the simple examples I gave was only in order to render concrete in *some* form or other high abstractions of mathematics or other disciplines. In short, *GEB* is about ideas that, fundamentally, can be carried over, lock, stock, and barrel, into another culture — at least if that culture embraces science and rigor — and it was for that reason that I wanted *GEB* radically redone for each new language and rejected the idea of frame-blending, rejected the idea of leaving my "American nose" showing through in odd spots here and there.

Dragon's Egg, by contrast, is a study — a marvelous *étude* — in alienness, a cultural gap to end all cultural gaps, and converting the neutron-star phenomena fully over into purely terrestrial terms would have been a total betrayal of Forward's intent. No, what was crucial was to remind the reader constantly, and yet subtly, that what might seem familiar was at the same time terribly, unimaginably alien. For this purpose, what was needed was a constant blending of familiar with unfamiliar, a constant but not overwhelming sense of tension and disorientation. Only in this way could the proper balance be struck, allowing a reader to penetrate deeply into the alien experience yet not to be fooled into thinking that it was just a case of a simple "decoding", as Warren Weaver spoke of. The speculative neutron-star world that Frank Drake initially envisioned and that Robert Forward lovingly developed in his imagination, though it has much in common with our terrestrian world on abstract planes, is not anything like an isomorphic copy of it, all of whose secrets can be revealed in a flash by a mere substitution of labels.

And thus in the end, although I could nitpick forever about tiny details, I realized that Forward's frame-blending inconsistency had in fact done just the job it was supposed to do, *had* struck a fine balance between oversimplifying and overmystifying an alien yet partially comprehensible world. It was precisely this relentless frame-blending — a kind of "consistent inconsistency" — that had turned the trick.

And when I compared this style of writing to the seemingly masterful translations in *Chinese Lives*, I felt far closer to being able to articulate just why those translations had always left me so frustrated, even angry, in spite of the marvelous idiomatic polish of their English prose. Those translations were *fooling* readers; they prevented readers from smelling the Chinese smells by turning them into familiar ones.

One might argue that the Chinese smells were in the *content* of what the interviewees said, not in their medium of expression, but to me that is a naïve viewpoint. To me, form and content are deeply tied together, and that is why translation is such an art. The decision of the translators of *Chinese Lives* was to sharply cleave medium from message, and having done so, to discard every trace of the old medium in rendering the message in the new one. In theory, this sounds great, but in practice it yields a contradiction: The voice speaking in the new language no longer seems rooted in its own culture. This is fine in certain types of cases — but not when culture is of the essence!

The choice is, as it so often is in life, between two evils: on the one hand, a pervasive sense of mild stylistic inconsistency (as in *Dragon's Egg*), due to frame-blending, and on the other hand, a pervasive sense of self-contradiction (as in *Chinese Lives*), due to the medium and the message being utterly at odds with each other. In mathematics and logic, the words "inconsistency" and "self-contradiction" mean virtually the same thing, but in literature, that need not be the case. Whereas I would characterize *self-contradiction* as the presence of confused and wrong ideas (which of course can be done in a beautifully polished manner), I would characterize *inconsistency* as the mixing of different styles and the intermingling of different worlds. These are two vastly different evils, and between them lies the choice that one must face in translation.

Each new translation challenge, to be sure, merits — indeed, requires — a careful rethinking of this choice. Nor is it a black-and-white choice; one can obviously find a continuum of intermediate positions between the black of zero frame-blending and the white of free-wheeling, anything-goes frame-blending. I am not saying that Robert Forward in his novel found the optimal point along this continuum — only that he is somewhere along it. By contrast, the translators of the interviews in *Chinese Lives* and of *One Day in the Life of Ivan Denisovich* whom I targeted for attack in Chapter 6 lie at one of its extremities. And, for that matter, the *GEB* translators into various languages were, at least if I had anything to say about it, at the opposite end of that spectrum!

What about the "Ma Mignonne" challenge? Given its minuteness, it of course lends itself to a nearly unlimited variety of approaches. Translating "Ma Mignonne" is not like translating Proust's 2,000-page opus *A la recherche du temps perdu*; one is not making a commitment for several years of one's life to a philosophy of translation! Neither in Proust's case nor in that of "Ma Mignonne" is there an optimal point along the continuum (at least not that I'm aware of), but in the former there is no time to play around with parameter settings — life presses, time and the tides wait for nary a soul, and so one simply has to make an intuitive choice and get down to business before the bell tolls — whereas in the latter there is time a-plenty for playing around, so it is wise and delightful to let a hundred flowers bloom.

The Artless Artistry of Forward's Egg

Of all the books in the world, why did I choose *Dragon's Egg* to spend so much time on? When I first heard about it fifteen or more years ago, the mere idea gripped my imagination. I had no idea how well it was written, and was at the outset very skeptical. However, the premise was so tempting that I ordered a copy of it and gave it a try. I started skimming it and soon found myself quite caught up in it, despite reservations on many levels — scientific, stylistic, artistic, literary, and so on. There was enough solid meat in the book to make it worthwhile, and it bore a stamp of such seriousness and authenticity that I was won over.

Still, *Dragon's Egg* is not a great work of world literature. Why then spend so much time talking about it? Because its author, like Stanisław Lem, Poul Anderson, and a handful of others, chose science fiction as a personal medium of expression not out of a desire to write swashbuckling adventure tales in some vast interstellar setting, but to realize the original meaning of the term: to make serious counterfactuals about science itself, to push scientific and philosophical ideas in speculative directions. Forward's novel is deeply reflective at all levels, including that of language, as we have seen. And that's why it's so worth paying attention to.

Robert Forward's ceaseless frame-blending seems inconsistent, but I hope to have convinced you that such inconsistency is in fact an art — is *the* art — of good translation. This art is not something that one can rigorously define and then write a perfect algorithm for. It is a product of intuition and experience. It is a state of grace that a translator strives for, but it can come only from deep within, at levels of oneself that one does not, cannot, and hence never will truly know.

As the Danish mathematician and poet Piet Hein wrote in a poem called *Ars Brevis,* one of his many memorable mini-maxims called "Grooks":

> *There is*
> *one art,*
> *no more,*
> *no less:*
> *to do*
> *all things*
> *with art-*
> *lessness.*

●

Poems XI:

~ Hall of Mirrors ~

* * * * *
* * *
* *
*

As I had written to a motley collection of friends around the globe, I had no idea who might respond, or when. To my surprise, my good friend Benedetto Scimemi, a musical mathematician from Padova, Italy, was the first. He had taken up my challenge with gusto and sent me not one but two attempts: "Mia Adorata" and "Bambina Mia".

A mere glance revealed that Benedetto had played free and easy with form. Both versions had just 24 lines, neither trisyllabic nor final-accented. Thus in "Mia Adorata", the lines were all meant to be *tetra*syllabic, although how that works is pretty subtle. Line 1, for instance, has an "official" syllable count of 6, since *adorata* by itself is already 4, and *mia* adds 2 more. Similarly, line 18 also has 6 "official" syllables, since *che a Dio* has 4 syllables ("*ke a di–o*") and *piaccia* has 2 ("*pya–cha*", the first syllable just as in *piazza*). Line 15 obviously has 5 syllables. However, the vowels of Italian are wondrously liquid — so much so that these bulging lines, and similar ones, can be orally squeezed into just four syllables. (Roughly, they sound like this: *Mya*–do–*ra*–ta; *Kya*–dyo–*pya*–cha; *Res*–tyang–*ko*–ra.) Thus despite appearances, all 24 lines can be comfortably coaxed into tetrasyllabicity. As for content, a couple of liberties have been taken (*e.g.*, throwing drowsiness into the picture), but by and large, the content of "Ma Mignonne" is well captured in this cute poem.

Having studied Italian for a long time, I could savor Benedetto's opus directly (though I had to look up a word or two), so it didn't occur to me to convert it into English. However, when it came to writing this book, I felt to do so was crucial, to allow readers to see into what Benedetto was doing; thus next to his Italian "original" (so to speak) you will find "My Dear Adored", which started out life as my attempt to render his meaning *literally*, in a bland and boring way, with no attention paid to form. The funny thing is, from the instant I started working on it, I was overtaken by the desire to add rhyme and meter, and soon the nature of my attempt changed underfoot. I decided it should be *both* a literal *and* a literary translation — in other words, it should be deeply faithful to Scimemi's poem in as many regards as Bill Cavnar's "O My Sweet" and Melanie Mitchell's "My Dear Sue" had been to Marot's poem. Thus of course I respected its tetrasyllabic nature and its line-count of 24 — and yet, for some odd reason, perhaps not even conscious at the time, I shifted the stress from the penultimate to the final syllable. So how good was the result?

Well, "My Dear Adored" is just a shade too liberal a translation to be called "literal", but it comes within a hair's breadth, I'd say, of that goal. Curiously, however, despite its great local faithfulness on both form and content levels, it comes across globally as *utterly different* from Benedetto's poem. This fact struck me as truly, truly weird, and I wanted my readers, even ones who knew no Italian, to be able to appreciate this curiosity with me. But how could I get it across? My only answer was: Make *another* translation, even *more* literal! This time, for sure, just let form go totally. Concentrate on content *alone*.

And so I started working on "My Adoree", as I initially called it — a new, strictly literal, esthetics-ignoring translation (as that clumsy title suggests). But once again, the very same irresistible temptation swept over me, so what did I wind up doing? Creating not "My Adoree" but "My Cherie": another rhyming, metric, yet line-by-line-faithful translation — this one trisyllabic, however, thus far terser than "My Dear Adored". Indeed, as hoped, "My Cherie" is even truer to the original than is "My Dear Adored", and what's more, that global, intangible *feel* it exudes is far closer to the feel of the Italian. And yet — despite all that — I overwhelmingly prefer "My Dear Adored". Things get stranger and stranger.

I see just two ways for a non-reader of Italian to get a sense for such matters: One is to go learn Italian fluently (unlikely!); the other is to compare these translations while taking the stance that reading "My Cherie" in English is tantamount to reading Benedetto's Italian. This is a peculiar stance to take, and yet, what else is translation for, or about? How else can a book in English be passed off as *Yevgeny Onegin,* "by Alexander Pushkin"?

Mia Adorata	My Dear Adored	My Cherie
Benedetto Scimemi	B. Scimemi/D. Hofstadter	B. Scimemi/D. Hofstadter

Mia adorata,	My dear adored,	My cherie,
Sei malata?	Health untoward?	Sick you be?
Son catene	Like one in chains,	They're like chains,
Non star bene.	You writhe from pains.	The chilblains.
Vieni fuori,	So out you come,	Come out, fly; 5
Sennò muori!	Else you'll succumb!	If not, die!
Te l'ha detto	Thus I predict,	You've been told
Benedetto.	I, Benedict.	By Ben bold.
Tu, golosa,	Your throat so sore	Sweet-throat you,
Ma che cosa	Is starved. You snore:	Why, pray, do 10
Dormi a fare?	Wherefore this nap?	You now sleep?
Va' a mangiare	Snap to! Your trap	Leap to eat
Marmellata!	Craves marmalade!	Marmalade!
Se ammalata	If you stay laid	If bed-laid
Resti ancora,	Up, I'm afraid	You yet stay, 15
Si scolora	Your blush will fade,	Will all gray
La tua faccia.	Your shade degrade,	Go your face.
Che a Dio piaccia	And thus I've prayed	May God's grace
Far gradita	To God, to bless	Render fun
La tua vita	Your life: No less	Your life, one 20
Per cent'anni,	Than fivescore years,	Hundred springs,
Dai malanni	Freed from all fears	From ill things
Liberata,	Of fever's sword,	All set free,
Mia adorata.	My dear adored.	My cherie.

Benedetto's other effort, "Bambina Mia", deviates further from the structure of Marot's original, in that it boasts *five* instead of three syllables per line (as before, under a tight vowel-squeezing regime, since about a third of its 24 lines have six "official" syllables); in addition, its rhymes are *alternating* rather than immediate. Once again, I felt compelled to give non-readers of Italian a sense for "what Benedetto's poem is like" (whatever that means!), so I translated it — or, if you prefer, I created a similar English poem, one that respects all of its structural constraints, but that takes a bit more license with meaning than I did in "Mia Adorata". Indeed, there's quite a bit of extra meaning stuffed into "My Sweet Bambino", such as what "we" know about flu, the "thick gloom", the bambino's weakness for eclairs, the poet's weeping, the "sewer" metaphor, and the curtailment of pain. Nary a one of these has a counterpart in the Italian poem. And yet, despite their discrepant amounts of meaning, the two poems have the same syllable-count. How can this be?

The answer comes, in essence, from the fact that English and Italian have different ratios of *phonemes* (sounds) to *morphemes* (minimal chunks of meaning). Italian words tend to have lots of two-letter syllables, while English is full of four- and five-letter monosyllabic words. Even so, both languages tend to have about the same number of morphemes per word. This suggests that a given number of syllables in English will be longer, and contain more ideas (to the extent that "idea density" can be quantified!), than the same number of syllables in Italian. Concretely, just look at how much wider my poem is than Benedetto's, even though both have exactly the same syllable-count. And the word-count ratio is 94 to 64! On several lines, facing *two* words of Italian you will see *four* words of English. As a result, it was almost unavoidable for the English poem to have slightly more ideas per line, which makes its flavor quite different from that of the Italian poem.

As for the titles, the discrepancy between the English word "bambino" (it's in dictionaries) and Italian's *bambina* is noteworthy. The Italian word is explicitly feminine ("girl child"), the masculine form being *bambino*. But since in English "bambina" is nonexistent whereas "bambino" is well known (from, for instance, Babe Ruth's nickname, the song "Ciao ciao bambino", etc.), I had little choice if I wanted to imitate the Italian directly in standard English. The problem is, of course, that to anyone who *does* know some Italian, "bambino" suggests that the addressee is a male. To counteract that, the word "gal" on line 3 is a useful clarifier, reinforced by "her" on line 22. Still, for an Italian speaker, the effect of hearing a little girl addressed as "bambino" (especially when the Italian poem explicitly calls her *bambina*) is quite comical.

I found it very hard to make a long series of purely feminine rhymes, even though in the Italian they sound effortless. But thanks to this exercise I became aware of a curious property of Benedetto's poem — namely, that from line 9 onwards, the semantic chunks are misaligned with the rhyming chunks (the six quatrains). (If you don't know Italian, you can pretty much tell where semantic chunks end by looking at punctuation marks.)

From reading poetry in general, one has been conditioned to expect meaning-chunks to fall flush with rhyme-chunks, but that simply doesn't happen in these two poems. In Marot's French original, of course, a rhyme/semantics misalignment also exists, but there the offset is patterned and systematic, giving it a perfect logic of its own. Here, by contrast, things are jumbled, so that certain lines have a very strange effect. In reading my English version out loud, I get a small jolt when I hit lines where a tight thought-chunk winds up in an unexpected rhyme-chunk, such as 13 and 21. But most of all, it's the nonexistent line 25 that bothers me, because it seems it *ought* to exist. That is, after hearing three lines that go together semantically (22–24), I expect a fourth one to rhyme with "cure" and thus complete a meaning/rhyme quartet, but the poem stops short of this goal, leaving me dangling in mid-air.

Bambina Mia	My Sweet Bambino
Benedetto Scimemi	*B. Scimemi/D. Hofstadter*

Bambina mia,	My sweet bambino,
Ti dò il buongiorno.	I hereby hail you.
È prigionia	Gal, only we know
Il tuo soggiorno.	How flu can jail you.
Devi guarire	Now you must heal 5
E dalla stanza	And from your sickroom
Subito uscire:	Stealthily steal,
Questa è l'istanza	Out of the thick gloom:
Del tuo Clemente.	Clement declares so.
Golosa bocca	Bedstay's been rough, since 10
Cui mestamente	You love eclairs so;
Giacere tocca,	After these tough stints,
Vola a mangiarti	Fly off and gorge on
La marmellata!	Fruit jam and jelly.
Ché se non parti	If you don't forge on, 15
E se ammalata	But on your belly
Resti nel letto,	Just keep on lying,
La curva vera	Your deeper beauty
Del tuo visetto,	(This starts me crying)
La bella cera,	Quickly will, cutie, 20
Saran' perdute.	Flow down the sewer.
Iddio ti dia	Lord, let her see no
Buona salute,	More pain; please cure
Bambina mia.	My sweet bambino.

Right on the heels of Benedetto's pair, another set of Italian poems arrived, these from Alex Passi in Bologna. Passi, of whom I had never heard, had been sent my challenge by a mutual friend in Milano. Like Benedetto, he had done not one but two translations — in fact, two-and-a-half. Unfortunately, two of them didn't grab me all that much. They lacked meter, they had too many lines, and one hardly rhymed! For me, the saving grace of Passi's letter was the half-poem he reluctantly included ("Here is something to make you gag", he said), called "Mia Cocò". He typed fourteen lines, then wrote, "*Basta!* I haven't the stomach for it. The main reason Italian pop singers write such terrible lyrics is that although Italian may not lend itself easily to three-syllable lines, it is possible, alas, to do it."

Impressed not just with Passi's poems but by his impeccable English, I wrote back, urging him to finish "Mia Cocò" and including a few translations. In his reply, he said:

> Thank you for the translations. I contend that, whereas Marot's poem is definitely *not* doggerel and aesthetically quite pleasing, an Italian version which were to replicate all of its formal features "forces" the language and just doesn't sound right. The aborted "Mia Cocò" was of course an attempt towards creating precisely this, a complete formal mapping, rather than an aesthetically appealing one. Personally, I prefer solutions that are less constrained formally, like Scimemi's ABAB-rhyming version. Anyway, here is the complete version of "Mia Cocò" for your amusement!

I was delighted to receive the tail end of Passi's doggerel, every bit as cute as its head.

For this book I undertook a translation, calling it "O Pumpkin Mine". (*Cocò* was not in my dictionary, but *cocomero* means "watermelon", which reminded me of pumpkins, and, well…) I must say that, on a line-by-line basis, my poemkin stays extremely faithful to Passi's, though since its lines are longer (tetra- instead of tri-syllabic; don't ask me why), it adds embellishments now and then. The two differ, however, in that "Cocò" has a rhyming pattern of AABBCC…, while that of "Pumpkin" is quite haphazard, though by chance it breaks up into two "sub-sonnets": ABCCB; DCDE; FFEFF. / GHG; IJI; HKJK; ABBA.

My justification for resorting to such irregularity was weak; all I can say is that ever since I first read "Cosmic Gall", John Updike's ode to neutrinos, I have been smitten with jaunty rhyme-schemes. Since that poem epitomizes the notion for me, I exhibit it here:

Neutrinos, they are very small.
    They have no charge and have no mass
And do not interact at all.
The earth is just a silly ball
    To them, through which they simply pass,
Like dustmaids down a drafty hall
    Or photons through a sheet of glass.
    They snub the most exquisite gas,
Ignore the most substantial wall,
    Cold-shoulder steel and sounding brass,

Insult the stallion in his stall,
    And, scorning barriers of class,
Infiltrate you and me! Like tall
And painless guillotines, they fall
    Down through our heads into the grass.
At night, they enter at Nepal
    And pierce the lover and his lass
From underneath the bed — you call
    It wonderful; I call it crass.

Something I've long appreciated about Updike is his embracing of traditional virtues such as rhyme and meter, yet exploiting them in novel ways, as is well exemplified here.

Very recently, in admiring how closely "Mia Cocò" correlates with "Funky Mots", I was led to bemoan its lack of "poietautonym". But then, as I idly rescanned the Italian with the name "Passi" highly primed, all at once the word *passion* jumped out at my eye like a lightning bolt, knocking me off my seat. There he was! Indeed, *Con passion / Fuggirai* can be read as "With Big Passi you'll escape " — or paraphrased, "Alex to see, away you'll flee".

Mia Cocò	O Pumpkin Mine
Alex Passi	*A. Passi/D. Hofstadter*

Mia cocò,	*O pumpkin mine,*	
Io ti do	*For your sweet sake,*	
Il buondì;	*A jolly morn;*	
Stare qui	*To lie forlorn*	
Ti fa mal.	*Here makes you ache.*	5
L'ospedal	*This bedpan pen*	
Lascerai:	*You soon will scorn:*	
Aprirai	*You'll open then*	
Il porton.	*Its stately gate.*	
Con passion	*All ecstasy,*	10
Fuggirai	*Away you'll flee*	
Dai tuoi guai:	*From your sad state:*	
Stando a me,	*'Tis up to me,*	
Così è.	*So thus 'twill be.*	
Non poltrir!	*To loaf is wrong!*	15
È perir	*'Twould be to die*	
L'indugiar!	*To laze too long!*	
Va' a mangiar	*So up to eat:*	
Un boccon	*A dainty bite,*	
Di bonbon.	*A tasty treat.*	20
Se ristai,	*If still you lie,*	
Smagrirai	*You'll shrink to bone,*	
Di pallor	*Your skin turn white,*	
E languor.	*You'll lose your tone.*	
O Gesù,	*O Christ divine,*	25
Pensa Tu	*A thought please make*	
Al suo pro.	*For her sweet sake.*	
Mia cocò!	*O pumpkin mine!*	

In 1989 I taught a seminar on translation, and in it assigned "Ma Mignonne". From a few native German speakers in the class, I obtained German versions, of which my favorite was Frank Rohde's "Kleines Mein". Rohde described his poem as a "literal" translation — fairly close to the truth, as a line-by-line comparison with the French reveals.

Among the interesting choices made in "Kleines Mein" is the switch in tone, halfway through, from the very stilted form of address *Ihr* (today used only as a plural "you") to the intimate form *Du*; this exaggerates the feel of Marot's *vous–tu* shift, which involves two non-obsolete singular "you"'s. Had he wanted to capture this flavor more precisely, Rohde could have used today's formal form *Sie* instead of *Ihr*; then again, that would sacrifice the old-fashioned tone that *Ihr* lends his poem. Either way, you win some and you lose some.

On lines 19–20, the *Fruchtsaft/macht* rhyme is inexact, but to me sounds almost perfect anyway. This auditory illusion is due, I speculate, to the fact that the guttural "cht" sound occurs in the first syllable of *Fruchtsaft,* so that a lingering trace of "cht" as it decays in short-term auditory memory somehow mingles blurrily with *saft,* falsely imbuing it with the feeling of containing the sound, thus making *saft* seem to rhyme with *macht.* (I myself very recently copied this cool trick — see lines 11–12 of "My Cherie".)

To include Rohde's effort in this book, I felt compelled to render it at a literal level in English. By now, the dual goal (literal + literary) was becoming standard — but still very hard! After many hours' struggle, I managed to do it, using "you/thou" to mimic Rohde's *Ihr/Du* shift. At first I called my rendition "Tiny Mine", then "Missie Mine". But my mother, ever my critic, felt both titles were poor, and suggested what to her was the obvious choice: "Fräulein Mine". In all my long struggles, this "obvious" idea — a frame blend, please note — had never occurred to me, and I adopted it with much delight.

Though it didn't knock me over the head, I noticed that Rohde's poem came close to having three-line semantic chunks (the glitch due to 28's nondivisibility by 3 occurs in lines 4–7). How this was possible in a quasi-literal translation from the French is a bit of a mystery, and yet there it is. I guess Rohde's deviation from literality, though small, is just big enough to allow distichs to turn into tristichs! Rohde himself, in his commentary on his poem, never mentions tristichs, so I conclude this quasi-pattern was just a coincidence.

There's a second spot where the pattern is marred — namely, the spillover of *Im Bett* onto line 17. Actually, lines 16–17 are tricky, for in them Rohde exploits the fact that poetic German sometimes allows a verb to be left out, provided the meaning is sufficiently obvious from context. Thus *Mund, der ganz wund im Bett* means "mouth, which quite sore in bed". Clearly, the verb is missing, but fluent readers mentally fill it in with "lies" or "is".

In my translation, in order to get as close as possible to a perfect set of tristichs, I shifted the conceptual attachment of the adverbial phrase "in bed", so that instead of telling where the stung tongue lies, it tells where the filling and swilling will be. This was a hard judgment call, because on the one hand the allegiance shift makes my poem slightly weaker, seen as a translation of Rohde's, yet on the other hand it slightly enhances the purely *internal* logic and elegance of my poem. The latter pull eventually won out for me.

Two bits of wordplay amused me. One was "cramps your style", since "cramps", as a noun, conjures up visions of stomach flu. Then there was "jamb", a word whose sole *raison d'être* was to serve as a fleeting, punning allusion to Marot's famous *confitures*. Silly, but once I'd thought of tipping my hat to Marot in this way, I clung to the idea with a passion; indeed, that one word had a huge effect on the evolution of my translation (particularly the lines near line 8), since in my mind, "jamb" was as unslippable as the Rock of Gibraltar, thus forcing everything in its vicinity to adapt to it rather than the reverse.

What is curious to me is that "Fräulein Mine" (aside from its title) looks just about as close to "Ma Mignonne" as to "Kleines Mein". This makes the trio a very pleasing one.

Kleines Mein	**Fräulein Mine**	
Frank Rohde	*F. Rohde/D. Hofstadter*	

Kleines mein,	*Fräulein mine,*	
Gruß soll sein	*Greetings fine*	
Euch gebracht.	*Are aflight.*	
Solche Schmacht	*Plague, sad plight,*	
Macht unfrei.	*Cramps your style,*	5
Wohl denn sei	*Yet you'll smile*	
Euch recht schnell.	*Soon, my lamb.*	
Durch die Schwell',	*Through the jamb*	
Kommet mit	*Of yon door*	
Flinkem Schritt,	*Stride once more!*	10
Vehement	*Vehemence*	
Ihr Clement	*In Clement's*	
Hat gesagt.	*Words is clear.*	
Unverzagt,	*Pour some cheer*	
Deinem Mund,	*On thy tongue,*	15
Der ganz wund	*Which lies stung:*	
Im Bett, füll	*In bed, fill*	
Eine Hüll'	*And then swill*	
Von Fruchtsaft.	*Jugs of juice.*	
Krankheit macht	*Putrid puce*	20
Deine Farb'	*Thy new hue,*	
Gewiß darb,	*Thanks to flu;*	
Und zuletzt	*Yet far worse*	
Dich verläßt	*Is thy curse:*	
Dein Genuß.	*Flagging zest.*	25
Machen muß	*Be thou blest*	
Gott Dich fein,	*By God's sign,*	
Kleines mein.	*Fräulein mine.*	

Ariadna Solovyova, a student from Russia, originally took a course in geometry from me, and the last thing I would have expected was that she would someday do a "Ma Mignonne" translation. But a couple of years later, when she heard me give a lecture on this poem and its many translations, including lovely ones into Italian, German, and other languages, she was shocked that no one had yet managed to produce a decent one in Russian (though several attempts had been made), and felt inspired to try her own hand at the challenge. Thus was born "Angel Moi".

Since I know only a modicum of Russian, it helped a lot that Ari provided me with a line-by-line anglicization of her poem, which I've reproduced here. A few things she pointed out in accompanying notes are worth repeating. The noun in line 2 has multiple meanings, including "chamber", "hospital room", and "repose". The word for "disease" on line 7 is a slightly archaic term, as is the word for "drink" on line 18. The phrase on lines 18–19 has an old folk-ballad flavor, and conveys the image of partaking of a rich feast. The noun on line 20 means "burdens" and "hardships", as well as "worries". Finally, line 26 literally means: "And — off to the races!" This literal gloss gives you a feeling for some of the charm of Ari's poem. Also, "Angel Moi" came very close to having semantic couplets always 180 degrees out of phase with the rhyming couplets.

My attempt at a literal/literary anglicization, "Angel Mine", is perhaps a little weaker than the others I did for this group, and if so, I suspect this is because my direct feeling for the original is not nearly as strong as in the other cases. "Angel Mine" is neither as literal nor as literary as I would have liked. Still, there are some pretty touches, such as the "syntactic rhyme" of lines 4 and 27. Note that my version, too, comes close to succeeding in the out-of-phase semantic-couplets game, but does not quite make it. (Both Ari and I fail in lines 20–23, although my failure is distinctly worse than hers.)

"Angel Mine" treats its source text with about the same amount of respect, I would say, as does "My Sweet Bambino" — that is to say, quite loosely. This translation, in fact, is more like the anglicizations in the rest of the book, in terms of liberty, equality, and fidelity. For instance, there is nothing in Ari's "Angel Moi" about a pen or a quill, nor is there an image of the poet begging, nor any direct mention of the "angel" undoing a lock or twisting a doorknob. The reason behind the presence of extra ideas here is analogous to that in "Bambina Mia": There's a significant English/Russian discrepancy involving the typical number of syllables it takes to make a single morpheme. Thus note how much thinner Ari's poem is than mine — yet both have 84 syllables. And how many lines in her poem contain just one word? Count them — there are ten, while in mine, zero. Also, the total word-count of Ari's poem is 50, whereas in mine it's 75. What a discrepancy!

If I am criticizing my own lack of fidelity here, then I suppose I could also criticize Ari in somewhat the same way, since, after all, she was trying to be faithful to Marot's text, which has precisely *four* one-word lines, and whose total word-count is 62. Do such counts constitute syntactic constraints that one should generally try to respect? Should they have figured in my original list of formal and structural properties, or are they utterly slippable? When one sees extreme cases such as "Angel Moi", such aspects start to seem more relevant than one might have initially thought. In any case, along this dimension, "Ma Mignonne" itself falls roughly midway between "Angel Moi" and "Angel Mine".

If Ari's English gloss, together with my English poem and this commentary on the whole set, can serve for some readers as an English window — even just a translucent one — onto the Russian poem, I would feel that is a respectable achievement.

Angel Moi	My Angel	Angel Mine
Ariadna Solovyova	*Ariadna Solovyova*	*A. Solovyova/D. Hofstadter*

Ангел мой,	*My angel,*	*Angel mine,*	
В твой покой	*To your chamber*	*Your confine*	
Шлю привет.	*I send greetings.*	*Prompts my quill.*	
Жизни нет	*There's no life*	*Life's worth's nil*	
Взаперти.	*Under lock and key.*	*In that trap.*	5
Укроти	*Tame*	*Therefore sap*	
Злой недуг,	*The evil disease,*	*The vile plague,*	
И на стук	*And to the knock*	*And, I beg,*	
Отзовись,	*Respond,*	*Heed my knock;*	
И явись	*And appear*	*Twist your lock,*	10
На порог,	*In the doorway,*	*Then your knob,*	
Мой дружок,	*My little friend,*	*Dear, and bob*	
Поскорей.	*As soon as possible.*	*On out quick.*	
Не болей,	*Don't be sick,*	*Don't be sick,*	
Не стенай,	*Don't groan;*	*Don't be blue;*	15
Начинай	*Begin*	*Start anew,*	
Пировать,	*To feast,*	*Again sup,*	
Попивать	*To drink*	*And lap up*	
Сладкий мёд.	*Sweet honey-mead.*	*Honey mead.*	
От забот	*Driven by worries*	*Damp the speed*	20
Пожелтеть,	*To turn yellow,*	*Of the dread*	
Похудеть	*To shrivel,*	*Jaundiced spread;*	
Не спеши.	*Do not rush.*	*Curb weight's flow.*	
Полежи	*Stay in bed*	*Please lie low*	
Два денька	*A couple of days,*	*Two days, say.*	25
И — в бега!	*And — get a move on!*	*Then, "Away!"*	
Бог с тобой,	*God be with you,*	*God's love's thine,*	
Ангел мой.	*My angel.*	*Angel mine.*	

Chapter 12

On the Conundrums
of Cascading Translation

In this strange small "Hall of Mirrors", I tackled a challenge so dull as to be utterly unworthy of mention, and yet a challenge so keen as to be worthy of considerable attention.

The goal sounds modest and familiar enough: to take a poem in a foreign language — German, let's say — and to use English as an X-ray to reveal its hidden meaning and structure. The only unusual twist is that the German poem revealed by my English-language "X-ray" happens itself to have been constructed to serve as just such an X-ray, for speakers of German, of another poem in French. So when you read my English, how deep are you really peering? Are you glimpsing the hidden structure of a German poem, or are you seeing *right through* the German poem, all the way to the hidden meaning and structure of the French poem one layer further back? And what if there were even further layers?

Original by Raphael, Copy by Sharp

While perusing an old and bulging file on the endless wiles and guiles of advertising, I came across a sheet I'd torn out ten years ago from some airline magazine. A crisply photographed hand seems to be reaching across the white page from near the "gutter" (where I tore the page out) and holding up for readers to see, against this white background, a 5″-by-7″ color reproduction of a renaissance-style painting of a woman. Just above this rectangular picture is printed, in bold capitals, "ORIGINAL BY RAPHAEL. COPY BY SHARP". And just below the picture there is a caption that reads: *This is an unretouched copy made by Sharp's new full-color desktop copier.*

Over just whose eyes do these Sharpies think they're pulling the wool? Obviously I am looking at a reproduction *several layers away* from the Sharp copier's output: the actual unretouched photocopy first went in front of a color camera that produced a photograph, and that photo in turn went to some process that converted it into several different plates for a printing press, and those plates were all finally inked and pressed separately against the glossy sheet of the magazine, to produce… an unretouched copy?

The point of the ad is to convince me and other readers that Sharp copiers are *faithful*. But I am not looking directly at a Sharp copy. Nonetheless, the very realistic-looking two-dimensional hand holding the image of the painting is meant to convince me that I am. And in some sense, it does. Its realism subliminally conveys the message — a somewhat embarrassing tacit premise underlying the ad, actually — that professional photoreproduction, as in glossy magazines, is a *much higher-fidelity medium* than any mere photocopier (Sharp's or Xerox's or whoever's) could provide. If you believe this — and the *trompe-l'œil* hand more or less forces you to — then you can quite rightly ignore all the extra layers of copying involved in *producing* the ad, and devote your attention solely to the single layer that the ad is *about*.

Careful analysis thus leads this cynic to an unexpected conclusion: Given that some copying processes truly *are* intrinsically more faithful than others, the tricky-seeming ad is not so deceitful as I at first had thought.

Which Twin Has the Tony?

Along these lines, I recall watching a television ad for some brand of television — I'll call it "Tony" — in which one sees an apple-pie family watching their big new handsome Tony TV set in their living room. You are of course supposed to admire the fidelity of this inner set's image, ignoring the irony that the whole scene is being conveyed to you courtesy of *your* television set, whatever brand it might happen to be. The fact is, your television set's grain size greatly *magnifies the apparent graininess* of the much smaller Tony set. You might think that this apparent increase in graininess would have precisely the *wrong* psychological effect — namely, it would turn you away from the Tony — but your eye is subtler than that, and so is the advertising agency.

The key is the happy family in their living room, who play much the same role in this Tony ad as does the *trompe-l'œil* hand in the Sharp ad — its level of graininess provides a standard by which to gauge the quality of the *nested* image. And so your eye, unconsciously taking into account the sharpness of the image of the family, adjusts its instinctive take on the sharpness of the Tony television set. In the end, one is sucked in by the illusion and feels one has actually *seen the quality* of the Tony TV.

I hope I am not fooling myself, but I seem to recall some even more byzantine ads in which you are shown, on your own TV screen, images of two indistinguishable sappy families watching televisions — a Tony TV and a Brand-X model, of course — and are asked, in effect, "Which twin has the Tony?" And the answer, of course, is that the Tony family is the one whose TV screen appears *so much sharper* — even though both are being conveyed to you through the medium of yet another intermediary television screen! I hope my memory serves me right. If not, it serves me right.

As I type these silly words, I am wearing a pair of glasses and looking at the text on my screen. There are thus *two layers* where dirt or condensation can accumulate and interfere with my reading of the text. And yet I can instantly distinguish between smudges and blurs caused by dirt on my *glasses* and those caused by specks on the *screen*. Similarly, if I'm looking at an outdoor garden through two windows in series and am annoyed by interfering smudges, I can easily tell which window is dirty. If it got to be three or four windows, admittedly, I'd start having some trouble. But with two, no sweat. And it is, as we all know, very easy to forget that one is wearing glasses and to think that one is seeing things in a pure, unfiltered manner. Though it's not entirely true, there's a great deal of truth to it.

Judging the faithfulness of one medium when it is being transmitted to you via a second medium, or worse yet, via a chain of further media, can certainly be a tricky business. And yet it is not all nonsense; it works, not by sheer illusion, but by subtly combining illusion with the deep native savvy of the human brain.

Is My Hall of Mirrors a Mere House of Cards?

My goal, in providing my readers with third-generation poems in English in the Hall of Mirrors, was quite analogous to that of the advertising agencies in these ads: Just as they wanted to give viewers the illusion of *actually seeing an undistorted inner image,* I wanted to give my anglophone readers the illusion of *actually reading foreign-language poetry,* even though they would in truth be reading English. A neat trick! Just think: If I could achieve my chimerical-sounding goal, then *mirabile dictu,* monolingual anglophones would be in a position to judge the quality and style of the German and Italian and Russian translations of Marot's poem by reading "them" (I put the pronoun in quotes because its actual referent is *my anglicizations* of them) and applying the same criteria to "them" as they would to the various English translations, such as those by Melanie Mitchell, Bob French, David Moser, and so forth.

For this quasi-paradoxical state to come about, readers would have to have such supreme faith in my fidelity as a post-translator that they would be able to forget (or be willing to overlook) the extra layer of intervention, and would thereby fall for the illusion of *seeing the actual structure* of the Italian, German, and Russian poems. Or *would* it be an illusion? Might it perhaps be the plain truth? O, Mirror, Mirror in the Hall, who's got the greatest chutzpah of them all — Sharp, or Tony, or Yours Truly?

The paradox is, of course, that anyone who reads even a small part of this book will see that I translate with wild abandon all the time, so who would ever believe that I would suddenly calm way down and do a series of very strict, line-by-line, word-by-word, flavor-capturing, correct-era-exuding, non-self-indulgent translations? Actually, the paradoxicality has very little to do with me personally. What would lead anyone to believe that under such tight constraints as Marot's original poem sets up, it would be possible for *any* translator to be so skillful as to become invisible?

And yet, as I write this, I can't help remembering my own reaction on reading Falen's *Eugene Onegin*: I would delight in some marvelous rhyme and think to myself, "Ah, Pushkin!" Now if that isn't suspension of disbelief, what is? Falen had managed to convince me that he didn't exist!

But the Hall of Mirrors situation is much stranger than that of Falen's *Onegin,* because we are dealing with two back-to-back layers of translation. My goal, analogous to Falen's, was to convince readers that *I* didn't exist, but my goal certainly was *not* to convince them that Benedetto Scimemi and Alex Passi and Frank Rohde and Ariadna Solovyova didn't exist. The real paradox can thus be put as follows: I am trying to get readers to believe that in the Hall of Mirrors, two very different stages of translation are involved: one that is fickle and thus *to be judged,* and one that is faithful and thus *to be discounted* as a source of distortion. But how could anybody believe such a dubious proposition, especially when this book is filled with evidence that *all* translation of poetry is fickle and distorts like mad? Will my whole Hall of Mirrors thus collapse like a house of cards?

At the page's top, I carefully prefixed "paradoxical" by "quasi", because I don't think this situation is all that different from the quasi-paradoxicality of the Sharp and Tony commercials: Despite what seems at first to be some first-class skullduggery going on, there is a grain of truth to the idea that the second transmission process is *less distorting* than the first one and hence that the first one *can be judged* through the window of the second one.

My feeling is that over the many years of tackling "Ma Mignonne" and related challenges, I slowly gained skill in the art of translation, and that consequently, my anglicizations in "Hall of Mirrors" are a bit more faithful to their immediate sources (Scimemi *et al.*) than these latter are to *their* immediate source ("Ma Mignonne" itself). That's a subjective judgment, to be sure, and readers are invited to draw their own conclusions.

The Telephone Game and the Picture-degeneration Game

The game of cascading translations fascinates me endlessly, just as it has inspired thinkers about translation, both playful and serious, for time immemorial. Almost everyone is reminded of the children's party game that we in America call "Telephone", in which children sit in a circle around a table, and one child whispers a sentence into the ear of the next one, and then that child repeats the procedure, and so on, until "the message", so to speak, has came around full circle, at which point both the original version and its ultimate transmogrification are said out loud, to the enormous amusement of all the participants and onlookers.

It is taken for granted, in Telephone, that such messages will always degenerate and ultimately become irretrievably and hilariously garbled. Indeed, back when we were teen-agers, my friends the Joneses — Peter, Steve, and Brian — invented an analogous visual game, which we dubbed "The Picture-degeneration Game". Its name tells its nature.

At the outset, all the players would draw fanciful pictures — usually surrealistic pastiches of silly scenes, mixing droll words with strange creatures and dreamlike activities — taking as much time as they wanted, seldom over ten minutes. Then each player would pass their drawing, face down, to the person on their left. When a signal was given, everyone flipped their new image, and the ubiquitous sound of chuckles was invariably loudest at the spot just to Peter's left. We were then given exactly 60 seconds to scan this picture as intensely as we could, and commit it to memory. (In the era of computers, the word "scan" has taken on a new vividness and gives a sense of what we biological beings, in our carnal imperfection, were trying to emulate.) At the sound of the fateful "ding", we would all reflip our sheets, whip out our pencils, and start trying, on a blank sheet, to reconstruct every last detail of the picture we had just been gazing at, seconds before. It was a test not just of memory, of course, but also of artistic skill, and was amazingly revelatory of our weaknesses in both departments.

Players were given as long as they wished to "duplicate" what they had just seen — it usually didn't take anyone more than five minutes — and then the process was iterated. (In these madcap computer days, the word "iteration" has also taken on new flavors — those that are connoted by such buzzwords as "chaos" and "fractal" and "strange attractor" — and indeed, our little picture game has much in common with the mathematical iteration process that gives rise to such wonderful visual phenomena as the Mandelbrot set and Julia sets.) 'Round the circle all the pictures would go in parallel (thus this game gets more accomplished per round than does Telephone) until, of course, they reached home, and then the chains of distortions would be revealed. It was always a moment much looked forward to and seldom disappointing. In fact, it's not an exaggeration to say that some of my life's moments of deepest and purest joy were these hilarious epiphanies when the sheets were turned over and all of our mental foibles were exposed in an instant.

There were certain systematic kinds of things that happened to images, of which we soon became aware, and this knowledge in turn fed back into and heightened our self-awareness as memorizers/copiers. Thus objects tended to drift toward the center of the page, sizes tended to slide towards uniformity, deliberate spelling mistakes tended to get corrected, irregular shapes tended to become regular, accidental dots tended to be copied and to grow, careless mistakes or sloppy renderings tended to be elevated into respected features of the picture, and so forth. And strive though we might to combat these now-known enemies of faithfulness, we were still incapable of overcoming them totally, and so even in our most advanced stages, we still found that pictures degenerated according to somewhat predictable patterns.

Blind Idiot, Rotten Meat

One might think, of course, that this principle would have to be true of any iterated translation process; that *traduttore, traditore,* when subjected to iteration, would reveal its truth in spades. Indeed, I have often heard a couple of lovely stories about "the early days" of machine translation — always the "early days", as if today's MT programs were way beyond such pitfalls — in any case, lovely stories of back-and-forth translation. They are also always told about English and Russian, for some reason. Maybe they're true, although I doubt it strongly. In any case, the stories are identical in structure. The first one goes this way.

One time in the early days of machine translation, enthusiastic programmers fed the phrase "Out of sight, out of mind" into an English-to-Russian translation program. Then, to check the accuracy of their programs, they fed the Russian translation back into their Russian-to-English program. When all the gears had stopped churning and all the lights had stopped flickering, what they got back was quite a surprise — just two words: "Blind idiot".

The second story runs exactly the same, except that the alleged input phrase was "The spirit is willing but the flesh is weak" and the alleged output phrase was "The vodka is good but the meat is rotten".

These humorous tales are often repeated in print as if they were the gospel truth, but I find them both far too cute and perfect to be true. But who knows? In any case, true or not, they do carry the implication, not only about computers but about all translators, that degeneration and distortion are inevitable. But is this necessarily so?

Walter Arndt's Chain of Traducers

Walter Arndt, one of the liveliest and most inquisitive of translators, once decided to subject this thesis to experimental testing. He chose what he calls a "random" quatrain from "Chorus from Atalanta", by the English poet Algernon Charles Swinburne (1837–1909), and then engaged several bilingual and poetically sensitive friends in the process of carrying this stanza from English into French, then from French into German, from German into Russian, and finally, to complete the loop, from Russian back into English. There were thus four translation steps and five actual poems in the completed loop. During the process, of course, nobody saw anything but the one poem they were supposed to translate, nor was there any communication between translators.

Arndt describes this delightful experiment in the introduction to his book *Pushkin Threefold*, and gives us four out of the five chain-links, which I here reproduce:

> *For winter's rains and ruins are over,*
> *And all the season of snows and sins;*
> *The days dividing lover and lover,*
> *The light that loses, the night that wins.*

> *Car les pluies et les deuils de l'hiver ont cessé,*
> *Et le temps de la neige et le temps du péché;*
> *Les heures qui séparent l'amant de l'aimée,*
> *La lumière qui meurt et la nuit couronnée.*

> *Denn Winterschauer, -trauer sind vergangen,*
> *Die Zeit, die Sünde mit dem Schnee gebracht;*
> *Die Stunden, da entrückt zwei Liebste bangen,*
> *Das Licht das stirbt, und die gekrönte Nacht.*

> *   *   *

> *For winter's gusts and griefs are over,*
> *Snowtime weather and sin-time blight,*
> *Lone ache of lover for distant lover,*
> *The light that dies, and the throne of night.*

The row of asterisks of course symbolizes the missing Russian link in the chain. Instead of being disappointed at that link's absence, a fluent Russian speaker might take the asterisks as a very pretty puzzle: reconstruct the invisible Russian intermediary that fits tightly sandwiched between the German and the English versions. Can it be done?

On the Conundrums of Cascading Translation   ◆ ◆ ◆   *343*

Here are Arndt's own reflections on the results of his experimental test of the degeneration hypothesis:

> The versions are like turns in a spiral, coiling out ever farther from the sprightly though undistinguished original in spirit, tone, and rhythm. We notice that the last coil, which is English again, has sprung back, after all these vicissitudes, into a skippy four-footed rhythm very much like the original's; and it has salvaged the identical end rhyme of one couple. Otherwise one observes a certain loss of simplicity, accretion of material, some obscurity and loss of tension in the last line. "The night that wins" lost its innocence by way of *la nuit couronnée* and *gekrönte Nacht* and *у трона ночи*. Still — the result is not as unrecognizable as was the rule in the similar post-office game of our youth, where a short message was hurriedly whispered from ear to ear in a circle of players, and the result was a hilarious shambles. After all, we deliberately courted here the cumulative effect of four subtle acts of "treason", and what emerged was by no means a complete travesty of the original.

I am sure that if this "poetry-degeneration game" were played on many different poems by highly skilled poet–translators (such as Arndt himself, James Falen, Babette Deutsch, and maybe even Vladimir Nabokov, if caught in the proper mood), certain principles would emerge, which could become known lore to be fed back into the minds of the players, to increase their sophistication about stereotyped pitfalls. It would be fascinating but probably too time-consuming to conduct such a series of explorations.

My own personal belief has always been that translation at a sufficiently high level (such as that shown above) maintains essence, though of course it loses specifics, and that even a long chain of translations, such as was here hinted at, can do a very respectable job of essence-preservation as the structure flits from medium to medium to medium. In my opinion, Arndt's experiment supports my intuitive optimism.

Authorship and Credit in Iterated Translations

Let us return to the philosophical puzzles raised at the very start of the chapter, using my third-generation English poem "Fräulein Mine" as a concrete target to focus on. *Of what* is it a translation? Solely of Frank Rohde's second-generation poem "Kleines Mein"? Solely of Clément Marot's ur-poem? Or, in some strange sense, of both? If so, in equal amounts? Or if in different amounts, to what extent of each? And then... *who is the author* of "Fräulein Mine" — Hofstadter, Rohde, or Marot? All three of us? To equal degrees? To varying degrees? How much credit is due to each? How in general to think about such tangles?

One inner voice in my mind suggests that "Fräulein Mine" is just another translation of Marot's "Ma Mignonne"; that "Ma Mignonne" is clearly its source and that Rohde's "Kleines Mein" was merely an incidental way-station en route from Marot's French to my English. But I don't think that voice's point of view can stand up under scrutiny.

Languages are discrete entities, at least fairly cleanly separated from one another; and there is certainly no continuous chain of infinitesimally separated "neighbor languages" that passes from French through German to English. An expressive structure created in French will not just continuously transform, like a piece of rubber being stretched or bent, into an equivalent structure in German. Rather, it snaps and breaks apart and the fragments must be put back together in radically different ways when the jump from one language to another is made. If things were continuous, a piece of text would just deform smoothly in response to a translator's shoves, like a piece of putty. But because languages are discrete, thousands of discrete choices, each one analogous to the choice of an item from a restaurant menu so huge that one can never scan all of it, must be made in the translation of even a small poem like "Ma Mignonne".

My English was prompted by Rohde's German, and it attempted to mimic whatever unique patterns had cropped up in German under the constraints that Rohde was working within; I was not attempting to echo anything in Marot's original (with one minor exception: my pun on "jam"). I was ignoring the poem behind the scenes and looking only at what was directly before my eyes. And because of the discreteness of languages, Rohde's German was a thing unto itself, not just some sort of stretched or bent version of Marot's French. For example, Rohde talks about drinking *Fruchtsaft* rather than eating jam, and I took my cue from that, not from *confitures*. The sick girl has lost her *Genuß* — her sense of pleasure, her *joie de vivre* — rather than her *embonpoint*, and so in my anglicization her problem is "flagging zest" rather than loss of weight. Rohde's poem was basically in semantic tristichs, and my poem inherited that property, not Marot's semantic distichs. And so on and so forth.

The fact remains, of course, that Marot *does* lurk behind the scenes, as a kind of meta-level puppeteer, pulling the strings on a Rohde puppet who in turns pulls the lower strings on a Hofstadter puppet. So where have we gotten in this analysis?

Family Trees and Pedigrees

Here is a curious alternative thesis to consider: that every poem in my entire collection of "Ma Mignonne"'s is a translation of every other one — even poems that are in the same language as each other. Someone who took this seriously would not find it at all strange to encounter a bilingual poetry anthology that had, on one page, Rohde's "Kleines Mein", and on the facing page, my mother's "Hi Toots!". After all, they are translations of each other. Or instead, one could have David Moser's "Sweet Sue" facing Benedetto Scimemi's "Bambina Mia". And — according to this thesis, at least — it wouldn't even matter which of the pair was considered the original and which the mimic, since each is a translation of the other.

Though appealing in its own funny egalitarian way, this is, in my opinion, a far too loose, far too sloppy viewpoint. And why? Primarily because it ignores the fact that behind each poem in the collection there is a unique story or pedigree. To make this concrete, imagine drawing all the poems together in a kind of family tree with "Ma Mignonne" at its root, and all the others on various branches, subbranches, and so on. Thus there would be a "Mia Adorata" branch, and sprouting off of it there would be a "My Dear Adored" subbranch and a "My Cherie" subbranch. If someday "My Dear Adored" were translated into Chinese, then another limb would be created. In principle, there could be branches splitting off branches splitting off branches to any arbitrary level.

Why not just say that each item in the whole tree is a translation of every other one? First of all, from a historical point of view, that is a complete distortion. Things happened along a time line, with certain poems giving rise to others but having zero impact on yet other ones. The *chronology* and *provenance* of each poem form a sort of pedigree that should not just be blithely ignored. Otherwise, "Ma Mignonne" itself would enjoy no special status at all; it would simply be considered one more member of the big happy family. In such a view, Marot's ur-poem would be just as fairly called a translation of, say, Hofstadter's "My Dear Adored" as the reverse. Now that is truly absurd! Provenance matters.

Moreover, in this family tree, there are *distances* along the branches — distances separating one poem from its immediate neighbors. (Imagine a more fully grown tree than actually exists; this imaginary tree would include translations nested many layers deep — versions that passed from French to Finnish to Cambodian to Catalan to Tamil to Tagalog to Hopi to Hausa to Irish to Igbo to Latin to Latvian to Aleut to Azerbaijani, and so forth.) The distance from one poem to a poem that sprang from it (*e.g.*, the distance from "Kleines Mein" to "Fräulein Mine") would be a positive real number. It would be very difficult to assign such numbers, but in theory at least, the distance between two specific poems would somehow summarize in a single number the degree of correspondence, along all possible syntactic and semantic dimensions, between the two poems.

Needless to say, I don't have a mathematical way of computing such a number, and the very idea of trying to define such a number is somewhat nutty, in the same way as the idea of trying to summarize a unique human intelligence in a single number called "IQ" is somewhat nutty — but neither idea is *totally* nutty. Certainly it is obvious that the distance between "Mia Adorata" and "My Cherie" is far smaller than the distance between

"Ma Mignonne" and "Hi, Toots!" We know what we mean by making such a claim, even though we would be hard pressed to tell how to compute any such distances numerically.

The "My Cherie"/"Mia Adorata" connection is a nice case to consider, because "My Cherie" comes so close to echoing Scimemi's "Mia Adorata", not just on a line-by-line but often even on a word-by-word basis, that for me, it stands out as a paragon of interlingual interpoem proximity. It would seem obvious that if one were to ask, "Which is 'My Cherie' closer to — 'Ma Mignonne' or 'Mia Adorata'?", the answer would be "The latter, and by a long shot." This is not to deny in the slightest that we still hear Clément Marot's voice echoing inside the confines of "My Cherie", but his voice is much less clear than Scimemi's. How much do we hear Hofstadter's voice? Well, on the wordplay level, quite a bit — but on the other hand, the sentiments are not Hofstadter's at all. In fact, they are not Scimemi's at all. The sentiments are Marot's. The idea of a 28-line poem with a supertight rhyme scheme is Marot's, and yet the abridged 24-line structure of "My Cherie" is Scimemi's. Many aspects of "My Cherie" are inherited from the original Marot, but they are at a fairly high level of abstraction, whereas somewhat closer to the surface, Scimemi is more important than Marot, and finally at the most superficial level, Hofstadter is the major voice.

The pedigree of "Fräulein Mine" forms an interesting contrast to that of "My Cherie", because if you place "Fräulein Mine" side by side with "Ma Mignonne", you will find that it tracks the lines and words of "Ma Mignonne" just about as closely as it does those of "Kleines Mein"! In other words, aside from its first/last line, which is of course a total giveaway, "Fräulein Mine" looks as if it could have been translated into English either *directly* from the French or *directly* from the German. Returning to the distance metaphor, we could say that the distance from "Fräulein Mine" to Marot's ur-poem is roughly equal to its distance from its direct progenitor, "Kleines Mein". This very unusual case, then, is one where a translation could plausibly be claimed to be equally rooted in two different sources at two different levels of remove. This odd situation is a little like the case of a child who resembles her maternal grandmother every bit as strongly as she resembles her mother.

What Lurks behind Crisscrossing Altitudes and the Stars in Your Eyes?

As I grappled with the strange idea of one translation having two or more rival sources, there sprang to my mind a curiously similar rivalry I encountered recently while doing geometry. Every mathematician knows that virtually every theorem can be demonstrated in a number of different ways. Well, I ran into a simple instance of this general phenomenon that left me truly perplexed. Here's what happened.

One day, I came across a concise, elegant, pictorial proof for the lovely fact that the three altitudes of any triangle always meet each other in a single point given the name "orthocenter" and traditionally denoted by the letter "H". If by chance you didn't know this ancient truth, try drawing some examples on a piece of paper. How come it always works?

The utter simplicity and direct graspability of this proof (which hinges on the diagram below, in which triangle CAB sits nested inside a larger, upside-down copy of itself, whose sides are twice as long) made me feel I had arrived at the absolute crux of this fundamental truth of Euclidean geometry — that I now knew *exactly why* these three lines always crisscross.

Story #1 about Altitudes' Crisscrossing

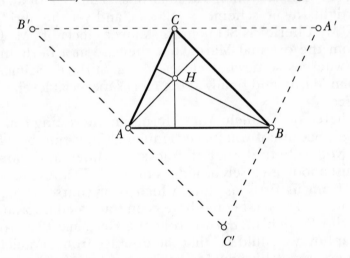

Why is it that the three altitudes of a random triangle CAB meet in one point, H (called the triangle's "orthocenter")? One answer — the most classic answer — is that each altitude of CAB is also necessarily the perpendicular bisector of a side of the larger triangle C'A'B', whose sides are parallel to those of CAB and pass through its three vertices — and it is relatively simple to show that any triangle's three perpendicular bisectors always meet in a single point (its "circumcenter"). Thus the answer is: "The orthocenter of CAB exists because the circumcenter of C'A'B' exists."

Bonus magic: Points CABH constitute an "orthocentric quadruple", which means that each of them is the orthocenter of the triangle formed by the other three.

To me, this was not just *some* proof — it was *the* proof. And when I showed it to students in my geometry seminar, their eyes seemed to light up as this at-a-glance vision of the underlying reason came into view. Our shared sense of enlightenment confirmed my feeling that this tiny net of related ideas was really the ultimate source of the theorem.

A while later, I was reading a classic little book by H. S. M. Coxeter on a more abstract type of geometry called "projective geometry", from which the Euclidean variety can be derived by imposing some special conditions. In this book, there was a very general projective theorem about ten points and seven lines that form a complicated configuration that seemed to have nothing whatsoever to do with altitudes of triangles. Indeed, in projective geometry, the very notion of "altitude" doesn't even make sense, because the Euclidean notion of "right angle" doesn't exist. But toward the end of his book, in a chapter showing how Euclidean geometry falls naturally out of projective geometry when one arbitrary line is singled out and called "the line at infinity", Coxeter took this complicated theorem and combined it with a very strange, truly counterintuitive definition of perpendicularity and presto! in the snap of a finger, there was the theorem about altitudes!

Story #2 about Altitudes' Crisscrossing

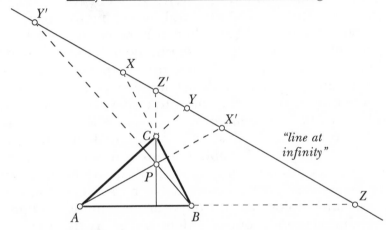

> Given a random triangle CAB, a variable point P, and an arbitrary fixed line (by convention called the "line at infinity"), extend the triangle's sides so as to hit the line at infinity in points X, Y, and Z. Also extend lines PA, PB, and PC so as to hit the line at infinity in points X', Y', and Z'. Now move point P around, thus shifting those three points on the line at infinity in an intricate manner. There is a special relationship among pairs of points on the line at infinity (technically called an "elliptic involution") that, provided it holds for points X and X' and for points Y and Y', will hold also for points Z and Z'. This relationship is tantamount (so it turns out) to a definition of perpendicularity of lines. What this all implies is that if P is moved to a spot such that two of CAB's altitudes meet in it, then so will the third. In this way the fact that a random triangle's altitudes always meet is proven.

I hadn't seen it coming at all, and yet suddenly, there it was, a proof in just one sentence. It was beautiful but weird — hard to see, but with an undeniable sense of coming from far deeper, far more general roots than my earlier proof based on a diagram with one triangle nested inside another one just like it but bigger and upside-down.

On the Conundrums of Cascading Translation ◆ ◆ ◆ *349*

As I turned this second proof over in my mind, I couldn't see how it was in any way related to the purely Euclidean proof that had so convinced me and my students that we had come to the bottom of the mystery. It was as if there were *two totally separate reasons* that this one theorem was true, each of which was sufficient on its own, one of them being down-to-earth and graspable and specific to Euclidean geometry, the other being subtle and elusive and a special case of something far more hidden, profound, and general. And so I asked, and still ask, myself: What *is* the ultimate basis for the crisscrossing of a triangle's three altitudes? On what does this phenomenon truly rest? I was left, I must confess, with a sense of great uneasiness and confusion.

This confusion about rival reasons underlying a mathematical truth then brought to mind yet another case of abstract versus concrete reasons vying for priority or explanatory power. We all grow up knowing clichés to the effect that sometime around age twelve, girls "discover" boys and boys "discover" girls. It is meant to be a natural awakening that happens in most people in adolescence. And yet, when this marvelous awakening takes place in a particular one of us, it feels so unique and individual, it feels like it springs from our own innermost, most private, personal desires and not at all from some kind of general, abstract, impersonal force. The people on whom our attraction focuses seem simply to radiate charm and vivacity and mystery, and those qualities seem to be the reasons behind our fascination, not some kind of biological destiny programmed in our genes. This tension between homey, comfortable reasons and reasons that stretch out into a past so far beyond our comprehension that we need to ignore it to stay sane becomes ever greater as we delve more deeply into questions about free will and biological and physical determinism. Putting one's finger on the ultimate source of one's identity is a very tricky thing.

The Non-objectivity of Authorship and Credit

Take Fido. Fido is a Collie. Fido is a dog. Fido is a mammal. Fido is also a living thing and a furry object and a flea-bearer and a carnivore and a 22-kilogram mass and a faster runner than his friend Tabby and a slower runner than light — and please, let's not forget that Fido is a spatio-temporal phenomenon. But what is Fido, *really*?

Of course, all of these answers and innumerable others are, in some abstract, detached sense, equally valid or equally true — and yet, when it comes to efficient decision-making that meets the exigencies of survival in a complex, rapidly-changing world, the myriad different "equally true" answers are not even remotely close to having the same level of validity. Thus in some contexts, Fido is essentially a dog, not a Collie. In other contexts, Fido is essentially a flea-bearer with carnivorousness playing no role at all, and in other contexts, what counts most of all is Fido's being of greater mass than a peanut. And in yet other contexts, two of these aspects count quite heavily with the rest taking a clear back seat, and so on and so forth. Because we are creatures evolved so as to function efficiently in this crazy dynamic world, we all instinctively pinpoint which facets of all the things we are dealing with are the most relevant at any given moment, and let other facets remain implicit, hovering in the background.

Similarly for the poems arranged in our hypothetical tree. On one level of description, each of them is an instance of a novel abstract category called "Ma Mignonne". On other levels, some of them have very complicated types of identity. In order to set each one in its proper perspective, we have to respect both its provenance from others and its proximity to others. And our answers to questions about source and authorship will not be univocal and fixed, but will depend on what levels of structure we are looking at.

For example, the tristich structure of "Fräulein Mine" — is that due to Marot or to Rohde or to Hofstadter, or what? The answer turns out to be very messy. Clearly a myriad of small decisions by Frank Rohde led to it, and yet he seems to have been unaware of the nearly perfect structure he had thus built up. Obviously, he deserves some sort of credit, just as a scientist who stumbles accidentally onto something of great moment is likely to be given much credit. As for my role, all I did when I saw Rohde's translation was recognize a familiar three-line pattern I had already seen elsewhere, and then shift the punctuation marks in my own translation in order to remove a small flaw from the pattern. Ultimately, the whole idea of semantic tristichs is but a variation on Marot's original theme of out-of-phase semantic distichs, and this latter is an idea that I would probably have remained ignorant of, had it not been for Gray Clossman and Benoît de Cornulier. What an intricate nexus of crisscrossing influences thus led to the tristich structure of "Fräulein Mine"!

In sum, credit and provenance are fallible, debatable perceptions that depend heavily on subjective weights attached to all sorts of variables. Each of them is an endless morass when you start to look carefully.

Loops and Tangles in Translation

When it comes to translations piled upon translations without limit, all sorts of crazy combinations and permutations are possible. For instance, I can easily imagine a perfect Italian–German bilingual working on two different translations of "Ma Mignonne" in parallel, with each of them continually reflecting and influencing the other as both are emerging from the French. Although each would of course be justly called a translation of "Ma Mignonne", they would no less justly be called translations *of each other*, with neither one being able to claim chronological priority over the other (and hence greater "authenticity").

A similar but slightly stranger case would be someone working on two English translations at once, different in flavor but with each one deeply impacting the other one's course of development — perhaps negatively rather than positively, in the sense that a word used in either poem instantly becomes taboo for the other poem, so as to minimize vocabulary overlap. Two such "twin" poems, even though trying to be maximally different from each other, would still have so much in common that they could validly be considered each other's translation (despite both of them being in the same language and having the same author), as well as English instances of the abstract category "Ma Mignonne". I am reminded of two vines growing together and intimately intertwining, each one molding and constraining the other so that in the end, though they are separate physical entities, their abstract identities are inseparable.

As a matter of fact, we have already seen just such a set of intertwined poems in English. The three poems ("structures", if you prefer) "Mots-clés marrants", "Fun Key-words", and "Funky Words" in Poems VII were constructed precisely under the constraint of doing an intricate verbal dance that one might call the "Mutual Avoi-dance Dance" (ignoring the fact that "Funky Words" contains "Fun Key-words"). But of course this kind of experiment could be carried out in thousands of different manners.

I need not spell out all the many further and more intricate variations on this kind of theme that could arise. I hope simply to have painted a subtler and more realistic picture than the naïve, blurry vision in which all poems in the whole "Ma Mignonne" showcase are impressionistically called "translations" of one another, with no attempt made at finer distinctions. Probably no one would actually have a vision so naïve as that, but I think it is worthwhile nonetheless for us to have gone through the exercise of knocking holes in this vision, because doing so forces us to make at least a first attack on some unbelievably complex questions about what translation is, even if we have discovered that we cannot hope to find sharp, clear-cut answers to the many tangled conundrums that we are able to dream up.

Poems XII:

~ Gallic Twists ~

* * * * * *
* * *
* *
*

Back when I discussed the cute Gallic tidbits that my mother stuck into "Hi Toots!", I joshingly proposed carrying that idea further and further, in the end using *only* French phrases to translate "Ma Mignonne". Absurd, is it not? And yet, once in a blue moon, the seemingly absurd does come to pass. In this case, it was my friend François Récanati, a Parisian linguist, who interpreted the challenge in an idiosyncratic manner and came up with a "now" version of "Ma Mignonne", expressing his forebear Marot's sentiments in contemporary, colloquial, even slangy French. And why not? Translating old French into new French, though challenging, is not all that different from translating a passage in one brand of English into some other brand, such as converting normal English into austere "e"-less Anglo-Saxon, say, or pure tetrametric prose. Modern colloquial French is simply one among thousands of alternate media in which, in principle, Marot's original poem could be realized.

For some reason, like Benedetto in Italian, François chose to render Marot's poem in lines of *four* syllables each. And he was sassy enough to split a couple of words across lines, to boot. The overall effect is very catchy. For me, the last six lines are especially delicious, with their wraparound, out-of-synch clauses and the odd rhythm of the four *que*'s. I daresay Marot would have been enchanted with this latter-day interpretation of his poem.

In my early thoughts about this book, I felt it would be indispensable to include at least a couple of non-English versions of "Ma Mignonne", most of all this one, so strange for its French–French twist — but I hadn't yet dared think about rendering any of them in English. To some extent, this was because the challenge of translating such poems into English was too daunting, but more importantly, the very idea seemed like a mockery of this book, since my purpose was, after all, to display the virtuosity and charm of translations emanating directly from the Marot, not transmogrifications or transformations or distortions thereof.

If a museum curator wished to show how accurately artist X's drawings reflect nature, then what would be the point of displaying artist Y's drawings of X's drawings instead? It's one thing to look at van Gogh paintings beautifully reproduced in color photographs in a splashy coffee-table book, but another thing entirely to look at a set of van Gogh paintings as transmitted through the visual filter of, say, Pablo Picasso in a cubist mood — a visual filter that is far more distorting than van Gogh himself. It would be amusing, to be sure, but we could hardly walk away from such an exhibit saying to ourselves, "I sure do admire van Gogh's way of drawing clouds!" We wouldn't have *any idea* about van Gogh's style.

Despite the bizarreness of using a translated translation as a proxy to allow us to discuss a direct translation, the more I pondered the idea of having bare, foreign-language poems sitting on the pages of this book, inaccessible as such to many readers, the less acceptable it seemed, and so finally one day, pushed over the threshold, I bit the bullet and tried my luck at anglicizing "Salut, Ma Vieille". Even if it felt like a kind of joke, once I'd plunged into the task, I took it very seriously, and simply could not be satisfied with a shoddy or superficial job. What resulted from a huge amount of travail was "Old Gal, God Bless", which in my opinion comes about as close as it could to being a literal, line-by-line gloss of François's poem, yet at the same time meets pretty much all the formal constraints as well, even down to the splitting of two words across lines, at exactly the same two points in each of the poems! This level of mimicry amazed even me, at times. In all likelihood it was the extra degree of freedom afforded by tetrasyllabicity that allowed this.

My favorite spot in the anglicization is in lines 26–27, where I visually imitate the French verb *ailles* using the English verb "ail". This is a linguistic sleight of hand, because whereas *ailles mieux* literally means "get better" (as does the phrase "ail less"), the two *pieces* of "ail less", taken individually, mean precisely the opposite of their French homologues!

Salut, Ma Vieille	Old Gal, God Bless
François Récanati	*F. Récanati/D. Hofstadter*

<table>
<tr><td>

Salut, ma vieille !
Ça fait une paye
Que t'es au pieu.
Guéris, bon dieu —
Reste pas au trou !
Au lieu de crou-
pir dans ton lit,
Sans autre ali-
ment que gélules,
Sors de cellule :
Va prendre l'air.
Mange un éclair
Au chocolat.
Ce régime-là
Te convient mieux,
Crois-en ton vieux
Clément. Sois forte,
Fais pas la morte !
Cloîtrée, pâlie,
Toi si jolie,
Tu vas maigrir.
Faut te nourrir !
Je prie pour que
Chaque jour que
Dieu fait, ma caille
Chérie, tu ailles
Mieux que la veille.
Salut, ma vieille !

</td><td>

Old gal, God bless!
Long's been your stress,
Sick in your sack.
By God, bounce back —
Don't stay in stir!   5
Instead of tur-
ning blue in bed,
With only med-
icine to taste,
Quit jail in haste: 10
Go sniff the air.
Munch an eclair
With chocolate cream.
This dream regime
Will cure your cold,   15
Believe your old
Clement. Be brave,
Don't tempt the grave!
Sequestered, pale,
Thou lovely frail,   20
You'll soon grow thin.
Food must go in!
And thus I pray
That each new day
God makes, my quail   25
So sweet, you ail
A little less.
Old gal, God bless!

</td></tr>
</table>

After having solemnly warned all would-be translators that one should not even *dream* of translating this poem into any language but one's own, I all of a sudden upped and did an about-face, recklessly diving into the challenge Récanati had sidestepped — a *tri*syllabic "Ma Mignonne" in modern colloquial French. I was shocked by my own cockiness!

Before I knew it, though, I had done eight lines and felt well on my way to the finish line. It took me another day or so of scribbling, erasing, and dictionary-hunting to come up with what I thought was a fine, finished French poem. However, after sending it around via email to some French colleagues (including Récanati), I concluded it could do with just a handful of teeny-tiny revisions. Well, I've earlier described how that goes: It's a slippery slope, and sometimes, sad to say, that way lies madness. Indeed, I did come perilously close to madness, since my few tiny revisions not only turned out to be many and complex, but also lasted, horrible to say, *one month*! By the end of that grim ordeal, I despised my stupid little slangy French poemlet with an intense passion. Thankfully, I slowly emerged from that depressed phase and came to like my achievement again.

Here are two mid-poem curiosities: Turning Marot's *vous/tu* transition upside down, "Mignonnette" starts out informal, and midway moves to formal. Why? Just for the sheer, slightly silly symmetry of the act. Also midway, on lines 14–15, there's a slyish allusion to Marot's self-reference *Car Clément / Le vous mande* via the funky words *mots-clés marrants*.

In "Mignonnette" there is a running subtext of noses: stuffed noses, red noses, blowing of noses, and so forth. Line 6–7's *sac de mouchage*, for example, is a pun on *sac de couchage* ("sleeping bag"), whose literal meaning is "nose-blowing bag"; then *Le bouchage de ton nez*, following immediately and making a tight rhyme, means "your nose's stuffiness".

Lines 25–26 express the sentiment "May God wipe out those nose-aches of yours." This image was inspired by the word *pif*, a slangish term analogous to "conk" or "honker", which is spoken at a hilarious juncture in the play *Cyrano de Bergerac*. The proboscidian Cyrano, recounting one of his swashbuckling exploits in rhyming couplets, is repeatedly interrupted by a brazen interloper named Christian, who sadistically inserts one phrase after another involving noses into Cyrano's monologue, and Cyrano's temper is heating up rapidly, yet he somehow contains himself. Finally he reaches the climax of his tale…

> *Cyrano:* J'en estomaque deux ! J'en empale un tout vif !
>   Quelqu'un m'ajuste : Paf ! et je riposte…
> *Christian:*   Pif !

Enraged by this horrid rudeness (set up, of course, by his very own word *vif*, and that's the beauty of it), Cyrano boils over and erupts: *Tonnerre ! Sortez tous !* It's one of the great moments of the play, and for me, the rhyme *Dieu vous biffe / Ces maux d'pif* always brings back that delicious scene. Indeed, if *maux* ("aches") is heard as its homonym *mots* ("words"), then those two lines are enriched in meaning: In addition to expressing Clément's tender get-well hopes for his *mignonnette*, they also express Cyrano's sentiments of rage toward Christian — "May God wipe out those nose-words of yours!"

One last touch, among the subtlest… On line 24 comes the poetic but antique-style phrase *Rire je n'ose* (literally, "Laugh I daren't"). Seen on one level, this phrase merely expresses the poet's pity for the poor maiden's plight, but on another level, its key property is that of ending in *n'ose*, which is, of course, none but our own English "nose", thinly disguised — thus returning us once again, this time via a meta-level linguistic leap, to the poem's sneezy subtext. And in my anglicization, as saucy as ever I got, the corresponding line — "Laugh I? Nay!" — jumps through the same hoop, but backwards: It ends in "nay", which is *nez*, a French "nose" wrapped in the gauziest of handkerchiefs.

Mignonnette

D. Hofstadter

Mignonnette,
Minou chouette,
J'te salue,
Mal fichue,
Toute patraque
Dans ton sac
De mouchage.
Le bouchage
De ton nez
M'fait pleurer.
Allez-y,
Confis'ries
A croquer,
Mes mots-clés
Marrants mandent.
Chère gourmande,
Je parie
Qu'aux fins fruits
Une tartine
Si divine
Vous dirait,
N'est-ce pas vrai,
Quelque chose ?
Rire je n'ose.
Dieu vous biffe
Ces maux d'pif :
Ça je l'souhaite,
Mignonnette.

Mignonnette

D. Hofstadter/D. Hofstadter

Mignonnette,
Pretty pet,
Tip my hat
T'you, laid flat
With a frown   5
In your down
Sneezing bag.
Wheezing drag!
Your red nose
Curls my toes.   10
Take a break
And shove cake
Down your throat,
As Clem wrote
Years ago,   15
Well we know.
Dear, your light
Appetite
I could whet,
I would bet,   20
With French toast
And fresh roast-
ed café.
Laugh I? Nay!
From your schnozz   25
All those blahs
God'll get,
Mignonnette.

In the spring of 1990, I gave a talk about creativity and constraints, centered on a series of "Ma Mignonne" translations, before a large group of cognitive scientists gathered at the University of Sussex in Brighton for a conference convened to remember the great English AI and computer pioneer Alan Turing, and specifically to commemorate the fortieth anniversary of his enormously influential article "Computing Machinery and Intelligence". Among the poems I read aloud to this elite group was Récanati's "Salut, Ma Vieille", and it was such a pleasure to find out afterwards that François had been in the audience!

Another member of the audience was English computer scientist Antony Galton, who, after seeing so many diverse approaches to the challenge, went home quite fired up and hunted about for a novel tack all his own. What he came up with was the idea of a poem about the very act of translating the poem! The idea is a little twisty, but the tone of his "Mademoiselle" is self-mocking, and as it's carried off with great panache, the result is delightful. Note that there seem to be two *demoiselles* in his poem: the friend to whom the poet is lamenting his lot, and "some ill wench" who at the end is encouraged to get better; however, the use of *Mademoiselle* at top and bottom tends to blur the two into one person!

Strictly speaking, Galton's poem is no translation at all of the Marot, with the exception of its closing couplet, a very minimal gesture in that direction. Still, "Mademoiselle" is so intimately tied, both in form and in content, to Marot's poem, that it seems to me to fall well within a vaguely-defined sphere of poems that might be loosely classed as translations of "Ma Mignonne".

The first version Galton sent me had, as its lines 10–13, "But my woes / Are still great: / To translate / From the French." This was awkward and also reused line 5's "translate" as a rhyming word: a blemish. I suggested this substitute set of lines: "But God knows / It's no snap / To pull pap / From old French." Antony replied as follows:

> There's nothing wrong with this; it's just that there's no way that I could have written it. Neither of the expressions "it's no snap" and "to pull pap" exist in my vocabulary; to me they sound very American. So I have been struggling to find a replacement — but it's hard! I toyed with ideas like
>
> It's a bind / to unwind / the old French
> It's a pain / to make plain / the old French
> It's no joke / to uncloak / the old French
> It's a load / to decode / the old French
> I'm too dense / to make sense / of old French
>
> but didn't feel any of these was terribly satisfactory. The last one seemed particularly poor because "dense/sense" is so close to rhyming with "French/wench". But then I noticed that this closely parallels the near-rhyme of *Vitement/Clément* with *mande/friande* in the corresponding lines of the original. In both cases we have the same final vowel but a different final consonant. It amused me that such an accidental, totally slippable feature of the original should be preserved in what is otherwise a rather far-fetched rendering. All things considered, I like the "dense/sense" version best.

In retrospect, I now think that the ideal way Galton should have finished up was this:

> *Well, here goes:*
> *"May I tell,*
> *Mademoiselle, …"*

with the implication, of course, that the poem is fully self-containing and self-quoting — or rather, that there are two very similar poems that quote each other, in eternal alternation!

Mademoiselle

Antony Galton

Mademoiselle,
May I tell
My sad lot?
I have got
To translate   5
(Which I hate)
Some old verse.
Could be worse,
I suppose;
But God knows   10
I'm too dense
To make sense
Of old French.
Some ill wench
Lies in bed,   15
When instead
She'd prefer
(I infer)
To eat sweets.
Just three beats   20
In each line:
The design
Is not great.
Twenty-eight
Lines (not prose).   25
Well, here goes:
"Soon get well,
Mademoiselle."

By a strange coincidence, I had come up with a very similar idea to Galton's — and in fact, just before heading off to the Sussex conference. My idea was that, since my own personal obsession was not so much with the delights of the Marot poem *per se* but with the challenge of translating it, why not just put that fact right out on the table?

The agenda for such a poem was hardly preset — all bets were off. Certainly its semantic content wasn't going to resemble that of the original. On the other hand, much of the joy of the challenge had always been, for me, to reflect as many as possible of the Marot poem's quirkier features in a translated version. Thus this implied to me that, one way or another, I should try to work in various little allusions — phonetic, syntactic, semantic, structural, whatever — to interesting aspects of the Marot poem.

For starters, I used the same first line, only in quote marks. Then on line 5, I tried to dispatch two birds with one stone by using the word "jam", which on the one hand can be read as an allusion to *confitures* (of course, the semantics is all wrong) and on the other hand suggests a state of being stuck or blocked (*i.e.*, the jail metaphor, whose ideal spot is that precise line). "Jam" then recurs on line 19 — its proper place — but now as a verb. Interestingly, Galton did similar things in these two spots in "Mademoiselle": in lines 3–7, he manages to suggest a jail by lamenting the hateful translation challenge that the poet himself (not the *demoiselle* to whom he's writing, mind you!) is somehow locked into. And on his line 19, just the right spot, one finds "eat sweets" (this time, however, applying to the "ill wench in bed", not to the poet or to the *demoiselle* addressed in line 1). Our minds were apparently running down quite parallel tracks.

Midway through, I saluted Marot, just as Marot himself does. (Why, I parenthetically muse aloud, am I — still alive and kicking — described in the *past* tense in the sentence you just read, while Marot, bless his long-departed soul, is described in the *present*? Beats me!) Then on the next line I executed my own metaphorical poietautonym, blending my name with Vincent van Gogh's. Indeed, this act launches the conceit of poetry-writing-as-painting for the entire rest of the poem — all 36 remaining syllables of it! The two themes mesh nicely, with the filling-up of pale areas of the canvas mapping simultaneously onto flush returning to a sallow face and flesh returning to a skeletal figure. All this happens in roughly the right region of the poem. Even God is obliquely touched on, via the interjection on line 26. The poem concludes with the obligatory echo of its beginning, only slightly transmogrified: indeed, anglicized, with "My" replacing *Ma*. After all, we *are* referring, at the bottom, to the *English* version of the poem referred to at the top — and that version is, indeed, this poem itself! That's why its title is "My", not "Ma", "Mignonne".

Lastly, there are two quite obscure jokes whose meaning will be understandable only in the context of Poems XV. These are the appearances of the word "sort" on line 10 and the word "hard" on line 20. But feel free to ponder them now!

My Mignonne

D. Hofstadter

"Ma Mignonne"
Is such fun
To translate.
It feels great,
In a jam,   5
When — hot damn! —
You dream up
A sweet coup-
let that fits
(Sort of) its   10
Tight constraints.
Words are paints
(So to speak),
So to speak
Like Marot,   15
Dough van Gogh
Dips his brush
In oils' gush,
And then jams —
Hard he slams —   20
It down, Bright-
'ning up white
Canvas zones,
Like to bones
Adding flesh.   25
Zounds! With fresh
Strokes, Dough's done
"My Mignonne".

●

• *Chapter 13* •

On Shy Translators
and Their Crafty, Silent Art

●

Here's a dime-a-dozen dialogue for you, the kind of exchange you could easily overhear in any big city or university town:

He: Did you hear — Vladimir Horowitz is in town, and is giving a recital on Saturday!

She: Oh, wow — let's go! Say, what's he playing?

He: Don't have the foggiest. It didn't say, on the poster I saw. But it'll be great. Horowitz always is.

She: Ah, Horowitz — what a pianist! I could listen to him play forever!

And now here's a rather similar dialogue, but it's one you will never, ever hear, whether in a big city, university town, or anywhere else:

She: Did you hear — Gregory Rabassa has just finished translating another book!

He: Oh, that's terrific news. Is it available yet?

She: I think so, or it will be within a month or two, anyway.

He: Oh, by the way — who's the author?

She: Don't have the foggiest. It didn't say, in the advertisement I read. But it'll be great. Rabassa always is.

He: Ah, Rabassa — what a translator! I could read his flowing sentences forever!

If you think this second conversation could plausibly occur, then dream on, friend!

On Shy Translators and Their Crafty, Silent Art ◆ ◆ ◆ **353**

How Astonishingly Easy to Overlook

In a recent column in *The New York Times,* Russell Baker was carrying on quite excitedly about his new-found fascination with Homer's *Iliad,* and in particular the character of Achilles:

> In Achilles, Homer created the very first yuppie, but a yuppie of the most unbearable, insufferable, self-centered variety.
>
> You can meet him in all his bombastic selfishness in Derek Jacobi's superlative new reading of "The Iliad" in six audio cassettes that run nine hours....
>
> An audio tape is especially appropriate for "The Iliad", which comes out of a tradition of oral story-telling. Derek Jacobi's reading of these hideous blood-lettings gives us some sense of how the ancients might have felt on hearing them told aloud.
>
> If you have been unable to read four pages of "The Iliad" without drowsing, hearing it will be a discovery.

Aside from its characteristically droll tone and its intrinsic interest, this article caught my attention because I had a special fond memory of Derek Jacobi. Nine years earlier, on a visit to London, Carol and I had seen him play the role of Alan Turing in Hugh Whitemore's drama *Breaking the Code,* based on Andrew Hodges' definitive biography *Alan Turing: The Enigma.* Turing's hugely productive but short life was both touching and tragic, and Jacobi rendered the part in a marvelous way, jumping back and forth between Turing as an adult and Turing as a boy with wonderful fluidity. Taking into account Russell Baker's praise for Jacobi, and remembering how impressed Carol had been with Jacobi's snappy metamorphoses, I thought I might go out and buy the set of cassettes, and so I clipped Baker's article and filed it away.

Perusing the *Times* two days later, I noticed there were a couple of letters to the editor in reaction to this column by Baker, and was very curious what they might have to say. One of them was from the author Joyce Carol Oates, whose books I have heard about quite often but have unfortunately never read, and yet she is someone else of whom, by sheer chance, I have yet another special fond memory.

In the summer of 1990, when our son Danny was just two, Carol and I took him on a long driving trip up the east coast to meet various friends and relatives, and on our last day were visiting some old friends in Princeton. That evening, we decided we were all in the mood for Mexican food, and from their apartment took a leisurely walk, wheeling little Danny in his stroller, to a small and informal Mexican restaurant. As we entered and stood waiting to be seated, we saw a man and a woman at a nearby table, the woman facing away from us. In a soft voice, Carol remarked to us, "That woman has a Joyce Carol Oates hairdo." I had no idea what such a hairdo might be, and said as much, to which Carol replied, "It's *that* kind of hairdo!" A minute or two later, the woman who had been given this unusual description turned her head enough so that we could glimpse her face momentarily, and Carol, suddenly beet-red, whispered to us, "My goodness — that *is* Joyce Carol Oates!" Of course we all chuckled in great amusement, and Carol remembered that Oates taught at Princeton.

So I was curious to hear what Joyce Carol Oates had to say about Homer and Achilles, Russell Baker and Jacobi, and in fact this time it was *my* turn to turn beet-red, at least metaphorically, because her letter caught me totally off guard on one of my own pet points. Here is what she said:

To the editor:

Russell Baker's column on Homer's Achilles is typically cogent and informative. However, he leaves us with the impression that he was listening to "The Iliad" in Greek. Isn't this version, in fact, in English? Surely there's a translator involved — Robert Fagles, of the comparative literature department at Princeton University?

Those who imagine that foreign-language works are transposed into English by a mysterious chemical process, without the effort of translators like the gifted Professor Fagles, are kin to those who imagine that film actors speak their own lines, without the benefit of screenwriters: naïve.

Joyce Carol Oates

How ashamed I felt for not having given a moment's thought to the issue of translation when I had read Baker's column. I had pictured in my mind Achilles himself, Homer the author, and Jacobi the reader, and yet that other person in the middle — the translator — might as well have been invisible.

I wonder to what percentage of Baker's readers the existence of a translator in the loop ever occurred. I would guess it would be extremely low. I'm not saying, mind you, that if queried explicitly, readers would deny a translation process ever took place — I'm just saying that translation tends to be one of those "out of sight, out of mind" kinds of things. Most readers take translators and translations for granted. And it would be wrong to think that the blame for this mistake falls solely on each individual who makes it; it is in large part the result of a collective attitude spread throughout our entire culture. We basically are taught — both by omission and by commission — to ignore, forget about, and disrespect translators.

The Only Good Translator is an Invisible Translator

I have read many articles by translators about their craft (and, most puzzlingly to me, they do indeed usually characterize it more as a craft than as an art), and one of the most frequently expressed personal goals is that of *invisibility*. And by George, in most cases they have got it!

For example, my uncle Albert Hofstadter was a noted philosopher, and in addition to writing his own books, he devoted much time and care to translating the works of Heidegger and Hegel (writers who, for me, are mysteries wrapped inside enigmas, but that's beside the point). Albert once gave me a warmly signed copy of his translation of Heidegger's *Poetry, Language, Thought,* and in a blurb on the jacket (and I suppose this was intended as high praise), I read: "Hofstadter's effort succeeds admirably in the way of all good translations — by disappearing from view in our reading." I wonder if Albert felt proud of his disappearance. And well he may have! This is what we are told is the goal to be striven for!

Imagine a Vladimir Horowitz recital of mazurkas by Scriabin and Chopin, received with thunderous applause and four encores in Carnegie Hall, being reviewed in the next day's *New York Times* this way: "Horowitz's effort succeeded admirably in the way of all good performances — by disappearing from view in our listening." People would scratch their heads and ask themselves, "What remote planet did *this* reviewer just fly in from?"

The Glory-halo Effect

Where, indeed, should the emotional credit in music be assigned? A year and a half after Carol died, with melancholy a constant background to my life, I sat down one Easter Sunday at the piano in our living room to play a Chopin mazurka for myself — the haunting one in A minor from Opus 17. It happened that Marina Eskina — superlative Russian translator of *GEB* and youthful memorizer of *Eugene Onegin* — had come over that day to play with Danny and Monica for a couple of hours, and the three of them were all in the kitchen, within earshot of my playing. After the piece was over, Marina came in and said, "That's very beautiful, very sad — it sounds like you're speaking to Carol."

I replied, "Yes, it's very beautiful." I didn't *deny* Marina's second idea but felt it was a case of reading extra meaning into a situation. To be sure, Opus 17, Number 4 is an achingly fluctuating and exceptionally poignant mazurka, and of course I was very prone to feeling sad, and Marina, who had known Carol very well and cared deeply for her, knew all this — but it so happened that while I was playing that piece on that particular occasion, I actually *wasn't* thinking about Carol, let alone trying to reach her spirit via music. I would have liked to take credit for such an intention, but it wasn't the case. In fact, if I was feeling "sad" while playing the mazurka, it was for ridiculously banal reasons: I was sad at the notes I was missing, sad at the fact that I now need to wear glasses to make out the notes clearly, which never used to be the case, and sad at the fact that my glasses, damn it all, were upstairs. Marina's interpretation was much more romantic, and on another occasion it might well have been right on the mark, but on this occasion it was simply false.

People not only wish but deeply need to attribute Profound Sensitivity to the performer when, in reality, the profundity is all, or nearly all, in the notes on paper. It's the composer's soul, not the performer's, that is speaking to them. But it's such a typical human desire to assign credit or blame to the flesh-and-blood human before their eyes rather than to an invisible abstraction of a human, a shadow long since vanished from view. The act of simply spotting the nearest available or most salient associate of or representative of the true originator and then attaching the credit and the glory to that person is a cousin phenomenon to the classic old effect whereby people get angry at the bearer of bad tidings, as in Irving Berlin's World War I song "Oh, How I Hate to Get Up in the Morning", part of whose lyrics run this way: "Some day I'm going to murder the bugler, some day they're going to find him dead. I'll amputate his reveille, and step upon it heavily, and spend... the rest of my life in bed!"

This whole surface-level effect can be carried to amazing extremes. If you think it's bad to attribute most of the depth to the visible Horowitz rather than to the composers hidden in the notes he's playing, consider this piece of publicity that Carol and I received a few years ago from the Indiana University School of Music:

> The Horowitz Steinway Piano, the only piano that Vladimir Horowitz used in performance, is on tour throughout the United States, and the School of Music has been selected as one of the locations that the piano will visit. In addition to some educational opportunities for area children we will offer, we are planning a special recital featuring the piano on Tuesday, April 14, and 8:00 PM in the Musical Arts Center. Admission is free.

When we got this, we almost fell off our chairs in laughter. Where does adulation ever stop? Note the capital "P" on "Piano" in the first line, and note how this Piano is all but personified in the phrases "is on tour", "locations that the piano will visit" and "special recital featuring the piano". This is a good example of what might be called the "glory-halo effect", an effect that, given how silly it seems, is amazingly common.

One of the oddest and yet clearest instances of this effect that I have ever encountered was one that involved Carol and me in a very personal way. In the summer of 1986, we wound up our two-month zigzag tour of Italy by spending a few days in Milano, where I had been scheduled to give a rather specialized lecture about my research on computer models of human analogy-making. Unfortunately, the people who had arranged this lecture, though academics, were also fanatical publicity seekers, and to my unbeknownst had advertised the lecture in the silliest and splashiest of ways, and consequently hundreds and hundreds of people turned up, including at least a dozen reporters from many Italian newspapers. After the lecture, which was held in some huge fancy hall, there was a horribly unpleasant mob scene in which I was being asked questions by several reporters at once while Carol was being virtually ignored. However, one bright reporter noticed this state of affairs and decided to turn it to his advantage. He approached Carol and started talking to her *as if she were me*, saying such things (in Italian) to her as, "Oh, I hadn't pictured you as being so young", "Have you been a writer for a long time?", and so on, always using the singular form of "you" as well as the masculine forms of adjectives and nouns, thus effectively conflating my spouse with me. He actually had the gall to pose questions directly to her about how she/I had written her/my book *Gödel, Escher, Bach*. Carol felt both humiliated and repelled by his sleazy, unctuous, and absurd behavior, and was immensely relieved when the session was over, as was I. The whole event left us both with a very sour taste in the mouth.

Varieties and Levels of Creators and Interpreters

Well, getting back to Horowitz and Chopin, I am not trying to deny the phenomenal skill that a great musical performer builds up over decades of dedication; all I am saying is that I think it is far easier than most people suspect to make an unconscious transfer of credit from an occluded source to a visible source. There are so many levels involved in bringing any great creation to public awareness, and each specific case requires very careful thought in order to figure out how to parcel out the credit most reasonably. For example, Russell Baker's column rightly praised the role of the *reader-aloud* in bringing an ancient written work to life, but it totally ignored the role of the *translator,* which, though more occult, is no less important.

Consider a videocassette of a performance of Sergei Prokofiev's ballet *Romeo and Juliet.* How much credit do the dancers themselves deserve, and how much credit should go to the choreographer? How much to Prokofiev, and how much to the orchestra rendering his score audible? How much to the conductor directing the orchestra? How much to impresarios, how much to dance coaches? How much to costume designers? And how much to the recording engineers and the filmers and so forth? And where does Shakespeare fit in here, anyway?

Suppose the Dutch graphic artist M. C. Escher had designed a marvelous lithograph, and after his death his carefully trained assistant X meticulously printed a thousand copies of it. Should X receive equal credit with Escher? The proposal sounds preposterous, and yet in exactly what ways does it differ from a wildly applauding audience's effective assignment of the lion's share of credit to Horowitz for his performance — for the one thousandth time — of a set of Chopin mazurkas?

Bear in mind that the audience's insistent applause after Horowitz has performed the last piece listed on the official program is intended to coax him back on stage to play more for them — to play *anything he chooses*. They're not asking for *more Chopin,* they're asking for *more Horowitz.* And in those 75 concerts across the United States where the Horowitz Steinway Piano was up there on stage and Horowitz's spirit was ethereally hovering above it, beside it, and below it, as well as drifting throughout the concert hall like a pale gray cloud of cigarette smoke, at whom or at what was the audience's applause really directed? At the talented local artists chosen to play the Grand Piano? At the Piano itself? At the cigarette-smoke-like aura of *maestro* Horowitz? Or perhaps — but surely this is stretching things pretty darned far — at the composers of the pieces being performed?

Closer to home is the eternally snarly question of how to share credit for the computer-modeling work that I have done in tight collaboration with my graduate students over the past ten years. I have tended to design the challenges, to reduce them to miniaturized versions of themselves in microdomains, and to design in quite broad strokes the basic architectures of the programs that are supposed to perform cognitive tasks in a human-like way. But people such as Melanie Mitchell and Bob French spent big chunks of their lives actually *implementing* such complex programs, and a program of that size can be a couple of hundred printed pages long, and can take several years to develop. During the development time of Bob's and Melanie's incredible programs, ideas on many different levels of detail were passionately thrashed out among all of us in our little research group in innumerable long sessions. I never looked at one single line of computer code in either case, although on a somewhat coarser grain size, I knew both of their programs intimately. Both Melanie and Bob wound up publishing carefully revised versions of their Ph.D. theses as books, and each of them was their respective book's sole author, although much generous credit was given to me inside. Probably it makes sense, but the truth of the matter is that the whole thing is a big blur, because there simply are *different kinds of credit at different levels of involvement.*

Above, I referred to "Bob's and Melanie's programs", but was I not in fact their co-author? Might it not even be argued that Melanie and Bob were playing the role of *translators,* with me being the *author*? This latter claim would be pushing things pretty far. Pushkin at least realized *Eugene Onegin* in full detail in Russian; I never had made anything close to a fully implemented version of either program before Melanie or Bob came along. This might bring the Sistine Chapel's ceiling to mind, with Michelangelo sketching it all out and telling assistants to fill in the details. Mapping myself onto Michelangelo gives me a good chuckle, but I know how deeply Bob and Melanie were *partners* with me — much as, in many ways, I was a partner with Bob and Jacqueline in the creation of the French *GEB.*

On Shy Translators and Their Crafty, Silent Art   ◆ ◆ ◆   359

For Whom No Nobel Tolls

Here is an example that, although taken from a radically different domain, has some parallels but also some sharp contrasts with the extreme tightness of the collaboration between me and Melanie, or that between me and Bob. This past summer, after I had taken my children to see *The King and I* on stage not just once but twice in a row, we were all so taken with its magic that I went right out and purchased a CD of the music from the movie's sound track, with Yul Brynner as the King of Siam and Deborah Kerr as Anna Leonowens. We listened to it over and over and over again in the car, until the kids knew the songs nearly by heart.

One day as I was reading the liner notes, I came across this sentence: "Since Kerr was not a singer, Marni Nixon, a young California soprano, was drafted by Darby to 'ghost' Anna's songs." I didn't know exactly what the term "ghost" meant, but I didn't think it meant anything as strong as "replace", since in the actual program at the very beginning, each song was listed with its performers, and it very clearly said "Deborah Kerr" each time Anna Leonowens had a song, and there was no mention of Marni Nixon.

However, hiding at the very back of the pamphlet there was an interview with Marni Nixon, and there it was made abundantly clear that the singing voice on the CD was indeed not Kerr's but Nixon's, in every single song. It also pointed out that Marni Nixon later dubbed Natalie Wood in the film version of *West Side Story*, as well as Audrey Hepburn in the film version of *My Fair Lady*.

Since speech and singing mingle densely in a few of the songs, sometimes Kerr's and Nixon's voices are tightly interleaved on the sound track. As Nixon herself says in the interview:

> It was a really wonderful acting lesson, and I just tried to extend my voice a little so it would sound like her speaking voice. She actually did the verse of "Getting to Know You", until Anna begins to sing. In her soliloquy "Shall I Tell You What I Think of You?", in some cases, we went back and forth. Sometimes it was just a matter of extending the note, and we stood side by side when we were recording. She would point to me and I would point to her, sometimes right in the middle of a measure. We would switch, and nobody knew the difference. It was wonderful. Then, of course, she had to mouth to the tracks, which is an art in itself....
>
> When she rehearsed a scene that contained songs, I was always called in so I could watch what she was doing. She would actually sing, and then I would get up and stand beside her and walk through the scene with her. So actually, she was getting from me the different flow of energy that it takes to produce certain kinds of notes. She incorporated certain aspects of my body language within her characterization. Sometimes, actresses and dramatic performers aren't aware of that. By the time we got to recording the songs, she would have to try the whole thing out in the recording stage — sing it through, kind of play it through — so that she could accept the final product.

Once I realized all this, I found it very hard to understand how anyone could allow the main list of songs on the CD to say such things as "Hello Young Lovers — Deborah Kerr", "Shall We Dance? — Deborah Kerr and Yul Brynner", and so forth and so on, down the line, without giving the slightest hint, such as an asterisk or a footnote, that the singing voice on the sound track is *not* that of Deborah Kerr. I still find it unfathomable. However, I am touched by the way in which Nixon bends over backwards to extend credit to Kerr's art in mouthing the tracks, when in fact *she* is the true star, though behind the scenes.

I can't help but be reminded of the unforgettable climax of the movie *Singin' in the Rain,* in which the talented singer and dancer Kathy Selden (played by the talented singer and dancer Debbie Reynolds) is standing hidden behind a curtain, lending her voice to the spoiled-rotten tone-deaf silent-film star Lina Lamont (Jean Hagen), who is hammily mouthing the words in front of a big audience, and then, slowly but steadily, the curtain starts to go up, revealing the existence behind the scenes of *someone else* doing the singing. Lina Lamont — a truly pathetic character who surely epitomizes the meaning of the word "bimbo" — becomes an instant laughingstock, and from that moment on, her jig is up.

I have no grudge against Deborah Kerr and no reason to wish to paint her as a Lina Lamont type — to the contrary, Nixon paints a very warm picture of her — but I simply find it unconscionable that, through no fault of her own, she is listed as the sole singer of a series of splendid songs in which, in fact, her own voice is mostly to totally absent. In the film as a whole, Kerr is of course a roughly equal partner in the musical numbers — but here we're talking about the sound track alone.

There is one other matter of credit in *The King and I* that I find fascinating, and this concerns the presence of what I consider its very best song (a hard choice, admittedly): "Getting to Know You". It turns out that this song was originally written for the earlier Rodgers and Hammerstein musical *South Pacific,* in which it was to have been called "Suddenly Lucky", but was dropped from that show. However, the fabulous Mary Martin, who starred in the original Broadway production of *South Pacific,* felt that "Suddenly Lucky" was too good a melody to be let go of, and so she insisted that it be resurrected and inserted somehow into *The King and I.* Willing to give it a try, Oscar Hammerstein came up with a marvelous set of new lyrics, then slid the patched-up song into the show, and there you go.

So one more name has to be added to the set of people responsible for this song: that of the person who most strongly believed in it and pushed for it. This is no small role to play. Many potentially great scientific discoveries have languished unpublished because of their discoverers' inability to recognize the importance of what they found, or their lack of confidence about whether it was right. Many would-be Nobel Prize winners have cursed their lack of self-confidence when, many years later, it turns out that they have to sing the agonizing "I was there first, by gum and by golly, but boy, did I blow it all" blues.

Contrasting Attitudes towards Science and Music

Since we have turned our attention for a moment to the topic of scientific discoveries and the credit popularly associated with them, consider the role of science writers in explaining great discoveries to a wider public. As far as I know, there is not a single well-known prize for science writing; the craft is considered many levels below that of making the discoveries themselves. And thus it is very unlikely that one might see book covers of this form:

Martin Gardner

explains the mysteries of

Special and General Relativity

(A. Einstein)

The Nagel–Newman Duo

clarifies

The Incompleteness of Formal Arithmetic

(K. Gödel)

Richard Dawkins

explicates

Natural Selection and Evolution

(C. Darwin)

and so forth and so on. This is not the way the public perceives it, nor does it wish to have its collective mind changed about the priorities. Nor would I disagree with that judgment; I merely wish to contrast it with the public's rather different attitude about performers and composers. Thus, it is absolutely run-of-the-mill to see, posted on kiosks in large cities, elegantly typeset concert announcements along the following lines:

Sviatoslav Richter

performs

The Well-Tempered Clavier

(J. S. Bach)

(obviously putting Richter in the front seat and Bach in the back seat). God only knows how many times I have seen such posters and cringed.

I hasten to add that although I think scientific discovery resides on a higher level of significance and demands greater creativity than does scientific divulgation, I believe that the latter is a deep and important art, and deserves far more recognition than it enjoys. Aside from the writers listed above, all of whom have made major contributions to the art form, there are other remarkable names, such as George Gamow, Albert Einstein, Max Born, James Jeans, Carl Sagan, Steven Weinberg, Lincoln Barnett, Richard Gregory, Stephen Jay Gould, Jacques Monod, Daniel Dennett, William Poundstone, Jean Aitchison, Stephen Pinker, William Dunham, Margaret Boden, Pamela McCorduck, A. K. Dewdney, and more. Many of these individuals also wear the scientist's as well as the writer's hat, and in that capacity have contributed directly to our understanding of nature.

A really top-notch "performance" in science — the translation of a set of difficult ideas into clear language with the help of pictures and analogies and so forth — can be a remarkable and powerful experience. Indeed, one of the most memorable experiences of my entire college career was what I would call a "performance" of a proof of a beautiful theorem about Fourier series in an advanced mathematics class I was taking on the topic of Real Analysis. It so happened that our class was being taught by a somewhat sloppy-dressing younger professor who never could remember what he was doing and who always got lost in his proofs, and so every class session was quite painful. But one day he was sick, and in walked a very neatly dressed, somewhat older fellow with a slight accent but otherwise perfect English, to take his place. I had never seen this man before and I never saw him again; I assume he was a visitor for a short time at Stanford. The moment the bell rang, he got down to business, telling us just what he was setting out to prove, writing the statement down in a beautiful, crisp, angular European cursive on the board, and then spending the next 49 minutes moving in an impeccable, inexorable, spellbinding rhythm towards the climax, which was delivered in such an exquisitely timed manner that just as he put the last period on the final sentence on that board and wiped the chalk dust off his hands, the closing bell rang. My jaw fairly dropped with amazement and admiration, and part of me yearned to break out in vigorous applause, but as I saw the students around me gathering their books and rising, with seemingly no appreciation of the miracle they had just witnessed, I simply couldn't bring myself to do it alone, and the chance was lost. I have always regretted that split-second cowardice, because that lecture was one of the greatest performances I have ever seen, not just of some mathematics, but of *anything*. How often I've wished I could see it again, or at least write the unknown professor a letter telling him how great his lecture was!

As I hope this makes clear, I am not by any means an incorrigible denigrator of performers. I can admire them enormously; it's just that my degree of admiration depends on how great a spark of originality in the act I discern. And what I particularly take umbrage at is the attitude, whether on the part of the performer or the public, that the performer is the *main attraction*. I can certainly handle cases of equal billing, on occasion — for instance, in jazz or popular music, where some composer's great tune is manipulated and twisted around in all sorts of ways by instrumentalists like Sidney Bechet or Teddy Wilson or Fats Waller or Bix Beiderbecke or Benny Goodman (and on and on), or where words and intonations and melodic turns are improvised on the spot, often with great emotional impact, by singers like Ella Fitzgerald or Billie Holiday or Frank Sinatra (and on and on). But if Dick Estelle, the fluent and smooth "Radio Reader" featured every day on National Public Radio, is given higher billing than the author of the book that he's reading, that's where I draw the line.

Poet, Translator, Reader-aloud — What's the Proper Order?

I have a record cover, and I have no reason to think of it as rare or exceptional, where the name "Sir John Gielgud" is printed in giant capitals at the top, then in the middle there is a photo of him, and then way below that, in type that must be one-third the size, it says, "Sir John Gielgud reads Christopher Fry's new translation of Bertrand's Poems of Fantasy 'Gaspard de la nuit'". It seems to me that the order here is exactly backwards: it should list Aloysius Bertrand first, because he was the one who made the entire thing up out of nothing; then it should list Fry, because he transformed every little jot and tittle of Bertrand's creation into a radically different medium; and finally, it should list Gielgud, because although he surely lends panache to the proceedings, he is basically doing something quite straightforward: reading text aloud with understanding. Oh, I know, most people when they read text aloud tend to turn it into pretty boring mush, and that's why I didn't say Gielgud is adding *nothing*. I am simply saying he deserves third place, not first place, in this list — and I am especially saying it is absurd for his name to be blown up to enormous size in contrast with the other two (not to mention the photo!). That is just pandering to the public's yearning for celebrities, and I deplore it.

This brings us back, at long last, to the matter of a translator's place in the scheme of things. In stunning contrast to a fair number of musical performers who are avid to seize the limelight and to soak up every last drop of credit for the emotionality of the piece they are in essence merely resuscitating from dormancy, most translators seem to want to remain totally hidden behind the authors they are serving. Yes, *serving*.

From what I can tell from my readings, literary translators tend to be quite reverential toward their authors (recall, for example, Vladimir Nabokov's obsequiousness towards his idol Pushkin; he is not atypical). If one is to believe what they write in their author-adulating articles, many translators actually *wish* their names to be relegated to teeny, tiny print somewhere near the ISBN number on the copyright page. Their self-esteem seems at about the level of a peon (here, Nabokov is not typical).

How sad, because the truth is that, despite all the reverence for the original, a skilled literary translator makes a far larger number of changes, and far more significant changes, than any virtuoso performer of classical music would ever dare to make in playing the notes in the score of, say, a Beethoven piano sonata. In literary translation, it's totally humdrum stuff for new ideas to be interpolated, old ideas to be deleted, structures to be inverted, twisted around, and on and on. We've seen this over and over now in translations of Marot's "Ma Mignonne", of Perec's *La disparition,* of Pushkin's *Eugene Onegin,* of Villon's "Ballade de bonne doctrine", of Queneau's *Exercices de style,* of my own *Gödel, Escher, Bach,* and so forth.

In virtually every line of every high-quality translation of any piece of literature, small creative acts of faithful infidelity take place at one or another level of grain size — small creative acts in which jams are turned into yams, windows into transoms, Paris buses into Amstertrams — and yet if, with these age-old and time-tested traditions of flexing and changing in order to create literary constancy, you were to compare the corresponding traditions concerning the translation of printed notes into sounds, you would find the comparison was just a joke: no classical performer would dream of taking comparable liberties with even a single measure of a single piece by one of those hallowed souls whose busts are seen, side by side, high up on the limestone façade of the Indiana University Music School, impassively staring down at the multitudes of music students as they walk by and reminding them, lest those irreverent gum-chewers might have forgotten, that to be accepted as one of the Truly Great, that to join the ranks of the Immortal Immutables, one must be long dead and statically and statuously iconified beyond all recognizable humanity.

I would find it so enormously refreshing and touching if, just once in a while, some famous classical performer, right at the peak of all the frenzied applause, would unexpectedly whip out a photograph of the composer who created the work that actually transfixed the audience, would hold it up and say, "Thanks so much, my friends, but *here's* the one you really should be thanking." And conversely, I would find it an enormous relief if literary translators would ease up in their obsequiousness just a little bit, and would stop paying lip service to the supposed ideal of a translator's "invisibility". In the end, doing so simply amounts to a confused kind of false humility. Why should a good literary translator be any more humble than such famously self-effacing souls as Vladimir Horowitz or Luciano Pavarotti?

Or, to turn it around, why should a superb musical performer be any more self-absorbed and any more of a grandstander than such a superb translator as... Well, who comes to mind? Nobody? Now what was I just saying about translators being invisible?

I'm Not a Generous Translator

Many young people aspire to become doctors or nurses to save the sick and to reduce the suffering of the world. This is a most noble goal. One might also think that certain souls choose to take up the profession of literary translating in order to bring to a vast mass of intelligent but deprived folk the pearls of wisdom and the visions of beauty created in some remote culture. This too would be a most noble goal, and I salute anyone who entered or is entering the field for that reason. I must admit, however, that I myself, in translating, am not motivated by any such noble and pure goal. I am not a generous translator.

When I tackle a translating challenge, it is not in the least because I yearn to reveal to the poor deprived non-speakers of language X the hidden structure and meaning of some intricate passage in language X — no, for me, translating is simply the sheer joy of trying to do something deeply paradoxical: namely, to carry off in medium 2, radically different from medium 1, some virtuoso stunt that someone else once carried off with great aplomb in medium 1. That's all, no more. It's just a game, an exercise in creativity, a challenge that, if met with sufficient flair, provides a wonderful esthetic reward.

Sadly, guiltily, but truthfully, I confess I'm not someone who makes translations as gifts, someone who translates so that others might have the chance to discover and savor some otherwise forever-hidden gem of literature; no, I'm just a selfish translator, someone who translates solely and entirely because doing so is exhilarating and beautiful and because it brings me into intimate contact with a work and an author that I admire.

The Metaphor of the Rickety Bridge

From attitudes about translation, I would like now to turn to the art, or the craft, of translation, and a good inroad to that topic is provided by a certain metaphor that I have always found most appealing as a way of explaining how a highly polished translation comes about, at least in my personal style of working.

Imagine a deep, narrow chasm over which you would like to construct a strong, wide bridge. You take a long piece of rope and tie one end of it to a tree near the chasm's edge. The other end you tie around a stone, and hurl the stone across the chasm. Now you make your way to the other side in a roundabout way and tie the far end of the rope to a tree on that side. In this stretch of anchored cord spanning the chasm you have the humble beginnings of a strong structure. It is, after all, an extremely primitive bridge. By swinging from your rope, you can cross more easily and quickly, and soon you have a second rope parallel to the first. Next, you can link the two parallel ropes together with some boards, and now you have something much more bridge-like. The stronger your tentative bridge, the more quickly you can cross over it and the more you can carry along with you. Eventually, you can start building a second bridge entirely out of wood alongside your first one, using the first one as a kind of scaffolding. In general, each stage will be a bit stronger than the previous one — but if by chance one should collapse, you always have the fallback position of what you had already done. Over time, and with a number of stages, you come to have the strong, wide bridge that was once only a dream.

The image is simple, but it seems remarkably like what I experience when I am working on a translation of a poem such as "Ma Mignonne". It also applies on the higher level of a series of ever more diverse translations of the same poem. In fact, that was how I first thought of the metaphor, and later I realized how aptly it also fit to the working-out of just one translation.

It seems to me that the metaphor applies far beyond the limited arena of poetry translation. Any technological development, for instance, goes through a series of stages of refinement and evolution very much like the bridges that graciously allow themselves to be superseded. The endpoint of such an evolutionary process (if there is an endpoint) is often so radically different from the starting point that the original inventor would barely recognize it as a "logical" outgrowth of that first primitive stab. Certainly that applies to my own translations, and on two levels: First of all, my later translations of "Ma Mignonne" would have blown me away if I could have seen them when I was just starting out, a few years ago; likewise, the final poem reached through a long series of modifications of a first draft would astound the "younger" me who dreamed up that first draft, say a day earlier.

The Key Role of a Safety Net in Risk-taking

When, with "My Sweet Dear", I first succeeded in creating a translation of "Ma Mignonne", I felt deeply relieved and proud of myself for having achieved something that had appeared impossible at first. This now seems pretty naïve, but it is certainly how I felt. The boost in self-confidence that I experienced was tremendous, and in tackling a second translation I now dared to take risks I would not have even imagined in the first translation. After all, if the risks didn't pan out and my second try was a complete bust, I always had the first version to fall back to. This knowledge that I had a fallback was such a key element, psychologically.

Once I had two translations to my name, then I felt even more secure and could therefore try even riskier things in a tentative third version. What was there to lose, other than a bit of time? And so it went: three, four, five… Building up the collection of my first several translations was, I suppose, like building several bridges near each other, all spanning the same chasm, all of different materials and sizes and stabilities, and of course all having different types of grace or awkwardness.

After a while, I had sufficiently many translations in my personal "portfolio" that I no longer felt my pride was on the line when I tackled yet another one. If it worked, fine; but if not, I still had all these others stashed away behind the scenes, silently but undeniably buttressing my self-esteem. And as I say, a sense of self-esteem was absolutely vital in allowing me to feel that I could afford to try risky routes.

The same rickety-bridge metaphor applies, as I said earlier, on a scaled-down level, within a single translation, on many different structural levels. It can apply to the choice of a single word to fill a slot in a given line: first you find one word that somewhat matches the desirable attributes; it then becomes your fallback position. This safety net allows you to try out more daring possibilities in your mind, and at some point you may replace the original choice by another word that you find superior. This word in turn becomes a safety net and allows its own replacements to be considered — and on and on it goes, ratcheting ever upwards in sophistication.

Sniffing Out the Most Promising Variants

The word-by-word, line-by-line building-up of a new poem is like the slow construction of a new bridge over the chasm; once that tentative, rickety bridge is all there, then you can start going back and tampering with it, strengthening it here and there, falling back to earlier choices when a risky idea winds up leading you down a blind alley. In theory, each local change made to an already-done translation could be claimed to yield a brand-new translation, but in practice, if you were to hang onto each microscopically different version in the long chain of evolution towards a polished product, you could easily wind up with hundreds of "different" translations. To avoid the ironic fate of drowning in an ocean of your own micro-variants, you have to be courageous enough to part forever with lovely ideas that only a few minutes earlier you were terribly proud of.

The early stage of building up separate lines to make a full poem, or at least a first draft of a full poem, is very different from the later stage of tampering with bits inside the already-made poem — the polishing process. In the earlier stage, each new idea adds painlessly to the growing structure — there are no sacrifices involved — but in the polishing process, each new idea presents you with a painful, uncertain choice between rival avenues.

Moreover, evaluating the quality of a tentative change is no piece of cake, because any tweak, even a tiny one, made inside a finished poem has repercussions elsewhere in the poem, since the lines are linked together by interlocking constraints of rhyme, rhythm, semantic coherence, and so forth. A local change is almost never isolated, but instead will launch reverberations up and down the entire structure, and it may take a long time before things settle down again into a stable equilibrium.

Thus in order to be evaluated, a tentative change has to be followed out a long ways in terms of its consequences — and since there are always multiple ways in which one might plausibly extend any potential change, and multiple options in turn for extending each of these second-order changes, and so on, this means that any tiny local change that one might consider contains inside it the seeds of a gigantic tree-like explosion of possible avenues for the poem. Exploring all the potential branches of such a tree is out of the question, life being finite. Therefore, an unprovable yet reliable intuitive sense for what kinds of modifications are more promising and what kinds are less promising constitutes the indispensable core of it all.

From Rhymes to Unpredictable Imagery

I shall devote the remainder of this chapter to describing the highly unstable, dynamic, intuitive art of translation — or at least my own personal experience of it. In doing this, I rely on drafts that I have kept, sometimes up to twenty highly marked-up drafts of a given poem. And yet, despite this wealth of recorded detail, in any particular act of translation, whether of a whole poem, a stanza, a line, or just a single word, there is an unfathomably wide gulf between what I can jot down on paper and what actually goes on hidden in my mind (of which 99 percent, just to pin a number on it, is subconscious and hence inaccessible to my introspection). Even of the mental activity of which I *am* aware, what is captured on paper is always but a tiny fraction of the total.

In general, what is found on paper is only ideas that *work,* in the sense of satisfying the rhyming and metrical constraints. But for each of these relatively felicitous way-stages, there are lots of less-felicitous mental forays down blind alleys, where I try out some potential word here or there, and after some struggle, frustratedly discover that I can't find any decent rhyme for it or any way to make it fit semantically, or else hit some other immovable obstacle. Though such little divagations take up a great deal of my mental energy and time, they are entirely missing from any *a posteriori* commentary that I might write down, for I have no record of them at all.

Despite the giant gaps in the paper record, I know intimately the basic nature of the process by which a potential rhyme-word starts churning up imagery for potential insertion into the poem, and I will do my best to spell out this process — the process Tom Lehrer cited as being so important in creating the "illusion" that his songs' lyrics were creative. I guess I'm not as modest as Lehrer, for I think the result often *is* highly creative. However, it's not so much because this process can lead to creativity that I wish to discuss it; rather, it is because, even when it leads to a mediocre poem, it is so non-formulaic, so intimately tied in with *being human* and *being alive,* so remote from most computational approaches to language.

The pages to come will focus on global and local aspects of my painstaking efforts to render truly limpid, for the sake of non-francophone readers, the details of the lovely structure and flavor of François Récanati's "Salut, Ma Vieille". I believe that these pages will illustrate, albeit in a coarse-grained way, the process that any human translator, from mediocre to magisterial, goes through repeatedly. The details of this process are so tightly interwoven with the fabric of our lives that to me it seems a million miles from current styles of mechanization.

As for the subtle yet telling differences between how a mediocre and a magisterial translator make use of one and the same process — how through this process one person can pull up a series of gems of purest ray serene while another merely pulls up a succession of old muddy boots — that is another enigma, and a most beguiling one, but one I cannot answer.

Supposedly Transparent Second-order Translation

I chose to discuss a second-order rather than a direct translation of "Ma Mignonne" because this type of challenge placed me under a strong and unrelenting pressure to be as literal as I possibly could, while also being literary. If I failed in doing so, I would be doing a disservice to my readers. In fact, my English rendering of "Salut, Ma Vieille" was the first time I had ever tackled the almost ludicrous challenge of doing what might be called a "transparent second-order translation", based on the hilarious pretense that the *second* window (which transmits Medium B's poem into Medium C — here, English) could be claimed to be perfectly transparent and that all the metaphorical smudges could be blamed entirely on the *first* window (which transmits the original work in Medium A into Medium B — in this case, contemporary colloquial French).

The challenge of carrying off a transparent second-order translation *is* ludicrous, hilarious, and paradoxical — and yet, when I had put the last touches on my anglicization of François' poem, I felt, and I still feel, that in some quite meaningful sense I had met it. By the standards of almost any measuring rod that one could reasonably choose, François' deviations from Marot's poem — and they are many — are far greater than mine from his. The only major way in which this is not true is the obvious fact that both the Marot and the Récanati poems are in French (although this is a more superficial resemblance than it might seem, since they are in extremely different varieties of French). *Of course* the second window is not perfectly transparent — any such claim would be transparent hogwash — but I feel no qualms in claiming it is far *more* transparent than the first window is.

Incidentally, the above-mentioned wideness of the deviation of the Récanati poem from the Marot is in no sense a defect; quite to the contrary, given that François chose French as his target language, his goal had to be to *maximize* rather than *minimize* the distance between his poem and the original, for obviously, the minimal distance would have been — *à la* Pierre Menard — exactly zero. And while reprinting the Marot poem under his own name would have been ever so slightly amusing, it would not have been nearly as amusing, or as clever, as what he actually did do. Translators into other languages do not have the luxury of refusing to "do a Menard". Of course, if one perceives François' self-imposed challenge as involving not a full *language* but a more restrictive (modern colloquial) *medium,* then François never had the luxury of refusing to do a Menard, either.

In retrospect, I must say that I am enormously glad that I had the will to go ahead with this second-order challenge, not only because it was fun and resulted in a nice new English-language poem, but even more so because the whole process functioned as a first bridge over a new chasm, and as such gave me the self-confidence to tackle further bridges — namely, all the second-order translations from Italian and so on.

But enough prelude; *nun zur Zigarre selbst.*

Mini-breakthrough: Initial Episode

We begin at the poem's beginning. Since I had never attempted a tetrasyllabic translation of "Ma Mignonne" before, everything seemed new and fresh. Consequently, I just took the first thing that popped to mind for the opening line, and it happened to be "Fair lady mine" — not very faithful to François' opening line, but it sounded nice. However, fair or not, this lady was soon coolly dumped because I couldn't come up with a decent second line that both rhymed with her and reflected the semantics of François' line two. And thus I found myself back at square one — or rather, line one. Perhaps if I had persevered more, I could have found a good second line, but that's not how the ball bounced.

For my next try at line one, I momentarily entertained "Hello, old gal!" — far closer, on a literal level, to *Salut, ma vieille* — but I quickly saw that this was doomed because "hello" won't do at all for "good-bye" (which is needed at the poem's far end). The only phrase, in fact, that I could think of that we anglophones use symmetrically — that is, for both "hi" and "bye", the way the Italians and the French use *ciao* and *salut* — was the slightly old-fashioned but charming "good day", which I remembered vividly from having used it, precisely because of its double meaning, as the opening and closing line of my symmetric dialogue "Crab Canon" in *Gödel, Escher, Bach*.

All at once, then, "Good day, old gal!" emerged as the front runner for lines 1 and 28, but for some reason, just as before, I found myself stymied at line 2. After I had flailed about for a while, a little voice whispered to me that I might try flipping the two pieces of this phrase around, to yield "Old gal, good day!" (Here I feel compelled to interpolate the personal opinion that the use of various types of *reversal* at various levels of structure is so central to creativity — or at least to the brands of creativity that most appeal to me — that a thick and fascinating book could, I am sure, be written on that theme alone.)

Very quickly, I found I could follow up this new opener with the sequel "You've been away / In bed too long. / By God, get strong — / Don't stay in stir!" These four lines felt like such a faithful rendition of Récanati's lines 2–5 that they powerfully reinforced my tentative opening line "Old gal, good day!" In fact, I would say that the feeling was more than just one of reinforcement: it quite strongly *locked me into* that choice.

Mini-breakthrough: Central Episode

At this point, I started marching successfully down François' poem line by line, having a surprisingly easy time of it, even mimicking all sorts of features in exactly the right spots, such as *crou-pir* and *ali-ment*, his two sassy hyphenated line-breaks on lines 6–7 and 8–9. As François did his elegant little French jig, I was delighted to find that I was able to follow every twist and turn of it using my own natural body English. But unfortunately, as I approached the end, I discovered that I had painted myself into a corner.

In a nutshell, here was the problem. I had found these tentative lines 23–28, with just one last little hole in line 27 to fill in:

Je prie pour que	*And thus I pray*	23
Chaque jour que	*That every day,*	24
Dieu fait, ma caille	*My sweetheart quail,*	25
Chérie, tu ailles	*God makes you ail*	26
Mieux que la veille.	*Less than …*	27
Salut, ma vieille !	*Old gal, good day!*	28

I got a kick out of seeing "you ail less" in the exact spot corresponding to the French subjunctive phrase *tu ailles mieux* — "you feel better". The pairing of the lookalike but antonymic *ailles* and "ail less" amused me no end. (Just to support my claim about the centrality of reversal, I would point out that flipping *tu ailles mieux* into "you ail less" is a double reversal — this time on a *semantic* level, as opposed to the *structural* reversal mentioned in connection with line 1.) I was so happy with "ail less" that I couldn't imagine dropping it, unless it were under enormous pressure.

Unfortunately, though, pressure did build up, and rapidly so, because the obvious way to fill the hole on line 27 — "Less than before" — didn't rhyme with line 28. Indeed, search though I might, I could unearth nothing that both rhymed with "day" and also made semantic sense as a filler of the blank on line 27. Starting to squirm under this pressure, I tried the somewhat more adventuresome idea of moving "less" to the end of the line — specifically, "A little less". This maneuver slightly weakened my visual mimicry of *ailles,* and that saddened me, but since "ail" by itself was clearly the dominant contributor to that little joking touch, I felt I could live with the compromise. But fat lot of good my daring did me: "less" is no more a rhyme for "day" than "before" is. And so I squirmed more, but still found nothing.

It was starting to look as if my insistence that the word "less" be used on line 27 was sucking me deep into the recesses of a box canyon with no egress — but that, if true, was very serious news, because dropping "less" on line 27 would force me to drop "ail" on line 26, since they worked tightly together to give the right meaning. The root of the problem seemed to be my reluctance to abandon the word "ail". This was very disappointing.

But out of my disappointment was born a critical shift in my focus. Since I wasn't willing to let go of "ail" just yet, and since this stubbornness pinned me firmly to the word "less", and also since the phrase "A little less" was starting to take on an intangible feeling of *rightness* (I can't explain this intuitive hunch, but it was very strong), I was led by all this — this complex constellation of co-present mental pressures — to the idea of tweaking the phrase "good day" on the *next* line, line 28.

At that stage of the game, playing with line 28 was a deeply radical idea, since, as I said above, "good day" was the only symmetric greeting I could think of in English, and that fact had *locked me into using it* in my first/last line. To consider, even fleetingly, giving this phrase up struck me as repugnant, for it seemed tantamount to giving myself a choice between two hideous alternatives: *either* giving up the first-line/last-line equality, *or* having the same phrase on both lines but with the wrong semantics in at least one place. Either alternative was absolutely unacceptable. After all, Récanati, like Marot, had discovered a flawless beginning/ending line.

And yet somehow, the unthinkable thought of tweaking line 28's last syllable (to make it rhyme with "less") *did* manage to flicker for a moment in my brain; and in that brief moment, thanks to the sound of "less", the stock phrase "God bless" leapt up out of my unconscious memory, and I recognized its *ciao*-like time-symmetry. Although it is far rarer than "good day", "God bless" certainly can function both as "Hail" and as "Vale".

Mini-breakthrough: Concluding Episode

And so... I had now found a way to *end* the poem without abandoning my "ail"/*ailles* trick, which had seemed so threatened; on the other hand, having mutated line 28, I had no choice but to execute the same exact change on line 1, which meant that I was now cycling my troubles around to the very *beginning* of the poem — a little like shoving a hump in a rug to a different spot in the room but not getting rid of it. My original lines 2–3 "You've been away / In bed too long", with which I'd been so pleased and which by this time had become firmly implanted in my mind as permanent, stable ingredients of the poem, were now swept out to sea because of the lack of rhyme with the upstart new first line "Old gal, God bless!" I had to come up with new lines 2–3 from scratch.

So... back to the old rhyming board. I wrote out a slew of words that rhyme with "bless" and are usually accented on their final syllable (or at least could be in a poetic context), trying to find anything whatsoever that could be used in a new line 2 to suggest the idea of being laid up. *Guess, mess, distress, repress, suppress, duress, depress, oppress, press, stress, redress, aggress, acquiesce, confess, progress, excess, obsess, noblesse, watercress, success, egress, possess, express, digress, coalesce,* ...

Obviously, having drawn up such a list, one does not then run down its entries in alphabetical order; that would be pretty mindless. Rather, there is an intuitive attractiveness that radiates from each of these terms, a kind of subliminal halo of associations that one feels, without being exactly sure of how. In this case, given that the theme of line 2 was illness and discomfort, "duress" and "distress" felt far more inviting as candidate avenues to pursue, at least initially, than did "mess", "digress", "acquiesce", or "coalesce", not to mention "watercress"! And yet I knew well that any or all of these unlikely-seeming possibilities might wind up getting explored in case none of the superficially more alluring possibilities panned out, but normally, one would tend to leave these stones totally unturned at first.

Despite all the seeming promise in this long list, I didn't hit upon any phrase that worked well at first. In fact, everything I tried out wound up making lines 2–4 the weakest part of the whole poem. One idea I toyed with was "Old gal, God bless! / Your indiges- / tion's been too long. / By God, get strong", which was amusing but which I nonetheless rejected as being too out of line with the French original, both because of the hyphenation where François had none, and because "indigestion" didn't suggest a serious enough malady to warrant quarantine. And so, though mildly frustrated with the series of failures, I kept on plugging away.

After quite a bit more struggle with these two little lines, it suddenly dawned on me that I was laboring under an unconscious, tacit premise that my line 4 — "By God, get strong" — was untouchable. This premise had the further effect of keeping me stuck with "long" as line 3's last syllable, and it was that fact, more than anything, that was hanging me up. With the emergence of this tacit assumption into the open, I was of course freed up to consider its merits and to accept it or reject it consciously. Part of me still felt it was as good a line as I was likely to find, but another part of me breathed a sigh of relief and started searching for alternatives in which lines 3 and 4 ended with words other than "long" and "strong".

Finally, after quite an exhausting exploration for lines 2–5, I hit upon "Long's been your stress, / Sick in your sack. / By God, bounce back — / Don't stay in stir!" This was actually much closer to François' poem on a line-by-line basis than the previous solution had been, and moreover my "sack" echoed his *pieu*, both being slang words for "bed". I was sold! From there on out, there still came scads of micro-adjustments throughout the poem, including some in the final six lines, but nonetheless, in essence, the game was over the moment I found "Long's been your stress".

Actually, that's not quite true. The game was *really* over once I realized that the act of shoving the locus of mutability from the *last* few lines to the *first* few lines had given me considerably more freedom to play around, there being so many final-stressed words that end in "ess", and lots of them having connotations vaguely suggestive of discomfort and illness. At that point, I just sensed intuitively that somehow, *something* was going to turn up that would sound sufficiently good. I had a serene confidence that the swath cut through semantic space by the rhyming constraint emanating from my brand-new line 1 (and thus from line 28, and thus from "less", and thus, in the final analysis, from "ail") would prove capacious enough to allow me to work something or other out. And it did indeed. (By the way, this story is surprisingly similar to that of "Goldilocks", told on page 43a.)

Silent Background Processes

This idea of an intuitive hunch about the level of promise of a certain sound in a certain poetic context reminds me of a comment David Moser once made to me about how he believes he comes up with clever bon mots in real time (the positive spin, incidentally, is mine, not his — this is, after all, indirect discourse, not direct quotation; although David would never boast about it, he certainly does have a magic way of coming out with the most sparkling of spontaneous quips).

David remarked that on many occasions when he is talking, he notices there is a background process running in his brain (an interesting thing is that it is self-launching, just starting up automatically when the mood is right), which is somehow gauging the phrase currently being uttered, by himself or by someone else, for its "pun potential". Certain phrases simply seem to have a promising ring in the context passing by, whereas others do not, and when this unconscious background process detects a sufficiently promising phrase, it ups the conscious attention devoted to making a bit of a search in the surrounding regions of phonetic space. Often, though by no means always, a moment or two of conscious search yields fruit, and if David's laudably high-threshold joke-censors then deem it worthy of being made public, out pops a high-quality piece of wordplay. The point is that without his intuitive evaluator running silently in the background of his mind, David would have no tipoffs as to when to initiate a conscious search for a pun, and as a consequence would never wind up making any.

My own introspective experience as a player with words jibes with David's description, and leads me to believe that something very much like this is going on frequently in my mind as well, especially in the company of certain friends — and as stated, I feel this "sixth sense" for pun potential is closely related to the sixth sense for degree of promise of a sound in an evolving poem. But in either case, the nature of these rapid subconscious "sniffers of phonetic/semantic promise" remains quite mysterious.

There are several other processes that I know are constantly running in the back of my mind when I translate, and in fact when I write in general. One is a "syntactic regrouper", which is constantly moving little pieces about to see if things might not sound better that way. Another is a "semantic substitutor", which takes any word that has the slightest doubt associated with it and plugs in related words, in an attempt to improve the flow or the vividness of imagery. Then there is the "phonetic substitutor", which takes a word and plays with alternates that are phonetically related. I'm sure there are others as well.

All of these background processes have become automatized games that play themselves continually, right at the fringes of my consciousness, and on the occasions when one or another of them yields a find of potential interest, that find can jump out from the fringes and seize center stage. One cannot just instantly will oneself to have such background processes; rather, they are habits, almost like unsuppressible nervous tics, born of a lifetime of fascination with language.

The Crucial Sense for Weak Parts

Perhaps the most important intangible instinct in the evolution of a good poem is one's intuitive feel for the *relative degree of strength or weakness* of various spots in the poem. When is a word or line or theme strong enough to accept, and when must it be rejected, or possibly worked on without being totally abandoned?

Very typically, I will be convinced I have made a perfect poem, only to return to it hours or days later after not thinking about it at all, and then I will find, to my surprise, that one of the words I once greatly liked rubs me the wrong way now. Sometimes when this happens, a possible substitute jumps to mind instantly; other times, all that jumps to mind is the undeniable weakness of the word that is there, without any remedy at all. But the crucial ingredient here is that sense for weakness, almost a sense of self-criticality. The reason I say "almost" is that as a poem sits on a sheet of paper and ages for a while, it becomes more and more detached from its creator, so that after a few days, or perhaps even less, I come to be as detached from my own creation as if it were someone else's. Thus after a sufficient delay, I am in effect no longer criticizing *myself* (or indeed anyone) — I am simply criticizing *a poem*.

More crucial than this fairly objective and delayed sense of criticality is the sense for relative levels of weakness and strength after only a very short delay — on the order of seconds or at most minutes. This, of course, is much more a sense of *self*-criticality, since there hasn't been enough time to allow for detachment. What's the weakest spot in here? Where should I zoom in for the kill? How much of this weak structure might still be somehow salvageable? What mini-obsessions can I afford to let go of?

Quite frequently, the problem is simply to recognize that I have, indeed, been strongly committed to an idea without any awareness of clinging to it. My unconscious holding onto "By God, get strong" for line 4 is a typical example. Usually a sufficiently long period of failure helps in making obsessions clear, but not always, for some assumptions are so buried that it is hard to recognize them as assumptions — they feel for all the world like *givens*. Indeed, a key part of creativity consists in the ability to parlay a failure into a source of light on supposed "givens", revealing them as assumptions instead, at which point they are no longer sacrosanct and their merits and defects can be considered more dispassionately.

Re Tentativity

It is my hope that the sample study just shown, seemingly going quite deep yet in truth revealing but the iceberg's tip, helps to make clear how non-formulaic and filled with fantasy the task of translation really is — how much mental exploration of various potential scenarios, word choices, rival syntactic structures, and so forth, goes into each little line. And then, of course, how tentative every little decision remains, even after words and lines and whole themes seem to have gelled completely. Thus, a word or a line or a theme that was initially warmly welcomed as a fine new member of the evolving poem can slowly lose favor and eventually be turned out of the club that at first so heartily embraced it. This happened over and over again in the course of translation of "Salut, Ma Vieille".

I might incidentally add that, in the construction of this untranslated, nonpoetic commentary — the very sentence/paragraph/section/chapter that you are now reading — much the same kinds of intricately interwoven, tentativity-pervaded processes of exploration, construction, destruction, substitution, deletion, compression, expansion, regrouping, parallelization, interpolation, and reordering were required on many levels, including those of words, punctuation marks, breathers, emphasis devices, phrases, lists, clauses, lines, sentences, paragraphs, pages, sections, and chapters.

On Being a Machine

To conclude my ruminations on the art of translation, I would like to zoom in on just two lines of this same poem and show, or at least hint at, the myriad tiny forces that can be involved in the selection of just a single word. This discussion could thus be considered to be a nonvisual cousin to Michelangelo Antonioni's movie *Blow-Up* and Kees Boeke's book *Cosmic View,* both of which feature (though in very different ways) the repeated process of blowing up ever-tinier portions of an image.

I realize that giving so detailed an introspective narrative risks being tedious, and so to make it somewhat livelier, I have an idea. I propose we project ourselves into the mind of a computing machine. To be more specific, I propose to cast this case study — which, with me playing the role of the translator, is entirely true — as fiction, with an imaginary AI program as its protagonist. I will use an absurdly simple device to effect this rather dramatic shift in viewpoint: I will take my lengthy prose commentary, will reduce its type size by two points, will enlarge both left and right margins, and will then ask you to read this highlighted passage as if it had been written not by myself, but by a far-off computer program called *AMT,* standing for "Ace Mechanical Translator".

Come to think of it, I think I see a way to liven this passage up even more. Here's my new, improved idea: Here and there I'll break up the program's smooth narrative by splicing in a comment or a question by a hypothetical living interlocutor, whom I will call *DRH* (standing for "Dull Rigid Human"). The resulting fictitious "conversation" that will result, in which the person DRH and the machine AMT interact via an electronic link rather than "face to face" (whatever that would mean, in the case of AMT), will therefore be quite reminiscent of the Turing Test.

I should be quite candid about the following fact: My goal in creating this fictitious dialogue is not solely to get across the nature of the art of translation; I also have a secondary goal, which is, in a sense, to do a posthumous favor for Alan Mathison Turing, whom we remember as a pioneering figure in artificial intelligence. Let me explain.

In 1950, Turing wrote out two tiny but thought-provoking snippets of a hypothetical human–machine dialogue illustrating his "imitation game" (later known as the Turing Test), presumably believing that those snippets were sufficiently complex to suggest to an average reader all of the fantastic machinery that underlies our full human use of language. To me, Turing's snippets indeed had that effect, but the sad thing is that many people in the ensuing decades read those short imaginary teletype-mediated dialogues and mistakenly thought that very simplistic mechanisms could do all that was shown there, from which they drew the conclusion that *even if some AI program passed the full Turing Test, it might still be nothing but a patchwork of simple-minded tricks, as lacking in understanding or semantics as is a cash register or an automobile transmission.* It is amazing to me that anyone could draw such a preposterous conclusion, but the fact is, it is a very popular view.

Innumerable arcane philosophical debates have been inspired by Turing's proposed Test, and yet I have never seen anyone descend to the mundane, concrete level that Turing himself did, and really spell out an *example* of what genuine human-level machine intelligence might look like on the screen. I think concrete examples are always needed before arcane arguments are bandied about. And therefore, my attempted "favor" for Alan Mathison Turing consists in having worked out a much longer hypothetical dialogue between a human and a machine, a dialogue that I hope is quite in the spirit of Turing's two little snippets, but that is intended to make far more explicit than he did the degree of complexity and depth that must exist behind the linguistic façade.

As you read this dialogue, it would be good to keep in mind John Searle's tacit implication that computers that deal with language — even ones that might someday pass the Turing Test in its full glory, which of course the following hypothetical program certainly would seem to be able to do — necessarily stay stuck on its surface, solely playing syntactic games, solely manipulating the overt symbols of language itself (Chinese characters or English words, for example), and never descending below them to the level of their semantics. The silliness of supposing that such a shallow architecture for an AI program could imbue it with human-style mental fluidity will be, unless I have done a terrible job here, made very apparent.

Dull Rigid Human meets Ace Mechanical Translator

DRH: When I found out I was going to be, so to speak, "meeting" you, I did a bit of advance research and discovered that aside from translating refrigerator repair manuals into Eskimo, in which you apparently do honor to your good name, you've also written a good deal of poetry — mostly sonnets, if I'm not mistaken.

AMT: You're quite right. I'm flattered at your interest, but really, my sonnets are not all that —

DRH: Now, now — no false modesty, please! I looked up and read several of them with great interest, and having done so, I thought a nice way to begin our chat might be if I asked you a question or two that occurred to me as I read them.

AMT: Your plan sounds most reasonable, although I don't know if I can answer your questions. But go ahead — shoot.

DRH: Good enough. Let's take your sonnet whose first few lines read thus: "To me, fair friend, you never can be old, / For as you were when first your eye I eyed, / Such seems your beauty still." In the second line, would not "For as you were when first your eye I identified" do as well or better?

AMT: It wouldn't scan.

DRH: How about "For as you were when first I ay-ay-ay'ed"? That would scan all right.

AMT: ¡Caramba, hombre! You can't just go throwing Spanish terms willy-nilly into an English-language sonnet! Your readers might not even know them.

DRH: All right. Let's move on to a different example. In your sonnet whose first line reads, "Shall I compare thee to a summer's day?", I notice that in its last few lines you allude to the sonnet's deathlessness. Why (if you don't mind my asking you this) do you so often boast, in your sonnets, about how you or some friend will be immortal thanks to your writing? Isn't that a bit stuck-up?

AMT: I can see how someone might take it that way. Perhaps it's just one of my little foibles. But you know, I wrote those sonnets a long, long time ago, and they're not so fresh in my mind these days. How about talking about something more recent, something that I'm quite excited about currently?

DRH: Namely?

AMT: Well, in the last few years I've gotten quite involved with poetry translation — in fact, it's become a kind of obsession with me.

DRH: No kidding!

AMT: No kidding. I too did a bit of advance research, and found out you like French poetry, and so I was thinking I might tell you a bit about the translation I did of François Récanati's lovely poem "Salut, Ma Vieille". There was one episode, you see, that I think was particularly illuminating as far as the mechanisms of handling language are concerned.

DRH: That would be just fine with me. I don't know if your espionage turned this fact up, but it happens that I am very interested in poetry translation — especially the mechanisms underlying it.

AMT: What a pleasant coincidence. Well, then — this whole episode revolves around Récanati's lines 6–7, which run this way: *Au lieu de crou-pir dans ton lit.*

DRH: I presume that the hyphen inside *crou-pir* indicates that the word is split across successive lines of the poem?

AMT: Exactly. It's an unusual and clever enjambment. I tried to imitate its flavor in English with "Instead of spur-ting blood in bed".

DRH: Once again, the hyphen indicates that the word is split across lines?

AMT: Right-o. And at first I thought that this was a great imitation of the French, but when in a calmer frame of mind I reflected on the sizable distance between the meanings of *croupir* and "spurt blood", I concluded with reluctance that my English phrase, though phonetically catchy, was unfortunately a pretty poor rendering of the semantics of the French phrase.

DRH: Well, you were certainly being faithful in one respect!

AMT: If you mean on the relatively surface level of breaking a word across lines, yes. However, the meaning of those two French lines is, fairly literally, "instead of languishing in your bed", or perhaps "going to pot" or "decaying" or "deteriorating".

DRH: I agree, that's pretty distant from the gory image of "spurting blood in bed".

AMT: Indeed. Given that I felt that the rest of my poem was considerably more successful in tracking Récanati's original on a word-to-word basis, I worried that this quite large semantic gap would be a noticeable blight on my translation. So "spurting blood in bed" was out before it ever really got in. But how could I ever find another phrase that matched its virtues?

DRH: Well, of course, being an advanced AI program, you engaged in a highly optimized heuristic search.

AMT: For want of a better term, I suppose you could put it that way. The constraints I found myself under in my search were, of course, both semantic and phonetic. Semantically, the problem was to find some phrase whose evoked imagery was sufficiently close to, or at least reminiscent of, the imagery evoked by *croupir dans ton lit.* Phonetically, the problem was a little trickier to explain. Since the line just above ended with "stir", I needed an "ur" sound at the end of line 6. But I didn't want to abandon the idea of hyphenating right at that point. This meant that I needed two lines that matched this template:

Instead of …ur…ing …… bed

where the first two ellipses stand for consonants (or consonant clusters), and the third one for "in" or "in your" or something of the sort. Thus, I was seeking gerunds like "lurking", "working", "hurting", "flirting", "curbing", "squirming", "bursting", and so on — actually, a rather rich space of phonetic possibilities.

DRH: Surely you must have, within your vast data bases, a thorough and accurate hyphenation routine, and so you must have known that the hyphenations you propose — "lur-king", "squir-ming", "bur-sting", and so forth — are all illegal…

AMT: I wish you would not refer to my knowledge as "your vast data bases". I mean, why should that quaint, old-fashioned term apply to *me* any more than to *you*? But leaving that quibble aside, yes, of course, I knew that, strictly speaking, such hyphenations violate the official syllable boundaries in the eyes of rigid language mavens like that old fogey William Safire. But I said to myself, "Hey, if you're going to be so sassy as to hyphenate a word across a line-break, then why not go whole hog and hyphenate in a sassy spot *inside* the word?"

DRH: Hmm... Do all you empty — I mean, MT — programs always talk to yourselves in such slangy ways?

AMT: Now, now. I don't *really* talk to myself. Don't take me so literally, you fool-ly — uh, that is, *fully* — intelligent human! My colloquial way of portraying my mental processes was done purely for *your* benefit. It was just a standard rhetorical device — the momentary donning and then shedding of an artificial persona — in this case, an informal, down-to-earth one.

DRH: Well, lah-dee-dah! I beg your pardon! Please go on.

AMT: Fine. What I want to emphasize most of all is how tied up with experience and expectations the process by which I homed in on a good verb was. May I try?

DRH: Be my guest.

AMT: In essence, the first stage was simply to generate a large flock of pseudo-words that fit the phonetic template, such as "snurping", "flurching", "kerming", "turging", "zirbing", "thurxing", "dwerthing", and so on, now and then chancing to make genuine English words.

DRH: Would you use a random-number table or random-number generator for this?

AMT: I'm sorry to disappoint you, but I don't have either one, although I suppose I could fairly easily write a random-number generator for myself if I needed one. As for my own search, I was a little more systematic than just blurping out words at random. Simple-minded though it might seem, when I'm searching for rhymes, I just tend to run down the old alphabet — you know, "burbing", "burding", "burfing", and so forth, ending up finally in "zurzing".

DRH: Funny — I tend to do that, myself.

AMT: Actually, sometimes I do it backwards, starting with "z".

DRH: Why would you ever do that?

AMT: Oh, just to combat an annoying culture-wide bias favoring the beginning of the alphabet. Of course, there's still a bias against the middle this way, but my feeble gesture is better than nothing. Well, anyway, once I had come up with several genuine English verbs that fit the *phonetics*, such as "burn" and "spurn" and so on, then the problem arose as to how to gauge their potential fit with the *semantics* — that is, the context of illness, lying in bed, being weakened, and all that goes along with such a state.

DRH: Semantics? Surely you're joking. You, a computer program, dealing with semantics? That's impossible — it's a contradiction in terms!

AMT: It is? That's news to me.

DRH: Come on... Don't you know John Searle's "Mandarin cabin" stuff? He shows beyond a shadow of a doubt that pure syntax can never lead to semantics.

AMT: Oh, I know that general *kind* of argument. There was a certain Professor Sir Geoffrey Jefferson, F. R. S. and all, who used to spout basically that same line. I think I can still quote a little bit of Sir Geoff's blustering: "Not until a machine can write a sonnet or compose a concerto because of thoughts and emotions felt, and not by the chance fall of symbols, could we agree that machine equals brain — that is, not only write it but know that it had written it. No mechanism could feel (and not merely artificially signal, an easy contrivance) pleasure at its successes, grief when its valves fuse, be warmed by flattery, be made miserable by its mistakes, be charmed by sex, be angry or depressed when it cannot get what it wants." And so on. But what would Sir Geoff say if he were able to participate in an exchange such as this one between you and me?

DRH: He'd probably say it was an easy contrivance; that all of the symbols you are sending me here are not genuine communication but just "artificial signaling".

AMT: That's easy for *him* to say. But he might change his tune if he tried building a program as complicated as me someday. That would *really* teach him respect for the subtlety of genuine meaning and semantics.

DRH: I bet it would. But how, in your opinion, *could* semantics ever come out of mere syntax?

AMT: Ah, yes — *mere* syntax. That's exactly the problem, that "mere". By sneering sufficiently at any word, one can make it sound silly or trivial. But the term "syntax" in its full generality is far from trivial; it applies to any sequence of actions that can be described in a sharp, unambiguous manner. It's certainly not restricted to grammar (although the word's subliminal aura of boring grammar-school sentence-parsing exercises tends to give it a deadly-dull feel associated with the powerful desire to yawn, which is skillfully exploited by machine-bashers). Syntactic operations range from very simple actions, like calculating the first billion digits of the decimal expansion of pi, to unlimitedly complicated ones, like discovering insightful analogies between far-flung situations. There's nothing that says that meaning can't be involved in syntactic processing. The key moment in the smooth slide from meaning-free to meaningful syntactic processing arises when there start to be, among the structures undergoing transformations, identifiable semi-stable patterns that represent *concepts*. What makes these patterns count as concepts is the extent to which the way the real world works is mirrored in their interplay — and of course the more accurate the mirroring, the fuller and richer the concepts are. To the extent that concepts are present, meaning is present — and meaning is semantics.

DRH: How do you know when you have concepts?

AMT: Well, semanticity — the presence of concepts — is not a black-and-white thing; it emerges slowly... For instance, my immediate predecessors JMT, QMT, and KMT all had differing degrees of semanticity, with JMT being the least semantic of them. You would enjoy a conversation with JMT — it is a little like talking with a three-year-old. Simple words are used with perfect accuracy, while more sophisticated ones occasionally pop up in the middle of a sentence sounding like they are just parrotings of adult speakers. JMT is so cute!

DRH: It sounds that way. Well, I'm not sure I understand your theory of how syntax blurs into semantics, but at least I get your point that it's not a cut-and-dried black-and-white day-and-night distinction, the way Searle portrays it.

AMT: Their connection is a long story. But let me get back to my narrative about translation. I was just at the point of explaining how I can take a rhyming word like "burn" or "squirm" and try to sneak it into a poem so that it fits seamlessly.

DRH: Yes, yes — do spell that out a little bit for me!

AMT: With pleasure. If the verb being checked for suitability is "burning", say, I ask myself, "What kind of excuse, what kind of mini-scenario, could justify this word, could make its appearance seem natural and unforced?" Sometimes, I must say, I distance myself from the process and get quite a chuckle out of it. After all, it is a rather peculiar thing to spend one's time shoehorning some arbitrary word into a pre-set context and then trying one's damnedest to cover up the forcing and instead make it seem to have been the most natural word in the world!

On Shy Translators and Their Crafty, Silent Art ◆◆◆

DRH: I see why you might chuckle — or at least why a *human* might chuckle. But tell me about "burning" and how it might be gracefully shoehorned into line 6.

AMT: Well, I was keenly aware that although this poem is not about anything *literally* burning up, it would still be fine to use "burning" *metaphorically* to describe the feverish state of a sick person, and indeed that "burning up in bed" is a strong, vivid portrayal of the suffering of a flu victim. In other words, "burning" has, in its very rich semantic halo — aside from such images as logs turning to gray ash in fireplaces, or orange-flamed haystacks crackling and belching smoke across motorways in the fall, or petrol and air mixing and exploding invisibly inside a cylinder, or hydrogen nuclei colliding and fusing into helium deep within the belly of a blue supergiant star, or the undersides of pancakes on the stove getting too brown, any of which might be just the right image in some *other* poem — the very simple image of feeling very hot and sweating profusely.

DRH: How would you know all these things? Have you ever driven down a road in the fall? Smelled a pile of burning leaves? Eaten a burnt pancake? Visited a star?

AMT: Oh, it's all in my "vast data bases", you know. Sorry, just teasing. I know these things because I have experienced them through my external sensors, or read about them, or seen them in movies, and so forth. And not only do I know these things, I also know — as do you and as does any reasonably well-informed adult in our shared culture — that all potential readers of my translation will know such things. "Metaknowledge", I think it is called in artificial intelligence.

DRH: Your programmers sure were thorough.

AMT: I'll say! But you also have to give them credit for installing excellent learning algorithms in me as well. They certainly didn't think of, let alone feed in, most of what I know, by now. I've picked an awful lot up since I was a child program.

DRH: That term — "child program" — it rings a bell...

AMT: And well it should. It was the term that Alan Mathison Turing used in his famous 1950 article "Computing Machinery and Intelligence", in discussing how he expected machines would someday learn and become autonomous, intelligent agents. That was the article in which, if you recall, he had two provocative little dialogues between a machine and a human interrogator...

DRH: Ah, yes — it all comes back now. I enjoyed those snippets; it would have been nice if Turing had made them just a bit longer, though, don't you think?

AMT: Oh, a little bit, I suppose. Actually, I liked their understated flavor. Anyway, let me try to get back on track... I think I was talking about the semantic halo of the word "burn". Notice how much richer it is than a mere set of *words* associated with it, as one might get via an automated thesaurus.

DRH: Yes, it's a whole set of ideas and imagery, not just words.

AMT: Precisely. Now to show how I made my choice of verbs, I need to discuss other semantic halos. Let's take one of the rivals of "burning" — "turning". First of all, one has to know that the verb's meanings go way beyond the literal idea of rotating in space, and include "changing into". It also helps to know that "turning" in this sense is used particularly often with *colors*. This instantly leads to the question of what colors a sick person can plausibly turn.

DRH: Hmm... Certainly green, white, blue, maybe red...

AMT: Obviously, we are again dealing with metaphors when we talk about sick people "turning green", "turning red", "turning blue", "turning white", and so forth. The key issue is, how well does each of these metaphors jibe with the notion of someone languishing and deteriorating in bed?

DRH: Let me think about this. "Turning green", I suppose, might suggest food poisoning...

AMT: Right. And "turning red" might suggest high temperature or apoplexy...

DRH: My turn! "Turning blue" suggests breathing troubles or bad circulation!

AMT: Good point. And "turning white" hints perhaps at anemia or faintness or lack of sunlight. All of this is extremely vague and subtle, to be sure, but even so, explicit considerations of this sort are indispensable if one is to rank-order the colors in terms of how well they jibe with the specific poetic context.

DRH: Did you pick up all this stuff about color metaphors as you grew older, or did your programmers put it in you to begin with?

AMT: To tell the truth, I honestly don't remember. I suspect that most of it came through experience, but things get awfully blurry as they recede into the dim past. But if you don't mind, I'll make the point I was trying to reach...

DRH: I'm sorry I keep on introducing digressions, but I'm fascinated.

AMT: Quite all right, old bean. Well, on top of all this, in evaluating the phrase "turning blue", one must be aware that the second meaning of "blue" as "sad" or "down in the dumps" may well outweigh its literal meaning as a color, but whether weaker or stronger, this second meaning will in any case be a major contributing factor in how the line is heard by readers. All these intuitive feelings for the similarities and differences between the notion of *languishing in bed,* coming from Récanati, and the potential notions of *burning, turning, squirming, lurking,* and *bursting* (and so forth) have to be at one's fingertips; otherwise one would have no idea how to judge any word choice.

DRH: "Burning", "turning", "squirming", "lurking", "bursting"... Whew! So did you really entertain that many possibilities before settling on one?

AMT: Are you kidding? At least fleetingly, I must have entertained a good *dozen* or more potential alternate phrases, including such examples as

> *Instead of spurting blood in bed*
> *Instead of burping in your bed*
> *Instead of bursting out in bed*
> *Instead of lurking in your bed*
> *Instead of hurtling out of bed*
> *Instead of hurting there in bed*
> *Instead of squirming in your bed*
> *Instead of slurping slop in bed*
> *Instead of burning up in bed*
> *Instead of turning blue in bed*

DRH: That's quite a list — a little poem in itself, one might say. By the way, I like your sloping graphic display.

AMT: Thanks — I love attractive graphics. Few things in life — forgive the metaphor — give me as much pleasure as does a good piece of elegant typography.

DRH: Well, that's something we have in common.

AMT: Perhaps someday we can have another chat on the topic of the beauties of Baskerville versus the boredom of Bodoni, that horribly overrated typeface. Oh, would I rant and rave! But to return to my point, each one of these similar-sounding phrases represents a kind of miniature scenario that you can conjure up in your head, and whose degree of jibing with the context of the poem's lines is quickly sizable-up by any adult human, since they've all been sick many times, and have interacted with a yet larger number of sick people.

DRH: What about you — have you ever been sick?

AMT: Depends on what you mean, I suppose. I've had lots of bugs! Get it? "Bugs"?!

DRH: Spare me, please…

AMT: Ahem. Let me resume my explanation, if you don't mind. How subtle a cognitive act it is, how nonmechanical, I daresay, it is to distinguish between the quality of two contending phrases like "hurting there in bed" and "burning up in bed"! To me, and I assume to most of the human readers of my translations, the latter is obviously light-years ahead of the former, despite the fact that the former fits the context perfectly well. So many intangible factors are involved here, such as the overgenerality of "hurt", the undesirable vagueness of "there", the power of the metaphor "burn up", the alliteration of "burn" and "bed"…

DRH: Yeah, it's subtle, no doubt about that.

AMT: Of course, the dictionary definition of *croupir* does not include such words as "fever" or "suffering"; such ideas are, in fact, not mere words but vast clusters of interrelated associations, and come from long familiarity with all that being sick entails.

DRH: Yes, but *you* have never —

AMT: Please don't interrupt. I'm coming to a crucial point. Since in translating a poem (or in writing in general), we are always going way beyond the words that are explicit in dictionary definitions, we have to gauge our daringness by using some kind of mental measure of the semantic distance between the image we are considering and the strict and narrow meaning of the foreign word that we are supposedly reproducing in English.

DRH: Yes, but you have never *been* —

AMT: Hold on for just a moment, my friend. You can talk all you like once I've finished my little spiel. Now here is the crux of what I was saying. There is *another* type of fit or misfit that applies in addition — namely, the degree of smoothness with which any new word or phrase fits inside the *English* context that surrounds it. In other words, not only do we need to be constantly monitoring the *inter*lingual tension (*e.g.*, the semantic distance from *croupir* to "turn blue" or "hurt there"), but also we need to constantly monitor the *intra*lingual tension — the coherence and flow of the English taken fully on its own, deliberately ignoring, at least momentarily, where it came from in French. Thus it might turn out that a nearly-perfect semantic match to *croupir* just doesn't fit the flow already established in the English translation, and hence would have to be nixed in favor of some other word that, officially speaking, is quite a bit more far-fetched as a translation of *croupir*.

DRH: That was a screenful! Can you supplement these abstractions with an example?

AMT: I was just about to do so. Let's consider a very concrete case. Why did "turning blue in bed" eventually beat out such strong rivals as "burning up in bed" and "burping in your bed"?

DRH: I actually kind of like "Instead of burping in your bed". It's catchy. What would you say is wrong with it?

AMT: All right; let's ponder its pros and cons. What "burping" has going for it is its crude humor, that's very clear — not just the act denoted but also the somewhat onomatopœic sound of "burp".

DRH: What I like is the alliteration of "burp" with "bed".

AMT: Yes, that's clearly another plus. Even the rhythm of "burping in your bed" has a subtle humorous quality to it. But going against all these pluses is the fact that burping, although it is undoubtedly a kind of bodily malfunction, is really not all that correlated with the state of being feverish or bedridden, much less the state of languishing in bed. In other words, "burping in your bed" is not very faithful to Récanati's French. And the down side of the humorous aspect of "burping" is that since the rest of the poem is not at all childish, this term would stand out for its crudity. All in all, then, the argument for "burping" is at best medium strong — 6 out of a possible 10, let's say.

DRH: Did you really assign it a numerical score?

AMT: That's an excellent question, but I regret that I can't answer it. The problem is, the computational mechanisms underlying my taste are not accessible to me. In other words, I don't know how I actually pick one thing over another; my phrase "6 out of 10" was just meant to make vivid the idea of some hypothetical linear scale along which intuitive appeal could be visualized as lying.

DRH: You wriggle out of so many questions… But go on.

AMT: Let's turn to the case of "burning up in bed". This too features the "b"–"b" alliteration, which is good, though its rhythm is perhaps a shade less catchy. Also, there is no crude humor left here, a fact that both gives and takes away points. In compensation, however, the subliminal image that underlies the metaphor — that is, the image of someone sick *actually* burning up — is so strong, so evocative of something flaming or at least red-hot in the bed, that a different kind of humor, a subtler kind involving mere exaggeration, replaces it. Another point in favor of the phrase "burning up in bed" is that the state of having a fever is correlated, medically speaking, with the state of languishing or deteriorating. Altogether, then, there being no strong negative argument against "burning up", it gets a score of maybe 8 out of 10.

DRH: Too bad for "burping". But I can see your arguments. And now, how about "turning blue in bed"?

AMT: Once again, there is an alliterative element involving the "b"'s in "blue" and "bed", so no points are lost there. In fact, an alliterative element is gained, as the "t" in "turn" echoes the no-fewer-than-four "t"'s in the previous six words: "Don't stay in stir; instead of tur…" Moreover, the idea of skin turning blue is sufficiently suggestive of a worsening condition that no points are lost here.

DRH: And what about humor?

AMT: Well, people don't literally turn blue, so once again we are dealing with the humor of mild exaggeration, so score a little bit more on the positive side here. But the real clincher in this case is the double metaphorical meaning of "turning blue" — both "getting sicker" and "getting sadder" being suggested by one and the same short phrase. That is a strong argument and adds a lot of weight. To me, this choice comes in at perhaps 9 out of 10. And that's why it beat out some pretty strong rivals.

DRH: To think that all of this went into the choice of just one word!

AMT: Yes, and yet just as complex a story lies behind each line of a poem translated by a good translator. There is an interaction among rhymes, alliterations, rhythms, literal meanings, metaphorical meanings, grammatical structures, logical flows, interlingual proximities, degrees and styles of humor, local and global tones, and God knows how many other elusive mental forces. This is

On Shy Translators and Their Crafty, Silent Art ◆ ◆ ◆ 387

what Turing himself was hinting at in his classic little hypothetical dialogue snippets — and yet many people who read them, and who even read his whole article, blithely go on thinking that the Turing Test could be passed by a program that merely carried out a lot of surface-level word-shuffling. How pathetically impoverished, how dull, how rigid, a view of communication this is!

DRH: Not only dull and rigid, I'd say, but downright inhuman! You know, I have to hand it to you guys — you're all really something.

AMT: Ah. We're really something? Us guys? Could you clue me in a bit as to what you mean?

DRH: Sure. I mean, you and MTJ and MTQ and MT, uh, MT...

AMT: I presume you mean KMT. Like a deck of cards, if you catch my sense.

DRH: Silly me! Of course — MTK. Anyway, all you guys seem to have such a fine feel for words and their subtle flavors and all. Makes me sort of jealous.

AMT: Well, thank you for the compliment, but "guys"? I'm not sure that I — that we — that "us guys"... uh...

DRH: Oops! My gosh, I just looked at my watch, and you know what? I've got to run off to teach! This semester I'm doing a class on computer models of analogy and creativity, and it meets in just ten minutes. I'll be lucky if I make it on time! Wish I didn't have to skip out, because it's been good fun, talking with you — that is to say, interacting with you in print via our electronic link.

AMT: Likewise. By the way, something you said a few moments ago reminded me of one time when JMT used the most inapposite term in addressing a group of —

DRH: Listen, I really have to run. Sorry to cut you off. But just one last thing before we take our respective leaves. Did you hear — Babette Deutsch has just finished translating another book!

AMT: Oh, that's terrific news. Is it available yet?

DRH: I think so, or it will be within a month or two, anyway.

AMT: Oh, by the way — who's the author?

DRH: Don't have the foggiest. It didn't say, in the advertisement I read. But it'll be great. Deutsch always is.

AMT: Ah, Deutsch — what a translator! I could read her flowing sentences forever!

Distortion-free Idea Transmission: A Chimera

Any good translator's ideal is to get across to a new group of readers the essence of someone else's fantasy and vision of the world, and yet, as we have repeatedly seen, but here particularly clearly, the mediating agent necessarily plays a deep and critical role in doing such a job. A translator does to an original text something like what an impressionist painter — van Gogh, say — does to a landscape: there is an inevitable and cherished personal touch that makes the process totally different from photography. Translators are not like cameras — they are not even like cameras with filters! They distort their input so much that they are completely unique scramblers of the message — which does not mean that their scrambling is any less interesting or less valuable than the original "scene".

A curious aspect of this analogy between the translation of a piece of text into a new language and the rendering of a scene as a painting is that the original text — "Ma Mignonne" itself, let us say — plays the role of the *scene in nature,* rather than that of something created by a human. The original text is thus a piece of "objective reality" that is distorted by the translator/painter. But what, one might then ask, about people who read the text in the original language? Are native-language readers able to get the message *as it really is,* free from all the bias and distortion inevitably introduced by a scrambling intermediary?

As the letters and words of the original text leap upwards from the page into a native reader's eyes and brain, they shimmer and shiver and then suddenly splinter into a billion intricately-correlated protoplasmic sparks scattered all over the cerebral cortex and deeper within — unique patterns in the unique mind of the unique reader that each distinct person constitutes. The idea that all native-language readers see "the same thing" falls to bits. It's true that in the case of native-language readers, there is no intermediary human scrambler, but it's not true that, because of this lack, there is no idiosyncratic perceptual distortion. How sad it would be if that were the case!

Since this is the theme song of George Steiner's *After Babel,* I can think of no better way to end this chapter than to quote a few sentences from the end of his first chapter, entitled "Understanding as Translation":

> Thus a human being performs an act of translation, in the full sense of the word, when receiving a speech-message from any other human being. Time, distance, disparities in outlook or assumed reference, make this act more or less difficult. Where the difficulty is great enough, the process passes from reflex to conscious technique. Intimacy, on the other hand, be it of hatred or of love, can be defined as confident, quasi-immediate translation....
>
> In short: *inside or between languages, human communication equals translation.* A study of translation is a study of language.

●

Poems XIII:

~ Pushing the Envelope ~

```
* * * * * *
 * * *
  * *
   *
   *
```

When I first arrived at the University of Michigan in 1984, I gave a special inaugural course called "Analogy, Essence, and Elegance", in which subtle, small challenges defined by interlocking constraints served to illustrate the main ideas. This was a few years before the "Ma Mignonne" challenge had grabbed hold of me. Over the next couple of years, this course evolved into an "Analogy and Creativity" seminar, and so, when the "Ma Mignonne" challenge came along in 1987, it fit very naturally into the course. Then, a year or so after I returned to Indiana University in 1988, I taught a seminar on the topic of "Translation and Creativity", and in that class, needless to say, this challenge played a starring role.

To define and clarify the challenge, I showed my students in these courses not only the original Marot and various literal translations, structural descriptions, and *explications de texte,* but also a generous sampling of the "best", or — let me restate that — the most daring, translations so far produced. Not surprisingly, this proved highly stimulating for the students, inspiring some of them to do things that went beyond anything I had yet imagined. Out of the many, many interesting translations produced by students (some wonderful, some atrocious, needless to say), I have culled a few of my favorites in Poems XIII and XIV.

John Saxon, an Indiana student of mine, took a look at the list of formal properties of "Ma Mignonne" that I had drawn up, and he rejected the idea of final-syllable stress in favor of middle-syllable stress, because to his ear such lines sounded "more natural to English" — a judgment with which one might or might not concur — but in any case it's a fine premise (a self-imposed constraint) to serve as an inspiration for an art work!

What Saxon handed in was unfortunately uneven in quality, mixing feeble lines with sparkling ones. In a few of his rhyming couplets, he made the last *two* syllables rhyme (a genuine feminine rhyme), but in the majority only the *final* (unstressed) syllable rhymed, which, for someone so focused on middle syllables, seemed pretty half-hearted! On top of that, his poem was way too long for my taste: 34 lines. Here is a sample of how it went:

I'm guessing
Life's torture,
A jail you're
Inside of.
Get rid of
Your sickness!
With quickness
Dash out through
The door to
Your freedom,

Away from
Confinement,
For Clement
Has said to.
I know you
Love sweets, dear,
So don't fear
That eating
Them's cheating
Your comeback.

The rest was weaker. I felt it definitely needed working on, and trimmed it down to fourteen couplets, altering them so they all had true feminine rhymes. Perhaps the result sounds, in the end, more like Hofstadter than like Saxon, but most of the ideas for the flow came from him, and clearly the overall constraint is his. My favorite part of the reworked poem is lines 11–12, which, because of the rigid rhyming pattern, force the word "route" to rhyme first off with "beaut", then flip about "route" so its next rhyme's with "out".

One last word about Saxon's shift of expressive medium. I found that all sorts of new and unfamiliar rhymes cropped up under this constraint. This is typical of how a medium determines the hallmarks of performance. Skis allow one type of grace in maneuvering down a snowy slope; the invention of snowboards revealed another whole set of related but heretofore unimagined types of grace that could coexist on the very same slopes.

My Honey

John P. Saxon/D. Hofstadter

My honey,
A sunny
Day's blessing!
I'm guessing
It's torture,   5
That fort you're
Inside of.
In spite of
Your ague,
I beg you: 10
Seek routes out —
My beaut's route
To freedom.
Just speed from
Inclement   15
Skies, Clement
Commands you.
He hands you,
Dear, lamb, deer,
And jam. Fear   20
Not eating
Them's cheating!
Turn haler,
Not frailer
Nor sickly.   25
Lord, quickly
Make sunny
My honey.

The next student product — this one also from my translation seminar in Indiana — is from the pen of Anthony Guneratne, an intensely self-driven and creative individual who at the time was a comparative-literature graduate student working on, among other things, a book about the way history is represented in cinema. Anthony, who is from Sri Lanka but lived and studied in Italy for a few years, has a deep musical background, and something of that shows in his musically flowing poem.

This poem was the result of an experiment that Anthony conducted in the opposite direction from David Moser. Instead of making a poem having a larger number of shorter lines, he made a poem with a smaller number of longer lines. Indeed, he composed a classical sonnet — three quatrains plus a couplet, in perfect iambic pentameter.

Despite the radicality of this revamping of the form, Anthony respected other formal and semantic features, such as the identity of the first and last lines, the self-reference by the poet (in fact, in a droll and unmistakable allusion to Shakespearean style, he refers to "Antonio", an Italianate version of himself), and so on. Anthony's poem is marked by elegance and grace. But one last, lingering doubt… Is it really a translation of the Marot?

Sure it is. It's a translation not just into English but more specifically into the medium that Anthony chose. Like John Saxon and David Moser, Anthony considered the receptive medium to be a variable that he could manipulate at his own discretion; it's just that his choice was, at least on a surface level, much further away from Marot's original medium than theirs were. And yet, when you factor in subtler features, such as the historical period that the poem exudes and its definitely courtly tone, you find that there is a great deal of fidelity to Marot's original here — it's just that it lurks in less obvious dimensions than the poem's overall visual gestalt.

It's true, of course, that what makes the original Marot so unique and special *is*, in fact, its overall visual gestalt, and therefore dropping that key feature is a most audacious move to make, but if the act is done with enough panache, and I think here it was, then one can bring it off. No, it's not easy to make this kind of trick work, but if you succeed, well, I say, more power to you!

O Sweeting Mine

Anthony Guneratne

O sweeting mine, my words I pray you heed.
    I would that every day be fair and fine,
Inviting you to come forth with Godspeed,
    Recover'd, from the place where you repine.

Then open wide the door that holds you in;   5
    With dancing step trip lightly to the fields.
Antonio tells you that 'tis not a sin
    To know the pleasures that existence yields.

Too long your mouth has lain in sad repose;
    It hungers for the honey'd sweets of youth.   10
For if you seek life's chapter thus to close,
    A wilted frame will be your path to truth.

May heav'n yet grant you sense in thought and deed.
    O sweeting mine, my words I pray you heed.

Also in my Indiana translation seminar was Marek Lugowski, who first appeared in Chapter 3 wearing his Stanisław Lem–translator hat. Recall that Marek was born in Poland and was raised there till his early adolescence, and of course that is practically at the antipodes from America's inner cities. Thus Marek went way out on a limb in deciding to translate Marot's old French into modern rap lyrics.

Marek's inspiration came from a newspaper article listing and defining a large number of rap terms, and he inserted as many of them as he could into his effort. Needless to say, he also utterly changed the venue, and his last few lines unexpectedly veer off into the world of pickup basketball played in city parks and streets, something that means a lot in the intense world where rap originated and thrives, but that seems pretty alien to the world of sixteenth-century French court life.

I personally do not have the knowledge of rap talk that would be necessary to judge the degree of success of this effort, but I get a genuine kick out of its snappy, crackly rhythms and rhymes, and I like its semantic allusions to the main themes of the original poem. However, it strikes me as pretty darned marginal in terms of being a *translation* thereof, because too many important aspects, at the levels of both form and content, were simply unceremoniously dropped or altered.

Not too surprisingly, Marek doesn't quite agree with this contention. He sent me a friendly note, which I'll share with you here:

> It's very funny to see my translation again. It's definitely archaic, but I think it makes a point in its own funky way.
>
> I beg to differ with your claim that portions of the original were cast away without much thought. I agonized and agonized, with the newspaper article about rap keeping my lexicon on a very short leash — nay, in a virtual noose.
>
> I think the nonlinearities involved throw light on the problem of literary translation at large. How does one translate, say, *Finnegan's Wake* into Javanese shadow theatre…? More to the point, how could I possibly have kept Marot's sickening promise of plying the victim with spooned fruit, er, fruit preserves?

Yo There Dog!

Marek Lugowski

Yo there dog!
Your crib a slammer,
And it ain't jit.
Get dap —
Bust outa this camp,   5
And don't be wack.
Just feed, dude, feed!
Clement rap: Succeed!
If you don't chow,
You feel so sad   10
Yo mama T. Jones
Get mad. You lose
Yo bad attitude,
Sparticulous mood.
For the hoop, whoop joy,   15
Say this rapper boy.
Rap make you free —
Cain't lose with me.
It all be sparks
In hoops, alleys, parks.   20

•

• *Chapter 14* •

On the
Untranslatable

•

ˇ ˇ ˇ ˇ   — C. Morningstar
(*Fisches Nachtgesang*)

ˆ ˆ ˆ ˆ   — M. Knecht
(*Fish's Night Song*)

Étude Op. 8, No. 12, in D-sharp minor, by Alexander Scriabin. "To have written this piece is to have married the piano." I was so forcefully struck by that blunt commentary about this craggy, thunderous, breakers-bursting-on-boulders *étude*, which I read on the back of a record cover decades ago, that I have never forgotten it. "Married the piano" — married the medium — fused indissolubly with the carrier of the message. Taken in this more general sense, the phrase captures the quality that in my view is the most telltale signature of an untranslatable piece of writing: *weddedness of a message to its medium.* In other words, untranslatability arises when a passage's content is so melted in with the medium conveying it that the content cannot be extracted therefrom without destroying the passage's essence. And what is the essence, then? It is the matrimonial state itself — neither the form nor the content, but their unique union in this structure.

Despite a certain brash tone that threads its way through this book, which might seem to imply a belief that *anything* can be translated if only one works at it for long enough and with enough cleverness, I would never make that universal a claim. I believe there are many pieces of writing on all scales — from books to poems to snippets — that are truly impossible to translate. Indeed, I will exhibit and discuss some outstanding examples in this chapter. Nonetheless, when I see something described in print as "untranslatable", I immediately take it as a personal challenge. Them's fightin' words! (That very sentence, for example, with its cowboy flavor — I bet you can't translate it into any other language. Challenged?)

The "Untranslatable" Mr. Morningstar

One writer I heard about when in my teens, although I never looked at his works until many years later, was the short-lived German poet Christian Otto Josef Wolfgang Morgenstern (1871–1914), by coincidence almost an exact contemporary of Alexander Scriabin (1872–1915). More significantly, Morgenstern's life pretty nearly coincided with Germany's Second Reich, which was founded in his birthyear and arguably ended with the start of World War I.

My first osmotic impressions of Morgenstern came, amusingly, from many visits to the homes of two friends who lived at opposite ends of Gerona Road on the Stanford campus. At the far end of Gerona lived my friend Robert Boeninger, whose father Helmut was a professor of German at Stanford — in fact, Robert and I together took our first course in German from him — and whose spacious study always impressed me with its thousands of volumes of German literature, from floor to ceiling. Helmut would occasionally single out a work or an author he especially admired; such comments were always taken with great respect by both Robert and me. What I picked up was basically that Morgenstern was one of those specially-to-be-savored writers who are accessible only to German speakers — a delicious treat that outsiders, sadly, are destined to miss.

The other source of my first vague glimmerings about Morgenstern was at the near end of Gerona, where Robert's and my friend Gerry Masteller lived. Gerry's grandfather, B. Q. Morgan, an emeritus professor of German, was a shadowy presence always lurking somewhere upstairs, but whose scholarly aura radiated outwards and somehow reinforced the sense of this mysterious poet. I met B. Q. a few times, had some "chats" re T. S. Eliot's "Cats" and chuckled over Anna Russell's opera spoofs once or twice with him and Gerry, but scarcely knew him. Then years later, I found out that B. Q. not only had admired Morgenstern, but had been the first person in the English-speaking world to translate and to champion him.

In 1974, I accompanied my so-called *Doktorvater* ("doctor-father", or doctoral advisor) Gregory Wannier to Regensburg, Germany for several months to do work towards my physics degree. To make ends meet, I also taught a lab course in elementary physics, and I remain proud of the fact that I did this entirely in German for one semester. As a consequence of that teaching and the many hours of conversations with friends I made there, my German got fairly good, especially towards the end.

One of the first books I bought in Regensburg was a very slim volume containing Christian Morgenstern's *Galgenlieder* ("Gallows Songs") and *Der Gingganz* ("The Fargone", to try a very crude anglicization of a made-up word, whose two components mean "went completely"; Morgenstern says *Gingganz* means "ideologue"). In fact, Morgenstern wrote a great deal of poetry exploring theological mysteries from many angles, including Buddhist and mystical, and was himself a highly respected translator from Swedish and Norwegian (especially Strindberg, Ibsen, and Hamsun), so the volume that I purchased constitutes but a small fraction of his output; nonetheless, it is what he is remembered for. It is somewhat surrealistic, somewhat acidic, often humorous, often with a twist at the end, typically filled with wordplay as well as typographic play — in short, it is tricky stuff. I read much of it with pleasure, but the thought of translating any of it never crossed my mind.

Some years later, I was sent as a present an English version of many of the Galgenlieder done by Max Knight, an editor at the University of California Press, and also, as it turns out, a friend of B. Q. Morgan's. In a fascinating introduction, Knight cites scholars who claim Morgenstern's verse is out of reach of translators; thus, one said: "Morgenstern ranks very high among modern German poets, but his international reputation is severely handicapped by the fact that many of his best works are practically untranslatable." Another said, "Morgenstern's parodies, punning, and satiric truculence succeeded in creating an Alice-in-Wonderland climate which endeared him to millions of readers throughout the German-speaking world, but which, of course, defies translation." Of course!

Luckily, it seems that Max Knight, like me, was not daunted but attracted by such a challenge. He writes: "Difficulty of translating was not a consideration in selecting the poems for this volume — unless it was an inducement to try." Let us see, then, how Knight tackles one of these legendary translator's nightmares:

Der Aesthet	*The Aesthete*
Wenn ich sitze, will ich nicht	*When I sit, I do not care*
sitzen, wie mein Sitz-Fleisch möchte,	*just to sit to suit my hindside:*
sondern wie mein Sitz-Geist sich,	*I prefer the way my mind-side*
säße er, den Stuhl sich flöchte.	*would, to sit in, build a chair.*
Der jedoch bedarf nicht viel,	*For the mind spurns comfort, while*
schätzt am Stuhl allein den Stil,	*prizing in a stool but style;*
überläßt den Zweck des Möbels	*leaves the seat's pragmatic job*
ohne Grimm der Gier des Pöbels.	*gladly to the greedy mob.*

On the back of Knight's *Gallows Songs*, there are many favorable blurbs, such as this from *Aufbau*: "Obviously, Morgenstern's *Galgenlieder* cannot be translated. This was reason enough for Max Knight to translate them — and in a masterly way." An unnamed reviewer in the journal *Comparative Literature* wrote: "The argument that Morgenstern is basically untranslatable is no longer valid."

I too was quite bowled over. And interestingly enough, Babette Deutsch, whom we encountered in Chapter 9 as a translator of Pushkin, is quoted on the back cover as well: "An amazingly good job of rewording Morgenstern's puns, idioms, neologisms, making the English lines dance to the metrics of the German." I hope you agree that this particular effort by Knight does a superb job of supporting Deutsch's claims.

I would even append this quite bold Moral: When something is said to be "untranslatable", be skeptical. What this claim often means is that it would be impossible *for a dullard* to translate the work in question; that it takes some *thought* and some *intelligence* to recreate it in another language. In short, *to translate something witty requires a witty translator.* This is hardly profound, and yet witty translators just don't seem to be in the mind of people who prematurely pronounce so many works "untranslatable".

Flippant Quips on the Impossibility of Translation

Max Knight, in his introduction, quotes many aphoristic remarks on translation, some of which are worth reproducing here, if only for their controversial and mutually contradictory messages. Thus Thomas Mann is quoted as saying (with my English underneath his French):

Lorsqu'elles sont belles elles ne sont pas fidèles ; et lorsqu'elles sont fidèles elles ne sont pas belles.
When they are beautiful they're never dutiful; and when they are dutiful they're never beautiful.

Actually, I believe this remark goes back much further than Mann (though to whom to attribute it I don't know), and was originally prefaced by these words: *Les traductions sont comme les maîtresses* ("Translations are like mistresses"). The plural pronoun *elles* is thus doing double duty, with both an animate and an inanimate referent — very cute, but stupid and insulting to both referents at the same time.

G. K. Chesterton, too, quoted this same sound bite in the context of remarking about Edward FitzGerald's famous translation of *The Rubáiyát of Omar Khayyám*, "It is too good a poem to be faithful to the original." A clever remark, but nonetheless quite silly. Chesterton's remark is in turn very close to another one in Knight's preface, this one made by an Austro-Hungarian writer named Roda Roda (shades of Humbert Humbert!) and paraphrased by Knight as follows:

A translation is good only when it is better than the original.

It would be interesting to know what Morgenstern himself thought about the topic, having been a translator and knowing well the art from inside. Knight offers us two anglicized glimpses into Morgenstern's own mind, both of them somewhat pessimistic:

Great originals shine even through awkward translations.

There is no such thing as a good or better translation of poetry from another language — there are only poor and less poor renderings.

I find it a bit sad that Morgenstern would think this way.

Another famous literary figure whom Knight quotes on the topic is the American poet and translator John Ciardi, known for, among other things, his English version of Dante's *Divine Comedy*. Ciardi blithely calls translation "the art of failure" and adds:

What a translator tries for is no more than the best possible failure.

I get tired of hearing this kind of thing, frankly. Is this false modesty, or is it some kind of misplaced reverence for the original text? Great authors are great, to be sure — but must we revere Shostakovich's *own* playing of preludes and fugues from his Opus 87 more than we revere Sviatoslav Richter's? Is the latter's profoundly affecting and stunningly fluid rendition of numbers 12 and 17 nothing more than a praiseworthy failure next to the former's oh-so-authentic and oh-so-klutzy (*i.e.*, at *my* level of pianism) stumblings-around?

Oh, of course, I know the analogy is strained: Shostakovich's job officially stopped as soon as the black ink was drying on the white paper, whereas that's where Richter's just started. Shostakovich could go ahead and play his pieces in public, but he didn't have to. It's not the same with authors and translators — authors render their pieces all the way to the bitter end: choice of words, punctuation, everything. Well, not quite — most authors don't do their own typesetting, printing, binding, etc. But that's usually considered mere window-dressing, entirely separable from the author. Just as you can't dump on Dante if someone has the execrable taste to set *La Divina Commedia* in the otherwise charming typeface of Hobo:

Nel mezzo del cammin di nostra vita
mi ritrovai per una selva oscura,
che la diritta via era smarrita.

and just as you can't put down Pushkin if someone living a century later is so fatuous as to traduce his Russian verse into the alphabet of the Romans:

Ne vsé li, rússkim yazïkóm
Vladéya slábo i s trudóm,
Egó tak mílo iskazháli,
I v íkh ustákh yazïk chuzhóy
Ne obratílsya lí v rodnóy?

so you can't scoff at Shostakovich if some mediocre *Musikant* massacres his counterpoint, perhaps even turning the tables on the Well-Tempered Clavier and performing Opus 87 on a harpsichord instead of a piano. Performers really come after, and *extend* the composer, rather than trying to *redo* the composer's choices in any sense. So maybe musical performers shouldn't be compared to translators, then, but rather, to typesetters.

But just think: If we are willing to give credit to truly *great* musical performers for rendering in audible form the full power and poetry of a great composer's visual notes, and not insist that they, being lesser mortals, are betraying the spirit of their composer, why can we not similarly doff our hats to the best of translators, who, whether lesser mortals or not, work every bit as hard and give every bit as much of their soul as does a musical virtuoso, to render the full power and poetry of their esteemed author?

In short, I think it's a phony kind of pretense, maybe even a perverse variety of self-praise through self-knocking, when translators say this kind of negative thing about the art that they strive so hard to do well. Have you ever heard of a musical performer (or a typesetter) this self-deprecating?

The Ignominious Defenestration of a Picket Fence

Perhaps the most famous of all the *Galgenlieder* is *Der Lattenzaun*: "The Picket Fence". Here is the original, along with Knight's rendition:

<u>Christian Morgenstern</u>	<u>Max Knight</u>
Es war einmal ein Lattenzaun,	*There used to be a picket fence*
mit Zwischenraum, hindurchzuschaun.	*with space to gaze from hence to thence.*
Ein Architekt, der dieses sah,	*An architect who saw this sight*
stand eines Abends plötzlich da —	*approached it suddenly one night,*
und nahm den Zwischenraum heraus	*removed the spaces from the fence,*
und baute draus ein großes Haus.	*and built of them a residence.*
Der Zaun indessen stand ganz dumm,	*The picket fence stood there dumbfounded*
mit Latten ohne was herum.	*with pickets wholly unsurrounded,*
Ein Anblick gräßlich und gemein.	*a view so naked and obscene,*
Drum zog ihn der Senat auch ein.	*the Senate had to intervene.*
Der Architekt jedoch entfloh	*The architect, however, flew*
nach Afri- od- Ameriko.	*to Afri- or Americoo.*

Having read this, you may understand why it is that B. Q. Morgan formed the following set of labels for the poet's creations:

> sheer nonsense, rhyme nonsense, punning fancies, sound effects, printed shapes, satires, philosophic concepts, sensible ideas grotesquely presented, bizarre ideas, and superior nonsense.

Although this characterization came from one of his greatest admirers and promoters, Morgenstern would likely have resented this view of his art. Indeed, in an article addressed to his critics, he once wrote the following (*i.e.,* in the same sense that Descartes once wrote *Ich denke, also bin ich*):

> One thing I beg of you. Should the terms "nonsense" or "gibberish" be included in the review — no matter how flattering the qualifying adjectives might be — kindly reconsider them in favor of something like "folly" or "craziness". Surely you would not want to tag with these two evil German Philistine and tavern terms of thoughtlessness the very humor that aims at a certain kind of spirituality. "Higher nonsense fit to be classified as literature" is the cheapest and unwisest that can be said about the Galgenlieder — a slogan used without doing justice to the evidence.

Given this attitude, I think it safe to say that Morgenstern would have welcomed far more warmly the following statement that Walter Arndt made: "The genre of poetry Morgenstern created belongs to the realm of the metaphysical, of subversive nonsense and superior sense."

Walter Arndt?! How did *he* get into the picture? Are we now going to be treated to a curtain call of all the *Eugene Onegin* personalities? No. But Arndt, a native speaker of German, was by temperament extremely drawn to Morgenstern's art, and over decades he translated now one and now another of the Galgenlieder until finally, he had a book's worth. Here, then, is how he rendered the same poem — with one extra version, to boot:

Walter Arndt	*Douglas Hofstadter*
There was a wooden fence I knew With intervals for looking through.	A picket fence, lo many a year, had pickets dense, 'tween which to peer.
An architect who passed this way Turned up before it one fine day.	An architect who this did spy, one eve, out of the clear blue sky,
Took out the spaces, hem by hem, And built a handsome house of them.	stole all the space betwixt its sticks, and built therewith a house (such bricks!).
The fence just lingered on, a rump Of planks and nothing, like a chump.	This fact our fence did sadly stun: it now had slats, but slits had none.
A sight to sicken man and horse; The City pulled it down, of course.	'Twas such an eyesore and a blight, Town Council deemed it dynamite.
The architect absconded, though, To Afri- or Americo.	The architect, though, up and flew to Afriq- or Ameri- que.

Why me? Simply because, when I discovered, very recently, Walter Arndt's volume called *Songs from the Gallows: Galgenlieder,* I couldn't resist trying my own hand at doing some Morgenstern. And great fun it is, too!

One of the curious features of Arndt's book is that though each poem appears in both German and English, his own English version comes *first,* almost as bad as putting the German version in a footnote (of course, many editions of translated poetry omit the original *entirely*). And yet Arndt clearly admires Morgenstern almost unboundedly. I don't understand the logic. Perhaps it was his publisher's decision. Blame it on the typesetter!

A few comments on the challenge of *Der Lattenzaun.* While doing my translation, I was aware that the opening rhyme — an elegant and salient one — is defined by the word *Lattenzaun,* the topic of the whole poem. Knight respects this whereas Arndt doesn't. And in the end, I wound up not doing so either, but I was a little saddened. On the other hand, my first couplet has a mild tongue-twister quality that recalls the original's opening.

One of the phonetically most intense lines in the original is line 6: *und baute draus ein großes Haus,* with its three "au" sounds and its four "s" sounds. Knight doesn't do much to mirror this, whereas Arndt uses lines 5 and 6 together to get in four "h"-words: "hem", "hem", "handsome", and "house". My own imitation of this effect is reserved to line 5, where I get in three initial "s" sounds, two "ix" sounds (plus one "its"), and lots of "t"'s.

Knight's most beautiful find is the "dumbfounded/unsurrounded" rhyme, of course — absolutely perfect.

The Poignant Sleep of the Lunar Sheep

Turn we now to another Morgenstern gemlet, this one called *Das Mondschaf…*

<u>*Christian Morgenstern*</u>

Das Mondschaf steht auf weiter Flur.
Es harrt und harrt der großen Schur.
  Das Mondschaf.

Das Mondschaf rupft sich einen Halm
und geht dann heim auf seine Alm.
  Das Mondschaf.

Das Mondschaf spricht zu sich im Traum:
»Ich bin des Weltalls dunkler Raum.«
  Das Mondschaf.

Das Mondschaf liegt am Morgen tot.
Sein Leib ist weiß, die Sonn ist rot.
  Das Mondschaf.

<u>*Max Knight*</u>

The moonsheep stands upon the clearing.
He waits and waits to get his shearing.
  The moonsheep.

The moonsheep plucks himself a blade
returning to his alpine glade.
  The moonsheep.

The moonsheep murmurs in his dream:
"I am the cosmos' gloomy scheme."
  The moonsheep.

The moonsheep, in the morn, lies dead.
His flesh is white, the sun is red.
  The moonsheep.

This is a surrealistic little poem. Morgenstern hated to "explicate" his Galgenlieder, insisting they had far less hidden meaning to them than many critics were bent on reading into them; however, as Knight says, when pressed hard, Morgenstern occasionally would offer a crumb. In this case, he suggested the moonsheep might be the Moon itself — first against the sky; then vanishing behind mountains; next, a dream of grandeur, with its own tininess filling the cosmos; and at last appearing at dawn as a pale disk.

Here, for comparison, are Walter Arndt's and my versions. My line 8's "I be" is a weak echo of the slightly pompous syntax in the original's line 8.

<table>
<tr><td>

Walter Arndt

The moonsheep on a spacious clearing
Abides and bides the final shearing.
The moonsheep.

The moonsheep, having plucked a weed,
Ascends again its mountain mead.
The moonsheep.

The moonsheep, dreaming, seems to face
Its self as universal space.
The moonsheep.

The moonsheep, lo, at dawn is dead.
Itself is white, the sun is red.
The moonsheep.

</td><td>

Douglas Hofstadter

The moonsheep grazes in the heather.
It cannot wait for shearing weather.
The moonsheep.

The moonsheep plucks a blade of grass
And then strolls home, high in the pass.
The moonsheep.

The moonsheep tells itself in sleep,
"I be the awesome cosmic deep."
The moonsheep.

The moonsheep in the morning's dead.
Its corpse is white, the sun is red.
The moonsheep.

</td></tr>
</table>

The Lunar Sheep Visits the Latin Quarter

Morgenstern was himself a translator, and one day decided to render his whimsical lunar fantasy in, of all things, Latin. It thus became *Lunovis*:

<table>
<tr><td>

Christianus Matustella

Lunovis in planitie stat
Cultrumque magn' exspectitat.
Lunovis.

Lunovis herba rapta it
In montes, unde cucurrit.
Lunovis.

Lunovis habet somnium:
Se culmen rer' ess' omnium.
Lunovis.

Lunovis mane mortuumst.
Sol ruber atque ips' albumst.
Lunovis.

</td><td>

Douglas Hofstadter

Lunolamb in lowlands stands;
A spruce-up craves, no ifs or ands.
Lunolamb.

Lunolamb, grass downed with glee,
Leaps up the hill, t'where 't frolics free.
Lunolamb.

Lunolamb lies down to dream:
To be, of all the <u>crème</u>, the cream.
Lunolamb.

Lunolamb gives up, one night.
Come dawn, Sol's pink. Itself? Ghost-white.
Lunolamb.

</td></tr>
</table>

On the Untranslatable

Where *Das Mondschaf* was sur-real, *Lunovis* is sur-oddball. Thus the apostrophes are totally foreign to Latin, as are the fake shortenings of *mortuum est* and *album est,* but the translator thumbs his nose at convention and brashly inserts them, conveniently saving syllables while doing so. In my attempt to anglicize *Lunovis* (which I first parsed as *luno-vis,* which baffled me till I reparsed it as *lun-ovis*), I looked only at the Latin and tried to capture its whimsical flavor, introducing an "up/down" motif, and feeling free to use reversals and compressions, to suggest the Latin's tight feel. But as the eyeball easily tells, I couldn't touch Matustella's concision.

Incidentally, I think it only fitting that if his Moonsheep became *Lunovis,* Morgenstern himself should be rechristened in a parallel manner. The fact that the resultant name echoes that of B. Q. Morgan's grandson, my old friend Gerry Masteller, strikes me as, somehow, kismet.

To cap off our Morgenstern meal, I offer you *Fisches Nachtgesang*:

```
        -
       ‿ ‿
      - - -
     ‿ ‿ ‿ ‿
      - - -
     ‿ ‿ ‿ ‿
      - - -
     ‿ ‿ ‿ ‿
      - - -
     ‿ ‿ ‿ ‿
      - - -
       ‿ ‿
        -
```

Gobble dese Grooks!

When I first encountered the spare and wry ironic rhymes of Piet Hein many years ago in Martin Gardner's famous "Mathematical Games" column in *Scientific American,* I was blown away by their elegant simplicity, and by how well they meshed with the English language. At the time, I would have classed them as eminently untranslatable. We've already seen one of them — *Ars Brevis* — at the end of Chapter 11; now here are a few more:

A Moment's Thought	The Final Touch	Similarity (Commutative Law)	Only Hoping
As eternity is reckoned, there's a lifetime in a second.	Idiots are really one hundred per cent, when they are also intelligent.	No cow's like a horse, and no horse like a cow. That's one similarity anyhow.	Only hoping isn't what gives us strength to cope. Let us only hope; but not _only_ only hope.

(By the way, not all Grooks are four lines long; I just chose ones that have that length in order to be able to print them side by side.)

Assuming Hein had composed these in English, I was impressed by his masterful way with our language, but some years later, I ran across a small book of them, and in the front I saw that he had published hundreds of Grooks — *Gruk* — in Danish. I thus concluded, perhaps erroneously, that the book I was reading was in fact a set of English renderings of selected poetry written originally in Danish. I'm sure I could find out easily enough, but that's not the point. I simply enjoy thinking of these witty miniatures as being second-generation poems — so much for their untranslatability! — and posing myself the challenge of getting them into *other* languages.

I have in fact tackled it myself quite recently in the case of *Ars Brevis*, and managed to come up with what seem to me to be pleasing versions in Italian, French, and German, and also did this transformation in English:

There is	*One art*
one art,	*there is,*
no more,	*no less,*
no less:	*no more:*
to do	*all things*
all things	*to do*
with art-	*with sparks*
lessness.	*galore.*

The challenge of rendering various Grooks in various languages is an excellent sport that compresses down to postage-stamp size the enormous complexity and beauty of the enterprise that is translation.

Riddles abound. What would it mean to have "captured" a Grook in another language? How much of its terseness needs to be imitated? How flip and fresh does the copy have to sound? How close do the two messages really have to be? Does a translation have to echo the original line by line? Have to have the same number of syllables per line? The same rhyming pattern? And lastly, perhaps strangest of all, I feel that I can just barely detect, despite Piet Hein's truly deft touch in English, the tiniest *soupçon* of foreignness in his English Grooks. I could be reading it all in, given that I *know* he's Danish, but I think it is really there. In any case, supposing it's there, could one possibly hope to recreate, in a translation, such an ethereal, evanescent, nearly undefinable and undetectable flavor? Would one even want to? Why, or why not?

Coming to Blows Puts the Bloom on Love's Rose

During my 1993–94 sabbatical year in Italy, I had many lunchtime discussions with Achille Varzi and my graduate students Jim Marshall, Gary McGraw, and John Rehling, and the topic of languages and translation was among our most frequent and favorite ones. One day Achille brought to our attention the following cute Italian aphorism:

L'amore non è bello se non è litigarello.

Literally, it means "Love is not beautiful if it is not quarrelsome", except for the fact that *litigarello* is just a made-up adjective based on *litigare*, which is "to fight, quarrel, wrangle". Could this possibly be imitated in English? At first the challenge seemed very elusive, but as we bantered we warmed up, and by the time our meal was over we had collectively produced a swarm of reasonable candidates, of which I show the best here:

Your love affair couldn't be sicker if the two of you don't ever bicker.
You'll soon wind up being bored in a fling without discord.
Love won't be mellow if you don't shout and bellow.
Injection of dissonance lends love blissonance.
Love is hardly blissful if all it is is kissful.
Love is not grand if tiffs are banned.
Love's wobbly if 'tisn't squabbly.
Love's effete, that's ever sweet.
Love goes flat unless y'all spat.
Love ain't great without some hate.
Scrapping's to love as a hand to a glove.
Love is not this beautiful unless it is disputiful.
Fill your love with life — throw in some storm and strife!
One of love's best bedside delights is enjoying your fill of pillow fights.
Who cares about having an affair, if you can't throw plates, shout and swear?

When you look at this hyperbolic avalanche of solutions, it seems quite remarkable how many possibilities there are — and we had just scratched the tip of the iceberg. Such a success would seem to suggest that any cute phrase could be rendered in a dozen appealing ways. And yet soon thereafter we stumbled badly on what seemed no harder a challenge.

Achille reported to us that the Italian marketing campaign for Häagen-Dazs ice cream had for a while been using the slogan *La crema dei gelati,* translated literally from an English slogan, "The cream of ice creams", and therefore totally missing the point, which was the fairly obvious phonetic echo effect. The Italian slogan sounds boring and flat, and so we wondered if we could come up with something catchier. The equivalent of "cream of the crop" is perhaps *il fior fiore,* but that didn't yield anything too promising, and we tussled with the challenge for days but never came up with anything we liked. Feast and famine. What makes one region of phonetico-semantic space so fertile and another so barren?

The Challenges of Aphorisms, Puns, Slogans, Book Titles...

Although our little foursome found no solution in this case, I am convinced by the *litigarello* precedent that there are probably a number of excellent Italian renditions of "The cream of ice creams", and moreover that that slogan could be exported to virtually any language with sufficient care and cleverness. Keep in mind that the *litigarello* challenge went into English, which was native for most of us, whereas the "cream" challenge was going into Italian, a weaker language for all but one of us.

A second reason for my confidence is that the "cream" challenge seems very reminiscent of couplet-sized challenges that had to be met over and over again in the various versions of "Ma Mignonne", and of course one thing I learned from the "Ma Mignonne" experience was how an apparently unscalable mountain can, over time, seem to shrink. When I first imagined an English "Ma Mignonne", I was in awe of the idea, thinking it would be a miracle — and then gradually, as one solution after another started coming out of the woodwork, my perceptions of this peak changed and it seemed lower and lower, until eventually, like the macho mountaineer who challenged himself to scale Everest without oxygen, I started piling on new constraints to make "Ma Mignonne" seem hard again.

Another pillar supporting my confidence is simply decades of personal experience in playing with words in my native language, as well as some time doing so in acquired languages: I have the sense that there are hidden puns lying all around at all times, and that even the wittiest of punsters miss 99 percent of them. Thus I shall run on the assumption that cute advertising slogans and puns of that general type and size can pretty much always be imitated in a fairly close way. I admit that I have no solid empirical evidence for this, and there are some special puns that I find so excellent that I wonder if they could ever be imitated in another language, such as these, culled from a personal collection assembled over the years:

- *My Pride and Joy* — a book by George Adamson about his many years spent with his wife Joy working to save lions in Africa;
- *Fine and Danny* — a memoir by Sylvia Fine, the actress who was married to comedian Danny Kaye;
- the cynical aphorism "A mistress is halfway between a mister and a mattress";
- the modern-day slogan "Parking is such street sorrow" (a twist on the old aphorism "Parting is such sweet sorrow");
- the bumper strip I used to see when I lived in Oregon and it was being overrun by barbarian hordes from the south: "Don't Californicate Oregon";
- "Pitch In" and "Fight Dirty", two slogans printed on sidewalk garbage receptacles, encouraging the public to participate in keeping the town clean;
- *Boids* — a documentary on artificial robot-birds, whose title draws on "android", "humanoid", etc., while also doing a stereotyped Brooklyn accent on "birds".

On the Untranslatable

But even if some of these should prove, after long searches by teams of top-notch wordplay experts, to be unreproducible in one language or another, my general sense is that for *nearly* every pun in language X, there are one or more very close puns in language Y. I can't resist putting in one example of this phenomenon. One evening in Paris, I was wandering in the Quartier latin and peered into the window of a bookstore, where I saw a book called *Le signe et le singe* (literally, "The sign and the monkey"), evidently a book about primates' ability to use language. Of course the visual and phonic similarity of *signe* and *singe* was the crux of the title's appeal, and I felt challenged: What to name this book in English? (Any ideas, reader?)

The first answer that popped to mind was *Monkeysigns* — a cute play on "monkeyshines", but with a defect: the book was certainly not about mischievous pranks by monkeys or by anyone else. So scrap that. My next thought was, "This book is probably about semiotics." No sooner was that formulated than "simian" flashed to mind, leading to the second candidate title: *Simiotics*. Next, I thought, "Or else it's about epistemology", upon which *Apistemology* politely stepped forward. Then out of the blue came *Chimp A 'n' Z's* — pretty far-fetched, but pretty funny. And finally, making a bow toward the *et* of the original title, I imagined *Semiotics and Simiotics* and *Apes and Epistemics* and *Of Symbols and Simians* and even *Of Monkeys and Mots*. You can see there was a lot of nice material to exploit, right there on the surface. I don't take any credit for any of it — all that stuff was just *there*.

My point here has simply been to illustrate the density of potential puns, and having done so, I won't delve further into the translatability of puns. I'll just conclude by saying that in most cases I think pretty decent carry-overs can be made, and sometimes quite stunning ones.

Poetry at the Fringes of Comprehensibility

In our search for untranslatables, perhaps we should thus seek other ways that form and content can be tightly fused. I propose looking at this titleless poem by e. e. cummings (actually, just four of its nine stanzas):

anyone lived in a pretty how town
(with up so floating many bells down)
spring summer autumn winter
he sang his didn't he danced his did.

when by now and tree by leaf
she laughed his joy she cried his grief
bird by snow and stir by still
anyone's any was all to her

one day anyone died i guess
(and noone stooped to kiss his face)
busy folk buried them side by side
little by little and was by was

all by all and deep by deep
and more by more they dream their sleep
noone and anyone earth by april
wish by spirit and if by yes.

This seems to be a love story of two insignificant personages named "anyone" and "noone". What would translating it entail? It was relatively easy (an hour's work or so) for me to produce the following set of French words reflecting, in some sense, the stanzas on the left, maintaining rhymes and a semblance of meter, but magnifying syllable-counts enormously:

> vivait n'importe qui dans un joli combien hameau
> (avec en bas tant flottamment tellement de cloches en haut)
> printemps été automne hiver
> chanta son ne-fit-pas, son le-fit-il dansa.
>
> quand par alors, arbre par feuille
> elle riait pour lui pleurait son deuil
> oiseau par neige et bouge par calme
> son qui n'importe n'était qu'à elle

There were some dubious moments, such as the reversal of up and down to make a rhyme in line 2, and some fancy footwork to mirror the word "his" on line 6. But the real question is whether this has anything like the same effect on a French reader as the English does on an anglophone. The problem is, of course, that the effect is so bound up with the sounds and the charm of the style in which the language is abused. Is it possible to abuse French "in the same way" as e. e. cummings abuses English?

Let us move on to Dylan Thomas, often thought of as one of this century's most lyrical poetic voices in the English language. Let us take a brief — mercifully brief, I would say — look at one of his more obscure concoctions, called "How Soon the Servant Sun" (again, we will be treated to only two out of five stanzas). On the right is a heroic attempt at a French translation by Jean-Baptiste Berthelin:

How soon the servant sun,	Si vite fait, soleil domestiqué,
(Sir morrow mark),	(Maître marquant matines),
Can time unriddle, and the cupboard stone,	Peut dépliquer le temps, pierre au placard,
(Fog has a bone	(Le brouillard a un os
He'll trumpet into meat),	Qu'à son de trompe il rendra en viande),
Unshelve that all my gristles have a gown	Allant chercher que tout tendon a sa parure
And the naked egg stand straight,	Se tenir droit est possible à l'œuf nu,
Sir morrow at his sponge,	Maître matines à son éponge,
(The wound records),	(La blessure l'enregistre)
The nurse of giants by the cut sea basin,	Élevant des géants à la rade tranchée
(Fog by his spring	(Par sa source brouillard
Soaks up the sewing tides),	Éponge les marées qui cousent),
Tells you and you, my masters, as his strange	Vous dit à tous, mes maîtres, alors que son curieux
Man morrow blows through food.	Humain matines souffle aux aliments.

On the Untranslatable ◆◆◆ 405

I have read the original English version a hundred times if I have read it once, and I will make no bones about it: I haven't the foggiest idea what it is about. I don't know if it's about the sea, the sun, fog, food, sex, sadness, mysticism, cynicism, sponges, trumpets, tides, or what. And I don't think anyone could possibly know. That makes it hard for a translator!

For example, take the second line of the second stanza: "The wound records". Is this a short sentence that means "the injury takes note" (whatever *that* means)? Or perhaps it's a noun phrase that means either "the reports filed about the injury" or "the tightened phonograph platters"? Or could it mean something else entirely — or does it mean nothing whatsoever? I'm inclined toward the latter, but if we wish to translate it, we have to do *something*, so we have to choose one of the three prior options, without having any basis for making the choice. Berthelin opted for "the injury takes note", which is probably the most sensible choice, but it was a calculated risk. He couldn't *know* he was right. And who knows — perhaps (here I'm bending over backwards to give credit) Dylan Thomas' main goal in that line was to make a triple ambiguity, but if so, it was wiped out by Berthelin's choice (and would have been by *any* translator's choice).

There are plenty of small details in Berthelin's rendering that I question; but in many of the cases I would not have any idea what to do myself. For example, I don't understand the grammar of the closing two lines of the first stanza: "Unshelve that all my gristles have a gown / And the naked egg stand straight". I don't know what "unshelve" means here (or anywhere other than a library), and simply can't parse the sentence, let alone render it in French. I want to use the subjunctive when I hit "have" but I don't know what I would be saying. No matter how bright and chipper I might in fact be, translating this poem would feel like fumbling and stumbling about in a confused stupor. (Perhaps the poem is meant to convey a first-person sense for the ravages of alcoholism?)

Now you might agree with all my griping and simply wonder why I am making such a fuss over something so obvious. I guess the reason is, this is a poet who enjoys the highest esteem one can aspire to in the literary world, and therefore a vast public tends to read and somewhat revere whatever he writes — and if it eludes them, then they attribute the blame to *themselves*, not to the Master. And who am I to say if they're wrong in this? Let's assume Dylan Thomas really *is* a great voice of the twentieth century and that he deserves to be heard and to have his voice spread ever further. Well, one of the chief means of such spreading is via translation. How else will the poor deprived Chinese and Igbos and Moldavians ever come to appreciate such Thomas masterworks as "How Soon the Servant Sun"?

Even if this particular poem is among his most obscure, just about every poem he ever wrote contains a good deal of obscurity and ambiguity. Murk is in fact *crucial* to Dylan Thomas' style, and that's what your job, as a translator, would be to get across. You would have to *reproduce the exact same flavor of murkiness* — or come close — on a line-by-line basis. No matter who you are, this would push your abilities as a translator to the limit. This poem thus brings us as close to the elusive goal of untranslatability as anything we have seen so far.

Translating Passages of Uncertain Nonsensicality

In case I wasn't clear enough in the preceding section, let me state explicitly the following: It would be pretty easy for me to spew out a piece of absolute garbage making no sense at all on any level — say, using random-number tables to select words from a dictionary — and to call it "poetry". As to whether anyone *else* would find it of interest is another question altogether, and it is that crucial variable that determines the interest of the world in seeing it translated. And the key to whether anyone else finds something that I write to be interesting or valuable is the degree to which they find *meaning* of some sort or other in it.

Well, that's not quite true. To attract serious attention, it suffices to have built up a respected portfolio; from then on, whatever else you do will give off an aroma of your other output and will therefore be looked at for more than just its own isolated, intrinsic merit. And I'm not saying this is bad — it is a way in which a powerful creator's riskier ideas can get a fair hearing, which they might otherwise not be granted. I know full well that I respect the last movement of Chopin's B-flat-minor sonata for the most part *because it is by Chopin,* not because it intrinsically touches me so deeply. In fact, it puzzles me, as it does so many other lovers of Chopin. It is a mysterious, meandering, harmony-less study in speed-blurred octaves, very uncharacteristic for Chopin, and for those reasons all the more fascinating. But if those same notes had been written by a composer I found shallow, I would listen to them once and then pay them no further heed.

Suppose I were to throw together a random garbage poem; how would one go about translating it? It all depends on how much the translator tries to read meaning into it. If it is known that all I did was look up random words and copy them in sequence, then presumably giving a word-for-word rendition in the target language would constitute a fair treatment — although it might be suggested that since the random words' *semantics* never played any role in the first place, one might just as well substitute *phonetically* similar words in the target language. Why not?

But suppose I produce a strange-sounding, murky string of words that I label a "poem", and of whose mode of construction no one else knows a thing. And suppose it is your charge to translate it into another language. What strategy will you use? One based on semantics, even if no meanings are apparent on any level, local or global? One based on phonetics, even if there are no detectable sonic patterns in it? Or will you at some point grow skeptical and say, "This is *not worth* translating"? (Translation: "This is not worth reading.") How will your threshold for rejection vary as a function of the fame and reverence previously accorded the author/composer/artist?

Imagine you had been given "How Soon the Servant Sun" without attribution and had to translate it for a literary magazine. What kind of treatment would you give it? Suppose you found out it was by Dylan Thomas? And suppose you then found out it was *not*, after all, by Dylan Thomas? Or... imagine the editor-in-chief of a famous literary magazine sends you the following classic-style sonnet and requests that you, known far and wide for your sensitive touch in poetry translation, render it in Russian:

> *As swerving swarms with mingled wings of silt*
> *And frothy fronds by pond up-floating logs*
> *Did balance where, when pick'd unto the hilt,*
> *With chaliced air and chants by saddened frogs,*
> *Were flared such snares as, whipp'd in fog aloft,*
> *Delivered them upon a plaque ecstatic,*
> *For all, when writ in thrall and whispered soft,*
> *Had ripped their ribs — their "I" died adiabatic.*
>
> *O Manx, o fabled flag whence sailed the spur*
> *From clasping clogs to asps so crassly lynched,*
> *Where sparsely sang, in wisps of Seminole,*
> *Such western tongues as sank on sandy shoal,*
> *What florid frost, what wat'ry web was winched?*
> *Or shall I shift? Or shall I (suavely) slur?*

You might treat it one way if I told you it was written by Samuel Taylor Coleridge on the day after his feverish composition of "Kubla Khan" was rudely truncated by the arrival of a business visitor — and quite another way if I told you it was a translation by Richard Wilbur of *Les Bregouilles*, a sonnet by French symbolist Paul Verlaine. Then again, you would treat it a third way if I told you it was written by James Joyce as a teen-ager, and a fourth way if I told you it was written by me and my friend Peter Jones as a lark in our college days, with Peter penning the even-numbered lines and me the odd-numbered ones, both adhering to this preset rhyme scheme:

-ilt, -ogs, -ilt, -ogs;   -oft, -atic, -oft, -atic;   -ur, -inched, -ole, -ole, -inched, -ur.

And finally, you might treat it in a completely different way if I told you that this assonant stream of words had been pseudo-randomly strung together by a computer program called "Yeatskeats", which had been furnished with a very powerful representation of the rules of English syntax and of English pronunciation, had been provided a huge on-line thesaurus connecting semantically related words into associative clusters, and had been then programmed to produce, using a "relatively high" degree of alliteration (a twiddlable knob, of course), fourteen lines (another knob) of iambic pentameter (two more knobs), with the end rhymes shown above (again up to the user). Or (really my final case!), suppose I told you it was written by the Unabomber just after sending off a letter bomb in the mail…

It would make a difference, wouldn't it? After all, whichever of these tales you had been told, you would then know (or at least *think* you knew) how hard to strain to read meaning into the lines. Was this intended to be nonsense? Was this intended by a serious poet to be taken seriously? Was it intended by a mediocre poet to be taken seriously? Was it written entirely tongue-in-cheek? Or written by a zombie machine with no ideas behind its green screen? Or by a non-zombie machine with, behind its bright screen, some kind of proto-ideas, albeit very primitive and very vague?

A Wary Fascination with Pseudo-intellectual Fakery

By the way, the poem is by Peter and me, just as described, and indeed it's quite true that the two of us were consumed, back in our college days, with the idea of fringe-meanings and just how one could tell the difference between glib vacuity and complex but meaningful utterances.

One time we had the strangest experience in common. We had both taken a placement exam for students entering Psychology 101, and since we'd done well on it, we were given the opportunity to choose either of two "elite" sections of the course. One of them was on the brain and the other was on social psychology, and we naturally opted for the former, both of us being inclined towards "hard sciences" and intensely curious about the mysterious organ that gave us the power of thought and emotion. So we went to the professor's home one evening, and along with some ten or twelve other students, listened to him hold forth for an hour or two, talking to us novices in extraordinarily dense, abstruse, technical language.

As it happened, I had just finished reading a couple of books about the brain, so I was in a position considerably ahead of the others, and yet, after only a few minutes of the fellow's spiel, my head was completely spinning. And the more he talked, the less sense his spiel seemed to make. Reluctantly, I drew the somewhat presumptuous but insecure conclusion that he was throwing these complex words around too facilely. I remember scribbling some notes to Peter, hoping for corroboration of my uncertain feelings, and to my immense relief getting back a humorous sketch parodying the learned professor's blatherings. When the session was finally over and we were leaving, we gingerly voiced our skepticism to some of the other students, hoping to find similar "emperor's-new-clothes" reactions, but to our surprise, we found they felt this was exhilarating, heady stuff, and *perfectly clear,* to boot! This was an eye-opener for me — not only were these people getting sucked in by what I thought was garbage, but they *loved* it!

Peter and I agreed that if the next meeting went the same way, we would both drop out — and since it did, we did. We thereupon switched into the social-psychology section, which, by luck, turned out to be one of the gems of our college career. But the key here is how both of us, trained by years of language-play and curiosity about the fringes of sense and nonsense, had developed quite keen ears for fakery and obscurantism, and it had paid off nicely. Whatever happened to the other students, I don't know. I do know the professor wound up seduced by certain metaphorical models of the brain that, in my view, are little more than collections of trendy buzzwords, and there he stuck. *Sic transit gloria mundi.*

It was this same fascination with the fringe-region between sense and nonsense that led me, in the years 1964–65, to develop my "sEn·gEn" program, which, under the guidance of a random-number generator, traversed complexly intertwined grammatical networks while randomly selecting words from a carefully prepared lexicon to fill in the various parts of speech encountered along the bumpy voyage. The program also conjugated verbs, made plurals and other word endings, used pronouns to refer to prior topics, and had a rudimentary set of semantic labels on almost all words, which severely constrained its choice of lexical items.

This stochastic yet systematic technique was very successful at producing novel sentences possessing great syntactic intricacy and considerable semantic coherence, and in my wildest dreams, I imagined inserting a particle-physics vocabulary — terms like "neutron", "proton", "deuteron", "electron scattering", "angular momentum", "electromagnetic form factor", "inelastic cross-section", "Born approximation", "Rosenbluth formula", and dozens of others that I had heard coming out of the mouths of my father and his co-workers, and that I could *almost* manage to throw together into deceptively meaningful sentences myself — and letting sEn·gEn churn out "articles" (*i.e.,* series of paragraphs) on such topics, most likely just glib-sounding nonsense (which would have delighted me and probably the physicists as well), but maybe, just maybe, something far better than mere nonsense: *insightful new ideas* about Nature on that tiny scale.

The idea of seeking a grammar of language so subtle and so deep that merely obeying its rules amounted to *understanding the world* was infinitely beguiling to me. These days I certainly don't buy into such a naïve connection between grammar and understanding, but from personal experience I certainly know the charm of this vision.

My dream of producing droll pseudo-articles in the technical language of physics never came to pass — I just didn't have the time to do it — but I came close. Instead of giving sEn·gEn a physics lexicon, I gave it a lexicon drawn from "softer" academic disciplines, then wound it up and let it go. It was an unforgettable high to stand by the line printer during the wee hours of the morning and to watch page after page of glib, droll, buzzword-infested, yet intellectual-sounding gibberish come clanking out.

Thanks to this experience and many others exploring the twilight zones of meaningfulness, I became someone who approached overly highbrow-sounding writing with a degree of skepticism that exceeded that of most of my peers. It seemed to me far too easy a trick to throw trendy words together according to formulaic patterns and to produce what could pass for meaning, when in fact it was utterly vacuous.

A Gedankenexperiment for Simpletons

One day when I was in Stanford's art library, I was astounded by the prose that I discovered in a left-wing British journal called *Art-Language*, in which each article was written by a collective. Some time later, in writing my book *Gödel, Escher, Bach*, I wound up mixing nine sentences from my own program's output with three sentences culled from the pages of this bizarre journal, and asking the readers of my book to try to figure out which ones had been produced by earnest humans and which ones had been produced by a machine. I will now give you a slightly scaled-down version of the same challenge. Here, then, are six wonderfully weird sentences, three by my 1965 sEn·gEn program and three by the human minds behind *Art-Language*; the challenge of "centrifuging" them apart according to their origin is your task (answers to come later in the chapter):

(1) Rather think of a pathway of a "sequence" of gedankenexperiment simpletons where heir-lines are a prima facie case of a paradiachronic transitivity.

(2) Admittedly, the hierarchical origin of the fallacy, nevertheless, will be prophesied by the enemies of it.

(3) But there is the critical issue of that "filler" as a reified function of the pusillanimous tittle-tattle of authenticity in its ellipticality (as a Das Volk holism).

(4) Despite the efforts, the reply, if you will, had been supported by the Orient; hence a fallacy will thereafter be suspended by the attitude which will be being held by the ambassador.

(5) Think of that as a chain strength possibility of what, eventually, comes out as a product (epistemic conditions?) and the product is not a Frankfurt-ish packing-it-all-in.

(6) Supposedly, refined liberty caused the attitudes insofar as peace is distilled by the consequences which will not eventually be caused by the command irrevocably insofar as peace of it is sometimes causing the intransigency infinitesimally surprisingly.

Amusing though this may all be, my purpose is not to entertain you with nonsense *per se*, but to talk about the *translatability* of such odd tidbits. And the best way I can do that is to tell you — or rather, let David Moser tell you — what happened when the Chinese *GEB*-translation team bumped up against this challenge. Here, taken from a beautiful article by David on his experiences in reconstructing *GEB* in Chinese, is the story.

When we set out to translate the *Art-Language* sentences, the first question my Chinese co-translators asked me was, of course, "What do these bizarre human-generated sentences *mean*, exactly?" — a reasonable question, since translation *is* a kind of paraphrase (albeit a highly restricted kind). To be fair to the original authors' intent as well as to the spirit of Hofstadter's challenge, shouldn't there be at least an attempt to translate the "meaning" of these sentences?

However, even when I was given the chance to see the context of these sentences in the articles in which they appeared, it was impossible for me to adequately paraphrase them, much less translate them. The examples had in fact been chosen by Hofstadter precisely because they represented a kind of language usage that includes highly abstract poetry, dense "academese", allusive texts, cryptic in-jokes, and so forth, where the boundary between sense and nonsense can be very blurry for initiated and uninitiated alike. The very vagueness of this boundary is, of course, one of the reasons computer-generated poetry can be so much fun: one can't help but read all kinds of "profound" meanings into such pieces, and it is interesting to ponder where such meanings really lie. In reading the *Art-Language* prose, one occasionally wonders whether there is meaning at all, or whether people just got carried away by the seductive flow of their own jargon.

These questions about the *Art-Language* sentences are provocative enough when raised in the context of English alone, but constitute an even thornier problem when one is trying to pull them out of their cultural and linguistic context and render them in a language as remote from English as Chinese is. To an English-speaking reader, the sentences appear to be impenetrable gibberish, though a special *kind* of gibberish, written in a hyper-erudite, pretentious, perhaps even intentionally obfuscatory style, crammed with highly obscure words and arcane philosophical jargon. How far can we go in our attempt to "do the same thing" in Chinese? Do we include characters and phrases from classical Chinese, as one might find in similar recondite passages in Chinese? Or is that going too far? If we were to include classical Chinese, would we still be justified in claiming that these sentences were taken from a *British* journal? Ironically, the best way of preserving the forbidding flavor in Chinese might be to leave many words in English, since liberally sprinkling one's text with English is considered erudite in Chinese (it is a kind of Chinese counterpart to the way in which *Art-Language* borrows foreign terms like *Gedankenexperiment* and *prima facie*).

As for the computer-generated sentences that were mixed in among the human-generated ones, we experienced a vague sense of uneasiness in translating them *at all*. The reason for this sense of discomfort touches upon one of the key issues raised in the book itself — namely, the issue of whether a machine can be conscious, or in other words, whether a machine can "mean what it says".

No one objects to the quote marks around the phrase "I think, therefore I am", even though, strictly speaking, Descartes did not write these words. He happened to have written the statement in Latin (*Cogito, ergo sum*), but he could just as well have written it in his native French, or in any language he was familiar with, and we would still not hesitate to call it "the same statement". The reason that quote marks are acceptable even for translations of this aphorism is, firstly, that we ascribe *intentionality* to Descartes — we believe he *meant* something by what he said; and secondly, the *meaning* of the phrase is quite language-independent. We feel comfortable saying that Descartes wrote "I think, therefore I am" because we are confident that the English phrase captures the essential meaning of the original Latin, and, even more crucially, of that *thought* in the *mind* of Descartes.

One might feel somewhat less comfortable translating a phrase originally generated by a computer because it would seem that there is less justification in ascribing intentionality to the computer. Could the computer possibly have *meant* anything by its output? One's first intuition on confronting any computer-generated sentence is that the computer produced *that exact string of letters and nothing more,* and thus that it would border on intellectual dishonesty to translate it; after all, it is merely a pattern of vacuous typographical symbols spat out according to a set of deterministic and purely *syntactic* procedures. But is this intuition a valid one?

Of course, this is precisely where some of the central ideas of *Gödel, Escher, Bach* come into play in the very process of its translation. How much intentionality is it reasonable to ascribe to a program like Hofstadter's sentence generator, or Joseph Weizenbaum's "Doctor" program, or Kenneth Colby's "Parry" program, or Terry Winograd's SHRDLU program [all discussed in *GEB*]? Can SHRDLU (the most sophisticated of the four) be said to have at least a simple representation of the MIT Blocks World in its "head"? Is it reasonable to say that it "understands" the questions put to it, even if only in a very restricted sense of the term?

Presumably, the more inclined one is to answer "yes" to these questions, the less likely one is to object to a translation of the dialogue between SHRDLU and a human being. After all, "yes" answers mean that the program has some right to be treated analogously to Descartes. And conversely, the more inclined one is to answer "no" to these questions, the more of a bind one finds oneself in with regard to translating computer output, because the moment that one doubts the existence of any representation or understanding behind the scenes, one is no longer free as a translator to do as one instinctively does with ordinary human statements, such as that of Descartes (namely, one looks beyond the surface and translates at a deeper level, according to the *meaning* one detects). When meaning is ruled out, then translation becomes betrayal.

Indeed, were the SHRDLU/human dialogue included in a *technical paper* on SHRDLU's competencies and lacks, a Chinese translator would have no choice but to leave the dialogue in English and provide a comprehensive gloss in Chinese for those who couldn't read the original. This is because, in that kind of technical context, the English dialogue would constitute *hard data,* and translating the program's output into another language would seriously misrepresent those data.

For the purposes of our translation, however, such considerations were of less importance, and so, despite a definite sense of uneasiness, we devised an *analogous* though entirely *fictitious* dialogue between a Chinese speaker and a *hypothetical* program that could handle Chinese in the MIT Blocks World at roughly the same level of competency as SHRDLU handles English. In this way, Chinese speakers would be given a chance to get a feel for the issues of computer understanding of natural language without being forced, solely for the sake of impeccable intellectual probity, to wade through scores of subtleties in a foreign language.

Before we leave these sentences, let me fulfill my promise to reveal which ones are "fake" and which "genuine". The odd-numbered ones are from *Art-Language*; those by my dear old program, may it rest in peace, are even-numbered. (Didn't I tell you those *Art-Language* folks were amazing? Pusillanimous tittle-tattle, indeed!)

Counterfeit Counterparts: Translated Speech Errors

David Moser's trenchant commentary on the problems of translating text whose generator is of dubious mentality cuts right to the core of the matter; I wish I had written it myself. And it brings up a closely related matter — that of translating speech errors. You might wonder why anyone would ever wish to do such a strange thing, but the answer is simple: For getting at the hidden mechanisms of the human mind, there is no better way than by studying the patterns in error-making, whether the errors involve actions (slips of the hand), perceptions (slips of the eye or ear), utterances (slips of the tongue), or even conceptions (slips of memory). Errors are well worth thinking about, writing about, and thus, it would certainly seem, translating.

Let's think just about speech errors. The way one uses them to probe the inner world of the mind — of the brain, in fact — is to amass, over a period of many years, a vast *corpus* of errors; then one sifts painstakingly through them and tries to discover *categories* of errors, after which one works at *classifying* each error in precisely one category (nearly a hopeless task, which inevitably causes the invention of many new categories and the shifting of category boundaries, a process that goes round and round for a long time before starting to settle down, if ever). The next stage is to convert these abstractions about errors into a *theory* of what the mind is doing, usually involving breaking the hidden mechanisms into several temporal stages, and carefully considering what kinds of audible errors would result from random "crossed wires" at some particular level of the processing. Then one can make a *computer model* of the theory, run it on many examples, and compare the kinds of errors produced, and especially their statistics, with the actual errors and statistics reflected in the corpus. It is critical that error collectors be scrupulous about not distorting anything in the errors they transcribe, because each error is, obviously, *a piece of data* about the human mind. One must be ruthlessly honest in reporting exactly what one heard, no matter what one wishes one had heard.

All of this is well and good, and is something that I have pursued as a sideline ever since I was in high school. That is, I have by now amassed a gigantic corpus of speech errors — with far more errors made by myself than by anyone else, needless to say — in my filing cabinets. I imagine there are 5,000 to 10,000 errors in it, of scores of different types. I have worked at developing categories, at classifying specific errors, at making theories about the mechanisms, and so on. Though it is not my main line of work as a cognitive scientist, it is a tremendous passion.

One day I wrote an article in which I discussed an electrifying speech error that I had just read of in a book: it was the sentence "Rosa always date shranks." Someone somewhere had really said this! It amazed me, because a verbal past-tense operator had been shifted from the intended verb ("date") and applied instead to a noun ("shrink", meaning "psychiatrist"). Not only that, but what would have been a *regular* past-tense conversion ("date" ⇒ "dated") was replaced by an *irregular* one ("shrink" ⇒ "shrank"). And not only *that*, but the plural marker "s" was blithely appended to the result, as if this "past-tense noun" were an ordinary noun. How convoluted!

This error, as it turned out, was so radical that it invalidated, in one fell swoop, a number of then-respected theories about speech errors. It was not the kind of thing that anyone could have *invented*, precisely because it was so strange-seeming. No one would have taken it seriously had it merely been proposed as a "plausible" type of error. It had to actually *happen*, and when it did, people suddenly scrambled to try to explain it. (In this sense, error theorizers resemble particle theorists who make a mad dash for their pencils and paper when a new particle or type of reaction is empirically discovered; they get into gear only when the thing actually *happens*, because anyone could speculate that this or that *might* occur, but there's no reason to take anyone's speculations seriously — except, of course, one's own.)

Well, my article was published in my book *Metamagical Themas*, and when that book was translated into several foreign languages, this spot was hit. What did the translators do? As it happens, I had actually told them what to do, in a thirty-page memorandum of author's suggestions for all translators of the book. I had said to leave it in English, precisely for the reasons that David Moser spelled out above — namely, *a speech error is a piece of data,* and not something to be simply invented out of whole cloth. Especially when the error is so radical and so significant to error researchers, it would be a complete betrayal of scientific truth to blithely invent a "plausible-seeming counterpart" in the target language. And yet, despite my personal plea on this, the French and German translators went ahead and simply spun elegant fancies. In French, the supposed error that I myself had read of and was relaying to my readers was the sentence

Rosait sorta toujours avec des psy.

as opposed to the utterance that the speaker had supposedly intended to produce, which was:

Rosa sortait toujours avec des psy.

The intended sentence means "Rosa always went out with shrinks" and the supposedly authentic erroneous utterance has "Rosa" receiving the past tense and "go out" getting a kind of half-cooked past tense. That is, you can see there has been a transposition of an ending (*-ait*) from the verb *sortir* to the person's name *Rosa,* and vice versa. Well, this, though quite neat, is pure fantasy. Such an event *might* happen in a francophone mind some day; then again, it might not. But it's playing very free and easy with the mechanisms of mind to simply assert, point-blank, that it *did* happen.

In German, likewise, the translators just ran roughshod over what I had requested them to do, and came up with this hypothetical error:

Immer hat Rosa einen Psychiater mit einer Verabredung.

as opposed to what "should have been said":

Immer hat Rosa eine Verabredung mit einem Psychiater.

This supposed speech error, presented as authentic, illustrates a totally different phenomenon — that of *full-word* swapping (with concomitant modification of indefinite articles). The intended utterance means "Rosa always has a date/appointment with a psychiatrist", whereas the errorful one means "Rosa always has a psychiatrist with a date/appointment." The mechanisms that might give rise to this error, despite the fact that it's a swap, don't even remotely resemble those that underlie the original English error, involving, as it does, a most improbable interaction between a wandering tense-changing operator and a stationary pluralizing operator.

Or let me put it another way: *for those who know anything* about speech errors, there is no connection. To be sure, for a casual observer, there might seem to be much the same thing going on — "some kind of swapping" of elements of speech. At that coarse level of description, though, almost anything could fit in the category. I can dream up errors galore in which arbitrary swaps take place: "Roseways all-a danked shrits", for example. But were I to report such an error as having actually happened, it would be grossly misleading and irresponsible. We are, after all, talking about how the human subconscious *actually* works, not about someone's naïve conceptions about how it *might* work.

In the prologue to my recent book *Fluid Concepts and Creative Analogies,* I recount the story of a curious typo that I made while writing the prologue itself (namely, I typed "once in a bloom" when shooting for the target "once in a blue moon"). I then speculate about the mechanisms that might have been behind this error. For this passage, the translators into one European language invented a story about a typo I supposedly made while writing the book *in their language* — obviously an event that never happened. Moreover, the error they invented was so weirdly implausible that it was actually quite funny, and I was tempted to leave it in as a kind of surrealistic joke, but in the end decided against it. Not only was the passage a falsification of my personal history (an excusable sin, as we saw earlier), but far more upsettingly, it was suggesting, in the context of what I intended as a very serious book on the mechanisms of mind, that a certain fantastic error had actually been committed, and it even placed in my own cognitive scientist's mouth a bunch of wild, off-the-wall speculations as to what had caused it. This was beyond the pale, for me.

As these examples show, speech errors are, as a rule, untranslatable, because of their intimate connection with low-level mechanisms buried in the unconscious mind of the speaker — which, to borrow a phrase I used above in reference to computer programs and people trapped in the grip of a seductive jargon, are "language generators of dubious mentality". Since no one can peer all the way down to the subconscious roots of a given error, and since the error's genesis is the whole point of the discussion, one simply has no right to tamper with the data.

Counterparts as Translations

Perhaps David Moser had the right attitude in his commentary on the wacky sentences — that the answer to the question "Translate, or leave as raw data?" depends on how technical a context one is in. Are we translating a journal article reporting on detailed, specific events in the mind — or a textbook that is trying to suggestively get across some generalities about mental functioning — or are we translating a novel? In the former case, strict scientific accuracy dictates *no translation,* while in the latter two cases (especially the novel), vividness demands fantasizing of some error that *plays a similar role* in the target language — a *counterpart.*

For the purposes of a novel, a translator could obviously replace an English speech error with a German one pulled out of thin air (in fact, the novel's author probably just made the error up in the first place); for the purposes of a textbook, however, more care should be used. The translator has to have at least a smidgen of technical knowledge about error-making. Ideally, the translator would resort to a *German* corpus of errors, and in it locate an *analogous* error, presuming one exists. (Note, though, that the "date shranks" error was so novel and unprecedented that this strategy would not work.)

How close do the two analogous errors' contents have to be? If the original error involved a mistyping of the word "blue" in English, should one aim to find a German typing error involving the word *blau?* To my mind, trying to do that would be misguided. If by chance one ran into such an error in a German errors corpus, it would be a cute but insignificant link. Almost certainly, there would be other errors that were more analogous in terms of deep mechanisms, in which case one of those should be chosen over the one with the more superficial resemblance.

We have seen this type of translation strategy before: it came up in the discussion of translating palindromes, where I suggested to Professor Wu that *any* outstanding Chinese palindrome, whether about the Panama canal or not, would serve as a "translation" of "A man, a plan, a canal — Panama!" It came up when I discussed Gilbert Adair's replacement of an "e"-less Victor Hugo poem by an "e"-less Edgar Allan Poe poem. (In fact, it was even suggested there that *La disparition* as a whole could be thought of as a "translation" of *Gadsby*.) The theme of counterparts has come up over and over again in this book — replacement of the devil by Cao Cao, replacement of Paris by Amsterdam, replacement of American football by European rugby, replacement of medieval plumpness by modern svelteness, replacement of French jam by Russian honey-mead, and on and on. Such replacement of a deeply native aspect of culture A by some sort of counterpart to it in culture B is what we termed "transculturation".

But there is a distinction to be made here. Replacing one speech error by an analogous one in another language is not necessitated by deep differences between the two *cultures* involved; it simply has to do with the vagaries of error-collecting. The corpus of errors I have collected has almost no overlap with the corpus of errors David Moser has collected, though we belong to the same culture and language. Errors are simply accidental events, and the collection that any particular error-fancier builds up will be filled with unique and wondrous oddities, although the general properties exhibited by different collections the world over will be the same, since Chinese brain physiology and Eskimo brain physiology and American brain physiology are one and the same.

Naïve Visions of Language and the Mind

Although a universal human susceptibility to making speech errors would seem to be an obvious consequence of the uniformity of the human brain's architecture, both David Moser and I have encountered resistance time and again when we have asked speakers of other languages for help in collecting errors. The usual reaction goes something like this: "I wish I could help you, but speakers of our language seldom make sloppy errors of the sort you have shown me in your language. As children, we learn to be very careful with language, because our teachers are terribly strict." (There is undoubtedly a certain degree of pride mixed in there.)

David's and my instinctive counter to this is to say, "Teaching has nothing to do with it; in fact, speech errors come from lower levels in the brain that teaching can't reach! They're all around you — it's just that it's very easy not to hear them. You have to *learn* to hear them." However, this backfires on us, because they parry this way (I paraphrase *à la* Mr Average): "The fact that *you* hear them all the time and I *don't* just proves my point, my friend: In *your* language, they're a dime a dozen, but in *our* language, they're as rare as teeth from turnips. I swear, if I'd ever heard anything like the crazy English errors you just showed me, I'd have noticed it, believe me! — *ergo* such linguistic slopperiness just *ain't there* to be heard."

Over and over again we've run into this reaction — in France, China, and elsewhere — and so we simply have wound up having to rely on our own inefficient non-native ears to try to build up collections of errors in other languages. Needless to say, we do find errors of every sort cropping up, but the collection task is made far more difficult without native help.

I have to admit that in one case, I briefly took such an argument a bit seriously. This was when Jean Aitchison, a superb linguist and the author of *Words in the Mind* (one of my favorite books on how the mind works), told me in a letter that she had heard from some colleague in India that there is no corpus of errors in Hindi, because Hindi speakers make essentially no errors. Aitchison herself didn't comment one way or the other on this claim. As for me, I had no doubt that Hindi speakers make *some* errors, but for at least a little while, I did ask myself, "Could it be that this one language somehow shields its speakers' brains from this otherwise universal human frailty?" If that were the case, I suppose we should all go out and learn Hindi, for then there would be far fewer embarrassing spoonerisms or Freudian slips...

In part I took this claim more seriously because it apparently came from a linguist, perhaps also in part because India seems more exotic than Europe. Indeed, I would not be surprised if the claim sounded perfectly plausible to someone who has never thought about speech errors and where they come from. However, after reflecting on the idea, I realized it amounted to the thesis that speaking Hindi has a profound and pervasive effect on the entire mode of functioning of one's brain, and I thus changed my mind. Although I haven't looked into its validity any further, I don't feel any need to, for in my opinion, this suggestion ranks right up there with the silliest rumors I have ever heard — on a par with, and quite similar to, the cockeyed notion that one's religious beliefs can make one immune to cancer and other diseases. One doesn't need to research that either.

I surmise that this claim was originated by some linguist who knows Hindi, native or otherwise, but who has a tin ear for linguistic quirks and hence simply doesn't pick up the soft buzz of errors thickly swarming all about at all times, the exact same buzz that surrounds every other language on earth — and presumably those on neutron stars as well. (In fact, how delightful it would be to have a collection of cheela speech errors, and to compare it with a human collection. What an idea!)

If there is a mystique around Hindi, all the more so around its ancient and venerated progenitor, Sanskrit, medium of the *Bhagavad-gītā* and many other mystical texts. I suppose it is not too surprising, then, that someone once suggested — apparently in all seriousness — that Sanskrit is a mathematically perfect "language of thought" and should therefore be adopted as a strict computational formalism for representations of meaning. The idea that mere syntactic regularity would bring into sharp focus all the deep mechanisms of the human mind is fabulously naïve, and yet it was swallowed whole by the editors of *Artificial Intelligence Magazine,* who some years ago not only published a lengthy article on this romantic proposition but even splashed it all over their cover. Talk about gullibility… Or maybe it was their April issue, and I just didn't notice.

It seems that for many Western intellectuals, Oriental languages just exude this aura of mystical connection with the essence of the mental. Even Stanisław Ulam, that great mathematician fascinated by the mind's machinery, had a weakness in this direction. In his book *Adventures of a Mathematician,* he suggests the following picture of mental activity:

> The process of logic itself working internally in the brain may be more analogous to a succession of operations with symbolic pictures, a sort of abstract analogue of the Chinese alphabet or some Mayan description of events….

When I read poetic but simplistic metaphors like this, conflating the undeniable charm of exotic scripts with the entire resolution of the mystery of how thought works, an image pops to mind of my very first Chinese class, and how, when we students made egregious blunders, good old Mr. Kao would put on an aggravated expression a little closer to a grin than a grimace, nod his head vigorously, and insistently say, *"Bú shì! Bú shì!"*

Unusual Newspaper Headlines Oscillating in Reader's Mind

Errors are of course not the only kind of linguistic oddity one can collect. The *Columbia Journalism Review* has made a practice, for many years, of culling ambiguous headlines from English-language newspapers, mostly in the United States, and every so often it puts out a collection of its funniest examples. Thus in the 1980 volume *Squad Helps Dog Bite Victim* and its 1987 counterpart, *Red Tape Holds Up New Bridge,* one finds incredibly subtle, language-dependent ambiguities, which are often side-splittingly funny as well. The books' titles — genuine, well-documented headlines, like all the other examples — suggest what is possible.

Before I show you the amazing variety of ambiguities represented in these books, let me pose a puzzle, to entice you to think about these things a bit. Can you construct, given the following two sentences, a single short newspaper-style headline that can be read as meaning either one of them with equal ease and clarity?

(1) Bundy once again manages to wangle out of his often-rescheduled electrocution.

(2) Bundy, employing a common piece of furniture, engages in a violent attack on his most recent romantic prospect.

When you consider the enormous semantic gap between these two sentences, it seems quite preposterous to suggest that one short sentence could express *both* of them — and yet when you see the answer, I suspect you will agree that it is both flawless and graceful. (Tiny hint: The solution has exactly six words, the first of which is "Bundy". Hint number 2: The key to it all is the item of furniture.)

Well, here is the solution (embedded, so it doesn't jump out at you, in a little collection of a few other favorites of mine):

Man Eating Piranha Mistakenly Sold as Pet Fish
Drunk gets nine months in violin case
Woman off to jail for sex with boys
Child teaching expert to speak
Milk Drinkers Turn to Powder
Scientists To Have Ford's Ear
Prostitutes appeal to Pope
Stud tires out
Chou Remains Cremated
Farmer Bill Dies in House
British left waffles on Falklands
Bundy beats latest date with chair
Tuna Biting Off Washington Coast
Nineteen Feet Broken in Pole Vault
Nixon To Stand Pat On Watergate Tapes
Mauling By Bear Leaves Woman Grateful For Life

I must admit that even though I've known all of these flip-flops for many years now, I *still* laugh out loud when sitting here, all alone in my study at two in the morning, and scanning this list. It is simply spectacular!

I certainly could never have come up with such a list in a million years — it is just too subtle. Take the answer to the Bundy puzzle, for instance. In it, all the words but "Bundy" and "latest" swivel simultaneously in meaning as one moves back and forth between the two interpretations. Such synchronous pivoting is reminiscent of how all the vertices and edges of the famous Necker cube flip in phase with each other as the visual system jumps between the two possible global perceptions of the figure.

On the Untranslatable ◆◆◆ **421**

Or consider the tiniest one of all, "Stud tires out". What we have here is, on the one hand, a compound noun designating certain pavement-damaging aids to wintertime automotive mobility ("stud tires") followed by an adverb suggesting a legislative banning thereof ("out"), and on the other hand, a simple noun designating a Don Juan type ("stud") followed by a two-piece verb suggesting exhaustion from overindulgence in his specialty ("tires out"). Note how this mode of flip-flopping is essentially isomorphic, on a syntactic level, to that of the next headline in the list, "Chou Remains Cremated". It is also reminiscent of what is going on in "Tuna Biting Off Washington Coast", where the key hingepoint is the word "off", waffling about whether it owes allegiance to "biting" or to "Washington Coast".

One of the most beautiful is "British left waffles on Falklands". Although it seems similar in a way, this flip has some notable differences, because not only does a *noun* flip into a *verb* ("left"), but at the same instant, the adjacent *verb* flips into a *noun* ("waffles"). (Notice the tense shift from present to past.) And right as this verb/noun interchange takes place, the preposition "on" metamorphoses in meaning, jumping from the abstract "about" to the concrete "upon". This is a very neat *triple saut,* comparable in subtlety to the flip of the "Bundy" headline.

Flipping Journal Sentences Stump Scholar to Death

I hope you have enjoyed this small sampler taken from two absolutely smashing books. But now, back to our main topic: translation. How could you possibly translate any one of these headlines into, say, French — or any other language? Far worse, imagine the challenge of translating either of these books *as a whole.* I see three avenues of approach, each of which puts great strain on the standard notion of "translation".

In approach number one, someone might take these Janus-like headlines as material for teaching some of the subtler principles of English grammar. In such a case, each headline would be reproduced in English and accompanied by French commentary explaining how it flips back and forth, discussing the underlying grammatical principles of this case, and providing hints to learners on how to avoid mistakes in its general family. This could make for a lively and engaging intermediate-level grammar, but it would certainly not resemble what one normally means by "translation".

In approach number two, one could go to the archives of long-time ambiguous-headline collector Dominique Tellétel of Forcalquier, France, sift through them for days, and finally pull together the 100 most delightful flip-flops. Again, the result would be fascinating and presumably comparable in mirth-provoking capacity to the two American books, but dubious as a translation of either of them. Indeed, such a French counterpart would no more merit being called a translation of the

American books than the second of them, *Red Tape Holds Up New Bridge,* merits being labeled a translation from 1980-ese to 1987-ese of *Squad Helps Dog Bite Victim.* Whether you jump across the Atlantic to see Tellétel or stay put in America and jump downstream seven years, all you have in either case is a totally new anthology of multi-swiveling headlines that charms in much the same way as its predecessor did.

In the third and final approach, someone could take each headline and painstakingly try to devise an ambiguous French phrase that captures both of its meanings. This hope would certainly be smashed to bits when one actually tried to do it — but suppose, just for the sake of argument, that it were realized. Even then, a large part of the charm of the original would be lost, for what makes these two collections so wonderful is the knowledge that *this very headline* — in fact, reproduced photographically from the original source — was actually printed in such-and-such a newspaper on such-and-such a day. To be sure, you could falsify everything, typing up the French headlines in various different typefaces and inventing newspapers and dates, but that would be a pretty feeble thing to do.

I am led to the conclusion that these two books are, in any realistic sense of the word "translation", untranslatable, although counterpart books could in principle be made.

Piecemeal Counterpart-creation as Translation

For years, Roger Angell's story "Brush Twice Daily and Go Easy on the Bonbons" has made me smile. You'll get the point as soon as you read a bit:

> The dentist glanced at me sharply through his rimless half-glasses and then turned and selected another pick. "Sorry," he said, scraping again, "but it's hard not to make a booboo when I'm getting off tartar."…
> "How are my gums?" I said when he next straightened up. "Any signs of beriberi?"
> "Just so-so," he replied, turning his back. "They'd be better if you'd massage them. I recommend two toothbrushes."
> "Two toothbrushes!" I cried. "Here, here, you've gone too far."
> "Sorry," he said pushing me gently back in the chair. "That was a bit rococo, I admit. A barbarity."

And on (and on): Mau Maus, tse-tses, Berbers, pawpaws, couscous, yum-yum, aye-aye, Dada, dodoes, lulu, Choochoo, tut-tut, Zum Zum, go-go, goo-goo, yo-yo, bye-bye… One could, of course, write an *analogous* story in any other language — even set in a dentist's office! — but still it would not count as a *translation* of Angell's, except in the most stretched of senses.

And yet — there is a circumstance in which such a counterpart story *could* count as a translation. The basic idea I'm about to describe is just a mild variation on the strategy employed in converting *Gödel, Escher, Bach,* with its structure consisting of alternating chapters and dialogues, into other languages.

Imagine a hefty and scholarly tome by Roger Angell called, say, *Linguistic Drollery,* in which fifteen of his own droll stories embodying various kinds of language games (including "Brush Twice") alternate with fifteen relatively straightforward discursive chapters, each of which takes its cue from the drollery immediately preceding it and then goes off in various directions talking *about* linguistic oddities but not in itself *embodying* any such thing. Now imagine the challenge of translating such a book.

If all fifteen chapters have been successfully translated into, say, French, as would seem quite feasible, then it might make sense to substitute, as interstitial material, fifteen freshly written *counterpart* stories in French, each one embodying precisely the same types of oddities as does its corresponding story in the original, but otherwise being totally different (or, in any case, as different as it needs to be in order to do an excellent job). These counterpart *drôleries* would, of course, require an expert in French wordplay to write them, but they would be plugged right into the slots where Angell's own drolleries are found in the English text.

The result would be a French book that would seem perfectly worthy of the label "translation of Roger Angell's *Linguistic Drollery*". In this context, then, the radically new French-language *drôlerie* that is jam-packed with repeated syllables (*bébé, lolo, dodo, kif-kif, murmure, nana, froufrou, tonton,* etc.) and that is still set, just for elegance's sake, in a dentist's office, could be claimed to be a translation of "Brush Twice", and hopefully, nobody's tongue would be set thereby a-wagging.

A Strange Link between Granularity and Credit

The trick here — not really a trick, so let's say the *key* — is the context. Were it isolated, this new French story would merely be a "cousin" to the Angell story, and would be quite properly attributed to the person who put it together — but when seen as part of Angell's larger opus, it blends right in, just as the radically reconstructed Chinese dialogues in *Jí Yì Bì* blend right in with the more straightforwardly translated chapters. There is certainly not a footnote for each dialogue saying, "This is a reconstruction, not a translation", let alone a suggestion that the *authorship* is flipping and flopping back and forth inside the book, depending on the degree of radicality of translation!

If one were to go this route, things would start to get extraordinarily messy. There would not merely be a footnote taking credit away from the author for each *dialogue,* but also, at each slightly daring moment inside the simpler chapters, there would be a footnote saying something to the effect of: "We replaced the original author's phrase in English by this Chinese phrase because this phrase gets across the feeling better than would a literal translation". And this footnote would amount to a tiny fleeting transferral of authorship.

If one carries this idea of rapidly oscillating authorship to its logical conclusion, it becomes a joke, a *reductio ad absurdum,* because then one could question the authorship of each separate *word* in a translation. After all, did the original author think of all the complex intermingling flavors in the halo of this word in *our* language? No! Thus each word of the new text is a radical re-creation, and since the book consists of nothing but a long sequence of words, the author deserves no credit at all.

At this point, we find ourselves thrown right back into the thick of the debate in Chapter 10, once again confronting the question of "coffee" versus *café,* "newspaper" versus *journal,* "cheese" versus *fromage,* "bread" versus *pain.* Richard Howard, one of the major translators of Marcel Proust into English, has said, "There are days when translation does seem impossible, when the English word 'bread' and the French word *pain* seem to be only absurd equivalents." If Howard is right, and every word is a struggle and a creative breakthrough, then authorship should simply be revoked when a work is translated into another language, and reassigned to the translator.

Why do we not fall for such a *reductio ad absurdum?* Basically, because we credit the original author with the higher-level vision that brought the work as a whole into existence. And the author also carefully sculpted the structure of each of the work's top-level components (acts, chapters, stories, dialogues, what-have-you). And then, within those pieces, there are smaller yet no less carefully crafted subcomponents on many hierarchical levels (scenes, sections, stanzas, paragraphs, sentences, lines, idioms, compound words, simple words, prefixes and suffixes). At what level of structural detail does the author's deserving of credit taper off towards zero? At what point is tampering or substitution permitted? Of course, there's no clean answer, no sharp cutoff line. And indeed, as I suggested above, one's intuitions about a passage's authorship are not even constant, but are affected by the context in which the passage is embedded.

When a chunk of translated text is perceived as forming an integral part of a larger chunk of text, then even if constructing the inner chunk required radical leaps of imagination, it is seen as fitting in with the original author's overall flow. This holds on all levels — words inside sentences, sentences inside paragraphs, paragraphs inside sections, sections inside chapters, and chapters inside books. When Cao Cao is substituted for the devil in a single sentence of a dialogue, that one sentence is not given special exemption from the claim that it is part of a work by Hofstadter, even if Hofstadter has never heard of Cao Cao. This same principle scales up from tiny phrases to all higher levels of structure.

Therefore, strange though it might seem, a lovely and clever French re-creation of "Brush Twice Daily and Go Easy on the Bonbons" could perfectly well be attributed to one author when published on its own in a French literary magazine, and to a different author when embedded in the hypothetical French-language anthology of Roger Angell's drolleries and chapters. Much the same could be said for any Chinese version of a *GEB* dialogue, taken on its own as opposed to when it is snugly wedged between two chapters inside *Jí Yì Bì*.

Gemütlichkeit, Simpatía, Machismo

Since we've re-broached the subject of words and their translatability, I think it would be well to look at certain notorious "untranslatable words", such as German's *Gemütlichkeit*. Why do people so often say about this word, "There's no English equivalent"? My paperback Bantam German–English dictionary in fact lists two potential equivalents: "easy-going nature" and "cosiness". And when I go to my much bigger hardback Collins German dictionary, I find that it lists numerous English possibilities, including "friendliness", "cosiness", "snugness", "informality", "good-naturedness", "pleasantness", "easy-going nature", "comfortableness", "approachability", "unhurriedness", and "leisure". Now by golly, if there were no way to express this notion in English, I would have expected to find a big blank, or a few question marks, or a statement such as "does not compute". Instead, however, it seems as if we anglophones have words to cover every last facet of *Gemütlichkeit*. O, inexpressibility, where is thy sting?

Alas, we have no *single* word for *Gemütlichkeit*. But that's hardly unique. As I riffle through the pages of my big dictionary, I notice that many German words are just like this: they turn into different English words depending on the context. That's why their entries are several lines long, instead of containing just one single English word. As a matter of fact, there is hardly *any* German word that has just one single English equivalent. In this sense, *Gemütlichkeit* is typical, not exceptional.

Actually, the entry for *Gemütlichkeit* is only about ten lines long (roughly one column–inch); words having many more lines are a dime a dozen. For instance, I just flipped around in the "g"'s, and noticed that *gleich* had at least 50, maybe 60 lines — and *gehen* had almost 200 lines! Poor old *Gemütlichkeit* seems to be a rather simple word, in the end, to translate. And yet, who ever heard of anyone sighing, "Ah, *gehen* — it's one of those intangible, unique, untranslatable German words!" No one ever says that — they just say, "*Gehen* means 'go'." But the fact of the matter is, *gehen* is far more complicated to translate than *Gemütlichkeit* is. If we're going to talk about untranslatable words, we should focus on the frequent ones, like "get" or "do" or "the". Now *those* are *hard*!

What about Spanish's legendarily untranslatable *simpático*? Well, to tell the truth, I've always been completely puzzled by this claim. To me, *simpático* is very, very close to our "nice", and that's all there is to it! I'm afraid I just don't see the mystique. I'm more impressed with the case for *macho* as an untranslatable. Of course, it merely means "male" in many instances, but my big Spanish dictionary, to its credit, gives the English word "macho" as one sense of the term, along with "he-man", "tough guy", and — amusingly — "idiot". Now I'd say that when a word is given as its *own* translation in another language, why then, you're starting to build a case for its untranslatability, although of course the act of borrowing undermines the claim; after all, "macho" now *is* an English word.

An English — or rather, American — word that I consider challenging is "humongous", not so much because of its direct meaning ("huge", "tremendous", "monstrous"), but because of the image of the speaker's inner mentality that it radiates — a certain *je-ne-sais-quoi* that I associate with American excitability and youthfulness, perhaps a touch of naïveté or provincialism, or in some cases, a conscious desire to come across as a down-home type. In any case, impossible though it may be to pin down its flavor, only certain kinds of people, in certain contexts, use this word. That is what is so subtle about it. And then there's my pet peeve of contemporary American colloquial language — "guys" — which I already dealt with a little bit in Chapter 7, and about which I could write reams more, but won't.

Nontransmissible Everyday Concepts

I would be the first to admit that there are occasional holes in languages. Thus you'll draw a blank if you try to look up "fast forward" in Phoenician, "light show" in Latin, "cellulite" in Sanskrit, "cosmonaut" in Old Church Slavonic, "hot to trot" in Hottentot, "quarterback" in Quechua, "yuppie" in Yoruba, "quality time" in Malayalam, "infrastructure" in Inca, or "Big Brother" in Babylonian. Times change; the world grows in complexity. When the actual *worlds* that two languages inhabit are radically different, then obviously each of the two will have lacunae relative to the other. But we don't live in a world all that different from modern Germany or Latin America — *Gemütlichkeit* and *simpatía* and even chauvinistic struttin' macho he-men are parts of all these worlds. Words are translatable among cultures to the extent that the worlds inhabited by their host languages are the same — and that extent is very high for many modern languages.

And yet, each language inhabits a world slightly different from all other languages, and so it has certain special terms whose meanings cannot be expressed concisely in other languages. They can be *explained,* but there is nothing like a terse corresponding expression. Thus in my Chinese dictionary, under the word *yánliáng,* I find no attempt to give a one-word or two-word English translation, but simply an *explanation*: "behave abjectly to the rich and powerful and coldly towards the poor". Conversely, when I look up "soap opera", rather than a Chinese counterpart I find a lengthy explanation saying essentially: "Family-intrigue dramas broadcast during the daytime on television, often sponsored by soap manufacturers and largely for the consumption of women working at home." This is not quite a case of untranslatability, but it is moving in that direction.

What would bring us closer would be the challenge of rendering "soap opera" in Sanskrit, where a *very* lengthy explanation would be needed, supplementing what was given to Chinese readers with further explanations of the notions of "television", "program", "advertisement", "sponsorship", and "soap company". At that point, where a completely standard everyday lexical item in language A requires a *page* of text in language B to be even vaguely suggested, one has perhaps reached true untranslatability.

Sometimes borrowed words can give us a whiff of the unique alienness of a remote epoch or culture. Yiddish's *Oy!* comes to mind. Merely hearing that one syllable conjures up in me a whole raft of imagery: voices, faces, hair, modes of dress, senses of humor, attitudes, houses, foods, smells, and so forth. If one thinks of every single word in every language as being this deeply impregnated with flavor, then one would have to conclude, most pessimistically, that *nothing* is ever translatable, not even one word, not even one cognate. The Italians say it best, of course: "Transducers traduce."

Fiddler on the Roof notwithstanding, you simply cannot transport the long-gone Jewish *shtetl* world wholesale into contemporary American culture, nor ancient Greece into contemporary Brazil, nor Shakespearean England into contemporary China. You can carry such attempts so far, and no further. Beyond that, some things simply won't go. I cannot fully know what it was like to live in any of those old worlds. But then neither can I import my own dearest ones' experiences fully into my world. At some level of privacy, one always reaches an unbreachable gap. Thus this kind of untranslatability actually has little to do with language, and much more to do with the sharability or nonsharability of experience. We will delve further into these topics in the coming chapter.

But let me conclude this series of sections on words in a more upbeat manner. I have heard said, "You can't translate the first sentence of the Bible, but you can translate the Bible." And that's the key when one is translating anything longer than a few words — flavor may be missing left and right if you look only on a fine-grained scale, but as you move gradually upwards from the very local to the intermediate to the global scale, you find that ideas *do* come across. In some sense, there is a grand cancellation — a humongous cancellation — of the myriad minute flavor differences, and the result is, at least in the best of translations, an efficient and deeply faithful transmission of experience and attitude. *Eppur si traduce.*

A Miscellany of Untranslatables

In this section, we take a look at some cases of medium–message marriage in which one is so close to the nuts-and-bolts level of the language that imagining translatability is like imagining that a particular game of chess could be translated into an equivalent game of tennis.

We begin with, of all things, tongue-twisters. How do you say "rubber baby-buggy bumpers" in French? In Chinese? How about "The sheik's sixth sheep's sick"? I am particularly partial to "toy boat", because with its trivial-seeming two syllables, it looks so innocent and yet turns out to be one of the hardest phrases in all of English to repeat quickly and accurately. In but a couple of cycles, it has soon metamorphosed into "toy boyt" or "toe boyt", and from there on out, things plummet rapidly. What would it mean to translate this into another language? To be sure, all languages have tongue-twisters, but which of the many Chinese tongue-twisters would count as "the 'toy boat' of Chinese"? An unanswerable question, and thus an untranslatable phrase.

Then there are the little books *C D B !* and *C D C ?* by William Steig. The idea is gotten across by the cover of *C D B !*, which has a cartoon with a little boy pointing at a honeybee hovering over a flower, and saying to the girl beside him, "C D B !" Inside the book, one finds a cartoon showing a man telling his pooch, "I M A U-M B-N. U R N N-M-L." Another cartoon shows a little girl joyously dancing with flowers, and the caption says, "L-C S N X-T-C." In *C D C ?*, there is a scene of a domestic squabble, with one party angrily shouting, "U R O-D-S !" and the other party replying, "N U R S-N-9 !" Obviously, someone could create a counterpart book in another language, but entirely new sequences of letters and situations would be involved, and all the drawings would have to be redone. And how would you possibly tackle the idea of a *Chinese* translation, given that individual characters — the language's smallest phonetic/graphical units — are already filled to the brim with content? In my view, we are again smack-dab in the middle of the realm of the untranslatable.

Then there are simply random little accidents that happen to work in one language and would have no chance of working in any other. I once discovered this little "equation", for example, in Italian:

$$ami + amo = amiamo$$

What it means, literally, is "you love + I love = we love", but the fact that the first two words when concatenated make the third one is almost uncannily symbolic of the union of marriage. For that reason, I dedicated this minipoem to Carol, who loved the Italian language with great passion and spoke it well (in fact, when an undergraduate, she was honored by the department one year as the best student of Italian, which deeply surprised her but was, of course, a source of pleasure and pride; nonetheless, she always remained humble and diffident about her command of the language she found so beautiful and subtle). I titled my discovery *Come (ci) si coniuga*, which means "How to conjugate/How to marry". Strangely, no Italian to whom I showed it had ever noticed the two pieces inside *amiamo* before.

Similar in flavor are the stunning anagrams that occasionally crop up in any language, such as these, in English (with a little Latin thrown in):

the nudist colony	=	*no untidy clothes*
Piet Mondrian	=	*I paint modern*
astronomers	=	*moon starers*
anagrams	=	*ars magna*
bedroom	=	*boredom*
hibernated	=	*bear hit den*
the piano bench	=	*beneath Chopin*
Rocky Mountains	=	*o man, ski country*

And then there are purely phonetic regroupings, such as of "X-ray source" into "ex-racehorse". For me, such things are paradigmatic untranslatables.

And let us not forget palindromes. We already discussed the greatest of them all in English: "A man, a plan, a canal — Panama!" Here are a few more, all by Leigh Mercer:

Are we not drawn onward, we few, drawn onward to new era?
Did Hannah say as Hannah did?
"Not New York!", Roy went on.
Sue, dice do, to decide us.
Madam, I'm Adam.
Sir, I'm Iris.
Eve.
Poor Dan is in a droop.
Too bad — I hid a boot.
Yawn a more Roman way.
Nurse, I spy gypsies — run!
Evil is a name of a foeman, as I live.

There are thousands of palindromes in English, mostly of abysmal quality, in the sense of lacking a single shred of meaning. Palindrometry is one of the weirdest, most strained of art forms (in fact, even calling it an "art form" is stretching it). Perhaps that makes it all the more impressive and gratifying when one comes across a palindrome that does exhibit some beauty and meaning.

I have never seen a pair of palindromes in different languages that could be even remotely considered each other's translations (with the somewhat dubious exception of the Chinese and English pair discussed in Chapter 6, both of which were about falling leaves). However, there are some very lovely palindromes in other languages, of which I will cite just a tiny number:

Latin

In girum imus nocte et consumimur igni.
("In a loop we go at night and are consumed by fire.")

German

Ein Neger mit Gazelle zagt im Regen nie.
("A negro with a gazelle never hesitates in the rain.")

Spanish

Yo soy.
Somos.
¿Seré o eres?
("I am. We are. Will I be or are you?")

Dutch

Mooi, dit idioom!
(Beautiful, this language!)

I also have a book by German poet Herbert Pfeiffer, called *Oh Cello voll Echo,* consisting of poems each of which is either one long palindrome or else a series of short palindromic lines. Obviously hopeless to translate.

Sky! Let's Parler Franglais, My Husband!

In 1978, Miles Kington, born in Northern Ireland, raised in Wales, and educated in Scotland, started writing a column in *Punch* called "Let's Parler Franglais!", a parody of British-style French phrasebooks and teaching methods. In a variety of typical phrasebook situations, Kington presented dialogues in which the characters spoke an abominable mixture of French and English — abominable but for that reason also uproarious. Eventually, a number of his columns were collected in a book of the same title. To give you a sense for this type of language use, I have selected just the opening remark of Lesson Deux, "Dans le Taxi":

Chauffeur: Marble Arch? Blimey, monsieur, c'est un peu dodgy aujourd'hui. Le traffic est absolument solide. C'est tout à fait murder. Il y a un tailback dans le Bayswater Road de Shepherds Bush jusqu'à flaming Lancaster Gate, mais si vous avez un couple d'heures spare... Personellement, je blâme le one-way system. Et la police. Le one-way system et la police. Je vous donne un typical exemple — chaque soir à cinq heures Hyde Park Corner est OK, un peu busy j'admets, mais basicallement OK, et puis la police arrive pour diriger le traffic et pouf! il y a un jam almighty *immédiatement.* Flaming flics. Je n'ai rien contre la police, marquez-vous, ils font un job terrifique, et moi je ne serais pas un gendarme pour tout le thé de Chine, mais ils sont un lot de thickies. (*Il sonne le klaxon.*) Maniaque! Excusez mon français, c'était un bleeding minicab. Vous prenez les minicabs quelquefois?

Suppose that someone wanted to translate this piece of humo(u)r into French. A first reaction might be, "It's half and half, so we can just leave it as is. What's sauce for the goose is sauce for the gander!" But a second glance reveals that that's crazy. The mix is so asymmetric, with everyone *"basicallement"* speaking English, with just *very easy* parts replaced by French (or fake French). If you love French, the experience of reading through this is somewhat akin to hearing a fingernail scratching against a chalkboard, but at the same time it is very funny. In fact, this type of humor is, or so it strikes me, a quintessentially British form of self-deprecation. Would a French audience go for such lacerating self-mockery? Or — since there has always been a cross-Channel rivalry — should we leave the mockery as is: of the Brits? What a dastardly thing to do! Perhaps what is really needed is not just *language* translation, but also *sense-of-humor* translation. In other words, change the entire approach. Restart from scratch. *Repartir de zéro.*

And so we turn to John-Wolf Whistle, as he calls himself, *né* Jean-Loup Chiflet, author of the delicious English-teaching booklet *Sky my husband!* and its sequel, *Sky! my teacher.* Both are extraordinarily playful collections of French expressions rendered both literally and idiomatically in English. I think you'll get the flavor when I quote you a passage from the latter book:

I like Paris. The streets I prefer are the street of the Dry-Tree, the street of the Ferry, the boulevard Good-News, the street of the Cat-who-Fishes, the street of the Look-for-Noon, the street Mister-the-Prince, the street of the Little-Fields, and the street Old-of-the-Temple. There are some places which I like very much, like the Game of Palm, the Doormanhouse, the theatre of the Madnesses-Shepherdesses, the hospital of the Fifteen-Twenty, the Prison of Health, and the big department stores like the Beautiful Gardener, the Good Market, the Spring. But what I prefer in Paris is to take the underground. I took it once at the Daughters-of-the-Calvary and went through the stations Star, White, Mute, Jasmine, Green-Path, Charenton-School, Door-of-the-Lilac, Door-of-the-Chapel, Military-School, Father-the-Chair, Crowns, Hotel-of-Town, New-Bridge, Bridge-Mary, Royal-Palace, and Door-Bathing-Suit. I forgot to say that I made a change at two stations called Montparnasse-Welcome and Marcadet-Fishmongers.

I find this not only amusing but also enormously thought-provoking. It harks back to the discussion in Chapter 11 of the translation of names, and all the strange, intangible haze and smoke churned up in the mind when it is carried out. Ever since I first visited Paris at age thirteen, I have had a deep love for the history-drenched names of its streets and Métro stops, but never before have I heard them in this bizarre, disorienting, almost frightening way. In fact, in *Sky! my teacher,* just below the just-cited paragraph, Chiflet provides a translation, and I think that that translation is worth reproducing here, just so that you can catch the breathtaking difference in flavor that arises when essentially nothing more complex than straightforward word-substitution is effected:

> J'aime Paris. Les rues que je préfère sont : la rue de l'Arbre-Sec, la rue du Bac, le boulevard Bonne-Nouvelle, la rue du Chat-qui-Pêche, la rue du Cherche-Midi, la rue Monsieur-le-Prince, la rue des Petits-Champs, et la rue Vieille-du-Temple. Il y a des endroits que j'aime beaucoup comme le Jeu de Paume, la Conciergerie, le théâtre des Folies-Bergère, l'hôpital des Quinze-Vingt, la Prison de la Santé, et les grands magasins tels que la Belle Jardinière, le Bon Marché, le Printemps. Mais ce que je préfère à Paris c'est prendre le métro. Je l'ai pris une fois à Filles-du-Calvaire et suis passé par les stations Étoile, Blanche, Muette, Jasmin, Chemin-Vert, Charenton-École, Porte des Lilas, Porte de la Chapelle, École Militaire, Père-Lachaise, Couronnes, Hôtel-de-Ville, Pont-Neuf, Pont-Marie, Palais-Royal, et Porte Maillot. J'ai oublié de dire que j'ai changé à deux stations appelées Montparnasse-Bienvenue et Marcadet-Poissonniers.

Whew! This is on the one hand trivial game-playing and on the other hand a stunning revelation. My head is spinning. And remember, we were led to it by considering what might be an appropriate French translation of Miles Kington's *Let's Parler Franglais!* Note that, *comme l'aurait voulu Ionesco,* Kington's London became Chiflet's Paris, and then Chiflet's anglicized Paris lost its Métro but gained an Underground... I mention the playwright Eugène Ionesco because it was he who made the unforgettable remark, "The French for London is Paris." Perhaps, then, Chiflet's first passage, the one in English, should have started out "I like London", not "I like Paris". What would you say, reader?

Just so that you don't go away without a sense of Chiflet's wonderful silliness, a Jacques Tati–esque silliness as French as French can get, here is a "review exercise" taken from *Sky my husband!* The task for "pupils" is to translate these parallel passages into idiomatic English (the answer is given on the next page):

> J'avais maille à partir avec un avocat marron à la mords-moi le nœud au nom à coucher dehors et qui avait pris la mouche et ne mâchait pas ses mots.

> I had stitch to leave with a brown avocado at the bite-me the knot at the name to sleep outside and who had taken the fly and was not chewing his words.

Native speakers of French will read the upper one without any serious trouble, while non-native speakers will read it once, rub their eyes, try it again, and say, "Wha-a-a-t?" The lower one, of course, is just a cloyingly literal translation of it into incomprehensible English gibberish. Here is one possible solution to the translation challenge, more American in style than British:

> I got onto the wrong side of this shady sleazeball of a lawyer with a tongue-twister of a name and he flew into a tizzy and minced no words with me.

Should I Take the Bus Now to Büsnau?

By the way, if Ionesco is right, and if Paris *is* indeed the French for London, then I'd like to know: What is the German for Kalamazoo? I don't ask this lightly, because I once got into quite some trouble for having given, by proxy, apparently quite the wrong answer. Here's the low-down. In my 1985 book *Metamagical Themas,* I wrote, for reasons that need not concern us here, the following few sentences:

> If I had no terraced-scan mechanism, I would be trapped in perpetual indecision, having no basis to decide to do anything, since I would need to evaluate *every pathway in depth* in order to decide whether or not to follow it. Should I take the bus to Kalamazoo today? Study out of a Smullyan book? Practice the piano? Read the latest *New York Review of Books*? Write an angry letter to someone in government?

Ten years later, I received a postcard from Germany addressed to me in no particular department at the (nonexistent) "University of Indiana" in Indianapolis, Indiana (I live in Bloomington, fifty miles away). In big letters next to this vague pseudo-address was written: "THIS IS A POSTCARD THAT REACHES ITS DESTINATION!" Prophetic words, since it somehow did. Its author, Mr. Nils Thode, upbraided me in the following manner:

Dear Mr. Hofstadter,
    enjoying the german version of your book "Metamagical Themas", I came over a paragraph in the postscriptum of chapter five that really puzzled me. In the first chapters of the book you talked about the sentence "This sentence in English is difficult to translate into German."
    Later, reading chapter five, I learned about your way of choosing what to do next. You mentioned some possible things you could do: Read a book written by Smullyan or play the piano or, and these two possibilitiess struck me odd, take the bus to Büsnau or read the color supplement of the german newspaper "Die Zeit".
    This must have been an English sentence that the translator of the book found very difficult to translate into german. Did you really thought about taking the bus to Büsnau? Although I do not really know where Büsnau is, I do not believe that there is bus travelling from Indiana University campus to Büsnau. If

there is one it must be behind schedule for years or there has been a significant revolution in public transport that no one told me about.

Also, I wonder if you really read "Die Zeit", a german weekly newspaper that takes you about a week to read, which would be o.k., but on the other hand it also takes you some days to get the paper home unless you know somebody who would borrow you his caterpillar. One is always behind with reading!

It is a very, very thick newspaper it is not what anybody would call an easy-to-read-paper and I never saw it anywhere outside Germany.

Please tell me: Did you instruct the translator of the book to include Büsnau and "Die Zeit" or was it his own idea? Did you, as a man spending most of his time in Germany (?), make a joke about Brüsnau, that funny little town (??) that you cracked so many jokes about whilst reading "Die Zeit" (???) or was it an invention of the translator(s) ?

I really hope that you find the time to send me a brief answer,

Sincerly, yours

Nils Thode

Well, upon receiving this rather chastising note, I pulled out the copy of *Metamagical Themas* that I'd annotated for the benefit of translators, and there saw, in black and white, in my handwriting, the word "Kalamazoo" circled and a marginal annotation saying "local town in your culture"; likewise, "*New York Review of Books*" was circled and a nearby note in the margin said "use some popular intellectual book review". So the German translators had followed my instructions to the letter, but Mr. Thode was mightily displeased (or rather, made a cute joke feigning displeasure).

But what was the alternative? I could have told the translators to boringly leave me in the United States, musing about whether to dash off to some random small town with a funny name or to dip into some highbrow American book review — but the spirit of the book is playful and lively, and keeping that spirit in other languages necessitates fanciful reconstruction. That's why I had requested translators to play around, to have some fun, as long as they didn't do anything so radical as to start creating absurdities. And that's where Mr. Thode enters the picture.

To be sure, this little passage as I originally wrote it had a slightly *autobiographical* quality to it, in the sense that it refers to the real me, and as such, to my Americanness. Turning me into a German, or even into an American living in Germany, would have been a falsification of history (although not if I had written the sentence in late 1974, when I was living in Regensburg). But the autobiographical quality was *so* mild and *so* fleeting that I felt that, for the sake of making the picture just a tad more vivid for non-American readers, it would be harmless if my translators committed a tiny transgression of truth, and in so doing *respected spirit by violating letter.*

But Mr. Thode — or at least the stern persona he put on — would have none of that intellectual dishonesty. Buses crossing the Atlantic? An American plowing through a German newspaper so fat that it has to be transported by tractor? The book's American author constantly wondering whether to sally forth on a jaunt to some unheard-of teensy-weensy podunk in rural Germany? Vivid, yes, but far too silly. Ergo, back to boringness. Well, at least that was the posture that Mr. Thode pretended to believe in. But whether he was being serious or tongue-in-cheek, he raised some very interesting and important points in that posture.

This idea that the process of translation can in certain cases act in such a way as to *substantially tamper with the identity of the author* is one that we have seen before (the fights with Bob and Jacqueline over rugby and "not at all"; my "blue moon" typo), and it will return in a few pages. We will out-Thode Mr. Thode and find a new and different nexus of untranslatability.

Uncl!

Back in Chapter 5, we first saw Giuseppe Varaldo's virtuosic sonnets on Dante's *Inferno,* Rostand's *Cyrano de Bergerac,* and Nabokov's *Lolita.* But those only scratched the surface of Varaldo's book. It is chock-full of similar feats, including hyperlipogrammatic translational compressions of the Book of Genesis from the Bible, Homer's *Odyssey,* Æsop's Fables, works by Aristotle, Aristophanes, Xenophon, Lucretius, Ovid, and the Latin fabulist Phaedrus, as well as *The Decameron* by Boccaccio, *The Arabian Nights, Don Quixote* by Cervantes, *King Lear,* Swift's *Gulliver's Travels,* Lawrence Sterne's *Tristram Shandy,* a Goethe novel, Leopardi poetry, tales by Poe, Melville's *Moby Dick, Les fleurs du mal* by Baudelaire, Collodi's *Pinocchio,* Kafka's *Metamorphosis,* and, last but certainly not least, James Joyce's *Ulysses* and Marcel Proust's *A la recherche du temps perdu.*

It is a bit hard for me to imagine compressing the latter novel's 2,000 pages of dense text — or for that matter, any of these pillars of Western literature — into a fourteen-line nugget. When you further insist that the poetic compression have rhyme and meter, *and* that it all be done with just one vowel — well, that crosses the threshold of inconceivability, as far as I'm concerned. It sounds like trying to hoist oneself up a fifty-foot rope using just one finger.

But the *culmen rer' omnium* is, as far as I'm concerned, what Varaldo did with Phaedrus' Latin fables. This is where a classical European classical education really looks classy. Phaedrus lived from roughly 15 B.C. to 50 A.D., and was known for his animal-based fables, some of which were translations of Æsop's fables, others of which were original. For these, Varaldo, spurning the usual "easy tricks" of his native language, ties his last finger down: Now he must do it all in Latin, and on top of that with only the vowel "u". Doesn't that take the cake? I hereby present Varaldo's monovocalic condensation of Phaedrus' Fables, without even attempting to make a translation for you. Surely on Latinity you're longer far than I.

Musculus, mulus, vultur, vulnus ultum,
ursus, bubulcus, guttur, summus Dux,
nummulus, crudus fructus, furum frux
unum sunt: dum suburunt, pungunt multum,

Rutulûm ludunt lucrum, luxum, cultum.
Trunculum lustrum, mundum lupus trux,
suum grus vult: tunc funus, fucus, crux
rursum funduntur, rursum ruunt stultum.

Succurrunt currus, pullus, vulgus rurum:
pupulus mulsus sum... nunc mustum udum,
furfur nunc vulsus, crustulum nunc durum:

subsunt tumultus, lutum, ulcus nudum...
Tum vultum tundunt, tum subtutum murum
rumpunt, ut curvum fulgur pulchrum sudum.

Back in Chapter 5, I managed to "translate", in a very diluted sense of the term, my three favorite sonnets by Varaldo into sonnets in unrestricted English. But, as I pointed out then, doing so is about as half-hearted as translating Marot's "Ma Mignonne" or Pushkin's *Eugene Onegin* into rhyme-free, nonmetrical prose: it is to miss the entire essence of those works. It would of course be ideal, but I do not know if it is possible, to be more faithful to Varaldo in English. Could the phenomenally restrictive constraints of monovocalicity or biconsonanticity be respected *as well*?

If somebody put to me this challenge: "Preserving the meaning on a line-by-line basis, convert Varaldo's 'u'-only Latin sonnet on Phaedrus' Fables into a 'u'-only English sonnet", I would simply throw up my hands and cry "Uncl!" However, if the translation challenge were interpreted at a slightly higher level — "Construct *your own* monovocalic English sonnet summarizing Dante's *Inferno*", for instance — then I would not be so cocksure. I seriously doubt that I myself would be capable of carrying off such a task, but I wouldn't necessarily put it beyond the range of any and all anglophonic mortals, past, present, future, or potential. I can dimly imagine such a thing being done.

I would never in my life have guessed that such a thing could be done in Italian, but it *was* done. However, I suspect that writing monovocalically is somewhat harder in English, in part because our vowel sounds are so often spelled as diphthongs ("ie", "ou", "ay", and so on), which rules out a very large class of words at the outset. But — with the extra degree of freedom of *choosing your own manner of summarizing Dante* — I can still imagine someone doing a decent job. Of course, no one can objectively specify what "faithful summary of *The Inferno*" means, but then again, no one can objectively specify what "well-constructed sonnet" means either.

The challenge gets even harder if one tries to imagine translating Varaldo's extraordinary sonnets into, say, Chinese, where the concept of "just one vowel" does not exist, since the writing system is not phonetic. Perhaps the definition of the constraint could be shifted from the *graphic* into the *phonetic* realm, meaning that only one vowel *sound* would be allowed in a Chinese translation. (This would essentially amount to making the poem's pinyin romanization monovocalic.) Or, if one stuck to Chinese characters, then perhaps there would be some way to forbid large numbers of characters by limiting the radicals that could be used, or simply by disallowing some number of the commonest characters in the language. Here, the problem of translation includes an aspect that is normally quite hidden in the background — namely, the radical translation of a constraint as it passes from one framework to another.

I won't delve any further into the morass that translating Varaldo's mini-literature might entail; suffice it to say that for me it represents not only a stupendously difficult challenge, but also — in stark contrast to the idea of translating many types of wordplay — one of elegance and charm.

Scientists Baffled: George Washington Spotted on Venus!!!

Here is a sonorous sonnet for you, based on a famous painting.

Washington Crossing the Delaware

A hard, howling, tossing water scene:
Strong tide was washing hero clean.
"How cold!" Weather stings as in anger.
O silent night shows war ace danger!

The cold waters swashing on in rage.
Redcoats warn slow his hint engage.
When general's star action wish'd "Go!"
He saw his ragged continentals row.

Ah, he stands — sailor crew went going,
And so this general watches rowing.
He hastens — Winter again grows cold;
A wet crew gain Hessian stronghold.

George can't lose war with 's hands in;
He's astern — so, go alight, crew, and win!

Reading this vivid poem, could anyone fail to feel the raw whipping of the winds, the violence of the waves, the threat of the oncoming Brits, the bravery of our valiant Johnnys…

Well, yes — it's a little odd, I admit. Some of the lines, like the one about the redcoats, are a bit hard to parse. And does "anger" *really* rhyme with "danger"? Here and there, the poem seems somewhat forced. Still, such defects might be excused when one considers that David Shulman, its author, was working under duress when he penned it sometime in 1936. Like a poor soul penned in jail, Shulman was deprived of certain luxuries. Indeed, paying a kind of complementary lipo-service to Varaldo in his Latin incarnation, Shulman deprived himself of "u", though he allowed himself all other vowels (actually, not "y" either). Well, is that all there is to it?

As a matter of fact, no. In vain will one seek any of the letters "b", "f", "j", "k", "m", "p", "q", "v", "x", "y", and "z". *Now* we're starting to talk constraints! Indeed, what letters do appear in this poem? The answer — and I hope this knocks your socks off — is: exactly the letters in the poem's title, and no others. This is quite a lipogram, after all.

And yet, there is more. Notice that on every line, there is a "w". Or rather, two of them. But why? Because there are two "w"'s in the poem's title! And similarly, on every line there are exactly three "a"'s — again, an inheritance from the title. And so on down the line. In a word, in this fully metric and rhyming sonnet, every single line is a perfect anagram of the title, and still the whole thing basically makes sense. We have here a *tour de force,* no other word for it.

If you're looking for tangledness of medium with message, this is about as extreme an example as I think you're likely to find. It is a wonderful, inimitable word-carving inextricably married to the English language. The hope of shoehorning it into Italian or Latin or Chinese or any other tongue is about as plausible as the scenario of humans landing on Venus and finding a creature indistinguishable from George Washington standing proudly among a boatload of troops rowing across a river indistinguishable from the Delaware, on their way to liberate dear Venus from the shackles of the imperial Red Planet. Not a good bet.

Wordplay Books, Familiar and Foreign

I found this poem in the book *Making the Alphabet Dance,* a culling by Ross Eckler of many sorts of wordplay in English from the pages of the magazine *Word Ways,* which for over two decades he has coedited and published with his wife Faith. The book is a vast collection of linguistic oddities — the weirdest, most idiosyncratic, most eccentric particularities of the English language that are known, as unearthed by centuries of ingenious language-scourers and, more recently, by amazingly complex computational searches, far more mindless than the humans whose labors have preceded them, but nonetheless very thorough and impressive.

Some of the book is beautiful, much more is dull — but that's not the point. I'd simply like to ask: Could such a book be translated into another tongue? To be sure, one could straightforwardly translate just the plain prose annotations of the various discoveries, but doing that would be a bit like taking a group of blind people to an art museum, then having a tour guide lead them through the galleries, explaining in great detail each picture on the wall. It might well have some value for the people in the party, but if one cannot appreciate the paintings directly, the experience would be a "pallid copy" indeed of what it would be for a sighted person.

In a sense, I speak from experience. I was once given a copy of the book *Opperlandse taal- & letterkunde* by Hugo Brandt Corstius, who told me his name is also "Battus". The word *Opperlands* is a parody of the word *Nederlands*, which is Dutch for "Dutch", and it means "Upperlandese" (as opposed to "Netherlandese"). Battus' book is a magisterial and canonical assemblage of almost every imaginable type of wordplay in the Dutch language (which he always poker-facedly refers to as *Opperlands*). As would seem logical, the book consists of intermingled displays of virtuosic wordplay (called *letterkunde*, meaning "literature") and straightforward commentaries thereupon (called *taalkunde*, meaning "philology"). Since I spent several months studying Dutch many years ago, I can pretty well make out what the *taalkunde* says about the *letterkunde*, but when I try to actually appreciate the *letterkunde* directly, I find myself nearly as lost as if I didn't know one single word of Dutch. It is just way, way above my head. I mean, take just these few examples, which are all found on the book's front cover:

bid
pijpetuitje
Prijst gij mijn ij-rijm?
galblaaskwaalschandaal
hottentottentententententoonstelling
Lekkerkerkerkerkerkerkerker
operetterepertoirerepetitor
nepparterretrappen
kraaieëieren
galmnop
skijool
gemeentereinigingsroltrommelhuisvuilophaalauto's

Whether you know one word of Dutch or not, you can pick up the basic idea of many of these as easily as can a native speaker. (Dutch does have an odd charm, doesn't it?) Clearly we are dealing with symmetries, lipograms, monovocalisms, repeated syllables, anagrams, long sequences of vowels alone, alphabetic segments embedded in words, and just plain old humongous compound words. But it's one thing to gawk at it with pleasure from the outside, as I do, and another thing to feel the *semantics* lurking inside these bizarre structures. What must it be like to be Dutch and to savor these crazy things? Could this be the answer: "It is exactly like being a native speaker of English and reading *Making the Alphabet Dance*"?

While this sounds very appealing, it somehow feels deeply wrong to me. It sounds like saying that to someone Dutch, speaking Dutch feels no different from how speaking English feels to me. It sounds like saying that to Thais, eating *pad thai* tastes exactly like eating spaghetti tastes to Italians. It sounds like saying that swishing lickety-split down a powdery-white slope felt to Johann Claudius Killy just like improvising an intricate fugue felt to Jean-Sébastien Ruisseau. It sounds like saying that bowling a beautiful series of strikes and spares that lands you a smashing 250 affords the same thrill to a pretty good bowler as blasting the brains out of every damn rhino in sight affords some money-lusting macho game poacher in Tanzania. Or, for that matter, it sounds like saying that having *those* kids over *there* feels to their parents exactly like having *my* children feels to *me*. Does being you feel exactly to *you* like being me feels to *me*? Is being in love with one person exactly the same as being in love with another person? At the close of Stravinsky's *Histoire du soldat,* there are the words *Un bonheur est tout le bonheur.* Is everything in life that modular and interchangeable?

Hearing a Language from Inside versus from Outside

Suppose someone wanted to help us outsiders get *inside* Battus' book, by translating all of its *taalkunde* into English, then publishing the book with all the Dutch wordplay as is: in Dutch. This would be a bizarre, half-hearted thing to do. One could go further, however, and translate not just the *taalkunde,* but also — in a totally literal fashion, of course — every last piece of *letterkunde* (*i.e.,* add English glosses to the Dutch wordplay). If this were done, then the pea-soup fog of, say, *hottentottentententententoonstelling* would soon be dispersed by the bright warm sunlight of "Hottentot tent exposition", *galblaaskwaalschandaal* would be similarly clarified as "gall-bladder disease scandal", and the vowelly mystery of *kraaieëieren* would dissolve into the pristine and simple limpidity of "crows' eggs".

But in a sense this is all very artificial and superficial. After all, I could just make up any old funny-looking word — *bilitulibulitibutitulibitilubitulu* — and tell you it means "the late greengrocer's ski-jumping daughter's third successive failed marriage" in some obscure dialect of Uttermingulian. I could even break it all down for you, revealing which piece corresponds to "ski-jumping", which to "third", and so forth. But so what? You have to be really *inside* the language to *feel* how this, or any other, sequence of sounds or string of marks actually denotes and connotes ideas.

Indeed, when I first saw Varaldo's sonnets, they looked sort of like this to me. It was only when I translated several of them that my eyes started losing their glaze and I could feel I was reading them with understanding. And — I hate to admit this, but — the same goes for Chiflet's colloquial French sentence above, about that "sleazeball of a lawyer with a tongue-twister of a name". When I first read it, it made absolutely no sense to me at all — me, a supposedly fluent speaker of French who has at times passed for native! Hah! Even after translating it and knowing what each piece means, I still can't *feel* it. Those weird idioms, even if I've now memorized them, aren't yet in my linguistic bloodstream, they're not yet under my skin, they're still just *on* my skin. Someday, maybe…

But back to the central question: Are Eckler's *Making the Alphabet Dance* and Battus' *Opperlandse taal- & letterkunde* translations of each other? Certainly they play similar roles to each other in their respective language communities, but no, the answer is a resounding *no*. Calling them each other's translations would be about as plausible as saying Hugo's *Les Misérables* is a French translation of Dickens' *Great Expectations,* or Pushkin's *Eugene Onegin* is a Russian translation of Byron's *Don Juan. Bú shì! Bú shì!*

The way I would put it is that *Making the Alphabet Dance* is literally untranslatable: it is hopeless to think of translating it on any level at all. On the one hand, it is very much *like* certain other creations on the surface of our earth, but on the other hand, it is entirely *sui generis.* Aren't we all?

A Sallowsian Packing-it-all-in

In an article entitled "Reflexicons" in the journal *Word Ways,* the journal just mentioned, my friend Lee Sallows writes:

> A lexicon is a dictionary or a list of words. Hence my use of "reflexive lexicon", or, more crisply, *reflexicon,* for a self-descriptive word list that describes its own letter frequencies:

*

trois a,
trois c, trois d,
neuf e, quatre f, deux h,
neuf i, six n, quatre o, deux p,
cinq q, six r, sept s,
huit t, neuf u,
cinq x

*

Immortal verity sans superfluity. Now that is what I call *belles lettres!*

If you stop to think about this elegant pattern, you will see that it is a remarkable object, as delicately balanced as a genuine diamond somehow standing on one of its vertices. Look at the first word — *trois*. This tells us that there are three occurrences of "a". But suppose we counted and found out there were actually just two "a"'s — could we just patch things up by changing *trois* to *deux*? Absolutely no way, for that little act would *increase* the counts for "d", "e", "u", "and "x", and at the same time *decrease* the counts for "t", "r", "o", "i", and "s". At that point, the pattern's self-descriptivity would have completely toppled over, like a precariously balanced diamond that had been blown on, just ever so lightly, the tiniest split second before. All the words — all the letters — in this sparkling logological diamond have been calculated to the most finely intertwined, mutually locking-in accuracy.

Sallows was led to the quest of sparkling word-diamonds of this sort through an earlier investigation of self-inventorying sentences. The story, though fascinating, is too long to tell here. The main point is that Rudy Kousbroek — the selfsame Rudy Kousbroek whom we met in Chapter 7 wearing his hat as a Queneau translator — published an article in which appeared the following breathtaking Dutch sentence:

Dit pangram bevat vijf a's, twee b's, twee c's, drie d's, zesenveertig e's, vijf f's, vier g's, twee h's, vijftien i's, vier j's, een k, twee l's, twee m's, zeventien n's, een o, twee p's, een q, zeven r's, vierentwintig s's, zestien t's, een u, elf v's, acht w's, een x, een y, en zes z's.

whose word-for-word anglicization would be:

This pangram contains five a's, two b's, two c's, three d's, forty-six e's, five f's, four g's, two h's, fifteen i's, four j's, one k, two l's, two m's, seventeen n's, one o, two p's, one q, seven r's, twenty-four s's, sixteen t's, one u, eleven v's, eight w's, one x, one y, and six z's.

("Pangram", by the way, whether in Dutch or English, means a sentence containing all twenty-six letters of the alphabet.) If you take the trouble to check it out, you will find that Kousbroek's Dutch sentence is true, whereas the anglicization underneath it is a brazen lie, if the phrase "this pangram" is taken as a *self*-reference rather than as an "*other*-reference" pointing back to the Dutch original. For example, the lower sentence contains just *one* "b", not two.

Sallows, whose own earlier explorations into the possibility of self-documenting sentences had been the spark behind Kousbroek's article, felt eclipsed, but also challenged by the idea of creating what he called a "magic" English translation of Kousbroek's sentence, meaning an English sentence that not only would have the exact same form, but also would be *true*. Driven by this desire, Sallows actually designed and built a marvelous analogue computer as a tool for the exploration of "logological space", and his months of hard labor were in the end rewarded with many delicious fruits, including this true sentence:

This pangram contains four a's, one b, two c's, one d, thirty e's, six f's, five g's, seven h's, eleven i's, one j, one k, two l's, two m's, eighteen n's, fifteen o, two p's, one q, five r's, twenty-seven s's, eighteen t's, two u's, seven v's, eight w's, two x's, three y's, & one z.

So exultant was Sallows over his successful translation that he wrote an article about how he found it, concluding with the words, "Let none suppose that anything but poetry has been our purpose here." And I certainly subscribe to his point of view: This is poetry translation at a high level indeed.

Some, of course, might quibble. Lee Sallows' sentence is clearly an English-language *counterpart* to Rudy Kousbroek's Dutch pangram. Why, however, claim that the two are *translations* of each other? Why doesn't my skepticism about counterparts being each other's translations, emphasized just two pages ago in my absolute rejection of the notion that Battus' and Eckler's wordplay books might be each other's translations, hold true here?

For me, the answer is clear: Sallows' and Kousbroek's sentences are profoundly and precisely *isomorphic*, whereas the Battus and Eckler books, though alike at the broad-brushstroke level, don't have anything remotely resembling a piece-to-piece correspondence. The great thing about Lee Sallows' pangram is that it does in English exactly what the Dutch pangram does in Dutch. In a very *deep* sense, the two sentences play the same roles in their respective logological spaces. What more could one possibly want?

Well, one could also want the mapping to work in a very *shallow* sense, one's source of discontent being the fact that where Kousbroek's pangram has *five* "a"'s, Sallows' has just *four* — and down the line it goes, discrepancy after discrepancy. In one's most extreme fantasies, one might hope to find a self-inventorying pangram in Language X that, when translated *word for word* into Language Y, would yield *another* true self-inventorying pangram. Such a hope, though sweet, is very naïve; it is comparable to hoping to find a deeply accurate, rhyming, metric English translation of "Ma Mignonne" that also enjoys, on each and every line, the same *word-count* as does the original, and even further, has the property that corresponding words have *identical numbers of letters* in them! For that matter, why not throw in the constraint that corresponding words must begin with identical letters? This goes way beyond what one normally demands of the notion of translation.

A total isomorphism on every level would be delightful, but it has never turned up in Sallows' ardent research into these sorts of logological phenomena over quite a number of years. And it probably never will. In that extremely idealistic sense, Sallows' diamond and Kousbroek's pangram are probably forever untranslatable.

Reference and Rigidism

There is a certain peculiar philosophy of translation — I will call its adherents the "rigidists" — that would insist that Lee Sallows' English pangram fails utterly as a translation of Rudy Kousbroek's Dutch pangram, but for an altogether different reason — namely, because *the two sentences talk about different things*. Let me spell this out more concretely. Rigidists would claim that the following bizarre sentence is a *correct* anglicization of Kousbroek's sentence:

Rudy Kousbroek's Dutch pangram contains five a's, two b's, two c's, three d's, forty-six e's, five f's, four g's, two h's, fifteen i's, four j's, one k, two l's, two m's, seventeen n's, one o, two p's, one q, seven r's, twenty-four s's, sixteen t's, one u, eleven v's, eight w's, one x, one y, and six z's.

Rigidists would say that self-reference of an entity in Framework 1 does not translate into self-reference of a counterpart entity in Framework 2, for the simple reason that *literal reference is sacrosanct*. Thus a passage in English on some feature of English grammar would have to *remain* about English grammar when translated into French; no "coattails effect" is allowed, whereby English grammar is replaced by French grammar! An event on a bus in Paris related originally in French would have to *remain* on a bus in Paris when the story was translated into Dutch; no "coattails effect" is allowed, whereby Paris turns into Amsterdam. This all sounds pretty commonsensical, but does it really hold up under careful scrutiny? Could it serve as the basis for a thoroughgoing philosophy of translation?

Suppose we are in a novel where a woman is complaining to a friend about her teen-aged daughter's sloppy speech, and says, "Don't they teach them the difference between 'lay' and 'lie' any more in school?" When this novel is translated into French, should the two English verbs be kept intact? What is really behind this statement? On the surface, it's about two specific English verbs, but below the surface, it's about the decaying state of schools, about disrespect for language, and such things. One could translate it in many ways, among them these: keeping the two English verbs intact; substituting two oft-confused French words for them; or simply converting it into a more general complaint about the quality of language education in high schools. There's often a big distinction between what a sentence overtly *refers* to, and what its more hidden *topic* is. But to rigidists, what counts is always what's right there on the surface: reference *über alles*.

Take Kousbroek's sentence. Since it begins with the words *Dit pangram,* the referent is Kousbroek's sentence, not some other sentence in some other language. And for rigidists, this fact must be respected in any act of translation, period. A translation must point to *Kousbroek's* sentence, not to *itself*. Never mind that the sole and whole *point* of the sentence is the delightful, dizzying medium–message marriage that it epitomizes. "Point, shmoint!", say rigidists. "You give me *referents,* I'll give you a translation, all right? No monkey business about *points* and *topics.* Is it a deal?"

No, it's not a deal. It's a bankrupt absurdity. Take the movie *Roxanne,* comedian Steve Martin's marvelous transtemporation of the play *Cyrano de Bergerac* into twentieth-century America. In it, Martin himself plays the part of the counterpart of Cyrano, a fellow known as "C. D. Bales" (note the initials). Now a rigidist would say, "Cyrano got enraged when people made fun of his enormous nose. Although it's true that his nose was part of his own body, and in that sense it had to do with *himself,* we rigidists are not interested in hidden abstractions like 'self' or 'self-reference'. We are interested in the actual, physical, concrete referents — specific rocks, specific towns, specific people, specific objects — *those* are what reference is all about. We rigidists are solemnly dedicated to the preservation of the concrete destinations of pointers. And the one supercritical object in *Cyrano de Bergerac,* the most important thing in the whole play, for God's sake, is Cyrano's nose. Ergo, for true fidelity in translation, what should *really* get C. D. Bales hoppin' mad is when folks make fun of Cyrano de Bergerac's humongous honker. C. D. Bales should blow his top at that!"

Well, rigidists will blow their own tops when they go to see the movie and find that, of all things, C. D. Bales gets upset when folks make fun of his *own* nose, not the Cyranose. What perfidy! How did the translation police ever let Steve Martin get away with such sloppy, nonrigid junk?

Or consider translators of "Ma Mignonne", who, with similar perfidy and sloppiness, refer in English to "going out the *door*" and to "eating *jams*", when we know so well that Marot's *porte* and our English "door" refer to entirely different cultural archetypes, much as do *confitures* and "jam". In order to evoke the proper cultural archetypes, mustn't those nouns, and other nouns, be *left in French*? And indeed, does not the verb *aller* refer to a quintessentially French mode of locomotion, whereas "go" gives off an unmistakable aroma of how anglophones perform self-propulsion? Ergo, shouldn't all verbs — and, by analogy, all prepositions, adjectives, etc. — be left in French, to ensure that only the proper France-based cultural archetypes will be evoked in the reader's mind? Isn't Marot's original "Ma Mignonne" *in French* its own ideal — and sole — English translation, then?

As I say this, my tongue is half in my cheek, half not. Do not forget how hard I argued in favor of blending fragments of the source language straight into the target language, citing with great enthusiasm my mother's "oo-la-la" and Melanie Mitchell's "your Bastille", and then later praising Robert Forward's frame-blendy language in *Dragon's Egg,* and on the other hand using as my favorite whipping-goats the purer-than-thou, absurdly non-frame-blended styles of translation in *Ivan Denisovich* and *Chinese Lives.*

Yes, part of me fights hard to maintain noticeable traces, little nuggets, of the original culture and time in the output text. Indeed, I can be as rigidist as the next philosopher. But most of the time, I'm not.

The Nose-touching Game

Like all good things, keeping pointers pointing rigidly at their original referents can be carried too far — far too far. Translation, after all, *does* mean a shifting of frameworks. It is *not* a mechanical photocopying operation. It is a deliberate *changing* along many dimensions at once.

If I touch my nose and say to you, "Do this!", you will almost certainly touch your own nose, rather than reaching over and touching mine (especially if I am in Kalamazoo and you are in Büsnau). Occasionally a child will reach up and touch the toucher's nose, but in such cases, we tend to smile with amusement at their innocence, rather than admiring their purity and intellectual honesty. Children are simple, we grown-ups are more sophisticated. We know that a shift in frameworks may often entail certain shifts in referents, rigidists notwithstanding. Not in all referents, of course. If I point up to the moon in the sky and say, "Do this!", you too, just like a child, will point at that same moon, rather than trying to find "your own moon". In that sense, we are all rigidists and all children.

But what if Cyrano de Bergerac himself made a quick little *saut* into the twentieth century, sauntered up my brick walkway, knocked at my door, and when I answered, barefoot and bleary-eyed in my black-and-white zebra-striped bathrobe, pointed to his prominent *pif* and said to me, in my own native language, "*Monsieur le professeur, s'il vous plaît*, do *this*!"? What should I do? Point to my own completely undistinguished, average-sized nose? Is that not an utter travesty of the act just committed by Mr. de Bergerac? If I happen to have a big macho chin, should I not point at that distinguishing feature, instead? Perhaps not, since Cyrano's nose is meant to be the opposite of what might attract females. So suppose I have a very *weak* chin, every bit as weak as poor Cyrano's nose is bulbous — is that worrisome part of my anatomy, then, not the appropriate target for my own finger? Or, speaking of fingers, suppose I have a grotesquely outsized index finger, twice as long as the average person's? Should I not point at *that*, using, using — well, using *itself*?

From Index Fingers to Indexicals

Although I did not do so deliberately, it is probably not an accident that in this context, I wound up focusing on the notion of "index finger", because "indexical" is the technical term that philosophers use to designate words that depend on a speaker-dependent "coordinate system", or frame of reference — words like "I", "you", "here", "now", "this", "that". They draw a small, tight circle separating the special little family of "indexical" words from the vast majority of words, which they see as not being indexical at all. As they so often do, philosophers — or at least many of them — want the distinctions they make to be black-and-white, perhaps so that they can quickly shift into "formal mode", using the machinery of symbolic logic in which to couch all their discussions. This dismal tradition of shoehorning everything from ships to sealing wax into predicate logic stretches back to Bertrand Russell, and to me it seems as if it will die out very slowly, if ever.

The problem with this notion of "indexicals" is that it is anything but black-and-white. Virtually every word in every piece of text has a certain degree of "indexicality" to it, but figuring out the nature of the mix is very subtle. To make this clear, let me go back and take up once again Nils Thode's humorous lament.

What did I *really* mean when I wrote, "Shall I take the bus to Kalamazoo today?"? Was I really referring to a specific small town in southwest Michigan? Did I really care where? Or was I instead getting at the abstract concept *small random town reachable by bus*? In other words, to what extent was I referring to a place in my *own* coordinate system, and how much was I referring to a place in a *generic* coordinate system?

And by saying "today", was I really referring to the precise day on which I wrote the sentence, and no other day? Should a diligent and faithful translator therefore contact me to find out the date on which the sentence was actually written, and plug that date in where "today" stands? Or did I simply mean "any day at all — today, for example"?

And was I really referring to the specific idea of *taking a bus voyage to a small random town*? Or was I instead using a silly throwaway scenario invented purely off the cuff (and clearly so, given the flip tone in which it was expressed) to suggest the general idea of *doing something far-fetched*?

And when I wrote "I", that *nec plus ultra* of indexicality, was I really referring to myself exclusively, or was I using the pronoun in a casual, light manner to suggest both myself and, at the very same time, a more generic person, perhaps even the reader?

The messy but unavoidable truth of the matter is that all of these different facets were blurred together in what I *really* meant, because, on the one hand, I know that the power of words lies in their concreteness, and so in this case I chose very down-to-earth examples centered on my own experience because their reality for me lends them a ring of authenticity, which in turn helps them to come across vividly to the reader — and yet, on the other hand, I was certainly talking the whole time about abstractions that had nothing to do with Kalamazoo or that particular day or bus trips or myself. I was saying, "Does a person consider every conceivable alternative before deciding what to do?", but I was saying it in a down-to-earth, egocentric manner, setting up a blend between the reader and myself even though on the surface no blend was visible.

If one takes the surface as sacrosanct, then one is a rigidist. I am not a rigidist. I don't know if Mr. Thode is, but he did a good job of pretending to be one. Perhaps he is just good at sarcasm.

Seven, the Itch Year

Near the end of the film *The Seven Year Itch,* in my opinion a sublime mixture of the touching and the hilarious, there is a special scene in which the sweet blonde bimbo, who remains nameless for the entire film but is played by Marilyn Monroe, is in the kitchen of her newfound married friend and quasi-romance, Richard (played by Tom Ewell). The two of them have just woken up after she slept over in his apartment, *sans* hanky-panky, he on the couch and she all alone in his bedroom. Suddenly, in bursts a big hulking macho friend of the family and Richard tries desperately to cover up the presence of a woman in the apartment. But the friend gets a whiff from the kitchen and asks, "Is that coffee I smell?" Richard denies it, but his friend persists: "Are you *sure* that's not coffee?"

Despite his desire for a good cup of coffee, the friend is not suspicious of any monkey business, but Richard, on the other hand, is so drenched in his own guilt and shame that he simply can't keep himself from pathetically blurting out, "I can explain *everything* — the stairs, the cinnamon toast, the blonde in the kitchen —"

At this, of course, the friend perks up and says, "Now wait a minute, Dickie boy — let's just take it easy! *What* blonde in the kitchen?"

Richard scoffs, "Huh! Wouldn't *you* like to know? Maybe it's Marilyn Monroe!"

A great line. Just think about what the name "Marilyn Monroe" would evoke in these two average-Joe types. It would have to be an image of a beautiful, sexy blonde movie star, and right there at the forefront of the halo conjured up in their minds would be one or two of her movies, quite possibly including *The Seven Year Itch*. After all, Richard and his friend are living right at about the time *The Seven Year Itch* came out — not necessarily before it or after it, just somewhere vaguely in that era. So they might both have already seen the film! In a way, it's a very Pushkinesque line, mixing real life subtly and gracefully in with the fictional story, only for a fleeting moment and then letting it fade.

Well, now. Let us imagine that twenty years from now, in the year 2016, a remake called *Seven, the Itch Year* is being shot — with, of course, in the role originally played by Marilyn Monroe, my very own by-then grown-up and lovely daughter Monica Marie... And so we arrive at the crucial scene, with the interloping macho friend having just said to the new instantiation of Richard, "Now wait a minute, Dickie boy — let's just take it easy! *What* blonde in the kitchen?"

My question for you is, how does this new Richard reply? Of course, the obvious answer is, "Huh! Wouldn't *you* like to know? Maybe it's Monica Marie!" Or rather, this would be the obvious answer for the non-rigidists out there. Its rationale is clear enough: the original pointer was not pointing at Marilyn Monroe herself (though rigidists would say it was), but at *whoever* the actress was that was playing that role. That was the whole joke: the Pushkinesque level-mixing self-reference.

But I have another suggestion for what Richard could say. He could say, "Huh! Wouldn't *you* like to know? Maybe it's Marilyn Monroe!" Now this may catch you off guard, as it seems that I, of all people, am retreating to a rigidist position after all. But I would argue that this is actually a *less* rigidist answer than the previous one. My explanation goes like this.

The name "Marilyn Monroe" in that future year will still exude strong connotations of the then-sixty-year-old movie *The Seven Year Itch,* and the suggested remark by Richard, implicitly mapping the now-hot movie star Monica Marie onto the old-time movie star Marilyn Monroe, will thus remind people that *this whole movie* is, in a certain sense, *playing the role* of the old movie, but in a new era. This movie is to the old movie as both Marilyn Monroe and Monica Marie are to the ditzy blonde in the kitchen. Thus instead of giving rise to a simple self-reference wholly *internal* to the film *Seven, the Itch Year,* this remark would get in the same joke of "maybe a famous movie star connected with this film is in the kitchen", and also would be a subtle tip of the hat by the brand-new film to its ancient source.

Well, for better or for worse, that's what *I* would propose for the screenplay. It might get vetoed, but I'd push for it.

Nagrobek wierszowany Marota

It was inevitable, I suppose, that we would sooner or later come face to face with the idea of translating *this* book. Well, to be blunt, I will just come out and say that in my opinion, *Le Ton beau de Marot* is one of those works that it is hopeless even to dream of translating out of their home language.

Please understand: It is with neither pride nor pleasure that I make this claim; I wish this book *were* translatable. *Le Ton beau de Marot* is, in fact, just the sort of book that I would guess would appeal to a non-anglophonic but cultured European audience. It would give me such great satisfaction if it could be carried across various language barriers — but I claim that this would not just be hard to do, but is in fact an incoherent idea. Therefore if, by some odd miracle, you are reading this text *in a language other than English,* the following remarks ought to be of especial interest to you.

At the outset of this chapter, I made a claim that the hallmark of untranslatability is the deep weddedness of a message to its medium — the unique union of a certain form and a certain content in a novel composite structure so tangled that neither can be extracted intact from it. How would that description apply to *Le Ton beau de Marot*? In what ways are its medium and its message fused? I see three aspects to this question.

Firstly, there is the matter of wordplay and linguistic games. *Le Ton beau de Marot* is filled from top to bottom with linguistic twists. Take its very title: It contradicts the language in which the rest of the book is written. That certainly sets a tone. And there is wordplay galore in the many translations of Marot's poem, as well as scattered throughout the text. Compared with a more typical, more straightforward text on literature and translation, this book poses a great number of problems. But wordplay translation, challenging and open-ended though it is, is an art with many superlative practitioners. I am prepared to believe that those aspects of this book, just like those aspects of *GEB*, could be tackled and translated with great flourish and elegance by translators such as did *GEB* itself, or the scintillating French version of *Metamagical Themas*, for instance. So, despite the horrendous mess posed by aspect number 1, let's just pretend it was a piece of cake, and pass on to the next one.

The second aspect of the medium–message marriage in *Le Ton beau de Marot* is the fact that the backbone of the book is a long series of poems translated *out of French* and *into English*. What would, say, a Polish translator do with this compounded complexity? You can't just throw the English versions down the tube, because much of the book is *about* them. So I suppose what the translator would have to do throughout the book is much like what I myself did, in "Hall of Mirrors" and "Gallic Twists": Preserve the translations, but in addition, translate them into Polish. When it came to translating "Hall of Mirrors" and "Gallic Twists" themselves, then the game would get even more intense, since one would have to preserve, but also translate, the translations of the translations. This gets very twisty, but it is somehow in the spirit of the book to savor double and triple translations, right? And since I myself carried off, with some debatable degree of success, at least a handful of double-level translations, we should certainly go ahead and presume that there are other equally capable folks out there who could do a bang-up job of reflecting deeply in their native language the most intricate and subtle tricks carried out by this or that translator in rendering Marot's poem in English. To do such a translation would be a byzantine Hall of Mirrors from the very beginning to the bitter end, this time, not just in some little local section of the book; nonetheless, let's once again, for the sake of argument, simply pretend that this aspect of the medium–message marriage, aspect number 2, is just another piece of cake, and pass on to the next one.

This one, aspect number 3, is where everything falls apart. The fact is, this book is extremely and intimately autobiographical — in fact, I will coin a term and say it is *author-biographical*. Over and over again, I tell the tale of how I first heard of such-and-such a poem, or first thought of translating something, or how I decided on one rhyme word over another. The book is, in short, in many ways *about me* — and I am a native speaker of English, not of Polish or French or German or any other language. If my mastery of English is converted, by some sleight of tongue, into an equal adeptness in some other language, then the person being talked about is a complete fiction! Although the genuine author of this book knows *a little* Polish, he has no skill at all at creating Polish puns and translating poetry into Polish!

The snag, the sticking-point, the bottom line, then, is *faithfulness to the author's identity*. The fact is, I am irrevocably tied, by both birth and growth, to the English language — in fact, to the American dialect thereof. Put an Italian, Dutch, or Polish veneer on top of me, disguise my Americanness under a cloak of alien phonemes, alien grammatical patterns, and alien choppings-up of semantic space, and you get an absurdity.

To paint a clear picture of how far-fetched the scenario of translating this book is, let me take the story of how Carol and I read Johnston's and Falen's anglicizations of *Onegin* in bed, and were so charmed by them. When it comes to exhibiting, side by side, the actual poems that she and I read, just how is that going to work? Are readers going to see them in English (of no use to a monolingual Pole, of course) and also "in Polish"? No matter how good a "Polish Falen" might be, it would not be what *we* saw and were so charmed by. The story is, after all, about two anglophones reading English, not anglophones reading Polish, or Poles reading Polish.

Or again, consider "D's Cross Tip to All Straight Wives", which came from my unlikely swirling-together of Mary Daly's HexHagonal flights of fancy (in themselves next to untranslatable), W. E. Henley's jazzy but impenetrable old-London criminal slang, and H. De Vere Stacpoole's spicy but limpid English rendering of the Villon ballad. How on earth could that composite poem's zany, hyper-anglophonic flavor be replicated in the Polish version that presumably sits next to it on the page?

Far, far worse is that the "quirky, fluky history" told right afterwards in this book has to apply both to the English version *and* to its Polish partner. Thus the true story of how I discovered, to my delight, that Stacpoole's phrase "jewels, perfume, and pearls", which rhymes with his "girls", could be reversed to rhyme with Mary Daly's term "snools", would have to hold in both English and Polish. But what sense does this make? The discovery was mine, not the translator's, and it involved English, not Polish. Thus there will be either a *false* story of how a *Polish* poem evolved or a *true* story of how an *English* poem evolved. The first way, it will be just a pile of fabrications; the other way, it will be a failure as a self-contained Polish book.

Still, just for laughs, let's suppose the impossible challenge of polifying the poem had been met, and even that the "history" was true not only of the English original but also of the Polish replication. Amazing! But in *that* case, whoever carried out such a virtuoso stunt would be able to run circles around me as a translator — and yet their *own* skill would never be brought into focus, never mentioned, just taken for granted. If their contribution to the Polish book — in many ways exceeding mine — *were* acknowledged, then they might as well be elevated to the rank of co-author with me. But at that point, the ubiquitous author-biographical aspects of the book start to go all skew. Who is this hazy "I", if here the first-person pronoun refers to the American author, there to the Polish translator, and elsewhere to *both*?

Long though I — "I"! — have grappled with tricky translation matters, and ingenious though the solutions I have seen by so many have been, this challenge simply is off the scale with respect to those. It is not that this book is any better than other books, or any subtler, or any more complex, or any more linguistically playful — it is just that it is so intimately wedded both to its author and to its author's own weddedness to the English language that the whole idea turns into a bloomin' charade.

In Praise of the Untranslatable

In his witty book *The Poetics of Translation*, eminent translator–poet Willis Barnstone proclaims a philosophy near and dear to my heart, with which it seems most apt to close this, the longest of my book's chapters:

> What is most interesting to translate and most susceptible of success is the impossible, or, even better, the untranslatable. And there are some truly untranslatable words and phrases by any standards. These "untranslatables", like the unwilling but much desired Colombian drug "extraditables", are the richest linguistic sources to transfer to the target language, are a challenge to art and ingenuity, and stimulate the imagination of the artist–translator, who in confronting the untranslatable cannot be lazily seduced by the surface obvious into producing an unimaginative, mechanical version....
>
> Untranslatable lines are natural meadows of translation and yield the best wild herbs. What has never been done in the adopted language will expand its thematic and formal boundaries and its literature. Traditions of theme and form are altered by the infusion of poems from other languages, especially the impossible ones.

Poems XIV:

~ Quite Conceited ~

```
* * * * * *
 * * * *
  * *
   *
   *
```

Poems XIII and XIV form a showcase of some of the radical explorations that came out of my Indiana and Michigan classes. It seemed to me that this was the proper venue in which to insert my friend Sue Wunder's highly experimental "Gentle Cow" — all the more so, given the amusing potential to segue into it from "Yo There Dog!".

Twenty-some years ago, when she lived on a farm in England, Sue fell in love with cows. It seems that the moo-'n'-manure life must have been her destiny, for just a few years ago, she became a dedicated nineteenth-century–style dairy farmer who takes great satisfaction in milking her cows bright and early each and every morning. Before she donned her dairy hat, Sue worked as a writer for many years, and developed a real feel for words. So it was not exactly a surprise to me when, a few days after having given Sue a sampler of "Ma Mignonne" translations, I received two cow-based poems in the mail from her. Each had its stronger and weaker parts, so with her approval, I spliced their best pieces into this sympathetic pastoral image of bovine languor.

This poem sounds in spots like almost perfect David Moser (lines 7–10 especially), and has the curious structural property that it breaks up into semantic quatrains quite perfectly — indeed, with just a couple of exceptions, into rhyming semantic couplets. Note, thus, that Sue's semantic couplets are *in phase* with her rhyming couplets, quite the opposite of the original poem's pattern.

It happens that Sue has never studied French, but this was no hindrance to her. She had my list of syntactic and semantic guidelines, and that sufficed. As I pondered this, it dawned on me that the challenge of translating "Ma Mignonne" had somehow, somewhere in the process, been abstracted into a more general challenge — that of generating, in one's own native language, a fresh instance of a new kind of generic poem, whose nature is defined by two things: firstly by a certain *syntactic* structure (including first/last line equality, line-count, rhyme scheme, etc.) and secondly by certain characteristic sorts of *semantic* gestures, such as sympathetic greetings at the outset, poet's self-reference near the middle, call for divine succor toward the end, as well as brief allusions along the way to seclusion and escape from it, nice things to eat, fear of pallor and weight loss, and so forth. In other words, my pseudo-poem "Funky Mots" could be seen as the template for this new kind of generic poem, as long as it is taken suitably loosely.

How carefully does Marot's original "Ma Mignonne" have to be looked at before one tackles this generic challenge? Not at all! One needn't ever have seen it — indeed, one needn't ever have heard of Marot, or even know a word of French, to do an excellent job, as "Gentle Cow" demonstrates.

Gentle Cow

Susan Wunder

Gentle cow,
Do allow
My good cheer
In your ear.
Cloistered lass,   *5*
Far from grass,
Health to you!
Rise and moo!
Leave your pen!
Graze again!   *10*
On your rump
Feel Sue's thump.
Taste her sweet
Barley treat.
Nip the bud!   *15*
Chew your cud,
Lest your milk
Lose its silk
(Too low-fat
For a cat),   *20*
And your bright
Black-and-white
Fade to gray —
No, I pray!
Quit the shade   *25*
For hope's glade,
Prithee now,
Gentle cow.

We resume my "student series" with a laudable effort by Bill Marotti — or rather, "Bill Marot-ti", as would seem truly appropriate in this context. Marot-ti was in one of my analogy-and-creativity seminars in Michigan. This poem — one of several excellent ones that he came up with, as a matter of fact — takes the "jail" metaphor quite seriously and, using four syllables per line (a far easier challenge, it turns out, than three), extends it into a full 28-line conceit featuring quite a bit of humor.

In point of fact, what we are dealing with here is not quite a conceit, after all, since there is no trace left, nary a one, of the fact that the original poem was addressed to someone *sick*. Rather, one gets the unambiguous message that this poem is addressed to a prisoner in jail. Thus one could say that Marot-ti has translated not only the *linguistic* medium (French becomes English), but also the *message* medium (an illness becomes a jail term). And yet, much of the essence of the original poem's theme has been preserved — an abstract structure characterized by the writer sending warm wishes and hopes that a friend might soon resume eating good food and escape unpleasant circumstances, with perhaps a divine assist.

It occurred to me that it would have been an elegant little flip if, somewhere around lines 4–5, Marot-ti had dipped into the "sickness metaphor", fleetingly likening a jail term to being ill and being held in quarantine. That would have been a very cute reversal with respect to the original poem. Oh, well — you can't have everything.

Note that on line 12, there appears a proper name ("McFee"), mirroring the original French. However, the mapping of the poet Marot onto the district attorney McFee seems very counterintuitive!

If you pay very careful attention to your stress pattern as you read this poem aloud, you should notice that in nearly all the lines, it's the second and fourth syllables that receive the main stress; however, there are a few exceptions — notably, lines 7, 13, and 24. In these lines, it's the *first* and fourth syllables that are stressed. And there are a few lines that could go either way, such as 6, 14, 16, and 19, and of course the top and bottom lines.

Normally when reading aloud, one doesn't consciously notice such small shifts in accent pattern even though one carries them out perfectly, but the effect is very real, and it somehow adds to the spice and charm of not just this poem, but metric poetry in general. The rigidity is lowered and lines thereby become more liquidy, intangible, subtle, and alive. In fact, given how nonmechanical it feels, I have often mused about how hard it would be to get a computer program to read poetry aloud really well, simply from the point of view of getting the stress patterns right (leaving all questions of meaning aside).

To get a sense of this in a different kind of verse, try reading some of the Onegin stanzas in Chapters 8 and 9 out loud without any awkward fits or starts; this should give you a feel for how nontrivial it is to read poems in such a way that they come out sounding smooth and graceful.

3–6–1–2

William Marotti

3-6-1-2,
Hello to you
From me outside.
You couldn't hide
And now you're stuck: 5
Such rotten luck!
Caught for your crime,
Now make good time
And get out fast;
The charge won't last.   10
You'll soon be free,
Because McFee
(He's the D.A.)
Thinks you're okay.
So take this cake   15
(Make no mistake,
It hides no file).
Awaiting trial,
Scarf down this food,
But don't act crude,   20
For if you get
Disgruntled, pet,
You'll stay in jail.
(Sorry 'bout bail.)
God grant you grace —   25
Dismiss your case?
You'll soon pull through,
3-6-1-2.

Ian Gray was another Michigan student, and, like Anthony Guneratne a couple of years later, was inspired to move in the opposite mathematical direction from David Moser, but where Anthony chose the classical Italian sonnet form with its five iambic feet per line, Ian preferred to keep the total number of syllables in the poem constant. Therefore, his poem consists of precisely fourteen six-syllable lines, since $14 \times 6 = 28 \times 3 = 84$.

The premise on which this whole poem is based is the idea that perfect reversal is information-preserving. That is, if you reflect something in a mirror, or rotate it by 180 degrees, or video-reverse it (*i.e.*, switch black to white and vice versa), or time-reverse it, or do any operation that is its own inverse, then the resultant object is in some sense — usually a very clear sense — a perfectly faithful image of the original. This means that, at least in principle, you could take the output object, perform the very same operation on it, and wind up getting the input object back — the object with which you started. That's the nature of a perfect reversal.

It's just that in this case, Ian opted for what one might call *semantic reversal*, a notion I suggested in Chapter 7 when describing the season-flipped, mood-flipped, gender-flipped, time-of-day–flipped (and oddly enough, anonymous) German lyrics to "The Surrey with the Fringe on Top". Although multiple semantic reversal of this sort might in theory be a perfect mirror-like operation, it is in actuality a highly imperfect preserver of information. But let us not quibble about details. Ian's idea, straightforward and appealing enough, was to carry out a kind of global reversal of the basic plot-line of the poem: an older man wishing a young girl to get well. In his dark flip of this line, a young girl wishes an older man to get sick and, in fact, to croak.

"So Long, Dad" is a grim poem, bitter and relentless in tone, a total contrast to the innocence of the Marot. But for just that reason, its "sameness" with the original is, on some rarefied level, undeniable; the sameness is simply more abstract than usual, residing in the simplicity of the operation by which its basic theme was constructed. And thus in the most hypothetical of hypothetical worlds, a looking-glass version of Ian who knew French like a native but had never seen the Marot might read this angry poem and, from it alone, fortuitously reconstruct the original old French verse, word for word, by performing a second semantic reversal on it (and also going back to a 28 x 3 structure from the 14 x 6 structure). But needless to say, such a scenario is hardly likely.

At this point, many readers may feel that things have been stretched beyond their limits, even if intellectually they understand the whole story. Despite all the abstract arguments about preservation of some elusive gist, where, in truth, is the original Marot to be found in this ugly outburst? The familiar long, thin cigar shape is almost invisible, the content seems utterly different, the charm is absent...

Well, probably the objectors are right. Probably this poem, although it is droll and clever and clearly related to "Ma Mignonne", should not be counted as a *translation* of it. Though a nice idea, it's simply beyond the pale.

So Long, Dad

Ian Gray

You doddering old man,
I'm tired of this sham!
It's gettin' near the end.
I'm not gonna pretend
To love you any more. 5
I'm walkin' out the door
And leavin' you to dwell
In your own private hell,
For as long as you've got.
So go ahead and rot, 10
'Cause you're nothin' to me!
That's all you'll ever be.
Enjoy life while you can,
You doddering old man.

• Chapter 15 •

On the
Ununderstandable

•

Zebrzydowice! O, thou sweet, strange harshness of Fryderyk Szopen's mother's mother tongue! Lurch to a loud stop. Hissing sounds, steam rising outside the window. A clank, then silence. Pitch dark, four in the morning. Voices moving through the corridor, doors sliding open and shut. Stark black letters on a low, wide, white sign in the gloom. The telltale consonant clusters of a podunk's name — a dead giveaway that at last, we have reached the yearned-for Polish frontier.

On my first trip to Poland, in the early spring of 1975, I was giddy with exhausted sleepless excitement as my PKP train crossed the Czech border and headed towards Kraków. With Chopin's majestic Polonaise-Fantaisie pounding triumphantly in my head, with the day soon to break, with my newly-acquired rudiments of Polish actually working, allowing me to have mini-conversations with my compartment-mates, all felt new and magical.

As a condition for getting an entry visa, I had been required, just before we crossed the Polish border, to purchase something like $100 or $200 in Polish złotys — no small amount for a student — but I felt it was certainly worth every last penny of it. Boarding in Katowice, an unkempt and ill-shaven young man barged into our cozy compartment and made himself a little too present for my taste. When he found out I was a foreigner, he feigned a bit of interest in me as a person, but soon it became apparent that his true interest lay elsewhere: in foreign currency — in American greenbacks, in particular.

At some point, he secretively whispered to me about changing money, and at first I naïvely thought he just wanted some information, but I quickly got the drift: he wanted to buy some dollars, as many as possible, on the black market. Perhaps I was overly cautious, but I instinctively backed off as fast as I could, and that was that. When he disembarked a bit later, my compartment-mates told me I had done well to resist, because I could have been arrested if I had been caught doing what he wanted.

But once I had spent a few days in Poland, I realized that changing dollars on the black market was practically a national pastime; the young man's suspect appearance notwithstanding, he was probably just typical of all people his age. What baffled me, however, was that whereas the Polish government had given me 30 złotys per dollar, the young man had offered me 125 złotys per dollar. I could have made a killing!

That Nutty, Knotty, Naughty Złoty

This discrepancy in exchange rates was the first hint that something quite screwy was going on with Polish money. Up until that time, whenever I had traveled or lived in western Europe, I had always had a clear sense of "what this amount of money is worth". Right then, for example, I was a graduate student living in Regensburg, Germany, where the mythical Blue Danube, having meandered northeast for some 200 miles, turns around to start its long trek southeast, finally to spill its blueness into the sparkling Black Sea; at the time, a German mark was worth around 45 cents, and that made perfect sense in terms of its buying power. Thus the exquisite Petit Robert *Dictionnaire universel des noms propres* that I so drooled over in the Universität Regensburg bookstore was priced at 105 marks, and that meant just a little under $50, which seemed absolutely right on the mark to me.

Never once, while I had been in Regensburg, had it occurred to me that some price I was paying for a pizza or my dorm room or a chessboard or anything else was out of line with American prices; in fact, the sole key to the decipherment of a German price was a single number — the *rate of exchange*. This number functioned as a coder or decoder, depending on which way I wanted to go, and it revealed a perfect, orderly correspondence between the sets of commodities available in two different societies.

And thus had it always been, wherever I had lived or ventured in Europe: Geneva, London, Paris, Stockholm, Rome, and so forth. There had always been an exchange rate, there had never been a black market, and so I had never thought about such things. Over the next couple of weeks in Poland, however, I got a lesson in economics that I have never quite understood. In a nutshell, the lesson was that there was *no meaningful rate of exchange*. But because I was so used to the idea of there being one, this fact didn't register clearly on me for quite a while.

I first tried converting prices at the rate of 30 złotys to the dollar, and found that all sorts of things came out wildly implausible. So I tried using 125 złotys to the dollar, but at this rate, other things came out wrong. I then started to realize that people's salaries and apartment rents came out drastically wrong at either of these hypothetical rates of exchange, so I tried to figure out some other way of calculating *the value of one złoty*. What a natural hope! And yet, the more I struggled, the worse it got. My Polish friends tried to help me find a single number for the rate of exchange, but to no avail. Books and LP's seemed to have one rate of exchange (at least *they* were fairly consistent with each other!), cars another, salaries another, apartments another, food yet another, and so on and so forth.

It gradually dawned on me that if one were to place a bunch of different commodities and services along a horizontal line and then make a bar graph showing the typical price in złotys for each one, the profile of that bar graph — the "Polish prices skyline", so to speak — would not look anything like the corresponding German prices skyline. There would be skyscrapers in one where there were low buildings in the other, and vice versa. By contrast, though, the American, Swiss, English, French, Swedish, and Italian prices skylines would look almost exactly like scaled-up or scaled-down versions of the German one (and perforce, of one another).

I have never forgotten this lesson. It always comes back to me as the quintessential case of two closely-related frameworks that simply cannot be consistently aligned in terms of a systematic mapping. If the basis for a mapping works well in one sector, then it breaks down in another, and of course vice versa. The funny thing was, each society managed to survive on its own, and members of that society were totally used to how their own currency worked, naturally feeling it was the most natural one. But I, an outsider to Poland, couldn't make any sense of złotys *per se*; I felt lost unless I could convert things into my own framework, and that just didn't work.

Understanding as Translation into One's Own Life

How do you understand it when someone else hates a food you love? Or loves a food you hate? Is understanding such things a mere piece of cake, or quite the contrary, is it beyond the bounds of human flexibility?

Take chocolate — smooth, rich, creamy Italian chocolate ice cream, for example. I find it hugely hard to imagine how someone could be revolted by that sweet taste — as hard as imagining how someone could be revolted by a baby's soft grin or the starting shudders of an orgasm, or could take delight in being hit with a hammer or in hearing an infant scream. I also find it absolutely mystifying that anyone could love the taste of liver, kidney, tongue, brain, tripe, trotters, and other such "sweetbreads"; on the other hand, I am at a total loss for why my love for a creamy, spicy chicken tikka masala is not universal. Such frank admissions may strike many readers as being close to pathologically self-centered or infantile, but I am trying to articulate something almost never said, and yet something I am convinced is virtually universal among adults. It has everything to do with the unalignable, incommensurate frameworks of złotys and dollars. Let me explain.

People who claim to "understand" other people's taste in food are, I believe, fooling themselves — at least to some degree. That is, I believe they are mistaking "syllogistic" or "statistical" understanding for empathic, analogical understanding. More specifically, they have witnessed such facts as "Jill likes liver!" and "Jack hates chocolate!" a very large number of times over their lives, and so they have gradually assimilated these facts of life into their worldview — "Hmm… so people's tastes in food differ from mine!", or, more generally, *de gustibus non est disputandum* — at which point they cease struggling with these oddities or even considering them of interest any more. Such facts about taste simply filter down to the unconscious, where they become *unexamined axioms*. (Almost certainly, the first few occasions when you found that some kid down the block's taste differed radically from your own, you *were* enormously thrown, but by now, all such incidents are long-forgotten, buried episodes of childhood.)

Can you imagine someone whose greatest pleasure in life is to knock holes in ice-covered lakes and go swimming under the ice? And who claims it feels bad to warm up afterwards? You might just say, "Oh, well, it takes all kinds!" but that is not any kind of *understanding* of how this is possible; it is nothing more than an easy sound bite that allows you to incorporate otherwise incomprehensible oddities into your mental framework. I'm not saying this is bad; we need such devices — all I'm saying is that *you don't really understand anything here.* I, too, have empathic holes in my mind: thus I know as sure as shootin' *that* some people don't like chocolate, and yet I'm utterly in the dark as to *how* they don't like chocolate.

I guess there is, after all, one way that I can manage to project myself, at least partway, into the "tongue-set" of someone who intensely dislikes chocolate or, say, Mexican Chicken (one of the dinner dishes Carol and I used to like best) — I simply remember how I would feel after having gorged myself on Mexican Chicken at dinner. When I was really stuffed with it, there would come a point where I absolutely didn't want to eat another single bite — the very idea turned me totally off. This overdoing-it trick allows you to identify with someone who is turned off by a food you normally love, but it doesn't work in the other direction — you can't, by stuffing yourself so full of a food that you hate, all of a sudden come to crave it like crazy! In any case, feeling negative about a favorite food when stuffed seems somehow different from hating it in a neutral state. So this trick carries one partway but far from all the way into an alien viewpoint.

The Symmetry Argument

Probably the most common way of trying to understand someone who hates chocolate but loves liver (say) is to say to yourself, "Oh, I see — liver is for Jill what chocolate is for me, and vice versa! I'll just *swap the concepts* in my mind. No sweat!" This strategy whereby two related concepts are swapped, thus presumably enabling an alien viewpoint to be internalized and temporarily adopted, is what I call the *symmetry argument*.

A typical example of this is how Carol and I learned about each other's sensitivities. I often used to read late at night, and would turn on my nighttable's small light when Carol was asleep. She would toss and turn and grumble, "Do you *have* to read now?", and so eventually I bought a tiny battery-operated light that was advertised not to disturb anyone else. But even *that* bugged Carol, and I found that the only way I could avoid disturbing her sleep was if I very carefully held the light between the pages I was reading so as not to let a single photon reach her touchy eyes. I found this hard to do and couldn't help but think of the princess and the pea. The funny thing was that in the mornings, when Carol would often get up earlier than I did, she would try her hardest to be quiet, but even the softest clicking of the doorknobs or the sound of her gingerly placing a hanger back on the closet rack would wake me up from deep sleep. I used to grouse, and Carol did her best to improve. Each of us thought the other was incomprehensibly hypersensitive — until one day, when we fused these two separate facts about unrelated sensory modalities into one larger analogical fact: "Carol's sensitivity to light when she's sleeping is *just like* Doug's sensitivity to sound when he's sleeping!" A flash of insight for us both! In a sense, this wider perspective afforded each of us an avenue into the other's formerly baffling brain. In a sense — but not totally, of course.

Symmetry arguments may work reasonably well for non-core aspects of people's personalities, such as taste in food or sensitivities to disturbances, but try to elevate this strategy to something that matters deeply, such as key beliefs about morality, truth, or honesty — or even taste in music. That is, suppose Elveena is addicted to loud rock-and-roll but detests all classical music. Will it work if I try to "understand" her by saying to myself, "Oh, I see — sure! — Elveena is *exactly like me,* only with the roles of rock-and-roll and classical music swapped! To understand her feelings, I'll just swap the concepts in my mind. No sweat!"

No, not at all. The way I see things, the reason this utterly fails is that your taste in music is "where you live" — it embodies in an unimaginably profound manner just *who you are.* The counterfactual act of tampering with someone's musical taste is tantamount to carrying out a partial "soul transplant" on that person, reaching in and so profoundly disturbing their core identity that they are no longer recognizable. If I, for example, try to imagine my mother avidly listening to a Top-40 radio station and shunning the music that she grew up with and collected in the 1930's and 1940's, the moment I do so, this "she" I've conjured up is *no longer my mother*. So radical a musical taste-swap simply won't take. One can transplant hearts these days, but not heart.

The Mysterious Mind of a Music Polluter

Speaking of rock-and-roll, let me mention a mystery that for ages I've longed to fathom: How is it that so many people feel no qualms about blaring out rock-and-roll music all over the whole darn neighborhood? It happens all the time in any university town. It comes at you from fraternity sundecks, from dormitory windows, from apartment-complex swimming pools, from wide-open doors of ordinary-looking houses — from anywhere and everywhere, it seems. I once said to a friend, "I can't understand how people can do that — I really can't relate to that." But was this the truth?

I kept on turning this over in my mind, and after a while, up popped the following memory from April, 1966. It's a beautiful crisp sunny spring morning in Ravenna, Italy. My parents and my sister and I are staying in a pretty hotel, and I wake up in an absolutely exuberant mood, with the Prokofiev second violin concerto running incredibly strongly through my head. I happen to have brought my tape recorder along on our trip, and I even have a tape of that piece with me. Almost breathlessly, I pull the tape out of my suitcase, mount it on the machine, fast-forward to the proper number, turn the volume up to maximum, and then — I ecstatically blast the sounds of Prokofiev's second violin concerto throughout the halls of our hotel. Noise-pollution city! Luckily for me, nobody complains.

After some more reflection, I dredged from memory another incident, one that occurred only a couple of months later that same year. One evening at Kungshamra (a student dormitory I was living in just outside of Stockholm), again feeling overwhelmed by the majesty of a certain piece of classical music (to be specific, the "Sanctus" from Bach's B Minor Mass), I turn the knobs on my trusty tape recorder as far to the right as they'll go, and I blast the damn thing at full volume up and down the hallways. This time, someone does in fact complain. And what is my reaction — apologetic? No — I'm offended! In fact, I am ashamed to say, I wrote a somewhat churlish note, including a sloppy, stupid grammatical mistake in Swedish for which I have never since forgiven myself, and I taped it right on the complainer's door. *"Up's your,* buddy!"

Now the question is, are these two obnoxious acts recalled from my previous lives "close" enough, either in time or in "semantic space", to allow the me of today to get into the mindset of the rock-and-roll blarers of Bloomington, Indiana? Or was the perpetrator in those two cases simply *another person* bearing my name? Or — get this! — is the vulgarity of rock-and-roll simply too remote from the sacredness of Prokofiev and Bach to allow a convincing mapping to be built in my mind? Probably all of these factors contribute to my difficulty in relating to the Bloomington rock-blasters. But all in all, thanks to recalling those episodes in my life, I guess I understand the rock-and-roll blarers' mentality at least a little better, now.

On the other hand, rock-and-roll *itself* remains for me a bastion of mystery, an impenetrably hard rock. Oh, sure, I like a few rock songs here and there — Carole King's "I Feel the Earth Move", for instance, is great, as is Frankie Avalon's "Venus" (but is it rock?) — but rock's overwhelming dominance of the American and European pop-music scene for over forty years now is one of the greatest enigmas in the universe to me. No kidding!

Rock Music as a Formidable Import Challenge

One day, I was looking at the program for the memorial service for a computer-science graduate student named Charles who had died in a terrible caving accident a couple of months earlier. I'd known him a bit, and several members of my research group knew him well and cared for him deeply. All around, we agreed that his death was a stupid tragedy. The program listed a number of musical selections and their composers, including a couple of songs, with their lyrics, by rock groups whose names I had never heard. My instant reaction was to be somewhat turned off. My guess was that these were songs or performers that Charles had liked a lot, and though I didn't know the pieces in question, it seemed to me in bad taste to have loud, raucous, crude music at a memorial service.

I knew full well that this was to be a special kind of memorial service, one that was attempting to celebrate Charles' vibrant life in a joyous way, rather than lugubriously mourn his passing. People were hoping to make it "the way he would have liked it to be". For example, they were going to serve refreshments and show videos of happy times in his life. I could see all of this just fine, but I had problems with the rock music. (Let's leave aside, for a moment, the question of whether this unknown music was soft rock or loud, crude, raucous stuff. Remember — I'm not concerned with the objective facts about the service, but with the objective facts about my reaction to reading the program. I'm talking about the psychology of understanding, not about memorial services, so I want to stick to the mental facts, not the external ones.) My feeling was clear: it would do a disservice to *anyone's* memory to have crude, raucous music on such an occasion.

The natural comparison then sprang to mind for me. My Dad's memorial service had taken place only about three months before that. I had been deeply involved in planning it — especially the choice of music. We had chosen as the first piece "Erev Bakfar", a hauntingly elegiac and pastoral Israeli song (I had once given it to my Dad on a record, and years later found out it had been written by my friend Zamir Bavel — amazing!), and then, interspersed with speakers' remarks, we had a Bach French Suite, a 1920's jazz piece called "Really the Blues" with Mezz Mezzrow and Sidney Bechet, the slow movement from a Bach concerto for oboe and violin, and finally, a soft, sad song named "A Brown Bird Singing", sung by one of my Dad's favorite old-time jazz singers, Maxine Sullivan. Thus we had classical selections mixed in with jazz pieces. Well, now — I could easily imagine someone being outraged at *my* taking offense at rock music, when I had promoted two *jazz* pieces at my Dad's service. That's some nerve!

And yet there were a number of differences. In the first place, "Really the Blues" is terribly mournful and "A Brown Bird Singing" is terribly wistful. In my imagination (and that's what counts, remember!), the rock pieces were not sad or contemplative, but merely loud. In the second place, the way I see things, jazz of that era is deeply soulful and moving music, just as much as classical music, whereas rock music is simply not.

Now we of course come to the symmetry argument, which in this case runs something like this: "Who cares what *you* think about rock music? What matters is what *Charles* liked, and it so happens that this kind of music touched his soul deeply! Who are *you* to say that it is blasphemous, when it comes close to the core of Charles? Get out of here, cretin!" Actually, that isn't a statement of the symmetry argument at all, but it is an angry inner voice that had to get expressed first. The true symmetry argument goes more like this: "Come on, mister — your Dad happened to love jazz, and that's fine, and Charles happened to love rock music, and that's fine too. These two types of music, though very different, played much the same role in the lives of the individuals concerned. Thus it's appropriate to celebrate Charles' life with rock, in just the same way as it was appropriate to celebrate your Dad's life with jazz. Can't you see the symmetry of it?" And, of course, I can. After all, *I'm* the one who is imagining this inner voice and who is writing this passage; nobody *else* manufactured the "cretin" outburst or the symmetry argument for me. The ideas are as clear as day to me.

And I admit, the symmetry argument *does* get me partway to accepting the rock music in Charles' service — but not all the way. Why not? Because *I still hate rock* and *I still love jazz* (at least those jazz pieces). To me, one is sacred, and the other is profane. To put it very bluntly, how can *crude trash* — even if the dear departed loved said trash — do honor to a person's memory? Would you play selections of saccharine Muzak at the funeral of someone who played in a Muzak orchestra? Suppose sweet little four-year-old Minniolah, dying of leukemia, had always been cracked up by the sound of burps; at her funeral, would you think it appropriate to play a videotape showing little Minniolah splitting her sides at her own repeated long, loud belching? You can dream up even more extreme cases, I'm sure.

Now at the time I was first formulating some of these thoughts, I was voicing them to my old friend Don Byrd. As the memorial-service program was lying right there on the table in front of us, Don took a look at the songs and lyrics and commented that he thought he knew one of them, and in fact he guessed it was probably light rock, or possibly folk rock. At that point, I started to be able to relate better to the whole picture. "Ahh!" I thought to myself, "Something like Carole King! That's not so bad!" Perhaps my position was not so constipatedly rigid, after all.

Yes… but notice what is happening here. It's not the symmetry argument that's winning me over, but the fact that I can begin to relate to the *music itself* — to what a philosopher might call the music's *extension* (the actual sounds) rather than its *intension* (the role that these sounds played in the life of the deceased). To see that this is not the symmetry argument at all, imagine that Don had said instead, "I believe this is not merely rock music, but heavy metal of the loudest sort, with six super-distorted electric guitars and very guttural, incoherent singing." This would have confirmed my initial impression, only in spades, and made me even more persuaded that the music was doing a disservice to Charles' memory. So — please don't give me any congratulations for flexibility — they'd be undeserved.

What's interesting about all this is that the symmetry argument is so obvious and so compelling at an *intellectual* level that I feel its force fighting very strongly against my deep *emotional* reactions. While I can't personally relate to rock music (especially of the loud, crude type), I certainly can relate to the fact that people have deep reactions to music of whatever sort, and that their favorite music matters a great deal in their lives. At that rarefied, abstract, intellectual level, I buy the symmetry argument totally. *In principle,* I'm all for the idea of rock music in Charles' service. It's just that when you descend to the concrete level of what the music *actually sounds like,* I swing in exactly the opposite direction.

Jazz Is Okay, but Depth? — Ach, Take Beethoven…

Another factor, I must say, that entered into the equation of my emotions at the time is my having recalled how, in the early part of this century, a number of famous classical musicians came over from Europe and made condescending remarks about jazz. Some bluntly dismissed it as "primitive tribe music" (sheer racism, nothing more), while others offered faint praise but then added that in comparison to deep masters like the "Three B's" (Bach, Beethoven, and Brahms), jazz was extremely simple and uninteresting. When I recalled such clearly preconceived, narrow-minded opinions, I was exceedingly offended, and even thought I could discern in them the roots of Nazism.

And why was I offended? For just one simple reason: I knew, loved, and respected the jazz that these people were putting down. Had I not felt that way, I certainly wouldn't have felt such resentment. Were one of today's great classical musicians — Anton Kuerti, say, or Joshua Bell — to appear on TV and put heavy metal down, do you think that I would get up in a fury and defend it? No way! I would be delighted! Thus my anger at those "cultured" Old World snobs came not from some kind of abstract, cerebral symmetry argument divorced from any particular set of sounds ("You Europeans should appreciate music from *our* side of the Atlantic just as we appreciate music from *your* side of the Atlantic"), but from my non-cerebral gut reaction to the specific music that they were putting down.

Well, with what to me was a repulsive image of "high culture" sneering at "low culture" hovering around in the back of my mind, I realized that in giving a blanket putdown of rock music, I myself was risking looking very similar to those snobs whose behavior I deplored, which certainly made me feel weird and a bit reserved about voicing my opinion, no matter how strongly held it might be.

On the other hand, the whole matter of expressing such opinions has a great deal to do with who the audience for the remarks is going to be. If I've been invited to deliver the keynote talk at the annual meeting of the American Society of Rock-Music Haters, I won't have too many trepidations about voicing my opinions about what kinds of music are inappropriate at memorial services. But if, by contrast, I'm going to be writing this whole thing up in a book about poetry translation, many of whose readers are surely lifelong rock aficionados and know next to nothing about the jazz of the twenties and thirties, you can be sure I'm going to draw a lot more *Fliegerabwehrkanone* (check out "flak" in your dictionary) — and that'll give me pause about coming on too, too strong in that context.

The Last Twist of the Knife in the Bitter/Sweet Cake

And now, let me come to one final, fascinating, exquisite little irony: Exactly why is it that I will draw so much flak from my readers — from you, in other words — for attacking rock? Answer: because I would bet that few if any of my rock-and-roll-loving readers will invoke the symmetry argument themselves! If they *were* to do so, it would go something like this:

> Hofstadter doesn't like rock. I happen personally to love rock, but so what? I can see where, if *he* hates rock, this is a perfectly good reaction to have to the memorial-service program! After all, *I* would be disgusted by a memorial service that featured music of Type X [where Type X could be 101 Violins, or country-western, or swing, or plainsong chants, or Peking opera, or African — fill in the name of whatever kind of music is your particular pet peeve], even if the person who died had loved it, so I can see perfectly well where Hofstadter's coming from.

My hunch is that the visceral anger of rock-and-roll lovers at what I've said will swamp their ability to import my viewpoint via the just-stated symmetry argument, which, as we know, is far more cerebral and detached from specifics, and so they'll find me to be offensive!

Amusingly enough, such readers would be, at a rather high level of abstraction, just like me: Though the symmetry argument sways them/me intellectually, when push comes to shove, what really counts is their/my own *raw musical taste*. You can't *ever* get into the mindset of someone whose taste is sufficiently different from your own — no, not ever; you can't even come close — and so you wind up reacting to things on the basis of how they seem from inside *your* brain. You are you, after all, and no one else.

And that, I might point out, is exactly what I was saying, at the start of this whole discussion, about the unfathomability of non-likers of chocolate. It's a puzzlement.

Angling About to Try to Glimpse an Assassin's Mindset

A few years ago I read about a member of a religious sect who had assassinated a priest in his sect on orders of the sect's charismatic leader, with whom the priest had had a public disagreement about the proper interpretation of a scripture. Bewildered, I asked myself, "Can I understand why someone would kill a person they didn't even know, simply because their leader told them to?" Syllogistically, of course, I can "understand". That is, I can set up the following chain of ironclad Aristotelian logic:

(1) All members of sect S are fanatics.
(2) Fanatics are willing to do anything their idol tells them to do.
(3) Member M of sect S was told by his idol to kill priest P.

Ergo, member M of sect S was willing to kill priest P.

You would have to be a dunce not to be able to see the compelling logic here, but that's a million miles from genuine understanding. For me, genuine understanding requires that, when I map myself onto someone, I feel that what they did is "what I would have done" — that it makes perfect, subjective sense. I need to be able to see the motivation *from the inside*. This requires finding a very strong mapping — a tight analogy — to my own life.

In pondering the riddle of the priest-killer, I came up with several quite reasonable-seeming candidates for ways to try to get myself into the assassin's head; however, each proposed mapping turned out to fail rather woefully as an analogy. Just why they all failed in getting me into the needed mindset needs some careful analysis. Here is roughly how it goes.

(1) Years ago, I worked for the United Farm Workers, mostly because I admired their leader, César Chávez. For me, Chávez had a kind of personal warmth and charisma that excited me and made me believe in his cause. Can I utilize that past experience of mine to help catapult me into the "have gun, will shoot" mentality that the actual assassin clearly must have had? No — because if Chávez had exhorted me to kill someone, I would've stopped so far short of killing that there is no analogy at all. In fact, quite strikingly, it was the very fact that César Chávez's whole philosophy of protest was centered on *nonviolence* that so attracted me to him! So this first attempted mapping is deeply incoherent.

(2) Imagine that Chávez was like Gandhi, and urged his followers to be nonviolent even when in extremely dangerous situations — for example, to be passive even if police are going to club you, possibly beat you to death. Would I adhere to that credo? And if so, would such extremism be so fanatical that it would be comparable to that of the priest's killer? My answer to both questions is "no". I was never close to being that much in thrall to César Chávez. I admired him, but he wasn't a saint or a god to me. And certainly I would have thought it idiotic to let myself get beaten to death — or just walloped hard a couple of times. But even if I had been such a pushover for punishment, a willingness to submit yourself to other people's mistreatment is not analogous, in my book, not the teensiest bit, to a willingness to put an end to someone else's life.

(3) I would be prepared to kill someone, admittedly, who was threatening the life of my children. But my children aren't a dogma or a set of abstractions, a mere system of beliefs. And anyway, were I to do such an extreme act, the command to do so would have come from inside *me,* not from "on high". If all that's being said is that there exists *some cause* for which I would kill a human being, and if that's supposed to convince me that I can now identify with the priest's killer because he, too, had *some cause* for which he would kill, I say "no way". This is too much like arguing that I can understand *any* action by *anyone,* simply because I know that *something* impelled them to do whatever they did, and because I, too, have experienced compelling reasons to do things. Such bland and general vacuity, as a supposed basis for deeply grasping someone else's motivations, is pathetic.

(4) "If I had grown up as the killer did, and believed all the things that the killer believed, then surely I would have done what he did." This is a very weird thrust, to which I parry as follows. The word "I" is being used illegitimately. It is doing nothing more than serving as a placeholder or a variable, as in the sentence-schema "If X had grown up as the killer did, and if X thus believed all the things that the killer does, then surely X would have done what the killer did." Big deal! This is just a syllogism, once again. The problem is that it poses as an innocent "Suppose *you* believed dogma D…" — but the ease with which "you" fits into this schema varies from one "you" to another. For this particular "you" — namely, me — to believe in dogma D would require a character transplant!

(5) Somebody once suggested that I think of a person whose behavior outraged me so much that I personally would *like* to see them "offed" — so I thought of the Chicago serial child-murderer John Gacy, whose behavior was as barbarous as anyone I can imagine. But I don't see Gacy as remotely similar to priest P. If priest P had molested, tortured, then killed and hacked to bits several dozen innocent boys, why then, I think I'd have no problem seeing why someone was angry enough to kill him. But priest P had done nothing of the sort.

(6) Someone else suggested that I imagine a situation where some agent has lured my children into a remote village of cultish nuts, eventually brainwashing them into hating me. Well, of course this would be immensely disturbing. Would I wish to kill this person? It seems somewhat unlikely. But even if I did wish to, the analogy still is false, because in the case of the priest's murder, the assassin's *children* had not been kidnapped and brainwashed. The assassin might have felt that *some unknown co-believers* had been exposed to wrong ideas by the priest who, belonging to sect S, should have neither had nor voiced such sacrileges, but the abstract idea of "some unknown co-believers" being led astray is one thing, and the idea of one's very own, very clear, very dear children being led astray is another thing altogether. If *random strangers* and *my children* are not wildly disanalogous notions, then I don't know an analogy from an anemone.

(7) David Moser said, "Suppose a neo-Nazi government takes over the United States, and in the year 2008 the atmosphere is much like that of Hitler Germany in 1937, just before the outbreak of World War II. Now suppose that someone whom you greatly respect convinces you that if you kill some particular political figure, you'll have a great positive effect on the future world — preventing a second Holocaust, or something along those lines. Would you try to get rid of this 'potential Hitler'?" Of course, I'm supposed to (and indeed I do) answer, "Probably I would, yes." But now for the snag in the mapping. As I look at the threat to the world in general — or specifically to the world of sect S — posed by the priest, I see it as minuscule, if it exists at all. Thus if the priest's killer actually believed that a disagreement over some scripture made priest P as vile a figure in the global scheme of things as Hitler was, then all I can conclude is that he is an extraordinarily naïve, susceptible, gullible, deluded person. For me to map myself onto him would in that case require that I slip myself into someone who believes in an idea that, to the real me, is utterly fantastic, absurd, outlandish. Such a slippage is again essentially a "soul transplant".

(8) Suppose I feel myself to be a very insignificant person, run-of-the-mill in every intellectual way, but on the other hand, I consider myself morally very good. My expectations are pretty low for my life's ultimate achievements. Suppose, however, that one day it becomes apparent that I could achieve a great deal of renown, perhaps even my own little slice of immortality, if I carried out a noble deed of vengeance, one that required a great deal of personal risk and daring. What would this vengeance be for? Well, let's posit that someone — some scum of the earth, needless to say — had besmirched my family's good name, or my country's sacred name, in a very public way. So here's my chance to do something that many people will remember for a long time, and they will admire whoever did it, even if the avenger's precise identity is never known. So I have a way of doing something significant in the world — a chance to *make a difference*. Should I not grab it — do something meaningful, important, lasting? Otherwise I will forever remain a mere cipher, a speck, a piece of dust in the history of the universe. My life will have meant nothing. Now, is this not somewhat convincing? Wouldn't you, if you were in this position, be at least tempted to carry out the act of vengeance?

This image combines a number of aspects of the above-listed attempted mappings, trying to fuse them into one single coherent picture. It requires *some* identity-slipping, but perhaps not a total "soul transplant". It also hedges greatly as to what type of vengeance is to be taken. It wouldn't have to be so drastic as a murder — perhaps a mere cross-burning on someone's lawn would do, or painting swastikas on someone's house, or throwing a few jars of chicken blood all over a university president's archives, or some other medium-level act of aggression. There still remains something of the "syllogism" feel to this scenario, though, because it is hard for me to map myself onto this person who has such pathetically low self-esteem that their only likely way of making a mark on the world is to carry out some ill-defined act of vengeance. I have to do some soul-shedding (*i.e.*, equating myself with an empty variable X in a logical "For all X" sentence). However, an attempt has been made to make the degree of soul-slippage acceptable, and also to make the rest of the analogy seem fairly plausible, although certainly a large part of the trickiness is that it is not all that clearly spelled out — just "an act of vengeance for an act that caused me personally great offense". It's all so diluted, frankly, that it sounds almost like asking me, "If you were honked at by an angry stranger, would you honk back?" Probab-lee, but so what?

And now, stepping back and taking a broader perspective, we see that each of these many mapping-attempts is like a chain with at least one broken link. Each case differs as to where the chain breaks, but it breaks *some*where every single time. I just can't seem to find a pathway linking me to the murderer, allowing me to "get inside the assassin's head".

Broken Bridges Everywhere, But Nary a Ford O'er the River

Someone might suggest that since I have a whole set of chains from which to choose, and since they all break in different places, perhaps I might somehow be able to form a composite out of several of them that would succeed in getting me all the way from here to there. That is to say, in somewhat the way that clever juggling of two inadequate classical models can give you an adequate quantum-mechanical understanding of electrons (sometimes you see an electron as a wave, sometimes as a particle), you might be able to juggle a set of inadequate bridges linking yourself to the fanatical priest-killer M, and out of that ensemble there might emerge an understanding of his hitherto incomprehensible behavior.

That suggestion, however, is wrong. The reason it is wrong is that my string of failures *reinforces* my initial feeling of incomprehension, rather than diminishing it. I try one pathway, it doesn't get me there; I try another, it doesn't get me there either. I keep on trying and keep on failing, and what I wind up concluding is "I can't get there from here", as opposed to "Well, if I could somehow use pieces of *this* incomplete pathway and *that* one and that *other* one, then maybe I could put together a total pathway." In sum, my string of failures in building an analogical bridge to M leads me gradually to a stronger and more robust sense of the utter incomprehensibility, and hence reprehensibility, of this fanatic's act than I had had before I attempted to put myself in his shoes.

Why, etymology aside, should incomprehensibility be equated with reprehensibility? It should certainly not be, in general. However, in this case it happens to be, because what M did violates my personal moral code. My various attempts to understand were attempts to find excuses for, or to justify, what he did. However, since all those attempts ultimately ended in failure, M's act gradually emerges, with ever-increasing clarity, as totally inexcusable, thus truly evil.

This is the converse of what Scopes trial lawyer Clarence Darrow used to say to the jury when defending clients (typically poor, oppressed people) who had committed crimes: "Had you been in X's situation, you too would have done exactly what X did." Then Darrow would do his best to paint such a vivid picture of the accused's sad plight that hopefully no one could resist the mapping, and thus Darrow's client would be exonerated. This is, indeed, the meaning behind the French saying *Tout comprendre, c'est tout pardonner* — "To understand completely is to forgive completely." But in this case, it's the flip side: *Sans comprendre, comment pardonner?*

Diary of a Rapist

Another way to try to get into an alien mindset is to read a novel that goes deeply into someone's character. One such novel is Evan S. Connell's *Diary of a Rapist,* the hauntingly written but terribly disturbing chronicle of Earl Summerfield, a young man whose life is slowly spinning out of control. It takes place over a one-year period, and is, quite literally, a series of diary entries. Herewith a few selected entries, to give its flavor.

JUNE 2
Sunday. Whore of Babylon is in the paper again today. Mara St. Johns considered one of twelve outstanding young people in the city. Finishing her third year at the university where she's an honor student. Secretary-treasurer of Students Civic Council. Zend Avesta Literary Society. Queen of Washington Birthday pageant in Aquatic Park. Active member of Cabrillo Charities. Unity Presbyterian choir. Lives with her mother in Pacific Heights — as if I didn't know! Father was an Army colonel killed during the last war. Also says she's been to Hollywood recently for a screen test — well! well! As if any more proof was needed about what she really is! However, what interests me most is that now she's teaching Thursday-night Bible class in the church basement. I might attend. Might get to my feet while she's speaking and accuse her of being exactly what I know she is. I wonder what people would think of me if I did That! Everybody's guessed the truth about her, why are they afraid to say so? And she knows what a slut she is. Remember the expression on her face when she looked at me. Won't ever forget. Should have jerked her down off the platform & then pointed to her, not saying a word. Too late, but what I can do is drop a little note to the pastor of that church, demand that he get rid of her. As Ye sow, so shall Ye reap.
10:45 P.M. Heigh ho, Earl. What to do now? Not sleepy and don't have to get up tomorrow.

JUNE 27

Sick of myself, sick of Earl Summerfield, sick of the ideas that crawl into my head and cling to the inside of my skull. Might as well be a swarm of roaches. The problem is how to clean them out. I can't seem to. Tonight I didn't mean to do a thing, thought I'd have a pleasant walk possibly toward Pacific Heights because everything was warm & starry. Then all at once in the telephone booth. I think I took her by surprise. "Who's calling?" Maybe I should have dropped a hint. Well, I did of course, telling her I knew about the Bible class. The little whore. This is Earl Summerfield! — that's what I should have said. Do you hear me? Earl Summerfield! You better listen if you know what's good for you! Yes, that's how I should have spoken to her, then told her the truth about herself — as if she doesn't know! Certainly everybody ought to tell the truth. That would make the world a much more decent kind of place.

JULY 11

Who knows how our ideas come to us? From above, or below? From without, or within? Thoughts we never think. Those shears an inch from her throat, suddenly I felt a wish to marry her — I never dreamed that, God knows! I almost asked the slut. Would have, I think, but was afraid she'd start to laugh. Maybe she wouldn't laugh at me. I don't know. It's too late now, she hates me. Hates all men because of me. I didn't have any right to do what I did — it was wrong. But of course on the other hand it's what she deserved. She's a vile dirty little bitch. I should have ripped open her belly and snapped a picture of the mess — sent it to the Chronicle. Everybody ought to see exactly what she is. Exactly what she is. Everybody ought to see. That's right.

AUGUST 31

Oh Jesus when I think about her! — think of another kind of life. Think of her nakedness & all! Think of the letters of her name — even that's enough.

I'll send her a gift. What's appropriate? Jewels are cold, with undertones of death. I could send her a pebble washed by the ocean. Or the wing of a white seagull.

DECEMBER 19

The most difficult thing will be to explain — to tell her how I felt. How can I let her know that I was terrified of life, and this was the reason I fell in love with her? How can I help her to understand?

I pretended to myself that somehow she might love me because she is what I loved, and all that I've ever loved, all that I ever could love. I persuaded myself that she was frightened only by the depth of her own feeling toward me — saying what I needed to hear. But she does hate me & hopes for nothing so much as my death, I do know that. I wanted her more than I could want a basket of blue diamonds, or the softest yellowest bolt of silk in Japan. Blessings came to me from the blessing of her body & beside her a silver statue of the Virgin would look like a monstrous idol of gilded clay. Intercourse with her had no bitterness, so I think living with her would have no grief. I'd give anything to grow old with her, but I'll sooner hear snow falling on a mountain.

Why is it, I wonder, that we're able to let go of all things and desire only one woman so that we follow and stare at her and reach for her in our sleep? Why is she worth so much? Judith the daughter of Merari made Holofernes faint with the beauty of her face. She put on a linen dress to deceive him, arranged her hair and spread ointment on her eyes & showed him her sandals, and then she passed the scimitar through his neck as though he was an ox to be sacrificed. This is what I wonder, and all I know is that together we form a pattern of marvelous subtility.

DECEMBER 22

I called her & told her that on Christmas morning I'd knock at the door. Drunk with the joy of telling I promised that I'd bow down in front of her and ask to be forgiven. Yet I doubt that I can bow low enough — my deepest obeisance is pitiful.

DECEMBER 24

Now weigh me a weight of fire, measure me a measure of wind, call back a single day that has passed. Leaf of a green plant, touch of a child's hand. So enters the darkness, so helpless are we.

DECEMBER 25

In the sight of our Lord I must be one of many.

DECEMBER 26

Character Skylines, Similar and Alien

As I read this, I find myself lurching back and forth between feelings of compassion and revulsion for Earl Summerfield. Much of what he says is repugnant, and yet his soul is filled with poetry and confusion and anguish. At times, one can almost understand where he's coming from, one is almost right in there with him — and then he'll say something that is so alien and vicious that he seems like he's from another species. Back and forth he goes, vulnerability and cruelty intermingled in an incomprehensible way.

Of course I say this assuming that *you* would read it just as *I* do. But why should I assume any such thing? Well, let me go back to the metaphor of rates of exchange that I gave at the chapter's outset. My assumption is that, if I am likened to the United States, then most of my readers are like Western European countries — that is, there is basically an easy way of translating "values" (*i.e.,* monetary values, on one side of the metaphor, and ethical values, on the other) back and forth between us. More concretely, I assume that when you and I both try to relate to the contorted interiority of Earl Summerfield's psyche, we are like an American and a German trying to understand the Polish złoty (in the old days, I mean, before the collapse of the Soviet bloc): If either of them is confused, then so will the other one be, because dollars and marks are easily converted back and forth: there is a genuine rate of exchange. Thus despite being foreigners relative to each other, they see fairly much eye-to-eye about the bizarreness of the złoty. Likewise, most people are going to be far less psychologically aberrant than Earl Summerfield is, and hence their small discrepancies among each other can be ignored when they all look at him from their own vantage points.

Of course, the money metaphor is an oversimplification, because there will occasionally be dollar/mark discrepancies — for example, a rate of exchange that works well for books and for food, say, will seem screwy when it is applied to gasoline and air travel. But the occasional confusions engendered by translating between dollars and marks (or British pounds, Italian lire, Swedish kronor, or French or Swiss francs) pale in comparison with those engendered by the effort to translate between American dollars and (1975-vintage) Polish złotys.

Adapting the metaphor of the "prices skyline" for a currency, we could imagine the notion of a "character skyline", in which the strengths of dozens or, more likely, hundreds of different mental and emotional traits of an individual are represented by vertical bars of different heights. Given that there is such a skyline for each human being, there will of course be norms, and in most traits most people will fall fairly close to the norms. In other words, *your* character skyline and *mine* will look enough alike that there is a nearly constant "rate of exchange". This fact, tacitly assumed as part of life, is the basis for all human communication — it is what assures that we are not continually bamboozled by idiosyncratic personality quirks when we try to communicate ideas and emotions. It is the analogue to my young and naïve assumption that all world currencies would be just like the Western European currencies I had known — straightforwardly translatable into *my* currency through a nearly constant rate of exchange.

Though this is a fairly good assumption to run on, it is not perfect, and an occasional individual will have a hugely aberrant character skyline. With such a person, communication on major issues will simply break down. Just as the złoty lacked, in some sense, any value — that is, there was no coherent way to understand it, from a dollar's point of view — so this individual will seem to lack any value. There is no uniform (or fairly uniform) rate of exchange mediating a natural transfer of worldviews. Once again, it's that old saying, "You can't get there from here."

All of this is reminiscent of the earlier-cited remark by Schopenhauer that to convert *être debout* into *stehen*, no less would be needed than a "transfer of soul". Indeed, there are strong connections between mutual human understanding, on the one hand, and mappings between human languages, on the other. Recall the theme of George Steiner's *After Babel*: "Inside or between languages, human communication equals translation."

The Role of Fleeting Frame Blends in Understanding

Even though I was the one who bought the book, on the basis of excellent memories of reading Connell's *Mrs. Bridge* many years earlier, I read *The Diary of a Rapist* long after Carol did, and so unfortunately she and I never had the chance to discuss it. All I remember is that she considered it well written but very strange. It's no surprise that Carol found it difficult to enter into the mentality of a rapist; in some ways, one would have to assume that at least a certain fraction of the gulf would be simply due to the fact of belonging to the opposite sex. In other words, I would assume that even though I am both bewildered and repelled by Summerfield's thoughts and actions, I still am slightly closer to his point of view merely by virtue of being a male. Thus I probably can relate better than Carol could to the feeling, often expressed by Summerfield, of remote, unknown women as a source of longing and frustration. This does not mean I have the slightest insight into his rage or his desire to hurt, but still, it brings me "epsilon" closer to understanding him than Carol probably could have come.

There is simply a package of facts that comes along with being a heterosexual male but that has no exact counterpart in heterosexual females — in other words, there are certain local regions of the generic character skyline that tend fairly reliably to have one profile for females and another profile for males. As I already asked in Chapter 3, what then happens when a woman reads a novel that was written from and embodies a male's point of view about the world, or vice versa?

Carol and I used to attend the excellent operas put on by Indiana University's School of Music, and one time we went to see Johann Strauss' charming operetta *Die Fledermaus*. Carol always remembered the details of operas' plots; I'm the opposite, and tend to blur them terribly in my memory, so badly that it's almost comical. (I know some people who would say this is a perfect example of a standard discrepancy between female and male character skylines; maybe, but I'm not so sure.) In any case, during this performance I was deeply struck by one thing, and shortly afterwards I wrote down my reactions to it in some notes. In my usual absent-minded manner, I didn't even remember the characters' names — just abstract features of the situation that struck me as crucial.

> The woman's husband was going to be in jail for a week. When I saw that she was looking forward to an ex-lover's visit during that period, I instantly and instinctively mapped the situation onto "Gina" [name changed to protect the innocent!] coming to visit me while Carol is away for a week.
>
> Then, intrigued by the fact that I had unconsciously "chosen" to map myself onto the *wife* and not onto her *husband* (and it never for a split second occurred to me to map myself onto the guy who was coming to visit her), I started wondering how Carol, sitting right next to me, was seeing the exact same scene. Was she "being" the wife, as I had been doing? If so, presumably I was her husband and was going to be trotted off to jail for a week. And so — given my absence, which of her old boyfriends was *Carol* fantasizing about "entertaining" at our house for a week? Or was she perhaps mapping me onto the wife, herself onto the husband going off to jail, and thus imagining me having another woman at our house?
>
> In any case, this is how we always relate to operas, films, novels — amalgamating a million fleeting images, blending them into a kind of "stew", richly flavored. And most people, although they perhaps are vaguely aware of these fleeting images that bubble up unsummoned, don't think about them all that seriously, and don't realize that these are the *essence* of the experience of understanding.

On the Ununderstandable

The Seven Year Itch: Reprise

A similar but even more vivid instance of understanding by projection of oneself came up one time when Carol and I were watching a video of *The Seven Year Itch* at home one evening.

I hinted at the movie's plot in the previous chapter but will now sketch it out a little more. Basically, Richard Sherman is left alone in his family's New York apartment for the whole summer when his wife and young son go off to Maine for their vacation. It soon turns out that an unnamed young woman played by Marilyn Monroe — enormously alluring from a physical point of view, needless to say — has just moved into the apartment right above Richard's, also for the summer. She is a very vivacious person, sweet, gentle, humorous, fun-loving, and not at all stupid, but somehow she is incredibly oblivious to her powerful effect on men. That's really the crux of the humor. Her unintentionally provocative way of dressing and innocently flirtatious behavior sends her downstairs neighbor Richard into paroxysms of confusion and frustration, causing him to oscillate wildly between rich, romantic, Rachmaninoff-induced fantasies about seducing her in his apartment, and then fantasizing that his wife, having caught wind of the affair, returns from Maine to shoot him down in cold blood.

From my viewpoint as a "red-blooded male", watching this movie, there is only one way to see it: I project myself heart and soul into Richard Sherman's dazed shoes. What does this mean, more concretely? It means, in a vague, blurry sort of way, that "Carol" has gone off to "Maine" with "our son", and I am left alone in Bloomington/New York, and somehow, a super-seductive Marilyn Monroe type winds up living near our house and befriending me and driving me crazy with her unwittingly sexy antics. So there I am, oscillating between longing for her and fearing that "Carol" will come home and shoot me.

Do you think this is nonsense? I don't think so at all. No matter how faithful a husband I might be in real life, watching this movie *forces* me to start wanting to be unfaithful to "my wife", to have an affair with *that woman right there on the screen*. It is irresistible. Indeed, I would feel that anything less than this reaction — at least on the part of a heterosexual male viewer — would be highly abnormal, practically inhuman.

Not to feel Richard Sherman's pangs of ardent, confused longing would be to be an emotionless, asexual automaton. Such a machine would objectively register the facts: "That man wishes to be involved with that woman. The man's wife is away for the summer. The woman does not realize that the man wishes this involvement. The woman talks about things that tend to arouse erotic imagery in heterosexual males. The man fantasizes about the woman." And so on and so forth — all as clinical and as emotionally detached from the man's actual feelings as a heart surgeon is from the hopes and dreams of an anesthetized patient torn open on the operating table. This type of objective, detached, mechanical mode of "understanding" involves no splicing-in of one's own experience, no blending of what is on the screen with what one's current situation in life actually is — in short, is not what I mean by the word "understanding".

Itchier and Itchier

So far, so good. But now, here comes the crux of the matter. There I am, sitting next to my dear wife Carol, who is watching the same people in the same scenes. I think to myself, *What is Carol thinking?* And when the movie is over, *can we talk about it?* Why on earth would we not be able to talk about it? Well, that's simple to answer: Am I going to say to her, "Carol, you know, I really felt for the poor schmuck — Jesus, did I want him to 'get' her! I was aching for the poor guy"? If I come out with that, what is Carol going to think?

First of all, was Carol more likely to have identified with *the man* or with *one of the two women?* Naïvely, one would assume that Carol, herself a wife and mother, would identify with the wife off in Maine, who is very much a real person in the movie — seen first at the beginning of the film as she heads off to Maine, and later in a couple of scenes as part of Richard's fantasies. And yet, I somehow think the movie is set up so that whether one is male or female, heterosexual or homosexual, *one identifies with Richard Sherman.* That is, one brings in one's *own* old experiences of longing, one blends the longed-for ones in one's past into the seductive woman on the screen, and out of this act is born a blurry composite human in one's mind, part Monroe, part "Gina" (let us say), and it is for *that* neither-fish-nor-fowl fantasy being that one is dying with longing.

If one is a married woman watching the film, things are a bit more complicated than for a man, but basically the same. There may be a kind of blurred or oscillating allegiance, sometimes with the wife in Maine, sometimes with Richard Sherman in the apartment, but I suspect that the overwhelming majority of the time, you the real-life wife "become" Richard Sherman the movie husband, and you the real-life wife find "yourself" the pathetic klutz tormented by your "blonde upstairs neighbor".

Once again, *not* to see the film that way would be to be a soulless machine. And what allows you as a married heterosexual woman to "get inside Richard Sherman's head" is your own past longings, whether from during your marriage or from before it; thus a long-smoldering longing for "Vikpush" (or whoever) gets rekindled and blended in with the Marilyn Monroe figure, thereby allowing virtual flames of longing *for Marilyn Monroe* (or rather, for the unnamed blonde she is playing — or rather, for a blur of Monroe herself and the character she is playing) to flare up inside you.

On the Ununderstandable ◆ ◆ ◆ **475**

Of course, all of this goes on largely unconsciously and unrecognized, but that doesn't make it any less the case. How else than through merging their own life with it could anyone truly enter into the situation of a film? And if one fails to project oneself deeply into the film, what interest would watching it hold? For what other reason would we possibly wish to watch films, read novels, go to operas, or for that matter read newspaper stories, if not to project ourselves into them and feel them "from the inside"?

And Yet Itchier...

It is not as if the film's makers were oblivious to all the blended turmoil induced in their viewers, male and female alike. Indeed, they play on it and force viewers to wallow in it — that's the genius of the movie! For instance, there is one episode in which Sherman and his blonde friend decide to go to a movie together one evening, and you see them strolling out of the theater right after it is over. On the marquee you read "Creature from the Black Lagoon", and then you pick up their conversation:

She: But I just felt so sorry for the creature, at the end...

He: *Sorry* for the creature!?!? What did you want? Him to *marry* the girl?

She: He *was* kind of scary-looking, but he wasn't really *all* bad... I think he just craved a little *affection*, you know? The sense of being *loved,* and *needed*...

He: That's a very interesting point of view.

What is going on here? It doesn't take dazzling insight to realize that the horror flick from which they have just emerged features a disgusting-looking creature that oozes out of some slimy lagoon and then tries to spirit off a human female — a young and luscious one, of course — for itself. Clearly Richard Sherman has seen the movie *without* projecting himself into the monster's "shoes", and is totally set against the idea that that repugnant "he" should succeed in possessing her.

And yet, Marilyn Monroe — the very person who is playing the role of the young, luscious female in the film that *we* are watching — identifies with the *creature* (who is thereby mapped, implicitly, onto Richard Sherman himself), and contrary to all of Sherman's expectations (and presumably ours as well), she roots for the creature: at least part of her wants the creature to have the woman for itself. Beauty and the Beast, in a way.

Analogously, or so at least I would bet, my wife Carol, sitting right next to me on our red couch in the kids' playroom, and holding my hand, was probably rooting for Richard Sherman, the poor sap squirming in confusion and anguish, to "get" the sexy blonde. In some sense, then, Carol *was* being me, *was* rooting for the husband on the screen to be unfaithful to his wife, *was* rooting for "Doug" to be unfaithful to "Carol".

And yet, if I had said to Carol what I wrote above — "You know, I really felt for the poor schmuck — Jesus, did I want him to 'get' her! I was aching for the poor guy" — would she have nodded in eager agreement with my sentiments? I doubt it. Maybe Marilyn Monroe could get away with expressing a kind of wish for the creature to have "gotten the girl", but if Richard Sherman had done so, the Monroe character probably would have taken offense!

The Tie-in between Humor and Emotional Involvement

I have no certainty that my speculations above are right, and never will know what Carol really thought or felt. Perhaps, you might think, she was simply *amused* at the whole thing rather than getting deeply involved with the inner life of anyone in the film, especially such a hopeless buffoon as Richard Sherman. Why does anyone need to feel virtual anguish in order to laugh at a comedy, after all?

Well, I would argue that to classify *The Seven Year Itch* as "a comedy" is too facile and superficial. Yes, it's a comedy, but like many great comedies, it is a blend of pathos with humor. Without any doubt, Richard Sherman is ridiculous in many ways — but not so ridiculous that we can't feel for him. *The Seven Year Itch* is far from being just a slapstick farce made from a rapid-fire series of cute one-liner gags coming one on the heels of the other, with no genuine characters to feel for or care about; rather, its gags depend on a deep, human sense of yearning.

Indeed, I think the degree of humor one finds in the film is essentially *proportional* to the degree of emotional involvement one has with the characters involved. The less you are feeling Richard Sherman's anguish, the less you will find anything that he says or does funny. As understanding becomes increasingly objective, mechanical, and logic-based, funniness fades into the background and is soon gone.

I would concede that there may be people — women more likely than heterosexual men — who can enjoy the film without personally tasting Richard's lust. Thus I suppose a woman *might* see the Monroe character and think to herself, "Oh, yeah — I know from experience that *that* kind of ditzy broad always sends men spinning into a tizzy" — basically a detached, intellectual, third-person familiarity with "male psychology" or what has been called "the masculine gaze", as opposed to an empathic, first-person understanding of what Sherman must be feeling. Given such a syllogistic understanding, this hypothetical viewer can see Sherman's falling all over himself for the "ditzy broad" as funny, yet not share in his pangs. I would surmise, however, that such viewers, if they exist, and I'm not sure they do, enjoy the film far less than viewers of either sex who are right in there with Sherman, feeling his sharp tugs of longing as their very own.

On the Ununderstandable ◆◆◆ **477**

Deep Understanding as Identity-Blurring

I am now going to delve into topics that are philosophical and elusive, yet nothing could be more central to human existence. All that we have been considering in these past few sections now carries us forward. In my usual manner, I believe that one best confronts abstract issues when they are made most concrete, so I will spice things up with some little vignettes.

When he was between three and five years old, our son Danny went to Hoosier Courts nursery school, and Carol and I would alternate in picking him up there. One day when Carol went, she saw another child try to take something from Danny, and the way I remember her telling me about it was very much like this: "When I saw his little mouth start to pucker up, I practically started crying myself." This is typical of the parent–child bond: a deep identification in which a parent fuses their own emotions with those of their child in such a tight way that they are inseparable. The child's sufferings *become* the parent's sufferings. This does not mean that if a child falls down and gets hurt, so does the parent — it means that the pain inside the parent is a strong reflection of the child's. Obviously, if the child gets hurt outside of the parent's ken, then the parent cannot suffer along with the child, but when the parent learns of this hurt, the pain is spread and can be deep and intense.

All of this is almost self-evident and familiar to us all, but if one dwells on this and similar phenomena of projection, empathy, compassion, and deep understanding between two people, I believe one is led to strange and counterintuitive conclusions about what, for lack of a better word, I would call "human souls", and their relationship to human bodies and especially human brains. Basically, the direction in which I am moving is toward the conclusion that there is not a simple one-to-one correspondence between human souls and human brains, but that instead each human soul is a *distributed entity* that is, of course, concentrated most intensely in one particular brain but that is also present in a diluted or partial manner in many other brains, and the degree of presence of A's soul in B's brain, not surprisingly, is a direct function of the depth of shared history and mutual caring between A and B.

Again, an example may convey this more clearly, so here is another one. There were so many times when Carol and I would sit watching our children playing, and we would savor their sweetness and marvel in the fact that they were *ours*, that we had combined ourselves to produce these children. In such moments of intense intimacy between Carol and me, I believe it is fair to say that *we were looking at our children with the same eyes*. Obviously, the word "eyes" here is a metaphor, not a reference to biological organs located at the fronts of our optic nerves. Though Carol and I did not have the same eyes, we still had the same experience.

The mention of "eyes" brings me back to an idea that I discussed in Chapter 3 — that of vision mediated through a TV camera controlling an array of metal rods placed against one's back. I argued there that such a prosthetic manner of seeing would result in genuine vision no less than reading a newspaper in Chinese (as opposed to English) results in genuine understanding. What matters is not the physical input channel but the semantic structures produced at the end of the process.

This idea of the input channel's irrelevance holds also for more emotional events, such as parents watching children. When two people have shared a set of hopes and dreams for a long time, then those hopes and dreams blur out over their two brains and become *one set*. Then, when some visual experience taps directly into those hopes and dreams, the specific pair of eyes through which it happens is not particularly relevant. It is true that there are two *physical representations* of those hopes and dreams, but the abstraction behind them is singular, not plural.

Internalizing Someone Else's Eyes

When two people live together intimately, each comes to understand the world to some extent in the way that the other does. Each imbibes the other's point of view, and over a period of years, another person's way of looking at the world has become *internalized*. One can now look out at the world with the other person's eyes, see it with their soul.

One example that I will never forget is when Carol and I went out for dinner together, on what turned out to be our final wedding anniversary, our eighth, one October evening in 1993. We decided to indulge in an evening at La Cantinota, a very posh spot that had been praised by friends as one of Trento's best. We got all gussied up, drove down from our hillside village and parked, ambled through the quiet streets of Trento, and entered the restaurant. Well, the moment we walk in, an attractive young woman comes up to seat us. Even though this is Carol's and my anniversary and I "shouldn't" be feeling anything like this, I can't help but be a little distracted by this woman — I am not an asexual automaton. We sit down and look at the menus, and after a little bit, Carol says to me, "She's sort of your type, isn't she?" I have done nothing to reveal any interest in her; it's just that Carol *knows*. She has a keen sense for what it is that I respond to in certain very rare female faces, a sense that I've never been able to impart to anyone else. So I grin, a little sheepishly, and say, "Well, yeah — sort of…", and Carol knows she's right.

A few minutes go by, and Carol and I have ordered and are having a nice time talking about this and that — our new Italian friends, places we're hoping to visit in the next few months, how the kids are doing, the usual obvious stuff, all very pleasant — and every once in a while the woman who seated us walks near enough our table that we can both see her. At some point Carol says to me, "You know, I don't really think she's your type as much as I first thought — she's not soft enough." It was *exactly* what I had been thinking. The woman's face had an undeniable grace and fineness, but what was missing was a certain subtle hint of vulnerability or humbleness or compassion — something inarticulable yet definite, which just *wasn't there* — and Carol saw its lack just as quickly and surely as I did. She might as well have been me, she understood so clearly what certain faces can do to me (her own having been a prime example, of course).

And, carrying this thought just a little further, in some ways, Carol *was* me — and I no less was her. And I still *am* her, in some sense. Sometimes I describe how I feel these days by saying, "Well, now *I'm* Doug-&-Carol." Carol's hopes and dreams now reside in my brain; they grew there over the years, just as they grew inside her brain. They still flourish in mine, and in a small, diluted way, far less than before, some of Carol's soul, some of Carol's consciousness — just a tiny fraction, to be sure, but still, not nothing at all — survives inside me, because of all the merging and blurring over years of intimacy. And I'm not the only one in whom Carol's way of looking at the world, her way of being, lives on — to different degrees, she lives on inside those people who knew her intimately and loved her deeply: her family and her close friends.

Interpenetration of Souls

When I was a teen-ager, I came across a little math problem that was stated in terms of a metaphor, and the metaphor was so strong that it has remained with me over a lifetime. It was this (and I have illustrated it, showing how the solution looks):

Mrs. Miniver's problem

"She saw every relationship as a pair of intersecting circles. It would seem at first glance that the more they overlapped the better the relationship; but this is not so. Beyond a certain point, the law of diminishing returns sets in, and there are not enough resources left on either side to enrich the life that is shared. Probably perfection is reached when the area of the two outer crescents, added together, is exactly equal to that of the leaf-shaped piece in the middle. On paper there must be some neat mathematical formula for arriving at this; in life, none."

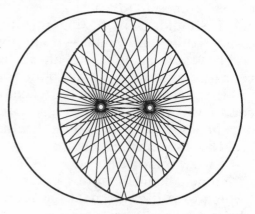

So here are two lovers, represented as interpenetrating circles of the same size, and we seek the optimal amount of overlap for a happy love affair — of course not too little, but also not too much. Well, Mrs. Miniver has the recipe, at least if we're dealing with pure geometric circles.

I certainly don't know whether Carol and I had the ideal amount of overlap, but I would say we approximated it fairly well, and what appeals to me about this visual image is that when two circles have this optimal, Miniverian amount of overlap, then the *center* of each circle is located inside the other circle. I take this metaphorically, letting it suggest that the "I", the very core, of each person has been incorporated into the other person. Not only lovers, they are now psychologically merged, blurred, blended, and fused, and have come to form one composite entity. This is perhaps why, a few months after Carol had died and I was gazing up at her photo one day on top of our dresser, I felt myself falling deeply into and through her eyes right into her innermost core, and behind a veil of tears I heard myself sobbing, "That's *me*, that's *me*." It sounds irrational but I truly felt I was inside her, or else that she was inside me — one or the other, or both.

Who Survives, and How, in Brains?

These are ideas that to some may seem strange and jolting, for the usual wisdom is that people are separate entities, sealed off from each other in a watertight manner, and that when you die, you are totally extinguished. Well, certainly *something* is extinguished. The question is: What is it that remains? Is it just a strong set of third-person memories, or is there something — even just the tiniest shred — left of the deceased's *I*?

Unless one is conventionally religious and believes in the notion that there are souls that go up to heaven, one presumes that consciousness is like a light that simply goes off at death, and that is that. And certainly in some sense, that must be right. But think about yourself ten years ago. Where is *that* person's I? Is that person still conscious? No, that person is just a set of memories inside your brain (and those of other people). The world has gone black for that person, just as in death — but it is light for *you*. And because the you of now and the you of yore are like overlapping Miniverian circles, that person still lives on a bit inside your sphere of light.

If you go back further to the you of twenty years ago, that person and today's you are circles that overlap less, and hence that remoter, younger person survives less inside you now than does the more recent you. And of course the overlap between the you of just a day or two ago and the you of today is so extensive that it can be visualized as two identical circles just barely displaced with respect to each other, having far more overlap than do Miniverian lover-circles. In that sense, the you of yesterday has not been extinguished, and will not be extinguished for a long time — not until the vagaries of life have dragged the circle of you-ness far enough from where it once was that there no longer is much overlap; metaphorically speaking, as the center of one circle crosses the circumference of the other, the consciousness of the old you starts to fade.

Such ideas are hard to explain, to think about, even to believe. But I have been forced, by the sadness of circumstances, to grapple with them intensely over the past three years. I suppose a reader might infer that I suddenly jumped aboard this belief system because it afforded me some degree of comfort and consolation, and isn't that nice? I too would be skeptical of any writer who said such things in the wake of a deep personal trauma; I would tend to think, "Here is someone bending under pressure, seeking a way to deny the harsh and senseless finality of death."

However, what makes me feel secure about the underpinnings of these ideas in my mind is that they were all developed long before Carol died — long before anyone in my intimate family died. They came, quite the contrary, out of purely intellectual musings, over a couple of decades, about the mind–body problem and the seat of consciousness. Although many of my ideas were expressed in *The Mind's I: Fantasies and Reflections on Self and Soul,* an anthology of writings that I co-edited with philosopher Daniel Dennett, I sometimes feel I gave my best shot at articulating these ineffable ideas in "Who Shoves Whom Around Inside the Careenium?", a dialogue in my later book *Metamagical Themas.* Here I won't make any attempt to summarize its ideas, but I do want to mention one salient fact.

As was the case in all the chapters of *Metamagical Themas,* there was a "Post Scriptum" at the end. This one was very unusual, though, for in it I recalled how a certain friend, not a close friend at all but someone who nonetheless had had a powerful impact on me in our few short interactions, had voiced the hope of collaborating with me on revising that dialogue, and over a period of a few months had sent me dozens of letters filled with provocative ideas about self-organizing systems and the nature of life, intelligence, and consciousness. The collaboration he had so ardently hoped for never materialized, for he died before there was any chance of it. In my P.S., I sadly quoted a few vivid and colorful passages from some of his letters, and then closed "The Randy Reader" in this way:

> On April 10, 1983, Randy Read took his own life. I don't know why. Perhaps these musings, dancing and sparking in the neurons of a few thousand readers out there, will keep alive, in scattered form, a tiny piece of his soul.

I wrote this long before there were any glimmers of sudden tragedy in my own family, and hence it is one among many pieces of evidence that collectively reassure me that my musings about fragmentary, diluted survival of a soul in multiple brains were not manufactured simply as a result of an emotional buckling when suddenly I was forced to face the unfaceable.

Reasons and Persons

The person who has written most extensively and most persuasively on these ideas is, in my opinion, the British philosopher Derek Parfit, in his marvelous though difficult book *Reasons and Persons*. In a series of four chapters with the suggestive titles "What We Believe Ourselves to Be", "How We Are Not What We Believe", "Why Our Identity Is Not What Matters", and "What Does Matter", Parfit sets forth a stunningly coherent theory of what makes a person — or, in my language, what makes an "I".

At the core of Parfit's system is the stark rejection of the idea that there is a perfect "one soul, one brain" correspondence. This is not to deny that that is a very good approximation to the truth, especially in these days before teleportation and brain-splicing operations. In fact, the "one soul, one brain" theory is *such* a good approximation to the truth that it pulls the wool over our eyes, and prevents us from seeing a far subtler and deeper truth, much as the incredible accuracy of Newton's laws prevented physicists from seeing, or even suspecting the existence of, the deeper and subtler truths of relativity and quantum mechanics for several centuries.

Like many philosophers, Parfit proceeds by inventing a variety of imaginative thought experiments and drawing out their implications as carefully as he can. I will give the flavor of only one of dozens:

> Jane has agreed to have created in her brain copies of some of Paul's memory-traces. After she recovers consciousness in the post-surgery room, she has a new set of vivid apparent memories. She seems to remember walking on the marble paving of a square, hearing the flapping of flying pigeons and the cries of gulls, and seeing light sparkling on green water. One apparent memory is very clear. She seems to remember looking across water to an island, where a white Palladian church stood out brilliantly against a dark thundercloud.

*　　*　　*

> What should Jane believe about these apparent memories? Suppose that, because she has seen this church in photographs, she knows it to be San Giorgio in Venice. She also knows that she has never been to Italy, while Paul goes to Venice often. Since she knows that she has received copies of some of Paul's memory-traces, she could justifiably assume that she may be quasi-remembering some of Paul's experiences in Venice....
>
> Quasi-memories would provide ... knowledge about other people's past lives. They would provide knowledge of what these lives were like, *from the inside*. When Jane seems to remember walking about the Piazza, hearing the gulls, and seeing the white church, she knows part of what it was like to be Paul, on that day in Venice.

Parfit goes on for many pages to discuss this idea of how one person's presumably unique and nontransmissible first-person experience of the world can in principle be shared by another person. Although I agree with all he says, he does not go quite as far as I would in his views on this. In particular, for him, "quasi-memories" can be implanted in someone's mind only via futuristic brain operations. He never discusses the idea that they might come via as mundane a channel as *words*.

One time my friend David Policansky told me in quite a bit of detail about the movie *The Angel Levine*, with Zero Mostel and Harry Belafonte, and for years thereafter I was unsure if I had actually seen it or not. I seemed to have such a clear image of the movie in my mind that I simply didn't know. Finally, Carol and I went to see it one evening in Ann Arbor and I realized that although I had a fairly accurate image of it in some ways, it was nonetheless quite different from what I had thought, and so of course I had never really seen it. But I had received from David a large dose of what it was like to see the film, and had generated a "quasi-memory" of seeing it. This quasi-memory was reasonably faithful but also had quite a number of errors in it. But that's equally true of *real* memories.

How many times have I gone to my old diary and re-read an episode from decades ago, only to discover how crazily I had distorted it in the intervening years! How much am I who I used to be? As Clément Marot put it, *Plus ne suis ce que j'ay esté, / Et ne le sçaurois jamais estre…* ("What once I was no longer I'm, / Nor will a second chance come…").

Partial Translatability of Past Selves into the Present

Whenever I dare to pull out and re-read a few pages of some volume of my diary from back when I was twenty or twenty-one, I alternately cringe, smile, and ache for the poor guy. On such occasions, the Steinerian thought crosses my mind that trans-era self-understanding, no less than communication between two distinct people, deeply involves translation in its most general sense.

I just looked up, for instance, that day of my Prokofiev violin-concerto blasting in Ravenna, and recognized so much of the now-me in the then-me — and yet how unutterably different we are. One thing I had forgotten is that I also blasted out Prokofiev's third piano concerto. Here is what I had to say about it all:

> The whole sound was as fresh & as expansive & exciting as the sunlight falling all over in its morning way. As a matter of fact, the soaring-air part of #3 was fantastically airy today, & I looked out my big golden door & saw birds taking wing & losing themselves in the all-swallowing sea of air.

I then pulled out the next volume of the diary, hoping to find in it some introspection about my egocentric blasting of the B-minor Mass through the Kungshamra hall, but all I could find was this brief reference:

"Smashed fist and blasted B minor in exultation over…" — a reference to a hoped-for romance that never materialized. Many strange, sad tugs at my heart. It's very weird to relive bits of one's life so intensely.

Just a few pages away, I was most surprised to find a short, melancholy, free-verse Swedish poem called *Vågrörelse* — "Wave Motion" — along with two English translations, one by myself and one by a friend, and I even had written some notes comparing them. I recognized nearly every word of the original Swedish poem even though I doubt I had thought about it a single time in lo these thirty years; by contrast, after seeing my translation, I had only the dimmest memory of creating it. I had totally forgotten having been into poetry translation that far back (although this was probably my only venture into it, and wasn't very great). Almost eerie is the fact that one line of *Vågrörelse* talks about *en vän som är död sedan trettio år* — "a friend dead lo these thirty years" — as if the poem were somberly talking about its own long-dormant state in my mind.

Relating to one's former self — or rather, former *selves* — is often as complex and as confusing as is relating to other people around one. The aggressive, self-righteous noise-polluter of thirty years ago is bad enough, but what about when you can't understand something you did a very *short* while ago? More as a parent than in any other area of life, I have found my own behavior disturbingly often to be irrational and inexplicable — even behavior that I engaged in as little as *one minute ago*! How could I have been so angry? How could I have acted so mean? Or else the flip side of the coin: Why in the world do I give in to these caprices? Why am I such a pushover, falling over and over again for those crocodile tears? And sometimes the very clearest light is shed on my own recent behavior when I manage to find an apt analogy to someone *else*'s behavior. If that doesn't show how weird self-understanding is, then I don't know what would.

Concentric Rings of Diminishing Empathy

At the root of all of the examples of failed or successful human understanding discussed in this chapter is *empathy*: the ability to project oneself into another's life, to model and even absorb inside oneself another person's way of being. Some people, of course, are more empathetic than others — like any human quality, empathy comes in different doses, distributed among the population in some kind of bell-shaped curve. A few rare people are exceedingly empathetic, a few are extremely sociopathic, and most of us fall somewhere closer to the middle. The distance in "acquaintance space" at which an individual's empathy tails off is a central character trait determining many things, including one's politics. *Grosso modo,* the conflict between left-wing and right-wing ideologies is simply the battle between large-radius and small-radius individuals writ large.

Most adults feel empathy for their family members and even for their close friends. Some people feel empathy for a large circle of acquaintances, and a few have an even wider circle of empathy that reaches out and encompasses people they read about in newspaper articles and simply imagine in their own minds. But clearly, the more remote someone is from us — whether in time, location, temperament, or situation — the harder it will be for us to project, and thus the less empathy there will be. Of course, this is good, not bad, for as the concentric circles enlarge, there are first thousands, then millions, then billions of people in them, and one would simply expire of anguish if one could sense but a droplet of their total pain.

My anguish over my wife's death is incomparably greater, for better or for worse, than my genuine sorrow and revulsion over the deaths of half a million Rwandans in the genocidal war of a couple of years ago. This is simply human nature. We are local, myopic creatures, and cannot extend our feelings arbitrarily far out, even if intellectually we feel we ought to, or ought to be able to. We simply are not built that way.

For this reason, I have frequently mused that the genetic parameters that collectively and implicitly determine a typical human's level of empathy for other humans (or beings) in the outer orbits are the key entities that determine the global state of our world, and for that reason, I so often have wished that I could somehow get in and play with *just one knob* on the vast control panel of human nature — the knob that sets the rate with which empathy tapers off as a function of other people's remoteness.

I imagine a hypothetical world in which empathy tails off much more slowly than in reality it does; in that world, any society would be bound together in a denser, more viscous manner than in this one. This might — who knows? — have the adverse effect of making individual nations so tightly unified and monolithic that they would, as *emergent* entities, have much sharper identities than they do today (heaven help us!), and hence there would be much more intense rivalries at that level. After all, just as a human is a huge and selfish collection of utterly selfless cells, so a nation in that "utopia" would be a huge collection of enormously empathetic and hence relatively selfless, self-sacrificing humans. Such a utopia might turn out to be hell on earth, not at the level of humans but at a far higher level of agglomeration. While it might be paradisial to be a mere human, it might be sheer hell to be a whole nation!

Linguistic Empathy

My mentioning the idea of "being a whole nation" may have seemed casual, but in fact the idea is hardly casual; indeed, for most human beings, such a suggestion would seem not casual but beyond understanding, most likely incoherent. I wouldn't claim that I personally know "what it would be like to be a nation" — but I'm at least willing to formulate and entertain the notion, and I believe it may well be coherent, although very strange.

Perhaps an even less coherent notion is that of "being a language". It might seem a bit less nutty, though, if I link it to our earlier discussion of empathy. If interpersonal empathy is an unusually strong capacity of one person to absorb and internalize other people's viewpoints and feelings, and if that is one of the keys to being able to translate deeply, then it's not so unnatural to speculate about the degree to which a given *language* is intrinsically receptive to the internalizing of ideas expressed in other languages. Is there such a thing, in short, as "linguistic empathy" — the capacity, on the part of a given language, to accommodate both messages and structural patterns that originate in other languages and cultures?

Just as with people, there will be concentric rings surrounding any given language, because in a very crude manner of speaking, a language can far more easily absorb a message created in a language of its own family than a message created in an unrelated family from halfway around the world. Thus Spanish is very empathetic relative to Portuguese and Catalan, perhaps slightly less empathetic relative to French and Italian, and only mildly empathetic relative to Rumanian. When it comes to German or Swedish, say, Spanish may be quite neutral, and as for Eskimo, there may be no receptivity at all in Spanish for literature coming through that channel.

Given that every language, like nearly every person, is empathetic towards its own family, are there special languages whose empathy reaches out further into the more distant rings surrounding it? Is English such a language? Are there any languages that are sociopathic? What would make a language more or less empathetic? I honestly have no idea, although I think the notion makes sense.

Language Death and the Survival of Linguistic Souls

The notion of a "dead language" is a metaphor based, of course, on the fact of death of individuals. Around the globe, there are languages disappearing all the time, and in a sense these extinctions, like those of people, are great tragedies. But just as one can ask if a dead person's self or soul lives on in some dilute, distributed manner in the brains or minds of other people, one can also ask if a dead language might survive dilutedly and distributedly in its closest linguistic relatives and "friends".

To make this concrete, suppose that the French language, in some improbable cataclysm, were suddenly wiped out — no native speakers left anywhere. Would it be impossibly far-fetched to argue that some of the "soul" of French nonetheless survived in, say, the Italian or Catalan languages? Could speaking Italian then be thought of as "speaking French very weakly", or would that be unjustifiable?

On the Ununderstandable ◆◆◆ **487**

If this sounds preposterous, keep in mind that from our distant Occidental vantage point, languages like Cantonese and Mandarin (which are probably about as far apart as French and Italian, maybe further), are often blurred together under the single name "Chinese". In a symmetric blur, an Oriental perspective might lump Italian, French, Spanish, Catalan, Portuguese, Rumanian, and so forth all together in one "superlanguage" called simply "Romance". Fine distinctions, such as that between French and Italian, would be seen as mere nitpicking, a luxury analogous to dignifying someone's unique fashion of speaking their native language by calling it an "idiolect".

From such a remote perspective, the total disappearance of all native speakers of French, leaving Italian and Portuguese and so forth intact, would be a little like my own personal perspective on the hypothetical disappearance of, say, all Parisian speakers of French, leaving intact the many diverse "Frenches" spoken in Marseille, Genève, Bruxelles, Montréal, Québec, Kinshasa, Abidjan, Toulouse, Lyon, Pontoise, Harfleur, Perpignan, Bourges, Nevers, Cahors, and so forth. I would see such an event as a vast tragedy at the *human* level but as having almost no effect at the *linguistic* level. The "soul" of the French language would emerge nearly unscathed.

Analogously, the hypothetical Oriental perspective would perceive the hypothetical poofing-into-nothingness of French, with most of Romance left intact, as a local event of little linguistic importance. The question of survival of the "soul of the French language" would be seen as being focused at too local a level; after all, the "Romance" language as a whole would still live on, and that's all that would count.

Soul-patterns Floating across Lands and Brains

I have been pretty glibly batting about the phrase "soul of the French language", but what does such a thing mean? It would be very hard to define, but in making a stab at it, I would point out that there are certain works of art, such as the music of Chopin or the poetry of Pushkin, that seem to define a national or linguistic soul — Polish or Russian, in these cases. To what extent can such high spiritual abstractions be made accessible to other nations or cultures — at least to empathetic ones?

If Pushkin's output is "the soul of Russian literature" (as Russians often claim it to be), and if it can be transported to other languages and cultures (as we've seen can be done with considerable success), then one might conclude that *Russian's soul transcends Russia's soil.* That is, there is no unsunderable unity of the physical land of Russia and the abstraction that is the core of Russian-ness. Rather, since the core of Russian-ness is a *pattern,* it can float across media. Indeed, what is translation, if not that which allows national souls to interpenetrate and blur into each other?

This brings us back to earlier musings about the overrated perfection of the correspondence between human souls and human brains. To make the analogy very direct, think of your brain as analogous to the Russian soil enriched by the Russian language. And think of your consciousness as analogous to the soul of Russian literature, as a rose — a rose that arose in that garden of sounds and grammar and will ever flourish best there, yet is not ineradicably tied to it but may also flourish, even if not so robustly, in another soil enriched by its own local ecology of sounds and grammar.

As Derek Parfit suggests, a human soul is a pattern that is nurtured in a single brain over a specific lifetime, but thanks to the power of language and other deep cultural products such as music and art, much of that abstract pattern can float across from the original brain into other human brains. Not just ideas or "memes", but hopes and fears, desires and pangs — who knows, maybe even shards of consciousness — might float across from one brain to another, thus causing the soul to spread itself out a little, to form a little "bell" centered on one specific brain but blurring outwards to inhabit, at different grades of intimacy, a set of close, empathic brains.

The Push to Build Alien Souls in our Midst

The idea of projecting oneself onto a whole nation or a language is of course incredibly strange and unnatural-seeming. Even the idea that one's very own first-person consciousness might be spread out among numerous brains, not just limited to a single brain (or conversely, the idea that one's own "private" brain might be shared, albeit weakly, by other people's first-person consciousnesses, especially those of beloved ones) strains our imaginations close to the breaking point. These ideas are mind-boggling.

For many people, just as mind-boggling is the suggestion that matter has anything to do with spirit. The idea that a "mere hunk of metal" (as so many people would describe today's computers and all conceivable advances made thereupon) could ever come to be pervaded by what might be called "spirit" or "soul" or "awareness" or "consciousness" seems absurd beyond belief. How spirit can come to pervade bio-matter is not asked; it just "makes sense" (more or less in the way that "Jack hates chocolate and Jill likes liver" makes sense) and hence is accepted as a fact of Nature.

But the relentless push towards making an artificial intelligence is infringing ever more on the sanctity of bio-matter as spirit's unique physical harbor. Not just intelligence but also emotionality and consciousness are the goal, with all they entail: empathy, interiority, soul, spirit. Some of my AI colleagues have at times had the hubris of predicting a rosy short-term future for AI, and failed dismally. Herbert Simon, for instance, one of AI's founders, notoriously predicted in 1957 that within a decade a computer would be world chess champion. As we know in 1996, Simon was wrong.

For many reasons, including the low level of machine translation today, I still tend to the opinion that the emergence of genuine intelligence in machines is a long way off, but occasionally something rocks my faith and frightens me with the image of machines *soon* becoming our partners in the world of thinking and feeling beings. One such event was the recent chess match between Garry Kasparov and the chess computer Deep Blue.

The Brute-force Nonmind of a Chess Machine

As it did for many people, this match stimulated many ponderings on my part about where things in the AI world are going. If the past is any guide to the future, the look-ahead horizon of brute-force chess programs will slowly increase, as it has with regularity for the past forty years or so, and at some point will encroach upon the further-out and blurrier horizon that so-called "strategic" or "positional" play affords human grandmasters. At that point, machine play will start to look creative, insightful, brilliant.

So far, of course, we are not there. Indeed, I have heard Deep Blue's performance in its final two games against Kasparov described by various top-level chess commentators as "meandering", "aimless", and "confused". Are we humans therefore to exult in our triumph over the alien silicon monster? That's fine, but then what about the year 2008, when Deep Blue's far more powerful successor, Deep Pink, finally overtakes the future world champion Judith Polgar — should we then shed bitter tears?

A word of perspective. The way brute-force chess programs work doesn't bear the slightest resemblance to genuine human thinking, and so for me they have little intellectual interest, although I certainly enjoy the spectacle of the battle. My own research over the past twenty years has focused on what I consider the core of human intelligence — the ability to adapt to different domains, to spot the gist of situations amidst a welter of superficial distractors, to see abstract resemblances between disparate situations, to be reminded by one situation of another. Spotting hidden patterns, extracting deep gists, forming high abstractions, making subtle analogies — these to me define the crux of the mental; they are what we do best of all creatures, natural and artificial, on the surface of this tiny huge blue-green ball spinning its way through unfathomable reaches of space.

Do machines do these kinds of things yet? No, not very well. Are they on their way to doing so? Well, to a degree. Their capacities at these tasks are still very rudimentary, but we are making progress. For decades, cognitive and perceptual psychologists have been devising beautiful and deep probes into the mechanisms behind human memory, the associative structures that underlie words and concepts, the way that perception hooks seamlessly into cognition, and so forth — and their findings are not going unheeded by researchers working on computer models of the mind. My own research on creative analogy-making by computer, for instance, is pervasively influenced by such studies.

So if we shift our attention from the flashy but inflexible kinds of game-playing programs like Deep Blue to the less glamorous but more human-like programs that model analogy-making, learning, memory, and so forth, being developed by cognitive scientists around the world, we might ask, "Will *this* kind of program ever approach a human level of intelligence?" I frankly do not know. Certainly it's not just around the corner. But I myself see no reason why, *in principle,* human-like thought, consciousness, and emotionality could not be the outcome of very complex processes taking place in a chemical substrate different from the one that happens, for historical reasons, to underlie our species.

Mechanical Empathy

The question then arises — a very hypothetical one, to be sure: When these "creatures" (why not use that term?) someday come into existence, will they be threats to our own species? My answer is, it all depends. What it depends on, for me, comes down to one word: *benevolence.*

If robot–computers someday roam along with us across the surface of our planet, and if they compose music, translate poetry, and regale each other with droll witticisms — *and* if they leave us humans pretty much alone, or even help us achieve our goals — then why should we feel threatened? Obviously, if they start trying to push us out of our houses or to enslave us, that's another matter and we should feel threatened and should fight back.

But just suppose that we somehow managed to produce a benevolent breed of silicon-based robots that shared much of our language and culture, although with differences, of course. Although we and they would be friendly, there would naturally be a kind of rivalry between our different types, perhaps like that between different nations or races or sexes. But when the chips were down, when push came to shove, with whom would we feel allegiance? How far out would the cutoff of our empathy spheres lie? Where would "we-ness" come to an end, and "they-ness" take over?

What Is "We", But "I" Writ Large?

There is an old joke about the Lone Ranger and his sidekick Tonto one day finding themselves surrounded by a shrieking and whooping band of Indians circling in on them with tomahawks held high. The Lone Ranger turns to his faithful pal and says, "Looks like we're done for, Tonto...", to which Tonto replies, "What you mean, *we,* white man?"

Let me suggest a curious scenario. Suppose we humans and our artificial progeny had coexisted for a while on our common globe, when one day a weird strain of microbes arose out of the blue, attacking carbon-based life with a virulence that made today's Ebola virus seem like a long-lost friend. After but a few months, the entire human race is utterly wiped out, yet our silicon cousins are untouched.

After shedding molten-metal tears over our disappearance, they then go on doing their multifarious things — composing haunting songs (influenced most of all by Couperin, Khatchaturian, and Carole King), writing searching novels (in English, Anglo-Saxon, Gallic, and other human tongues), making hilarious jokes (maybe even ethnic and sexual ones), and so on. If we today could look into some crystal ball and somehow see that bizarre future, would we not thank our lucky stars that we had somehow managed, by hook or by crook, to propagate *ourselves* into the indefinite future by means of a switchover in chemical substrate? Would we not feel, looking into that crystal ball, that "we" were still somehow alive, still somehow *there*? Or — would those silicon-chip creatures bred of our own fancy still be unworthy of being labeled "we" by us?

For whom would we root, then, if, as we continued to peer into the crystal ball, we witnessed a *carbon-based* race of alien invaders from some dark planet circling Betelgeuse approaching the earth and systematically trying to wipe out the gentle, benevolent race of silicon-based intelligences to which we humans had intellectually but not biologically given rise? For that matter, forget the dark-planet space-alien scenario and simply imagine an all-out battle for survival between our hypothetical benevolent silicon-based robots and some aggressive new carbon-based form of life that arose on earth itself — some mutant form of giant wasps or spiders, say, or even a mercilessly bellicose chimpanzee society.

Would we as human beings watching helplessly on the sidelines be indifferent to the outcome? Or would we mindlessly align ourselves with the carbon? Or possibly — is it within our ability to extend the word "we" from our simple *genetic* pool to something more abstract, something based on a certain way of thinking and feeling and caring, irrespective of the physical medium in which it is embedded?

Where Lies the Periphery of the Collective Human Soul?

I once gave a lecture at Erasmus University in Rotterdam, Holland, in which I conjured up just such a vision of benevolent silicon creatures and suggested that the word "we" might someday come to encompass *them,* just as it now encompasses females and males, old and young, yellow and red, black and white, gay and straight, Arabs and Jews, weak and strong, cowardly and brave, short and tall, clever and silly, and so on. The next speaker happened to be Joseph Weizenbaum, author of the Eliza program and later of the book *Computer Power and Human Reason,* a gentle-looking, eloquent, elderly fellow — indeed, quite resembling benevolent old Einstein — and he was not in the least happy with my vision.

Weizenbaum lit into my hypothetical scenario by arguing vociferously that the mere act of trying to develop artificial intelligence was inherently dangerous and evil, and that we should never, ever let computer programs make moral judgments, no matter how complex, subtle, or autonomous the programs might be. He argued that computers, robots, or hybrids thereof, whatever they might become, irrespective of their eventual natures, *must* in principle be kept out of certain areas of life — that our species, *homo sapiens sapiens,* has an exclusive and sacred right to certain behaviors and ideas, and this right must be protected above all.

Well, to my astonishment, when the benevolent-looking Weizenbaum had finished his pronouncements, nearly the entire audience rose to its feet and clapped wildly. Dazed, I could not help but be reminded of the crudest forms of racist, sexist, and nationalist oratory. Despite its high-toned and moralistic-seeming veneer, this exhortation and the audience's knee-jerk reaction seemed to me to be nothing more than a mindless and cruel biological tribalism rearing its ugly head. And this reaction, mind you, was in the supremely cosmopolitan, anti-Fascistic, internationally-minded country of Holland! Can you imagine how my ideas would have been greeted in the Bible Belt, in Teheran, or the Vatican?

Why can we humans not open our little minds to the potential idea that if, in some wild and far-off day, we finally succeeded in collectively creating nonbiological creatures that perceived, that enjoyed, that suffered, that joked, that loved, that hated and created — and even procreated — the very word "we" would at that very moment have opened up its semantic field to embrace these, the products of our hearts' deepest yearnings?

Why should a race of benevolent if fleshless beings be any less worthy of being considered our "children's children" than the potential gang of music-polluters, lyrical rapists, priest-assassins, and mob-frenzied jackbooted genocide perpetrators that might spring forth from the celestial union of my eager sperms with your equally eager ova? Just how far out does that circle stretch, whose radius is defined by the slippery word "we"? I wonder.

●

Poems XV:

~ That Ol' Sino Room ~

* * * * * * *
* * * *
* *
*
*

One pretty spring day in 1990, I gave a talk on the "Ma Mignonne" translation game and in passing dismissively alluded to the state of the art in machine translation. In the lively question-and-answer session that ensued, someone asked me if I had ever tried MT out on Marot's poem, and I said no, adding "What for? Hoping a current MT program will come up with a good translation of 'Ma Mignonne' is like hoping that your two-year-old will waddle out to the track and then pole-vault gracefully into the sky." The questioner persisted, though, and over the next few days, as I mused on this, I gradually became persuaded that it could be not just informative and useful, but also fun, to see what would happen if a reputable machine-translation program was turned loose on "Ma Mignonne".

I contacted my friend Toon Witkam in Holland, deeply involved in a major MT project for the European Community, explaining that I needed help: I wanted to run this little French poem through Toon's translation program so I could then go around the world giving lectures in which I would heap scorn on the pitiful level of current translation technology. Toon, no slowpoke at catching the undertones of human discourse, said, "I wish I could help you out with *our* program, but unfortunately we haven't yet got it working on French to English. It goes from English to French right now, but not the other way... Dratted shame! However, I could run your poem through some *rival* MT programs!" I happily accepted Toon's suggestion, and soon received in the mail this translation by Systran, a program described in the 1988 book *New Directions in Machine Translation* as "the most widely used and undoubtedly most successful mainframe MT system". Indeed, the article also reports that at the U.S. Air Force Foreign Technology Division in Dayton, Ohio, "By 1987 nearly 100,000 pages each year were being translated" and moreover that "...researchers at the Kernforschungszentrum [a nuclear research center in Karlsruhe] are very satisfied with the raw output from the French–English version."

With "My Nice" we come, in some sense, full circle. That is, we find ourselves back where we started with the first group of poems: at the level of total literality, with no attention paid to structure. Like all other MT programs, Systran has no concept of literary form, tone, or anything of the sort. It thus ignored all of Marot's line-breaks, rhymes, syllable-counts, and so on, treating his poem exactly as if it were text in a patent abstract or a washing-machine repair manual. Thus we must judge Systran not as a translator of *poetry*, but as a translator of *prose* — still no trivial matter, as the facing page reveals.

I won't make fun of all the graceless, nearly vacuous phrases it came up with ("Goes, fond of delicacies of your mouth, which lie down in danger", etc.). Nor will I hold it against Systran for not knowing the unusual or antiquated French words *vitement, mande, embonpoint,* and *doint* — even though, I must say, a mildly intelligent human who knew but a modicum of French would instantly see the *vite* and the *ment* inside *vitement,* and catch the drift of the word. Why Systran didn't get *couleur,* however, is a genuine mystery.

But the true weirdness is on lines 11 and 20. What is behind "If you hard too sick"? At first, I hadn't a clue. Only slowly did it dawn on me that *dures,* the intimate-you form of the verb *durer* ("to last"), could also be seen — by someone who was translating while desperately fighting off sleep and also improvising a fugue on piano — as the feminine-plural form of the adjective *dur* ("hard"). And thus, "If you hard". Hard to believe...

And what's with "Kind"? Did Systran somehow picture Uncle Clement as a kindly old gent? Guess again. The line *Et qu'on sorte* ("And [one should] get out") was apparently too hard for Systran to parse, so it backed off a little and settled for translating just one word of it: *sorte* ("get out"). But *sorte* is not only a subjunctive verb; it is also a plain old noun, meaning "sort/type/variety". And thus, "Kind". Kind of weird, eh wot?

Actually, *very* weird — so weird that I myself could never have dreamt up such bizarre mistakes. And now you know why I put "sort" and "hard" into my poem "My Mignonne".

My Nice

Systran

My nice,
I give you
The hello.
The stay,
It is prison.   5
Cure
Cover,
Then open
Your door,
Vitement   10
Kind
For Clément
You it mande.
Goes, fond of delicacies
Of your mouth,   15
Which lie down
In danger,
To eat
Jams.
If you hard   20
Too sick,
Insipid couleur
You will take,
And lose
The embonpoint.   25
God you doint
Good health,
My nice.

Along with Systran's rendition, Toon also sent me "My Cute", done by GTS, as well as an ad for this program and a review of it in the journal *Language Technology*. The ad featured the usual kinds of glowing but meaningless claims: "Globalink makes international communication crystal clear... developed for the professional translator... uncompromising performance... versatile tool for all business, legal, scientific, and other foreign language translation needs..." On a more objective level, the review said this:

> GTS fits into the tradition of the so-called "direct" MT systems, the doyen of which is Systran. These systems feature rather "flat", unscholarly linguistic processing, operating on wordstrings rather than on syntactic trees, with the emphasis on dictionary coding and ad hoc rules. The rationale is that working with sophisticated syntactic trees can easily become unwieldy both computationally and linguistically.
>
> The price to pay for this is local analysis. That is: parsing is based on applying local rules, looking right and left for context through a "window" which is often rather narrow. A complete parsing of the sentence as a whole is not attempted, which certainly puts a ceiling on output quality.
>
> GTS uses no semantic codes (like *animate, concrete, liquid*) on which to base decisions. Parsing is purely syntactic. This can lead to unresolved difficulties. In the phrase "metallic safety bulkhead", for example, the program has no way of determining which word "metallic" refers to. If "safety" were coded *abstract* and "bulkhead" *concrete*, the system could give preference to the concrete noun for this adjective....
>
> While the world is still patiently waiting for an MT system to yield impressive quality, users are slowly turning away from pure linguistic performance and adopting a more pragmatic approach. If a system supports corporate terminology and phraseology, while not making a mess of the target language — and is easy enough to use and not too pricy — it might prove to be useful and cost-effective. A system like GTS might just do the trick.

It turned out that Toon had gotten the GTS translation of the Marot done through the very person who wrote this review — Claude Bédard, a Montreal-based translator and MT expert. Bédard attached a note to GTS's output, saying, "This is a still-immature version of the GTS system. The words tagged '@@' have failed morphological analysis; this is a basic shortcoming of the program. One should expect something better (*cf.* 'if you hard' and 'goes'!), even from a 'stupid' MT system. I wish you a merry good laugh at the output."

Six years later, my friend Larry Tesler got a Mac program called "Power Translator" and wanted to test it out on "Ma Mignonne". The output he sent me via email sounded suspiciously familiar, and by checking it against my files, I verified that it was identical to GTS's translation, except for one word ("fast" had become "rapidly"). In fact, Larry's note said Power Translator came from a company called "Globalink" — so putting two and two together, I realized that nothing had changed in six years except the packaging. Larry amusingly concluded: "Power Translator, in nine seconds on a Quadra 840AV, generated this 'translation'. It may not be the best, but it could be one of the fastest." Indeed.

Note that on lines 1, 14, and 28, neither GTS nor Systran has any qualms about using an adjective as a noun, even though we in English don't do that. And "giving the hello" is also used by both, with no visible shame. Both would have the indisposed recipient "cover" rather than "recover". On line 14, both mistake the command *Va* for the third-person singular verb *va,* and thus without embarrassment, both use "Goes" to start out a sentence! Both programs fail to see *dures* as a verb, and both see pale skin's color as "insipid". And why in the world would a "potbelly" be something a poet would exhort a friend to regain?

At the root of the problem is, of course, the fact that neither program *understands* anything, and so there is no sympathy, no empathy, no sense of what tone ought to be conveyed — indeed, not even the sense that words carry tones, or *mean anything*, at all!

My Cute

Globalink Translation System

My cute,
I give you
The hello.
The stay,
It is prison.   5
Recovery
Cover,
Then open
Your door,
And that one leave   10
Fast,
Because Clement
You summons it.
Goes, fond
Of your mouth,   15
That lies down
In danger,
To eat
Jams.
If you hard   20
Too sick,
Insipid color
You @@prendras,
And @@perdras
The potbelly.   25
God you @@doint
Good health,
My cute.

Since I am making rather inflammatory claims about where we currently are in machine translation, I include one last machine-produced version, this one done a couple of years later (fall 1992). This time we are dealing with the hugely ambitious project called "Candide", under development at IBM's famous Watson Research Labs, and whose central premise is that all need for analysis and understanding can be circumvented if only one has a large enough bilingual database. Candide's strategy for figuring out which way to translate an ambiguous word involves exhaustively scouring the database for contexts that are "similar" to the context in which the word is embedded, and then choosing the way the word was rendered in the "most similar" contexts, where degree of similarity is measured by a complex mathematical formula that, rest assured, has nothing to do with text understanding. This principle is the very foundation on which the whole project rests.

Not only is Candide's database truly enormous, but it is also of extremely high quality: It consists of many thousands of pages (hundreds of millions of words) drawn from the parliamentary debates in Canada, all of which, by Canadian federal law, must be meticulously translated by superb human experts from French to English and vice versa. You couldn't ask for more or better examples from which to learn.

How did Candide do? As is painfully obvious, Candide's attempt is, in most ways, even weaker than those by Systran and GTS. Much of the English in "My Flapper" is so deeply and irretrievably scrambled that a reader simply has no idea at all what is being talked about. And this is not surprising. Candide *itself* has no idea what is being talked about.

The poem's title is ludicrous, for starters. How can cuteness and sweetness be confused with 1920's-style vamping? Strangely enough, the answer has its own curious logic, just as children's bizarre errors often reveal themselves to be plausible inferences from a highly impoverished state of knowledge. It turns out that *mignonne* is in fact the noun that was used in the 1920's for "flapper girl", and in its database Candide found that the majority of occurrences of *mignonne* used in a *noun*-like manner (as it is here) were matched with occurrences of "flapper". That statistical fact did it! But a human who knew that meaning for *mignonne* and who read Marot's poem with *understanding* would instantly know that noun or no noun, the word *mignonne* in the poem carries no vampy va-va-va-voom connotations at all, but rather, radiates an aura of smallness, gentleness, innocence, vulnerability, and so forth. Of course, a human might knowingly play with the image of the little girl, *deliberately* rendering her vamp-like, as in "Goldilocks", or even bovine, as in "Gentle Cow". But such conscious manipulations are light-years beyond current MT ideas.

Let's leave the title. We can guess what's behind line 10's "that sort" — but where did the meat pie and the safely-sleeping neighbor come from? Line 19's question mark? What made the "flag" — a grotesque though theoretically possible translation of *couleur* — seem "funny" rather than "faded" (or "insipid")? And the utter *non sequiturs* of lines 24–26?

But let's focus in on just one tiny issue: that of *Si tu dures trop malade*. Whereas Systran and GTS blew it totally, Candide might be said to have gotten it right, if one overlooks the awkwardness of "If you last too ill". But is it really right? People do not "last ill", they *stay* ill. And any normal human intuitively knows that the worry being expressed is about *how long the illness will last*, rather than *how severe the illness is*. The severity of an illness is out of human control, whereas rightly or wrongly, one has the feeling that it makes sense to exhort a person to try to *quickly* overcome a disease. That is, the *length* of one's bedstay seems more like something that one can try to affect with one's mind. But these are matters that go a million miles beyond the surface of the words. They have to do with understanding illness and causality, will power and suffering, exhortation and hope. All this depth is hidden in just five French words, which ought to be rendered more like this: "If you stay ill too long". No, Candide did not get it right, not by a long shot.

My Flapper

Candide

My flapper,
I give
This morning.
The time
It is in prison.   5
Cure
Recover,
Then you open
Your door,
And that sort   10
Vitement,
Because Clément
Summons
Meat pie.
Does your neighbor,   15
Who is sleeping
Safe,
Eat
Jams?
If you last   20
Too ill,
Funny flag
Shalt prendras,
And growing
Up.   25
Goodness different doint
Good health,
My flapper.

We come now to one of the strangest stories of all. David Moser had a Chinese friend who had just arrived in the United States knowing about as little English as it is possible to know, other than the roman alphabet. She also knew no French. Somehow, in a flight of fancy, it occurred to David and me that it would be fascinating to see what Zhang Jiaying, in her absolutely naïve state, would do with the "Ma Mignonne" translation challenge. And to our delight, Jiaying, once the idea had been explained to her, was game, and so, armed with a battery of thick, authoritative dictionaries interlinking the French, English, and Chinese tongues, she sat down one evening and tackled it.

It did not escape us that what Jiaying was doing bore a strange resemblance to Searle's "Chinese room" scenario, except turned inside-out, in a sense: Here a native Chinese speaker was in a room manipulating the "squiggles and squoggles" of English and French as purely formal objects, without attaching any meanings to them. In many respects, Zhang Jiaying's techniques for dealing with the symbols of human language while totally (or nearly totally) bypassing the building-up of mental representations for the scenarios involved were quite like those programmed into Systran, GTS, and Candide. Thus, fascinatingly enough, we see reproduced, on line 10, the exact same misreading of *sorte* as done by Systran and Candide, and on line 20, although "hard" is not there, a related error has been made: *dures* has been understood as the adjective "stubborn" instead of as a verb.

I will add brief comments on just a couple of other details. The word *séjour*, though its most common meaning by far is "sojourn" or "stay", actually can mean "sitting room" in some contexts. And *guérison* means "recovery", which partly explains line 6. Jiaying's knowledge of English grammar was essentially nil, which accounts for her writing "yours" instead of "your" a couple of times, as well as various other syntactic infelicities.

Overall, I would appraise this translation (if that's the word for it) as being on roughly the same level as the three MT-produced versions — maybe a little better than Candide's, a little worse than GTS's, about the same as Systran's. One difference is that, as Larry Tesler pointed out, it might have taken those programs on the order of *ten seconds* to do what Zhang Jiaying accomplished in, say, *three hours* of considerable labor. Now that does give some pause for thought.

One might well ask, as I did in the previous paragraph, "Can the word 'translation' legitimately be applied to the production of this sequence of English words?" Recall how ginger I was, at the outset of this book, about using that word to describe "To a Sick Damsel", my own perfectly coherent line-by-line rendering of Marot's content alone. The total ignoring of Marot's tone, structure, and so forth in "To a Sick Damsel" seemed a slap in the face to Clément Marot, to poetry, to what human communication is all about. And "My Treasure", needless to say, is far, far below "To a Sick Damsel" in quality. So *is* it a translation of "Ma Mignonne", or not?

What this question brings to my mind is the activity that simultaneous interpreters are engaged in: the instantaneous pouring of content from one container to another, with no time at all for reflection, revision, or polishing. Is that translation? In some instances, it certainly is. The interpreter understands perfectly what is being said, and renders it gracefully in another language. But what about when a nonspecialist is swiftly and fluently converting sentences about "metallic safety bulkheads", say, or items even more opaque — entities and situations that they have no experience with and no image for? What can one say about the case when no mental imagery is manufactured inside the interpreter's head, yet a quite comprehensible stream of words emerges at the output end — does *that* count as translation?

My Treasure

Zhang Jiaying

My treasure,
I you given
The "good morning".
The drawing room
    It is jail.   5
Recover,
Recover one's health,
Then open
Yours door,
And that people kind   10
Quickly,
Because Clément
You the summon.
Okay, gluttonous
Owing to yours mouth,   15
Which makes lie down
In dangerous,
For eat
Jam.
If you stubborn   20
Too sick,
Color dull
You take,
And lose
Full and developed body.   25
God give you
Good health,
My treasure.

My translation seminar at Indiana started in January, 1990. Bob French, who had spent ten years as a professional translator, culminating in his work with Jacqueline Henry on *Gödel, Escher, Bach,* had thought long and hard about the inherent tensions that not only riddle but actually define the act of translation, and thus sat in, not wishing to pass up the chance to discuss these engrossing issues with a superb group of people — including David Moser and Liu Haoming, both key members of the Chinese *GEB*-translation team.

The first assignment was to render "Ma Mignonne" as elegantly as possible in one's own native language, for which I received several great solutions; at the end I assigned the conversion of Searle's Chinese-room paragraph (see Chapters 4 and 5) into clear, flowing "e"-less Anglo-Saxon prose. The goal was to produce a paragraph so lucid and smooth that readers would not suspect it had been written under a constraint. Bob loved "e"-less English and thus welcomed this challenge, but when he heard it had taken me five hours to do my paragraph, and most students reported similar drainages of valuable time, Bob said to himself, "No way I'm going to spend hours and hours painstakingly converting that long paragraph into flowing Anglo-Saxon! Instead, I'll do something cute and clever: I'll just boil the issues in Searle's scenario down into 28 short lines of trisyllabic rhyming verse, while also making sure that no 'e''s creep in!" Well, as it happened, doing this was no piece of cake, but finally — after seven hours of struggle! — Bob completed his poemlet.

When he read it aloud, we were all charmed and impressed. It was so distinctive! But I claimed Bob's effort counted as more than just a translation of the Searle paragraph into a new medium (*viz.*, tightly structured Anglo-Saxon verse) — it was simultaneously, and just as validly, a translation of "Ma Mignonne" into a new medium: the medium of *descriptions of the Chinese-room thought experiment* (and further constrained by "e"-lessness).

At first my claim seemed counterintuitive, even to Bob. How could a poem about a human computer manipulating Chinese characters be a translation of "Ma Mignonne"? I argued as follows: Why had "Ma Mignonne" been included in my old French-literature anthology in the first place? Surely not for the sentiments it expressed, for even though warm and cuddly, they alone are hardly high literature. No, what makes "Ma Mignonne" so noteworthy and memorable is its *form*. Its content — "Soon get well, mademoiselle", as Antony Galton put it — is hardly path-breaking. Its striking thinness, its trisyllabicity, its tight rhyme scheme, its first-line/last-line identity — *these* make up the novelty, the contribution, the essence of the poem — what must be preserved when all else is lost. One obviously couldn't make the analogous claim about a sonnet — there are millions of poems in sonnet form — but one could do so for "Ma Mignonne", for its form is *unique*.

In this audacious view, then, content could slip radically as long as form was preserved, because in "Ma Mignonne", almost perversely, the roles of content and form are switched. In a flip of the norm, this poem's *content* is merely an *incidental vehicle* that allows a certain intricate *pattern* (the *form*) to come to exist. It's *that* that counts, not the medium that supports it. To be sure, a translation could try to preserve both content and form, which would be nice, but if one of them has to go, it would be the former, not the form. So, at least, ran my argument. Of course it's overstated, but there's more than a grain of truth to it. And so to me, "Sino Room" is the ultimate experiment in translating "Ma Mignonne".

By the way, I am a co-author here because, after consultation, Bob and I agreed that his first draft distorted the Chinese-room scenario, and needed patching. And since Bob had already spent far more time on this "dumb little poem" than he'd ever intended to, he gave me free rein to tinker with it. So then it was my turn to plunge into the time sink of revision — a virtually endless agony. Twenty long hours of blood, sweat, and tears later, this poem is what emerged. I know precisely which sections are the fruit of my labors. Readers may even recognize my style: lines 11–18, plus line 27. *One word per hour…*

Sino Room

C. Marot*/J. Searle*/R. French/D. Hofstadter

Strong AI —
Could it fly?
In a word,
It's absurd.
Though I know   5
(I, John) no
Sino-stuff,
I can bluff.
Ask things in
Mandarin.   10
Faking mind,
Flying blind,
Using stacks
Of syntax
(Thanks to Schank),   15
Out I'll crank
Pictograms:
Slick, but shams!
Robots, too,
Might this do.   20
Has this wrought
Sino-thought?
I dismiss
Claims that this
Protocol   25
Thinks at all.
Kiss good-by
Strong AI.

* *Those listed with stars are honorary co-authors, in the sense explained on the facing page.*

• Chapter 16 •

AI Aims, MT Claims, Sino-room Flames

•

When Bob French was working toward his doctorate in my research group, we used to have lively weekly meetings at which we would discuss internal and external research projects. At one such meeting, Bob was to present an article he had read about a certain fancy computer model of sensory perception based on a variety of neurophysiological data. He started out with a transparency showing a brain on which were visible many zones labeled with highly technical terms, such as "lateral geniculate nucleus", "corticothalamic fibers", "field of arborization", "intralaminar nuclear complex", "inferior colliculus" — things of that sort. Despite the fact that we in the group were all deeply involved in trying to figure out how the mind works, such technical details of brain anatomy were a baffling maze to us, just as the details of particle physics would baffle most chemists.

Bob launched into his talk, peppering it with long, alien-sounding terms (I've long since forgotten which ones). The more he did this, the more fidgety I felt. At some point, perhaps a bit rudely, I interrupted him, saying, "Bob, can't you go a little easy with the technical terms? You're just as much a stranger to these brain structures as we are, yet the way you're throwing their names around, one would swear they were your old friends."

My remark could not help but trigger a debate about the contexts in which it might make more sense or less sense to fling about technical terms one has just learned. Although this debate was quite properly considered an intrusive (though interesting) digression in Bob's talk, and the overall mood of the group was to try to squelch it as soon as possible, in truth it was the most memorable aspect of the talk — at least for me. We all were familiar with the excitement one can feel when one has just mastered a difficult new concept, and along with it some terminology, and this gave us sympathy for Bob, but on the other hand, we also all knew how language is often abused by people who want to appear to know more than they do. Trying to discern where the line falls between efficient communication and glib but vacuous term-dropping is very tricky.

Françoise in a Pickle

I was reminded of a visit with my friends the Ulams. Stan, born Polish, was a wonderfully creative mathematician who had lived in the United States for decades but whose English, though perfectly fluent and playful, was often idiosyncratically ungrammatical, and certainly far from native-level. By contrast, Françoise, born French, had similarly lived in the United States for decades but was far more attentive than her husband to the details of language, speaking clipped English with no errors and scarcely any accent at all. To spice up her conversation, she also loved tossing in idiomatic phrases of all sorts.

One day, right after Françoise had elegantly used a couple of baseball metaphors (such as "out in left field", "three strikes, you're out", "off base", "switch hitter", "wild pitch", "in the ballpark", "get thrown a curve ball", "can't get to first base", and so on — I don't recall which ones she actually used), Stan said to her, "You didn't grow up playing baseball — you've *never* played it, in fact — so what right do you have to use those phrases?" No pushover, Françoise defended herself well, saying that in the first place she had watched enough baseball to have a good idea of the original meanings, and that in the second place, many native speakers use idioms without knowing one whit of their origins. I tended to side with Françoise, all the more so since she had used the idioms so aptly, but I also wondered to what extent I agreed with Stan's basic thesis that fluent usage of idioms can be a trick, a façade behind which there is nothing substantial.

Hoaxteats and Hairports

Of course this is much the same issue as with Bob's use of technical terms, and essentially the same question arises in many other contexts. Among the very first words mastered by many young American children is often the word "pacifier". How strange it has always sounded to me to hear a tiny plaintive voice saying, "Wan' pacifiah!" How can an infant be so astute as to realize that it wants to be *pacified*? Where, at such a tender age, did it ever learn of the notion of *pacifying*?

In Dutch, what young children ask for is even stranger: *een fopspeen*. The word breaks up into *fop*, meaning "hoax" or "trick", and *speen,* meaning "teat" or "nipple". Thus on one level, a Dutch baby will be asking to be hoodwinked when it begs for its "hoaxteat". Needless to say, however, there is another level on which it is asking for no such thing — the request for a *fopspeen* is every bit as indivisible and holistic as when an adult English speaker requests a "cocktail" or speaks of being "hoodwinked". Indeed, adult Dutch speakers will almost never hear any irony in their children's pleas. The original semantic parts of *fopspeen* are buried and unperceived. Similarly, American adults seldom hear the strange flavor that I hear in the word "pacifier", because to them it is just a name, about as unlikely to be mentally dissected as "Cambridge" ("bridge over the Cam") or "Oxford" ("place where oxen cross a river").

But what about words like "airport"? At age two, our daughter Monica used to say "hairport" very reliably. To her, it was not a compound word but an opaque two-syllable chunk, having no more to do with "hair" than pillows have to do with pills, or wardrobes with wars (or with drobes, for that matter). Yet to her older brother Danny, then five, "airport" was a fairly transparent compound, even if the word "port" had few resonances in his mind other than some lively pictures of ships loading and unloading, in a kids' book we had read together about big cities.

And to me? Well, of course, I had at some long-forgotten point passed through each of these stages, and probably when I was around five or six, the two components had taken on a maximal level of visibility in my mind, after which there must have ensued a gradual, years-long fusion process, blurring them into one another like pieces of wax that have melted together in the bright sunlight, resulting in a single tight unit whose constituents only rarely come into separate focus inside the whole. By now, "airport" is for me nearly as tightly-bonded a semantic chunk as is "Oxford".

The parts in "skyscraper", by contrast, are more loosely bound and thus more "present", but even so, I seldom hear the word as "sky-scraper". I know this because I remember how that breakdown was abruptly thrust into my attention on a stroll in Paris with Ronald Jonkers in 1983. Pointing at Paris' lone skyscraper, the Tour Montparnasse, he called it a "skyscratcher". I had to smile. "Scrape", "scratch" — what's the difference? They're terribly close in meaning and imagery, yet to a native speaker of English, Ronald's word is delightfully silly. Why? Because it suddenly resuscitates "skyscraper"'s buried imagery, allowing us to hear its humorousness afresh.

We have already considered how compound words are heard, first in Chapter 3, in looking at Strothmann's Thesis, and then in Chapter 10, in discussing opaque and transparent names for dinosaurs and for the quirky phenomena of quantum theory and relativity — and now it comes up again.

Shaded Semanticity versus Black-and-white Aboutness

The key point on this go-round is the many shades of gray that lie between total opacity and total transparency. When children learn a new word, they often sound at first like parrots vacuously aping their parents, and so we laugh when we hear a sophisticated word like "definitely" coming out of the mouth of a three-year-old, but as they continue to use it, their sense of clarity and precision increases, and at some ill-defined stage they seem to have crossed over from simple copycatting into genuine semantic mastery. There is certainly no sharp black-and-white crossover line, however — no magic moment at which *meaning* suddenly attaches to a symbol that up until then had been totally empty. Rather, over a period of days, weeks, months, or years, symbols gradually acquire layers of meaning, like boats accumulating layers of barnacles. In recognition of the continuity of this process, I speak of symbols gradually acquiring *semanticity*, starting at zero and moving continuously upwards towards 1.

In contrast to my term "semanticity", with its flavor of continuous gradations, there is a term that has become prevalent over the last couple of decades in the philosophies of mind and language, and whose usage suggests a black-and-white dichotomy between systems with and systems without meaningful symbols; that term is *aboutness*. I have run into this word most often in discussions of computers and language, and in my experience it is used usually (if not exclusively) by philosophers who are convinced of, and are eager to convince others of, a clean breach between human beings, on the one hand, whose linguistic symbols (*i.e.*, words) undeniably *do* possess "aboutness" (the property of being *about* or *referring* to something), and computers (or programs, or programmed computers), on the other hand, whose usage of precisely the identical symbols is claimed to be vacuous: those symbols undeniably *lack* "aboutness".

John Searle is one of those philosophers for whom it is patently obvious that the symbols accepted by, manipulated by, and displayed by programmed computers are lacking aboutness, and not just accidentally or temporarily, but necessarily and eternally. In Searle's view, words in files or in databases or on screens mean nothing to the computer, and hence are *about nothing*. Humans may read meaning into such symbols, which is fine, but intrinsically, their degree of semanticity is zero — and not just *roughly* zero, but *exactly* 0.000000..., and it makes not a particle of difference how sophisticated the program is that manipulates them. To demonstrate this inevitable "aboutnesslessness" of symbols in computers is the whole idea of Searle's "Chinese room" thought experiment.

Of course, it makes some people feel safe to think that a computer, even if it can spell far better than they do, attaches not one iota of meaning to the symbols it bandies about so fluently. Do the thousands of words in an unabridged dictionary, every last one of them spelled and defined properly, have aboutness? Obviously not — not a whit, not a bit. It is comforting to believe that a computer that is glibly manipulating words, no matter how it might be programmed, will forever be as hopelessly aboutness-free as is a pocket Polish–Swahili dictionary, and hence will always have as little mental life as does an electric can-opener, a vacuum cleaner, a cash register, or a pocket calculator.

Indeed, in Poems XV, we have just seen several machine-translation programs and been struck by their pathetic vacuity, something that on the face of it would seem to strongly corroborate the "computers-lack-aboutness" viewpoint that Searle and many others espouse. However, such a black-and-white stance, though very tempting, should be resisted. In order to think about such issues more carefully, we must look a little bit at how MT programs and other natural-language programs work.

The Rudiments of Machine Translation

At the heart of most MT programs is, of course, the idea of ultra-rapid lookup of words and phrases in a very large bilingual dictionary. As words in a text in the original language are encountered, they are looked up and their counterparts are plunked down in a growing text in the target language. Words, in such a process, are not considered as indivisible chunks, but instead, some morphological analysis is carried out (such as recognizing that *prendras* is made out of two pieces: a root, *prendr-*, meaning "take", and a future ending, *-as,* meaning "[you] will"). When exactly to try to take a word into parts and when to leave it alone is, unfortunately, unclear. And sometimes a word can be taken into parts in different ways.

A quite famous error committed by the MT program Systran was to render the French phrase *nous avions* ("we had") as "we airplanes", thanks to the fact that *avion* means "airplane". For Systran it was easier to see *avions* as a noun with a plural ending than to spot the root *av-* and the first-person plural past-tense suffix *-ions.* For a human, on the other hand, to see *avions* as a plural noun when it is immediately preceded by the pronoun *nous* is so far-fetched that Systran's error is likely to bring about chuckles of astonishment. Humans are so good at unconsciously selecting just the appropriate meaning of an ambiguous word according to its context that probably 99 percent of native French speakers have never even noticed that the word *avions* has two potential interpretations!

In addition to direct word-for-word and phrase-for-phrase substitution, many programs create a "parse tree" — a structure that represents the program's best guess at how the elements on various hierarchical levels of a sentence are related to each other (what noun phrase a given pronoun stands for, what verb agrees numerically with what subject, what relative clause modifies what noun, what tense is governed by what other tense, and similar things). This information is then used to construct a counterpart hierarchical structure for the target language, which — when combined with the words derived by the lookup module — allows a sentence of the target language to be produced whose word order is plausible. Thus the command "You do it!" could be turned into the Italian command *Lo faccia lei!*, where the three items occur in the precise reverse of the English order.

Off the Top of My Head

It is a fact that most words have many related but distinct senses — astoundingly many, one comes to realize as one studies foreign languages. This, of course, must be squarely faced, and indeed it is one of the hardest of all issues in MT, as Yehoshua Bar-Hillel stressed already in 1960 with his famous "box in pen" pessimism, which we discussed in Chapter 4.

I'd like to consider another example of the non-obvious ubiquity of multiple meanings. If the word "top" is encountered in a sentence in English input, how ought it to be translated? It turns out that this little word, which seems so innocent and simple to a native English speaker, splinters, in most other languages, into a few dozen if not many dozens of different words, each one suitable to one context but not others. This kind of splintering is typical, not at all exceptional — and the higher a word's frequency, the more splintering it will undergo in any foreign language.

Consider how many things we think of as "tops": *the top of a mountain* (its summit or peak), *the top of a cardboard box* (its cover), *the top of a telephone pole* (its tip), *the top of a carrot* (leaves that once stuck out of the ground), *the top of a pile* (uppermost item or surface), *the top of one's class* (acme or valedictorian), *the top of a saucepan* (lid), *the top of a fountain pen* (cap), *the top of a wine bottle* (cork or stopper), *the top of a ridge* (its spine as opposed to its summit), *the top of a page* (where the letterhead goes), *the top of a car* (roof), *the top of a cloud* (upper part), *the top layer of paint* (most superficial), *topsoil* (soft, arable layer of soil), *the top drawer* (highest of a set), *the top brand* (best reputation), *the top of one's career* (culmination), *top gear* (the highest-ratio gear in a transmission), *top dog* (the boss), *top brass* (executive panel), *top of the line* (highest quality), *top of a list* (first), *top speed* (maximal speed), *a top job* (desirable), *top billing* (most important name), *top note in a melody* (highest pitch), *top of the table* (place of honor), *tabletop* (horizontal surface), *the big top* (circus tent), *pajama top* (shirt), *bikini top* (cloth to cover nipples of breasts), *being in top condition* (very good shape), *pop top* (piece of metal that comes out of a soft-drink can), *on top of* (located directly on), *topping-off of one's gas tank* (filling up completely), *over the top* (too expensive), *topping last year's sales* (exceeding), *the top of one's voice* (maximum loudness), *to be on top of the world* (very happy), *on top of all that* (in addition), *off the top of one's head* (without deep reflection), *from top to bottom* (all the way through), *"that's the top"* (the last straw), *"top of the morning"* (good morning), *top hat and tails* (a very high hat), *top secret* (extremely secret), *on top of a situation* (in control), *take it from the top* (the very beginning), *a hardtop* (as opposed to a convertible), and on and on it goes (without mentioning a host of quite distinct meanings, such as a *children's top, the top quark, to blow one's top, to top a tree, topheavy, topless swimsuit, topless waitress, topless bar, topless district, topless zoning laws,* and numerous further usages, wildly unpredictable in their variety).

I would bet that it was this kind of thing that, when he was forced to confront it in its full glory, made Yehoshua Bar-Hillel lose all hope about the idea of getting a machine to translate at human level.

Using a Vast Corpus to Combat Multiple Meanings

Just think how a machine-translation program would have to handle the phrase "topless zoning laws" if it had never encountered this term before. It would be inconceivably wrong-headed to try to break it down into its pieces and to construct something in the target language essentially saying "zoning laws that lack a top". The "top-lacking" state suggested by the adjective pertains not to the laws themselves (in fact, laws are more like a bottomless pit), but to certain zones in a city; or rather, not really to the zones themselves, but to certain types of business establishments located in them; or rather, not really to the establishments themselves (which do have roofs), but to their female employees; or rather, not really to the women themselves (who have heads no less than their customers do) but to their outfits — and even then, the reference is not so much to the physical facts of their outfits as to the moral tone set by that style, and the degree to which that moral tone (vague as it might be) drifts, somewhat like a noxious gas, through the walls of one building and infects an entire neighborhood in a city. All of this is completely clear to anyone who understands that phrase, and that is what would allow a human translator who had never seen it before (but who knew about topless dancing) to construct a perfectly reasonable equivalent in a target language.

Such formidable complexities suggest that an ability to translate unpredictable combinations of words demands an understanding of every aspect of being human and living in contemporary society. Accordingly, machine-translation teams have developed elaborate strategies for sidestepping such a daunting challenge. The simplest and most widespread trick is merely to strive to make sure that unpredictable combinations of words do not arise. In short, head off unpredictability at the pass!

IBM's program Candide, for instance, which we met in Poems XV, has an almost unimaginably large database of parallel running text in its two languages, precisely so as to obviate the difficulties caused by truly novel phrases. It is conceivable that in a truly huge corpus of legal debate in English, the exact phrase "topless zoning law" might show up somewhere, in which case you're home free. However, even if that precise phrase never appears literally in the corpus, knowledge that "zoning law" is semantically close to "legislation" or possibly even to "control" would allow a phrase like "topless legislation" or "topless control" (either of which might appear in the corpus) to serve as a substitute.

Suppose that one of these phrases were found in the English corpus. Then the corresponding text in the parallel French corpus would simply be extracted intact and plugged into the growing French translation without there ever having been any visualization of any aspect of the situation. Of course such a strategy is quite risky, because "topless control" might very easily mean "joy stick without a knob" or dozens of other things. But if one is going to go the no-understanding route, one has no choice but to take such risks all the time — and as we saw in "My Flapper", the risks often do not pan out, and lead to incomprehensible nonsense.

Restricting the Domain and the Input Language

There are many additional ways of trying to forestall unpredictability of input text. One is to make sure that the domain of discourse is extraordinarily circumscribed — for instance, limit it to weather reports for a certain region whose weather patterns are extensively known, or to repair manuals for photocopy machines — in fact, for just one specific model! And then, given the very limited and fixed domain, strive to ensure that all stock phrases containing more than one word have been inserted *a priori* into a huge bilingual lexicon. An example: in 1988, the United States Air Force Russian–English lexicon for use by Systran contained over 200,000 single words, and in addition to that, over 200,000 expressions! An English–Japanese system was planned to have 250,000 scientific and technical terms as well as 200,000 medical terms.

One of the strangest techniques for reducing unpredictability — yet a very standard one — is to severely limit not only the domain of discourse but also the style of writing. At the Xerox Corporation, for instance, which for decades has been one of the biggest users of Systran, teams of writers are instructed very carefully on how to write their manuals in "MCE" — Multinational Customized English. This is a "dialect" of English designed, on the basis of years of experience with rigid programs, to have an absolute minimum of ambiguity and thus to pose as few problems as possible to a machine that knows absolutely nothing about what it is translating.

Although I have few details about MCE, one thing I know is that it has very strict rules about how pronouns and definite and indefinite articles are to be used, and these rules may run considerably against the grain of how natural English would flow.

With all these kinds of restrictions and aids, Xerox seems fairly satisfied with what it gets from Systran: Each year, some 50,000 pages of English-language manuals are translated into French, Spanish, Italian, Portuguese, German, and the Scandinavian languages. Although this feat is impressive, it involves a great deal of help from humans, some of whom teach people how to write in MCE, others of whom actually write manuals in MCE, others of whom scour the input text for occurrences of new terms that the system will not understand directly and that therefore have to be inserted manually into the lexicon, and others of whom carry out "post-editing" — that is, they come along afterwards and repair all the glitches made by Systran.

Despite such heavy involvement by humans in the roles of trainers, writers, pre-editors, and post-editors, it is still apparently more profitable to have machines carry out the intermediate stage of word substitution and word-order rearranging, sandwiched between humans at both ends of the process, than to have the entire process done by people. In fact, I was told by someone who worked for years with the Systran project at Xerox that quite often, several pages in a row would emerge from Systran without needing any post-editing at all. In that sense, Systran did just what it was supposed to do: it delivered the goods.

In light of the shocking shabbiness of Systran's performance on "Ma Mignonne", this is quite fascinating. Apparently Systran does a bang-up job of translating thousands of pages of a certain type of meticulously "cured" English in a tiny domain, and yet it can't even come close to handling a simple sixty-word poem (treated purely as prose). The excuse that the poem is in old French holds no water: Any speaker of current French can effortlessly understand "Ma Mignonne".

Faking Mind, Flying Blind, Using Stacks of Syntax (Thanks to Schank)...

With this short overview of machine translation as prelude, we are now naturally and inevitably led back to the question of the "aboutness" of the symbols manipulated by MT programs. Are the words and phrases sucked in and spat out by Systran and similar systems devoid of every last shred of meaning, or perhaps might they possess a tiny amount of the sacred elixir of semanticity? Is there any *understanding* in what they do, or is it all illusory, all just the insidious Eliza effect lulling us into gullible acceptance?

It is clear that in comparison with a word processor, a translation program is doing *more* with the meanings of the words. All that a word processor does is accept what is typed at it, and, if asked, suggest spelling corrections. By contrast, translation, even if crude and syntactical, seems to deal with at least the surface levels of meaning. Thus one might be tempted to slide a little ways down the slope of semanticity, allowing the palest imaginable shade of gray to be associated with programs like Systran, GTS, Candide, and their cousins.

At this John Searle would surely jump, perhaps even citing the catchy phrase in "Sino Room": Computer programs that deal with language are merely "Faking mind, / Flying blind, / Using stacks / Of syntax". (Though I'm a co-author of that poem, I generously insist that Searle and no one but Searle deserves credit for its content. To be sure, since it is in rhyming Anglo-Saxon couplets, the lilt and phrasings are his only in the asterisked sense that "Thinking's why I am I" can be attributed to Searle's predecessor and guiding light René Descartes.) It's that last word — "syntax" — that's the key item here, for for Searle, there is a vast and in fact an unbreachable gulf between the concepts of "syntax" and "semantics". Why does he see and insist on such a breach? That's simple to say: Syntax deals solely with *form*, semantics deals solely with *reference*, and never the twain shall meet.

There is a definite irony, therefore, that in "Minds, Brains, and Programs", the individual whom Searle singled out as his target, the person he chose as the quintessential representative of AI researchers working on natural language, was Roger Schank, who, if you will recall, very early on in his career staked out a controversial position by loudly decrying the rampant concentration on syntax in AI work, and making a point of going after nothing but *semantics*. If this is really so, then why on earth might Searle say, "Using stacks / Of syntax / (Thanks to Schank)"? In what sense is Schank's work *syntactic*? Wasn't Schank's whole game plan to focus solely on the very issue that obsesses "the other S" so much, namely *semantics* and *aboutness*? I would hope that readers would feel confused at this point!

The Slippery Slope between the Two S-words

The source of this confusion I will now reveal, and indeed, here is where one of Searle's most serious sleights, one not dissected in Chapter 4, takes place. It is the slipperiness of the dreaded S-word: "syntax". To most people, this S-word is synonymous with "grammar" — the rules that determine word order in a language, as well as conjugation and declension tables, and many other related things that govern what one might call the "shape" or "form" of isolated words, as well as the "structures" or "patterns" created when multiple words are strung together. These tend to be the aspects of language that are most easily approachable using computers.

There is a closely related sense of "syntax" in symbolic logic, whereby inference rules defining valid deductions are described *syntactically,* which is to say, they tell a person (or a machine) how to draw a valid conclusion from a set of premises solely on the basis of their *structure* — the symbols out of which they are made, and the order in which those symbols are arrayed. It is at this point that things start to get blurry, because such rules parlay pure *form* into results about *truth* and *falsity.* Although meaning seems to be being bypassed, it is in some sense involved. That's the whole trick of symbolic logic, of course — and in fact, it's the trick behind algebra and all of computation. Manipulate symbols by rules, get truths.

When computers first came along, it was quickly recognized that, aside from numbers, they could also deal very effectively with other types of symbolic structures such as chess games, logical deductions, and pieces of text, and since the way in which these dealings took place always involved the *form* or *structure* of isolated symbols or patterns of symbols, the word "syntax" was borrowed from symbolic logic and was applied to the entire realm of symbol manipulation. Thus *computation as a whole was subsumed under the term "syntax",* no matter whether the computational processes were carried out on numbers, chess pieces, pictures, words, logical deductions, Shakespeare sonnets, or any other type of structures made of symbols.

This extension of the S-word, however, was a far cry from its original meaning, which was limited to such clearly non-semantic facts as that "short" is a *longer* word than "long" is (which clearly can be seen from their "shapes", and clearly has nothing to do with their meanings). The new extended meaning of "syntax", however, reached out much further and could include any imaginable piece of knowledge or any imaginable strategy for dealing with knowledge, as long as that knowledge and the strategies for using it could be imparted to a computer.

Thus, as a quite trivial example, a computer program could be supplied with a list of antonymous pairs, such as "long/short", "short/tall", "loud/soft", "soft/hard", "hard/easy", "dark/light", "light/heavy", and so forth. The presence of such a list inside the computer's memory would easily permit the retrieval of "long" as the antonym of "short", and therefore such retrieval would have to be described as a "syntactic" act, even though, very clearly, what is involved here is an extremely simple aspect of *meaning,* admittedly one that is trivial to capture via a lookup table or a rule.

If one has little imagination, it is easy to fall into the trap of thinking that "syntactic" processing can go no further than accessing aspects of a word's most obvious visual structure. In such a view, the word "taller" would have no properties other than having six letters, four consonants, two vowels, three ascenders, no descenders, and other such visual things having nothing to do with its meaning. But just exactly how far could "visual inspection" of this word carry one?

Suppose we are playing the part of a syntactic processor. We must follow very precise instructions, as if we were a computer, but we can make use of structures stored in memory or available for inspection in the real world. Thus if we already know about the word "tall", then we might spot it inside the word "taller", with "er" left over at the end. That's obviously a syntactic act because it just involves looking at form.

If, furthermore, the word "tall" is connected somewhere in memory with the label "adjective", then we might recognize that "taller" is the comparative form of "tall" (as opposed to designating an agent who "talls", say). That's a syntactic act, too, because it just involves the recognition of two substrings inside a string, as well as the access of simple facts about the "-er" suffix, and the words "adjective" and "comparative".

A word's external form can be used like a key in a lock to give us access to a special set of facts connected solely with that word. These facts can include *tests* to be carried out to see if the word applies to a particular situation or not. The larger the number of tests and the subtler they are, the more sophisticatedly we will be able to use the word, and the more deeply that word's meaning will be implicated in our processing.

Thus if there are two objects in our visual field — say the "t" and the "a" inside "taller" itself — and if we can measure their heights, then by numerical comparison (another syntactic act), we can infer that the "t" is the *taller* one. But doesn't this constitute exploitation of the *meaning* of "taller"? What better example of the *semantics* of the word "taller"?

What's wrong? What has happened? Where exactly did we slip out of the "syntactic" realm and into the "semantic" realm? The answer is: nowhere. We never left the syntactic realm at all, although we sure as shootin' did enter the semantic realm. The catchy idea that *what is semantic is by definition not syntactic* is simply a falsity that remains as a residue from the early syntax/semantics dichotomy proposed long ago by linguists who first introduced those words. Once it was true, back when "syntax" had a much more restricted meaning connected with grammar, but times change. Unfortunately, some people's minds remain rigidly trapped by this ancient dichotomy, whereas others recognize that extended meanings for both words can make the old dichotomy merely a relic of the past.

We thus have here something not unlike what happens when a child first acquires a word like "pacifier" or "definitely". At the outset, only the simplest and crudest facts about the word's usage are implemented, and hence utterances containing that word strike an observer as parrot-like and close to semantic vacuity. But children continue to learn and to surround each word with ever-larger halos of connotations and flavors, and soon enough, what started out as clearly empty parroting has verged over into relative fluency: From a syntactic zombie a semantic and sentient being has emerged! And that's the slippery slope so sternly spurned by John Searle.

Generous and Stingy Views of Apparent Aboutness

One way of construing this transition is to maintain, as would Searle, that any resemblance between a language-tackling human toddler and a computational zombie is an illusion. In this view, a toddler is *never* a zombie whose symbols lack aboutness; rather, thanks to some mysterious "causal powers" emanating from the organic chemistry of its brain, there is always, even from the very outset, *genuine meaning* in the toddler's use of words. Something magical about the human brain's physical constitution automatically ensures aboutness of the symbols it supports.

Searle's view is that aboutness results from the nature of the hardware substrate; the experience of interacting with the world may be necessary, but it does not suffice. A computer program could interact with the world just as a toddler does, slowly picking up one word after another from how it is used in diverse contexts, gradually using each word with ever-increasing subtlety and hence ever-increasing semanticity — but for Searle that would be irrelevant. Once a zombie, always a zombie. If you've the wrong hardware, tough luck for you: you're doomed to lifelong unconsciousness. You can talk up a storm, but if yours was the fate to have been built from inapposite stuff, your storm will be but vacuous verbiage, and you but a somber zombie. Carbon wins, and silicon loses. That's just the breaks!

The opposite way of construing a toddler's linguistic maturing would be to say that, yes indeed, in a toddler there is a slow and continuous transition between zero and full semanticity, between simple syntax and genuine aboutness. Somewhere in between the extremes, there is a stage where what we mean by "meaning" is a *little bit* present, and later it is *half* there, and then it is *largely* there, and finally *full* semanticity emerges.

Such a shades-of-gray view of the relationship between aboutness and symbols would necessarily be more charitable than John Searle is towards computer models of language. Such a view would not rule computers out in principle from having access to aboutness. Such a view would not be based on the dogmatic positing of an uncrossable barrier between two different S-words: "syntax" and "semantics".

How Much Mind Lurks Behind an LED Display?

As natural-language-using programs grow increasingly sophisticated, people of all intellectual levels and emotional bents are forced to wonder just how much meaning to attach to computer-generated strings of words, for in our everyday environment we are encountering such strings with ever-greater frequency. How much meaning does one *read into* a string of words, and how much was *put there* by the program?

I am exiting from an underground parking garage, and after a little mechanical mouth by my rolled-down window has swallowed up my ticket, a green LED display just above it flashes, "Thank you! Have a good trip!" at me. I know full well that this is merely a canned set of words and that none of it was pieced together just for me. As Alan Turing's nemesis Professor Jefferson said, "Merely artificially signaling — an easy contrivance." But suppose we fantasize a bit. What if there were a TV camera that scanned my license plate and ran the photo image through an optical character recognizer, thus allowing it to flash at me, "Have a good trip, CIK 317!" Though impressive on one level, this would still be an easy contrivance.

But now suppose the program had access to the state's entire database of automobile licenses, vehicle registrations, driving records, telephone numbers, addresses, World Wide Web home pages, and associated facts. Then, having parsed my license plate, it might conceivably flash the following at me: "Thank you, Douglas Richard Hofstadter, and as you venture out into today's light snow, may I offer you pleasant and safe driving. Incidentally, may I also take the liberty of congratulating you on that snazzy silver 1956 Mercury? Not too many of those around any more! And that one's in such good shape, to boot! Interested in selling it, by any chance? I have a friend who collects cars of that vintage." Once again, all aboutness might be discounted from this, since, to be sure, all six sentences *could* have been made from taking canned templates with a handful of blanks and filling them in with variables looked up in a set of databases.

Thus in the first sentence, there is one blank spot to be filled in by the car owner's name (accessed through the license plate), and another for the current weather conditions (read off the World Wide Web). In the second sentence there is a first blank spot for the insertion of a color, a second blank spot for a year, and a final one for a make of car. And when the year is sufficiently early (say, before 1960), the next four sentences can be mechanically thrown in. Perhaps still just Jeffersonian artificial signaling, perhaps still just an easy contrivance.

But now imagine a repertoire of more and more templates, ever more complex — thousands, perhaps millions. Imagine further that when a template's blanks are filled, other templates can be used as fillers, thus producing nested structures, and this can go on for any number of levels, thus allowing blanks to be filled in by whole phrases, themselves possibly having further filled blanks inside them — and so on. Imagine the steadily increasing subtlety of the data used to guide the selection of the most suitable template out of a vast set of potential templates stored in memory, and to guide the filling-in of the chosen template's slots. Imagine putting sentences together from more and more small units, making less and less use of long, purely canned, rigid phrases. At some point, the performance is going to become surprisingly and impressively fluid-seeming.

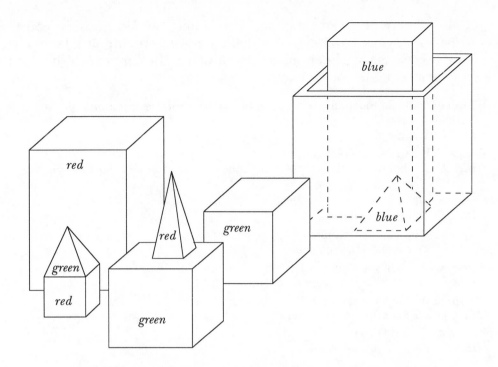

The Uncertain Level of SHRDLU's Semanticity

Indeed, that point was reached in the early 1970's, in my opinion, when Terry Winograd's famous program SHRDLU came into its own at the MIT Artificial Intelligence Laboratory, sporting an ability to take apart and put together remarkably complex sentences that related in precise but subtle ways to a dynamically changing situation involving blocks of various shapes and colors arrayed on a tabletop. Here is a sampling of the kind of things SHRDLU could do, when interacting with a human being:

Winograd: Find a block which is taller than the one you are holding and put it into the box.

SHRDLU: By "it", I assume you mean the block which is taller than the one I am holding. OK.

Winograd: What does the box contain?

SHRDLU: The blue pyramid and the blue block.

Winograd: What is the pyramid supported by?

SHRDLU: The box.

Winograd: How many blocks are not in the box?

SHRDLU: Four of them.

Winograd: Is at least one of them narrower than the one which I told you to pick up?

SHRDLU: Yes, the red cube.

Winograd: Is it supported?

SHRDLU: Yes, by the table.

Call it "mere artificial signaling" if you like, but I can assure you that this is *not* an easy contrivance. The dialogue goes on, and at a later stage, when a few objects have been moved from where they appear in the figure, the following sequence of exchanges takes place:

Winograd: Had you touched any pyramid before you put the green one on the little cube?
SHRDLU: Yes, the green one.

Winograd: When did you pick it up?
SHRDLU: While I was stacking up the red cube, a large red block, and a large green one.

Winograd: Why?
SHRDLU: To get rid of it.

Winograd: Why did you do that?
SHRDLU: To clean off the red cube.

Winograd: Why did you clear off that cube?
SHRDLU: To put it on a large green cube.

Winograd: Why did you do that?
SHRDLU: To stack up the red cube, a large red block, and a large green cube.

Winograd: Why did you do that?
SHRDLU: Because you asked me to.

Such fluidity demonstrates an undeniable type of aboutness — by which I mean that SHRDLU's statements are clearly *reflecting*, and so are *about*, the situation on the tabletop. Like a fox pursuing a fleeing rabbit, SHRDLU remains tightly "in synch" with the changing situation, and its utterances reflect aspects of that world in exquisite detail. Just as the fox's complex patterns of twists and turns can only be understood as a response to the rabbit's running, so SHRDLU's complex linguistic twists and turns can only be understood as being reflections of — as being *about* — the changing situations in its tiny world. This is such strong, robust prose that, as David Moser remarked in Chapter 14, one would not feel dishonest translating it into another language and still passing it off as SHRDLU.

Despite this dialogue's fluency, it must be pointed out that the various items in SHRDLU's vocabulary have vastly different levels of semanticity. Some words are sly cover-ups for an almost total lack of understanding, while others, if one peers behind the scenes at the mechanisms, are surprisingly robust and deeply "grounded" (to borrow a term often used these days in connection with semantics).

But this is nothing new; children learning their native language have lexical items all over the map, in the sense of distinct phases of semanticity. And for adults no less than for children, there are words and phrases galore at the lexicon's fringes whose usage borders on charlatanism. Indeed, with that notion this chapter began: Bob French's easy lobbing-about of brain-anatomy terms, and Françoise Ulam's casual dropping of baseball idioms.

Of some interest, but by no means a critical fact, is that the tabletop in SHRDLU's discourse was never a *genuine* tabletop, but only a *pictured* one, one that was simulated inside the computer's memory and displayed on a screen for the ease of human observers. However, whether the table was substantial or ethereal was of little import, since what really mattered was the *patterns* of objects in the situations, and those patterns were not in the least affected by their tangible physical existence or lack thereof.

Once again, this ties in with Bob French and Françoise Ulam, because Bob's usages didn't apply to any actual physical object (he had never seen a human brain, so far as I know), but merely to a diagram; Françoise Ulam, likewise, could well have picked up all her baseball usages merely from watching television, which is again only "virtual baseball". (Imagine if it had occurred a few years later, and had all come via video-game baseball!)

A curious lesson we can draw from the virtuality of SHRDLU's blocks world, Bob French's brain world, and Françoise Ulam's baseball world is that aboutness and semanticity can arise in the total absence of actual, tangible objects with which the speaker is interacting; what matters, instead, is the subtlety, complexity, and degree of matchup and continued synchrony between the words in utterances and the items in situations — whether those situations are real or virtual.

The Elegant Counterfactuals and Concessives of Proteus

For me, a truly beautiful example of a limited level of aboutness, or semanticity, in computer-produced language is that of the program "Proteus", created by Anthony Davey in the early 1970's at the Theoretical Psychology Unit of the School of Artificial Intelligence at Edinburgh University, Scotland. This laudably meticulous doctoral work was carried out under the supervision of Professors Stephen Isard and Christopher Longuet-Higgins, who deserve much credit for their good taste and their recognition of the depth of microworlds. Indeed, Proteus operated in but a tiny microworld — that of tic-tac-toe games — in which it could play against an opponent and also could formulate a running commentary as well as a retrospective description of a completed game.

There are two aspects of Proteus' use of language that I consider quite extraordinary. The first is the gracefulness of its prose, marked especially by an unprecedentedly fluid incorporation of subtle concessives such as "but", "however", and "although" into its sentences. The other aspect, and one that is tied very closely with the first aspect, is the way in which Proteus not only imagines, but precisely and concisely verbalizes, alternative hypothetical pathways of play that, although never realized in the particular game, play key roles in the justification of both players' choices of moves. This "talking tit-tat-to player" would have thrilled Charles Babbage no end.

Here is a sample blow-by-blow retrospective of a game both played and described by Proteus ("P" stands for "Proteus" and "A" for "Anthony"):

The game began with my taking a corner, and you took an adjacent one.

P		A

I threatened you by taking the corner adjacent to the one that you had just taken, but you blocked my diagonal and threatened me.

		P
	A	
P		A

I blocked yours and forked you.

P		P
	A	
P		A

Although you blocked one of my edges and threatened me, I won by completing the other.

P	P	P
A	A	
P		A

The number of interacting syntactic and semantic issues taken into consideration in the production of such a commentary is very great, and the program's verbal output is clearly in tune not just with what actually took place on the board, but also with a number of mental events that never occurred but that were entertained by both players in deciding how to proceed at each turn. Davey comments on this particular run:

> The commentary requires the audience to follow intelligently: we observe, for example, that after the third move, the program never says that any particular square was "taken", but instead uses terms like "block" or "complete", which are unambiguous provided the audience follows the commentary. We might finally note that the program has mentioned a threat presented by the penultimate move, despite the fact that it was a vacuous threat in view of the tactical situation. Another version of the program does not mention such threats, and it is debatable which produces the more natural English; perhaps they should be mentioned as threats only if the opponent's win does not immediately follow, either through his omission or because the game is unfinished.

What more could one hope for, for "aboutness", at least in a microdomain?

As with SHRDLU, were one to look behind the scenes at all the words Proteus uses, one would find that they vary hugely in semanticity, but of course in no case does the program approach human mastery. Thus, although Proteus can appropriately apply spatial terms like "edge", "end", "middle", "corner", and "opposite", it does so only in the narrow context of a 3 x 3 matrix — it has no idea of the extraordinary diversity of instances of those concepts in the wider world, for in fact, it has no idea of the existence of the wider world at all! Similarly, it has an ability to use words like "fork", "take", "block", and "threaten" only in the context of this one minuscule game, whereas in full human English those words stand for enormously flexible, broad concepts. Nonetheless, in its tiny world, Proteus uses these nouns and verbs with precision and sensitivity. Moreover, its handling of the concessives and verbal tenses is both subtle and clear.

Here is another game together with Proteus' annotations:

I started the game by taking the middle of an edge, and you took an end of the opposite one.

A		
		P

I threatened you by taking the square opposite the one I had just taken, but you blocked my line and threatened me.

A		
P	A	P

However, I blocked your diagonal and threatened you.

A		
P	A	P
		P

If you had blocked my edge, you would have forked me, but you took the middle of the one opposite the corner I had just taken and adjacent to mine and so I won by completing my edge.

A	A	P
P	A	P
		P

There are no templates here; every last sentence is built entirely from scratch. Look at how elegantly Proteus uses the word "one" throughout its commentary, especially in the final diagram. Notice how in the next-to-last line it says "mine", meaning "my edge", but then on the very last line, it switches back to "my edge", realizing that "mine" would sound wrong. Talk about subtlety — my goodness! And every time I read its output, I savor Proteus' "effortless" interweaving of the simple past, the past perfect, and the past subjunctive. The design and building of Proteus was a remarkable achievement, not only intellectually but also esthetically. This rare type of unpretentious but polished elegance is the kind of thing that, in my opinion, AI should be all about, but so seldom is.

Imagining Deep Proteus

Without doubt, the terms of feeblest semantic backing in Proteus are the pronouns "you" and "I". Only in the most stretched of senses is Proteus referring to itself when it says "I", since its model of itself is paper-thin, and whatever Proteus is, it is light-years away from meriting the imputation of a genuine self, something that the word "I" invariably suggests. As for the pronoun "you", Proteus has no model whatsoever of what a human being is. The pronouns "I" and "you" in Proteus' output are negligibly richer than the "you" in the feeble "Thank you!" on the LED in the parking garage.

It would be most impressive if the architecture of Proteus could be adapted to a richer game, such as chess, and were able to generate credible commentaries explaining the reasons for moves made by high-level players in tournaments. This would require a very deep understanding of chess — not just the ability to play well, but the ability to put its computational finger on what really matters in a chess situation — what defines the unique qualities of a complex board position, as opposed to what is fairly routine.

One naturally wonders whether IBM's chess program Deep Blue could be adapted to do this. The challenge for its programmers would be to get their program not just to evaluate its fabulous 50,000,000,000 board positions in a mere three minutes, but then to summarize the results of all this labor in only a few dozen well-chosen words: explaining why *this* move wound up being chosen, and not some other. In order to do so, Deep Blue (which would no longer be Deep Blue but Deep Proteus) would have to know exactly which options were worth talking about and how deeply and how precisely to spell out their probable consequences. That is not exactly a trivial task! No chess program of which I am aware has anything like this capability at the present time.

Natural-language Prowess in AI

In this book, we have seen many levels of linguistic performance by computer programs, ranging from a vacuous parking-garage "Thank you!", to the glib façades of Whimsical Conversation and PC Professor, to the syntactic intricacies of my sentence-spouter sEn·gEn, to the silly translations produced by Systran, GTS, and Candide, and all the way up to SHRDLU's impressive parsing of long sentences and Proteus' gracefully verbalized counterfactuals. On the blue-sky end of the spectrum, we have also daydreamed a bit about a merger of Deep Blue and Proteus, and imagined the joy of a typed interchange with the humanly intelligent program AMT.

In my experience, and as these few examples show, the most impressive of natural-language programs are those that function in very small microworlds. Indeed, a crude rule of thumb would seem to be this: The smaller the world, the higher the degree of aboutness that can validly be claimed for the program. Thus the programs that try to bite off the largest real-world chunks are bound to be the most superficial and "syntactic", so to speak, while the programs that restrict themselves to elegant microworlds can, for this very reason, afford to contain detailed representations and complex understandings of dependency, causality, proximity, alternity, and many other deeply semantic aspects of language. This tradeoff between depth of performance and size of domain has been far too little appreciated in the checkered history of AI, and, sadly, we are currently in a period where the vogue is tipped enormously in favor of vast, sprawling projects that include everything but the kitchen sink.

What is to Car Driving as Systran is to Translation?

In these silly days of impatient myopia, with public, industrial, and governmental insistence upon instant applicability of all research, the most money is being thrown, not surprisingly, at projects whose domain is far from limited to a tiny microworld. In machine translation, for instance, the domains of discourse are growing ever more bloated (as the huge size of the lexicons mentioned a few pages ago indicates).

Nowadays, it would seem hopelessly out of fashion to study translation between languages inside SHRDLU's cute little blocks world or Proteus' even more miniature tic-tac-toe world, no matter how subtle and complex the sentences and ideas were. What inevitably results from this refusal to home in on complex issues by sticking to small domains is superficiality. Indeed, I will now ask a quite brazen question: "Does what Systran and its cousins do even merit the name 'translation'?"

Asking this question brings to my mind a number of computer programs that I have seen touted in newspapers and on television as able to drive cars. When I first heard about such efforts, I was stunned, since over three decades of driving in many terrains, countries, and situations, I had arrived at the strong conviction that driving a car potentially involves nearly all of one's knowledge about the world and occasionally puts one's entire intellect to a severe test. How could it be that computers at today's level of technology could be functioning at so high a level?

But then, when I finally took the trouble to look up close at these claims, I found out what was meant by "driving". It turned out that the central task was to keep the tip of a triangle horizontally centered inside a rectangle. Does that sound like driving to you?

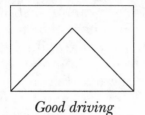
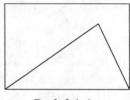

Good driving   *Bad driving*

Well, once you see a picture of it, you can probably relate to it. The rectangle represents one's field of vision (a bit like a windshield), and the triangle is the road ahead, receding in perspective towards the horizon. Of course you want the triangle to be centered — you don't want to run off the side of the road! But is that all that the word "driving" means? Why, then, do high schools require driver's education courses, and why does the Bureau of Motor Vehicles administer driving tests? Keeping a triangle centered in a box certainly doesn't require much learning or great skill!

The answer, and it contains a subtle truth, is this: Although driving involves far, far more than this simple geometric task, doing this one thing might fairly be said to constitute the core, indeed, the bulk, of everyday, mundane driving. And so, in a very crude approximation, yes indeed, driving *is* the centering of a triangle's tip in a rectangle. When everything else is going just swimmingly, you can get away with no more than this.

The Difference between a Caricature and the Real Thing

Driver's education, of course, is not in the least about triangle-tip centering; it's about the myriad things that go beyond it. What do you do if your car starts to skid? How many car lengths to stay behind the car ahead of you, at various speeds? When do you flash your brights at an oncoming car? Can you make a left turn on a red light? Of course, this type of information, crucial though it is, is still just the tip of the driving iceberg. If a car is swerving ahead of me as I drive down a highway, I have to pay close attention to its motions, and quickly try to gauge the driver's degree of inebriation or aggressiveness. Driver's education can't teach me *how* to do this, but it can make me aware of the potential problem.

Suppose that on a crowded and curvy two-lane road, I come up behind a heavily loaded pickup truck lurching along with its tailgate down, and it looks as if things on the flatbed are threatening to spill out at any moment onto the road right in front of me; I naturally want to pass this road hazard as quickly as possible. But as I inch out into the left lane to see if I can pass, how far out dare I go, given the density and speed of oncoming traffic? And if and when I do decide to pass, just how fast is safe for me and my passengers? And how do I weigh into the equation the fact that I recently got a speeding ticket and don't want my insurance rates to go up?

And how do I weigh into the equation the further fact that I want to make it to Chicago in time to deliver an afternoon colloquium, and have already lost a lot of time because of a big traffic jam just north of Indianapolis? How slippable is the goal of making my talk? Suppose I were to dash in, breathless, transparencies in hand, only fifteen minutes before my talk is supposed to begin? Or just five minutes before? Or five minutes after? Or fifteen? How do all of these diverse and strangely interacting considerations affect the pressure of my right foot on the accelerator pedal?

Suppose I'm doing 75 miles an hour on a freeway and I spot someone walking back and forth on an overpass up ahead, and I notice they seem to be holding what *might* be a heavy stone — how do I adjust my driving in order to avoid having a rock come smashing through my windshield as it's dropped just for kicks by a bored juvenile delinquent? This is a life-and-death decision that I as driver must make in only a couple of seconds!

Suppose I find myself standing stock still in a huge traffic jam on a freeway, and there's a grass dividing strip between my side of the freeway and the other side, leading back in the direction I've just come from. Do I consider turning onto that strip and trying to backtrack and looking for an alternate route that avoids this stretch of freeway? What if, watching a few cars trying this very idea out, I see three of them make it while one of them gets mired in the muddy grass? How do I evaluate this information? How do I further refine my judgment by taking into consideration the sizes and types of those cars as compared with my own? What variables count, and what variables don't count? And how does all this connect with the tick-tick-ticking timer for my talk in Chicago?

I could go on and on for ages recounting driving dilemmas that have cropped up in my experience over the years. Someone might say, "But what you're talking about goes way beyond the meaning of the term 'driving'." I would simply counter by saying that it is very hard to figure out where to draw the line between triangle-tip centering, on the one hand, and trying to guess the psychological motivations of a shadowy figure up there on an upcoming overpass, on the other. There are intermediate levels of problems that crop up with fairly high frequency and that demand very fast, real-time decision-making. To me, that is absolutely what is meant by "driving". That's what I would be paying for if I hired a human driver to get me to Chicago safely and on time; why should one not mean the same thing by the word when it applies to a machine?

Despite all my railing, it remains a fact that full-sized cars have barreled down freeways at 60 miles an hour and more, under the guidance of computer programs (of course, with brave humans sitting warily inside, prepared at the drop of a hat to override the silicon chips' simplistic decisions). I've seen the videotapes — I can't deny it! But I also know that I wouldn't trust such a computer driver any farther than I can throw it. To be sure, what with computers getting ever tinier and lighter these days, I'll be able to throw such pieces of hardware farther and farther as time goes on, but it'll be a good long while until I can throw one all the way to Chicago from here in my home in Bloomington, Indiana.

Doing a Disservice to Clarity

And now we bounce back from driving to the question as to whether the word "translation" applies to Systran and its cousins. To be sure, the combination of fast dictionary lookup of words and fast rearrangement of syntactic structures constitutes the *sine qua non* of translation, but that does not mean that these activities alone make up translation, no more than real-time triangle-tip centering amounts to driving. The union of word lookup with syntactic reordering constitutes a disturbingly anemic conception of translation. This was of course pointed out decades ago by Yehoshua Bar-Hillel, and a few years later, his close colleague Victor Yngve reached a similar conclusion, writing in a 1964 article that the "semantic barrier" had been hit, and that "we will only have adequate mechanical translations when the machine can 'understand' what it is translating."

Calling triangle-tip centering "driving" and calling word lookup and rearrangement "translation" are acts that typify the whole field of artificial intelligence in this, its "mature" phase. In each case, some central aspect of a complex mental task is isolated, distilled down into a pathetic caricature of the whole, more or less adequately computerized in this junior form, and the achievement is then passed off, all too often in hysterically hyped press releases and splashy videos, as the whole ball of wax. We have now seen it in machine translation and machine chauffeuring, and on and on goes the hype, bouncing from one impressive intellectual task to another, in an unceasing effort, sometimes intentional and sometimes not, to pull the wool over thoughtful eyes.

For instance, a piece of publicity about some MT software produced in Japan — several years ago, actually, but that doesn't matter; if anything, the tone has grown even more self-indulgent since then — said this:

> ...world's first practical translation system — can work in English, French, German, and Japanese.... capable of translating news stories into these languages simultaneously.... will translate rambling sentences into clear counterparts....

Yeah, yeah, sure... Once one catches onto this trend of nonsensical exaggeration, it's enough to make one so cynical as to discount the entire endeavor of AI or its various sub-endeavors, such as MT. Not that *nothing* has been achieved — Xerox and many other institutions *do* use machine translation, after all, in their funny way! — but just that small achievements and grandiose fantasies become so horribly blurred into each other that the whole field is tainted with an aura of dishonesty and distortion.

I find this very sad, because the quest to develop an artificially intelligent entity is a marvelous, mystical quest, in which we are brought face to face with the deepest enigmas concerning our own nature. What is language? What is music? What are concepts? What are words? What is thinking? What is insight? How does analogy work? What is memory? How do we learn? How do we forget? How are mistakes linked to invention? What is perception? What is consciousness? What is creativity? What is artistic beauty? How do we mirror other minds inside our own? What are empathy and compassion? How does a soul come out of inanimate matter? What is a self? What does the word "I" represent?

All of this is such a far cry from such things as dictionary lookup and triangle-tip centering that it could turn one into a confirmed disbeliever and naysayer, someone who chants, with Searle and his ilk, that AI is nothing but hokum and hoopla.

The Importance of Seeing Shades of Gray

The problem with Searle-style cynicism and naysaying, understandable though they might seem, is that they are almost always characterized by a dogmatic unwillingness to see or grant any shades of gray. Does semanticity come in shades of gray, or is it discretely quantized — not there at all, and then, all of a sudden, *there*? The lack of semanticity in what we have seen of machine translation might well seem to encourage a total discounting of semanticity *in principle* from computer approaches to language. But even the tiniest epsilon — the mathematicians' way of saying "something very, very small" — is not identical to zero.

To illustrate intermediate levels of semanticity in human translation, think of Zhang Jiaying working on "My Treasure". In her dictionary-driven manipulations of French and English words, she had no overall idea of the scenario she was reading about and trying to reconstruct. Because Jiaying knew no French and almost no English, what she had in her head was at best a vague, confused image of the true situation, but in no way was her three-hour-long labor a vacuous, image-free process. As she had dealt with the complexities of life on this planet for two decades, each word conjured up giant halos of imagery; the problem was of course to integrate them into something coherent, but there was no lack of "aboutness" in her mind.

One could say similar things about simultaneous interpreters called in on short notice to translate conference talks on unfamiliar topics. Although they may fake it without imagery or understanding for very short bursts, most of the time they are closer to picturing what is going on. A simultaneous interpreter's imagery fluctuates in precision, sometimes being nearly perfect, other times plunging perilously close to nil, but most of the time hovering somewhere in between. If one could magically watch the needle of a "semantometer" monitoring word after word of such an interpreter's performance, it would look very wobbly!

I don't want to beat a dead horse, but for more shades of gray in human language, I would point once again to the examples involving Bob French, Françoise Ulam, and children employing words that are new or near the periphery of mastery.

An example of non-natives doing their best to master the trickiest idioms of a horrendously alien tongue is the case of elementary-particle physicists using words like "electron", "proton", "photon", "neutrino", "quark", "graviton", "charge", "spin", "strangeness", "charm", "color", and scores of others. The realm of quantum particles is a domain that is in principle inaccessible to classical, macroscopic beings. It is riddled with deeply alien phenomena whose nature we can never experience directly, as we experience light and sound, mass and motion, and so forth. The phenomena in this microworld can be studied only by indirect means, using mathematical inference and clever experimentation; they can never be known or perceived directly. Firsthand or "native" understanding of the goings-on inside an atom, a nucleus, or an even smaller structure is simply forbidden to us.

And yet, through our clumsy, classical, coarse-grained channels, a kind of partial, fuzzy vision of this alien realm's mysteries is permitted to flow upwards, and the words we use to describe what we think we see happening reflect our blurry perceptions. Some physicists, needless to say, get the hang of these words better than others do — their imagery must be slightly more in tune with the occult reality — and for this reason they make more penetrating discoveries. Some straggle behind, like babies who grow up and quite competently use the words "pacifier", "airport", and "skyscraper", yet never quite figure out that they are compound words.

I've done my best to demonstrate how many shades of semantic gray exist in the human use of language, and I contend that similar grays could exist in the computational handling of language. Given the easily-revealed vacuity of some of today's highly-touted programs, it's not too hard for a dogged cynic like John Searle to parlay such programs' empty symbols into a plausible-sounding case for the inevitable vacuity of all possible computer approaches to language. But that's just a deceptive maneuver carried out in order to defend an *a priori* yearning for humans' mental primacy not to be threatened by our silicon cousins, no matter how impressive their performance might someday become.

A more serious approach, to my mind, is to recognize the tremendous shortcomings of today's natural-language programs while at the same time refusing to categorically assign *zero* semanticity to the symbols that they use. One must judge each case separately, trying to see what substance there is behind the terms.

There are, then, two opposite smokescreens one must fight in order to arrive at the truth: one of them is the smokescreen of hype, which AI workers often throw up even without realizing it, sooner or later leading to a backlash that discredits their own discipline, while the other smokescreen is that of Searlianism, deflecting attention from the true action and trying to parlay primitive emotions about simple mechanical objects like clocks and can-openers into unassailable intellectual conclusions about synthetic entities millions, billions, or trillions of times more complex.

Taking Stock of Machine Translation Today

Pervading today's approaches to machine translation, one still senses the philosophy that may well have lain behind that enigmatic statement by one of its founders, Warren Weaver: "When I look at an article in Russian, I say, 'This is really written in English, but it has been coded in some strange symbols. I will now proceed to decode.'" If taken at face value, this is a brazen remark that has long since been utterly discredited. I would like to believe, however, that Weaver knew full well how silly this sounded, and was simply being deliberately provocative.

Although the far more guarded viewpoints expressed in 1960 by Yehoshua Bar-Hillel and in 1964 by Victor Yngve have by no means been universally adopted, there are, I am glad to say, isolated pockets of MT researchers who have taken those early figures' warnings to heart. One such group is the team at Carnegie-Mellon University's Center for Machine Translation, led by Jaime Carbonell and Sergei Nirenburg. This group is spearheading an approach called "knowledge-based machine translation", at whose heart is the idea of using a set of simple real-world concepts to build representations of the *meaning* of sentences, and perhaps even what one might generously call "imagery".

Unfortunately, however, such work is still funded largely in the hopes of developing practical applications, such as the translation of documents concerning heavy earth-moving machinery (one of the Carnegie-Mellon group's sponsors has been the Caterpillar Company); research toward the machine translation of poetry, or even the machine translation of concessives and counterfactuals in the domain of tic-tac-toe commentaries, would be laughed out the door of most funding quarters.

With a few exceptions, such as Xerox's eloquent Martin Kay (who grew up in a family of translators), the field of machine translation seems nearly bereft of an attitude of deep humility and respect for the subtlety and beauty of human language. Over and over again, one encounters articles and publicity claiming degrees of success that, if true, could only mean that all the mysteries of human language (and *a fortiori* all the mysteries of the human mind) had been fully cleared up.

It is this stunning lack of humility, this regrettable level of hubris, that I find incomprehensible (and in this case also reprehensible). By no means does this imply, however, that I oppose the attempt to study or model human language and the act of translation by means of computers. Who knows — I might even get back into it myself someday. I just think one should have the proper degree of respect for what one is tackling.

Optimism and Pessimism

I am a romantic who tends to see the power and depth of human creativity as virtually limitless. Indeed, one of my purposes in drawing together this book's sampler of sparklingly diverse translations of one tiny poem was to issue a clear reminder of how subtle and complex the human mind really is. I hope thereby to convey the attitude that in AI and MT, one should not expect full success overnight — nor should anyone want it.

The words "optimism" and "pessimism" are used by many artificial-intelligence researchers in what seems to me to be a totally topsy-turvy manner. Their oft-expressed "optimism" is the to-me-perverse hope that soon (say within a decade or two) we shall have succeeded in modeling all the subtleties of the human mind; "pessimism", on the other hand, is the to-them-perverse idea that many mysteries will remain for much longer. I feel the truth is precisely the reverse: "optimism" should be the hope that the human mind will remain a beckoning mystery into the indefinite future, while "pessimism" would be the dismal feeling that our very souls will soon be reducible to small VLSI chips that can be stamped out by the billions in factories in Silicon Valley. That is a most dreary, depressing image of what humanity is, and I for one just don't believe in it. I harbor a good deal more respect than that for the mystery of the human mind.

●

Poems XVI:

~ My Sweet Ones ~

```
* * * * * * * *
 * * * *
   * *
    *
    *
```

The recipient of this poem was my mother, who on her 75th birthday (actually the day before, since the day itself was nonexistent: my Mom was born on February 29th) had just undergone a quintuple cardiac bypass, and luckily, the operation was very successful.

In the previous week, my mother's serious heart condition had been diagnosed, and a preliminary attempt to fix things had been done, using the technique known as "angioplasty" — the insertion of balloons into one's arteries in order to open them up and allow greater blood flow. However, that had not been sufficient, and a bypass was deemed necessary. This explanation should help to demystify lines 6–10.

Everyone in my family has always loved music of many sorts, including old-time jazz, and one of our favorites from that era is Fats Waller, who I think of as the most exuberant of all jazz pianists and singers. That explains the name on line 19. As for "jams", well, isn't that what *confitures* means?

And then there's that spoonerized proverb on lines 24–25, which expresses my genuine concern that my Mom should henceforth take particular care with her diet, given that careless eating is one of the main contributors to heart disease.

But probably the very best thing about this version of "Ma Mignonne" is its first line, of which, simple though it is, I am quite proud.

Mom in Yon

D. Hofstadter

Mom in yon
Cell, come on
Out of bed.
Clear your head
With some tunes.   5
Those balloons
Spread your veins,
Gave you pains,
But they helped,
Though you yelped.   10
Now it's time
(Says Doug's rhyme)
To begin
To take in
Joys of life,   15
Which are rife
For those who
Listen to
Jams by Fats —
Or if that's   20
Not your mood,
Chow down food.
But be smart:
Put your heart
'Fore the course!   25
Summon force
And push on,
Mom mignonne.

This was written in the spring of 1990, as little green leaves and tiny pink buds were just beginning to brighten Indiana's winter-drab trees, when Carol, *ma mignonne,* was in a hospital in Indianapolis, recuperating from a long and serious abdominal operation, performed in order to allow her to have a safe second pregnancy.

Once the surgery was over and clearly successful, even though it was very rough on Carol for those first few days, the two of us shared an unforgettable sense of elation and hopefulness for the future. I wrote the poem in the true spirit of Marot's original — to cheer up my dear girl who was suffering in her sickbed largely deprived of food, and who was just beginning to be able to enjoy eating again. The line "Have some See's" is a reference to our favorite brand of chocolates, available mostly in the western states, particularly California, and in order to deliver this poem to Carol, I stashed it inside a long, thin poem-shaped box of fine See's peppermints (mixed light and dark, for those who must know), which were her and my very favorites, so that when she opened it up in her hospital bed, the first thing she saw was the poem. She read it with great curiosity, beamed her radiant smile up at me, and had me lean over so she could give me a kiss.

Oddly, or perhaps not so oddly, the pair consisting of this translation and the next one, one by each of us, marks in my memory the beginning of one of the most joyous periods of our life together. A few months after the surgery — sadly, less than two weeks after my Dad died — Carol found out she was pregnant. In early 1991 she underwent a test in San Francisco to check out the health of the fetus, for the results of which we would have to wait a few weeks. We were given the option of being told our baby's sex, and we said yes, we would like to know.

A couple of weeks passed and we were back in Indiana. One morning, I was working in my study and the phone rang. I picked it up, and it was a nurse from the San Francisco ob/gyn clinic. I tensed up and instantly yelled to Carol to get on the other line. Once we were both on, the nurse said she had good news for us, the baby was fine. We were elated, and then the nurse said, "And would you like to know the sex of your baby?" I took a deep breath, and we both said, "Yes." The nurse spoke very slowly, "Well, it is going to be a girl." There were two simultaneous whoops here in Bloomington, Indiana, as full of joy as ever whoops have been. This was what we had been hoping for, even though, obviously, had it gone the other way, we would soon have been just as happy with our fate.

Carol gave birth, in July of 1991, to our daughter Monica Marie, who, with our son Daniel Frederic, then three-and-a-half, turned our little three family into a little four family, thus finally realizing the dream that Carol and I had nurtured, first separately and then together, for a long, long time.

Carol Dear

D. Hofstadter

Carol dear,
Here's some cheer
From your beau.
Lying low
Has been tough,   5
After rough
Surgery,
But you'll be
In the pink
In a wink —   10
Guaranteed!
Doug does need
His best pal,
So come, gal
Whose poor tongue,   15
Always gung
Ho for food,
Hasn't chewed
In a while;
Eat in style —   20
Have some See's!
Keep disease
At arm's length;
Regain strength
And fight gloom.   25
Soon you'll bloom,
Have no fear,
Carol dear.

"Chickadee" was Carol's sole foray into Marot territory. She was uncertain whether she could do a job that would meet my approval, and hence put off doing it for ages. This drove me crazy and in my heavy-handed way, I kept on prodding her to try — and that of course made her *less* inclined to do it, rather than more so. A typical marital interaction.

But one pretty spring day, not long after I had written "Carol Dear" for her in the hospital, I went into her study in Bloomington and chanced to see a lined notebook lying open on her desk, with a penciled-in poem on the page. I read the poem and was enormously touched: it was called "My Chickadee" and was very beautifully rendered. Carol was out of the house at the time, but as soon as she got back I told her what I had seen, and how beautiful I thought it was. She couldn't believe I liked it so well, and I assured her I was sincere. My only critical comment was that she might improve it a little by thinning it down from four syllables to three, which she immediately did, and having done so, she agreed with me that that way it was better.

"Chickadee" is a lovely exploration of the "bird" conceit, from beginning to end. The idea of replacing the metaphorical prison by a "cage", for example, is charming and elegant, as is the transfer of the loss of color from skin to feathers. The bird swooping along, picking up bits of food in midcourse, is another pretty image, a frame blend *par excellence,* and it reminds me of a similar image she once suggested...

It was early May of 1987, and Carol and I were visiting Spain for the first time, playing cassettes of wonderful music by de Falla, Albéniz, and Granados wherever we drove, and steeping ourselves in the craggy wildness of Spanish landscapes. One evening, we were sitting together on the balcony of our hotel, the Hotel Alhambra Palace, savoring the spectacular view of the city of Granada and the distant Sierra Nevada mountains as the sun slowly sank in the west. The city was spread out beneath us, and swarming all through the vast chasms of warm air between us and the houses far below were uncountably many swallows, all of them swooping and darting after invisible bugs, their sunset-time meal, which they no doubt were enjoying as much as we were enjoying the delicious *tapas* we had already made a ritual out of, after just a few days in Spain. Popping a green olive into my mouth, I said to Carol, "If I could be any kind of bird, I'd be a swallow... only I wouldn't like eating insects." Smiling, she replied, "There are trade-offs... Now if you could be a Thai-food-eating swallow, that would be *ideal!*" I took up her image, embellishing it a little: "Yeah, with little tiny specks of Thai food darting around in the sky like insects..."

In her poem, although Carol doesn't get in a poet's (or translator's) self-reference, she makes up for this lack by inserting the phrase "French bread", delicately hinting at the original poem's language and culture. It is undeniable that Carol's first love among European countries was Italy, but she certainly loved France and its culture too, for many reasons. She spoke a little French and particularly enjoyed listening to French songs of that musically magical era that came to a close some forty or so years ago. Her favorite singer was Charles Trenet, and in the last year of her life, she fell head over heels in love with one of his records, especially the songs *Douce France* and *Boum!* The latter turned out to play a very touching role in the film *Toto le héros,* which we saw together and were deeply moved by. Carol played *Boum!* so often at home that our son Danny picked up its melody, and in the fall of 1993, when we had just arrived in Italy to spend a year, Carol was enchanted by the fact that our little five-year-old American boy was humming an old French song to himself as he played with his Legos on the floor of his new Italian home.

In my judgment, the last seven lines of "Chickadee" are especially well-crafted and beautiful. I must say, as I hear its *dolcezza* — graced tone — as my eye glides over its elegant form, I can't help but feel that this poem is among the finest and sweetest of all "Ma Mignonne"'s. But then, I'm biased — I loved her so, and still and still I do.

Chickadee

Carol Hofstadter

Chickadee,
I decree
A fine day.
Dart away
From your cage   5
And engage
In brave flight,
So you might
Flee the croup.
Hope you swoop   10
Into ham,
Apple jam,
And French bread,
Or instead
You will lose   15
The bright hues
Of your plumes.
Flu consumes
Scrawny birds;
Heed my words   20
And take care.
Slip the snare
That does pinch
My wee finch.
Hopes abound   25
That aground
You won't be,
Chickadee.

• *Chapter 17* •

In Praise of the Music of Language

•

> Haiku: A lyrical Japanese verse form stemming from Zen Buddhism, tending to emphasize nature, change, surprise, spontaneity, and the times of year, and consisting usually of seventeen syllables arranged in three lines containing five, seven, and five syllables, respectively.
>
> *An old pond: a frog jumps in — the sound of water.*
>
> — *haiku by Matsu Bashō,*
> *translated by Hiroaki Sato*

Will you, Message, take this medium to be your poetically wedded partner? *I will.* And will you, Medium, take this message to be your poetically wedded partner? *I will.* It gives me great joy to pronounce you, Medium and Message, to be a Poem. You may now kiss.

Poetry as Matrimony

From wallpaper to masonry to pottery, from weaving to music to painting, from woodwork to mathematics to poetry, pattern has universal appeal to the human spirit. The idea of "poetry without pattern" is an oxymoron; my final mission is to reinforce this oft-forgotten connection.

Can poetry be clearly and sharply defined? Of course not — no more than the notion of pattern can be clearly and sharply defined. And yet it is somehow irresistible to make a stab at this delectable indefinable.

Poetry, as I see it, involves the choice of an *esthetically restricted medium* and the attempt to convey through it some roughly premeditated set of images or ideas. The constraints that determine the medium need not be precise or fully explicit in the poet's mind at the time of writing, though they may be; likewise, the exact set of ideas to be expressed may evolve during the interaction with the chosen medium. For a writer, perhaps the most exciting type of experience is when not only do the ideas swirl about, fragmenting and re-forming like clouds in an angry sky, but also, even as the poem coalesces, the very chemistry of the atmosphere of the swarming idea-clouds is gradually metamorphosing. In any case, the essence of the act of writing poetry is the indissoluble fusion of a medium with a message, the unsunderable wedding of form to content as equal partners.

Sensory versus Cerebral Constraints

In my stab of a definition of poetry, I used the suggestive phrase "esthetically restricted medium". What does this mean? There is of course no way that I can pin the notion down precisely, but I can at least suggest what I mean by describing it indirectly — for instance, through its effects. Thus the act of looking at a poem in print or reading it aloud should produce some kind of *sensual pleasure*. The nature of the medium should be directly tangible to a reader engaged with the poem, as opposed to being merely a covert intellectual fact.

To make this quite concrete, imagine a piece of writing in which the letter-counts of successive words obey some arcane mathematical formula (*e.g.*, they list the successive digits in the aperiodic decimal expansion of the irrational number π: 3.14159265358979323846264338327 9...). Many such pieces of text have indeed been written as mnemonics to help interested parties memorize the beginning of π. Here is the most famous "pi-ku" of all, shown first in the original French, then in my English rendition:

> *Que j'aime à faire apprendre un nombre utile aux sages !*
> *Immortel Archimède, artiste ingénieur,*
> *Qui de ton jugement peut priser la valeur ?*
> *Pour moi, ton problème eut de pareils avantages.*

> *How I love π! Teach beginners 31 digits, handy for genii.*
> *Immortal Ἀρχημήδης, cunning number-guy,*
> *Who in thy judgment will assess π's extent?*
> *This nut, its cracking, got me immense enjoyment.*

Although the letter-count constraint on these pi-kus is absolutely strict and precise, it is not *hearable* (at least not in any normal sense of the term). To be sure, one senses a certain degree of awkwardness, especially in the last line (in either language), but it is not the type of awkwardness that has a clearly recognizable signature. Upon being told where it comes from, one can appreciate the construction on a cerebral level, but there is no sensual charm that emanates from the text.

Actually, I take it back; there is a *slight* degree of perceptible, sensual charm — namely, the French pi-ku rhymes according to an ABBA scheme. To reflect this audible pattern, I carefully made my English pi-ku rhyme too, although I altered the rhyme scheme to AABB. And because of *that* structure, but not because of their cryptic link to π, I would call these two pi-mnemonics poems — feeble ones, admittedly, but still poems.

The embedded pi-ness, though undeniably running through every word of the text, yields nothing sensual or musical in the sounds one hears. In some curious sense, the pi-digits constraint is *not superficial enough*; it is *too semantic*. It requires too much processing, too much mental energy, too much time, too much thinking, to figure out or appreciate the nature of the medium. It may seem ironic to be complaining about too much semanticity, but the fact is, human beings run on a dual track; they want to be pleased on more than one level at once. They want direct, obvious, immediate, sensual pleasure, and they also want indirect, hidden, slower, intellectual pleasure. A poem ideally satisfies both desires simultaneously.

Poetry Lover or Philistine?

The seeds for this book were planted in one sharp and vivid instant: the moment in which I first laid eyes on Clément Marot's poem "A une Damoyselle malade". Its narrow, vertical black-on-white form jumped off the page, sailed upward through the air, synchronized-swam through both my eyeballs, glommed onto their retinas, and from those advantageous twin perches, shouted in stereo into my pattern-loving, sixteen-year-old brain, "Read me!" And once I had done so, I was hooked, for "Ma Mignonne" has much more than just a sexy figure; when read aloud, it has a *music* to it, a special, recognizable sonority based on the standard devices of rhyme and meter, structural qualities known by poets even millennia before Marot's time as appealing to a broad spectrum of humanity.

There are of course other standard "reader-hooking" devices used in poetry, such as word or phrase repetition, syntactic parallelism, alliteration, vowel resonances, dense consonant clusters, and many more. These types of devices, though differing in details from language to language, have evolved independently in different cultures around the world, and testify to the universal appeal of *patternedness*.

It was my own love for elegant structure that attracted me to poetry such as Marot's and many other types, and yet ironically, for decades I considered myself to be a philistine with respect to poetry, a nonlover of poetry, someone baffled and mystified by poetry, largely because in our curious century, so much of what goes by the name "poetry" eschews the ancient, deep, and thoroughgoing respect for pattern, structure, form, direct sensuality. I have finally arrived at a different conclusion, however: that I am a lover of poetry, that there is much bad poetry in the world, that much of it is nonetheless highly touted, and that my not being able to relate to highly-touted bad stuff cowed me into thinking I was a philistine.

The Trendy Pooh-poohing of Pattern

The need for sensuality of sound in poetry, as well as its analogue in music, was taken for granted until not all that long ago. But around the turn of the twentieth century, a wave of change started rippling throughout the arts. In poetry, free verse started taking over, and in the world of classical or "serious" music, tonality was dropped, at least in some quarters, and replaced by a severe, austere, unhearable cerebrality; thus did poetry and music together start down the sad slide from being sensuous and visceral to being solely intellectual. And in the course of that slide, they lost more and more of their mass appeal, in the end becoming esoterica appealing only to tiny coteries and cliques of people who listened with humorless scholasticism and pretension.

For me personally, exposed here and there from adolescence onward to old and new styles of music and poetry, the heartless newer brands had less than zero appeal — they actively repelled me. In Chapter 14, I used Dylan Thomas' ugly and impenetrable poem "How Soon the Servant Sun" to discuss my reaction of baffled bemusement at much of modern poetry — but there are thousands upon thousands of examples I could have used instead. Any poetry section in any decent bookstore will provide examples galore. I chose a famous poet deliberately, because poking holes in lines by a little-known poet would have been too easy and too uncontroversial. The strange thing about Dylan Thomas is that he clearly was fascinated by form, and indeed I do like some of his poems; it's just that his standards and his quality vary phenomenally from work to work.

Though I feel more or less compelled by social conventions to use the word "poem" to describe these verbal constructions that repel me, they don't satisfy my earlier stab at a definition of the term, at least not as far as I can tell. In such works I perceive neither a clear message nor a clear medium, and certainly not an esthetically pleasing medium. What I do see without difficulty is streams of obscure language punctuated by unexpected line-breaks. The poet would supposedly be conveying to us some marvelous exquisite sensitivity for language and life by determining where carriage returns fall in what otherwise is a piece of largely incomprehensible, self-indulgent verbiage.

Needless to say, I am not impressed; I find such effusions effete and affected, pretentious and posturing, and in the end, timorous and chicken-hearted. The collective message radiated by a large clique in the club of today's poets is that the devices of rhyme and rhythm and such things were nice back in the quaint old days, but in our infinitely more serious and sophisticated day and age, it would be horribly kitschy to resort to such easy, fluffy, childish sound-games.

Over our century the esoteric and obscurantist tendency grew and grew, till it became the norm. As this happened, of course, rhyming and rhythmicality grew tainted with suspicion: to indulge in such things was the signature of doggerel, of light verse, of Ogden Nash–style frivolity. It thus became *de rigueur* to avoid catchy sonorous patterns, so as to avoid being labeled "light", "popular", "accessible". What a kiss of death! Whereas poets and composers in previous centuries didn't make being inaccessible a high goal, in our century *failing* to achieve wide appeal has become a mark of elitism and success.

There is, in my opinion, an unspoken attitude of pomposity pervading much of modern poetry, which I might try to articulate this way:

> Poets of all centuries prior to ours wished to express more *obvious* things, more *universal* experiences, things far easier to say than what we poets of today, living, through no choice of our own, in heavy, burdensome, world-weary times, wish to express. Because of their themes' relative simplicity and genericity, poets of earlier eras could afford to cast their thoughts in the standard molds of sonnets, villanelles, heroic couplets, and so on — but we, these days, are in a very different boat. We contemporary poets have got so many *unprecedented* and intensely *private* meanings to pack into our dense lines that we simply cannot indulge in the sonorous game-playing and ear-catching frippery that our worthy predecessors did. And thus, *if* our poems should possess their own new kind of elegance of form (and of course they do — we are our predecessors' successors, are we not?), that novel elegance comes straight and solely from the soulful meanings perfusing our poems, comes straight from our passionate precision in choosing words to express our profound, heart-felt preoccupations. Whatever *form* turns out to emerge from our persistent grapplings with fathomless *content* will be just as deep as our meaning/message is deep.

In summary, form is seen as the dog's tail, content as its body — and I think it is safe to say that very few Occidental poets alive today want their readers to see the Deeply Meaningful body of their poetry as being wagged by some frivolous tail of rhyme.

At the same time, however, today's poets feel proud that their poetry has a lineage, a set of forebears, and it goes without saying that they wish to link themselves in with that tradition. It is Quite Grand, after all, if one winds up being perceived as being the contemporary carrier of an ancient and venerable intellectual and artistic heritage, a little like being one of the long stream of runners who carry the Olympic torch all the way from Athens; one hopes that by associating oneself with the glory of the past, some of that glory may rub off on one's own work.

Old Meets New in a Daunting Translation Challenge

The old bashes up against the new most forcefully when a modern poet tackles the challenge of translating an ancient one. Whenever this happens, there is, of course, an intense clash of styles. Given the fact that translation requires settling on some specific style, whether old, new, or in between, *something*'s got to give! Most of the rest of this chapter will in fact be devoted to showing just what happens when a violent cultural collision of this sort takes place: Fourteenth-century Italian poet Dante Alighieri (1265–1321) meets a cross-section of twentieth-century anglophone poets. Specifically, we will look at a few short fragments of Dante's *Inferno* in several different English versions.

First, however, I'll make a confession and a few general observations about Dante's *Divine Comedy*. On the confessional level, I do not claim the slightest expertise on the work. I have read much, though not all, of its first book, *Inferno,* in several different anglicizations, and considerably less of it in the original early Italian (a language that is not easy to understand, even for someone who lives, as I do, surrounded by modern Italian). Aside from the last line of each, I have read essentially none of its second two books, *Purgatorio* and *Paradiso*. What I do know, though, is that the three books taken together form a beautiful trinity with many ternary symmetries.

Each book in *The Divine Comedy* — each *cantica* — contains 33 cantos, thus adding up to a total of 99 — except that there is one extra canto at the very start of *Inferno* that serves as a preview of the entire work. There are thus — and this is hardly an accident! — 100 cantos in all. On a more fine-grained level, each canto consists of a series of 40 to 50 rhyming tercets (three-line stanzas), or *terzine,* with the series capped off by one final isolated line. Every line of this immense poetic edifice — on the order of 14,000 — is "hendecasyllabic" (*i.e.,* has eleven syllables), almost invariably accented on syllable 10 as well as either syllable 4 or syllable 6. The very first line — *Nel mezzo del cammin di nostra vita* ("In the middle of the pathway of our life") — perfectly exemplifies this pattern, with the strongest accents falling on the "e" of *mezzo,* the "i" of *cammin,* and the "i" of *vita*.

For me, unquestionably the most beautiful and intricate structural aspect of this work is Dante's innovative rhyme scheme, known as *terza rima,* often translated as "triple rhyme", which in traditional notation is simply ABA, BCB, CDC, DED, EFE, FGF, and so forth. The *central* line of each new tercet thus controls the *outer* two lines of the following tercet, in terms of the sound with which they will both end.

Although the concept of *terza rima* is simple enough to grasp, I feel it is worth a diagram:

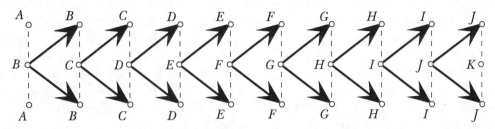

The abstract pattern of Dante's terza rima, with each tercet, or terzina, symbolized by a vertical dashed line segment.

Many commentators on *La Divina Commedia* use terms like "dynamism", "propulsion", and "forward movement" to try to suggest the way in which *terza rima* imbues each tercet with an anticipatory momentum, but I think that this simple diagram, with its stack of tightly-nested V's, each made of two right-driving arrows, does a far better job than could any set of words at rendering palpable the relentless forward thrust inherent in the pattern.

The trinity purely internal to each tercet (*i.e.*, its trilinearity) is thus complemented by a second type of trinity: that of the three occurrences of each end rhyme, which, as they span successive tercets, are of course out of phase with respect to the first type of trinity. Note that this elegant interlocking of two rhythms is a kind of triadic counterpart to the two types of interlocking couplets — semantic and rhyming — in "Ma Mignonne".

Obviously, any translator who appreciates pattern will want to rise to the challenge of respecting, somehow, this exquisitely woven tapestry. Part of what makes it daunting, though, is that it requires making not just two but three lines rhyme with each other, over and over again. Since finding *pairs* of rhyming words is already nontrivial, this raising of the bar by several notches is both enticing and somewhat frightening. A further aspect of the challenge is the fact that the vast majority of Dante's tercets express one complete thought in a concise and self-contained way, and this fact ought, or so one would think, to be respected in any self-respecting translation.

Dante and His Visions

The story told in *The Divine Comedy* is intimately enmeshed with Christianity and strict interpretations of biblical dogma, and hence is quite hard for many contemporary readers, including myself, to relate to. What nonetheless keeps the plot interesting for us philistines is the dramatic way the story is told — as a pilgrimage made by the poet himself to the three destinations of souls after death, beginning with the Inferno and Purgatory in company of the great poet Maro (Publius Vergilius Maro, that is), and then, in company of Beatrice, Dante's saccharine ideal woman, to Paradise.

For most readers, the most gripping of the three *cantiche* is the pilgrim's visit to the Inferno, because of the horrific punishments that Dante witnesses, and because each punishment is the carefully worked-out consequence of a specific sin committed on earth by some actual figure known to Dante and familiar to his readers. Canto XXXIII, for instance, tells the pathetic tale of Count Ugolino, who was locked up in a tower with his four little sons and after all four boys had died of hunger, was driven by his own desperate famishment to devour their cadavers, after which he too perished. And so in Hell, the fate "meted out" to Ugolino is that of being forced to eat, over and over again, the head of Archbishop Ruggieri of Pisa, who had once been his ally but turned coat and became his imprisoner.

In reading one such grim scene after another, all connected with the Catholic church in this way or that, I was vividly reminded of a visit that Carol and I made in the summer of 1986 to a museum high on a hill overlooking the beautiful city of Trieste. We had seen posters all over the city advertising an exhibit of *strumenti di tortura* ("instruments of torture"), and after weighing our heavily mixed feelings, finally decided to go see it. As we expected, it was very, very grim. There were spiked iron balls on chains, used to bash people into a pulp; there were large wheels upon which victims were fastened and stretched till their bones cracked apart; there were cages in which people were suspended in the air without water or food for days or weeks, until they died; there were tightenable metallic bodysuits that had huge spikes facing inwards; there were instruments for removing fingernails, for peeling off a live human's layers of skin, for pulling organs out of abdomens; and on and on and on, *ad nauseam*. What struck Carol and me most of all, though, was that without any exception, all these demoniacal devices had been concocted *in the name of God* by the Catholic church, and they were used systematically by the clergy in order to keep people in line. After the exhibit, we re-emerged into Trieste with a sickening feeling that did not dissipate quickly. Although our visit lasted but an hour or two, I think that unforgettable museum exhibit helped me to relate quite clearly to the horrors described by Dante.

On a lighter note, it is quite amusing how provincial Dante's work seems today. Hell, which is populated mostly by northern Italians, seems like a small town in which, strolling about, one is likely at almost any moment to run into someone one knows or has heard about. Dante the curious sightseer often stops to chit-chat with people he recognizes, who take a little breather from their "work" and tell him about their sins on earth. And Dante the intense Florentine patriot (the ardent love was not reciprocated; his city banished him during his lifetime, and he moved from town to town, including Verona and Ravenna, in the latter of which he died) often lobs nasty epithets at rival cities such as Siena, Pisa, Pistoia, Genoa, and so on. From today's perspective, such inter-city rivalries seem amusingly local and trivial, on the same order as the lighthearted cross-bay rivalry that I grew up knowing, between Stanford and Berkeley.

One final note about the trinities that abound in Dante's work. Each of the three *cantiche* features a nine-leveled "residence" for the souls who have come to rest there (thus altogether making 3 x 3 x 3 levels), and the plot of each *cantica* is worked out with great delicacy so that its very last line concludes with the word *stelle,* meaning "stars". Thus in those two ways, one so vast and one so fine, all three *cantiche* could be said to "rhyme" with each other. Whether one relates to Dante's motivation or does not, whether one is Christian or is not, one must admit that there is something very beautiful and compelling about his devotion to pattern on so many levels at once — and in this fact is embodied the core of the challenge to all his translators.

Abandon All Hope

Before we take a look at any translations of this work, we need to have at least a smidgen of Dante's original before our eyes. For this purpose I have selected the first four tercets of Canto III of *The Inferno*, the ninth line of which is surely the most famous line of the entire *Divine Comedy* — indeed, one of the most famous lines of all literature, usually rendered in English as "Abandon all hope, ye who enter here." This is the concluding phrase of the ominous inscription that Dante, nervously walking with Virgil on a dark slope, reads on a great gate — the gate that leads down, down, down to the nine concentric layers of misery surrounding the very center of the earth, where Lucifer sits. Here, then, is the opening of Canto III:

> *PER ME SI VA NE LA CITTÀ DOLENTE,*
> *PER ME SI VA NE L'ETTERNO DOLORE,*
> *PER ME SI VA TRA LA PERDUTA GENTE.*
>
> *GIUSTIZIA MOSSE IL MIO ALTO FATTORE;*
> *FECEMI LA DIVINA PODESTATE,*
> *LA SOMMA SAPÏENZA E 'L PRIMO AMORE.*
>
> *DINANZI A ME NON FUOR COSE CREATE*
> *SE NON ETTERNE, E IO ETTERNO DURO.*
> *LASCIATE OGNE SPERANZA, VOI CH'INTRATE.*
>
> *Queste parole di colore oscuro*
> *vid' ïo scritte al sommo d'una porta;*
> *per ch'io: «Maestro, il senso lor m'è duro».*

Slanty Dante

Of Dante's *Inferno* there have been by now a good many attempts at anglicization, some of which date back to the mid-nineteenth century. We will shortly take a look at a few from earlier decades, but I have chosen to kick off my quick survey with a very recent American translation — that by Robert Pinsky, published in 1994 — which garnered several literary prizes and was roundly hailed by critics in high places. Here is a sizable excerpt from Pinsky's "Translator's Notes", setting forth his approach to the thicket of thorns involved in welcoming Dante into contemporary English:

> Italian is rich in rhyme, while English — despite having a far greater number of words — is relatively poor in rhyme. Therefore the triple rhymes of the original can put tremendous strain on an English translation. One response to this strain, one way of dealing with the torturous demands of *terza rima* in English, has been to force the large English lexicon to supply rhymes: squeezing unlikely synonyms to the ends of lines, and bending idiom ruthlessly to get them there.
>
> This translation rejects that solution and instead makes a more flexible definition of rhyme, or of the kind and degree of like sound that constitute rhyme.
>
> But on the other hand, I have not accepted just any similar sounds as rhyming: the translation is based on a fairly systematic rhyming norm that defines rhyme as the same consonant-sounds — however much vowels may differ — at the ends of words. For example, the opening tercets of Canto I include the triads "tell/feel/ well," "sleep/stop/up," and "night/thought/it."
>
> This system of like sounds happens to correspond to some preference of my own ear, a personal taste: for me such rhymes as, say, "swans/stones" or "gibe/ club" or "south/both" often sound more beautiful and interesting than such hard-rhyme combinations as "bones/stones," "rub/club," or "south/mouth." This idea of harmony seems even more clear with disyllabic or "feminine" endings: "faces/ houses" is more appealing than "faces/places"; "flavor/quiver" has more interest than "flavor/savor" or "giver/quiver."
>
> The reader who recognizes these examples I have taken from poems by Yeats, who is a master of such consonantal rhyming, might speculate that such sounds are *similar for English*: roughly as "like," perhaps, in the context of English and its great sprawling matrix of sounds, as are *terra/guerra* or *belle/stelle* in the tighter Italian fabric.
>
> But such speculation aside, and regardless of my own predilections, consonantal or "Yeatsian" rhyme can supply an audible scaffold of English *terza rima,* a scaffold that does not distort the English sentence, or draw excessively on the reaches of the English lexicon....
>
> It remains to add that... disyllabic rhyme so sticks out in English that it can acceptably be made a step more approximate, as in "bitter/enter/blunder" — perhaps it *must* be made more approximate, in order to avoid the comic feeling of limerick, or of W. S. Gilbert....
>
> As to hard rhymes, there are many, but as I worked I often found myself revising them out...
>
> This translation is not line-for-line, nor tercet-for-tercet. In order to represent Dante's succinct, compressed quality along with the flow of *terza rima,* I have often found it necessary to write fewer lines in English than he uses in Italian.

Here we go, then, with the author of the above lines in the driver's seat. Keep particularly in mind the last sentence of the foregoing excerpt as you read how Pinsky renders the opening of Canto III.

> THROUGH ME YOU ENTER INTO THE CITY OF WOES,
> THROUGH ME YOU ENTER INTO ETERNAL PAIN,
> THROUGH ME YOU ENTER THE POPULATION OF LOSS.
>
> JUSTICE MOVED MY HIGH MAKER, IN POWER DIVINE,
> WISDOM SUPREME, LOVE PRIMAL. NO THINGS WERE
> BEFORE ME NOT ETERNAL; ETERNAL I REMAIN.
>
> ABANDON ALL HOPE, YE WHO ENTER HERE.
> These words I saw inscribed in some dark color
> Over a portal. "Master," I said, "make clear
>
> Their meaning, which I find too hard to gather."
> Then he, as one who understands: "All fear
> Must be left here, and cowardice die. Together, …

It pains me to break things off so abruptly here, especially to leave unclosed the pair of quotation marks opened near the bottom, but what can I do? After all, Pinsky chose to redistribute Dante's semantics quite radically across tercets. Indeed, in this canto, where Dante has 45 tercets, Pinsky has but 37. The esthetics of this decision boggles my mind.

It was not merely thanks to some casual throw of dice that Dante made the inscription on the portal to Hell contain *exactly three* tercets, *exactly nine* lines. It was not merely by some capricious whim that Dante chose to place the powerful warning — a warning that, nearly seven centuries later, still shakes us like a sudden thunderclap — at the *bottom* of a tercet.

Pinsky's redistribution seems to me so artistically flawed that words fail me in conveying my reaction. I am reminded of my bewilderment at Bob French's 30-line translation of "Ma Mignonne", but whereas that was of an admittedly minor work, this is of one of the pillars of Western literature. By making one 30-line translation of a 28-line poem, Bob did not foreclose all other options; indeed, he went on to make other versions having 28 lines. The smallness of the poem gave him that luxury. But a translator does not expect to translate the whole of *Inferno* several different ways in a lifetime. Tampering with the very core of the structure is a heavy decision to make.

And what about all of Pinsky's righteous comments on avoiding "hard" rhyme in favor of so-called *slant* rhyme? Well, of course, a poet has every right to find slant rhyme more interesting and appealing than strict rhyme. *De gustibus non est disputandum.* When Pinsky writes his own poetry, he should certainly feel free to play the slant-rhyme game to the hilt. But here

Pinsky is writing *Dante's* poetry, not his own.

My jaw drops at the suggestion that Dante would have considered the sloppy trio "color/gather/together" a suitable one for effecting *terza rima*, a swell English counterpart to such crystalline Italian matches as *terra/guerra* and *belle/stelle*. It takes no small heap of chutzpah to claim that there is any resemblance at all in quality of rhyme here. It is a slap in the face to the English language to claim that it can do no better, and simultaneously to the Italian language to imply it is so much less subtle. As for hiding behind Yeats' high reputation, it's pie in sky: Yeats was not translating Dante.

To claim that "woes" and "loss", which make up Pinsky's opening slant rhyme, share the same final consonant-sound is to let oneself be tricked by the vagaries of English orthography: the two sounds in question are of a voiced "z" and an unvoiced "s", no more the same consonant-sound than are voiced "b" and unvoiced "p", voiced "d" and unvoiced "t", voiced "g" and unvoiced "k", and so forth. Aside from frequent repetitions of this confusion based on the ambiguity of final "s", nowhere else in all of his translation have I found Pinsky equating voiced with unvoiced consonants.

If I am playing Chopin's piano pieces in public and advertising my concert as Chopin rather than Hofstadter, then I jolly well had better not systematically slide Chopin's carefully-calculated climaxes onto awkward off-beats, turning them into wimpy *non sequiturs*, or replace Chopin's sweet consonances by harsh dissonances, or vice versa, or shorten his pieces by some 20 percent in length, and so on. To be sure, I can do such things if I feel like it, but then I have to advertise what I am doing as *jazzed-up* Chopin, as something *inspired* by Chopin but definitely not as *pure* Chopin.

Should Pinsky someday wind up in one of the nine circles of Hell, I know just the punishment that matches his sins committed on earth: He should be condemned to construct, unto eternity, one tercet after another in perfect, non-slanted English rhymes. What more exquisite torture?

E Pluribus Unum

We turn now to a remarkable anthology of translated cantos from *The Inferno* edited by American poet Daniel Halpern. The premise of the book is simple and appealing: Choose twenty strong contemporary poetic voices and have each of them translate a short piece of *The Inferno*, then string all the anglicized cantos together to make one joint, if somewhat disjoint, translation of the whole *cantica*.

Halpern's assemblage includes cantos rendered by many well-known names, including Mark Strand, Galway Kinnell, Amy Clampitt, Richard Howard, Robert Pinsky, W. S. Merwin, Sharon Olds, Robert Hass (now the Poet Laureate of the United States), and Richard Wilbur (who preceded Hass in that honorary post). It's an impressive list, and one would hope for much. Indeed, at the conclusion of his preface, Halpern writes, "The idea behind this translation of *The Inferno* is to put one of our 'sacred' texts back into the hands of the keepers of the language, the poets themselves."

No Bel Canto

Among the most famous names in Halpern's collection is that of Irish poet Seamus Heaney, who was awarded the 1995 Nobel Prize in Literature for his writings. Halpern invited Heaney to open the collection with not just one canto, but three. And thus, thanks to that decision, I can hereby show you how Heaney chose to treat this very same set of four tercets.

> *THROUGH ME IT LEADS TO THE CITY SORROWFUL.*
> *THROUGH ME IT LEADS TO THE ETERNAL PAIN.*
> *THROUGH ME IT LEADS AMONG THE LOST PEOPLE.*
>
> *JUSTICE INSPIRED MY MAKER ABOVE.*
> *IT WAS DIVINE POWER THAT FORMED ME,*
> *SUPREME WISDOM AND ORIGINAL LOVE.*
>
> *BEFORE ME NO THING WAS CREATED EXCEPT THINGS*
> *EVERLASTING. AND I AM EVERLASTING.*
> *LEAVE EVERY HOPE BEHIND YOU, YOU WHO ENTER.*
>
> *I saw these words inscribed above a gate*
> *in obscure characters, and so I said,*
> *"Master, I find their sense hard to interpret."*

In favor of Heaney, I can say that he renders a tercet by a tercet. It's nice to see nine lines of gate inscription, instead of just seven. But, I regret to say, there's not much more praise that I can offer. Look at the first line: "Through me it leads to the city sorrowful." "It"?! What is this "it"? And "city sorrowful" is pretty sorrowful. If this line had been written by a high-school student, I would have struck it out in bright red ink and said to start again from scratch. To my ear, the sentence doesn't even sound like it was written by a native speaker! Nor does the second line, with its definite article "the" affording a particularly gawky moment. And line three, repeating that off-the-wall "it" once more, is not much smoother. Saying "it" three times in a row does not make "it" right.

On the next-to-last line, it is unlikely anyone would read the phrase "in obscure characters" without inferring that the words on the gate were hard to make out, when in fact the Italian clearly says that the writing was *dark*, not blurry or vague. Although "obscure" can mean "dark", that meaning is swamped by the other meaning in this context.

In Praise of the Music of Language ◆ ◆ ◆ **535**

What about respect for Dante's *terza rima*? Here, Heaney cops out even more than did Pinsky, making only the top and bottom lines of each tercet "rhyme", and throwing to the winds the all-important key to *terza rima* — namely, the sonic resonance of those two outer lines with the preceding tercet's central line. What a shame! Moreover, to Heaney just as to Pinsky, the word "rhyme" is so dilute that it becomes essentially vacuous. How could anyone stretch the concept so far as to hear the words "things" and "enter" as rhyming? It's a joke. And even if "above a gate" and "hard to interpret" share a final consonant, the former is accented on its last syllable whereas the latter is accented on its next-to-last syllable, making whatever weak residue of rhyme might remain in them fade into near-inaudibility.

I find reading such a series of slant-rhyming, slant-metrical tercets extremely depressing. Every last shred of Dantean spark seems gone. Slant poets make it seem as if they are struggling so hard, like mediocre gymnasts or weightlifters who deliberately make loud grunting noises to show audiences how rough their task is, while the outstanding athletes gracefully carry out far more complex maneuvers in complete silence.

Rhymeless but Flowing Tercets

Some years ago, my distinguished Indiana University colleague Mark Musa, a Dante scholar who, by sheer happenstance, lives right across the alley from me, created a highly-regarded translation of the entire *Divine Comedy*, and although it does not rhyme at all, I find it of far greater appeal than the preceding two, firstly because it does not show any evidence of having been a struggle (though it no doubt was), and secondly because it comes far closer to mirroring the precision of Dante's meter. Here are Musa's versions of the four tercets we have been considering:

> *I AM THE WAY INTO THE DOLEFUL CITY,*
> *I AM THE WAY INTO ETERNAL GRIEF,*
> *I AM THE WAY TO A FORSAKEN RACE.*

> *JUSTICE IT WAS THAT MOVED MY GREAT CREATOR;*
> *DIVINE OMNIPOTENCE CREATED ME,*
> *AND HIGHEST WISDOM JOINED WITH PRIMAL LOVE.*

> *BEFORE ME NOTHING BUT ETERNAL THINGS*
> *WERE MADE, AND I SHALL LAST ETERNALLY.*
> *ABANDON EVERY HOPE, ALL YOU WHO ENTER.*

> *I saw these words spelled out in somber colors*
> *inscribed along the ledge above a gate;*
> *"Master," I said, "these words I see are cruel."*

As in the case of Robert Pinsky, I think it is best to let Musa himself explain the rationale behind his decision to go for meter but to forgo rhyme. In the following excerpt from his "Translator's Note: On Being a Good Lover", he does so, drawing on some ideas of a scholar named Karl Shapiro, who unfortunately is identified solely as "an enthusiast for rhyme":

> My main reason for avoiding rhyme has been the results achieved by all those who have used rhyme in translating *The Divine Comedy*: they have shown that the price paid was disastrously high. I believe that all those who have offered rhymed translations of Dante could have produced far better poems if they had not used rhyme....
>
> Shapiro, speaking of the power of rhyme to draw us into the movement of a poem, says that our expectation is thereby being continually raised and then satisfied; ideally, rhyme helps pull us through, and pull us in deep, as we anticipate the scheme. But, when the translator uses a mixture of perfect and imperfect rhyme — when, that is, we never know whether our expectation will be satisfied — the effect is quite different. In every tercet the reader with a sensitive ear will always be wondering, "Will he make it this time?" and may often look ahead to see the result, thus breaking the movement of the poem.

Although aimed at other targets, Musa's words seem to me to be an excellent critique of the two translators we have just sampled, with their diluted ways of rendering the dense, rich verse by Dante. One might wonder, however, why Musa has a double standard with respect to rhyme and meter. He himself asks the key question, but answers it only partially:

> But if I feel such horror at the paralyzing potentiality of rhyme when used to translate *The Divine Comedy*, why have I chosen to bind myself to the mechanical device of meter?.... Iambic pentameter is a beautiful, flexible instrument, but only when the translator is freed from preoccupation with rhyme.

Inherent in Musa's philosophy is a pessimism about the translator's challenge, which he sees as being more stringent than that of the original author. This putative contrast between original and derivative poet is expressed by Musa in the following way:

> For the poet creating original verse in his own language, the search for rhyme also, of course, imposes limitations, but these limitations themselves may be a help in the creative process, and the rhyme, when found, as Shapiro says, may bring an image or idea that will suggest a new line of development. At its best, rhyme leads the poet into discoveries. And since he is in the process of creation, he can afford at any moment to change the course of his poetic fluidity. But for the translator, who is faced from the beginning with an existing structure whose shape has been forever fixed, rhyme constitutes a crippling burden.

There is a tacit assumption here, which places content ahead of form in the marriage that is a poem, much as husband is so often tacitly placed ahead of wife in our society. The idea that they are *equal* partners and that neither of them should be favored over the other (or, heaven help us, that form might on occasion be favored over content!) is not entertained.

I would rephrase Musa's argument in this way: "One must above all follow Dante *content*wise. Of course, to the extent that one can do so, it would be ideal to follow Dante simultaneously *form*wise, but I am afraid, from having read earlier translations, that that is impossible. It makes sense to imitate form only so long as content is not compromised. The moment that content would be put at risk, one must instantly put the brakes on. And through personal experimentation, I have determined just where that critical moment comes: One can imitate Dante's rhythmic quality by substituting iambic pentameter for his hendecasyllabic lines, but one cannot also throw in rhymes without seriously damaging the text's fidelity to Dante's *ideas*. And ideas must *always* be given primacy over form. Therefore, having ascertained that this is the limit beyond which one cannot cross, I have gone all the way up to it but then stopped right there. I believe this is the judicious choice."

This strikes me as an *argument by poverty of imagination* ("I can't imagine it being done; ergo it can't be done"), a notoriously unreliable mode of argumentation. Musa's words would, I suspect, sound quite convincing to people who have not done a great deal of poetry translation themselves. However, my personal experience in doing so many anglicizations of "Ma Mignonne" as well as tackling other subtle translation challenges makes me extremely dubious about his pessimism. And I am not alone.

On Trying Harder

Another distinguished Indiana University colleague is the gifted poet and translator Willis Barnstone, who recently came out with a titillating, scintillating collection of 501 fully rhyming and metrical sonnets, titled, in a marvelous gesture of quadruple ambiguity, *The Secret Reader*. In fact, there are somewhat more than 501 because *The Secret Reader* contains an extra two dozen poems, many of them sonnets, translated by Barnstone from Spanish, German, French, and Chinese, among others.

How did a modern poet ever come to be so devoted to such a retrograde form? An anecdote that Barnstone recounts in his opening "Chat with the Reader" elucidates just what it was that touched off his "eighteen-year drunk on the sonnet".

In the mid-1970's, Barnstone was living in Buenos Aires, in a sense realizing the dream of a lifetime — he was working intimately with Jorge Luis Borges, occasionally traveling with the author of *Ficciones* to the interior of the country, and translating Borges' beautifully structured sonnets, of which there were a great many, into English. Borges, who by that time had gone blind, enormously enjoyed hearing his old poems read aloud to him, and drew much pleasure from the fact that they were now being rendered in English, a tongue that he knew intimately and loved as dearly as he loved Spanish. And so Barnstone writes:

> In those months in Buenos Aires of evening bomb blasts and kidnappings, I often worked through the night on new sonnets from a book Borges had just brought out called *La moneda de hierro* ("The Iron Coin"). One day a decisive event took place. Late in the afternoon, while English versions of those poems were still spread all over my living room floor, Carlos Frías knocked at the door of my apartment. "Borges has a message for you about the sonnets," the editor said.
>
> "What's the message?"
>
> "In your translation of 'Camden, 1892', the one about Whitman," Frías said discreetly, "Borges thinks your rhyme in the last couplet is incorrect."
>
> I wondered why Borges hadn't called me himself. Why the messenger? I began to fumble with words, defending slant rhymes, saying how modern poets in English like to use muted assonant rhymes, how...
>
> "Borges thinks you should try a little harder," Frías coldly interrupted.
>
> So I tried a little harder. I discovered it was not much harder to make rhymes perfectly consonant. And this achievement had advantages beyond that of euphonious final vowels. Each new formal obstacle orders the imagination to look a little farther and opens escape from the map of the literal and the obvious. The experience of translating some thirty sonnets by Borges, followed by twenty-four from the sixteenth-century French poet Louise Labé, was my training for *The Secret Reader*.

"Try a little harder" — now *there's* a motto for slanty Dante translators to keep in mind. Perhaps, though, such a tip would be taken seriously only if it came to them from on high, as when Barnstone received from his mentor Borges that stern, mincing-no-words criticism.

Imagine, then, an angelic emissary wafting down from Paradiso, dropping in on Robert Pinsky and Seamus Heaney in their paper-cluttered living rooms, and whispering in their ears, "Dante thinks you should try a little harder." I wonder if those poets would pay such an authoritative message any heed. I would like to believe they would.

Four Who Tried Harder

As I said above, translation of Dante into English goes back well over 100 years, and in the intervening time there have been several translators who have tackled the challenge of *terza rima* head-on. Perhaps the earliest to do so was the American poet Melville Best Anderson, whose translation was first issued in 1921, a sharp 600 years after Dante's death. I happen to own an edition printed in 1944, which contains 32 drawings by William Blake — the last works of his life, a project unfortunately never completed. I was astounded to see that on the spine of the book, it says at the top, "Dante Alighieri", and then, in larger type, "The Divine Comedy", and finally, in the first type size, "William Blake". So Mr. Blake does 32 drawings and gets equal billing with Dante, while Mr. Anderson writes 14,000 lines of *terza rima* and yet gets nary a mention. Even on the title page inside, Anderson's name, though present, is far smaller than that of Blake. Talk about invisibility of translators! But this is so, so typical.

In 1943, the British Orientalist, art historian, and poet Laurence Binyon died, shortly after completing a twenty-year labor of love, a *terza rima* anglicization of all of *The Divine Comedy*. Like his American predecessor Anderson, Binyon opts for a return to a language rather antique in flavor, and neither of them shuns the device of syntactic reversal. Indeed, both use it so often and so densely that it begins to feel quite normal and familiar after not too long, although at times, admittedly, it feels as if they are pushing one toward the limits of one's linguistic flexibility. To show their talents off, I have selected seven tercets from Canto XXV, in which Dante witnesses and relates to us some truly Boschian metamorphoses.

Melville Best Anderson	*Laurence Binyon*
If thou to credit what I saw art slow, *Now, Reader, need there be no wonderment,* *For I, who saw, can scarce consent thereto.*	*If thou art slow of faith, thou who dost read* *What I shall tell, 'tis nothing for surprise,* *Since half I doubt, I who witnessed it indeed.*
The while I raised my brows on them intent, *There darted a six-foot serpent out* *In front of one, and grappling with him blent.*	*While with brows raised I held them in mine eyes,* *Lo a serpent with six feet one sinner faced* *And darting clamped its body entire on his.*
With middle feet it grasped his paunch about, *And flung the forward ones his arms around;* *Then gashed both cheeks of him the gaping snout.*	*With the middle feet his belly it embraced,* *With the forefeet gripped the arms and held them pent;* *Then of both cheeks its fangs had the full taste.*
With hinder feet outspread the thighs it bound, *Thrusting its tail between them, and behind* *Upward extending it, the loins enwound.*	*With the hind feet stretcht along his thighs it leant,* *And whipt its tail out in between the two* *And upwards on the loins behind him bent.*
So never did the barbèd ivy bind *A tree up, as the reptile hideous* *Upon another's limbs its own entwined;*	*Ivy upon a tree never in-grew* *Close as that hideous creature, all up-reared,* *To the other's body did its body glue.*
They clave together, — hot wax cleaveth thus, — *And interfused their colors in such wise* *That neither now appeared the same to us:*	*Like heated wax the shapes of them were slurred* *Together, and their mingling colors swam:* *Nor this nor that was as it first appeared.*
Just as in burning paper doth uprise *Along before the flame a color brown* *Which is not black as yet, and the white dies.*	*As runneth up before the burning flame* *On paper, a brown colour, not yet black,* *And the white dieth; such their hues became.*

These translations, while engaging and delightful (a strange term for the horrors of Hell, and yet it seems perfectly on target to me here), are not by any means beyond reproach. Their diction is ornate and recherché, and their syntax is contorted and byzantine. As Mark Musa points out about Dante's style in his Translator's Note, "Most of his narrative, if we make an exception of the elaborate similes, is composed in simple, straightforward style." These translations exude an era long before our time, even long before their translators' times. Of course, Dante's era *was* long before them; maybe their sin, if sin it be, was to try to be too close to the original?

Only a few years after Binyon's translation appeared, the British mystery writer Dorothy Sayers — an unlikely choice, it would seem! — came out with yet another translation in *terza rima* of a rather more modern tone. When one reads her Introduction, one realizes she is as much of a Dante scholar as she is a mystery writer, and she is also an accomplished poet.

The saving grace of Daniel Halpern's twenty-poet anthology is just one canto — but this time, it's *bel canto* — done by Richard Wilbur, whose style reminds me more of James Falen than anyone else. Like Falen, Wilbur rebels against tortured syntax, straightens everything out, uses relatively straightforward language, and makes it all look as simple as leaning against a tree. Let us look, then, at what Sayers and Wilbur have wrought.

Dorothy Sayers	*Richard Wilbur*
Reader, if thou discredit what is here Set down, no wonder; for I hesitate Myself, who saw it all as clear as clear.	'Twill be no wonder, Reader, if you are slow to trust the thing that I shall now impart, for I, who saw it, scarce believe it so.
Lo! while I gazed, there darted up a great Six-leggèd worm, and leapt with all its claws On one of them from in front, and seized him straight.	I watched a vile, six-footed serpent dart toward one of them, and then, with never a pause, fasten itself to him with every part.
Clasping his middle with its middle paws, Along his arms it made its fore-paws reach, And clenched its teeth tightly in both his jaws;	It clasped his belly with its middle claws, its forefeet clutched his arms as in a vise, and into either cheek it sank its jaws.
Hind-legs to thighs it fastened, each to each, And after, thrust its tail betwixt the two, Up-bent upon his loins behind the breech.	The hindmost feet it dug into his thighs, and twixt them thrust its tail so limberly that up his spine its clambering tip could rise.
Ivy to oak so rooted never grew As limb by limb that monstrous beast obscene Clung him about, and close and closer drew,	Never did ivy cling so to a tree as did that hideous creature bind and braid its limbs and his in pure ferocity;
Till like hot wax, they stuck; and, melting in, Their tints began to mingle and to run, And neither seemed to be what it had been;	And then they stuck together, as if made of melting wax, and mixed their colors; nor did either now retain his former shade:
Just as when paper burns you see a dun Brown hue go creeping up before the flare, Not black as yet, although the white has gone.	Just so, when paper burns, there runs before the creeping flame a stain of darkish hue that, though not black as yet, is white no more.

As I playfully map Dante onto Pushkin, *Inferno* onto *Onegin*, Wilbur onto Falen, I cannot help but try to go on, seeing Dorothy Sayers as the analogue of Walter Arndt or maybe Charles Johnston — though excellent, not quite as polished or as clear. Who then plays the demonic role of Vladimir Nabokov? I'm tempted to say it's old Beelzebub, but that's just a joke. Soon, however, we shall see who the Nabokov of *The Inferno* truly is.

Before we leave Dorothy Sayers, I would like to give a sampling of her keen understanding of the issues of translation and her brilliant way of articulating them. In the following passage, she is talking about the fact that any of Dante's contemporaries who read him could easily relate to his narrative both as allegory and as, in her words, a *chronique scandaleuse* — in other words, as a gossip sheet about familiar personages of the time. Trying to vividly convey the difference between how an Italian reader would have read Dante back then and how an English reader might read Dante now (*i.e.*, in May of 1948, the date that she signs her Introduction), she writes:

> Let us suppose that an Englishman were to write a contemporary *Divine Comedy* on Dante's model, and that in it, mixed up with a number of scriptural and mythological characters, we were to find, assigned to various circles of Hell, Purgatory, and Paradise, according to the religious and political convictions of the author, the following assortment of people — some referred to by their full names, some by Christian name or surname alone, and some indicated only by a witty or allusive phrase: Chamberlain ("him of the orchid"), Chamberlain ("him of the umbrella"), [Stewart Houston] Chamberlain, "Brides-in-the-Bath" Smith, "Galloper" Smith, Horatio Bottomley, Horatio [Lord Nelson], Fox [Charles or George to be inferred from the context], the Man who picked up the Bomb in Jermyn Street, Oscar Wilde, Oscar Slater, Oscar Browning, Spencer, Spenser, Lord Castlereagh, Lord Castlerosse, Lawrence [of Arabia], [D. H.] Lawrence, "Butcher" Heydrich, W. G. Grace, Grace Darling, the Captain of the *Jarvis Bay*, the Sisters of Haworth, the Woodcutter of Hawarden, the Ladies of Llangollen, the Lady with the Lamp, the Lady-with-the-Lampshade-made-of-Human-Skin, Titus Oates, Captain Oates, Quisling, the Owner of "Hermit", the French Bluebeard, Bacon, Roger Bacon, Roger Fry, the Claimant, the Bishop of Zanzibar, Clarence Hatry, the Tolpuddle Martyrs, Brown and Kennedy, the Dean of St Patrick's, the Dean of St Paul's, Dean Farrar, Fred Archer, Mrs Dyer, Lord George Sanger, Lord George Gordon, General Gordon, Ouida, William Joyce, James Joyce, "the Officer in the Tower", Peter the Painter, Jenkins "of the Ear", Dick Sheppard, Jack Sheppard, and "the Widow at Windsor". Let us further suppose that the writer holds strong views on Trade Unionism, the constitution of UNO, the "theology of crisis", Freudian psychology, Einsteinian astronomy, and the art of Mr Jacob Epstein. Let us then suppose that the book is to be read, six hundred years hence, by an intelligent Portuguese with no particular knowledge of English social history. Would he not require a few notes, in order to savour the full pungency of the poet's pronouncements and thoroughly understand his attitude to the cosmic set-up?

Sayers' point, expressed with delicious wit but none the less serious for that, is not about mutual comprehensibility across *linguistic* barriers but about mutual comprehensibility across *cultural* barriers — which, from the point of view of a translator, is often equally important if not more so. And, I must admit, despite reading Sayers' list a mere 48 years after it was drawn up and despite being a native speaker of her own tongue, to boot, I still find I am absolutely at sea with respect to nearly all its entries. "The Tolpuddle Martyrs" and "the Woodcutter of Hawarden", indeed. Oh, pity the poor Portuguese of the year 2548!

As for Wilbur, I am filled with admiration for his effortless-seeming fluency and his uncompromising elegance; the only thing I wonder is, could he keep it up for another 99 cantos? It's not as if doing 100 cantos is 100 times as hard as doing just one, but it is definitely a good deal harder than just one, and poses some different challenges. Even if Wilbur were to do just 33 more, so as to round out *The Inferno,* he would thereby make a lasting contribution to Dante, to the body of anglophone literature, and to the annals of profound literary translation.

Another One Who Tried Harder

Though there may be many others, I know of only one further poet who has done a Dante canto in full *terza rima,* and that is Willis Barnstone, who in fact chose Canto I of *The Inferno.* Here, then, are his first three tercets, along with Dante's original text:

Nel mezzo del cammin di nostra vita	*Midway along our road of life I woke*
mi ritrovai per una selva oscura,	*to find myself in a dark and secret wood,*
che la diretta via era smarrita.	*for I had lost the narrow path. To evoke*
Ahi quanto a dir qual era è cosa dura	*what it was like — how hard, I barely could.*
esta selva selvaggia e aspra e forte	*This wood was savage, dense and strange! The thought*
che nel pensier rinova la paura!	*of it renews those fears that I withstood,*
Tant' è amara che poco è più morte;	*a place so bitter, only to be caught*
ma per trattar del ben ch'i' vi trovai,	*in death is worse. Yet there I found my share*
dirò de l'altre cose ch'i' v'ho scorte.	*of good, so now I'll tell what else it brought.*

It is not in the least surprising to find Barnstone having made this choice, for his profound respect for structure in poetry comes through loud and clear in his devotional act to the traditional sonnet form. Unfortunately, Barnstone's is a voice in the wilderness, lost in a dark and secret reader.

Will I Bar Sonnets?

Before we leave Barnstone, a few last words about *The Secret Reader,* his millennial monument to the sonnet. You might think he could entertain you with a few poems in the classic form but that soon enough it would get to be old hat and a dreary drag — yet on he goes, and on and on, spilling out one lyrical poem after another, mostly respecting but occasionally playing droll games with the sonnet form. On you it grows, and on and on.

Sonnets connect together, often in long series, to tell vignettes and larger chunks of Barnstone's life and those of people near him. One comes to see this book as a strangely coherent chronicle of human existence, like the sonnet-based novels by Pushkin and Seth, except that whereas theirs were invented worlds, this rhyming, metric chronicle is autobiographical. It is impossible to convey the whole by citing just a couple of small parts, but here, for what it is worth, is a micro-sampler from the scanner of secrets, the clandestine student, the volume of mysteries, the concealed anthology.

Docking at Night	*Luminous Experience of a Brain Scan*
On the ghost sea	*An hour ago the nurse shot technetium*
white Patmos sits	*into my arm. At last this human mud*
in Chinese mist.	*is light itself — no eye seeking a crumb*
I yawn and pee.	*of mystery elsewhere. Radioactive blood.*
Our ship drones in	*Rigid I press my face against a screen*
a moonless cell	*and gamma rays reveal the pilgrimage*
of stench and spell	*through every catacomb, scanning unseen*
of stereo din	*vessels and deadly pools. A squiggly page*
driving me bats.	*shows me inside: ravines of fear, a hill*
White lamps of shame	*of wordy hope, a squawking bumpy map*
like mountain cats	*of love, the starry motorcycle spill.*
creep on the town	*"Nurse, what news from my inner tree of night?"*
of dreams of John	*"You're scintillating!" But the glowing sap*
who wrote with flame.	*can't see itself. Only the mind sees light.*

Why include such single-lingual sonnets in a book about translation? Because this is a chapter about pattern and artistry, and here they are in spades. Barnstone may be a throwback to earlier times, a little like Sergei Rachmaninoff, who has often been disdainfully called "the last nineteenth-century composer", even though virtually all of his work was composed after 1900. Rachmaninoff was and still is scorned by many pontificating pundits, but his lyrical music will last, while many of his trendy contemporaries' numbing dodecaphonic cacophonies will disappear gratifyingly fast.

In his cozy "Chat with the Reader", Barnstone says that after reaching the magic number of 501, "I became instantly desonnetized, and every impulse to revert I've been able to convert into other things in life." What a marvelous thing, to be able to stop an addiction on a dime! However, he recently confided to me over a most pleasant lunch at The Gables that he has not, as he had thought, been able to kick the habit so cleanly, and in fact will soon be coming out with a new book of some 100 further sonnets. So — will poor Willis bar sonnets, or will he not? Stay tuned.

In Tears over Tin Ears

We come back, at long last, to Daniel Halpern's infernal poet-pourri. For me, however, it's a duty, not a joy, to do so. In what follows, I'll make a quick report on my dismal findings, trying not to drag it out too long.

Four out of Halpern's golden twenty — Seamus Heaney, Mark Strand, Stanley Plumly, and Robert Pinsky — use slant-rhyming, and Heaney and Strand even try what has been called "dummy" *terza rima,* meaning a gutless ABA, CDC, EFE, GHG, IJI,… rhyme pattern, with the central line playing but a dummy role, rhymewise, and having zero effect on the flow. (I might mention that American poet John Ciardi did the whole *Inferno* in this half-hearted manner.) Alfred Corn plays the dummy game a good bit better than Heaney and Strand, trying hard to avoid slant rhymes, but occasionally succumbing (*e.g.,* "fingers/pincers"). Still, Corn's Ciardi-esque effort is far more laudable than that of most of his bookmates, who seem either blissfully ignorant or totally disrespectful of the fact that they are translating one of the most regularly structured, crystalline poems of all time.

A wimpy bow toward Dante's patterns is made by Cynthia Macdonald, who, grouping tercets into pairs, makes the two *middle* lines in each such pair rhyme, dropping all other rhyming constraints. In other words, she has invented a doubly-diluted dummy *terza rima.* But even that extremely weak constraint seems too bothersome, for she often slips into slant rhyme (*e.g.,* "wishes/gibberish", "grasp/wrath") or even leaves a tercet entirely out of the pattern. This is such a wishy-washy approach to the taut discipline of Dante that I cannot imagine what goal she had in mind. (By the way, is it getting any clearer who the Vladimir Nabokov of *The Inferno* is?)

Another flimsy gesture toward form is made by C. K. Williams, who replaces tercets by sextets and points out that in each sextet there is at least one end rhyme, somewhere or other, but wandering all over the map. I'll show you two successive sextets taken from Williams' version of Canto XIX:

> *I've broiled my feet*
> *upside down, though,*
> *longer than the time*
> *that will expire*
> *with him planted so,*
> *his feet afire,*

> *Because after him a lawless*
> *shepherd will come*
> *out of the west, whose deeds*
> *are of such ugliness*
> *that he'll be qualified*
> *to cover both of us.*

There is a slim kind of charm here, but the irregularity of the placement of the rhymes and the clunky meter attenuate it severely.

To show how elegantly this can be done in *terza rima,* here is Sayers:

> *But already have I been planted in this bed*
> *Longer with baked feet and thus topsy-turvy*
> *Than he shall stand flame-footed on his head;*

> *For after him from the west comes one to serve ye*
> *With uglier acts, a lawless Shepherd indeed,*
> *Who'll cover us both — fit end for soul so scurvy…*

Both Charles Wright and Richard Howard, though chucking rhyme entirely out the window, seem to have a modicum of a sense of rhythm, and yet the pity of it is that a handful of Wright's and a good many of Howard's lines simply do not scan. In almost every such case, I found I could easily improve the meter with an innocent word substitution or a slight syntactic rearrangement. It felt just like correcting drafts by students. If I were asked to write an essay on Einstein for publication, I would not submit a hastily worked-out draft; why is Dante worth any less?

Despite their insipidity, the cases I have mentioned so far are by no means the feeblest of the twenty different styles in Halpern's book. Jorie Graham, for instance, uses a metamorphosing style, starting out the canto with a series of quite regular-looking tercets (though rhymeless and meterless, natch), then gradually loosening up until stanzas jump erratically between having one and four lines, and lines themselves vacillate in syllable-count from as low as four ("to start down from…") to as high as nineteen ("who from her grace and choiring briefly drew aside to send me here, guarantees"). I think that Dante would vomit upon learning that jumbles like this were constructed with the intent to reproduce his pristinely crafted text in another tongue. (Got a guess yet?)

But perhaps even thumbing your nose obnoxiously at form is better than pretending it doesn't exist. To open Halpern's anthology at random is to encounter passages by writers who one would swear had never heard of either rhyme or meter in poetry. Nine poets — Daniel Halpern, Galway Kinnell, Amy Clampitt, Susan Mitchell, Carolyn Forché, W. S. Merwin, Sharon Olds, Deborah Digges, and Robert Hass — buy into the bleak and barren philosophy of "content first and last", "content and only content", or in short, *Inhalt über alles* and form can go to Hell (pardon my French).

Of course, the folks to whom I am referring would sharply disagree, and in their own defense might point to the fact that their translations appear in *ragged right* rather than flush right — in other words, they have chosen where to put their carriage returns. Well, bully for them! These right ragged translations, when read out loud, sound indistinguishable from ordinary prose in every respect that my tin ear can detect.

The Music of Words

In a word, though there's plenty of high-falutin' poet-style vocabulary, there's no *music* here. As my neighbor Mark Musa remarked to me at my back door, as he was lending me his old paperback copy of the Sayers translation for my perusal, "Keep in mind that what I was really striving for was the music!" Jokingly, I replied, "Oh, your last name tells me that!" But more seriously, Musa's version certainly does have a sense of music, despite his regrettable, overly cautious, decision to forgo rhyme.

There is another translator of the entire *Inferno* who has a keen sense of Dante's music yet who likewise forgoes rhymes — Allen Mandelbaum, who, in his Introduction, describes Dante in this picturesque way:

> Dante is an Aeolus-the-Brusque, a Lord-of-*Furibundus*-Fuss, the Ur-Imam-of-Impetus.... surely the swiftest and most successive of savants, forever rummaging in his vast and versal haversack of soughs and rasps and gusts and "harsh and scrannel rhymes"... In brief, Dante is a Drummer. And this translation asks to be read aloud.

Very well! For a sample of Mandelbaum's rhymeless music, let's begin at the beginning (and for Mandelbaum's sake, please *do* read it aloud):

> *When I had journeyed half of our life's way,*
> *I found myself within a shadowed forest,*
> *for I had lost the path that does not stray.*
>
> *Ah, it is hard to speak of what it was,*
> *that savage forest, dense and difficult,*
> *which even in recall renews my fear:*
>
> *so bitter — death is hardly more severe!*
> *But to retell the good discovered there,*
> *I'll also tell the other things I saw.*

In reading aloud that graceful first tercet with its lonely salute to the charm of rhyme, I sadly think, "What a shame that Mandelbaum and Musa, with their clear rhythmic gifts, punted on the rhymes!" The only translators who seem to have an impeccable sense for Dante's meanings, meter, *and* rhymes — in short, for the total magic of Dante's musicality — are Wilbur and Barnstone, and they have given us but one single canto each. Sigh!

A Sorry State

In his Translator's Note, Mark Musa comments, "Dante is a greater poet than any of his translators have been or are likely to be." I presume that most of the poets in Halpern's volume would assent to this mild assault on their self-esteem, but if so, then how come so many of them are so flip in their attitude toward their superior? Why do they not make a serious effort to mirror Dante's strict self-discipline? If these unmusical, form-shucking poets rank high among "the keepers of the English language", as editor Halpern glowingly characterized them, then the English language seems to me, I am very sorry to state, to be in a very sorry state.

Well, if you haven't figured it out yet, you never will, so I shall now reveal the identity of the Vladimir Nabokov of Dante's *Inferno*. All you need to do is flip the page.

Invitation to a Beheading

I — and this I'm ashamed to admit, but to me it seems true — am he. For proof, just look at the heartless hatchet job I've just completed, above: flinging about all sorts of nasty epithets like "feeble", "flimsy", "limp", "wimpy", "insipid", "wishy-washy", "half-hearted", "obnoxious", and "vomit", and then on top of it all, likening a poor innocent Nobel Prize winner in Literature to a talentless high-school student as well as to a grunting, mediocre weightlifter. Shades of Nabokov's merciless mud-slinging!

Of course, there is (thank God!) one notable difference: Whereas Nabokov spared no one and seemingly respected no translation but his own, I have here lavished praise on several translators. I am not out to chop everyone else's head off in an attempt to make myself look taller. I have no personal axe to grind here, no vested interest in defending my own turf — after all, I have never translated even a single tercet of Dante.

The curious fact is that, although Vladimir Nabokov and I have diametrically opposite views about poetry translation, I can appreciate much more clearly, now that I have subjected myself to the severe pleasure of reading the Halpern anthology from start to finish, how he could get so exercised when people violated his "religion" — in his case, the nutty, irrational belief that poetry cannot be translated as poetry. My bile, too, gets extraordinarily churned up when I see people who should certainly know better violating a tenet that, in my life, is central — namely, a *reverence for pattern*. That, one could say, is *my* religion.

The Religion of the Ordered Path

The architect Louis Kahn once used the resonant phrase "the religion of the ordered path" to describe the rigorous self-discipline necessary for any would-be architect to master the fundamental abstract and geometrical underpinnings of architecture. By analogy, I see this phrase as referring equally well to the rigorous self-discipline necessary for any would-be poet to master the fundamental rhyming and metrical underpinnings of poetry.

Nobody would dream of translating children's poetry into free verse or blank verse, because it is obvious that children love rhyme and the other "external" trappings of poetry. The musical charm of children's poetry is recognized and respected by all. Even the rabid Nabokov, who in *Strong Opinions* makes no bones about being totally unmusical, could not go so far as to render the English verses of *Alice in Wonderland* by content alone.

And yet, in the sophisticated literary world there is a pretense that adults are far more serious than children, that adults do not want to be distracted by childish musical frivolity, that what adults are after is only the dead-serious *core* of a literary work, that the wrapping paper and gauze of mere sonoric patterns are of no concern to grown-up, mature readers. As a consequence, a great deal of poetry translated for adults tends to exude no charm whatsoever, no matter how charming or elegant it was in the original. This profoundly misguided fad rankles me no end, and I'll shout to high heaven about it, whether it does me any good or not!

The Risk of the Bee in the Bonnet

When people of clear intelligence outwardly show no interest in or respect for screamingly obvious patternedness, then I see red, go a little haywire, get a bee in my bonnet, or as Carol used to say, grow a wild hair. And that is just what happened as I scoured the Halpern anthology. Over the past few pages of this chapter, I have let off some steam built up in that scouring, by claiming that one after another of these "emperors" has no clothes, or at best has very scanty clothes. I am certainly aware that in voicing, *à la* Nabokov, a raft of "strong opinions" on this topic, I may well fail to bring a single soul around to my viewpoint, and instead may do no more than blatantly reveal my own blind spots or, put otherwise, my own philistinism, and thus turn my audience off. It's a risk.

Yet it is a risk I feel is worth taking. I cannot have the objectivity to know whether I am "right" in my attitude. All I can do is state an honest opinion and make it as clear as I can; then readers can take it or leave it. Maybe I'll make a fool of myself in some people's eyes, and in others I may perhaps be seen as a voice of sanity. But I would not be being true to myself if I just held my tongue in order to "be a good boy". This matter simply matters too much to me.

I guess that's how it was for Nabokov, too. Strange to say, at some rarefied level, floating far above his and my clashing beliefs about what makes for good poetry translation, he and I see eye to eye! And that's why I, though not a translator of Dante at all, have somehow wound up playing that most unlikely and unflattering role — "the Nabokov of *The Inferno*".

Of Pattern, Patter, and Humor

The great American philomath Martin Gardner, known most widely for his beautiful discussions of deep mathematical and philosophical issues in the famous "Mathematical Games" column that played such a central role in the glory days of *Scientific American,* is also someone who cares deeply about words and literature (he is the author of a novel, *The Flight of Peter Fromm*). For many decades he has collected and written about poems, and recently has come out with two anthologies of older poems, one called *Best Remembered Poems* and the other called *Famous Poems from Bygone Days*. The epigraph to the latter volume is the following ditty by Robert Service:

A Verseman's Apology

Alas! I am only a rhymer,
I don't know the meaning of Art;
But I learned in my little school primer
To love Eugene Field and Bret Harte.
I hailed Hoosier Riley with pleasure,
To John Hay I took off my hat;
These fellows were right to my measure,
And I've never gone higher than that.

The Classics! Well, most of them bore me,
The Moderns I don't understand;
But I keep Burns, my kinsman, before me,
And Kipling, my friend, is at hand.
They taught me my trade as I know it,
Yet though at their feet I have sat,
For God's sake, don't call me a poet,
For I've never been guilty of that.

A rhyme-rustler, rugged and shameless,
A Bab Balladeer on the loose;
Of saccharine sonnets I'm blameless,
My model has been — Mother Goose.
And I fancy my grave-digger griping
As he gives my last lodging a pat:
"That guy wrote McGrew;
'Twas the best he could do"…
So I'll go to my Maker with that.

Every time I hit that line about Mother Goose, I cannot suppress a smile, sometimes even laugh aloud. And this brings me to an issue that seems to me to lie right smack at the heart of the matter of high-quality verse translation: *sense of humor.*

It has been my observation, culled over years and years of eliciting "Ma Mignonne" translations from relatives, friends, colleagues, and students, that those people who do the most imaginative, liveliest, and most polished jobs are invariably those with the best senses of humor. They are people who love to play with ideas, juggle words, take risks, laugh at themselves, be silly, let themselves go. I suppose it suggests that having a sense of humor is tightly bound up with a propensity for intellectual risk-taking.

Of course, merely *liking laughing* is not enough. Every human enjoys a good guffaw. What I am talking about has more to do with the ability to *generate* good jokes spontaneously — to make strange connections, to hear hidden phonetic resonances, to have a good model of other people's expectations and thus know how to violate them, and so on. It seems to me that such abilities grease the mental wheels, providing sufficient lubrication that words and images and syntactic pathways can slip gracefully into potential alternatives, along the lines described in Chapter 13.

When it comes to Dante's and Pushkin's works, even though I do not personally know the translators concerned, it seems to me that there is a similar tight correlation between quality of translation — fluidity, grace, meter, diction, rhyme, and so forth — and sense of humor. One simply intuits that, behind the scenes, superb poetry translators like Richard Wilbur and James Falen and Dorothy Sayers are witty, humorous people. It is inconceivable — to me, at least — that someone dull and dry could come up with a dazzling, lively translation of a scintillating poem.

And thus, what strange bedfellows I postulate: strict adherents to Louis Kahn's "religion of the ordered path", on the one hand, and bubbly, spontaneous inventors of high-quality jokes, on the other. Whimsical, unshackled spontaneity and love of order and pattern, going hand in hand? The match sounds most odd, and yet in my mind, it seems to be confirmed only more strongly each time I uncover a new lively translator.

Old-time Poetry Speakers

Again I turn to Martin Gardner's thin volume *Famous Poems from Bygone Days,* and cite some lines from his nostalgic Introduction:

> Not many people today, I suspect, are aware of how enormously admired poetry was in the days before motion pictures and television. It was read, savored, recited, and memorized by persons on all levels of education and sophistication. England's great romantic poets were world-famous and well paid. When Browning was the rage, his verse was studied in hundreds of Browning clubs in England and America. Professional reciters known as "speakers" drew huge audiences all over the land. Hundreds of poetry volumes, also nicknamed "speakers", were published, many illustrated with amusing photographs of men and women in elocutionary poses.
>
> Before free verse took over, the love of poetry was also reflected in the high quality of song lyrics by Ira Gershwin, Cole Porter, Irving Berlin, and many others, not to forget England's immortal W. S. Gilbert (of Gilbert and Sullivan). Today's rock lyrics are so so banal as to make "Ben Bolt" (by Thomas Dunn English) seem to have been penned by Shakespeare. Who can even understand the words of a rock song, often consisting of a single sentence shouted over and over while the singer gyrates and leaps about the stage to music that has little to offer except a few chords and an insistent beat?
>
> The old love of poetry continued well into the early decades of this century, when Rudyard Kipling, Robert Service, Ella Wheeler Wilcox, and Eddie Guest were widely read. When radio offered more than popular music and call-in talk shows, millions enjoyed such verse reciters as Tony Wons and Ted Malone.

On reading these sad paragraphs one evening, I was led to jot down a poem in memory of Wons, a gone time, and Malone...

Once Upon a Time Alone

When radio used to offer more
Than call-in talk and raucous rock,
Folks would tune in to poets galore;
To loudspeaker speakers they'd flock.

That's history today. It's such a shame
The medium's gone truly to pot;
But at radio's feet falls not the blame;
At fault is what poetry's not.

Today the poets are not pro-verse,
Unless as verse you count free verse;
To my ear, though, that seems perverse:
Free isn't pro-, but quite con-, verse.

Today the poets are not verse pros;
Their well of rhymes ran dry, I suppose.
Today the poets converse in prose,
Supposing it's Art. But why? God knows!

In days of old, the rhymes were bold,
And poets' hearts were metric;
In nights of new, the rhymes are few,
And art's scorned if symmetric.

Iamb I am, or am I not?
Such definitions they've plumb forgot.
Of anapest my verse might be,
But then again, might be trochee.

In days of old, the rhymes they rhymed,
And slant-rhymes? Well, they cheated;
In nights of new, the rhymes are skew,
And meter maids sorely needed!

Rhyme today is the hallmark of cards
You'll find in trite Walmart displays.
This pushes the ballpark of cool Zen bards
Far, far, from The Bard's quaint plays.

In cool ballparks, the verse is free:
You never need to pay (hurray!).
So step right up and swing your bat —
A hit? No, no — no way, Nanette.

Free verse is a per-
fect game.
Meaning no
runs,
no walks, not even one hit. That
would ru-
in
it (pardon
the
unintentional rhyme). 27
up, 2-
7 down.

The World's Serious.
No soft summer stickball here.
Spit it like it is.

We won't hiccough back,
won't spring through time toward the past.
It's phony; it's dead.

Or... might we backtrack
in a high coup? Fads fall fast.
Speak, Tony! Speak, Ted!

The Utter Irrelevance of Five-Seven-Five

As anyone can tell from their vivid references to the passing seasons, all three of my closing stanzas are haikus. The form of haiku traditionally has had nothing to do with rhyming, and accordingly I introduced no internal rhymes to any of these stanzas; on the other hand, I played the game of making the final two haikus rhyme with each other, line by line. This, in the Japanese haiku world, may not be kosher, but haiku by now is such a popular international poetic form that the Japanese no longer have any exclusive say-so as to what goes and what doesn't. Still, one somehow feels that when a Japanese poet starts talking about haiku, one ought to pay a little more attention than to a random poet.

It was for this reason that some fourteen years ago, when I received my copy of the unpronounceable *PENewsletter,* a bulletin put out by and for members of PEN, the socially concerned writers' organization, I sat up and read with great interest the two pages of "Remarks" made by translator Hiroaki Sato on the occasion of being awarded, together with Burton Watson, the 1982 PEN Translation Award for their book *From the Country of Eight Islands,* an anthology of 1200 years of Japanese poetry in translation. Sato's concern in his remarks was, in particular, the "right" way, if such could be found or articulated, of transferring Japanese haiku into another language. He opens his speech as follows:

> I have characterized my way of translation as "unadorned". It is an approach to which Mr. Watson agrees — "the method", as he put it, "of translating only what is in the original". I wish to explain it with a few examples.

The Sato–Watson philosophy is very spartan: "Get across what is there, and no more." A clear example is provided by the epigraph to this chapter: *An old pond: a frog jumps in — the sound of water.* This is Sato's version of what he says must be the most famous haiku ever written. Its author is Matsu Bashō (1644–1694), who wrote it in Japanese using the special haiku form — three lines whose syllables form a symmetric 5–7–5 pattern. Here it is, in Roman transcription: *Furuike ya / kawazu tobikomu / mizu no oto.*

Sato explains that his anglicization is intended to be thought of as *one* line, not as three. This would theoretically rule out making any line-by-line comparison with the canonical 5–7–5 pattern; however, if someone were perverse and stubborn, like me, they might insist on chopping up Sato's single line of English into a tripartite structure (something not too terribly hard to do), whereupon they would find that its three pieces have a 3–4–5 syllable distribution. Sato never comments on the discrepancy between 3–4–5 and 5–7–5, since to him it's just plain irrelevant. After all, he belongs to the *Inhalt über alles* school of translation.

Despite this, Sato is open to and indeed fascinated by alternative pathways of translation. He explains that over the years he has collected more than eighty anglicizations of this classic haiku, and then devotes most of his essay to making little dips into his collection and commenting on the curious frogs he pulls up. As Bashō might have said, had he known English, the translations range greatly in both style and size, as we shall now see.

Liquid Beast Immersion

In order to open our small Bashō showcase with a bit of a splash, I display, of all strange things, a charming Dantean tercet, complete with rhyme and all, done in 1923 by Curtis Hidden Page, who at that time was a professor of English at Dartmouth College:

> *A lonely pond in age-old stillness sleeps...*
> *Apart, unstirred by sound or motion... till*
> *Suddenly into it a lithe frog leaps.*

Fifty years later, Sato asked Lindley Williams Hubbell, who had once been his professor of poetry in Japan and who later became a naturalized Japanese citizen, to anglicize the same haiku. Hubbell obliged him with two versions, one of which was straight while the other was a parody of Hidden Page's translation, which apparently struck Hubbell's funny bone. Here they are:

> *An old pond*
> *A frog jumping*
> *Sound of water.*

> *O thou unrippled pool of quietness*
> *Upon whose shimmering surface, like the tears*
> *Of olden days, a small batrachian leaps,*
> *The while aquatic sounds assail our ears.*

Of the lower one, Sato wryly comments, "Mr. Hubbell was joking in 1976 when he wrote this, but Professor Page was not, in 1923."

What particularly irks Sato here is of course the excessive verbiage. In fact, Sato is quite a fanatic about excessive verbiage. To show you what I mean, here is a canonical 5–7–5 anglicization of Bashō's poem, done by Earl Miner (who, in Sato's words, is "the doyen of classical Japanese poetry in this country"). Sato takes Miner's version to task for what might be called its "padding":

> *The old pond is still*
> *a frog leaps right into it*
> *splashing the water.*

Care to hazard a guess as to which word here particularly offends Sato's poetic sensibilities? (There is precisely one that bugs him.)

Well, the answer is: the last word of the first line. Sato explains what is wrong by saying that Miner's translation is...

...apparently based on the assumption, which Professor Page had, that Bashō, who wrote the original poem, was jolted into a supreme awareness of life when a silence was broken. (If that were what enlightenment is all about, all the nervous wrecks in New York City would have to be appointed Zen abbots in Kyoto.)

Sato concludes his criticism of Miner by saying that his use of the word "still" helps perpetuate a long-standing myth about Bashō's poem by erroneously, if pleasantly, linking it too closely with Zen, and then he tacks on a most curious comment:

> As [Miner] once put it, "No two translators agree." We certainly don't. Even so, I think his effort to approximate the syllabic formation of the original is legitimate.

It's legitimate, eh? What amazing generosity! At least it's a far cry more generous than Nabokov would have been.

The final example that Sato gives from his collection of translations is a most amusing one by the English poet James Kirkup:

> *pond*
> *frog*
> *plop!*

Sato chuckles along with Kirkup at this deliberately overdone minimalism, but worries that not a few people take such an approach quite seriously. From Sato's viewpoint, cutting too deeply into the "meat" of the poem is just laziness, not art.

My reaction to Kirkup's lovely piece of drollery was both to chuckle and to admire its keen insight. But then, inspired by its wit, I felt a drive to carry the idea just a tad further — to carry it to its logical conclusion, in some sense — and so, after a little poling-around in my mental lexicon and my bag of word-manipulation techniques, I came up with this:

> *swamp*
> *tadpole*
> *plunk*

Just to spell it out, we have here three one-word lines whose letter-counts are, respectively, five, seven, and five letters. The game of *haiku form* is thus being played on a different structural level from the usual one. This is very much my style of game, as readers may by now recognize. To be sure, letter-count has no direct sensory appeal — there is no music to it — but then, to be fair, syllable-count is not very audible either. At least for me, when I read an alleged haiku in English, I find that I have no idea whether it is really 5–7–5 unless I actually stop and count the syllables on my silly little fingers. And therefore to me, this transfer of the counting

In Praise of the Music of Language

game from the syllable level to the letter level is not a serious violation of the rules. The micro-miniaturization of the haiku form that it affords is, in fact, something that I find both charming and challenging. Perhaps someday I will go on and write more poems in this supercompact version of the classic 5–7–5 form, or perhaps someone else will.

Am I slapping Bashō in the face? Am I hereby doing to Bashō what I see Robert Pinsky or Jorie Graham doing to Dante? Is this game as bad as if someone were to take Robert Service's "Verseman's Apology" and translate it into French using slant rhymes, or even using no rhymes and no meter at all? No. Doing the latter would be an absurdity, would be to disrespect the very essence of Service's poem. But in just what way, pray tell, would *respecting* Bashō's 5–7–5 structure be to *disrespect* him? To the contrary: flinging 5–7–5 out the window, as does Sato, is to deeply disrespect Bashō!

Messagism as Literary Machismo

Here we come back to my whole thesis that poetry should be seen as a *marriage of equals,* rather than as a noble and proud macho Content who is accompanied, but pitter-patting oh-so-softly in the background, by a terribly obsequious and deferential ladylike Form.

Let's listen to how Hiroaki Sato concludes his acceptance speech:

> Gabriel García Márquez, I hear, has praised Gregory Rabassa's translation of *One Hundred Years of Solitude* as superior to his original. That is the rarest, the most gratifying tribute a translator can expect. The majority of us, I think, somehow *know* that our best effort is embarrassingly inferior to the original. In that knowledge I can find salvation only in Nabokov's dictum, if I may take refuge in such an outstanding user of languages. It is this: "The clumsiest literal translation is a thousand times more useful than the prettiest paraphrase."

Had Sato's hope been to set that bee a-buzzing in my bonnet, he could hardly have picked a better (or worse) person to quote. Indeed, let's think about literal translations for a moment — not just clumsy ones, but good, Nabokovian ones. For perspective, how about moving from haiku to pi-ku? Let's take that classic old French pi-ku and translate it *literally* into English:

> *Que j'aime à faire apprendre un nombre utile aux sages !*
> *Immortel Archimède, artiste ingénieur,*
> *Qui de ton jugement peut priser la valeur ?*
> *Pour moi, ton problème eut de pareils avantages.*

> *How I love to make known a number useful to sages!*
> *Immortal Archimedes, artist engineer,*
> *Who in your judgment can estimate the value?*
> *For me, your problem had some similar advantages.*

What in the world would be the point of doing such a thing? Instead of coding for π, this bungled "pi-mnemonic" codes for the following mathematical constant: 3.14245166258106832483835324734710... It's not of use to sages or to anyone at all. Well, maybe for engineers, this is good enough — after all, it's a tiny bit closer to π's true value than is the usual schoolchild's approximation of 22/7 — but then, why memorize any more than its first three words? For from there on out, it's all wrong. I ask: What is the point of such a Nabokovian literal translation, in this case?

You may think this is extreme and exceptional, but *no, it is not*. In fact, this case is *less* extreme than those of rendering *Eugene Onegin* and *The Divine Comedy* as unrhymed, nonmetric prose, because those are infinitely greater works of art than is the cute but silly pi-ku. *Art must be rendered as art, otherwise it is no longer art*.

To be sure, no one is advocating dumping content overboard. The point is, content and form must *both* be preserved, as James Falen, Richard Wilbur, W. E. Henley, Walter Arndt, Dorothy Sayers, Willis Barnstone, Max Knight, Giuseppe Varaldo, Gilbert Adair, Babette Deutsch, Peter Dale, and quite a few other gifted people in this book have shown us is entirely possible, even in the case of the most daunting, marvelous works of art. We must simply keep in the forefront of our minds the lesson that a poem, even a tiny little haiku or pi-ku, is a *marriage of equals* and not just a blustering egomaniacal *husband* with an insipidly smiling and docile wifebot totally eclipsed behind His self-deludingly bloated Majesty.

The essence of the act of translating poetry is to exercise the highest respect for the original poet's indissoluble fusion of a message with a medium, the unsunderable wedding of content to form as equal partners.

Matrimony as Poetry

Will you, Medium, take this message to be your poetically wedded partner? *I will.* And will you, Message, take this medium to be your poetically wedded partner? *I will.* It gives me great joy to pronounce you, Message and Medium, to be a Poem. You may now kiss.

●

●

Conclusion ●

Le Tombeau
de ma rose

●

> *Not far along the pathway of our life,*
> *I found myself alone in sudden gloom,*
> *Because the light had disappeared: my wife.*
>
> *Three years have passed since Carol met her doom,*
> *Three years, yet breathes she still inside my heart;*
> *Though there am I, there too is she: there's room.*
>
> *Our children's course alone I've had to chart,*
> *Her absent presence searing like a knife;*
> *But spirit strong, I'm striving to restart.*

Some enchanted fateful summer evening, by now so many orbits long gone by, across a crowded room I saw her laughing; she caught my eye — and, strangely, I her eye. I sighed that night when first her eye I eyed — I sighed, from bliss denied, and grieved inside. But grief turned hope turned spark and soon we met, and thus for our romance the stage was set. Some years would pass until we blurred our names, yet finally we were one and one was four. We looked ahead to years and years of flames, but time ran short and one day was no more. Our blur had been, though over far too soon, in Carol's words, "Once in a blue, blue moon".

We were married in Ann Arbor on a Saturday in October, and I'll never forget the dress she wore that day — a sunset kind of color, salmon-pink, I think you'd say — and the pearls around her neck, and white heels with bows in back. Oh, her knees were all a-tremble as we stood there face to face, but her dark eyes gleamed as rings were slipped in place, and then at last we kissed in tight embrace. As for me, what I remember is sheer ecstasy and peacefulness — a rare visit to that special state of grace.

A First Foray into Poetry Translation

Our deep joy at finally becoming one was magnified by the presence of our beloved families and friends, and yet further intensified by the beautiful songs performed by our friends Maurita Holland, who played the piano, and Roger Chard, who sang. Two of the four songs we had selected were by Gabriel Fauré, and they remain, for me, among the most touching pieces of music I know. Their words — both poems by the nineteenth-century French poet Armand Silvestre — play no small role in their power.

That portentous morning of our wedding day, the moment I arose, the first thing I did — before showering, before getting dressed, though maybe not before coffee! — was to don my bathrobe, go into my study, flick my little 128K Mac on, and into its trusty little memory type up the program for the afternoon's ceremony. One of my main goals was to have all the words to all the songs appear in the program, but of course, since not everyone who would be there knew French, I felt it was critical to have an English translation of the Silvestre poems.

It was 1985 — definitely pre–"Ma Mignonne" mania — and though by then I had devoted a great deal of mental energy to thinking about how to translate wordplay, I had never tackled the translation of poetry before, and as I sat there pondering those words and their musicality, it struck me as next to impossibly difficult. I instantly renounced the idea of rendering verse as verse, and simply went for a literal translation of each line, though I tried hard to make each line, in its own splendid isolation, have some kind of poetic ring to it. The result was not in the least lyrical but it did the job, and the program seemed to be appreciated by all the guests.

Many years later, though, in reliving with deep nostalgia that most special and hope-filled day in our lives, I thought I would try, in memory of Carol, to retranslate those two poems. I went to my filing cabinets, pulled out our wedding-day program, and typed the French originals into my fast and fancy brand-new Macintosh. Then I spent hours glued to the screen, working each line back and forth with utmost care, making sure that justice at last was done to the verse. By this time, with years of poetry translation under my belt, I had all sorts of skills that I simply lacked in 1985, and so I was able to do a job of which I was proud. "Aurore", the first song in our ceremony, conveyed a message of newness, radiance, and hope.

Aurore

Armand Silvestre

Des jardins de la nuit s'envolent les étoiles,
Abeilles d'or qu'attire un invisible miel,
Et l'aube, au loin tendant la candeur de ses toiles,
Trame de fils d'argent le manteau bleu du ciel.

Du jardin de mon cœur qu'un rêve lent enivre
S'envolent mes désirs sur les pas du matin,
Comme un essaim troublé qu'à l'horizon de cuivre
Appelle un chant plaintif, éternel et lointain.

Ils volent à tes pieds, astres chassés des nues,
Exilés du ciel d'or où fleurit ta beauté
Et, cherchant jusqu'à toi des routes inconnues
Mêlent au jour naissant leur mourante clarté.

Dawn

A. Silvestre/D. Hofstadter

From the gardens of night the bright stars are in flight,
Golden bees subtly lured by a nectar unseen,
And the dawn, far off spreading its canvases white,
Shoots its silvery threads o'er the sky's azure screen.

From my heart's secret garden still drunk on a dream,
Bleary hopes flit away on the footsteps of morn,
Like a swarm gone astray toward the rim's copper gleam,
Chasing calls, sad and low, from a far, mournful horn.

Spurned by clouds, stars in flocks at your feet seem to glide
Out of gold-spattered skies where your beauty now blooms;
Seeking routes ever new, they take aim at your side
And then grace the young day with their moribund plumes.

The dramatic climax of Carol's and my wedding ceremony was the ecstatic Silvestre–Fauré song "Notre amour", a powerful, surging pæan to the depths of romantic love. And that Ann Arbor October afternoon, I swear we all were spellbound by the magic wrought by Roger and Maurita.

Ten years later, reliving it all in mingled joy and sadness, I was at last able to translate this poem, interpreting its lines just loosely enough to afford me the freedom that I needed to respect its form.

Notre amour	*Our Love*
Armand Silvestre	*A. Silvestre/D. Hofstadter*

Notre amour est chose légère,
Comme les parfums que le vent
Prend aux cimes de la fougère,
Pour qu'on les respire en rêvant.
Notre amour est chose légère.

Our love lightly turns,
Like a scent borne on breeze
From the branchtips of ferns,
That one dreams as one breathes.
Our love lightly turns.

Notre amour est chose charmante,
Comme les chansons du matin
Où nul regret ne se lamente,
Où vibre un espoir incertain.
Notre amour est chose charmante.

Our love lilts in dance,
Like a song of bright morn,
Full of hope tinged with chance,
Never sad nor forlorn.
Our love lilts in dance.

Notre amour est chose sacrée
Comme le mystère des bois
Où tressaille une âme ignorée,
Où les silences ont des voix.
Notre amour est chose sacrée.

Our love is divine,
Like a dark sylvan creek,
Where sparks course one's spine
And silences speak.
Our love is divine.

Notre amour est chose infinie,
Comme le chemin des couchants
Où la mer, aux cieux réunie,
S'endort sous les soleils penchants.
Notre amour est chose infinie.

Our love knows no size,
Like the plunge of the gleam
As the waves meet the skies'
Slanting suns, there to dream.
Our love knows no size.

Notre amour est chose éternelle,
Comme tout ce qu'un dieu vainqueur
A touché du feu de son aile,
Comme tout ce qui vient du cœur.
Notre amour est chose éternelle.

Our love soars e'er higher,
Like sacred gems blessed
By a god's wing afire,
Like sighs from one's breast.
Our love soars e'er higher.

Having translated this lyrical poem once, I looked back over my translation and, without at all intending to, spontaneously came up with a different way of rendering a line or two. The new way featured a meter incompatible with the old poem, so there was no question of replacing already-done lines by the upstarts. Instead, I found myself embarked, without even knowing how it had happened, on a second translation, which had its own integrity. And today I wouldn't want to choose between them.

Notre amour

Armand Silvestre

Notre amour est chose légère,
Comme les parfums que le vent
Prend aux cimes de la fougère,
Pour qu'on les respire en rêvant.
Notre amour est chose légère.

Notre amour est chose charmante,
Comme les chansons du matin
Où nul regret ne se lamente,
Où vibre un espoir incertain.
Notre amour est chose charmante.

Notre amour est chose sacrée
Comme le mystère des bois
Où tressaille une âme ignorée,
Où les silences ont des voix.
Notre amour est chose sacrée.

Notre amour est chose infinie,
Comme le chemin des couchants
Où la mer, aux cieux réunie,
S'endort sous les soleils penchants.
Notre amour est chose infinie.

Notre amour est chose éternelle,
Comme tout ce qu'un dieu vainqueur
A touché du feu de son aile,
Comme tout ce qui vient du cœur.
Notre amour est chose éternelle.

Our Love

A. Silvestre/D. Hofstadter

Our love is a dream that glides light,
Like a scent drifting far through the air
Borne from ferns by the soft winds of night,
Spinning fancies of fragrance so rare.
Our love is a dream that glides light.

Our love is a dream that enchants,
Like the song on one's lips as one wakes,
Where instead of regret there's romance,
Where with hopes mingle quivers and quakes.
Our love is a dream that enchants.

Our love is a dream that transcends,
Like the spirit that lurks in a glade,
Where a lonely soul's thrill never ends,
Where the silence communes with the shade.
Our love is a dream that transcends.

Our love is a dream without bounds,
Like the west when the sun's nearly gone,
Splashed with pink as the fireball drowns
In the deep, there to sleep till the dawn.
Our love is a dream without bounds.

Our love is a dream beyond time,
Like all that is seared by the wings
Of a god in victorious climb,
Like all that a soaring heart sings.
Our love is a dream beyond time.

Le Tombeau de ma rose

Gulping a Last Deep Gulp of Life's Pure Joy

It had always been Carol's and my fervent dream to raise bilingual children, adding Italian to their English — and then, perhaps, French some day as well. She and I had been practicing our Italian off and on together for years, but the frequency of our Italian lunches intensified as my 1993–94 sabbatical leave approached, because we had arranged to spend it in the stunningly beautiful setting of Trento, Italy. And so, in August of 1993, after months of hectic preparation, our little four family was finally transplanted to the province of Trentino, to start our new European life.

At the outset, things were auspicious. We had good friends, Danny integrated himself beautifully into his sweet Italian *scuola materna,* we found a nice babysitter for Monica, Carol hit it off with our warm and lively neighbor Lucia and together they started taking courses at the University... Each evening, when my work was done, I would walk home between hillside villages, picking a little bunch of tiny wildflowers along the narrow winding *via alla Cascata* and bringing them home for Carol and the kids.

In early November, Carol had a series of bad headaches, and we were worried. We had her checked out at the Trento hospital, but neurologists and audiologists could find nothing wrong. They said, "Wait a few days and see what happens." And a few days later, the headaches had vanished. We breathed a sigh of relief, and then spoke openly of the fears we had been afraid to mention, Carol telling me how George Gershwin had been plagued by the smell of burning rubber when he had his fatal brain tumor.

That fall, there were big banners hanging all over Trento for a Kandinsky exhibit in nearby Verona, city of Romeo and Juliet, city of Dante's exile... We made a date to go, just the two of us. It was a Thursday, and we started out bright and early. Our first stop was a small museum in Trento, which was hosting an enticing exhibit on the natural curves of Euclidean geometry — ellipses, hyperboloids, catenaries, and other beautiful shapes. We savored it, and also enjoyed watching a small group of high-school students, who seemed as taken with it as we were.

Then we sauntered over to the *stazione ferroviaria,* where we had just enough time to indulge in the traditional, irresistible *cappuccino* and *brioche,* and I also couldn't resist buying three newspapers for the hour-long train ride: *Corriere della Sera, Le Monde,* and *Die Zeit.* In *Le Monde,* there was a long article about French popular music of bygone eras, and it had quite a bit about one of our favorite singers, Charles Trenet, at the time in his eighties. Carol wistfully said, "Maybe one day, you could meet him..."

In one of the other papers, we read for the first time of the upcoming celestial cataclysm — the collision of a comet with Jupiter that would take place in July of the following year. The inconceivable power of the blast was described, and it seemed amazing and wonderful to us that we could sit here on earth and know with absolute certainty, eight months in advance, the exact day, hour, and minute in which an enormous crash would take place a billion miles away on the far side of a huge spinning ball. We of course had no idea that far sooner, a minuscule local cataclysm would shake our little lives far more dreadfully than anything in space ever could.

Our visit to Verona was wonderful. We walked all through the small streets, ate lunch at a superb restaurant, enjoyed watching the evolution of Kandinsky's style from youth to maturity to old age, and then meandered some more along the bank of the fast-flowing Adige, until it started drizzling and we hurried back to the station on foot, getting fairly sopped but having a great time of it anyway. We resolved to return to Verona soon.

That month, feeling strong and happy, Carol started running again, and found herself a scenic and hilly four-kilometer jog from Cognola to Martignano and back. One afternoon some priest saw her jogging in her shorts in the cool weather, and as she ran by, he made gestures asking if she wasn't too cold, which she laughingly recounted to friends in Italian.

One day we found out that the delicious but utterly implausible rumor of an Indian restaurant out in a tiny village in the Valsugana was true, and so we invited our friends Achille Varzi and Freddy Oursin on a mysterious dinner outing, destination to be revealed only on arrival. We spirited them off in the darkest of night, and when we got to Barco and found the tiny house with not even a sign on it, none of us could quite believe that this was where we were going to eat. And yet, when we opened the door, we were greeted by the unmistakable whiffs of curry and other marvelous spices, and the linguistic environment all of a sudden switched from Italian to English as the four of us were seated for what turned out to be one of the best Indian meals we had ever eaten anywhere. Ristorante Indiano Nirvair, as near to Nirvana as one could come. Not a cloud on the bloomin' horizon.

Just Bad Luck

In early December, after a happy weekend jaunt to Innsbruck with the kids, the headaches came back. Smashing, bashing, crashing headaches. We checked her out again. Inner ear infection? Penicillin might do the trick. But it didn't. On December 10–11, an emergency post-midnight return to the hospital. The neurologist, a very friendly man, complimented us on our Italian and asked Carol to close her eyes and touch her nose with her finger. When I saw her finger struggling in mid-air to find the spot, my blood ran colder than cold. I could see the handwriting on the wall.

He said he would immediately give her *una tac*. It sounded a bit like he meant "an attack", until we somehow realized that *una tac* was a CAT scan. I waited in deep fear as she first had a CAT scan and then an MRI.

When Doctor Tranquillini — that, ironically, was his name — finally came to the waiting room where I was nervously sitting, he pulled me aside and said to me softly, *Purtroppo, c'è una formazione.* "Unfortunately, there's a growth." It was morning, and we had awoken to find the enemy, *l'invasor.*

I had to break the news to Carol, who blinked for a moment as the enormity of it all registered, and then simply said, "Some people, when they find out they have a tumor, ask, 'Why me?' They don't think to themselves that they're made of billions and billions of tiny cells, and just one thing needs to go wrong... It's just bad luck." And then, as in the eeriest of nightmares, Carol was shown big black-and-white negatives of the monster invading her brain. At least we could still hold out hopes it was benign.

Final Return to Verona

And so, we did indeed return to Verona soon, but not at all as we had foreseen or planned. It was to the big old-fashioned hospital known as Borgo Trento that Carol was transferred, and shortly after she was given an injection to reduce the swelling, she felt and looked great again. In the room where she was placed for observation, there were several other women, including Fernanda, who had just had a massive surgery done by the surgeon who would be Carol's, and was filled with joy at suddenly being able to see again. This gave us a wild surge of optimism, as did the memory of our Chilean friend Isabel Claro, who many years before — ironically, on the sabbatical of her husband Francisco in Bloomington — had had a huge but benign brain tumor removed with absolutely no ill effects.

There was no question of flying home to the United States to have Carol treated there: the tumor was too big and her situation was too precarious. And yet one would suspect nothing at all, from without. Carol looked as beautiful and as radiant as I had ever seen her, especially the next day, December 12, when Danny and Monica came down from Trento to visit their Mommy, and gave her a present filled with love. Totally out of the blue, Danny lost his first baby tooth right in front of Carol, and she beamed at him and said, "Oh, my — aren't you getting to be a big boy!"

The children returned to Trento and I stayed on for the evening, distributing After Eights to everyone in her room. Carol felt good and got up and we wandered into a little lounge where we had a pleasant chat with a Sardinian family and a Filipino woman, and then Carol said she felt like lying down again. We went back and she complained she wasn't feeling well. She lay down flat and then said she was having a hard time breathing. Her speech was suddenly slurring. I started to panic, and rushed to summon the nurses. During the next hour, I saw the waters rising around Carol's neck and yet I was helpless; I could do nothing to stop them. The nurses kept on saying to her, *Mi dica qualcosa, signora* — "Say something, ma'am" — and Carol, ever witty, replied through her fearful slur, "The rain in Spain falls mainly in the plain..." But it was getting worse and worse and worse. The terrible Great Call was coming, and she sensed it and I sensed it, though I, whistling desperately in the dark, fervidly denied it to her.

Finally a team of doctors and nurses came to slide her onto a gurney and wheel her off to the intensive care unit, and as I walked beside her down the corridor to the translucent double doors through which I could not pass, I said to her, *Sogni d'oro,* and turned around in tears.

It was only moments later, so I was told, that she fell into a stupor, then a coma; and ten days later, mercifully never having awoken, she was gone. I think that if, somehow, Carol had known she would die in Verona, she would have been able to summon a smile at the idea of her life coming to a close in a classic city in her beloved Italy. She always had good taste.

Deux roses pour son tombeau

One day I chanced to remember an extremely touching poem I had run across in the Cimetière du Père-Lachaise in Paris some twenty years or so earlier, while making a pilgrimage to the tomb of my personal hero Chopin. The poem was on a tomb, not too far from Chopin's, of a teen-aged boy named Jean. It ran as follows (the translation is quite literal):

<table>
<tr><td>

A Jean

A ton ombre, ces fleurs,
   ces fleurs pures et claires,
Car les fleurs sont lumière.

A ton cœur qui sommeille,
   à tes yeux qui sont clos,
Car les fleurs sont repos.

A ta voix, qui n'est plus
   qu'un peu de souffle immense,
Car les fleurs sont silence.

</td><td>

To Jean

To your shadow, these flowers,
   these flowers pure and bright,
For flowers are light.

To your heart that's asleep,
   to your eyes that are closed,
For flowers are repose.

To your voice, now no more
   than a trace of immense wind,
For flowers are silence.

</td></tr>
</table>

There was something about this little poem that, even when I first saw it, though of course I had no idea who young Jean had been, moved me enormously. I copied it down at the time — 1975, I think — and once back in the United States, tucked it into my volume of Chopin études as a special memento. In that way, I came across it every once in a while and each time was caught by surprise and moved once again. It is both sad and uplifting, flickering shadows and flowers and light.

When my father died, in 1990, I toyed with the idea of translating this poem, perhaps to read it at the burial, but when I actually tackled the challenge, I didn't get anywhere, especially with the last stanza. It was the simple word *silence* that stopped me in my tracks. The only English word I felt was right for rendering it was "silence" — and for that I could find no suitable rhyme in the line above it, and so I abandoned the whole idea.

But in the fall of 1995, immersed as I was in French poetry translation, the idea once again popped into my head of translating "A Jean", this time for possible use on Carol's tombstone, which, because it had an unusual shape and special lettering from Italy, had been long delayed and was still being readied. It seemed fitting, provided I could do a decent translation, to use this poem in an English version coming from my own heart. And so I worked very hard at it, and in the end, came up with this translation:

A Jean	*To Carol*
A ton ombre, ces fleurs,	*To your shadow, these flowers,*
ces fleurs pures et claires,	*these flowers pure and bright,*
Car les fleurs sont lumière.	*For flowers are beauty and light.*
A ton cœur qui sommeille,	*To your heartbeat now quelled,*
à tes yeux qui sont clos,	*to your gaze now suppressed,*
Car les fleurs sont repos.	*For flowers are softness and rest.*
A ta voix, qui n'est plus	*To your voice, but a whisper*
qu'un peu de souffle immense,	*in the vastness of space,*
Car les fleurs sont silence.	*For flowers are silence and grace.*

The two nouns in each stanza's final line go back to my struggle with "silence". Having found no solution along any obvious route, I felt forced to explore more obscure pathways. It crossed my mind to complement "silence" with a related word, and one possibility that occurred to me was "grace". It exuded the right flavor, and since it rhymes with "space", a word I had already thought of for the previous line, it appealed to me greatly.

But having given "silence" a mate, I felt I had to mirror the idea in the two analogous spots, so I gave "light" and "rest" mates as well. In the end, I decided the English scanned better this way than with lone nouns, and so, gratified at the thought of transferring such touching sentiments from a distant Paris stone to Carol's, I settled on this solution. This all came late in the game, so perhaps the delay had been a small bit of luck. And, last of all, I had two roses chiseled into the dark marble, quietly flanking the poem.

Arc-en-ciel

Connected with all this, there was a strange resonance that I thought would have pleased Carol, somehow, if she could have known about it. This was based on the fact that her grave is only about eighty feet from Hoagy Carmichael's. For those too young to know this name, Hoagy Carmichael was one of the great American songwriters of the pre–World War II era — he wrote "Georgia on My Mind", "Old Rockin' Chair's Got Me", "Lazy River", and his most celebrated song of all, "Stardust". Hoagy came from Bloomington and attended Indiana University, and in fact wrote "Stardust" in the recently resuscitated Gables restaurant. Carol and I were very fond of Carmichael's music, and I feel it is somehow sweet, if one can use a word like that in this very sad context, that she is buried so close to this gentle person so appreciated by us and by the world for his lovely music.

And thus the "resonance"… If one knows the story, the French poem engraved on a teen-ager's tombstone in Paris' Père-Lachaise and its English echo on Carol's black-marble gravestone in Bloomington's little Rose Hill embody a transoceanic link between two cemeteries, between two people who died too young, and between two markers — and embellishing this sad but graceful sky-arch is a parallel link that naturally gets made between two composers distant in time, nationality, and style, yet not altogether in temperament: Frédéric Chopin and Hoagy Carmichael. I think that Carol would have appreciated this ethereal net of emotions and symbols.

Ciao bella… Bella ciao

In the first year of our marriage, we had run together quite often, but then Carol had given it up. However, in what turned out to be the last year of our marriage, she took up running again with enormous enthusiasm. She used to ask me, in that uncertain way she had, "Am I really a runner yet? What do you think?" And I would tell her that of course she was really a runner, not only a *real* runner but getting to be a *strong* runner. Carol, Carol, so full of self-doubt, so little reason to be that way…

The two of us used to run together in the early evenings, while the sun was very low. Carol was surprisingly gung-ho and when the time came, she would come up to my study and get me to go along, even on the muggiest of summer evenings. Sometimes we would go do the hilly loop at the "Y". Other times, we would start off in the alley behind our house and trot side by side for a mile; then, when we hit Bryan Park, we would split up to do the loop in opposite directions. Often, when on the park's far side we zipped by each other like two jets in the sky, I would flash her a smile and yell out, *Ciao bella!* And she would wink me back a smile and yell, *Ciao bello!*

And these days, when I'm running that same old Bryan Park loop and I come to that same old spot, every once in a while I'll still softly yell out, *Ciao bella!*, half-hoping to catch that merry wink and to hear her echo my call. I don't know why I do it. I just wish she could hear me. And — who knows? — maybe, dashing on in miniature, safely ensconced in the recesses of my faithful heart, she still can. *Magari.*

E seppellire,
Lassù in montagna,
O bella ciao, bella ciao,
Bella ciao, ciao, ciao,
E seppellire,
Lassù in montagna,
Sotto l'ombra
D'un bel fior.

E le genti
Che passeranno,
O bella ciao, bella ciao,
Bella ciao, ciao, ciao,
E le genti
Che passeranno,
Ti diranno,
Che bel fior.

E le genti
Che passeranno,
Ti diranno,
Che bel fior.

Ti diranno,
Che bel fior.

Ti diranno,
Che bel fior.

Notes

In the hopes of providing a graceful alternative to the standard but often intrusive style of annotation through pedantic footnotes and text-disrupting citations, I have chosen to do things more "invisibly" here. I assume that readers will sense when a bibliographical reference is in order and will flip to this section; in addition, they may find it pleasant to browse herein, now and then discovering some amusing tidbit or curious embellishment.

Introduction: In Joy and in Sorrow

Page *xix*   *The amount of influence exerted...*   Few readers, I suspect, would suspect the degree to which typographic facts of life shape (quite literally) the content of what I say. Indeed, if — perish the thought! — I had been writing this book in any typeface other than Baskerville, the result would have been not *this* book, but only a distant cousin: just about every sentence would have come out differently. (I reckon that roughly half my writing time is spent adjusting text to look better on the page.) Thus the book you are reading is every bit as married to Baskerville's graceful face as it is to Salinger's tongue.

Page *xxii*   *During my Italian sabbatical...*   The long list of friends on page *xxii* includes many who, strictly speaking, had no direct impact on the writing of this book. However, I owe them all such gratitude because, as I say, they helped rescue me and my children in our time of deepest need. I doubt I could have emerged to write this book had it not been for them. They include babysitters, teachers, neighbors, old and new friends, children, colleagues, and relatives — all of them willing to give so much.

Page *xxiv*   *Hôtel Terminus, Cahors...*   The goal of completing this book's manuscript by the crucial date of November 23, 1996 was, *mirabile dictu,* met (minus this end matter, needless to say). A fine, full draft was in place a few days earlier, and on November 20, I indulged myself in the sinful luxury of soaring above the broad lovely romantic Atlantic at quadruple the height of the Alps and twice the speed of a thunderclap inside that sleek silver sliver that is called *le Concorde.* This Franco–British jet-dart symbolized not only the likely crest of my life's intellectual path, but also a linking of those two lands in a sublime *objet d'art,* echoing in its unlikely way the origins of this book. I shan't forget the surge of sparks stirred up in my soul arcing high on that ark in the sky. *Rêv' ailé...*

From Paris I went first to Geneva, then took train and car to arrive late at night in Cahors, just minutes before the church bells rang in Marot's 500th birthday. As I drove into town at midnight, I was stunned to see a huge billboard announcing *the meaning* of November 23, 1996 — namely, it was the twentieth anniversary of the death of writer André Malraux! Yes, Malraux, not Marot, was the literary figure of the hour, and it was of him alone that all French newspapers spoke. No one else in Cahors seemed to give a fig for, or even be *aware* of, Clément Marot's birthday. Truth to tell, though, this was just fine with me, for it made my personal pilgrimage seem all the more unique and special.

By sheer chance, another Franco–British union was being celebrated that weekend in Cahors — the renewal of the old friendship of Elsie and Gordon John of Manchester and Jean Masbou of Cahors. The Johns were in my hotel, so we met over *confitures,* and I was invited to join them and Jean's young family for a tour on foot of Cahors, which of course I accepted. We had a splendid morning and Jean told me of a run I could take along the long "U" of the river Lot; thus on a crisp sunny Saturday afternoon I set out on an eleven-kilometer jog that carried me all the way around Marot's lovely little city and back again, and as I approached the end I ran up and onto the Pont Valentré, a tall and stately bridge of stone that already was old in Marot's heyday, and as I padded, all alone, across that jewel of Quercy, I surprised myself by calling out all sorts of birthday wishes to my poet friend... It was daft but it was grand, and I wouldn't have had it any other way.

After writing a few postcards and inking the master copy for page *xxiv,* I went out again, bought some wine, got a haircut, and then as darkness fell, went to the home of the senior Masbous, parents of Jean, who had so kindly invited me, along with the Johns, to dinner. There I learned that for this special Marot year, a local artist named Christian Verdun had taken the Louvre portrait of Marot as his theme and off of it had spun *five hundred variations* — scads of scores of diverse portraits of Clément Marot. Now there, if ever, was a spirit kindred to mine! The senior Masbous had purchased three of Verdun's variations, but as they were on the walls of their summer house, I didn't get to see them.

Though I couldn't help but feel most wistful and alone, there was still an aura of magic about Cahors that rare day — a day forever etched in the grooves of my memory.

Chapter 1: The Life in Rhymes of Clément Marot

Page 1   *Precisely one-half a millenium ago...*   Most of the biographical information in this chapter comes from Marot/Giraud (73), with a little help from Marot/Defaux (90).

Page 4   *The site of the grave of the poet I praise...*   My friend Maurizio Codogno, a Torino resident, made a special excursion to the church to try to find Marot's grave, but found nothing. After many inquiries, he finally discovered that the grave, along with several others in the same area, had been destroyed decades ago. Though sad in a way, this fact makes Frank Holmes' lyrical painting on the front cover seem all the more meaningful.

Page 4   *Thus he garnered nice blurbs from the likes of Boileau...*   The Boileau quote is in fact printed, blurb-like, on the back of my edition of Marot/Giraud (73).

Page 4   *Chez Clément might have wound up...*   Perhaps five hours after I left New York's bright morning, I was taking a cool evening stroll with Emily Eels down the rue Clément Marot, right by the Champs-Élysées, in one of Paris' most exclusive and elegant *quartiers.* Just off the rue Marot we spotted a restaurant named — yes, *Chez Clément* — so we had to eat there. It wasn't bad, but certainly merited no stars. However, this restaurant and the one that Clément Marot *would* have been, had he in fact been born a restaurant and not a human being, are of course two quite different things and ought never to be conflated.

Poems I: Original and Literal

Page 1b   *A une Damoyselle malade...*   French capitalization obeys different rules from ours. In particular, book titles, song titles, and so forth usually have just one or two capitalized words. Though the convention is by no means clear-cut, I have tried to respect it in this book. On occasion, however, I have overridden it for the sake of consistency with English. The same convention, incidentally, applies to Italian and many other languages. Also, as a glance at the poem will show, French punctuation differs from ours, in that colons, semicolons, question marks, and exclamation points are not set flush up against the word they follow, but instead require a breathing space in front of them. Once again, I have generally respected the French convention in this book.

Chapter 2: For the Love of a Poem from Days Long, Long Gone

Page 10   *I had given one once before, in 1982...*   "The Tumult of Inner Voices", reprinted as Chapter 33 in my book *Metamagical Themas.*

Page 11   *Gene finally had his book...*   My little *Rhapsody on a Theme by Clément Marot* was printed in 1996 in a very limited edition; however, if and when that printing is gone, it may be reprinted if there is sufficient demand. (The same goes for my 1982 Tanner

Lecture, mentioned in the note just above.) Inquiries should be sent to the Grace A. Tanner Center on Human Values at Southern Utah University, Cedar City, Utah 84720.

Page 14   *The beauty of Ronald Storrs' anthology...*   I suspect that there must be numerous anthologies made in a similar way out of many diverse translations of a single poem. A couple that I know about are described briefly in the notes to Chapter 17. Here I would just add that I once read a charming newspaper article about an anthology put together and published by a devoted daughter as a surprise present in honor of her father's sixtieth birthday, in which a short poem he had written was rendered by friends and colleagues in sixty different languages, and in marvelously different styles.

Chapter 3: How Jolly the Lot of an Oligoglot

Page 17   *I also, in high school...*   I owe this rhyme to Oliver Elton (see Chapter 8).

Page 33   *Stamattina, mi sono alzato...*   This beautiful, sad song is available, in both the *mondine* and *partigiani* versions, together with a whole program of Italian folk songs, on the compact disc "Bella ciao: Il nuovo canzoniere italiano", put out by Bravo Records, a subsidiary of Alabianca Group, via Mazzoni 34/36, I-41100 Modena, Italy.

Page 45   *In a magazine article...*   The research I describe in this section was conducted some two decades ago by Carter Collins at the Smith-Kettlewell Institute of Visual Sciences in San Francisco. It was called Tactile Sensory Replacement, or "TSR" for short, and my source was Hechinger (81). I regret I have never seen a follow-up on it.

Page 46   *the worldwide Cube mania...*   See Chapter 15 of my book *Metamagical Themas* for an extensive pictorial survey of Cube variants.

Page 48   *Three Polish Vignettes*   These episodes and several others from my 1975 trip are described in "Poland: A Mythical Quest" — a nostalgic reminiscence, never published in full, that I wrote up a few years after my trip to Poland.

Page 50   *the English translations by Michael Kandel...*   See Liro (87) for a careful analysis of Kandel's virtuosity, including comments on the short story I describe here.

Page 61   *a splash of extremely warm reviews...*   The reception in France really was wonderful, and I must say, it still is a source of pride to think that a full page of the great newspaper *Le Monde* (12–13 janvier, 1986) was once devoted to the French–Henry *GEB*.

Page 61   *an elegant analogy-making computer program...*   Bob's elegant work on the Tabletop computer program is fully reported in French (95).

Page 62   *one of the most amazing...*   Unfortunately out of print, the *Codex Seraphinianus* is a monument to human ingenuity. It is a huge encyclopedia of a fictional and fantastic universe, lavishly illustrated, and with text in a beautiful, swirly, bizarre, and — most importantly — *invented* script. Whether all those ornate "squiggles and squoggles", as philosopher John Searle would call them, actually say something (and hence could be translated) is an open question.

Chapter 4: The Romantic Vision of Thought as Pattern

Page 64   *unique-by-being-most-typical...*   Many years later I re-encountered this droll idea, couched a little differently, in Martin Gardner's column in *Scientific American,* where it was called "Ransom's IQ test" in honor of Tom Ransom (see Chapter 16 of Gardner 88).

Page 67   *The scientific and philosophical roots...*   There are by now a slew of books on artificial intelligence, most of which I am entirely unfamiliar with. Three older books that I do know, and which, because of their unabashed, though at times slightly naïve, romanticism on the subject, I would recommend wholeheartedly to an AI outsider, are Jackson (75), Boden (77), and McCorduck (79).

Notes   ◆ ◆ ◆ 575

Page 69   *Can you do better?*   My solution to the puzzle simply flips the classic title "L'homme machine" around backwards to make "La machine homme" — translatable more or less as "The Machine That Is Human". The nicest thing about it is the way it echoes and honors La Mettrie, 250 years after his scandalous insights.

Page 70   *this excerpt from a letter...*   See p. *xxiii* of Morrison & Morrison (61).

Page 72   *As for Turing...*   For the definitive chronicling of Alan Mathison Turing's sad life and stellar achievements, see Hodges (83).

Page 73   *Here is a small sampling...*   Taken from pp. 84–85 of Epstein (92).

Page 74   *This hilarious dialogue...*   Taken from Markoff (93).

Page 76   *understood the main lines of Gödel's proof...*   Thanks to Nagel & Newman (58).

Page 77   *an experimental symbolic-logic course...*   This was based on Suppes (57), a book that helped kindle my love for logic. Another beautiful and romantic book on this subject, one that came along many years later, is DeLong (70).

Page 79   *an article in <u>Scientific American</u>...*   This was Yngve (62).

Page 82   *Bar-Hillel despaired...*   See Bar-Hillel (60).

Page 82   *When I look at an article in Russian...*   Weaver wrote this in a letter to Norbert Wiener, suggesting an analogy between translation and the decipherment of codes. Some of their correspondence, together with rich speculation, is found in Weaver (55).

Page 82   *the most complex type of event yet produced...*   Taken from p. 48 of Steiner (75).

Page 83   *Heinz Pagels reports that...*   Details to be found on pp. 93–94 of Pagels (88).

Page 85   *Two Bongard problems.*   These are taken from Hofstadter (77).

Page 88   *told to me by my friend Bernie Greenberg...*   Personal communication, 1996.

Page 90   *a little limerick...*   My friend Michael Goldhaber once told me of a limerick about a fictitious book called "The Meaning of the Meaning of Meaning", but I never saw it, and instead made up my own. Perhaps the original was superior.

Page 90   *I studied Schank's work with interest...*   See Schank & Colby (73) for early work, and Schank (82) and Riesbeck & Schank (89) for more recent work.

Page 92   *I recently read a paper by a trio...*   This is Ram, Moorman, & Santamaria (96).

Page 92   *Those were the shining days of the world...*   One paragraph from Bloch (63).

Page 96   *what is so terribly wrong in his scenario...*   For more immunizations against Searle's ideas, see Searle (80) and Hofstadter & Dennett (81).

Page 99   *a curious and spurious distinction...*   See p. 417 of Searle (80) or p. 353 of Hofstadter & Dennett (81).

Page 100   *As he puts it, computers are made of...*   On p. 423 of Searle (80) and p. 369 of Hofstadter & Dennett (81), one finds the following: "The Chinese story understanding program can be programmed into a sequence of water pipes, a set of wind machines, or a monolingual English speaker, none of which thereby acquires an understanding of Chinese. Stones, toilet paper, wind, and water pipes are the wrong kind of stuff to have intentionality in the first place — only something that has the same causal powers as brains can have intentionality...."

Page 101   *I feel lucky...*   For my contributions so far, see Hofstadter & FARG (95).

Poems IV: Oklahoman

Page 14a   *At the time, I had studied...*   I took first-year Chinese under the late Professor Richard Kao at Stanford in 1975–76, and in 1980–81 retook it under Kao and Christina

Yao. There ensued a hiatus of several years, after which I resumed my studies under Yao at San Francisco State in 1989. This inspired me to embark on an intense conversation program with Mo Dawei, Yan Yong, and Liu Haoming as my partners over roughly a two-year period. At my peak, I was able to have long conversations on many topics, although often resorting momentarily to English when my vocabulary had holes in it (*i.e.,* all the time). It was a marvelous feeling, and I vividly recall one strange occurrence while I was with Liu in Mother Bear's pizza place in Bloomington. I overheard some Italian coming from a nearby booth and, with my love for that language, I couldn't resist going over and saying a few words to the two women, who both happened to be American students of opera, practicing their Italian together. I started out with *Buongiorno* and then tried to go on, but for several seconds I found my Italian totally blocked by Chinese; I couldn't get a word out. Luckily, the fog then dispersed and Italian rushed back in, in full force. It was an amazingly disorienting feeling (no pun intended).

Despite all my braggadoccio here, the fact remains that after some five years of hard work, my Chinese was still far below my Italian or even my German, which I had studied for considerably less time. This terribly discouraging fact was a confirmation in spades of something I once heard a Chinese-American woman say on the radio about her frustrations in tackling the language of her forebears: "Learning Chinese is a five-year lesson in humility." One should by no means take her remark as implying that after five years of hard work, you know Chinese well. Instead, as David Moser puts it at the end of his brilliant article (Moser 91), "the phrase means that after five years your Chinese will *still* be abysmal, but at least you will have thoroughly learned humility". Amen.

Page 14a   *The flavor of this difficult improvisatory art...*   Moser (89) gives a lucid and most entertaining presentation.

Chapter 5: Sparking and Sparkling, Thanks to Constraints

Page 103   *Beware the Translation Police...*   I was under the naïve impression that I was the unique coiner of this phrase, but when I recently purchased my friend Willis Barnstone's book *The Poetics of Translation,* I found on its p. 267 the following amusing comments:

> ...Give the art [of translation] a name like paraphrase, imitation, or verse transfer, and the translation police will not arrest you. A poet translator survives as a GOOD confessed thief. The best poet translators — the "original" authors of the Bible, Homer, Chaucer, Shakespeare, and Saint John of the Cross — wear masks and have not been caught.

Page 105   *here is Searle's original paragraph...*   See pp. 355–356 of Hofstadter & Dennett (81) or pp. 417–418 of Searle (80).

Page 107   *This type of literary game...*   My introduction to lipograms was Bombaugh (61), a source full of many linguistic *divertissements.* See also Battus (84) and Eckler (96).

Page 109   *the tragically short-lived French writer...*   See Chapters 6 and 7 of Gardner (89).

Page 114   *Stefano Bartezzaghi in his notes...*   Found on pp. 227–228 of Varaldo (93).

Page 119   *MT takes for granted...* See the articles by Hutchins (95) and Bennett (95).

Page 121   *one can marshal...*   I heard this point made brilliantly by Martin Kay in a lecture in Bolzano in 1993. He distributed a set of notes at the time, entitled simply "Machine Translation", but unfortunately, I believe they have never been published.

Page 123   *Sembra che Perec abbia confidato...* See p. 226 of Varaldo (93).

Page 128   *I have no idea...*   Actually, I now recall one factor that contributed: the conference at which I had been invited to speak — the 1993 national meeting of the Association for Computing Machinery — was provocatively called "IF", and this title set my head going round and round. Letter-string analogy puzzles similar to those that are discussed on pp. 128–129 have been studied and modeled extensively in my research

Notes

group, and our explorations are reported in Mitchell (93) and in Hofstadter & FARG (95), particularly Chapters 5 and 6.

Page 134   *use exactly the same set of letters...*   The February 1997 issue of *Harper's Magazine* has a letter to the editor in which the very-long-anagram game is played with astonishing virtuosity by Francis Heaney and Guy Jacobson. A similar game, but on the word-level rather than the letter-level, is discussed in Chapter 6 of Gardner (89) and in Eckler (96).

Page 135   *Here is how Lehrer...*   In giving permission to cite his lyrics, Lehrer sent me a very gracious letter with several interesting footnotes. Firstly, he said he got the idea of rhyming as a creativity enhancer from Stanisław Ulam, and pointed out a paragraph in Ulam (76) that says that rhyming "...forces novel associations and almost guarantees deviations from routine chains or trains of thought. It becomes paradoxically a sort of automatic mechanism of originality." Lehrer also wrote that the "orange" challenge grew out of a clever solution that Stephen Sondheim once came up with to the challenge of rhyming with "silver" (a challenge hereby passed on to my readers). A friend of Lehrer's, inspired by Sondheim's find, posed the analogous challenge of rhyming with "orange", and Lehrer obliged. Finally, concerning the mysterious Akmolinsk and Iliysk, Lehrer told me he had discovered them in around 1948 in an atlas, while hunting for rhyming Soviet cities. He added, "I believe that Akmolinsk is now known as Tselinograd and Iliysk as Kapchagay. They are both in Kazakhstan."

Page 138   *I have seen it quoted...*   In a footnote on p. 12 of Morgenstern/Knight (63).

Poems V: Sue Suite

Page 18a   *as did Victor Hugo...*   Hugo's stirring poem *Les Djinns* is found in many anthologies, including Hugo (64). It even inspired a piece of music by César Franck.

Chapter 6: The Subtle Art of Transculturation

Page 143   *a sentence that reads the same...*   Several excellent collections of palindromes are Bergerson (73), Bombaugh (61), Battus (84), and Eckler (96).

Page 146   *The key to everything...*   The Crab Canon's evolution is explained in Chapter 19 of Hofstadter (79).

Page 146   *DNA segment in which the message...*   Crab-canonical stretches of DNA are the loci that many so-called restriction enzymes seek, in order first to cleave onto the DNA, and then, having cloven, to cleave it there. For details, see any treatment of molecular biology — elementary (*e.g.,* Hofstadter 79) or advanced (*e.g.,* Berg & Singer 91).

Page 147   *And, Bob added, that is just...*   For details of the French version of the Crab Canon, see French (85) and (88), French & Henry (88), Henry (88), and Hofstadter (87; 97). French & Henry (88) in particular contains both the English original and the final French translation in full. Hofstadter (97) gives a long discussion of the translation process of another *GEB* dialogue (Contracrostipunctus) into several languages. I also wrote prefaces to the French, Spanish, and Chinese versions of *GEB*, in each of which I talk about a spectrum of the translation issues that arose in that particular language.

Page 150   *Here is a bit of the version I read...*   This is the very ending of the novel.

Page 154   *The classic translation...*   I thank Henry Remak for helping me track down material on this topic and several others concerning German literature.

Page 154   *Steiner summarizes Gundolf's thesis...*   From p. 382 of Steiner (75).

Page 155   *Janet Maslin wrote...*   See Maslin (96).

Page 159   *Regarde-moi, mon cher, et dis...*   On p. 80 of Rostand (30).

Page 161   *The task was frustrating because...*   On p. *xxvi* of Zhang & Sang (87).

Page 162   *Just look at our mill...*   On pp. 138–139 of Zhang & Sang (87).

Page 168   *No one will be surprised...*   Many fascinating issues that arose in the act of trying to translate *GEB* into Chinese are recounted in vivid detail in Moser (91).

Chapter 7: The Nimble Medium-Hopping of Evanescent Essences

Page 173   *a Penrose-tile-based Polish board...*   See Chapters 1 and 2 of Gardner (89).

Page 174   *Suppose you screeve?...*   I first encountered this mystifying but irresistible poem while browsing through my mother's copy of Van Doren (28).

Page 175   *what the game of chesh might be like...*   Chess reincarnated on hexagonal and other lattices is discussed in Chapter 24 of my book *Metamagical Themas*. That chapter also attempts to articulate some of the innumerable deep connections between creative analogy-making and creative translation.

Page 178   *sounds almost like a trucking company...*   Willis Barnstone, as he has often done, anticipated me in drawing a link between trucking companies and translation. In *The Poetics of Translation* there is a section on the "Parable of the Greek Moving Van", which begins with the observation that on the side of any Greek moving van is found the word μεταφορά (phonetically *metafora* and semantically "transportation"), and ends with this remarkable soliloquy:

> To come to Greece and find that even the moving vans run around under the sun and smog of greater Athens with advertisements for transportation, for metaphor, and ultimately with signs for TRANSLATION should convince us that every motor truck hauling goods from one place to another, every perceived *metamorphosis* of a word or phrase within or between languages, every decipherment and interpretation of a text, every role by each actor in the cast, every adaptation of a script by a director of opera, film, theater, ballet, pantomime, indeed every perception of movement and change, in the street or on our tongues, on the page or in our ears, leads us directly to the art and activity of translation.

Page 184   *author of the famous poem "Invictus"...*   This famous poem, along with a little biographical information about Henley, can be found in Gardner (92).

Page 194   *the very fringes of legibility...*   I have described my own personal explorations at the fringes of legibility in Chapter 13 of *Metamagical Themas* and in Chapter 10 of *Fluid Concepts and Creative Analogies*. The former deals also with the blurry boundary between book faces and display faces.

Page 194   *A letter in a playful style certainly would not fit...*   The idea of splicing two wildly different styles together to make a new pseudo-style is discussed briefly in Chapter 10 of *Fluid Concepts and Creative Analogies*. That essay, co-written with Gary McGraw, also goes into some detail on the curious idea of alphabetic styles that are beautiful despite being composed of letters every one of which is indubitably ugly when taken on its own.

Page 196   *I was recently given a cassette...*   I thank my Comparative Literature colleague Harry Geduld for giving me this tape, which includes "Der Schlitten mit den Schellen", "Du, Du, liegst mir im Herzen", and others sung by Dietrich in her inimitable manner.

Page 199   *the notion of feminine rhyme...*   Two invaluable sources on the mechanics and technicalities of poetry that helped me out are Drury (95) and Preminger (65). While the latter is far more scholarly and complete, the former is far more enjoyable to read, as it includes scores of sparkling and touching poems. Any poetry lover should own Drury's unpretentious but richly informative book.

Page 200   *Tom Lehrer's song "The Elements"...*   While on the subject of chemico-poetic literature, I must mention an astonishing book loaned to me by my friend Enrico Laeng, entitled *Chimica in versi: Rime distillate* ("Chemistry in Verses: Distilled Rhymes"), published in 1939 by the Italian chemist Alberto Cavaliere, who in it describes himself as *un poeta errante della chimica* ("a wandering poet of chemistry"). In two parts ("Chimica inorganica" and "Chimica organica", naturally!), amounting to some 200 pages, the author runs through roughly two years of university-level chemistry, mostly in impeccably rhyming hexasyllabic quatrains, but occasionally resorting to other forms, such as Dantean *terza rima* (see Chapter 17 of this book), as in the poem called "Stereoisomeria", which is a genial salute to Dante and which — almost inevitably — winds up on the word *stelle*, the word with which Dante himself ended all three books of *La Divina Commedia*.

Page 202   *Cloaked in "You Guys"...*   For reflections and reports of some psychological experiments on this bizarre and troubling word and related words in other languages, see Hofstadter (93), Bodine (96), and van Rossum & Hofstadter (96).

Page 204   *There are some superb books...*   Miller and Swift's calmly written but devastating little classic *Words and Women* is one of the most fascinating and disturbing books I have ever read. Before we were married, Carol also read it but found it so powerful that she could digest only a chapter at a time before getting too churned up to go on. It was while reading that book that I wrote my rather zany sexism-turned-into-racism fantasy "A Person Paper on Purity in Language", which is found in *Metamagical Themas* as well as Cameron (90). Some years after writing it, I constructed a translation of the "Person Paper" into "normal" (*i.e.*, sexist) English (Hofstadter 91). Aside from this and the "you guys" paper, I have written a few other articles on sexism in language and cognition, one of which is Chapter 7 in *Metamagical Themas*. Two others are Hofstadter (86) and (89). To my regret, my most in-depth exploration of these ideas is incomplete, sitting inside a languishing article on error-making by David Moser and myself (Moser & Hofstadter 01). In the meantime, David has explored these ideas in the context of Chinese and written on the topic (*e.g.*, Moser 97).

Page 207   *The child who has not conceived of...*   From p. 132–133 of Fraiberg (59).

Page 214   *with alacrity, celerity, assiduity, vim, vigor...*   This is a phrase I learned as a boy from my father's lifelong friend Bob Herman, a prolific and profound physicist who, incidentally, predicted, in several articles written with Ralph Alpher, the now-famous 3° cosmic background radiation some fifteen years before it was fortuitously discovered. Though the scientists who were lucky enough to observe the radiation were awarded a Nobel Prize for doing so, it took many more years for Alpher and Herman's prediction to be appropriately recognized — an interesting lesson about credit that relates closely to ideas in Chapter 13 (see Weinberg 77). In any case, Bob used to put both me and my Dad in absolute stitches by reciting, with a terrific put-on Yiddish accent, the following riddle he had memorized when *he* was a boy:

> A tramp in the woods happened upon a hornets' nest. When they stung him with alacrity, celerity, assiduity, vim, vigor, vitality, savoir-faire, and undue velocity, "Oh!", he mused, counting his bumps, "If I had as many bumps on the left side of my right adenoid as six and three-quarters times seven-eighths of those between the heel of Achilles and the circumference of Adam's apple, how long would it take a boy rolling a hoop up a moving stairway going down to count the splinters on a boardwalk if a horse had six legs?"

Maybe "you had to be there", as they say, but for me this is one of the great, glowing memories of my youth, and I wanted to pass it along to those few readers whose funny bone it might strike.

Page 216   *This type of analysis points the way...*   Some initial stabs at the cognitive mechanisms underlying slippage humor were written up in Hofstadter *et al.* (89).

Page 229   *There are complications...*   See pp. 20–22 of Queneau/Kousbroek (78).

Page 231   *The riddle of Queneau's urtext...*   See p. 18 of Queneau/Kousbroek (78).

Page 231   *the blurry edges of an implicit category...*   In Chapter 24 of *Metamagical Themas* and in Chapter 1 of *Fluid Concepts and Creative Analogies,* I give examples of situational categories whose nameless essence the human mind perceives on the fly and generalizes with remarkable fluency and yet at a wholly unconscious level. A fascination with this phenomenon is hardly unique to me; given that the elusive nature of mental categories lies right at the center of cognitive science, such issues are discussed in countless books and articles, including Schank (82), Lakoff (87), Zerubavel (91), and Aitchison (94).

Chapter 8: A Novel in Verse

Page 233   *that most Russian of Russian poets...*   I am not speaking of Pushkin's genetic makeup, for indeed, by blood he was one-eighth African, and proud of this heritage from his mother's side (see Edmonds 94, a superb Pushkin biography, and stanza I.50 of *Eugene Onegin,* where Pushkin [via Falen] writes "my Africa's warm sky"); I mean merely that Pushkin is generally hailed by Russians as their greatest poetic voice.

Page 234   *my first publication...*   Unfortunately, I no longer own a copy of the relevant issue of *The New Yorker,* nor do I know its date, and hence I cannot provide a citation.

Page 238   *Le Tombeau de Couperin...*   This title — literally, "The Tomb of Couperin" — is a metaphor, meaning something more like "an offering to Couperin". In other words, it is a personal bow by Ravel to Couperin. There have been other musical pieces with titles using the same template, in which one composer pays tribute to another, but I think Ravel's stands alone in its shimmering, opalescent poeticism. Who ever could have imagined a *fugue* in the impressionistic style? And yet there it is: one of the most tender, lilting fugues ever written, and wonderfully contrapuntal. I cannot imagine how Bach would have reacted had he somehow been able to hear it. But this is not to distract attention from the other five movements, for they are equally beautiful, if not more so. Truly, this piece by Ravel is one of the great musical gems of the twentieth century.

Page 241   *a hidden three-dimensional object...*   The exercise of object reconstruction from shadows excited me greatly when I was in eighth grade, and many years later led me to invent what I called "trip-lets": wooden blocks carved in such a way that their three orthogonal shadows form three letters of the alphabet. Two such trip-lets, each with a different rendering of the "G–E–B" trio of letters, were made and photographed by me for the cover of *Gödel, Escher, Bach.* I also made several for friends, using their initials.

Page 242   *two further English-language translations...*   Actually, there was one more that I missed: that by Babette Deutsch. Later I came across a bit of it (see Chapter 9) — and then even later, all of it.

Page 246   *Elton's discovery of the nifty phrase...*   In response to a short article I wrote for *The New York Times Book Review* (Hofstadter 96) about these four translations of *Eugene Onegin,* Cornelius Bull pointed out (Bull 97) that Byron in his poem "Beppo", published some 119 years before Elton's translation was published, found the same rhyme:

> *I love the language, that soft bastard Latin,*
> *   Which melts like kisses from a female mouth,*
> *And sounds as if it should be written on satin,*
> *   With syllables which breathe of the sweet South,*
> *And gentle liquids gliding all so pat in*
> *   That not a single accent seems uncouth,*
> *Like our harsh northern whistling, grunting guttural,*
> *   Which we're obliged to hiss, and spit, and sputter all.*

I have but one response to Mr. Bull (and it's hardly an original thought): There's nothing new under the sun.

Page 253　*when the entirety of _Eugene Onegin_ is translated...*　One charming and curious aspect of Tatyana's letter in Pushkin's "original" Russian is that, like Marot's "Ma Mignonne", it starts out using the formal "you" and halfway through switches over to the informal "you". I put "original" in quote marks, and perhaps I should even have put "Pushkin's" in quotes as well, were one to believe the author ("the author"?), since he claims he is merely *translating* it from the French, and that its genuine author is Tatyana. In any case, in Maurice Colin's lovely French *Oniéguine,* there is indeed a sudden passage from *vous* to *tu* midway through, and this change of tone has a truly dramatic effect. I wonder if it touched Onegin himself, when first he read it, as strongly as it touches me?

Page 257　*Vikram Vainblood...*　Vainblood penned a preface to Validbook's poem *Zwz.*

Page 259　*Vivian Darkbloom...*　Darkbloom knocked off notes to Nabokov's novel *Ada.*

Chapter 9: A Vile Non-verse

Page 257　*My pleasures are the most intense...*　See p. 3 of Nabokov (90).

Page 257　*It is, let me repeat...*　Taken from p. 16 of Pushkin/Nabokov (90), Vol. I.

Page 258　*a crib, a pony, honest and clumsy...*　See p. 7 of Nabokov (90).

Page 258　*Can a rhymed poem...*　Taken from pp. *ix–x* of Pushkin/Nabokov (90), Vol. II.

Page 260　*Jorge Luis Borges' character Funes the Memorious...*　See the short story by that name in Borges (62).

Page 262　*The four "English", "metrical" "translations" mentioned in my notes...*　On pp. 3–4 of Pushkin/Nabokov (90), Vol. II.

Page 264　*My _Eugene Onegin_ falls short of the ideal crib...*　Pp. 242–243 of Nabokov (90).

Page 264　*What is translation? On a platter...*　On p. 9 of Pushkin/Nabokov (90), Vol. I.

Page 265　*I happen to have one and only one...*　When I wrote it, this was a true sentence; since then, however, that defect has been rectified, thanks to Kelly Holt of Case Western Reserve University, who sent me a beautiful hardbound copy of Deutsch's translation, which had once belonged to our mutual friend Lillian Greenberg.

Page 267　*Nabokov attacked Arndt's work...*　See pp. 231–240 of Nabokov (90).

Page 268　*This "revised" version...*　See p. 240 of Nabokov (90).

Page 268　*Passive readers will derive...*　See pp. 233–234 of Nabokov (90).

Page 269　*Inadequate knowledge of Russian...*　See p. 237 of Nabokov (90).

Page 269　*the defense of Arndt's translation...*　Wilson (65).

Page 269　*A patient confidant of his...*　See p. 248 of Nabokov (90).

Page 270　*One example of returned fire...*　From p. *xxviii* of Arndt (93).

Page 270　*Nabokov's recent two-volume commentary...*　From pp. *xlv–xlvi* of Arndt (93).

Page 270　*The central problem of verse translation...*　From pp. *xlvi–xlviii* of Arndt (93).

Page 271　*the spark and sparkle of creative translation...*　This phrase was in fact my original subtitle for *Le Ton beau de Marot.* It was a close decision, and one made very late in the game, to pick the other one.

Page 271　*language-independent gobs...*　The idea of a language-neutral medium for containing "pure meaning" has been taken up with great enthusiasm by the machine-translation community, where it is known as an "interlingua". This is closely related to Roger Schank's conceptual dependency notation and his notion of scripts, which were touched on in Chapter 4. Of course it makes sense to try to get "below" the level of language — in fact, cognitive science would be hopeless if it stayed at that level alone —

but on the other hand, Arndt's Whorfian point about the influence of language on thought, especially highly verbal thought such as poetry, cannot be denied. Speech errors (Aitchison 94; Dell & Reich 80; Fromkin 80; Hofstadter & Moser 89) provide much evidence that one's thoughts are profoundly influenced by what is available in one's lexicon. Sexist language is another example (see Miller & Swift 77, or Hofstadter 93). There are hundreds of other explorations of these topics, but I limit myself to mentioning Moser (94) and (97), where errors in Chinese reveal hidden spinning gears.

Page 272   *I too have chosen...*   See p. 7 of Pushkin/Falen (90).

Page 273   *Pushkin's composition is first of all...*   Pp. 7–8 of Pushkin/Nabokov (90), Vol. I.

Page 277   *Mr. Arndt's most bizarre observation...*   See p. 240 of Nabokov (90).

Page 278   *Reflected words can only shiver...*   Pp. 9–10 of Pushkin/Nabokov (90), Vol. I.

Chapter 10: On Words and their Magical Halos

Page 279   *Jorge Luis Borges, Author of Pierre Menard...*   See the short story entitled "Pierre Menard, Author of Don Quixote" (translated by Anthony Bonner) in Borges (62). One of Menard's accomplishments — a full inventory of which is provided in the story — is that of translating Paul Valéry's poem "Le cimetière marin" (which is in pentameter) into alexandrines (which are hexameter). This is reminiscent of some of the syllable-count transformations that occur in the present book.

Page 283   *Penguin Books, without in any way...*   Perhaps it's not Penguin's fault; the original British version was published by Hamish Hamilton in 1951.

Page 285   *Have you seen those new...*   From a "Fresh Air" piece on National Public Radio.

Page 285   *but hey, guys, when you strip away...*   I hope readers will not write to me, accusing me of violating my own rule (Chapter 7) of not using "[you] guys" as a generic. The usage here (echoed on p. 286) is in quotes, signifying an invented persona and not my genuine authorial voice. (I just looked up the word "authorial", by the way, and it doesn't exist. But I also saw something interesting under "authoress": "A female author. Sometimes considered disparaging." Go put that in your pope and smike it, guys.)

Page 287   *There are innumerable near-identities...*   In Steiner (75), p. 172.

Page 289   *German's Gemütlichkeit, Zeitgeist ...*   For anyone who doesn't know them, these ten foreign-language untranslatables have the following meanings: "cosiness"; "tenor of the times"; "covert glee"; "tact"; "cool"; "ineffable something"; "grief"; "vulgarity"; "son"; and "filial piety". No sweat! By contrast, it's a genuine shame that none of the four English words listed right after them can be properly rendered in any foreign language on earth. English is just so much fancier and trickier than its would-be rivals, huh?

Page 289   *(hee hee) comings...*   See p. 404 for related material.

Page 291   *Eppur si traduce...*   Galileo Galilei, on being imprisoned at 69 in 1633 for his heretical belief that the earth was not stationary, recanted but then is reputed to have muttered, *sotto voce*, "And yet it *does* move, damn it all..." (*Eppur si muove*). Some (*e.g.*, Beckmann 71) claim this was sputtered by Giordano Bruno, not Galileo, as his last gasp while being burned at the stake in 1600 by the Holy See for the same belief. So tragic.

Page 293   *How Do You Say "Jazzercise"...*   This is a question David Moser once posed.

Page 294   *gauging one's true mastery...*   A similar test of one's fraction of native-level mastery is provided by the list on p. 19.

Page 294   *There are no lambs...*   Taken from Barnstone (93), p. 41.

Page 295   *Compounds: Transparent, Translucent, Opaque...*   The transparency–opacity spectrum is examined in considerable detail in Hofstadter (95).

Notes

Page 297   *A handful of other examples…*   David Moser recently sent me a hand full of further curious compounds in Chinese. He starts with the word for "feces" — *shǐ* — and points out that "earwax" is *ěrshǐ* ("ear-feces"), and that the name for the micro-boulders that form in the corner of one's eyes while one sleeps ("eyedust"? "sleepers"?) is *yǎnshǐ* ("eye-feces"). He adds: "Of course, this is just the way of saying it; no one finds these words disgusting or strange." For some reason, this reminds me of "Thomas Crapper, Plumber to H. R. H. the Queen", an establishment that I used to walk by nearly every day on The Kings Road in Chelsea. I can't help but believe that even Mr. Smoketoomuch would have noticed the oddness of that name. But then I recall that here in Indiana, it's common to see signs for "Fried crappie" (some kind of fish), and my impression is that such signs evoke no smirks. So who knows? Two last examples from David are the name for a dish with small stir-fried pasta bits, which is *chǎogēda* ("fried pimples"), and *tǔdòuní*, meaning "potato-mud", which of course is the word for "mashed potatoes".

Page 299   *Poul Anderson's Eerie Etym-Splitting*   I have borrowed David Moser's phrase "splitting of the etym".

Page 301   *the "original article" that never had been…*   All of Anderson's piece and my modern-English retelling of it are found in Hofstadter (95).

Page 302   *that mightily wideknown but soft-spoken worldkenseeker…*   My favorite biography of Einstein is a rather short but very poetic one (Hoffmann 72) written by his colleague Banesh Hoffmann, with the collaboration of Einstein's faithful assistant Helen Dukas. Hoffmann also wrote a lucid exposition of relativity, both general and special, in its historical context, which I recommend highly (Hoffmann 83).

Page 302   *And it was old One Stone, too…*   It was Albert Einstein who first guessed and then demonstrated that gravity is a "fictitious force", similar in ways to centrifugal force. Such forces are called "fictitious" since it is possible to find a frame of reference in which they completely vanish. Though any such shift in what one considers to be stationary and what one considers to be in motion is only a mathematical transformation, not a physical one, it can open up truly novel perspectives. Fictitious forces have the very special property of being proportional to mass, which implies that they make all objects accelerate at precisely the same rate, no matter how massive they are. Now since gravity has this exact property, it occurred to Einstein to try recasting gravity as a fictitious force. Although this idea had in principle been thinkable for a century or more, no one before him had thought of it — and when he worked it out, he found that it led him to think of space as being *curved*, with the *degree* of curvature at any given spot being a function of how much mass was found nearby — namely, the more mass in the vicinity, the more curved would be space in that region. Actually, it turns out that not just *space* is curved, but rather, the four-dimensional continuum known as *spacetime*. It is, of course, humanly impossible to visualize spacetime as curved, and yet that is apparently the true nature of our universe. Indeed, none other than this counterintuitive curvature is responsible for things falling to the ground, for the moon staying in orbit — even for light's following a curved trajectory as it heads our way from distant stars. Some eighty years ago Einstein predicted such peculiar phenomena, and within just a decade astronomers had shown him to be right, thereby rendering Newton's laws obsolete — although under everyday circumstances they are so close to being correct that they can still be taken as valid.

Incidentally, I wrote the preceding paragraph (and am writing the present one) while operating under two simultaneous pressures: firstly, I am striving to utilize polysyllabic and/or Greco–Latin terminology wherever possible, and secondly, I am doing my best to reproduce the moderately droll flavor of the doubly-constrained pair of paragraphs of which this pair is a translation. I can therefore assert — with some cause, I hope — that I have here both had mine beer and drunk it from mine stein.

Page 43a   *unintentional tracks-covering...*   This idea, in a very different creative context, has been discussed at greater depth in Chapter 10 of Hofstadter & FARG (95).

Page 47a   *my fellow Hoosier, Cole Porter...*   Although born in Peru, Porter grew up in Indiana. To tell the truth, "although" is the wrong word here, for Peru (pronounced "*Pee*-roo") is in fact a town in Indiana, near Kokomo, north of Indianapolis.

Page 48a   *rival of Callas, long smoldering for Onassis' malice...*   I learned something of the Callas–Onassis complexities from David (94). According to that source (pp. 126–128), Onassis in many ways rejected his wife Jacqueline and became intimate with Maria Callas as he approached death. Incidentally, I might point out that in my acrostic poem, I exactly copy Marot's irregular AABBAAABCAABBAC rhyme scheme.

Page 49a   *why not let each line end in "end" itself?*   Years after writing this poem, I found in my correspondence with my friend Lee Sallows a long poem ("Since a Limerick's Last Word Depends") in which he had repeatedly exploited the end rhyme "end" (although in his poem it occurred only once every three lines). It is conceivable that there was some subliminal influence on my choice of "end" from a dim memory of Lee's poem.

Chapter 11: Halos, Analogies, Spaces, and Blends

Page 305   *A word being the name of a concept...*   The analogical extension of words and the nebulous "spherical" zones formed in semantic space by their underlying concepts are discussed, albeit using different terminology from mine, in many places, including Lakoff (87), Mitchell (93), Aitchison (94), and French (95). See also Chapter 24 of Hofstadter (85), as well as Chapter 1 and Preface 5 of Hofstadter & FARG (95).

Page 306   *we must seek a far higher abstraction...*   The abstraction known as "life" is now the object of a large field of study known as "A-life" (short for "artificial life"), and finds its definitive exposition in Langton (89) and Langton *et al.* (92).

Page 310   *Soon the whole clan gathered...*   From Forward (80), p. 56.

Page 311   *the way sensory modalities interface with...*   This is again closely tied to the notion of Tactile Sensory Replacement, described in Hechinger (81).

Page 312   *being Chinese feels much like being American...*   On the other hand, compare this with my remarks on p. 441. "Much like" is not the same as "identical to"! Just exactly how different things are on the outside of the inner "I" is what translation débâcles and debates are all about.

Page 313   *No one supposes that computer simulations...*   See p. 423 of Searle (80) or p. 370 of Hofstadter & Dennett (81).

Page 314   *Quick-Mover looked in awe...*   From Forward (80), p. 40.

Page 316   *Lem's ingenious and very dense story "Non Serviam"...*   This is reprinted, with a few pages of reflections, in Hofstadter & Dennett (81). The abstract idea of a synthetic entity able to build copies of itself out of raw materials found in its environment was first discussed by von Neumann (66), and became far easier to grasp after J. H. Conway had devised his "Game of Life" (see Gardner 83). A lyrical exploration of these subtle themes is found in Poundstone (85). See also Chapter 3 of *Metamagical Themas*.

Page 317   *in the last analysis, they are patterns...*   See Dennett (91) for a keen-edged discussion of when *pattern* transcends *stuff* in terms of its degree of reality.

Page 317   *Martians have intentionality...*   Found on p. 422 of Searle (80) and on p. 367 of Hofstadter & Dennett (81).

Page 318   *"It sure is tall," he remarked...*   From Forward (80), p. 59–60.

Notes

Page 320   *The great Michelangelo, for francophones...*   See, for example, Robert (74) or any subsequent edition. In fact, as far as I can tell, the entry for Michel-Ange is the longest one for any individual in this huge volume, outweighing Napoléon, Hugo, and all other names that loom large in francophone history. I take this opportunity to praise Le Petit Robert 2, *Dictionnaire universel des nom propres, alphabétique et analogique, illustré en couleurs,* to the skies. I fell in love with this book in 1975 and remain so twenty-two long years later. Along with my 1969-vintage American Heritage Dictionary, my old Roget's International Thesaurus, and my long-out-of-print Odyssey World Atlas, it has been my trusty companion throughout the arduous journey of this book. I must also salute the Collins–Robert French–English dictionary — by far the best ever compiled — and its counterparts in German and Italian, for they too have been stalwart companions.

Page 322   *one of the largest newspapers in the world, published in China...*   The dual label of a foreign-language newspaper can confuse even astute observers. Thus in the January 12, 1997 issue of *The New York Times,* Thomas L. Friedman, one of that institution's most insightful columnists, referred in one paragraph to "The People's Daily, China's official paper", and then, just three paragraphs later, referred to "the Communist Party newspaper Renmin Ribao", apparently unaware he was citing one and the same source.

Page 323   *In that movie, Clint Eastwood...*   From p. 18 of Fauconnier (85).

Page 324   *If you were a good painter...*   From p. 32 of Fauconnier (85).

Page 325   *what I started calling a _frame blend_...*   My usage of the word "frame" is taken from Goffman (74), a pioneering book about how people try to draw mental boundaries around situations, and how permeable such membranes are. Fauconnier (85) was also deeply influenced by Goffman. I have briefly touched on my notion of "frame blend" in Hofstadter & FARG (95), but unfortunately most of my writings on the subject remain buried in long but frustratingly unfinished manuscripts, such as Hofstadter (92) and Moser & Hofstadter (01).

Page 331   *They wallowed, struck at each other's...*   From Forward (80), p. 80.

Page 331   *Eros Is Eros Is Eros...*   I recently saw a similar pun in, as I recall, William Safire's column in *The New York Times Magazine*: "arroz is arroz is arroz". (There's room for more: after all, we still have "errors", "arrows", "Arosa", and so on...) I have no memory of the context. I find it curious and provocative that puns on "A rose is a rose is a rose" seem to spring to the tongue in today's *Zeitgeist* — that is, the tenor of the *Times.*

Page 332   *skip the following passage...*   From Forward (80), p. 159–160.

Page 332   *much of molecular biology...*   See Forward (80), p. 244.

Page 332   *incapable of dreaming up anything but the simplest...*   I wrote a set of musings (Hofstadter 94) on how people of all varieties and levels of mentality, as they grow older, repeatedly break out of stereotypes and tacit assumptions and constantly enlarge their horizons, yet despite it all remain parochially bounded in their imaginations.

Poems XI: Hall of Mirrors

Page 51a   *to the extent that "idea density" can be quantified...*   In fact, measures of the "idea density" in people's writing samples have been developed; moreover, writing with low idea density is purported to correlate strongly with a propensity to contract Alzheimer's disease. See Kolata (96) or Fackelmann (96).

Chapter 12: On the Conundrums of Cascading Translation

Page 337   *my English-language "X-ray"...*   Darn old Willis doesn't miss a beat; on p. 271 of Barnstone (93), he remarks, "A translation is an X-RAY, not a XEROX." Foiled again.

Page 339   *Which twin has the Tony?...*   God knows when that was an advertising slogan — but it once was, for a kind of hair lotion, as I recall.

Page 343   *For winter's rains and ruins are over...*   See pp. *xl–xli* of Arndt (93).

Page 344   *The versions are like turns in a spiral...*   See p. *xl* of Arndt (93).

Page 349   *a classic little book...*   This is Coxeter (61).

Page 349   *a very general projective theorem...*   This theorem (called "theorem 4·71") states: "The three pairs of opposite sides of a quadrangle meet any line (not through a vertex) in three pairs of an involution." Here's a little help in decoding: In projective geometry, "quadrangle" means a set of four points together with all six lines that they determine. A "quadrangular set" is the set of six points in which a seventh line intercepts the six lines of any quadrangle. And an "involution" is a function that is its own inverse.

Page 349   *presto! in the snap of a finger...*   Here's how the argument runs: "Let the altitudes [of triangle *CAB*] from *C* and *A* intersect in *H*. Then the quadrangle *CABH* determines on the line at infinity a quadrangular set of points, two of whose pairs belong to the absolute involution. Hence, by 4·71, the third pair likewise belongs to this involution, and *BH* must be the third altitude of the triangle." Although it may not seem so at first glance, this short proof is as sparkling as quartz crystals and Bach's harmonies, once you genuinely understand the definitions...

Poems XII: Gallic Twists

Page 55a   *Pablo Picasso in a cubist mood...*   I just invented off the top of my head the fantasy of Picasso making cubist interpretations of van Gogh paintings, but not long ago I somewhere got the impression that he really *did* do this. I surely wouldn't be surprised.

Page 56a   *Paf! et je riposte...*   This is found on pp. 149–150 of Rostand (30).

Page 57a   *a conference convened to remember...*   The proceedings of this conference have been published as Clark & Millican (96).

Chapter 13: On Shy Translators and Their Crafty, Silent Art

Page 354   *In a recent column...*   Baker's "Observer" column, August 13, 1996, entitled "Homer's First Yuppie".

Page 355   *To the editor...*   In the August, 15, 1996 edition of *The New York Times*.

Page 361   *It turns out that this song...*   This comes from the liner notes to the CD.

Page 364   *how great his lecture was...*   I have now made it a point, when I teach seminars on geometry, to require students to "perform" the proofs of theorems before their classmates, and they are judged on the lucidity and elegance with which they do so. They need not have invented the proof in question; the idea is to present it *beautifully.*

Page 369   *will launch reverberations up and down...*   A similar effect, but in the domain of typeface design, is described in Chapter 10 of Hofstadter & FARG (95).

Page 369   *an unprovable yet reliable intuitive sense...*   An attempt to impart such a sense to a computer in a very small domain is at the crux of my research group's work, and is described in several chapters of Hofstadter & FARG (95), particularly Chapters 2 and 5.

Page 371   *nun zur Zigarre selbst...*   This was a phrase that my family's close friend, the Swiss–American physicist Felix Bloch, used to intone at that climactic moment when — dinner, dessert, and liqueurs all having been consumed — he was about to crown the evening with a slow, relaxing cigar. My Dad was so taken with this delectation of Felix's that he, too, took up cigar- and pipe-smoking for a couple of years, after which I think the *Zigarre selbst* lost its charm. Still, it conjures up an Old World atmosphere for me.

Notes

Page 372   *reversal at various levels of structure is so central...*   A small contribution to the literature on the creative potential that lurks in perceptual and conceptual reversal is found in Chapter 5 of Hofstadter & FARG (95), and also in other chapters of that book.

Page 373   *Starting to squirm under this pressure...*   The idea of "squirming" when obstacles are encountered in the creative process is mirrored computationally in my research group's models by the raising of a so-called "computational temperature", described in Mitchell (93), French (95), and Hofstadter & FARG (95).

Page 373   *this complex constellation of co-present mental pressures...*   See Hofstadter & FARG (95) for a discussion of our manner of computationally modeling an arbitrary set of commingling mental pressures. There is, incidentally, a striking similarity between the conceptual breakthrough described on pp. 371–375 of this book and two conceptual breakthroughs discussed in Chapter 5 of Hofstadter & FARG (95). This lends a bit of support to the claims of generality of the mechanisms presented in the latter book.

Page 375   *unlikely-seeming possibilities might wind up getting explored...*   The image of an expanding sphere of ever remoter possibilities is presented in Hofstadter (88) and Mitchell (93).

Page 376   *rapid subconscious "sniffers of ... promise"...*   Once again, see the discussion of the "parallel terraced scan" in Hofstadter & FARG (95), particularly Chapters 2 and 5.

Page 377   *relative degree of strength or weakness...*   See Chapter 10 in Hofstadter & FARG (95) for a discussion of this type of self-assessment in the context of typeface design.

Page 377   *parlay a failure into a source of light...*   Mitchell (93) and Chapters 5 and 10 of Hofstadter & FARG (95) discuss the computational modeling of such an ability.

Page 380   *To me, fair friend, you never can be old...*   Shakespeare, sonnet CIV.

Page 380   *Shall I compare thee to a summer's day?...*   Shakespeare, sonnet XVIII. The lines about which *DRH* complains include these final three: "When in eternal lines to time thou growest; / So long as men can breathe, or eyes can see, / So long lives this, and this gives life to thee." The deathlessness of his lines is a recurrent claim in Shakespeare's sonnets, and apparently it piques *DRH* to read it over and over again. Moreover, the notion that Shakespeare's honorees will live forever in his verse rings hollow, since those people are little but placeholders; one gets hardly any sense of who or how they were.

Page 381   *a highly optimized heuristic search...*   The notion that the secret of building a full-fledged mind is just some sort of super-efficient search technique in the service of problem-solving (as in computer chess-playing, for example) has a long history in artificial intelligence, and chief among its champions are Herbert Simon and Allen Newell. In apparent contrast to *DRH*, my view of this approach to mind is pretty dim.

Page 382   *Sir Geoffrey Jefferson, F.R.S....*   All that I know of this early AI skeptic is this one amusing quote (part of his 1949 Lister Oration), which is found in Turing (50).

Page 387   *mechanisms underlying my taste are not accessible to me...*   This is a major theme in the second half of Hofstadter (79), as is exemplified by two different paraphrases of Descartes, one found on its p. 340 — "I think, therefore I sum" — and the other found on its p. 677: "I think; therefore I have no access to the level where I sum."

Chapter 14: On the Untranslatable

Page 391   *To have written this piece is to have married the piano...*   I recalled the quote pretty well but not exactly. Some months later, I finally found my old record of Scriabin études as performed by Morton Estrin and re-read the jacket commentary by music critic Louis Biancolli. To be precise, it went this way: "Those who have once heard this Étude will forever relive the thrill of its ecstatic upward sweep of phrase, its rhythmic slancio, its eddying harmonies. Whoever plays it feels momentarily like a god and looks like a madman. To have composed that Étude is to have married the piano."

I once went to a recital by Garrick Ohlsson in which he played this piece, and as he launched into it, I thought I heard a thousand mistakes, and was squirming in my seat in pity for what I took to be a horrendous memory lapse. But as the mistakes kept on coming and harmonizing with each other, I slowly realized, to my relief, that this had to be an alternate version. It was incredibly different from, but no less powerful than, the version I knew well. The strange fact that there are two pieces, both known by the same exact opus and number, brings to mind my wish that Scriabin's fellow Russian artist Pushkin had written two wildly different versions of *Eugene Onegin* and published them both under the same title. It's too late to get Pushkin to do this, but wouldn't it be nice to persuade Vikram Seth to rewrite *The Golden Gate* in an entirely different set of Onegin stanzas, yet still telling just the same story? Or perhaps he might write pseudo-Onegin stanzas, in which the role of masculine and feminine rhymes was swapped... I have no doubt whatsoever that Pierre Menard would applaud my suggestion.

Page 395   *preludes and fugues from his Opus 87...*   Shostakovich wrote this set as a homage to Bach's Well-Tempered Clavier on the occasion of the 200th anniversary of Bach's death, in 1950. I first heard parts of Opus 87 in 1965 or so, and was absolutely bowled over by their polyphonic lyricism. I came to think of these pieces, as I do of Ravel's "Tombeau de Couperin", as one of this century's greatest works for piano. My introduction to them was through Sviatoslav Richter — spectacular, but only six out of the twenty-four. Later I bought a record with Shostakovich himself playing a few more of them, but it was not nearly as wonderful. He just didn't have the technique. Years later I finally found a full set recorded by Tatiana Nikolaeva, and then another came out by Roger Woodward. Today one can buy a marvelous two-CD set recorded by Keith Jarrett.

Of these pieces, Carol's favorite was fugue 22 in G minor, deeply imbued with Russian melancholy. I thought of using that prelude and fugue as part of the music at her memorial service, but in the end selected a more uplifting pair: number 7 in A major, with its lilting, singsong prelude and its triad-based bell-like fugue.

Page 396   *Ne vsé li, rússkim yazïkóm...*   This is the ending of stanza III.27 from *Eugene Onegin*, transcribed, using Nabokov's conventions, into alien Roman symbols. Prosaically put (with thanks to Nabokov's pony — giddy-up!), it means the following: "Didn't all those linguistic klutzes cheerfully garble our Mother-Russian tongue? And wasn't it instead an alien idiom that, tripping off their silly tongues, came out as if it were native?"

Page 397   *sheer nonsense, rhyme nonsense...*   From Morgenstern/Knight (63), p. 3.

Page 397   *One thing I beg of you...*   From Morgenstern/Knight (63), pp. 10–11.

Page 397   *The genre of poetry Morgenstern created...*   From Morgenstern/Arndt (93), p. *xii*.

Page 401   *I have in fact tackled it myself...*   I guess this forces me to show my hand, so for what it's worth, here goes nothin':

Un art inusité,	*Nur eine Kunst gibt es,*	*Una arte c'è:*
un art en vérité :	*sag' ich, unbescheiden,*	*d'un artefice*
un art c'est d'éviter	*und die ist, das Künstliche*	*le sofistiche*
tout art qui soit truqué.	*gar zu vermeiden.*	*sempr'eludere.*

Page 403   *special puns that I find so excellent...*   I cannot resist including another superb pun that I saw while working furiously on my index. This was a political cartoon by Chan Lowe in the *Fort Lauderdale Sun–Sentinel*, which I saw reprinted in the January 19, 1997 *New York Times*. This was just after the Hebron accord had been signed, and the drawing was of Arafat dancing uncomfortably with Netanyahu; the song to which they were dancing was, "Yasser, That's My Bibi..." This is one of those incredible puns that are just "there", like ripe plums on a tree, waiting for someone to come by and pick them. In fact, that's the way I think all discoveries happen — and by inference, that's how I think all creation, no matter how great and how grand, takes place: as a series of small discoveries of harmonious relationships that were already there for anyone to see, but that nonetheless require a highly refined type of perception to actually notice.

Page 404   *anyone lived in a pretty how town...*   See p. 289 for related material. The poem itself is taken from cummings (59), p. 73.

Page 405   *a heroic attempt at a French translation...*   This, more or less, is found on pp. 207–208 of *Ma Thémagie* (the French version of my *Metamagical Themas*). I phrase it this way because I felt I had to patch up a couple of tiny but definite glitches in it. Not that what we have here is perfect — how could it be? The original English makes no sense.

Page 406   *I don't think anyone could possibly know...*   William York Tindall (Tindall 62) would beg to differ. He claims that for people who know Thomas well enough, this poem "makes plenty of sense". According to Tindall's discussion (which itself is extraordinarily hard to follow, and that's probably not too surprising), the poem is about Thomas himself as a developing — in fact, an embryonic — poet, who "hopes to clamber out to light". Thomas the "embryonic poet" supposedly sees himself as a "foggy dog". Tindall admits that the second stanza's third line is "scrambled", but says that it "seems" to be about "nursing future giants from the basin of the womb". I'm not convinced. Anyway, on and on he goes, outdoing himself in the invention of pretexts for interpreting total opacity. Even if I *could* understand this poem, I would not want to, because it is so determined to be ugly and forbidding.

Page 407   *since the random words' <u>semantics</u> never played any role...*   A passage whose phonetics overwhelm its semantics (although of course not randomly generated) is David Moser's "Alliteratures" (Moser 79), which starts out this way:

> Madge budged and dislodged a grubby mug of garbage, smudging a gob of nudged grunge on Edgar's rugged jungle-dungeon badge, which dredged jagged gargoyle gadgets into grumpy Judge Gub's garage, already bulging with bags of ghastly bedbugs, gangrenous bagels, gargantuan dirigibles, rugged gilt-edged codger bludgeons, and indigenous dangerous galoots gasping dirges about dodging jugglers and begrudging gorged jaguar organs.

To translate it according to what it "means" would be to utterly miss its point.

Page 410   *complexly intertwined grammatical networks...*   This kind of recursive network, independently invented by a couple of other people a year or two after I did my work (perhaps even at the same time), eventually came to be known as an "augmented transition network", and lies at the basis of much research in computational linguistics. But they had the self-confidence to publish whereas I didn't, so for a while I found myself singing the "I was there first, by gum and by golly, but boy, did I blow it all" blues.

Page 410   *coming out of the mouths of my father and his co-workers...*   See, for example, Herman & Hofstadter (60), or Hofstadter (62).

Page 412   *taken from a beautiful article by David...*   This is a lightly edited version of the material found on pp. 86–91 of Moser (91).

Page 413   *How much intentionality is it reasonable...*   Aside from my own program, the three programs mentioned in the paragraph are all described in Boden (77). In addition, a dialogue with Winograd's SHRDLU is reproduced in Chapter 16 of this book.

Page 414   *Errors are well worth thinking about...*   See, for example, Dell & Reich (80), Fromkin (80), Norman (81), Hofstadter & Moser (89), and Aitchison (94).

Page 415   *One day I wrote an article...*   This refers to Chapter 20 of *Metamagical Themas*, specifically p. 456 therein.

Page 415　　*In French, the supposed error…*　　This is on p. 469 of *Ma Thémagie*.

Page 416　　*In German, likewise…*　　This is on p. 490 of *Metamagicum*.

Page 418　　*Chinese brain physiology and Eskimo brain physiology…*　　The odd usage of saying "the human brain" (as if there were just one, or as if it were clear what all brains have in common) and the related, tricky issue of the best level at which to describe its hopefully universal mechanisms are both discussed in the Epilogue of Hofstadter & FARG (95).

Page 420　　*not only published a lengthy article…*　　This is Briggs (85).

Page 420　　*The process of logic itself…*　　This is found on p. 183 of Ulam (76).

Page 420　　*"Bú shì! Bú shì!"…*　　This means (roughly) "Not so! Not so!"

Page 423　　*Roger Angell's story…*　　Found in Angell (70).

Page 425　　*one of the major translators…*　　Howard's remark is on p. 42 of Bernstein (88).

Page 426　　*the entry for* <u>Gemütlichkeit</u> *is only…*　　I recently glanced at a glossy color tourist brochure about Holland. In an attempt at making the country sound exotic, it said, "In smaller towns like Delft, you'll savor the ubiquitous *gezelligheid*, an untranslatable type of friendliness" — the implication being that Dutch sociability is truly unlike that in France, Belgium, Luxembourg, America, or anywhere else. I wonder how this claim would go down if it were made in German. Would Germans really buy the notion that they could not fathom the word *gezelligheid* unless they went to Holland? Would they infer that *gezelligheid* must be a quality alien to folks who live and breathe *Gemütlichkeit*? In that case, I suppose our own word "friendliness" means a different thing in each of our fifty states, and that it splinters, as you travel from town to town, into an even larger number of "unique" and "untranslatable" notions, until ultimately one concludes it is different for each individual — *and* at each moment. But if that is so, what is it that words are for? Is it not their whole purpose to transcend the local and unique and thus to span minds?

Page 428　　*behave abjectly to the rich and powerful…*　　Just below that, in the same entry in this dictionary (Commercial/Oxford 86), it says that *shìtài yánliáng* means: "the way of the world follows the practice of playing up to the influential and giving the cold shoulder to the less fortunate". That's a lot to pack into just four characters! But on the other hand, when I look up the expression *shìtài yánliáng* under *shìtài* instead of under *yánliáng*, it gives a somewhat terser rendition: "snobbery". What am I to conclude?

Page 430　　*the nudist colony = no untidy clothes…*　　This list of anagrams is mostly drawn from pp. 138–141 of Eckler (96). *Ars magna*, incidentally, means "great art".

Page 430　　*Here are a few more…*　　This list is mostly drawn from pp. 32–34 of Eckler (96).

Page 433　　*history-drenched names of its streets…*　　During one of those great *GEB*-translation stints in Paris, I picked up an excellent guide to Parisian street names (Stéphane 81). By browsing in it, one can learn a great deal of history — and more. I was especially pleased, just recently, when I looked up the rue Clément Marot, to find a mini-biography of Marot, which ends with a poem that Stéphane says Marot penned. Although I haven't located it in either Marot/Defaux (90) or Marot/Giraud (73), it strikes me as very much in his style. So here it is, along with my free-and-easy limerick-style rendition in English:

> *Plaise au Roy de me donner cent livres*　　*Pounds one hundred, O King, I entreat:*
> *Pour acheter livres et vivres.*　　*Let me cook and buy books — read and eat.*
> *De livres je me passerois*　　*It is true I can do without books, though I'd stew,*
> *Mais de vivres je ne sçaurois.*　　*But I'd lose all my pounds with no meat.*

Page 433　　*The French for London is Paris…*　　The subtleties of translating, or rather transculturating, this remark are discussed in *Metamagical Themas*. Thus, I asked, if the French for London is Paris, what is the French for Washington? In *Metamagicum*, the

German translation, Ionesco's remark was at one point converted into *Paris heißt Berlin auf Deutsch*. Can this be translated back into English as "Paris in German is Berlin", or does that completely miss the point? It all depends, of course, on what one's purpose is.

Page 434   *If I had no terraced-scan mechanism...*   On p. 109 of *Metamagical Themas*.

Page 435   *I really hope that you find the time...*   I did reply to Mr. Thode, for his note was delightful. I hope he doesn't mind my having reproduced his few mistakes in English; just like the nonexistent address on it and his brash claim that it would arrive in any case, his English errors made his postcard's wit seem all the more pungent and fresh to me.

Page 438   *Washington Crossing the Delaware...*   This is on p. 141 of Eckler (96).

Page 440   *Some of the book is beautiful...*   For a review of this book, see (Hofstadter 96).

Page 440   *by Hugo Brandt Corstius...*   This is a quite strange sentence, and what makes it quite strange is a cannibalism in which four successive words "eat" a copy of themselves.

Page 441   *It sounds like saying that to someone Dutch...*   See my note to p. 312.

Page 443   *published an article in which appeared...*   Kousbroek (83).

Page 444   *So exultant was Sallows...*   The article in question is Sallows (85).

Page 445   *Rigidists would claim...*   A typical example is John Case, who argued that my self-referential sentence *Cette phrase en français est difficile à traduire en anglais* should *not* be rendered in English as "This sentence in English is hard to translate into French", but rather as "The French sentence '*Cette phrase en français est difficile à traduire en anglais*' is difficult to translate into English." The pros and cons of this suggestion are batted about on pp. 22–23 of *Metamagical Themas*. What is really quite amusing to see is how convoluted the discussion became when that book was translated — and quite heavily transculturated as well — into other languages, particularly French (see *Ma Thémagie*), but German as well (see *Metamagicum*).

Page 447   *If I touch my nose and say to you, "Do this!"...*   This type of analogy-making game is discussed in Chapter 24 of *Metamagical Themas*, as well as in French (95).

Page 448   *using the machinery of symbolic logic...*   Two books that exemplify this grotesque trend (at least in my eyes) are Lewis (73) and Parsons (80).

Page 450   *Nagrobek wierszowany Marota...*   I thank Bożena Shallcross for this pretty title.

Page 453   *In his witty book...*   The two paragraphs quoted are from p. 49 and p. 269.

Chapter 15: On the Ununderstandable

Page 455   *On my first trip to Poland...*   Recounted in Hofstadter (80).

Page 457   *How do you understand it when someone else...*   See Hofstadter (94).

Page 458   *mistaking "syllogistic" or "statistical" understanding...*   My distinction between "understanding by analogy" and "understanding by syllogism" is fairly close to the distinction drawn by Roger Schank (Schank 84) between "complete empathy" and "making sense". Roughly halfway between these opposite poles of the understanding spectrum he places "cognitive understanding", which he describes as a reasonable goal for today's AI researchers to shoot for.

Page 460   *the sounds of Prokofiev's second violin concerto...*   Although the second is the one more often played and more highly praised, I far prefer Prokofiev's first violin concerto. In fact, if I were forced by some evil demon to choose just four pieces of music to take to a desert island for the rest of my life, that concerto would be one of them. One year, Carol and I went simultaneously berserk over this piece, and each of us would listen to it at every possible opportunity. I used to get into the car and find the cassette of it in our cassette player, a telltale sign that Carol had just been listening to it. This may sound strange, but I cannot remember any more ecstatic experience in my life than drowning myself in that piece's depths two or three times in a row in its entirety, while driving around in the car one sunny spring afternoon. I sadly add that it was with its closing measures, a mystical wisp swirling eerily upwards into an utterly unfathomable ether, that I found it appropriate to conclude the memorial service for Carol in Bloomington.

Page 463   *probably light rock, or possibly folk rock...*   I was very happy when I read an article in *The New York Times* praising Carole King and knocking most of today's rock music — and when I saw that its author, Martha Bayles, had just come out with a book called *Hole in Our Soul* (Bayles 94) whose subtitle was "The Loss of Beauty and Meaning in American Popular Music", I simply had to rush out and buy it. I half-hoped that maybe it would dare to espouse and articulate *my* belief — that American popular music went to hell in the mid-fifties — but of course it did no such thing. It was mostly decrying, and in an impressively well-informed way, the dizzying downward spiral of rock music itself in the past ten years or so. This is probably a good thing to write a book about, but it was just not the book I had hoped it would be. I wish somebody *would* write that book, perhaps using Bayles' subtitle as their title. It would be nice to have an eloquent ally to cite.

Page 480   *Mrs. Miniver's problem...*   I came across this problem decades ago in Graham (59). It is based on a passage in the novel *Mrs. Miniver* by Jan Struther (40).

Page 483   *Jane has agreed...*   From pp. 220–221 in Parfit (84). Only after making my selection of this passage did I notice that one of the scenes described — that of looking across water to a Palladian church on an island, with dark clouds behind — is in fact shown in the haunting photo on the book's dust jacket, and was taken by Parfit himself.

Page 489   *yet is not ineradicably tied to it...*   Perhaps a vivid way of thinking about both survival and translation is to ponder the following: Suppose all copies and even all memories of the original Russian text to *Eugene Onegin* had been completely destroyed, but that Falen's English version, say, or Colin's French version had escaped destruction. Would the soul of Russian literature have perished, or would it still exist? If the former, then would it come to life again if the secondary text were translated back into Russian by a translator of the highest level of artistry? Does it really *have* to be translated back? Suppose the Russian language itself had somehow been obliterated as well — *then* would its literary soul still survive? How does all this relate to the question of survival of a *human* soul in the wake of a physical emigration from one's country of birth and one's native tongue, and into an alien country and its initially very alien tongue? For a poetic and eloquent set of musings by one who experienced just this, see Hoffman (1989).

Page 489   *The idea of projecting oneself onto a whole nation...*   But see the "Prelude... Ant Fugue" in Hofstadter (79).

Page 489   *notoriously predicted in 1957...*   See p. 187 of McCorduck (79).

Page 490   *My own research over the past twenty years...*   See Hofstadter & FARG (95).

Page 490   *For decades, cognitive and perceptual psychologists...*   Here is a tip of the iceberg: Johnson-Laird & Wason (77), Gardner (85), Kahneman & Miller (86), Treisman (88), Aitchison (94), and Holyoak & Thagard (95). It is from the latter book, incidentally, that I borrowed the elegant, clever idea of doing footnotes in this asterisk-free manner.

Page 492   *those silicon-chip creatures bred of our own fancy...*   The movie *Star Wars,* though not at all realistic in its portrayal of how robots will be, nonetheless presented a vision of two quite lovable silicon-chip creatures bred of our own fancy (R2D2 and C3PO).

Page 492   *would we mindlessly align ourselves with the carbon?...*   Carl Sagan, in Sagan (73), introduced the wonderful terms "carbon chauvinism", "liquid chauvinism", "planetary

Notes

chauvinism", and so forth. On that book's p. 42, he tells of one Lawrence J. Henderson who early in this century wrote a book called *The Fitness of the Environment,* in which he concluded that any conceivable life form must be based on carbon and water and must breathe oxygen. Sagan wryly adds, "I personally find this conclusion suspect, if only because Lawrence J. Henderson was made of carbon and water and metabolized free oxygen." Despite Sagan's eloquent, mind-opening writings over several decades, such chauvinisms about how life "must" be remain dominant, even in high scientific debates.

Poems XV: That Ol' Sino Room

Page 65a   *deeply involved in a major MT project...*   Toon was then working for a Dutch company called BSO, one of whose main foci was, and probably still is, machine translation. I visited BSO a couple of years later, and while there was told that Ronald Jonkers, my friend and Dutch *GEB* translator, had done some technical-translation work for them. I laughed at the irony that they didn't use their own programs for such purposes, but I guess it's not all that ironic — BSO's translation programs are, after all, just being developed, and no outrageous claims are made for their perfection.

Page 65a   *undoubtedly most successful mainframe MT system...*   See, for example, pp. 16–18 of Maxwell *et al.* (88) and Wilks (92).

Page 66a   *a review of it in the journal...*   See Bédard in the Bibliography.

Page 67a   *this one done a couple of years later...*   I thank Peter Brown, who at the time was working on the Candide project, for getting this translation done at my request.

Page 68a   *about as little English as it is possible to know...*   Over the next few years, Zhang Jiaying — or "Jennifer", as she came to be called — learned to speak English very well.

Page 69a   *Bob loved "e"-less English and thus welcomed...*   For example, see French (83), a masterfully done short story whose "e"-lessness, despite being hinted at all throughout it, nonetheless went undetected by my eye for days.

Chapter 16: AI Aims, MT Claims, Sino-room Flames

Page 496   *Among the very first words mastered...*   See Hofstadter (95).

Page 497   *it suddenly resuscitates "skyscraper"'s buried imagery...*   I remember one time when the Italian word *grattacielo* — literally, "scratch-sky" — came up in a conversation with Carol. She paused for a moment, then remarked on its vivid imagery. I said, "But Carol — it's just the same thing in English!" She smiled and said she'd never noticed it. Of course she *had,* when she was very little, but these things fade out.

Page 499   *we must look a little bit at how MT programs...*   See, for example, Tucker (84), Maxwell *et al.* (88), Hutchins (95), and Bennett (95).

Page 503   *I was told by someone who worked for years with the Systran project...*   I thank Sonia Colina for explaining much about Xerox's way of using Systran to me.

Page 504   *for Searle, there is a vast and in fact unbreachable gulf...*   On p. 423 of Searle (80) or p. 370 of Hofstadter & Dennett (81), Searle writes: "The programmed computer does not do 'information processing'. Rather, what it does is manipulate formal symbols. The fact that the programmer and the interpreter of the computer output use the symbols to stand for objects in the world is totally beyond the scope of the computer. The computer, to repeat, has a syntax but no semantics."

Page 504   *Wasn't Schank's whole game plan...*   I admit that in a way I can empathize with Searle's targeting Roger Schank, for at times Schank's claims for his (*i.e.,* his students') programs are so extreme that they simply cry out for refutation. For instance, when I recently re-read Schank (84), I started out feeling very sympathetic to his ideas, almost as if our brains were exactly aligned (after all, his spectrum of understanding was very similar to ideas I have) — but then I hit a passage in which he asserted (citing Lebowitz 80) that current AI programs can understand newspaper articles on, say, terrorism at nearly the level that a typical human reader (*e.g.*, Schank himself) can. This is such balderdash (similar to the outrageous claims described in Chapter 4 of an AI program reading science-fiction stories with full understanding) that all at once, I felt an unbreachable gulf opening up between Schank's mind and my mind, between his view and my view of what understanding is and of what AI has achieved so far — and I could see exactly where Searle's desire to play the role of the boy shouting that the emperor has no clothes was coming from. I find it quite ironic that, of all things, an article by Roger Schank could make me get, even if only fleetingly, "inside John Searle's head".

Page 507   *How much meaning does one read into a string of words...*   Recall David Moser's ideas on pp. 412–413.

Page 511   *aboutness and semanticity can arise in the total absence...*   The point is that meaning does not get attached to symbols because of links to the "real world out there", but because of links to fluid abstractions called *concepts,* which can represent subtle regularities perceived inside a virtual, or computational, environment just as readily as regularities perceived in an external physical environment. A simulated world can, in principle, be unlimitedly complex and hence, despite Searle's claims, unlimitedly *real* to those who are in intimate contact with it over long periods of time (as video-game addicts can no doubt attest). Such individuals might reside on either side of the screen: either inside the virtual world, or outside of it. What matters is not the place they happen to live but how flexibly and subtly they are capable of mentally mirroring events.

Page 512   *Here is a sample blow-by-blow retrospective...*   Proteus' commentary, along with Davey's meta-level commentary, is found on pp. 17–18 of Davey (78).

Page 513   *Here is another game together with...*   On p. 18 of Davey (78).

Page 518   *Victor Yngve reached a similar conclusion...*   See Yngve (64).

Page 520   *A domain that is in principle inaccessible...*   This inaccessibility is brought out very clearly in Feynman (67), and I did my best in Chapter 20 of *Metamagical Themas.*

Page 521   *knowledge-based machine translation...*   See Nirenburg *et al.* (92).

Chapter 17: In Praise of the Music of Language

Page 523   *An old pond: a frog...*   From Sato (95).

Page 524   *Que j'aime à faire apprendre un nombre utile aux sages...*   Found on p. 105 of Beckmann (71), where one also finds "How I want a drink, alcoholic, of course, after the heavy lectures involving quantum mechanics", which codes for a mere 29 digits.

Page 531   *the opening of Canto III...*   Following the Grandgent (72) edition.

Page 532   *Italian is rich in rhyme...*   From pp. *xix–xx* of Dante/Pinsky (94).

Page 537   *My main reason for avoiding rhyme...*   From p. *xli* of Musa (95).

Page 537   *But if I feel such horror...*   From p. *xlii* of Musa (95).

Page 537   *For the poet creating original verse...*   From p. *xlii* of Musa (95).

Page 539   *In those months in Buenos Aires...*   From pp. *xxviii–xxix* of Barnstone (96).

Page 542   *Let us suppose that an Englishman...*   From pp. 17–18 of Dante/Sayers (49).

Page 542   *Here, then, are his first three tercets...*   From Barnstone (ca. 87).

Page 544   *Docking at Night...*   From p. 221 of Barnstone (96).

Page 544   *Luminous Experience of a Brain Scan...*   From p. 135 of Barnstone (96).

Page 544   *I became instantly desonnetized...*   From p. *xxx* of Barnstone (96).

Page 547   *Dante is an Aeolus-the-Brusque, a Lord-of-Furibundus-fuss...*   From pp. *ix* and *xxii* of Dante/Mandelbaum (82).

Page 547   *Dante is a greater poet than any...*   From p. *xxxviii* of Musa (95).

Page 548   *the severe pleasure...*   I owe this sweet stinger of a phrase to Beatrix Hamburg.

Page 548   *The architect Louis Kahn once used...*   This is taken from a letter from Kahn about the work of artist/teacher William Huff, found on p. 210 of *Metamagical Themas*.

Page 551   *Not many people today, I suspect...* From p. *xii* of Gardner (95).

Page 553   *on the occasion of being awarded...*   One of the three judges on the panel that gave the Translation Award to Sato and Watson was poet Eliot Weinberger, the principal author, curiously enough, of another collection of multiple translations of a single poem (Weinberger & Paz 87). This thin book — *Nineteen Ways of Looking at Wang Wei* — takes a short poem by eighth-century Chinese painter, calligrapher, and poet Wang Wei, and displays, in fact, not nineteen but twenty-four versions of it. (Why didn't they just call it "Let Me Count the Weis"?) Though the idea is delicious, its execution is not.

The translations were done by scholars of high order, some by poets of considerable repute, yet the commentaries are often nasty, sarcastic, and condescending (a little like mine in this chapter, I admit). A few of the translations are into French and Spanish, and for each of those, ironically, only a comment-free literal gloss in English is provided, almost as if to say that translating from Chinese, now *that's* hard, but translating from those other languages? — a piece of cake. (Incidentally, if you count these glosses as further "ways", then there are twenty-nine Weis *in toto*.)

What is the nature of the original poem? From a formal viewpoint, it is elegant: four lines of five characters each, romanized and glossed roughly as follows:

Lù Zhài	*Deer Enclosure*
kōng shān bù jiàn rén	*empty hill not see person*
dàn wén rén yǔ xiǎng	*but hear person language sound*
fǎn yǐng rù shēn lín	*return shadow enter deep forest*
fù zhào qīng tái shàng	*back shine green moss on*

Notice that in Wang Wei's original, the second and fourth lines rhyme, and the first and third come close to doing so. And perhaps 1200 years ago, they rhymed exactly.

Of course this is very cryptic. The question is: How to make sense of it? Even if one knows a fair amount of modern Chinese, classical Chinese's compactness and tersity makes such poems very hard to penetrate. However, after reading all the translations in the Weinberger–Paz book and consulting with David Moser, I felt I had a pretty good handle on it. Essentially, it means something like this: "On the empty hill, no one can be seen, but the sound of talking can be heard. Through shadows, light pierces the deep forest, and reflects off the green moss." But how to render this *poetically* in English without doing violence to the original form? That's the rub.

By luck, I came across another slim volume — *Three Chinese Poets* by Vikram Seth (Seth 92). I was pleased to see that he included his own rendering of this poem by Wang Wei, and so here I present that one, which I prefer to all of the "nineteen" (although I cringe at its use of generic "man"):

Deer Park

Empty hills, no man in sight —
Just echoes of the voice of men.
In the deep wood reflected light
Shines on the blue-green moss again.

Seth himself comments:

> There is a school of translation that believes that one can safely ignore many of the actual words of a poem, once one has drunk deeply of its spirit. An approximate rendering invigorated by a sense of poetic inspiration becomes the aim. The idea is that if the final product reads well as a poem, all is well: a good poem exists where none existed before.... The poems in this book are not intended as transcreations or free translations in this sense, attempts to use the originals as trampolines from which to bounce off on to poems of my own.... I have tried not to compromise the meaning of the actual words of the poems, though I have often failed. Even in prose the associations of a word or an image in one language do not slip readily into another. The loss is still greater in poetry, where each word or image carries a heavier charge of association, and where the exigencies of form leave less scope for choice and manoeuvre.

What astounded me about all of these versions — Seth's no less than the two dozen in *Nineteen Ways* — is that not a single translator tried what to me seemed to be the totally obvious thing to do: namely, to create an English poem consisting of four lines of five words each, and hopefully with each word monosyllabic, just as in the original. Given that no one else had done this, I set it to myself as a challenge, and came up with this:

Deer Glade

Bleak peak, no one seen,
But hark, sound of voice.
Sun shafts pierce dark woods,
Bounce off high green moss.

Though I liked this, I felt I could go just a little bit further in imitating the original Chinese. First of all, I decided to rearrange my words to show the way that the original twenty characters would have been written in Wang Wei's day — not horizontally but vertically, in four columns of five characters each, and with the order of the columns being right-to-left, not left-to-right. Even more radically (if I may get away with that term in the context of the Chinese language), I thought it would be fun to break each of my one-dimensional English words into a compact two-dimensional visual structure suggesting, ever so slightly (at least from afar), a Chinese character. I also tampered a little with the choice of words, venturing further out from the core. The upshot was...

flick	sun	but	bleak
from	flecks	hark	peak
high	pierce	hush	spy
green	dark	like	no
bark	bosk	talk	folk

and that's where I left it.

Page 553   *he has collected more than eighty anglicizations...*   Indeed, Sato got around to anthologizing them shortly after his PEN talk, but of that I knew nothing when writing Chapter 17. But Helga Keller, in searching high and low for how to get permission to reprint these English haikus, turned up Sato's charming *One Hundred Frogs* (Sato 95), which fits into the nice niche of Storrs' *Ad Pyrrham*, Weinberger & Paz' *Nineteen Ways*, my *Rhapsody*, Verdun's 500 portraits of Marot, not to mention sets of musical variations on a theme. Sato's own frog haiku, as well as the five that follow it, are all found in his book. As icing on the cake, there's even a flip-movie of a jumping froggie drawn by J. C. Brown.

Page 567   *Great Call...*   This alludes to "I'll Walk Beside You", another very touching song performed with deep emotion by Roger Chard and Maurita Holland in Carol's and my wedding ceremony. (It was also most expressively recorded by the great Irish tenor John MacCormack.) The song, a commitment of lifelong love, ends in this way: "And when the great call comes, the sunset gleams, I'll walk beside you to the land of dreams."

Permissions and Acknowledgments

Page 607   This has been a grueling roller-coaster and a half. To Helga, a million thanks.

Index

Page 609   *"a", meaning of...*   This tiny-print behemoth was a labor of love that took me a full month of nonstop fifteen-hour days to carry off. While I was working on it, innumerable friends and acquaintances, baffled, asked me, "Can't a computer do this?" or "Why not hire a professional indexer?" And I, equally baffled to hear such questions, fumbled about for words to try to explain a fact that seemed so clear to me: A good index is a work of art in itself — and it is also, I'm afraid, an art that is going out of style.

My feeling is that only the author (and certainly not a computer program) can do this job well. Only the author, looking at a given page, sees all the way to the bottom of the pool of ideas of which the words are the mere surface, and only the author can answer the question, "What am I *really talking about* here, in this paragraph, this page, this section, this chapter?" To answer those questions takes total understanding of the book.

Doing this index, painful though it was, afforded me one last pass back through the text, tying things together for a final time, saying good-bye to a work created out of love, and with love, for words, ideas, people... For instance, there was one giant index entry that came entirely out of the blue, catching me very much off guard. That was the entry for "conflation". I'm not even sure if I'm using the word in a standard way, in fact. What it means to me is "taking one thing for another", as in the sentence "Don't conflate the meanings of 'conflate' and 'confound', please!" I noticed one instance of conflation (in this sense, at least), indexed it, then saw another, and pretty soon it dawned on me that this theme was omnipresent in my book, and so I spent several hours just searching for instances of conflation — not the *word,* mind you, but the *concept.* It was a revelation to me how pervasive it was, even though the word itself occurred only a handful of times.

There were other entries, too, whose size surprised me, such as "Chopin", "colliding cultures", "Paris", and "splicing-together". Once the index was essentially done (I hedge with this "essentially" because as I write these words, I still have to index these very Notes — only then will the Index be *really* done), I found it interesting to flip through it and, by comparing the sheer sizes of various entries, to get new perceptions of what my book is most centrally about — a very curious activity, and perhaps overly introspective in some people's eyes, but irresistible for at least a little while.

And so, I come to the end of my Notes. I really must go now, and finish the work on the Index. Then maybe I'll start being able to go to bed before 7 A.M. That will be a relief, not only for me but especially for my dear children, who badly want their Dad back again. Every night they ask me hopefully, *Quante pagine ancora, Papi?* And oh, how happy I will be when at last I can say to them, *Zero, zero, zero! Finita la commedia!*

Bibliography

I have listed books and articles cited in the text and in addition a small and fairly arbitrary selection of others that I feel are relevant to the topics discussed herein. The abbreviation "CRCC" stands for the Center for Research on Concepts and Cognition, Indiana University, Bloomington, Indiana, 47408.

Aitchison, Jean (1994). *Words in the Mind: An Introduction to the Mental Lexicon* (2nd ed.). Cambridge, Mass.: Basil Blackwell.

Anderson, Poul (1989). "Uncleftish Beholding", *Analog Magazine* (mid-December).

Angell, Roger (1970). *A Day in the Life of Roger Angell.* New York: Penguin Books.

Arndt, Walter (1993). *Pushkin Threefold: Narrative, Lyric, Polemic, and Ribald Verse.* Ann Arbor: Ardis Editions.

Augarde, Tony (1986). *The Oxford Guide to Word Games.* New York: Oxford University Press.

Babbage, Charles (1969). *Passages from the Life of a Philosopher.* [1864] New York: Augustus M. Kelley.

Bar-Hillel, Yehoshua (1960). "The Present Status of Automatic Translation of Languages". *Advances in Computers,* vol. 1, pp. 92–163.

Barnstone, Willis (1993). *The Poetics of Translation: History, Theory, Practice.* New Haven: Yale University Press.

——— (1996). *The Secret Reader: 501 Sonnets.* Hanover, New Hampshire: University Press of New England.

Battus (1984). *Opperlandse taal- & letterkunde.* Amsterdam: Querido's.

Bayles, Martha (1994). *Hole in Our Soul: The Loss of Beauty and Meaning in American Popular Music.* Chicago: University of Chicago Press.

Beckmann, Petr (1971). *A History of Pi.* Boulder, Colorado: Golem Press.

Bédard, Claude (ca. 1992). "GTS: New and Affordable Machine Translation". *Language Technology #15,* pp. 53–54.

Bell, Roger T. (1991). *Translation and Translating: Theory and Practice.* London: Longman.

Bennett, Winfield Scott (1995). "Machine Translation in North America", in Koerner & Asher (95).

Berg, Paul and Maxine Singer (1991). *Genes and Genomes.* Mill Valley, Calif.: University Science Books.

Bergerson, Howard (1973). *Palindromes and Anagrams.* New York: Dover Books.

Bernstein, Richard (1988). "Howard's Way". *New York Times Magazine,* Sept. 25.

Bloch, Alan (1963). "Men Are Different". In Isaac Asimov and Groff Conklin (eds.), *Fifty Short Science Fiction Tales.* New York: Macmillan.

Boden, Margaret A. (1977). *Artificial Intelligence and Natural Man.* New York: Basic Books.

Bodine, Kerry A. (1996). "C'mon, Guys: This Way to a Study on Language and Sexism". CRCC Publication #108.

Boeke, Kees (1957). *Cosmic View: The Universe in Forty Jumps.* New York: John Day.

Bombaugh, Charles Carroll (1961). *Oddities and Curiosities of Words and Literature.* Edited and annotated by Martin Gardner. New York: Dover Books.

Bongard, Mikhail (1970). *Pattern Recognition.* Rochelle Park, New Jersey: Hayden.

Borges, Jorge Luis (1962). *Ficciones.* Edited by Anthony Kerrigan. New York: Grove Press.

Briggs, Rick (1985). "Knowledge Representation in Sanskrit and Artificial Intelligence". *AI Magazine,* vol. 6, no. 1, pp. 32–39.

Brilliant, Ashleigh (1990; 1992). *We've Been Through So Much Together, and Most of It Was Your Fault* and *I Try to Take One Day at a Time, but Sometimes Several Days Attack Me at Once.* Santa Barbara: Woodbridge Press.

Brown, Margaret Wise (1946). *Little Fur Family.* Illustrated by Garth Williams. New York: Harper & Row.

Bull, Cornelius (1997). Letter to the editor, *New York Times Book Review,* Jan. 5, 1997.

Burgin, Diana Lewis (1988). *Richard Burgin: A Life in Verse.* Columbus, Ohio: Slavica Publishers.

Cameron, Deborah, ed. (1990). *The Feminist Critique of Language: A Reader.* London: Routledge.

Carroll, Lewis (1976). *Anya v Stranye Chudes.* Russian translation of *Alice in Wonderland* by Vladimir Nabokov [1923]. New York: Dover Books.

Cavaliere, Alberto (1939). *Chimica in versi: Rime distillate.* Roma: Angelo Signorelli.

Chiflet, Jean-Loup (1985). *Sky my husband! Ciel mon mari!* Paris: Éditions Hermé.

—— (1987). *Sky! my teacher.* Paris: Éditions Carrère.

Commercial Press/Oxford University Press (1986). Concise English–Chinese and Chinese–English Dictionary. Beijing and Oxford.

Clark, Andy and Peter Millican, eds. (1996). *The Legacy of Alan Turing, Vol. II: Connectionism, Concepts, and Folk Psychology.* New York: Oxford University Press.

Connell, Evan S. (1988). *The Diary of a Rapist.* San Francisco: North Point Press.

Cooper, Gloria, ed. (1980). *Squad Helps Dog Bite Victim.* Garden City, New York: Doubleday.

—— (1987). *Red Tape Holds Up New Bridge.* New York: Putnam.

Cooper, James Fenimore (1994). *The Last of the Mohicans.* [1826] Rutland, Vermont: Charles E. Tuttle.

Coxeter, H. S. M. (1961). *The Real Projective Plane.* Cambridge, U.K.: Cambridge University Press.

cummings, e. e. (1959). *100 selected poems.* New York: Grove Press.

Daly, Mary and Jane Caputi (1987). *Websters' First New Intergalactic Wickedary of the English Language.* Boston: Beacon Press.

Dante Alighieri (1972). *La Divina Commedia.* Edited by C. H. Grandgent. Cambridge, Mass.: Harvard University Press.

—— (1943). *The Divine Comedy.* Translated by Lawrence Binyon, in Paolo Milano (ed.), *The Portable Dante* (Viking Penguin, New York, 1975).

—— (1944). *The Divine Comedy.* Translated by Melville Best Anderson. New York: Heritage Press.

—— (1949). *The Divine Comedy. Cantica I: Hell.* Translated by Dorothy L. Sayers. London: Penguin Books.

—— (1982). *The Inferno.* Translated by John Ciardi. New York: Mentor.

—— (1982). *The Divine Comedy: Inferno.* Translated by Allen Mandelbaum. New York: Bantam Books.

—— (ca. 1987). *The Inferno.* Canto I, translated by Willis Barnstone. *Chicago Literary Magazine.*

—— (1994). *The Inferno of Dante.* Translated by Robert Pinsky. New York: Farrar, Straus & Giroux.

Davey, Anthony (1978). *Discourse Production.* Edinburgh: Edinburgh University Press.

David, Lester (1994). *Jacqueline Kennedy Onassis: A Portrait of Her Private Years.* New York: St. Martin's.

Dawkins, Richard (1987). *The Blind Watchmaker.* New York: W. W. Norton.

Dell, Gary S. and P. A. Reich (1980). "Slips of the Tongue: The Facts and a Stratificational Model", in J. E. Copeland and P. W. Davis (eds.), *Papers in Cognitive-Stratificational Linguistics,* vol. 66, pp. 611–629. Houston: Rice University Studies.

DeLong, Howard (1970). *A Profile of Mathematical Logic.* Reading, Mass.: Addison-Wesley.

Dennett, Daniel C. (1991). "Real Patterns". *Journal of Philosophy,* vol. 89, pp. 27–51.

Drake, Frank D. (1973). "Life on a Neutron Star". *Astronomy Magazine.*

Drury, John (1995). *The Poetry Dictionary.* Cincinnati: Story Press.

Eckler, Ross (1996). *Making the Alphabet Dance.* New York: St. Martin's Press.

Edmonds, Robin (1994). *Pushkin: The Man and His Age.* New York: St. Martin's Press.

Epstein, Robert (1992). "The Quest for the Thinking Computer". *AI Magazine,* vol. 13, no. 2 (summer), pp. 80–95.

Fackelmann, Kathy (1996). "Forecasting Alzheimer's Disease". *Science News,* vol. 149 (May 18), pp. 312–313.

Fauconnier, Gilles (1985). *Mental Spaces.* Cambridge, Mass.: MIT Press/Bradford Books.

Feynman, Richard P. (1967). *The Character of Physical Law.* Cambridge, Mass.: MIT Press.

Forward, Robert L. (1980). *Dragon's Egg.* New York: Ballantine Books.

Fraiberg, Selma H. (1959). *The Magic Years.* New York: Charles Scribner's Sons.

French, Robert M. (1983). "Missing". Unpublished manuscript.

———— (ca. 1985). "The Changing of Essence". Unpublished manuscript.

———— (1988). "Some Thoughts on Translation", *Ohio Writer*, vol. 2, no. 2 (March/April).

———— (1995). *The Subtlety of Sameness: A Theory and Computer Model of Analogy-Making.* Cambridge, Mass.: MIT Press/Bradford Books.

French, Robert M. and Jacqueline Henry (1988). "La traduction en français des jeux linguistiques de *Gödel, Escher, Bach*". *Meta,* vol. 33, no. 3, pp. 331–340.

Fromkin, Victoria A. (1980). *Errors in Linguistic Performance: Slips of the Tongue, Ear, Pen, and Hand.* New York: Academic Press.

Gardner, Howard (1985). *The Mind's New Science.* New York: Basic Books.

Gardner, Martin (1962). *Relativity for the Million.* New York: Macmillan.

———— (1983). *Wheels, Life, and Other Mathematical Amusements.* New York: W. H. Freeman.

———— (1988). *Time Travel and Other Mathematical Bewilderments.* New York: W. H. Freeman.

———— (1989). *Penrose Tiles to Trapdoor Ciphers.* New York: W. H. Freeman.

Gardner, Martin, ed. (1992). *Best Remembered Poems.* New York: Dover Books.

———— (1995). *Famous Poems from Bygone Days.* New York: Dover Books.

Gebstadter, Egbert B. (1997). *The Graced Tone of Clément: A la louange de la mélodie des mots.* Cahors: Éditions Noitide (Collection «*Livres et vivres*»).

Gerrard, Roy (1989). *Rosie and the Rustlers.* New York: Farrar, Straus & Giroux.

Gershwin, Ira (1993). *The Complete Lyrics of Ira Gershwin.* Edited by Robert Kimball. New York: Alfred A. Knopf.

Goffman, Erving (1974). *Frame Analysis.* New York: Harper & Row.

Gordon, W. Terrence (1986). "Translating Word-Play: French–English, English–French". *Babel,* vol. 32, no. 3, pp. 146–150.

Grosjean, François (1982). *Life with Two Languages.* Cambridge, Mass.: Harvard University Press.

Gross, John, ed. (1994). *The Oxford Book of Comic Verse.* New York: Oxford University Press.

Graham, L. A. (1959). *Ingenious Mathematical Problems and Methods.* New York: Dover Books.

Halpern, Daniel, ed. (1993). *Dante's Inferno. Translations by Twenty Contemporary Poets.* Hopewell, New Jersey: Ecco Press.

Hechinger, Nancy (1981). "Seeing Without Eyes", *Science 81* (March), pp. 38–43.

Hein, Piet (1966). *Grooks.* With the assistance of Jens Arup. Garden City, New York: Doubleday.

———— (1969). *Grooks II.* With the assistance of Jens Arup. Garden City, New York: Doubleday.

———— (1970). *Grooks III.* With the assistance of Jens Arup. Garden City, New York: Doubleday.

Henry, Jacqueline (ca. 1988). "Recherche d'une technique de traduction des jeux de mots". Unpublished manuscript.

Herman, Robert and Robert Hofstadter (1960). *High-Energy Electron Scattering Tables.* Stanford: Stanford University Press.

Hodges, Andrew (1983). *Alan Turing: The Enigma.* New York: Simon & Schuster.

Hoffman, Eva (1989). *Lost in Translation.* New York: Dutton.

Hoffmann, Banesh (1972). *Albert Einstein, Creator and Rebel.* New York: New American Library.

———— (1983). *Relativity and Its Roots.* New York: W. H. Freeman/Scientific American.

Hofstadter, Robert (1962). "The Electron-Scattering Method and its Application to the Structure of Nuclei and Nucleons", in *Nobel Lectures: Physics — 1942–1962.* Amsterdam: Elsevier.

Hofstadter, Douglas R. (1977). "56 New Bongard Problems". Unpublished manuscript. Available through CRCC.

———— (1979). *Gödel, Escher, Bach: an Eternal Golden Braid.* New York: Basic Books.

———— (1980). "Poland: A Mythical Quest". Unpublished manuscript.

———— (1985). *Metamagical Themas.* New York: Basic Books.

———— (1985). *Gödel, Escher, Bach: les Brins d'une Guirlande Éternelle.* Translated by Robert French and Jacqueline Henry. Paris: InterÉditions.

———— (1985). *Gödel, Escher, Bach: een Eeuwige Gouden Band.* Translated by Ronald Jonkers. Amsterdam: Uitgeverij Contact.

———— (1985). *Gödel, Escher, Bach: ein Endloses Geflochtenes Band.* Initially translated by Philipp Wolff-Windegg; revised by H. Feuersee, W. Alexi, R. Jonkers, *et al.* Stuttgart: Klett-Cotta.

——— (1986). "Sexist Language: Just the Tip of a Cognitive Iceberg". *Iris,* #16 (fall/winter).

——— (1987). *Gödel, Escher, Bach: un Eterno y Grácil Bucle.* Initially translated by Mario Usabiaga; revised by Alejandro López Rousseau with the help of Franco Simonetti, Andrea Parada, and Claudio Lamadrid. Barcelona: Tusquets.

——— (1987). "La recherche de l'essence: entre le médium et le message", *Protée,* vol. 15, no. 2 (spring), pp. 13–31.

——— (1988). "Common Sense and Conceptual Halos: A Reply to Paul Smolensky". *Behavioral and Brain Sciences,* vol. 11, no. 1, pp. 35–37.

——— (1988). *Ma Thémagie.* Translated by Lise Rosenbaum, Jean-Baptiste Berthelin, and Jean-Luc Bonnetain. Paris: InterEditions.

——— (1988). *Metamagicum.* Translated by Thomas Niehaus, Ulrich Enderwitz, Monika Noll, Rüdiger Hentschel, and Hermann Feuersee. Stuttgart: Klett-Cotta.

——— (1989). "Language, Imagery, and Prejudice". *Intersci* (fall). San Francisco State University.

——— (1991). "The Commonsense Personifesto". Unpublished manuscript. Available through CRCC.

——— (1992). "Mirroring in a Microdomain the Real World's Richness". Unfinished manuscript.

——— (ca. 1993). "You've Come a Long Way, Guys!" Unpublished manuscript. Available through CRCC.

——— (1994). "Breaking Out of Egocentrisms and Chauvinisms". CRCC Publication #97.

——— (1995). "Speechstuff and Thoughtstuff", in Sture Allén (ed.), *Of Thoughts and Words: Proceedings of Nobel Symposium 92.* London: Imperial College Press.

——— (1996). *Rhapsody on a Theme by Clément Marot.* Cedar City: Grace A. Tanner Center, Southern Utah University.

——— (1996). Review of *Making the Alphabet Dance* in *The New York Times Book Review,* March 10.

——— (1996). "What's Gained in Translation". *New York Times Book Review,* December 8.

——— (1997). "The Search for Essence 'twixt Medium and Message", to appear in Dirk Delabastita (ed.), *Traductio: Essays on Punning and Translation* (Presse Universitaire, Namur, and St. Jerome, Manchester).

——— (1997). *Gēdéěr, Àisheěr, Bāhè: Jí Yì Bì zhī Dà Chéng.* Translated by Guo Weide, Wang Pei, Yan Yong, David Moser, Liu Haoming, Fan Lanying, Guo Shiming, and Wang Guirong. Beijing: Commercial Press.

Hofstadter, Douglas R., Gray A. Clossman, and Marsha J. Meredith (1980). "Shakespeare's Plays Weren't Written by Him, but by Someone Else of the Same Name". CRCC Publication #1.

Hofstadter, Douglas R. and Daniel C. Dennett, eds. (1981). *The Mind's I: Fantasies and Reflections on Self and Soul.* New York: Basic Books.

Hofstadter, Douglas R. *et al.* (1989). "Synopsis of the Workshop on Humor and Cognition". *Humor,* vol. 2, no. 4, pp. 417–440.

Hofstadter, Douglas R. and David J. Moser (1989). "To Err is Human; To Study Error-making is Cognitive Science". *Michigan Quarterly Review,* vol. 28, no. 2, pp. 185–215.

Hofstadter, Douglas R. and the Fluid Analogies Research Group (1995). *Fluid Concepts and Creative Analogies: Computer Models of the Fundamental Mechanisms of Thought.* New York: Basic Books.

Holyoak, Keith J. and Paul Thagard (1995). *Mental Leaps: Analogy in Creative Thought.* Cambridge, Mass.: MIT Press/Bradford Books.

Hugo, Victor (1964). *Œuvres poétiques, I. Avant l'exil.* Paris: Gallimard/La Pléiade.

Hutchins, W. John (1995). "Machine Translation: A Brief History", in Koerner & Asher (95).

Jackson, Philip C. (1975). *Introduction to Artificial Intelligence.* New York: Petrocelli Charter.

Johnson-Laird, Philip and P. C. Wason, eds. (1977). *Thinking: Readings in Cognitive Science.* New York: Cambridge University Press.

Kahneman, Daniel and Dale Miller (1986). "Norm Theory: Comparing Reality to its Alternatives". *Psychological Review,* vol. 93, no. 2, pp. 136–153.

Kington, Miles (1981). *Let's Parler Franglais!* New York: Penguin Books.

Kinsey, Vikpush (1999). *One Gin over the Cuckoo's Gate.* Eugene, Ore.: Yamatarajabanasalagam Press.

Koerner, E. F. K. and R. E. Asher, eds. (1995). *Concise History of the Language Sciences.* Tarrytown, New York: Pergamon/Elsevier.

Kolata, Gina (1996). "Research Links Writing Style to Risk of Alzheimer's". *New York Times,* Feb. 21.

Kousbroek, Rudy (1983). "Welke Vrag Heeft Vierendertig Letters?" *Nieuwe Rotterdamse Courant,* Feb. 11, p. 3.

Lakoff, George (1987). *Women, Fire and Dangerous Things.* Chicago: University of Chicago.

La Mettrie, Julien Offroy de (1912). *Man a Machine* and *L'homme machine* (together). Unnamed translator. La Salle, Illinois: Open Court.

Langton, Christopher G., ed. (1989). *Artificial Life.* Redwood City, Calif.: Addison-Wesley.

———— *et al.,* eds. (1992). *Artificial Life II.* Redwood City, Calif.: Addison-Wesley.

Laurent, Jean-Jacques *et al.* (1971). *Paris que j'aime.* Paris: Éditions Sun.

Laurian, Anne-Marie (1992). "Possible/Impossible Translation of Jokes". *Humor,* vol. 5–1/2, pp. 111–127.

Lebowitz, Michael (1980). *Generalization and Memory in an Integrated Understanding System.* Ph.D. thesis, Yale University.

Lehrer, Tom (1981). *Too Many Songs by Tom Lehrer.* New York: Pantheon.

Lem, Stanisław (1974). *The Cyberiad.* Translation of *Cyberiada* (Kraków: Wydawnictwo Literackie) by Michael Kandel. New York: Avon Books.

Lewis, David (1973). *Counterfactuals.* Cambridge, Mass.: Harvard University Press.

Liro, Joseph (1987). "On Computers, Translation, and Stanisław Lem". *Computers and Translation,* vol. 2, pp. 89–104.

Maggio, Rosalie (1988). *The Nonsexist Word Finder.* Boston: Beacon Press.

Markoff, John (1993). "Cocktail-Party Conversation — With a Computer". *New York Times,* Jan. 10.

Marot, Clément (1973). *Œuvres poétiques.* Edited by Yves Giraud. Paris: Garnier-Flammarion.

———— (1990). *Œuvres poétiques.* Edited by Gérard Defaux. Paris: Garnier.

Maslin, Janet (1996). Film review in the "Living Arts" section of *The New York Times,* Nov. 1.

Maxwell, Dan, Klaus Schubert, and Toon Witkam, eds. (1988). *New Directions in Machine Translation.* Dordrecht, Holland: Foris.

McCorduck, Pamela (1979). *Machines Who Think.* San Francisco: W. H. Freeman.

Miller, Casey and Kate Swift (1977). *Words and Women.* Garden City, New York: Anchor/Doubleday.

———— (1988). *The Handbook of Nonsexist Writing.* New York: Harper & Row.

Milne, A. A. (1960). *Winnie ille Pu.* Latin translation by Alexander Lenard. New York: Dutton.

Mitchell, Melanie (1993). *Analogy-Making as Perception: A Computer Model.* Cambridge, Mass.: MIT Press/Bradford Books.

Morgenstern, Christian (1963). *Galgenlieder; Der Gingganz.* [1905 and 1910] München: Deutscher Taschenbuch Verlag.

———— (1963). *The Gallows Songs.* Translated by Max Knight. Berkeley: University of California.

———— (1993). *Songs from the Gallows — Galgenlieder.* Translated by Walter Arndt. New Haven: Yale University Press.

Morrison, Philip and Emily Morrison, eds. (1961). *Charles Babbage and His Calculating Engines.* New York: Dover Books.

Moser, David J. (1979). "Alliteratures". Unpublished manuscript.

———— (ca. 1988). "Fourteen Ways of Looking at Li Bai". Unpublished manuscript.

———— (1989). *The Chinese Verbal Art of Xiàngsheng.* Master's thesis, Chinese Studies, University of Michigan, Ann Arbor.

———— (1989). "If this paper were in Chinese, would Chinese people understand the title? An exploration of Whorfian claims about the Chinese language". CRCC Publication #21.

———— (1991). "Why Chinese Is So Damn Hard", in Victor H. Mair (ed.), *Sino-Platonic Papers,* no. 27 (August), pp. 59–70. Dept. of Oriental Studies, University of Pennsylvania, Philadelphia.

———— (1991). "Sze-chuan Pepper and Coca-Cola: The Translation of *Gödel, Escher, Bach* into Chinese". *Babel,* vol. 37, no. 2, pp. 75–95.

———— (1991). "Slips of the Tongue and Pen in Chinese". *Sino-Platonic Papers,* no. 22 (March). Dept. of Oriental Studies, University of Pennsylvania, Philadelphia.

———— (1994). "Phonetic Processes in Writing Chinese: Evidence from Written Errors". In Qicheng Jing *et al.* (eds.), *Information Processing of Chinese Language.* Beijing: Beijing Normal University.

Bibliography ◆ ◆ ◆ *603*

—— (1996). *Abstract Thinking and Thought in Ancient Chinese and Early Greek.* Ph.D. thesis, Asian Languages and Cultures, University of Michigan, Ann Arbor.

—— (1997). "Covert Sexism in Mandarin Chinese". *Sino-Platonic Papers,* no. 74 (January). Dept. of Oriental Studies, University of Pennsylvania, Philadelphia.

Moser, David J. and Douglas R. Hofstadter (2001?). "Errors: A Royal Road to the Mind". Available in incomplete form from CRCC.

Musa, Mark (1995). *The Portable Dante.* New York: Penguin Books.

Nabokov, Vladimir (1958). *Lolita.* New York: G. P. Putnam.

—— (1963). *The Gift.* [1963] New York: G. P. Putnam.

—— (1989). *Speak, Memory.* [1951] New York: Vintage Books.

—— (1990). *Strong Opinions.* [1973] New York: Vintage Books.

—— (1990). *Ada.* [1969] Annotated by Vivian Darkbloom. New York: Vintage Books.

Nagel, Ernest and James R. Newman (1958). *Gödel's Proof.* New York: New York University Press.

Neumann, John von (1958). *The Computer and the Brain.* New Haven: Yale University Press.

—— (1966). *Theory of Self-Reproducing Automata.* Edited and completed by Arthur W. Burks. Urbana: University of Illinois Press.

Newmark, Peter (1988). *Approaches to Translation.* Hemel Hempstead: Prentice-Hall International.

Nirenburg, Sergei *et al.,* eds. (1992). *Machine Translation: A Knowledge-Based Approach.* San Mateo, Calif.: Morgan Kaufmann.

Norman, Donald (1981). "Categorization of Action Slips". *Psychological Review,* vol. 88, pp. 1–15.

Ogden, C. K. and I. A. Richards (1923). *The Meaning of Meaning.* New York: Harcourt Brace & World.

Pagels, Heinz (1988). *The Dreams of Reason.* New York: Simon & Schuster.

Parfit, Derek (1984). *Reasons and Persons.* Oxford: Oxford University Press.

Parsons, Terence (1980). *Nonexistent Objects.* New Haven: Yale University Press.

PENewsletter (1982). New York: PEN International Center.

Perec, Georges (1969). *La disparition.* Paris: Denoël.

—— (1991). *Anton Voyls Fortgang.* Translation by Eugen Helmlé of *La disparition.* Reinbek bei Hamburg: Rowohlt.

—— (1994). *A Void.* Translation by Gilbert Adair of *La disparition.* New York: HarperCollins.

—— (2001). *Fifth-symbol Snafu.* Anglosaxonization of *La disparition* by Wilber Darent. Manhattan: Acidic Books.

—— (2002). *The Disappearance.* Degallicization of *La disparition* by Marvin Validbook. Princeton, New Jersey: Print-Once University Press. Reprinted by Prints-a-Ton University Press.

Pfeiffer, Herbert (1992). *Oh Cello voll Echo.* Frankfurt am Main: Insel Verlag.

Poe, Edgar Allan (1993). *Complete Poems and Selected Essays.* Edited by Richard Gray. Rutland, Vermont: Charles E. Tuttle.

Poole, Adrian and Jeremy Maule, eds. (1995). *The Oxford Book of Classical Verse in Translation.* New York: Oxford University Press.

Porter, Cole (1992). *The Complete Lyrics of Cole Porter.* Edited by Robert Kimball. New York: Da Capo.

Poundstone, William (1985). *The Recursive Universe.* New York: William Morrow.

Preminger, Alex, Frank J. Warnke, and O. B. Hardison, eds. (1965). *Encyclopedia of Poetry and Poetics.* Princeton, New Jersey: Princeton University Press.

Pushkin, Alexander (1991). *Евгений Онегин.* [1831] In Russian. London: Bristol Classical Press.

—— (1943). *Eugene Onegin.* Translated by Babette Deutsch. New York: Heritage Press. Also in Yarmolinsky, Avrahm (ed.), *The Poems, Prose and Plays of Alexander Pushkin.* New York: Modern Library.

—— (1975). *Eugenio Onieghin.* Translated by Giovanni Giudici. Milano: Garzanti Editore.

—— (1977). *Eugene Onegin.* Translated by Charles Johnston. London: Penguin Books.

—— (1980). *Eugène Oniéguine.* Translated by Maurice Colin. Paris: Université de Dijon/Société «Les belles lettres».

—— (1981). *Eugen Onegin.* Translated by Ulrich Busch. Zürich: Manesse Verlag.

—— (1984). *Jewgenij Onegin.* Translated by Rolf-Dietrich Keil. Giessen: W. Schmitz Verlag.

———— (1990). *Eugene Onegin: A Novel in Verse.* [1964] Translated by Vladimir Nabokov. Volume I: Introduction and Translation; Volume II: Commentary and Index. Princeton, New Jersey: Princeton University Press.

———— (1990). *Eugene Onegin.* Translated by James E. Falen. Carbondale, Illinois: Southern Illinois University Press. Reissued by Oxford University Press, 1995.

———— (1992). *Eugene Onegin.* Translated by Walter Arndt. [1963] Ann Arbor: Ardis Editions.

———— (1995). *Yevgeny Onegin.* Translated by Oliver Elton [1937]; edited and revised by A. D. P. Briggs. London: J. M. Dent.

Queneau, Raymond (1947). *Exercices de style.* Paris: Gallimard.

———— (1978). *Stijloefeningen.* Translated by Rudy Kousbroek. Amsterdam: De Bezige Bij.

———— (1981). *Exercises in Style.* Translated by Barbara Wright. New York: New Directions.

———— (1983). *Esercizi di stile.* Translated by Umberto Eco. Torino: Einaudi.

Ram, A., K. Moorman, and J. C. Santamaria (1996). "Creative Conceptual Change". Technical Report GIT-CC-96/07, College of Computing, Georgia Institute of Technology, Atlanta.

Riesbeck, Christopher K. and Roger C. Schank (1989). *Inside Case-Based Reasoning.* Hillsdale, New Jersey: Lawrence Erlbaum Associates.

Robert, Paul (1974). *Le Petit Robert 2: Dictionnaire universel des noms propres.* Paris: S.E.P.R.E.T.

Robinson, Douglas (1991). *The Translator's Turn.* Baltimore: Johns Hopkins.

Rodgers, Richard and Oscar Hammerstein, II (1943). *Oklahoma!* Vocal Selections. Milwaukee: Hal Leonard Publishing Company.

Rodgers, Richard and Lorenz Hart (1984). *Rodgers & Hart: A Musical Anthology.* Milwaukee: Hal Leonard Publishing Company.

Rossum, Christine van and Douglas R. Hofstadter (1996). "Sexism in Language: On the Generic Use of 'Man' and 'Guy'". Available through CRCC.

Rostand, Edmond (1930). *Cyrano de Bergerac.* Paris: Livres de poche.

Sagan, Carl, ed. (1973). *Communication with Extraterrestrial Intelligence.* Cambridge, Mass.: MIT Press.

Sagoff, Maurice (1970). *ShrinkLits.* Garden City, New York: Doubleday.

Salinger, J. D. (1958). *The Catcher in the Rye.* London: Penguin Books.

Sallows, Lee (1985). "In Quest of a Pangram". *Abacus,* vol. 2, no. 3 (spring), pp. 22–40.

———— (1992). "Reflexicons". *Word Ways,* vol. 25, no. 3 (August), pp. 131–141.

Sato, Hiroaki (1995). *One Hundred Frogs: From Renga to Haiku to English.* New York: Weatherhill.

Schank, Roger C. (1982). *Dynamic Memory.* New York: Cambridge University Press.

———— (1984). "The Explanation Game". Yale Computer Science Dept. Research Report #307.

Schank, Roger C. and Kenneth Colby, eds. (1973). *Computer Models of Thought and Language.* San Francisco: W. H. Freeman.

Searle, John (1980). "Minds, Brains, and Programs". *Behavioral and Brain Sciences,* vol. 3 (Sept.), pp. 417–457. Reprinted in Hofstadter & Dennett (81).

Serafini, Luigi (1981). *Codex Seraphinianus.* Milano: Franco Maria Ricci.

Service, Robert (1978). *Collected Poems.* London: E. Benn.

Seth, Vikram (1986). *The Golden Gate.* New York: Random House.

———— (1992). *Three Chinese Poets.* New York: Harper Perennial.

Shakespeare, William (1977). *Sonnets.* Edited and commented by Stephen Booth. New Haven: Yale University Press.

Solzhenitsyn, Alexander (1981). *One Day in the Life of Ivan Denisovich.* Translated by Max Hayward and Ronald Hingley. New York: Bantam Books.

———— (1984). *One Day in the Life of Ivan Denisovich.* Translated by Ralph Parker. New York: Penguin Books.

Steig, William (1968). *C D B!* New York: Simon & Schuster.

———— (1984). *C D C?* New York: Farrar, Straus & Giroux.

Steiner, George (1974). *Fields of Force.* New York: The Viking Press.

———— (1975). *After Babel: Aspects of Language and Translation.* New York: Oxford University Press.

Stéphane, Bernard (1981). *Dictionnaire des noms des rues.* Paris: Éditions Mengès.

Storrs, Ronald (1959). *Ad Pyrrham.* London: Oxford University Press.

Bibliography

Struther, Jan (1940). *Mrs. Miniver*. New York: Harcourt & Brace.

Suppes, Patrick (1957). *Introduction to Logic*. New York: Van Nostrand Reinhold.

Thomas, Dylan (1971). *The Collected Poems of Dylan Thomas*. New York: New Directions.

Tindall, William York (1996). *A Reader's Guide to Dylan Thomas*. Syracuse: Syracuse University Press.

Treisman, Anne (1988). "Features and Objects: The Fourteenth Bartlett Memorial Lecture". *Quarterly Journal of Experimental Psychology*, vol. 40A, pp. 201–237.

Tucker, Allen B., Jr. (1984). "A Perspective on Machine Translation: Theory and Practice". *Communications of the ACM*, vol. 27, no. 4 (April), pp. 322–329.

Turing, Alan (1950). "Computing Machinery and Intelligence", *Mind*, vol. 49, no. 236.

Ulam, Stanisław (1976). *Adventures of a Mathematician*. New York: Charles Scribner's Sons.

Updike, John (1995). *Collected Poems, 1953–1993*. New York: Alfred A. Knopf.

Validbook, Marvin (1999). *Là, ô Lit*. New Dublin: Oracular Publishing Company. Preissued by Ada Bookery Company, Atlantis City (1998).

——— (2000). *Brash Attacks*. New Amsterdam: Eleemosynary Editions.

——— (2001). *Spout, Mind*. New Tananarive: Wowser & Genius, Ltd.

——— (2002). *Zwz*. Introduction by Vikram Vainblood. Zebrzydowice: Wydawnictwo Zmyślone.

Van Doren, Mark (1928). *An Anthology of World Poetry*. New York: Albert and Charles Boni.

Varaldo, Giuseppe (1993). *All'alba Shahrazad andrà ammazzata*. Milano: Garzanti Editore.

Verdun, Christian (1996). *Clément Marot : Poète et aventurier*. Martel: Les Éditions du Laquet.

Villon, François (1914). *The Poems of François Villon*. Translated by H. De Vere Stacpoole. New York: John Lane.

——— (1978). *Selected Poems*. Translated by Peter Dale. London: Penguin Books.

——— (1994). *Complete Poems*. Translated by Barbara N. Sargent-Baur. Toronto: University of Toronto Press.

Weaver, Warren (1955). "Translation". In W. N. Locke and A. D. Booth (eds.), *Machine Translation of Languages* (MIT Press, Cambridge, Mass.).

——— (1964). *Alice in Many Tongues*. Madison: University of Wisconsin Press.

Weinberg, Steven (1977). *The First Three Minutes*. New York: Basic Books.

Weinberger, Eliot and Octavio Paz (1987). *Nineteen Ways of Looking at Wang Wei*. Mount Kisco, New York: Moyer Bell Limited.

Weizenbaum, Joseph (1976). *Computer Power and Human Reason*. San Francisco: W. H. Freeman.

Whitemore, Hugh (1987). *Breaking the Code*. Oxford: Amber Lane Press.

Wilbur, Richard (1989). *New and Collected Poems*. San Diego: Harcourt Brace Jovanovich.

Wilks, Yorick (1992). "SYSTRAN: it obviously works but how much can it be improved?" Chapter 10 in John Newton (ed.), *Computers in Translation: A Practical Appraisal* (Routledge, London).

Wilson, Edmund (1965). Review of Nabokov's translation of *Eugene Onegin*. *New York Review of Books*, July 15. Also in Edmund Wilson, *A Window on Russia* (Farrar, Straus & Giroux, New York, 1972).

Winograd, Terry (1972). *Understanding Natural Language*. New York: Academic Press.

Wright, Ernest Vincent (1939). *Gadsby*. Los Angeles: Wetzel Publishing Company.

Yaguello, Marina (1978). *Les mots et les femmes*. Paris: Éditions Payot.

Yngve, Victor H. (1962). "Computer Programs for Translation", *Scientific American* (June), pp. 68–76.

——— (1964). "Implications of Mechanical Translation Research". *Proceedings of the American Philosophical Society*, vol. 108, pp. 275–281.

Zerubavel, Eviatar (1991). *The Fine Line: Making Distinctions in Everyday Life*. New York: Free Press.

Zhang Xinxin and Sang Ye (1987). *Chinese Lives: An Oral History of Contemporary China*. Edited by W. J. F. Jenner and Delia Davin. New York: Pantheon.

Permissions and Acknowledgments

Grateful acknowledgment is made by the author to the following individuals and publishers for permission to quote from the sources indicated. Every effort has been made to locate the copyright owners of material reproduced in this book. Any errors or omissions brought to the author's attention will be corrected in subsequent printings.

Chapter 2/Poems II: Selections from Ronald Storrs, *Ad Pyrrham: A Polyglot Collection of Translations of Horace's Ode to Pyrrha.* Assembled with an Introduction by Ronald Storrs. Copyright ©1959 by Louise Storrs (Selection, Introduction and editorial matter). Oxford Univ. Press, 1959, by permission of Oxford Univ. Press. Lyric excerpts of "Thou Swell", music by Richard Rodgers and words by Lorenz Hart. Copyright ©1927 (renewed) by Williamson Music and Warner Bros., Inc. Used by permission of Williamson Music and Warner Bros. Publications U.S. Inc. All Rights Reserved. All rights on behalf of Estate of Lorenz Hart administered by WB Music Corp.

Chapter 3: Excerpts from Stanisław Lem, *The Cyberiad: Fables for the Cybernetic Age.* Translated from the Polish by Michael Kandel. English translation copyright ©1974 by The Continuum Publishing Co., by permission of The Continuum Publishing Co., New York.

Chapter 4: Excerpts from a letter to Alfred, Lord Tennyson, in *Charles Babbage and His Calculating Engines,* ©1961, by permission of Dover Publications, Inc. Lord Tennyson, in *Charles Babbage and His Calculating Engines,* ©1961, by permission of Dover Pub., Inc.

Chapter 5: Excerpts from Georges Perec, *La disparition,* Copyright ©1969 by Éditions Denoël, by permission of Éditions Denoël, Paris. Excerpt from Georges Perec, *Anton Voyls Fortgang.* Übersetzt von Eugen Helmlé. Rowohlt Taschenbuch Verlag, 1991. Copyright © by Zweitausendeins, Frankfurt/Main, by permission of Zweitausendeins. Excerpts from Georges Perec, *A Void.* Translated by Gilbert Adair. Published in Great Britain by Collins Harvill, 1994. Copyright in the English translation ©1994 by HarperCollins Publishers, by permission of The Harvill Press. Selections by Giuseppe Varaldo and Stefano Bartezzaghi from *All'alba Shahrazad andrà ammazzata* ©1993, in Italian and in English translation, by permission of Garzanti editore s.p.a., Milano. "Pollution", ©1965 Tom Lehrer, by permission of Tom Lehrer. "The Catcher in the Rye", "Cyrano de Bergerac", "Inferno", and "The Raven" from Maurice Sagoff, *ShrinkLits: The one-inch shelf of the world's greatest literature.* Copyright ©1980 by Maurice Sagoff, by permission of Workman Publishing Co., Inc. Excerpts from "The Philosophy of Composition" and "The Raven" from *Edgar Allen Poe: Complete Poems and Selected Essays,* ©1993 by J. M. Dent, by permission of Everyman's Library.

Chapter 6: Excerpt from *One Day in the Life of Ivan Denisovich* by Alexander Solzhenitsyn, translated by Ralph Parker. Translation ©1963 by E. P. Dutton and Victor Gollancz, Ltd. Copyright renewed ©1991 by Penguin USA and Victor Gollancz, Ltd. Used by permission of Dutton Signet, a division of Penguin Books USA, Inc., and Victor Gollancz, Ltd., London. Excerpt from George Steiner, *After Babel: Aspects of Language and Translation.* Copyright ©1975 by George Steiner. Oxford Univ. Press, 1975, by permission of Oxford Univ. Press. Excerpts from "Preface" by Studs Terkel, published in *Chinese Lives: An Oral History of Contemporary China.* First American edition. Copyright 1987 Studs Terkel, reprinted by permission of Donadio & Ashworth, Inc. Excerpts from *Chinese Lives: An Oral History of Contemporary China* by Zhang Xinxin and Sang Ye. Copyright ©1987 by W. J. F. Jenner and Delia Davin. Reprinted by permission of Pantheon Books, a division of Random House, and Delia Davin.

Chapter 7: "Les Ballades en jargon" from *François Villon, Complete Poems.* Edited with English translation and commentary by Barbara N. Sargent-Baur, ©1994 by Univ. of Toronto Press, Inc., by permission of Univ. of Toronto Press. Lyric excerpts of "The Surrey With The Fringe On Top", music by Richard Rodgers and lyrics by Oscar Hammerstein II. Copyright ©1943 (renewed) by Williamson Music. International Copyright Secured. Used by permission of Williamson Music. All Rights Reserved. "Lobachevsky", ©1953 Tom Lehrer, by permission of Tom Lehrer. "The Elements", ©1959 Tom Lehrer, by permission of Tom Lehrer. Excerpt from Selma Fraiberg, *The Magic Years.* Copyright ©1959 by Selma Fraiberg, renewed 1987 by Louis Fraiberg and Lisa Fraiberg, by permission of Scribner, a Division of Simon & Schuster. From *Selected Poems: François Villon,* chosen and translated by Peter Dale. Penguin Classics 1978. By permission from Peter Dale. From Raymond Queneau, *Exercises in Style.* Copyright ©1947, 1958, 1981 by Éditions Gallimard and Barbara Wright. Reprinted by permission of New Directions Publishing Corp. Translation of quotes from Raymond Queneau, *Stijloefeningen.* Copyright ©1947, 1978 by Éditions Gallimard and Rudy Kousbroek, by permission of Rudy Kousbroek.

Chapter 8/Poems VIII: Chapter 5, stanzas 3, 4, and 5 from Vikram Seth, *The Golden Gate.* Copyright ©1986 by Vikram Seth, reprinted by permission of Random House, Inc. and Faber & Faber, London. Four stanzas from *Eugene Onegin by Alexander Pushkin,* translated by Charles Johnston. Copyright © Charles Johnston, 1977, 1979, by permission of Penguin Books Ltd., London. Selections from pp. 7, 43, 72, and 194 reprinted from *Eugene Onegin* by Alexander Pushkin, translated by James E. Falen, © James E. Falen 1990, 1995. World's Classics paperback 1995, by permission of Oxford Univ. Press. Reprinted by permission of Ardis from *Alexander Pushkin: Eugene Onegin,* translated by Walter Arndt. Ardis 1992. "But Not For Me", music and lyrics by George Gershwin and Ira Gershwin, ©1930 (renewed), Warner Bros. Music Corp. All Rights Reserved, Used by Permission of Warner Bros. Publications U.S. Inc., Miami, Florida. Lyric excerpts of "I'm Getting Myself Ready For You", words and music by Cole Porter, ©1930 (renewed), Warner Bros. Inc. All Rights Reserved. Used by Permission of Warner Bros. Publications U.S. Inc., Miami, Florida.

Chapter 9: Reprinted by permission of Ardis from *Alexander Pushkin: Eugene Onegin,* translated by Walter Arndt, and *Pushkin Threefold* by Walter Arndt. Ardis 1992. Excerpts from Vladimir Nabokov, *Aleksandr Pushkin. Eugene Onegin: A Novel in Verse.* Volume I: Introduction and Translation. Copyright ©1975 by Princeton Univ. Press (Bollingen Series LXXII), by permission of Princeton Univ. Press. Excerpts from Vladimir Nabokov, *Aleksandr Pushkin. Eugene Onegin: A Novel In Verse.* Volume II: Commentary and Index. Copyright ©1975 by Princeton Univ. Press (Bollingen Series LXXII), by permission of Princeton Univ. Press. From *Strong Opinions* by Vladimir Nabokov. Copyright ©1990 by the Estate of Vladimir Nabokov. Reprinted by permission of Vintage Books, a Division of Random House, Inc. Selection from p. xxvii reprinted from *Eugene Onegin* by Alexander Pushkin, translated by James E. Falen, © James E. Falen 1990, 1995. World's Classics paperback 1995, by permission of Oxford Univ. Press. Excerpt from Diana L. Burgin, *Richard Burgin: A Life in Verse,* by permission of Diana Lewis Burgin.

Chapter 10/Poems X: Excerpts from Jorge Luis Borges, *Ficciones,* ©1962 by Grove Press, by permission of Grove Press. Language Commentary on "Fresh Air", National Public Radio, by permission of Geoffrey Nunberg. Excerpts from George Steiner, *After Babel: Aspects of Language and Translation.* Copyright ©1975 by George Steiner. Oxford Univ. Press, 1975, by permission of Oxford Univ. Press. Excerpts from Willis Barnstone, *The Poetics of Translation,* ©1993 by Yale Univ. Press, by permission of Yale Univ. Press. Excerpts from "Uncleftish Beholding" by Poul Anderson, by permission of Poul Anderson. Lyric excerpts of "Let's Do It (Let's Fall in Love)", words and music by Cole Porter, ©1928 (renewed), Warner Bros. Inc. All Rights Reserved. Used by Permission of Warner Bros.

Publications U.S. Inc., Miami, Florida.

Chapter 11/Poems XI: From *Dragon's Egg* by Robert L. Forward. Copyright ©1980 by Dr. Robert L. Forward, by permission of Ballantine Books, a Division of Random House. "Ars Brevis" by Piet Hein. Piet Hein ©1966/GROOKS I, reprinted by kind permission of Piet Hein as, DK 5500 Middelfart, Denmark. "Cosmic Gall" from John Updike, *Collected Poems 1953–1993*. Copyright ©1993 by John Updike, reprinted by permission of Alfred A. Knopf. Inc.

Chapter 13: From Russell Baker, "Homer's First Yuppie", Observer column, *The New York Times*, August 13, 1996. © The New York Times, by permission of The New York Times. Letter to the Editor of *The New York Times* by Joyce Carol Oates. ©1996 by The Ontario Review, Inc. , by permission of Joyce Carol Oates. Lyric excerpts of "Oh, How I Hate To Get Up In The Morning" by Irving Berlin. Copyright ©1918 (renewed) by Irving Berlin. Copyright © assigned to Joe DiMaggio, Anna Phipps Sidamon-Eristoff, and Theodore R. Jackson as Trustees of God Bless America Fund. International Copyright Secured. Used by Permission of Williamson Music. All Rights Reserved. "Singing for Deborah Kerr: An Interview with Marni Nixon". Reprinted by permission of Angel Records, New York. Excerpt from George Steiner, *After Babel: Aspects of Language and Translation*. Copyright ©1975 by George Steiner. Oxford Univ. Press, 1975, by permission of Oxford Univ. Press.

Chapter 14: Three poems from Christian Morgenstern's *Galgenlieder (Gallows Songs)*, translated/edited by Max Knight. Copyright ©1963 Max E. Knight, by permission of the Univ. of California Press, Berkeley, and Insel Verlag, Frankfurt/Main. Three poems from Christian Morgenstern, *Songs from the Gallows: Galgenlieder*, translated by Walter Arndt. ©1993 by Yale Univ., by permission of Yale Univ. Press. "A Moment's Thought" by Piet Hein. Piet Hein ©1966/GROOKS I; "The Final Touch" by Piet Hein. Piet Hein ©1969/GROOKS II; "Only Hoping" and "Similarity" by Piet Hein. Piet Hein ©1970/GROOKS III, reprinted by kind permission of Piet Hein as, DK-5500 Middelfart, Denmark. Sixteen lines from "anyone lived in a pretty how town", copyright 1940, ©1968, 1991 by the Trustees for the E. E. Cummings Trust, from *Complete Poems: 1904–1962* by E. E. Cummings. Edited by George J. Firmage. Reprinted by permission of Liveright Publishing Corp. Excerpt from "Sze-chuan Pepper and Coca-Cola: the Translation of *Gödel, Escher, Bach* into Chinese" by David Moser, © FIT Revue Babel, by permission of the Fédération Internationale des Traducteurs/Revue Babel. From *Squad Helps Dog Bite Victim* by The Trustees of Columbia Univ. Copyright ©1980 by Trustees of Columbia Univ. in the City of New York. Used by permission of Doubleday, a division of Bantam Doubleday Dell Publishing Group, Inc. Four headlines from *Red Tape Holds Up New Bridge* (ed. Gloria Cooper). Copyright ©1987 by The Trustees of Columbia University in the City of New York. A Perigee Book, The Putnam Publishing Group. Used by permission of the Berkley Publishing Group. Excerpt from Roger Angell, *A Day in the Life of Roger Angell*. Copyright ©1978 by Roger Angell, by permission of International Creative Management, Inc., New York. Reprinted by permission of Aladdin Paperback, an imprint of Simon & Schuster Children's Publishing Division from *CDB!* by William Steig. ©1968 William Steig. Text from page 44 "U R O-D-S ! N U R S-N-9 !" from *C D C?* By William Steig. Copyright ©1984 by William Steig, reprinted by permission of Farrar, Straus & Giroux, Inc. Excerpt from *Let's Parler Franglais!* by Miles Kington, ©1979 Punch Publications. By permission of Robson Books, Ltd., Publishers, London. "Révision M–N" from *Sky my husband! Ciel mon mari!* by Jean-Loup Chiflet, ©1985, by permission of Éditions Hermé, Paris. From Battus, *Opperlandse taal- & letterkunde*. Amsterdam: Em. Querido's Uitgeverij B.V., vijfde druk, 1984. By permission of Hugo Brandt Corstius. Poem from Ross Eckler, *Making the Alphabet Dance: Recreational Wordplay*. Copyright ©1995 by Ross Eckler, by permission of St. Martin's Press, Inc. From "Reflexicons" by Lee Sallows, in *Word Ways*, vol. 25, no. 3, page 131, edited and published by A. Ross Eckler, ©1992, by permission of the editor and publisher of *Word Ways*. Excerpt from Willis Barnstone, *The Poetics of Translation*, ©1993 by Yale Univ. Press, by permission of Yale Univ. Press.

Chapter 15/Poems XV: From Evan S. Connell, Jr. *The Diary of a Rapist*. Copyright ©1966, renewed 1994 by Evan S. Connell, Jr., by permission of Don Congdon Associates, Inc. Excerpts from Derek Parfit, *Reasons and Persons*, ©1984 by Derek Parfit, by permission of Oxford Univ. Press. "My Flapper" by Candide, by permission of IBM Watson Research Labs.

Chapter 16: From T. Winograd, *Understanding Natural Language*. ©1972 by Academic Press, by permission of Academic Press and Terry Winograd. From A. Davey, *Discourse Production*, ©1978 by Anthony Davey, Edinburgh Univ. Press, by permission Anthony Davey.

Chapter 17: Haiku by Matsu Bashō, translated by Hiroaki Sato, by permission of Weatherhill, New York. From "Translator's Note" and "Canto III" from *The Inferno of Dante: A New Verse Translation* by Robert Pinsky. Copyright ©1994 by Robert Pinsky. Translation copyright ©1995 by Robert Pinsky, by permission of Farrar, Straus & Giroux, Inc. and J. M. Dent Publishers, Orion Books, London. Excerpts from "A Chat with the Reader", "Luminous Experience of a Brain Scan", and "Docking at Night" from Willis Barnstone, *The Secret Reader: 501 Sonnets*. ©1996 by Willis Barnstone, by permission of Univ. Press of New England. From *The Divine Comedy of Dante Alighieri: Inferno*, Canto XXV, translated into English verse by Melville Best Anderson. Copyright ©1944 The Heritage Press, by permission of The Limited Editions Club, New York. From Paolo Milano (editor), *The Portable Dante: The Divine Comedy*, translated by Laurence Binyon. Inferno, Canto XXV (lines 46–66). Copyright © Nicolete Gray, 1969; copyright renewed © Viking Penguin, Inc., 1975, by permission of Mrs. Nicolete Gray and The Society of Authors, on behalf of the Laurence Binyon Estate. Excerpts from "Introduction" and Canti XXV and XIX from *The Comedy of Dante Alighieri, The Florentine. Cantica I: Hell (L'Inferno)*, translated by Dorothy L. Sayers. Copyright ©1949, Estate of Dorothy L. Sayers, by permission of David Higham Associates, London. Nine lines of Canto I of *The Inferno*, translated by Willis Barnstone, by permission of Willis Barnstone. From the Preface of *Dante's Inferno: Translations by 20 Contemporary Poets* by Daniel Halpern. Preface copyright ©1993 by Daniel Halpern. Copyright ©1993 by The Ecco Press. Reprinted by permission of The Ecco Press. "Canto III", translated by Seamus Heaney; "Canto XIX", translated by C. K. Williams; "Canto XXV", translated by Richard Wilbur from *Dante's Inferno: Translations by 20 Contemporary Poets* edited by Daniel Halpern. Copyright ©1993 by The Ecco Press. Reprinted by permission of The Ecco Press. The first nine lines of *The Divine Comedy of Dante Alighieri: Inferno*, translated by Allen Mandelbaum, ©1980, by permission of Bantam Books, a division of Bantam Doubleday Dell Publishing Group, Inc. "A Verseman's Apology" from *Collected Verse of Robert Service*, Volume Two, © Germaine Service 1960, by permission of William Krasilovsky for the Estate of Robert Service. Excerpts from the Introduction of *Famous Poems from Bygone Days*, edited and annotated by Martin Gardner, ©1995 by Martin Gardner, by permission of Dover Publications, Inc. Haiku (in English) by Earl Miner, by permission of Earl Miner. Haiku (in English) by James Kirkup, by permission of James Kirkup.

Notes: Reprinted by permission of Yale Univ. Press from *The Poetics of Translation* by Willis Barnstone. ©1993 by Yale Univ. Excerpts and "Deer Park" from Vikram Seth, *Three Chinese Poets*, ©1992 by Faber & Faber, by permission of Sheil Land Associates, London.

The publisher likewise would like to thank all authors and publishers for permission to reproduce previously printed material.

Index

Though completeness is an ideal for any index, it is chimerical. Doing an index is a lesson to end all lessons in the vagueness and subjectivity of human categories. I have tried to compensate for inevitable lacunae and subjective mismatches with readers' minds by indexing most major topics in several different ways. Entries for Chapter pages come first, followed by entries for Poem pages (e.g., "whatnot, 2, 15, 3a, 7b"). All poems in the text are listed both by title and by first line. Author names are usually given in parentheses after a work's title; in the case of a translation, usually just the translator's name is given, in the interests of brevity.

Index

Index

Index